The Oxford Handbook of Sport and
Performance Psychology

OXFORD LIBRARY OF PSYCHOLOGY

OXFORD LIBRARY OF PSYCHOLOGY

Editor in Chief PETER E. NATHAN

The Oxford Handbook of Sport and Performance Psychology

Edited by

Shane M. Murphy

OXFORD
UNIVERSITY PRESS

OXFORD
UNIVERSITY PRESS

Oxford University Press is a department of the University of Oxford. It furthers the University's objective of excellence in research, scholarship, and education by publishing worldwide.

Oxford   New York
Auckland   Cape Town   Dar es Salaam   Hong Kong   Karachi
Kuala Lumpur   Madrid   Melbourne   Mexico City   Nairobi
New Delhi   Shanghai   Taipei   Toronto

With offices in
Argentina   Austria   Brazil   Chile   Czech Republic   France   Greece
Guatemala   Hungary   Italy   Japan   Poland   Portugal   Singapore
South Korea   Switzerland   Thailand   Turkey   Ukraine   Vietnam

Oxford is a registered trademark of Oxford University Press in the UK and certain other countries.

Published in the United States of America by
Oxford University Press
198 Madison Avenue, New York, NY 10016

Library of Congress Cataloging-in-Publication Data
The Oxford handbook of sport and performance psychology / edited by Shane M. Murphy.
  p. cm. — (Oxford library of psychology)
  ISBN 978-0-19-973176-3
1. Performance—Psychological aspects—Handbooks, manuals, etc.   2. Sports—Psychological aspects—Handbooks, manuals, etc.   3. Attitude (Psychology)   I. Murphy, Shane M., 1957–
BF637.S4O954 2012
617.1'027—dc23
2012004840

9 8 7 6 5 4 3
Printed in the United States of America
on acid-free paper

SHORT CONTENTS

Oxford Library of Psychology   vii–viii

About the Editor   ix

Contributors   xi–xiv

Table of Contents   xv–xvii

Preface   xix–xxiv

Chapters   1–754

Index   755

OXFORD LIBRARY OF PSYCHOLOGY

The *Oxford Library of Psychology*, a landmark series of handbooks, is published by Oxford University Press, one of the world's oldest and most highly respected publishers, with a tradition of publishing significant books in psychology. The ambitious goal of the *Oxford Library of Psychology* is nothing less than to span a vibrant, wide-ranging field and, in so doing, to fill a clear market need.

Encompassing a comprehensive set of handbooks, organized hierarchically, the *Library* incorporates volumes at different levels, each designed to meet a distinct need. At one level are a set of handbooks designed broadly to survey the major subfields of psychology; at another are numerous handbooks that cover important current focal research and scholarly areas of psychology in depth and detail. Planned as a reflection of the dynamism of psychology, the *Library* will grow and expand as psychology itself develops, thereby highlighting significant new research that will impact on the field. Adding to its accessibility and ease of use, the *Library* will be published in print and, later on, electronically.

The *Library* surveys psychology's principal subfields with a set of handbooks that capture the current status and future prospects of those major subdisciplines. This initial set includes handbooks of social and personality psychology, clinical psychology, counseling psychology, school psychology, educational psychology, industrial and organizational psychology, cognitive psychology, cognitive neuroscience, methods and measurements, history, neuropsychology, personality assessment, developmental psychology, and more. Each handbook undertakes to review one of psychology's major subdisciplines with breadth, comprehensiveness, and exemplary scholarship. In addition to these broadly conceived volumes, the *Library* *also* includes a large number of handbooks designed to explore in depth more specialized areas of scholarship and research, such as stress, health and coping, anxiety and related disorders, cognitive development, or child and adolescent assessment. In contrast to the broad coverage of the subfield handbooks, each of these latter volumes focuses on an especially productive, more highly focused line of scholarship and research. Whether at the broadest or most specific level, however, all of the *Library* handbooks offer synthetic coverage that reviews and evaluates the relevant past and present research and anticipates research in the future. Each handbook in the *Library* includes an introductory and concluding chapters written by its editor to provide a roadmap to the handbook's table of contents and to offer informed anticipations of significant future developments in that field.

An undertaking of this scope calls for handbook editors and chapter authors who are established scholars in the areas about which they write. Many of the nation's and world's most productive and best-respected psychologists have agreed to edit *Library* handbooks or write authoritative chapters in their areas of expertise.

For whom has the *Oxford Library of Psychology* been written? Because of its breadth, depth, and accessibility, the *Library* serves a diverse audience, including graduate students in psychology and their faculty mentors, scholars, researchers, and practitioners in psychology and related fields. Each will find in the *Library* the information he or she seeks on the subfield or focal area of psychology in which he or she works or are interested.

Befitting its commitment to accessibility, each handbook includes a comprehensive index, as well as extensive references to help guide research. And because the *Library* was designed from its inception as an online as well as a print resource, its structure and contents will be readily and rationally searchable online. Further, once the *Library* is released online, the handbooks will be regularly and thoroughly updated.

In summary, the *Oxford Library of Psychology* will grow organically to provide a thoroughly informed perspective on the field of psychology, one that reflects both psychology's dynamism and its increasing interdisciplinarity. Once published electronically, the *Library* is also destined to become a uniquely valuable interactive tool, with extended search and browsing capabilities. As you begin to consult this handbook, we sincerely hope you will share our enthusiasm for the more than 500-year tradition of Oxford University Press for excellence, innovation, and quality, as exemplified by the *Oxford Library of Psychology*.

Peter E. Nathan
Editor-in-Chief
Oxford Library of Psychology

ABOUT THE EDITOR

Shane M. Murphy

Shane M. Murphy, Ph.D., is a licensed psychologist and Professor in Psychology at Western Connecticut State University in Danbury, Connecticut, where he teaches sport, health, and performance psychology. Dr. Murphy served as head of the United States Olympic Committee's Sport Psychology Department from 1987 to 1994, and from 1992 to 1994 he was Associate Director of its Division of Sport Science & Technology.

Shane is a past-President and also a fellow of the Division of Sport and Exercise Psychology of the American Psychological Association. His books include *Sport Psychology Interventions, The Sport Psych Handbook, The Achievement Zone,* and *The Tears and the Cheers*. He has published 17 book chapters on sport psychology and human performance, and over 30 refereed articles. Shane serves on the Editorial Boards of the *International Review of Sport and Exercise Psychology*, the *Journal of Clinical Sport Psychology*, and the *Journal of Media Psychology*. His research includes the study of imagery and performance, the assessment of psychological skills for managing high performance, and analysis of the psychology of participation in video game play.

In addition to working with the world's top athletes, Shane is a performance consultant to many companies and organizations and has worked with Royal Bank of Scotland, Pepsi, Bristol-Meyers-Squibb, Siemens-Rolm, Deutsche Bank and with a number of performing artists, directors, musicians, and arts groups. He is married to wife Annemarie, and has two children.

CONTRIBUTORS

Bruce Abernethy
Faculty of Health Sciences
The University of Queensland
Brisbane, Australia

Mark B. Andersen
Institute of Sport, Exercise and Active
Living
Victoria University
Melbourne, Australia

Mark R. Beauchamp
School of Kinesiology
University of British Columbia
Vancouver, British Columbia, Canada

Stuart J. H. Biddle
School of Sport, Exercise, and Health
Sciences
Loughborough University
Loughborough, United Kingdom

Nicole D. Bolter
Department of Kinesiology
San Francisco State University
San Francisco, California

Charles Brown
Director, Get Your Head in the Game
Charlotte, North Carolina

Christopher M. Carr
St. Vincent Sports Performance
Indianapolis, Indiana

Sam Carr
Department of Education
University of Bath
Bath, United Kingdom

Albert V. Carron
University of Western Ontario
London, Ontario, Canada

Kathleen V. Casto
Department of Graduate Psychology
James Madison University
Harrisonburg, Virginia

Packianathan Chelladurai
School of Physical Activity and Educational
Services
The Ohio State University
Columbus, Ohio

Dave Collins
Institute of Coaching and Performance
University of Central Lancashire
Grey Matters Performance
Lancashire, United Kingdom

Jean Côté
School of Kinesiology and Health Studies
Queen's University
Kingston, Ontario, Canada

Jennifer Cumming
School of Sport and Exercise Sciences
University of Birmingham
Birmingham, United Kingdom

Julie P. Douglas
School of Sport, Exercise, and Health
Sciences
Loughborough University
Loughborough, United Kingdom

Kate I. Goodger
English Institute of Sport
The High Performance Centre
Bisham Abbey National Sports Centre
Nr Marlow, Buckinghamshire

Trish Gorely
School of Sport, Exercise, and Health
Sciences
Loughborough University
Loughborough, United Kingdom

Daniel Gould
Institute for the Study of Youth Sports
Michigan State University
East Lansing, Michigan

Christy Greenleaf
Department of Kinesiology, Health
Promotion, and Recreation
University of North Texas
Denton, Texas

Douglas M. Hankes
Student Counseling Services
Auburn University
Auburn, Alabama

Robert J. Harmison
Department of Graduate Psychology
James Madison University
Harrisonburg, Virginia

Chris G. Harwood
School of Sport, Exercise, and Health
Sciences
Loughborough University
Loughborough, United Kingdom

Antonis Hatzigeorgiadis
Department of Physical Education and
Sport Sciences
University of Thessaly
Trikala, Greece

Kate F. Hays
Director, The Performing Edge
Toronto, Ontario, Canada

John Heil
Psychological Health Roanoke
Roanoke, Virginia

Tom Hildebrandt
Appearance and Performance Enhancing
Drug Use Program
Mount Sinai School of Medicine
New York, New York

Ben Jackson
School of Sport Science, Exercise and
Health
University of Western Australia
Perth, Australia

Graham Jones
Top Performance Consulting, Ltd.
Wokingham, United Kingdom

Marc V. Jones
Centre for Sport Health and Exercise
Research
Staffordshire University
Staffordshire, United Kingdom

Martin I. Jones
Department of Sport and Exercise
Psychology
University of Gloucestershire
Gloucestershire, United Kingdom

Sara Kamin
From The Heart Psychotherapy
Toronto, Ontario, Canada

Maria Kavussanu
School of Sport and Exercise Sciences
University of Birmingham
Birmingham, United Kingdom

Lindsay E. Kipp
School of Kinesiology
University of Minnesota, Twin Cities
Minneapolis, Minnesota

Anthony P. Kontos
UPMC Sports Medicine Concussion
Program
Department of Orthopaedic Surgery
University of Pittsburgh School of
Medicine
Pittsburgh, Pennsylvania

Alan S. Kornspan
Department of Sport Science and Wellness
Education
University of Akron
Akron, Ohio

Justine K. Lai
Appearance and Performance Enhancing
Drug Use Program
Mount Sinai School of Medicine
New York, New York

Barbi Law
Schulich School of Education
Nipissing University
North Bay, Ontario, Canada

Todd Loughead
Department of Kinesiology
University of Windsor
Windsor, Ontario, Canada

Luc Martin
Department of Kinesiology
University of Western Ontario
London, Ontario, Canada

Rich Masters
Institute of Human Performance
University of Hong Kong
Hong Kong SAR, China

Sean McCann
Senior Sport Psychologist
United States Olympic Committee
Colorado Springs, Colorado

Penny McCullagh
Department of Kinesiology
California State University, East Bay
Hayward, California

Nikola Medic
School of Exercise and Health Sciences
Edith Cowan University
Perth, Australia

Joseph P. Mills
Faculty of Physical Education and
Recreation
University of Alberta
Edmonton, Alberta, Canada

Antoinette M. Minniti
School of Science and Technology
Nottingham Trent University
Nottingham, United Kingdom

Zella E. Moore
Department of Psychology
Manhattan College
New York, New York

Aidan Moran
School of Psychology
University College Dublin
Dublin, Ireland

Katie L. Morton
Department of Public Health and
Primary Care
University of Cambridge
Cambridge, United Kingdom

Bryan P. Murphy
University of Connecticut
Storrs, Connecticut

Shane M. Murphy
Department of Psychology
Western Connecticut State University
Danbury, Connecticut

Sanna M. Nordin-Bates
Department of Performance and Training
Swedish School of Sport and Health Sciences
Stockholm, Sweden

Kirsten Peterson
Performance Psychology
Australian Institute of Sport
Canberra, Australia

Albert J. Petitpas
Department of Psychology
Springfield College
Springfield, Massachusetts

Trent A. Petrie
Department of Psychology
University of North Texas
Denton, Texas

Leslie Podlog
Department of Exercise and Sport Science
University of Utah
Salt Lake City, Utah

Emily A. Roper
Department of Health and Kinesiology
Sam Houston State University
Huntsville, Texas

Martyn Standage
Department for Health
University of Bath
Bath, United Kingdom

Diane Ste-Marie
School of Human Kinetics
University of Ottawa
Ottawa, Ontario, Canada

Joachim Stoeber
School of Psychology
University of Kent
Canterbury, United Kingdom

William B. Strean
Faculty of Physical Education and
Recreation
University of Alberta
Edmonton, Alberta, Canada

Yannis Theodorakis
Department of Physical Education and
Sport Sciences
University of Thessaly
Trikala, Greece

Taunya Marie Tinsley
Department of Counselor Education
California University of Pennsylvania
California, Pennsylvania

Eleanna Varangis
Appearance and Performance Enhancing
Drug Use Program
Mount Sinai School of Medicine
New York, New York

Amy S. Walker
Independent Practice Success in a Different
Language
Rockville, Maryland

Maureen R. Weiss
School of Kinesiology
University of Minnesota, Twin Cities
Minneapolis, Minnesota

Sarah E. Williams
University of Birmingham
Birmingham, United Kingdom

Mark R. Wilson
University of Exeter
Exeter, United Kingdom

E. Missy Wright
Institute for the Study of Youth Sports
Michigan State University
East Lansing, Michigan

Bradley W. Young
School of Human Kinetics
University of Ottawa
Ottawa, Canada

Nikos Zourbanos
Department of Physical Education and
Sport Sciences
University of Thessaly
Trikala, Greece

CONTENTS

Preface   xix

Part One   •   The Nature and Scope of Sport and Performance Psychology

1. History of Sport and Performance Psychology   3
   Alan S. Kornspan
2. The Psychology of Performance in Sport and Other Domains   24
   Kate F. Hays
3. Sport and Performance Psychology: Ethical Issues   46
   Douglas M. Hankes
4. The Role of Superior Performance Intelligence in Sustained Success   62
   Graham Jones
5. Performance Psychology in the Performing Arts   81
   Sanna M. Nordin-Bates

Part Two   •   Individual Psychological Processes in Performance

6. Concentration: Attention and Performance   117
   Aidan Moran
7. Conscious and Unconscious Awareness in Learning and Performance   131
   Rich Masters
8. Emotion Regulation and Performance   154
   Marc V. Jones
9. Anxiety: Attention, the Brain, the Body, and Performance   173
   Mark R. Wilson
10. Cognitions: Self-Talk and Performance   191
    Yannis Theodorakis, Antonis Hatzigeorgiadis, and Nikos Zourbanos
11. The Role of Imagery in Performance   213
    Jennifer Cumming and Sarah E. Williams
12. Motivation: Self-Determination Theory and Performance in Sport   233
    Martyn Standage
13. Modeling and Performance   250
    Penny McCullagh, Barbi Law, and Diane Ste-Marie
14. Efficacy Beliefs and Human Performance: From Independent Action
    to Interpersonal Functioning   273
    Mark R. Beauchamp, Ben Jackson, and Katie L. Morton
15. Perfectionism and Performance   294
    Joachim Stoeber

Part Three • Social Psychological Processes in Performance

16. Teamwork and Performance 309
    Albert V. Carron, Luc J. Martin, and Todd M. Loughead
17. Leadership and Manifestations of Sport 328
    Packianathan Chelladurai
18. The Psychology of Coaching 343
    Daniel Gould and E. Missy Wright
19. Moral Behavior in Sport 364
    Maria Kavussanu
20. Gender, Identity, and Sport 384
    Emily A. Roper
21. Relationships and Sport and Performance 400
    Sam Carr
22. Culture/Ethnicity and Performance 418
    Anthony P. Kontos

Part Four • Human Development and Performance

23. A Developmental Approach to Sport Expertise 435
    Jean Côté and Bruce Abernethy
24. Training for Life: Optimizing Positive Youth Development through Sport and Physical Activity 448
    Maureen R. Weiss, Lindsay E. Kipp, and Nicole D. Bolter
25. Talent Development: The Role of the Family 476
    Chris G. Harwood, Julie P. Douglas, and Antoinette M. Minniti
26. Expert Masters Sport Performers: Perspectives on Age-Related Processes, Skill Retention Mechanisms, and Motives 493
    Bradley W. Young and Nikola Medic
27. Transitions: Ending Active Involvement in Sports and Other Competitive Endeavors 513
    Albert J. Petitpas, Taunya Marie Tinsley, and Amy S. Walker

Part Five • Interventions in Sport and Performance Psychology

28. Counseling Performers in Distress 527
    Zella E. Moore
29. Appearance- and Performance-Enhancing Drug Use 545
    Thomas B. Hildebrandt, Eleanna Varangis, and Justine K. Lai
30. Burnout: A Darker Side to Performance 562
    Kate I. Goodger and Martin I. Jones
31. The Body and Performance 581
    William B. Strean and Joseph P. Mills
32. Injury and Performance 593
    John Heil and Leslie Podlog
33. Pain and Performance 618
    John Heil and Leslie Podlog

34. Eating Disorders in Sport   635
    Trent A. Petrie and Christy Greenleaf
35. Physical Activity Interventions   660
    Stuart J. H. Biddle and Trish Gorely
36. The Role of the Sport and Performance Psychologist with the
    Coach and Team: Implications for Performance Counseling   676
    Christopher M. Carr
37. The Performance Coach   692
    Dave Collins and Sara Kamin
38. Optimal Performance: Elite Level Performance in "The Zone"   707
    Robert J. Harmison and Kathleen V. Casto
39. Supervision and Mindfulness in Sport and Performance Psychology   725
    Mark B. Andersen

Part Six   •   Future Directions
40. Sport and Performance Psychology: A Look Ahead   741
    Kirsten Peterson, Charles Brown, Sean McCann, and Shane M. Murphy

Index   755

PREFACE

From 2009 to 2011, my scholarly life [SM] has revolved around editing this volume, *The Oxford Handbook of Sport and Performance Psychology*. It has been a very exciting time. From the beginning, the Handbook was built on the principle of examining the broad spectrum of research and practice on the psychology of excellent performance, in sport and in many other domains. To my knowledge, this is the first volume to attempt such an enterprise, and I owe my contributing authors an enormous debt of gratitude for tackling this project with such enthusiasm, perseverance and, yes, excellence. I am sure they began to tire of my hands-on approach as I questioned, probed, and pushed them to address the broadest possible range of performance psychology issues. They answered the challenge magnificently, and my excitement grew as I read each new chapter and realized the great depth and scope of the research being presented. There are so many chapters in this Handbook that are truly groundbreaking, bringing together knowledge from a variety of domains and sources and looking at the question of the psychology of excellent performance in innovative ways. I am confident that you will experience this tangible sense of excitement as you read the chapters of the Handbook.

As I look back over the past two decades of work in sport and performance psychology, it is interesting to note the gradual focusing of attention on performance issues. As the field has matured, there has been a surge of interest in the psychological factors that influence performance and enable high levels of performance to occur. As a result, there has been much debate over the essence of the field and appropriate areas of emphasis. Where once an interest in sport and physical activity chiefly defined the field, a movement has been under way to instead define sport and performance psychology as primarily reflecting interest in issues of performance, in sport and other domains. This trend can clearly be seen in several recent developments. For example, within the Oxford Library of Psychology, a separate volume is being published under the editorship of my colleague Ed Acevedo, *The Oxford Handbook of Exercise Psychology*. Publishing separate volumes on exercise and on sport and performance reflects the reality that research in these fields has focused on different issues and that there has been such a great amount of research in both areas that trying to combine them would do a disservice to both. Another example is the appearance of the new *Journal of Sport, Exercise and Performance Psychology*, due to begin publication by the American Psychological Association in 2012, under the editorship of Jeffrey Martin. This is the first academic journal to use the title "performance psychology," and although it includes all three interest areas, it acknowledges that: "The third and unique branch of *Sport, Exercise and Performance Psychology* reflects the growing interest in performance with strong physical elements by individuals who cannot be viewed as either athletes or exercisers" (Martin, 2011, p. 1).

In researching the debate on the appropriate focus for our field, I find it fascinating that I first addressed this issue in print 16 years ago, when I edited *Sport Psychology Interventions* (Murphy, 1995) for Human Kinetics Publishers. In my introductory chapter to that volume, I discussed proposals that practitioners move away from defining themselves as "sport psychologists" and establish a separate field of "performance enhancement." I concluded that there was little to be gained from such an approach and much to be lost. My summary of the argument is still convincing to my modern self:

> It seems unwise to deny the historical and theoretical roots of such [performance enhancement] approaches. The danger of "reinventing the wheel" is apparent. As this book illustrates, there

is much more to be gained from recognizing the intellectual roots of the field and drawing on them in fresh and creative ways. The variety of intervention models described in this book is a testament to the vibrancy of the field of psychology and to the opportunities for incorporating a variety of approaches into the applied practice of sport psychology.
(p. 11)

It seems clear that the resolution of this issue, established in the following years, has indeed been to reject dividing sport psychology and performance psychology into separate fields, and instead a consensus has emerged among researchers and practitioners that the best approach is to regard sport and performance as complementary foci of attention. Thus, the term "sport and performance psychology" has gained widespread acceptance. For those readers who wish to consider these issues in greater depth, many excellent discussions are contained in this volume. I especially recommend the wonderful overview chapter by Kate Hays, and the critical analysis offered by Dave Collins and Sara Kamin in *The Performance Coach* chapter.

I believe we still have work to do in bringing clarity to these issues. One issue I encourage researchers and practitioners to consider is the question of the primacy of performance as a focus of both research and intervention. There are those who argue that a focus on improving performance is the defining feature of sport and performance psychology (Newburg, 1992), those who see performance as just one possible focus of intervention (along with others such as health or happiness, c.f., Whelan, Meyers, & Donovan, 1995), and those who see a focus on performance as a dead end for the field, one that distracts us from helping the whole person (Andersen, 2009). Having spent much of the past 2 years considering this issue, I believe that there may be more agreement among these competing viewpoints than is recognized. Simply put, I think that a focus on performance *is* the central focus of sport and performance psychology, but that there is no reason to think that such a focus is antithetical to a consideration of the needs of the individual in the context of his or her entire life. Sport and performance psychology has evolved toward a holistic approach that considers the life of the whole person while nonetheless maintaining the central focus on performance itself. There are no life issues than cannot potentially impact performance for good or ill, and therefore there are no issues that are out of bounds for consideration by the effective sport and performance psychology practitioner. For example, important issues such as injury, an eating disorder, a troubled family relationship, or a deleterious tendency toward perfectionism (all of which are covered in chapters in this Handbook) may all interfere with an athlete's or performing artist's performance. Thus, the skilled sport and performance psychology practitioner will identify the key issues and intervene appropriately in each such situation. In some cases, this may result in a referral out or bringing a colleague into the consultation. In some cases, the resulting interventions may include some or many aspects of traditional psychotherapy. Yet, I would maintain that performance issues can remain the focus of intervention. There are many intervention approaches and strategies that the skilled performance consultant can utilize to effect change—but it is not the techniques and strategies that define performance psychology. I have seen the argument that consultations can move from a performance focus to a clinical focus and back again, and that such moves are reflected in changes from using psychological skills training (PST) to doing psychotherapy, but I reject this argument. Psychological skills training is simply a collection of intervention techniques, not a framework for consultation. If issues (e.g., alcoholism, obsessive-compulsive disorder, marital distress) arise that interfere with performance, they must be dealt with, and psychotherapy may be the best technique to employ to improve performance. Thus, it is not a matter of moving from a focus on performance to a focus on health or vice versa, but a matter of moving between different techniques in the pursuit of improved performance.

We believe there are strong theoretical and historical justifications for this approach. From the beginning, history's great thinkers have always considered worldly performance as an important part of a complete human life; it is difficult to find a great thinker who has scorned performance. Even the Eastern traditions, often regarded as antithetical to achievement and worldly striving, offer support for one who believes in the importance of human performance. Siddhartha Guatama, the Buddha, who is widely misperceived in the West as advocating a recluse's detachment from worldly things, joyfully propounded the central importance of human performance. Right Effort, the energetic will to perform rightly in the world, is one of the spokes of the central Eightfold Path. Further, the Buddha maintained that one of the four keys to a layperson's happiness in life is excellent accomplishment born of persistent effort—that by "whatsoever activity a householder earns his living [...] at that he becomes skillful [...and knows and performs] the proper ways and means." Not even the Buddha, then, who said that all attachment and desire is *dukkha* [suffering] and should be eliminated (which seems so shocking to anyone with the Western "thirst to win" mentality) was opposed to the study and improvement of human performance (Rahula, 1974).

The great scholar Confucius, whose ideals have shaped world history in inestimable ways, was not a particular fan of athletic performance, castigating in his Analects two Chinese princes who focused their efforts on the disciplines of archery and rowing, respectively (Confucius, 1995). Yet, although he disdained sport, Confucius considered human performance so important that he flatly decreed that "if a man has reached forty or fifty without being heard of [acquired a good reputation through his performance in proper duties], he, indeed, is incapable of commanding respect!"

If we look to the Western philosophical traditions, it is even harder to find a great thinker who would say that human performance is not of central importance. Perhaps the closest we can come are the Greco-Roman philosophers of the Stoic school, famous for their assertion that virtue alone is sufficient for happiness and that all worldly goods, honors, and accolades are unnecessary. But even among the Stoics, the absolute importance of hard-won exceptional performance was accepted. Epictetus, the liberated slave whose handbook is one of the most widely read reviews of Stoic philosophy, tells us that we must not only engage in but succeed in what we turn our efforts toward in this world, for it is "impious for a man to withdraw himself from being useful to those who have need of our services." The key, Epictetus asserts, is that we must execute our performances mindfully, as he makes clear when he says, "A man wishes to conquer at the Olympic Games. I also wish indeed, for it is a fine thing. But observe both the things which come first, and the things which follow; and then begin to act." In fact, Epictetus the Stoic delivers one of the most remarkable defenses of hard-won, true-grit performance in the history of early Western thought. Epictetus tells us that we must pursue our loftiest, most difficulty won ideals "as if they were laws, as if you would be guilty of impiety if you transgressed any of them." He then goes on to tell his reader that:

> You are no longer a youth, but already a full grown man. If then you are negligent and slothful, and are continually making procrastination after procrastination, and proposal after proposal, and fixing day after day, after which you will attend to yourself, you will not know that you are not making improvement, but you will continue ignorant both while you live and till you die. Immediately then think it right to live as a full-grown man, and one who is making proficiency, and let every thing which appears to you to be the best be to you a law which must not be transgressed. And if anything laborious, or pleasant or glorious or inglorious be presented to you, remember that now is the contest, now are the Olympic Games, and they cannot be deferred; and that it depends on one defeat and one giving way that progress is either lost or maintained. (*Epictetus*, 2004, p. 21)

If we can find such a rousing defense of the importance of performance in the writings of Epictetus, how much more support can a proponent of performance find in the writings of Aristotle? Aristotle indisputably places the centrality of performing well in all the activities of our lives at the very center of his philosophy. Action and performance is key to the

Aristotelian worldview; "activities are, as we have said, what really matters in life," Aristotle writes in his *Nicomachean Ethics*, and Aristotle means not only activities, but excellently performed activities. Aristotle is willing to say that "without qualification, in the same way in every case" the only path to goodness for a man is to excel in performance. He explains, "for the characteristic activity of the lyre-player is to play the lyre, and that [the characteristic activity] of the good lyre-player to play it well." For Aristotle, mere possession of superior skills is an irrelevant distinction; one must perform well in the world to win happiness. Echoing our quote of Epictetus, Aristotle writes that, "As in the Olympic Games it is not the most attractive and the strongest who are crowned, but those who compete (since it is from this group that winners come), so in life it is those who act rightly who will attain what is noble and good" (Aristotle, 1962).

The Greco-Roman philosophical tradition has strongly influenced European and American psychology, and the Aristotelian concept of doing well and living well (*eudaimonia*, sometimes translated as human "flourishing") as the goal of life permeates many psychological theories. Abraham Maslow placed the esteem needs, such as achievement, on the second highest rung of his hierarchy of needs, below only that of self-actualization. In recent times, the positive psychology movement has re-emphasized the centrality of achievement and success within psychology: "[Positive psychology] provides a means of looking at the people in organizations that is grounded in the strengths that enable those people to succeed in what they do, the well-being that they achieve through doing so, and the meaning and fulfilment that gives coherence and direction to their activities along the way" (Linley, Harrington, & Garcea, 2010, p. xxiii).

But perhaps the simplest argument we can propose is that human performance is still the essential feature that determines the success of our society. Our performance as individuals, families, organizations, communities, and as a nation will determine our success in dealing with the most important issues of our day, such as social justice, global warming, the fossil fuel crisis, the health threat of pollution, and developing a sustainable approach to resource and ecosystem management. It is not hyperbole to suggest that our success or failure in tackling these challenges will determine the future of our culture and, perhaps, our very existence as a species.

The organization of this Handbook is, I hope, simple and straightforward. Part one, The Nature and Scope of Sport and Performance Psychology, contains the most general overview chapters, addressing the wide range of performance psychology issues being studied today. Alan Kornspan provides an interesting overview of the historical development of the field; Kate Hays has written the foundational chapter of the Handbook, incisively delineating the nature and scope of sport and performance psychology; Doug Hankes contributes an immensely practical guide to the many ethical issues that arise from practice in our field; the chapter from Graham Jones is unique, an original piece of research examining the proposed concept of Superior Performance Intelligence as an explanatory and unifying concept in performance psychology; and the final chapter in this section is a wonderful contribution to the field, Sanna Nordin-Bates' truly comprehensive review of the psychological literature on performance psychology in the performing arts.

Part two of the Handbook deals with Individual Psychological Processes in Performance. It includes chapters on most of the individual difference variables that have been widely studied for their relationship with performance. Aidan Moran's chapter on concentration is typically thoughtful and complete; Rich Masters provides a fascinating and provocative chapter studying the role of awareness in consciousness and performance; Marc Jones contributes a concise and up-to-the-minute report on the role of emotional control in performance; Mark Wilson tackles the issue of anxiety by examining its role in attentional processes; Yannis Theodorakis, Antonis Hatzigeorgiadis, and Nikos Zourbanos give us a splendid overview of the research on the concept of self-talk; Jennifer Cumming and Sarah E. Williams have written a timely review of the role of imagery in performance, utilizing the latest research from cognitive neuroscience to bring together the many research strands in this area; the meta-theory of self-determination theory (SDT) provides the unifying framework for Martyn Standage's excellent critique of current research and practice in motivation; Penny McCullagh, Barbi Law, and Diane Ste-Marie have contributed an important chapter on the too-often understudied topic of modeling and performance; Mark R. Beauchamp, Ben Jackson, and Katie L. Morton provide an informative synthesis of the research on self-efficacy and performance; and Joachim Stoeber concludes this section with his own research and that of many others on the role that perfectionism plays in excellent performance.

Part three of the Handbook addresses Social Psychological Processes in Performance, covering those topics that deal with performance in groups, teams, relationships, and even cultures. Albert V. Carron, Luc Martin, and Todd Loughead lead off this section with a definitive chapter on the issue of teamwork; Packianathan Chelladurai provides a fresh look at the issue of leadership with his chapter; Dan Gould and E. Missy Wright have written an extensive and eminently accessible chapter on the psychology of coaching; Maria Kavussanu brings clarity to the very important issues of moral behavior in sport; Emily Roper makes a superb contribution, bringing together scholarship from a wide variety of sources in her chapter on gender, identity, and sport; Sam Carr provides a much-needed examination of the role of relationships in performance, offering several fascinating approaches to this area, including attachment theory, transference, and actor–partner models; and Anthony Kontos concludes this section by discussing the many significant issues raised when a cultural/ethnic perspective is taken toward performance.

Part four of the Handbook, Human Development and Performance, looks at human performance from a developmental perspective, considering such topics as expertise, talent development, and training throughout the lifespan. Jean Côté and Bruce Abernethy provide their usual masterful review of the varied literature on sport expertise; Maureen Weiss, Lindsay Kipp, and Nicole Bolter give us a thoughtful, well-supported chapter on positive youth development via the pathways of sport and physical activity; Chris Harwood, Julie Douglas, and Antoinette Minniti provide a thorough and thought-provoking examination of the role of the family in talent development across performance domains; Bradley Young and Nikola Medic review a sometimes-neglected literature on expert master-level athletes and provide a clear pathway for future researchers to follow; and Albert Petitpas, Taunya Tinsley, and Amy Walker give us a thoughtful reflection on the issue of career transitions in sports and other competitive endeavors.

Part five of the Handbook addresses Interventions in Sport and Performance Psychology. Too often, review handbooks of this type offer up the same predictable menu of intervention chapters. This Handbook instead offers a wide-ranging set of chapters that deal with the real issues faced by consultants who work in high-performance fields in sports, the arts, and business. Each author is not only a recognized leader in his or her field, but has also faced the hands-on issues engendered by working in his or her field of expertise. Zella Moore bats lead-off in this section and delivers a hit, a concise and lucid roadmap to counseling performers in distress, containing a practical dimensional classification system for performers; Thomas Hildebrandt, Eleanna Varangis, and Justine Lai next provide a compelling account of appearance- and performance-enhancing drug use in sport, describing a research base that many psychologists are unfamiliar with; Kate Goodger and Martin Jones examine the issue of burnout in sport and performance, highlighting key areas in which new applied research is desperately needed; Billy Strean and Joe Mills contribute a groundbreaking chapter that steps outside the prevailing zeitgeist to examine the phenomenology of the body in physical activity and suggests how adopting this perspective offers a pathway to better health and happiness; next comes two chapters authored by John Heil and Leslie Podlog—the first is a comprehensive overview of the psychological issues of injury and performance, while the second is another innovative and groundbreaking chapter, one of the first ever to deal with the psychology of pain and performance; Trent Petrie and Christy Greenleaf next contribute a sensitive and practical chapter dealing with eating disorders in sport; Stuart Biddle and Trish Gorely review the research on behavior change in physical activity in a terrific chapter that bridges the gap between exercise and sport psychology; Chris Carr has written a very practical, systems theory–based guide to organizational consulting with high-performance teams, utilizing his extensive experience in this area; Dave Collins and Sara Kamin took on one of the toughest assignments in the Handbook, discussing the objectives, knowledge base, and best practices for "performance coaches"; Bob Harmison and Kathleen Casto do a great job describing the extensive research on optimal performance; and Mark Andersen concludes this section in his inimitable style, exploring supervision issues in sport and performance psychology from a mindfulness perspective.

The final section of the Handbook, Part six, Future Directions, includes only one chapter, but it is a special surprise. Three of the most experienced sport and performance psychologists in the world, Kirsten Peterson, Charles Brown, and Sean McCann, gamely agreed to peek into the crystal ball and provide a look at the future of sport and performance psychology. Their answers to the questions I posed yield some of the most thought-provoking discussions in the entire Handbook.

Finally, a very big thank you to all who made this Handbook possible. Peter Nathan, the Editor-in-Chief of the Oxford Psychology Library, has my gratitude for asking me to guide such an ambitious project. All the staff at Oxford have been wonderfully supportive during this long and tiring process; I wish to thank Mariclaire Cloutier, who provided invaluable feedback during the planning process, and especially my editor-extraordinaire, Chad Zimmerman, without whose quiet encouragement and dry wit I might not have survived this experience. My colleagues at Western Connecticut State University have been understanding and encouraging throughout, and granting me a sabbatical for a semester was a godsend. And, of course, my wonderful family: my caring wife Annemarie, the best psychologist I know; my son Bryan, who co-wrote this Preface; and my wonderful daughter Theresa, the best scientist in the family. I love you very much.

Shane M. Murphy
Bryan P. Murphy
Danbury, Connecticut
November 2011

References

Andersen, M. (2009). Performance enhancement as a bad start and a dead end: A parenthetical comment on Mellalieu and Lane. *The Sport and Exercise Scientist*, *20* (June), 12–14, British Association of Sport and Exercise Sciences.

Aristotle. (1962). *Nicomachean ethics*. Translated by Martin Ostwald. Indianapolis, IN: The Bobbs-Merrill Company.

Confucius. (1995). *The Analects*. Translated by William Soothill. New York: Dover Publications.

Epictetus. (2004). *Enchiridion*. Translated by George Long. Minneola, NY: Dover Publications.

Linley, P. A., Harrington, S., & Garcea, N. (2010). Preface. *Oxford handbook of positive psychology and work*. New York: Oxford University Press.

Martin, J. (2011). Welcome. *Sport, Exercise and Performance Psychology*. *1*(Suppl), 1–2.

Murphy, S. M. (1995). Introduction to sport psychology interventions. In S. M. Murphy (Ed.), *Sport psychology interventions* (pp. 1–15). Champaign, IL: Human Kinetics.

Newburg, D. (1992). Performance enhancement: Toward a working definition. *Contemporary Thought on Performance Enhancement*, *1*, 10–25.

Rahula, W. (1974). *What the Buddha taught* (2nd edition). New York: Grove Press.

Whelan, J. P., Meyers, A. W., & Donovan, C. (1995). Competitive recreational athletes: A multisystemic model. In S. M. Murphy (Ed.), *Sport psychology interventions* (pp. 71–116). Champaign, IL: Human Kinetics.

PART 1

The Nature and Scope of Sport and Performance Psychology

History of Sport and Performance Psychology

Alan S. Kornspan

Abstract

This chapter presents an overview of the history of sport and performance psychology. First, the chapter will highlight the beginnings of sport psychology in the 1890s, when psychology was first applied to sport in laboratory settings. The applications of the "new psychology" applied to sport and the first sport psychology congress held in Lausanne, Switzerland, in 1913, are described. The chapter describes how psychologists began testing athletes in psychology laboratories using experimental psychology methods during 1920–1940. The development of sport psychology laboratories worldwide and the work of Coleman Griffith are highlighted. Next, the chapter explains the beginnings of the use of psychology for performance enhancement purposes between 1940 and 1965. The growth of sport psychology literature during this time is discussed. The chapter then focuses on sport and performance psychology from 1965 to 1980, including the development of sport psychology organizations. The chapter concludes by providing an overview of sport and performance psychology from 1980 to today. The modern period is characterized by an increasing application of sport and performance psychology knowledge across a variety of performance domains.

Key Words: History, sport psychology, time periods, application, historical development

Researchers in the fields of sport psychology and the history of psychology are increasingly interested in the historical development of sport and performance psychology (Green & Benjamin, 2009). Work on the historical development of the field of sport psychology has been published since at least the late 1970s (Feige, 1977), but recent analyses have provided a more thorough understanding of the development of the field.

Recent literature in the history of sport psychology has discussed the development of sport psychology from 1890 to1965, focusing on the development of the profession of sport psychology during this time. Although the field of sport psychology compromises various areas, including exercise, health, and participation and motivation, the focus of this chapter is on the historical aspects of using psychology and mental skills training to help enhance athletic performance. First, a historical overview of the development of sport psychology from 1890 to 1920 will be detailed. This will be followed by information about how psychological testing began to be used by psychologists and coaches between 1920 and 1940, and this section also presents an overview of the laboratories developed specifically for sport psychology research. The third section, focused on 1940–1965, provides a discussion of the development and use of psychology and mental skills training to help athletes enhance performance. Historical developments that occurred in the field of sport and performance psychology from 1965 to 1980 are discussed, and the chapter concludes by providing an overview of the development of sport and performance psychology between 1980 and 1989, and from 1990 to the present.

The New Psychology: Sport and Performance Psychology from 1890 to 1920

Few details about sport and exercise psychology between 1890 and 1920 appeared in the literature until now, when recently published literature has provided a more detailed understanding of this period (e.g., Bäumler, 2009). For example, influential physical educators and psychologists began to teach psychology as part of the training of physical directors; William James, author of the 1892 *Principles of Psychology* taught a psychology course to students in the physical training program at Harvard (Kornspan, 2007a). Additionally, in 1891, Luther Gulick, the director of the YMCA training school in Springfield, Massachusetts, began teaching a new seminar in psychology for students studying to be physical training directors (Naismith, 1941). This first psychology seminar included James Naismith and legendary football coach Amos Alonzo Stagg.

During this seminar, Gulick challenged the physical directors he was training to create a sport or game that would be interesting, fun, and could be played inside during the winter; James Naismith rose to the challenge and presented his ideas for a new indoor sport. Months later, Gulick assigned Naismith the task of developing this new game by stating, "Naismith, now would be a good time for you to work on that new game that you said could be invented" (Naismith, 1941, p. 37). Thus, it was during the psychology seminar of 1891 that Naismith originally was influenced to develop the new game of basketball. Additionally, it appears that Naismith was so influenced by the field of psychology that he gave a commencement address at the YMCA Training School, in 1891, titled the "Psychology of Exercise," and he taught a psychology course in the YMCA training school after graduation (Slayer, 2009).

In addition to Gulick, James, and Naismith teaching psychology courses in physical director training schools during this period, E. W. Scripture became interested in the applications of psychology to daily life (Scripture, 1895). Scripture referred to this area of the field as the "New Psychology." Historically, psychology was at a crossroads: some individuals believed that psychology should be based on philosophical thought, whereas others, such as Scripture, believed that psychology should be based in scientific evidence gained from studies conducted in the laboratory (Kornspan, 2007a). Scripture brought attention to these ideas in his 1895 text, *The New Psychology*, which provided examples of how psychology could improve life in a variety of different

ways (Fuchs, 1998) using examples of his work and the research that he conducted in the psychology laboratory. One example of his research included an experiment on the reaction time of fencers, conducted in December 1893. Interestingly, at about the same time, at Harvard University, G. W. Fitz was also studying the reaction time of athletes (Kornspan, 2007a).

In perhaps one of the first experiments conducted studying sport in a psychology laboratory, Scripture designed an experiment to determine if there were differences between expert and novice fencers (Scripture, 1894a). It is noteworthy that Scripture's work was conducted with W. G. Anderson; Anderson was an influential physical educator and the founding president of the Association for the Advancement of Physical Education, in 1885 (Kornspan, 2007a). In addition to the sport of fencing, Scripture also studied runners and boxers in the Yale psychology laboratory during the 1890s (Scripture, 1894b).

Clearly, from Scripture's writings, he believed that psychology could have an influence on sport performance. He also believed that his work could influence physical educators to investigate and apply psychological findings to the field of sport and physical training (Kornspan, 2007a). Apparently, Scripture also had the opportunity to influence physical educators through the teaching of psychology, since he was part of the faculty of the Anderson Normal School for Gymnastics (Anderson School of Gymnastics, 1896). Additionally, as a professor of psychology at Yale University, Scripture taught the course "Psychology (Elementary Laboratory Course)," which was specifically recommended to students who had an interest in the psychology of exercise or physical training (Yale University, 1898/1899). For an in-depth description of Scripture's work at the Yale psychology laboratory, see Kornspan (2007a) and Goodwin (2009).

In addition to recent literature discussing the work of E. W. Scripture and the "new psychology" as applied to sport, recent researchers have written about the work of Norman Triplett (e.g., Davis, Huss, & Becker, 2009; Strube, 2005; Stroebe, 2012; Vaughan & Guerin, 1997), who published an experimental investigation related to the psychology of sport and social psychology (Triplett, 1898). This study, often referred to as the first experimental study in sport psychology, has been considered by some as the birth of the social psychology discipline (Brehm, Kassin, & Fein, 1999). Triplett's (1898) study was a part of his master's degree thesis at Indiana University (Strube, 2005) and was completed under the direction of professors W. L. Bryan and J. A. Bergstrom (Triplett, 1898). Triplett was interested in studying the performance of cyclists: He wanted to know if cyclists were more likely to cycle faster if they were riding against a competitor, if they were paced, or if they were riding alone. Interestingly, one of the first Europeans to study the psychology of sport during the same period, Phillipe Tissie, was also studying the psychological aspects of cycling (Bäumler, 2009).

Researchers have recently reanalyzed the results of the Triplett (1898) study (Strube, 2005). Strube has suggested that, based on the results of Triplett's study, there was very little evidence to suggest that social facilitation existed based on his (2005) reanalysis of statistical data using contemporary statistical methods. Fascinatingly, Triplett's study of cyclists would not be the only study of athletics and games completed in the psychology department at Indiana University during this period. Claude E. Price completed a master's degree thesis titled, "The relation of athletics to scholarship at Indiana University: A statistical study." Additionally, Robert E. Newland completed a master's degree thesis titled, "The psychology of a game—Checkers" (Indiana University, 1905; Hearst & Capshew, 1988).

Recent sport psychology literature has also begun to discuss one of the first sport psychology events to be organized by the International Olympic Committee, the International Congress of the Psychology and Physiology of Sport (Bäumler, 2009; Kornspan, 2007b; Kornspan, 2009b; Silva, 2002). This event was developed through the efforts of the founder of the modern Olympic Games, Pierre de Coubertin, who organized the modern Games in the early 1890s. He believed that the Olympic Games should include an educational component and not be simply focused on watching and participating in sports (Kornspan, 2007b). Thus, he developed educational congresses to be part of the Olympic Games. The first congress to have a psychological component was held in Le Havre, France, in 1897. A part of the congress held in Le Havre focused on the "Psychology of Exercise" (Kornspan, 2007b).

A comparison of the works by Scripture and Coubertin shows that, whereas Scripture was very interested in bringing psychology into the laboratory and taking scientific measurements in order to make data-based recommendations, Coubertin viewed psychology from a philosophical point of view. This would be a significant distinction as Coubertin developed and planned the International Congress of the Psychology and Physiology of Sport.

Throughout the early 1900s, Coubertin wrote philosophical essays related to the psychology of sport, and a collection of these articles would later be published as a book, *Essais de psychologie sportive*, in 1913 (Coubertin, 1913). These essays were mainly developed and published in the *Olympic Review* to help individuals consider the psychology of sport as a lead-up to the International Congress of the Psychology and Physiology of Sports. A review of this book appeared in the *American Physical Education Review* (Meylan, 1917).

Coubertin described the sports psychology congress in his *Olympic Memoirs*. He organized the congress because he believed that the medical profession had been too focused on the physiology of sports, and he wanted to see the medical profession focus additionally on psychology related to sport. Coubertin presented the idea to develop a sport psychology congress in 1909 (Coubertin, 1936/1979), and he received permission to hold the congress in 1911, at the Budapest meetings. After receiving permission to assemble the congress, Coubertin focused on convincing the medical profession of its importance (Coubertin, 1936/1979).

The International Congress of the Psychology and Physiology of Sport, or what Coubertin has referred to in his Olympic memoirs as the *Sports Psychology Congress*, took place from May 8 to May 10, 1913 (Kornspan, 2007b). Approximately 400 individuals from throughout the world attended the congress. Many of the reports were related to philosophical or introspective psychology. For example, presentations were provided by elite athletes who discussed what they were thinking during high-level performance. Paul Rousseau, a famous cyclist, discussed how positive thoughts could help him overcome fatigue while performing. In addition to these introspective reports, a presentation was provided by Jean Phillipe (Kornspan, 2007b), who called for the psychology of sport to be studied in psychological laboratories. Although many of the presentations focused on the mental aspects of sports, a main critique of the congress by those in attendance was related to insufficient scientific evidence presented to support the statements made. Despite the critics, Coubertin would later refer to this event as "the birth of the psychology of sport" (Müller, 1997, p. 54).

As recent literature in the history of sport psychology demonstrates, the works of E. W. Scripture, Pierre de Coubertin, and Norman Triplett are an important part of the early history of the field. An additional important aspect of this period is the interest psychologists showed in the area of sport, physical activity, and human performance. Wilhelm Wundt, who is considered the father of modern experimental psychology, was the major professor for 16 American doctoral students who went on to work as professors of psychology in the United States (Benjamin, Durkin, Link, Vestal, & Acord, 1992). Eight of the 16 American psychologists whom Wundt trained would go on to either conduct research in physical training/athletics or write or work in the field of athletics. These psychologists included Frank Angell (who became an athletic director at Stanford University), James Cattell, Lightner Witmer, Charles Judd, Edward A. Pace, Walter Dill Scott, E. W. Scripture, and Harry Kirke Wolfe.

James McKeen Cattell conducted a study of how individuals practiced running 3 miles (Fuchs, 1998). E. W. Scripture, along with writing various books and conducting studies related to sport and physical activity, was an active presenter at American Physical Education Association conferences. An abstract of his presentation, "The Psychological Aspects of Physical Education" was published in the *American Physical Education Review* in 1901 (Scripture, 1901). Lightner Witmer, the founder of the first psychology clinic and the first individual to use the term "clinical psychology" (Watson, 1956), presented a paper at the National Education Association conference and at the Philadelphia Physical Education Society in 1898 titled, "The Mental Factor in Physical Training" (Kuhn, 1898; Stoneroad, 1898). Witmer also published an experimental study of his work titled "The Special Class for Backward Children." A main part of this study was to observe how physical training and exercise affected those children who participated in the study (Witmer, 1911).

Additionally, Edward A. Pace was part of the gymnasium committee at Catholic University ("Report of the Temporary Committee on the Gymnasium," Catholic University Bulletin volumes 21–23). Walter Dill Scott completed laboratory studies of athletes (Scott, 1917); Scott was interested in whether coaching could improve the performance of athletes. Harry Kirke Wolfe had an interest in athletics because he served on the faculty athletics committee helping to oversee athletics at the University of Nebraska. Additionally, Wolfe may have been one of the first to propose the creation of a laboratory specifically to study the psychology of football (Brannon, 1913).

It also should be noted that early psychologists were actively involved in committee membership for the American Physical Education Association during this time. The Committee of Nineteen (originally the Committee of Fifteen) was formed by the Advancement of the American Physical Education Association in 1899. The purpose of this committee was to focus on helping elementary, secondary, and higher education institutions understand the important role of physical training in education (American Physical Education Association, 1900). Psychologists who were a part of the Committee of Nineteen included G. Stanley Hall, Joseph Jastrow, E. W. Scripture, James M. Cattell, and William James.

In summary, the early years of sport psychology saw psychologists and physical educators becoming interested in applying psychology to physical training and sport. From the beginning of the experimental study of psychology, psychologists and physical educators collaborated to determine how psychology could be applied to sport and physical education. It is noteworthy that many individuals trained directly by Wilhelm Wundt had an interest in writing about, researching, or working in sport-related jobs. It should be noted that other areas of performance psychology also began to be studied and written about during this period (e.g., Carl E. Seashore's study of the psychology of music [Seashore, 1919]; Walter Dill Scott's application of psychology to business [Scott, 1917]).

As this period progressed, suggestions were made to create laboratories to study the psychology of football and to study athletes directly in psychology laboratories. The next phase of the development of the field of sport psychology saw the actual creation of laboratories specifically devoted to sport psychology.

1920–1940: Development of Sport Psychology Laboratories and Psychological Testing Applied to Sport

During the decades between 1920 and 1940, psychologists and physical educators began to study the psychological aspects of athletics utilizing experimental laboratory methods. Individuals with an interest in applying psychology focused on the use of psychological testing and measurement to identify highly skilled athletes. Thus, testing that took place at psychology laboratories involving athletes often focused on identifying those psychological attributes that helped athletes become successful (e.g., Fuchs, 1998).

There was a worldwide development of sport psychology laboratories in which athletes were tested during this time. In 1920, Robert Werner Schulte, a former student of Wilhelm Wundt, became the director of the sport psychology laboratory at the German High School for Physical Exercise in Charlottenburg, Germany (Bäumler, 2009; Seiler & Wylleman, 2009; Tenenbaum, Morris, & Hackfort, 2008). This laboratory tested athletes in order to analyze their psychological skills and various attributes (Bäumler, 2009). In addition to his research, Schulte began to provide lectures on sport psychology to students, and he also published *Body and Mind in Sport* in 1921 and *Aptitude and Performance Testing in Sport* in 1925 (Bäumler, 2009). Schulte's work was documented in the Grandenwitz (1923) *Scientific American* article, "Making Sport a Science" and in a 1922 article titled, "The Psychology of Sport" in the *Journal of the American Medical Association*.

In Russia, the first sport psychology department was developed by P. A. Rudik, in 1920, in Moscow, at the State Central Institute of Physical Culture (Rudik, 1962; Seiler & Wylleman, 2009). Bäumler (2009) reported that the type of research conducted by Rudik used experimental methods to test various aptitudes. Rudik conducted studies related to reaction times of runner, boxers, and wrestlers (Rudik, 1962), and he also investigated whether specific types of training could help athletes react more quickly. In explaining the type of work that he and his colleagues were conducting during this period, Rudik (1962, p. 557) stated, "Special attention of the psychologists in this period of the development of the psychology of sport was directed to the study of the psychological laws connected with the latent period of motor reactions." For a detailed description of the history of sport psychology in Russia, see Rodionov (2010).

In addition to the advent of sport psychology departments and laboratories in Germany and Russia, in Japan, in 1924, the National Institute of Physical Education was established by the ministry of Education in Tokyo (Fujita, 1987). A specific section of the institute was devoted to the study of psychology applied to sport and physical education (Fujita, 1987). Mitsuo Matsui, who had majored in aviation psychology at Tokyo University, was appointed director of the sport psychology section for the institute (Fujita, 1987). Matsui completed sport psychology research from 1924 until the beginning of World War II (Fujita, 1987).

In the United States, the first sport psychology laboratory opened in September 1925, at the University of Illinois (Kroll & Lewis, 1970). The laboratory was in existence from 1925 until 1932. Early reports of Coleman Griffith's work with the University of Illinois athletic department began in the fall of 1921, when it was reported that Coach Zuppke changed the colors of the school's football team uniforms from traditional blue to orange based on his consultations with Griffith (Eckersall, 1921). Griffith appears to have begun teaching a psychology of athletics class in the early 1920s. By 1922, a description of Griffith's course is provided in the University of Illinois *Bulletin* (University of Illinois, 1922). In March 1922, it was reported that Coleman Griffith had been added to the faculty advisory staff for the University of Illinois football team ("Psychologist to Aid Selection of Illini Athletes," 1922; "Psychology of Athletics Will be Tried," 1922). As part of the faculty advisory staff, Griffith hoped to aid coaches in selecting athletes for the team. Apparently, having Griffith as part of the advisory staff was effective: according to Brichford (2008, p. 48), "the Zuppke-Griffith collaboration contributed to the national championships the Illini won in 1923 and 1927."

Griffith viewed his research as important since it provided him with scientific evidence to teach his course, "Psychology and Athletics." It appears also that Griffith was very proud of his research work and of how it had influenced the teaching of sport psychology. In fact, Griffith stated: "When this course was first started, it was the only one of its kind; but other schools have seen the advantage of such a course and the idea has now spread to other parts of the country. Illinois still has, however, the only laboratory devoted exclusively to the study of psychological problems in athletic competition" (Griffith, 1928, p. 10). In addition to sport psychology classes being taught at the University of Illinois in the 1920s, the *Daily Illini* reported that courses related to the psychology of sport were being taught at the State University of Iowa and at Cornell University and that these universities were also using Griffith's book, the *Psychology of Coaching* ("Griffith to teach coaching course," 1926). Not only was Griffith's work influential in the United States, it appears that it was also influential worldwide. According to Lidor, Morris, Bardaxoglou, and Becker (2001), Herbert Niiler, an instructor at Tartu University in Estonia, was influenced by Griffith's work on various publications he produced about sport between 1930 and 1932. Griffith was also aware of the work in sport psychology being conducted worldwide. According to Kremer and Moran (2008), Griffith visited both

Schulte's and Sippel's sport psychology laboratories in Berlin, Germany.

Although systematic research in sport psychology appears to have begun in laboratories started in the 1920s in Germany, Russia, Japan, and the United States, historians of sport psychology have recently published detailed accounts of other laboratories and individuals conducting sport psychology research during this period. Fuchs provided an example of the testing of elite-level athletes at the Columbia University Laboratory (Fuchs, 2009), and he recounted the story of Babe Ruth, an elite athlete in the sport of baseball and playing for the New York Yankees, being tested in the Columbia University Psychology Laboratory. After a baseball game during the 1921 season, Hugh Fullerton (a well-known sportswriter) took Ruth to the Columbia University Psychology laboratory to be tested by psychologists Albert Johanson and Joseph Holmes (Fuchs, 2009). Ruth was tested on a variety of psychological tests that included tests of reaction time, intelligence, auditory speed, visual processing, the speed his swing, and perception. In most of the tests, the Babe scored well above average (Fullerton, 1921).

Another example of research studying the psychology of human sports performance was the work conducted by Walter Miles and John Lawther. Miles, a psychology professor at Stanford University, had a graduate student in the psychology department, B. C. Graves who was also a coach with the school's football team. Miles and Graves published two studies together during the early 1930s related to tests of the charging time of athletes on the Stanford football team, which was coached by Pop Warner (Baugh & Benjamin, 2009). Lawther, while coaching basketball and serving as the chair of the department of psychology at Westminster College, studied athletes' reaction times in his school's psychology laboratory during the early 1930s ("Big Athletes Alert," 1931).

Psychologists during the 1920s and 1930s were interested in providing psychological tests to athletes related to speed of movement, reaction time, vision, concentration, tapping, and physical strength. Additionally, some psychologists began to use inventories that measured psychological qualities such as the personality, intelligence, and aggression of athletes (Graef, Kornspan, & Baker, 2009). Paul Brown, in consultation with Ross Stagner and Robert Henderson, designed a battery of tests that Brown could utilize to gain more knowledge about his athletes (Graef et al., 2009). In addition to psychomotor tests, such as tests of reaction time, Brown tested various psychological variables including intelligence, aggression, personality, and character (Graef et al., 2009).

By the end of the 1930s, psychologists were consulting with coaches and providing psychological testing for athletes. A noteworthy example of consultation during this period is the work of Coleman Griffith and Jack Sterrett with the Chicago Cubs professional baseball team. For a detailed account of Griffith and Sterrett's work, see Green (2003; 2011).

An important aspect of the new psychology during this period was to create a scientific discipline of the field of sport psychology. Because this was such a significant aspect of this period, it is important to recognize the International Federation of Sports Medicine's defining the purpose of their organization in their first constitution in 1928. This organization proposed that one of its main purposes was "to inaugurate scientific research on biology, psychology, and sociology in relation to sports" (LaCava, 1956, pp. 1109–1110). Additionally, in 1928, Coubertin formed the International Bureau of Sport Pedagogy; one of the purposes of this association was to provide a sport-related organization that would welcome psychologists as members of the sport science team interested in the study of sport (Kornspan, 2007b).

As Benjamin and Baker (2003) pointed out, during the 1920s, the general public became more interested in consulting with psychologists. Businesses and families wanted the services of psychologists to help improve their situations. Donald Laird, director of the Colgate Psychology Laboratory, consulted with large corporations and businesses and promoted psychology to improve business (Laird, 1936).

Additionally, by 1939, the field of psychology in the United States was organizing psychologists to prepare for the possibility of psychology professionals being needed to assist the military during World War II (Benjamin & Baker, 2003). Consultation with the military would continue into the next decade as psychologists and physical educators contributed their knowledge to helping address military problems. For example, individual psychologists who contributed to the development of sport psychology also consulted with the military during World War II. Walter Miles investigated adaptation to darkness and found that a pilot who wore red goggles under normal light conditions was able to adapt to working in the dark immediately

(Goodwin, 2005). Also, Coleman Griffith served as the director for specialized training programs for military students attending the University of Illinois (Franch, 2007).

Psychology of Sport 1940–1965

In addition to recent sport psychology literature that has provided insight into the historical development of the field between 1890 and 1940, recent sport psychology research has provided more detail about how psychology was used with athletes between 1940 and 1965. In the 1940s and 1950s, psychologists and physical educators began to discuss ways that psychology could be applied specifically to work with athletes to help improve performance. During this period, individuals such as Dorothy Yates, Richard Paynter, and Bud Winter were involved in researching and applying psychology to sport to enhance athletic performance (Kornspan, 2009b). What is interesting about the literature from the 1940s is that individuals began to discuss their consultations with athletes in which they applied cognitive-behavioral methods. Additionally, professionals during this period, such as Anna Espenschade and Franklin Henry, suggested ways that mental practice and visualization could be helpful to athletes (Kornspan, 2009b).

Research into the history of sport psychology has begun to examine the application of psychology to sport during this period, including the work of Dorothy Yates with boxers at San Jose State College (Kornspan & MacCracken, 2001; Vealey, 2006), the work of David F. Tracy with the St. Louis Browns (Kornspan & MacCracken, 2003), the use of hypnosis with athletes during the 1950s and 1960s (Kornspan, 2009a), and the work of A. C. Puni in applying psychology to sport in Russia in the 1950s and 1960s (Ryba, Stambulova, & Wrisberg, 2005).

In the early 1940s, Dorothy Yates, a clinical psychologist at San Jose State College, became interested in applying psychology to athletics (Kornspan & MacCracken, 2001). Yates, who was a professor of clinical psychology at San Jose State College, was asked by an athlete on the boxing team to help him with the mental aspects of boxing. Thus, she began helping athletes by using a combination of progressive relaxation and positive affirmations (Yates, 1943). Riley (1943) wrote:

> Dr. Yates has applied psychological treatment to every man coming out for boxing. The team is undefeated this year…. All of the men on the team,

with the exception of one have had no previous experience, and yet all are fighting like veterans. (p. 95)

Dewitt Portal told his friend Bud Winter, the track and field coach at San Jose State College, about the work that Yates was conducting with the boxing team (Kornspan, 2009a). Winter had planned to have his athletes start to work with Yates, but enlisted in the Navy before this could begin. When Navy officials learned that he knew about the work that Yates was conducting at San Jose State College, they asked Winter to take charge of a relaxation research committee at the Navy preflight school in Del Monte, California (Winter, 1981). The Navy had been having issues with aviators not being relaxed enough while flying combat missions. Thus, Yates was part of a committee that researched the effects of relaxation on naval aviators. Edmund Jacobson, the developer of progressive relaxation, a commonly used technique in sport psychology today, was also part of the same research committee (Jacobson, 1962; Winter, 1981). According to Winter (1981), the research was very successful, and it showed the importance of relaxation for the successful performance of both athletic and nonsport activities.

Another example of psychology applied to sport during this period was the work of David F. Tracy (Kornspan & MacCracken, 2003). Tracy was interviewed by a reporter in 1949, and he suggested that he could help the St. Louis Browns improve their performance. The St. Louis Browns hired him to work with the team during the 1950 spring training session. Tracy gained much media attention for applying psychology with the St. Louis Browns baseball team, and he worked with the team through the end of May 1950 (Kornspan & MacCracken, 2003). Tracy's work received a great deal of attention throughout the United States; thus it would seem reasonable to hypothesize that many psychologists heard about Tracy's work and may have begun to consider applying psychology to work with athletes (Kornspan, 2009a).

In the 1950s, other individuals who began applying psychology in their work with athletes included Bruce Ogilvie and Burt Giges (Simons & Andersen, 1995), both of whom used their clinical backgrounds to work with individual athletes. In Brazil, a psychologist was working with the national soccer team as early as 1958 (Salmela, 1992). Antonelli was involved with the Italian Olympic committee in helping to select athletes for the 1956 Olympic

Games in Melbourne, Australia. In Japan, another example of applying psychology to athletic performance was provided by Naruse (1965), who, in a published article, described examples of helping athletes deal with performance anxiety.

In addition to examples of psychology being applied in the United States, Italy, Japan, and Brazil, reports of the use of psychology to enhance sport performance were seen in England (Kornspan, 2009b), Australia (Phillips, 2000), and the Soviet Union ("Russia eyes hypnotism in sports," 1957) during this same period. In Australia, Phillips (2000) provides credit to Forbes and Ursula Carlile for applying psychology with Olympic swimmers. According to Phillips (2000), Forbes Carlile was one of the first coaches to use hypnosis in Australia to prepare athletes for competition. Additionally, the Soviet Olympic team at the 1952 Olympics worked with sport science professionals including sport psychologists (Ryba et al., 2005). According to Seiler and Wylleman (2009), the use of psychology to help enhance athletic performance was also being applied in Germany during this period.

Coaches in the United States and other parts of the world learned that sport science and sport psychology methods were being used in the Soviet Union to train athletes during this period ("Russ clinic at Stanford," 1961). Payton Jordan, coach of the Stanford University track and field team, maintained a correspondence with the national coach for the Russian track-and-field team, Gabriel Korobkov. Korobkov described to Jordan the various training techniques they were using to train their athletes and that the Russian athletic teams had psychologists who were analyzing sport performance. Jordan stated, "By studying these things, including the particular emotions of the individual athletes, they often avoid the trial and error which many of our athletes often go through before they find the events for which they are best suited" ("Russ clinic at Stanford," 1961, p. 22). Ryba, Stambulova, and Wrisberg (2009) have recently detailed A. C. Puni's theoretical concepts of preparing athletes mentally, which were used to guide the work of sport psychology professionals working with Russian athletes during the period. Rodionov (2010) also described the growing use of psychology in preparing athletes for competition.

The research on psychological factors involved in successful performance was moving out of the research laboratory and was being applied in the field. In a 1963 *Life* magazine article, "Athletes Get Help from Hypnotists," Moser (1963) explained that high-level athletes in the United States were being provided with hypnosis interventions to aid them in enhancing performance. He describes how a hypnotist and a psychologist provided a hypnosis intervention to Bill Faul, a rookie baseball pitcher with the Detroit Tigers. Moser (1963) suggested that the use of hypnosis in athletics was becoming much more common, citing the University of Arizona football team and professional golfers as among those who were using hypnosis for performance enhancement purposes.

In addition to the beginnings of the application of sport psychology to help athletes improve performance, researchers were continuing to study performance and to produce research related to the psychology of sport during these decades. An effort was made to encourage researchers to become actively involved in conducting psychological research related to sport and physical education. Johnson (1943), a professor of physical education at the University of Denver, published an article titled, "The Opportunity for Psychological Research in the Field of Physical Education"; in analyzing the current state of the psychology of physical education and sport literature, Johnson believed that there was great opportunity for those in the physical education profession to study psychological issues. Additionally, researchers made an effort during this time to summarize current knowledge in the field of sport psychology.

Cureton (1949) and Henry, Espenschade, Hodgson, Karpovich, Steinhaus, and Jarrett (1949) reviewed the literature on psychology related to physical education and sport. Cureton (1949), a professor at the University of Illinois, analyzed the research in the field of physical education between 1930 and 1946. Of the 3,426 master's degree theses completed in this period, Cureton coded 129 or 3.8% of these studies to be related to psychological issues. Of the 416 doctoral dissertations completed, Cureton identified 22 or 6.3% of the physical education doctoral dissertations as having a focus on psychology. Finally, Cureton analyzed *Research Quarterly* between 1930 and 1946 and identified 830 published articles. Of these, Cureton identified 21 or 2.5% as being focused on psychology related to sport and physical education.

In addition to describing the amount of studies related to psychological issues in physical education, Cureton (1949) also provided a narrative of what he referred to as "applied psychological studies" (Cureton, 1949, p. 39). He noted that the research literature contained reports on the relationships between athletic performance and intelligence, emotional aspects of sport participation, and personality and sports participation in relation to achievement in physical education activities. Additionally, Cureton reported that studies had been made in relationship to relaxation and tension and performance.

Coleman Griffith also summarized the research and literature in sport psychology in his chapter, The Physical Educator, in the *Handbook of Applied Psychology* (Griffith, 1950). He noted the long collaboration between physical educators and psychologists, and explained that coaches had asked psychologists to conduct tests of athletes' reaction times, to determine the best ways to mentally prepare athletes for competition, to discover the best tests to use in selecting athletes for the team, and to detail the best way to develop leadership in athletes involved in team sports.

An interesting development in sport psychology in the United States during the 1950s and 1960s was the reinstitution of the sport psychology laboratory at the University of Illinois in 1951 (Kornspan, 2012; Staley, 1952). While Coleman Griffith was the provost, Alfred W. Hubbard was asked by Seward Staley, the director of the school of physical education, to submit a proposal to restart the university's sport psychology laboratory. After gaining approval, the sport psychology laboratory was officially created in September 1951, thus illustrating the apparent influence of Coleman Griffith (Cureton, 1969; Kornspan, 2012; Staley, 1952). In the early years of this sport psychology laboratory, Coleman Griffith and Alfred W. Hubbard corresponded, and Griffith requested that Hubbard respond to a few requests for information that he had received related to specific sport psychology questions (Kornspan, 2012). In discussing the work of the sports psychology laboratory, Cureton (1954, p. 5) wrote: "The Sports Psychology Laboratory is new and no theses show from that Laboratory until the last three years."

C. H. McCloy (1958), who, along with Alfred W. Hubbard (at the University of Illinois) was researching the science of sport at the State University of Iowa, provided some insights into the then current state of the field of sport psychology in his literature review in the area of sports medicine. Based on his readings of bibliographies and a study of sports medicine curricula, McCloy divided the field of sports medicine into 17 different areas of study. One of the 17 areas that he identified was sport psychology. Within the sport psychology area, McCloy categorized the research that he had reviewed into 17 topic areas. For example, topic areas identified by McCloy included understanding mental aspects of optimal performance, influence of mental aspects on endurance sports, effects of fatigue on sport performance, how rewards and punishments affect sport participation, emotional aspects of sport, personality and character in sport, and improving sport performance through the use of psychology.

During the 1960s, Morgan Olsen analyzed the progress of sport psychology literature throughout the world from 1890 to 1963 (Olsen, 1966). He found that, from the 1890s to 1923, fewer than 10 published works were identified as dealing with sport psychology in six consecutive 5-year periods. However, Olsen found that between 1924 and 1948, growth occurred in sport psychology publications throughout the world. During this time, for each 5-year period, he found between 30 and 50 publications. Growth in the nascent sport psychology literature more than doubled for the two periods 1948–1953 and 1954–1959. Finally, he reported extreme growth in the amount of sport psychology literature produced globally from 1959 to 1963 (Olsen, 1966). Apparently, the efforts of individuals such as Cureton (1949), Henry et al. (1949), Griffith (1950), McCloy (1958), and Rudik (1962) were having a profound effect on other researchers worldwide. In addition, sport-specific mental training books were beginning to be made available to the general public during the early 1960s (Kornspan, 2009a).

During this period, individuals who were consulting with athletes demonstrated an awareness of how their performance enhancement work might benefit from the cross-fertilization of ideas in other performance domains. For example, David Tracy, who worked with the management of the St. Louis Browns in the 1950s, believed that because psychological techniques were already being used to enhance performance in other industries, applying these techniques to sport would be also prove successful (Kornspan & MacCracken, 2003). Additionally, Dorothy Yates, who applied psychology with boxers in the early 1940s, went on to apply psychological techniques to help aviators achieve relaxation when flying combat missions during World War II (Winter, 1981). *Human factors psychology* became a main aspect of military psychological consultation as psychologists helped the military during World War II to more effectively design equipment (Benjamin & Baker, 2003) and to prepare individuals to more effectively handle stress and to increase relaxation (Neufeld, 1951).

Although mental training techniques were used in the 1940s and early 1950s, the development of the theory of self-actualization by Abraham Maslow was important to the growth and development of performance enhancement interventions. Maslow's theories emphasized that all humans have the potential to improve, in order to reach our ultimate goals (Benjamin & Baker, 2003). As his theory became more well known in the field of psychology, popular approaches to enhancing performance began to emerge within society. One approach that popularized the technique of visualization was psychocybernetics, developed by Maxwell Maltz (1960). Maltz's (1960) book brought attention to mental training techniques such as visualization and goal setting within society.

Sport Psychology from 1965 to 1980

By the mid 1960s, worldwide interest in sport psychology had reached a critical mass, leading to organized efforts to form institutions to bring together like-minded individuals in the field. In 1963, Fernanando Antonelli, at a sports medicine conference in Barcelona that included a session on sport psychology (Antonelli, 1989), discussed sport psychology with three other attendees, Jose-Maria Cagigal and Jose Ferrer-Hombravella, from Spain, and Michel Bouet, from France (Salmela, 1992; Cei, 2011). They proposed inviting individuals with an interest in sport psychology from all over the world to a scientific meeting focused exclusively on sport psychology. The idea of a world congress of sport psychology was credited to Jose Ferrer-Hombravella. After this meeting, Antonelli began to organize such a conference.

At the congress, 148 presentations were provided by 237 authors. The congress was important because it subsequently led to the founding of the International Society of Sport Psychology (ISSP), with Antonelli elected the president of the organization (Antonelli, 1989). The formation of the ISSP served as a model for many nations to found their own sport psychology organizations, including the North American Society for the Psychology of Sport and Physical Activity (NASPSPA) in the United States in 1966, the British Society of Sports Psychology (in 1967), the French Society of Sport Psychology (in 1967), the Canadian Society for Psychomotor Learning and Sport Psychology (in 1969), and the Association for Sport Psychology in Germany (in 1969). The European Federation of Sport Psychology was founded in 1968 (Seiler & Wylleman, 2009). For detailed information about the early history of the ISSP and the influence of Ferruccio Antonelli on the discipline of sport psychology see Cei (2011).

During this period, professional organizations began to focus on the application of psychology to sport. Through the Division of Men's Athletics of the Alliance for Health, Physical Education, and Recreation, a sports psychology task force was developed. This task force included John Lawther, Reuben Frost, Harry Fritz, and Walter Schwank. One of the main projects that the task force organized was a national sports psychology conference, held in Buffalo, New York, in May 1973. The main focus of this conference was the practical applications of psychology to the coaching of sports (Schwank, 1974, p. 7).

Interest in applications of psychology to improve athletic performance continued to grow among individual practitioners as well. Ogilvie and Tutko published an influential text titled, *Problem Athletes and How to Handle Them,* in 1966. Williams and Straub (2010) pointed out that these psychologists worked with many professional and college teams during this period, and they believed that Ogilvie and Tutko's sport psychology work in the United States created great interest in the application of psychology to sport performance (Williams & Straub, 2010). Examples of that interest include the various media reports that chronicled the work of Ogilvie and Tutko; for example, an article in *Sports Illustrated* featured their work (Jares, 1971).

Many other professionals began to work extensively with athletes at this time (Simons & Andersen, 1995). In preparation for the 1968 Olympics, Mirsoluv Vanek conducted psychological testing for the Czechoslovakia national team (Kremer & Moran, 2008). Ema Geron encouraged the use of psychological training for athletes in her manuscript prepared for the Bulgarian Olympic Committee titled, "Psychological Conditioning for the Sportsman" (Olympic Review, 1968). According to Straub, Ermoleava, and Rodionov (1995), Antoli V. Alekseev was working with the Russian national shooting team between 1967 and 1971 to develop a psychological preparation system that would aid athletes in obtaining an optimal state for competition. Albert Rodionov (Straub et al., 1995), well-known in the Soviet Union, began working with the Soviet men's and women's basketball teams in 1969 (Rodionov, 2005). Additionally, it was reported in sports medicine journals that Russian athletes had psychologists who traveled with their teams (Gold, 1968).

Many of the leaders in the field of applied sport psychology of the past few decades began their consulting work in the 1970s (Simons & Andersen, 1995). Individuals beginning their consulting during this period included Ron Smith (in 1971), Bob Rotella (in 1972), Ken Ravizza (in 1973), Bob Nideffer (in 1974), Jim Loeher (in 1974), Gloria Balague (in 1976), Betty Wenz (in 1976), and Dan Gould (in 1978) (Simons & Andersen, 1995). Also in 1970, the Kansas City Royals began a baseball academy that incorporated a role for a psychologist, Ray Reilly, who was focused on completing testing of baseball players ("Using Royals heads," 1970; McCarthy & Clayton, 1973; Peurzer, 2004). The purpose of Reilly's work was to create norms that would aid in the selection of players. Reilly was conducting tests related to vision, reaction time, coordination, and balance.

Richard Suinn began providing consulting services to U.S. Olympic athletes in 1972 (Epstein, 1999). Interestingly, Jares (1971) reported that Ogilvie and Tutko had been very interested in working with the U.S. Olympic team as consultants but were not given serious consideration or were told that there was not enough money to fund their services. Although they did not work directly with Olympic teams in the 1960s and early 1970s, they did provide psychological testing to the U.S. national swimming team, under the direction of James "Doc" Counsilman and George Haines (Jares, 1971).

Richards Suinn appears to be the first sport psychology professional to be part of the U.S. Olympic Committee's (USOC) sports medicine team (Epstein, 1999). Additionally, Suinn was team psychologist for the U.S. Nordic ski team and the U.S. biathlon team at the 1976 Olympics (Suinn, 1985). Interestingly, Suinn reported that he was credentialed as a press photographer and not as part of the sports medicine team (Suinn, 1985). In addition to Suinn, other professionals would work with the U.S. Olympic Committee at their Olympic Training Centers. Jerry May, of the University of Nevada, was appointed to the sports medicine staff for the Squaw Valley Olympic Training Center as the first director of sport psychology in 1977 (Murphy & Ferrante, 1989). May served in this role for the U.S. Olympic Committee from 1977 to 1980 (May, 2009). During this time period the United States Olympic Committee sport psychology subcommittee worked toward developing an organizational structure to provide sport psychology services to coaches and athletes training at the national level throughout the Unites States (United States Committee, 1979).

Dorothy Harris, from Penn State University, would become the first resident sport psychologist for the U.S. Olympic Training Center in Colorado Springs in 1980 (United States Olympic Committee, 1979). Harris also worked with college sports teams at Penn State University (Kaup, 1979).

Applied sport psychology work in the Soviet Union also increased during the 1970s (Stambulova, Johnson, & Stambulov, 2008). Gregory Raiport, who moved to the United States in the late 1970s, provided an overview of the work that sport psychologists in Russia were conducting in a 1978 *New York Times* article titled, "The Sports Psychologist Gives Russians an Edge." Raiport's work at the National Institute of Physical Culture in Moscow included the use of psychological tests with athletes to determine how an athlete's personality might affect his or her performance (Raiport, 1978). Additionally, Raiport discussed the use of computers to analyze an athlete's personality in comparison with those of a champion's profile.

In Canada, sport psychology professionals began consulting with Olympic athletes during the 1970s (Halliwell, 1989). Halliwell credits Brent Rushall as the first sport psychology consultant to work with the Canadian Olympic teams in 1976. "Starting with Brent Rushall's pioneering work at the 1976 Olympic games in Montreal, sport psychology consultants have been actively involved in enhancing performance in amateur sport" (Halliwell, 1989, p. 39). At the 1976 Olympics, Rushall was the team psychologist for the Canadian swim and wrestling teams (Rushall, n.d.). Rushall also served as the sport psychologist for the Canadian National Swimming team at the 1978 Commonwealth games and at the 1978 World Championships (Rushall, n.d.). Also, in Sweden, during the early 1970s, Lars Eric Uhenstahl provided mental training programs to prepare the Swedish national and Olympic teams (Scandinavian International University, 2011).

In addition to the worldwide growth of the practice of applied sport psychology in the 1970s, this decade also saw the growth of sport psychology graduate programs in the United States (Landers, 1995). Graduate programs in sport psychology were begun at schools such as Florida State University, Penn State University, the University of Illinois, and West Virginia University (Salmela, 1981). Generally, the focus of academic sport psychology during this period was on the social psychology of sport (Gill, 2009). Students were being trained to conduct research to prepare for academic positions, so that they could help develop the science of the field of sport psychology. In fact, although there were more individuals beginning to practice sport psychology, individuals in academic settings appear to have been discouraged to practice applied sport psychology (Williams & Straub, 2010). However, it should be pointed out that students in graduate school in physical education and coaching were now given more opportunities to enroll in sport psychology courses. Thus, sport psychology was beginning to make an impact on the development of future coaches. Pete Carroll, a highly successful collegiate coach for the University of Southern California, and now coach of the Seattle Seahawks, has recently written about how his sport psychology graduate class taken at the University of the Pacific in the early 1970s impacted his coaching philosophy (Carroll, Roth, & Garin, 2010). This experience was likely repeated for hundreds if not thousands of future coaches as sport psychology became a mainstream part of coaching education and sport science curricula.

By the end of the 1970s, it was clear throughout the world that psychology was an important part of the sport training process (Tuccimei, 1978). Tuccimei stated (1978, p. 526): "Ideally an Olympic delegations medical team should be composed of a general physician, a specialist in traumatology, and a psychologist. The psychologist is particularly needed by both technicians and athletes, and many NOCs have already included a specialist in their medical units."

As mental training was becoming more popular for athletes during the late 1960s and 1970s, peak performance concepts from the general field of psychology became a focus of interest. Maslow (1968) provided a description of the concepts of peak experiences, and Csikszentmihalyi (1975) began to study a similar concept of peak experience that he termed the *flow state*. Peak performance psychology research would be a major focus of the field of sport and performance psychology during the next four decades (for a detailed look at optimal performance research, see also Chapter 38, this volume).

It is interesting to note that individuals involved in sport psychology realized that the skills they were teaching to athletes to achieve peak performances and achieve flow were applicable to a variety of additional performance domains. According to Lars-Eric Unestahl (2011), in 1977, Sweden was the first country to form a society focused on the general aspects of mental training. Swedes were already using sport psychology techniques that were being used by athletes in other populations. The Mental Training organization in Sweden was divided into five main sections focused on sport and the performing arts, clinical and health areas, business, education, and research and theory (Unestahl, 2011).

During this period, many women contributed to the growth of sport psychology. According to Gill (1995), it is important that researchers review our past history to better understand the various contributions that women have made to the development of sport psychology. In the athletic research laboratory directed by Coleman Griffith at the University of Illinois, Minnie Giesecke conducted reaction time testing of athletes during the 1920s (Giesecke, 1930; University of Illinois, 1930). Additionally, prior to the 1970s, individuals such as Dorothy Yates (San Jose State College), Anna Espenschade (University of California, Berkeley), and Olive G. Young (University of Illinois) were teaching sport psychology courses (Kornspan, 2012; Kornspan & MacCracken, 2001; Park, 1994). Additionally, women were studying under the supervision of Alfred W. Hubbard at the University of Illinois and were also conducting research in the University of Illinois sport psychology laboratory; these included Florence Patricia Cullen, Phyllis Day, Sherry Lyn Bovinet, and Mary Hoke Slaughter (Kornspan, 2012). Women worldwide were also influencing the development of the sport psychology profession at this time.

Gill (1995) noted that individuals such as Emma McCloy Layman, Dorothy Harris, Evelyn Bird, and Ema Geron provided presentations at the second International Sport Psychology Congress in 1968. In addition, Phyllis Day, who had studied in the sports psychology laboratory under Alfred W. Hubbard, attended the conference as a faculty member of Temple University (Kenyon & Grogg, 1970). The organizing committee for the 1968 second ISSP included Anne G. Ingram (social committee), a professor of physical education at the University of Maryland (Kenyon & Grogg, 1970; University of Maryland, 2011), and Frances Cumbee (scientific committee), professor at the University of Wisconsin, Madison (Kenyon & Grogg, 1970; University of Wisconsin, Madison, 2005).

As a sport psychology professional in Bulgaria, Ema Geron had an impact on the development of the profession of sport psychology (European Federation of Sport Psychology, 2011). Geron published influential books related to the psychology of sport in the late 1950s and early 1960s (Tenenbaum,

Lidor, Bar-Eli, 2011). Additionally, she attended the first ISSP conference and took a leadership role in the development of a sport psychology professional organization. Geron organized a sport psychology professional conference in 1968, the International Scientific conference on the problems of the psychological preparation of athletes, which was held in Bulgaria. In addition to organizing this conference, Geron was the first president of the European Federation of Sport Psychology from 1969 to 1973 (European Federation of Sport Psychology, 2011). She started the Israeli Society for Sport Psychology and Sociology in 1974, and was also the first president of this organization (European Federation of Sport Psychology, 2011). Geron became part of the managing council for the International Society of Sport Psychology in 1968 (Morris, Hackfort, & Lidor, 2003).

In addition to Ema Gerron and her influential work in the field of sport psychology, Dorothy Harris from Penn State University also began consulting with athletes during the 1970s and was influential in the United States, becoming the first resident sport psychology professional at the U.S. Olympic Center (Kaup, 1979). In addition to Harris, other women focused on sport psychology interventions during the 1970s included Gloria Balague and Betty Wenz, who began working with athletes in the mid 1970s (Simons & Andersen, 1995). Wenz and Harris were part of the U.S. Olympic Committee's Sport Psychology Advisory Panel between 1982 and 1984 (Clarke, 1984; Granito, 2002). Additionally, various women published influential textbooks in sport psychology during the 1970s. For example, Dorcas Susan Butt published the *Psychology of Sport: The Behavior Motivation, Personality, and Performance of Athletes* (Butt, 1976).

Recently, Krane and Whaley (2010) have described the contributions of women who have helped develop the field of sport psychology from the 1970s to the present. Krane and Whaley (2010) reviewed contributions made to the profession of sport psychology by Joan Duda, Diane Gill, Tara Scanlan, Maureen Weiss, Carole Oglesby, Jean Williams, Penny McCallaugh, and Deborah Feltz. Krane and Whaley found that a common theme among the individuals they interviewed was that, although they were initially not trained in consulting with athletes on mental skills training, they learned this information and developed course work so that their students could gain this knowledge. Also, both Gill and Weiss have contributed greatly to an understanding of the history of sport psychology. For an in-depth analysis of 75 years of sport psychology research published in the *Research Quarterly for Exercise and Sport*, see Weiss and Gill (2005).

Sport Psychology's Growth from 1980 to 1989

Williams and Straub (2010) described this period (1980–1989) as a time in which sport psychology research increased greatly and applied sport psychology became more accepted in the United States. In fact, the U.S. Olympic Committee (USOC) created the elite athlete project in order to incorporate sport psychology into the process of helping elite athletes prepare for international competition. As part of the project, a committee was organized that included Richard Suinn, Daniel Landers, Denis Waitley, Bruce Ogilvie, and Jerry May (Suinn, 1985). The purpose of this committee was to analyze the needs of the various National Olympic sports teams and to match that team with someone who could apply sport psychology to the team. Eleven sport psychology professionals were placed with teams in preparation for the 1984 Olympics. The mental training services provided included such interventions as visualization, concentration, relaxation, goal setting, and self-talk. Also, a few professionals provided crisis intervention services (Suinn, 1985).

Although these individuals were working with the teams in preparation for the Olympics, these professionals were not credentialed for the 1984 Olympics. In fact, Ogilvie (1989, p. 6) wrote "at the Los Angeles Olympics, it was necessary for me to dress in a women's volleyball sweatsuit and to cover my head so that I could sneak into the stadium with the team in order to provide services that the team had requested." This was similar to Suinn's recounting that, for the 1976 games, he had to receive credentials as a press photographer rather than as part of the sports medicine staff.

The USOC Sports Medicine Committee recommended that credentials for sport psychology professionals working at the Olympic Games be provided at future events. Another important recommendation was that a full-time sport psychologist was needed at the U.S. Olympic Training Center (Suinn, 1985). The individual hired was Shane Murphy, the first full-time USOC sport psychologist, who provided sport psychology services for the USOC from 1987 to 1994 (Murphy, 1995). Murphy functioned as an integral member of the USOC Sport Science Division, which also included sports physiologists and sports biomechanists, and he provided sport psychology services to several U.S. Olympic Festivals and also at the 1988 Summer Games in Seoul with Alfred "Bud" Ferrante (Murphy & Ferrante, 1989) and at the 1992 Winter Games in Albertville. Ogilvie (1989, p. 6), in reflecting on the growth and acceptance of sport psychology in North America stated that, "The installation of Shane Murphy as the resident sport psychologist at the United States Olympic Training Center and the credentialing of him as a bona fide member of the United States Sports Medicine Staff in Seoul, Korea, is a major accomplishment." In 1992, Murphy became Deputy Director of the USOC Sport Science Division. Today, five full-time sport psychologists work for the USOC.

With this greater acceptance and growth of applied sport psychology taking place, professional organizations in the United States saw the need to address professional issues, and the USOC led the way in addressing these issues during the 1980s. The USOC organized a meeting for August 1982, the purpose of which was to help define the practice of sport psychology in the United States (Sport Psychology Today, 1983). Three main areas of sport psychology practice were defined including educational, clinical, and research-based sport psychology. Criteria were created to identify an individual as an educational sport psychologist, research sport psychologist, or clinical sport psychologist. Additionally, the USOC developed a registry in which sport psychology professionals identified as having the requisite training and experience could be listed (Clarke, 1984). This registry was then used to help national governing bodies (NGBs) of sport in the United States identify potential consultants for their coaches and athletes.

In the United States during this period, two major sport psychology organizations were formed to address professional, research, and applied issues—the Association for the Advancement of Applied Sport Psychology (originally AAASP, changed to AASP in 2006) and the Division of Exercise and Sport Psychology of the American Psychological Association (APA). The impetus for the APA organization was provided at an APA convention in 1974, at which Richard Suinn and Bill Morgan discussed the idea of creating an interest group related to sport psychology (Swoap, 1999). A special interest group (SIG), the Exercise and Sport Psychology SIG, was formed at the APA conference in 1982, largely due to the organizational efforts of William Morgan, Steve Heyman, David Brown, Deborah Feltz, Richard Suinn, and Eugene Levitt

(Swoap, 1999). Morgan became the first president of the new division when it was officially recognized as APA Division 47 in 1986, and Heyman its first secretary-treasurer (Swoap, 1999). At about the same time, the formation of an organization devoted to the applied aspects of sport psychology that would bring together professionals from the fields of sport science, physical education, and psychology was being discussed by leaders in the field who felt dissatisfied with the lack of an applied focus within NASPSPA (Silva, 1989). These leaders held their first organizational meeting October 4–6, 1985, in Nags Head, North Carolina (Williams, 1985); thanks to the tireless efforts of John Silva of the University of North Carolina, the Association for the Advancement of Applied Sport Psychology (AASP) was founded and held its first annual conference in Jekyll Island, Georgia, in October 1986 (Association for the Advancement of Applied Sport Psychology, 1986). Silva became the first AASP president (Williams, 1985). For historical documentation of the formation of AAASP, the reader is referred to the organization's online archives, which provide the minutes of its meetings from 1985 to 1997 (Bowling Green State University, 2011) and the article "A Primer on the Development of SEP in North America vs. Europe: Comparing the Developmental Paths of FEPSAC and AASP (Quartiroli & Zizzi, 2011). Both Division 47 and AASP are thriving organizations today.

The sport psychology literature now began to highlight the application of mental skills to other performance domains. For example, the work of Orlick and Partington, who used mental training with the Canadian military's tank team, was highlighted (Salmela, 1987). Salmela (1988) reported that many sport psychology professionals were beginning to consult with corporations on issues related to enhancing performance in the business setting. There was concern, however, that the field might lose sport psychology professionals to corporations who provided a much higher salary.

As individuals in the field of sport psychology consulted in other performance domains, sport psychology professionals realized the need to not only have professional organizations focused on the psychology of sport, but to also have a more inclusive professional organization, separate from sport psychology–specific organizations (Unestahl, 2011). Thus, an international professional organization, the International Society for Mental Training and Excellence, was formed in 1989 (Journal of Excellence, 1998). Well-known sport psychology professionals would lead the organization into the 1990s as the first president of the organization, Lars Eric Unestahl organized its first world conference in 1991. Terry Orlick became the second president of the organization and organized its world congress in 1995 (Journal of Excellence, 1998). In the 1990s and 2000s, individual consultants trained in sport psychology would continue to use their skills with athletes and in other related performance domains.

Sport Psychology: 1990s to the Present

As more professionals applied sport psychology theories and methods to performance concerns in areas such as business and the performing arts (Hays & Brown, 2004), issues of professional practice and ethics rose to the forefront. In the United States, AASP created a certification program in which an individual with a doctoral degree who met a set of defined criteria could be provided with consultant certification from the association. Although an individual receiving this title cannot call him- or herself a sport psychologist solely based on this credential, he or she is able to use the designation "certified consultant" (CC-AASP). Although this certification was created almost 20 years ago, there still seems to be uncertainty and debate about who can practice in the field. To try to clarify this issue in the United States, the AASP has recently published a position paper in 2006 titled, "How to choose a Sport Psychology Consultant" (Association for the Advancement of Applied Sport Psychology, 2006). In another recent major change to the certification process, an individual can become a certified consultant AASP with a master's degree rather than having to obtain a doctoral degree to achieve this credential. Division 47 of APA also addressed professional practice concerns when it developed and was granted recognition in 2003 of a proficiency in sport psychology by the APA (American Psychological Association [APA], 2009). The recognition of a proficiency, which provided guidelines for the specialized knowledge necessary for practice in this area, addressed what Division 47 saw as two main concerns. First, the proficiency provided a way to protect the public from psychologists who are not qualified or trained to provide sport psychology services. Second, the proficiency provided guidelines for the type of training psychologists should have in order to practice sport psychology (APA, 2009). Throughout the world, these professional issues in sport psychology continue to be addressed (see, for example, Morris, Alfermann, Lintunen, & Hall, 2003).

In addition to the debate on establishing practice, education, and training standards in sport psychology, a related issue throughout the 1990s to the present has been program accreditation in the United States (Kornspan, 2009b). It is believed that a program accreditation or approval process in applied sport psychology could help assure students who went through an accredited program in applied sport psychology that they would have the opportunity to become a certified consultant after program completion. Thus, an applied program would provide master's-level students and doctoral students with the course work and applied practical experiences that would give them the opportunity to meet national organization certification requirements. Although a graduate training committee has recommended that the AASP create a program approval process, the executive board of the Association has decided not to pursue this at present.

As the field of sport psychology has become more defined, students have become interested in providing performance enhancement services, as well as clinical and counseling services (Kornspan, 2009b). To meet this need and advance the field of sport psychology, some graduate programs have begun to offer multidisciplinary training programs in which students can develop expertise in providing mental training services and also receive training to practice counseling or clinical psychology (Kornspan, 2009b). Examples of these schools include West Virginia University, Boston University, Argosy University, and JFK University.

Interest and practice in the field of applied sport psychology, especially in areas related to performance enhancement, are growing. An example of this growth was provided by USOC sport psychologist Jim Bauman, who noted that, before 2000, the USOC had one sport psychology professional on staff to attend the Olympic Games; by 2008, the USOC had five full-time sport psychology professionals on staff (Kornspan, 2009b). Professionals from a diverse set of backgrounds, including licensed psychologists, educators, "mental skills" coaches, and executive coaches provide services focused on increased performance to individuals, teams, coaches, and organizations in a great variety of settings (Hays, 2009), including collegiate sports, professional sports, dance, music, theater (Greene, 2001; Kenny, 2011), business (Elko & Beausay, 2009), medicine, military, trading (Hirschorn, 2011), and with police (Asken, 2005) and firefighters (Palmer, 2007). As Kornspan (2009b) pointed out, individuals today are applying sport psychology or mental training with professional sports organizations, college and university athletic departments, college counseling centers, in private practice, and as full-time consultants in sport academies and with national Olympic committees and national sports governing bodies. Some sport psychology professionals are working for sport agents providing services directly for the agencies' athletes (Kornspan, 2009b). Additionally, students who are being trained in sport psychology are entering fields related to student-athlete services and working with nonprofit sport organizations that provide academic and life skills programming through the use of sport. Others are working with college athletes as Challenging Athletes Minds for Personal Success (CHAMPS)/life skills directors, performance lifestyle coordinators for elite national-level athletes, and as player development specialists for professional sports teams and organizations (Kornspan, 2009b). Sport and performance psychology today has become a multidisciplinary field, as acknowledged in the APA Division 47 proficiency description: "Sport psychology is a multi-disciplinary field spanning psychology, sport science, and medicine" (APA, 2009).

Williams and Straub (2010) have suggested that it will be necessary for new students trained in the field of sport psychology to use their sport psychology training in other performance domains. The AASP performance excellence movement was developed by Rob Fazio and Michelle Coleman in 2001 to address this issue (Association of Applied Sport Psychology, 2011). The goal of this special interest group is to educate students, professionals, and the general public about how sport psychology can be used in other performance domains. Sport psychology concepts continue to be applied in novel and interesting ways. For example, students and professionals trained in sport psychology and who have AASP certification are being hired to work with individuals who are returning from military obligations overseas. In the United States, the Army has created several Centers for Enhanced Performance; according to Williams and Straub (2010), the eventual goal of these centers is to employ over 400 individuals who are trained in either sport psychology, performance psychology, or a related field and also have AASP certification.

To support this growth in performance psychology, the *Journal of Excellence* was inaugurated in 1998 (Zitzelsberger, 1998). Additionally, a new journal *Sport, Exercise and Performance Psychology*, published by the APA, will begin publication in the spring of 2012 with Jeffrey Martin as the editor

(Chamberlain, 2011). Two recent books published by the APA illustrate the professional development of performance psychology: *You're On! Consulting for Peak Performance* (Hays & Brown, 2004), and *Performance Psychology in Action* (Hays, 2009).

Additional organizations related to performance psychology have been formed during this period, such as the Society for Performing Arts Psychology, formed in 2005 (Society for Psychology in the Performing Arts, 2011). Research laboratories are also being developed to focus on performance psychology. One such laboratory is the Performance Psychology Laboratory at the University of Florida (University of Florida, 2007).

Conclusion

This chapter has provided an overview of the development of the field of sport psychology, with a special emphasis on human performance issues. Performance, its measurement, the psychological factors that influence it, and methods to improve it, has been a central focus of sport psychology research since its earliest days, beginning with the work of E. W. Scripture and Norman Triplett. Understanding the history of sport psychology helps provide a deeper understanding of the development of the contemporary field of sport psychology. Some areas deserve further attention: much of the recent research on the history of sport psychology has analyzed historical developments before 1965, but less research has focused on the development of the field after 1965. Few studies have provided oral histories from sport psychology professionals related to the development of the field of sport psychology; for example, little is known about how various graduate training programs in sport psychology developed. Interviewing individuals about the development of these programs and interviewing individuals who developed applied sport psychology practices would help to provide a more thorough understanding of the field's development. Additionally, hopefully, researchers in the history of sport psychology will continue to provide overviews of how sport psychology has developed throughout the world.

Over 37 years ago, G. H. Sage (Sage, 1974, p. 113), a professor at the University of Northern Colorado stated: "What does the future hold for sports psychology? I think the prospects are quite exciting, and I fully expect that it will become one of the most significant forces in directing sports in the next couple of decades." Indeed, the field of sport psychology has developed greatly in its first 100 years and today encompasses a wide variety of issues and concerns. The professionalization of sport and performance psychology and the application of psychological approaches to performance enhancement is an interesting development over the past two decades, and it will be fascinating to see if the field further clarifies the issue of practice in the field and how the job market will develop for those with an interest in the field of sport and performance psychology.

References

American Physical Education Association. (1900). Official announcement. *American Physical Education Review, 5,* 331–332.

American Psychological Association. (2009). *APA Proficiency in sport psychology.* Retrieved April 2, 2011, from http://www.apa47.org/pracExSpPsych.php

Anderson School of Gymnastics. (1896). *Mind and Body, 27*(3), 68.

Antonelli, F. (1989). Applied sport psychology in Italy. *Journal of Applied Sport Psychology, 1,* 45–51.

Asken, M. J. (2005). *Mental toughness skills for the police officers in high stress situations.* Camp Hill, PA: Mindsighting.

Association for the Advancement of Applied Sport Psychology. (1986, October 9–12). Conference program and abstract from the *Association for the Advancement of Applied Sport Psychology Annual Conference, Jeckyll Island, GA.* Retrieved March 31, 2011, from http://www.bgsu.edu/downloads/lib/file59668.pdf

Association for the Advancement of Applied Sport Psychology. (2006). *How to choose a sport psychology consultant.* Retrieved September 12, 2010, from http://appliedsportpsych.org/files/file/position-papers/choosing-consultant.pdf

Association of Applied Sport Psychology. (2011). *Performance excellence movement.* Retrieved April 3, 2011, from http://appliedsportpsych.org/students/pem

Baugh, F. G., & Benjamin, L. T., Jr. (2009). An offensive advantage: The football charging studies at Stanford University. In C. D. Green & L. T. Benjamin, Jr. (Eds.), *Psychology gets in the game: Sport, mind, and behavior, 1880–1960* (pp. 168–2001). Lincoln, NE: University of Nebraska Press.

Bäumler, G. (2009). The dawn of sport psychology in Europe, 1880–1930. In C. D. Green & L. T. Benjamin, Jr. (Eds.), *Psychology gets in the game: Sport, mind, and behavior, 1880–1960* (pp. 20–77). Lincoln, NE: University of Nebraska Press.

Benjamin, L. T., Jr., & Baker, D. B. (2003). *From séance to science: A history of the profession of psychology in America.* Belmont, CA: Wadsworth/Thomson Learning.

Benjamin, L. T., Jr., Durkin, M., Link, M., Vestal, M., & Acord, J. (1992). Wundt's American doctoral students. *American Psychologist, 47,* 123–131.

Big athletes alert, speedy as small men, coach proves. (1931, January 9). *The Charleston Gazette,* p. 2

Bowling Green State University. (2011). *Center for archival collections: Association for Applied Sport Psychology.* Retrieved March 30, 2011, from http://www.bgsu.edu/colleges/library/cac/ms/page42832.html

Brannon, E. W. (1913, December 14). The psychology of football: Dr. Wolfe of the University of Nebraska illustrated his new theory using three 1913 Cornhuskers stars to prove it. *Lincoln Daily Star,* p. 14.

Brehm, S. S., Kassin, S. M., & Fein, S. (1999). *Social psychology* (4th ed.). Boston, MA: Houghton Mifflin.

Brichford, M. (2008). *Bob Zupke: The life and football legacy of the Illinois coach.* Jefferson, NC: McFarland & Company Publishers.

Butt, D. S. (1976). *Psychology of sport: The behavior, motivation, personality, and performance of athletes.* New York: Van Nostrand Reinhold.

Carroll, P., & Roth, Y., & Garin, K. A. (2010). *Win forever: Live, work, and play like a champion.* New York: Penguin.

Cei, A. (2011). Ferrucio Antonelli: His work and legacy. *International Journal of Sport and Exercise Psychology, 9,* 356–361.

Chamberlain, J. (2011). In the game: Jeffrey Martin will edit APA's first sport psychology journal. *APA Monitor, 42,* 62.

Clarke, K. S. (1984). The USOC Sports Psychology Registry: A clarification. *Journal of Sport Psychology, 6,* 365–366.

Coubertin, P. (1913). *Essais de psychologie sportive.* Lausanne, CH: Payot.

Coubertin, P. (1979). *Olympic memoirs.* Lausanne, CH: International Olympic Committee. (Original work published 1936)

Cureton, T. K. (1949). Nature and scope of research in health, physical education, and Recreation. In G. Scott & T. K. Cureton (Eds.), *Research methods applied to health, physical education, and recreation* (pp. 20–41). Washington, DC: American Association for Health, Physical Education, and Recreation.

Cureton, T. K. (1954). *University of Illinois abstracts of graduate theses in physical education, recreation and health education 1923–1954.* Urbana, IL: University of Illinois.

Cureton, T. K., Jr. (1969). I have learned that.... In D. B. Franks (Ed.), *Exercise and fitness 1969: A tribute to Thomas K. Cureton, Jr.* (pp. 11–20). Champaign, IL: Athletic Institute.

Csikszentmihalyi, M. (1975). *Beyond boredom and anxiety: Experiencing flow in work and play.* San Francisco: Jossey-Bass.

Davis, S. F., Huss, M. T., & Becker, A. H. (2009). Norman Triplett: Recognizing the importance of competition. In C. D. Green & L. T. Benjamin, Jr. (Eds.), *Psychology gets in the game: Sport, mind, and behavior, 1880–1960* (pp. 98–115). Lincoln, NE: University of Nebraska Press.

Eckersall, W. H. (1921). Psychology of the gridiron. *Illustrated World, 36,* 350–352.

Elko, K., & Beausay, B. (2009). *True greatness: Mastering the inner game of business success.* New York: AMACOM.

Epstein, R. (1999). Helping athletes go for the gold. *Psychology Today.* Retrieved September 11, 2010, from http://www.psychologytoday.com/articles/199905/helping-athletes-go-the-gold

European Federation of Sport Psychology. (2011, March 21). *Ema Geron.* Retrieved March 31, 2011, from http://www.fepsac.com/?akbNewsID=22&akbNewsAction=single

Feige, K. (Ed.). (1977). *The development of sport psychology: A synopsis of its research, application and organization in different countries.* Germany: Arbeitsgemeinschait fur Sportpsychologie in derBuderrepublik Deutschland.

Franch, J. (2007). *The University of Illinois goes to war.* Retrieved April 1, 2011, from http://www.library.illinois.edu/archives/slc/researchguides/oralhistory/WWII/WWIIHistory.pdf

Fuchs, A. (1998). Psychology and "The Babe". *Journal of the History of the Behavioral Sciences, 34,* 153–165.

Fuchs, A. (2009). Psychology and baseball: The testing of Babe Ruth. In C. D. Green & L. T. Benjamin, Jr. (Eds.). *Psychology gets in the game: Sport, mind, and behavior, 1880–1960* (pp. 144–167). Lincoln, NE: University of Nebraska Press

Fujita, A. H. (1987). The development of sport psychology in Japan. *The Sport Psychologist, 1,* 69–73.

Fullerton, H. (1921). Why Babe Ruth is the greatest home run hitter. *Popular Science Monthly, 99,* 19–21, 110.

Giesecke, M. (1930). Diagnostic value of reaction time tests in the athletic coaching school. *Transactions of the Illinois State Academy of Science, 23,* 560–562.

Gill, D. L. (1995). Women's place in the history of sport psychology. *The Sport Psychologist, 9,* 418–433.

Gill, D. L. (2009). Social psychology and physical activity: Back to the future. 2008 C. H. McCloy lecture. *Research Quarterly, 80,* 685–695.

Gold, A. A. (1968). A team manager's view. *Bulletin of the British Association of Sports Medicine, 3,* 118–120.

Goodwin, C. J. (2005). An insider's look at experimental psychology in America: The diaries of Walter Miles. In D. Baker (Ed.), *Thick description and fine texture: Studies in the history of psychology* (pp. 57–75). Akron, OH: The University of Akron Press.

Goodwin, C. J. (2009). E. W. Scripture: The application of "new psychology" methodology to athletics. In C. D. Green & L. T. Benjamin, Jr. (Eds.), *Psychology gets in the game: Sport, mind, and behavior, 1880–1960* (pp. 78–97). Lincoln, NE: University of Nebraska Press.

Graef, S., Kornspan, A. S., & Baker, D. (2009). Paul Brown: Bringing psychological testing to football. In C. D. Green & L. T. Benjamin, Jr. (Eds.), *Psychology gets in the game: Sport, mind, and behavior, 1880–1960* (pp. 230–252). Lincoln, NE: University of Nebraska Press.

Grandenwitz, A. (1923). Making sport a science: Devices and tests which determine the individual fitness of candidates. *Scientific American, 129,* 392, 445.

Granito, V. (2002). Excellence is a journey, not a goal: The historical significance of Betty J. Wenz (1934–2001). *The Sport Psychologist, 16,* 291–295.

Green, C. D. (2003). Psychology strikes out. Coleman Griffith and the Chicago Cubs. *History of Psychology, 6,* 267–283.

Green, C. D. (2011). The Chicago Cubs and the headshrinker: An early foray into sports psychology. *Baseball Research Journal, 40*(1), 42–45.

Green, C. D., & Benjamin, L. T. (Eds.). (2009). *Psychology gets in the game: Sport, mind, and behavior.* Lincoln, NE: University of Nebraska Press.

Greene, D. (2001). *Audition success: An Olympic sports psychologist teaches performing artists how to win.* New York: Routledge.

Griffith, C. (1928, October 20). Illinois Psychological Lab Devoted to Sports is Only One in Country. *Daily Illini,* p. 10.

Griffith, C. (1950). The physical educator. In D. H. Fryer & E. R. Henry (Eds.), *Handbook of applied psychology* (pp. 658–664). New York: Rinehart and Company.

Griffith to teach coaching course. (1926, January 28). *Daily Illini,* p. 5.

Halliwell, W. (1989). Applied sport psychology in Canada. *Journal of Applied Sport Psychology, 1,* 35–44.

Hays, K. F.,& Brown, C. H. (2004). *You're on! Consulting for peak performance.* Washington, DC: American Psychological Association.

Hays, K. F. (Ed.). (2009). *Peak performance psychology in action.* Washington, DC: American Psychological Association.

Hearst, E., & Capshew, J. H. (1988). *Psychology at Indiana University: A centennial review and compendium.* Retrieved April 2, 2011, from http://psych.indiana.edu/tradition/Hearst_and_Capshew_1988.pdf

Henry, F., Espenschade, A., Hodgson, P., Karpovich, P., Steinhaus, A.H., & Jarrett, R. F. (1949). Psychological laboratory research In G. Scott, & T. K. Cureton (Eds.), *Research methods applied to health, physical education, and recreation* (pp. 275–300) Washington, DC: American Association for Health, Physical Education, and Recreation.

Hirschhorn, D. (2011). *Welcome to DrDougHirschhorn.com.* Retrieved March 31, 2011, from http://www.drdoug.com/

Indiana University. (1905). *Indiana University Bulletin.* Bloomington, IN: Author.

Jares, J. (1971). We have a neurotic in the backfield, doctor. *Sports Illustrated, 34(3),* 30–34.

Jacobson, E. (1962). *You must relax: A practical method of reducing the strains of modern living.* New York: McGraw-Hill.

Johnson, G. B. (1943). The opportunity for psychological research in the field of physical education. *The Physical Educator, 4,* 55–56.

Journal of Excellence. (1998). About the International Society of Mental Training and Excellence. *Journal of Mental Excellence, 1,* 96–97.

Kaup, G. (1979, August 10). Rose to widen scope for lady volleyballers. *Penn State Daily Collegian,* p. 8.

Kenny, D. T. (2011). *The psychology of music performance anxiety.* Oxford: Oxford University Press.

Kenyon, G. S., & Grogg, T. M. (Eds.). (1970). *Contemporary psychology of sport.* Chicago: Athletic Institute.

Kornspan, A. S. (2007a). E. W. Scripture and the Yale PsychologLaboratory: Studies related to athletes and physical activity. *The Sport Psychologist, 21,* 152–169.

Kornspan, A. S. (2007b). The early years of sport psychology: The work and influence of Pierre de Coubertin. *Journal of Sport Behavior, 30,* 77–93.

Kornspan, A. S. (2009a). Enhancing performance in sport: The use of hypnosis and other psychological techniques in the 1950s and 1960s. In C. D. Green & L. T. Benjamin, Jr. (Eds.). *Psychology gets in the game: Sport, mind, and behavior, 1880–1960* (pp. 253–282). Lincoln, NE: University of Nebraska Press.

Kornspan, A. S. (2009b). *Fundamentals of sport and exercise psychology.* Champaign, IL: Human Kinetics Publishers.

Kornspan, A. S. (2012). *Alfred W. Hubbard: The sport psychology laboratory at the University of Illinois, 1950–1970.* Manuscript under review.

Kornspan, A. S., & MacCracken, M. J. (2001). Psychology applied to sports in the 1940s: The work of Dorothy Hazeltine Yates. *The Sport Psychologist, 15,* 342–345.

Kornspan, A. S., & MacCracken, M. J. (2003). The use of psychology in professional baseball: The pioneering work of David F. Tracy. *Nine: A Journal of Baseball History and Culture, 11,* 36–43.

Krane, V., & Whaley, D. E. (2010). Quiet competence: Writing women into the history of U.S. sport and exercise psychology. *The Sport Psychologist, 18,* 349–372.

Kremer, J., & Moran, A. (2008). Swifter, higher, stronger: A history of sport psychology. *The Psychologist, 21,* 740–743.

Kroll, W., & Lewis, G. (1970). America's first sport psychologist. *Quest, 13,* 1–4.

Kuhn, E. (1898). Philadelphia Physical Education Society. *American Physical Education Review, 3,* 139.

LaCava, G. (1956). The International Federation of Sports Medicine. *Journal of the American Medical Association, 162,* 1109–1111.

Laird, D. (1936). *How to use psychology in business.* New York: McGraw-Hill.

Landers, D. M. (1995). Sport psychology: The formative years, 1950–1980. *The Sport Psychologist, 9,* 406–417.

Lidor, R., Morris, T., Bardaxoglou, N., & Becker, B., Jr. (Eds.). (2001). *The world sport psychology sourcebook.* Morgantown, WV: Fitness Information Technology.

Maltz, M. (1960). *Psycho-cybernetics: A new way to get more living out of life.* Englewood Cliffs, NJ: Prentice Hall.

Maslow, A. (1968). *Toward a psychology of being* (2nd ed.). New York: Von Nostrand Reinhold Company.

May, J. (2009). The hidden secret of success: The fun factor. *Coleman Griffith Lecture Keynote.* Association of Applied Sport Psychology. Retrieved September 11, 2010 from http://appliedsportpsych.org/conference/2009/keynotes

McCloy, C. H. (1958). What is sports medicine? *Journal of Health, Physical Education, and Recreation, 29,* 45–48.

McCarthy, J., & Clayton, R. D. (1973). Baseball academy: Implications for professional preparation. *Journal of Health, Physical Education, and Recreation, 44*(6), 6–7.

Meylan, G. (1917). Review of *Essais de psychologie sportive* by P. Coubertin. *American Physical Education Review, 22,* 58.

Morris, T., Alfermann, D., Lintunen, T., & Hall, H. (2003). Training and selection of sport psychologists: An international review. *International Journal of Sport and Exercise Psychology, 1,* 139–154.

Morris, T., Hackfort, D., & Lidor, R. (2003). From Pope to hope: The first twenty years of ISSP. *International Journal of Sport and Exercise Psychology, 1,* 119–138.

Moser, D. (1963, June 7). Athletes get help from hypnotists: Svengali comes to sport. *Life* pp. 71–72.

Müller, N. (1997). The Olympic Congresses in Lausanne. *Olympic Review, 16,* 49–59.

Murphy, S. (Ed.). (1995). *Sport psychology interventions.* Champaign, IL: Human Kinetics Publishers.

Murphy, S. M., & Ferrante, A. P. (1989). Provision of sport psychology services to the U.S. team at the 1988 summer Olympic Games. *The Sport Psychologist, 3,* 374–385.

Naismith, J. (1941). *Basket ball: It's origins and development.* New York: Association Press.

Naruse, G. (1965). The hypnotic treatment of stage fright in champion athletes. *International Journal of Clinical and Experimental Hypnosis, 13,* 63–70.

Neufeld, W. (1951). Relaxation methods in U.S. Navy air schools. *American Journal of Psychiatry, 108,* 132–137.

Ogilvie, B. C. (1989). Applied sport psychology: Reflections on the future. *Journal of Applied Sport Psychology, 1,* 4–7.

Olsen, A. M. (1966). *Sports psychology in the literature.* In F. Antonelli (Ed.), *Psychology of sports: Proceedings of the 1st International Congress of Sport Psychology* (pp. 1220–1224). Rome: International Federation of Sports Medicine.

Olympic Review. (1968). Some aspects of training for sport. *Olympic Review, 9,* 227.

Palmer, C. (2007). *Fired up! The optimal performance guide for wildland firefighters.* Roseville, MN: Birch Grove Publishing.

Park, R. J. (1994). A long and productive career: Franklin M. Henry—scientist, mentor, pioneer. *Research Quarterly for Exercise and Sport, 65,* 295–307.

Peurzer, R. J. (2004). The Kansas City Royals' Baseball Academy. *The National Pastime: A review of baseball history, 24,* 3–13.

Phillips, M. G. (2000). *From sidelines to centre field: A history of sports coaching in Australia.* Sydney, AU: Australian Coaching Council.

Psychologist to aid selection of Illini athletes. (1922, March 24). *Washington Post,* p. 14.

Psychology of athletics will be tried at Illinois. (1922, April 2). *New York Times,* p. 30.

Quartiroli, A., & Zizzi, S. J. (2011). A primer on the development of SEP in North America vs. Europe: Comparing the developmental paths of FEPSAC and AASP. *Athletic Insight, 3,* 1–16.

Raiport, G. (1978, February 19). The sports psychologist gives Russians an edge. *New York Times,* p. S2.

Riley, B. G. (1943). Boxing and psychology. *Physical Educator, 3,* 95–96.

Rodionov, A. (2005). *Mental conditioning before the game.* Retrieved September 12, 2010, from http://www.fiba.com/asp_includes/download.asp?file_id=453

Rodionov, A. (2010). *History of sport psychology.* Retrieved September 17, 2011, from http://systempsychology.ru/journal/2010_1_2/39-rodionov-va-istoriya-sportivnoy-psihologii.html using http://translate.google.com/

Rudik, P. A. (1962). The psychology of sport. In *Psychological science in the USSR* (Distributed by the Office of Technical Services, U.S. Department of Commerce). Washington, DC: U.S. Joint Publications Research Service.

Rushall, B. (n.d.). Practical consultations (national and international) for Brent S. Rushall. Retrieved September 11, from http://coachsci.sdsu.edu/rushall/consulpr.htm

Russ clinic at Stanford. (1961, December 14). *The Times,* p. 22.

Russia eyes hypnotism in sports. (1957, September 15). *New York Times,* p. S11.

Ryba, T. V., Stambulova, N. B., & Wrisberg, C. (2005). The Russian origins of sport psychology: A translation of an early work of A. C. Puni. *Journal of Applied Sport Psychology, 17,* 157–169.

Ryba, T. V., Stambulova, N. B., & Wrisberg, C. (2009). Forward to the past: Puni's model of volitional preparation. *International Journal of Sport and Exercise Psychology, 7,* 275–291.

Sage, G. H. (1974). Teaching sports psychology: Problems and prospects. In W. C. Schwank (Ed.), *The winning edge* (pp. 110–114). Washington, DC: American Alliance for Health, Physical Education.

Salmela, J. H. (1981). *The world sport psychology sourcebook.* Ithaca, NY: Mouvement Publications.

Salmela, J. (1987). Bulletin board. *The Sport Psychologist, 1,* 267–274.

Salmela, J. (1988). Bulletin board: Industry borrows sport psychologists: Our gain or loss. *The Sport Psychologist, 2,* 88.

Salmela, J. H. (Ed.). (1992). *The world sport psychology sourcebook.* Champaign, IL: Human Kinetics Publishers.

Scandinavian International University. (2011). *Mental training programs.* Retrieved March 31, 2011, from http://www.siu.nu/page_sub.asp?apid=13

Schwank, W. (1974). Foreword. In W. Schwank (Ed.), *The winning edge* (pp. 6–7). Washington, DC: American Alliance for Health, Physical Education, and Recreation.

Scott, W. (1917). *Increasing human efficiency in business: A contribution to the psychology of business.* New York: The McMillan Company.

Scripture, E. W. (1894a). Tests of mental ability as exhibited in fencing. *Studies from the Yale Psychological Laboratory, 2,* 122–124.

Scripture, E. W. (1894b). Reaction-time and time-memory in gymnastics work. In *Report of the ninth annual meeting of the American Association for the Advancement of Physical Education*. New Haven, CT: Press of Clarence H. Ryder.

Scripture, E. W. (1895). *Thinking, feeling, doing*. Meadville, PA: The Chautauqua Century Press.

Scripture, E. W. (1901). The psychological aspects of physical education. *American Physical Education Review, 6,* 298–299.

Seashore, C. E. (1919). *The psychology of musical talent*. Boston: Silver, Burdett and Company.

Seiler, R., & Wylleman, P. (2009). FEPSAC's role and position in the past and in the future of sport psychology in Europe. *Psychology of Sport and Exercise, 10,* 403–409.

Silva, J. M. (1989). The evolution of the Association for the Advancement of Applied Sport Psychology and the Journal of Applied Sport Psychology. *Journal of Applied Sport Psychology, 1,* 1–3.

Silva, J. M. (2002). The evolution of sport psychology. In J. M. Silva & D. E. Stevens (Eds.), *Psychological foundations of sport* (pp. 1–26). Boston: Allyn and Bacon.

Simons, J. P., & Andersen, M. B. (1995). The development of consulting practice in applied sport psychology: Some personal perspectives. *The Sport Psychologist, 9,* 449–468.

Slayer, J. (2009). James Naismith papers. Retrieved September 14, 2010, from http://www.spfldcol.edu/homepage/library. nsf/8E05E26111B1DC7C85257632005BD970/$File/ MS-506-James-Naismith-Finding-Aid.pdf010

Society for Psychology in the Performing Arts. (2011a). *About SPPA*. Retrieved April 2, 2011, from http://www.artspsych. org/index.php?option=com_content&view=article&id=44 &Itemid=27

Sport Psychology Today. (1983). US Olympic Committee establishes guidelines for sport psychology services. *Journal of Sport Psychology, 5,* 4–7.

Staley, S. C. (1952). School of physical education. In V. L. Nickell (Ed.), *Forty-ninth biennial report of the superintendent of public instruction of the State of Illinois, July 1, 1950–June 30, 1952* (pp. 68–69). Circular Series A, No. 88. Springfield, IL: State of Illinois.

Stambulova, N., Johnson, U., & Stambulov, A. (2008). Sport psychology consulting in Russia and Sweden. In R. J. Schinke & S. J. Hanrahan (Eds.), *Cultural sport psychology* (pp. 125–139). Champaign, IL: Human Kinetics Publishers.

Stoneroad, R. (1898). News notes: National Education Association. *American Physical Education Review, 3,* 313–314.

Straub, W. F., Ermolaeva, M. V., & Rodionov, A. V. (1995). Profiles and professional perspectives: Ten leading former Soviet Union sport psychologists. *Journal of Applied Sport Psychology, 7,* 93–11.

Stroebe, W. (2012). The truth about Tripplet (1898), But nobody seems to care. *Perspectives on Psychological Science, 7,* 54–57.

Strube, M. J. (2005). What did Triplett really find? A contemporary analysis of the first experiment in social psychology. *The American Journal of Psychology, 118,* 271–286.

Suinn, R. (1985). The 1984 Olympics and sport psychology. *Journal of Sport Psychology, 7,* 321–329.

Swoap, R. A. (1999). A history of division 47: Exercise and sport psychology. In D. Dewsbury (Ed.), *Unification through division: Histories of the divisions of the American psychological association, (*Vol. 4, pp. 151–173). Washington, DC: American Psychological Association.

Tenenbaum, G., Morris, T., & Hackfort, D. (2008). Sport and exercise psychology. In J. Borms (Ed.), *Directory of sport science* (pp. 209–235). Champaign, IL: Human Kinetics Publishers.

Tenenbaum, G., Lidor, R., & Bar-Eli, M. (2011). Obituary: Ema Geron (1920–2011). *International Journal of Sport and Exercise Psychology, 9,* 99–101.

The psychology of sport. (1922). *Journal of the American Medical Association, 78*(5), 368.

Triplett, N. (1898). The dynamogenic factors in pacemaking and competition. *American Journal of Psychology, 9,* 507–533.

Tuccimei, G. (1978). The Olympic medical team. *Olympic Review, 130,* 526.

Unestahl, L. E. (2011). *The International Society of Mental Training and Excellence*. Retrieved March 31, 2011, from http://www. worldcongressonexcellence.com/display.asp?apid=100

United States Olympic Committee. (1979). *Minutes of the Sports Psychology Subcommittee, Colorado Springs, CO, July 13–15*. In Dorothy V. Harris Papers, Pennsylvania State University, State College, PA.

University of Florida. (2007). *Performance psychology lab*. Retrieved April 2, 2011, from http://www.hhp.ufl.edu/apk/ ces/affil/pp/index.php

University of Illinois. (1921). *University Bulletin, 19*.

University of Illinois. (1922). *University Bulletin, 19* (29).

University of Illinois. (1930). *Transactions of the board of trustees*. Urbana, IL: University of Illinois.

University of Maryland. (2011). *University of Maryland Women*. Retrieved April 1, 2011, from http://lib.guides.umd.edu/ content.php?pid=126002&sid=1091405

University of Wisconsin, Madison. (2005). *Memorial resolution of the faculty of the university of Wisconsin Madison on the death of professor emerita Frances Z. Cumbee*. Retrieved April 1, 2011, from http://www.secfac.wisc.edu/ senate/2005/0502/1847(mem_res).pdf

Using Royals' heads. (1970, May 23). *The Sporting News*, p. 37.

Vaughan, G., & Guerin, B. (1997). A neglected innovator in sports psychology: Norman Triplett and the early history of competitive performance. *The International Journal of the History of Sport, 14,* 82–99.

Vealey, R. (2006). Smocks and jocks outside the box: The paradigmatic evolution of sport and exercise psychology. *Quest, 56,* 128–159.

Watson, R. I. (1956). Lightner Witmer: 1867–1956. *The American Journal of Psychology, 69,* 680–682.

Weiss, M. R., & Gill, D. L. (2005). What comes around goes around: Re-emerging themes in sport and exercise psychology. *Research Quarterly for Exercise and Sport, 76*(supplement), S71–S87.

Williams, J. M. (1985). *Organizational meeting minutes of the Association for the Advancement of Applied Sport Psychology*. Retrieved September 12, 2010, from http://www.bgsu.edu/ downloads/lib/file61131.pdf

Williams, J. M. (1986). *Executive board meeting minutes of the Association for the Advancement of Applied Sport Psychology*. Retrieved September 12, 2010, from http://www.bgsu.edu/ downloads/lib/file61132.pdf

Williams, J. M., & Straub, W. F. (2010). Sport psychology: Past, present, and future. In J. M. Williams (Ed.), *Applied sport psychology: Personal growth to peak performance* (pp. 2–11). McGraw-Hill: Boston.

Winter, B. (1981). *Relax and win: Championship performance*. San Diego: A. S. Barnes.

Witmer, L. (1911). *The clinic class for backward children.* Philadelphia: The Psychological Clinic Press.

Yale University. (1898/1899). *Catalogue of the officers and graduates of Yale University.* New Haven, CT: Yale University.

Yates, D. H. (1943). A practical method of using set. *Journal of Applied Psychology, 27,* 512–519.

Zitzelsberger, L. (1998). Editorial statement. *Journal of Excellence, 1,* 95.

The Psychology of Performance in Sport and Other Domains

Kate F. Hays

Abstract

This chapter addresses the psychology of performance in domains including sports, the performing arts, business/executive coaching, and high-risk professions. Performance psychology and sport psychology are described as interrelated fields. At the same time, with its long history of research as well as practice, sport psychology holds a particular, privileged position within the broader field of performance psychology. The roots of performance psychology lie in the fields of applied sport psychology, psychotherapy, and consultation or coaching. The chapter reviews critical issues in the psychology of performance: standards and excellence, competition, emotion, temporal factors, audience, pressure, performance consequences, and performers' developmental trajectories. Issues of appropriate preparation for performance psychology practice and performance psychologists' roles and ethics are briefly addressed. In the various domains of performance psychology, clients' attitudes toward consultants may vary. Further research, training, and practice implications are reviewed.

Key Words: Performance psychology, sport psychology, performing arts, executive coaching, excellence, competition, pressure, consultant, coach

The psychology of performance addresses the ways in which performers think, feel, and behave so as to obtain optimal results in their particular domain. Performance psychology addresses both the processes involved in developing performers' knowledge, skills, and abilities and the execution of those skills during a discrete performance event (Aoyagi & Portenga, 2010). Performance psychology, thus, can be characterized in terms of both process and outcome. In turn, performance psychologists are "defined by what we do (i.e., performance enhancement), not whom we do it with (e.g., athletes)" (Aoyagi & Portenga, 2010, p. 254). As will be described further, the psychology of sport, or sport psychology, holds a privileged position within performance psychology: It is one of the major performance domains, offers a long history of research into psychological factors influencing performance, and provides a rich resource of research and example.

In the sections that follow, I will examine the psychology of performance from a number of different angles: definitions of performance psychology and sport psychology, the sources for or roots from which performance psychology emerges, the conceptual relationship between performance psychology and sport psychology, the significant issues that are addressed within the psychology of performance, and a brief overview concerning consultants' appropriate training and application. The chapter concludes with some suggestions regarding future directions for the field.

Definitions of Performance Psychology and Sport Psychology

In its broadest definition, performance psychology might be viewed as the psychology of performance—that is, what people do when they are behaving purposively. The common features of performance psychology, however, are more specific and targeted: Performance psychology refers to the mental components of superior performance, in situations and performance domains where excellence is a central element. Performers "must meet certain performance standards: They are judged as to proficiency or excellence, there are consequences to poor performance, [and] good coping skills are intrinsic to excellent performance" (Hays & Brown, 2004, p. 19).

A temporal dimension is critical as well: A performer's particular talents and skills must be delivered at a specific point in time (Brown, 2001). Performance includes the achievement of competence at a particular activity in which performance before others is a central defining feature (Emmons & Thomas, 1998).

Although performance itself is defined by its outcome, sport and performance psychologists focus particularly on the processes that affect those performance outcomes. Performance can be viewed as a combination of the development and execution of knowledge, skills, and abilities in a given performance domain (Aoyagi & Portenga, 2010).

Four general areas or domains of performance—sports, the performing arts, business, and high-risk professions—have been the focus of both research and application. Although seemingly diverse, these four areas share certain characteristics. In particular, high levels of performance in these areas are both critical and, often, difficult to maintain (Hays & Brown, 2004). The task of the performance consultant is to assist in the development of more effective performance within the particular domain (see Chapter 37, this volume; Kampa & White, 2002).

In the process of defining the field of performance psychology, it is important to highlight the domain of sport psychology in particular. Sport psychology is in itself an academic discipline, typically, although not always, housed within departments of physical education or kinesiology. Sport psychology addresses the interaction of mind and body to produce highly skilled sport performance. Sport psychology includes such areas as learning, performance, and skill; developmental issues and youth sports; mental/psychological skills; counseling; group dynamics; and well-being (Singer, Hausenblas, & Janelle, 2001). Issues of injury and recovery are critical to performers whose body is their performance tool (see also Chapter 31, this volume).

With its long history based primarily within the sport sciences, but increasingly recognized and valued within psychology, sport psychology has been clustered and subdivided in a number of ways. As an amalgam of psychology and sport sciences, in this chapter, and indeed throughout this Handbook, the focus is on ways that sport psychology addresses sport performance and the psychological (cognitive, affective, and behavioral), interpersonal, and systemic elements that contribute to excellent sport performance. As this chapter explores more fully, it can be debated whether sport psychology is the basis for performance psychology or whether it should be subsumed within a broader category of performance psychology.

The Roots of Performance Psychology

Three general sources inform the overall field of performance psychology: applied sport psychology, psychotherapy, and consultation and coaching. Each offers a somewhat different framework, with distinct bases of history, knowledge, practice, application, and assumptions. Applied sport psychology contributes a long-established and well-defined field of quantitative and qualitative research with regard to one specific domain: performance excellence in athletes. Systems of psychotherapy, especially those that emphasize practical, present-focused, active, and affirmative treatment, have direct relevance to performance. Consultation and coaching emphasize the contextual and systemic knowledge that form a vital complement—or antidote—to the sometimes intra-individual focus of psychotherapy.

In general, each of the four principal performance domains draws from slightly different elements of these roots. Professionals working with athletes primarily make use of sport psychology research, some of which comes from concepts and research in the general field of psychology. Those working with business leaders in executive coaching often look to an equally long and separate tradition of research and practice emanating from industrial-organizational consulting. Performing arts consultation (see also Chapter 5, this volume) derives from a mix of applied sport psychology, psychotherapy, and performing arts medicine. Performance psychology with professionals in high-risk professions has thus far been derivative, although the bulk of available information appears to come from applied sport psychology.

Applied Sport Psychology

Psychological historian E.G. Boring identified Coleman Griffith as one of a select number of individuals with the potential to influence the entire field of psychology (Boring, 1950). A psychologist active during the 1920s and 1930s, Griffith conducted laboratory and field research with athletes while at the University of Illinois and subsequently as a performance consultant. Griffith can be considered the consummate (pre-Boulder) scientist-practitioner, setting the standard for integrating laboratory findings with practical application to real-world situations (Carron, 1993; Gould & Pick, 1995; Singer, 1989). In spite of Boring's prediction, it would be another 30 or more years until practitioners once again began assisting athletes regarding the psychology of their performance.

The academic discipline of sport psychology has until recent years been of little interest to psychologists (Brewer & Van Raalte, 2002; Murphy, 1995; Petrie & Diehl, 1995). Despite its name, sport psychology research was located within university departments of physical education; its application by psychologists to athletes' performance only began to be used systematically in the 1960s, with an initial clinical focus on personality variables and the psychological management of the elite athlete (e.g., Ogilvie & Tutko, 1966).

The public became more aware of sport psychology during the 1984 Olympic Games, when televised coverage included several features on the mental aspects of sport. This same period saw the development of applied sport psychology organizations, relevant journals, and graduate programs—the latter still within sport sciences departments (Williams & Krane, 1997; Smith & Christensen, 1995; see also Chapter 1, this volume).

As key peak performance skills were identified, efforts in the field immediately focused on how best to facilitate these abilities (known as psychological skills training [PST] or mental skills training [MST]). Rapidly, a set of cognitive-behavioral intervention techniques became the typical methods used with competitive athletes (see meta-analyses and reviews by Greenspan & Feltz, 1989; Meyers, Whelan, & Murphy, 1995). This PST "canon" (Andersen, 2000) focuses on the psychological processes that govern performance, such as arousal management, concentration and attention, motor control and rehearsal, goals, and motivation, and these topics are addressed in Part Two of this Handbook. Applied research examining interventions designed to change performance has been augmented by research in the neurosciences concerning the brain mechanisms that underlie performance (e.g., Decety, 1996; Jeannerod, 1997).

Psychotherapy

With some notable exceptions, the techniques of much of applied performance psychology are consonant with a number of current methods of psychotherapy practice. Contemporary psychotherapy often attends to individuals' interests in and ability to grow and change, to solve problems, and to become increasingly effective. Cognitive-behavioral therapy (CBT) and solution-focused methods in psychology seem to provide a particularly good "fit" with performance consultation. Cognitive-behavioral methods offer relevant tools that have regularly been applied in working with athletes. "These PST interventions come directly from CBT...and have been modified to address sport performance issues" (Andersen, 2009, p. 12). Solution-focused techniques (De Shazer, 1985; O'Hanlon & Weiner-Davis, 1989) share with performance consultation an emphasis on present behavior and practical solutions to problems.

More recently, researchers and practitioners have been adapting mindfulness, acceptance, and positive psychology in their work with performers (Gardner & Moore, 2007; Park-Perin, 2010). These techniques focus in particular on the present and can assist performers in such essential performance methods as nonjudgmental attention and concentration. Positive psychology, focusing on "what works, what is right, and what is improving" (Sheldon & King, 2001, p. 216), was developed by Martin Seligman and others (Seligman & Csikszententmihalyi, 2000) in large part as an antidote to a disease- or pathology-focused understanding of human beings. Interestingly, this approach has also long been championed by sport psychologists working on performance enhancement:

> In most cases, psychologists are helping unhappy, dysfunctional people to be normal. That is not what we're trying to accomplish at all. The people I work with want to be the best.
> (*Bob Rotella*, quoted in Newburg, 1992, pp. 16–17)

> The problem is that over time psychology has become the study of abnormal human behavior. That's clearly not what a sport psychologist does. What is so attractive about sport psychology is that we're not dealing with people who are having psychological difficulties. We're dealing with generally healthy people....
> (*Linda Bunker*, quoted in Newburg, 1992, p. 17)

These theoretical perspectives and their accompanying methodologies, techniques, and exercises have immediate applicability to performance psychology in their directed attention to the constructive elements within individuals and situations (Meyers et al., 1995; Murphy, 1995). Clinical and counseling psychologists, proficient in various methods of psychotherapy, use their knowledge, training, and experience in mechanisms of change to help athletes and other performers with performance issues. Within the domain of sport psychology in particular, various educators and practitioners have engaged over many years in lively debate on the validity of a psychotherapeutic as compared with an enhancement perspective; that is, healing or amelioration versus education and skill development (Aoyagi & Portenga, 2010).

In the final analysis, performance psychology is probably evolving toward a field that requires either a breadth of knowledge from multiple domains or a team of experts with diverse proficiencies who can work together to support high-level performance. An educational and strength-based perspective may be most effective and useful for the majority of performance interventions. A lack of grounding in theories and practice in counseling and psychotherapy may become a limiting factor in some situations, however, especially those in which psychological barriers limit performance (Aoyagi, Portenga, Poczwardowski, Cohen, & Statler, 2012; see also Chapters 28 to 34 of this volume). Practitioners from noncounseling backgrounds may lack the sequenced training of counseling skills and supervised practice that would effectively prepare them for a range of clientele and situations. Also, without a broader background and perspective, sport science–trained practitioners may be somewhat hampered in their capacity to generalize performance psychology theory and techniques to other domains. On the other hand, those unfamiliar with motor skill development, physiology, biomechanics, and peak performance may be limited in truly helping performers achieve their personal best. This may be especially true for the most elite performers: Competing at a world-class level means a full integration of mental and physical skills (see also Chapter 23, and 25, this volume).

Division 47 of the American Psychological Association (APA) developed the Proficiency in Sport Psychology (Public description of sport psychology, n.d.) to underscore the specialized, sport-specific knowledge that psychologists need, beyond that necessary for licensure.

Consultation and Coaching

The roots of consultation and coaching lie in such diverse areas of theory and practice as industrial-organizational psychology, family and systems psychology, and community psychology. All focus in one way or another on the recognition that individuals do not operate in isolation and that there is a powerful interaction between the person and his or her environment. This systemic perspective informs such issues as gaining access or "entry" into a system, formal and informal power, strategic interventions, role function, situational determinants, a focus on solutions to current issues, and a collaborative perspective (Kampa-Kokesch & Kilburg, 2001; Newman, Robinson-Kurpius, & Fuqua, 2002; Sarason, 1967; Wynne, McDaniel, & Weber, 1986). Industrial-organizational psychology, with its roots in organizational theory, human motivation, learning theory, and problem identification and analysis, can provide a strong initial base for coaching (Caironi, 2002).

An athletic coach—or for that matter, an acting coach—works with the performer to build or strengthen already existing skills. The term "coach" (derived from the sport setting, activities, and relationship) thus implies that, although the coach trains, directs, and assists, it is the performer who undertakes the action.

Certain techniques, such as reframing, active listening, empathy, and a focus on solutions, are the province of both coaching and psychotherapy. Coaching has been described as differentiated from psychotherapy in that the focus is on building on a person's strengths, resources, and passions to actualize growth and potential rather than on treating psychopathology (Dean, 2001; Harris, 2002; Levinson, 1996).

Work between an athlete and sport psychologist is usually described as "consultation"—perhaps to differentiate the role and activity from athletic coaching. In the business context, however, "coaching" is the more common term (Jones, 2002). Coaching has been described as linking "industrial-organizational skills with counseling skills" (Dingfelder, 2006). "Goal-oriented and collaborative" (Foster, 1996), the goal of executive coaching is to assist executives in improving overall performance, with a consequent improvement in the performance of the larger organization (Kilburg, 1996). Typically, an outside consultant is hired by a business organization to meet at regular intervals with a company executive to "improve the executive's managerial skills, correct serious performance problems, or facilitate long-term development" (Witherspoon & White, 1996, p. 125).

The Relationship Between Performance Psychology and Sport Psychology

As indicated in the preceding section, some elements of performance psychology derive from sport psychology. In turn, sport psychology has evolved out of various avenues of knowledge. Differing Venn diagrams can illustrate the complex interrelationship between performance psychology and sport psychology: Varying size circles overlap in some instances, whereas in other cases, the circles are nested. I will approach an analysis of the connection between the two fields in the following ways: psychology dominant, with sport psychology a subset; sport psychology as dominant in relation to performance psychology; a disconnect between sport psychology and other areas of performance psychology; or, in occasional instances, an active rejection of sport psychology within performance psychology.

Sport Psychology Informed by Mainstream Psychology

Although the academic and research housing of sport psychology has often been within university sport science departments, much of the practice of sport psychology derives from other areas in human performance. Perhaps the most obvious of these is the "final common path" of cognitive-behavioral theory and techniques, as applied both in clinical contexts and in the development of PST with athletes. The work of Lazarus (e.g., Lazarus, 1991, 1999; Lazarus & Folkman, 1984), for example, has informed much of the research and practice regarding stress and stress coping among athletes.

The research and analyses of goal setting effects in enhancing performance in organizational and industrial settings forms another example (e.g., Locke & Latham, 1990). Burton's application of these findings to the sports arena, and others' subsequent work in the area (e.g., Burton, Naylor, & Holliday, 2001), has offered a rich stream of research and practice. Despite its promise for sport, however, it has been noted that goal setting is more effective in enhancing performance in the world of work than in the sports domain (Burton, Naylor, & Holliday, 2001).

A number of other psychological theories and research applications were initially directed to the broader arena of psychology and subsequently applied to the sports context. Disparate examples would include educational research regarding achievement motivation in school children (e.g., Dweck, 1999) that has been applied to sports (Duda & Hall, 2001); research dating back to mid 20th century industrial-organizational psychology on leadership and team cohesion (e.g., Festinger, Schachter, & Back, 1950; Sherif & Sherif, 1969) with direct application to sport psychology (Paskevich, Estabrooks, Brawley, & Carron, 2001); the general work on the theory of flow (Csikszentmihalyi, 1990) that has been specifically applied to understanding peak performance in sport (Jackson & Kimiecik, 2008); or research and theory concerning talent development and expertise in sport and other domains (Ericsson, 1996).

Sport Psychology Informs Performance Psychology

As indicated earlier, sport psychology is one of the fundamental strands in the development of performance psychology. Framing their research as a measure of the consonance of sport psychology in relation to other performance domains (performing arts, business, and high-risk professions), Hays and Brown (2004) found many areas of similarity. As a female musician who was an avid golf player commented, "I am finding it really fascinating to see the parallels between athletic performance and what musicians do. We both have to practice skills until things become automatic; then we have to get out of our own way to show them to others" (p. 3).

Many business executives experience a face-valid connection between focus on athletic peak performance and that within business (Jones, 2002; McCann, 2009; Strauss, 2001; see also Chapter 4, this volume).

Interestingly, the "aha!" of connection has at times been appreciated by someone in another area of performance and then thrust on the sport psychology professional. Graham Jones, for example, a university academic who conducted research and consulted with elite athletes, was approached by a senior executive in a large business firm. The executive wanted to make use of Jones' knowledge of high-level performance. "This was a very responsive environment ready to experiment with many of the key principles of elite sport performance, and the important factor was that the majority of the key principles seemed to apply well to the business environment" (Jones, 2002, p. 269). Jones noted a variety of parallels between sports and business: organizational constraints, stress resulting from the high visibility and public nature of performance outcomes, transformational leadership, and the importance of team functioning. Similarly, a number of well-known sport psychologists have adapted their research and practice to the world of business. Robert Nideffer, for instance, widened his research and procedures regarding concentration and attention from the initial sports application (1970s) to evaluation methods within military and business settings (1990 and subsequently) (EPS history, n.d).

Parallel interests in the psychology of excellence in sports and in business in the 1980s and 1990s, and anecdotal reports of the connections and similarities between successful leadership in sports and the business world, resulted in a proliferation of popular books and motivational speeches by big-name sport coaches (Weinberg & McDermott, 2002). A preliminary investigation, comparing sport and business leaders' perceptions of critical aspects of organizational effectiveness in regard to group dynamics, suggested a close, although not exact, relationship between perceived characteristics of success in the worlds of business and sport (Weinberg & McDermott, 2002).

Sport psychology techniques are being applied in ever-broadening areas of performance, such as work with public safety officers and those in other high-risk professions (Le Scanff & Taugis, 2002; Newburg, Kimiecik, Durand-Bush, & Doell, 2002; Seligman & Matthews, 2011). A French sport psychologist, for example, was approached by that country's police Special Forces to design a stress management program. The organization turned to the sport psychologist specifically because the focus of mental skills training was on performance improvement, education, and behavioral control rather than recovery from psychopathology (Le Scanff & Taugis, 2002).

Performing artists have made use of applied sport psychology to some degree. The unanticipated transition from sport psychology consulting to business coaching, described earlier, is paralleled in published reports by some sport psychology practitioners who were approached by musicians for performance enhancement training (e.g., Emmons & Thomas, 1998; Greene, 2001). As sports medicine informed performing arts medicine, so sport psychology has informed performing arts psychology. Although artistic performance evaluation tends to be more subjective than objective, both sport and the performing arts "involve socially evaluated performances of motor skills" (Poczwardowski & Conroy, 2002, p. 315). Drawing on the literature in sport psychology, Hays (2002) suggested that performing arts psychology could benefit from research and practice, particularly with regard to performance enhancement, developmental issues, injury and retirement, and eating disorders (see also Chapter 5, this volume).

Performance Psychology Disconnected from Sport Psychology: Other Sources of Information and Knowledge

The well-established field of industrial-organizational psychology and/or business management, with its own traditions and literature, exists entirely separate from sport psychology. The website for the Society for Industrial-Organizational Psychology (SIOP) notes that "Industrial-organizational (I-O) psychology is the scientific study of the workplace. Rigor and methods of psychology are applied to issues of critical relevance to business, including talent management, coaching, assessment, selection, training, organizational development, performance, and work-life balance" (What is I-O?, n.d.) The website further indicates that industrial-organizational psychology is directed toward "the application of psychology to all types of organizations providing goods or services, such as manufacturing concerns, commercial enterprises, labor unions or trade associations, and public agencies."

Even though sport psychologists have become involved in business coaching, whether through their own interest and instigation or on invitation from people in the business world, it is important to recognize the prior legitimacy, research base, and separate field of industrial-organizational psychology. Not to learn from this field is somewhat equivalent to practitioners who become engaged in working with athletes without knowing about the field of sport psychology.

Although public safety and health-related high-risk professions are age-old, the systematic provision of psychological services to these professionals has occurred fairly recently (Scalora, 2009). Much of the research that informs such work comes from applied psychology, psychology and the law, and the literature on occupational stress. A proficiency in Police Psychology within APA, for example, was approved in 2008. This domain consists of "the application of the science and profession of psychology in four primary domains of practice: assessment, clinical intervention, operational support, and organizational consulting" (Public description of police psychology, n.d.).

Sport Psychology Eschewed by Performance Psychology

Are there domains of performance psychology in which the two Venn circles (performance psychology and sport psychology) are not only entirely disconnected but actively separate, in which the sport psychology paradigm does not work? In my experience, some performing artists intentionally reject information that might be useful to their domain if they see it as derived from sport psychology.

Performing artists may perceive sport psychology as irrelevant at best, or antithetical at worst, if they do not understand the commonalities. Further, for some performing artists, the sport domain is a direct competitor, whether for visibility, glamor, prestige, recognition—or financial support (Hernandez, Russo, & Schneider, 2009). Performing artists may, additionally, assume that there are fundamental differences between the arts and sports in regard to values, systems, and goals. They may view sport as, in essence, focused on competition and the dichotomy of winning or losing, while seeing the arts as centered on aesthetics and beauty. That both performance processes share similarities may clash with the worldview of these artists (Hays, 2002).

To some degree, this separation can be overcome by careful attention to the language and culture of performing artists. The popular phrase "mental toughness," for example, has been well-researched in sport psychology (e.g., Gucciardi, Gordon, & Dimmock, 2009a,b; Jones, Hanton, & Connaughton, 2007). In teasing out the elements of mental toughness, Jones, Hanton, and Connaughton characterize top-level sport as consisting of "a demand to excel at optimal levels while performing under conditions that are considered extremely demanding" (2007, p. 243). Many in business or high-risk professions can easily adapt this concept and related research to their domains, even if mental toughness is "one of the most used but least understood terms" (Jones et al., 2007, p. 244). Performing artists may be less willing to strive for "mental toughness" but much more willing to accept a comparable term, such as "resilience," a mainstay of positive psychology (e.g., Fredrickson, 2001).

This cautionary note should be taken as just that: a caution. It can serve as a reminder that consultants need to maintain "contextual intelligence" (Brown, Gould, & Foster, 2005) in working within different performance domains. Among others who have embraced the connection between sports and the performing arts, for example, double bass player Barry Green joined with Timothy Gallwey to extrapolate the "inner game" principles from sport to instrumental music (Green & Gallwey, 1986).

Critical Issues in the Psychology of Performance

Do the various performance domains I have discussed share similar critical processes regarding the psychology of performance? Or, are there significant differences that require further study? By "comptrasting," that is, comparing and contrasting, it becomes possible to understand more about performance in general, as well as the similarities and differences between particular performance domains.

Because elite sport performance is public, popular, and universal, with outcomes that have both intrinsic and extrinsic consequences, "sport provides the ideal laboratory for examining the stress response and its effects" (Jones, 2002, p. 271). At the same time, direct applications to other performance domains may require careful examination. For example, although considerable research has been conducted regarding coping in sport, a qualitative comparison of athletes' and performing artists' coping strategies concluded that coping taxonomies are probably oversimplified: "Sport psychology consultants delivering performance-enhancement services to nonathletic performers should consider domain-specific examinations of the performance demands, language, and other attributes of respective subcultures" (Poczwardowski & Conroy, 2002, p. 326).

The key issues that will be discussed here include standards and excellence, competition, emotion, temporal factors, audience, pressure, performance consequences, and performers' developmental trajectory. A number of these issues are examined in greater depth in subsequent chapters of this Handbook.

High Standards and Excellence

One of the defining characteristics of performance, as has been noted, is the development and maintenance of high standards, with a focus on excellence.

> A perfect 10! Go for the gold! You're on! Break a leg! Have a good one! No mistakes! [sic] Such demands set the stage for a perfect performance. For dancers, musicians, and actors, meeting exceptionally high standards is a way of life. For elite athletes and surgeons performing life-threatening operations,

flawless, human-powered precision is expected; perfection is the goal.
(*Mainwaring*, 2009, p. 139)

Considerable research and theoretical framing underlies concepts of adaptive and maladaptive perfectionism, applied to sports and the performing arts (e.g., Flett & Hewitt, 2005; Gould, Diefenbach, & Moffet, 2002; Hamilton, 2008). Mainwaring suggested that the term "performance perfection" be used to denote "the aspiration for perfection in a particular domain of functioning" (Mainwaring, 2009, p. 142). In his own research and in his review of research in this field, Stoeber (see Chapter 15, this volume) has partially resolved the perfectionism dilemma by differentiating two main dimensions of perfectionism—perfectionistic strivings and perfectionistic concerns. In general, Stoeber finds that studies indicate that perfectionistic strivings are positively associated with performance; perfectionistic concerns are not consistently negatively associated with performance. The research is complex, however, and further information regarding the interrelationship of performance and perfectionism is available in Chapter 15, Perfectionism and Performance.

Often internally fueled but with external expectations, the primary psychological issue for performers involves a sustained drive toward perfection. How does the performer maintain that energy without becoming beset by maladaptive perfectionist characteristics? Expectation of the self does not stand alone. It is linked to individual characteristics, whether those be personality traits or performance states. It is also dependent on the systemic factors or milieu in which performance is conducted.

Various studies have pointed to the interaction between ego orientation and perfectionism. To the extent that one is predisposed to seek external validation rather than growth, there are threats to self-worth and a greater likelihood of anxiety, depression, or generally poor functioning (Duda & Hall, 2001).

To some degree, domains with long performance traditions may accentuate the external demand for perfection; classical ballet offers a particularly rich example of this set of beliefs and practices (Hamilton, 1997). Cultural changes also influence performers' and audiences' expectations: running or swimming records that are routinely broken add pressure to the performer; musical recordings (comprising carefully spliced snippets from hours of performance recording, designed to obtain a "perfect"

sound) lead both performer and audience to expect that live performance should be equally flawless (Hays & Brown, 2004).

These challenges are difficult to resolve. Writing of sports, Botterill suggested that "excellence should be the goal; perfection by definition is impossible" (2005, p. 39). Striving toward excellence, that is, adaptive achievement, involves persistence even in the face of mistakes or perceived failures (Duda & Hall, 2001).

A perfectionistic equestrian, learning to manage her unrealistic self-expectations, reflected on a recent event in which she had participated in a horse show. "It's a great goal to strive for," she commented, speaking of her expectations about her performance, "but I shouldn't set it as a standard."

The high-stakes world of high-risk professions would seem to demand an expectation of perfection. Intriguingly, and perhaps because of a cultural recognition that perfection is not possible for human beings engaged in challenging activities, the potential for "medical errors" is recognized and tracked. Similarly, it is noteworthy that for 20 years, the Army's recruiting slogan was not "Be all that anyone could possibly be" but rather, "Be all you can be."

The mental skills particularly applicable to standards and expectations may include:

• Recognition and appreciation for achievement strivings that motivate the performer toward excellence
• Recognition that focusing on perfection may in fact subvert excellent performance
• Understanding the historical, institutional, and systemic forces that set expectations of perfection
• Regulation of arousal levels in order to be able to manage appropriate cognitions, affect, and behavior
• Effective goal setting and evaluation
• Ultimately, creating a balance of thoughts, feelings, goals, and expectations so that the performer can perform at an optimal, rather than "perfect," level

Competition

Competition is one of the hallmarks of performance. It is important, however, to distinguish between competitive situations and competitive motivation. Sports, for example, is in many ways defined by the competitiveness of the event, whether that be competing against the clock (striving for a particular time), competing against a standard (ranking), or contending against a competitor directly for a win. Other performance domains are often rife with competitive events and fierce competition, yet in these other arenas, "winning" is generally seen as a means to an end, rather than the end in and of itself. Musicians audition for orchestral positions; actors audition for parts in a play; law school students strive for clerkships. Achieving that coveted spot then allows the "winner" to perform; it is not the ultimate performance itself.

Primarily, competition is viewed as rivalry against another, a strong desire to win. This immediately implicates motivation and achievement. "Competition can trigger the drive to excel, to be our best, but it can also make us afraid, envious, and self-centered. It can push us to achieve more than we thought possible, but it also can make us fearful that we will lose what we have" (Balague, 2009, p. 163).

Although the term "competition" immediately suggests contention and triumph over another, in fact the word itself derives from Latin, and means "to come together," or "to strive together." Viewed from this perspective, competition becomes an enabling force that encourages drive, focus, and achievement.

The business world is rife with competition; one of the striking and complicating characteristics of competition within business is the rapid pace of change (Hays & Brown, 2004). Recently, the increased salience of electronic communications has, for example, meant that business professionals have extended their work day well into the night and weekend, in order to "stay competitive." The continuous interruptions of e-mails, tweets, and other forms of social media may feel necessary, but at the same time disruptive and unproductive. How does an individual business executive adapt to these changes? What pressures and demands are exerted? How does this shift in work–life balance affect the person's family relationships? Does this person respond to these changes with interest and excitement or dread and foot-dragging?

Competition within the high-risk domains may be more varied, subtle, and indirect. Competition to gain entry to medical school is often fierce; once in, competition between students continues, whether for prize placements or specialty training. Medicine is hierarchical. Likewise, the armed services and public safety systems operate within hierarchical structures, ones that imply and sustain competition.

Whereas competition is understood within business or sports to be one of the defining features, for the performing arts, "the competitive milieu…is sometimes unrecognized, overlooked, or minimized" (Hays & Brown, 2004, p. 58). The milieu and expectation, nonetheless, involve competition. There are labeled hierarchies and, often, auditions at every level of skill and competence. Acknowledging the amount of performance anxiety that is endemic to auditions, a jury panelist at the famous music school commented: "I hate audition time at Juilliard. The whole building shakes" (Kogan, 1989, p. 14).

Goal orientation has been identified as a key aspect of the motivational factors involved in competition. (For more on this subject, see Chapter 24, this volume.) "Task orientation is self-referenced; the focus is on mastery, and success is viewed as resulting from the exertion of effort. In contrast, ego orientation anchors performance in relation to others" (Balague, 2009, p. 163). Both motivational climate (the performance environment) and personality predispositions (achievement goal orientations), as well as their interaction, are relevant to determining attitudes and goals in competition.

Considerable research, particularly in sport, has examined the relative value of task and ego orientation both with regard to the achievement of success and the avoidance of failure. High ego orientation increases confidence, satisfaction, and energy when a performer is doing well. If other performers are perceived to be doing better, however, ego orientation can threaten the performer's sense of self-worth. Because of the other-focused nature of this type of motivation, protection of the sense of self becomes more central. An athlete high in ego orientation facing defeat may choose to invest less effort in order to avoid looking incompetent, a process known as *tanking* (Harwood, 2005).

A balance of both high task and high ego orientation may best serve an athlete in competition. The athlete maintains a fierce desire to win, at the same time sustaining effort and persistence, even if the situation becomes challenging. A high-task/high-ego motivated self-statement might be: "It's about performing to the best of your ability, being competitive and hungry, and learning about why you might have won or lost on that particular day" (Harwood, 2005, p. 30).

This perspective, one that values the optimal qualities of both types of orientation, can serve as a model not only for sport but for other performance domains. Since Western society in general and performance situations in particular tend to emphasize ego orientation, it is often useful for those around the performer, and the performer him- or herself, to attend to and reinforce those aspects that are most task-oriented. Particularly relevant mental skills may include:

• Awareness of one's personal tendency toward ego or task orientation
• Maintaining a daily or weekly achievement log, focused on goal setting in relation to process or performance, rather than outcome, goals
• Post-competition analysis, focusing in particular on questions "that relate to technical, physical, tactical, or mental skills" (Harwood, 2005, p. 35); this can apply to coaches, teachers, and parents, as well as performers themselves

The Role of Emotion in Performance

The topic of emotion, as a concept in psychology as well as sport psychology, has had a checkered existence. At different moments in history, its importance has been valued and denigrated, equally. Cognitive processes at times have been dominant or at the forefront. The current wave sees attention to emotion as not only pertinent but critical (Algoe & Fredrickson, 2011; Botterill, 2005; Greenberg, 2002). The interaction and balance of cognition, affect, and behavior, and their multiple ways of influencing one another, has become relevant.

In the popular mind, Daniel Goleman's *Emotional Intelligence* (1995) was a significant turning point in recognizing emotional awareness as valuable in many areas of performance, especially the world of business. Emotional intelligence (EI) "involves both awareness/perception of emotions and the effective management of those emotions" (McCann, 2009, p. 36). In addressing the role of emotion in performance, it becomes useful to distinguish between these two elements of emotion. Emotional awareness, knowledge, facility, and flexibility form one aspect; choice regarding the use or deployment of emotion during performance is another.

The Comprehensive Soldier Fitness (CSF) program, developed by researchers associated with Martin E. P. Seligman's positive psychology program at the University of Pennsylvania, is designed to measure the psychological strengths, assets, and problems of all members of the U.S. Army, in addition to offering programs intended to increase resilience and foster post-traumatic growth (Seligman & Matthews, 2011). In many respects, CSF is a quintessentially cognitive-behavioral program, writ

large. One component that is included recognizes "emotional fitness" and "emotional resilience" as teachable skills, akin to cognitive or physical fitness (Algoe & Fredrickson, 2011). "Basic training" is designed to assist soldiers in recognizing that emotions are ubiquitous; soldiers learn the full emotional spectrum, in order to increase their functional and adaptive use of emotion. Based on research developed by Fredrickson and colleagues over the past decade, the "broaden-and-build" theory posits the importance of a range of positive emotions to individual and group functioning, general well-being, and the development of resilience.

Training in emotional fitness for soldiers appears designed in particular to assist soldiers in the management of emotion in their everyday life both within their unit and in their family relationships (Algoe & Fredrickson, 2011). Although each of these might be considered "performance" opportunities, soldier "performance" as defined in the present chapter refers more to the specifics of battle. It is here that emotional regulation becomes especially relevant. The interaction of personal style, comfort with emotional expression, and the demands of the particular domain will all influence the emotion that becomes projected at this moment. For example, a professional sniper recognized that, although he was an "emotional" person, he tended to perform in role better when he focused on a variety of mental tasks and distanced himself emotionally from the situation. He knew that he functioned optimally, in role, when he was able to "kind of stand outside of the emotional sphere" (Hays & Brown, 2004, p. 179).

In some areas of performance, then, emotion regulation means maintaining control over either awareness or expression of emotion, whether during or outside of performance. (For further discussion of emotion regulation, see Chapter 8, this volume.) In general, traditionally "macho" areas of performance, whether military or contact sports, tend to see emotion as something to be ignored or suppressed. Performers may be reluctant or actually resistant to paying attention to emotion, assuming that it will imply weakness or vulnerability. "A business executive is more likely to admit to a bad decision than to a bad temper" (McCann, 2009, p. 37). For some, emotional expression may become a deliberate (even if unconscious) decision to express an acceptable rather than unacceptable emotion. Anger may be seen as an "acceptable" emotion. Smashing one's racket or throwing one's golf club may help an athlete feel strong—and (temporarily, at least) able to bypass the primary emotion of embarrassment over a poor play (Balague, 2009; Greenberg, 2002).

Similarly, in police work, "emotions are carefully separated from operational thinking.... Work performance is privileged, and affective maturity is left behind" (Le Scanff & Taugis, 2002, p. 331). The professional, physical, and psychological costs of this stance, however, can mean decreased professional efficiency, increased stress, poorer coping mechanisms, and distance from self-understanding and from emotionally engaged relationships (Le Scanff & Taugis, 2002).

Some performance domains, in contrast, are defined in part by the deliberate use of emotion and emotional expression. Method acting is perhaps the quintessential embodiment of this perspective. A trial lawyer, "playing to the audience" (i.e., the jury) may perform in as theatrical a fashion as a professional actor. Actors describe a flat, emotionally disengaged performance as one that has been "phoned in" (Hays & Brown, 2004). "The artist's emotional self-expression must evoke the kind of emotional response in the audience that convinces it of the performer's authentic artistic talent" (Kogan, 2002, p. 4).

One approach to integrating an understanding of emotions into performance consulting is *resonance theory*. This paradigm, and the *resonance performance model* heuristic, is based on an assumption that expert performers in all fields seek resonance, "a seamless fit between how they want to feel (internal) each day and the environment (external) in which they live" (Newburg et al., 2002, p. 252). The model has been applied to athletes, performing artists, business people, and those in medicine. Awareness of the "positive lived feelings," and the intention to elicit these feelings, gives performers the opportunity to manage potentially negative emotional responses to their striving. Performers then can engage in emotional reappraisal and self-regulation. Newburg and colleagues would describe this as "revisiting the dream" (Newburg et al., 2002). Within Resonance Theory, shifting from "what do I have to *do* today?" to "how do I want to *feel* today?" can allow an ongoing awareness and intentionality to performers' cognitions and actions.

Understanding the expression of the interrelationship between affect, cognition, and behavior in a particular domain is often key. As was noted regarding competition, contextual intelligence should guide the consultant. In the business world, "A consultant who describes EI as a means of enhancing productivity is much more likely to achieve behavior change than a consultant who frames some of the same issues as happiness, balance, or emotional well-being" (McCann, 2009, p. 37). In other domains, the opposite presentation would be experienced as authentic: Achieving balance, rather than producing more widgets, could well be a desired outcome.

The role of emotion in performance, then, varies from one domain to another and needs to take individual differences into account as well. Some of the relevant mental skills with regard to emotion in performance may include:

• Differentiation between felt emotion and its expression in the particular performance domain
• Language that conveys the value and utility of emotional knowledge within that domain
• Recognition that emotional awareness and expression can be taught, practiced, and used
• Individualized appreciation for the type and amount of emotional awareness and expression for optimal performance functioning (Hanin, 1999)

The Temporal Dimension

Delivering one's skill at a particular moment in time, being "on," is one of the central characteristics of performance. It is one of the elements that differentiates performance from practice (which could, at least hypothetically, occur at any time). It is the moment, whether the 21 seconds of hurdling or the 6 hours of neurosurgery, when all of one's mental skills need to be fully available. Extended focus, in the present, is particularly critical during performance. As a pianist noted:

> When you practice, you're always editing and you're always thinking backward, you're always evaluating. If you play a phrase, you stop and think back: "What can I fix, what would be better there?" But if you do that while you're performing, then at the moment that you're thinking backward you're not thinking about the music that you're playing at the moment.
> (*Hays & Brown*, 2004, p. 184)

The multidimensional construct of attention includes three elements: selective attention, actively divided attention, and concentration, deliberately investing "mental effort in information that seems most important at any given time" (Moran, 2010, p. 501). Robert Nideffer developed a model that looked at situational characteristics for performance and personal preference regarding attention. He suggested that attentional focus varies along two orthogonal dimensions: breadth (narrow or broad) and direction (internal or external). According to this model, different performance activities require differing attentional foci, and performers vary in their preferred attentional focus (Nideffer & Sharpe, 1978).

Because the temporal dimension defines the moment of performance, and because focused attention is so critical, the development of a "pre-performance routine" is a standard element of PST training. Changes to the performance time frame can be especially challenging. An outdoor event may be delayed by weather conditions; technical problems may beset the most seemingly performance-ready venue. Delays happen. Optimal performance preparation takes into account the potential for shifts of time and timing.

A collegiate gymnast who trained to be a member of Cirque du Soleil noted the temporal difference between the two roles: "The biggest difference is you know how to get up for the NCAAs and Big Tens, but [in] Cirque...you have to be at a peak performance 10 shows per week, 300 shows per year. You can't have an off-night, because that may be the only night somebody comes to see the show. It requires a different type of sports psychology" (Gerstner, 2010).

The relevant mental skills and processes related to attention, concentration, and the temporal dimensions of performance are discussed in detail in Chapter 6, and 7, this volume.

Audience

Within some domains, the people who observe and engage with the performer form a central, defining feature of that performance. Within other domains, spectators are at most implied. "Although the audience may be an important or even (financially) necessary element of sport performance, a sense of connection with the spectators is not essential to the activity itself. In contrast, one of the central purposes of the performing arts is presentation to an audience—that is, sharing one's art with others" (Hays, 2002, pp. 300–301).

Even for the same person using some of the same skills, yet in a different milieu or domain, "audience" can have very different meaning. This is vividly illustrated by the gymnast-turned-Cirque performer: "He never saw himself as a theatric performer though. McCarthy knew how to perform as a gymnast, playing to the judges and nobody else. Now, he's learning how to express himself as a character, such as an insect, animal or a mythical creature, to judging strangers in an audience" (Gerstner, 2010).

For a business executive, audience may comprise a "360" dimension. The executive is being watched and judged directly by supervisors, boards of directors, peers, and "reports." At a more abstract level, shareholders or customers become the implied audience, the ones to whom the performer feels accountable. A trial lawyer will definitely have an audience: Most directly, the lawyer will address the jury. At the same time, the lawyer will also be playing to the judge, opposing counsel, spectators, and journalists as well.

Issues of audience engagement and interaction are intricately tied in with levels of arousal and perfectionism. Playing in front of a large crowd, in front of a hostile crowd, or in front of an audience for the first time, can all greatly increase arousal and anxiety. Thinking about being observed and judged can trigger concerns about being perfect and increase internal monitoring of mistakes. In order to deal with unwanted and interfering negative emotions and cognitions, performers often need to have self-talk and other CBT strategies readily at hand. Some critically important mental skills will include:

• Arousal management strategies that can be used during performance
• Methods for focus, concentration, and refocus
• Relevant self-talk strategies that, adapted to the individual, the environment, and the demands of the domain, make constructive use of the performer's awareness of audience or assist the performer in minimizing focus on audience

Pressure

Perhaps above all, the multiple elements of optimal performance involve the experience of pressure. No other factor appears to be as universally identified among performers and observers as contributing to poor performance than this culminating sense of pressure that can interfere with well-learned performance. The performer must have enough confidence—or enough capacity to act "as if"—to be able to manage that pressure. The interaction of confidence, mental toughness, and competence all can directly impact the performer's response to pressure.

Competence is one of the central underlying elements of performance. It is only gained through knowledge and the accretion of experience. It is fundamental to a secure sense of confidence. In a series of semi-structured, in-depth interviews with high-level performers in various domains, the one necessary mental skill that all performers endorsed was "confidence" (Hays & Brown, 2004). These performers invariably defined confidence as a product of both thorough preparation and cumulative experience.

This personal confidence bears close connection to a number of other theoretical frames, in particular, self-efficacy (Bandura, 1986), mental toughness, and resilience. When Australian football coaches conceptualized mental toughness, the first-ranked construct was "self-belief" (Gucciardi & Gordon, 2008).

When performers high in ego orientation are not succeeding, they tend to focus on avoiding the demonstration of lack of competence; they work hard to avoid being wrong (Skaalvik, 1997). In and of itself, this self-protective shift adds pressure to the performer; it moves the performer's focus away from the goal of ultimate competence and does not give the performer information that will help the person refocus.

Situations that are likely to require high levels of mental toughness include preparation for training and competition, repeated failure, both personal and professional challenges, peer and social pressures, internal and external pressures, and the management of injury (Gucciardi & Gordon, 2008). The key mental toughness characteristics include self-belief, work ethic, personal values, self-motivation, a tough attitude, concentration and focus, reticence, capacity to handle pressure, emotional intelligence, sport intelligence, and physical toughness (Gucciardi & Gordon, 2008; see Jones, 2012). As was noted earlier, it is possible that many if not all of these characteristics could be identified among performers in other domains, if some relabeling were considered.

In general, at the time of performance, focusing on one's experience of pressure is likely to interfere with the performance itself. The key issues, thus, will be ways in which self-confidence can be sustained and task focus enhanced. In order to manage and counteract the experience of pressure, the full panoply of mental skills may be relevant:

• The experience of performance pressure arises from many sources and is to some extent domain-specific. Awareness and identification of that experience is necessary in order to select the appropriate response(s). A general schematic assesses the perceived demands and supports, the level of uncertainty, and the importance of the outcome. In general, performers will do best by decreasing the perceived demand, increasing perceived supports, handling uncertainty, and managing the perceived importance of the outcome (McGrath, 1970; Weinberg & Gould, 2011).

• Self-regulatory methods are critical. For any one individual, a specific combination of PST is likely to be most effective, e.g., arousal management (via diaphragmatic breathing or progressive muscle relaxation), cognitive restructuring (positive self-talk, countering, reframing), imagery, and an effective pre-performance plan.

• Methods for responding to affective as well as cognitive activation will be critical.

Performance Consequences

Expectations concerning performance, to some degree, affect performance itself. Performance is stressful in part because it does not exist only for its autotelic properties, the intrinsic pleasure of doing the particular activity (Csikszentmihalyi, 1990). The consequences to the performer's actions are, in fact, part of what defines performance.

The effect of consequence in relation to performance is particularly relevant in high-risk occupations: consequences may be a matter, literally, of life or death, whether in relation to oneself or others. A surgeon's knowledge, abilities, and skills must come together from the initial slice through the last stitch. Military personnel decisions may affect the lives of their platoon as well as of civilians or military, whether allies or enemies.

When contrasted with these absolutes, the performance consequences for an actor flubbing a line or a swimmer 1/10th of a second slow would seem to diminish in importance. But if it's a command performance, or if it's the Olympics, those consequences have great significance both in and of themselves and potentially in regard to that performer's professional future as well. *The Bone Cage* by Angie Abdou (2007) offers a detailed fictional account of process and outcome for Olympic-level contenders in swimming and wrestling.

In the business world, although financial loss may loom as a very large and real threat, often it is the potential loss of prestige among others and self-esteem within oneself that becomes threatened by inferior performance (Balague, 2009).

These demands are external; they are the outcome against which performance is judged. In some domains, performance outcome is (to some degree) linear: A successful business transaction may well augur promotion. In the performing arts, on the other hand, a successful "gig" often stands alone rather than being predictive of future roles or recognition (Kogan, 2002).

The relevant mental skills with regard to consequences may include:

- Attention to the ways in which the performer handles judgment about proficiency
- Cognitive control
- Structured opportunities for deliberate reflection
- Appropriate goal setting and evaluation

Pacings: Performance Development, Challenges, and Career Completion

For people whose sense of self is closely, if not inextricably, connected to their professional identity, a number of issues are tied to their performance trajectory. Here, I will look briefly at beginnings: performance development; middle challenges, such as injury, illness, and burnout; and endings, that is, performance limits. Part Four of this volume expands in much greater detail on issues of performance development and career limits.

The various elements that form the arc of a performer's career are interrelated. As Kierkegaard noted, life must be lived forward but can only be understood backward.

FAMILY AND THE DEVELOPMENT OF EXPERTISE

The performer's family of origin may have a marked influence on the entrance and development of the performer into his or her profession. The intra-individual differences that comprise personality are shaped—and equally, shape—those around them. This developmental trajectory is most visible for those whose performance careers start in early childhood or adolescence. A gymnast who begins her performance life at 6 and ends it on graduation from high school or college will be different from a pianist whose career also begins at 6 but ends in his 70s. In turn, these will differ from a surgeon whose career begins, develops, and continues in adulthood.

Research with children, parents, and coaches has resulted in a three-stage model of talent development in regard to athletes, tied closely to the family and the demands of the sport: the sampling years (ages 6–13), specializing years (13–15), and investment years (15 and up) (Côté, 1999; see

also Chapter 23, this volume). Family support for professional development involves various costs, including time, psychic energy, and actual finances. This in turn can be strongly influenced by socioeconomic status.

Although Côté's work has been specific to athletes, it has applicability to other areas of performance, perhaps most obviously for performing artists whose physical activity requires early learning (e.g., ballet; Hamilton, 1997) or musical specialization, such as the violin or piano (Davidson, Howe, Moore, & Sloboda, 1996). Even if not tied to specific ages, the construct sequence of sampling, specializing, and investment offers a broad perspective that can be applied to professional development in any area of performance.

OVERUSE AND BURNOUT

Burnout, classically including symptoms of emotional exhaustion, depersonalization or devaluation, and lack of personal accomplishment (Maslach, 1982; see also Chapter 30, this volume), has been posited as occurring in various areas of performance.

This framework may apply particularly in relation to those in professions, such as business and some high-risk professions, that have some longevity. At the same time, early sport specialization—and presumably, early specialization in other performance areas—can result in early burnout (Gould, Udry, Tuffey, & Loehr, 1996a,b). Especially in areas of performance involving physical activity, overtraining or overuse may become interpreted as burnout (Peterson, 2009).

Not surprisingly, burnout is also intimately interrelated with injury and illness. A track-and-field athlete returned to training after injury had forced her to discontinue the prior season. Her new coach, eager to train her for optimal performance in the new season, relentlessly increased training. Because he was concerned that the athlete would not be fully prepared without an uncompromising practice routine, he was loath to recognize symptoms of overtraining: her tiredness, sleep problems, irritability, and sense that her body just could not respond. At a meeting between the athlete, coach, and sports medicine physician, the coach relented and the athlete became a more effective advocate for her own recovery.

INJURY, ILLNESS, AND CAREER COMPLETION

Career limits, whether internally or externally imposed, are important aspects of performance.

Many sports have physical limitations; the wear and tear on the body mean that, for the most part, athletes will need to develop subsequent careers. Dancers experience medical issues and career limits similar to athletes; for other performing artists, however, age and physical limits may be less determinative (Hamilton, 1997; Mainwaring, Krasnow, & Kerr, 2001; Sataloff, Brandfonbrener, & Lederman, 2010).

There may be more similarity between than within performance domains. In some ways, the defining feature centers on the physical limits of the human body. For example, ballet has been called "the butterfly profession" (Kaye, 1998, p. AR1), in recognition of the way in which typically, by around age 30, a dancer will need to develop another career, whether within the field (e.g., as a teacher) or entirely outside of it. Similarly, gymnasts' careers end early.

On the other hand, athletes in some sports can extend their sports careers for many years. Shooting is a sport that sees Olympians in their 50s. Likewise, musicians' careers extend through a long life; opera singers' voices only mature in their late 20s. Soprano Sondra Radvanovsky had been singing professionally for 20 years before she felt prepared to take on the lead role in Verdi's *Aida*. "It's not an easy feat, so I waited until I was ready. As you age, you have greater stamina and can push your voice more" (The mega-soprano, 2010, p. 50). Famed cellist Pablo Casals performed well into his 70s and conducted other musicians in his 90s. For most business executives and high-risk performers in non–physically demanding roles, age means advancement and further career development (for a discussion of the role of age-related processes on performance, see Chapter 26, this volume).

Illness or injury (see Chapter 32, this volume) may sideline a performer or put that person's career on hold for some period of time. Although considerable research on the psychological aspects of injury and retirement has been conducted regarding athletes, the subject is only beginning to be addressed among performing artists (Hays, 2002). Dedicated performers who work in a group environment (e.g., team or company) will often feel a sense of separation, isolation, guilt, or ostracism when sidelined with injury or illness (Hays & Brown, 2004; Peterson, 2009).

Whether injury does or does not end the performing career, in those professions in which the performer's life has been consumed by this domain, especially from a young age, issues of identity foreclosure may need to be addressed (Murphy, Petitpas, & Brewer, 1996). Similarly, deselection may disrupt or end a performer's career path (Brown & Potrac, 2009).

In the management of burnout, overtraining syndrome, or illness or injury, effective methods of recovery can be critically important. Additionally, effective methods of recovery are crucial, ultimately, to the prevention of those aspects that limit the performer's optimal functioning. A model of systematic recovery, developed in relation to upper echelon executives, is applicable to all areas of performance that involve high levels of unremitting stress (Loehr & Schwartz, 2001).

Thus far, this chapter has considered definitions of performance psychology and sport psychology, the development of these fields, and a variety of critical issues that influence performance across all domains. Because these fields are above all interactive, it is critical to address the other side of the equation: not just the performer but also the consultant who works with the performer. What training is necessary for consultants? How are they perceived and experienced by performers? These two issues are addressed next.

Sport and Performance Psychology Consultants
Preparation and Application

In the same way that one would examine the question of knowledge, skill, and abilities among performers, especially within emergent fields of practice, it is important to consider these issues among practitioners (Aoyagi & Portenga, 2010; Aoyagi et al., 2012; Brown, 2009). By analogy with the field of nuclear physics, one can consider the "half-life" of knowledge and skill: In 1972, Dubin suggested that the half-life of the doctoral degree in psychology was about 10–12 years. Given the rapid pace of knowledge development and dissemination over the subsequent 40 years, professional obsolescence, or the half-life of a professional's knowledge, may now be considerably shorter (Wise, 2010), especially in new and emerging fields (Neimeyer & Taylor, 2011). This suggests the necessity of ongoing learning, particularly as sport and performance psychology develops.

TRAINING

Within the larger field of sport and performance psychology consulting, the overall picture includes a mixture of both formal and informal knowledge and skill. Among the formal elements are those developed during academic degree preparation and subsequent structured training. Informal preparation may include performance experience, informal training opportunities, and pertinent formative life experiences (Hays & Brown, 2004).

The field of sport psychology is in some ways separate from the other areas of performance psychology, since graduate programs, standards, and criteria have been developed with regard to competent practice (Association for Applied Sport Psychology, n.d.; Sachs, Burke, & Schweighardt, 2011; American Psychological Association [APA], 2002; Association for the Advancement of Applied Sport Psychology, n.d.; APA, n.d.). At the same time, the integration of sport and exercise psychology into graduate training in mental health practice is still markedly limited (Pasquariello, 2011). Practitioners interested in sport psychology should at the very least be cognizant of the resources and expectations concerning the practice of sport psychology.

Executive coaching has become very big business: It is estimated that companies spend around $1 billion each year, worldwide, on executive coaches (Dingfelder, 2006). The field, however, is only marginally regulated, with a nearly chaotic mix of charlatans, undertrained professionals, and skilled coaches vying for coveted and lucrative positions.

Practitioners interested in coaching in business settings may come to that work through a variety of training methods; for example, through general training as a psychology practitioner, sport psychology grounding with further applications in the business world, training in consulting psychology or industrial-organizational psychology (see O'Roark, Lloyd, & Cooper, 2005), or coach training (e.g., International Coaching Federation, n.d.). Any of these routes may be supplemental to one's initial training and practice.

Consulting work with performing artists and high-risk professionals is still in its nascent stages and, as a result, training to work with these types of performers may be more idiosyncratic. It is likely to rely on practitioner interest or expertise in the domain in question, along with informal training subsequent to professional training. This route will seem familiar to those who conducted performance enhancement work with athletes in the early years of the development of applied sport psychology.

Especially within an emergent area of practice, informal preparation takes on more significance (Belar et al., 2001; Brown et al., 2005; Glueckauf, Pickett, Ketterson, Loomis, & Rozensky, 2003; Hays & Brown, 2004). Relevant reading, observation, or direct experience in the domain may all become a central part of one's additional learning. Interacting with others, whether through being coached, mentored, or supervised, allows further individualized learning and application.

Ongoing informal learning often occurs through the development of a network of colleagues. These colleagues can serve as sounding board, resource, or means of peer review when the consultant encounters challenging situations.

Interest in a domain, although important, does not in and of itself suffice for adequate training or self-labeling. Professional arrogance, ignorance, or hubris at times stands in the way of further specialized training (Hays & Brown, 2004). Charles Brown (personal communication, February 28, 2011), for example, has commented on not knowing what he didn't know until he obtained sport psychology training, subsequent to his formal training in counseling and family systems work.

ROLE

As previously noted, sport and performance psychology can be defined by both process and outcome, the development and execution of knowledge, skills, and abilities (Aoyagi & Portenga, 2010). Aoyagi and Portenga differentiate between the activity of performance enhancement and the particular population with whom it is applied. These authors further contend that doing psychotherapy with an athlete is not sport psychology, as it "does not directly improve people's ability to perform a desired skill" (2010, p. 254). It is worth noting that others, however, would consider this definition more arbitrary than either performers want or need, or practitioners deliver.

It is also important to reflect on the distinction between generalist and specialist. In some ways, it can be argued that a performance psychologist can provide performance enhancement services regardless of performance domain. A more nuanced perspective suggests that contextual intelligence will be critically important to effective service delivery (Aoyagi et al., 2012; Hays & Brown, 2004).

Performance psychologists practice in a number of different settings and take on a variety of roles. Services typically range from educational to clinical to systems consultation—and with all points in between. Depending on the domain, performance consultants may work within university counseling centers, be employed by organizations on a contractual basis, teach classes or workshops, offer consultation in a private practice office, or go on the road, whether literally or figuratively (i.e., electronically) (Brown, 2009).

ETHICS

Successful professionalization of a field is defined in part by the presence of an ethics code (Whelan, Meyers, & Elkins, 2002). One of the initial tasks following the founding of the Association for the Advancement of Applied Sport Psychology (now the Association for Applied Sport Psychology; AASP) was the development of a code of ethics for the practice of sport psychology (Ethics code, n.d.). Similarly, the International Coaching Federation has developed an ethics code (International Coach Federation, n.d.). Psychologist members of the APA maintain an obligation to understand and abide by that organization's ethics code (APA, 2002).

Ethics can be understood as encompassing more than just the application of a specific code. Ethics includes both responsiveness to specific documents and a "continuing process of attending to one's knowledge, beliefs, values, and practices" (Hays, 2006, p. 224). This latter, "positive ethics," emphasizes the practitioner's full ethical or moral development (Aoyagi & Portenga, 2010). A number of ethical issues in sport and performance psychology are especially relevant, including competence, multiple role relationships, confidentiality, boundaries, and self-regulation (Aoyagi & Portenga, 2010; Hays, 2006; Stapleton, Hays, Hankes, & Parham, 2010). A more extensive discussion of issues in regard to ethics can be found in Chapter 3, this volume.

Client Attitudes Toward Consultants in Sport and Performance Psychology

Because coaching and consultation in sport and performance psychology are interactive processes, consultants' knowledge, training, and skills need to be matched to some degree by client interest and willingness to engage. Along with clients' own personality and situation, their attitudes toward working with a sport or performance consultant is critical to the effective functioning of that relationship.

Historically, performers in settings that have been male-dominated and where the role of emotion is minimized during performance, such as sports, business, medicine, and the law, have been somewhat cautious about seeking performance services. The notion of working with a "shrink" seemed to indicate weakness or vulnerability (Linder, Pillow, & Reno, 1989). Practitioners can also tackle this issue from the marketing side of the field, as with the clever adage of baseball performance consultant Harvey Dorfman, who told skeptics: "I'm not a shrink; I'm a stretch" (Shapiro, 2011).

As the domain of applied sport psychology becomes better known, team consultation at both the collegiate and professional level has been increasing (Kornspan & Duve, 2006)—and increasingly well received (Wrisberg, Loberg, Simpson, Withycombe, & Reed, 2010; Wrisberg, Simpson, Loberg, Withycombe, & Reed, 2009). For example, collegiate coaches whose teams had met with a sport psychology consultant more than five times were likely to be supportive of further contact with sport psychology consultants. The topics in which they were interested included managing pressure, confidence development, focus, communication (coaches and teammates), and the management of emotion during competition (Wrisberg et al., 2010). Likewise, media more frequently report high-profile athletes' use of sport psychology services for performance enhancement, not just treatment of emotional problems, whether collegiate, Olympian, or professional athletes. Many athletes themselves seem more comfortable today discussing their consultations with a sport or performance psychologist or consultant. In her autobiography, Monica Seles described her work with sport psychologist Jerry May after she was stabbed on court in 1993 (Seles, 1996); after winning the 2011 British Open, Darren Clarke discussed with the media his work with Bob Rotella. Perhaps because they are paying attention to this behavior as it is modeled by their sports heroes, adolescent athletes increasingly seek out sport psychology services (Hays & Lesyk, in press).

For at least the past 80 years, business leaders have encountered various types of consultants. Although executive coaching is a recent phenomenon, the legitimacy of consultation and coaching in business is well established, as compared with domains unaccustomed to consultants. Given the wide variability in skills, knowledge, and credentials of consultants and coaches in the field, however, performance coaches may encounter both more competition and more skepticism (Hays & Brown, 2004).

Partly because it is newer and still being defined, and partly because of a culture that eschews neediness, consultation to professionals in or training to be in high-risk professions may be especially challenging. Credibility is often gained through informal knowledge, whether that is a similarity of lived experience or willingness to "hang out" and learn the culture from within (Hays & Brown, 2004). "Walkabouts" at military bases and the front-line allow soldiers to make meaningful connections with military psychologists (Moore & Reger, 2006). This tactic seems reminiscent of sport psychologists' actions and methods at Olympic venues (Haberl & Peterson, 2006).

Since performing artists are often interested in matters of cognition and affect, one might think that entrée into consultation with performing artists would be especially easy. There are a few stumbling blocks, however. Performing artists may assume that if they were to work with a psychologist, this would mean engaging in traditional psychotherapy (i.e., that, by definition, it would be long-term, depth-focused, expensive, and therefore unaffordable; Hays, 2002). They may think that performance enhancement training would imply that their performance or ability was in some ways ineffective (Schoen & Estanol-Johnson, 2001). Different from other, seemingly more resistant, performers, those in the performing arts may need particular information and education as to the methods and usefulness of performance psychology (Hays & Brown, 2004).

Conclusion

This chapter has been designed to open the door to the central purpose of the Handbook: exploring the yin and yang of sport psychology and performance psychology. How does each inform the other? Where are the gaps? What are the differences? Does one need to be subsumed within the other?

These questions and possibilities have been raised since the late 20th century, yet it is now, in the second decade of the 21st century, that they are actively being addressed. Courses, workshops, practice, and organizations recognize these intersecting fields. Performance psychology is formally acknowledged through such mechanisms as the *Journal of Sport, Exercise, and Performance Psychology*, whose inaugural issue appears in 2012. Similarly, this Handbook reflects the knowledge base necessary for initial delineation of this field. New leaders in the field call for a training model in which sport psychology is incorporated into a broader framework of performance psychology (Aoyagi et al., 2012). New answers emerge—and along with them, new questions arise.

From this overview of the psychology of performance in sport and other domains, some conclusions seem warranted:

- To the extent that performance psychology is a field in development, sport psychology has provided a model that offers strengths as well as its own challenges: a strong body of research; divergent means and entry points to practice; training models that have some inherent limitations for the full practice of sport psychology, let alone performance psychology; and unresolved tensions between the academic fields of sport sciences and psychology.
- If all you have is a hammer, everything looks like a nail: Because it is a field unto itself, sport psychology often does not take into account other models of training and research, and other means to the practice of performance psychology.
- Performance psychology is not a unified field. Different domains of performance are at different stages of development with regard to research, education, practice, and performers' receptivity to practitioners.
- On the one hand, there are a number of commonalities among domains in the field of performance psychology. Researchers and practitioners should be mining those connections, similarities, and convergences. The richness and challenges of the critical issues in the psychology of performance, briefly reviewed earlier in this chapter, offer many opportunities for learning and sharing. Performance psychology will do best if it is not practiced in silos nor decimated by turf wars. This has implications for research, practice, education, and community among organizations.
- On the other hand, we should be informed by significant variations between the different domains of performance. These domains have vastly diverse histories, reasons for being, goals, and cultures. Those differences, both subtle and vast, need to be appreciated by researchers, practitioners, and educators.

Future Directions

As the practice of applied sport psychology moves into "adulthood," its strengths and limitations have become clearer. Whether at the individual or organizational level, the value and utility of a broader perspective, focused on human performance, holds great appeal and promise.

Education is critical along a number of dimensions, particularly if viewed broadly and addressing many types of stakeholders:

- At the graduate level, programs need to be developed that enhance student learning and opportunities, rather than the piecemeal, often random, and undirected experience that students frequently encounter.
- Perhaps this systematic training will occur within sport sciences departments, perhaps in psychology. The broader focus on the psychology of performance may support more creative and interdisciplinary connection.
- As a discipline, psychology continues to need to learn about, embrace, and help define performance psychology.
- Because performance psychology is emergent, those who have already completed formal education and who approach performance psychology from within an already-established career form a distinct cohort. Their needs for further education and support should be addressed.
- Standards of competency, guidelines for practice, and ethical standards will need to be further developed.

Ironically, the public may be ready to embrace performance psychology; it is we who are professionals in the field who may need the greatest amount of education. Interpreted at an individual, organizational, systemic, and cultural level, we may best be guided by the words of the sage, Hillel, speaking to us across two millennia:

If I am not for myself, who will be for me?
If I am only for myself, what am I?
If not now, when?

References

Abdou, A. (2007). *The bone cage*. Edmonton, AB: NeWest Press.

Algoe, S. B., & Fredrickson, B. L. (2011). Emotional fitness and the movement of affective science from lab to field. *American Psychologist, 66*, 35–42.

American Psychological Association (APA). (2002). Ethical principles of psychologists and code of conduct. *American Psychologist, 57*, 1060–1073.

American Psychological Association (APA). (n.d.). *Public description of police psychology.* Retrieved from http://www.apa.org/ed/graduate/specialize/police.aspx

American Psychological Association (APA). (n.d.). *Public description of sport psychology.* Retrieved from http://www.apa.org/ed/graduate/specialize/sports.aspx

Andersen, M. B.(2000). Introduction. In M. B. Andersen (Ed.), *Doing sport psychology: Process and practice* (pp. xiii–xvii). Champaign, IL: Human Kinetics.

Andersen, M. B. (2009). The "canon" of psychological skills training for enhancing performance. In K. F. Hays (Ed.), *Performance psychology in action* (pp. 11–34). Washington, DC: American Psychological Association.

Aoyagi, M. W., & Portenga, S. T. (2010). The role of positive ethics and virtues in the context of sport and performance psychology service delivery. *Professional Psychology: Research and Practice, 40*, 253–259.

Aoyagi, M. W., Portenga, S. T., Poczwardowski, A., Cohen, A., & Statler, T. (2012). Reflections and directions: The profession of sport psychology past, present, and future. *Professional Psychology: Research and Practice, 53*, 32–38.

Association for Applied Sport Psychology. (n.d.). *Become a certified consultant.* Retrieved from http://appliedsportpsych.org/consultants/become-certified

Association for the Advancement of Applied Sport Psychology. (n.d.). *Ethics code.* Retrieved from http://appliedsportpsych.org/about/ethics/code

Balague, G. (2009). Competition. In K. F. Hays (Ed.), *Performance psychology in action* (pp. 161–179). Washington, DC: American Psychological Association.

Bandura, A. (1986). The explanatory and predictive scope of self-efficacy theory. *Journal of Social and Clinical Psychology, 4*, 359–373.

Belar, C. D., Brown, R. A., Hersch, L. E., Hornyak, L. M., Rozensky, R. H., Sheridan, E. P., et al. (2001). Self-assessment in clinical health psychology: A model for ethical expansion of practice. *Professional Psychology: Research and Practice, 32*, 135–141.

Boring, E. G. (1950). *A history of experimental psychology.* New York: Appleton-Century-Crofts.

Botterill, C. (2005). Competitive drive: Embracing positive rivalries. In S. M. Murphy (Ed.), *The sport psych handbook* (pp. pp. 37–48). Champaign, IL: Human Kinetics.

Brewer, B. W., & Van Raalte, J. (Eds.). (2002). *Exploring exercise and sport psychology* (2nd ed.). Washington, DC: American Psychological Association.

Brown, C. H. (2001). Clinical cross-training: Compatibility of sport and family systems psychology. *Professional Psychology: Research and Practice, 32*, 19–26.

Brown, C. H. (2009). The consultant as performer. In K. F. Hays (Ed.), *Performance psychology in action* (pp. 309–327). Washington, DC: American Psychological Association.

Brown, C. H., Gould, D., & Foster, S. (2005). A framework for developing contextual intelligence (CI). *The Sport Psychologist, 19*, 51–62.

Brown, G., & Potrac, P. (2009). "You've not made the grade, son": De-selection and identity disruption in elite level youth football. *Soccer Society, 10*, 143–159.

Burton, D., Naylor, S., & Holliday, B. (2001). Goal-setting in sport: Investigating the goal effectiveness paradox. In R. Singer, H. A. Hausenblas, & C. M. Janelle (Eds.), *Handbook of research on sport psychology* (2nd ed., pp. 497–528). New York: Wiley.

Caironi, P. C. (2002). Coaches coach, players play, and companies win. *The Industrial-Organizational Psychologist, 40*, 37–44.

Carron, A. V. (1993). Toward the integration of theory, research, and practice in sport psychology. *Journal of Applied Sport Psychology, 5*, 207–221.

Côté, J. (1999). The influence of the family in the development of talent in sport. *The Sport Psychologist, 13*, 395–417.

Csikszentmihalyi, M. (1990). *Flow: The psychology of optimal experience*. New York: Harper & Row.

Davidson, J. W., Howe, M. J. A., Moore, D. G., & Sloboda, J. A. (1996). The role of parental influences in the development of musical performance. *British Journal of Developmental Psychology, 14*, 399–412.

Dean, B. (2001, January/February). The sky's the limit. Retrieved from http://www.mentorcoach.com/coaching/sky.html

Decety, J. (1996). The neurophysiological basis of motor imagery. *Behavioural Brain Research, 77*, 45–52.

De Shazer, S. (1985). *Keys to solution in brief therapy*. New York: Norton.

Dingfelder, S. F. (2006, November). Postgrad growth area: Executive coaching. *GradPSYCH, 4*(4). Retrieved from www.apa.org/gradpsych/2006/11/coaching.aspx

Duda, J. L., & Hall, H. (2001). Achievement goal theory in sport. In R. N. Singer, H. A. Hausenblas, & C. M. Janelle (Eds.), *Handbook of sport psychology* (2nd ed., pp. 417–443). New York: Wiley.

Dweck, C. S. (1999). *Self-theories and goals: Their role in motivation, personality, and development*. Philadelphia: Taylor & Francis.

Emmons, S., & Thomas, A. (1998). *Power performance for singers: Transcending the barriers*. New York: Oxford.

Enhanced Performance Systems. (n.d.). *EPS history*. Retrieved from http://www.epstais.com/history.php

Ericsson, K. A. (Ed.). (1996). *The road to excellence: The acquisition of expert performance in the arts and sciences, sports and games*. Mahwah, NJ: Erlbaum.

Festinger, L., Schachter, S., & Back, K. (1950). *Social pressure in informal groups*. New York: Harper & Row.

Flett, G. L., & Hewitt, P. L. (2005). The perils of perfectionism in sports and exercise. *Current Directions in Psychological Science, 14*, 14–18.

Foster, S. (1996). Healing work-related trauma. *At Work, 5*, 7–9.

Fredrickson, B. L. (2001). The role of positive emotions in positive psychology: The broaden-and-build theory of positive emotions. *American Psychologist, 56*, 218–226.

Gardner, F. L., & Moore, Z. E. (2007). *The psychology of enhancing human performance: The Mindfulness-Acceptance-Commitment (MAC) approach*. New York: Springer.

Gerstner, J. C. (2010, Aug. 11). Ryan McCarthy: From national champion to Cirque de Soleil. *Men's Gymnastics*. Retrieved from http://www.mgoblue.com/sports/m-gym/spec-rel/081110aaa.html

Glueckauf, R. L., Pickett, T. C., Ketterson, T. U., Loomis, J. S., & Rozensky, R. H. (2003). Preparation for the delivery of telehealth services: A self-study framework for expansion of practice. *Professional Psychology: Research and Practice, 34*, 159–163.

Goleman, D. (1995). *Emotional intelligence*. New York: Bantam.

Gould, D., Diefenbach, K., & Moffet, A. (2002). Psychological characteristics and their development in Olympic champions. *Journal of Applied Sport Psychology, 14*, 172–204.

Gould, D., & Pick, S. (1995). Sport psychology: The Griffith era. *The Sport Psychologist, 9*, 391–405.

Gould, D., Udry, E., Tuffey, S., & Loehr, J. (1996a). Burnout in competitive junior tennis players: I. A quantitative psychological assessment. *The Sport Psychologist, 10*, 322–340.

Gould, D., Udry, E., Tuffey, S., & Loehr, J. (1996b). Burnout in competitive junior tennis players: II. Qualitative analysis. *The Sport Psychologist, 10*, 341–366.

Green, B., & Gallwey, T. (1986). *The inner game of music*. New York: Doubleday.

Greenberg, L. S. (2002). *Emotion-focused therapy: Coaching clients to work through their feelings*. Washington, DC: American Psychological Association.

Greene, D. (2001). *Audition success*. New York: Routledge.

Greenspan, M. J., & Feltz, D. L. (1989). Psychological interventions with athletes in competitive situations: A review. *The Sport Psychologist, 3*, 219–236.

Gucciardi, D. F., & Gordon, S. (2008). Personal construct psychology and the research interview: The example of mental toughness in sport. *Personal Construct Theory and Practice, 5*, 119–130.

Gucciardi, D. F., Gordon, S., & Dimmock, J. A. (2009a). Evaluation of a mental toughness training program for youth-aged Australian footballers: I. A quantitative analysis. *Journal of Applied Sport Psychology, 21*, 307–323.

Gucciardi, D. F., Gordon, S., & Dimmock, J. A. (2009b). Evaluation of a mental toughness training program for youth-aged Australian footballers: II. A qualitative analysis. *Journal of Applied Sport Psychology, 21*, 324–339.

Haberl, P., & Peterson, K. (2006). Olympic-size ethical dilemmas: Issues and challenges for sport psychology consultants on the road and at the Olympic Games. *Ethics and Behavior, 16*, 25–40.

Hamilton, L. H. (1997). *The person behind the mask*. Greenwich, CT: Ablex.

Hamilton, L. H. (2008). *The dancer's way*. New York: St. Martin's Press.

Hanin, Y. L. (Ed.). (1999). *Emotions in sport*. Champaign, IL: Human Kinetics.

Harris, E. (2002). *Risk management for therapists who coach*. Retrieved from www.MentorCoach.com

Harwood, C. (2005). Goals: More than just the score. In S. M. Murphy (Ed.), *The sport psych handbook* (pp. 19–36). Champaign, IL: Human Kinetics.

Hays, K. F. (2002). The enhancement of performance excellence among performing artists. *Journal of Applied Sport Psychology, 14*, 299–312.

Hays, K. F. (2006). Being fit: The ethics of practice diversification in performance psychology. *Professional Psychology: Research and Practice, 37*, 223–232.

Hays, K. F. (Ed.). (2009). *Performance psychology in action*. Washington, DC: American Psychological Association.

Hays, K. F., & Brown, C. H. (2004). *You're on! Consulting for peak performance*. Washington, DC: American Psychological Association.

Hays, K. F., & Lesyk, J. J. (in press). Incorporating sport and exercise psychology into clinical practice. In J. Van Raalte & B. Brewer (Eds.), *Exploring exercise and sport psychology* (3rd ed.) Washington, DC: American Psychological Association.

Hernandez, D., Russo, S. A., & Schneider, B. A. (2009). The psychological profile of a rock band: Using intellectual and personality measures with musicians. *Medical Problems of Performing Artists, 24*, 71.

International Coach Federation. (n.d.). *ICF code of ethics*. Retrieved from www.coachfederation.org/ethics

Jackson, S. A., & Kimiecik, J. C. (2008). The flow perspective of optimal experience in sport and physical activity. In T. S. Horn (Ed.), *Advances in sport psychology* (pp. 377–399). Champaign, IL: Human Kinetics.

Jeannerod, M. (1997). *The cognitive neuroscience of action*. Oxford, UK: Blackwell.

Jones, G. (2002). Performance excellence: A personal perspective on the link between sport and business. *Journal of Applied Sport Psychology, 14,* 268–281.

Jones, G., Hanton, S., & Connaughton, D. (2007). A framework of mental toughness in the world's best performers. *The Sport Psychologist, 21,* 243–264.

Kampa, S., & White, R. P. (2002). The effectiveness of executive coaching: What we know and what we still need to know. In R. L. Lowman (Ed.), *Handbook of organizational consulting psychology* (pp. 139–158). San Francisco: Jossey-Bass.

Kampa-Kokesch, S., & Kilburg, R. R. (2001). Executive coaching: A comprehensive review of the literature. *Consulting Psychology Journal: Practice and Research, 53,* 139–153.

Kaye, E. (1998, May 24). At the end of a brief, brilliant turn. *The New York Times,* pp. AR1, AR27.

Kilburg, R. R. (Ed.). (1996). Executive coaching [Special issue]. *Consulting Psychology Journal, 48*(3).

Kogan, J. (1989). *Nothing but the best: The struggle for perfection at the Juilliard School.* New York: Limelight.

Kogan, N. (2002). Careers in the performing arts: A psychological perspective. *Creativity Research Journal, 14,* 1–16.

Kornspan, A. S., & Duve, M. A. (2006). A niche and a need: A summary of the need for sport psychology consultants in collegiate sport. *Annals of the American Psychotherapy Association, 9,* 19–25.

Lazarus, R. S. (1991). *Emotion and adaptation.* New York: Oxford University Press.

Lazarus, R. S. (1999). *Stress and emotion: A new synthesis.* New York: Springer.

Lazarus, R. S., & Folkman, S. (1984). *Stress, appraisal, and coping.* New York: Springer.

Le Scanff, C., & Taugis, J. (2002). Stress management for police Special Forces. *Journal of Applied Sport Psychology, 14,* 330–343.

Levinson, H. (1996). Executive coaching. *Consulting Psychology Journal, 48,* 115–123.

Linder, D. E., Pillow, D. R., & Reno, R. R. (1989). Shrinking jocks: Derogation of athletes who consult a sport psychologist. *Journal of Sport and Exercise Psychology, 11,* 270–280.

Locke, E. A., & Latham, G. P. (1990). *A theory of goal setting and task performance.* Englewood Cliffs, NJ: Prentice-Hall.

Loehr, J., & Schwartz, T. (2001). The making of a corporate athlete. *Harvard Business Review, 79,* 120–128.

Mainwaring, L. M. (2009). Working with perfection. In K. F. Hays (Ed.), *Performance psychology in action* (pp. 139–159). Washington, DC: American Psychological Association.

Mainwaring, L. M., Krasnow, D., & Kerr, G. (2001). And the dance goes on: Psychological impact of injury. *Journal of Dance medicine and Science, 5,* 105–115.

Maslach, C. (1982). Understanding burnout: Definitional issues in analyzing a complex phenomenon. In W. S. Paine (Ed.), *Job stress and burnout: Research, theory, and intervention perspectives* (pp. 29–40). Beverly Hills, CA: Sage.

McCann, S. M. (2009). Emotional intelligence. In K. F. Hays (Ed.), *Performance psychology in action* (pp. 35–56). Washington, DC: American Psychological Association.

McGrath, J. E. (1970). A conceptual formation for research on stress. In J. E. McGrath (Ed.), *Social and psychological factors in stress* (pp. 19–49). New York: Holt, Rinehart and Winston.

Meyers, A. W., Whelan, J. P., & Murphy, S. (1995). Cognitive behavioral strategies in athletic performance enhancement. In M. Hersen, R. M. Eisler, & P. M. Miller (Eds.), *Progress in behavior modification* (pp. 137–164). Pacific Grove, CA: Brooks/Cole.

Moore, B. A., & Reger, G. M. (2006). Clinician to frontline soldier: A look at the roles and challenges of army clinical psychologists in Iraq. *Journal of Clinical Psychology, 62,* 395–403.

Moran, A. (2010). Concentration/attention. In S. J. Hanrahan & M. B. Andersen (Eds.), *Routledge handbook of applied sport psychology* (pp. 500–509). New York: Routledge.

Murphy, G. M., Petitpas, A. J., & Brewer, B. W. (1996). Identity foreclosure, athletic identity, and career maturity in intercollegiate athletes. *The Sport Psychologist, 10,* 239–246.

Murphy, S. M. (1995). Introduction to sport psychology interventions. In S. M. Murphy (Ed.), *Sport psychology interventions* (pp. 1–15). Champaign, IL: Human Kinetics.

Neimeyer, G. J., & Taylor, J. M. (2011, August). *The half-life of professional knowledge in psychology.* Presented at APA Convention, Washington, D.C.

Newburg, D. (1992). Performance enhancement—Toward a working definition. *Contemporary Thought on Performance Enhancement, 1,* 10–25.

Newburg, D., Kimiecik, J., Durand-Bush, N., & Doell, K. (2002). The role of resonance in performance excellence and life engagement. *Journal of Applied Sport Psychology, 14,* 249–267.

Newman, J. L., Robinson-Kurpius, S. E., & Fuqua, D. R. (2002). Issues in the ethical practice of consulting psychology. In R. L. Lowman (Ed.), *The California School of Organizational Studies handbook of organizational consulting psychology: A comprehensive guide to theory, skills, and techniques* (pp. 733–758). San Francisco: Jossey-Bass.

Nideffer, R. M., & Sharpe, R. (1978). *A.C.T.: Attention control training.* New York, Wyden Books.

Ogilvie, B. C., & Tutko, T. A. (1966). *Problem athletes and how to handle them.* London: Pelham Books.

O'Hanlon, W., & Weiner-Davis, M. (1989). *In search of solutions.* New York: Norton & Company.

O'Roark, A. M., Lloyd, P. J., & Cooper, S. E. (2005). *Guidelines for education and training at the doctoral and postdoctoral level in consulting psychology/organizational consulting psychology.* Retrieved from http://www.apa.org/about/governance/council/policy/div-13-guidelines.pdf

Park-Perin, G. (2010). Positive psychology. In S. J. Hanrahan & M. B. Andersen (Eds.), *Routledge handbook of applied sport psychology* (pp. 141–149). New York: Routledge.

Paskevich, D. M., Estabrooks, P. A., Brawley, L. R., & Carron, A. V. (2001). Group cohesion in sport and exercise. In R. N. Singer, H. A. Hausenblas, & C. M. Janelle (Eds.), *Handbook of sport psychology* (2nd ed., pp. 472–494). New York: Wiley.

Pasquariello, C. D. (2011). *Let's get physical: The role of physical activity in the training of graduate mental health students.* Master's thesis, Virginia Commonwealth University, Richmond, VA.

Peterson, K. M. (2009). Overtraining, burnout, injury, and retirement. In K. F. Hays (Ed.), *Performance psychology in action* (pp. 225–243). Washington, DC: American Psychological Association.

Petrie, T. A., & Diehl, N. S. (1995). Sport psychology in the profession of psychology. *Professional Psychology: Research and Practice, 26,* 288–291.

Poczwardowski, A., & Conroy, D. E. (2002). Coping responses to failure and success among elite athletes and performing artists. *Journal of Applied Sport Psychology, 14,* 315–329.

Sachs, M. L., Burke, K. L., & Schweighardt, S. L. (2011). *Directory of graduate programs in applied sport psychology* (10th ed.). Madison, WI: Association for Applied Sport Psychology.

Sarason, S. B. (1967). Toward a psychology of change and innovation. *American Psychologist, 22*, 227–233.

Sataloff, R. T., Brandfonbrener, A. G., & Lederman, R. J. (Eds.). (2010). *Performing arts medicine* (3rd ed.). San Diego: Singular.

Scalora, M. (2009). Hierarchical public safety organizations. In K. F. Hays (Ed.), *Performance psychology in action* (pp. 289–305). Washington, DC: American Psychological Association.

Schoen, C., & Estanol-Johnson, E. (2001, May). *Assessment of the applicability of sport psychology implementation to ballet and dance.* Paper presented at the 10th World Congress of Sport Psychology, Skiathos, Greece.

Seles, M., & Richardson, N.A. (1996). *Monica: From fear to victory.* New York: HarperCollins.

Seligman, M. E. P., & Csikszentmihalyi, M. (2000). Positive psychology. *American Psychologist, 55*, 5–14.

Seligman, M. E. P., & Matthews, M. D. (Eds.). (2011). Special issue: Comprehensive soldier fitness. *American Psychologist, 66* (1).

Shapiro, T. R. (2011). Harvey Dorfman, psychologist to top baseball stars, dies at 75. *The Washington Post.* Retrieved from http://www.washingtonpost.com

Sheldon, K. M., & King, L. (2001). Why positive psychology is necessary. *American Psychologist, 56*, 216–217.

Sherif, M., & Sherif, C. W. (1969). *Social psychology.* New York: Harper.

Singer, R. N.(1989). Applied sport psychology in the United States. *Journal of Applied Sport Psychology, 1*, 61–80.

Singer, R. N., Hausenblas, H. A., & Janelle, C. M. (2001). Prologue. In R. N. Singer, H. A. Hausenblas, & C. M. Janelle (Eds.), *Handbook of sport psychology* (2nd ed.) (pp. xiii–xix). New York: Wiley.

Skaalvik, E. M. (1997). Self-enhancing and self-defeating ego orientation: Relations with task and avoidance orientation, achievement, self-perceptions, and anxiety. *Journal of Educational psychology, 89*, 71–81.

Smith, R. R., & Christensen, D. S. (1995). Psychological skills as predictors of performance and survival in professional baseball. *Journal of Sport and Exercise Psychology, 17*, 399–415.

Society for Industrial and Organizational Psychology. (n.d.). *What is I-O?* Retrieved from http://www.siop.org/topminds.aspx

Stapleton, A. B., Hays, K. F., Hankes, D. M., & Parham, W. D. (2010). Ethical dilemmas in sport psychology: A dialogue on the unique aspects impacting practice. *Professional Psychology: Research and Practice, 41*, 143–152.

Strauss, G. (2001, March 6). "Corporate athletes" hit the mat: LGE Performance applies sports-style training principles to business. *USA Today*, p. 18.

The mega-soprano: Sondra Radvanovsky finally takes on *Aida*—and the COC. (2010, October). *Toronto Life.* Retrieved from http://www.torontolife.com/daily/hype/print-edition/2010/09/30/the-mega-soprano-sondra-radvanovsky-finally-takes-on-aida%E2%80%94and-the-coc/

Weinberg, R., & Gould, D. (2011). *Foundations of sport and exercise psychology* (5th ed.). Champaign, IL: Human Kinetics.

Weinberg, R., & McDermott, M. (2002). A comparative analysis of sport and business organizations: Factors perceived critical for organizational success. *Journal of Applied Sport Psychology, 14*, 282–298.

Whelan, J. P., Meyers, A. W., & Elkins, T. D. (2002). In J. Van Raalte & B. W. Brewer (Eds.), *Exploring sport and exercise psychology* (2nd ed., pp. 503–523) Washington, DC: American Psychological Association.

Williams, J., & Krane, V. (1997). Psychological characteristics of peak performance. In J. Williams (Ed.), *Applied sport psychology: Personal growth to peak performance* (pp. 137–147). Mountain View, CA: Mayfield Publishing Company.

Wise, E. H. (2010). Maintaining and enhancing competence in professional psychology: Obsolescence, life-long learning, and continuing education. *Professional Psychology: Research and Practice, 41*, 289–292.

Witherspoon, R., & White, R. P. (1996). Executive coaching: A continuum of roles. *Consulting Psychology Journal, 48*, 124–133.

Wrisberg, C. A., Loberg, L. A., Simpson, D., Withycombe, J. L., & Reed, A. (2010). An exploratory investigation of NCAA Division-I coaches' support of sport psychology consultants and willingness to seek mental training services. *The Sport Psychologist, 24*, 489–503.

Wrisberg, C. A., Simpson, D., Loberg, L. A., Withycombe, J. L., & Reed, A. (2009). NCAA Division I student-athletes' receptivity to mental skills training by sport psychology consultants. *The Sport Psychologist, 23*, 470–486.

Wynne, L. C., McDaniel, S. H. & Weber, T. T. (1986). *Systems consultation: A new perspective for family therapy.* New York: Guilford Press.

Sport and Performance Psychology: Ethical Issues

Douglas M. Hankes

Abstract

The psychology of human performance, which includes the domains of sport and other performance areas such as dance and music, offers a unique and complex environment in which to engage in ethical practice. Regardless of what "type" of psychology the practitioner is providing, the American Psychological Association's General Principles and Ethics Code guides the psychologist and consultant in their work with performers and the organizations to which they belong and interact within. Much of the work that sport and performance psychologists and consultants provide is done outside of traditional practice models, so a commitment to ethical practice is imperative.

This chapter discusses some of the fundamental elements that may serve to encourage and nurture ethical practitioners, including the development of sound clinical judgment, utilization of personal skill inventories, adoption of a lifelong learning attitude, incorporation of peer supervision, and the selection of a decision-making model for ethical questions. The different training backgrounds of sport and performance psychologists and consultants, including certification and proficiency standards, are also explored. Finally, the three major areas of ethical issues in the practice of sport and performance psychology are examined, including competence and training, confidentiality and informed consent, and multiple relationships and boundaries. Case examples and vignettes are provided to illustrate the relevant ethical considerations.

Key Words: Competence, confidentiality, decision making model, ethics code, informed consent, multiple relationships, personal skill inventory, supervision

On his business website, Dr. G.O. Flow identifies himself as a sport psychologist specializing in competitive performance enhancement. His terminal degree is stated to be a Ph.D. in sport psychology from a well-respected university's kinesiology department. Dr. Flow's website prominently displays the names of many professional athletes that he has taught "how to choose success to reach their highest potential." Dr. Flow is savvy in his use of social media and regularly tweets. A talented but underachieving professional tennis player, P.O. Tential, wins an important tournament leading up to the year's first Grand Slam event. Dr. Flow tweets, "Wow! P.O. wins! Dr. Flow strikes again! Can't wait to travel with P.O. to the Grand Slam tournament next week to help him prepare 4 more success!"

Kate Hays, in Chapter 2, this volume has expertly described the evolving field of the psychology of human performance. The bedrock forming the foundation that guides the practice of the field remains the same, the American Psychological Association (APA) General Principles and Ethics Code (American Psychological Association [APA], 2002). Whether one is providing sport or other performance psychology services, the APA General Principles and Ethics Code applies to the psychologist's work. First, irrespective of the specific field of performance psychology, it is primarily a collaborative effort between two entities—one expert by training, and the other expert in their inner world and life experiences—to assist the client in making changes to improve performance (Andersen, 2009). Second, the collaborative effort is guided by the APA General Principles and Ethics Code, regardless of the "type" of psychology that the professional is practicing. The focus of this chapter is to explore some of the unique aspects of sport and performance psychology that make the ethical practice of the domains complex, challenging, and infinitely fascinating.

Although this chapter is directed more toward an audience of psychologists and psychologists-in-training, it is important to acknowledge the contributions that the field of kinesiology and sport sciences (formerly most frequently referred to as physical education) has made (and will continue to make) to the domain of sport and performance psychology. It is only in the past two decades that we have seen the exponential increase in the number of psychologists providing applied sport and performance psychology services. Initially, these psychologists often developed an interest in working with athletes and coaches as part of their more general focus on improving resilience and coping in all clients (Murphy, 1995). Prior to the 1990s, most professionals working in sport psychology and performance domains were trained in kinesiology and sport science departments with a primary focus in conducting research and teaching in an academic setting (Straub & Hinman, 1992). Because of their content knowledge, many of these kinesiology and sport science–trained professionals were frequently asked to apply their research findings and knowledge to assist athletes, coaches, and teams improve performance. The work focused on sport-specific interventions including goal setting, motivation, confidence building, imagery, team dynamics, and arousal management. These sport-specific interventions were often referred to as *peak performance* or *psychological skills* training, and the individuals who taught or provided the information have been called sport psychology consultants, mental skills or mental toughness coaches, performance enhancement experts, and the like. These professionals did not typically address decrements in performance caused by personal problems or clinical issues, and most were not trained to provide such services. Thus, sport performance issues gradually came to be addressed by two sets of professionals, those from sport science backgrounds and those from psychology training

programs, and, initially, their approaches may have seemed to share little common ground.

Petrie and Harmison (2011) have detailed the sometimes acrimonious debates between sport science- versus psychology-trained professionals concerning who is best trained and qualified to provide what type of applied sport and performance psychology services to what populations. A major point of contention concerns the belief as to whether clinical or personal issues (the primary training and domain of psychologists) can be separated from performance enhancement issues (the area of expertise of sport science–trained professionals). One view is that applied sport and performance psychology consulting may be seen as running along a continuum anchored on one end by performance enhancement issues and on the other end by clinical or personal issues. The most strident proponents of this view would argue that professionals should choose to work on one end of the continuum or the other. In the Afterword to Andersen's *Sport Psychology in Practice*, Ecklund (2005) addressed the book's examination of counseling and clinical concerns of athletes and the ethics of professional practice by writing:

> I find it unsettling, however, when the truth is employed as a bludgeon to belittle the merits and potential results of professionals whose training in sport and exercise science has not been primarily focused on detection and treatment of the underlying possibilities for these difficulties. The unspoken but implied agenda in raising this truism is that those whose training focused on the detection of underlying but unspecified difficulties are the ones with the best competencies for preaching ethical service to the field.
> (p. 301)

Another view is that this approach offers a false dichotomy, one that oversimplifies a complex process. Most applied sport and performance psychology consultation probably falls in the middle of the continuum, where personal and performance issues overlap and are intimately intertwined (Andersen, 2005; Hankes, 2009). For example, if a marriage fails or an individual becomes depressed, these events are likely to impact one's ability to perform optimally (Gardner & Moore, 2006). Conversely, if the performance of an Olympic athlete or ballerina in a national dance company declines precipitously, then this may affect different areas of their personal lives, exacerbate mental health issues, and impact core issues of self-worth, self-identity, interpersonal relationships, and family dynamics (Barber & Krane, 2005). Hays and Brown (2004) have posed the question of whether a psychologist can ethically provide both psychotherapy and performance consulting services to the same individual. The delicate issue of dual or multiple relationships will be considered later in the chapter. This is why some in the field have called for interdisciplinary graduate training that allows professionals to work holistically with athletes and performers (e.g., Petrie & Harmison, 2011; Stapleton, Hankes, Hays, & Parham, 2010). In sum, the field is currently a hybrid of professionals with varying training backgrounds providing a constellation of applied sport and performance psychology services in numerous and varied settings. It is in this historical context that the ethical practice of sport and performance psychology must take place. Although this discussion focuses on interventions and practice in the sport and exercise domain, other areas of human performance are now confronting similar issues of practice and ethics, as this Handbook makes clear. Such practice areas include working with artists, musicians, dancers, and performers in fields as varied as business, medicine, and education. When it is appropriate, the implications of the lessons learned in the practice of sport psychology for other performance domains will be addressed.

Most psychologists approach ethics with a paralyzing, nauseous combination of dread, fear, apathy, and boredom. Feelings of dread are rooted in the irrational fear of making an ethical mistake unintentionally, and, if getting caught, being punished swiftly, harshly, ultimately resulting in loss of one's license to practice. The topic of ethics conjures feelings of apathy and boredom and is also a function of an irrational belief that "I am, of course, an ethical practitioner of psychology." Perhaps this can be illustrated humorously. What psychologist acknowledges being a poor driver? Likewise, who admits to being ethically challenged? Perhaps a primitive rationalization for some of us follows along the lines that "the APA Code of Ethics has been in place in sport consulting since 2002, and I have not been charged with being unethical. Therefore, I have been and will continue to be an ethical psychologist." Consider the last ethics presentation that you voluntarily attended at a professional conference. How many were in attendance, if continuing education credits were not being given? Of course, neither fear nor boredom should be the primary motivators for those who are truly committed to the ethical practice of psychology. One should not approach ethics with foreboding and the fear of making a mistake, getting caught, and being punished. Instead, ethics should be about doing right with the best interests of your client always in mind. Those psychologists who take for granted or simply assume that they are ethical practitioners are the scariest drivers on the road.

Ethical practice is defined and guided by the Ethics Code, but as the code's Introduction and Applicability section states, other resources must be considered. These include applicable laws, psychology board regulations, professional psychological organizations' guidelines, consultation with others in the field, and the dictates of one's own conscience. Are there key, fundamental elements that encourage and nurture psychologists and consultants toward ethical practice? A review of the literature suggests there are activities, behaviors, and approaches that are important for psychologists and consultants to engage in and that support the ethical process. The practice of sport and performance psychology varies widely from traditional practice, so it behooves professionals working in these domains to be even more vigilant about these key, fundamental elements. The following list, comprehensive if not exhaustive, offers a solid framework to improve the chances of ethical practice. First and foremost, a thorough knowledge of the Ethical Principles of Psychologists and Code of Conduct is imperative. Although commonsensical, a simple commitment to rereading the General Principles and Ethical Standards at least once a year is an excellent starting place.

Behnke (2006) has suggested three metaphors to teach the APA Ethics Code that goes beyond mere compliance and the avoidance of ethical allegations and prohibitions: the stoplight, the moon, and the airplane ride. The Ethics Code can serve as a stoplight. There are certain behaviors (e.g., sexual involvement with a client) that the code flags as a red light that demands the psychologist to stop and not proceed. Or, the light may turn yellow to serve as a reminder to slow down and cautiously continue only after thoughtful contemplation (e.g., entering into a multiple relationship with a client). Travel to the moon is unobtainable for most of us, yet, it serves an aspirational purpose as we strive to reach our maximal potential. The General Principles serve as aspirational goals, but the standards put the principles into practice. The Ethics Code is less abstract than the principles and lies somewhere in the clouds beneath the moon. The gap between the moon and clouds is filled with the psychologist's clinical judgment. Another analogy is that the Ethical Principles are the ceiling to which psychologists aspire while the standards are the floor that psychologists do not fall below. The final aspect of the metaphor is the airplane ride. There have been ten revisions of the Ethics Code, and although the words of the current code stay the same, forces behind the code continue to bubble and foment. From 35,000 feet in the airplane, the ocean appears calm, but as the airplane descends and moves nearer the surface, the waves and troughs become apparent. The metaphor underscores that the churning forces are not a sign of problems, but a reminder that the code is always evolving and in motion.

Second, the ethical practice of psychology is a lifelong process, and a personal skills inventory can fuel that process (Bennett et al., 2006). As John Wooden, the former, great University of California, Los Angeles (UCLA) basketball coach stated, "When you stop learning, you're done." A personal skills inventory refers to a psychologist's knowledge, skills, past experiences, and emotional competencies. It also suggests that self-awareness is integral to development. Unfortunately, the accuracy of a psychologist's personal skills inventory is only as good as the individual's self-awareness. Not surprisingly, many of us overestimate our personal skills compared to our actual skill inventories. This underscores the importance of utilizing trusted peers and colleagues for consultation and critical, honest feedback. The psychologist who is professionally isolated increases the chances of becoming obsolete as his or her skills diminish and his or her ethics are unmonitored. As part of this lifelong process, the commitment to self-care and a strong, healthy personal life is also critical. Psychologists who don't relax and recharge themselves make mistakes with clients. "It is a pleasant paradox that those psychologists who are most able to distance themselves from work and immerse themselves in family, friends, or avocations are most able to return to work with curiosity, vigor, and a sense of optimistic challenge" (Bennett et al., 2006, p. 15).

Finally, identifying, learning, and adhering to an ethical decision-making model provides structure and guidance when dealing with the ambiguity that is embedded in applying ethics to the messy realities of life. It is rare that the psychologist has a lack of ethical information; instead, the lack is absence of a coherent framework or model to organize and make sense of the information that is available. Choosing an ethical decision-making model requires intentionality and forethought. As the agrarian adage states, "When you're at the barn, no one believes the horse will run away until it runs away." In the next section, several ethical decision-making models are described that sport and performance psychologists might effectively use to guide their work.

Ethical Decision-Making Models

In addition to the fundamental elements that might nurture and encourage psychologists and consultants toward ethical practice of their profession, it is important to consider what one's general approach or stance to ethics will be. Historically, ethics and ethics codes have been taught in graduate school as obligations and prohibitions that the psychologist must abide by, sometimes with minimal acknowledgment of the ambiguity involved. In essence, the Ethics Code is viewed as written in black and white, quasi-legal language, and psychologists are expected to focus on avoiding mistakes and rule-breaking. This "follow the principles" approach to ethics has recently been questioned, and more recently admonished, as being relatively ineffective in its appreciation for the complexity, ambiguity, and nuances of real-world psychology (Campbell, Vasquez, Behnke, & Kinscherff, 2010; Gottlieb & Younggren, 2009).

Other general approaches to ethics include risk management (Bennett et al., 2006), personal values (Koocher & Keith-Spiegel, 2008), virtues (Fisher, 2009), positive ethics (Aoyagi & Portenga, 2010), and even the premise that ethics and morality are an evolutionary process that may be hardwired in humans (Pinker, 2006). Although all of these approaches have merit, they seem to fall short of providing a comprehensive approach to ethics when only viewed through each of these particular lenses. In revisiting the premise of multiple relationships as a slippery slope, Gottlieb and Younggren (2009) discussed an *ethics acculturation model* that attempted to incorporate personal, ethical, and value traditions and the interface with professional psychology. As metaphor, this is a saltwater tide meeting the fresh water of an inland river. In essence, the psychologist's personal values come together with the profession's norms and values (ethics). Ideally, the best possible outcome is that psychologists embrace their profession's ethics while maintaining and nurturing their own personal values. This, of course, assumes that those personal values (virtues) are positive, healthy, and embedded because the question as to whether they can be taught is unknown. Similar to the search for the individual who acknowledges difficulties driving a car, rare indeed is the individual or psychologist who states that her personal values are questionable and her virtues lacking. Gottlieb and Younggren (2009) concluded that it is time for researchers to test this and other models in different ways, including whether all relevant variables have been identified. Behnke (2008) has also put forth the idea that the ethical analysis of the relationship among the private and professional lives, values, and virtues of psychologists is a critical and fascinating area for research. "If the highest standards of professional conduct come from within," then this relationship between personal and professional becomes critical (Bennett et al., 2006). This may be especially true of the field of sport and performance psychology, given the youth of our field, its relatively loose organizational structures, and the ongoing discussion in the field of what constitutes appropriate, adequate, or exceptional training and preparation for practice.

The ethics literature is replete with numerous ethical decision-making models, some more lengthy and complex than others. Campbell, Vasquez, Behnke, and Kinscherff (2010) offer a straightforward four-step process that includes (1) gathering the facts of the ethical matter at hand and determining what is believed to be fact and what is speculative, (2) identifying the relevant ethical principles and standards that bear on the ethical dilemma and exploring the text and language of the Ethics Code that speak to the specific situation, (3) moving beyond what the psychologist must consider to focus on how the situation is to be resolved by weighing and balancing the competing interests and values, and (4) consolidating the first three steps in order to generate concrete and explicit options to resolve the ethical dilemma. This includes weighing the risks and benefits of the possible courses of action.

Fisher (2009) suggests a slightly more detailed model that explicitly outlines some steps that are implied or assumed in the Campbell et al. model. Fisher's model incorporates eight steps: (1) developing and sustaining a professional commitment to do what is right, (2) being sufficiently familiar with the Ethics Code General Principles and Ethical Standards, (3) gathering additional facts relevant to the specific ethical situation, (4) making efforts to understand the perspectives of different stakeholders who will be affected by the decision and consulting with colleagues, (5) applying steps 1–4 to generate ethical alternatives and evaluate each alternative, (6) selecting and implementing an ethical course of action, (7) monitoring and evaluating the effectiveness of the course of action that was initially decided upon, and (8) modifying and continuing to evaluate the ethical plan if necessary.

A final example is provided by the Canadian Psychological Association's (CPA) ten-step model and is presented as another alternative when ethical dilemmas present themselves (Canadian Psychological Association [CPA], 2000). The CPA model starts very differently from the two previous models by beginning with (1) identifying those who are likely to be affected by the decision, (2) identifying the relevant ethical issues and practices, (3) considering one's own personal biases and self-interests, (4) developing alternative courses of action, (5) analyzing the risks and benefits of each of the options, 6) applying the ethical standard and principles and choosing a course of action, (7) taking action, (8) evaluating the outcome, (9) assuming responsibility for consequences, and (10) taking action to prevent future occurrences of the dilemma.

These three ethical decision-making models offer a sampling of approaches that a sport or performance psychologist or consultant might implement when facing an ethical dilemma such as that described at the beginning of the chapter. Each has merit; however, whatever ethical decision-making model a sport or performance psychologist or consultant selects is not as important as the fact that one is selected. A structured, well-learned ethical decision-making model allows the psychologist (and other professionals consulting the psychologist) to approach ethical dilemmas in a confident, organized manner that facilitates the process of working toward the best possible solution.

The remainder of the chapter will build on what has been conveyed thus far; that is, that ethics is complex, and that the ethics practiced in sport and performance psychology adds an additional layer of complexity. Although this labyrinth can heighten the personal anxiety and tax the intellectual endurance of the sport and performance psychologist or consultant, it is hoped that this path is considered a challenge rather than an obstacle or something to be feared and avoided in our work with athletes and performers. After all, isn't this the same attitude that we try to foster in our athletes and performers as they pursue excellence?

Three major ethical issues seem to arise most frequently in the practice of sport and performance psychology: competence and training, confidentiality and informed consent, and multiple relationships and boundaries. Each of these issues will be discussed, with examples presented to highlight specific parts of the Ethics Code. There are

89 ethical standards in the Ethics Code, all of which are potential sources of complex, slippery, and nuanced dilemmas. It is not the intention of this chapter to address all standards, situations, and settings, but to simply give a representative sampling of the most common challenges that face sport and performance psychologists.

Competence and Training

Although much has been written in the extensive sport psychology literature (Andersen, Van Raalte, & Brewer, 2001; Aoyagi & Portenga, 2010; Brown, 2001; Brown & Cogan, 2006; Etzel & Watson, 2007; Etzel, Watson, & Zizzi, 2004; Hack, 2005; Hays, 2002; Packard, 2007; Roche & Hankes, 2009; Stapleton et al., 2010) and growing performance psychology literature (Hays & Brown, 2004; Hays, 2006) concerning competence and training, contention and confusion remains concerning who can legally and ethically call him- or herself a "sport" or "performance" psychologist. Although the confusion can be addressed by education, the contention is more difficult to surmount. Title, credentialing, and misrepresentation of competence and training all entail strong emotions, turf issues, and financial ramifications.

The Ethics Code is clear in stating that psychologists must only engage in practice and professional activities for which they are competent. Behnke (2006) and Hack (2005) have identified the common practice of psychologists who describe themselves as a "licensed (fill-in-the-blank) psychologist," especially in those states that do not have license subspecialties. It has been argued that this practice is acceptable because it simply provides information regarding a psychologist's area of specialized training and expertise. Although few states license the subspecialties of sport or performance psychology, there are specific avenues by which a psychologist can gain expertise above and beyond the typical training of a counseling or clinical psychologist.

To call oneself a sport psychologist, which implies specialized training and demonstrated competence, two primary, more structured, avenues should be considered. First, APA Division 47 (Exercise and Sport Psychology) created a Sport Psychology Proficiency in 2003 that delineated two major requirements that must be completed before a psychologist can legitimately add "sport" to his or her title: (1) the psychologist must acquire supervised experience in applying sport psychological principles in sport settings, as well as understand the special needs of this population; and (2) the

psychologist must acquire knowledge and expertise on the research in sport psychology and, more broadly, the exercise and sport sciences, to be considered knowledgeable and competent to practice applied sport psychology (APA, 2008).

A second avenue to gain training and competence in order to use the title sport psychologist is to pursue credentialing through the Association for Applied Sport Psychology (AASP) certification process. Application requirements include completion of three sport and exercise psychology courses (two at the graduate level), as well as graduate courses in professional ethics; biomechanics; exercise physiology; historical, philosophical, social, or motor behavior bases; counseling; psychopathology; and other additional courses. The applicant must also demonstrate competence with skills, techniques, and analysis in sport or exercise. Finally, 400 hours of supervised experience in the preparation and delivery of sport and exercise psychology services under the supervision of an AASP-approved supervisor, preferably an AASP-certified consultant, is required. This certification is a daunting task for those psychologists who chooses to pursue this post-doctoral training; however, this certification provides the only credential from an established professional organization. Psychologists who choose to follow the APA Division 47 guidelines do so under their own oversight and personal ethics. Neither the APA Division 47 Sport Psychology Proficiency nor the AASP Certification process was specifically created to allow individuals to use the title "sport psychologist"; however, meeting those requirements does imply an effort to gain specialized training in the domain.

Hays and Brown (2006) have done an excellent job of organizing the education and training experiences for those psychologists who choose to expand their scope of practice to sport and performance psychology without following the more structured APA Division 47 proficiency guidelines or AASP certification process. These training and education experiences must meet the standard of those who are already established and active in sport and performance psychology consulting. Hays and Brown (2006) recommended a solid foundation in either psychology or exercise science as essential, and this should be supplemented with additional relevant training. This can be achieved by formal academic training, structured post-degree training, sport or other performance experience, informal training (e.g., learning through reading, personal experiences in the domain), and formative life experiences (e.g., the use of oneself, personality, values, perspectives). In contrast, competency in sport or performance psychology is not achieved solely by having a passionate interest in sport or a performance domain, being a fan, having a subscription to *Sports Illustrated* or the theater season, a computer tab linked to ESPN or Pitchfork, or a membership in a professional organization.

Standard 2.01 (a), Standard 2.01 (c), and Standard 2.01 (e) are three pertinent standards to consider when establishing boundaries of competence in sport and performance psychology. Consider the following situations.

Standard 2.01 (a) Competence

Psychologists provide services, teach, and conduct research with populations and in areas only within the boundaries of their competence, based on their education, training, supervised experience, consultation, study, or professional experience (American Psychological Association [APA], 2002).

> Dr. Rock Star has played guitar since he was big enough to hold a Fender Stratocaster. Before becoming a psychologist, Dr. Rock Star even toured professionally as a member of a moderately successful indie punk band. Currently, he plays acoustic guitar in local coffee shops. In an effort to grow his private practice, Dr. Rock Star added "Licensed Performance Psychologist" to his business cards, signage outside of his office, and on his business website. He distributes the business cards to local music shops, bars where musicians congregate, and local community schools with band programs.

Despite Dr. Rock Star's extensive background in music, he may have placed himself in a tenuous position with regards to the title "Performance Psychologist" as it is not clear that he has completed the more formal education and training necessary to document competency. Dr. Rock Star should also review his state's laws relevant to psychologists and licensure. It is unlikely that his state lists a performance psychology subspecialty. Although he may be a licensed psychologist, using the modifier "performance" in front of "psychologist" is misleading to the public.

Standard 2.01(c) Competence

Psychologists planning to provide services, teach, or conduct research involving populations, areas, techniques, or technologies new to them undertake relevant education, training, supervised experience, consultation, or study.

Dr. Speedo recently attended a sport psychology workshop to gain more practical experience to enhance his work with athletes, an expanding part of his private practice. During the workshop, the presenter emphasized the importance of "hanging out" in the athletic environment, so that athletes become more comfortable with the sport psychologist and more likely to utilize services. Dr. Speedo serves as a consultant to the university's swimming and diving team, and suggested to the head coach that he spend more time on the pool deck with the team, including swimming with the team during the warm-up and warm-down segments of practice.

Dr. Speedo should be commended for his pursuit of additional training in the domain of sport psychology since he is working with athletes in his practice; however, his suggestion to the swimming coach that he "hang out" more with the team may need to be more carefully considered. The concept of "hanging out" is one that has been discussed in the professional literature (Andersen, 2000). Dr. Speedo's suggestion to swim with the team during parts of practice would clearly be labeled as a significant boundary crossing by most psychologists. It would likely be viewed even by sport psychologists with an understanding of the "hanging out" concept as unorthodox. In a university setting, his actions might also create issues with the school's compliance officer and National Collegiate Athletics Association (NCAA) regulations. All of this suggests that it would behoove Dr. Speedo to pursue supervised experience and consultation when he attempts a new technique—"hanging out" in this case.

Standard 2.01 (e) Competence

In those emerging areas in which generally recognized standards for preparatory training do no exist, psychologists nevertheless take reasonable steps to ensure the competence of their work and to protect clients/patients, students, supervisees, research participants, organizational clients, and others from harm.

> Dr. T.E. Bag is vaguely aware that sport and performance psychology exists as emerging areas of psychology; however, she passionately believes that government and licensure bodies should not interfere or infringe on her right to market her services as she sees fit. She talks to another psychologist at a professional luncheon and comments, "Labeling areas of sport and performance as unique domains of psychology is just a way to take money out of my

pocket. I'll ethically practice psychology the way I deem fit."

Dr. Bag's cavalier comments are concerning. As she has acknowledged that she is aware of sport and performance psychology as emerging areas of psychology, she should not ignore the need to pursue steps to gain competence if she chooses to make this part of her private practice services. Although Dr. Bag is free to express her personal feelings about the perceived infringement on her rights to market and provide services, she is not absolved from her professional obligations.

Confidentiality and Informed Consent

Confidentiality has been described as "a cornerstone of the helping relationship" (Koocher & Keith-Spiegel, 2008, p. 115). Behnke (2005) has even more viscerally described the importance of confidentiality as "a core value of our profession. It is, as they say, bred in our bones" (p. 76). And yet, despite this emphasis on confidentiality as a critical and fundamental aspect of psychologists' work, it creates more ethical problems and dilemmas than any other aspect of professional practice. When establishing policies about confidentiality, psychologists must consider 28 specific ethical standards, plus nine other ethical standards that are directly relevant to, but do not actually use the word, confidentiality (Fisher, 2008). For example, confidentiality is not specifically mentioned, but is implied, in ethical standards relevant to multiple relationships, consultation, and documentation. In an intraorganizational sport and performance environment that includes a sport or performance psychologist, Hays (2006) has suggested that confidentiality may be most relevant to the type and scope of information that is being shared rather than whether information is being shared or not. Information will be shared in this environment, but it should be done intentionally, with the best interests of the athlete, performer, and organization in mind.

Several aspects of the sport and performance environment make confidentiality and informed consent even more challenging. First, unlike traditional office-based psychologist–client counseling relationships that take place in a quiet, controlled environment, applied sport and performance psychologists and consultants often work with their clients, teams, and organizations as they train, practice, and perform. Consultations may include holding team or group meetings in a locker room or performance venue; counseling athletes on a

training table in the sports medicine complex; traveling with a ballet troupe or orchestra in vans, buses, or planes; working out or practicing with an athlete; or scrubbing in and observing a surgeon in an operating room. Although these behaviors might seem foreign to many psychologists in traditional practices, Andersen (2000) has suggested that being able to "hang out" with athletes in their environment is a critical aspect of developing a strong consultative relationship. Interventions, consultations, and counseling that take place in the client's environment place obvious and subtle limitations on confidentiality. For example, if a psychologist travels with a team or works with a performer during a practice or competition, interactions are very likely to occur in public settings. In such situations, it will be obvious to teammates, coaches, spectators, and opponents that these performers are receiving services "under the care of" a sport or performance psychologist (Linder, Pillow, & Reno, 1989). Second, athletes and performers seeking performance excellence have often chosen a public life, and, in a sense, are always auditioning (Fowler, 2009). Frequently, these athletes and performers are celebrities, perhaps famous, and highly visible in their local community, whether they are the conductor of a metropolitan orchestra or the starting point guard for the local college. Given the public life they lead, whether chosen or bestowed, it is imperative that psychologists be extra cautious in not betraying their client's confidence, as well as not falling under the tempting assumption that the psychologist, too, somehow deserves attention for his or her work with the athlete or performer.

Finally, it is important to recognize that athletes and performers function in organizations and systems in which information is frequently shared freely and often. To outsiders, the sport environment, CEO's conference room, or the theater backstage may seem closed and off limits, but from within, it is a very open and fluid system in which coaches, athletic trainers, physicians, directors, teammates, managers, and administrators talk directly with one another about practices, training, performances, physical condition, and personal lives and concerns. Therefore, psychologists who work in these environments may experience considerable pressure to share information regarding their work with athletes, performers, sport teams, and organizations. For example, a referral within an NCAA Division I-A athletic department to a sport psychologist might originate from a coach, teammate, athletic trainer, team physician, academic advisor, compliance officer, or nutritionist. Because these athletes are part of a big business in which their performances can have significant financial repercussions (Etzel & Watson, 2007; Sperber, 2000), all of the referral sources are likely interested and invested in how the athlete is doing, and they may want information or updates on their progress with the sport psychologist. A basic premise that differentiates sport and performance psychology from traditional clinical practice is the emphasis on and criticality of outcomes and competition (Brown, 2001). In an environment that provides easily measurable feedback and is focused on results, this combination of factors places pressure on all of those who are involved with the athlete, including the psychologist.

Although the simple question, "Who is the client?" lies at the heart of confidentiality and informed consent, it can still be difficult when others do not assume or treat information in the same way as psychologists. In the example of the athletic department and its organizational structure, some in the field have argued that the athletic director is the applied sport psychologist's client (if the client is paid by the athletic department) since the athletic director is the organization's official representative and final authority (Portenga & Aoyagi, 2007). Applied sport and performance psychologists and consultants would be well served to consider the explanation of informed consent as an active, ongoing process rather than a passive, one-time event in which the psychologist only gives required information to the client to make an informed decision about treatment or consultations (Bennett et al., 2006). Furthermore, when beginning sport or performance psychology relationships with organizations or individuals who are an active part of an organization, having a discussion about confidentiality and its limits is crucial. In the sport and performance environments, as previously discussed, these limits to confidentiality should extend beyond those typically discussed in a beginning therapy relationship (e.g., danger to self or others, child or elderly abuse). In conclusion, applied sport and performance psychologists and consultants need to carefully reflect on the realities of working in the sport and performance environments, how these realities (external and self-imposed) affect confidentiality, and clearly communicate those limits to clients at the beginning of the counseling/consulting relationship. The consultant should also keep monitoring confidentiality issues, as such consulting situations are dynamic, and maintain excellent communication about these issues with his or her client(s).

Consider the following situations that address confidentiality and informed consent.

Standard 4.05 (b) Disclosures

Psychologists discuss confidential information without the consent of the individual only as mandated by law or where permitted by law for a valid purpose such as to provide needed professional services; obtain appropriate professional consultations; protect the client/patient, psychologist, or others from harm; or obtain payment for services from a client/patient, in which the instance disclosure is limited to the minimum necessary to achieve the purpose.

> Dr. Get A. Long has worked on a college campus for many years and has successfully established working relationships with many individuals in the athletic department. She has been very successful in her ability to engage coaches, who subsequently refer their athletes to Dr. Get A. Long. Even though the coaches are aware of confidentiality (Dr. Get A. Long reviews it at the beginning of each year during the athletic department's compliance meetings), they occasionally ask how an athlete they've referred is doing, or what Dr. Get A. Long has done that has positively impacted their athlete's recent performance.

To Dr. Get A. Long's credit, she has gone the extra step of educating her frequent sources of athlete referrals about confidentiality on an ongoing basis. No doubt due to her warm, collaborative relationships with the coaches, they still feel comfortable asking about how their athletes are doing or complimenting Dr. Get A. Long on her successful interventions. In this situation, Dr. Get A. Long should refrain from simply stating that she cannot talk to the coaches. A gentle reminder of confidentiality and encouragement to directly discuss how things are going with the athlete should satisfy all of those involved. For clients who are athletes and performers, and whose actions and performances are visible and on public display, the conviction that confidentiality and privacy are being adhered to provides the necessary environment to engage in the work that will positively impact performance.

Standard 4.05 (a) Disclosures

Psychologists may disclose confidential information with the appropriate consent of the organizational client, the individual client/patient, or another legally authorized person on behalf of the client/patient unless prohibited by law.

Dr. Twinkle Toes provides psychological consulting services for a national ballet company. Her services are a standing line item in the ballet company's budget. She has done team building and other team activities, as well as individual work with the troupe. The CEO of the ballet company has requested that Dr. Twinkle Toes provide a monthly summary of her work, including each ballet dancer's attendance and progress. The CEO emphatically reminds Dr. Twinkle Toes that he signs the checks for the company, so it is quite obvious to him that the company should have documentation for what they're getting out of their money.

Standard 3.11 (a) Psychological Services Delivered To or Through Organizations

Psychologists delivering service to or through organizations provide information beforehand to clients and, when appropriate, to those directly affected by the services about the nature and objectives of the services, the intended recipients, which of the individuals are clients, the relationship the psychologist will have with each person and the organization, the probable uses of services provided and information obtained, who will have access to the information, and the limits of confidentiality. As soon as feasible, they provide information about the results and conclusions of such services to appropriate persons.

It appears that Dr. Twinkle Toes did not adequately address confidentiality and informed consent early and/or adamantly enough in her relationship with the ballet company. She may still be able to rectify the situation; however, it will likely require patience and delicacy on her part. She should initially continue to communicate with the CEO concerning the pros and cons that providing the requested information might have on the effectiveness of her work with the troupe. Should the CEO continue his demand for information, Dr. Twinkle Toes will need to discuss the request with her ballet dancer clients before determining her willingness to provide it.

Standard 4.04 (b) Minimizing Intrusions on Privacy

Psychologists discuss confidential information obtained in their work only for appropriate scientific or professional purposes and only with persons clearly concerned with such matters.

Dr. Life O. Party loves to tell stories about the clients, athletes, and entertainers that he works with in his private practice. He will do this at parties with friends, as well as casually with colleagues at conferences and workshops. Dr. Life O. Party believes he hides identifying information so that the client's privacy is protected. In addition to his joy in entertaining others, he believes these stories destigmatize his work with athletes and performers, so others will see the value in the field. At least one of his former clients is an ex-NFL (National Football League) quarterback who Dr. Life O. Party said had given his permission to share his story for the same purpose of destigmatizing sport psychology.

It is difficult to see the value in Dr. Party's behavior. In fact, if he were completely honest with himself, it would appear that Dr. Party is putting his needs in front of his clients'. Whether or not he is being successful in de-identifying his clients is beside the point. In this case, the standard is clear that this is not an appropriate environment in which to share client information, whether de-identified or not, and regardless of whether he has a former client's permission. Although this is an obvious error on the part of Dr. Party, the reader should guard against rushing to judgment as many psychologists are lax, if not so obviously, in this area.

Multiple Relationships and Boundary Issues

Perhaps the signature ethical issue for psychologists who work in sport and performance arenas, multiple relationships and boundary issues consistently perplex the most conscientious psychologist. Multiple relationships (or, in the past, frequently referred to as *dual relationships*) are not in and of themselves unethical or prohibited as long as they "would not reasonably be expected to cause impairment or risk exploitation or harm" to the client (APA, 2002). Psychologists are expected to put the needs of their clients before their own, and clear boundaries assist in holding them to this tenet. It is an unreasonable expectation for psychologists to be egoless, but awareness that our own needs for gratification are part of being human should be acknowledged. When multiple relationships are present, a key to keeping these needs in check is hypervigilance and acceptance of our ability to cause harm or exploit our clients. That said, it should be noted that humans also have an infinite capacity for self-deception (Moorehead-Slaughter, 2006).

Sport and performance organizations have been described as small communities of individuals, largely self-contained, insular, and often focused on a common goal or worldview (Moore, 2003). Often compared to military or rural communities, the sport and performance realms foster frequent contact, and the sport and performance psychologist and consultant should prepare him- or herself for both the planned and unplanned interactions and multiple relationships that will occur. For example, a sport psychologist might be providing individual counseling with an athlete, working with that same athlete's team to improve cohesion, and consulting with the coach to assist her in becoming a better leader and communicator. Not only are there obvious multiple relationships present, but this brief example also highlights the previously discussed importance of identifying the primary client. It also conveys the multiple levels of interventions and the possibility of competing interests to develop. Finally, it should be noted that the sport or performance psychologist or consultant is likely the only individual in the organization who is aware of the complexity of the situation and has special knowledge and expertise (and obligations) concerning ethical practice (although public examples abound of coaches, leaders and CEOs who have experienced career-ending complications as a result of abusing such situations). It is a heavy burden to shoulder and requires great personal oversight to successfully see the process through. The most conservative psychologist or consultant might view multiple relationships and boundary crossings as something to simply avoid. Others have taken the more extreme position that multiple relationships should be encouraged, viewed more broadly as beneficial therapeutically, and a sign of the psychologist becoming fully engaged in the community (Behnke, 2008; Lazurus & Zur, 2002). Instead of hiding behind a cloak of pseudo-professionalism and attempting to avoid all multiple relationships, psychologists should consider a more flexible approach, one that athlete and performance clients are more likely to trust. A psychologist who is comfortable and familiar with the increased encounters and interactions that occur in the intimate sport and performance psychology environment will likely facilitate better working relationships with clients and be more successful.

Younggren and Gottlieb (2004) delineated a number of considerations that help guide psychologists in managing potential multiple relationships. Their conservative stance advocated a decision-making model to assist the professional in his or her evaluation of whether to enter a multiple relationship. Entering a multiple relationship significantly increases the number of boundary crossings that are likely to occur, and they argue that this also increases the likelihood of a boundary violation occurring. Their model suggests that the psychologist first assesses the risk of damage or disruption to the relationship. Is the multiple relationship necessary? Second, assess one's objectivity in the evaluation of the multiple relationship. The question of objectivity might best be answered by consulting other professionals. Third, adequately document the decision-making process that was undertaken when deciding to enter a multiple relationship. "If it isn't written down, it didn't happen" is a trite but potent truism. Because applied sport and performance psychology is so complex by nature, documenting the decision-making process can be a helpful way to clarify decisions and also benefits the psychologist by providing a record to utilize if decisions are questioned. This includes the contacts, the progress, and the results of consultation. Even the best work of a sport or performance psychologist can be subject to question if it was not documented, or poorly or inadequately documented. Finally, ensure that the client was allowed to give informed consent regarding the risks of engaging in this multiple relationship. Although the psychologist cannot possibly address all of the possible risks and dilemmas, the client should be given access to the psychologist's thought process as much as possible. In the best situation, documentation should include a signed informed consent. This may seem contrived and time-consuming to some, but it protects both the client and the psychologist. Too frequently, athletes and performers who are part of larger organizations surrender their rights to privacy without much thought, with the perhaps implicit understanding that this is part of membership in the organization. A mindful, careful explanation of informed consent can empower the client in the collaborative, working relationship. For example, the performance psychologist who will be working with a theater cast as a group, but who is also available to individual actors for one-on-one work, should inform the actors that he or she will likely interact with them not only in the confines of the office, but also during practices, set design, dress rehearsals, and perhaps, during actual productions, as part of the work with the larger ensemble.

Gottlieb and Younggren (2009) have since revisited multiple relationships and risk management and concluded that boundary management is an even more complex and nuanced process than even they previously thought. They conclude that their earlier recommendations remain necessary but are not necessarily sufficient and require elaboration. Additional suggestions include utilization of peer consultation groups as an excellent means to assist professionals to perform at higher levels, especially in guarding against the effects of practitioners who are personally distressed; documentation of consultations when boundary management issues have been identified; development of the psychologist's own practice ethics policy (Gottlieb, 1997); consideration of boundary crossings in light of multicultural contexts; and encouragement of psychologists to pursue doing right (practicing positive ethics) rather than functioning in fearful avoidance of sanctions.

Boundary crossings are defined as departures from accepted practice standards and can range from the most extreme behaviors, such as sexual violations and exploitation, to those that are nonsexual boundary crossings (NSBCs) and might be considered innocuous, such as nonsexual touch with a client (handshake or hug), crying in the presence of a client, accepting a token gift, exchanging holiday cards, or self-disclosure of a personal stressor. Interest in NSBCs was initially based on the premise that those boundary crossings may be related to sexual boundary crossings (Lamb & Catanzaro, 1998). This relationship and the resultant outcome is commonly referred to as the "slippery slope" (Gutheil & Gabbard, 1993). The reality is that most NSBCs do not necessarily lead to sexual exploitation but are often simple benign departures from traditional settings or constraints. They may actually increase familiarity, understanding, and connection, and can positively impact meaningful work with clients (Lamb, Catanzaro, & Moorman, 2003). That said, sexual relationships between psychologists and clients always start with a boundary crossing, and some practitioners are more susceptible to poor boundary management than others. Special circumstances can also lead some psychologists and consultants to be at high risk for a boundary violation (e.g., increased personal stress).

In the more open, flexible, and casual world of sport and performance psychology, both chance and purposeful NSBCs occur frequently. In fact, the current practice of applied sport and performance psychology encourages and actually promotes NSBCs. For example, a sport psychologist might be present during a conditioning session in a weight room when an athlete might ask to be "spotted" while he completes a lift. Such interactions could easily involve the sport psychologist touching the athlete. A performance psychologist working backstage for a theater company might be present in the midst of a client's quick costume change during a performance. Gottlieb and Younggren (2009) have adamantly stated that appropriate NSBCs are not tantamount to stepping onto the slippery slope—NSBCs do not automatically lead to boundary violations. Given the variety of services that psychologists offer in diverse, contemporary practice, practitioners working in the field of sport and performance psychology should be prepared to answer for their decision-making if they choose to enter these complex relationships with clients. Those individuals with both a low identification with personal values and a superficial internalization to professional culture and ethics may be unsuited for work in sport and performance psychology.

Working with athletes and performers who frequently receive considerable attention and glory for their accomplishments may lead some professionals to experience what has been referred to as BIRG (basking in reflected glory), the Zsa Zsa Zsu effect, hero worship, or more simply, overidentification with a famous client (Andersen, 2005). Because NSBCs can contribute to this phenomenon, sport and performance psychologists and consultants need to carefully self-monitor as they work with athletes, performers, and organizations. Psychologists and consultants who become too emotionally invested in a client or organization's performance, regardless of outcome, can undermine their effectiveness as a consultant and counselor (Andersen et al., 2001). Taking credit for an organization's or a client's performance is clearly problematic. In fact, the applied sport or performance psychologist and consultant should almost always be in the distant background and never on a stadium's HD video screen or taking a bow during a curtain call with the ensemble. Athletes compete, performers execute, and sport and performance psychologists merely assist in the process. Similarly, if a sport or performance psychologist becomes unreasonably upset about a performance or competition outcome, then he or she is not likely to be present and emotionally available when the athlete or performer needs support.

Given the general acceptance of NSBCs as part of doing business in applied sport and performance psychology, Hankes (2002) offered several recommendations for those working in this field: personally assess why the NSBCs are occurring and the purpose they may serve in their work with the performer or team; consistently question whose needs are getting met by the NSBCs; be aware of, and acknowledge when necessary, identification with attractive, fit, talented, and famous clients; and monitor the occurrence of NSCBs and possible overidentification with clients, and discuss these issues in ongoing supervision or consulting relationships with trusted colleagues. This last recommendation is most important. Applied sport and performance psychologists and consultants who work in isolation (by choice, geography, or professional field), practicing alone without peer supervision and consultation, are most frequently the professionals who find themselves in unfortunate ethical dilemmas. Seeking out nurturing and honest relationships with professional colleagues who have similar professional interests in sport and performance psychology, and who have a strong commitment to ethics, can go a long way toward establishing consistent ethical practice. The ideal situation occurs if these colleagues are capable of providing open, critical feedback,

Consider the following situations that contain multiple relationships and boundary issues.

Standard 3.05 (a) Multiple Relationships

A multiple relationship occurs when a psychologist is in a professional role with a person and (1) at the same time is in another role with the same person, (2) at the same time is in a relationship with a person closely associated with or related to the person with whom the psychologist has the professional relationship, or (3) promises to enter into another relationship in the future with the person or a person closely associated with or related to the person.

A psychologist refrains from entering into a multiple relationship if the multiple relationship could reasonably be expected to impair the psychologist's objectivity, competence, or effectiveness in performing his or her functions as a psychologist, or otherwise risks exploitation or harm to the person with whom the professional relationships exists.

Multiple relationships that would not reasonably be expected to cause impairment or risk exploitation or harm are not unethical.

> Dr. Who's My Boss has been hired by an athletic department to be their full-time, in-house sport psychologist. Dr. Boss's overarching goal is to create an environment of trust in which athletes, coaches, and administrators are all equally comfortable coming to him for assistance. Dr. Boss has been asked by the athletic director to mentor a coach who has had an average record (and is in jeopardy of losing her job at the end of the season) and who has marginal interpersonal skills. Dr. Boss and the coach

work diligently to improve her interactions with her athletes, but Dr. Boss is not optimistic that she will be able to change. The coach's student-athletes are frustrated with her negative and confrontational leadership style and meet with Dr. Boss. They request direction as to whether they should approach the athletic director with their concerns. Dr. Boss is also currently seeing several of these same student-athletes in individual therapy.

Obviously, Dr. Boss is in a quandary. It appears that he entered into his position as the in-house sport psychologist with the hopes that he could be available as a resource to everyone in the athletic department. His intentions were good, if not realistic. In this situation, it is not clear who Dr. Boss considers to be his primary client. In hindsight, he should have clarified what his primary role would be in the department. If the athletic director is Dr. Boss's primary work supervisor, then this further complicates the situation as Dr. Boss undoubtedly would feel pressure to respond to his request to "mentor" the coach. As difficult as the conversation might have been, perhaps Dr. Boss should have discussed with the athletic director the potential conflicts of interest that might occur if he entered into the mentoring role with the coach.

Standard 3.05 (b) Multiple Relationships

If a psychologist finds that, due to unforeseen factors, a potentially harmful multiple relationship has arisen, the psychologist takes reasonable steps to resolve it with due regard for the best interests of the affected person and maximal compliance with the Ethics Code.

> Dr. Goes D. Extra Miles has served as a performance psychology consultant for a local theater company for many years. On occasion, he provides team-building exercises, primarily as a means to remind actors that he is available for individual work. He has worked with the leading actress in the company since he began the consultative relationship. The actress is deeply grateful for the help she has received and has shown her appreciation by giving Dr. Miles tickets to other productions in the community. Occasionally, Dr. Miles has shared drinks with the actress and other actors in a group setting. This usually occurred in celebration at the close of a successful run of shows. After several drinks, the actress tells Dr. Miles that she has begun an affair with another member of the company. Dr. Miles suspects that he is seeing the spouse of the actress's new partner in his private practice.

Clearly, Dr. Miles has engaged in NSBCs with the actress and the theater company. As discussed, this is not unusual for a performance psychologist, especially in light of his lengthy relationship with the theater company. That Dr. Miles chose to be present at the celebration of the theater company might not be unusual in the context of a performance psychology consultative relationship, and, in fact, his refusal to attend could be construed as negatively impacting the relationship. On the other hand, Dr. Miles' decision to consume alcohol with the theater company, even in a celebratory environment, is questionable. One wonders if the actress would have shared the information if she had not been drinking. Regardless, Dr. Miles now has the information and must determine how to resolve it in the best interest of all of those involved. It is not clear whether the actress is currently in therapy or in a performance relationship with Dr. Miles. Dr. Miles may want to strongly consider referring the actress to another professional if there is a desire on her part to address further issues that might arise.

Standard 3.06 Conflict of Interest

Psychologists refrain from taking on a professional role when personal, scientific, professional, legal, financial, or other interests or relationships could reasonably be expected to (1) impair their objectivity, competence, or effectiveness in performing their functions as psychologists; or (2) expose the person or organization with whom the professional relationship exists to harm or exploitation.

> Dr. Pain N. The Head is a sport psychologist who specializes in the neuropsychology of concussions. He has a lucrative contractual relationship with several professional football teams to provide predraft psychological evaluations for the purposes of assisting the NFL teams in determining who they will draft. Dr. Head has also established a reputation as a "go-to" consultant for a local Division I-A university. Dr. Head is working with the quarterback of the university's football team who has had a very successful career and desires to play in the NFL when his football eligibility ends. The quarterback confides to Dr. Head that at times he has struggled with blurred vision, headaches, and dizziness during his senior year. He has not shared this information with the team physician or coaches. Dr. Head suspects that the quarterback's symptoms are the result of a concussion that has not been treated. The quarterback refuses Dr. Head's recommendation

that he submit to a complete neuropsychological evaluation because he fears that the findings could affect his draft status. Subsequently, two professional football teams interested in drafting the quarterback contact him and Dr. Head to set-up a pre-draft psychological evaluation.

Dr. Head's successful work as sport psychologist with expertise in neuropsychology has contributed to this ethical dilemma occurring. Where performance outcome is critical, as it is in the world of professional sport, it is not unusual for an individual with a reputation for success to be contacted by multiple entities to request services. It is not clear in the current situation whether Dr. Head could have seen the likelihood that this conflict might occur. If the university athletic department, and specifically the football team, he consults with is historically one that competes successfully at the highest level, then he might have considered discussing and considering this conflict with the NFL teams he contracted with. Obviously, Dr. Head cannot provide the pre-draft psychological evaluation of the quarterback that is being requested by the NFL teams; however, he will need to be creative in how he explains this to the teams, so that the quarterback's confidentiality is protected. In addition to the conflict of interest issue, Dr. Head will need to consider how he will deal with the issue of the quarterback's concussion symptoms. Dr. Head should insist on a special counseling session with the quarterback to make certain that the athlete understands the potential risks to his health if he remains untreated and without an accurate neuropsychological assessment of his condition. Dr. Head may also want to consider the question of whether the quarterback's symptoms warrant an assessment for imminent risk of harming of himself.

Conclusion

Providing ethical services in the evolving fields of sport and performance psychology is a challenging endeavor that requires critical thinking, personal introspection, creativity, and flexibility. This chapter has discussed the continuum of clinical and performance issues, the systemic and organizational factors that are involved in work with athletes and performers, ethical decision-making models and the lifelong process of ethics, and common ethical dilemmas that permeate sport and performance psychology. No chapter can fully cover this important topic; however, it hopefully provides a framework for those who desire to work ethically and effectively in the complex, exciting domain of the psychology of human performance.

References

American Psychological Association (APA). (2002). Ethical principles of psychologists and code of conduct. *American Psychologist, 57,* 1060–1073.

American Psychological Association (APA; Division 47). (2008). *A proficiency in sport psychology.* Retrieved October 31, 2008, from http://www.apa47.org

Andersen, M. B. (2000). Beginnings: Intakes and the initiation of relationships. In M. B. Andersen (Ed.), *Doing sport psychology* (pp. 3–16). Champaign, IL: Human Kinetics.

Andersen, M. B. (2005). "Yeah, I work with Beckham": Issues of confidentiality, privacy and privilege in sport psychology service delivery. *Sport & Exercise Psychology Review, 1*(2), 5–13.

Andersen, M. B. (2005). Coming full circle: From practice to research. In M. B. Andersen (Ed.), *Sport psychology in practice* (pp. 287–298). Champaign, IL: Human Kinetics.

Andersen, M. B., Van Raalte, J. L., & Brewer, B. W. (2001). Sport psychology service delivery: Staying ethical while keeping loose. *Professional Psychology: Research and Practice, 32,* 12–18.

Andersen, M. B., & Van Raalte, J. L. (2005). Over one's head: Referral processes. In M. B. Andersen (Ed.), *Sport psychology in practice* (pp. 159–169). Champaign, IL: Human Kinetics.

Andersen, M. B. (2009). The "canon" of psychological skills training for enhancing performance. In K. F. Hays (Ed.), *Performance psychology in action: A casebook for working with athletes, performing artists, business leaders, and professionals in high-risk occupations* (pp. 11–34). Washington, DC: American Psychological Association.

Aoyagi, M. W., & Portenga, S. T. (2010). The role of positive ethics and virtues in the context of sport & performance psychology service delivery. *Professional Psychology: Research and Practice, 41,* 253–259.

Barber, H., & Krane, V. (2005). The elephant in the locker room: Opening the dialogue about sexual orientation on women's sports teams. In M. B. Andersen (Ed.), *Sport psychology in practice* (pp. 265–285). Champaign, IL: Human Kinetics.

Behnke, S. (2005). Ethics rounds: Disclosing confidential information in consultations and for didactic purposes. *Monitor on Psychology, 36,* 76–77.

Behnke, S. (2006). Beyond mere compliance: Three metaphors to teach the APA Ethics Code. *Monitor on Psychology, 37,* 54–55.

Behnke, S. (2008). Reflections on training ethical psychologists. *Monitor on Psychology, 39,* 58–59.

Behnke, S. (2008). Multiple relationships: A vignette. *Monitor on Psychology, 39,* 62.

Bennett, B. E., Bricklin, P. M., Harris, E., Knapp, S., VandeCreek, L., & Younggren, J. N. (2006). *Assessing and managing risk in psychological practice: An individualized approach.* Rockville, MD: The Trust.

Brown, C. H. (2001). Clinical cross-training: Compatibility of sport and family systems. *Professional Psychology: Research and Practice, 32,* 19–26.

Brown, J. L., & Cogan, K. (2006). Ethical clinical practice and sport psychology: When two worlds collide. *Ethics and Behavior, 16*(1), 15–23.

Campbell, L., Vasquez, M., Behnke, S., & Kinscherff, R. (2010). *APA Ethics Code commentary and case illustrations.* Washington, DC: American Psychological Association.

Canadian Psychological Association (CPA). (2000). *Canadian code of ethics for psychologists* (3rd ed.). Ottawa, ON: Author.

Ecklund, R. C. (2005). Afterword. In M. B. Andersen (Ed.), *Sport psychology in practice* (pp. 299–304). Champaign, IL: Human Kinetics.

Etzel, E. F., & Watson, J. C. (2007). Ethical challenges for psychological consultations in intercollegiate athletics. *Journal of Clinical Sport Psychology, 6,* 210–222.

Etzel, E. F., Watson, J. C., & Zizzi, S. (2004). A web based survey of AAASP member ethical beliefs and behaviors in the new millennium. *Journal of Applied Sport Psychology, 16,* 236–250.

Fisher, C. B. (2009). *Decoding the ethics code: A practical guide for psychologists* (2nd ed.). Thousand Oaks, CA: Sage Publications.

Fisher, M. A. (2008). Protecting confidentiality rights: The need for an ethical practice model. *American Psychologist, 63,* 1–13.

Fowler, R. D. (2009). Forward. In K. F. Hays (Ed.), *Performance psychology in action: A casebook for working with athletes, performing artists, business leaders, and professionals in high-risk occupations* (pp. ix–x). Washington, DC: American Psychological Association.

Gardner, F. L., & Moore, Z. E. (2006). *Clinical sport psychology.* Champaign, IL: Human Kinetics.

Gottlieb, M. C. (1997). An ethics policy for family practice management. In D. T. Marsh & R. D. Magee (Eds.), *Ethical and legal issues in professional practice with families* (pp. 257–270). New York: John Wiley.

Gottlieb, M. C., & Younggren, J. N. (2009). Is there a slippery slope? Considerations regarding multiple relationships and risk management. *Professional Psychology: Research and Practice, 40,* 564–571.

Gutheil, T. G., & Gabbard, G. O. (1993). The concept of boundaries in clinical practice: Theoretical and risk-management dimensions. *American Journal of Psychiatry, 150,* 188–196.

Hack, B. (2005). Qualifications: Education and experience. In S. Murphy (Ed.), *The sport psych handbook* (pp. 293–304). Champaign, IL: Human Kinetics.

Hankes, D. M. (2002). *Boundary crossings in applied sport psychology consultation: Assessing ethical risks in service delivery and training.* Paper presented at the 17th annual meeting of the Association for Applied Sport Psychology, Tucson, AZ.

Hankes, D. M. (2009). Adolescent performers and the family system. In K. F. Hays (Ed.), *Performance psychology in action: A casebook for working with athletes, performing artists, business leaders, and professionals in high-risk occupations* (pp. 247–267). Washington, DC: American Psychological Association.

Hays, K. F. (2002). The enhancement of performance excellence among performing artists. *Journal of Applied Sport Psychology, 14,* 299–312.

Hays, K. F. (2006). Being fit: The ethics of practice diversification in performance psychology. *Professional Psychology: Research and Practice, 37*(3), 223–232.

Hays, K. F., & Brown, C. H. (2004). *You're on! Consulting for peak performance.* Washington, DC: American Psychological Association.

Koocher, G. P., & Keith-Spiegel, P. (2008). *Ethics in psychology and the mental health professions: Standards and cases* (3rd ed.). New York: Oxford University Press.

Lamb, D. H., & Catanzaro, S. J. (1998). Sexual and nonsexual boundary violations involving psychologists, clients, supervisees, and students: Implications for professional practice. *Professional Psychology: Research and Practice, 29*, 498–503.

Lamb, D. H., Catanzaro, S. J., & Moorman, A. (2003). A preliminary look at how psychologists identify, evaluate, and proceed when faced with possible multiple relationship dilemmas. *Professional Psychology: Research and Practice, 35*, 248–254.

Lazurus, A. A., & Zur, O. (Eds.). (2002). *Dual relationships and psychotherapy.* New York: Springer Publishing Company.

Linder, D. E., Pillow, D. R., & Reno, R. R. (1989). Shrinking jocks: Derogation of athletes who consult a sport psychologist. *Journal of Sport and Exercise Psychology, 11*, 270–280.

Moore, Z. E. (2003). Ethical dilemmas in sport psychology: Discussion and recommendations for practice. *Professional Psychology: Research and Practice, 34*, 601–610.

Moorehead-Slaughter, O. (2006). *The ethics of athletic excellence: More than just a competitive edge.* Paper presented at the 21st annual meeting of the Association for Applied Sport Psychology, Miami, FL.

Murphy, S. M. (1995). *Sport psychology interventions.* Champaign, IL: Human Kinetics.

Packard, E. (2007). Sports authority. *Monitor on Psychology, 38*, 62–63.

Petrie, T. A., & Harmison, R. (2011). Sport psychology in the field of counseling psychology. In E. Altmaier & J. I. Hanson (Eds.), *Oxford handbook of counseling psychology* (pp. 780–806). New York: Oxford University Press.

Pinker, S. (2006). Evolution and ethics. In J. Brockman (Ed.)., *Intelligent thought.* New York: Vintage.

Portenga, S. T., Aoyagi, M. W. (2007). *Ethical practice for consultants working directly for university athletic departments.* Paper presented at the 22nd annual meeting of the Association for Applied Sport Psychology, Louisville, KY.

Roche, D. N., & Hankes, D. M. (2009). Consultation in intercollegiate athletics. In. E. F. Etzel (Ed.), *Counseling college student-athletes: Issues and interventions* (3rd ed., pp. 51–84). Morgantown, WV: Fitness Information and Technology, Inc.

Sperber, M. A. (2000). *Beer and circus: How big-time college sports is crippling undergraduate education.* New York: Henry Holt and Company.

Stapleton, A. B., Hankes, D. M., Hays, K. F., & Parham, W. B. (2010). Ethical dilemmas in sport psychology: A dialogue on the unique aspects impacting practice. *Professional Psychology: Research and Practice, 41*, 143–152.

Straub, W. F., & Hinman, D. A. (1992). Profiles and professional perspectives of 10 leading sport psychologists. *The Sport Psychologist, 6*, 297–312.

Younggren, J. N., & Gottlieb, M. C. (2004). Managing risk when contemplating multiple relationships. *Professional Psychology: Research and Practice, 35*, 255–260.

The Role of Superior Performance Intelligence in Sustained Success

Graham Jones

Abstract

This chapter introduces a new theoretical concept, *superior performance intelligence* (SPI), to help organize and understand the psychological research on sustained success. It describes an interview-based investigation of top performers from a variety of performance fields. The findings reveal a common critical awareness and know-how among top performers, from athletes to business leaders to cardiologists to performing artists to military leaders to entrepreneurs, that enables them to apply their minds, skills, techniques, strategies, and tactics to the same high standard every time they perform. This chapter proposes that a high level of SPI is at the core of high performance delivered on a consistent basis and comprises three components: knowing how to maximize your potential; knowing how to *work with your environment*; and knowing how to deliver high performance. The introduction of a new concept into the performance psychology literature suggests a number of potential research and applied directions; a small number of the more pressing ones are identified in this chapter.

Key Words: Multiple intelligences, superior performance, maximizing potential, environment, sports, business, military, performing arts, medicine, entrepreneurs

Do you remember Andrea Jaeger? She was the 15-year-old American tennis teenage prodigy who, in 1980, became the youngest player to be seeded at Wimbledon, and then became ranked World Number Two at age 16. Jaeger reached two Grand Slam finals and three semi-finals but never got to win the "big one." She was lost to the sport at an early age, partly through injury, but largely as a result of never coming to terms with the pressure-cauldron environment she was performing in. Perhaps fittingly to some, Jaeger eventually sought solace as a nun.

Golf's John Daly is another who features in the ranks of sports' underachievers. Although Daly *has* achieved the ultimate prize, the two Major wins he has to his name are a poor return indeed for someone with such enormous talent. Unfortunately, Daly is better known for his almost embarrassing ability to publically self-destruct. His well-documented problems with substance abuse and troubled relationships make Daly a prime example of how a promising career can be hurt by a failure to come to terms with and master what it takes to perform at the highest level.

Of course, athletes whose achievements have not lived up to their enormous potential exist in all sports. These are the athletes who are among the most technically gifted in their sports, yet are renowned for their inability to live up to their obvious talents. On their day, these performers are a match for anyone, but some days—often when it matters most—they have just not been able to deliver. And their careers have often been short and stormy, the opposite of the long, consistent records of success sustained by athletes such as Michael Phelps, Michael Jordan, Steffi Graf, Wayne Gretzky, Martina Navratilova,

Pele, Babe Ruth, Magic Johnson, Lance Armstrong, Michael Johnson, Annika Sorenstam, Carl Lewis, Michael Schumacher, Joe Montana, Muhammad Ali, Usain Bolt, Alex Rodriguez, Brett Favre, Roger Federer, and Tiger Woods.

These athletes are famous not only for their incredible talent, but also for their consistency in delivering the goods time and time again. Yet, even this list of sporting icons throws up some examples—Tiger Woods being the most prominent—of how athletes can run into tremendous difficulties in sustaining success if they violate the principles discussed in this chapter.

Putting these "blemishes" to one side, what is it about champions like these that enables them to perform at their peak, day-in-day-out, while many other hugely talented athletes never seem to know how they are going to perform until the competition begins?

Sports provide the highly visible arena that attracts huge attention and debate over such questions. People have a fascination with watching how athletes who perform at the very highest level deal with the immense demands placed on them. The performance environment is a cauldron of fierce competition in which victory comes often by the smallest of margins. Their lives are dominated by hard work, perseverance, determination, achieving the highest goals and targets, teamwork, dealing with success, and recovering from failure. Underpinning their success is the ability to continually move performance to higher levels—what you achieve this year is never going to be good enough next year. Goals and standards move onward and upward, resulting in an incessant demand to find new means and methods to ensure the delivery of performance curves that at times can seem tantalizingly, and at other times impossibly, out of reach. And all of this occurs under an intense media spotlight that searches for every frailty and any indication of not being able to cope (Connaughton, Hanton, & Jones, 2010; Jones, 2010; Jones & Moorhouse, 2008).

In applying the learning from elite athletes to the business world over the last several years, I have discovered that this type of pressure-cooker environment is by no means exclusive to sports (see Jones, 2002, 2008). I have witnessed pressure levels in some companies that rival the most extreme in elite sports. And it's getting worse. These are turbulent economic times, in which big companies are failing more frequently and performance slumps are proliferating. The uncertainty and apparent lack of total control over corporate destiny creates enormous pressure.

There is a subtle difference, though, between sports and business in this respect. In sports, dealing with pressure is part of the "test" that performers *choose* to participate in; however, in the business context, this type of pressure is not something to which most people would actually choose to subject themselves. Instead, it is often an unwanted distracter, and sometimes detractor, from individual, team, and organizational performance. And the consequences of failure are potentially more catastrophic at the personal level, with redundancy, demotion, severance, burnout, and ill health lurking around the corner.

In some high-performance environments, the price of failure is even greater. A few years ago, I worked closely with Royal Marines trainers and recruits who were pushing themselves to the limit to earn the right to wear the coveted Green Beret. Here, the consequences of being overwhelmed by what can be a very intimidating training environment were severe enough, but for those recruits who were successful in coming through the intense examination of their physical and mental endurance, an even more demanding environment awaited them. Many of them soon found themselves in the heat of battle or on peace-keeping duties, life-threatening situations in which the consequences of failing could quite literally be deadly.

There are also many less hostile, but still potentially overpowering and draining professional environments in which performers have little or no apparent control, perhaps through resource shortages or inefficient processes that serve as constraints that frustrate highly skilled and committed personnel from delivering the service they know they are capable of providing (see also Chapter 30, this volume). Examples include health care organizations where resources are continually being stretched and government agencies where processes are often in disarray and employees are under the continual spotlight of government opposition and the media. And what about the world of education, where teacher assessments, student performance appraisals, and school reviews and ratings have increased the visibility of schools and their staff to levels never witnessed before?

Organizations and individuals in these environments are held accountable to the bottom-line standard of performance, and all of them require people to excel to meet the enormous demands that face them. They also require high levels of performance that are sustainable. Excelling in these types of environments on a regular basis requires more than talent alone. Indeed, a number of well-read popular psychology books published in the last few years argue that "talent is overrated" (Colvin, 2008; Gladwell, 2008; Syed, 2010). These books focus heavily on research by Ericsson, Krampe, and Tesch-Romer (1993) that showed the importance of deliberate (quantity and quality) practice in predicting who will make it to the top. Specifically, it was estimated that experts spend typically 10 years or 10,000 hours in deliberate practice to attain exceptional performance. These works further sought to minimize the role talent plays in reaching the top by emphasizing other factors such as birth dates (Musch & Grondin, 2001) and citing case studies on people of the likes of Bill Gates and the Beatles to show how "being in the right place at the right time" is also a crucial factor.

However, the narrow environmentalist position these popular works are based on reflects only half of the opposing nurture versus nature views that have dominated the scientific literature on expertise development. The opposing genocentric position is similarly limited, so that neither is sufficient in isolation to explain how people get to the top of their professions and stay there (see Phillips, Davids, Renshaw, & Portus, 2010, for a review).

Even when you combine these positions, something is still missing. Indeed, Côté and Abernethy provide a convincing rationale for a much more holistic perspective on the development of expertise in Chapter 23 of this volume. Talent, hard work, and luck are important in helping performers reach the top, but are insufficient to enable people, in any domain, to deliver high performance on a consistent basis once they get there.

Having studied and worked with high performers in a variety of arenas over several years, I have come to realize that the missing ingredient in this "sustained success cocktail" is what I believe to be a form of intelligence. It is very evident among the world's best athletes, and I have also witnessed it among the best performers in work and military settings. Since this intelligence is about delivering superior performance on a consistent basis, I did not deliberate for too long over naming it *superior performance intelligence* (SPI).

The aim of this chapter is to explore the concept of SPI from the same perspective that I and my research colleagues have approached the study of mental toughness. It has been known for a long time that mental toughness exists and is a fundamental feature of delivering top performance under pressure, but it has only recently been the subject of scientific rigor to establish what it is and what it comprises. This has emanated from qualitative methodologies using purposive sampling to first ask participants to define the concept and then to identify the key components underlying it (Connaughton et al., 2010; Jones, Hanton, & Connaughton, 2002, 2007).

This chapter provides a brief overview of the notion of different types of intelligence, before describing interviews I carried out with high-level performers from a number of performance domains. The findings are encapsulated in the form of a proposed framework of SPI. Future research directions are then explored.

Different Types of Intelligence

The notion that there are different types of intelligence is founded on the proposition that intelligence conceived as constituting solely traditional IQ is too limited and fails to explain how humans are capable of extraordinary creativity and ingenuity without necessarily possessing a high IQ.

One of the early approaches was Sternberg's (1985) *triarchic model,* which proposes that intelligence comprises three primary components. *Analytical intelligence* closely resembles the traditional concept of "intelligence," referring to skills such as reasoning and analyzing. *Creative intelligence* involves the ability to combine seemingly unrelated information to form new ideas. *Contextual intelligence* is about practical know-how and is an interactive process with the external environment.

Howard Gardner's work on multiple intelligences (MI; 1983, 1999) also identified a number of different intelligences to account for a broader range of potential in people.

- *Linguistic intelligence:* Words and language
- *Logical-mathematical intelligence:* Logic and numbers
- *Spatial intelligence:* Images and space
- *Bodily kinesthetic intelligence:* Body movement control
- *Musical intelligence:* Sound and rhythm
- *Interpersonal intelligence:* Other people's feelings
- *Intrapersonal intelligence:* Self-awareness
- *Naturalistic intelligence:* Environmental awareness

This work has attracted considerable ongoing debate, particularly in the educational psychology literature (Allix, 2000; Chen, 2004; Waterhouse,

2006). Antagonists' main argument is that MI theory has no validating data (Allix, 2000; Waterhouse, 2006), pointing instead to a general intelligence function that is identified by an IQ test factor. Protagonists, on the other hand, argue that intelligence is not necessarily a tangible object that can be measured (Chen, 2004). Furthermore, even if intelligence is measurable, most tests of intelligence focus only on the first two—linguistic and logical—and fail to measure a whole array of other capacities and capabilities that underpin human potential.

It is not my intention to assess the relative merits of these positions here; rather, it is to acknowledge the fact that the notion of MI is not universally accepted. For the purposes of this chapter, the following quote by Gardner (2004) is especially pertinent: "the notion of multiple intelligences is hardly a proven fact; it is, at most, an idea that has.... the right to be discussed seriously" (p. 11).

A number of researchers and writers believe firmly in the existence of MI and its potential to contribute significantly to understanding people and performance. The notion of *emotional intelligence* (EI) was first outlined by Salovey and Mayer (1990). A version of their construct was popularized by Daniel Goleman in 1995, and it attracted widespread interest in a number of fields at both practical and research levels. Goleman articulated five domains of EI as knowing your emotions, managing your emotions, motivating yourself, recognizing and understanding other people's emotions, and managing relationships. Goleman (1998, 2001; Goleman, Boyatzis, & Mckee, 2002) later expanded this model and redefined EI as competence in four areas: self-awareness, self-management, social awareness, and relationship management.

There have been a number of adaptations of emotional intelligence in recent years, some of which offer conflicting constructs (Matthews, Roberts, & Zeidner, 2004). However, they all essentially comprise what Gardner referred to as "personal intelligences"—interpersonal and intrapersonal—and these constructs are argued to be better predictors of success in the workplace than academic or cognitive ability (see Joseph & Newman, 2010; O'Boyle, Humphrey, Pollock, Hawver, & Story, 2010), as well as being predictors of achievement in leadership (George, 2000) and sport (Lane et al., 2010; Meyer & Fletcher, 2007). As such, EI is about understanding and managing yourself and relationships with others.

Goleman (2006) later proposed that the notion of EI was unable to explain many of the specific details and nuances of interpersonal relationships and proposed a further dimension of intelligence—*social intelligence*. According to Goleman, social intelligence comprises two broad categories: "social awareness"—what we sense about others; and "social facility"—what we then do with that awareness.

Other forms of intelligence have also been identified. Nelson (2009) argued for the existence of what she termed *physical intelligence* based on her experience as an elite college basketball player and the toll the intense training, practicing, and competing had on her body. Physical intelligence is the ability to listen to the body's subtle signals and respond wisely to them. *Cultural intelligence* is defined as the ability to deal effectively with people from a different cultural background and understanding (Earley & Ang, 2003). Finally, Albrecht (2002) presented seven dimensions of *organizational intelligence*: strategic vision, appetite for change, alignment and congruence, performance pressure, knowledge deployment, heart, and shared fate.

Two things are evident about the work on MI. First, it is unclear how many different intelligences exist. Second, the lack of coherence among the approaches and methodologies adopted to conceptualize and study MI has resulted in significant overlap and commonality across the different intelligences identified.

Investigating Superior Performance Intelligence

Of the intelligences identified to date, some are clear prerequisites for achieving a high level of performance. In sports, for example, athletes will not get very far without high levels of spatial and bodily kinesthetic intelligences—these are the very underpinning of the physical and perceptual abilities required to compete at the top level in any sport. Exceptional levels may actually be enough to sometimes ensure a one-off performance that is good enough to win on the day. But they are intelligences that every performer must possess to make them competitive and are insufficient on their own to enable the world's best performers to deliver success on a consistent basis. In fact, none of these intelligences, either in isolation or in combination, is able to fully explain why some elite athletes are able to reach the top and stay there, whereas others with the same ability and talent do not.

My research and experience of working with elite athletes and performers from other domains point strongly to the existence of another, previously unidentified type of intelligence—SPI—that lies at the core of being able to deliver high levels of performance on a consistent basis. The interviews conducted were designed to examine this form of intelligence.

PARTICIPANTS

Consistent with qualitative methodologies (Lincoln & Guber, 1985; Patton, 1990), purposive sampling was employed to select the study participants. The major criterion that determined the selection of the participants was that they had achieved the highest levels of performance on a demonstrably sustainable basis. This did not necessarily have to be demonstrated in the same performance arena. Indeed, of particular interest to the author were participants who had achieved the highest success in one domain and had clearly transferred their learning and mindset to enable high performance in another.

The 12 participants who agreed to participate were informed of the nature of the study and comprised the following:

- Five people who had achieved the highest levels of performance over a minimum period of 10 years in their chosen field. They comprised the most senior leader in an elite fighting force, an entrepreneur who was renowned for being innovative and successful in the financial sector, a performing artist (ballet dancer) who had danced at the highest level, and two chief executive officers, one of whom led a large global charity and the other in the postal service industry.
- Seven people who had been successful in more than one performance domain. Three of these participants were Olympic Gold Medal winners (rowing and track and field) before being successful in the world of professional services. Two other participants had achieved success in American football (one a Super Bowl winner and the other an All-America college player) before moving into careers that ultimately resulted in achieving senior leadership status in large global commercial organizations. The All-America college player had also had a successful career in the military before moving into the commercial world. Another participant in this category had won an Olympic Gold Medal (modern pentathlon) before pursuing a successful career as a medical doctor. The final participant in this category was the head of a heart surgery team in a leading hospital before becoming a senior leader in a large pharmaceutical company.

The participants included nine males and three females. Seven of the participants were from the United Kingdom, while the remaining five were from North America.

INTERVIEWS

All participants were interviewed using a semi-structured technique. Participants were briefed as to the purpose of the research prior to the interview and were informed that all data would be reported anonymously unless permission was granted to reveal their identity for the purpose of specific dissemination. All interviews were tape-recorded and conducted by the same individual, and lasted between 30 and 60 minutes. Five of the interviews were conducted over the telephone and seven were conducted in person. Weinberg, Butt, and Knight (2001) have previously showed no differences in findings resulting from these different forms of interviewing. Core questions that formed the foundation of all the interviews included: "When I refer to the notion of 'Superior Performance Intelligence,' what does it bring to mind?"; "Are there any examples of when SPI has been important in your own career?"; and, "What advice would you offer people who want to develop SPI?"

DATA ANALYSIS

The interview data were analyzed using content analysis in which quotes were grouped into themes if they logically fitted together. The protocol used in analyzing and reducing the data was as follows:

1. All interviews were tape-recorded and transcribed.
2. Two researchers read the transcripts and familiarized themselves with the content.
3. Data themes were then identified by each of the researchers. Consensus was achieved by the researchers as a result of subsequent discussions.
4. After establishing these themes, the participants were given the opportunity to comment on the themes identified, and their view given as to whether they felt the themes were representative of their responses. Where there was disagreement, discussions were held with the participant and the researchers until consensus was gained.[1]

FINDINGS

Three major themes emerged from the data analysis, which are presented as comprising the major components of SPI and are labeled as follows:

- Knowing how to maximize your potential
- Knowing how to work *with* your environment
- Knowing how to deliver high performance

These themes form the basis for an understanding of SPI and the starting point for future research. The following sections are organized around the three themes. Brief quotes taken directly from the interview transcripts are included to enable an in-depth understanding of the themes and associated dimensions and subcomponents that emerged (see Table 4.1).

Table 4.1 A framework of superior performance intelligence

Knowing How to Maximize Your Potential

Knowing Yourself

Knowing *who* you are

Knowing *how* you are

Stretching Yourself

Wanting to be the best you can

Having a personal vision

Being a sponge for information and learning

Having a fundamental belief in yourself

Sustaining Yourself

Keeping the bigger picture in mind

Dealing with pressure

Achieving a good life balance

Recovering from failures and setbacks

Celebrating successes

Switching off

Knowing How to Work *with* Your Environment

Knowing Your Environment

Knowing your controllable environment

Knowing your uncontrollable environment

Shaping Your Environment

Defining and communicating the vision and goals

Surrounding yourself with the right people

Fostering collaboration

Challenging orthodoxy

Using your emotional intelligence

Being in Tune with Your Environment

Being agile

Building and maintaining relationships

Staying humble

Knowing How to Deliver High Performance

Planning and Preparing

Defining success

Making sure everything has a purpose

Planning for every scenario

Optimizing your emotional state

Delivering

Performing under pressure

Trusting yourself

Controlling the critical controllables

Seizing opportunities

Knowing when to alter course

Evaluating

Comparing against measurement criteria

Picking out the good bits

Identifying what needs work

Knowing How To Maximize Your Potential

This theme split into three dimensions that reflected a self-knowledge and ability to self-regulate in order to realize one's capability and potential: "knowing yourself," "stretching yourself," and "sustaining yourself."

Knowing Yourself

This dimension represented how well the participants understood what drove them and their behaviors, and further divided into knowing "who" and "how" you are.

KNOWING WHO YOU ARE

This subcomponent is best captured in the quotes of three participants who stated separately: "knowing who I am, I think, is around value sets," "it's about understanding who you are and understanding what is important to you and not compromising on the things that are important," and "knowing deeply who you are and sticking with that and being comfortable with that." Another of the participants went to great lengths to gain this level of understanding:

> I spent five years in West Africa living in small villages with no running water, no electricity, no water, no phones... there was a huge amount of time alone and I had to get comfortable with who I am and really know myself and be satisfied with myself. It was a painful and lonely process but I felt the luckiest person in the world I was able to do it.

KNOWING HOW YOU ARE

The participants made a clear distinction between knowing *who* you are and knowing *how* you are: "knowing how you are is more about knowing yourself in a social context... I've always been very aware of the impact I have on other people." One participant stated that "it helps me to understand how I think, behave, and manage, and it enables me to think about how other people might be thinking about how I'm behaving and managing." Another participant emphasized the importance of knowing how you are in enabling regulation of behavior:

> I'm not that different at work than I am at home and I don't have a strain about putting on a guise. It can be confusing to the boys because I'm a General and I often don't behave quite like one. I behave like a General when I know I need to.

SUMMARY

"Knowing Yourself" comprises knowing "who" and "how" you are. "Knowing how you are" relates closely to EI in terms of being aware of your emotions and behaviors and how they impact on other people. "Knowing who you are" is about personal values and not compromising on the things that are important to you. As such, this represents an additional component of self-knowledge that is based on self-discovery. This self-knowledge is fundamental to knowing what you are capable of and of knowing the second dimension, "stretching yourself," in order to achieve it.

Stretching Yourself

This dimension reflected a continual striving for self-improvement in the participants' quest to satisfy their personal aspirations. Four subcomponents comprised this dimension: "wanting to be the best you can," "having a personal vision," "being a sponge for information and learning," and "having a fundamental belief in yourself."

WANTING TO BE THE BEST YOU CAN

The desire to be the best you can was critical to one of the participants, who was unequivocal in having a conviction that "if you don't have that (desire) then you're not going to be the best you can." Another participant who had achieved in more than one performance domain provided more context: "Even now, I want to be the best doctor that I can be. I want to know that I'm doing the right thing for my patients."

HAVING A PERSONAL VISION

If "wanting to be the best you can" drove these highest achievers on a daily basis, then "having a personal vision" provided them with the long-term aspirations that kept them heading in the right direction. Some of the participants were clear about their personal vision at a relatively early stage in their careers. For example:

> I had an epiphany when I was about 20 that there was injustice in the world and my vision was to dedicate my life to doing something about injustice, whatever form that takes, and my personal vision has been to make a difference. And then I had a moment in my late 20s when I said I'm pretty good at leading people and I want to inspire and motivate people and I want to lead an organization, lead on an issue, and that was when I wanted to be a CEO of an organization dedicated to fighting injustice.

They were also clear about the consequences of not having a personal vision: "a lack of vision hurts... you can't plan if you don't have a vision... lots of people don't have an idea of what they're trying to do and so have no chance of getting there."

BEING A SPONGE FOR INFORMATION AND LEARNING

All of the participants talked passionately about their desire and commitment to learning and being a sponge for new information, and not being afraid to admit what they do not know:

Our reputation is such a guarded sovereign thing, over 20 or 30 years in any environment your reputation is the most important thing you have, and sometimes it's quite difficult to damage it and sometimes it's quite easy and sometimes catastrophically, particularly with the intrusiveness of the media. People get so scared that they're not prepared to try new things, you know the more senior they become the more cautious and guarded they become because they're always worried about being seen to be foolish…I always ask questions about the things I don't understand, and very often lots of people don't understand as well and they go "thank goodness the General doesn't understand."

Further insight into this subcomponent is captured by the brief quotes from four different participants whose passion for learning was clear: "Continuous learning…never stop, even if you don't have a goal to aim for"; "I read about new things that will give me new knowledge and continuously reinforce my excitement about the job"; "I love constantly learning and growing and developing"; "I read a lot, I share a lot of articles with people here…I love to sit down with three or four big thinkers and see what we can learn from one another."

The importance of seeking and accepting feedback was raised by a number of the participants, best characterized in the following quote:

I once read a quote that "feedback is the breakfast of champions," and I fully believe that. One of the biggest pitfalls I see in senior leaders is that they become incapable to take constructive criticism. They've created these barriers to negative feedback and they have this open door to positive feedback so that they end up losing touch with reality…to me, feedback keeps you in touch with reality and the higher you go in an organization the more you have to seek feedback because it won't be given to you voluntarily.

HAVING A FUNDAMENTAL BELIEF IN YOURSELF

A deep belief in yourself emerged as an important factor in enabling the participants to stretch themselves to achieve their success. One participant emphasized the importance of belief in delivering sustainable success: "once you're at the top, it's having the belief and confidence that you can deliver repeatable top performance, a belief that enables you to keep stretching yourself." Other participants were more specific in identifying a

"confidence to be relaxed in your own skin" and having a mindset of "*knowing* you can win versus *hoping* you can win."

SUMMARY

"Stretching yourself" draws together a number of different factors that have been identified in the performance psychology literature as being important predictors of success. Wanting to be the best you can on a daily basis reflects an internalized motivation that is well-documented in the literature (Ryan & Deci, 2006; Ryan, Lynch, Vansteenkiste, & Deci, 2011). Striving for a personal vision, which participants often identified at a relatively young age and which kept them headed in the right direction, was a strategy advocated strongly by Covey (2004) in his popular writing. This drive was underpinned by a self-belief that has been identified as fundamental to achieving sustained success (Connaughton & Hanton, 2009; Jones, 2010) and a mindset for continuous personal growth (Dweck, 2006; Jones & Spooner, 2006). In order to maintain this commitment to strive for high performance on a consistent basis, the participants identified a third dimension, "sustaining yourself."

Sustaining Yourself

The final dimension in "knowing how to maximize your potential" divided into five subcomponents that highlighted how the participants sustained themselves during the process of delivering high performance on a consistent basis: "keeping the bigger picture in mind," "achieving a good life balance," "recovering from failures and setbacks," "celebrating successes," and "switching off."

KEEPING THE BIGGER PICTURE IN MIND

All of the participants identified how important keeping the bigger picture in mind was in helping them to deliver sustainable high performance. The quotes below speak for themselves in encapsulating the essence of this subcomponent:

Whether you're in sport or in a business, you're going to have high highs and low lows and it's important to keep perspective of the big picture…there are going to be highs and there are going to be lows and that's what makes you stronger over time. Don't let the lows get you down too much, don't let the highs make you too cocky.

I raced in Lucerne recently and have never won there in my previous career. It was playing on my mind in the warmup and I recognized the bigger picture and that Lucerne was a step in a journey and not the be-all-end-all. London was the bigger picture.

That's one of the reasons I travel...I want to get out and remind ourselves what the bigger picture is and why you sit in this glass office and do what you do.

The headlong rush for material gain strikes me for its hollowness and I know because of the environment I work in, because of the direness of bereavement, the yin and the yang, I know what's important, and over the years I have made some sometimes difficult and hard corrections to my life.

You get sucked down so much into the detail sometimes, and crises that come up, that reminding yourself of the bigger picture helps to pull you out of it.

I keep coming back to the bigger picture about who I am in terms of values and balance and that kind of thing and it helps get me back on track when I'm veering off.

It is striking to note the consistency of the clear message that these performers across a variety of performance domains were delivering: "keeping the bigger picture in mind" is fundamental to the need to be able to keep things in perspective during both highs and lows.

ACHIEVING A GOOD LIFE BALANCE

This appeared to be a critical factor for the participants, especially in light of the many demands placed upon them in different aspects of their lives. They emphasized the importance of achieving a good life balance not only for themselves but also for the other people in their lives. A selection of quotes presented below highlight the importance these participants placed on getting this balance right:

I'm a better doctor for having the time out with my children. If I was consulting full-time I just couldn't do that, I think my patients benefit because I get a better balance in terms of life.

It's important to have more than your sport or business as your driving factor in life and get satisfaction out of a broader range of things. My family is deeply important, faith, giving back to the community...I play the guitar, to me music is emotion...it's an important part of my balance.

It's about recognizing that there are other things going on as well as my rowing, recognizing that there

are really important things in my life as well as trying to row fast.

It's having ways of contextualizing what you do and not being so busy making a living that you've failed to make a life. You can quite easily become completely absorbed. When you have a responsibility for people, it's an unlimited liability.

I failed at this during my 20s and 30s...I was really driven and was a workaholic. It's much better now and there's two reasons. One is a self-awareness. I realized that I was on a gerbil's wheel and that I needed to find something much more internal to be happy with my reason to be and that I didn't have to just define myself by myself and by my work...I found a way to define myself with work as part of that but not the sum of it. And the other one is now I have a family. Having a family is something that pulls you out of work, I can't wait to get home to see my kids now.

I work hard at achieving the right balance between putting the time and energy and attention into my family, my pharmaceutical services job and balancing that with the need to do the hospital/academic job within cardiology.

Take care of your body, eating, sleeping properly, resting, maintaining balance outside of work...when I'm at my best all of these things have been in place.

I work as hard out of work and that's how I get my balance.... my children, writing my sermons for Sunday...I'm as busy out of work but things are so completely different.

Again, the consistency of the performers' sentiments about "achieving a good life balance" is striking, showing that it is important in all performance domains.

RECOVERING FROM FAILURES AND SETBACKS

Of course, the world of high achievers is not always about succeeding. The participants identified the importance of accepting that failure is inevitable:

You have to be prepared to lose, you have to be prepared to tough it out when things are down.

I think part of the willingness or the ability to be flexible is also recognition that you don't have enough wisdom and it's all right to fail. It's all right to fail and to be seen to fail, people want to be led by human beings.

Be prepared for setbacks, that's just part of the job and take it in your stride.

The importance of having an attitude that emphasized learning and moving on from failure and setbacks was also a common thread among the participants:

> I sometimes think I personalize it too much but I also think I'm able to move on pretty quickly...I absorb it and then I get rid of it pretty quickly.

> I learn from them. I take accountability and then change things.

CELEBRATING SUCCESSES

The participants emphasized that dealing with success was as important as dealing with setbacks in enabling them to deliver sustainable high performance:

> When we won in Bled, the opposition was not too strong, but I got the crew together and said "we've got to enjoy when we win races no matter who we've just beaten"...an important part of my awareness over the years is that I should recognize and celebrate and enjoy success.

However, the participants also highlighted the importance of knowing when to refocus on the next challenge:

> When we have a huge win here, I celebrate big time with people on a Friday evening, but Monday morning I'm thinking "back at it." There are things and moments where I want to share in that glory but it's crucial to know when to refocus on the challenges ahead.

SWITCHING OFF

In achieving a good life balance, the emphasis of the participants was on spreading themselves across the various elements of their lives and working hard at each. "Switching off" is essentially about slowing down so that vital energy resources required to deliver high performance on a consistent basis can be replenished. This is highlighted in the following quotes:

> It would be so intense you'd wear yourself into a frazzle...there's a time when you need to rest and to refresh...there's a time when there's just pure performance and emotion, and there's a time to back off and let things settle and reflect.

> Really addressing the "switch off" time and having other things to do which still allow effective recovery but that allow the brain to stop thinking about that

last session...I go off and do something that I like to do but doesn't require much effort.

> You have to have time to replenish and relax and regroup for the next fight.

SUMMARY

"Sustaining yourself" is very much about knowing how to achieve a personal equilibrium that enables you to deal effectively with the demands, pressures, and potential distractions that are inherent in the process of delivering high performance on a consistent basis. In particular, all of the participants emphasized the importance of "achieving a good life balance," a demand that is worthy of greater research attention going forward (Grzywacz & Carlson, 2007; Waulmsley, Hemmings, & Payne, 2010). "Keeping the bigger picture in mind" bears a striking resemblance to Covey's (2004) "begin with the end in mind" advice to prospective high achievers. "Recovering from failures and setbacks" and "switching off" are well-documented as being important contributors to being mentally tough (Jones et al., 2002, 2007). "Celebrating successes" is something that appears more prominent among athletes—individuals in other performance domains characterized by intense pressure could learn an important lesson from them.

Knowing How to Work *with* Your Environment

This theme also split into three dimensions and related to the participants' ability to shape and use the performance environment to their advantage. As one of the participants stated, "I use that word 'with' because it means you're never a victim of your environment." The three dimensions were: "knowing your environment," "shaping your environment," and "being in tune with your environment."

Knowing Your Environment

This dimension reflected a detailed awareness of the performance environment and comprised two subcomponents that distinguished separate aspects of that environment: "knowing your controllable environment," and "knowing your uncontrollable environment."

KNOWING YOUR CONTROLLABLE ENVIRONMENT

Participants distinguished between two aspects of the performance environment. The first included those factors over which they were able to exert a significant degree of control. Sample quotes include:

> You can sometimes feel isolated and removed as a leader. I ask a lot of questions. I want to know what's going on, to take the pulse of the organization and morale, purpose, etc., to see how and where I can help.

> I'm in a very busy GP practice…you know you're going to be under pressure, running late, receptionists hassling you for this and that. It's about knowing that that is the situation…you have to find your own ways of getting things done, prioritizing things, time management, delegation.

KNOWING YOUR UNCONTROLLABLE ENVIRONMENT

The second aspect of the performance environment comprised factors that participants required detailed knowledge of but had little control over:

> In football, knowing the competition, knowing the game, even the stadium and where you're playing, whether it's hostile or not…those things were all very important. In business, obviously you've got to know your market, your customers, your competitors, the environmental regulations and governmental constraints, knowing the rules which you've got to play by and how the game's going to be played is absolutely critical to setting strategy and being successful.

One participant commented on the importance of not focusing on what you cannot control but "know everything about what's out there and what you're up against…don't get surprised…don't lose sleep over it but use that knowledge when the time comes."

SUMMARY

"Knowing your environment" involves having a deep knowledge and awareness of the performance environment. This has been identified as important in developing contextual intelligence (Brown, Gould, & Foster, 2005; Sternberg, 1985; Terenzini, 1993). However, this investigation shows that the highest achievers are careful to distinguish between knowledge and information about controllable and uncontrollable aspects of the performance environment. This knowledge is fundamental to the next dimension, "shaping your environment."

Shaping Your Environment

This dimension covers the ability to create and shape the performance environment that will deliver sustained success and comprised five subcomponents: "defining and communicating the vision and goals," "surrounding yourself with the right people," "fostering collaboration," "challenging orthodoxy," and "using your emotional intelligence."

DEFINING AND COMMUNICATING THE VISION AND GOALS

Having a deep awareness of what's going on around you provides a foundation for defining what is possible. One of the participants referred to an ability to "see around corners and what can be rather than what is." Another of the participants described how:

> I've always worked hard at defining and communicating a vision that people buy into and creating a culture and belief that you can win, will win, and here's why, how, and when. Once you create that, people not only buy into it, they take the extra steps to get the skill sets, the mental toughness to be successful, and that organization can go anywhere because it has that capability of truly rising above any competition.

Underpinning the vision is a series of clearly defined goals that map out how it will be achieved. One of the participants described how "I use the classic goal setting tree framework where I set outcome, performance, and process goals to push myself…I need a focus, a goal to work toward which everyone's bought into."

Having interconnecting goals was reinforced by a large number of the participants and is best captured in the following quote: "Plan for the end result and work backward. It won't happen just through raw talent. You have to have those stepwise goals to be able to get there."

SURROUNDING YOURSELF WITH THE RIGHT PEOPLE

These high achievers mentioned the need to have the right people around them if they are to deliver high performance over an extended period; they are unable to do this on their own. One of the participants highlighted the need to "have players that can be successful in different types of situations—a diversified team." Two other participants described how "I was truly blessed with having several great people who coached me, and their belief in me was huge," and "it's critically important to have trusted advisors and people you can go to when times are tough." Being surrounded by people with the appropriate expertise was also a big factor: "you want to surround yourself with people who have the know-how, knowing you have access to the best advice, and apply it."

FOSTERING COLLABORATION

Collaborating with teammates and colleagues emerged as a key strategy for ensuring a positive interaction with the performance environment. Alignment with others' goals was of particular importance among the participants: "if the desire to win is not in alignment against a common vision, a personal win will create ill-will or harm the overall team." This was especially important for leaders in large organizations: "If you're the CEO you have to be aligned with the shareholders' goals, the customers' goals, the employees' goals, and the community goals and have to get everybody working toward those goals."

Of course, there are situations in which performers are in competition with colleagues and it can be beneficial, but ultimately it is unlikely to lead to sustained high performance:

> Coming out of the NFL [National Football League] into the business world was one of the things that I had to truly learn to balance. In pro football, unlike business, every year your employer brought in 45 additional guys to come take your job, so part of your focus had to be against your internal competition and, until you were designated as a team, you were trying to protect your role. It was great for competition but in business that level of intensity can be detrimental to an organization and to an individual. When you start seeing your workmates as your competition it creates an unhealthy atmosphere. So I had to learn to deal with that intellectually. I had to learn to channel against the external competition and not internal competition.

CHALLENGING ORTHODOXY

One of the participants referred to the old adage "If you always do what you've always done, then you'll always get what you've always got," reflecting that people who deliver sustained high performance are always striving to do things differently and better. The same participant also commented on how "a head hunter once wrote that I had a healthy sense of frustration...you don't have to accept stuff, and you should always push back on stuff that you think it isn't right." Another participant reinforced this by stating:

> We all get into ruts, and if you want to truly outperform what everybody else is doing then you

have to do something different and that means stretching out beyond what's normal. If you don't do that, you're not going to be the best.

USING YOUR EMOTIONAL INTELLIGENCE

Some of the participants used the phrase "emotional intelligence," describing how it helped them to "read emotion in my colleagues" and "know what's going on around me, what's going on for the people around me so that we're in sync with one another." Other participants described how they used their EI to "get the environment to adapt to me," "get the most out of the people around me," and "influence people to do things sometimes they don't want to do or are very difficult to do, but doing it in a way that makes them want to do it."

SUMMARY

"Shaping your environment" is largely about ensuring you have the right people around you who are committed to working together toward a common vision and are striving constantly to find new and better ways of delivering success. This supports Jones, Gittins, and Hardy's (2009) work on how to create a high-performance environment, with an addition being the explicit use of EI as a key part of the process. Once the performance environment has been shaped to be conducive to sustained high performance, the next dimension, "being in tune with your environment," describes how it requires continual attention.

Being in Tune with Your Environment

The final dimension of the "working *with* your environment" theme related to the day-to-day interaction with the performance environment and comprised three subcomponents: "being agile," "building and maintaining relationships," and "staying humble."

BEING AGILE

This subcomponent highlighted the often fast-moving circumstances surrounding the highest achievers and how they needed to be resourceful and adaptable:

> You've got that horse and you've got to work with it. You have 20 minutes with a strange horse before you're in a show jumping ring. You're not able to change the horse in any way so you've got to be able to alter and adapt and go with the horse.

Being agile is critical but a challenge in a business, where you've got governance, processes, etc., as a really big deal, but you have to be, otherwise you get caught up in it and don't move the business on.

Some of the participants also stated how they thrive on the need to be agile:

> Dealing with a whole range of issues that are bombarding you at the same time... I love that laterality and having to see connections between seemingly unrelated events and actions.

BUILDING AND MAINTAINING RELATIONSHIPS

All of the participants identified the importance of building and maintaining day-to-day relationships in being able to deliver sustainable high performance. The sample quotes below capture the essence of this subcomponent:

> I gravitate toward certain sorts of people and with those other people I don't necessarily gel with, I make huge efforts to build and maintain those relationships whether inside or outside work.

> Success in business is all about relationships, it's critical. It's also critical in sports... relationships with teammates, your relationship with your coaches.

> The unique dynamic with others like coaches and the interactions... they need to be effective, the communication, the whole dynamic I think is really important to success.

STAYING HUMBLE

There was strong agreement across the participants about the importance of staying humble: "you're not the only one that matters—"we" is the key word," "everybody's perspective is important," and "it's really important, it gives people space to propose ideas and be excellent." One of the business leaders in the sample stated:

> Humility is so important. You have to create the situation where people can feel comfortable telling you what they think or giving you their ideas. A lot of this comes from acknowledging that you might be the boss but that doesn't make you any better than them.

SUMMARY

"Staying in tune" with your performance environment requires a continual focus and involves "being agile," akin to Sternberg's (1985) notion of creative intelligence, so that you can react quickly to changing circumstances that often characterize high-performance environments. Also important is the maintenance of supportive relationships,

which appears to be facilitated by demonstrating humility, similar perhaps to the concept identified by Collins (2001) as an important component of Level 5 Leadership.

Knowing How to Deliver High Performance

This final theme represented the know-how required to deliver sustainable high performance. Like the previous two themes, this one split into three dimensions: "planning and preparing," "delivering," and "evaluating."

Planning and Preparing

This dimension covered the meticulous planning and preparation that typifies sustained high performance and comprised four subcomponents: "defining success," "making sure everything has a purpose," "planning for every scenario," and "optimizing your emotional state."

DEFINING SUCCESS

Being clear about what constitutes the performance you are trying to deliver was emphasized by several of the participants. For example, "I prioritize the winning and the performance bits. Sometimes it's about winning and nothing else. Other times, it's about getting the performance right... practicing the bits that need to be right when it really matters and I need to raise my game... and if I win it's a bonus." Another participant reinforced this sentiment: "You've always got to think about the bigger picture, the end goal, and the milestones along the way. Winning isn't always the most important thing."

Some of the participants were keen to benchmark their performance against the competition: "You know your game plan is better than the competition's and if you execute it, you know we'll win," and "where was the competition this year and where will they be this time next year... that add-on factor as well."

References to colleagues and teammates were also prominent, especially to their perceptions of high performance and to the concept of everyone working toward the same goals: For example, "You may know what high performance is but you have to be sure your team knows as well."

MAKING SURE EVERYTHING HAS A PURPOSE

These highest achievers did not want to waste any time: "Everything you do should have a purpose. If you have a vision and a plan, then everything has a purpose so what you do ends up being much more efficient." One of the participants referred to "mindfulness or purposefulness":

> It's important not to get into the rut of going through the motions in training. Mindfulness or purposefulness is giving some thought to each session—what do I want to get out of it so that (a) I've achieved something and (b) it focuses me. I come into contact with so many people who've just done a training session and they don't know what they've just done.

The principle of everything having a purpose also applied at an organizational level:

> We're good at performance management so everyone has objectives which tie into the overall business objectives, and they're all shared and they go all the way down the organization so everybody knows what they're doing and how it fits into the overall picture.

PLANNING FOR EVERY SCENARIO

A number of the participants raised the importance of practice and repetition in addressing "what-if" scenarios: "In my day we rehearsed game plans for different weather conditions until we knew them inside out." The same applied in the business world:

> Before any big meeting, I will always have a pre-brief or a run-through because it gives you and the team the opportunity to test things…it's about second-guessing. One of the things we did at Company X was a "failure points analysis"…you always worked out what could go wrong and then you'd put it right before you did it so it didn't happen…it's about planning and preparing and is one of the most critical points of any success that I've had, trying to second-guess all the stuff that could go wrong and getting it right before you do it.

One participant described how planning for every scenario helped deal with the pressure of competition:

> Race day was always kept in perspective because we acknowledged that we had done it in training and under different conditions and this definitely reminded me that there was nothing to stop me from racing well and enable the thriving to happen.

OPTIMIZING YOUR EMOTIONAL STATE

All participants acknowledged the criticality of achieving an optimum emotional state prior to important events. The states differed across individual participants, ranging from wanting to be "emotionally on fire" to "cool as ice." One participant described how:

> I want to be totally present in the moment so I can respond to any challenge coming my way…there are rituals I'd go through to get myself into the right emotional state before a performance…if I missed some of those stages, I'm playing catch-up a little bit, I'm not saying I couldn't turn it on but it would be far more challenging.

Achieving an appropriate emotional state prior to a significant event was also raised as being important in the commercial world: "When I've got that big presentation and a lot rests on it…I've got to wow them…I disappear during those final few minutes before and try to get into what I call my 'control room'…I know what works for me, I want to be nervous but I want to be in control."

SUMMARY

Not surprisingly, "planning and preparing" meticulously is a key aspect of sustained success, and it begins with being clear about what success looks like. It is not always about winning, and SPI involves a deep understanding of the principle of outcome, performance, and process goals (Burton, Weinberg, & Yukelson, 1998) and how and when to implement them. "Making sure everything has a purpose" means that performers with high levels of SPI do not waste any time, and they are also careful to leave no stone unturned in planning for every "what-if." The notion of "mindfulness" was mentioned as helpful in this respect. Mindfulness has gained rapid interest and momentum in the health psychology literature (Cresswell, Way, Eisenberger, & Lieberman, 2007; Davidson et al., 2003) and has begun to attract attention in sport (Araya-Vargas, Gapper-Morrow, Moncada-Jimenez, & Buckworth, 2009). Knowing and achieving your optimal emotional state is also a critical element of preparing to perform, emphasizing the importance of individualized ideal performing states (Hanin, 1995, 2000) rather than a "one-size-fits-all" approach. The detailed "planning and preparing" forms the foundation for the next dimension, "delivering."

Delivering

Meticulous planning and preparation provide the strong foundation for performers to deliver sustained success. This dimension reflected several aspects of delivering high performance on a sustainable basis: "performing under pressure," "trusting yourself," "controlling the critical controllables," "seizing opportunities," and "knowing when to alter course."

PERFORMING UNDER PRESSURE

All of the participants referred to having an ability to deal with pressure in a positive way. Sample quotes that reflect this are: "I'm at my best when it really matters," "I have a mindset which is getting 'nervous and excited' and not 'nervous and scared,'" and "part of me says I cope but part of me says I get a big buzz out of pressure…I get a buzz out of a million things coming at me that I've just got to deliver on. I'm a pretty fast and lateral thinker and I get a huge adrenalin rush out of that."

Thriving on pressure is not always about being energized by it, and the participants identified the importance of staying composed when the pressure was at its most intense: "There's times when the intensity level is extremely high, when you're involved in important decisions, a key meeting, negotiating an acquisition…you're at the height of emotions but at the same time have to maintain control, stay cool under pressure."

A number of the participants used the phrase "mental toughness" to reflect a key attribute in helping them deal with pressure at its fiercest. They encapsulated mental toughness in a number of ways, including: "controlling what you're feeling, not letting that distract away from the job in hand, your focus, your preparation"; "keeping calm, composed, and focused during critical high pressure moments"; "life's a contact sport so you've got to be tough mentally to break through the barriers in front of you"; and "it's about being able to maintain equilibrium and equanimity in the face of trials, challenge, distress, and a whole raft of other things."

TRUSTING YOURSELF

Trusting yourself was raised by a number of the participants: "Sometimes people get inhibited by fear…no, not fear, they don't trust themselves in the moment…I have a great trust of myself, I back myself in the moment"; "one of the fundamental ingredients of success is that you have faith in yourself and trust you can do this and just let it happen"; "it was intuitive when I was at my best on stage…it was amazing, I just let go and it just seemed to happen"; and "having the confidence to apply your intuition as a leader."

One of the participants highlighted how this aspect of SPI is different from the traditional concept of intelligence:

I worked with a swimmer, one of the best at the moment, and the guy is not particularly bright, but just today one of the coaches said to me he has this incredible feeling for the water and intuition about his training and the way he races, and he is successful but I'm not sure he could explain why.

CONTROLLING THE CRITICAL CONTROLLABLES

"Control the controllables" is a popular sound bite in the world of performance psychology. The participants' responses reinforced this, but they were careful to emphasize that some controllables are much more significant than others:

My belief is that you quantify everything in business and then focus on the 20% that gets you the 80% leverage. And, as an athlete, you've got to know what you need to focus on. If you've got ten things to focus on, then work out which two are really going to propel your performance. Focusing on those leverage points is critical.

There's so much to do and so many initiatives I want to move forward…moving big organizations forward there's a couple of things you have to do really, really well rather than a lot of things half way and have them take 18 rather than 9 months.

The ability to compartmentalize your focus also emerged: "In cardiology you're focusing on the very specific problems of one particular patient and one particular disease that patient has and one specific procedure…nothing else matters."

SEIZING OPPORTUNITIES

"Making things happen to stay one step ahead of the competition," as described by one participant, depended on what another elucidated as "crystal-clear decision-making which enables you to increase performance…seize opportunities…that one critical crunch moment where the psychological momentum is either lost or gained, holding your nerve to seize that moment, and with consistency."

Other participants referred to "having a savvy which involves a cleverness, knowing where the boundaries are and in-the-moment thinking that enables you to use them to your advantage" and having "the ability to deliver at a crunch time…being able to bring it all together in what might be a millisecond."

KNOWING WHEN TO ALTER COURSE

The highest achievers have an ability to recognize quickly when executing the pre-agreed plan is not the best course of action: "Knowing when to stop persisting with Plan A because it isn't working or the conditions have changed and knowing whether to implement Plan B or Plan C."

They were also aware of when going all out for success may be futile in the longer term: "knowing when to push and when to back off…there are times when you just have to accept it's not happening and come back and fight another day…and not pushing yourself so that you risk not being able to come back and fight another day."

SUMMARY

"Delivering" involves knowing how to cope and hopefully thrive on the often intense pressure associated with elite-level performance and competition, and the term "mental toughness" was used in this context by several of the participants, emphasizing the importance of the growing body of literature in that area (Connaughton & Hanton, 2009; Gucciardi, Gordon, & Dimmock, 2008, 2009; Jones, 2010; Connaughton et al., 2010; Thelwell, Weston, & Greenlees, 2005; see also Chapter 38, this volume). The participants also highlighted trusting their intuition as key to delivering high performance, and their comments bore a strong resemblance to the concept of "flow," highlighting its prominence across a wide range of performance domains (Csikszentmihalyi, 1990, 2003; Jackson & Kimiecik, 2008). "Seizing opportunities" and "knowing when to alter course" reflect a know-how that encompasses a mental nimbleness involving rapid and accurate pattern recognition, quick and correct decision-making, and commitment to the required action. As such, this appears similar to Sternberg's (1985) notion of analytical and contextual intelligences. "Controlling the critical controllables" means that performers with high SPI know that some controllables are greater performance levers than others, and their focus is mainly on those. This resembles Koch's (2004) popular writing on the "80/20 principle": that 80% of results flow from 20% of causes. "Knowing how to deliver high performance" is not complete without the final dimension, "evaluating."

Evaluating

For high performance to be repeatable and sustainable, a process of evaluation is required and forms the basis of continued growth and improvement. This final dimension of the "knowing how to deliver high performance" theme comprised three subcomponents: "comparing against measurement criteria," "picking out the good bits," and "identifying what needs work."

COMPARING AGAINST MEASUREMENT CRITERIA

Measuring the degree of success was prominent among the participants: "It's a very obvious thing to say but it keeps you on the straight and narrow…you need a good balance scorecard in place"; "I call it 'watching the game film.' You have to know where you are, and that means constant evaluation and stepping back to look at what's going on"; and "always go back to the detailed goals you set in the planning stage…which goals did you hit, which didn't you hit?"

One participant was keen to also measure performance success against the bigger picture:

> I believe that we shouldn't just be looking at processes or outputs but outcomes…outcomes being lives saved or unwanted births prevented and things like that. If you push through the boundaries of what you evaluate…so you're not just evaluating efficiency or processes…too many people evaluate a snapshot of today instead of benchmarking that against what could or should be and what it's going to lead to tomorrow.

Another participant described how "record-keeping, making notes helps you to understand what you did that worked and didn't work and also helped to bring closure to my day."

PICKING OUT THE GOOD BITS

"People too often forget to celebrate the bits that went well and to learn from them" was a common sentiment expressed by the participants. They emphasized how "you need to notice the good stuff every day," with one participant elaborating as follows:

> It's too easy to focus only on what you can't do or what isn't going well and forget that there is a lot going well too. It's not about "today was a great day"…it should be "what was great about it?," really getting into the detail so that you repeat the good stuff again and again.

One of the athletes described how the ratio of recognizing "what went well" to "what needs work" altered as a function of training versus competition. In training, the ratio was one to three respectively, whereas in the competition phase it reverted to three to one respectively.

IDENTIFYING WHAT NEEDS WORK

All high achievers who sustain their success are constantly seeking to figure out "how would we do it better next time? ... It stops you getting complacent." The participants were clear that "this isn't about beating yourself up ... that serves no useful purpose ... it's about that constant urge to do things even better next time ... to keep moving forward so that you stay ahead of the competition." One of the participants highlighted how having things to work on "gives me that short-term focus and motivation that keeps me going day after day."

SUMMARY

Performance is not the end-point for performers with high SPI; a forensic evaluation is critical for sustained high performance and continued development. "Comparing against measurement criteria" emphasizes the importance of a detailed assessment of performance based on goals and benchmarks that enable progress to be monitored in the longer term. There always seem to be aspects of performance that "need work," often in the form of developmental feedback, even if it is just to prevent complacency creeping in, but SPI also involves "picking out the good bits," so that they are reinforced and replicable, as well as acting as motivational feedback. This aspect of SPI is akin to the notion of reflective practice (Hanton, Cropley, & Lee, 2009; Schon, 1983).

Conclusion

This chapter provides evidence for the addition of SPI to the list of MIs that have previously been identified. Superior performance intelligence is a critical awareness and know-how that enables top performers, from athletes to business leaders to cardiologists to performing artists to military leaders to entrepreneurs, to apply their minds, skills, techniques, strategies, and tactics to the same high standard every time they perform. A high level of SPI is at the core of high performance that is delivered on a consistent basis. It comprises three components that reflect a deep awareness and know-how regarding self-knowledge and regulation, using the environment to your advantage, and the process of delivering high performance.

As emphasized in the introduction to this chapter, the different MIs identified to date are characterized by significant overlap and commonality resulting from a lack of coherence among approaches and methodologies. Superior performance intelligence, as defined and identified in this chapter, draws upon some of the core components in other intelligences and brings them together in a framework that is applicable across numerous performance domains. There are links, in particular, with Sternberg's (1985) notion of contextual intelligence in the sense that they both incorporate a practical know-how and interactive process with the external environment. Aspects of the other two intelligences proposed by Sternberg, analytical and creative, are also evident in "knowing how to deliver high performance." Further, the interpersonal and intrapersonal intelligences identified by Gardner (1983, 1999) resemble several aspects of SPI. There are obvious links with EI (Goleman, 2001; Salovey & Mayer, 1990) in both the "knowing how to maximize your potential" and "knowing how to *work with your environment*" components in SPI, in the form of emotional self-awareness and regulation. Goleman's (2006) later work on social intelligence and, in particular, his social facility category, which is about what people do with that awareness, is captured in the "how to work with your environment" component of SPI. Finally, the links with the "strategic vision," "alignment and congruence," and "performance pressure" dimensions of organizational intelligence (Albrecht, 2002) are evident in several aspects of SPI, particularly in the context of high-performance leadership.

Future Directions

Superior performance intelligence underpins the reason that Andrea Jaeger and John Daly have been underachievers while athletes such as Wayne Gretzky, Martina Navratilova, and Michael Johnson were able to achieve long, consistent records of success. These great athletes possessed high levels of SPI, while one or more of the three components that comprise it has been lacking in the underachievers. The data from the investigation reported in this chapter show that this concept of SPI appears to apply across multiple performance domains, making SPI a worthy focus of both research and developmental attention.

In pursuing a deeper understanding of SPI, it is important not to confuse it with the central issues involved in the relative merits of different perspectives on the expert development debate (see Chapter 23, and 25, this volume). Superior performance intelligence is not necessarily about who will make it to the world's top stage. Superior performance intelligence *will* help performers get there, but more important is that, when they get there, it helps them deliver high performance on a consistent and sustainable basis rather than falling prey to the attractions, distractions, and pitfalls that serve as potential derailers of their careers.

The introduction of a new concept into the performance psychology literature is inevitably accompanied by a multitude of research and applied implications. A small number of the more pressing and interesting ones are identified here.

• The key priority is the further investigation of the concept and construct of SPI as part of the process of creating valid measures that can be employed to test its predictive validity. Practitioners will be keen to learn how to develop SPI in their clients. Research is required in this area, but the good news is that there is evidence that at least some of the key components of SPI can be developed—for example, emotional intelligence and mental toughness—and should be an important component of talent development programs.

• Drilling deeper into the make-up of some of the SPI components, two areas offer interesting avenues of investigation. First, "life balance" emerged as a particularly important area for all the participants; there is little research in this area in relation to performance. Second, the notion of "mindfulness" is receiving a considerable amount of attention in health psychology, and it would be interesting to examine its link to performance.

• Finally, and at a broader level, the content of this chapter provides further substance to the growing literature investigating links across a range of performance domains (Fletcher & Wagstaff, 2009; Gordon, 2007). Further research of the nature of SPI will allow a broader and deeper understanding of performance and its enhancement.

Acknowledgments

I am very grateful to Shane Murphy for providing the freedom and encouragement to indulge an interest and idea that has been intriguing me for some time.

Note

1. It was not possible to contact three of the participants for this stage of the protocol.

References

Albrecht, K. (2002). *The power of minds at work: Organizational intelligence in action*. New York: Amacom.

Allix, N. M. (2000). The theory of multiple intelligences: A case of missing cognitive matter. *Australian Journal of Education, 44*, 272–288.

Araya-Vargas, G. A., Gapper-Morrow, S., Moncada-Jimenez, J., & Buckworth, J. (2009). Translation and cross-cultural validation of the Spanish version of the Mindful Awareness Attention Scale (MAAS): An exploratory analysis and potential applications to exercise psychology, sport, and health. *International Journal of Applied Sports Sciences, 21*, 94–114.

Brown, C. H., Gould, D., & Foster, S. (2005). A framework for developing contextual intelligence (CI). *The Sport Psychologist, 19*, 51–62.

Burton, D., Weinberg, R., & Yukelson, D. (1998). The goal effectiveness paradox in sport: Examining the goal practices of collegiate athletes. *The Sport Psychologist, 12*, 404–418.

Chen, J. Q. (2004). Theory of multiple intelligences: Is it a scientific theory? *Teachers College Record, 106*, 17–23.

Collins, J. (2001). *Good to great*. New York: Random House.

Colvin, G. (2008). *Talent is overrated: What really separates world-class performers from everybody else*. London: Nicholas Brealey.

Connaughton, D., & Hanton, S. (2009). Mental toughness in sport: Conceptual and practical issues. In S. D. Mellalieu & S. Hanton (Eds.), *Advances in applied sport psychology: A review*. London: Routledge.

Connaughton, D., Hanton, S., & Jones, G. (2010). The development and maintenance of mental toughness in the world's best performers. *The Sport Psychologist, 24*, 168–193.

Covey, S. R. (2004). *The 7 habits of highly effective people*. New York: Simon & Schuster.

Cresswell, D., Way, B., Eisenberger, N., & Lieberman, M. (2007). Neural correlates of dispositional mindfulness during affect labeling. *Psychosomatic Medicine, 69*, 560–565.

Csikszentmihalyi, M. (1990). *Flow: The psychology of optimal experience*. New York: Harper & Row.

Csikszentmihalyi, M. (2003). *Good business: Leadership, flow, and the making of meaning*. New York: Penguin Books.

Davidson, R. J., Kabat-Zinn, J., Schumacher, J, Rosenkranz, M., Muller, D., Santorelli, S., et al. (2003). Alterations in brain and immune function produced by mindfulness meditation. *Psychosomatic Medicine, 65*, 564–570.

Dweck, C. (2006). *Mindset: The new psychology of success*. New York: Random House.

Earley, P. C., & Ang, S. (2003*). Cultural intelligence: Individual interactions across cultures*. Palo Alto, CA: Stanford University Press.

Ericsson, K. A., Krampe, R. T., & Tesch-Romer, C. (1993). The role of deliberate practice in the acquisition of expert performance. *Psychological Review, 100*, 363–406.

Fletcher, D., & Wagstaff, C. (2009). Organizational psychology in elite sport: Its emergence, application, and future. *Psychology of Sport and Exercise, 10*, 427–434.

Gardner, H. (1983). *Frames of mind: The theory of multiple intelligences*. New York: Basic Books.

Gardner, H. (1999). *Intelligence reframed*. New York: Basic Books.

Gardner, H. (2004). Audiences for the theory of multiple intelligences. *Teachers College Record, 106*, 212–220.

George, J. M. (2000). Emotions and leadership: The role of emotional intelligence. *Human Relations, 53*, 1027–1055.

Gladwell, M. (2008). *Outliers: The story of success*. New York: Little, Brown, and Company.

Goleman, D. (1995). *Emotional intelligence*. New York: Bantam.

Goleman, D. (1998). *Working with emotional intelligence*. New York: Bantam.

Goleman, D. (2001). Emotional intelligence: Issues in paradigm building. In C. Cherniss, & D. Goleman (Eds.), *The emotionally intelligent workplace* (pp. 13–26). San Francisco: Jossey-Bass.

Goleman, D. (2006). *Social intelligence: The new science of human relationships*. New York: Bantam Dell.

Goleman, D., Boyatzis, R., & McKee, A. (2002). *Primal leadership: Realizing the power of emotional intelligence*. Boston: Harvard Business School Press.

Gordon, S. (2007). Sport and business coaching: Perspective of a sport psychologist. *Australian Psychologist, 42*, 271–282.

Grzywacz, J. G., & Carlson, D. S. (2007). Conceptualizing work family balance: Implications for practice and research. *Advances in Developing Human Resources, 9*, 455.

Gucciardi, D. F., Gordon, S., & Dimmock, J. A. (2008). Towards an understanding of mental toughness in Australian football. *Journal of Applied Sport Psychology, 20*, 261–281.

Gucciardi, D. F., Gordon, S., & Dimmock, J. A. (2009). Advancing mental toughness research and theory using personal construct theory. *International Review of Sport and Exercise Psychology, 2*, 54–72.

Hanin, Y. L. (1995). Individual Zones of Optimal Functioning (IZOF) model: An idiographic approach to performance anxiety. In K. Henschen & W. Straub (Eds.), *Sport psychology: An analysis of athlete behavior* (pp. 103–119). Longmeadow, MA: Mouvement.

Hanin, Y. L. (2000). *Emotions in sport*. Champaign, IL: Human Kinetics.

Hanton, S., Cropley, B., & Lee. S. (2009). Reflective practice, experience, and the interpretation of anxiety symptoms. *Journal of Sports Sciences, 27*, 517–533.

Jackson, S. A., & Kimiecik, J. C. (2008). The flow perspective of optimal experience in sport and physical activity. In T. S. Horn (Ed.), *Advances in sport psychology* (pp. 377–399). Champaign, IL: Human Kinetics.

Jones, G. (2002). Performance excellence: A personal perspective on the link between sport and business. *Journal of Applied Sport Psychology, 14*, 268–281.

Jones, G. (2008). How the best of the best get better and better. *Harvard Business Review, June*, 123–128.

Jones, G. (2010). *Thrive on pressure: Lead and succeed when times get tough*. McGraw-Hill: New York.

Jones, G., Gittins, M., & Hardy, L. (2009). Creating an environment where high performance is inevitable and sustainable: The High Performance Environment Model. *Annual Review of High Performance Coaching And Consulting, 1*, 139–149.

Jones, G., Hanton, S., & Connaughton, D. (2002). What is this thing called mental toughness? An investigation of elite sport performers. *Journal of Applied Sport Psychology, 14*, 205–218.

Jones, G., Hanton, S., & Connaughton, D. (2007). A framework of mental toughness in the world's best performers. *The Sport Psychologist, 21*, 243–264.

Jones, G., & Moorhouse, A. (2008). *Developing mental toughness: Gold medal strategies for transforming your business performance*. Oxford, UK: Spring Hill.

Jones, G., & Spooner, K. (2006). Coaching high achievers. *Consulting Psychology Journal: Practice and Research, 58*, 40–50.

Joseph, D. L., & Newman, D. A. (2010). Emotional intelligence: An integrative meta-analysis and cascading model. *Journal of Applied Psychology, 95*, 54–78.

Koch, R. (2004). *The 80/20 principle: The secret of achieving more with less*. London: Nicholas Brealey.

Lane, A. M., Devonport, T. J., Soos, I., Karsai, I., Leibinger, E., & Hamar, P. (2010). Emotional intelligence and emotions associated with functional an dysfunctional athletic performance. *Journal of Sports Science and Medicine, 9*, 388–392.

Lincoln, Y. S., & Guba, E. G. (1985). *Naturalist inquiry*. Newbury Park, CA: Sage.

Matthews, G., Roberts, R., & Zeidner, M. (2004). Seven myths about emotional intelligence. *Psychological Inquiry, 15*, 179–196.

Meyer, B. B., & Fletcher, T. B. (2007). Emotional intelligence A theoretical overview and implications for research and professional practice in sport psychology. *Journal of Applied Sport Psychology, 19*, 1–15.

Musch, J., & Grondin, S. (2001). Unequal competition as an impediment to personal development: A review of the relative age effect in sport. *Developmental Review, 21*, 147–167.

Nelson, M. B. (2009). The damage I have done to myself: Physical intelligence among college athletes. *Journal of Intercollegiate Sports, 2*, 127–144.

O'Boyle, E. H., Humphrey, R. H., Pollack, J. M., Hawver, T. H., & Story, P. A. (2010). The relation between emotional intelligence and job performance: A meta-analysis. *Journal of Organizational Behavior, 32*, 788–818.

Patton, M. Q. (1990). *Qualitative evaluation and research methods*. Newbury Park, CA: Sage.

Phillips, E., Davids, K., Renshaw, I., & Portus, M. (2010). Expert performance in sport and the dynamics of talent development. *Sports Medicine, 40*, 271–283.

Ryan, R. M., & Deci, E. L. (2006). Self-regulation and the problem of human autonomy: Does psychology need choice, self-determination, and will? *Journal of Personality, 74*, 1557–1586.

Ryan, R. M., Lynch, M. F., Vansteenkiste, M., & Deci, E. L. (2011). Self-determination theory in counseling, psychotherapy, and behavior change. *The Counseling Psychologist, 39*, 193–160.

Salovey, P., & Mayer, J. D. (1990). Emotional intelligence. *Imagination, Cognition, and Personality, 9*, 185–211.

Schon, D. (1983). *The reflective practitioner: How professionals think in action*. New York: Basic Books.

Sternberg, R. J. (1985). *Beyond IQ: A triarchic theory of human intelligence*. New York: Cambridge University Press.

Syed, M. (2010). *Bounce: The myth of talent and the power of practice*. London: HarperCollins.

Terenzini, P. T. (1993). On the nature of institutional research and the knowledge and skills it requires. *Research in Higher Education, 34*, 1–10.

Thelwell, R., Weston, N., & Greenlees, I. (2005). Defining and understanding mental toughness in soccer. *Journal of Applied Sport Psychology, 17*, 326–332.

Waterhouse, L. (2006). Multiple intelligences, the Mozart Effect and emotional intelligence: A critical review. *Educational Psychologist, 41*, 207–225.

Waulmsley, J. A., Hemmings, B., & Payne, S. M. (2010). Work-life balance, role conflict, and the UK sport psychology consultant. *The Sport Psychologist, 24*, 245–262.

Weinberg, R., Butt, J., & Knight, B. (2001). High school coaches' perceptions of the process of goal setting. *The Sport Psychologist, 15*, 20–47.

Performance Psychology in the Performing Arts

Sanna M. Nordin-Bates

Abstract

In this chapter, a wide range of performance psychology–related topics are considered in relation to the performing arts. Existing research with musicians, dancers and, to a smaller extent, actors is reviewed and contrasted with sport research within a tripartite structure. In the first section, Exploring Convergence, topics with largely similar research results to sport are considered. These include expertise, talent, and deliberate practice; motivation; flow; perfectionism; disordered eating; and injury and pain. In the second section, Exploring Divergence, topics that have been tackled differently in the performing arts and sports are considered. These include psychological skills; personality; anxiety, stress, and coping; and self-confidence and self-esteem. In a third and final section, Exploring Novelty, topics that appear promising for an emerging psychology of performing arts, yet which have less precedent in sport research, are outlined. These comprise creativity and inspiration; memorization; emotional expression; and audience research.

Key Words: Dance, music, theater, acting, performing arts, artistry, psychology

Why Performance Psychology in the Performing Arts?

The central theme of this Handbook is that the psychology of human performance can be studied across multiple domains, not just sport and exercise, and this chapter examines the research base that exists in another performance area: the performing arts. It would be overambitious, perhaps impossible, to do justice to the enormous variety of psychology topics that have potential implications for the performing arts; as such, this chapter focuses on research based in performance psychology, putting the *performance* of performing artists, suitably, at center stage. Within the limitations of my own training and expertise, I also make links to other areas where I have found them especially appropriate. A key issue addressed in the chapter is whether the approaches and techniques of sport psychology can be successfully used in the domains of dance, music, and theater. In the last decade, a few papers (e.g., Hays, 2002), a couple of book chapters (Hanrahan, 2005; Hays, 2005), and one book (Hays & Brown, 2004) have been written on the topic of applying sport psychology to performing arts. As will become apparent, my conclusion is that, in some areas, sport psychology approaches dovetail well with the psychology of performing arts; in other areas, much work remains to be done; and in some key areas, the issues that arise are different, perhaps unique to each field.

The application of performance psychology to the performing arts makes sense, simply because *performing well* lies at the heart of both sports and artistic activities. At the same time, it is perhaps the definition of what constitutes "good performance" that has kept the areas largely separated. What, exactly, does successful performing entail? Differences commonly highlighted include competition, the notion of artistry, and the nature of audiences, and these will now be briefly outlined.

The notion of performing in a context not directly set up as a comparison between performers (i.e., competitions) is frequently mentioned as a key difference between performing arts and sports. However, there is growing recognition that the performing arts often *are* competitive, for instance in selection to schools, auditioning for jobs, casting for roles, and even getting attention from teachers (e.g., Hays, 2002; Hays & Brown, 2004; Kogan, 2002; Robson, 2004). Gardner (1993) argued that because of the difficulties of getting any recognition for one's efforts and of making a living in the arts, artists constantly compete for recognition in the social and cultural arena. Some performing artists also do compete: The rise of TV shows such as *X-factor, American Idol,* and their ilk is striking; competition is the default mode of performance for freestyle disco and ballroom dancers; and there are many competitions in art forms such as classical music and ballet, such as the Prix de Lausanne for young elite ballet dancers.

A second distinction often drawn between arts and sports is that of artistry, and several studies reviewed in this chapter testify to the importance of considering this factor in research. Still, not all who take part in the performing arts do so for artistic purposes (e.g., some dance simply because they enjoy moving to music), whereas aesthetic athletes, such as gymnasts and figure skaters, perform to music and get scored on artistic merit. Finally, it is notable that sports and arts are all frequently performed in front of audiences. The characteristics of sport and arts audiences usually differ, however, and the third section of this chapter presents an exploration of audiences as a research area.

Although some differences exist between performing arts and sports, many more similarities than differences are apparent: Artists and athletes alike are passionate about what they do, develop talent through hard training, seek coaching for further development, often work in teams or ensembles, need to stay motivated, and encounter obstacles and try to tackle them. They try to avoid injury, and need to cope with injuries and pain when they do happen. For all these reasons and more, the performing arts can benefit from an increased understanding of the psychological aspects of performance.

Chapter Overview

Performance psychology holds great potential for understanding many aspects of the performing arts. As yet, however, only music and dance can be said to have anything resembling a psychological literature, and even these two areas have seen limited performance-related research when compared to sport. It is encouraging that some movement is being made toward a better understanding of actors' health (Seton, 2009) but perhaps a little sad that Seton is forced to conclude that little change has taken place since Alice Brandfonbrener (founder of the Performing Arts Medicine Association) called actors "The Forgotten Patients" in a 1992 editorial, noting that, "Regarding the many areas of potential research in 'theatrical medicine' those in the psychological realm are particularly intriguing" (p. 101).

Publications in performing arts psychology sometimes have a different emphasis than those seen in sport psychology, and topics such as goal setting and self-talk have as yet seen no published papers in the performing arts domain. Much research to date has been problem focused (e.g., on anxiety and disordered eating), and less is known about performers' strengths, such as positive goal striving and concentration. An exception is the literature into expertise and talent, which is where this review will begin. The chapter is organized into three sections, based on the extent to which research issues seem to have a common focus in performing arts and sports. Several topics have been studied in similar ways in both arts and sport and these are reviewed first (Exploring Convergence). Other topics have been studied slightly differently in the two domains; these are reviewed next (Exploring Divergence). The third and final section outlines research topics that appear to hold promise for the performing arts, yet are rarely researched in sport (Exploring Novelty). Some future research recommendations and applied implications are suggested throughout.

Exploring Convergence: Research Topics Pursued Similarly in Sport and Performing Arts

This section reviews topics in which researchers have undertaken somewhat similar investigations with athletes and performing artists. As such, sport models may transfer well to performing arts domains. The selected topics include expertise, talent, and deliberate practice; motivation; flow; perfectionism; disordered eating; and injury and pain.

Expertise, Talent, and Deliberate Practice

Talent, like creativity, is according to folk psychology something mysteriously bestowed on a lucky few (e.g., Howe, Davidson, & Sloboda, 1998;

Sloboda, 1996). Studies are gradually demonstrating the limitations of such a belief (e.g., Ericsson, Krampe, & Tesch-Römer, 1993; Howe et al., 1998; Kemp & Mills, 2002; Smith, 2005), yet a variety of domains including sport, music, and dance all appear to be holding the same debate as to whether nature or nurture is most important in the development of talent (see, e.g., the special issue in *Behavioral and Brain Sciences*, 1998, 21(3)). Although the strongest proponents of each argument may be debating for some time yet, it seems clear that talent is a multidimensional construct (e.g. Csikszentmihalyi, 1998; Howe et al., 1998; Kemp & Mills, 2002; Walker, Nordin-Bates, & Redding, 2010; Warburton, 2002; see also Chapter 23, and 25, this volume) and that deliberate practice is crucial to the development of physical, technical and creative excellence (e.g., Csikszentmihalyi, 1996; Howe et al., 1998; Weisberg, 1998). It is also recognized that identifying talent is hard, that psychological aspects play a major part both in talent identification and development, and that nurture is crucial yet nature plays some part (e.g., Hays & Brown, 2004; Kemp & Mills, 2002; Walker et al., 2010; Warburton, 2002; Winner, 1996).

The influence of teachers in artistic talent development is recognized to be paramount (e.g., Csikszentmihalyi, Rathunde, & Whalen, 1993; Gembris & Davidson, 2002; Walker et al., 2010), and succeeding without family support is "possible but exceptional" (Gembris & Davidson, 2002, p. 23). In their landmark study, Csikszentmihalyi and colleagues (1993) examined, among other things, the family structure among youth talented in academics, sport, and the arts. It appeared that optimal talent development was associated with families balancing *integration* (e.g., support, stability) with *differentiation* (i.e., supporting independence, challenge). Termed *complex families*, this notion appears to have gained little research momentum and further investigation is encouraged (see also Chapter 25, this volume). Research by Manturzewska (1995, cited in Gembris & Davidson, 2002) into the characteristics of families that nurtured exceptional Polish musicians is also illuminating: The conclusion was that family background was the primary influence in developing a music career, and many of the factors identified match those appearing in recommendations from research into athlete motivational climates (e.g., encouragement and support, child-centered attitude, emphasis on process/enjoyment). Manturzewska also noted that parents of successful musicians managed to be highly involved, yet not overinvolved, which resembles findings with athletes (Carlsson, 1988; Côté, 1999). The achievement of this balance deserves further study in order to address the potential problems of what in the arts is called "stage parents" (see e.g., Hamilton, 1998) and, sometimes in American sports, "soccer moms" (Murphy, 1999).

It makes sense that parental support is important for all, but perhaps especially so in domains where training typically starts at a very early age (e.g., ballet) and where practicing long hours at home is seen as very important (e.g., violin). Accordingly, parental encouragement is crucial in getting young musicians to practice (Davidson, Howe, Moore, & Sloboda, 1996; Howe et al., 1998). The optimum amount of support likely depends on the age of the performer, however. Davidson et al. (1996) found that parental support for high-achieving musician children was high until age 11 and then dropped off in favor of intrinsic motivation and self-regulation. For lower achievers, the reverse was noted; this was interpreted as parents getting stricter in an attempt to "motivate" their children—albeit unsuccessfully. The interpersonal aspects of deliberate practice therefore seem crucial. Even being called "talented" can be either helpful (e.g., in promoting motivation and in boosting confidence; Van Rossum, 2001) or hurtful (e.g., by promoting an external locus of control; Walker & Nordin-Bates, 2010), suggesting that examination of the very term "talent" would be worthwhile. In fact, Smith (2005, p. 51) argued that "Musical talent is a vague concept of little practical value, and the role of education is to serve the musical development of every individual."

The deliberate practice framework has been consistently supported in several fields (Bonneville-Roussy, Lavigne, & Vallerand, 2011; Chaffin & Imreh, 2001; Ericsson, 1996; Gembris, 2006; Hallam, 2001; Lehmann & Gruber, 2006; Miksza, 2011; Nielsen, 1999; Sloboda, Davidson, Howe, & Moore, 1996; Ureña, 2004; Van Rossum, 2001; see also Chapter 23, this volume). Ericsson et al. (1993) created the framework based on work in multiple domains, including music. Of particular interest here is the notion of enjoyment. In the original framework, activities were judged to be deliberate practice if they were specifically designed to improve performance (i.e., highly relevant to performance), required a great deal of physical and/or mental effort (concentration), and were not inherently enjoyable (Ericsson et al., 1993). Sport researchers, however, have demonstrated that athletes often *do* enjoy their deliberate practice (e.g., Helsen, Starkes, & Hodges, 1998; Hodge & Deakin, 1998; Hodges & Starkes, 1996; Young & Salmela, 2002). It is possible that being alone makes a difference to the enjoyment felt. In many sports, athletes train together in groups and teams, and in most dance forms lessons are group-based even at the professional level (ballroom and Latin American being notable exceptions). In music, many practice in bands and orchestras, yet it is commonly accepted that one has to actually *learn* one's instrument and become technically proficient through solo practice. So strong is this demand that many spend several hours each day practicing on their own, even at young ages. Says a young man in an interview study:

> I started playing in bands at school and doing little gigs; it was really good fun. I made a lot of friends doing that, whereas the piano, it was always kind of by myself. With my bass I could play with others and that was always more fun.
>
> (*Papageorgi* et al., 2010, p. 170)

Papageorgi and her colleagues (2010) also found that, for their sample of university-level music students, solo practice was not seen as enjoyable now, nor had it been so in the past. As a result, parental support was especially important in getting them to practice. This raises the question of what constitutes healthy practice and healthy support. Research has demonstrated that enjoyment is an important component in nurturing adherence (Scanlan et al., 1993; Weiss & Amorose, 2008), and doing something for enjoyment is a key aspect of intrinsic motivation (Ryan & Deci, 2000). Moreover, as explained by Standage (Chapter 12, this volume), intrinsic motivation is typically the most adaptive form of motivation. At what point does parental support and encouragement to practice turn into pressure, fostering extrinsic motivation? How can we make sure that, even if in itself extrinsic, parental encouragement to practice alone is *a way of making possible* the parts of music learning that the young person does enjoy? These are important questions to address—perhaps especially because young people's perceptions of the support and pressure they are receiving can differ from what parents believe they are providing (Kanters, Bocarro, & Casper, 2008).

It is possible that motivation theories can help answer some of these questions. For instance, it would be valuable to examine the intrinsic motivation toward practice among young performing artists. Is it different between those practicing primarily alone versus in groups? If so, perhaps the lack of opportunity to develop positive peer relations during solo practice (e.g., Fredricks et al., 2002; Kamin, Richards, & Collins 2007; Patrick et al., 1999; van Rossum, 2001) and the consequent low sense of relatedness (Ryan & Deci, 2000) accounts for the observed difference?

Although deliberate practice is important, a criticism of the framework has been its emphasis on quantity over quality (e.g., Howe et al., 1998; Singer & Janelle 1999; Walker et al., 2010; Williamon & Valentine, 2000). The extent to which training constitutes deliberate practice likely depends on a range of factors, including the degree to which one is able to understand one's teacher, pedagogic effectiveness, time spent on- and off-task during a session (e.g., waiting for one's turn), and the quality of equipment (such as one's instrument). Music researchers have made more progress than either dance or theater researchers in considering practice quality. For example, differences in *approaches* to practice have been found between more and less accomplished musicians (Chaffin & Imreh, 2001; Gruson, 1988; Nielsen, 1999) and between those performing better and worse in intervention studies (Miksza, 2006, 2007, 2011). Professional string players appear to have greater self-awareness than novices (Hallam, 2001). Overall, then, musicians' talent development depends on a combination of practice quality and quantity. Although that is hardly a revolutionary conclusion, it is interesting that no research appears to have considered what constitutes quality practice in either theater or dance. Is it the dancers who are able to transform group class into individually relevant, "true deliberate practice" who progress the most while those who "go through the motions" progress less?

Several theorists have recognized that the wider social environment also plays a major part in the practice behaviors and talent development of performing artists (e.g., Csikszentmihalyi et al., 1993; Hallam, 1997, 2002; McPherson & Zimmerman, 2002). These concepts have developed in parallel with talent models in sport (Gagné, 1995; Henriksen, Stambulova, & Roessler, 2010; Williams & Reilly, 2000) and education (e.g., Subotnik, Olszewski-Kubilius, & Arnold, 2003) yet appear similar in many ways. For instance, there is usually recognition that intrapersonal, interpersonal, and wider environmental factors all matter and all interact. Accordingly, a recent review reported that, for dance, a large number of both relatively stable and more unstable factors interact in the development of talent (Walker et al., 2010). As Henriksen et al. (2010) note, the move toward a contextual approach is evident in several areas of contemporary literature, and they recommend looking to organizational psychology for guidance, given its focus on how organizations and cultures function. It seems beneficial for researchers in both performing arts and sports to take advantage of strides made in other domains, so that models created can be truly holistic in nature.

In summary, it appears that although talent in arts and sports take different expressions, their development seem to require similar factors. Although far from reviewed here in their entirety, these include a range of favorable intrapersonal, interpersonal, cultural, and environmental factors. In order to want to develop one's talent at all, however, motivation is clearly a key consideration and consequently is the next topic considered.

Motivation

Not all that long ago, expertise researcher Ericsson (1997) stated that "our knowledge about the gradual acquisition of expert performance during decades of high levels of daily practice is greatly increased, but the motivational factors that maintain the daily efforts to keep improving continue to be largely a mystery" (p. 45). It is therefore encouraging that more can now be said about the fundamental topic of motivation. Advances in dance and music are being made with the theories that have found most favor with sport researchers in recent years, namely *self-determination theory* (SDT) and *achievement goal theory* (AGT). Additionally, the allied concept of passion has attracted attention. This section therefore focuses mostly on findings related to those three theoretical frameworks.

PASSION

Imagine entering a field that promises a 10-year performing career, or in which the unemployment rate at any moment in time is on the order of 90% to 95%. Even if we had the requisite talents, how many of us would embark on either course? Yet, as we have seen, there are individuals for whom the passionate and persistent involvement in an activity is of such immense importance that the issues of career longevity or low odds of success are viewed as trivial. (*Kogan*, 2002, p. 15)

Passion is an intuitively attractive concept in explaining why people want to practice, perform,

and persist, and is often mentioned in performing arts contexts (e.g., Bonneville-Roussy et al., 2011; Fortin, 2009; Kogan, 2002; Manturzewska, 1990; Turner & Wainwright, 2003). Passion is the difference between just doing drama and *being* an actor, and between having a job as a dancer and *being* a dancer. It is precisely this *being* that means an activity has become such a part of the self that it is an inherent part of one's identity (Vallerand et al., 2003). Because the identity of performing artists is so often tightly bound to their activity (e.g., Aalten, 2005, 2007; Mainwaring, Krasnow, & Kerr, 2001; Wainwright & Turner, 2004; Wainwright, Williams, & Turner, 2005), passion may be a promising research topic in the performing arts.

A recent study with high-level musicians (Bonneville-Roussy et al., 2011) revealed that 99% of them fulfilled the passion criteria stipulated as part of the passion scale (Vallerand et al., 2003). Among expert dancers, similarly high levels of passion have been found (Rip, Fortin, & Vallerand, 2006). Vallerand et al. (2003) note that levels of passion are logically lower in nonexpert samples; however, Vallerand's group of researchers stipulate the activity for which participants score their passion (e.g., asking a group of musicians about their passion for music). Walker, Nordin-Bates, and Redding (2011) instead asked talented young dancers what their favorite activity was and had them complete the passion scale for that activity. Around 80% of participants put dance as their favorite activity and fulfilled the criteria for being passionate, whereas others were primarily passionate about some other activity—despite undertaking intense training in dance. This might be appropriate for young people, especially if early diversification versus specialization is of interest: that is, young people may be passionate about several activities and this, in itself, might be positive for the formation of a rounded identity. Further research is required to explore these ideas.

Research has demonstrated the utility of the passion framework with performing artists. For example, Rip et al. (2006) found that in a sample of dancers, those with higher rates of chronic injuries and greater use of health-threatening behaviors also reported higher levels of obsessive (rigid) passion. Dancers with better coping skills and those spending less time injured reported higher levels of harmonious (flexible) passion. Bonneville-Roussy et al. (2011) linked passion to AGT and deliberate practice, finding that higher levels of harmonious passion meant that musicians adopted mastery goals to a greater extent and reported greater well-being. The adoption of mastery goals was predictive of both deliberate practice behaviors and better performing. The pattern for obsessive passion was the reverse: Higher levels of this construct were associated with musicians reporting a higher rate of adoption of both performance-approach and performance-avoidance goals. Holding performance goals (whether approach- or avoidance-oriented) was negatively associated with performance attainment. Findings such as these provide a strong indication that harmonious passion is desirable for both well-being and performance.[1]

Given the positive outcomes associated with harmonious passion, it is a natural next step to examine ways in which this healthy passion can be nurtured. Bonneville-Roussy et al. (2011) suggest that training environments in which intrapersonal comparison is encouraged over social comparison would likely be helpful in this regard. On a related note, Fortin (2009) argued that the entire dance milieu is responsible for making dancers accept a culture in which obsessive passion is sometimes promoted and living with pain is normal. To examine issues like these, passion theory is usefully complemented by AGT (e.g., Ames, 1992) and its concept of motivational climates. Another promising avenue is SDT (Deci & Ryan, 2000; Ryan & Deci, 1985; see also Chapter 12, this volume), and SDT research with performing artists will be reviewed next, followed by research using AGT.

SELF-DETERMINATION THEORY

Although SDT research with performing artists is rare as yet, there is no shortage of indirect evidence that intrinsic and extrinsic motivation matter to artists. For example, the pursuit of enjoyment is often the primary reason for engaging in a performing art (e.g., Bond & Stinson, 2007; Houston, 2004; Papageorgi et al., 2010; Stinson, 1997). Enjoyment is also frequently sourced in the *giving* of music or communication of art, whether to an audience or through teaching (Hays & Brown, 2004; Papageorgi et al., 2010). Papageorgi et al. (2010) shared the following quote from a student musician: "There's no pleasure really in learning how to get better and better and being a good player without carrying it on to other people" (p. 171). Poczwardowski and Conroy (2002) gave examples of how artists sometimes deliberately "let their ego go" because they perceived their art to be more important than themselves as individuals. This aspect of intrinsic motivation is rarely discussed in sport, but warrants attention. Positive psychologists (Peterson, Park, & Seligman,

2005; Seligman, 2002) have explored differences in happiness orientation, distinguishing the pursuit of pleasure from that of engagement and that of meaning. Perhaps the sharing of artistic works and the associated meaning-making is one way of pursuing a life that is both engaging and meaningful in service to others?

Intrinsic motivation originates in basic needs satisfaction (Ryan & Deci, 2000). That is, when we feel autonomous, competent, and related, our intrinsic motivation toward an activity grows. Less than a decade ago, Kogan (2002) wrote that "It is important that we examine both the intrinsic and extrinsic influences that propel individuals into performing arts careers and provide the satisfaction that keep them there" (p. 15). It is encouraging, therefore, that SDT research is emerging in dance (Quested & Duda, 2009, 2010, 2011). In the most systematic series of studies into dance and motivation to date, Quested and Duda demonstrated that those interested in the well- and ill-being of dancers (including affect, burnout, body perceptions, and even hormonal responses) should consider issues of motivation and self-determination; from a practical point of view, environments supportive of basic psychological needs appeared paramount to well-being (e.g., teachers providing autonomy support and social support). Although novel, the clear similarities of these studies to those in sport and exercise are important as they indicate that the arts community can avoid "reinventing the wheel" by taking those larger, existing literatures into account.

Despite the shortage of SDT research in music, some studies suggest it to be a valid framework there, too. For example, Schmidt (2005) found that the more intrinsically motivated music band students were, the higher their teachers' ratings of both effort and performance achievement. A case study of a young clarinetist revealed that practice time for a self-chosen piece was 12 times greater than for pieces she was told to practice (Renwick & McPherson, 2002). The practice strategies she used were also more advanced. Thus, it appears that autonomy and intrinsic motivation can have an enormous impact, and it would be interesting to investigate the extent to which artistic practice is autonomous versus teacher-led. Certainly, there are accounts of the latter in the literature (e.g., Jørgensen, 2000; Persson, 1994), but how common are authoritarian styles now, in 21st-century studios and practice rooms? A longitudinal study by Brändström (1995) is also worth noting. He found that 80% of student musicians responded very well to being given freedom to set their own goals and practice schedules; among the remaining 20%, however, there was evidence of negative reactions, including anxiety. The study is a reminder that autonomy support is not as simple as just providing freedom. Studies into autonomy support and into the potential moderating and mediating variables in the autonomy–motivation relationship (e.g., age; level of expertise; personality factors) would be valuable. For now, it is notable that several authors have mentioned the idea of balancing structure and freedom. For example, Renwick and McPherson (2002) reported that successful music students were likely able to balance the playing of pieces assigned by teachers with pieces they enjoyed and had chosen themselves. Sloboda and Davidson (1996) found that high achievers not only do more formal practice but more informal playing as well. Balancing structure and freedom has also been suggested to nurture creativity in dance (Watson, Nordin-Bates, & Chappell, 2010).

ACHIEVEMENT GOAL THEORY

As with SDT, achievement goal theory (AGT; e.g., Ames, 1992) has begun to be applied to the study of performing artists. In the first study of its kind, Nieminen et al. (2001) found that university dance students all endorsed task-oriented goals (focused on effort and individual improvement) over ego-oriented goals (focused on social comparison and public demonstration of excellence), but that those training to be performers were more ego-oriented than those training to be teachers. More recent work indicates a trichotomous model of achievement goals (Elliot, 1997) to be useful in music (Bonneville-Roussy et al., 2011; Smith, 2005). Two other studies with performing artists have added a fourth component to the trichotomous model: intrinsic goals, conceived of as achievement goals focused on enjoyment (Lacaille, Koestner, & Gaudreau, 2007; Lacaille, Whipple, & Koestner, 2005). Lacaille et al. (2005) compared musicians with swimmers and found that when recollecting previous performances, swimmers held more performance-approach goals prior to peak than catastrophic performances, whereas for musicians the opposite was true. All performers reported holding more intrinsic goals prior to peak performances, but this was especially true for musicians.

In a second study, intrinsic goals again emerged as being important in a sample of music, acting, and dance students (Lacaille et al., 2007): It was the only goal type to significantly predict self-rated performance. Holding intrinsic goals was positively associated with well-being (life satisfaction) and negatively with the intention to quit. Performance goals were associated with negative outcomes whereas mastery goals were unrelated to all other variables. Importantly, items tapping intrinsic goals were expanded beyond a focus on enjoyment to include such goals as absorption and audience communication (as was the case in the first study; Lacaille et al., 2005). This forms an interesting link with the intrinsic motivation found in communicating art mentioned above. Qualitative support for intrinsic goals is also found in the following quote from a conductor, linking achievement goals with the purposes of artistic activity and several other constructs:

> People have all kinds of reasons why they do what they do. Some [reasons] are based on social concerns; some [people] are more concerned for themselves. If your purpose is to get a stamp of approval from somebody else, if your purpose is to be perfect, if your purpose is to get a good review or to be thought of as being more gifted than somebody else, if that's what you're all about, you're going to be a mess your whole life. . . . And it will all be suffering for you one way or the other, because I think you're not really fulfilling the purpose of art anyway. I think the main purpose of art is to be dramatic. That's it. To be dramatic and then beyond that, to stimulate people's thought processes and emotions and get their ideas going, to make them feel ultimately much more in love with life because of having contacted whatever it is you've intended for them.
> (*Hays & Brown*, 2004, p. 107)

As a final note, a few investigations have applied the evolving 2 × 2 achievement goal model (Elliot & McGregor, 2001) to music. In so doing, Miksza (2009a) found mastery-approach and performance-approach goals to be associated with positive music practice behaviors (e.g., time spent practicing, perceived efficiency), but correlations were small. In a second study, mastery-approach goals were associated with better achievement (Miksza, 2009b).

Overall, AGT has been used in few and rather disparate studies of the performing arts. Many findings are congruent with research in sport, suggesting that theoretical frameworks apply across domains, although others have produced divergent findings from those with athletes. Some caution should be taken in interpreting results, too, given that the measures used in several of these studies (Lacaille et al., 2005, 2007; Smith, 2005) have not undergone full psychometric evaluations. Future researchers should try to elucidate further whether intrinsic goals and intrinsic motivation concerned with giving and communicating artistic messages can find homes in the achievement goal frameworks of the future—or whether other frameworks, such as SDT, are better equipped to make sense of these issues.

BASIC NEEDS SUPPORT AND MOTIVATIONAL CLIMATES

Only a small number of studies have examined motivational climates in the performing arts, most of which have been in dance. From the earliest dance climate research (Carr & Wyon, 2003) through to more recent work (Quested & Duda, 2009, 2010; Nordin-Bates, Quested, Walker, & Redding, 2012), findings from dancer samples resemble those with athletes in highlighting the value of task-involving motivational climates. For example, in studies by Quested and Duda (2009, 2010), dancers' climate perceptions predicted basic needs satisfaction. Needs satisfaction was also predictive of positive and negative affective states. That is, dancers who perceived that their dance teachers focused on effort, individual improvement, and cooperation were more likely to report high levels of perceived autonomy, competence, and relatedness, and those with greater perceived needs satisfaction reported more positive and less negative affect. Other dance research has found that increased ego-climate perceptions over a 6-month period predicted increases in dancer anxiety (Nordin-Bates et al., 2012). Matthews and Kitsantas (2007) found that band musicians who perceived their conductors to be more task-involving were also more likely to rate them as supportive.

Although motivational climate studies are rare in the performing arts, the similarity of findings with domains such as sport, where such research is more plentiful, suggests that promoting task-involving climates is desirable also in artistic domain. With this in mind, it is positive to note that arts climates do appear to be perceived as highly task-involving and less ego-involving (Carr & Wyon, 2003; Matthews & Kitsantas, 2007; Nordin-Bates et al., 2012; Quested & Duda, 2009, 2010). Such findings contrast with the traditional view of dance and music instructors as demanding authoritarians (Buckroyd, 2000; Hays & Brown, 2004; Jowitt, 2001; Mackworth-Young, 1990; Persson, 1994; Renwick & McPherson, 2002; Smith, 1998; van Staden, Myburgh, & Poggenpoel, 2009). A recent small-scale study with ballet professionals tentatively suggests that differences may exist between schools

and companies, however, and/or between ballet and other forms of dance (van Staden et al., 2009). In their study, several examples of a highly rivalrous, competitive, and critical dance milieu are provided. Clearly, the dance and music domains, and their subdomains, are too complex and varied to be categorized simply. Both classical and contemporary training contexts are worth further examination so that adaptive motivational climates may be better understood and promoted.

BEYOND TEACHER-CREATED MOTIVATIONAL CLIMATES

In addition to teacher-created climates, it has been proposed that the emotional climate in the home is another crucial formative factor for young musicians (McPherson, 2006a,b). McPherson argues that authoritarian parents can inhibit performance, whereas the provision of meaning, rationale, and encouragement of independent learning encourages development. He also provides excellent suggestions for how parents may foster motivation and performance enhancement, all in line with SDT (providing support for autonomy/meaning, relatedness, and competence). This is an important line of research because, as noted above, much of music learning takes place in the home, thus heightening the need for self-regulatory strategies. It would be interesting to see the extent to which parental support for basic psychological needs is impactful in performing arts activities and whether this support decreases as a performer becomes more self-regulated and independent later in his or her teens (Davidson et al., 1996).

A broader look was taken by Papageorgi et al. (2010) in researching institutional culture. Defined as "the quality and way of life within the institution and the conduct of the institution itself" (p. 151), institutional culture was found to relate meaningfully to the way in which music students felt about their learning. Jørgensen (2000) similarly argues that "educational outcomes like independence and responsibility must not be looked at as a private matter, concerning only the individual student or teacher, but as official, institutional responsibilities" (p. 74). This has echoes of the contextual models-approach to talent development mentioned above, as well as of Fortin's (2009) argument that dance culture is responsible for what dancers come to see as acceptable. Taken together, it would be useful to combine research lenses from AGT (motivational climate) with an institutional culture view to get a better idea of how psychological characteristics, and ultimately performance and well-being, are affected by the training context (see also the discussion of leadership in institutions in Chapter 17, this volume). This is perhaps particularly warranted for acting, where there is a complete lack of research, but where concerns have been voiced:

> I know teachers of other disciplines tend to understand their pedagogy fairly well or it's being encouraged to understand their pedagogy. That, I haven't seen in actor training. . . . Because someone's a good actor doesn't mean they're a good teacher. . . . there are times when what's going on is suspect and could be dangerous, not just on a physical level but a mental one. There are too many people out there playing amateur psychologists.
>
> (*Actor trainer*, in Seton, 2009, p. 40)

Wider environments can perhaps also be examined as predictors of needs satisfaction, motivational regulations, and well-being outcomes. Hallam's (1997, 2002) model of musical practice and its outcomes, incorporating intrapersonal (e.g., motivation), interpersonal (e.g., teaching style), and environmental components (e.g., school ethos, home support) might be a useful starting point for such investigations.

Flow

Strongly related to the topic of motivation is the notion of *flow*, or optimal psychological experience (Csikszentmihalyi, 1975, 1990). The original work into flow comprised performers from a range of domains including sport, music, and dance. It is therefore somewhat surprising that only a handful of studies into flow in artistic performance exist. Those that do exist are spread across dance, music, and theater, and all indicate the importance of intrinsic motivation for flow to occur (Bakker, 2005; Hefferon & Ollis, 2006; Martin & Cutler, 2002). Bakker (2005) even found that the intrinsic motivation of teachers was positively related to their students' flow experiences. Factors found to promote and inhibit flow among dancers (Hefferon & Ollis, 2006) also appear broadly similar to those identified in athletic research (e.g., Jackson, 1995). Bakker (2005) found that situational conditions at music teachers' places of work (e.g., feeling autonomous and in receipt of appropriate feedback and support) were predictive of flow. Future research might consider using SDT to gain a better understanding of how performing artists can get into flow (Kowal & Fortier, 1999), and whether flow

results in better performances. Although flow is conceptualized as peak experience rather than peak performance (see Chapter 38, this volume, for a fuller discussion), a relationship has been found between flow and creativity as a performance outcome in composing (Byrne, MacDonald, & Carlton, 2003; MacDonald, Byrne, & Carlton, 2006). These researchers have also been part of developing applied work in music education based on the flow model (see also Byrne & Sheridan, 2000).

The links between flow and artistically valued concepts extend beyond creativity. In fact, it has been proposed that flow has significant conceptual overlap with the artistic notion of *presence* (Bradley, 2009). It is also possible that "being in a bubble" (i.e., completely absorbed) is more likely when a dancer is in character (Hefferon & Ollis, 2006; Walker & Nordin-Bates, 2010). In line with such speculation, one study reported that dancers were in flow more frequently during performances than during training (Jeong, Morris, & Watt, 2005). This makes sense in light of anxiety research, as reviewed below. It would be fascinating to better understand the role of characterization in the flow process.

As a final note, Hefferon and Ollis (2006) also highlighted how flow was unlikely when roles were easy; indeed, several dancers reported boredom when performing a particular role for the umpteenth time. It is a difficult but important job for the professional performing artist to try exploring variations in repetitive performing, and research into this notion would be most valuable—for instance, can imagery interventions be designed to increase the prevalence of engagement and flow?

Perfectionism

Especially in classical domains such as orchestral music and ballet, it is often said that performers are perfectionists—and perhaps need to be, in order to achieve high standards of excellence (e.g., Dews & Williams, 1989; van Staden et al., 2009). A music consultant interviewed by Hays and Brown (2004) considered musicians to be fearful of mistakes and driven to attain perfection; another interviewee described dancers as perfectionists, but actors as far more "laid back." Still, perfectionism prevalence has gained surprisingly little research attention. In a recent study of high-level dance students in ballet and contemporary training, most students could be categorized into clusters labeled as having *perfectionistic tendencies* or *moderate perfectionistic tendencies*; few students fell into the *no perfectionistic tendencies* cluster (Nordin-Bates, Cumming, Aways, & Sharp, 2011). However, such labels are based on averages and are data-driven; only a very small minority of participants reported agreement with each and every item on the questionnaire (i.e., were perfectionistic in every regard). Further research into artists' perfectionism is warranted—while keeping in mind that there are no "diagnostic criteria" helping us determine who can be labeled a perfectionist. It would also be worthwhile to further examine the finding from a qualitative pilot study that ballet dancers often report other-oriented perfectionism (van Staden et al., 2009).

More studies exist to indicate that perfectionistic cognitions are associated with experiences such as anxiety (Carr & Wyon, 2003; Kenny, Davis, & Oates, 2004; Mor, Day, Flett, & Hewitt, 1995; Nordin-Bates, Cumming et al., 2011; Stoeber & Eismann, 2007; Wilson & Roland, 2002). Work in music indicates that perfectionism may be incompatible, or at least unhelpful, when it comes to artistry. A conductor described it as follows:

> If your aim is to be perfect, then the moment you make any mistake, you've already failed. But for me, the main purpose of, let's say, my doing a Beethoven symphony is to deliver the intent of the music. The technique of the piece itself is there to serve the dramatic ends of it. Your focus as an artist should be to master the techniques sufficiently to live with that dramatic intent. There can still be mistakes in the performance, there can still be lack of perfection in performance, and yet you can still fulfill the purpose.
> (*Hays & Brown*, 2004, p. 190)

Thus, although much remains to be researched in regard to the correlates and outcomes of perfectionism, there is reason to believe that it is meaningfully related to variables commonly addressed in sport (e.g., anxiety) and more artistic ones (e.g., dramatic intent). How perfectionism is conceptualized and measured also matters greatly; as such, some studies appear to find perfectionism to have mainly negative correlates (e.g., Carr & Wyon, 2003; Kenny et al., 2004; Mor et al., 1995; Nordin-Bates, Cumming, et al., 2011; Nordin-Bates, Walker, & Redding, 2011; Wilson & Roland, 2002), whereas others have also identified some positive ones (e.g., intrinsic motivation; Stoeber & Eismann, 2007). Care is required in interpreting the findings from any given study, because there is no consensus as to what perfectionism actually is. This mirrors the debate around perfectionism in sport (see Chapter 15, this volume), but further study with performing artists

is especially warranted because some appear to take pride in being labeled perfectionists, overtly stating that they pursue perfection in their art. Is this use of the term compatible with the literature—and is it helpful or hurtful? Most theorizing is also based on group averages and correlations, but, as noted, there is no cutoff value beyond which an individual can be labeled a "true perfectionist." Case studies of pronounced perfectionists (and of nonperfectionist high achievers) would be particularly welcome for this reason.

The origins of perfectionistic beliefs would also be of interest for further research. This is because, although conceptualized as a trait, perfectionism is seemingly affected by environmental and interpersonal aspects such as feedback. Says a music consultant:

> If you look beyond the garage band, self-taught kind of musician, criticism has been an integral part of the music world since whenever. You have to do it right. If you listen to musicians talk to the conductor or their teacher or even their peers, the initial focus is always on "What did I do wrong?" or "How could I do better?" ...So kids come in, since childhood, with this perfectionistic kind of belief, and I work real hard at changing that. There's more to making music than just following the notes on the page.
> (*Hays & Brown*, 2004, p. 191)

Disordered Eating

Intimately related to perfectionism is disordered eating. In fact, perfectionism is both a risk factor for disordered eating development (Tyrka, Waldron, Graber, & Brooks-Gunn, 2002), and an intrinsic part of it (Forsberg & Lock, 2006; Halmi et al., 2000). In dance, this raises important questions in relation to the prevalence of both perfectionism and of disordered eating. That is, if perfectionism is more prevalent among high-performing dancers than in the average population, as is sometimes assumed, does this account for the increased prevalence of disordered eating in this same group (Garner & Garfinkel, 1980; Hamilton, Brooks-Gunn, & Warren, 1985; Ravaldi et al., 2006; Ringham et al., 2006; Thomas, Keel, & Heatherton, 2005; Tseng et al., 2007)?

The extent to which prevalence rates of disordered eating vary among studies is remarkable. Ranging from 1.6% (Abraham, 1996) to 25.7% (Garner, Garfinkel, Rockert, & Olmsted, 1987) even when focusing only on female ballet dancers and anorexia nervosa, there is clearly no way to characterize *dancers overall* in terms of relative risk—let alone performing artists. And, although dancers have been the focus of most disordered eating research to date, Seton (2009) mentions eating and body attitudes as potentially problematic among actors, especially if an attitude prevails that bodies are there to be molded into anything for the sake of a role, whether it be smaller, bigger, more muscular, or just "more beautiful." Thus, we must extend the study of disordered eating beyond dance—and certainly beyond females in classical ballet. But instead of focusing on prevalence using relatively small and homogeneous samples, it may now be time to direct research attention to the personal, interpersonal, and wider environmental and cultural factors contributing to disordered eating development and how they may be prevented or managed.

As noted, perfectionism is one such factor that appears to hold explanatory promise (de Bruin, Bakker, & Oudejans, 2009; Nordin-Bates, Walker, et al., 2011; Thomas et al., 2005). Other relevant intrapersonal variables include psychological aspects such as body image, self-esteem, achievement goals, and perceptions of personal control (e.g., de Bruin et al., 2009; Mor et al., 1995; Ravaldi et al., 2006; Tseng et al., 2007) and physiological aspects such as body mass index (BMI), age of menarche, and growth. These physical variables are relevant because early maturation is associated with being taller and heavier than one's later maturing peers (e.g., Malina, Bouchard, & Bar-Or, 2004) and, at least in ballet, late maturers are favored (Hamilton, Hamilton, Warren, Keller, & Molnar, 1997).

A number of studies have examined dancers' BMI in relation to disordered eating, with varied results (de Bruin et al., 2009; Neumärker, Bettle, Bettle, Dudeck, & Neumärker, 1998; Ravaldi et al., 2006; Thomas et al., 2005; Toro, Guerrero, Sentis, Castro, & Puértolas, 2009; Tseng et al., 2007). Given that most studies are cross-sectional, this is unsurprising: High BMI can be a risk factor for disordered eating in an attempt to slim down and cope with body-related pressures (e.g., Tseng et al., 2007), while having low BMI may be indicative of an existing disorder. In sum, it would be valuable for psychologists to engage in both interdisciplinary and longitudinal research to better understand disordered eating as a biopsychosocial phenomenon in performing artist populations.

Interpersonal variables indicated as playing a part in dancers' disordered eating include perceptions of pressure from significant others, such as teachers, parents, and peers (Berry & Howe, 2000; de Bruin, Oudejans, & Bakker, 2007; de Bruin et al., 2009; Garner & Garfinkel, 1980; McCabe & Ricciardelli, 2005; Reel, SooHoo, Jamieson, & Gill, 2005; Thomas et al., 2005; Toro et al., 2009), the motivational climate (de Bruin et al., 2009; Duda & Kim, 1997), and learning experiences regarding thinness in dance class (Annus & Smith, 2009). As an example of how intrapersonal and interpersonal variables have been examined together, de Bruin and her colleagues (2009) found that both ego-goal orientations and mastery (i.e., task-involving) climate perceptions predicted unique variance in dieting frequency. Thomas et al. (2005) speculated that perfectionism might represent a personality risk factor for eating disorder development regardless of dance school pressures, but that the latter may well enhance or lead to the expression of the former.

Even very important individuals, such as teachers, cannot be held solely responsible for something as complex as disordered eating attitudes, body dissatisfaction, or related variables; instead, the wider culture must be studied if we are to gain a holistic understanding. Indeed, whole institutions and inherited, passed-on beliefs about what is acceptable and valued have been associated with disordered eating in sociological studies (Benn & Walters, 2001; Gvion, 2008). In a qualitative study with students and professional dancers, it was noted that, "eating disorders may indeed be a form of adaptation to the ballet culture in which it appears that thinness is often interpreted by the institution as a sign of commitment or dedication and rewarded with advancement in the profession" (Benn & Walters, 2001, p. 146).

In summary, it appears that future research into disordered eating would benefit from considering a combination of intrapersonal, interpersonal, environmental, and cultural variables (see Chapter 34, this volume, for a fuller discussion of these issues in sport). As suggested in Chapter 29, this volume, appearance and performance-enhancing drug use is also a health concern that may be related to similar body image issues. In domains in which history, subjective criteria for success, and unpredictable feedback from teachers, directors, and the media may all influence how a performer comes to interpret his or her own adequacy, a multifactorial approach appears especially valuable. Notably, an intervention focused on creating a healthy school environment appeared to be effective in reducing the prevalence of disordered eating in an elite ballet school (Piran, 1999). In her intervention, Piran worked to create systemic change through sessions with not just students and teachers but also administrative staff; topics ranged from the intrapersonal (e.g., changing emphasis from weight to fitness) to the interpersonal (e.g., disallowing teachers from making comments on students' body shapes); and both psychological (e.g., body image) and physiological aspects (e.g., puberty) were addressed. It is encouraging to see such positive action being taken in a domain sometimes seen as old-fashioned and "closed" to outside influences.

Injury and Pain

Following logically from the discussion of disordered eating and perfectionism, we now turn to a discussion of the psychological aspects of injury and pain among performing artists. Dancers who are perfectionistic "high achievers" (Hamilton, 1998) or report more obsessive passion (Rip et al., 2006) have been suggested to suffer with more frequent and/or prolonged injuries. Those suffering from an eating disorder also run a greater risk of sustaining an injury (e.g., Kaufmann, Warren, & Hamilton, 1996; Liederbach & Compagno, 2001). Although not yet studied in music or theater, the same principle would most likely hold true also in those settings; that is, performers who are driven to attain an unrealistic goal or who simply cannot stand to give up their activity even in the face of negative outcomes may well go beyond what is sensible and healthy (e.g., pushing beyond fatigue), thus sustaining injury. They may also return from injury too early, thus heightening the risk of reinjuring themselves (Hamilton, 1998). These are valuable topics for further study with musicians and actors, too, because although there is research into musicians' injuries from a physiological perspective (e.g., Heinan, 2008), literature on how psychological factors may affect injury incidence or rehabilitation is almost nonexistent.

Again, such literature is at least emerging in the dance domain. Mainwaring, Krasnow, and Kerr (2001) reviewed the literature and concluded that dancers often accept pain as something normal, perform through pain, and are reluctant to seek medical attention. They describe dancers as subject to a "culture of tolerance" regarding pain and injury, and point out that those with an identity defined largely by their dance activity are especially likely to suffer more when injured. Seton (2009) describes a similar "culture of silence" among actors. Hence, it appears that just as cultural factors may contribute to the development of disordered eating, cultural expectations and norms encourage performing in pain and through injury in performing arts populations (Aalten, 2005; Fortin, 2009; Mainwaring et al., 2001; Seton, 2009; Turner & Wainwright, 2003). Studies have also reported that, perhaps as a result of a culture of tolerance, dancers often do not report their injuries for medical attention (Krasnow, Kerr, & Mainwaring, 1994; Mainwaring et al., 2001; Pedersen & Wilmerding, 1998; Robson & Gitev, 1991) and may be more interested in holistic therapies than traditional medical care. Mainwaring et al. (2001) note that this is at least in part due to a lack of confidence in the medical profession, with dancers feeling that they are not understood and that they may simply be told to rest—which they do not want to hear. The growth of dance science and medicine may have helped remedy this unfortunate situation for those lucky enough to have access to specialist care, but much remains to be done to optimize support in all performing arts domains. Nevertheless, it is positive to note that a recent study found that dancers did seem to follow advice given by health professionals after injury, and self-esteem was not lower among a group of injured dancers compared to their noninjured peers (Nordin-Bates, Walker, Baker, et al., 2011).

In the last decade, progress has also been made regarding how to help dancers prevent injury. A series of studies has examined how psychological skills and coping strategies are related to Korean ballet dancers' injuries (Noh, Morris, & Andersen 2003, 2005, 2007, 2009). In the first study, dancers' reported a wide range of dance-specific stressors, including competing for roles against friends and critical comments from directors. More than half of the sample (65%) reported some form of dysfunctional coping strategy (e.g., overeating) in response to such stress, indicating that further research into dancers' coping was warranted. A second study found that coping skills were related to injury frequency and duration. In particular, dancers with low levels of coping skills seemed to be injured more often and for longer than those with a better coping skills repertoire (Noh et al., 2005). Finally, an intervention study was designed, comprising autogenic training, imagery, and self-talk focused on stress reduction (Noh et al., 2007). Dancers undertaking this combination of psychological skills training not only enhanced their coping skills but also spent less time injured during a 48-week period, compared to dancers in either a no-intervention control group or a group undertaking only autogenic training. This work represents a step forward in terms of helping us understand dancer injuries and also represents the only published psychological skills training intervention study performed with dancers to date.

Studies by Noh and her colleagues (2005, 2007) combined with those by others (Liederbach, Gleim, & Nicholas, 1994; Mainwaring, Kerr, & Krasnow, 1993; Patterson, Smith, Everett, & Ptacek, 1998) show that the stress-injury model of athletic injury can be applied to dance. As a result, findings and recommendations from sport injury research are likely also relevant for intervention research and applied work with dancers (see also Chapters 32 and 33, this volume, on injury and performance and on pain and performance). Does the model have merit also in music and theater settings? The nature of musicians' injuries may differ from those of athletes and dancers, but the high prevalence of stress and anxiety in the music domain (see below) suggests that finding out more would be highly worthwhile.

Exploring Divergence: Research Topics Pursued Differently in Sport and Performing Arts

These topics have been grouped based on the different focus of studies performed in sport compared to the performing arts. As such, there may be more work to be done in bridging gaps between domains than in the areas previously discussed, but doing so may bring benefits to both "sides." The selected topics include psychological skills; personality; anxiety, stress, and coping; and self-confidence and self-esteem.

Psychological Skills

Although an extensive range of studies in sport have examined psychological skills such as imagery, goal setting, self-talk, and relaxation (see Chapter 8, 10, 11, and 14, this volume), the same cannot be said for the performing arts. Instead, there are growing literatures on imagery in music and dance, but no studies focused on goal setting, self-talk, or relaxation. The only exceptions are the mixed-skills intervention study mentioned above (Noh et al., 2007), a handful of studies aiming to combat musicians' anxiety in which self-talk and relaxation formed parts of interventions (e.g., Kendrick, Craig, Lawson, & Davidson, 1982; Stanton, 1994), and a discursive article on private speech in ballet and how its inhibition through authoritarian teaching may limit student learning (Johnston, 2006). Given

the positive outcomes associated with goal setting and self-talk in sport, research into these under-studied topics is warranted. Anecdotal evidence already attests to the potential benefits of such psychological skills in artistic domains (e.g., Hays & Brown, 2004); it is also logical that performers engage in mental rehearsal when learning a music piece, dance variation, or acting role. However, the arts add a complication for anyone wanting to undertake goal setting research in these domains; that is, they depend on subjective and varying performance standards. Moreover, feedback may be sparse or nonexistent in key evaluative situations, such as auditions (Hays & Brown, 2004), and in many dance forms, not even professional performers get individualized training, but practice in groups. These factors conspire to make the *specific* and *measurable* aspects of effective goal setting tricky, and it may be useful to work with tools such as goal attainment scaling (Kiresuk, Smith, & Cardillo, 1994)—or devise new, creative methods for research in this domain.

IMAGERY

The literatures on imagery in dance and music have numerous overlaps with that in sport, but differences exist: Dance studies in particular have tended to focus on artistic images based on metaphors, abstract notions, and descriptions of desired movement or sound quality (Franklin, 1996a,b; Hanrahan, 1995; Lewis, 1990; Minton, 1990; Purcell, 1990; Sweigard, 1974; Woody, 2002). Such artistic images all describe something that is not real, but it is a hugely varied category. For example, an actor may imagine conflicting emotions of joy and guilt as part of a role, a singer may imagine the tragic story of farewell that she is conveying to her audience, and a dancer that his movements are light and flowing, lifted up on a gust of wind. Artistic images such as these have been proposed to accomplish a variety of aims, including enhanced recall, body awareness, movement or sound quality, and even injury prevention through improved alignment. Anecdotal and qualitative evidence (Hanrahan & Vergeer, 2000; Nordin & Cumming, 2005; Woody, 2002) make it clear that performers and instructors alike do make use of a variety of artistic images, but the lack of research makes it equally clear that we have a long way to go before we achieve an in-depth understanding of artistic imagery. The idea that images should ideally be individualized for maximal effectiveness (e.g., Franklin, 1996a; Sweigard, 1974) makes researching their utility at the group level yet more difficult, but at least six studies have attempted to do just that.

These studies (all of which were with dancers and used metaphorical/abstract images and some of which were additionally based on anatomical principles) have been of mixed quality and resulted in mixed findings (Couillandre, Lewton-Brain, & Portero, 2008; Hanrahan & Salmela, 1990; Hanrahan, Tétreau, & Sarrazin, 1995; Krasnow, Chatfield, Barr, Jensen, & Dufek, 1997; Sacha & Russ, 2006; Sawada, Mori, & Ishii, 2002). Still, technical improvements were noted in two studies (Hanrahan & Salmela, 1990; Hanrahan et al., 1995), and, in two others, children learned better when imagery was part of their instruction (Sacha & Russ, 2006; Sawada et al., 2002). One study found changes in alignment following a combination of abstract imagery and verbal instruction (Couillandre et al., 2008).

In addition to artistic or abstract images, performers often engage in more concrete imagery, such as dancers going over movements and variations in their heads (Fish, Hall, & Cumming, 2004; Hanrahan & Vergeer, 2000; Monsma & Overby, 2004; Nordin & Cumming, 2005; 2006a,b,c, 2007, 2008; Overby, 1990; Overby, Hall, & Haslam, 1998). Similarly, musicians rehearse through imaging finger placements, passages, and whole pieces of music (Clark, Williamon, & Aksentijevic 2012; Godøy & Jørgensen, 2001; Holmes, 2005; Schoenberg, 1987). Some of the functions that imagery serves for performing artists also include those commonly noted in sport research, such as for learning, memorizing, and improving skills; boosting motivation and confidence; and managing anxiety (Clark et al., 2012; Clark, Lisboa, & Williamon, in press; Connolly & Williamon, 2004; Gregg, Clark, & Hall, 2008; Murphy, Nordin, & Cumming, 2008). For instance, Ross (1985) found that imagery improved trombone players' performance, and Holmes (2005) reported that auditory and kinesthetic imagery were especially important for learning and performance enhancement with string instrumentalists. Interestingly, Holmes (2005) cites the fact that music educationalist Seashore wrote of imagery as a necessity for memorization in 1938—but that few empirical studies have focused on the topic since then. Still, a review by Clark et al. (2012) demonstrates that those music interventions that do exist have perhaps shown more similarity to sport than to dance imagery interventions: Overall, these seem to indicate that, as in sport (e.g., Driskell, Copper, & Moran, 1994), a combination of imagery and physical practice is more advantageous than either practice method alone or than no practice.

Imagery can also be used as pre-performance preparation (e.g., Clark et al., 2012; Clark et al., in press; Vergeer & Hanrahan, 1998), and Hays and Brown (2004) provide a superb example of violinist and conductor Itzak Perlman doing a mock performance with as much detail as humanly possible—in his own house. In addition to dressing appropriately and other logistical aspects, the power of imagery was used to its full as he imagined his house as the Carnegie Hall. He even imagined announcements and a delay in the start of the performance, an approach consistent with the PETTLEP model of imagery (Holmes & Collins, 2001). However, performing artists also use imagery for a variety of purposes not typically discussed in sport, such as for exploring interpretive possibilities (Haddon, 2007), for inspiration, to get into character, and to convey emotion to an audience (Clark et al., 2012; Hanrahan & Vergeer, 2000; Nordin & Cumming, 2005). They also experience spontaneous imagery (Haddon, 2007; Nordin & Cumming, 2005).

Two of the first studies to start bridging the gap between imagery research in sport and dance used the Sport Imagery Questionnaire (SIQ; Hall, Mack, Paivio, & Hausenblas, 1998) with ballet dancers (Fish et al., 2004; Monsma & Overby, 2004). Together, they indicated that dancers' imagery experiences are related to their perceptions of anxiety and of self-confidence, but also that the SIQ may not be ideal for trying to capture the experience of dance imagery. Since then, a dance-specific imagery questionnaire has been developed (Nordin & Cumming, 2006c), and research with this instrument has extended the research relating to dancers' self-confidence and anxiety; moreover, the questionnaire may also be applicable to the aesthetic sports (Nordin & Cumming, 2008). Measurement of imagery in the performing arts has otherwise generally borrowed questionnaires from domains such as sport, although Clark et al. (2012) give examples of novel designs in music research, including behavioral tasks and chronometry.

Imagery research in the arts has begun to address questions that have been less addressed in sport. First, it has become clear that teachers matter in the development of performers' imagery experiences (Nordin & Cumming, 2006a,b; Persson, 1996; Woody, 2002). In fact, studies indicate that arts instructors use metaphorical images in their teaching not only frequently (e.g., Woody, 2002) but perhaps more often than do sports coaches (Overby, 1990; Overby et al., 1998). Second, dance researchers have found that not all imagery is helpful to performers (Nordin & Cumming, 2005) and that those with perfectionistic tendencies experience debilitative imagery more frequently (Nordin-Bates, Cumming, et al., 2011). Further research into this topic is warranted, so as to maximize our understanding of how imagery can best be made facilitative, in sport as well as in arts. Finally, it is noteworthy that the dance intervention studies cited above all focus on imagery *during* movement, something that is common in real-life dance settings (Nordin & Cumming, 2005, 2007). Although it stands to reason that similar uses of imagery would likely apply also in other domains, this aspect is rarely studied in sport, music, or theater. The findings therefore beg the question of whether imagery use during actual movement can enhance performance in other domains. Only a handful of studies have mentioned the use of metaphorical imagery in sport (Efran, Lesser, & Spiller, 1994; Hanin & Stambulova, 2002; Orlick & McCaffrey, 1991; Ruiz & Hanin, 2004), although Ahsen's (1984) triple code model, previously cited frequently in sport research, does mention metaphors in imagery. In sum, benefits may well be had not only for arts practitioners in learning from sport imagery, but also for sport practitioners in studying artistic imagery.

Imagery research appears well-developed in comparison to other topics, and we should therefore be closer to reaping benefits from it. For example, we may now be at a stage where evidence-based interventions can be designed to enhance artists' performance and well-being. As noted, a mixed psychological skills intervention was found to reduce the injury duration of dancers (Noh et al., 2007); a valuable next step would be to examine the extent to which imagery is impactful on its own versus in combination with other psychological skills. A final note concerning how imagery works is warranted. Studies have begun to examine how imagery, perception, observation, and action are linked in the brains of musicians in particular (for a review, see Clark et al., 2012) and also dancers (e.g., Calvo-Merino, Glaser, Grèzes, Passingham, & Haggard, 2005). This mirrors developments toward a neuroscientific functional equivalence understanding of imagery in sport (for a review, see Cumming & Ramsey, 2008). Such work is exclusively focused on concrete imagery (e.g., mental rehearsal of skills), however, and it would be illuminating to integrate this emerging understanding with one of how artistic imagery is made effective.

OBSERVATIONAL LEARNING

Despite the overlap between observational learning and imagery, the former (also known as modeling) is a psychological skill or method sometimes said to be overlooked in sport (McCullagh & Weiss, 2002; and see Chapter 13, this volume). Given that dance and music are commonly learned through visual observation and/or auditory modeling, studying these processes with artistic performers appears to be a fruitful avenue for research. To date, studies on observational learning appear to be more numerous in music (e.g., Dickey, 1992; Hewitt, 2001; Linklater, 1997) than in dance (Cadopi, Chatillon, & Baldy, 1995; McCullagh, Stiehl, & Weiss, 1990; Weiss, Ebbeck, & Rose, 1992), although studies exist in related areas such as expert–novice differences in how dance movements are perceived in the brain (Calvo-Merino et al., 2005) and the impact of mirrors on dancers' learning and feelings about themselves (Brodie & Lobel, 2008; Dearborn & Ross, 2006; Ehrenberg, 2010; Radell, Adame, & Cole, 2002, 2003). Interestingly, it has been argued that both modeling and metaphorical imagery are crucial for teaching expressivity in music (Davidson, 1989). Juslin and Persson (2002) also report that although modeling is used for this purpose, this is not always easy given that top-level performances (such as may be demonstrated by a teacher to a student) may seem "perfect" and do not reveal their constituent parts. Sport psychology research into the use of peers and/or coping models (McCullagh & Weiss, 2002) may be helpful in this regard, as might the use of a relatively new questionnaire focused on the functions of observational learning (Cumming, Clark, Ste-Marie, McCullagh, & Hall, 2005).

Personality

In recent years, many sport psychologists moved away from the assessment of athlete personalities, but an increase in personality research in other areas of psychology has been noted (Beauchamp, Jackson, & Lavallee, 2007; McAdams & Pals, 2006). Beauchamp et al. (2007) suggest that the personality paradigm does have merit in sport, although correlating performance and personality is likely to be futile. For instance, they highlight how the Big Five personality trait dimensions (extraversion, neuroticism, agreeableness, openness to experience, conscientiousness; McCrae & Costa, 1999) have potential for research. In the performing arts, researchers have demonstrated great interest in what makes artists "special" and different from nonartists. In some cases, different types of artist, such as actors and musicians, have been compared.

A number of studies have examined aspects of personality, such as extraversion-introversion, with findings that appear to vary with the samples studied (Bakker, 1988, 1991; Buttsworth & Smith, 1995; Cribb & Gregory, 1999; Dyce & O'Connor, 1994; Eysenck & Eysenck, 1975; Gillespie & Myors, 2000; Hammond & Edelmann, 1991; Kemp, 1981, 1996; Marchant-Haycox & Wilson, 1992; Nettle, 2006a; Reardon MacLellan, 2011; Stacey & Goldberg, 1953; van Staden et al., 2009; Wilson, 1984). Many researchers noted unfavorable personality findings for artists for traits such as neuroticism and emotionality (Bakker, 1988, 1991; Dyce & O'Connor, 1994; Gillespie & Myors, 2000; Hamilton, Kella, & Hamilton, 1995; Kemp, 1981; Marchant-Haycox & Wilson, 1992; Nettle, 2006a; Taylor, 1997; Wills & Cooper, 1988). These traits may well be worth further investigation due to their inherent link with stress and anxiety (McCrae & Costa, 1999). Some studies have found high levels of openness to experience among artists (Dyce & O'Connor, 1994; Gillespie & Myors, 2000; Nettle, 2006a). This makes sense, because art is often about seeing things in new ways and opening up possibilities. Openness to experience is also part of creativity (King, McKee Walker, & Broyles, 1996), as further outlined below.

Finally, conscientiousness, although less studied than the traits just mentioned, is intriguing because of its conceptualization as involving self-discipline, organization, and diligence (McCrae & Costa, 1999). Thus, it has overlap with descriptions of striving for perfection. It would be worthwhile to examine what the overlap is between personality approaches to conscientiousness (as part of the Big Five) and perfectionism research in sport and arts. For example, one pertinent question to the fostering of optimal performance and well-being is the degree to which characteristics such as the Big Five and perfectionism are trait-like or state-like. They are all conceptualized as traits, and so should not be particularly amenable to change; however, studies indicate that they can be associated with environmental aspects, such as the motivational climate (e.g., Carr & Wyon, 2003), and several studies attribute their findings of "specific personalities" in performance domains to a combination of self-selection and environmental impact (e.g., Bakker, 1988, 1991;

Kogan, 2002; Marchant-Haycox & Wilson, 1992; Wills & Cooper, 1988). Marchant-Haycox and Wilson (1992) explained it as follows:

> [W]e cannot be sure to what extent people (a) gravitate towards their speciality within the performing arts because of their personality, (b) survive within the profession because of their personality, or (c) have their personality shaped in a particular direction as a result of experience within that profession. Probably there is some truth in each of these hypotheses.
> (pp. 1066–1067)

If traits can be nurtured or diminished, then this would have implications for both research and applied practice: Indeed, perhaps it is time to move beyond the rather simplistic trait–state distinction and see personality characteristics as lying on continua of stability or adaptiveness. Alternatively, the concept of "characteristic adaptations" appears to have promise (McAdams & Pals, 2006).

Beauchamp et al. (2007) suspected that a key reason for the decline of personality research was researchers' disgruntled attitudes toward research trying to establish a "personality profile of the elite athlete" and examining whether a particular personality type was associated with success. It will be old news to readers of this book that such studies produced inconsistent findings and that no particular "elite athlete personality" was ever identified. Beauchamp et al. (2007) also criticize some studies with athletes for being atheoretical and purely descriptive. Most performing arts studies could be criticized on similar grounds. It is suggested, therefore, that personality research with artists should divert attention toward questions that are founded in conceptual arguments and that have clear implications for performance and/or well-being, instead of trying to characterize "artists" through small-scale descriptive studies. In particular, we must resist the temptation to generalize the findings of a single, small-sample study to other samples and genres, especially when the majority of dance and music forms, and almost the entire domain of theater, are so understudied.

Measurement approaches in this field also deserve mention. As noted by Marchant-Haycox and Wilson (1992), the move away from psychoanalytic personality approaches led to researchers finding far less psychopathology with artistic samples than in earlier studies. A similar shift appears to have taken place regarding dancers' self-esteem; that is, although personality studies (e.g., Bakker, 1988,

1991; Bettle, Bettle, Neumärker, & Neumärker, 2001; Marchant-Haycox & Wilson, 1992) and other writings (Buckroyd, 2000) state that dancers suffer from low self-esteem, that is not supported in recent research. This will be discussed more fully after the introduction of another topic related to personality, namely anxiety.

Anxiety, Stress, and Coping

Anxiety has been said to be "ubiquitous" in the performing arts (Hays, 2002) or at least very common (e.g., Bakker, 1988, 1991; Barrell & Terry, 2003; Kenny, 2005; Laws, 2005; Marchant-Haycox & Wilson, 1992; Papageorgi, Hallam, & Welch, 2007; Steptoe, 2001; Wills & Cooper, 1988; Wilson & Roland, 2002). In one study, musicians reported being affected by anxiety more frequently (47% of the time) than singers (38%), dancers (35%), and actors (33%; Wilson & Roland, 2002). Another reported higher, more frequent, and sometimes more debilitating anxiety among musicians than among athletes (Lacaille et al., 2005). Anxiety is the most studied performance psychology topic in music, which indicates the importance of the topic to those active in that domain. As a result, much of this section is devoted to studies with musicians, although the interested reader is directed to alternative sources for reviews (Kenny, 2005; Kenny & Osborne, 2006; Papageorgi et al., 2007; Salmon & Meyer, 1998; Steptoe, 2001; Taborsky, 2007; Wilson & Roland, 2002). Research with dancers is interspersed throughout, although almost no research with actors exists as yet.

CAUSES OF ANXIETY

Papageorgi and colleagues (2007) created a model of musicians' anxiety, attempting to integrate research in the field. This model makes it clear that musicians' anxiety is similar to that of athletes or dancers. For example, factors cited as influencing musicians' anxiety include individual differences and personality factors such as trait anxiety and perfectionism—factors that have also been studied in relation to anxiety in sport and, to a lesser extent, dance (Barrell & Terry, 2003; Mor et al., 1995; Walker & Nordin-Bates, 2010). Some less studied factors (e.g., insufficient development of metacognitive skills), were also suggested (Papageorgi et al., 2007). Altogether, a large number of personal, interpersonal, and environmental causes of anxiety were proposed. Among the personal causes, Papageorgi and colleagues (2007) identified a number of inherent aspects, such as age and sex; traits, such as introversion and trait anxiety; and environmental factors, such as occupational stress. Although a seemingly comprehensive list, many of the suggestions require more research attention before their model can be said to be conceptually thorough, evidence-based, and parsimonious.

Studies focusing on personal characteristics and anxiety have focused primarily on cognitions reflective of perfectionism and/or catastrophizing (Hays & Brown, 2004; Kenny et al., 2004; Kirchner, Bloom, & Skutnick-Henley, 2008; Mor et al., 1995; Lehrer, 1987; Sharp & McLean, 1999; Steptoe & Fidler, 1987; Wilson & Roland, 2002). Liston, Frost, and Mohr (2003) suggested that the large number of factors associated with performance anxiety among musicians in other studies (e.g., sex, trait anxiety, perfectionism) could be explained more parsimoniously in terms of two main cognitive aspects, namely catastrophizing and personal efficacy. It would be valuable to examine whether this proposal extends to other samples.

A number of additional personal sources of anxiety have been identified. Under-rehearsal, fear of injury or reinjury (Walker & Nordin-Bates, 2010), poor finances, job insecurity, and the strain of having to memorize large amounts of material (Hays & Brown, 2004) have been noted. The latter is obvious in acting, where performers typically must learn vast quantities of lines; it can also be important in music and dance, where long music or movement passages must often be retained. Particularly when performing at the last minute as a result of another's injury, there can be major stress in trying to memorize a performance; however, some find this *less* stressful than other work, because expectations are typically lower (Hays & Brown, 2004). Role type or focus can also play a part: When immersed in character roles or focusing entirely on the music rather than on oneself, there may be no room for anxiety (Hays & Brown, 2004; Walker & Nordin-Bates, 2010). It would be interesting to examine whether an intervention focused on characterization and absorption (e.g., via imagery) would help performers manage their anxiety—and perhaps reach flow.

Among the interpersonal and environmental factors proposed to affect anxiety are audiences, exposure, and performance conditions (Papageorgi et al., 2007; Walker & Nordin-Bates, 2010). But although early studies seemed to find that the very existence of an audience could induce anxiety in musicians, or that the size of the audience was important (for a review see Papageorgi et al., 2007), it now appears that the audience–anxiety relationship is more complex. For instance, the nature of the audience matters, with theater-goers being seen as more positive, and peers and professionals as more critical, with higher expectations (e.g., Hays & Brown, 2004; Walker & Nordin-Bates, 2010; Wilson & Roland, 2002). Helin (1989) found that dancers had higher physiological activation during final rehearsals than on stage, and a number of studies report that auditions are often the most anxiety-provoking performance situations (Hays & Brown, 2004; Seton, 2009; Wilson & Roland, 2002). As explained for acting auditions, "You put yourself in front of people on a regular basis and say 'choose me' and 9 times out of 10 they say 'no, thanks'" (Seton, 2009, p. 28). Altogether, studies suggest that studio, rehearsal, and audition anxiety are just as worthy of study as performance anxiety and that factors common to auditions such as negative feedback, critical comments, and lack of feedback should be the focus of initial research attention (Hays & Brown, 2004; Kogan, 2002; Phillips, 1991). Of course, performing in front of peers could also be a highly positive, supportive experience, and this likely depends on perceived supportiveness, as well as person-level variables such as concern about how other people react to one's performance (Lehrer, Goldman, & Strommen, 1990). Wilson and Roland (2002) proposed that audience composition (i.e., more or less knowledgeable) and proximity (e.g., being able to see facial expressions vs. pure darkness) are probably more influential in provoking an anxiety response than audience size.

As a related construct, performers' feelings of exposure are related to anxiety (e.g., Wilson, 1997). Increased exposure may help explain why anxiety is prevalent even among experienced performers—in crude terms, because making a mistake is more obvious as the lead violin than when part of a large orchestra. This may be similar in sport, where some roles (e.g., quarterbacks in American football) are more visible than others. Accordingly, studies indicate that experience often does not decrease anxiety intensity, although it may help with anxiety management (Fishbein, Middlestadt, Ottati, Strauss, & Ellis, 1988; Steptoe, 2001; Walker & Nordin-Bates, 2010; Wilson & Roland, 2002). It also stands to reason that having one's body exposed and scrutinized can be an additional source of anxiety in dance (e.g., Noh et al., 2009; Quested & Duda, 2011) and perhaps in theater.

Also related to audiences and exposure are expectations, whether from important others such as teachers and audiences or from the self. Therefore, expectations are both a personal and an interpersonal or environmental source of potential anxiety. Hays and Brown (2004) describe the case of an ex-dancer who struggled with expectations: "In my early years, I had the sort of success that was just astounding... [I] couldn't cope with the fact that people were expecting great things from me all the time" (p. 139). Walker and Nordin-Bates (2010) present a similar example, in which an experienced dancer felt anxious because of a perceived need to continuously prove that she could still perform at the top level. Hays and Brown suggest that performing artists often feel that they need to prove themselves and their worth as part of competing for attention and recognition. Feeling a need to prove oneself may be related to mastery avoidance goals, and as such the 2 × 2 theory of achievement goals (Elliot & McGregor, 2001) may provide a useful framework to understand these issues.

As a final note, a number of performance-related conditions can affect performer anxiety (Papageorgi et al., 2007). Air quality for singers and stage sizes for dancers might be two such conditions. Similarly, a study with dancers identified that to achieve flow (in many ways the antithesis of anxiety), a number of factors such as costuming and hair needed to be "right" (Hefferon & Ollis, 2006). Although research into such conditions might be valuable to each domain, they may be so specific that no cross-domain generalizations are possible. If so, a general category may be adequate for models of research, and applied practice must simply search out which factors impact any given individual.

ANXIETY MANAGEMENT

Because under-rehearsal is a common source of anxiety, overlearning is a strategy to cope (e.g., Walker & Nordin-Bates, 2010); even better, overlearning and subsequent automaticity can enable emotional communication (Hays & Brown, 2004). Other anxiety management and coping strategies noted in qualitative studies include a range of psychological skills (imagery, self-talk, relaxation and breathing techniques), social support, and other social strategies such as being silly and joking with colleagues (Hays & Brown, 2004; Walker & Nordin-Bates, 2010). Barrell and Terry (2003) found that dancers reporting the use of problem-focused coping strategies also reported lower trait anxiety; dancers using more maladaptive coping strategies were more anxious. As with most topics, however, the literature on coping in the performing arts is not as well established as in sport (see Chapter 8, this volume).

Alongside studies into spontaneous anxiety management, researchers in music have examined the effectiveness of various interventions. To date, no such studies exist in dance or theater. In a review, Kenny (2005) concluded that whereas both behavioral and cognitive interventions demonstrated some benefits, cognitive-behavioral approaches seemed most effective. However, conclusions were tentative due to the disparate nature of the studies and various methodological weaknesses. A number of other interventions not commonly examined in sport were also reviewed, with mixed evidence emerging for drug interventions, meditation, music therapy, the Alexander Technique, and other strategies. The mixed evidence and the differences in approach taken compared to sport psychology interventions suggest that all performance domains may benefit from learning from each other; indeed, even in a review as comprehensive as Kenny's (2005), no sport research is cited. Some studies do include strategies resembling psychological skills training, however (Stanton, 1994). For instance, Kendrick, Craig, Lawson, and Davidson (1982) found that both behavioral and cognitive-behavioral approaches had some impact on pianists' anxiety, although a cognitive-behavioral approach, called *attention training*, was superior. It comprised cognitive restructuring of self-talk from negative and irrelevant to positive, task-focused statements, as well as strategies to boost self-efficacy.

Much more research is required into psychological skills and other coping strategies as ways of managing anxiety. One approach could be listening to music, as has been suggested for athletes (Terry & Karageorghis, 2006). Given the inherent importance of music in many of the performing arts, studying this phenomenon with performers makes sense. For example, is it advantageous to listen to the same music you are about to perform, or are your own chosen songs that can calm you down or psych you up preferable? It would also be worthwhile to further examine somatic approaches commonly used for anxiety reduction (and general performance enhancement) in the arts, such as the Alexander Technique (Kenny, 2005; Wilson & Roland, 2002). In particular, it would be interesting to better document and understand what somatic approaches do, and do not, have in common with other techniques (see Chapter 31, this volume, for a discussion of somatic approaches in sport). Particular breathing techniques, for example, are emphasized in many somatic techniques, as well as in relaxation interventions.

Most studies concern themselves with over-arousal and anxiety as a negative phenomenon, but the opposite can also be a problem. For example, musicians need to make sure that repeated performances do not become "too relaxed" (Hays & Brown, 2004). Similarly, anxiety levels may be high for final rehearsals and at the start of a show run, but levels can decrease over time, and if a show run is very long (e.g., a ballet company performing Swan Lake 50 times, or musical theater artists performing in the same show for years), underarousal is a more pertinent issue (Helin, 1989; Noice & Noice, 2002; Walker & Nordin-Bates, 2010). To date, no studies have directly examined strategies used to manage underarousal or even to maintain optimal arousal.

In summary, anxiety appears to be a problem in performing arts settings and perhaps especially in music. But although anxiety may be the most studied topic in music performance psychology, the literature is nevertheless behind that in sport in at least four regards. First, many studies do not separate trait from state anxiety; second, cognitive and somatic symptoms are not always distinguished. Few studies consider anxiety direction (Kenny, 2005), and, finally, most lack theoretical foundations. Papageorgi et al. (2007) explain the effects of anxiety using inverted U (i.e., the Yerkes-Dodson law; Yerkes & Dodson, 1908) and catastrophe theory (Hardy & Parfitt, 1991); however, neither has much evidence to back up its utility in explaining music anxiety. Multidimensional anxiety theory (Martens, Vealey, & Burton, 1990) was not mentioned at all, but has some support from a study with dancers (Walker & Nordin-Bates, 2010). The behavior of leaders, peer interactions, rivalry and cooperation, and task demands have also not been studied in regard to performers' anxiety. For instance, would a drummer in a rock band not require different levels of arousal and anxiety compared to a harpist playing a requiem? Perhaps cognitive anxiety should remain low while somatic activation should vary according to situational demand? Hopefully, conceptually strong research will soon help answer some of these questions.

Self-Esteem and Self-Confidence

Performing artists, and dancers in particular, have often been said to suffer from low levels of self-esteem, self-confidence, or both (e.g., Bakker, 1988, 1991; Buckroyd, 2000; Hanrahan, 1996; Neumärker, Bettle, Neumärker, & Bettle, 2000;

Laws, 2005; Marchant-Haycox & Wilson, 1992). It is possible that factors such as feelings of exposure and vulnerability, having one's identity tightly bound to the performance activity, subjective and varying criteria for judging success, lack of feedback, and possibly personality traits such as perfectionism and introversion may contribute to such self-perceptions (e.g., Fortin, 2009; Hays & Brown, 2004). In contrast, it has been suggested that elite athletes often have high self-confidence and self-esteem (see Chapter 14, this volume). Before jumping to conclusions regarding domain differences, however, it is worth examining the nature of the evidence. In particular, those reporting less than positive feelings about the self among dancers have done so either based on work with ballet dancers (Bakker, 1988, 1991; Neumärker et al., 2000) via a small qualitative study (Hanrahan, 1996), single-item self-report (Laws, 2005) or anecdotally (Buckroyd, 2000).

More recent and larger scale studies report rather different findings; for instance, a group of young dancers in mixed styles reported moderately high self-esteem (Walker et al., 2011), as did a sample mixed both in regard to style, age, and level (Nordin-Bates, Walker, Baker et al., 2011) and a large sample of vocational school students (Quested & Duda, 2011). Similarly, Quested and Duda found that hip hop dancers (2009) and vocational dance students (2010) reported relatively high levels of perceived competence, as well as moderate to high levels of well-being. Domain-wide generalizations can therefore not be made, and further research is required to establish whether these constructs may be considered at healthy levels or problematic among performing artists—and how improvements may be made if and when the latter applies. Gender is also worth considering: Most dancers are female, and other research indicates that females usually report lower levels of both constructs than do males. The degree to which an activity like dance is gender stereotyped may also be important (Clifton & Gill, 1994).

There is a need for conceptual clarity when discussing these constructs because although everyday language often uses them interchangeably, self-confidence and self-esteem are conceptually distinct, with the latter more life domain- or situation-specific and the latter more enduring and generic. Sport research has typically focused more on self-confidence or self-efficacy, the most situation-specific form of feelings or evaluations of the self. Building on work done in sport, self-efficacy research may well deserve a more prominent place in performing arts research. It stands to reason that self-esteem may be more related to health and well-being, whereas self-efficacy is more related to performance. Additionally, the functional significance of self-confidence and self-esteem ought to be considered. Are they beneficial to performing artists? Studies addressing this question are limited, although it has been found that having high self-confidence can help performers interpret their anxiety as more facilitative (Papageorgi, 2007; Walker & Nordin-Bates, 2010). Hays and Brown (2004) labeled confidence "vital for performance excellence" in all domains. Still, performers sometimes say they do not want to be too confident, lest they become arrogant or complacent. An ex-dancer interviewed by Hays and Brown (2004) gave the following description of confidence-related problems in her domain while highlighting that confidence must be balanced by humility:

> I don't know if this is just in dance—it probably isn't. I'm sure in the acting profession it's kind of rampant too. Because of the kind of world it is, there are huge issues of insecurity and lack of confidence, and it's a very tricky balance to remain humble and open and to have confidence in yourself at the same time. (p. 66)

Although the idea of high self-confidence being problematic goes against the grain of most research (see Chapter 14, this volume), a recent study demonstrated that reduced self-confidence can in fact improve sport performance in some cases (Woodman, Akehurst, Hardy, & Beattie, 2010). The concepts of confidence, overconfidence, and their relationship to risk taking (Campbell, Goodie, & Foster, 2004) remain to be examined. In fact, risk taking is of particular interest in artistic domains given its link to creativity (e.g., Chappell, 2007; Simonton, 2000; Sternberg, 2006). But despite the value of examining these notions, it seems safe to assume that self-esteem is generally positive even if a lack of self-confidence can sometimes improve performance in the way Woodman et al. (2010) indicate.

Exploring Novelty: Non-Sport Topics with Promise for the Performing Arts

This third and final section briefly introduces four psychological topics not commonly researched or discussed in sport psychology but which appear to hold promise in helping us understand the performance and well-being of performing artists.

These include creativity and inspiration, memorization, emotional expressivity, and audiences.

Creativity and Inspiration

Although there is literature into creativity in arts education (e.g., Byrne et al., 2003; Chappell, 2007; Chappell, Craft, Rolfe, & Jobbins, 2009; Fleming, 2010; Odena, Plummeridge, & Welch, 2005; Running, 2008; Sawyer, 2003; Smith-Autard, 2002), and in mainstream and positive psychology (e.g., Csikszentmihalyi, 1996; Simonton, 2000; Snyder, 2002; Sternberg, 2006), it is not a topic that has captured many sport researchers' imaginations. This highlights that performance psychology in the performing arts should develop an identity of its own that serves its particular needs. And although not researched much in sport, creativity is related to many commonly studied concepts, including intrinsic motivation and flow (Amabile, 1983; Byrne et al., 2003; Csikszentmihalyi, 1996; Koestner, Ryan, Bernieri, & Holt, 1984; MacDonald et al., 2006), motivational climates (Hennessey, 2003; Hunter, Bedell, & Mumford, 2007), and well-being (Simonton, 2000; Snyder, 2002). These relationships, as well as the inherent value placed on creativity in arts, suggest that investing more research attention in creativity is worthwhile.

Psychology research into creativity has traditionally been person-centered, product-focused, and somewhat elitist (e.g., studying the outputs of genius-level creators like Igor Stravinsky and Martha Graham; Gardner, 1993). Recently, however, at least three parallel shifts in focus have occurred. First, there is growing recognition that creativity is collaborative (Craft, 2008; MacDonald, Miell, & Mitchell, 2002; MacDonald, Miell, & Morgan, 2000; Sawyer, 2003), communal (Chappell, 2007), social (Gardner, 1993; Hennessey, 2003), and culturally determined (Gardner, 1993; Glăveanu, 2010). Second, researchers have started to examine everyday or "small c" creativity (Chappell, 2007) as distinct from the "Big C" or genius-level creativity upon which much past writing was focused (Craft, 2008). Third, there is a move toward studying processes rather than just products. Studying processes appears at least as important as products, because it informs us of everyday lived experience (Sawyer, 2000). For instance, the creative process of a dancer or choreographer might be associated with flow and a positive sense of self, but she experiences self-consciousness and anxiety when performing (product). For a research area concerned as much with well-being as with performance, what could be more interesting? Sawyer (2000) also points out that in improvisation, the process *is* the product, and in the arts, improvising is often a part of training and sometimes of performance (e.g., in improvisational jazz ensembles and theater groups; Sawyer, 2003). The outlined shifts are of interest for two reasons. First, they highlight that creativity is worthy of study not only among the elite, but in performing arts generally. Second, they have implications for the study of group dynamics and leadership behaviors as factors that may affect creative processes, as well as products.

It is important to note that although creativity is an indicator of optimal functioning (e.g., Snyder 2002), associations between creativity and mental illness have also been found (Glazer, 2009; Nettle, 2006b). Nettle (2006a) points out that the personality traits of actors and other artists appear similar to those of individuals vulnerable to affective disorders (i.e., high levels of openness to experience and neuroticism). Presumably, we only want to encourage learning climates in which healthy creativity is nurtured even if ill health can also result in creative outputs. But what about creative performers with suboptimal functioning? How can the creativity of any "tortured geniuses" best be nurtured without exploiting their health? One suggestion emerges from the work of Barron (1972), who suggested that *ego strength* (resilience, self-control, and positive coping and well-being) is what makes the difference between certain traits (e.g., schizotypy and its associated high levels of unusual experiences) resulting in healthy or unhealthy creative products. Given the commonality between Barron's concept of ego strength and many sport psychology constructs (see especially the discussion of coping strategies in Chapter 8, this volume), there may be ways in which performers could be taught to be resilient and self-regulate so that well- rather than ill-being might accompany creativity.

INSPIRATION

Inspiration is intuitively linked with creativity, but it has only been researched systematically in the last few years. Thrash and colleagues have established that inspiration is three-dimensional, comprising transcendence, evocation, and approach motivation (Thrash & Elliot, 2003); that it has logical links to variables such as creativity, positive affect, and self-determination (Thrash & Elliot, 2003, Thrash, Maruskin, Cassidy, Fryer, & Ryan, 2010); and that it predicts well-being over time (Thrash, Elliot, Maruskin, & Cassidy, 2010). The potential implications of this research for the performing arts are many: For example, do personality constructs such as perfectionism impact inspiration and creativity? Can environmental influences including autonomy support promote higher levels of inspiration, creativity, and well-being?

Memorization

For many performing artists, memory is of paramount importance (e.g., actors learning lines; Kogan, 2002; Wilson, 2002), and, as noted above, having to memorize can be a source of stress. Accordingly, memory has been studied in music psychology (Aiello & Williamon, 2002) and in acting (Noice & Noice, 2002) but less so in dance (Starkes, Deakin, Lindley, & Crisp, 1987). Examples of memorizing strategies include counting beats aloud in music (Ginsborg, 2002), inferring meaning to text in acting (Noice, 1992; Noice & Noice, 2002; Schmidt, Boshuizen, & van Breukelen, 2002), and marking in dance (small hand or foot gestures used to simulate actual, full body movements; e.g., Starkes et al., 1987). Wilson (2002) outlines a range of memorization strategies, two of which form interesting overlaps with sport psychology: learning within context and overlearning. To learn within context, Wilson encourages the actor to learn his or her lines on the stage with props, costumes, and so on (see also Noice & Noice, 1997). This resembles PETTLEP guidelines for effective imagery (Holmes & Collins, 2001), with an emphasis on contextual factors and making imagery as realistic as possible. It would be interesting to examine whether the sport literature on imagery as a learning tool can be of use to actors, and whether the ways in which actors learn and recall material have implications for best practice in other domains. Cognitive neuroscience appears an obvious adjunct to sport psychology if we are to learn more about performers' memory encoding and retrieval; for instance, research has shown that high-level performers acquire highly specialized ways of encoding activity-specific information (Allard & Starkes, 1991; Calvo-Merino et al., 2005; Intons-Peterson & Smyth, 1987; Noice, 1991; Tervaniemi, Rytkönen, Schröger, Ilmoniemi, & Näätänen, 2001). Noice and Noice (2002) argued that actors employ "every strategy for facilitating recall that has been examined in cognitive psychology,", including depth processing and overlearning. The latter (learning until material is automatic) is said to be advantageous because attention can then be directed toward audience communication and artistry, with less risk of skill breakdown (Wilson,

2002). Interventions examining this point empirically would be most valuable.

Emotional Expression

References to artistic phenomena such as emotional expression, characterization, and audience communication have been interspersed throughout this chapter, but as topics in their own right they are not well researched—even though they are arguably the raison d'être of the performing arts. In this brief section, they are all referred to by the umbrella term *emotional expression* for simplicity.

Like memory, emotional expression has been studied in music (Juslin & Persson, 2002; Juslin & Sloboda, 2001) and acting (Noice & Noice, 2002) but less so in dance (Camurri, Lagerlöf, & Volpe, 2003). Still, dance and music both provoke emotional reactions by varying structural performance elements (Juslin & Persson, 2002), and so learning across domains may well be possible. Metaphorical images are logical aids to enhance emotional expressivity (e.g., Hanrahan & Vergeer, 2000; Juslin & Persson, 2002; Nordin & Cumming, 2005, 2006b; Woody, 2002). For instance, imagery-laden instructive terms such as "bouncy" have been said to be crucial in making music evoke emotion (Woody, 2002), and professionals are able to translate these into something perceived accurately and reliably by an audience (e.g., emotions such as joy; Gabrielsson & Juslin, 1996). In short, imagery appears to be an effective way of creating expressive musical performance (see also Clark et al., in press). Future research could help illuminate whether imagery interventions can be designed to improve expressivity.

Wilson (2002) touches on the subject of emotional expression within the context of actor training. In contrasting what he terms the "imaginative" approach (Method and Stanislavsky approaches) with its more "technical" counterpart (French and British schools), many links to performance psychology, and especially imagery, are evident. For instance, it is likely that a method actor (who focuses on the internal life of a character in order that true emotion be felt and expressed in a genuine way) employs different types of imagery than does a "technically" trained actor (who focuses on how he is being seen by an audience, without personally generating or imagining the relevant emotions). How realistic should imagery be, lest it takes over and the actor (or dancer) forgets his lines or movements as a result of overwhelming emotion—and is this necessarily a bad thing in a powerful performance? Indeed, the clarity with which emotions are communicated to an audience is what will be their (and the critics') measure of success; not the intensity with which the actor actually feels them (Juslin & Persson, 2002; Wilson, 2002).

Wilson highlights Bloch's method of training actors in emotional expression (entitled *Alba Emoting*), which is detached from inner sensation or emotional memory (Bloch, Orthous, & Santibáñez, 1987). Instead, it focuses on expressing emotions through adopting particular combinations of posture, facial expressions, and breathing patterns. Bloch and her collaborators have demonstrated that when actors replicate the breathing patterns associated with particular emotions, those emotions are partially experienced and are conveyed to observers (Bloch, Lemeignan, & Aguilera-Torres, 1991; Bloch et al., 1987). Interestingly, Bloch et al. (1987) found that actors trained in this detached manner were rated as *more* expressive than Stanislavsky-trained actors by independent judges. Bloch and her colleagues argue that their technique is healthier because it removes the need for reliving negative emotions from one's past, and that it may prevent anxiety by putting the actor in control. Psychologists might do well to study these suggestions further, including whether differences in well-being exist between actors trained in different traditions.

It is important to distinguish between emotions associated with a particular role or character and emotions felt by the performer: in fact, Bloch et al. (1987) suggested that actors trained to express emotions in a detached manner were rated as particularly expressive because emotions relevant to the character or role versus those of the actor her- or himself were clarified. Studying this distinction in a somewhat different way, Konijn (1991) found that while character emotion was often felt in rehearsals, performing in front of an audience was colored by feelings of anxiety for them as people. Thus, integrating research into emotional expression (e.g., conveying anxiety to an audience as part of a role) and psychological skills training (e.g., anxiety management for the self) seems appropriate. This is perhaps particularly important in art forms or pieces where *personal vulnerability* is seen as positive (see, e.g., Seton, 2006), given how different this appears to the mental toughness so often praised in sport.

There is much to be done before a comprehensive psychological understanding of emotional expression becomes a reality. Such work, integrated with research performed in sport psychology, could help make sure that emotion in performing arts psychology does not become the "missing link" it has been said to be in sport psychology (Botterill, 1997). The performing arts are sometimes insular (Hays & Brown, 2004) and may resist some terms commonly used in sport psychology (e.g., performance enhancement) because they do not seem aligned with the purposes of art. As a result, work with concepts such as inspiration, creativity, memorization, and emotional expression may help performing arts communities embrace performance psychology as something they want to be part of.

Audiences

As with emotional expression, references to audiences have been made throughout this chapter, yet the role of audiences is not well understood. Audiences are clearly important in the arts, whether as a source of stress and anxiety or as a valued and inherent part of art—after all, communicating to an audience is often what performing is about. Sport literature on fan behavior and sport spectators may not transfer logically to the arts, given the different roles of audiences in the two domains. Success in the performing arts is arguably more fickle than in sport due to its subjectivity, and audiences help determine success: jubilant reactions may extend a show run and empty seats shorten it, and critics can lift a performer to the skies with a rave review or "shoot them down" with vehement criticism. For all these reasons, the reactions that people have to the arts—both performers and audiences—are attractive study topics, and it is encouraging to see audience research emerging. One example is the Watching Dance project, in which researchers performed interdisciplinary inquiry around topics such as audience responses, kinesthetic empathy, emotion perception, and the mirror neuron system (Reason & Reynolds, 2010; Reynolds, 2010). Perception is also studied intensely in music psychology and even has its own journal (*Music Perception*). Reviewing such work is outside the scope of this chapter, but together with related studies (e.g., Calvo-Merino, Jola, Glaser, & Haggard, 2008; Hagendoorn, 2005), these writings indicate that an emerging psychology of the performing arts may have many parent disciplines outside of sport psychology, including cognitive neuroscience, aesthetics, positive psychology, and others. Integrating these fields will likely lead to the growth of a rich, broad-based field with great potential for enhancing the lives of performing artists both on and off stage.

Conclusion

This chapter has attempted to explore a range of performance psychology topics as they apply to the performing arts. A tripartite structure was employed, with topics grouped according to apparent similarity with research in sport psychology. The three components are illustrated in Figure 5.1.

Exploring Convergence presented topics that have been researched somewhat similarly in sport and art domains. Topics within Exploring Divergence were grouped based on differences in research emphasis (and sometimes findings) between sport and arts. Finally, Exploring Novelty introduced topics that seem to hold great potential for psychology research with artists, yet have attracted little or no research in sport. It has hopefully become evident that although research into the psychology of performing arts performance has lagged behind such research in sport, there are many areas in which the domains could learn from each other. For example, the aesthetic sports may be interested in the imagery and emotional expression research done in dance and music, and the situational motivation and focus of athletes could perhaps also benefit from considering intrinsic goals (Lacaille et al., 2005, 2007).

Key emergent messages, one for each section, have been illustrated in Figure 5.1. First, a notion that emerged repeatedly in the Exploring Convergence section was that environmental and cultural factors seem to matter greatly when working to understand performing artists. For example,

the social environment appears to play a part in the development of talent and passion, practice behaviors, disordered eating, and perhaps even affects performers' personalities (see also McAdams & Pals, 2006). The culture of institutions and of entire domains (e.g., ballet subculture) was also proposed to affect the likelihood of performers developing healthy or unhealthy attitudes toward their learning, bodies, eating, pain, and injury. As such, future research into these topics could usefully focus not only on individual or interpersonal factors but also on environmental and cultural ones. In this way, a more holistic picture of what promotes optimal performance and well-being in the performing arts is likely to be gained.

In the Exploring Divergence section, a more intrapersonal focus was notable. The main emergent message was that if we are to actively help performers help themselves (i.e., promote self-regulation), further research into strength building is necessary. This might include psychological skills training intervention studies, examination of anxiety management strategies, and studies into whether performers' feelings about their selves need to be improved; and if so, how. Combined with the message of the Convergence section, it seems that a particularly useful line of questioning might be to study the relative impact of intrapersonal, interpersonal, and environmental/cultural factors on well-being and performance outcomes. If considering, say, the experience of anxiety as a process, it would be

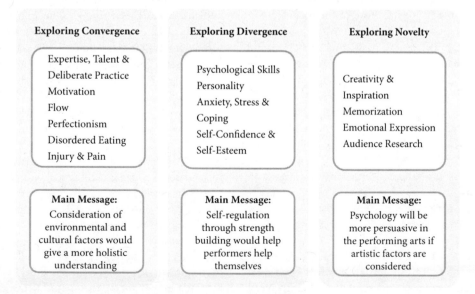

Figure 5.1 A tripartite overview of performance psychology in the performing arts.

valuable to better understand when, or under which conditions, intrapersonal and interpersonal aspects are most impactful. In this way, interventions could be designed in a more targeted and effective manner. For instance, if intrapersonal aspects were identified as influential sources of anxiety, then psychological skills training might be most pertinent; if teaching styles were the chief source of anxiety, then interventions focused on autonomy and social support may be better placed. Of course, these are highly complex questions and no single study could address them fully. Still, they represent a direction in which a series of studies may be able to build on each other to gradually develop momentum and understanding. If cultural factors are shown to be influential, a more complex question arises: Should the problem (e.g., increased prevalence of disordered eating in dance due to unquestioned assumptions that dancers must be underweight and of prepubescent shape) be accepted, and dancers taught coping strategies to manage? Or, should the ideals be challenged on a wider scale? Here, the issues clearly become more than psychological, related as they are to health and safety, politics, the history of the art form, and more.

The Exploring Novelty section highlighted that the fledgling field of performing arts psychology might do well to consider artistic aspects that can be conceptualized as psychological in nature. This includes creativity, inspiration, memorization, emotional expression, and audiences. Due to their lack of attention in sport research, there may well be a greater need to look to other "parent disciplines," such as positive and cognitive psychology, for background literature, inspiration, and applied implications.

As an overall conclusion, the domains of sport, music, dance, and theater have much in common and a psychological understanding of performance in these domains therefore logically shares much common ground. To date, research has to some extent progressed in parallel and more integration holds considerable promise for all concerned.

Note

1. For a more complete description of the Passion model, see Chapter 26, this volume.

References

Aalten, A. (2005). 'We dance, we don't live'. Biographical research in dance studies. *Discourses in Dance, 3*(1), 5–19.

Aalten, A. (2007). Listening to the dancer's body. *The Sociological Review, 55*(1), 109–125.

Abraham, S. (1996). Characteristics of eating disorders among young ballet dancers. *Psychopathology, 29*(4), 223–229.

Ahsen, A. (1984). ISM: The triple code model for imagery and psychophysiology. *Journal of Mental Imagery, 8*, 15–42.

Aiello, R., & Williamon, A. (2002). Memory. In R. Parncutt & G. E. McPherson (Eds.), *The science and psychology of music performance: Creative strategies for teaching and learning* (pp. 167–181). New York: Oxford University Press.

Allard, F., & Starkes, J. L. (1991). Motor-skill experts in sports, dance and other domains. In K. A. Ericsson & J. Smith (Eds.), *Toward a general theory of expertise. Prospects and limits* (pp. 126–153). Cambridge: Cambridge University Press.

Amabile, T. M. (1983). *The social psychology of creativity.* New York: Springer.

Ames, C. (1992). Achievement goals and the classroom motivational climate. In J. Meece & D. Schunk (Eds.), *Students' perceptions in the classroom: Causes and consequences* (pp. 327–348). Hillsdale, NJ: Erlbaum.

Annus, A., & Smith, G. T. (2009). Learning experiences in dance class predict adult eating disturbance. *European Eating Disorders Review, 17*(1), 50–60.

Bakker, F. C. (1988). Personality differences between young dancers and non-dancers. *Personality and Individual Differences, 9(1)*, 121–131.

Bakker, F. C. (1991). Development of personality in dancers: A longitudinal study. *Personality and Individual Differences, 12,* 671–681.

Bakker, A. B. (2005). Flow among music teachers and their students: The crossover of peak experiences. *Journal of Vocational Behavior, 66*, 26–44.

Barrell, G., & Terry, P. (2003). Trait anxiety and coping strategies among ballet dancers. *Medical Problems of Performing Artists, 18*(2), 59–64.

Barron, F. (1972). *Artists in the making.* New York: Seminar Press.

Beauchamp, M. R., Jackson, B., & Lavallee, D. (2007). Personality processes and intra-group dynamics in sport teams. In M. R. Beauchamp, & M. A. Eys (Eds.), *Group dynamics in sport and exercise psychology: Contemporary themes* (pp. 25–41). London: Routledge.

Benn, T., & Walters, D. (2001). Between Scylla and Charybdis: Nutritional education versus body culture and the ballet aesthetics: The effects of the lives of female dancers. *Research in Dance Education, 2*(2), 139–155.

Berry, T. R., & Howe, B. L. (2000). Risk factors for disordered eating in female university athletes. *Journal of Sport Behavior, 23*, 207–219.

Bettle, N., Bettle, O., Neumärker, U., & Neumärker, K. (2001). Body image and self-esteem in adolescent ballet dancers. *Perceptual and Motor Skills, 93*, 297–309.

Bloch, S., Orthous, P., & Santibáñez, G. (1987). Effector patterns of basic emotions: A psychophysiological method for training actors. *Journal of Social Biological Structure, 10*(1), 1–19.

Bloch, S., Lemeignan, M., & Aguilera-Torres, N. (1991). Specific respiratory patterns distinguish among human basic emotions. *International Journal of Psychophysiology, 11*, 141–154.

Bond, K. E., & Stinson, S. W. (2007). "It's work, work, work, work": Young people's experiences of effort and engagement in dance. *Research in Dance Education, 8*(2), 155–183.

Bonneville-Roussy, A., Lavigne, G. L., & Vallerand, R. J. (2011). When passion leads to excellence: The case of musicians. *Psychology of Music, 39*(1), 123–138.

Botterill, C. (1997). The role of emotion in sport performance: The missing link? *Journal of Applied Sport Psychology, 9*, 12.

Bradley, E. (2009, February). *Dancing in the moment: Dancers' flow experiences.* Presented at the Music and Dance Scheme Conference "Foundations for excellence: Promoting health and wellbeing in talented young dancers and musicians," Dartington, England.

Brandfonbrener, A. G. (1992). The forgotten patients. *Medical Problems of Performing Artists, 7*(4), 101–102.

Brändström, S. (1995). Self-formulated goals and self-evaluation in music education. *Bulletin for the Council of Research in Music Education, 127*, 16–21.

Brodie, J. A., & Lobel, E. E. (2008). More than just a mirror image: The visual system and other modes of learning and performing dance. *Journal of Dance Education, 8*(1), 23–31.

Buckroyd, J. (2000). *The student dancer: Emotional aspects of the teaching and learning of Dance.* London: Dance Books.

Buttsworth, L. M., & Smith, G. A. (1995). Personality of Australian performing musicians by gender and by instrument. *Personality and Individual Differences, 18*(5), 595–603.

Byrne, C., MacDonald, R., & Carlton, L. (2003). Assessing creativity in musical compositions: Flow as an assessment tool. *British Journal of Music Education, 20*(3), 277–290.

Byrne, C., & Sheridan, M. (2000). The long and winding road: The story of rock music in Scottish schools. *International Journal of Music Education, 18*(2), 173–185.

Cadopi, M., Chatillon, J. F., & Baldy, R. (1995). Representation and performance: Reproduction of form and quality of movement in dance by eight- and 11-year-old novices. *British Journal of Psychology, 86*(2), 217–225.

Calvo-Merino, B., Glaser, D. E., Grèzes, J., Passingham, R. E., & Haggard, P. (2005). Action observation and acquired motor skills: An fMRI study with expert dancers. *Cerebral Cortex, 15*(8), 1243–1249.

Calvo-Merino, B., Jola, C., Glaser, D. E., & Haggard, P. (2008). Towards a sensorimotor aesthetics of performing art. *Consciousness and Cognition, 17*(3), 911–922.

Campbell, W. K., Goodie, A. S., & Foster, J. D. (2004). Narcissism, confidence, and risk attitude. *Journal of Behavioral Decision Making, 17*(4), 297–311.

Camurri, A., Lagerlöf, I., & Volpe, G. (2003). Recognizing emotion from dance movement: Comparison of spectator recognition and automated techniques. *International Journal of Human-Computer Studies, 59*(1–2), 213–225.

Carlsson, R. (1988). The socialization of elite tennis players in Sweden: An analysis of the players. *Sociology of Sport Journal, 5*, 241–256.

Carr, S., & Wyon, M. (2003). The impact of motivational climate on dance students' achievement goals, trait anxiety and perfectionism. *Journal of Dance Medicine and Science, 7*(4), 105–114.

Chaffin, R., & Imreh, G. (2001). A comparison of practice and self-report as sources of information about the goals of expert practice. *Psychology of Music, 29*(1), 39–69.

Chappell, K. (2007). Creativity in primary level dance education: Moving beyond assumption. *Research in Dance Education, 8*(1), 27–52.

Chappell, K., Craft, A., Rolfe, L., & Jobbins, V. (2009). Dance partners for creativity: Choreographing space for co-participative research into creativity and partnership in dance education. *Research in Dance Education, 10*(3), 177–197.

Clark, T., Lisboa, T., & Williamon, A. (in press). The phenomenology of performance I: Preparing for performance, *Research Studies in Music Education.* Clark, T., Williamon, A.,

& Aksentijevic, A. (2012). Musical imagery and imagination: The function, measurement and application of imagery skills for performance. In D. Hargreaves, D. Miell, & R. MacDonald (Eds.), *Musical imaginations: Multidisciplinary perspectives on creativity, performance and perception* (pp. 351–368). Oxford, UK: Oxford University Press.

Clifton, R. T., & Gill, D. L. (1994). Gender differences in self-confidence on a feminine-typed task. *Journal of Sport and Exercise Psychology, 16*, 150–162.

Connolly, C., & Williamon, A. (2004). Mental skills training. In A. Williamon (Ed.), *Musical excellence: Strategies and techniques to enhance performance* (pp. 221–245). Oxford, UK: Oxford University Press.

Côté, J. (1999). The influence of the family in the development of talent in sports. *The Sport Psychologist, 13*, 395–417.

Couillandre, A., Lewton-Brain, P., & Portero, P. (2008). Exploring the effects of kinesiological awareness and mental imagery on movement intention in the performance of demi-plié. *Journal of Dance Medicine and Science, 12*(3), 91–98.

Craft, A. (2008). Studying collaborative creativity: Implications for education. *Thinking Skills and Creativity, 3*(3), 241–245.

Cribb, C., & Gregory, A. H. (1999). Stereotypes and personalities of musicians. *The Journal of Psychology, 133*(1), 104–114.

Csikszentmihalyi, M. (1975). *Beyond boredom and anxiety.* San Francisco: Jossey-Bass.

Csikszentmihalyi, M. (1990). *Flow: The psychology of optimal experience.* New York: Harper and Row.

Csikszentmihalyi, M. (1996). *Creativity: Flow and the psychology of discovery and invention.* New York: HarperCollins.

Csikszentmihalyi, M. (1998). Fruitless polarities. *Behavioural and Brain Sciences, 21*, 411.

Csikszentmihalyi, M., Rathunde, K., & Whalen, S. (1993). *Talented teenagers: The roots of success and failure.* New York: Cambridge University Press.

Cumming, J., Clark, S. E., Ste-Marie, D. M., McCullagh, P., & Hall, C. (2005). The functions of observational learning questionnaire. *Psychology of Sport and Exercise, 6*, 517–537.

Cumming, J., & Ramsey, R. (2008). Sport imagery interventions. In S. Mellalieu & S. Hanton (Eds.), *Advances in applied sport psychology: A review.* (pp. 5–36). London: Routledge.

Davidson, L. (1989). Observing a yang ch'in lesson: Learning by modeling and metaphor. *Journal of Aesthetic Education, 23*, 85–99.

Davidson, J. W., Howe, M. J. A., Moore, D. G., & Sloboda, J. A. (1996). The role of parental influences in the development of musical performance. *British Journal of Developmental Psychology, 14*(4), 399–412.

Dearborn, K., & Ross, R. (2006). Dance learning and the mirror: Comparison study of dance phrase learning with and without mirrors. *Journal of Dance Education, 6*(4), 109–115.

de Bruin, K. A. P., Bakker, F. C., & Oudejans, R. R. D. (2009). Achievement Goal Theory and disordered eating: Relationships between female gymnasts' goal orientations, perceived motivational climate and disordered eating correlates. *Psychology of Sport and Exercise, 10*(1), 72–79.

de Bruin, K. A. P., Oudejans, R. R. D., & Bakker, F. C. (2007). Dieting and body image in aesthetic sports: A comparison of Dutch female gymnasts and nonaesthetic sport participants. *Psychology of Sport and Exercise, 8*, 507–520.

Deci, E. L., & Ryan, R. M. (1985). *Intrinsic motivation and self-determination in human behavior.* New York: Plenum.

Dews, C. L. B., & Williams, M. S. (1989). Student musicians' personality styles, stresses, and coping patterns. *Psychology of Music, 17*(1), 37–47.

Dickey, M. R. (1992). A review of research on modelling in music teaching and learning. *Bulletin of the Council for Research in Music Education, 113,* 27–40.

Driskell, J. E., Copper, C., & Moran, A. (1994). Does mental practice enhance performance? *Journal of Applied Psychology, 79,* 481–492.

Duda, J. L., & Kim, M. (1997). Perceptions of the motivational climate, psychological characteristics, and attitudes toward eating among young female gymnasts. *Journal of Sport and Exercise Psychology, 19,* S48.

Dyce, J. A., & O'Connor, B. P. (1994). The personalities of popular musicians. *Psychology of Music, 22*(2), 168–173.

Efran, J. S., Lesser, G. S., & Spiller, M. J. (1994). Enhancing tennis coaching with youths using a metaphor method. *The Sport Psychologist, 8*(4), 349–359.

Ehrenberg, S. (2010). Reflections on reflections: Mirror use in a university dance training environment. *Theatre, Dance and Performance Training, 1*(2), 172–184.

Elliot, A. J. (1997). Integrating the 'classic' and 'contemporary' approaches to achievement motivation: A hierarchical model of achievement motivation. In M. Maehr & P. Pintrich (Eds.), *Advances in motivation and achievement* (Vol. 10, pp. 243–279). Greenwich, CT: JAI Press.

Elliot, A. J., & McGregor, H. A. (2001). A 2×2 achievement goal framework. *Journal of Personality and Social Psychology, 80*(3), 501–519.

Ericsson, K. A. (1996). *The road to excellence: The acquisition of expert performance in the arts and sciences, sports, and games.* Mahwah, NJ: Erlbaum.

Ericsson, K. A. (1997). Deliberate practice and the acquisition of expert performance: An overview. In H. Jørgensen & A. C. Lehmann (Eds.), *Does practice make perfect? Current theory and research on instrumental music practice* (pp.7–51). MNH-publikasjoner 1997:1. Oslo: Norges musikkhøgskole.

Ericsson, K. A., Krampe, R. Th., & Tesch-Römer, C. (1993). The role of deliberate practice in the acquisition of expert performance. *Psychological Review, 100*(3), 363–406.

Eysenck, H. J., & Eysenck, S. B. G. (1975). *Manual of the Eysenck personality questionnaire.* London: Hodder & Stoughton.

Fish, L., Hall, C., & Cumming, J. (2004). Investigating the use of imagery by elite ballet dancers. *Avante, 10*(3), 26–39.

Fishbein, M., Middlestadt, S. E., Ottati, V., Straus, S., & Ellis, A. (1988). Medical problems among ICSOM musicians: Overview of a national survey. *Medical Problems of Performing Artists, 3*(1), 1–8.

Fleming, M. (2010). *Arts in education and creativity: A literature review* (2nd ed.). London: Creativity, Culture and Education. Retrieved from http://www.creativitycultureeducation.org/data/files/arts-in-education-and-creativity-2nd-edition-91.pdf

Fortin, S. (2009). *The dominant artistic discourse as a health determinant.* Presented at the International Symposium on Performance Science, Auckland, New Zealand.

Forsberg, S., & Lock, J. (2006). The relationship between perfectionism, eating disorders and athletes: A review. *Minerva Pediatrica, 58*(6), 525–536.

Franklin, E. N. (1996a). *Dance imagery for technique and performance.* Champaign, IL: Human Kinetics.

Franklin, E. N. (1996b). *Dynamic alignment through imagery.* Champaign, IL: Human Kinetics.

Fredricks, J. A., Alfeld-Lido, C. J. Hruda, L. Z. Eccles, J. S. Patrick, H., & Ryan, A. M. (2002). A qualitative exploration of adolescents' commitment to athletics and the arts. *Journal of Adolescent Research, 17*(1), 68–97.

Gabrielsson, A., & Juslin, P. N. (1996). Emotional expression in music performance: Between the performer's intention and the listener's experience. *Psychology of Music, 24*(1), 68–91.

Gagné, F. (1995). From giftedness to talent: A developmental model and its impact on the language of the field. *Roeper Review: A Journal on Gifted Education, 18*(2), 103–111.

Gardner, H. (1993). *Creating minds: An anatomy of creativity seen through the lives of Freud, Einstein, Picasso, Stravinsky, Eliot, Graham, and Gandhi.* New York: Basic Books.

Garner, D. M., & Garfinkel, P. E. (1980). Socio-cultural factors in the development of anorexia nervosa. *Psychological Medicine, 10*(4), 647–656.

Garner, D. M., Garfinkel, P. E., Rockert, W., & Olmsted, M. P. (1987). A prospective study of eating disturbances in the ballet. *Psychotherapy and Psychosomatics, 48*(1–4), 170–175.

Gembris, H. (2006). The development of musical abilities. In R. Colwell (Ed.), *MENC handbook of musical cognition and development* (pp.124–164). New York: Oxford University Press.

Gembris, H., & Davidson, J. (2002). Environmental influences. In R. Parncutt & G. E. McPherson (Eds.), *The science and psychology of musical performance* (pp. 17–30). New York: Oxford University Press.

Gillespie, W., & Myors, B. (2000). Personality of rock musicians. *Psychology of Music, 28*(2), 154–165.

Ginsborg, J. (2002). Classical singers learning and memorising a new song: An observational study. *Psychology of Music, 30*(1), 58–101.

Glăveanu, V. -P. (2010). Principles for a cultural psychology of creativity. *Culture Psychology, 16*(2), 147–163.

Glazer, E. (2009). Rephrasing the madness and creativity debate: What is the nature of the creativity construct? *Personality and Individual Difference, 46,* 755–764.

Godøy, R. I., & Jørgensen, H. (2001). *Musical imagery.* Lisse, NL: Swets and Zeitlinger.

Gregg, M., Clark, T., & Hall, C. (2008). Seeing the sound: An exploration of the use of mental imagery by classical musicians. *Musicae Scientiae, 12*(2), 231–247.

Gruson, L. M. (1988). Rehearsal skill and musical competence: Does practice make perfect? In J. A. Sloboda (Ed.), *Generative processes in music: The psychology of performance, improvisation, and composition* (pp. 91–112). Oxford, UK: Clarendon Press.

Gvion, L. (2008). Dancing bodies, decaying bodies: The interpretation of anorexia among Israeli dancers. *Young, 16*(1), 67–87.

Haddon, E. (2007). *What does mental imagery mean to university music students and their professors?* Presented at the International Symposium on Performance Science, Auckland, New Zealand.

Hagendoorn, I. (2005). Some speculative hypotheses about the nature and perception of dance and choreography. *Journal of Consciousness Studies, 11*(3–4), 79–110.

Hall, C. R., Mack, D. E., Paivio, A., & Hausenblas, H. (1998). Imagery use by athletes: Development of the Sport Imagery Questionnaire. *International Journal of Sport Psychology, 23,* 1–17.

Hallam, S. (1997). What do we know about practising? Towards a model synthesising the research literature. In

H. Jorgensen & A. Lehman (Eds.), *Does practice make perfect? Current theory and research on instrumental music practice.* NMH-publikasjoner 1997:1 (pp. 179–231). Oslo: Norges musikkhögskole.

Hallam, S. (2001). The development of metacognition in musicians: Implications for education. *British Journal of Music Education, 18*, 27–39.

Hallam, S. (2002). Musical motivation: Towards a model synthesising the research. *Music Education Research, 4*(2), 225–244.

Halmi, K. A., Sunday, S. R. Strober, M., Kaplan, A., Woodside, D. B., Fichter, M., et al. (2000). Perfectionism in anorexia nervosa: Variation by clinical subtype, obsessionality, and pathological eating behavior. *American Journal of Psychiatry, 157*, 1799–1805.

Hamilton, L. H. (1998). *Advice for dancers: Emotional counsel and practical strategies.* San Francisco: Jossey-Bass.

Hamilton, L. H., Brooks-Gunn, J., & Warren, M. P. (1985). Socio-cultural influences on eating disorders in female professional dancers. *International Journal of Eating Disorders, 4*, 465–477.

Hamilton, L. H., Kella, J. J., & Hamilton, W. G. (1995). Personality and occupational stress in elite performers. *Medical Problems of Performing Artists, 10*, 86–89.

Hamilton, L. H., Hamilton, W. G., Warren, M. P., Keller, K., & Molnar, M. (1997). Factors contributing to the attrition rate in elite ballet students. *Journal of Dance Medicine and Science, 1*(4), 131–138.

Hammond, J., & Edelmann, R. J. (1991). The act of being: Personality characteristics of professional actors, amateur actors and non-actors. In G. D. Wilson (Ed.), *Psychology and performing arts.* Amsterdam: Swets & Zeitlinger.

Hanin, Y. L., & Stambulova, N. B. (2002). Metaphoric description of performance states: An application of the IZOF model. *The Sport Psychologist, 16*(4), 396–415.

Hanrahan, C. (1995). Creating dance images: Basic principles for teachers. *Journal of Physical Education, Recreation and Dance, 66*(1), 33–39.

Hanrahan, S. J. (1996). Dancers' perceptions of psychological skills. *Revista de Psicologia del Deporte, 9–10*, 19–27.

Hanrahan, S. (2005). On stage: Mental skills training for dancers. In M. B. Andersen (Ed.), *Sport psychology in practice* (pp. 109–127). Champaign, IL: Human Kinetics.

Hanrahan, C., & Salmela, J. H. (1990). Dance images—do they really work or are we just imagining things? *Journal of Physical Education, Recreation, and Dance, 61*(2), 18–21.

Hanrahan, C., Tétreau, B., & Sarrazin, C. (1995). Use of imagery while performing dance movement. *International Journal of Sport Psychology, 26*, 413–430.

Hanrahan, C., & Vergeer, I. (2000). Multiple uses of mental imagery by professional modern dancers. *Imagination, Cognition and Personality, 20*, 231–255.

Hardy, L., & Parfitt, G. (1991). A catastrophe model of anxiety and performance. *British Journal of Psychology, 82*(2), 163–178.

Hays, K. F. (2002). The enhancement of performance excellence among performing artists. *Journal of Applied Sport Psychology, 14*, 299–312.

Hays, K. F. (2005). Commentary on chapter 7. In M. B. Andersen (Ed.), *Sport psychology in practice* (pp. 129–134). Champaign, IL: Human Kinetics.

Hays, K. F., & Brown, C. H., Jr. (2004). *You're on! Consulting for peak performance.* Washington, DC: American Psychological Association.

Hefferon, K. M., & Ollis, S. (2006). 'Just clicks': an interpretive phenomenological analysis of professional dancers' experience of flow. *Research in Dance Education, 7*(2), 141–159.

Heinan, M. (2008). A review of the unique injuries sustained by musicians. *Journal of the American Academy of Physician Assistants, 21*(4), 45–51.

Helin, P. (1989). Mental and psychophysiological tension at professional ballet dancers' performances and rehearsals. *Dance Research Journal, 21*(1), 7–14.

Helsen, W. F., Starkes, J. L., & Hodges, N. J. (1998). Team sports and the theory of deliberate practice. *Journal of Sport and Exercise Psychology, 20*(1), 12–34.

Hennessey, B. A. (2003). The social psychology of creativity. *Scandinavian Journal of Educational Research, 47*(3), 253–271.

Henriksen, K., Stambulova, N., & Roessler, K. K. (2010). Holistic approach to athletic talent development environments: A successful sailing milieu. *Psychology of Sport and Exercise, 11*(3), 212–222.

Hewitt, M. P. (2001). The effects of modeling, self-evaluation, and self-listening on junior high instrumentalists' music performance and practice attitude. *Journal of Research in Music Education, 49*, 307–322.

Hodge, T., & Deakin, J. (1998). Deliberate practice and expertise in the martial arts: The role of context in motor recall. *Journal of Sport and Exercise Psychology, 20*, 260–279.

Hodges, N. J., & Starkes, J. L. (1996) Wrestling with the nature of expertise: A sport specific test of Ericsson, Krampe and Tesch-Römer's (1993) theory of 'deliberate practice'. *International Journal of Sport Psychology, 27*, 400–424.

Holmes, P. (2005). Imagination in practice: A study of the integrated roles of interpretation, imagery and technique in the learning and memorisation processes of two experienced solo performers. *British Journal of Music Education, 22*, 217–235.

Holmes, P. S., & Collins, D. J. (2001). The PETTLEP approach to motor imagery: A functional equivalence model for sport psychologists. *Journal of Applied Sport Psychology, 13*(1), 60–83.

Houston, S. (2004). The seriousness of having fun: The political agenda of community dance. *Animated, Winter 2004.* Retrieved from www.communitydance.org.uk/metadot/index.pl?id=22439&isa=DBRow&op=show&dbview_id=17860

Howe, M. J. A., Davidson, J. W., & Sloboda, J. A. (1998). Innate talents: Reality or myth? *Behavioral and Brain Sciences, 21*, 399–407.

Hunter, S. T., Bedell, K. E., & Mumford, M. D. (2007). Climate for creativity: A quantitative review. *Creativity Research Journal, 19*(1), 69–90.

Intons-Peterson, M. J., & Smyth, M. M. (1987). The anatomy of repertory memory. *Journal of Experimental Psychology: Learning, Memory, and Cognition, 13*(3), 490–500.

Jackson, S. A. (1995). Factors influencing the occurrence of flow in elite athletes. *Journal of Applied Sport Psychology, 7*, 138–166.

Jeong, E. H., Morris, T., & Watt A. P. (2005). *State and dispositional flow during training and performance in Korean dancers.* Presented at the 11th International Society of Sport Psychology (ISSP) congress, Sydney, Australia.

Johnston, D. (2006). Private speech in ballet. *Research in Dance Education, 7*(1), 3–14.

Jørgensen, H. (2000). Student learning in higher instrumental education: Who is responsible? *British Journal of Music Education, 17,* 67–77.

Jowitt, D. (2001). *Not just any body: Advancing health, well-being and excellence in dance and dancers.* Ontario, CAN: The Ginger Press.

Juslin, P. N., & Persson, R.,S. (2002). Emotional communication. In R. Parncutt & G. E. McPherson (Eds.), *The science and psychology of music performance: Creative strategies for teaching and learning* (pp. 219–236). New York: Oxford University Press.

Juslin, P. N., & Sloboda, J. A. (2001). *Music and emotion: Theory and research.* New York: Oxford University Press.

Kamin, S., Richards, H., & Collins, D. (2007). Influences on the talent development process of non-classical musicians: Psychological, social and environmental influences. *Music Education Research, 9*(3), 449–468.

Kanters, M. A., Bocarro, J., & Casper, J. (2008). Supported or pressured? An examination of agreement among parents and children on parent's role in youth sports. *Journal of Sport Behavior, 31,* 64–80.

Kaufmann, B. A., Warren, M. P., & Hamilton, L. H. (1996). Intervention in an elite ballet school: An attempt at decreasing eating disorders and injury. *Women's Studies International Forum, 19*(5), 545–549.

Kemp, A. (1981). The personality structure of the musician: I. Identifying a profile of traits for the performer. *Psychology of Music, 9,* 3–14.

Kemp, A. E. (1996). *The musical temperament: Psychology and personality of musicians.* Oxford, UK: Oxford University Press.

Kemp, A. E., & Mills, J. (2002). Musical potential. In R. Parncutt & G. E. McPherson (Eds.), *The science and psychology of music performance: Creative strategies for teaching and learning* (pp. 3–17). New York: Oxford University Press.

Kendrick, M. J., Craig, K. D., Lawson, D. M., & Davidson, P. O. (1982). Cognitive and behavioral therapy for musical-performance anxiety. *Journal of Consulting and Clinical Psychology, 50*(3), 353–362.

Kenny, D. T. (2005). A systematic review of treatments for music performance anxiety. *Anxiety, Stress and Coping: An International Journal, 18*(3), 183–208.

Kenny, D. T., Davis, P. J., & Oates, J. (2004). Music performance anxiety and occupational stress amongst opera chorus artists and their relationship with state and trait anxiety and perfectionism. *Journal of Anxiety Disorders, 18,* 757–777

Kenny, D. T., & Osborne, M. S. (2006). Music performance anxiety: New insights from young musicians. *Advances in Cognitive Psychology, 2*(2–3), 103–112.

King, L. A., McKee Walker, L., & Broyles, S. J. (1996). Creativity and the five-factor model. *Journal of Research in Personality, 30*(2), 189–203.

Kirchner, J. M., Bloom, A. J., & Skutnick-Henley, P. (2008). The relationship between performance anxiety and flow. *Medical Problems of Performing Artists, 23*(2), 59–65.

Kiresuk, T. J., Smith, A., & Cardillo, J. E. (1994). *Goal attainment scaling: Applications, theory, and measurement.* Hillsdale, NJ: Lawrence Erlbaum.

Koestner, R., Ryan, R. M., Bernieri, F., & Holt, K. (1984). Setting limits on children's behavior: The differential effects of controlling vs. informational styles on intrinsic motivation and creativity. *Journal of Personality, 52*(3), 233–248.

Kogan, N. (2002). Careers in the performing arts: A psychological perspective. *Creativity Research Journal, 14*(1), 1–16.

Konijn, E. A. (1991). What's on between the actor and his audience? Empirical analysis of emotion processes in the theatre. In G. D. Wilson (Ed.), *Psychology and performing arts* (pp. 59–74). Lisse, NL: Swets & Zeitlinger.

Kowal, J., & Fortier, M. S. (1999). Motivational determinants of flow: Contributions from self-determination theory. *The Journal of Social Psychology, 139*(3), 355–368.

Krasnow, D. H., Chatfield, S. J., Barr, S., Jensen, J. L., & Dufek, J. S. (1997). Imagery and conditioning practices for dancers. *Dance Research Journal, 29*(1), 43–64.

Krasnow, D. H., Kerr, G., & Mainwaring, L. (1994). Psychology of dealing with the injured dancer. *Medical Problems of Performing Artists, 9,* 7–9.

Lacaille, N., Koestner, R., & Gaudreau, P. (2007). On the value of intrinsic rather than traditional achievement goals for performing artists: A short-term prospective study. *International Journal of Music Education, 25*(3), 245–257.

Lacaille, N., Whipple, N., & Koestner, R. (2005). Reevaluating the benefits of performance goals: The relation of goal type to optimal performance for musicians and athletes. *Medical Problems of Performing Artists, 20,* 11–16.

Laws, H. (2005). *Fit to dance 2. Report of the second national inquiry into dancers' health and injury in the UK.* London: Dance UK.

Lehmann, A. C., & Gruber, H. (2006). Music. In K. A. Ericsson, N. Charness, P. J. Feltovich, & R. R. Hoffman (Eds.), *The Cambridge handbook of expertise and expert performance* (pp. 457–470). Cambridge, UK: Cambridge University Press.

Lehrer, P. M. (1987). A review of the approaches to the management of tension and stage fright in music performance. *Journal of Research in Music Education, 35,* 143–153.

Lehrer, P. M., Goldman, N. S., & Strommen, E. F. (1990). A principal components assessment of performance anxiety among musicians. *Medical Problems of Performing Artists, 5*(1), 12–18.

Lewis, N. G. (1990). Creative visualization: Maximising human potential. *Journal of Physical Education, Recreation and Dance, 61,* 30–32.

Liederbach, M., & Compagno, J. M. (2001). Psychological aspects of fatigue-related injuries in dancers. *Journal of Dance Medicine and Science, 5*(4), 116–120.

Liederbach, M., Gleim, G. W., & Nicholas, J. A. (1994). Physiologic and psychological measurements of performance stress and onset of injuries in professional ballet dancers. *Medical Problems of Performing Artists, 9,* 10–14.

Linklater, F. (1997). Effects of audio- and videotape models on performance achievement of beginning clarinetists. *Journal of Research in Music Education, 45*(3), 402–414.

Liston, M., Frost, A. A. M., & Mohr, P. B. (2003). The prediction of musical performance anxiety. *Medical Problems of Performing Artists, 18*(3), 120–125.

MacDonald, R., Byrne, C., & Carlton, L. (2006). Creativity and flow in musical composition: An empirical investigation. *Psychology of Music, 34*(3), 292–306.

MacDonald, R. A., Miell, D., & Mitchell, L. (2002). An investigation of children's musical collaborations: The effect of friendship and age. *Psychology of Music, 30*(2), 148–163.

MacDonald, R., Miell, D., & Morgan, L. (2000). Social processes and creative collaboration in children. *European Journal of Psychology of Education, 15*(4), 405–415.

Mackworth-Young, L. (1990). Pupil-centered learning in piano lessons: An evaluated action-research programme focusing on the psychology of the individual. *Psychology of Music, 18,* 73–86.

Mainwaring, L., Kerr, G., & Krasnow, D. (1993). Psychological correlates of dance injuries. *Medical Problems of Performing Artists, 8*(1), 3–6.

Mainwaring, L., Krasnow, D., & Kerr, G. (2001). And the dance goes on: Psychological impact of injury. *Journal of Dance Medicine and Science, 5*(4), 105–115.

Malina, R. M., Bouchard, C., & Bar-Or, O. (2004). *Growth, maturation, and physical activity* (2nd ed.). Champaign, IL: Human Kinetics.

Manturzewska, M. (1990). A biographical study of the life-span development of professional musicians. *Psychology of Music, 18*(2), 112–139.

Marchant-Haycox, S. E., & Wilson, G. D. (1992). Personality and stress in performing artists. *Personality and Individual Differences, 13*(10), 1061–1068.

Martens, R., Vealey, R. S., & Burton, D. (1990). *Competitive anxiety in sport.* Champaign, IL: Human Kinetics.

Martin, J. J., & Cutler, K. (2002). An exploratory study of flow and motivation in theater actors. *Journal of Applied Sport Psychology, 14*(4), 344–352.

Matthews, W. A., & Kitsantas, A. (2007). Group cohesion, collective efficacy, and motivational climate as predictors of conductor support in music ensembles. *Journal of Research in Music Education, 55*(1), 6–17.

McAdams, D. P., & Pals, J. L. (2006). A new big five: Fundamental principles for an integrative science of personality. *American Psychologist, 61*(3), 204–217.

McCabe, M. P., & Ricciardelli, L. A. (2005). A prospective study of pressures from parents, peers, and the media on extreme weight change behaviors among adolescent boys and girls. *Behavioural Research and Therapy, 43,* 653–668.

McCrae, R. R., & Costa, P. T., Jr. (1999). A five-factor theory of personality. In L. Pervin & O. P. John (Eds.), *Handbook of personality* (2nd ed., pp. 139–153). New York: Guilford Press.

McCullagh, P., Stiehl, J., & Weiss, M. R. (1990). Developmental modeling effects on the quantitative and qualitative aspects of motor performance. *Research Quarterly for Exercise and Sport, 61*(4), 344–350.

McCullagh, P., & Weiss, M. R. (2002). Observational learning: The forgotten psychological method in sport psychology. In J. L. Van Raalte & B. W. Brewer (Eds.), *Exploring sport and exercise psychology* (2nd ed., pp. 131–149). Washington, DC: American Psychological Association.

McPherson, G. E. (2006a). *The nature of musical giftedness and talent.* Keynote address at the Music Teachers National Association Leadership Summit, Cincinnati, OH. Retrieved from www. mtna.org/Programs/SummitforLeadership/Summit2006/ TheHomeEnvironmentandChildrensMusicalPracti/ tabid/258/Default.aspx

McPherson, G. E. (2006b). *The home environment and children's musical practice.* Keynote address at the Music Teachers National Association Leadership Summit, Cincinnati, OH. Retrieved from www.mtna.org/Programs/SummitforLeader ship/Summit2006/TheHomeEnvironmentandChildrens MusicalPracti/tabid/258/Default.aspx

McPherson, G. E., & Zimmerman, B. J. (2002). Self-regulation of musical learning: A social cognitive perspective. In R. Colwell & C. Richardson (Eds.), *The new handbook of research on music teaching and learning* (pp. 327–347). Oxford, UK: Oxford University Press.

Miksza, P. (2006). Relationships among impulsiveness, locus of control, sex, and music practice. *Journal of Research in Music Education, 54*(4), 308–323.

Miksza, P. (2007). Effective practice: An investigation of observed practice behaviors, self-reported practice habits, and the performance achievement of high school wind players. *Journal of Research in Music Education, 55*(4), 359–375.

Miksza, P. (2009a). An investigation of the 2 x 2 achievement goal framework in the context of instrumental music. In L. K. Thompson & M. R. Campbell (Eds.), *Advances in music education research* (Vol. 2, pp. 81–100). Charlotte, NC: Information Age Publishing.

Miksza, P. (2009b). Relationships among impulsivity, achievement goal motivation, and the music practice of high school wind players. *Bulletin of the Council for Research in Music Education, 180,* 39–57.

Miksza, P. (2011). Relationships among achievement goal motivation, impulsivity, and the music practice of collegiate brass and woodwind players. *Psychology of Music, 39*(1), 50–67.

Minton, S. (1990). Enhancement of alignment through imagery. *Journal of Physical Education, Recreation and Dance, 61*(2), 28–29.

Monsma, E. V., & Overby, L. Y. (2004). The relationship between imagery and competitive anxiety in ballet auditions. *Journal of Dance Medicine and Science, 8*(1), 11–18.

Mor, S., Day, H. I., Flett, G. L., & Hewitt, P. L. (1995). Perfectionism, control, and components of performance anxiety in professional artists. *Cognitive Therapy and Research, 19,* 207–225.

Murphy, S. (1999). *The cheers and the tears: A healthy alternative to the dark side of youth sports today.* San Francisco: Jossey-Bass.

Murphy, S., Nordin, S. M., & Cumming, J. (2008). Imagery in sport, exercise and dance. In T. Horn (Ed.), *Advances in sport and exercise psychology* (3rd ed., pp. 297–324). Champagne, IL: Human Kinetics.

Nettle, D. (2006a). Psychological profiles of professional actors. *Personality and Individual Differences, 40,* 375–383.

Nettle, D. (2006b). Schizotypy and mental health amongst poets, visual artists, and mathematicians. *Journal of Research in Personality, 40*(6), 876–890.

Neumärker, K. J., Bettle, N., Bettle, O., Dudeck, U., & Neumärker, U. (1998). The Eating Attitudes Test: Comparative analysis of female and male students at the Public Ballet School of Berlin. *European Child and Adolescent Psychiatry, 7*(1), 19–23.

Neumärker, K. J., Bettle, N., Neumärker, U., & Bettle, O. (2000). Age-and gender-related psychological characteristics of adolescent ballet dancers. *Psychopathology, 33,* 137–142.

Nielsen, S. G. (1999). Learning Strategies in instrumental music practice. *British Journal of Music Education, 16*(3), 275–291.

Nieminen, P., Varstala, V., & Manninen, M. (2001). Goal orientation and perceived purposes of dance among Finnish dance students: A pilot study. *Research in Dance Education, 2*(2), 175–193.

Noh, Y. E., Morris, T., Andersen, M. B. (2003). Psychosocial stress and injury in dance. *Journal of Physical Education, Recreation and Dance, 74,* 36–40.

Noh, Y., Morris, T., & Andersen, M. (2005). Psychosocial factors and ballet injuries. *International Journal of Sport and Exercise Psychology, 3*(1), 7–25.

Noh, Y. E, Morris, T, & Andersen, M. B. (2007). Psychological intervention for injury reduction in ballet dancers. *Research in Sports Medicine: An International Journal, 15*, 13–32.

Noh, Y. E., Morris, T., & Andersen, M. B. (2009). Occupational stress and coping strategies of professional ballet dancers in Korea. *Medical Problems of Performing Artists, 24*, 135–145.

Noice, H. (1991). The role of explanations and plan recognition in the learning of theatrical scripts. *Cognitive Science, 15*, 425–160.

Noice, H. (1992). Elaborative memory strategies of professional actors. *Applied Cognitive Psychology, 6*, 417–427.

Noice, T., & Noice, H. (1997). *Expertise of professional actors: A cognitive view.* Hillsdale, NJ: Lawrence Erlbaum.

Noice, T., & Noice, H. (2002). The expertise of professional actors: A review of recent research. *High Ability Studies, 13*(1), 7–19.

Nordin, S. M., & Cumming, J. (2005). Professional dancers describe their imagery: Where, when, what, why and how. *The Sport Psychologist, 19*, 395–416.

Nordin, S. M., & Cumming, J. (2006a). The development of imagery in dance: Part I. Qualitative data from professional dancers. *Journal of Dance Medicine and Science, 10*(1&2), 21–27.

Nordin, S. M., & Cumming, J. (2006b). The development of imagery in dance: Part II. Quantitative data from a mixed sample of dancers. *Journal of Dance Medicine and Science, 10*(1&2), 28–34.

Nordin, S. M., & Cumming, J. (2006c). Measuring the content of dancers' images: Development of the Dance Imagery Questionnaire (DIQ). *Journal of Dance Medicine and Science, 10*(3&4), 85–98.

Nordin, S. M., & Cumming, J. (2007). Where, when, and how: A quantitative account of dance imagery. *Research Quarterly for Exercise and Sport, 78*(4), 390–395.

Nordin, S. M., & Cumming, J. (2008). Exploring common ground: Comparing the imagery of dancers and aesthetic sport performers. *Journal of Applied Sport Psychology, 20*, 1–17.

Nordin-Bates, S. M., Cumming, J., Aways, D., & Sharp, L. (2011). Imagining yourself dancing to perfection? Correlates of perfectionism in ballet and contemporary dance. *Journal of Clinical Sport Psychology, 5*, 58–76.

Nordin-Bates, S. M., Quested, E., Walker, I. J., & Redding, E. (2012). Climate change in the dance studio: Findings from the UK Centres for Advanced Training. *Sport, Exercise, and Performance Psychology, 1*(1), 3–16.

Nordin--Bates, S. M., Walker, I., Baker, J., Garner, J., Hardy, C., Irvine, S., et al. (2011). Injury, imagery, and self-esteem in dance: Healthy minds in injured bodies? *Journal of Dance Medicine and Science, 15*(2), 76–85.

Nordin-Bates, S. M., Walker, I., & Redding, E. (2011). Correlates of disordered eating attitudes among male and female young talented dancers: Findings from the UK Centres for Advanced Training. *Eating Disorders, 19*, 1–23.

Odena, O., Plummeridge, Ch., & Welch, G. (2005). Towards an understanding of creativity in music education: A qualitative exploration of data from English secondary schools. *Bulletin of the Council for Research in Music Education, 163*, 9–18.

Orlick, T., & McCaffrey, N. (1991). Mental training with children for sport and life. *Journal of Sport Psychology, 5*, 322–334.

Overby, L. Y. (1990). The use of imagery by dance teachers—Development and implementation of two research instruments. *Journal of Physical Education, Recreation and Dance, 61*, 24–27.

Overby, L. Y., Hall, C., & Haslam, I. (1998). A comparison of imagery used by dance teachers, figure skating coaches, and soccer coaches. *Imagination, Cognition and Personality, 17*, 323–337.

Papageorgi, I., Hallam, S., & Welch, G. F. (2007). A conceptual framework for understanding musical performance anxiety. *Research Studies in Music Education, 28*(1), 83–107.

Papageorgi, I., Haddon, E., Creech, A., Morton, F., De Bezenac, C., Himonides, E., et al. (2010). Institutional culture and learning I: Inter-relationships between perceptions of the learning environment and undergraduate musicians' attitudes to learning. *Music Education Research, 12*(2), 151–178.

Patrick, H., Ryan, A. M. Alfeld-Lido, C. Fredricks, J. A. Hruda, L. Z., & Eccles, J. S. (1999). Adolescents' commitment to developing talent: The role of peers in continuing motivation for sports and the arts. *Journal of Youth and Adolescence, 28*(6), 741–763.

Patterson, E. L., Smith, R. E., Everett, J. J., & Ptacek, J. T. (1998). Psychosocial factors as predictors of ballet injuries: Interactive effects of life stress and social support. *Journal of Sport Behavior, 21*(1), 101–112.

Pedersen, M., & Wilmerding, V. (1998). Injury profiles of student and professional flamenco dancers. *Journal of Dance Medicine and Science, 3*, 108–114.

Persson, R. S. (1994). Control before shape—on mastering the clarinet: A case study on commonsense teaching. *British Journal of Music Education, 11*, 223–238.

Persson, R. (1996). Brilliant performers as teachers: A case study of commonsense teaching in a conservatoire setting. *International Journal of Music Education, 28*, 25–36.

Peterson, C., Park, N., & Seligman, M. (2005). Orientations to happiness and life satisfaction: The full life versus the empty life. *Journal of Happiness Studies, 6*, 25–41.

Phillips, E. M. (1991). Acting as an insecure occupation: The flipside of stardom. In G. D. Wilson (Ed.), *Psychology and performing arts.* Amsterdam: Swets & Zeitlinger.

Piran, N. (1999). Eating disorders: A trial of prevention in a high risk school setting. *Journal of Primary Prevention, 20*(1), 75–90.

Poczwardowski, A., & Conroy, D. E. (2002). Coping responses to failure and success among elite athletes and performing artists. *Journal of Applied Sport Psychology, 14*(4), 313–329.

Purcell, T. M. (1990). The use of imagery in children's dance-Making it work. *Journal of Physical Education, Recreation and Dance, 61*, 22–23.

Quested, E., & Duda, J. L. (2009). Perceptions of the motivational climate, need satisfaction, and indices of well- and ill-being among hip hop dancers. *Journal of Dance Medicine and Science, 13*(1), 10–19.

Quested, E., & Duda, J. L. (2010). Exploring the social-environmental determinants of well- and ill-being in dancers: A test of basic needs theory. *Journal of Sport and Exercise Psychology, 32*(1), 39–60.

Quested, E., & Duda, J. I. (2011). Antecedents of burnout among elite dancers: A longitudinal test of basic needs theory. *Psychology of Sport and Exercise, 12*(2), 159–167.

Radell, S. A., Adame, D. D., & Cole, S. P. (2002). Effect of teaching with mirrors on body image and locus of control in women college ballet dancers. *Perceptual and Motor Skills, 95*(2 pt 3), 1239–1247.

Radell, S. A., Adame, D. D., & Cole, S. P. (2003). Effect of teaching with mirrors on ballet dance performance. *Perceptual and Motor Skills, 97*(3 Pt 1), 960–964.

Ravaldi, C., Vannacci, A., Bolognesi, E., Mancini, S., Faravelli, C., & Ricca, V. (2006). Gender role, eating disorder symptoms, and body image concern in ballet dancers. *Journal of Psychosomatic Research, 61*(4), 529–535.

Reardon MacLellan, C. (2011). Differences in Myers-Briggs personality types among high school band, orchestra, and choir members. *Journal of Research in Music Education, 59*(1), 85–100.

Reason, M., & Reynolds, D. (2010). Kinesthesia, empathy, and related pleasures: An inquiry into audience experiences of watching dance. *Dance Research Journal, 42*(2), 49–75.

Reel, J. J., SooHoo, S., Jamieson, K. M., & Gill, D. L. (2005). Femininity to the extreme: Body image concerns among college female dancers. *Women in Sport and Physical Activity Journal, 14*(1), 39–51.

Renwick, J. M., & McPherson, G. E. (2002). Interest and choice: Student-selected repertoire and its effect on practising behaviour. *British Journal of Music Education, 19*(2), 173–188.

Reynolds, D. (2010). "Glitz and glamour" or atomic rearrangement: What do dance audiences want? *Dance Research, 28*(1), 19–35.

Ringham, R., Klump, K., Kaye, W., Stone, D., Libman, S., Stowe, S., et al. (2006). Eating disorder symptomatology among ballet dancers. *Eating Disorders, 39*, 503–508.

Rip, B., Fortin, S., & Vallerand, R. J. (2006). The relationship between passion and injury in dance students. *Journal of Dance Medicine and Science, 10*(1–2), 14–20.

Robson, B. E. (2004). Competition in sport, music, and dance. *Medical Problems of Performing Artists, 19*(4), 160–165.

Robson, B. E., & Gitev, M. (1991). In search of perfection. *Medical Problems of Performing Artists, 6*(1), 15–20.

Ross, S. L. (1985). The effectiveness of mental practice in improving the performance of college trombonists. *Journal of Research in Music Education, 33*(4), 221–230.

Ruiz, M., & Hanin, Y. (2004). Metaphoric description and individualized emotion profiling of performance states in top karate athletes. *Journal of Applied Sport Psychology, 16*(3), 258–273.

Running, D. J. (2008). Creativity research in music education: A review (1980–2005). *Update: Applications of Research in Music Education, 27*(1), 41–48.

Ryan, R. M., & Deci, E. L. (2000). Self-determination theory and the facilitation of intrinsic motivation, social development, and well-being. *American Psychologist, 55*(1), 68–78.

Sacha, T. J., & Russ, S. W. (2006). Effects of pretend imagery on learning dance in preschool children. *Early Childhood Education Journal, 33*(5), 341–345.

Salmon, P., & Meyer, R. G. (1998). *Notes from the green room: Coping with stress and anxiety in musical performance.* San Francisco: Jossey-Bass.

Sawada, M., Mori, S., & Ishii, M. (2002). Effect of metaphorical verbal instruction on modeling of sequential dance skills by young children. *Perceptual and Motor Skills, 95*(3 pt 2), 1097–1105.

Sawyer, R. K. (2000). Improvisation and the creative process: Dewey, Collingwood, and the aesthetics of spontaneity. *The Journal of Aesthetics and Art Criticism, 58*(2), 149–161.

Sawyer, R. K. (2003). *Group creativity: Music, theater, collaboration.* Mahwah, NJ: Erlbaum.

Scanlan, T. K., Carpenter, P. J., Schmidt, G. W., Simons, J. P., & Keeler, B. (1993). An introduction to the Sport Commitment Model. *Journal of Sport and Exercise Psychology, 15*(1), 1–15.

Schmidt, C. P. (2005). Relations among motivation, performance achievement, and music experience variables in secondary instrumental music students. *Journal of Research in Music Education, 53*, 134–147.

Schmidt, H. G., Boshuizen H. P. A., & van Breukelen G. J. P. (2002). Long-term retention of a theatrical script by repertory actors: The role of context. *Memory, 10*(1), 21–28.

Schoenberg, H. (1987). *Great pianists.* St. Louis: Fireside Books.

Seligman, M. E. P. (2002). *Authentic happiness: Using the new positive psychology to realise your potential for lasting fulfilment.* New York: Nicholas Brealey.

Seton, M. C. (2006). 'Post-dramatic' stress: Negotiating vulnerability for performance. *Proceedings of the 2006 Conference of the Australasian Association for Drama, Theatre and Performance Studies.*

Seton, M. C. (2009). *The Gilbert Spottiswood Churchill Fellowship to study holistic healthcare of actors in training and in the workplace.* Retrieved October 1, 2011, from http://www.churchill-trust.com.au/site_media/fellows/Seton_Mark_2009.pdf

Sharp, L. J., & McLean N. (1999). *Performance anxiety: The roles of perfectionism, anxiety sensitivity, and cognitive appraisal.* Unpublished masters thesis, University of Western Australia.

Simonton, D. K. (2000). Creativity: Cognitive, personal, developmental, and social aspects. *American Psychologist, 55*(1), 151–158.

Simonton, D. K. (2002). Creativity. In C. R. Snyder & S. J. Lopez (Eds.), *Handbook of positive psychology* (pp. 189–201). London: Oxford University Press.

Singer, R. N., & Janelle, C. M. (1999). Determining sport expertise: From genes to supremes. *International Journal of Sport Psychology, 30*(2), 117–150.

Smith, B. P. (2005). Goal orientation, implicit theory of ability, and collegiate instrumental music practice. *Psychology of Music, 33*(1), 36–57.

Smith, C. (1998). On authoritarianism in the dance classroom. In S. Shapiro (Ed.), *Dance, power and difference* (pp. 123–146). Champaign, IL: Human Kinetics.

Smith-Autard, J. M. (2002). *The art of dance in education* (2nd ed.). London, UK: AC & Black.

Sloboda, J. A. (1996). The acquisition of musical performance expertise: Deconstructing the "talent" account of individual differences in musical expressivity. In K. A. Ericsson (Ed.), *The road to excellence: The acquisition of expert performance in the arts and sciences, sports, and games* (pp. 107–126). Hillsdale, NJ: Lawrence Erlbaum Associates.

Sloboda, J. A., & Davidson, J. W. (1996). The young performing musician. In I. Deliège & J. Sloboda (Eds.), *Musical beginnings: The origins and development of musical competence* (pp. 171–190). Oxford, UK: Oxford University Press.

Sloboda, J. A., Davidson, J. W., Howe, M. J. A., & Moore, D. G. (1996). The role of practice in the development of performing musicians. *British Journal of Psychology, 87*(2), 287–309.

Stacey, C. L., & Goldberg, H. D. (1953). A personality study of professional and student actors. *Journal of Applied Psychology, 17*, 24–25.

Stanton, H. E. (1994). Reduction of performance anxiety in music students. *Australian Psychologist, 29*, 124–127.

Starkes, J. L., Deakin, J. M., Lindley, S., & Crisp, F. (1987). Motor versus verbal recall of ballet sequences by young expert dancers. *Journal of Sport Psychology, 9*(3), 222–230.

Steptoe, A. (2001). Negative emotions in music making: The problem of performance anxiety. In P. N. Juslin & J. A. Sloboda (Eds.), *Music and emotion: Theory and research series in affective science* (pp. 291–307). New York: Oxford University Press.

Steptoe, A., & Fidler, H. (1987). Stage fright in orchestral musicians: A study of cognitive and behavioural strategies in performance anxiety. *British Journal of Psychology, 78*(2), 241–249.

Sternberg, R. J. (2006). Creating a vision of creativity: The first 25 years. *Psychology of Aesthetics, Creativity, and the Arts, S*(1), 2–12.

Stinson, S. W. (1997). A question of fun: Adolescent engagement in dance education. *Dance Research Journal, 29*(2), 49–69.

Stoeber, J., & Eismann, U. (2007). Perfectionism in young musicians: Relations with motivation, effort, achievement, and distress. *Personality and Individual Differences, 43*(8), 2182–2192.

Subotnik, R. F., Olszewski-Kubilius, P., & Arnold, K. D. (2003). Beyond bloom: Revisiting environmental factors that enhance or impede talent development. In J. H. Borland (Ed.), *Rethinking gifted education* (pp. 227–238). New York: Teachers College Press.

Sweigard, L. E. (1974). *Human movement potential: Its ideokinetic facilitation.* New York: Harper and Row.

Taborsky, C. (2007). Musical performance anxiety: A review of literature. *Update: Applications of Research in Music Education, 26*, 15–25.

Taylor, L. D. (1997). MMPI-2 and ballet majors. *Personality and Individual Differences, 22*, 521–526.

Terry, P. C., & Karageorghis, C. I. (2006). Psychophysical effects of music in sport and exercise: An update on theory, research and application. In M. Katsikitis (Ed.), *Psychology bridging the Tasman: Science, culture and practice—proceedings of the 2006 joint conference of the Australian Psychological Society and the New Zealand Psychological Society* (pp. 415–419). Melbourne, VIC: Australian Psychological Society.

Tervaniemi, M., Rytkönen, M., Schröger, E., Ilmoniemi, R. J., & Näätänen, R. (2001). Superior formation of cortical memory traces for melodic patterns in musicians. *Learning and Memory, 8*, 295–300.

Thomas, J. J., Keel, P. K., & Heatherton, T. F. (2005). Disordered eating attitudes and behaviors in ballet students: Examination of environmental and individual risk factors. *International Journal of Eating Disorders, 38*(3), 263–268.

Thrash, T. M., & Elliot, A. J. (2003). Inspiration as a psychological construct. *Journal of Personality and Social Psychology, 84*(4), 871–889.

Thrash, T. M., Elliot, A., Maruskin, L. A., & Cassidy, S. E. (2010). Inspiration and the promotion of well-being: tests of causality and mediation. *Journal of Personality and Social Psychology, 98*(3), 488–506.

Thrash, T. M., Maruskin, L. A., Cassidy, S. E., Fryer, J. W., & Ryan, R. M. (2010). Mediating between the muse and the masses: Inspiration and the actualization of creative ideas. *Journal of Personality and Social Psychology, 98*(3), 469–487.

Toro, J., Guerrero, M., Sentis, J., Castro, J., & Puértolas, C. (2009). Eating disorders in ballet dancing students: Problems and risk factors. *European Eating Disorders Review, 17*(1), 40–49.

Tseng M. M. C., Fang D., Lee M. B., Chie W. C., Liu, J. P., & Chen W. J.(2007). Two-phase survey of eating disorders in gifted dance and non-dance high-school students in Taiwan. *Psychological Medicine, 37*, 1085–1096.

Turner, B. S., & Wainwright, S. P. (2003). Corps de ballet: The case of the injured ballet dancer. *Sociology of Health and Illness, 25*(4), 269–288.

Tyrka, A., Waldron, I., Graber, J., & Brooks-Gunn, J. (2002). Prospective predictors of the onset of anorexic and bulimic symptoms. *International Journal of Eating Disorders, 32*, 282–290.

Ureña, C. A. (2004) *Skill acquisition in ballet dancers: The relationship between deliberate practice and expertise.* Dissertation, Department of Educational Psychology and Learning Systems, Florida State University. Retrieved from http://etd.lib.fsu.edu/theses/available/etd-07122004-170955/

Vallerand, R. J., Blanchard, C., Mageau, G. A., Koestner, R., Ratelle, C., Léonard, M., Gagné, M., & Marsolais, J. (2003). Les passion de l'Âme: On obsessive and harmonious passion. *Journal of Personality and Social Psychology, 85*(4), 756–767.

Van Rossum, J. H. A. (2001). Talented in dance: The Bloom stage model revisited in the personal histories of dance students. *High Ability Studies, 12*(2), 181–197.

van Staden, A., Myburgh, C. P. H., & Poggenpoel, M. (2009). A psycho-educational model to enhance the self-development and mental health of classical dancers. *Journal of Dance Medicine and Science, 13*(1), 20–28.

Vergeer, L., & Hanrahan, C. (1998). What modern dancers do to prepare: Content and objectives of preperformance routines. *Avante, 4*(2), 49–71.

Wainwright, S. P., & Turner, B. S. (2004). Epiphanies of embodiment: Injury, identity and the balletic body. *Qualitative Research, 4*(3), 311–337.

Wainwright, S. P., Williams, C., & Turner, B. S. (2005). Fractured identities: Injury and the balletic body. *Health: An Interdisciplinary Journal for the Social Study of Health, Illness and Medicine, 9*(1), 49–66.

Walker, I. J., & Nordin-Bates, S. M. (2010). Performance anxiety experiences of professional dancers: The importance of control. *Journal of Dance Medicine and Science, 14*(4), 133–145.

Walker, I. J., Nordin-Bates, S., & Redding, E. (2010). Talent identification and development in dance: A review of the literature. *Research in Dance Education, 11*(3), 165–189.

Walker, I. J., Nordin-Bates, S. M., & Redding, E. (2011). Characteristics of talented dancers and age group differences: Findings from the UK Centres for Advanced Training. *High Ability Studies, 22*(1), 43–60.

Warburton, E. C. (2002). From talent identification to multidimensional assessment: Toward new models of evaluation in dance education. *Research in Dance Education, 3*(2), 103–121.

Watson, D., Nordin-Bates, S. M., & Chappell, K. (2010). *The experience and nurture of creativity in dance.* Presented at the 20th annual meeting of the International Association for Dance Medicine and Science, Birmingham, England.

Weisberg, R. B. (1998). Creativity and practice. *Behavioral and Brain Sciences, 21*(3), 429–430.

Weiss, M., & Amorose, A. (2008). Motivational orientations and sport behavior. In T. S. Horn (Ed.), *Advances in sport psychology* (3rd ed., pp. 115–155). Champaign, IL: Human Kinetics.

Weiss, M. R., Ebbeck, V., & Rose, D. J. (1992). "Show and tell" in the gymnasium revisited: Developmental differences in modeling and verbal rehearsal effects on motor skill learning and performance. *Research Quarterly for Exercise and Sport, 63*(3), 292–301.

Williamon, A., & Valentine, E. (2000). Quantity and quality of musical practice as predictors of performance quality. *British Journal of Psychology, 91*(3), 353–376.

Williams, A. M., & Reilly, T. (2000). Talent identification and development in soccer. *Journal of Sports Sciences, 18*(9), 657–667.

Wills, G., & Cooper, C. L. (1988). *Pressure sensitive: Popular musicians under stress.* London: Sage.

Wilson, G. D. (1984). The personality of opera singers. *Personality and Individual Differences, 5,* 195–201.

Wilson, G. D. (1997). Performance anxiety. In D. J. Hargreaves & A. C. North (Eds.), *The social psychology of music* (pp. 229–245). Oxford, UK: Oxford University Press.

Wilson, G. D. (2002). *Psychology for performing artists* (2nd ed.). London: Whurr.

Wilson, G. D., & Roland, D. (2002). Performance anxiety. In R. Parncutt & G. E. McPherson (Eds.), *The science and psychology of music performance: Creative strategies for teaching and learning* (pp. 47–61). New York: Oxford University Press.

Winner, E. (1996). The rage to master: The decisive case for talent in the visual arts. In K. A. Ericsson (Ed.), *The road to excellence: The acquisition of expert performance in the arts and sciences, sports and games* (pp. 271–301). Hillsdale, NJ: Erlbaum.

Woodman, T., Akehurst, S., Hardy, L., & Beattie, S. (2010). Self-confidence and performance: A little self-doubt helps. *Psychology of Sport and Exercise, 11*(6), 467–470.

Woody, R. H. (2002). Emotion, imagery and metaphor in the acquisition of musical performance skill. *Music Education Research, 4*(2), 213–222.

Yerkes, R. M., & Dodson, J. D. (1908). The relation of strength of stimulus to rapidity of habit-formation. *Journal of Comparative Neurology and Psychology, 18*(5), 459–482.

Young, B. W., & Salmela, J. H. (2002). Perceptions of training and deliberate practice of middle distance runners. *International Journal of Sport Psychology, 33,* 167–181.

PART 2

Individual Psychological Processes in Performance

<table>
<tr><td>CHAPTER

6</td><td></td></tr>
</table>

Concentration: Attention and Performance

Aidan Moran

Abstract

Concentration is an attentional process that involves the ability to focus on the task at hand while ignoring distractions. Cognitive research shows that it is vital for success in any field of skilled performance. The chapter begins by identifying three different dimensions of attention—concentration (or effortful awareness), selective perception, and divided attention (or the ability to perform two or more concurrent skills equally well). In the next section, three influential metaphors of attention are reviewed—the filter approach, capacity (or resource) theory, and the spotlight metaphor. Next, the relationship between people's attentional focus (i.e., whether they "shine" their mental spotlight externally or internally) and skilled performance is investigated. Then, the issue of why skilled performers appear to "lose" their concentration so easily (because of external and internal distractions) is examined. The next section of the chapter explains five research-based building blocks of effective concentration. The sixth section explains five practical techniques that can help people to improve their concentration skills. The final section of the chapter outlines some potentially fruitful new directions for research on attentional processes in skilled performers.

Key Words: Attention, concentration, skilled performance, selective attention, divided attention, sport

You are creating something within the stage, and the concentration has to be total, on what you're doing, all the way through. You can't let up for a minute.
—*The late Moira Shearer*, former ballet dancer and actress, cited in Roland, 1997, p. 32

On the days we're doing gigs, I'd visualise the venue all through the day; see myself sitting on the stage. That's the whole focus of the day, the gig...It's important to focus, to have a sense of occasion about performing.
—*Martin Hayes*, Irish traditional musician, cited in Boland, 1999, p. 6

I was so totally in the present.
—*Trevor Immelman*, South African golfer, on winning the 2008 U.S. Master's Championship; cited in McRae, 2008, p. 7

As the above quotations illustrate, "concentration" or the ability to focus effectively on the task at hand while ignoring distractions (Moran, 1996) is a crucial prerequisite of highly skilled performance in any field be it as dance, music, or sport. To illustrate, consider how a lapse in concentration can mean the difference between success and failure in competitive sport. For example, at the 2004 Olympic Games in Athens, the American rifle shooter Matthew Emmons missed an opportunity to win a gold medal in the 50 m three-position target event when he shot at the wrong target. Leading his nearest rival Jia Zhambo (China) by 3 points as he took his last shot, Emmons lost his focus momentarily and shot at the target of a *competitor* in the next lane—thereby squandering his chance of victory. Such attentional anomalies are difficult to explain in strongly motivated and highly trained elite performers. They also remind us that, despite over a century of psychological research on attentional processes, a number of issues remain unresolved in this field.

First, what exactly is "concentration," and how is it related to the broader construct of attention? Second, what are the most useful psychological theories and metaphors in helping us to understand attentional processes? Third, what do we know about the relationship between a person's attentional focus and his or her performance? Fourth, why do skilled performers appear to "lose" their concentration so easily? Fifth, what practical psychological techniques can help performers to achieve and maintain an optimal focus? Finally, what are the most fruitful new directions for research on concentration in skilled performers? The purpose of this chapter is to answer these six questions using the principles and findings of cognitive psychology—a discipline that studies mental activity in an effort to understand how the mind works (Smith & Kosslyn, 2007).

What Is Concentration? How Is It Related to Attention?

The topic of attention is central to cognitive neuroscience because it explores the mechanisms by which "voluntary control and subjective experience arise from and regulate our behaviour" (Posner & Rothbart, 2007, p. 1). But what exactly is "attention"? For psychologists, this term is inherently paradoxical because it is *familiar* and yet *mysterious*. It is familiar because it is used frequently in everyday discourse—as happens, for example, when a music teacher asks her students to "pay attention" to something important that she is about to

say or demonstrate to her class. Indeed, based on such apparent familiarity, William James (1890) remarked famously that

> Everyone knows what attention is. It is the taking possession by the mind, in clear and vivid form, of one of what may seem several simultaneously possible objects or trains of thought. Focalization, concentration, of consciousness are of its essence. It implies withdrawal from some things in order to deal effectively with others.
> (pp. 403–404)

But the term *attention* is also mysterious because it refers to many different types and levels of psychological processes ranging from biological arousal or alertness to high-level conscious awareness. For example, Ashcraft (2006) identified six different meanings of attention, including biological alertness or arousal (a state of readiness to respond to the environment), the orienting response (whereby attention is captured reflexively by an unexpected stimulus), visual search (a shift in attention toward a specific region of visual space), selective attention (the ability to attend to a particular source of information while ignoring other material), mental resources (a form of mental effort that fuels cognitive activity), and a supervisory process that regulates conscious cognitive activity. Commenting on this proliferation of definitions, Pashler (1998) subverted James' quotation by observing that perhaps "*no one* knows what attention is, and . . . there may not even be an 'it' to be known about" (p. 1; italics mine).

Despite such semantic confusion, significant progress *has* been made in at least three aspects of attentional research in recent years. First, most theorists now accept that the hallmark of attention is the *concentration of mental activity* (Matlin, 2009). Second, neuroscientific studies have identified a number of different brain regions that are activated during attentional processing. For example, Corbetta and Shulman (2002) concluded that the task of searching for a friend in a crowded room involves activation of frontal and dorsal parietal brain regions. By contrast, the act of redirecting one's attention to an unexpected stimulus (e.g., the sound of breaking glass) involves the activation of the ventral frontal cortex (Smith & Kosslyn, 2007). Finally, researchers agree on the *multidimensional* nature of this construct and can distinguish among at least three different types or dimensions of attention as follows (Moran, 2012).

The first dimension of attention is called "concentration" and refers to a person's deliberate decision to invest mental effort on what is most important in any given situation. For example, when rehearsing for a play, actors will listen intently to the director for advice or instructions about what is required of them. The second dimension of attention is "selective attention" or the perceptual ability to "zoom in" on task-relevant information while ignoring distractions. To test your skill in this area, can you focus only on the vocals of a song on the radio, disregarding the instrumental backing? Interestingly, research suggests that one way of capturing people's attention is through the use of sudden-onset stimuli and movement (Strayer & Drews, 2007). For example, the blinking cursor on a computer monitor makes it stand out from the static display of text that the user is typing on the screen. Internet "pop-up" advertising exploits this perceptual principle by trying to "steal" computer users' attention. The third dimension involves "divided attention" and refers to a form of mental time-sharing ability whereby performers learn, as a result of extensive practice, to perform two or more concurrent actions equally well. For example, whereas inexperienced motorists cannot drive and talk at the same time, experienced drivers have no such difficulty in doing so. But even experienced motorists have trouble in dividing their attention successfully between driving and using their mobile phones. To illustrate, Strayer, Drews, and Johnston (2003) discovered that drivers who had held conversations using their mobile phones either missed or had poor recall of billboard signs along their routes. In summary, the construct of attention refers to at least three different cognitive processes—concentration or effortful awareness, selectivity of perception, and/or the ability to coordinate two or more actions at the same time. Let us now consider the question of how psychologists have attempted to explain attention theoretically.

Explaining Attention: Theories and Metaphors

As scientists, psychology researchers use metaphors to explain the unknown in terms of the known. Adopting this strategy, Fernandez-Duque and Johnson (1999) reviewed a variety of metaphors of attention postulated by cognitive psychologists since the 1950s. Three of these conceptual approaches deserve special mention.

Filter Theory

The first modern theory of attention, proposed by Broadbent (1958), was based on a series of laboratory experiments on selective listening tasks. A key assumption of this theory was that people are limited in their ability to process information and that there must be a mechanism that facilitates the selection of some information while inhibiting the selection of competing information. To explain this mechanism, Broadbent drew an analogy between attention and a filtering device or bottleneck that screens and restricts the flow of information into the mind in accordance with a set of early perceptual or later semantic criteria. Put simply, just as the neck of a bottle restricts the flow of liquid, a hypothetical filter limits the quantity of information to which we can pay attention at any given time. Broadbent's (1958) model suggested that although multiple channels of information reach the filter, only one channel is permitted to pass through to the perceptual analysis stage of information processing. Selection by this filtering mechanism was believed to occur on the basis of physical characteristics, such as the pitch or loudness of the message being processed.

Although Broadbent's model was novel, it soon encountered many conceptual and methodological criticisms. For example, subsequent researchers failed to agree on either the location or timing of the filter. Another challenge to Broadbent's filter theory came from an everyday experience of attentional processing called the "cocktail party phenomenon"—an auditory perceptual effect associated with research by Cherry (1953). Imagine that you are at a noisy party and trying to pay attention to a conversation. Suddenly, you hear your name being mentioned in another conversation somewhere else in the room. How can Broadbent's theory explain the fact that you recognized your name? Clearly, if you heard your name being mentioned, then it could not have been blocked by the filter. Put differently, if your brain had previously selected the first conversation on the basis of physical features of the speaker's voice, how did it manage to process another set of sounds to which you had not been trying to pay attention? Interestingly, filter theory was incapable of accounting for the flexibility and sophistication of human attention, so, attention researchers abandoned signal-blocking filters in favor of other metaphors. Yet another factor that hastened the demise of filter theory was the switch from an auditory to a visual methodological paradigm in attention research. This switch occurred mainly because experimenters found it easier to measure the presentation times of visual stimuli than their auditory equivalents. Taken together, these developments paved the way for visual metaphors of attention such as the "spotlight" approach, which we explain shortly.

Capacity Theory

The "resource" or "capacity" theory of attention was developed by Kahneman (1973) in an effort to explain the mechanisms underlying divided attention or people's ability to perform two or more tasks at the same time. It suggested that attention resembles a pool of undifferentiated mental energy that can be allocated to concurrent tasks depending on various strategic principles—such as the influence of the performer's arousal level. Specifically, people have a greater amount of attentional capacity available when they are fully alert than when they are sleepy. Another strategic principle arises from the effects of task practice. For example, tasks that are highly practiced require less mental effort than novel ones and hence "free up" attentional resources (or spare mental capacity) to be devoted to other things. According to Kahneman (1973), the way in which a performer allocates his or her attentional capacity is determined by a combination of factors such as "momentary intentions" (i.e., factors that are deemed important at the time, like the decision to pay attention to whoever is speaking to you at a party) and "enduring dispositions" (i.e., factors that are always important to you, like the sound of your own name). Most resource theorists believe that divided attentional performance is regulated by a limited central capacity system, such as the "central executive" of the working memory model Baddeley, 2012). The extent to which two tasks can be performed concurrently depends on their combined demands on available attentional resources. A recurrent weakness of resource models of attention, however, stems from the possible circularity of some of their terminology. For example, as Eysenck and Keane (2010) have noted, there is a logical flaw in the "explanation" offered by resource theorists for people's inability to divide their attention successfully between two concurrent tasks. Specifically, the assumption in such cases that the resources of some central attentional capacity system have been exceeded by the joint demands of these concurrent tasks is circular in the absence of an independent measure of attentional resources. For a critique of resource models of attention, see Hancock, Oron-Gilad, and Szalma (2007).

Spotlight Metaphor

According to the spotlight metaphor (e.g., Posner, 1980), selective attention resembles a mental beam that illuminates a circumscribed part of the visual field and information lying outside the illuminated region is ignored. Spotlight theorists also suggested that the attentional beam can be redirected voluntarily to other locations in space. For psychologists, coaches, and performers, these visual metaphors have several advantages. For example, they show us that our mental beam of concentration is never truly "lost" but can be directed at the "wrong" target—something that is irrelevant to the task at hand, outside one's control, or located too far in the future. We shall return to this idea later in the chapter when we summarize some key principles of an effective focus for optimal performance. Incidentally, this idea of specifying a target for one's attentional spotlight is important because there are relatively few studies on the question of what exactly performers should actually focus on when they are exhorted to "concentrate" by their instructors (e.g., see Castaneda & Gray, 2007). A second benefit of the spotlight metaphor of attention is that it reminds us that performers have *control* over where they "shine" their concentration beam at all times. For example, at any given moment, when you shine your mental spotlight at a target in the world around you (e.g., as you look at your teammates before the start of a match), you have picked an *external* focus of attention. However, when you concentrate on your own feelings or bodily processes (e.g., in listening to your heart pounding with excitement before kickoff), you have switched to an *internal* focus of attention. In collective activities, an external focus of attention is required whenever you try to synchronize your movements with those of others (e.g., when rehearsing a dance formation). By contrast, an internal focus of attention is needed whenever you rehearse a skill in your mind's eye before performing it.

The assumption that one can control one's visual attention forms the basis of Nideffer's (1976) theory that expert performers in any field are adept at knowing which of four different types of attentional focus is required for a given task: "broad external," "narrow external," "broad internal," and "narrow internal." These different types of focus can be illustrated using the following examples. A broad external focus is required whenever a skilled performer has to assess a situation quickly to ascertain what options are available. For example, an ambulance driver called out to a motor accident needs to be able to scan the emergency scene rapidly before deciding whether or not to seek additional medical help. A narrow external focus involves a performer to "lock on" to a specific physical target in the immediate environment. For example, a novice actor struggling to overcome self-consciousness on stage may be advised to look over the audience's heads at a specific spot on the wall at the back of the theatre. A broad internal focus occurs whenever a performer (e.g., a dancer) goes through a sequence of movements in his or her imagination before actually executing them. For example, a ballet dancer may rehearse her dance movements in her "mind's eye" while sitting on a sofa before actually performing them on stage later that evening. Finally, a narrow internal focus involves concentrating on a single thought or image—as shown by our earlier example (see the beginning of this chapter) of the musician Martin Hayes' habit of visualizing his stage performance in advance of the event itself.

Of course, skilled performers in any field usually manage to switch between these different attentional foci as the situation requires. For example, a learner driver who is doing a driving test must be able to alternate effectively between going through the route in his or her mind (broad internal focus), scanning the environment for potential traffic hazards (broad external focus), looking in the rear view mirror (narrow external focus), and trying to stay calm (narrow internal focus). Interestingly, the question of whether one's focus is *appropriate* for the skill that one is performing is a very important issue. Thus, thinking too technically about your skills while performing can be counterproductive because it can induce "paralysis by analysis." Likewise, shining your spotlight on yourself is not a good idea as it makes you self-conscious and worried about making mistakes.

Unfortunately, although the spotlight metaphor of attention has been helpful in applied settings, it is plagued by at least three conceptual and empirical problems. First, spotlight theorists have not adequately explained the mechanisms by which executive control of attentional focus is achieved. Put simply, what processes govern direction of the spotlight? This question is difficult to answer without postulating some kind of homunculus—which invalidates the theory scientifically (but see Dennett, 1991, for an interesting philosophical critique of homunculi and the problem of consciousness). A second problem is that the spotlight metaphor neglects the issue of what lies outside the beam of our concentration. In other words, it ignores the possibility that *unconscious* factors such as "ironic" or counterintentional processes (Wegner, 1994; see below for further discussion) can affect people's attentional processes. Interestingly, such factors have attracted increasing scrutiny from cognitive scientists in recent years (e.g., Bargh & Morsella, 2008; Velmans & Schneider, 2007). Indeed, Nadel and Piattelli-Palmarini (2002) remarked that although cognitive science began with the assumption that cognition was limited to conscious processes, "much of the domain is now concerned with phenomena that lie behind the veil of consciousness" (p. xxvi). The third problem of the spotlight model of attention is that it neglects emotional influences on attentional processes. We shall return to this issue later when we summarize some key principles of effective concentration.

In summary, I have explored three different metaphors of attention: the filter, capacity (resource), and spotlight approaches. Whereas filter theories of attention were concerned mainly with identifying *how* and *where* selective attention occurred in the auditory information processing system, resource theories explored divided attention through dual-task interference methodology. Perhaps most persuasively, however, the spotlight metaphor has highlighted the way in which people control and focus their visual attention in everyday cognitive situations.

Attentional Focus and Performance

What exactly should people focus on in order to produce their best performance of a given skill? According to Wulf (2007) and Wulf, Shea, and Lewthwaite (2010), the accuracy and quality of skilled actions depend significantly on what the performer focuses on while executing the skill. More precisely, evidence is accumulating to show that an external focus of attention (i.e., one in which the performers concentrate on the effects of their movements on the environment) is usually superior to an internal focus of attention (in which performers focus on their own body or on the mechanics of the skill in question) in both skill learning and skilled performance. Wulf (2007) claimed that this principle is remarkably consistent across a variety of skills (e.g., balance tasks, jumping, golf, American football), levels of experience (i.e., whether the performers are experts or novices), and participant populations (including those with motor impairments). The domains of sport and the performing arts provide some anecdotal support for Wulf's (2007) hypothesis. To illustrate, consider the different types of attentional focus revealed by two experts as they prepared for important performances in their field—the former ballet dancer Deborah Bull and the golfer Paul McGinley. According to Bull, the fact that that she experienced "nerves from breakfast onwards" (cited in Brooks, 2001, p. 7) was the main reason for her retirement as a professional dancer in 2001. In particular, her fear of making mistakes dominated her thinking before a performance—an example of an unhelpful internal focus of attention. By contrast, when McGinley faced a putt to win the 2002 Ryder Cup match for Europe against the United States in the Belfry, he deliberately adopted an external focus of attention:

> At no time did I even consider the mechanics of the stroke. Of course, I knew what the putt meant and what it was for, but I became absorbed in the line of the putt. I could see it exactly from beginning to end. My only job at that moment in time was to set the ball off on the line that I had chosen. *That was the only thing I could control.*
>
> (cited in *Clarke*, 2002, p. 63; italics mine)

McGinley's insights are broadly in line with Wulf's (2007) research findings and reveal two practical concentration tips for elite performers in any field. First, a performer needs a *target* (in McGinley's case, the line of the putt) to focus on if he or she is to concentrate properly. In addition, optimal concentration requires focusing only on *actions that are under one's own control*. Of course, it is not always easy to concentrate on the right target in any performance situation because, although motor skills can become automatic through practice, a performer's train of thoughts (which require working memory—a cognitive system that stores and manipulates currently relevant information for short periods of time; Baddeley, 1986, 2012) can be derailed rather easily. For example, the pianist Louis Lortie explained how occasional attentional lapses impaired his performance on stage: "It could happen in the middle of a phrase. You have a silly thought, or you feel the instrument is not responding exactly as you'd like. Memory slips may result" (cited in Blau, 1998, p. 17).

Having sketched the relationship between attentional focus and performance, I now explore why people "lose" their concentration.

Why Do Skilled Performers "Lose" Their Concentration?

Have you ever discovered that you have been reading the same sentence in a book over and over again without any comprehension because your mind was "miles away"? If so, then you have first-hand experience of losing your concentration. But is concentration ever really lost? Instead, what probably happened was that you *distracted yourself* by allowing a thought, daydream, or feeling to become the focus of your attention. These could be classified as internal distractions, and psychologists generally differentiate these from more objective external distractions that divert attention away from a task-relevant focus (Moran, 2012). As we learned in our discussion of the spotlight metaphor, performers do not really "lose" their concentration at all. Instead, their attentional beam focuses on factors that are irrelevant to the job at hand, out of their control, or too far in the future.

Typically, external performance distractions include crowd movements, flash photography, and audience behavior. For example, the Brazilian marathon runner Vanderlei De Lima was leading the race in the 2004 Olympics in Athens when an unstable spectator suddenly jumped out from the crowd and wrestled him to the ground. Stunned and naturally distracted, De Lima eventually finished third in the event (Goodbody & Nichols, 2004).

By contrast, internal distractions could include a vast array of thoughts, such as wondering what might happen in the future, regretting what has happened in the past, or worrying about what other people might think, say, or do. Internal distractions may also be feelings (upset, angry) and/or bodily sensations (pain and fatigue) that impede efforts to concentrate on the job at hand. A classic example of a costly internal distraction occurred in the case of golfer Doug Sanders, who missed a putt of less than 3 feet that prevented him from winning his first major tournament—the 1970 British Open championship in St. Andrews, Scotland—and also deprived him of millions of pounds in prize money, tournament invitations, and advertising endorsements. Remarkably, Sanders' attentional lapse was precipitated mainly by thinking too far ahead and years later, he revealed what had happened: "I had the victory speech prepared before the battle was over...I would give up every victory I had to have won that title. It's amazing how many different things to my normal routine I did on the 18th" (cited in Moran, 2005, p. 21).

Unfortunately, despite the vivid testimonies of skilled performers, like Sanders, who have suffered dramatic attentional lapses, little research has been conducted to date on the phenomenology of internal distractibility—although Gouju, Vermersch, and Bouthier (2007) explored athletes' attentional experiences in a hurdle race. Specifically, these researchers investigated hurdlers' awareness of, and thoughts about, factors such as the presence of opponents (e.g., "I can feel him/her come closer"; pp. 181–182). Because of a dearth of research on internal distractions, the theoretical mechanisms by which people's own thoughts and feelings can disrupt their concentration were largely unknown until recently. Fortunately, Wegner (1994) developed a model that rectifies this oversight by attempting to explain why attentional lapses occur ironically—or precisely at the most inopportune moment for the person involved.

Wegner's (1994) theory proposed that the mind wanders *because* we try to control it. In other words, when we are anxious or tired, trying not to think about something may paradoxically increase its prominence in our consciousness. For example, if you try to make yourself fall asleep on the night before you are scheduled to take an early-morning flight, you will probably achieve only a prolonged state of wakefulness! Similarly, if you attempt to block a certain thought from entering your mind, you may end up becoming more preoccupied with it. This tendency for a suppressed thought to come to mind more readily than a thought that is the focus of intentional concentration is called *hyperaccessibility* and is especially likely to occur under conditions of mental load. Clearly, there are many situations in skilled performance in which such ironic self-regulation failures occur, and Wegner proposes theoretical mechanisms to account for this phenomenon.

According to Wegner (1994), when people try to suppress a thought, they engage in a controlled (conscious) search for thoughts that are different from the unwanted thought. At the same time, however, our minds conduct an automatic (unconscious) search for any signs of the unwanted thought. In other words, the intention to suppress a thought activates an automatic search for that very thought in an effort to monitor whether or not the act of suppression has been successful. Normally, the conscious intentional system dominates the unconscious monitoring system. Under certain circumstances (e.g., when our working memories are overloaded or when our attentional resources are depleted by fatigue or stress), however, the unconscious monitoring system prevails and an ironic intrusion of the unwanted thought occurs. Wegner attributes this rebound effect to the excessive cognitive load. Although this load is believed to disrupt the *conscious* mechanism of thought control, it does not interfere with the *automatic* (and ironic) monitoring system. Thus, Wegner (1994) proposed

that "the intention to concentrate creates conditions under which mental load enhances monitoring of irrelevancies" (p. 7). To summarize, Wegner's (1994) research helps us to understand why performers may find it difficult to suppress unwanted or irrelevant thoughts when they are tired or anxious. Perhaps not surprisingly, Wegner (2002) has investigated ironies of *action* as well as those of thought. For example, consider what happens when people who are asked *not* to overshoot the hole in a golf putt are given tasks that impose a heavy mental load on them. In such situations, the unwanted action (overshooting the hole) is exactly what happens. Interestingly, Woodman and Davis (2008) corroborated Wegner's (1994) theory that ironic processes impair skilled performance. Specifically, they discovered that the imposition of a cognitive load manipulation (based on the opportunity to win a financial prize for proficiency in putting) resulted in increased ironic errors in a golf putting task.

Having explored what concentration is and why we experience attentional lapses, it is worthwhile to consider some principles governing effective concentration or a focused state of mind.

Principles of Effective Concentration

At least five theoretical principles of effective concentration in skilled performance may be identified (Kremer & Moran, 2008), as shown in Figure 6.1. Each is examined in turn.

Decide to Concentrate—It Won't Just Happen by Chance

The first building block of effective concentration results from a deliberate decision to invest mental effort in performance. Just as researchers have differentiated between *deliberate* or mindful practice and casual or mindless practice (e.g., see Ericsson & Charness, 1994), we can distinguish between *preparing* to concentrate and simply hoping that it will happen by chance. Interestingly, this link between deciding to concentrate and subsequently performing to your full potential is well known in sport. For example, Ronan O'Gara, the Ireland and British and Irish Lions' rugby out-half, admitted that:

> I have to be focused. I have to do my mental
> preparation. I have to feel that I'm ready. I don't
> want to be putting myself out there for credit but
> I have a big impact on how Munster perform. When
> it's coming up to a big match, rugby is the only
> thing in my head. Driving around, I visualise certain

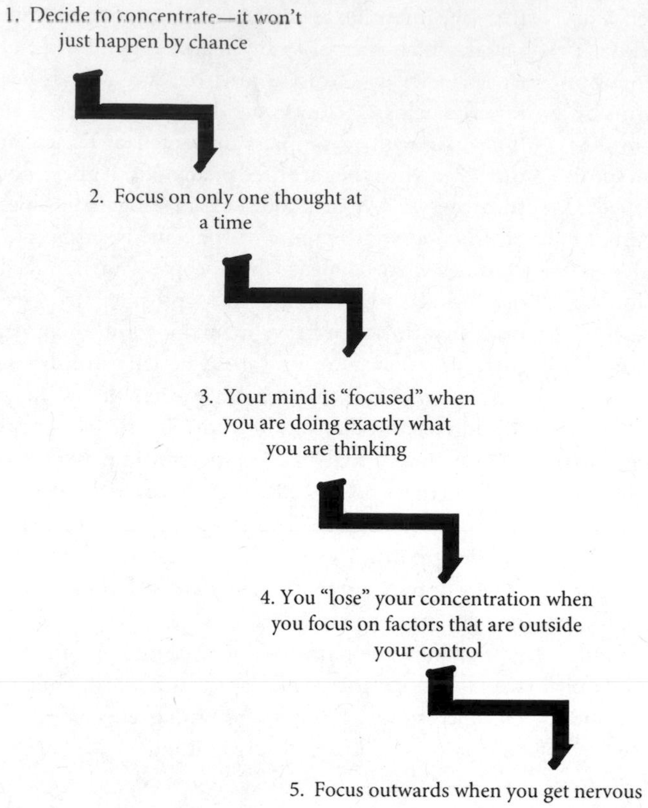

1. Decide to concentrate—it won't just happen by chance

2. Focus on only one thought at a time

3. Your mind is "focused" when you are doing exactly what you are thinking

4. You "lose" your concentration when you focus on factors that are outside your control

5. Focus outwards when you get nervous

Figure 6.1 Concentration principles. Based on Moran, A. P. (1996). *The psychology of concentration in sport performers: A cognitive analysis.* Hove, East Sussex: Psychology Press.

scenarios, different positions on the pitch, different times when the ball is coming to me.
(cited in *English*, 2006, p. 70)

In sport, many athletes establish imaginary "switch on" and "switch off" zones for their performance. For example, entering the locker room before a game reminds them to turn on their concentration switch. Likewise, some athletes associate "switching off" their concentration with stepping into the shower afterward. This idea of learning to turn one's concentration on and off as required was proposed by Garry Sobers, the famous cricketer, when he said: "Concentration's like a shower. You don't turn it on until you want to bathe. You don't walk out of the shower and leave it running. You turn it off, you turn it on. It has to be fresh and ready when you need it" (cited in White, 2002, p. 20).

Focus on Only One Thought at a Time

A second building block of effective concentration is the "one thought" principle—the idea that you can focus consciously on only one thing at a time. This idea is supported by research on the "bandwidth" of attention or the number of items

in working memory on which one can focus effectively. Specifically, Garavan (1998) and McElree (1998) tested people's ability to perform counting and retrieval tasks in working memory and concluded that the focus of attention is limited largely to just one item. Of course, as we mentioned earlier in our discussion of divided attention, people can perform several actions simultaneously—as long as one or more of these skills has been practised to the point at which it no longer requires conscious control (when the performer has achieved a state of automaticity).

Given the fragility and brevity of our attentional focus, it seems plausible that the ideal thought for a performer should be a single word triggering the appropriate feeling or tempo of the action to be executed (e.g., "smooth" or "flow") rather than a complex technical instruction (e.g., "bend your knees and go from low to high"). Evidence to support this idea comes from research by Hardy, Hall, and Hardy (2005) that showed that athletes' "self-talk" (what they say to themselves before or during their performance) tends to be abbreviated (e.g., "head" instead of "keep your head steady").

Do Exactly What You're Thinking

A third principle of good concentration is the idea that your mind is truly focused when there is no difference between what you are thinking about and what you are doing. This principle is derived from research on "flow states" and peak performance experiences in athletes (see reviews by Harmison, 2007; Jackson & Kimiecik, 2008) and musicians (Sinnamon, Moran, & O'Connell, 2012). To illustrate this principle, consider what Roger Bannister said about his achievement in running the first under 4-minute mile in May 1954 in Oxford: "There was no pain, only a great unity of movement and aim" (Bannister, 2004, p. 12).

To ensure a match between thought and action, the content of thoughts should be restricted to those that are highly relevant and positively phrased.

Focus Only on Factors Within Your Control

Fourth, extrapolating from recent literature reviews (e.g., see Chun, Golomb, & Turk-Browne, 2011), it is clear that performers' concentration tends to wander when their focus "shines" on factors outside their control, irrelevant to the job at hand, or located too far in the future. A dramatic example of this problem in horse racing occurred in 2005, when a young Irish jockey, Roger Loughran, finished third in a race that he should have won. Leading with a short distance to go and perhaps focusing on the thought of winning rather than riding, he misperceived a stick on the finishing straight as the winning post and began to celebrate his success prematurely. Punching the air in elation, he suddenly noticed two other riders passing him to claim first and second place (Muscat, 2005)!

Focus Outward when You Get Nervous

The final building block of effective concentration is the idea that a performer experiencing anxiety should focus *outward* on actions—not inward on doubts. This outward focus is necessary because anxiety tends to make people self-critical and hyper-vigilant (i.e., primed to detect any sign of what they may fear). As I explained at the beginning of this chapter, such advice is consistent with Wulf's (2007) review of research on the optimal attentional focus for skilled performance. Some performers have become so good at focusing outward that they become totally immersed in the present moment—a form of mindfulness (or present-centered attention) that is beginning to receive research attention in neuroscience (e.g., see Jha, Krompinger, & Baime, 2007).

Mindfulness training is an attentional focusing strategy that originated in the Buddhist meditative tradition (Erisman & Roemer, 2010). According to one of its leading proponents, Kabat-Zinn (2005), mindfulness involves "an openhearted, moment-to-moment, non-judgmental awareness" (p. 24) of oneself and of the world. This emphasis on adopting a nonjudgmental orientation to distractions is important because it distinguishes mindfulness training from more active cognitive control techniques such as thought suppression. By urging acceptance rather than attempted elimination of intrusive, unwanted thoughts and feelings, mindfulness training purports to help performers to concentrate on the here-and-now. In a recent experiment, Aherne, Moran, and Lonsdale (2011) investigated the effects of a 6-week, CD-based mindfulness training program on elite athletes' flow experiences in training. Results showed that athletes who underwent this training program experienced greater flow than did a control group that received no mindfulness instruction. Interestingly, an increasingly popular behavior-analytic program called *acceptance and commitment therapy* (ACT; Hayes, Luoma, Bond, Masuda, & Lillis, 2006) is based on mindfulness training principles and purports to help people to increase their ability to engage nonjudgmentally with the present moment. A recent review of the efficacy of this program was published by Coyne, McHugh, and Martinez (2011).

Concentration Techniques

Research psychologists have developed a variety of practical strategies that purport to improve concentration skills in performers (Greenlees & Moran, 2003). The purpose of these strategies is to help performers achieve a focused state of mind in which there is no difference between what they are thinking about and what they are doing (Kremer & Moran, 2008; Moran, 2012).

Specifying Performance Goals

Psychologists commonly distinguish between outcome goals (e.g., successful audition or competition victory usually linked with comparisons to others) and performance goals (achieving specific levels of performance that lie within the performer's control). Based on this distinction, it seems likely that the act of specifying performance goals can improve performers' concentration skills. For example, tennis players could improve their concentration on court by focusing solely on such performance goals as seeking increased accuracy (through better placement or achieving a higher percentage "in") on their first serves. This suggestion seems theoretically valid because performance goals encourage performers to focus on task-relevant information and on controllable actions. Additional support for this idea stems from studies on the correlates of people's best and worst athletic performances. For example, Jackson and Roberts (1992) found that collegiate performers performed worst when they were preoccupied by result goals. Conversely, their best displays coincided with an explicit focus on performance goals. In summary, there seems to be some support for the idea that performance goals can facilitate concentration skills in performers.

Pre-performance Routines

Most top-class performers display characteristic sequences of preparatory actions before they perform key skills. For example, dancers may go through the same physical stretching before going on stage. Similarly, rugby place kickers like to go through a systematic series of steps before striking the ball. These preferred action sequences and/or repetitive behaviors are called "pre-performance routines" and are typically performed prior to the execution of self-paced skills (i.e., actions that are carried out largely at one's own speed and without interference from other people).

Two main types of routines are commonly used by skilled performers. First, *pre-event* routines are preferred sequences of actions in the run up to important events (e.g., a concert for a musician). Included here are stable preferences for what to do on the night before and on the morning of the performance itself. In addition, *pre-performance* routines are characteristic sequences of thoughts and actions that performers adhere to immediately prior to skill execution.

Support for the value of pre-performance routines as concentration techniques comes from theoretical sources, case studies and interviews. Theoretically, pre-performance routines should help people to concentrate for several reasons. First, they are intended to encourage performers to develop an appropriate mental set for skill execution by helping them to focus on task-relevant information. For example, many soccer goalkeepers follow pre-kick routines in an effort to block out any jeering that is directed at them by supporters of opposing teams. Second, such routines may enable performers to concentrate on the present moment rather than on past events or on possible future outcomes. Finally, pre-performance routines may prevent performers

from devoting too much attention to the mechanics of their well-learned skills—a habit that can unravel automaticity (see Beilock & Carr, 2001).

Recently, Cotterill, Sanders, and Collins (2010) conducted in-depth interviews with a sample of amateur international golfers in an effort to understand the nature and perceived benefits of their pre-performance routines. Results showed that these golfers used routines for attentional purposes such as attempting to "switch on and off" (p. 55) and "staying in the present and not dwelling on the past or engaging in fortune telling" (p. 55). What theoretical mechanisms could explain the popularity of ritualized behavior (such as pre-performance routines) in sport? According to Jackson and Masters (2006), such behavior serves two purposes. On the one hand, it consumes working memory resources and hence prevents the performer from "reinvesting" conscious control over skills that are more effectively executed automatically (see Chapter 7 this volume, for a more detailed account of reinvestment theory). On the other hand, pre-competitive rituals may provide some temporary relief from excessive anxiety on the part of the performer. Unfortunately, pre-performance routines may lead to superstitious rituals on the part of some performers.

A "superstition" can be defined as the belief that, despite evidence to the contrary, certain behavior is causally related to certain outcomes. Athletes, actors, and musicians are notoriously superstitious—perhaps because of the capricious nature of success in their field. For example, tennis star Rafael Nadal must have two water bottles beside the court, perfectly aligned and with the labels facing the baseline, and golfer Tiger Woods typically wears a "lucky" red shirt on the last day of a golf tournament (Hyde, 2009). Interestingly, some evidence has emerged recently to suggest that despite their irrational origins, superstitions may sometimes be helpful to performers. Thus, Damisch, Stoberock, and Mussweiler (2010) conducted a series of intriguing experiments that appear to highlight some benefits of superstitions to motor and cognitive task performance. Specifically, they showed that playing with a ball described as "lucky" seems to improve participants' putting accuracy and that the presence of a personal charm enhances participants' performance on memory and anagram tests. In an effort to explain these results, Damisch et al. (2010) postulated that good luck superstitions may have increased participants' self-efficacy (or belief in their own ability to succeed on the tasks in question) which, in turn, may have improved their performance.

Psychologically, routines and superstitious behavior differ on two key criteria: control and purpose. The essence of superstitious behavior is the belief that one's fate is governed by factors that lie outside one's control. But the virtue of a routine is that it allows the player to exert complete control over his or her preparation. Indeed, players often shorten their pre-performance routines in adverse circumstances (e.g., if the performance event is delayed unexpectedly). Unfortunately, the converse is true for superstitions. They tend to grow longer over time as performers "chain together" more and more illogical links between behavior and outcome. The second criterion that may be used to distinguish between routines and rituals concerns the technical role of each behavioral step followed; whereas each part of a routine should have a rational basis, the components of a superstitious ritual may not be justifiable objectively.

Identifying these differences between routines and superstitions suggests that in developing routines performers should be encouraged to develop a routine that provides them with a sense of control over performance. They should also be instructed to practice varying their routine so that it can be used flexibly. Finally, regular review and revision of routines will help to reduce the likelihood of them forming the basis for superstition.

"Trigger Words" as Cues to Concentrate

It has long been known that skilled performers talk to themselves, either overtly or silently, before and during important action sequences (recall the earlier discussion of the importance of focusing on only one thought at a time). This "self-talk" is used both for motivational and instructional purposes (Hardy et al., 2005; see also Chapter 10, this volume).

To illustrate, the British Olympic athlete Paula Radcliffe, who won the 2007 New York City Marathon, reported counting her steps silently to herself in an effort to maintain her concentration in a race. As she explained afterward, "when I count to 100 three times, it's a mile. It helps me to focus on the moment and not to think about how many miles I have to go. I concentrate on breathing and striding, and I go within myself" (cited in Kolata, 2007, p. 1). Similarly, during the 2002 Wimbledon ladies' singles tennis final between the Williams sisters, Serena Williams (who defeated Venus 7–6, 6–3) was observed by millions of viewers to be reading something as she sat down during the change-overs between games. Afterwards, she explained that she had been reading notes that she had written to herself as trigger words or instructional cues to remind her to "hit in front" or "stay low" (Williams, 2002, p. 6). Interestingly, she used a similar strategy in 2007 in Wimbledon when she defeated Daniela Hantuchova in the fourth round of the tournament. On this occasion, she used phrases like "get low," "add spin," and "move up" (Martin, 2007). In a similar vein, many skilled performers talk to themselves either silently or out loud when they compete—usually in an effort to motivate themselves. This covert self-talk can involve instructional ("swing slowly") or motivational ("you can do this!") content, and both types of content can be phrased positively or negatively.

Mental Practice

The term *mental practice* (MP) or *visualization* refers to the systematic use of mental imagery in order to rehearse physical actions. It involves "seeing" and "feeling" a skill in one's imagination before actually executing it (Driskell, Copper, & Moran, 1994). Although there is considerable empirical evidence that mental imagery (see Weinberg, 2008) and MP facilitate skill learning and performance, their use as a concentration tool remains uncertain (but see Chapter 11, this volume). Anecdotally, however, mental imagery is used widely by performers for the purpose of focusing. Thus, Mike Atherton, the former England cricket captain, used to prepare mentally for test matches by actually going to the match venue and visualizing "who's going to bowl, how they are going to bowl . . . so that nothing can come as a surprise" (cited in Selvey, 1998, p. 2). From this quote, it seems that imagery helps performers to prepare for various hypothetical scenarios, thereby ensuring that they will not be distracted by unexpected events. However, this hypothesis has not been tested empirically to date. Therefore, despite the fact that mental imagery is known to improve athletic performance, its status as a concentration technique is uncertain.

Simulation Training

Simulation training (i.e., practising under conditions that replicate key aspects of an impending challenge) may help skilled performers to concentrate. For example, the renowned swimming coach Bob Bowman admitted deliberately breaking the goggles of Michael Phelps (who has won more Olympic gold medals than any other athlete) during practice so that he could learn to swim calmly without them if necessary in a competition. Remarkably, this later situation actually arose in the 2008 Olympics when Phelps won the 200 m butterfly event even though his goggles had been broken for the last 100 m of the race (Whitworth, 2008). Recently, Oudejans and Pijpers (2010) investigated whether simulation training helps to counteract choking behavior in athletes (i.e., a sudden and significant deterioration in athletic performance under conditions of perceived anxiety; Kremer, Moran, Walker, & Craig, 2012; see also Chapter 9, this volume). In this study by Oudejans et al. (2010), a sample of novices was assigned to one of two groups. In the experimental group, participants practiced darts throwing under experimentally induced levels of mild anxiety— achieved by requiring participants to hang high rather than low on an indoor climbing wall. In the control group, participants practised without any additional anxiety. Manipulation checks using heart rate (an index of arousal/anxiety) were conducted to ensure that the anxiety manipulation had been effective. After training, participants were tested under conditions of low, mild, and high anxiety. Results showed that despite systematic increases in anxiety, heart rate, and effort from low to mid to high anxiety, the experimental group (i.e., the one that had trained under mild anxiety) performed *equally well* on all three tests, whereas the performance of the control group *deteriorated* in the high anxiety condition. In summary, Oudejans and Pijper (2010) interpreted their results to indicate that training with mild anxiety may help to prevent performers from choking under pressure in conditions of high anxiety (see also Chapter 9, this volume).

New Directions for Research in Concentration

Based on the preceding theories, evidence, and examples, it is clear that successful skill execution in any domain requires optimal concentration on the part of the performer. What is equally clear, however, is that additional research is needed in sport and performance psychology in order to understand and develop effective concentration skills. In particular, four potentially fruitful new research directions can be specified. To begin, further research is required on the "meta-attentional" processes of athletes—their intuitive theories about how their own concentration systems work. Such research is important because concentration skills enhancement in sport psychology is really an exercise in meta-attentional training whereby athletes learn to understand, and gain some control

over, their apparently capricious concentration system. As yet, however, we know very little about the nature, accuracy, and/or malleability of athletes' theories of how their own mental processes operate. Next, we need to address the *type* of concentration skills required for success in various domains of skilled performance. Intuitively, the ability to sustain attention is vital, for example, for tennis players during a grueling match (e.g., at the 2010 Wimbledon tennis championship, the U.S.'s John Isner took 11 hours and 5 minutes to defeat France's Nicolas Mahut 6–4, 3–6, 6–7, 7–6, 70–68). A third fruitful avenue for research on attention in sport comes from cognitive neuroscience. Specifically, brain imaging techniques can provide vital insights into the neural processes that support high-level skilled performance in domains such as sport, music, and dance (e.g., see Yarrow, Brown, & Krakauer, 2009). Finally, additional theoretically driven research is needed to establish the precise mechanisms by which emotions (such as anxiety) affect athletes' concentration processes.

Conclusion

Attention, or the concentration of mental activity on the task hand, is a crucial prerequisite of success in any field of skilled performance. To begin, a distinction was made between three different cognitive dimensions of attention: concentration or effortful awareness, selective perception, and divided attention or the ability to coordinate two or more actions at the same time. Then, three key cognitive metaphors of attention were reviewed: the filter approach, capacity theory, and the spotlight metaphor. Next, the relationship between people's attentional focus (e.g., external, internal) and skilled performance was examined. After that, an investigation of why skilled performers seem to lose their concentration so easily as a result of external (i.e., environmental) and internal (i.e., self-generated thoughts and feelings) distractions was presented. Particular consideration was devoted to a theoretical model of how internal distractions arise to affect people's concentration and performance. Next, five key building blocks of effective concentration were identified. Then, five practical techniques that can help performers to improve their concentration skills were explained. Finally, I sketched some potentially fruitful new directions for research on attentional processes in skilled performers. Consideration of these new directions can enhance the progress of research in this field.

References

Aherne, C., Moran, A., & Lonsdale, C. (2011). The effects of mindfulness training on athletes' flow: An initial investigation. *The Sport Psychologist, 25*, 177–189.

Ashcraft, M. (2006). *Cognition* (4th ed.). Upper Saddle River, NJ: Pearson.

Baddeley, A. D. (1986). *Working memory*. Oxford: Clarendon Press.

Baddeley, A. (2012). Working memory: Theories, models, and controversies. *Annual Review of Psychology, 63*, 1–29.

Bannister, R. (2004, May1). "Fear of failure haunted me right to the last second." *The Guardian*, pp. 12–13 (Sport).

Bargh, J. A., & Morsella, E. (2008). The unconscious mind. *Perspectives on Psychological Science, 3*, 73–79.

Beilock, S. L., & Carr, T. H. (2001). On the fragility of skilled performance: What governs choking under pressure? *Journal of Experimental Psychology: General, 130*, 701–725.

Blau, E. (1998, October 2). Nervous issues. *The Guardian*, pp. 16–17 (Review).

Boland, R. (1999, December 4). Making magic. *The Irish Times* (Supplement), p. 6

Broadbent, D. E. (1958). *Perception and communication*. London: Pergamon Press.

Brooks, R. (2001, June 10). Nerves force ballet star Bull to quit dancing. *Sunday Times*, p. 7.

Castaneda, B., & Gray, R. (2007). Effects of focus of attention on baseball performance in players of differing skill levels. *Journal of Sport and Exercise Psychology, 29*, 60–77.

Cherry, E. C. (1953). Some experiments on the recognition of speech with one and two ears. *Journal of the Acoustical Society of America, 25*, 975–979.

Chun, M. M., Golomb, J. D., & Turk-Browne, N. B. (2011). A taxonomy of external and internal attention. *Annual Review of Psychology, 62*, 73–101.

Clarke, D., & Morris, K. (2005). *Golf—The mind factor* (p. 63). London: Hodder & Stoughton.

Cotterill, S. T., Sanders, R., and Collins, D. (2010). Developing effective pre-performance routines in golf: Why don't we ask the golfer? *Journal of Applied Sport Psychology, 22*, 51–64.

Corbetta, M., & Shulman, G. L,. (2002). Control of goal-directed and stimulus-driven attention in the brain. *Nature Reviews Neuroscience, 3*, 201–215.

Coyne, L. W., McHugh, L., & Martinez, E. R. (2011). Acceptance and Commitment Therapy (ACT): Advances and applications with children, adolescents, and families. *Child and Adolescent Psychiatric Clinics of North America, 20*, 379–399.

Damisch, L., Stoberock, B., & Musseweiler, T. (2010). Keep your fingers crossed! How superstition improves performance. *Psychological Science, 21*, 1014–1020.

Dennett, S. (1991). *Consciousness explained*. Boston: Little, Brown & Company.

Driskell, J. E., Copper, C., & Moran, A. (1994). Does mental practice enhance performance? *Journal of Applied Psychology, 79*, 481–492.

English, A. (2006). *Munster: Our road to glory*. Dublin: Penguin.

Ericsson, K. A., & Charness, N. (1994). Expert performance: Its structure and acquisition. *American Psychologist, 49*, 725–747.

Erisman, S. M., & Roemer, L. (2010). A preliminary investigation of the effects of experimentally induced mindfulness on emotional responding to film clips. *Emotion, 10*, 72–82.

Eysenck, M. W., & Keane, M. T. (2010). *Cognitive psychology: A student's handbook* (6th ed.). Hove, East Sussex, UK: Psychology Press.

Fernandez-Duque, D., & Johnson, M. L. (1999). Attention metaphors: How metaphors guide the cognitive psychology of attention. *Cognitive Science, 23*, 83–116.

Garavan, H. (1998). Serial attention in working memory. *Memory and Cognition, 26*, 263–276.

Goodbody, J., & Nichols, P. (2004, August 30). Marathon marred by invader's attack on race leader. *The Times*, p.1 (Sport).

Gouju, J. -L., Vermersch, P., & Bouthier, D. (2007). A psycho-phenomenological approach to sport psychology: The presence of the opponents in hurdle races. *Journal of Applied Sport Psychology, 19*, 173–186.

Greenlees, I., & Moran, A. (Eds.). (2003). *Concentration skills training in sport*. Leicester, UK: The British Psychological Society (Sport and Exercise Psychology Division).

Hancock, P. A., Oron-Gilad, T., & Szalma, J. L. (2007). Elaborations of the multiple-resource theory of attention. In A. F. Kramer, D. A. Wegmann, & A. Kirlik. *Attention: From theory to practice* (pp. 45–56). New York: Oxford University Press.

Hardy, J., Hall, C. R., & Hardy, L. (2005). Quantifying athlete self-talk. *Journal of Sports Sciences, 23*, 905–917.

Harmison, R. J. (2007). Peak performance in sport: Identifying ideal performance states and developing athletes' psychological skills. *Professional Psychology: Research and Practice, 37*, 233–243.

Hayes, S. C., Luoma, J., Bond, F, Masuda, A., & Lillis, J. (2006). Acceptance and Commitment Therapy: Model, processes, and outcomes. *Behaviour Research and Therapy, 44*, 1–25.

Hyde, M. (2009, July 1). Obsessive? compulsive? Order of the day at SW19. *The Guardian*, pp. 2–3 (Sport).

Jackson, R. C., & Roberts, G. C. (1992). Positive performance states of athletes: Toward a conceptual understanding of peak performance. *The Sport Psychologist, 6*, 156–171.

Jackson, R. C., & Masters, R. S. W. (2006). Ritualized behaviour in sport. *Behavioral and Brain Sciences, 29*, 621–622.

Jackson, S. A., & Kimiecik, J. C. (2008). The flow perspective of optimal experience in sport and physical activity. In T. S. Horn (Ed.), *Advances in sport psychology* (3rd ed., pp. 377–399, 474–477). Champaign, IL: Human Kinetics.

James, W. (1890). *Principles of psychology*. New York: Holt, Rinehart and Winston.

Jha, A. P., Krompinger, J., & Baime, M. J. (2007). Mindfulness training modifies subsystems of attention. *Cognitive, Affective and Behavioral Neuroscience, 7*, 109–119.

Kabat-Zinn, J. (2005). *Coming to our senses: Healing ourselves and the world through mindfulness*. New York: Hyperion.

Kahneman, D. (1973). *Attention and effort*. New York: Prentice-Hall.

Kolata, P. (2007, December 6). I'm not really running, I'm not really running… *The New York Times*. Retrieved from http://www.nytimes.com/2007/12/06/health/nutrition/06Best.html

Kremer, J., & Moran, A. (2008). *Pure sport: Practical sport psychology*. Hove, East Sussex, UK: Routledge.

Kremer, J., Moran, A., Walker, G., & Craig, C. (2012). *Key concepts in sport psychology*. London: Sage.

McElree, B. (1998). Attended and nonattended states in working memory: Accessing categorized structures. *Journal of Memory and Language, 38*, 225–252.

McRae, D. (2008, July 15). Even great players have tortured minds. *The Guardian*, p. 6 (Sport).

Martin, A. (2007, July 3). More than words: Book of Serena the answer to Williams' prayers. *The Guardian*, p. 5 (Sport).

Matlin, M. (2009). *Cognition* (7th ed.). New York: John Wiley.

Moran, A. P. (1996). *The psychology of concentration in sport performers: A cognitive analysis*. Hove, East Sussex, UK: Psychology Press.

Moran, A. P. (2003). The state of concentration skills training in applied sport psychology. In I. Greenlees & A. Moran (Eds.), *Concentration skills training in sport* (pp. 7–19). Leicester, UK: The British Psychological Society (Division of Sport and Exercise Psychology).

Moran, A. P. (2012). *Sport and exercise psychology: A critical introduction* (2nd ed.). London: Routledge.

Moran, G. (2005, July 12). "Oh dear, so near but yet so far away." *The Irish Times*, p. 21.

Muscat, J. (2005, December 28). House of horrors torments Loughran. *The Times*, p. 55.

Nadel, L., & Piattelli-Palmarini, M. (2002). What is cognitive science? In L. Nadel (Ed.), *Encyclopaedia of cognitive science* (Vol. 1, pp. xiii–xli). London: Nature Publishing Group.

Nideffer, R. (1976). Test of attentional and interpersonal style. *Journal of Personality and Social Psychology, 34*, 394–404.

Oudejans, R. R. D., & Pijpers, J. R. (2010). Training with mild anxiety may prevent choking under higher levels of anxiety. *Psychology of Sport and Exercise, 11*, 44–50.

Pashler, H. (1998). *The psychology of attention*. Cambridge, MA: MIT Press.

Posner, M. I. (1980). Orienting of attention: The VIIth Sir Frederic Bartlett lecture. *Quarterly Journal of Experimental Psychology, 32A*, 3–25.

Posner, M. I., & Rothbart, M. K. (2007). Research on attention networks as a model for the integration of a psychological science. *Annual Review of Psychology, 58*, 1–23.

Roland, D. (1997). *The confident performer*. London: Nick Hern Books.

Selvey, M. (1998, November 20). Getting up for the Ashes. *The Guardian*, p. 2 (Sport).

Sinnamon, S., Moran, A., & O'Connell, M. (2012). Flow among musicians: Measuring peak experiences of student performers. *Journal of Research in Music Education, 60*, 6–25.

Smith, E. E., & Kosslyn, S. M. (2007). *Cognitive psychology: Mind and brain*. Upper Saddle River, NJ: Pearson/Prentice-Hall.

Smith, M. (2002, February 15). Practice makes perfect. *The Daily Telegraph*, p. 3 (Sport).

Strayer, D. L., & Drews, F. A. (2007). Attention. In F. T. Durso, R. S. Nickerson, S. T. Dumais, S. Lewandowsky, & T. J. Perfect (Eds.), *Handbook of applied cognition* (2nd ed., pp. 29–54). Chichester, West Sussex, UK: Chichester.

Strayer, D. L., Drews, F. A., & Johnston, W. A. (2003). Cell-phone induced failures of visual attention during simulated driving. *Journal of Experimental Psychology: Applied, 9*, 23–32.

Velmans, M., & Schneider, S. (2007). *The Blackwell companion to consciousness*. Oxford: Blackwell.

Wegner, D. M. (1994). Ironic processes of mental control. *Psychological Review, 101*, 34–52.

Wegner, D. M. (2002). Thought suppression and mental control. In L. Nadel (Ed.), *Encyclopaedia of cognitive science* (Vol. 4, pp. 395–397). London: Nature Publishing Group.

Weinberg, R. (2008). Does imagery work? Effects on performance and mental skills. *Journal of Imagery Research in Sport and Physical Activity, 3*(1), 1–21.

White, J. (2002, June 10). Interview: Garry Sobers. *The Guardian*, pp. 20–21 (Sport).

Whitworth, D. (2008, September 13). On the waterfront. *The Times (magazine)*, pp. 20–25.

Williams, R. (2002, July 8). Sublime Serena celebrates the crucial difference. *The Guardian*, p. 6 (Sport).

Woodman, T., & Davis, P. A. (2008). The role of repression in the incidence of ironic errors. *The Sport Psychologist, 22*, 183–196.

Wulf, G. (2007). Attentional focus and motor learning: A review of 10 years of research. *Bewegung und Training, 1*, 4–14.

Wulf, G., Shea, C., & Lewthwaite, R. (2010). Motor skill learning and performance: A review of influential factors. *Medical Education, 44*, 75–84.

Yarrow, K., Brown, P., & Krakauer, J. W. (2009). Inside the brain of an elite athlete: The neural processes that support high achievement in sports. *Nature Reviews: Neuroscience, 10*, 585–596.

Conscious and Unconscious Awareness in Learning and Performance

Rich Masters

Abstract

William James stated that "every hour we make theoretic judgments and emotional reactions, and exhibit practical tendencies, for which we can give no explicit logical justification, but which are good inferences from certain premises. We know more than we can say. Our conclusions run ahead of our power to analyze their grounds" (1890, p. 168). The boundary between what is conscious and what is not conscious is often blurred, clouded by doubt. Never is this more obvious than in sport, where we learn to move and make decisions in the blink of an eye, often with little idea of whether we were even in control of what just happened. The aim of this chapter is to provide insight into the role of human consciousness in learning and performance in sport by synthesizing and contextualizing some of the relevant views of consciousness held by philosophers, psychologists, computer scientists, and neuroscientists over the years.

Key Words: Motor skill, knowledge, attention, implicit motor learning, conscious control, reinvestment, marginal perception, hypothesis testing

It is said that in 1962, as legendary Australian tennis player Rod "The Rocket" Laver was winning the Wimbledon Final, a low-flying jet roared over Centre Court, and that afterward, "The Rocket" asked "what jet?" Was his attention so focused that he was unconscious of the jet? Was he conscious of the jet, but unaware of it? Would he have become aware of the jet if it had been indicated to him? If he had been asked whether a jet had passed overhead, would he have answered yes, but thought he was guessing?

Even now, after 400 years or more of debate about the nature of human consciousness—if we date from the time of Descartes (1596–1650)—there is no unified theory of consciousness and, consequently, no single definition of what it is to be conscious: "consciousness is a word worn smooth by a million tongues" (Miller, 1962, p. 25), a "mongrel" concept (Block, 1995) that "leaves even the most sophisticated thinkers tongue-tied and confused" (Dennett, 1991, p. 21).

The language of consciousness has evolved many dialects, in literally thousands of papers that have been published on the topic. A quick search on Google Scholar (.12 sec to be exact) showed 2,100,000 articles that contained the term "consciousness" on February 17, 2012. So confused is our understanding (and I fully admit to being overwhelmed by the concept) that Miller (1962) proposed a ban on the word "consciousness" to allow our heads to clear. It is probably fair to say that discussion of consciousness in the context of sport has been trivial or at least superficial despite its obvious role in the way we acquire and perform our sport skills; however, the aim in this chapter is not to provide a detailed synopsis of consciousness in a sport context. Rather, the aim is to piece together (it would be misleading to use the term "integrate") relevant theories, views, or principles of consciousness in order to provide some insight into the role that consciousness plays in *learning* and *performance* in sport.

Early Views of Consciousness

Prior to Descartes, the ancient Greek philosophers thought that consciousness was a physical substance somewhere in the body (often the lungs) and even when it became apparent that mental processes were associated with the brain, the view persisted. Descartes, who is often described as the first of the "modern" philosophers, localized consciousness in a chamber of the brain, the pineal gland ("the seat of the soul"), but, in what has become known as mind–body dualism, he dissociated the two by conceiving the mind as a "thinking thing" and matter (i.e., the body) as an "extended thing" occupying space and consequently responsive to physical laws. In the "wax" argument, Descartes argued that the senses present us information about the characteristics of a piece of wax; it's texture, smell, and shape, yet when the wax melts, it is the mind that remains aware that it is wax despite the fact that the information from our senses no longer represents these characteristics.

William James debated the mind–body problem at length and eventually decided that consciousness does not exist as an entity, but that mental life is constructed of inner experiences that are manifested as a succession of constantly changing "states of mind" of which we can become aware—*the stream of consciousness.* James identified two important characteristics of the stream of consciousness: the ability to choose to which "objects-of-consciousness" to attend (selective attention) and *the fringe of consciousness,* in which feelings of rightness or familiarity can arise without selective attention processes. James acknowledged that introspection cannot access fully the stream of consciousness, in the same way that it is not possible to seize "a spinning top to catch its motion" (1890/1950, i, 244). In his seventh proof that unconscious mental states exist, James (1890/1950) stated that

> [M]ost of our knowledge is at all times potential. We act in accordance with the whole drift of what we have learned, but few items rise into consciousness at the time. Many of them, however, we may recall at will. All this co-operation of unrealized principles and facts, of potential knowledge, with our actual thought is quite inexplicable unless we suppose the perceptual existence of an immense mass of *ideas in an unconscious state*, all of them exerting a steady pressure and influence upon our conscious thinking. (p. 169)

Freud (e.g., 1915/1957, 1922) in many ways demoted consciousness to a "walk-on" role in human behavior by conceiving the unconscious as an active processor of repressed emotions, desires, and conflicts (especially, within the context of dreaming), allowing some and not others to reach consciousness.

Discussion stagnated until the 1970s, when Mandler (1975) is said to have reignited interest in the study of consciousness. Mandler restricted consciousness to "events and operations within a limited capacity system, with the limitation referring to the number of functional units or chunks that can be kept in consciousness at any one point in time" (p. 10). Mandler also defined attention processes more clearly as functionally specific mechanisms "that deal with the selection of objects or events that occur in consciousness" (p. 10). Mandler's views were extremely influential, providing in many ways the bedrock of the cognitive approach to consciousness—the processing of information.

Consciousness and Processing Information

Marcel (1983) conceptualized consciousness as "an attempt to make sense of as much data as possible at the most functionally useful level" (p. 238). One of the most well documented mechanisms by which it is thought that we make sense of data is a multiple component structure, *working memory* (e.g., Baddeley & Hitch, 1974),[1] which mediates thinking, reasoning, problem-solving, and hypothesis testing via rehearsal mechanisms that actively maintain information in an ordered form for brief durations or that update context and task-relevant information (e.g., Miyake & Shah, 1999; O'Reilly, Braver, & Cohen, 1999; Smith & Jonides, 1999). Working memory processes data via a central executive that directs attention,[2] and subsidiary systems that temporarily code, order, and rehearse verbal and acoustic-related information (the phonological loop); hold visual, spatial, and kinesthetic components of information (the visuospatial sketchpad); and integrate information from different sources by interfacing between the subsidiary systems and long-term memory (the episodic buffer) (e.g., Baddeley, 2000; see also Chapter 6, this volume).

Working memory is generally regarded as providing the best explanation of how we make sense of data, but it is thought of as a system that is conscious and intentional. Baars and Franklin (2003) claimed that all of the active operations of working memory are conscious, whether related to rehearsal or recall of information or its report. In most examinations of working memory, people are presented with explicit information that they are required consciously to manipulate (e.g., count, rehearse, add, subtract, etc.). Kintsch, Healy, Hegarety, Pennington, and Salthouse (1999; see also Churchland, 1995, and O'Reilly et al., 1999) argued that we are consciously aware of at least some of the information that is held in working memory at any one time, and Baddeley (2000) inferred that conscious awareness is necessary for retrieval of information from the episodic buffer when multiple sources of information are integrated during activities such as problem-solving or planning. Hassin, Bargh, Engell, and McCulloch (2009), however, used an implicit working memory paradigm to show that working memory can be used to actively extract and maintain pattern information without conscious awareness or intention.

Baars (e.g., 1997, 2003a) proposed a different architecture specifically to account for conscious and unconscious processes. *Global workspace theory* argues that the human brain has a multitude of unconscious information processors, specialized for problem-solving, language, decision-making, planning, perception, or goal setting and so on (Shanahan & Baars, 2005). The processors function independently but in parallel and can engage with other processors to access a global workspace via attention mechanisms. Information that reaches the global workspace is accessible by all of the specialist processors and is associated with consciousness. Baars argued that this architecture models the complexity of the human brain because many specialist processors can thus contribute to overall behavior. Global workspace theory is supported by imaging studies that show conscious processes cause widespread neural activation, whereas unconscious processes (such as highly automatic behaviors) cause more localized neural activation (e.g., Baars, 2002, 2003b; Dehaene & Naccache, 2001).

Surprisingly, models such as these have seldom been used as a theoretical underpinning for the study of learning and performance in sport (Memmert, 2010), although implicit motor learning theory (e.g., MacMahon & Masters, 2002; Masters, 1992), which will be discussed later in the chapter, is an exception.

Consciousness: More than Information Processing?

For many thinkers, consciousness as a reflection of merely processing data is an oversimplification. Computers process information, but they are not conscious. This is a problem that philosophers, in particular, have tussled with, and, more often than not, they have added an "extra ingredient" to the discussion, subjective experiences or *qualia* (e.g., Chalmers, 1996; Cleeremans, 2008; although Dennett, 1991, argued that consciousness arises from information processing functions alone). Block (1995), for example, proposed that perception, introspection, and recall often generate information that is access conscious (A-consciousness), available for reasoning and to control behavior. But Block included a distinction on the basis of phenomenal consciousness (P-consciousness)—"what it is like" to experience *qualia*, internal, subjective experiences of a property or perception, such as to smell cut grass or feel the pleasure of pain.[3]

It is relatively easy to conceptualize computational or neural mechanisms that attend, discriminate, integrate, order, and store information, but the "hard problem" of consciousness, as Chalmers (1995, 1996) described it, is to explain how subjective experiences are generated by these physical functions. No amount of information processing alone can fully recapture the feeling of clipping a perfect 5-iron to the heart of the green on a balmy summer evening or the experience of swishing the ball through the hoop for a 3-pointer in the dying moments of a game.

States of Consciousness

By now, it is obvious that there is more than one state of consciousness. Two modes of mental state have been discussed in the consciousness literature again and again.[4] Raichle (1994), for example, distinguished two processing pathways in the brain, one active when we learn consciously and one active when we perform automatically. Neisser (1967) described processes that are serial or parallel, and Bruner (1960) used the terms *analytic* and *intuitive* to distinguish between an easily reported step-by-step process of performance/thinking and a less progressive, unreportable process (see Dulany, 1991, 1996, for further discussion, or Tzelgov, 1997). Even Milner and Goodales' (1995, 2008; Goodale & Milner, 1992) popular view that there is one visual (ventral) system that mediates perception of objects (vision for perception) and another visual (dorsal) system that mediates visuomotor control of actions on objects (vision for action) incorporates elements of the distinction. The latter system allows remarkably accurate movement without conscious knowledge of the visual information that is used.

To trim to a manageable size discussion of these mental states (discussion of consciousness in general, in fact), this chapter takes for practical purposes the relatively loose view that there is a distinction between conscious awareness and unconscious awareness and that the influence of these states on learning and performance varies as a consequence of factors, such as individual propensity for their use, the relationship between the individual and the environment, external agencies such as the coach, and the quantity, complexity, and nature of the data to be made sense of (e.g., processed), as well as many other factors.

Dennett (1969) argued that conscious awareness occurs when the contents of consciousness can be accessed for verbal report, or at least be "made visible by language":

> [T]he improvements we install in our brain when we learn our languages permit us to review, recall, rehearse, redesign our own activities, turning our brains into echo chambers of sorts, in which otherwise evanescent processes can hang around and become objects in their own right. Those that persist the longest, acquiring influence as they persist, we call our conscious thoughts.
>
> (p. 155)

Indeed, the standard index of conscious awareness in psychology has always been our ability to *report* experiences. Conscious awareness in this context is defined by Baars (2003a) as experiences that "can be reported and acted upon...with verifiable accuracy...under optimal reporting conditions...and which are reported as conscious" (p. 4).

So, what is unconscious awareness? Mangan (2003) claimed that "at any moment, far more detailed information is potentially accessible *to* consciousness than, in fact, is actually *in* consciousness" (p. 743). This was not a new claim. Sperling's (1960) classic experiments on iconic memory attest to the possibility of unconscious awareness. Sperling presented rows of alphanumeric characters to participants, who typically could recall four or five of the characters (regardless of how many were displayed). Yet, instructions to report different portions of the display (e.g., the bottom row) indicated that many more than four or five characters were available to unconscious awareness, even if they could not be accessed in their entirety for conscious report.

The clinical condition of *blindsight* (e.g., Weiskrantz, 1986, 1997) also provides an example of what it means to be unconsciously aware. People with blindsight have lesion damage to the occipital area of the cortex, which causes them to report that they cannot see objects in sections of the visual field, yet often they can indicate the position or movements of the objects with surprising accuracy if encouraged.

Conscious or Unconscious Awareness: Which Is Better?

For many of us, complex decisions are best made on the basis of explicit, conscious deliberation and judgment, whereas for others it is better to incubate decisions (e.g., Woodworth, 1938). Incubation may be useful for a number of reasons, according to Rey, Goldstein, and Perruchet (2009). For example, interference from "wrong" solutions potentially lessens. Also, unconscious processes have an opportunity to work on the problem behind the scenes if consciousness is directed to the problem intermittently. Dijksterhuis and his colleagues argued that encouraging an "unconscious-thought effect" (e.g., Bos, Dijksterhuis, & van Baaren, 2008; Dijksterhuis, 2004; Dijksterhuis & Nordgren, 2006; Smith, Dijksterhuis, & Wigboldus, 2008) can improve complex decision-making. Typically, Dijksterhuis and colleagues present participants with a large amount of complex information that informs a number of different choices. After reading the information, participants either make a decision immediately, think consciously for a brief duration about what is the best decision, or perform a distractor task, such as counting backward, for an equivalent duration (e.g., unconscious thought condition). Dijksterhuis, Bos, van der Leij, and van Baaren (2009), for example, demonstrated that unconscious thought resulted in better predictions of soccer results by soccer experts than did conscious thought or immediate decisions.

Rey et al. (2009), however, and others (e.g., Lassiter, Lindberg, González-Vallejo, Belleza, & Phillips, 2009) queried whether Dijksterhuis' findings provide irrefutable evidence that unconscious awareness is such an effective deliberation mechanism. They found that participants asked to immediately make a decision were as accurate (or even better) than participants in an unconscious thought condition. Performance was worse when participants were required to consciously deliberate prior to making a decision than in either the immediate decision condition or the unconscious thought condition.

Why, then, might conscious deliberation disrupt performance? Some insight is gained from Wegner's concept of ironic processes of mental control (Wegner, 1994), in which people appear, much more often than might be expected, to behave contrary to their conscious intent. Wegner showed that instructions to consciously suppress a specific thought, most famously, "don't think about a white bear" (Wegner, Schneider, Carter, & White, 1987), resulted in an ironic increase in such thoughts. In numerous studies, Wegner and others showed that the thoughts lingered over hours or even days (e.g., Muris, Merckelbach, & Horselenberg, 1996; Trinder & Salkovskis, 1994; Wegner et al., 1987) and that some people were better than others at suppressing the thoughts (e.g., Nixon, Flood, & Jackson, 2007; Tolin, Abramowitz, Przeworski, & Foa, 2002). The problem, of course, is that, in order to avoid thinking of a particular subject, a person must hold knowledge of that subject in mind in order to know what thought it is that must be suppressed. For this reason, coaches should never shout "not like that" to an athlete, for the only way that the athlete can avoid "doing it like that next time" is to hold in mind what it is that he or she did wrong, which ironically increases the chances that it will occur.[5]

Wegner (1994) proposed that two mental processes are active during attempts to suppress thoughts. Conscious awareness maintains the goal of suppressing the thought (by focusing on distractions, for example), while unconscious processes monitor specifically for the unwanted thought. This system works well enough, according to Wegner (2009), until conscious awareness becomes distracted, a stressor arises, or another mental load occurs, at which point the unconscious processes actively remind us of the thought or behavior that we are supposed to be suppressing. Wegner and Erber (1992), for example, asked participants to avoid thinking about a specific target word during a word association task. Pressure to respond as rapidly as possible caused that very target word to be used as a response much more often than if participants had not been asked to avoid thinking about it. In sport performance, it is not uncommon for the same effect to occur in response to pressure to perform well. Although most golfers may be well aware of the dangers associated with an "out of bounds" fence that runs along a particular fairway, few have not at some point thought "I must not hit the ball anywhere near that fence" and few have not then struck the ball plum over the fence. Indeed, Wegner, Ansfield, and Piloff (1998) showed just this in golf putting. Golfers who were instructed not to putt past the target were more likely to do so when they tried to hold a six-digit number in conscious awareness than when they did not. Bakker, Oudejans, Binsch, and van der Kamp (2006) showed a similar phenomenon in penalty shooting in soccer, even showing

that gaze was greater to the area that participants were instructed not to think about shooting to, and Dugdale and Eklund (2002) showed that players and coaches (umpires, too) who were asked to view video of Australian Rules Football games were more likely to look at the umpire when instructed specifically to avoid doing so.

The Role of Conscious Awareness in Learning

Baars (1998) argued with considerable conviction that unconscious processes are better than conscious processes—at everything:

> Almost everything we do, we do better unconsciously than consciously. In first learning a new skill we fumble, feel uncertain, and are conscious of many details of the action. Once the task is learned, sometimes after only a few repetitions, we lose consciousness of the details, forget the painful encounter with uncertainty, and sincerely wonder why beginners seem so slow and awkward. (p. 73)

If the unconscious is so much better, it follows that consciousness should rapidly lose its hold on performance as skills are repeated, and this is typically what is seen and what most theories of learning imply (e.g., Anderson, 1982; Eversheim & Bok, 2001; Fitts & Posner, 1967; Hasher & Zacks, 1979; Kahneman & Treisman, 1984; Shiffrin & Schneider, 1977). William James (1890/1950) described this in his second proof of whether unconscious mental states exist:

> In all acquired dexterities and habits, secondarily automatic performances as they are called, we do what *originally* required a chain of deliberately conscious perceptions and volitions. As the actions still keep their intelligent character, intelligence must still preside over their execution. But since our consciousness seems all the while elsewhere engaged, such intelligence must consist of unconscious perceptions, inferences, and volitions. (p. 167)

Hasher and Zacks (1979) presented the case more simply. They argued that processing becomes less effortful and demands fewer attention resources as a consequence of learning, eventually reaching a stage of control that can occur automatically with little conscious effort and few demands for attention resources (Shiffrin & Schneider, 1977, used similar terms; controlled and automatic).[6] This final stage of learning[7] is perhaps best characterized by the fact that the "nuts and bolts" of performance can no longer be "made visible by language."[8] Kate Grenville (2005) captured the essence of automaticity in her Commonwealth Prize winning novel, *The Secret River*, when she described the life of William Thornhill, a bargeman on London's Thames River in 1806: "Sometimes he forgot that he'd ever had to learn all the things he knew" wrote Grenville (p. 28).

The involvement of consciousness in learning, especially early learning, seems to be a vital component of performance. The reason may be that conscious thought is necessary if we are to deal effectively with novel or unexpected events in the environment (Mandler, 2002), a view held by various researchers in sport (e.g., Baumeister, Hutton, & Cairns, 1990; Beek, 2000). Mandler argued that, although well-learned behaviors can be carried out without conscious involvement, conscious awareness can be invaluable if the behaviors are novel. Various studies have suggested that performers benefit from conscious awareness early in learning, but not late in learning (e.g., Beilock, Bertenthal, McCoy, & Carr, 2004; Beilock, Carr, MacMahon, & Starkes, 2002; Castaneda & Gray, 2007; Gray, 2004; Jackson, Ashford, & Norsworthy, 2006).

Hypothesis Testing

Poletiek (2001) argued that one role of consciousness is to help us "cope" with the environment, so a major function of consciousness must be hypothesis testing, the process of comparing internal thoughts with external facts in order to engage effectively with the environment. Consciousness is "a calculating machine capable of modeling or paralleling external events…, it is able to try out various alternatives, conclude which is the best of them, react to future situations before they arise, utilize the knowledge of past events in dealing with the future" (Craik, 1943, p. 61). In other words, consciousness allows us to envisage outcomes and test hypotheses about the impact of our actions on the environment, permitting "our hypotheses to die in our stead" to borrow Karl Popper's famous (1959) line.

In learning for sport, hypothesis testing occurs when learners generate movements to provide a solution to a motor problem (e.g., Guadagnoli & Lee, 2004; Miller, Galanter, & Pribram, 1960) and then evaluate the success of the solution using movement-related outcome feedback (e.g., Masters & Maxwell, 2004). Ineffective strategies are usually discarded or forgotten (although it is not uncommon in sport to see a golf swing that is a patchwork of undiscarded

movement strategies, which the owner has added one after another, each to rectify the one before). The result of all this hypothesis testing[9] is that rules and facts (explicit knowledge) accrue in long-term memory and can be reinstated in working memory (or possibly a global workspace) on future occasions to allow consciousness to control performance (Allen & Reber, 1980; Hayes & Broadbent, 1988; Maxwell, Masters, Kerr, & Weedon, 2001), often to its detriment.

The Problem with Conscious Control!

It is generally proposed that an executive mechanism directs conscious attention and has authority to override unconscious behaviors with conscious control when appropriate (e.g., Baddeley & Logie, 1999; Norman & Shallice, 1986; Schneider, Dumais, & Shiffrin, 1984). Various functions have been ascribed to the executive mechanism, including shifting, updating, and inhibition (e.g., Miyake et al., 2000; Was, 2007).

Reason and Mycielska (1982) suggested that it is oversights of inhibition that allow everyday slips-of-action to occur, in which inappropriate automated behaviors run their course. Inhibition is the deliberate suppression of automated responses (e.g., in the traditional Stroop [1935] color naming task, a person must suppress naming the color-word instead of the color of the word when the two are incongruent). In sport, David Gower, England's premier test cricket batsman during the 1980s, provides a potential example of oversights of inhibition. More often than by chance, he was "caught behind" after playing at a rising ball outside the off-stump. Gower had difficulty inhibiting this inappropriate behavior, a failing he described as "a case of acquiring more discretion with experience" (Wisden Cricketer's Almanac, 1979).[10]

It is appropriate deployment of conscious attention that prevents a catastrophe when, for example, "a person walks into the field of vision of a javelin thrower in mid throw" (Masters & Maxwell, 2008, p. 170), but equally it is inappropriate deployment of attention that can result in conscious control compromising unconscious performance. This proposition is very well documented.[11] The consensus is that, in order to gain control of performance, consciousness directs attention to the knowledge that underlies movement control, but cannot access enough of the underlying knowledge to produce efficient movement. Consequently, performance is compromised (Baumeister, 1984). This view is supported by evidence that disrupted performance is often associated with greater ability to describe low-level task-relevant knowledge (e.g., Beilock & Carr, 2001; Koedijker, Oudejans, & Beek, 2007; Liao & Masters, 2002; Poolton, Maxwell, & Masters, 2004; Smeeton, Williams, Hodges, & Ward, 2005). Additionally, Maxwell, Masters, and Eves (2000) showed that people with a personality disposition inclined toward conscious control stored a greater amount of task-relevant knowledge than did people disinclined toward conscious control.

Access to task-relevant knowledge may compromise performance by causing regression to earlier levels of control (e.g., Fitts, Bahrick, Noble, & Briggs, 1961; Fuchs, 1962; Jagacinski & Hah, 1988), possibly because only rudimentary knowledge can be recalled from storage in long-term memory and manipulated by working memory (e.g., Baddeley, 2007) to control performance.[12,13] Deschamps, Nouritt, Caillou, and Delignières (2004; see also Nourrit, Delignières, Caillou, Deschamps, & Lauriot, 2003), for example, showed that, under stress, some participants who had learned a ski simulator task temporarily regressed to a previous bistable stage of performance. Early in learning, participants typically increased the amplitude of their oscillations on the ski simulator, but the frequency of oscillations was low and injection of force in the oscillation cycle was early. With practice, participants increased the frequency of their oscillations, becoming less stiff but switching between early and late (bistable) injections of force in the oscillation cycle. Finally, as they became very skilled, participants used only late injections of force in the cycle, which conferred very large amplitude oscillations at a high frequency. Deschamps et al. (2004) showed that in some cases, stress (raising the ski simulator off the ground) caused a regression from the final stage of performance to the earlier, bistable stage.

Another way in which to conceptualize the possibility of regression is provided by *instance theory* (Logan, 1988). Initially, novices rely on unwieldy algorithms (a finite sequence of steps) to support performance, but repetition causes an accumulation of task-specific instances of performance in memory. These support fast, effortless performance because only a single step is needed to retrieve the information from memory—"there are no intervening steps or stages upon which to introspect" (Logan, 1988, p. 587). Conscious control may represent a switch from performance that is instance based to performance that relies on an algorithm.

The Theory of Reinvestment

The *theory of reinvestment*[14] (Masters, 1992; Masters, Polman, & Hammond, 1993; Masters & Maxwell, 2008) seeks to "bring under one roof" the many views of the impact of consciousness on performance (see Masters & Maxwell, 2008). The theory, which has also been called the *conscious processing hypothesis* (e.g., Hardy, Mullen, & Jones, 1996; Mullen & Hardy, 2000; Mullen, Hardy, & Oldham, 2007; Mullen, Hardy, & Tattersall, 2005; Pijpers, Oudejans, & Bakker, 2005; Pijpers, Oudejans, Holsheimer, & Bakker, 2003; Wilson, Smith, & Holmes, 2007),[15] suggests that unplanned use of task-relevant knowledge to control movement online is responsible for disrupted motor performance or deautomaticity (even in early learning, there are many automated components of a movement—e.g., Bernstein, 1969/1996; Logan, 1988; Schneider & Fisk, 1983; Schneider & Schiffrin, 1977; see also Note 7).

Operationalized as the "manipulation of conscious, explicit, rule based knowledge, by working memory, to control the mechanics of one's movements during motor output" (Maxwell & Masters, 2008, p. 208), the theory is unique in that it proposes that conscious access to task-relevant knowledge is a prerequisite for reinvestment, and that individual differences explain the proclivity to consciously access task-relevant knowledge in order to gain conscious control.

It is likely that self-regulatory mechanisms cause self-evaluations by performers of whether they are achieving personally desired standards of performance, at which point consciousness wins the competition "against other mental contents for domination in the control of behavior" (Dennett, 1996, p. 155) and gains conscious control of performance (e.g., Carver & Scheier, 1978, 1998; Duval & Wicklund, 1972; Mor & Winquist, 2002).[16] For some performers, reinvestment may be a maladaptive "problem-focused" coping method because it is used inappropriately to "manage specific external and internal demands that are appraised as taxing or exceeding the resources of the person" (Lazarus & Folkman, 1984, p. 141). For other performers, reinvestment may represent an inability to inhibit conscious control. Engle (2002) proposed that high working memory capacity is associated with greater ability to use central executive functions, such as inhibition, so it is possible that working memory capacity moderates the likelihood that reinvestment will occur. People who score high on the Reinvestment Scale or the Movement Reinvestment

Scale (Masters & Maxwell, 2008)[17] may be more vulnerable to conscious control if they have low working memory capacity and vice versa.

Evidence for reinvestment in sport and in other performance-related domains is plentiful. Pressure, derived from factors or combinations of factors that increase "the importance of performing well" (Baumeister, 1984, p. 610), has consistently been associated with reinvestment.[18] In addition, various studies have provoked reinvestment with interventions that draw attention to movements as they are performed. For example, Beilock, Carr, MacMahon, and Starkes (2002) asked golfers with highly automated putting actions either to verbally indicate the end of their putting movement or to verbally indicate when they heard a target sound that occurred randomly during the movement. Their performance was compromised by the requirement to become conscious of their movements in the former condition. Gray (2004), Ford, Hodges, and Williams (2005), and Jackson et al. (2006) showed similar effects in baseball, soccer, and hockey skills.[19]

Many other contingencies exist that can provoke reinvestment, including evaluation by others and self-presentational concerns (e.g., Baumeister, 1982; Butler & Baumeister, 1997; Law, Masters, Bray, Bardswell, & Eves, 2003; Schlenker, Phillips, Boniecki, & Schlenker, 1995), process goals (Jackson et al., 2006; Kingston & Hardy, 1994), and too much time in which to initiate performance (Liao & Masters, 2001; Singer, 2002). Beilock, Wierenga, and Carr (2002) showed that expert golf putters took longer when putting with an unusual putter, suggesting, not surprisingly, that aberrations in normally constant environmental constraints may initiate conscious control processes.

Errors in performance, even those that are trivial, also have potential to trigger conscious control processes. For example, David Gower had a reputation for batting "beautifully, until the moment he made a mistake." If England was lucky "sometimes, the mistake was put off long enough for him to play an innings of unforgettable brilliance" (Engel, 2007).

It is likely that in these circumstances conscious control processes are tripped by performers comparing their movement outcomes with their desired movement goals to identify discrepancies or errors.[20] When errors are detected, conscious processes, such as hypothesis testing, are used to explicitly modify future performance (Maxwell et al., 2001). Recent evidence supports this claim. For example, Koehn, Dickinson, and Goodman (2008) showed that processing error feedback was more cognitively demanding than processing success feedback, and Lam, Masters, and Maxwell (2010a) found that performers displayed slower probe reaction times (and longer completion times) on golf putting trials that were preceded by an error than on trials that were not preceded by an error, thus implying that consciousness was more involved in these trials. Additionally, Compton, Arnstein, Freedman, Dainer-Best, and Liss (2011; see also Carp & Compton, 2009) examined neural activity in the intertrial interval of a Stroop task following trials with correct responses or error responses. Alpha (α) power was significantly lower following trials in which errors occurred, suggesting that cortical activity was increased by processes of "mental adjustment." Cognitive demands have previously been shown to be higher for movement preparation than execution (e.g., Ells, 1973; Fischer, 1997; Holroyd, Yeung, Coles, & Cohen, 2005; see also Wilson et al., 2007), but importantly, Lam et al. found that probe reaction times were slower for both movement preparation and execution, suggesting that not only explicit hypothesis testing but also online conscious control occurs following error detection.

Other triggers of inappropriate conscious control potentially include gamesmanship (e.g., Fox & Evans, 1979; Moran, 1996; Potter, 1947); self-talk about "choking" (Leith, 1988); and injury, accident, or even boredom (Masters & Maxwell, 2008). People who are unsure of their action capabilities may also use conscious control (e.g., Heuninckx, Wenderoth, Debaere, Peeters, & Swinnen, 2005; Masters, Pall, MacMahon, & Eves, 2007), presumably to ensure that they move effectively or safely. This phenomenon generalizes to performance domains beyond sport. For example, Huffman et al. (2009) showed that conscious control was greater and modified posture more when postural threat was elevated by balancing on a high platform compared to a low platform. Additionally, Wong, Masters, Maxwell, and Abernethy (2008, 2009) showed that elderly people who had previously fallen had a much greater propensity for reinvestment, as assessed by the Movement Specific Reinvestment Scale. Similarly, Masters et al. (2007) and Orrell, Masters, and Eves (2009), respectively, found that duration of Parkinson disease and severity of stroke were associated with a greater propensity for reinvestment. Both conditions cause people to be unsure of their action capabilities. Performance history therefore plays a part in the likelihood of reinvestment. Skilled baseball batters, for example, are better at recalling the position of their bat in space following a random tone if they have a recent history of poor performance (a slump) than if they have a recent history of good performance (a streak) (Gray, 2004).

In recent work, Zhu, Poolton, Wilson, Maxwell, and Masters (2011a) claimed to have presented the first objective neuropsychological evidence for reinvestment, using electroencephalography (EEG) methodology. They showed that people with a high inclination for conscious control, as assessed by the "conscious motor processing" factor of the Movement Specific Reinvestment Scale (Masters & Maxwell, 2008) displayed significantly higher cortical co-activation (coherence) between the verbal-analytical region (T3) of the cortex and the motor planning frontal midline region (Fz) of the cortex than did people with a low inclination for conscious control. Low coherence indicates independence between regions of the cortex (e.g., Weiss & Mueller, 2003), whereas high coherence between the T3–Fz regions implies that verbal-analytical processes were actively contributing to motor performance in the high reinvesters.

Consciousness and Optimum Performance

Finding the right balance of consciousness during performance can be a constant challenge for performers. On occasion, the rawest of unconscious processes may provide a reflex volley at the net, but on the next shot a gentle lob may leave the door ajar for conscious introspection to what best shot to play and where or even how to play it most effectively. However, conscious control is often conspicuous by its absence when performers surpass their best. Csikszentmihalyi (1996) described states of "flow" in which performance is "an almost automatic, effortless, yet highly focused state of consciousness" (p. 110). Similar states have been described by Maslow (1959) and also by Tellegen and Atkinson (1974), using the terms "peak experience" and "absorption," respectively. Common characteristics are that these states involve deep immersion in performance, with no concern for success and little sense of time. The states tend also to be accompanied by positive emotional experiences (e.g., Snodgrass & Lynn, 1989; Wild, Kuiken, & Schopflocher, 1995) and low levels of self-reported conscious control (e.g., Ravizza, 1984).

Although little is known about the mechanisms that give rise to states of flow, Dietrich (2004) used the distinction between conscious and unconscious processes to explain the effortless nature of the

information processing states that are characteristic of flow during skilled performance, arguing that a conscious, explicit system has specifically evolved to provide cognitive flexibility (a similar argument is made by Baars, 1994), whereas an unconscious, implicit system has evolved to support skilled motor performance in a highly efficient manner that draws upon few cognitive resources. Dietrich argued that flow manifests as "a period during which a highly practiced skill that is represented in the implicit system's knowledge base is implemented without interference from the explicit system" (p. 746), but this only occurs when there is reduced activation of primarily the prefrontal cortex (hypofrontality). The prefrontal cortex superintends higher order cognitive control functions (e.g., Frith & Dolan, 1996; Fuster, 2000; Miller, Freedman, & Wallis, 2002), so its reduced activation causes temporary suppression of the analytical, meta-conscious capacities of the explicit system.

Suppression of the conscious, explicit system can be caused in one of two ways, according to Dietrich. On the one hand, a performer can use "volitional control over the executive attentional system...to narrow the focus of attention to exclusively buffer the task at hand" (p. 758), which reduces, but seldom eliminates, prefrontal involvement (i.e., interference from consciousness). As most performers know, whether they are athletes, musicians, surgeons, or even magicians, this is not an easy solution. On the other hand, competition for information processing (Miller & Cohen, 2001) may be so high during some performances that neural activity is inhibited in regions of the brain, such as the prefrontal cortex, to prevent unnecessary or irrelevant processing (Dietrich & Sparling, 2004)—thus, reducing interference from consciousness.[21]

Boyer and Liénard (2006) discussed the potential for suppression of prefrontal involvement in performance in a different context. Boyer and Liénard proposed that humans have evolved a "precaution system" that is designed to detect and respond to threats to fitness for survival. They argued that, in contrast to the more common view that rituals are simply routine acts performed without thinking, ritualized behaviors do not become automatic. That is, they are implemented via working memory and are "recognizable by their stereotypy, rigidity, repetition, and apparent lack of rational motivation" (p. 595). Consequently, ritualized behaviors can "swamp" working memory and provide temporary reprieve from survival debilitating conditions, such as state anxiety. Jackson and Masters (2006) extended this proposal to performance in sport by suggesting that ritualized behaviors are commonplace (often as pre-performance routines) in sport (e.g., Rafael Nadal elaborately positions and aligns his fluid bottles between games before returning to court). Jackson and Masters suggested that by swamping working memory, such rituals may provide temporary relief from competition anxiety and prevent unwarranted conscious control ("reinvestment").

A Balance Between Two Modes of Consciousness?

Baars (2003a) implied that the alliance between consciousness and unconsciousness is sometimes uneasy because we have not yet evolved an appropriate balance between two functions that are needed for survival. Consciousness is considered by many to be a valuable evolutionary adaptation that increases the human potential for survival (e.g., Baars, 1994; Freeman & Herron, 2007; see also Periera & Ricke, 2009), but it is a relatively young evolutionary characteristic (e.g., Dennett, 1991; Reber, 1992). Consequently, a seamless partnership between consciousness and unconsciousness may not yet have developed, and conscious processes may not have evolved as fully as unconscious processes. Reed, McLeod, and Dienes (2010) illustrated this lack of continuity very clearly in relation to catching a ball, which they used as a proxy for important survival skills during human evolution. They showed that catchers could not articulate why they moved backward (or forward) to make each catch, despite employing an interception strategy that changed the angle of gaze elevation by specifically moving backward or forward. Catchers were also poor at identifying descriptions of how the elevation of their gaze changed for catches, often displaying high confidence for descriptions of strategies that, if deployed, would, in evolutionary terms, have been a disaster for survival. Reed et al. concluded that "where simple solutions to important evolutionary problems exist, unconscious perception needs to be impervious to conscious beliefs" (p. 63).

Implicit Learning

Reber (1992) drew upon general heuristics of evolutionary biology (e.g., von Baer, 1828; Gould, 1977; Schank & Wimsatt, 1987) to suggest that unconscious processes are phylogenetically older than conscious processes[22] and therefore have the advantage of extended selection processes that have left them better at perceptual and cognitive functions needed for learning and performance. The advantages are that implicit (unconscious) processes are stable and robust, unrelated to age or IQ, and lower in variability than conscious processes.

On this basis, Reber (1967) proposed that unconscious learning should be possible, and advantageous, and coined the term *implicit learning*, which he defined as "the acquisition of knowledge that takes place largely independently of conscious attempts to learn and largely in the absence of explicit knowledge about what was acquired" (p. 5). Reber's classic work on artificial grammar learning, which has been replicated many times, suggested that participants' who rote-learned strings of letters generated by an underlying set of grammar rules could classify whether new strings were grammatically correct or incorrect at well above chance levels, even though they appeared to have no conscious awareness of the underlying rules (i.e., they could not report the rules). Some researchers have argued that participants do have some conscious awareness of the underlying rules, which is enough to make correct classifications (e.g., Perruchet & Pacteau, 1990). Nevertheless, Reber's work generated unprecedented interest in the role of unconscious awareness in learning, and subsequent paradigms that emerged included studies of how people learn to control complex systems (e.g., Berry & Broadbent, 1984) and how people learn repeating sequences (e.g., the serial reaction time task, Nissen & Bullemer, 1987).

Another paradigm, *continuous tracking*, has been used to examine implicit learning of motor tasks. Pew (1974) asked participants to track a target moving across a monitor in a waveform pattern that consisted of three segments of equal duration generated by a sine-cosine series function. Participants were not informed that the middle segment repeated for each trial, whereas the first and last segments were random. Participants displayed much better tracking performance on the repeated segment than on the random segments following practice, yet were not consciously aware of the repeating characteristics of the waveform, implying that they had learned implicitly (see, for replication of the findings, Boyd & Winstein, 2004; Shea, Wulf, Whitacre, & Park, 2001; Wulf & Schmidt, 1997; but see, for reappraisal of the findings, Chambaron, Ginhac, Ferrel-Chapus, & Perruchet, 2006).

Debate about implicit learning has been considerable (e.g., Cleeremans, 1993; Perruchet & Vinter, 1998, Reber, 1993; Stadler & Frensch, 1998),[23] but generally there is consensus that people can acquire knowledge of "underlying" features of a task without being aware that they are acquiring the knowledge and without therefore having conscious access to the knowledge. Reber's concept of implicit learning generates the intriguing prospect that it is possible to restrict the role of consciousness in learning and performance of ontogenetic skills in sport (and in other domains of human performance, such as surgery or music) far more than previously was thought possible.

Implicit (Motor) Learning

In early work, Masters (1992; and later Hardy et al., 1996; MacMahon & Masters, 2002; Mullen, Hardy, & Oldham, 2007, and others) used secondary task methodology to bring about implicit motor learning. By loading participants with a cognitively demanding secondary task while they tried to perform a new motor task, Masters (1992) argued that the attention and rehearsal processes of working memory would be unavailable for hypothesis testing (the primary mechanism by which task-relevant knowledge is acquired in motor learning). The secondary task paradigm restricted the temporal rate of learning, but participants displayed performance characteristics aligned with Reber's (1967, 1993) advantageous characteristics of implicit motor learning; they were able to report little about the knowledge underlying their skills, and their performance remained stable under pressure to perform well (suggesting immunity to inappropriate conscious control processes, such as reinvestment). In later work, secondary task transfer tests and probe reaction time tests were incorporated into many studies as important additional tests of the occurrence of implicit motor learning (e.g., Lam et al., 2010a; Lam, Maxwell, & Masters, 2010b; Maxwell, Masters, & Eves, 2003; Rendell, Masters, Farrow, & Morris, 2011). To rely solely on verbal reports of task-relevant knowledge as an indicator of implicit motor learning is insufficient. Shanks and St. John (1994), for example, argued that there is no convincing evidence that verbal reports index the full body of knowledge that underlies performance or that the relevant knowledge is even elicited by verbal report. Both probe reaction time tests and secondary task transfer tests provide an objective assessment of the involvement of processing resources (and thus working memory) in motor performance. Less disrupted motor performance when carrying out a secondary task and faster response times to random probes (e.g., tones) during motor performance indicates that processing resources are not so involved in conscious control of performance.

In more recent work, Masters, Maxwell, Poolton, and colleagues have examined a variety of paradigms designed to cause implicit motor learning and applied the paradigms not only to learning and performance in sport but to a variety of other domains, including surgery (e.g., Masters, Lo, Maxwell, & Patil, 2008; Masters, Poolton, Abernethy, & Patil, 2008; Zhu et al., 2011b), rehabilitation and movement disabilities (e.g., Masters, MacMahon, & Pall, 2004; Orrell, Eves, & Masters, 2006; Orrell, Eves, Masters, & MacMahon, 2007), and speech production (Tse, Masters, Whitehill, & Ma, 2012). Most of the paradigms take prevention of hypothesis testing as a departure point. For example, Maxwell et al. (2001), Masters et al. (2004), and Poolton, Masters, and Maxwell (2007) showed that motor learning is likely to be more implicit if practice at least initially occurs without errors. That is, consciousness is less likely to engage working memory in hypothesis testing if the motor solution appears to be successful. Similarly, Masters (2000) also argued that motor learning would be more implicit if a performer did not receive visual (or auditory) knowledge of results about the outcome of the movements. Maxwell et al. (2003) subsequently showed that it is not possible to test hypotheses about the effect of a particular motor solution on the environment if no information is forthcoming about its effect. In fact, in the absence of visual and auditory forms of feedback, participants became more consciously aware of kinesthetic, tactile, and proprioceptive feedback related to the success of their motor solutions (e.g., the sense of the strike or the shake in the shaft). Only when Maxwell et al. (2003) included a visual distraction task to be completed immediately subsequent to the end of each practice trial (to swamp working memory so that it could not be used to process the wealth of kinesthetic, tactile, and proprioceptive information available to the participant) did hypothesis testing diminish. Not surprisingly, given that there was no target, performance accuracy was poor. But what would happen if all-important information about the outcome of the movement (i.e., accuracy of a putt, for example, or the depth of a surgeon's incision) could be presented without reaching conscious awareness? Would consciousness be less likely to engage working memory in hypothesis testing, yet performance accuracy improve—surely resulting in a fundamental form of implicit motor learning? How might such information be provided?

Marginal Perception of Performance-Related Information

James (1890/1950) believed that what is often described as unconscious is in fact a lack of recall for conscious events that have passed too fleetingly. Humans have a remarkable ability to discriminate information provided by physical stimuli, such as weight, distance, size, light, or temperature. We can do this even when the stimuli are present beneath the threshold, or *limen*, of conscious awareness (e.g., Cheesman & Merikle, 1984, 1986). Pierce and Jastrow (1884) demonstrated this by reducing the pressure (or the brightness) of two different stimuli until people claimed to have no confidence that they could distinguish between them. Despite this apparent lack of conscious awareness of the differences in pressure (or brightness) of the stimuli, people were more accurate at distinguishing between them than expected by chance.

This phenomenon is evident in sport. Masters, van der Kamp, and Jackson (2007) found that when a soccer goalkeeper created space differences in the mouth of the goal by standing marginally off-center by as little as 0.5%,[24] penalty-takers nevertheless discriminated which side had more space at reliably above chance levels. Participants reported, however, that they were guessing. In another study, Masters et al. found that up to differences in space of approximately 3.0%, penalty-takers directed more kicks to the side with more space, without appearing to be consciously aware that the goalkeeper was standing marginally off-center. More remarkably, when Masters et al. examined video clips of penalties taken during international competitions, such as the World Cup, not only did goalkeepers inadvertently stand marginally off-center when receiving most of the penalties, but penalty-kicks were directed to the unintentionally larger space more than would be expected by chance.

Marginal Perception of Outcome Feedback During Motor Learning

It is generally accepted that information "perceived without awareness" influences how we respond to and experience subsequent stimuli (e.g., Cheesman & Merikle, 1984; Kemp-Wheeler & Hill, 1988; Marcel, 1983; Merikle, Smilek, & Eastwood, 2001; Neely, 1991). Cheesman and Merikle (1984, 1986) operationalized "awareness of a stimulus" as confidence of being able to distinguish it at greater than chance levels (i.e., not guess). They, and many others since (e.g., Greenwald, Klinger, & Schuh, 1995; Holender, 1986), demonstrated

that stimuli presented at a threshold of awareness at which participants believed that they had not detected information (i.e., a subjective threshold) influenced performance, whereas stimuli presented at an objective threshold, at which participants genuinely could not detect any information, had no influence on their performance. In typical studies, one of several target stimuli is presented for various durations using a tachistoscope. As the duration is reduced, confidence of having accurately detected the stimulus decreases until eventually observers report that they can no longer see the stimulus and are guessing its identity. At this subjective threshold, participants perform at above chance levels, despite their apparent lack of conscious awareness. If the stimulus duration is further reduced to the objective threshold, performance reduces to chance levels (the participant is truly guessing the identity of the stimulus).

Effective movement in the face of marginal or distorted (conscious) perception of the environment has been reported in different motor tasks. Mann, Abernethy, and Farrow (2010a,b; see also Mann, Ho, De Souza, Watson, & Taylor, 2007), for example, caused significant refractive visual blurring in skilled cricket batsmen (+3.00 D via contact lenses) before the batsmen displayed disrupted ability to intercept an oncoming cricket ball successfully. Additionally, Jackson, Abernethy, and Wernhart (2009) showed that, despite lacking confidence in their judgments, skilled tennis players were able to predict service direction (on a video display) even when the display was 40% blurred. People have also been shown to adapt their movements (e.g., pressure control, gait, rhythm) in response to subtle changes in load (Henry, 1953) or visual or auditory stimuli (e.g., Prokop, Schubert, & Berger, 1997; Thaut & Kenyon, 2003), of which they report a lack of awareness. Ghahramani, Wolpert, and Jordan (1996; see also Goodbody & Wolpert, 1999) used a virtual feedback system to introduce a 10 cm discrepancy between the true position of the hand and a target representing the hand's position. Participants adapted their movements to cancel out the discrepancy between visual and proprioceptive information, but postexperimental interviews revealed that they were unaware of the change in their true arm position.

Masters, Maxwell, and Eves (2009; see also Dienes & Berry, 1997) proposed that the subjective threshold may be a useful marker of implicit motor learning, demarcating a point at which explicit hypothesis testing becomes unlikely because there is no obvious external reference in the environment (i.e., target) upon which hypotheses can be tested. They asked participants to practice putting golf balls (500 trials) to a hidden target (thus removing visual knowledge of results). Knowledge of results was instead presented on a tachistoscope, which allowed the position of the final resting place of the ball relative to the hidden target to be presented for a duration that accessed conscious awareness (a supraliminal threshold, 100 ms), a duration that accessed unconscious awareness but not conscious awareness (the subjective threshold, ~11.71 ms), and a duration that was inaccessible (the objective threshold, ~7.33 ms). Participants showed significantly increased putting accuracy in the supraliminal condition, no change in the objective condition, and, remarkably, a significant increase in accuracy in the subjective threshold condition. Subsequently, the target was revealed and participants completed a transfer test, which showed that no differences in putting ability existed between those who had received knowledge of results of which they were consciously aware or of which they were consciously unaware (i.e., guessing). Participants in all conditions reported virtually no underlying knowledge of their putting performance, suggesting that even in the supraliminal condition conscious hypothesis testing was difficult (presumably because visual information about the relationship between the motor solution and the outcome was not veridically available; i.e., participants could not see the actual target).

Applications of Marginal Perception to Sport

Marginal perception potentially could be deployed for motor learning by using the phenomenon of "gradual" *change blindness*, in which observers fail to notice changes in stimuli (e.g., pictures), despite the change taking place continuously before them (e.g., Laloyaux, Devue, Doyen, David, & Cleeremans, 2008; Rensink, 2002; Rensink, O'Regan, & Clark, 1997; Simons, Franconeri, & Reimer, 2000). By adopting a constraints-led approach (e.g., Davids, Button, & Bennett, 2008), which holds that coordination patterns are a function of the unique interaction of constraints imposed on each of us by the information-rich environment with which we constantly interact, a coach might use gradual change blindness to cause unconscious (implicit) rather than conscious (explicit) adaptations of movement. For example, if a coach raises the net on a volley ball court in order to cause

an adaptation in the kinematics of the spike (e.g., to force greater vertical extension when jumping to smash the ball down over the net), players will be consciously aware that the height of the net is altered and will almost certainly engage in explicit hypothesis testing about the effects of the altered constraints on their actions. A coach could, however, raise the net marginally at each training session (using the just noticeable difference for change in the height of a volley ball net). The gradual change to this particular constraint would be likely to result in subtle adaptations of movement without conscious awareness of the underlying knowledge that drives the adaptations, and possibly without conscious awareness of the adaptations. By the time the players become conscious of the heightened net, their movements should have begun to automate.

A "Primer" for Learning and Performance in Sport

Another means by which learning and performance in sport potentially can be influenced unconsciously is by *priming*, in which residual effects of representations evoked by a prior stimulus influence behaviors (e.g., Bargh, 1994; Bruner, 1957; Ebbinghaus, 1885/1964; Higgins & 1981; Segal & Cofer, 1960). There are a variety of different forms of priming (i.e., sequential, conceptual, mindset), but one of the more common techniques (a form of conceptual priming) is the scrambled sentence test (Srull & Wyer, 1979), in which participants are asked to form grammatically correct four-word sentences from any five stimulus words. Within a portion of the sentences that they complete are target prime words designed to influence their behavior. For example, Bargh, Chen, and Burrows (1996) used target words related to being old to activate a representation of elderliness in participants. Participants were shown to walk significantly slower after priming than before priming. Importantly, participants in these tests are not aware of the potential to be influenced by the prime target words (and seldom notice that the target words are from a similar category). The primes can be presented supraliminally or subliminally, although the effects seem to be stronger for supraliminal presentation (e.g., Bargh & Chartrand, 1999). Ashford and Jackson (2010) have examined priming in sport. They used the scrambled sentence test to prime field hockey players with automaticity-related target words (e.g., movement-the-*smooth*-was-could; the movement was *smooth*). The hockey players, who were highly skilled, showed faster and more accurate dribbling performance following priming compared to both a skill-focused condition (in which their attention was directed to their movements) and a high-pressure condition. Ashford and Jackson speculated that the primes directed attention away from the mechanics of movement execution, thus reducing the likelihood that conscious control would compromise dribbling performance.[25] In a second experiment, they replicated this finding and also showed an opposite effect by priming participants to be more skill focused, using prime target words such as breakdown, poor, and slow. One implication of these findings is that priming potentially can be exploited by coaches to provide specific instructions of which performers are not consciously aware, without needing to engage the consciousness of the player by providing explicit instructions, such as "putt more fluently."

Conclusion

The intention when writing this chapter was to synthesize the literature on consciousness and summarize the role of both conscious and unconscious processes in learning and performance in sport. In retrospect, such an intention was ambitious. There simply has been too much said about consciousness, in too many ways. Consequently, there may be unintended misuse of terms within the chapter and possibly omissions, some of which I am consciously aware, some not. For example, I like to think that I consciously chose to make only fleeting reference to the rich modern literature dedicated to examination of neural correlates of consciousness—most modern scientists believe that consciousness emerges from complex patterns of neural activation (e.g., Crick, 1994; Crick & Koch, 1992; Frith & Frith, 1999; Hofstadter, 1979); "committees of cells" as Calvin (1996) describes them, overlapping and firing spatiotemporally.

What is very clear is that attempts to decipher consciousness by generations of thinkers have settled layer upon layer as sediment in the literature, each layer an archaeological time capsule rich in the thinking of that generation. This chapter almost certainly has stirred up sediment as it searches for an understanding of conscious and unconscious awareness in learning and performance, but hopefully Birkerts (1994) was correct when observing that: "a novel [chapter] . . . can become a blur to me soon after I've finished it. I recollect perfectly the feeling of reading it, the mood I occupied, but I am less sure about the narrative details. It is almost as if the book [chapter] were, as Wittgenstein said of

his propositions, a ladder to be climbed and then discarded after it has served its purpose" (p. 84).

Notes

1. The term "working memory" was first used by Miller, Galanter, and Pribram (1960) and then later by Atkinson and Shiffrin (1968) to describe a single component short-term memory store.

2. Neisser (1967) described attention as the "allotment of analyzing mechanisms to a limited region of the field" (p. 88). The term is generally used to describe selection (the processing or ignoring of specific data in the field) or alertness (readiness to act) and is viewed as being flexibly divisible among tasks if the general capacity is not exceeded (e.g., Abernethy, Maxwell, Masters, van der Kamp, & Jackson, 2007; Kahneman, 1973). The capacity is reduced dramatically if tasks require high cognitive effort (Tyler, Hertel, McCallum, & Ellis, 1979), as when we learn a new skill, which leaves only residual capacity that can be allocated to other tasks.

3. Block distinguished phenomenal consciousness from "monitoring consciousness," which is associated with thoughts about one's own thoughts or feelings or needs (similar to metacognition—Flavell, 1976).

4. Sidis (1898) may have been the first to examine the topic empirically.

5. Next time that you tell a golf partner to remember not to lift his head when teeing off, watch what happens.

6. This general argument is supported by evidence of brain activity. For example, Pascual-Leone, Grafman, and Hallett (1994; see also Raichle, 1994) used transcranial magnetic stimulation (TMS) to examine changes in the excitability of the motor cortex as people practiced a serial reaction time task (SRTT). Early in learning, the areas of cortex that showed excitability became larger as participants gained conscious control over performance, but as they became more skilled and performance became automatic, the active areas reduced dramatically.

7. Bernstein (1969/1996) was of the view that automaticity develops sooner than the final stage of learning and is followed by processes of standardization and stabilization of performance. Rapid development of motor automaticity makes sense from an evolutionary standpoint, as it would potentially free up resources for important survival-related aspects of performance, such as monitoring the environment for predators.

8. Studies using electroencephalography (EEG) power spectral analysis have shown that α power in the verbal-analytical left temporal region (T3) of the brain is higher in expert marksmen than in novices (Hatfield, Landers, & Ray, 1984; Haufler, Spalding, Santa Maria, & Hatfield, 2000) and increases with practice (Kerick, Douglass, & Hatfield, 2004), suggesting withdrawal of conscious, verbal-analytical processes as skill develops.

9. In the cognitive effort literature, this is sometimes referred to as "making decisions" in the context of deciding how to correct prior errors by adapting future movements (e.g., Lee, Swinnen, & Serrien, 1994; Sherwood & Lee, 2003).

10. A feature of attentional control theory (Eysenck, Derakshan, Santos, & Calvo, 2007) is that effective inhibition of attention can be disrupted if the efficiency of goal-directed attention is lowered by contingencies, such as pressure, which allows stimulus-driven attention to dominate performance. For the reader with a sense of déjà vu, Wegner (2009) proffers a similar explanation of how ironic processes of mental control occur, as was discussed in an earlier section.

11. For example, Bayley, Frascino, & Squire, 2005; Adam & van Wieringen, 1983; Baddeley & Woodhead, 1982; Baumeister, 1984; Baumeister & Showers, 1986; Beilock & Carr, 2001; Bliss, 1892; Boder, 1935; Dietrich, 2004; Eysenck & Keane, 1995; Freud, 1922; Gallwey, 1982; Green & Flowers, 1991; Henry & Rogers, 1960; Keele, 1973; Kimble & Perlmuter, 1970; Klatzky, 1984; Langer & Imber, 1979; Lewis & Linder, 1997; Masters, 1992; Masters & Maxwell, 2008; Masters, Polman, & Hammond, 1993; Moran, 1996; Reason & Mycielska, 1982; Schmidt, 1988; Schneider & Fisk, 1983; Singer, Lidor, & Cauraugh, 1993; Vallacher, 1993; Weinberg, 1978; Weinberg & Hunt, 1976; Willingham, 1998; Wulf, McNevin, & Shea, 2001; Wulf & Weigelt, 1997.

12. This logic may explain why novices appear to be unaffected by conscious control (e.g., Beilock et al., 2002, 2004; Castaneda & Gray, 2007; Gray, 2004; Jackson et al., 2006; but see Koedijker, Poolton, Maxwell, Oudejans, Beek, & Masters, 2011). Consciousness, restricted by a limited capacity (Baars, 1998), holds too little sophisticated knowledge to support expert performance but enough basic knowledge to support the performance of novices.

13. See also the concept of *overshadowing*, in which a requirement to describe from memory a perceptual experience (e.g., a face) disrupts later recognition of the face because verbalization relies on consciously accessible features to form the description—such features of consciousness have only limited utility for recognition performance (e.g., Melcher & Schooler, 1996; Schooler & Engstler-Schooler, 1990, see Flegal & Anderson, 2008, for a recent demonstration of overshadowing in golf putting performance).

14. *Reinvestment* is a term borrowed from Deikman (1969), who theorized that automatic, unconscious performance can be disrupted by "*reinvesting actions and percepts with attention*" (p. 31).

15. Two recent theories that are very similar are *constrained action hypothesis* (e.g., Wulf, McNevin, & Shea, 2001; see Wulf, 2007, for a review) and *explicit monitoring theory* (Beilock & Carr, 2001). The former suggests that an internal focus of attention to movements, instructed or otherwise (e.g., Landers, Wulf, Wallmann, & Guadagnioli, 2005), causes performers to "freeze" their motor system, which disrupts automatic control of the movements. The latter suggests that monitoring and controlling performance is useful in the early stages of learning but disruptive when performance has automated.

16. This process is different from distraction, during which attention becomes focused on stimuli or thoughts that are irrelevant or external to performance (e.g., Ashcraft & Kirk, 2001; Baumeister & Showers, 1986; DeCaro, Rotar, Kendra, & Beilock, 2010; Eysenck, 1979; Eysenck, 1992; Eysenck & Calvo, 1992; Kahneman, 1973; Sarason, 1980; Wine, 1971).

17. A number of psychometric instruments have been developed and validated for assessment of the proclivity for reinvestment. These include the Reinvestment Scale (Masters et al., 1993), the Movement Specific Reinvestment Scale (Masters & Maxwell, 2008), and the Decision-Specific Reinvestment Scale (Kinrade, Jackson, Ashford, & Bishop, 2010b). The Self-Consciousness Scale (Fenigstein, Scheier, & Buss, 1975), which played a prominent role in the development of all three scales, is also associated with conscious control processes.

18. For example, Baumeister & Showers, 1986; Hardy et al., 1996; Hardy, Mullen, & Martin, 2001; Huffman et al., 2009; Jackson et al., 2006; Kinrade, Jackson, & Ashford, 2010a; Kinrade, Jackson, Ashford, & Bishop, 2010b; Landers

& Boutcher, 1998; Lewis & Linder, 1997; Mullen, Hardy, & Oldham, 2007; Mullen, Hardy, & Tattersall, 2005; Pijpers et al., 2005; Pijpers et al., 2003; see Gucciardi & Dimmock, 2008; Mullen & Hardy, 2000, for exceptions.

19. Jackson et al. (2006) distinguish between the conscious monitoring of movements during performance and conscious control of the movements, suggesting that monitoring can occur independently of control. Monitoring without control may occur during episodes of "flow" (Csikszentmihalyi, 1996; Dietrich, 2004), which describe effortless yet focused performance undisrupted by consciousness.

20. See also *conflict monitoring hypothesis* (Botvinick, Nystrom, Fissell, Carter, & Cohen, 1999; Carter, Braver, Barch, Botvinick, Noll, & Cohen, 1998; MacDonald, Cohen, Stenger, & Carter, 2000).

21. Csikszentmihalyi (1996) described characteristics of flow that appear to reflect the potential suppression of prefrontal involvement. For example, states of "flow" are accompanied by reduced concerns about failing (the prefrontal cortex handles cultural values and belief systems), performers often have a distorted sense of time (temporal integration is a prefrontal function), and performers lose self-consciousness (a sophisticated function attributed to the prefrontal cortex).

22. There is little doubt that conscious processes have evolved recently. Archaeological studies show no evidence of metacognitive functions in the prefrontal lobe (e.g., planning, strategizing, attention, decision making, etc.) in prehistoric humans (Ardila, 2008), suggesting that these forms of consciousness are mediated by recent culturally developed "conceptualization instruments," language being the most obvious.

23. Frensch (1998) listed 11 different definitions of implicit learning.

24. This was the just noticeable difference (jnd) or difference limen, expressed using Weber's fraction; Δ in space between the two sides/total space × 100.

25. Donker, Roerdink, Greven, and Beek (2007) showed a similar effect in a postural sway task. Participants who were asked to stand with their eyes closed displayed less stability and greater center-of-pressure variability than when standing with their eyes open. However, when participants performed a cognitive secondary task while standing with their eyes closed, stability and center-of-pressure variability matched the eyes-open condition, reflecting normal, automatic postural control. Donker et al. argued that standing with eyes closed caused participants to consciously monitor and control their posture, but that this was prevented by the secondary task.

References

Abernethy, B., Maxwell, J., Masters, R. S. W., van der Kamp, J., & Jackson, R. (2007). Attentional processes in skill learning and expert performance. In G. Tenenbaum & R. C. Eklund (Eds.), *Handbook of sport psychology* (3rd ed., pp. 245–263). Hoboken, NJ: John Wiley.

Adam, J. J., & van Wieringen, P. C. W. (1983). Relationship between anxiety and performance on two aspects of a throwing task. *International Journal of Sport Psychology, 14*, 174–185.

Allen, R., & Reber, A. S. (1980). Very long term memory for tacit knowledge. *Cognition, 8*, 175–185.

Anderson, J. R. (1982). Acquisition of cognitive skill. *Psychological Review, 89*, 369–406.

Ardila, A. (2008). On the evolutionary origins of executive functions. *Brain and Cognition, 68*, 92–99.

Ashcraft, M., & Kirk, P. (2001). The relationships amongst working memory, math anxiety, and performance. *Journal of Experimental Psychology: General, 130*, 224–237.

Ashford, K. J., & Jackson, R. C. (2010). Priming as a means of preventing skill failure under pressure. *Journal of Sport and Exercise Psychology, 32*, 518–536.

Atkinson, R. C., & Shiffrin, R. M. (1968). Human memory: A proposed system and its control processes. In K. W. Spence (Ed.), *The psychology of learning and motivation: Advances in research and theory* (pp. 89–195). New York: Academic Press.

Baars, B. J. (1994). A global workspace theory of consciousness experience. In A. Revonsuo & M. Kamppinen (Eds.), *Consciousness in philosophy and cognitive neuroscience* (pp. 149–171). Hillsdale, NJ: Lawrence Erlbaum.

Baars, B. J. (1997). *In the theater of consciousness: The workspace of the mind.* New York: Oxford University Press.

Baars, B. J. (1998). *A cognitive theory of consciousness.* New York: Cambridge University Press.

Baars, B. J. (2002). The conscious access hypothesis: Origins and recent evidence. *Trends in Cognitive Science, 6*, 47–52.

Baars, B. J. (2003a). Introduction: Treating consciousness as a variable: The fading taboo. In B. J. Baars, W. P. Banks, & J. B. Newman (Eds.), *Essential sources in the scientific study of consciousness* (pp. 1–10). Cambridge, MA: Bedford Books.

Baars, B. J. (2003b). How brain reveals mind: Neuroimaging supports the central role of conscious experience. *Journal of Consciousness Studies, 10*, 100–114.

Baars, B. J., & Franklin, S. (2003). How conscious experience and working memory interact. *Trends in Cognitive Science, 7*, 166–172.

Baddeley, A. D. (2000). The episodic buffer: A new component of working memory? *Trends in Cognitive Sciences, 4*, 417–423.

Baddeley, A. D. (2007). *Working memory, thought and action.* Oxford, UK: Oxford University Press.

Baddeley, A. D., & Hitch, G. (1974). Working memory. In G. A. Bower (Ed.), *Recent advances in learning and motivation* (Vol. 8, pp. 47–90). New York: Academic Press.

Baddeley, A. D., & Logie, R. H. (1999). The multiple component model. In A. Miyake & P. Shah (Eds.), *Models of working memory: Mechanisms of active maintenance and executive control* (pp. 28–61). Cambridge, UK: Cambridge University Press.

Baddeley, A. D., & Woodhead, M. M. (1982). Depth of processing, context and face recognition. *Canadian Journal of Psychology, 36*, 148–164.

Bakker, F. C., Oudejans, R. R. D., Binsch, O., & Van der Kamp, J. (2006). Penalty shooting and gaze behavior: Unwanted effects of the wish not to miss. *International Journal of Sport Psychology, 37*, 265–280.

Bargh, J. A. (1994). The four horsemen of automaticity: Awareness, efficiency, intention, and control in social cognition. In R. S. Wyer, Jr. & T. K. Srull (Eds.), *Handbook of social cognition* (2nd ed., pp. 1–40). Hillsdale, NJ: Lawrence Erlbaum.

Bargh, J. A., & Chartrand, T. (1999). The unbearable automaticity of being. *American Psychologist, 54*, 462–479.

Bargh, J. A., Chen, M., & Burrows, L. (1996). Automaticity of social behavior: Direct effects of trait construct and stereotype activation on action. *Journal of Personality and Social Psychology, 71*, 230–244.

Baumeister, R. F. (1982). A self-presentational view of social phenomena. *Psychological Bulletin, 91*, 3–26.

Baumeister, R. F. (1984). Choking under pressure: Self-consciousness and paradoxical effects of incentives on skillful performance. *Journal of Personality and Social Psychology, 46*, 610–620.

Baumeister, R. F., Hutton, D. G., & Cairns, K. J. (1990). Negative effects of praise on skilled performance. *Basic and Applied Social Psychology, 11*, 131–148.

Baumeister, R. F., & Showers, C. J. (1986). A review of paradoxical performance effects: Choking under pressure in sports and mental tests. *European Journal of Social Psychology, 16*, 361–383.

Bayley, P. J., Frascino, J. C., & Squire, L. R. (2005). Robust habit learning in the absence of awareness and independent of the medial temporal lobe. *Nature, 436*, 550–553.

Beek, P. J. (2000). Toward a theory of implicit learning in the perceptual-motor domain. *International Journal of Sport Psychology, 31*, 547–554.

Beilock, S. L., Bertenthal, B. I., McCoy, A. M. & Carr, T. H. (2004). Haste does not always make waste: Expertise, direction of attention and speed versus accuracy in performing sensorimotor skills. *Psychonomic Bulletin & Review, 11*, 373–379.

Beilock, S. L., & Carr, T. H. (2001). On the fragility of skilled performance: What governs choking under pressure? *Journal of Experimental Psychology: General, 130*, 701–725.

Beilock, S. L., Carr, T. H., MacMahon, C., & Starkes, J. L. (2002). When paying attention becomes counterproductive: Impact of divided versus skill-focused attention on novice and experienced performance of sensorimotor skills. *Journal of Experimental Psychology: Applied, 8*, 6–16.

Beilock, S. L., Wierenga, S. A., & Carr, T. H. (2002). Expertise, attention, and memory in sensorimotor skill execution: Impact of novel task constraints on dual-task performance and episodic memory. *The Quarterly Journal of Experimental Psychology, 55A*, 1211–1240.

Bernstein, N. A. (1969/1996). On dexterity and its development. In M. L. Latash & M. T. Turvey (Eds.), *Dexterity and its development* (pp. 3–246). Mahwah, NJ: Lawrence Erlbaum.

Berry, D., & Broadbent, D. (1984). On the relationship between task performance and associated verbalizable knowledge. *Quarterly Journal of Experimental Psychology, 36(A)*, 209–231.

Birkerts, S. (1994). *The Gutenberg elegies: The fate of reading in an electronic age.* Boston: Faber & Faber.

Butler, J. L., & Baumeister, R. F. (1997). The trouble with friendly faces: Skilled performance with a supportive audience. *Journal of Personality and Social Psychology, 75*, 1213–1230.

Bliss, C. B. (1892). Investigations in reaction time and attention. *Studies from the Yale Psychology Laboratory, 1*, 1–55.

Block, N. (1995). On a confusion about a function of consciousness. *Behavioural and Brain Sciences, 18*, 227–247.

Boder, D. P. (1935). The influence of concomitant activity and fatigue upon certain forms of reciprocal hand movements and its fundamental components. *Comparative Psychology Monographs, 11*, 4.

Bos, M. W., Dijksterhuis, A., & van Baaren, R. B. (2008). On the goal-dependency of unconscious thought. *Journal of Experimental Social Psychology, 44*, 1114–1120.

Botvinick, M. M., Nystrom, L. E., Fissell, K., Carter, C. S., & Cohen, J. D. (1999). Conflict monitoring versus selection-for-action in anterior cingulate cortex. *Nature, 402*, 179–181.

Boyd, L. A., & Winstein, C. J. (2004). Providing explicit information disrupts implicit motor learning after basal ganglia stroke. *Learning and Memory, 11*, 388–396.

Boyer, P., & Liénard, P. (2006). Why ritualized behavior? Precaution systems and action parsing in developmental, pathological and cultural rituals. *Behavioral and Brain Sciences, 29*, 595–650.

Bruner, J. S. (1957). On perceptual readiness. *Psychological Review, 64*, 123–152.

Bruner, J. S. (1960). *The process of education.* Cambridge, UK: Harvard University Press.

Calvin, W. H. (1996). *How brains think: Evolving intelligence, then and now.* New York: Basic Books.

Carp, J., & Compton, R. J. (2009). Alpha power is influenced by performance errors. *Psychophysiology, 46*, 336–343.

Carter, C. S., Braver, T. S., Barch, D. M., Botvinick, M. M., Noll, D., & Cohen, J. D. (1998). Anterior cingulate cortex, error detection, and the online monitoring of performance. *Science, 280*, 747–749.

Carver, C. S., & Scheier, M. F. (1978). Self-focusing effects of dispositional self-consciousness, mirror presence and audience presence. *Journal of Personality and Social Psychology, 36*, 324–332.

Carver, C. S., & Scheier, M. F. (1998). *On the self-regulation of behavior.* New York: Cambridge University Press.

Castaneda, B., & Gray, R. (2007). Effects of focus of attention on baseball batting performance in players of differing skill levels. *Journal of Sport and Exercise Psychology, 29*, 60–77.

Chalmers, D. J. (1995). Facing up to the problem of consciousness. *Journal of Consciousness Studies, 2*, 200–219.

Chalmers, D. J. (1996). *The conscious mind: In search of a fundamental theory.* New York: Oxford University Press.

Chambaron, S., Ginhac, D., Ferrel-Chapus, C., & Perruchet, P. (2006). Implicit learning of a repeated segment in continuous tracking: A reappraisal. *Quarterly Journal of Experimental Psychology, 59A*, 845–854.

Cheesman, J., & Merikle, P. M. (1984). Priming with and without awareness. *Perception and Psychophysics, 36*, 387–395.

Cheesman, J., & Merikle, P. M. (1986). Distinguishing conscious from unconscious perceptual processes. *Canadian Journal of Psychology, 40*, 343–367.

Churchland, P. M. (1995). *The engine of reason, the seat of the soul.* Cambridge, MA: MIT Press.

Cleeremans, A. (1993). *Mechanisms of implicit learning: Connectionist models of sequence processing.* Cambridge, MA: MIT Press.

Cleeremans, A. (2008). Consciousness: The radical plasticity thesis. *Progress in Brain Research, 168*, 19–33.

Compton, R. J., Arnstein, D., Freedman, G., Dainer-Best, J., & Liss, A. (2011). Cognitive control in the intertrial interval: Evidence from EEG alpha power. *Psychophysiology, 48*, 583–590.

Craik, K. (1943). *The nature of explanation.* Cambridge, UK: Cambridge University Press.

Crick, F. H. (1994). *The astonishing hypothesis: The scientific search for the soul.* New York: Scribner.

Crick, F. H., & Koch, C. (1992, September). The problem of consciousness, *Scientific American*, 111–117.

Csikszentmihalyi, M. (1996). *Creativity.* New York: Harper Perennial.

Davids, K., Button, C., & Bennett, S. (2008). *Dynamics of skill acquisition: A constraints-led approach.* Champaign, IL: Human Kinetics.

DeCaro, M. S., Rotar, K. E., Kendra, M. S., & Beilock, S. L. (2010). Diagnosing and alleviating the impact of performance pressure on mathematical problem solving. *Quarterly Journal of Experimental Psychology, 63A*, 1619–1630.

Dehaene, S., & Naccache, L. (2001). Towards a cognitive neuroscience of consciousness: Basic evidence and a workspace framework. *Cognition, 79*, 1–37.

Deikman, A. J. (1969). Deautomatization and the mystic experience. In C. T. Tart (Ed.), *Altered states of consciousness* (pp. 23–43).New York: Wiley.

Dennett, D. C. (1969). *Content and consciousness.* London: Routledge.

Dennett, D. C. (1991). *Consciousness explained.* Boston: Little Brown.

Dennett, D. C. (1996). *Kinds of minds: Towards an understanding of consciousness.* New York: Perseus.

Deschamps, T., Nouritt, D., Caillou, N., & Delignières, D. (2004). Influence of a stressing constraint on stiffness and damping functions of a ski simulator's platform motion. *Journal of Sports Sciences, 22*, 867–874.

Dienes, Z., & Berry, D. (1997). Implicit learning: The subjective threshold. *Psychonomic Bulletin and Review, 4*, 3–23.

Dietrich, A. (2004). Neurocognitive mechanisms underlying the experience of flow. *Consciousness and Cognition, 13*, 746–761.

Dietrich, A., & Sparling, P. B. (2004). Endurance exercise selectively impairs prefrontal-dependent cognition. *Brain and Cognition, 55*, 516–524.

Dijksterhuis, A. (2004). Think different: The merits of unconscious thought in preference development and decision making. *Journal of Personality and Social Psychology, 87*, 586–598.

Dijksterhuis, A., Bos, M. W., Nordgren, L. F., & van Baaren, R. B. (2006). On making the right choice: The deliberation-without-attention effect. *Science, 311*, 1005–1007.

Dijksterhuis, A., Bos, M. W., van der Leij, A., & van Baaren, R. B. (2009). Predicting soccer matches after unconscious and conscious thought as a function of expertise. *Psychological Science, 20*, 1381–1387.

Donker, S. F., Roerdink, M., Greven, A. J., & Beek, P. J. (2007). Regularity of center-of-pressure trajectories depends on the amount of attention invested in postural control. *Experimental Brain Research, 181*, 1–11.

Dugdale, J. R., & Eklund, R. C. (2002). Do not pay any attention to the umpires: Thought suppression and task-relevant focusing strategies. *Journal of Sport and Exercise Psychology, 24*, 306–319.

Dulany, D. E. (1991). Conscious representation and thought systems. In R. S. Wyer & T. K. Srull (Eds.), *Advances in social cognition* (pp. 91–120). Hillsdale, NJ: Erlbaum.

Dulany, D. E. (1996). Consciousness in the explicit (deliberate) and the implicit (evocative). In J. Cohen & J. Schooler (Eds.), *Scientific approaches to consciousness* (pp. 179–212). Hillsdale, NJ: Erlbaum.

Duval, S., & Wicklund, R. A. (1972). *A theory of objective self-awareness.* New York: Academic Press.

Ebbinghaus, H. (1885/1964). *Memory: A contribution to experimental psychology.* Mineola, NY: Dover.

Ells, J. G. (1973). Analysis of temporal and attentional aspects of movement control. *Journal of Experimental Psychology, 99*, 10–21.

Engel, M. (2007). Player profile: David Gower. *Wisden Cricketer's Almanack.* London: John Wisden & Co. Retrieved

November 15, 2010, from http://www.espncricinfo.com/ci/content/player/13418.html

Engle, R. W. (2002). Working memory capacity as executive control. *Current Directions in Psychological Science, 11*, 19–23.

Eversheim, U., & Bok, O. (2001). Evidence for processing stages in skill acquisition: A dual-task study. *Learning and Memory, 8*, 183–189.

Eysenck, M. W. (1992). *Anxiety: The cognitive perspective*. Hove, UK: Lawrence Erlbaum.

Eysenck, M. W., & Calvo, M. G. (1992). Anxiety and performance: The processing efficiency theory. *Cognition and Emotion, 6*, 409–434.

Eysenck, M. W., Derakshan, N., Santos, R., & Calvo, M. G. (2007). Anxiety and cognitive performance: Attentional control theory. *Emotion, 7*, 336–353.

Eysenck, M. W., & Keane, M. T. (1995). *Cognitive psychology: A student's handbook* (3rd ed.). Hove, UK: Lawrence Erlbaum.

Fenigstein, A., Scheier, M. F., & Buss, A. H. (1975). Public and private self-consciousness: Assessment and theory. *Journal of Consulting and Clinical Psychology, 43*, 522–527.

Fischer, M. H. (1997). Attention allocation during manual movement preparation and execution. *European Journal of Cognitive Psychology, 9*, 17–51.

Fitts, P. M, Bahrick, H., Noble, M., & Briggs, G. (1961). *Skilled performance*. New York: Wiley.

Fitts, P. M., & Posner, M. I. (1967). *Human performance*. Belmont, CA: Brooks/Cole.

Flavell, J. H. (1976). Metacognitive aspects of problem solving. In L. B. Resnick (Ed.), *The nature of intelligence* (pp. 231–236). Hillsdale, NJ: Erlbaum.

Flegal, K. E., & Anderson, M. C. (2008). Overthinking skilled motor performance: Or why those who teach can't do. *Psychonomic Bulletin and Review, 15*, 927–932.

Ford, P., Hodges, N. J., & Williams, A. M. (2005). On-line attentional-focus manipulations in a soccer dribbling task: Implications for the proceduralization of motor skills. *Journal of Motor Behavior, 37*, 386–394.

Fox, A., & Evans, R. (1979). *If I'm the better player, why can't I win?* Kentfield, CA: Adidas Tennis Camps.

Freeman, S., & Herron, J. C. (2007). *Evolutionary analysis*. Upper Saddle River, NJ: Pearson Education.

Frensch, P. A. (1998). One concept, multiple meanings? On how to define the concept of implicit learning. In M. A. Stadler & P. A. Frensch (Eds.), *Handbook of implicit learning* (pp. 47–104). New York: Sage.

Freud, S. (1915/1957). The unconscious. In J. Strachey (Ed., Trans.), *The standard edition of the complete psychological works of Sigmund Freud* (Vol. 14). London: Hogarth Press.

Freud, S. (1922). *Introductory lectures on psychoanalysis*. London: George Allen & Unwin.

Frith, C. D., & Dolan, R. (1996). The role of the prefrontal cortex in higher cognitive functions. *Cognitive Brain Research, 5*, 175–181.

Frith, C. D. & Frith, U. (1999). Interacting minds: A biological basis. *Science, 286*, 1692–1695.

Fuchs, A. H. (1962). The progression-regression hypothesis in perceptual-motor skill learning. *Journal of Experimental Psychology, 63*, 177–182.

Fuster, J. M. (2000a). Executive frontal functions. *Experimental Brain Research, 133*, 66–70.

Gallwey, W. T. (1982). *The inner game of tennis*. New York: Bantam Books.

Ghahramani, Z., Wolpert, D. M., & Jordan, M. I. (1996). Generalization to local remappings of the visuomotor coordinate transformation. *Journal of Neuroscience, 16*, 7085–7096.

Goodale, M. A., & Milner, A. D. (1992). Separate visual pathways for perception and action. *Trends in Neuroscience, 15*, 20–25.

Goodbody, S. J., & Wolpert, D. M. (1999). The effect of visuomotor displacements on arm movement paths. *Experimental Brain Research, 127*, 213–223.

Gould, S. J. (1977). *Ontogeny and phylogeny*. Cambridge, MA: Harvard University Press.

Gray, R. (2004). Attending to the execution of a complex sensorimotor skill: Expertise differences, choking, and slumps. *Journal of Experimental Psychology: Applied, 10*, 42–54.

Green T. D., & Flowers, J. H. (1991). Implicit versus explicit learning processes in a probabilistic, continuous fine-motor catching task. *Journal of Motor Behavior, 23*, 293–300.

Greenwald, A. G., Klinger, M. R., & Schuh, E. S. (1995). Activation by marginally perceptible ('subliminal') stimuli: Dissociation of unconscious from conscious cognition. *Journal of Experimental Psychology: General, 124*, 22–42.

Grenville, K. (2005). *The secret river*. Edinburgh: Canongate.

Guadagnioli, M. A., & Lee, T. (2004). Challenge point: A framework for conceptualizing the effects of various practice conditions in motor learning. *Journal of Motor Behavior, 36*, 212–224.

Gucciardi, D. F., & Dimmock, J. A. (2008). Choking under pressure in sensorimotor skills: Conscious processing or depleted attentional resources? *Psychology of Sport and Exercise, 9*, 45–59.

Hardy, L., Mullen, R., & Jones, G. (1996). Knowledge and conscious control of motor actions under stress. *British Journal of Psychology, 87*, 621–636.

Hardy, L., Mullen, R., & Martin, N. (2001). Effect of task-relevant cues and state anxiety upon motor performance. *Perceptual and Motor Skills, 92*, 943–946.

Hasher, L., & Zacks, R. T. (1979). Automatic and effortful processes in memory. *Journal of Experimental Psychology: General, 108*, 356–388.

Hassin, R. R., Bargh, J. A., Engell, A., & McCulloch, K. C. (2009). Implicit working memory. *Consciousness and Cognition, 18*, 665–678.

Hatfield, B. D., Landers, D. M., & Ray, W. J. (1984). Cognitive processes during self-paced motor performance: An electroencephalographic profile of skilled marksmen. *Journal of Sport Psychology, 6*, 42–59.

Haufler, A. J., Spalding, T., Santa Maria, D. L., & Hatfield, B. D. (2000). Neuro-cognitive activity during a self-paced visuospatial task: Comparative EEG profiles in marksmen and novice shooters. *Biological Psychology, 53*, 131–160.

Hayes, N. A. & Broadbent, D. E. (1988). Two modes of learning for interactive tasks. *Cognition, 28*, 249–276.

Henry, F. M. (1953). Dynamic kinaesthetic perception and adjustment. *Research Quarterly, 24*, 176–187.

Henry, F. M., & Rogers, D. E. (1960). Increased response latency for complicated movements and a 'memory drum' theory of neuromotor reaction. *Research Quarterly, 31*, 448–458.

Heuninckx, S., Wenderoth, N., Debaere, F., Peeters, R., & Swinnen, S. P. (2005). Neural basis of aging: The penetration of cognition into action control. *Journal of Neurosciences, 25*, 6787–6796.

Higgins, E. T., & King, G. A. (1981). Accessibility of social constructs: Information-processing consequences of individual and contextual variability. In N. Cantor & J. F. Kihlstrom (Eds.), *Personality, cognition, and social interaction* (pp. 69–122). Hillsdale, NJ: Erlbaum.

Hofstadter, D. R. (1979). *Godel, Escher, Bach: An eternal golden braid*. New York: Penguin Books.

Holender, D. (1986). Semantic activation without conscious identification in dichotic listening, parafoveal vision, and visual masking: A survey and appraisal. *The Behavioural and Brain Sciences, 9*, 1–66.

Holroyd, C. B., Yeung, N., Coles, M. G. H., & Cohen, J. D. (2005). A mechanism for error detection in speeded response time tasks. *Journal of Experimental Psychology: General, 19*, 163–191.

Huffman, J. L., Horslen, B. C., Carpenter, M. G., & Adkin, A. L. (2009). Does increased postural threat lead to more conscious control of posture? *Gait & Posture, 30*, 528–532.

Jackson, R. C., Abernethy, B., & Wernhart, S. (2009). Sensitivity to fine-grained and coarse visual information: The effect of blurring on anticipation skill. *International Journal of Sport Psychology, 40*, 461–475.

Jackson, R. C., Ashford, K. J., & Norsworthy, G. (2006). Attentional focus, dispositional reinvestment, and skilled motor performance under pressure. *Journal of Sport and Exercise Psychology, 28*, 49–68.

Jackson, R. C., & Beilock, S. L. (2007). Performance pressure and paralysis by analysis: Research and implications. In D. Farrow, J. Baker, & C. MacMahon (Eds.), *Developing elite sports performers: Lessons from theory to practice* (pp. 104–118). London: Routledge.

Jackson, R. C., & Masters, R. S. W. (2006). Ritualized behavior in sport. *Behavioral and Brain Sciences, 29*, 621–622.

Jagacinski, R. J., & Hah, S. (1988). Progression-regression effects in tracking repeated experiments. *Journal of Experimental Psychology: Human Perception and Performance, 14*, 77–88.

James, W. (1890/1950). *The principles of psychology*. New York: Holt, Rinehart & Winston.

Kahneman, D. (1973). *Attention and effort*. Englewood Cliffs, NJ: Prentice-Hall.

Kahneman, D., & Treisman, A. (1984). Changing views of attention and automaticity. In R. Parasuraman & R. Davies (Eds.), *Varieties of attention* (pp. 29–61). New York: Academic Press.

Keele, S. W. (1973). *Attention and human performance*. Pacific Palisades, CA: Goodyear.

Kemp-Wheeler, S. M., & Hill, A. B. (1988). Semantic priming without awareness: Some methodological considerations and replications. *Quarterly Journal of Experimental Psychology, 40A*, 671–692.

Kerick, S. E., Douglas, L., & Hatfield, B. D. (2004). Cerebral cortical adaptations associated with visuomotor practice. *Medicine and Sciences in Sport and Exercise, 36*, 118–129.

Kimble, G. A., & Perlmuter, L. C. (1970). The problem of volition. *Psychological Review, 77*, 361–384.

Kingston, K., & Hardy, L. (1994). When some goals are more beneficial than others? *Journal of Sports Sciences, 10*, 610–611.

Kinrade, N. P., Jackson, R. C., & Ashford, K. J. (2010a). Dispositional reinvestment and skill failure in cognitive and motor tasks. *Psychology of Sport and Exercise, 11*, 312–319.

Kinrade, N. P., Jackson, R. C., Ashford, K. J. & Bishop, D. T. (2010b). Development and validation of the Decision-Specific Reinvestment Scale. *Journal of Sports Sciences, 28*, 1127–1135.

Kintsch, W., Healy, A., Hegerety, M., Pennington, B., & Salthouse, T. (1999). Eight questions and some general issues. In A. Miyake & P. Shah (Eds.), *Models of working memory: Mechanisms of active maintenance and executive control* (pp. 412–441). New York: Cambridge University Press.

Klatzky, R. L. (1984). *Memory and awareness: An information-processing perspective*. New York: W. H. Freeman.

Koedijker, J. M., Poolton, J. M., Maxwell, J. P., Oudejans, R. R. D., Beek, P. J., & Masters, R. S. W. (2011). Attention and time constraints in perceptual-motor learning and performance: Instruction, analogy, and skill level. *Consciousness and Cognition, 20*, 245–256.

Koedijker, J. M., Oudejans, R. R. D., & Beek, P. J. (2007). Explicit rules and direction of attention in learning and performing the table tennis forehand. *International Journal of Sport Psychology, 38*, 227–244.

Koehn, J. D., Dickinson, J., & Goodman, D. (2008). Cognitive demands of error processing. *Psychological Reports, 102*, 532–538.

Laloyaux, C., Devue, C., Doyen, S., David, E., & Cleeremans, A. (2008). Undetected changes in visible stimuli influence subsequent decisions. *Consciousness and Cognition, 17*, 646–656.

Lam, W. K., Masters, R. S. W., & Maxwell, J. P. (2010a). Cognitive demands of error processing associated with preparation and execution of complex movement. *Consciousness and Cognition, 19*, 1058–1061.

Lam, W. K., Maxwell, J. P., & Masters, R. S. W. (2010b). Probing the allocation of attention in implicit [motor] learning. *Journal of Sport Sciences, 28*, 1543–1554.

Landers, D. M., & Boutcher, S. H. (1998). Arousal-performance relationships. In J. M. Williams (Ed.), *Applied sport psychology: Personal growth to peak performance* (3rd ed., pp. 197–218). Mountain View, CA: Mayfield.

Landers, M., Wulf, G.,Wallmann, H., & Guadagnoli, M. A. (2005). An external focus of attention attenuates balance impairment in Parkinson's disease. *Physiotherapy, 91*, 152–185.

Langer, E. J., & Imber, L.G. (1979). When practice makes imperfect: Debilitating effects of overlearning. *Journal of Personality and Social Psychology, 37*, 2014–2024.

Lassiter G. D., Lindberg M. J., González-Vallejo C., Bellezza F. S., & Phillips N. D. (2009). The deliberation-without-attention effect: Evidence for an artifactual interpretation. *Psychological Science, 20*, 671–675.

Law, J., Masters, R. S. W., Bray, S., Bardswell, I., & Eves, F. (2003). Motor performance as a function of audience affability and metaknowledge. *Journal of Sport and Exercise Psychology, 25*, 484–500.

Lazarus, R. S., & Folkman, S. (1984). *Stress, appraisal, and coping*. New York: Springer.

Lee, T. D., Swinnen, S. P., & Serrien, D. J. (1994). Cognitive effort and motor learning. *Quest, 46*, 328–344.

Leith, L. M. (1988). Choking in sports: Are we our own worst enemies. *International Journal of Sport Psychology, 19*, 59–64.

Lewis, B. P., & Linder, D. E. (1997). Thinking about choking? Attentional processes and paradoxical performance. *Personality and Social Psychology Bulletin, 23*, 937–944.

Liao, C. H., & Masters, R. S. W. (2001). Analogy learning: A means to implicit motor learning. *Journal of Sports Sciences, 19*, 307–319.

Liao, C. M., & Masters, R. S. W. (2002). Self-focused attention and performance failure under psychological stress. *Journal of Sport and Exercise Psychology, 24,* 289–305.

Logan, G. D. (1988). Toward an instance theory of automatization. *Psychological Review, 95,* 492–527.

MacDonald, A. W., III, Cohen, J. D., Stenger, V. A., & Carter, C. S. (2000). Dissociating the role of the dorsolateral prefrontal and anterior cingulate cortex in cognitive control. *Science, 288,* 1835–1838.

MacMahon, K. M. A. & Masters, R. S. W. (2002). Implicit motor learning: A suppression solution? *International Journal of Sports Psychology, 33,* 307–324.

Mandler, G. (1975). Consciousness: Respectable, useful, and probably necessary. In R. L. Solso (Ed.), *Information processing and cognition: The Loyola symposium* (pp. 229–254). Hillsdale, NJ: Lawrence Erlbaum.

Mandler, G. (2002). *Consciousness recovered: The functions and origins of conscious thought.* Amsterdam, NL: John Benjamins.

Mangan, B. (2003). The conscious "fringe": Bringing William James up to date. In B. J. Baars, W. P. Banks, & J. B. Newman (Eds.), *Essential sources in the scientific study of consciousness* (pp. 741–760). Cambridge, MA: MIT Press.

Mann, D. L., Abernethy, B., & Farrow, D. (2010a). The resilience of natural interceptive actions to refractive blur. *Human Movement Science, 29,* 386–400.

Mann, D. L., Abernethy, B., & Farrow, D. (2010b). Visual information underpinning skilled anticipation: The effect of blur on a coupled and uncoupled in-situ anticipatory response. *Attention, Perception, & Psychophysics, 72*(5), 1317–1326.

Mann, D. L., Ho, N., De Souza, N., Watson, D., & Taylor, S. (2007). Is optimal vision required for the successful execution of an interceptive task? *Human Movement Science, 26,* 343–356.

Marcel, A. J. (1983). Conscious and unconscious perception: An approach to the relations between phenomenal experience and perceptual processes. *Cognitive Psychology, 15,* 238–300.

Maslow, A. H. (1959). Cognition of being in the peak experiences. *Journal of Genetic Psychology, 94,* 43–66.

Masters, R. S. W. (1992). Knowledge, knerves and know-how: The role of explicit versus implicit knowledge in the breakdown of a complex motor skill under pressure. *British Journal of Psychology, 83,* 343–358.

Masters, R. S. W. (2000). Theoretical aspects of implicit learning in sport. *International Journal of Sport Psychology, 31,* 530–541.

Masters, R. S. W., Lo, C. Y., Maxwell, J. P. & Patil, N. G. (2008). Implicit motor learning in surgery: Implications for multitasking. *Surgery, 143,* 140–145.

Masters, R. S. W., MacMahon, K. M. A., & Pall, H. S. (2004). Implicit motor learning in Parkinson's disease. *Rehabilitation Psychology, 49,* 79–82.

Masters, R. S. W., & Maxwell, J. P. (2004). Implicit motor learning, reinvestment and movement disruption: What you don't know won't hurt you. In A. M. Williams & N. J. Hodges (Eds.), *Skill acquisition in sport: Research, theory and practice* (pp. 207–228). London: Routledge.

Masters, R. S. W., & Maxwell, J. P. (2008). The theory of reinvestment. *International Review of Sport and Exercise Psychology, 1,* 160–183.

Masters, R. S. W., Maxwell, J. P., & Eves, F. F. (2009). Marginally perceptible outcome feedback, motor learning and implicit processes. *Consciousness and Cognition, 18,* 639–645.

Masters, R. S. W., Pall, H. S., MacMahon., K. M. A., & Eves, F. F. (2007). Duration of Parkinson disease is associated with an increased propensity for 'reinvestment'. *Neurorehabilitation and Neural Repair, 21,* 123–126.

Masters, R. S. W., Polman, R. C. J., & Hammond, N. V. (1993). "Reinvestment": A dimension of personality implicated in skill breakdown under pressure. *Personality and Individual Differences, 14,* 655–666.

Masters, R. S. W., Poolton, J. M., Abernethy, B., & Patil, N. G. (2008). The implicit learning of movement skills for surgery. *ANZ Journal of Surgery, 78,* 1062–1064

Masters, R. S. W., Poolton, J. M., & Maxwell, J. P. (2008). Stable implicit motor processes despite aerobic locomotor fatigue. *Consciousness and Cognition, 17,* 335–338.

Masters, R. S. W., van der Kamp, J., & Jackson, R. C. (2007). Imperceptibly off-center goalkeepers influence penalty-kick direction in soccer. *Psychological Science, 18,* 222–223.

Maxwell, J. P., Masters, R. S. W., & Eves, F. F. (2000). From novice to know-how: A longitudinal study of implicit motor learning. *Journal of Sports Sciences, 18,* 111–120.

Maxwell, J. P., Masters, R. S. W., & Eves, F. F. (2003). The role of working memory in motor learning and performance. *Consciousness and Cognition, 12,* 376–402.

Maxwell, J. P., Masters, R. S. W., Kerr, E., & Weedon, E. (2001). The implicit benefit of learning without errors. *The Quarterly Journal of Experimental Psychology, 54A,* 1049–1068.

Memmert, D. (2010). The role of working memory in sport. *International Review of Sport and Exercise Psychology, 3,* 171–194.

Merikle, P. M., Smilek, D., & Eastwood, J. D. (2001). Perception without awareness: Perspectives from cognitive psychology. *Cognition, 79,* 115–134.

Miller, E. K., & Cohen, J. D. (2001). An integrative theory of prefrontal cortex function. *Annual Review of Neuroscience, 24,* 167–202.

Miller, E. K., Freedman, D. J., & Wallis, J. D. (2002). The prefrontal cortex: Categories, concepts and cognition. *Philosophical Transactions of the Royal Society of London, Series B, Biological Sciences, 357,* 1123–1136.

Miller, G. (1962). *The science of mental life.* Gretna, LA: Pelican Books.

Miller, G., Galanter, E., & Pribram, K. H. (1960). *Plans and the structure of behavior.* New York: Holt, Rinehart & Winston.

Milner, A. D., & Goodale, M. A. (1995). *The visual brain in action.* Oxford, UK: Oxford University Press.

Milner, A. D., & Goodale, M. A. (2008). Two visual systems re-viewed. *Neuropsychologia, 46,* 774–785.

Miyake, A., Friedman, N. P., Emerson, M. J., Witzki, A. H., Howerter, A., & Wager, T. D. (2000). The unity and diversity of executive functions and their contributions to complex "frontal lobe" tasks: A latent variable analysis. *Cognitive Psychology, 41,* 40–100.

Miyake, A., & Shah, P. (1999). Toward unified theories of working memory: Emerging general consensus, unresolved theoretical issues and future directions. In A. Miyake & P. Shah (Eds.), *Models of working memory: Mechanisms of active maintenance and executive control* (pp. 28–61). Cambridge, UK: Cambridge University Press.

Mor, N., & Winquist, J. (2002). Self-focused attention and negative affect: A meta-analysis. *Psychological Bulletin, 128,* 638–662.

Moran, A. P. (1996). *The psychology of concentration in sport performance: A cognitive analysis.* Hove, UK: Psychology Press.

Mullen, R., & Hardy, L. (2000). State anxiety and motor performance: Testing the conscious processing hypothesis. *Journal of Sports Sciences, 18*, 785–799.

Mullen, R., Hardy, L., & Oldham, T. (2007). Implicit and explicit control of motor actions: Revisiting some early evidence. *British Journal of Psychology, 98*, 141–156.

Mullen, R., Hardy, L., & Tattersall, A. (2005). The effects of anxiety on motor performance: A test of the conscious processing hypothesis. *Journal of Sport and Exercise Psychology, 27*, 212–225.

Muris, P., Merckelbach, H., & Horselenberg, R. (1996). Individual differences in thought suppression. The White Bear Suppression Inventory: Factor structure, reliability, validity and correlates. *Behaviour Research and Therapy, 34*, 501–513.

Neely, J. H. (1991). Semantic priming effects in visual word recognition: A selective review of current findings and theories. In D. Besner & G. Humphreys (Eds.), *Basic processes in reading: Visual word recognition* (pp. 264–336). Hillsdale, NJ: Erlbaum.

Neisser, U. (1967). *Cognitive psychology*. New York: Appleton, Century, Crofts.

Nissen, M. J., & Bullemer, P. (1987). Attentional requirements of learning: Evidence from performance measures. *Cognitive Psychology, 19*, 1–32.

Nixon, R. D. V., Flood, J., & Jackson, K. (2007). The generalizability of thought suppression ability to novel stimuli. *Personality and Individual Differences, 42*, 677–687.

Norman, D. A., & Shallice, T. (1986). Attention to action: Willed and automatic control of behaviour. In R. J. Davidson, G. E. Schwarts, & D. Shapiro (Eds.), *Consciousness and self-regulation: Advances in research and theory* (Vol. 4, pp. 1–18). New York: Plenum.

Nourrit, D., Delignières, D., Caillou, N., Deschamps, T., & Lauriot, B. (2003). On discontinuities in motor learning: A longitudinal study of complex skill acquisition on a ski-simulator. *Journal of Motor Behavior, 35*, 151–170.

O'Reilly, R., Braver, T., & Cohen, J. D. (1999). A Biologically based computational model of working memory. In A. Miyake & P. Shah (Eds.), *Models of working memory: Mechanisms of active maintenance and executive control* (pp. 375–411). New York: Cambridge University Press.

Orrell, A. J., Eves, F. F., Masters, R. S. W., & MacMahon, K. M. A. (2007). Implicit sequence learning processes after unilateral stroke. *Neuropsychological Rehabilitation, 17*, 335–354.

Orrell, A. J., Eves, F. F. & Masters, R. S. W. (2006). Motor learning of a dynamic balancing task after stroke: Implicit implications for stroke rehabilitation. *Physical Therapy, 86*, 369–380.

Orrell, A., Masters, R. S. W., & Eves, F. F. (2009). Reinvestment and movement disruption following stroke. *Neurorehabilitation and Neural Repair, 23*, 177–183.

Pascual-Leone, A., Grafman, J., & Hallett, M. (1994). Modulation of cortical motor output maps during development of implicit and explicit knowledge. *Science, 263*, 1287–1289.

Pereira, A., Jr., & Ricke, H. (2009). What is consciousness?: Towards a preliminary definition. *Journal of Consciousness Studies, 16*, 28–45.

Perruchet, P., & Pacteau, C. (1990). Synthetic grammar learning: Implicit rule abstraction or explicit fragmentary knowledge? *Journal of Experimental Psychology: General, 119*, 264–275.

Perruchet, P., & Vinter, A. (1998). Learning and development. The implicit knowledge assumption reconsidered. In M. A. Stadler & P. A. Frensch (Eds.), *Handbook of implicit learning* (pp. 495–531). Thousand Oaks, CA: Sage.

Pew, R. W. (1974). Levels of analysis in motor control. *Brain Research, 71*, 393–400.

Pierce, C. S., & Jastrow, J. (1884). On small differences in sensation. *Memoirs of the National Academy of Sciences, 3*, 73–83.

Pijpers, J. R., Oudejans, R. R., & Bakker, F. C. (2005). Anxiety-induced changes in movement behaviour during the execution of a complex whole-body task. *Quarterly Journal of Experimental Psychology, 58A*, 421–445.

Pijpers, J. R., Oudejans, R. R., Holsheimer, F., & Bakker, F. C. (2003). Anxiety-performance relationships in climbing: A process-oriented approach. *Psychology of Sport and Exercise, 4*, 283–304.

Poletiek, F. (2001). *Hypothesis-testing behavior*. Hove, UK: Psychology Press.

Poolton, J. M., Masters, R. S. W., & Maxwell, J. P. (2007). Passing thoughts on the evolutionary stability of implicit motor behaviour: Performance retention under physiological fatigue. *Consciousness and Cognition, 16*, 456–468.

Poolton, J. M., Maxwell, J. P., & Masters, R. S.W. (2004). Rules for reinvestment. *Perceptual and Motor Skills, 99*, 771–774.

Popper, K. R. (1959). *The logic of scientific enquiry*. New York: Basic Books.

Potter, S. (1947). *The theory and practice of gamesmanship*. Harmondsworth, Middlesex, UK: Penguin.

Prokop, T., Schubert, M., & Berger, W. (1997). Visual influence on human locomotion. *Experimental Brain Research, 114*, 63–70.

Raichle, M. K. (1994). Images of the mind: Studies in modern imaging techniques. *Annual Review of Psychology, 45*, 333–356.

Ravizza, K. (1984). Qualities of the peak experience. In J. M. Silva & R. S. Weinberg (Eds.), *Psychological foundations of sport* (pp. 452–461). Champaign, IL: Human Kinetics.

Reason, J., & Mycielska, K. (1982). *Absent-minded? The psychology of mental lapses and everyday errors*. Englewood Cliffs, NJ: Prentice-Hall.

Reber, A. S. (1967). Implicit learning of artificial grammars. *Journal of Verbal Learning and Verbal Behavior, 6*, 855–863

Reber, A. S. (1992). An evolutionary context for the cognitive unconscious. *Philosophical Psychology, 5*, 33–51.

Reber, A. S. (1993). *Implicit learning and tacit knowledge: An essay on the cognitive unconscious*. New York: Oxford University Press.

Reed, N., McLeod, P., & Dienes, Z. (2010). Implicit knowledge and motor skill: What people who know how to catch don't know. *Consciousness and Cognition, 19*, 63–76.

Rendell, M., Masters, R. S. W., Farrow, D., & Morris, T. (2011). An implicit basis for the retention benefits of random practice. *Journal of Motor Behavior, 43*, 1–13.

Rensink, R. A. (2002). Change detection. *Annual Review of Psychology, 53*, 245–277.

Rensink, R. A., O'Regan, J. K., & Clark, J. J. (1997). To see or not to see: The need for attention to perceive changes in scenes. *Psychological Science, 8*, 368–373.

Rey, A., Goldstein, R. M., & Perruchet, P. (2009). Does unconscious thought improve complex decision making? *Psychological Research, 73*, 372–379

Sarason, I. G. (1980). Introduction to the study of test anxiety. In I. G. Sarason (Ed.), *Test anxiety: Theory, research, and application* (pp. 3–14). Hillsdale, NJ: Lawrence Erlbaum.

Schank, J. C., & Wimsatt, W. C. (1987). Generative entrenchment and evolution. In A. Fine & P. Machamer (Eds.), *PSA 1986: Proceedings of the meetings of the philosophy of science association* (Vol. 7, pp. 33–60). East Lansing, MI: Philosophy of Science Association.

Schlenker, B. R., Phillips, S. T., Boniecki, K. A., & Schlenker, D. R. (1995). Championship pressures: Choking or triumphing in one's own territory? *Journal of Personality and Social Psychology, 68*, 632–641.

Schmidt, R. A. (1988). *Motor control and learning: A behavioral emphasis* (2nd ed.). Champaign, IL: Human Kinetics.

Schneider, W., Dumais, S. T., & Shiffrin, R. M. (1984). Automatic and controlled processing and attention. In R. Parasuraman & D. R. Davies (Eds.), *Varieties of attention* (pp. 1–27). New York: Academic Press.

Schneider, W., & Fisk, A. D. (1983). Attention theory and mechanisms for skilled performance. In R. A. Magill (Ed.), *Memory and control of action* (pp. 119–143). Amsterdam: North-Holland Publishing.

Schneider, W., & Schiffrin, R. M. (1977). Controlled and automated human information processing: I: Detection, search and attention. *Psychological Review, 44*, 627–644.

Schooler, J. W., & Engstler-Schooler, T. Y. (1990). Verbal overshadowing of visual memories: Some things are better left unsaid. *Cognitive Psychology, 22*, 36–71.

Segal, S. J., & Cofer, C. N. (1960). The effect of recency and recall on word association. *American Psychologist, 15*, 451.

Shanahan, M., & Baars, B. (2005). Applying global workspace theory to the frame problem. *Cognition, 98*, 157–176.

Shanks, D. R., & St. John, M. F. (1994). Characteristics of dissociable human learning systems. *Behavioral and Brain Sciences, 17*, 367–447.

Shea, C. H., Wulf, G., Whitacre, C. A., & Park, J. H. (2001). Surfing the implicit wave. *Quarterly Journal of Experimental Psychology, 54A*, 841–862.

Sherwood, D. E., & Lee, T. D. (2003). Schema theory: Critical review and implications for the role of cognition in a new theory of motor learning. *Research Quarterly for Exercise and Sport, 74*, 376–382.

Shiffrin, R. M., & Schneider, W. (1977). Controlled and automatic human information processing: II. Perceptual learning, automatic attending, and a general theory. *Psychological Review, 84*, 127–190.

Sidis, B. (1898). *The psychology of suggestion: A research into the subconscious nature of man and society.* New York: Appleton.

Simons, D. J., Franconeri, S. L., & Reimer, R. L. (2000). Change blindness in the absence of a visual disruption. *Perception, 29*, 1143–1154.

Singer, R. N., Lidor, R., & Cauraugh, J. H. (1993). To be aware or not aware: What to think about while learning and performing a motor skill. *The Sport Psychologist, 7*, 19–30.

Singer, R. S. (2002). Preperformance state, routines and automaticity: What does it take to realise expertise in self-paced events? *Journal of Sport and Exercise Psychology, 24*, 359–375.

Smeeton, N., Williams, A. M., Hodges, N., & Ward, P. (2005). The relative effectiveness of various instructional approaches in developing anticipation skill. *Journal of Experimental Psychology: Applied, 11*, 98–110.

Smith, E. E, & Jonides, J. (1999). Storage and executive processes in the frontal lobes. *Science, 283*, 1657–1661.

Smith, P. K., Dijksterhuis, A., & Wigboldus, D. H. J. (2008). Powerful people make good decisions even when they consciously think. *Psychological Science, 19*, 1258–1259.

Snodgrass, M., & Lynn, S. J. (1989). Music absorption and hypnotizability. *International Journal of Clinical and Experimental Hypnosis, 37*, 41–54.

Sperling, G. (1960). The information available in brief visual presentations. *Psychological Monographs: General and Applied, 74*, 1–30.

Srull, T. K., & Wyer, R. S. (1979). The role of category accessibility in the interpretation of information about persons: Some determinants and implications. *Journal of Personality and Social Psychology, 10*, 1660–1672.

Stadler, M., & Frensch. P. (1998). *Handbook of implicit learning.* Thousand Oaks, CA: Sage.

Stroop, J. R. (1935). Studies of interference in serial verbal reactions. *Journal of Experimental Psychology, 18*, 643–662.

Tellegen, A., & Atkinson, G. (1974). Openness to absorbing and self-altering experiences ("absorption"), a trait related to hypnotic susceptibility. *Journal of Abnormal Psychology, 83*, 268–277.

Thaut, M. H., & Kenyon, G. P. (2003). Rapid motor adaptations to subliminal frequency shifts during syncopated rhythmic sensorimotor synchronization. *Human Movement Science, 22*, 321–338.

Tolin, D. F., Abramowitz, J. S., Przeworski, A., & Foa, E. B. (2002). Thought suppression in obsessive-compulsive disorder. *Behaviour Research and Therapy, 40*, 1255–1274.

Trinder, H., & Salkovskis, P. M. (1994). Personally relevant intrusions outside the laboratory: Long-term suppression increases intrusion. *Behaviour Research and Therapy, 32*, 833–842.

Tse, A. C. Y., Masters, R. S. W., Whitehill, T., & Ma, E. P. M. (2012). The use of analogy in speech motor learning. *International Journal of Speech-Language Pathology, 14*, 84–90.

Tyler, S. W., Hertel, P. T., McCallum, M. C., & Ellis, H. C. (1979). Cognitive effort and memory. *Journal of Experimental Psychology: Human Learning and Memory, 5*, 607–617.

Tzelgov, J. (1997). Specifying the relations between automaticity and consciousness: A theoretical note. *Consciousness and Cognition, 6*, 441–451.

Vallacher, R. R. (1993). Mental calibration: Forging a working relationship between mind and action. In D. M. Wenger & J. W. Pennebaker (Eds.), *Handbook of mental control.* Englewood Cliffs, NJ: Prentice Hall.

von Baer, E. K. (1828). *Entwicklungsgeschichte der thiere: Beobachtung und reflexion.* Königsberg, BY: Bornträger.

Was, C. A. (2007). Further evidence that not all executive functions are equal. *Advances in Cognitive Psychology, 3*, 399–407.

Wegner, D. M. (1994).Ironic processes of mental control. *Psychological Review, 101*, 34–52.

Wegner, D. M. (2009). How to think, say or do precisely the worst thing for any occasion. *Science, 325*, 48–50.

Wegner, D. M., Ansfield, M., & Piloff, D. (1998). The putt and the pendulum: Ironic effects of the mental control of action. *Psychological Science, 9*, 196–199.

Wegner, D. M., & Erber, R. (1992). The hyperaccessibility of suppressed thoughts. *Journal of Personality and Social Psychology, 63*, 903–912.

Wegner, D. M., Schneider, D. J., Carter, S., & White, L. (1987). Paradoxical effects of thought suppression. *Journal of Personality and Social Psychology, 53*, 5–13.

Weinberg, R. S. (1978). The effects of success and failure on the patterning of neuromuscular energy. *Journal of Motor Behavior, 10*, 53–61.

Weinberg, R. S., & Hunt, V. V. (1976). The interrelationships between anxiety, motor performance and electromyography. *Journal of Motor Behavior, 8*, 219–224.

Weiskrantz, L. (1986). *Blindsight: A case study and implications.* Oxford, UK: Oxford University Press.

Weiskrantz, L. (1997). *Consciousness lost and found.* Oxford, UK: Oxford University Press.

Weiss, S., & Mueller, H. M. (2003). The contribution of EEG coherence to the investigation of language. *Brain and Language, 85*, 325–343.

Wild, T. C., Kuiken, D., & Schopflocher, D. (1995). The role of absorption in experiential involvement. *Journal of Personality and Social Psychology, 69*, 569–579.

Willingham, D. B. (1998). A neuropsychological theory of motor skill learning. *Psychological Review, 105*, 558–584.

Wilson, M., Smith, N. C., & Holmes, P.S. (2007). The role of effort in influencing the effect of anxiety on performance: Testing the conflicting predictions of processing efficiency theory and the conscious processing hypothesis. *British Journal of Psychology, 98*, 411–428.

Wine, J. D. (1971). Test anxiety and the direction of attention. *Psychological Bulletin, 76*, 92–104.

Wisden Cricketer's Almanack. (1979). *Cricketer of the year, David Gower.* London: John Wisden & Co. Retrieved November 15, 2010, from http://www.espncricinfo.com/wisdenalmanack/content/story/154487.html

Woodworth, R. S. (1938). *Experimental psychology.* New York: Holt, Rinehart, Winston.

Wong, W. L., Masters, R. S. W., Maxwell, J. P., & Abernethy, B. A. (2008). Reinvestment and falls in community-dwelling older adults. *Neurorehabilitation and Neural Repair, 22*, 410–414.

Wong, W. L., Masters, R. S. W., Maxwell, J. P., & Abernethy, B. (2009). The role of reinvestment in walking and falling in community-dwelling older adults. *Journal of the American Geriatrics Society, 57*, 920–922.

Wulf, G. (2007). *Attention and motor skill learning.* Champaign, IL: Human Kinetics.

Wulf, G., McNevin, N., & Shea, C. H. (2001). The automaticity of complex motor skill learning as a function of attentional focus. *The Quarterly Journal of Experimental Psychology, 54A*, 1143–1154.

Wulf, G., & Schmidt, R. (1997). Variability of practice and implicit motor learning. *Journal of Experimental Psychology: Learning, Memory, and Cognition, 23*, 987–1006.

Wulf, G., & Weigelt, C. (1997). Instructions in learning a complex motor skill: To tell or not to tell. *Research Quarterly for Exercise and Sport, 68*, 362–367.

Zhu, F. F., Poolton, J. M., Wilson, M. R., Hu, Y., Maxwell, J. P., & Masters, R. S. W. (2011b). Implicit motor learning promotes neural efficiency during laparoscopy. *Surgical Endoscopy and Other Interventional Techniques, 25*, 2950–2955.

Zhu, F. F., Poolton, J. M., Wilson, M. R., Maxwell, J. P., & Masters, R. S. W. (2011a). Neural co-activation as a yardstick of implicit motor learning and the propensity for conscious control of movement. *Biological Psychology, 87*, 66–73.

Emotion Regulation and Performance

Marc V. Jones

Abstract

Sport is an ideal environment in which to explore the influence of emotion on performance and the efficacy of strategies to regulate emotions. In performance settings such as sport, emotions are important at a group level and at an individual level, influencing physical functioning, cognitive functioning, motivation, and, ultimately, performance. The emotional responses to performance settings can be aligned with specific cardiovascular changes into identifiable challenge and threat states with particular performance consequences. A number of strategies to regulate emotions are outlined based on Gross' model, and the development of the ability to regulate emotions is discussed along with individual differences that influence the use, and efficacy, of emotion regulation strategies. Although regulating emotions may help achieve the most suitable emotional state for competition, the possible cost of engaging in this process for performance on subsequent tasks is discussed. The chapter concludes with potential areas for future research.

Key Words: Affect, mood, regulation, challenge, threat, self-control, athletes, performers, arousal

Sport is an ideal performance environment in which to study emotion. The role emotion plays in sport is often illustrated by the archetypal image of an athlete *choking*—snatching defeat from the jaws of victory. But emotions can also help athletes perform well. Emotions also play a role in behavior away from the competition arena, influencing motivation and performance in training and how athletes experience and manage injury and retirement from their sport. For psychologists interested in helping athletes deal with the challenge of competitive sport and maximize potential, an understanding of emotion is clearly advantageous. Although helping athletes achieve their potential is a worthy endeavor in its own right, the study of emotion in sport is also important because it can provide lessons that are applicable to other performance settings in which tasks are also difficult and achievement is important to the individual, such as education, the performing arts, and business.

Sport is an ideal environment within which to study emotion for three reasons. First, the sporting environment creates intense emotions that may otherwise be difficult to manufacture. Athletes are typically highly motivated to succeed. However, success is not guaranteed, and the emotions experienced cover a spectrum from the joy of victory to the dejection of defeat. Second, with athletes often well matched on physical and technical aspects, the ability to regulate emotions is central to success (Uphill, McCarthy, & Jones, 2009). Third, sport has a wide range of performance environments that test abilities as diverse as physical prowess, effort, courage, technique, reaction time, and complex decision-making and is an excellent context within which to explore how emotions influence a range of performance aspects. Even minor fluctuations in each aspect may result in substantial changes in performance and outcome. For example, a slight alteration in a golfer's putting stroke from an increase in anxiety-induced muscular tension may be the difference between a successful or unsuccessful putt.

In summary, there is much to be gained from understanding how emotions arise and the impact they may have on performance in sport, and this knowledge is applicable to a wide range of performance environments. In the first part of this chapter, the nature of emotions is explored in detail; the second part outlines how emotions relate to performance; and the third integrates physiological responses to competition with emotions and performance consequences. The fourth section considers techniques for regulating emotions, discusses the development of strategies in this regard, and notes individual differences in emotion regulation ability. The fifth section explores how individuals deal with emotions after performance, and the chapter concludes with a consideration of areas for future research.

Understanding Emotion

Defining emotion is a difficult task, given the range and complexity of different states it must describe. Yet, having a clear definition of emotion, and in particular how it may differ from the similar constructs of mood and affect, is necessary to provide a framework for understanding how emotions influence performance and how emotions can be regulated.

What Is Emotion?

Emotion is a response to an event or stimulus, for example, pride at winning a gold medal, happiness at scoring a goal, anger at a barbed comment from an opponent. In contrast, *mood* is proposed to be a more enduring state, less intense than an emotion, in which the individual does not know the causes of feelings experienced (Jones, Mace, & Williams, 2000; Parkinson, Totterdell, Briner, & Reynolds, 1996). Despite these distinctions, the boundaries between mood and emotion are blurred, and, in particular, the experience of mood and emotion may be very similar to a person unable to distinguish between feelings triggered in response to specific events and those already present as part of an underlying mood state (Lane & Terry, 2000). Although mood and emotions describe specific feeling states, *affect* is typically used in the literature as a broad term referring to all valenced responses including preferences, emotions, and moods (Ekkekakis & Petruzzello, 2000; Rosenberg, 1998).

Although precise definitions of emotion vary among researchers, Fredrickson (2001) suggests there is a consensus that an emotion is a cognitively appraised response to an event, either conscious or unconscious, which "triggers a cascade of response tendencies manifest across loosely coupled component systems, such as subjective experience, facial expression, cognitive processing and physiological changes" (p. 218). Some researchers also emphasize a behavioral aspect (e.g., action tendencies) in the emotional response (e.g., Gross, 1998). To illustrate, imagine a soccer player who perceives he has been punished unfairly by the referee. The soccer player may experience an increase in heart rate, muscular tension, feel angry, scowl, and remonstrate with the referee.

Knowledge about the characteristics of emotion facilitates an understanding of how emotions may impact behavior and ultimately performance. Of particular importance in understanding emotional regulation is an awareness of how emotions arise. This makes it possible to prevent, or at least limit, the intensity of emotions unhelpful to performance while generating, and increasing the intensity, of those helpful to performance. A number of theories of emotion explain how emotions arise in sport settings (for reviews, see Crocker, Kowalski, Graham, & Kowalski, 2002; Jones & Uphill, 2004; Kerr, 1997; Vallerand & Blanchard, 2000). This chapter focuses on one specific approach; Lazarus' *cognitive-motivational-relational theory* (CMRT; Lazarus, 1991, 1999, 2000a,b).

Lazarus' CMRT was chosen as the illustrative approach for five reasons. First, CMRT outlines how discrete emotions arise, in contrast to the dimensional approaches of affect (e.g., Watson & Tellegen, 1985) that typically focus on the valence (i.e., pleasantness–unpleasant) and degree of arousal (i.e., high–low). This is important as the association between discrete emotions and performance may differ. To illustrate, anger may relate to performance in a different way to anxiety, which is also a high-intensity emotion of negative valance (Jones, Lane, Bray, Uphill, & Catlin, 2005). Second, CMRT provides a detailed description of the cognitive processes involved in generating specific emotions, such that each emotion has its own unique "cognitive blueprint." The role of cognition in emotion, and specifically whether cognition is necessary for an emotional response, has been the subject of debate with differences largely a result of the way in which the terms *cognition* and *emotion* are defined (see Ekman & Davidson, 1994).

It is difficult to conceive that an emotion may occur in an individual without some form of cognition because emotions do not occur in response to events perceived as meaningless. Indeed, growing neurobiological evidence supports the role of cognitive processes that both rapidly detect the emotional valence of an event, and some that provide a more elaborate context-dependent evaluation (Uphill et al., 2009). Third, CMRT outlines how the intensity of emotions may change with the importance of the event, which can help explain why emotions appear to play a more significant role in critical performances. Fourth, the role of coping is central to CMRT, and, as such, outlines how developing a robust and adaptive psychological approach to performance environments may contribute to emotion regulation. Finally, there is evidence that the central tenets of CMRT hold in athletes (Uphill & Jones, 2007).

LAZARUS' COGNITIVE-MOTIVATIONAL-RELATIONAL THEORY

In CMRT, emotions occur when events are appraised as having either a positive or negative significance for well-being (relational meaning) in relation to goals. Emotion is part of a changing person–environment relationship, and three components central to this process are motivation, appraisal, and coping. These combine and form core relational themes for each emotion that describes the transaction between the individual and environment. This is useful for practitioners because it can provide an explanation of how each emotion arises. The core relational themes for the eight emotions Lazarus (2000b) outlined as particularly relevant to sport are shown in Table 8.1.

Motivation covers both an individual's goals (e.g., to win a badminton match) and how psychological and behavioral responses may be mobilized to achieve a goal (e.g., increase effort). Events are appraised through two processes: primary and secondary appraisal. *Primary appraisal* is concerned with the relevance of an event to a person's well-being in terms of his or her goals. The three ways in which events are primarily appraised include goal relevance (is there anything at stake?), goal congruence or incongruence (is the stimulus beneficial or harmful?), and goal content (i.e., the kind of goal at stake, such as enhancing ego identity). An individual's goals are arranged hierarchically, and the more important the goal, the more intense the emotion. This is why more important performance environments tend to induce stronger emotional responses.

Secondary appraisal concerns coping options, which Lazarus defined as cognitive and behavioral efforts to manage demands that are appraised as taxing or exceeding the resources of that person. The three aspects of secondary appraisal include blame or credit (can responsibility for the harm or benefit be determined?), coping potential (is it possible to influence the person–environment relationship for the better?), and future expectations (whether things will improve or worsen). It is the combination of the elements of primary and secondary appraisal that explains how different emotions occur.

Because goals, appraisal of situations, and coping strategies may vary both between and within

Table 8.1 Core relational themes for sport-related emotions

Emotion	Core-Relational Theme
Anger	A demeaning offense against me and mine.
Anxiety	Facing uncertain, existential threat.
Shame	Failing to live up to an ego-ideal.
Guilt	Having transgressed a moral imperative.
Hope	Fearing the worst but yearning for better, and believing the improvement is possible.
Relief	A distressing goal-incongruent condition that has changed for the better or gone away.
Happiness	Making reasonable progress toward the realization of a goal.
Pride	Enhancement of one's ego-identity by taking credit for a valued object or achievement, either one's own or that of someone or group with whom one identifies.

Adapted from *Emotion and Adaptation* by Richard S. Lazarus, 1991. New York: Oxford University Press.

individuals, CMRT provides an explanation for the inter- and intraindividual differences witnessed among performers (Jones, 2003). For example, an actor who is anxious about performing in an unfamiliar theater, may find his anxiety reduce as he becomes familiar with the environment following rehearsals, thus lessening his uncertainty about the environment. A performer's commitment to multiple goals can also explain how the same event can generate more than one emotion. For example, a boxer may want to win a contest, look stylish in doing so, and not get hurt.

The central tenets of CMRT have been supported in athletes. Uphill and Jones (2007) interviewed 12 international athletes on the emotions experienced during competition. There was evidence of appraisals being central to emotion and the appraisal process as comprising primary and secondary aspects. The findings on core relational themes was mixed, with support for the core relational themes of guilt, relief and shame, partial support for anxiety, happiness and sadness, and no support for the core relational themes of anger and pride. It may be that the core relational themes account for some emotions better than others (Bennett, Lowe, & Honey, 2003) or that cognitive appraisals may be unconscious, and, as such, interviewing athletes may not yield a complete description of the appraisal process (Uphill & Jones, 2007).

In summary, CMRT may not provide a complete explanation of emotions, but it does provide a framework for research into performance emotions. Importantly, CMRT illustrates the complexity of the emotion process and the central role of cognition. That cognition is central to the emotion process is shared with many other theories of emotion (see Uphill et al., 2009) and is useful for understanding how emotions can be regulated in performance settings. By changing a performer's cognition, it is possible to change an emotional response. Before discussing how emotions can be regulated in performance settings, the social importance of emotion is outlined, followed by an analysis of the link between emotions and performance.

Emotions in Groups

Emotions are generally adaptive and, as such, crucial to our evolution and survival as a species (cf. Rolls, 2005). A key element of this adaptive function is the role that emotions play in social behavior, which is illustrated by the universality of some emotional expressions across cultures (Ekman, 1980). Emotions indicate to others how we feel, and displays of emotion may maintain, enhance, or destroy social relationships. For example, the look of anger on the face of a coach after an error by a senior member of a lacrosse team may lead to a breakdown in trust. A challenge in performance settings is to regulate displays of emotion to that which the performer desires. For example, a quarterback distraught at missing an open wide receiver for a game-changing touchdown may maintain an impassive, confident persona to show his teammates and opponents that he is in control and focused on the next play.

Although displays of emotion may influence how others see us, the emotions experienced may also influence social interaction. Specifically, positive emotions in particular may be important in social settings since a positive affective state is associated with the liking of self and others, sociability and activity (Lyubomirsky, King, & Diener, 2005), and prosocial behavior (Platow et al., 1999). *Emotional contagion* can also occur in social settings (Hatfield, Capcioppo, & Rapson, 1994), whereby an emotion is "transmitted" from one person to another via facial, verbal, and behavioral expressions of emotion (Jones & Uphill, 2004). To illustrate, during a cricket match there was a significant association between each player's levels of happiness (on the same team) that was independent of the match situation (Totterdell, 2000).

Emotions may also be influenced by significant others in performance settings (e.g., leader, coach). Behaviors reflecting a negative personal rapport positively predicted anxiety in varsity and regional athletes (Baker, Cote, & Hawes, 2000). Athletes recognize the influence of significant others and look to coaches to change emotions. Collegiate and varsity athletes indicated a preference for emotional content in a pre-game speech (e.g., arousing phrases, appeals to emotions such as pride or anger) before a championship game, when competing against a higher ranked opponent and when considered an underdog (Vargas-Tonsing & Guan, 2007). Interestingly, though, it was the informational content (e.g., game plans) and not the emotional content of coaches' pre-game speeches that changed competitive soccer players' emotional states (Vargas-Tonsing, 2009).

Research on mirror neurons may help explain why emotions are important socially. Originally discovered in relation to motor skill, it was observed that some neurons in the brain fired both when a motor skill was performed and when it was observed (Iacoboni, 2009). The strength of activity may vary as a function of expertise, with greater activity occurring when an individual is better able to relate to the action being observed. For example, the brain activity of professional and novice dancers was assessed when they observed dance moves, and the activation of the network of motor areas involved in preparation and execution of an action was stronger for the well-learned motor skills (Calvo-Merino, Glaser, Grezes, Passingham, & Haggard, 2005). There are also mirror neurons that fire in response to the facial expressions of others, triggering activity in the limbic areas of the brain and producing the emotions that the observed person is experiencing (Carr, Iacoboni, Dubeau, Mazziotta, & Lenzi, 2003; Iacoboni, 2009). In short, the brain activity in the observer is generating a similar emotion to that which is observed (see also Chapter 13, this volume).

Because we may experience the emotions of others, we desire to have our emotions influenced by others (e.g., coaches), and we may react to the emotional displays of others, the social role of emotions in performance settings is clear. In sport, a visibly angry player may cause fear in his opponents, a visibly anxious leader may increase the anxiety levels of her team, and a calm official may defuse a potentially explosive contest. Similar effects may be seen in other performance settings; for example, the important role of leaders in business is often highlighted (e.g., Harris & Kacmar, 2006). That emotions are affected by others is important because emotions influence performance, and the next section of the chapter describes why and how emotions are so crucial for performance.

Emotions and Performance

A substantial amount of research has explored the relationship between anxiety and performance (see Woodman & Hardy, 2001, for a review), and it informs much of the material covered in this section. However, the aim is to take a broader perspective and consider the relationship between a range of emotions (including anxiety) and performance.

Two approaches, the *mental health model* (Morgan, 1985), which admittedly is based on a measure of mood, and the *individual zones of optimal functioning model* (IZOF; Hanin, 2000) have made substantial contributions to the sport literature in describing whether a particular affective pattern is associated with good or poor performance. There is support for both the mental health model (e.g., Beedie, Terry, & Lane, 2000) and IZOF (e.g., Robazza, Bortoli & Hanin, 2004; Robazza, Pellizzari, Bertollo & Hanin, 2008). However, the

mental health model describes, rather than explains, the link between mood and performance, whereas the link between emotions and performance in the IZOF is idiosyncratic and therefore variable.

Collectively, researchers agree that emotions are important for performance because of changes in an individual's physical and cognitive functioning, along with motivation levels (Botterill & Brown, 2002; Jones, 2003; Lazarus, 2000b; Uphill et al., 2009; Vallerand & Blanchard, 2000). In the remainder of this section, how emotions influence performance on each of these aspects is discussed, with the performance effects of specific emotions outlined where evidence permits.

Emotions and Physical Functioning

A history of research outlines that physiological changes may be unique to specific emotions (e.g., Ax, 1953) and that activation of the sympathetic arm of the autonomic nervous system may be associated with intensity of feeling (Hohmann, 1966). In short, feedback from the autonomic nervous system is central to emotion (cf. Damasio, 1999), and this section outlines how it may influence performance.

Arousal, defined as the level of neural excitation (Malmo, 1959), may be increased with activation of the autonomic nervous system during an emotion. High levels of arousal can increase anaerobic power, which may enhance performance on simple physical tasks such as jumping (e.g., Parfitt, Hardy & Pates, 1995; Parfitt & Pates, 1999). The effect of arousal on performance may vary across emotions. For example, handgrip strength was significantly higher following imagery-induced excitement, compared with imagery-induced anxiety, which in turn was higher than a control condition (Perkins, Wilson, & Kerr, 2001). Imagery-induced anger, in contrast to imagery-induced happiness, was associated with enhanced muscular strength on an isometric extension of the right leg, and this effect was moderated by personality, with imagery-induced anger leading to a greater increase in muscular strength in extroverts than introverts (Woodman, Davis, Hardy, Callow, Glasscock, & Yuill-Proctor, 2009).

The implication of these findings is that an increase in arousal accompanying some emotions could be positive for performance settings requiring anaerobic power (see Tod & McGuigan, 2001, for a review). Yet, caution is warranted as anger and fear are not consistently associated with enhanced anaerobic power (e.g., Murphy, Woolfolk, & Budney, 1988). Also, there are very few tasks where the sole requirement is strength. Even tasks such as weight-lifting or scrummaging in rugby require coordination in order to be successful.

With regard to motor skill performance and coordination, increased arousal does not appear beneficial. Specifically, increased arousal has been shown to have a negative effect on fine motor control (e.g., Noteboom, Barnholt, & Enoka, 2001; Noteboom, Fleshner, & Enoka, 2001). Increased arousal may also result in difficulties with coordination (Oxendine, 1970) and has been shown to impact the fluidity of movement on motor tasks (Beuter & Duda, 1985; Collins, Jones, Fairweather, Doolan, & Priestley, 2001).

Emotions and Cognitive Functioning

Positive and negative emotions appear to serve complementary cognitive functions. Negative emotions are most beneficial and adaptive in situations requiring immediate action, whereas the benefits of positive emotions—and the broader process of creative thinking—emerge over time (Fredrickson & Losada, 2005). The complementary benefits of positive and negative emotions are not always clear-cut. For example, hope (a positive emotion) was associated with the immediate benefit of increasing reaction time in a computer-based soccer task (Woodman et al., 2009). Similarly, the pleasant experience of happiness experienced by a tennis player on reaching match point is not useful if he begins imagining what it would be like to win and not pay sufficient attention to receiving his opponent's serve. Differences in thinking and approaches to problem-solving are not only apparent across positive and negative emotions but also within negative emotions. For example, fearful people made pessimistic estimates of risk and risk-averse choices, whereas angry people made optimistic risk estimates and choices relating to risk-seeking (Lerner & Keltner, 2001). So, an angry golfer may be more inclined to play a risky approach shot to the green, and a fearful coach may adopt conservative tactics going into an important game.

Attention is influenced by emotion. Broadly, positive emotions broaden attention whereas negative emotions narrow attention (Fredrickson, 2001; see also Chapter 9, this volume). Not only do positive emotions, such as amusement and contentment, encourage a broader focus of attention, they also manifest more creative thinking and approaches to problem-solving (Fredrickson & Branigan, 2005). This may be useful in sport settings when a performer is trying to think of a novel game play or

approach to break down the defense of a determined opponent. Arousal is proposed to narrow attention (cf., Easterbrook, 1959), but the effect of high arousal emotions like anxiety on attention is not always so clear cut. *Attentional control theory* (ACT) outlines that a performer under high anxiety is more concerned with potential threats in the environment rather than striving for a goal (Eysenck, Derakshan, Santos, & Calvo, 2007). This is supported by research showing that rather than simply narrowing their attentional field, anxious gymnasts (Moran, Byrne, & McGlade, 2002) and footballers (Wilson, Wood, & Vine, 2009) fixate their vision on threatening cues in the environment. In ACT, worry is proposed to impair the efficiency of cognitive functioning but not necessarily its effectiveness, provided that the performer can respond to this processing inefficiency by using compensatory strategies, such as enhanced effort and use of processing resources. Enhanced effort may, however, lead to worse performance on motor skills if attention is directed inward in an attempt to consciously control the execution of a motor skill (Beilock & Carr, 2001; Masters & Maxwell, 2008; see also Chapter 7, this volume).

Emotions and Motivation

Emotions can mediate and energize subsequent behaviors by ensuring that people channel extra physical and psychological resources toward a task (Vallerand & Blanchard, 2000). For example, an individual feeling ashamed about an error during a basketball match may try to gain possession of the ball as much as possible in an attempt to improve performance and overcome feelings of shame. Positive affect was associated with higher levels of effort, higher levels of motivation, and greater persistence on cognitive tasks in a laboratory setting (Erez & Isen, 2002). In performance settings, a lack of perception of effort is observed in flow states, with movement often perceived as effortless (Jackson, 2000). More broadly, enjoyment is one of the most important predictors of sport commitment, and, accordingly, participation, in both youth athletes (e.g., Carpenter & Scanlan, 1998) and elite sport (e.g., Scanlan, Russell, Beals, & Scanlan, 2003). Emotions can also lead an individual away from an object (Vallerand & Blanchard, 2000). For example, an individual anxious about making an error during a basketball match may avoid calling for the ball, while feelings of depression may be associated with lower levels of adherence and effort during an injury rehabilitation program.

Perceptions of Emotional State

The emotion–performance relationship does not only depend on the intensity of felt emotion or associated autonomic arousal, but also how the emotions are perceived. The control model of debilitative and facilitative competitive state anxiety suggests that athletes with a positive belief in their ability to cope and attain their goals will interpret anxiety symptoms as facilitative (helpful), whereas those with negative expectancies will interpret their symptoms as debilitative (unhelpful) to performance (Jones, 1995). Research supports the tenets of Jones' theory and that athletes with a positive perception of anxiety symptoms perform better (see Hanton, Neil, & Mellalieu, 2008 for a review). Other negative emotions may also be perceived as helpful to performance, such as a boxer perceiving a high level of anger as useful for performance (Jones, Meijen, McCarthy, & Sheffield, 2009).

Emotions and Performance: A Summary

Positive emotions do not necessarily have positive effects on performance, and negative emotions do not necessarily have negative effects on performance. The valence of the emotion does not determine performance outcome. The performance consequences of emotional experiences depend on which aspects of performance are affected by the emotions. A comprehensive description of the performance consequences of a range of emotions is not available, although much of the research has focused upon the role of anxiety. To illustrate, emotionally induced arousal, which often accompanies anxiety, would appear to play a role in power, coordination, and motor control in performance settings. However, it is uncertain exactly how many emotions other than anxiety are accompanied by high levels of arousal and if emotions characterized by low levels of arousal, such as sadness, are associated with changes in coordination and motor control (Uphill et al., 2009).

Bringing it Together: Understanding Psychophysiological Responses to Performing

The *theory of challenge and threat states in athletes* (TCTSA; Jones et al., 2009), integrates research on the appraisal, emotional response (intensity and direction), autonomic arousal, and performance consequences of competition. The broad basis for this theory is that a dichotomy exists between individuals who perceive a competitive situation as a challenge (positively) and those who perceive it as a threat (negatively). This dichotomy is intuitively appealing because it supports the commonly held belief that some individuals will rise to the demands of competition and perform well, while some wilt and perform poorly.

The TCTSA (Jones et al., 2009) draws predominantly on the biopsychosocial model of challenge and threat (Blascovich & Mendes, 2000; Blascovich & Tomaka, 1996), the model of adaptive approaches to competition (Skinner & Brewer, 2004), and the control model of debilitative and facilitative competitive state anxiety (Jones, 1995) to understand athletes' responses to competition. The TCTSA is displayed graphically in Figure 8.1.

Of particular relevance to this chapter are the changes that occur in autonomic arousal and the emotions triggered by challenge and threat states, and these are discussed next. The overall theory is discussed in greater detail in Jones et al. (2009).

The cardiovascular responses described by Blascovich and colleagues (Blascovich & Mendes, 2000; Blascovich & Tomaka, 1996) in challenge and threat states are proposed to be indicative of differential activation of the sympathetic-adreno-medullary (SAM) and pituitary-adreno-cortical (PAC) axes. A challenge state is proposed to result from SAM activation producing greater cardiac activity (increased heart rate) and left ventricular contractility that increases stroke volume. The combination of increased heart rate and enhanced left ventricular contractility enhances cardiac output. SAM activation releases epinephrine, which causes vasodilatation (widening of blood vessels resulting from relaxation of the muscular wall) and a decrease in systematic vascular resistance. Together, these changes represent the efficient mobilization of energy for immediate action and coping (Blascovich, Mendes, Hunter, & Salomon, 1999) and consist of increased blood flow to the brain and muscles; higher blood glucose levels, which is the fuel of the nervous system; and an increase in free fatty acids that can be used by the muscles as fuel (cf. Dienstbier, 1989).

A threat state is proposed to result in an increase in both SAM and PAC activation. The activation of the PAC axis results in the release of adrenocorticotropic hormone that causes the adrenal cortex to secrete corticosteroids into the bloodstream. Thus, although cardiac activity increases similar to a challenge condition, there is no corresponding decrease in systemic vascular resistance, and it may even increase (Dienstbier, 1989). As a result, blood pressure typically increases (Blascovich & Mendes, 2000; Blascovich & Tomaka, 1996). The

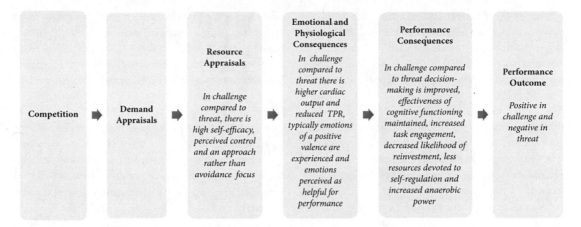

Figure 8.1 Comparison of challenge and threat responses in the theory of challenge and threat states in athletes. Adapted from Jones, M. V., Meijen, C., McCarthy, P. J., & Sheffield, D. (2009). A theory of challenge and threat states in athletes. *International Review of Sport and Exercise Psychology, 2,* 161–180.

combination of increased cardiac activity and stable or increased systemic vascular resistance represents a less efficient pattern for coping because, in this instance, the blood flow to the brain and muscles is not increased, and although stored fat and protein is converted into usable energy, it is done so over a longer period of time.

In the TCTSA, positive emotions will typically, but not exclusively, be associated with a challenge response and negative emotions will typically, but not exclusively, be associated with a threat response. Challenge and threat reflect motivational states (Blascovich & Mendes, 2000) and are independent to the valence of the emotion experienced (Mendes, Major, McCoy, & Blascovich, 2008). High-intensity emotions of a negative valence, like anger, that can serve motivational functions could therefore occur in a challenge state. To illustrate, cardiovascular responses consistent with a challenge state were associated with higher levels of anger in participants who experienced social rejection (Mendes et al., 2008). Athletes in a challenge state will perceive their emotions as helpful for performance and their emotions in a threat state as unhelpful for performance.

The TCTSA is a new approach yet to be fully tested in sport settings, although the cardiovascular responses aligned with challenge and threat states have been observed in baseball and softball athletes who provided a 2-minute speech about a specific playing situation (Blascovich, Seery, Mugridge, Norris, & Weisbuch, 2004). The participants who experienced a challenge state during this task performed better during the subsequent season compared to players who experienced a threat state. In contrast, Williams, Cumming, and Balanos (2010) were unable to find consistent differences in cardiac output between participants when using challenge or threat imagery, although the anxiety experienced during the challenge script was perceived as more helpful for performance. Additional physiological changes may also occur during performance settings not covered in the TCTSA. In particular, testosterone may be associated with a challenge state (Salvador & Costa, 2009), and this may be beneficial to performance (Neave & Wolfson, 2003).

Regulating the Responses to Performing on the Big Stage

Because emotions influence performance, and the more important performance environments are associated with the more intense emotions (cf. Lazarus, 1991), it is no surprise that understanding how emotions are regulated is of interest to psychologists.

Emotion Regulation or Coping?

A substantial amount of research has investigated coping in performance settings. Coping is defined as "constantly changing cognitive and behavioral efforts to manage specific external and/or internal demands that are appraised as taxing or exceeding the resources of the person" (Lazarus & Folkman, 1984, p. 141). In sport, coping is typically viewed as a dynamic process, as the type of coping strategies employed may differ according to the competition period (Gaudreau, Blondin, & Lapierre, 2002), the nature of the stressor, and whether the stressor is appraised as harmful, threatening, or challenging (Anshel, Jamieson, & Raviv, 2001). Research also suggests that situational factors, rather than personal disposition, best predict coping response (Anshel & Kaissidis, 1997).

Coping behaviors are typically classified into one of two categories (Lazarus & Folkman, 1984). *Problem-focused coping* involves taking action to change the person–stressor relationship. For example, warming up for an important soccer game away from the hostile fans of the opposing teams would be viewed as a problem-focused coping strategy to lessen pre-match anxiety. *Emotion-focused coping*, on the other hand, attempts to regulate the emotional states associated with or resulting from the stressor. For example, an athlete who is feeling particularly anxious may use progressive muscular relaxation in an attempt to reduce anxiety. Individuals do not typically rely on one strategy but rather combine problem- and emotion-focused coping when dealing with a stressor (Folkman & Lazarus, 1985), and a range of coping strategies have been reported in sport settings (see Nicholls & Polman, 2007, for a review).

Lazarus (1999) proposed that only appraisals of harm, threat, or challenge (which leads to negative emotions) warrant the use of coping resources. This may occur after "positive" events. For example, athletes report having to use coping strategies after winning an Olympic Gold medal (Jackson, Mayocchi,

& Dover, 1998). Performers may also want to be able to "cope" with positive emotions (Uphill & Jones, 2004). For example, athletes may actively seek to generate positive (and sometimes negative) emotions as an aid to performance in both training and competition.

A broader approach than just coping with emotions in performance settings comes from the emerging literature on emotion regulation. Emotion regulation refers to "the processes by which individuals influence which emotions they have, when they have them, and how they experience and express these emotions." (Gross, 1998, p. 275). As such, emotion regulation is considered distinct from coping in that the primary focus of coping is on decreasing negative emotional experience, whereas emotion regulation may include processes such as maintaining or augmenting positive emotions, as well as considering how these are displayed (Gross, 1998). The role of emotion regulation in sport has previously been outlined by Uphill et al. (2009) and forms the basis for the next section in which the application of emotion regulation strategies for performance settings are outlined.

Gross' Model of Emotion Regulation

Gross (1998) provides a model of emotion regulation, outlined in Figure 8.2. One proposition to emerge from this model is that antecedent-focused emotion regulation, which takes place before the emotion occurs, is the more efficient approach,

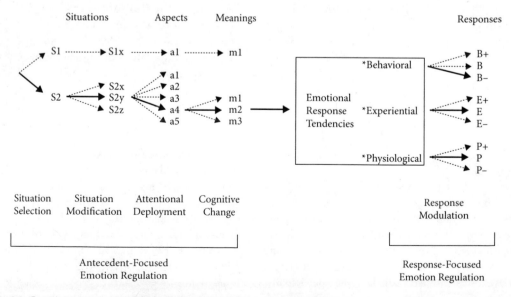

Figure 8.2 Gross (1998) process model of emotion regulation. From Gross, J. J. (1998). The emerging field of emotion regulation: An integrative review. *Review of General Psychology, 2,* 271–299.

whereas response-focused emotion regulation takes place after the emotion has occurred and is more cognitively "effortful," requiring greater resources to monitor and regulate emotion-expressive behavior (Richards & Gross, 2000).

SITUATION SELECTION AND MODIFICATION

Situation selection involves choosing to place oneself in a particular situation or not, whereas situation modification involves actively changing aspects of the situation (Gross, 1998). Both these techniques are similar to the problem-focused coping techniques outlined in the coping literature (Uphill et al., 2009) and are discussed together as it is sometimes difficult to draw boundaries between situation selection and situation modification (Gross & Thompson, 2007). To illustrate these strategies, one soccer player may choose not to take part in a penalty shoot-out to avoid the feelings of anxiety that she would experience (situation selection) while her teammate volunteers and chooses to take the first penalty to avoid having too long to dwell on the upcoming task (situation modification). One element that may be particularly useful for situation selection and modification is for performers to develop strategies for dealing with a range of potential scenarios, thus, in effect, "controlling the controllables" and changing either the situation or aspects of the situation (Uphill et al., 2009). Furthermore, as trying to anticipate every possible event is difficult, developing generic problem-solving skills may be a more parsimonious solution and help a performer's appraisals of his or her ability to cope with a situation, resulting in a more adaptive emotional response (Jones, 2003).

ATTENTION DEPLOYMENT

Some evidence suggests that directing attention to or away from emotion-inducing stimuli can be an effective way of regulating emotions (Ochsner & Gross, 2005). To illustrate, in the waiting area prior to an Olympic 100 m final, a sprinter may choose to close his eyes and focus his attention on imagining the perfect start out of the blocks rather than listen to his opponents' comments. A basketball player may choose to remind herself of derogatory comments made about her by an opponent as a means of increasing the anger and excitement about an upcoming game; emotions that she feels are necessary to do well.

COGNITIVE CHANGE

Cognitive change involves altering the meaning or significance of an event or situation (Uphill et al., 2009). The four basic psychological skills of imagery, relaxation, goal setting, and self-talk—the "workhorses in the applied sport psychology canon" (Andersen, 2000, p. ix)—may be useful in facilitating cognitive change, along with strategies that aim to change reappraisal.

Goal Setting

Aside from the simple proposition that achieving goals leads to positive emotions and failure to achieve goals leads to negative emotions, at first glance, the type of goal an individual has would seem unrelated to emotions. Yet, what a performer is striving for is crucial to the emotion process, and emotions arise because encounters with the environment are appraised as having either a positive or negative significance for well-being in terms of a person's goals. Thus, the importance of an individual's goal determines the intensity of the emotional response (Lazarus, 1991). The importance of goals in how emotions arise is supported by research (e.g., Graham, Kowalski, & Crocker, 2002). Of particular relevance are achievement goals. In general, there is a positive association between approach goals, in which the focus is on what can be achieved, and positive affect (e.g., Adie, Duda, & Ntoumanis, 2008, 2010). Individuals focused on gaining money on a cognitive task displayed cardiovascular responses consistent with a challenge state, in comparison to participants focused on not losing money (Seery, Weisbuch, & Blascovich, 2009). Consideration of achievement goals may also help explain why some emotions are considered helpful for performance. Participants playing a computer game had a stronger preference for fear when pursuing an avoidance goal, whereas excitement was the preferred emotion when adopting an approach goal (Tamir & Ford, 2009).

Self-Talk

Self-talk can be conceptualized as cognition (thinking) in its broadest sense, but more typically it is conceptualized more narrowly as athletes' overt (said out loud) and covert verbalizations. Self-talk could be used to regulate emotions in two ways (Jones, 2003). By replacing a maladaptive self-statement with a positive or neutral statement, a stimulus that may result in a negative emotional state is removed. In addition, certain self-talk statements may be used as stimuli to actively generate an appropriate emotional state for performance (e.g., "I have been performing so well in training" being used to generate excitement). Both of these strategies reflect cognitive changes that could equally be considered as attention deployment—that is, stimuli are generated to which an athlete pays attention. There is a growing body of evidence that self-talk can be used to regulate emotions (e.g., Hardy, Hall & Alexander, 2001; Hatzigeorgiadis, Zourbanos, Mpoumpaki, & Theodorakis, 2009; see also Chapter 10, this volume).

Imagery

Imagery involves the creation, or recreation, of an event in the mind and may involve some or all of the senses related to the event (see Chapter 11, this volume). Lang's *bioinformational theory* (1979) provides a framework for explaining how imagery can alter the emotional valance of an event. During imagery, a stimulus proposition is activated that describes the content of the image. For example, if an individual were to imagine taking a free throw in a basketball game, she may see the hoop and hear the crowd. Accompanying stimulus propositions are response propositions, which describe the individual's emotional, physiological, and behavioral responses. In this example, the basketball player may experience anxiety along with an increase in heart rate and muscular tension. Using imagery, response propositions can be changed from undesirable to desirable (Martin, Moritz, & Hall,1999), so that the basketball player may imagine feeling calm and relaxed when stepping up to take a free throw and so that the response (anxiety and tension) to a stimulus (taking a crucial free throw) is changed (to feeling calm and physically relaxed).

By imagining effectively coping and mastering a challenging situation, response propositions may also be changed. In our basketball example, if the player imagines not only feeling calm and physically relaxed but also executing the correct movement pattern associated with a free throw and seeing the ball go through the hoop, then the meaning of the event is likely to be changed and perceived as less threatening.

Imagery that represents specific goals and goal-oriented behaviors, such as imagining winning an important competition (and can be considered an example of attention deployment in Gross' model), may result in positive emotions. There are examples of imagery being used to change the emotional states of participants in sport settings (e.g., Jones, Mace, Bray, MacRae, & Stockbridge, 2002), and elite athletes reported using imagery to both increase excitement and maintain composure during competition (Munroe, Giacobbi, Hall, & Weinberg, 2000).

Relaxation

Relaxation techniques are used to reduce the autonomic arousal associated with emotional responses. They have been classified as *muscle-to-mind,* which are more physical in nature, or *mind-to-muscle,* which are more cognitive in nature (Harris, 1986). Relaxation is typically considered a response-focused strategy (e.g., Uphill et al., 2009). However, the use of relaxation may lead to cognitive changes. That the autonomic nervous system and cognitive aspects of emotion are linked is illustrated in research showing that an intervention designed to reduce somatic (physical) anxiety also reduced (albeit to a lesser degree) cognitive anxiety in soccer players (Maynard, Hemmings, & Warwick-Evans, 1995) and field hockey players (Maynard & Cotton, 1993).

Autonomic arousal may also guide decision-making. To explain, participants asked to choose a card from one of four decks displayed increased autonomic arousal when choosing cards from one of the two decks that will likely lose them money in the long term in comparison to cards from one of the two decks that are likely to gain them money in the long term (Bechara, Damasio, Tranel, & Damasio, 1997). This increase in autonomic arousal preceded participants' abilities to articulate which decks were best and also guided decision-making. Even when participants were unable to explain why, they still chose more cards from the "better decks." This illustrates how autonomic arousal can be a powerful driver for decision-making.

Reappraisal

Reappraisal involves reinterpreting a stimulus in ways that change its emotional "punch" and can either reduce or increase an emotion's intensity (Uphill et al., 2009). Reappraisal can not only change the intensity of emotions but also prevent emotions occurring or ensure that they do occur. For example, a field hockey player may perceive an umpire's error as a genuine mistake rather than an example of biased decision-making and accordingly not feel angry, while an athlete perceiving participating in the Olympic Games as a tremendous opportunity may feel excited rather than pressured. Reappraisal has been shown to be an effective strategy across a range of performance settings. Participants encouraged to view the autonomic arousal associated with taking a Graduate Record Examination in a positive light displayed physiological responses consistent with a challenge state and performed better in both practice and actual examination (Jamieson, Mendes, Blackstock, & Schmader, 2010). Similarly, experienced soccer players who used imagery to view a penalty kick as a challenge reported lower anxiety and a more positive perception of anxiety than did soccer players who used imagery to view the penalty kick as a pressure situation (Hale & Whitehouse, 1998).

Many cognitive strategies, such as imagery and self-talk, can be used for reappraisal in that they can be used to change how an event is viewed. In addition, Jones (2003) outlined six strategies that could be used by a consultant in dialogue with a client to reappraise an event. These included self-analysis, didactic approach, Socratic dialogue, cognitive paradox, reframing, and the use of storytelling, metaphors, and poetry.

RESPONSE MODULATION

Strategies to regulate emotions are focused on the physiological, behavioral, cognitive, and experiential aspects of emotions, with much of Gross' work focused on the use of suppression. Suppressing emotions can have important social consequences, although there is evidence that suppression may not be very effective and may even be costly as a strategy. To explain, Richards and Gross (2000) outlined that trying to suppress a display of emotion may hide one's feelings from an observer but not change how the participant feels (study 2), and participants engaging in suppression while watching a film (study 1) or series of slides (study 2) had a worse memory for the film's content than did participants who watched the film normally (study 1) or reappraised the content of the slides (study 2). It appeared that suppressing the emotion left fewer cognitive resources to process the viewing content. Suppressing thoughts may also have paradoxical consequences as, under cognitive load, attempting to suppress thoughts may exacerbate the very thoughts one is trying to suppress (Wegner, 1994; see also Chapter 7, this volume).

Other response-focused strategies may be more effective, however, and the proposition that response-focused emotion regulation is more cognitively "effortful" is a result of research focusing on one particular technique: suppression. For example, Schweiger Gallo, Keil, McCulloch, Rockstrock, and Gollwitzer (2009) asked participants to view pictures designed to induce disgust (study 1) and fear

(study 2). In both studies, participants who had an implementation intention (e.g., "I will not get disgusted—and if I see blood then I will stay calm and relaxed!"; "I will not get frightened—and if I see a spider I will remain calm and relaxed!") reported lower levels of the target emotion— either disgust or fear—than did participants who simply had a goal (e.g., "I will not get disgusted"; "I will not get frightened") and a control group. Further this type of cognitive regulation (implementation intention), despite being response focused, is considered cognitively efficient (Schweiger Gallo & Gollwitzer, 2007) and thus should be devoid of unwanted cognitive consequences (Schweiger Gallo et al., 2009).

Regulating the autonomic arousal accompanying emotions is one response strategy commonly employed in performance settings. A number of strategies have been proposed (e.g., progressive muscular relaxation, centering, up-beat music) that aim to regulate the physiological arousal of an individual and emotions (see Jones, 2003). However, some caution is warranted as increasing or decreasing physiological arousal would appear to have a blanket effect on the intensity of emotions experienced by the individual (e.g., Hohmann; 1966; Zillmann, Katcher, & Milavsky, 1972) and as such it may be difficult to target individual emotions without influencing others.

EMOTION REGULATION: SUMMARY

A number of strategies can be used to regulate emotions in performance settings. However, emotion regulation, just like coping, does change on the basis of individual differences. Higher self-esteem (Wood, Heimpel, & Michela, 2003), conscientiousness (Jensen-Campbell, Knack, Waldrip, & Campbell, 2007), and working memory capacity (Schmeichel, Volokhov, & Demaree, 2008) are all positively associated with better emotion regulation. Cultural differences may also influence which emotion regulation strategies are best employed. For example, individuals with Asian values may be more comfortable suppressing emotional responses, and doing so is a less negative experience than for individuals with Western-European values (Butler, Lee, & Gross, 2007).

The capacity for emotion regulation does develop over time, and this has implications for consultants working with youth athletes. As regions of the brain associated with emotion regulation (prefrontal cortex, anterior cingulate cortex, amygdala) mature through childhood and into adolescence, children appear to get better at emotion regulation

(Beauregard, Levesque, & Paquette, 2004). A consultant should be particularly aware of what psychological skills may be useful as young athletes mature. For example, children up to 12 years of age will have a poor understanding of time (Piaget, 1969), and, as such, having a "long-term goal" will have little meaning for the child. Thus, an adult may be able to understand that to achieve a long-term goal a series of smaller goals will be useful, but research suggests that younger children will find this concept problematic (Bandura & Schunk, 1981). With caution and consideration of developmental issues, there are examples of psychological skills being used to change emotions in youth athletes (e.g., McCarthy, Jones, Harwood, & Davenport, 2010).

Although emotion regulation strategies can be effective, it would be remiss not to consider one major issue emerging from the emotion regulation literature: emotion regulation strategies can, at times, be costly for the individual. These potential costs are outlined next.

The Cost of Emotion Performance

A consistent theme in the emotion regulation literature, echoed in the preceding section, is that it is better to perceive the performance environment positively than to try to eliminate or control unhelpful negative emotional responses once they occur (Jones et al., 2009). There is good reason for this. Self-control—that is, any attempt to override one's responses—draws on and depletes a limited pool of resources that is available for controlling all emotions, thoughts, and behaviors (Baumeister, Heatherton, & Tice, 1994; Baumeister & Heatherton, 1996). Of particular relevance to the performance environment is that depletion of this self-regulation strength in one area affects performance in another area. For example, participants required to suppress emotions performed worse on a subsequent anagram task (Baumeister, Bratslavsky, Muraven, & Tice, 1998, study 3), and exaggerating the expression of negative emotions reduced subsequent working memory span (Schmeichel, 2007, study 4). There may even be physical consequences from cognitive self-regulation (e.g., Bray, Martin-Ginis, Hicks, & Woodgate, 2008). Given that performance environments often involve significant others (e.g., managers, coaches, captains, and teammates), it is also interesting to note that simulating acts of self-control, which can occur when a person takes the perspective of a person engaging in an act of self-control, also depletes self-regulatory resources (Ackerman, Goldstein, Shapiro, & Bargh,

2009). So, viewing a coach actively trying to control anxiety may be costly to an athlete if she simulates what the coach is doing (i.e., imagines what it would be like to be the coach in that situation) as this simulation may trigger mental representations that are similar to those that occur when actually engaging in the actions.

Self-control as a limited resource was used as a metaphor to explain the deleterious effects of overriding responses (e.g., regulation of emotions) on the performance of subsequent tasks. However, self-control may indeed rely on an actual renewable energy source: glucose (Gailliot & Baumeister, 2007). This is important because the brain relies heavily on glucose for energy (Laughlin, 2004). Evidence across a range of tasks shows that acts of self-control deplete blood glucose levels and that low levels of blood glucose predict poor performance on subsequent self-control tasks. This effect can be eliminated by consuming a glucose drink (Gailliot et al., 2007). The ingestion of glucose is not the only way to counteract the negative effects of self-control depletion. Positive emotions induced by watching a comedy video or receiving a surprise gift were also found to alleviate the effects of self-control depletion from a previous task (Tice, Baumeister, Shmueli, & Muraven, 2007), although it was not possible to determine if the positive emotional state somehow replenished the self-control resource or if it served as a motivating, energizing, and creative impetus for performance on subsequent tasks (cf. Fredrickson, 2001).

Not only may glucose ingestion and positive affect help eliminate self-control depletion but evidence also supports the idea that self-control can be trained (Muraven, 2010). Participants' self-control was assessed on a "stop-signal procedure" whereby participants were asked to press a button to indicate the position of a square on the screen but to inhibit this response when a tone sounded, which it did on 25% of the trials. Participants practiced self-control over 2 weeks by either cutting back on sweets (resisting the urge to eat something pleasant) or holding a handgrip for as long as possible twice a day (regulating feelings of physical discomfort). Compared with participants who completed math tasks or a diary, the participants who practiced self-control (cutting back on sweets, holding a handgrip) performed better on the "stop-signal procedure" after 2 weeks.

Collectively, these findings illustrate how self-control, of which emotion regulation is one element, may be enhanced (ingestion of glucose), maintained (generation of positive emotions), and trained (practising self-control). Self-control, such as emotion regulation, can be developed in performers and explains why psychological toughness can develop over time (Dienstbeir, 1989). It also supports the widespread practice among performance psychologists of challenging performers by placing them in situations that require self-control (e.g., simulation training).

Although self-control can be replenished or trained, the findings also suggest that being able to regulate psychological responses with as few resources as possible (i.e., by perceiving the situation as a challenge) is helpful because it leaves sufficient self-regulatory resources available for other demands (psychological or physical) arising from the task. Perceiving a competitive situation as a challenge means that there is less need for regulation as this is an adaptive approach for competition. In short, when it comes to a psychological approach to performance environments, prevention is better than cure (Jones et al., 2009).

Reflecting Smartly on Performance

To this point in the chapter, emotion and emotion regulation have been discussed in the context of an upcoming or actual performance. However, the way in which individuals in performance settings reflect after the event is also important and can influence emotion in training and future performances (Allen, Jones, & Sheffield, 2010).

If the desire is to develop a positive emotional state after performance, then one strategy that may be effective is to ask participants to reflect positively on the performance. Although not based on data from performance settings, but from daily life, participants asked to write down three things that went well each day and to provide a causal explanation for each good thing experienced an increase in happiness and a decrease in depressive symptoms during the 6 months that symptoms were monitored (Seligman, Steen, Park, & Peterson, 2005). Developing a positive emotional state after a performance state may be effective as it can help individuals recover from negative emotional experiences (Tugade & Fredrickson, 2004).

Understanding how people make sense of performance has been the domain of attribution research (see Weiner, 1986). In sport, attributions predict post-competition emotions (e.g., Allen, Jones, & Sheffield, 2009) and so changing emotional state post-competition could be done by changing attributions. However, limited research has explored the impact of attribution retraining interventions on both attributions and emotions. In one study by Allen et al. (2010), participants were asked to complete a positive reflection exercise in which, similar to the intervention outlined by Seligman et al. (2005), they listed three things that went well during a recently completed golf putting competition, while a control group completed the concentration grid. Although the participants who completed the positive reflection task reported an adaptive series of attributions that were significantly more internal and personally controllable than participants in the control group, no differences were observed between groups on emotion.

Counterfactual thinking (i.e., generating thoughts of what might have been) may also play a role in post-performance emotions (Roese, 1997). For example, Olympic Bronze medalists who were not expected to medal were rated as happier than Olympic Silver medalists who were expected to have won gold, as the bronze medalists were likely to have made a downward counterfactual comparison (e.g., "I could have left with nothing") that resulted in a positive emotional response (McGraw, Mellers, & Tetlock, 2005). Typically, counterfactual thoughts are directed upward and consider how the situation could have been improved because negative affect, which is more likely to occur after a negative and unexpected outcome, is a principal trigger for counterfactual thinking (Roese & Olson, 1993). Upward counterfactuals were associated with negative emotions in athletes, whereas downward counterfactuals were associated with positive emotions (Dray & Uphill, 2009).

Conclusion

Participating in sport is emotional and thus sport provides an excellent context within which to explore how emotions arise and influence performance and the efficacy of strategies for emotional regulation. Findings from sport are applicable to other performance settings where tasks are also difficult and achievement is important to the individual, such as education, the performing arts, and business. Emotions play an important role in social settings and impact performers' motivation and physical and cognitive functioning. Although positive emotions are often considered beneficial in performance settings, the valance of the emotion and performance outcome are not the same. Positive emotions do not necessarily have positive effects on performance, and negative emotions do not necessarily have negative effects on performance. Moreover, negative emotions such as anxiety are often associated with substantial increases in performance levels.

The important role of cognition in the emotion process highlights why cognitive strategies (e.g., self-talk, imagery) may be effective in regulating emotions. However, there may be a cost to regulating emotions in that the limited pool of resources available for regulating all emotions, thoughts, and behaviors is thereby depleted, and this may have negative performance consequences on subsequent tasks. Given the importance of emotions for performance and the potential value of emotion regulation strategies in facilitating successful performance, it is no surprise that there is a large, growing, and complex literature on emotions and emotion regulation. Despite this substantial body of literature and the clear guidelines it provides for theoreticians and practitioners, there are a number of areas where further research is warranted and these are outlined in the next section.

Future Directions

With a topic as diverse as emotion and emotional regulation, a range of potential areas for future research is possible. In this section, some of these areas are outlined. It is not an exhaustive list, and, although grounded in the extant literature, the areas outlined, perhaps understandably, represent my own personal biases and interests. In total, eight areas for future research are identified.

Emotional responses, in the shape of autonomic arousal, may guide decision-making and performance in performance settings for reasons of which we are unaware (c.f. Bechara et al., 1997), yet there has been no research of that nature in performance settings. Exploring this area may help explain why performers often rely on their instinct (e.g., a poker player who just "feels" his opponent is bluffing). Unconscious processing of stimuli may help explain why athletes are not aware of why they respond emotionally. A second area of possible research is to explore the role of conscious and unconscious processing in emotion (Jones, 2003). To illustrate, although most people know that flying (statistically at least) is the safest form of travel, it does not stop some people being very anxious when they fly (Lazarus, 1991). The appraisal of stimuli at different levels may help explain why intervention techniques do not always work as they may change the conscious appraisal of a situation but do little to alter the subconscious appraisal of the stimulus that might determine the emotional reaction (Jones, 2003).

The third, fourth, and fifth areas for future research all focus on the area of self-regulation. Research could consider if using emotion regulation techniques that are well learned and automatic deplete the central resource for self-control in the same way that novel emotion regulation techniques do. And if emotion regulation techniques that are new and effortful deplete the central resource for self-control, but ones that are well learned do not, understanding at what point this change occurs would be useful. There is also a broader research question: If there are costs to emotion regulation, then it may not always be worthwhile to try to regulate emotions. For example, suggesting to an anxious athlete that efforts must be made to regulate anxiety may, at times, be worse for performance than simply allowing the anxiety to occur.

Response-focused regulation strategies are considered to be more effortful, yet this is likely because much of the research has focused on suppression. It may be that many response-focused strategies are effective in changing the emotional intensity and yet exert little cognitive cost, and this should be explored (cf. Schweiger Gallo et al., 2009).

Emotions serve a social purpose and are important to the way we interact and function in group settings. To complement the work of Butler et al. (2007), one possible area to investigate is if the culture or ethos of the sport, which defines acceptable or unacceptable behavior, also has a significant impact on the emotions experienced by athletes and the ways in which they are controlled (Jones, Lavallee, & Thatcher, 2004).

Finally, sport has led the way in research exploring perceptions of anxiety symptoms. Yet, the conceptual worth of this research has recently been questioned, and a positive perception of symptoms may simply represent the absence of any perceived anxiety (Lundqvist, Kentta, & Raglin, 2010). Attempting to replicate this approach and extending the research to other emotions (e.g., anger) would be a worthy addition to the literature.

References

Ackerman, J. M., Goldstein, N. J., Shapiro, J. R., & Bargh, J. A. (2009). You wear me out: The vicarious depletion of self-control. *Psychological Science, 20*, 326–332.

Adie, J. W., Duda, J. L., & Ntoumanis, N. (2008). Achievement goals, competition appraisals, and the psychological and emotional welfare of sport participants. *Journal of Sport and Exercise Psychology, 30*, 302–322.

Adie, J. W., Duda, J. L., & Ntoumanis, N. (2010). Achievement goals, competition appraisals, and the well- and ill-being of elite youth soccer players over two competitive seasons. *Journal of Sport and Exercise Psychology, 32*, 555–579.

Allen, M. S., Jones, M. V., & Sheffield, D. (2010). The influence of positive reflection on attributions, emotions, and self-efficacy. *The Sport Psychologist, 24*, 211–226

Allen, M. S., Jones, M. V., & Sheffield, D. (2009). Causal attribution and emotion in the days following competition. *Journal of Sports Sciences, 27*, 461–468.

Andersen, M. B. (Ed.). (2000). *Doing sport psychology.* Champaign IL: Human Kinetics.

Anshel, M. H., Jamieson, J., & Raviv, S. (2001). Cognitive appraisals and coping strategies following acute stress among skilled competitive male and female athletes. *Journal of Sport Behavior, 24*, 128–143.

Anshel, M. H., & Kaissidis, A. N. (1997). Coping style and situational appraisals as predictors of coping strategies following stressful events in sport as a function of gender and skill level. *British Journal of Psychology, 88*, 263–276.

Ax, A. F. (1953). The physiological differentiation between fear and anger in humans. *Psychosomatic Medicine, 15*, 433–422.

Baker, J., Cote, J., & Hawes, R. (2000). The relationship between coaching behaviours and sport anxiety in athletes. *Journal of Science and Medicine in Sport, 3*, 110–119.

Bandura, A., & Schunk, D. H. (1981). Cultivating competence, self-efficacy and intrinsic interest. *Journal of Personality and Social Psychology, 41*, 586–598.

Baumeister, R. F., Bratslavsky, E., Muraven, M., & Tice, D. M. (1998). Ego depletion: Is the active self a limited resource? *Journal of Personality and Social Psychology, 74*, 1252–1265.

Baumeister, R. F., & Heatherton, T. F. (1996). Self-regulation failure: An overview. *Psychological Inquiry, 7*, 1–15.

Baumeister, R. F., Heatherton, T. F., & Tice, D. M. (1994). *Losing control: How and why people fail at self-regulation.* San Diego: Academic Press.

Beauregard, M., Levesque, J., & Paquette, V. (2004). Neural basis of conscious and voluntary self-regulation of emotion. In M. Beauregard (Ed.), *Consciousnesses, emotional self-regulation and the brain* (pp. 35–59). Philadelphia: John Benjamins.

Bechara, A., Damasio, H., Tranel, D., & Damasio, A. R. (1997). Deciding advantageously before knowing the advantageous strategy. *Science, 275*(5304), 1293–1295.

Beedie, C. J., Terry, P. C., & Lane, A. M. (2000). The profile of mood states and athletic performance: Two meta-analyses. *Journal of Applied Sport Psychology, 12*, 49–68.

Beilock, S. L., & Carr, T. H. (2001). On the fragility of skilled performance: What governs choking under pressure? *Journal of Experimental Psychology-General, 130*, 701–725.

Bennett, P., Lowe, R., & Honey, K. (2003) Appraisals and emotions: A test of the consistency of reporting and their associations. *Cognition and Emotion, 17*, 511–520.

Beuter, A., & Duda, J. L. (1985). Analysis of the arousal/motor performance relationship in children using movement kinematics. *Journal of Sport Psychology, 7*, 229–243.

Blascovich, J., & Mendes, W. B. (2000). Challenge and threat appraisals: The role of affective cues. In J. P. Forgas (Ed.), *Feeling and thinking: The role of affect in social cognition* (pp. 59–82). Paris: Cambridge University Press.

Blascovich, J., Mendes, W. B., Hunter, S. B., & Salomon, K. (1999). Social "facilitation" as challenge and threat. *Journal of Personality and Social Psychology, 77*, 68–77.

Blascovich, J., Seery, M. D., Mugridge, C. A., Norris, R. K., & Weisbuch, M. (2004). Predicting athletic performance from cardiovascular indexes of challenge and threat. *Journal of Experimental Social Psychology, 40*, 683–688.

Blascovich, J., & Tomaka, J. (1996). The biopsychosocial model of arousal regulation. *Advances in Experimental Social Psychology, 28*, 1–51.

Botterill, C., & Brown, M. (2002). Emotion and perspective in sport. *International Journal of Sport Psychology, 33*, 38–60.

Bray, S. R., Martin-Ginis, K. A., Hicks, A. L., & Woodgate, J. (2008). Effects of self-regulatory strength depletion on muscular performance and EMG activation. *Psychophysiology, 45*, 337–343.

Butler, E. A., Lee, T. L., & Gross, J. J. (2007). Emotion regulation and culture: Are the social consequences of emotion suppression culture-specific? *Emotion, 7*, 30–48.

Calvo-Merino, B., Glaser, D. E., Grezes, J., Passingham, R. E., & Haggard, P. (2005). Action observation and acquired motor skills: An fMRI study with expert dancers. *Cerebral Cortex, 15*, 1243–1249.

Carpenter, P. J., & Scanlan, T. K. (1998). Changes over time in the determinants of sport commitment. *Pediatric Exercise Science, 10*, 356–365.

Carr, L., Iacoboni, M., Dubeau, M. C., Mazziotta, J. C., & Lenzi, G. L. (2003). Neural mechanisms of empathy in humans: A relay from neural systems for imitation to limbic areas. *Proceedings of the National Academy of Sciences of the United States of America, 100*, 5497–5502.

Collins, D., Jones, B., Fairweather, M., Doolan, S., & Priestley, N. (2001). Examining anxiety associated changes in movement patterns. *International Journal of Sport Psychology, 31*, 223–242.

Crocker, P. R. E., Kowalski, K. C., Graham, T. R., & Kowalski, N. P. (2002). Emotion in sport. In J. M. Silva III & D. E. Stevens (Eds.), *Psychological foundations of sport* (pp.107–131). Boston: Allyn & Bacon.

Damasio, A. R. (1999). *The feeling of what happens: Body and emotion in the making of consciousness.* San Diego: Harcourt.

Dienstbier, R. A. (1989). Arousal and physiological toughness: Implications for mental and physical health. *Psychological Review, 96*, 84–100.

Dray, K., & Uphill, M. A. (2009). A Survey of athletes' counterfactual thinking: Precursors, prevalence, and consequences. *Sport and Exercise Psychology Review, 5*, 16–26.

Easterbrook, J. A. (1959). The effect of emotion on cue utilization and the organization of behavior. *Psychological Review, 66*, 183–201.

Ekkekakis, P., & Petruzzello, S. J. (2000). Analysis of the affect measurement conundrum in exercise psychology I. Fundamental issues. *Psychology of Sport and Exercise, 1*, 71–88.

Ekman, P. (1980). *The face of man: Expressions of universal emotions in a New Guinea village.* New York: Garland STPM Press.

Ekman, P., & Davidson, R. J. (1994). *The nature of emotion.* Oxford, UK: Oxford University Press.

Erez, A., & Isen, A. M. (2002). The influence of positive affect on the components of expectancy motivation. *Journal of Applied Psychology, 87*, 1055–1067.

Eysenck, M. W., Derakshan, N., Santos, R. & Calvo, M. G. (2007). Anxiety and cognitive performance: Attentional control theory. *Emotion, 7*, 336–353.

Folkman, S., & Lazarus, R. S. (1985). If it changes it must be a process: Study of emotion and coping during three stages of a college examination. *Journal of Personality and Social Psychology, 48*, 150–170.

Fredrickson, B. I. (2001). The role of positive emotions in positive psychology—The broaden-and-build theory of positive emotions. *American Psychologist, 56*, 218–226.

Fredrickson, B. L., & Branigan, C. (2005). Positive emotions broaden the scope of attention and thought-action repertoires. *Cognition and Emotion, 19*, 313–332.

Fredrickson, B. L., & Losada, M. F. (2005). Positive affect and the complex dynamics of human flourishing. *American Psychologist, 60*, 678–686.

Gailliot, M. T., & Baumeister, R. F. (2007). The physiology of willpower: Linking blood glucose to self-control. *Personality and Social Psychology Review, 11*, 303–326.

Gailliot, M. T., Baumeister, R. F., De Wall, C. N., Maner, J. K., Plant, E. A., Tice, D. M., et al. (2007). Self-control relies on glucose as a limited energy source: Willpower is more than a metaphor. *Journal of Personality and Social Psychology, 92*, 325–336.

Gaudreau, P., Blondin, J. -P., & Lapierre, A. -M. (2002). Athletes' coping during a competition: Relationship of coping strategies with positive affect, negative affect, and performance-goal discrepancy. *Psychology of Sport and Exercise, 3*, 125–150.

Graham, T. R., Kowalski, K. C., & Crocker, P. R. E. (2002). The contributions of goal characteristics and causal attributions to emotional experience in youth sport participants. *Psychology of Sport and Exercise, 3*, 273–291.

Gross, J. J. (1998). The emerging field of emotion regulation: An integrative review. *Review of General Psychology, 2*, 271–299.

Gross, J. J., & Thompson, R. A. (2007). Emotion regulation: Conceptual foundations. In J. J. Gross (Ed.), *Handbook of emotion regulation* (pp. 3–24). London: Guilford Press.

Hale, B. D., & Whitehouse, A. (1998). The effects of imagery-manipulated appraisal on intensity and direction of competitive anxiety. *The Sport Psychologist, 112*, 40–51.

Hanin, Y. L. (2000). Individual zones of optimal functioning (IZOF) model: Emotions-Performance relationships in sport. In Y. L. Hanin (Ed.), *Emotions in sport* (pp. 65–89). Champaign, IL: Human Kinetics.

Hanton, S., Neil, R., & Mellalieu, S. D. (2008). Recent developments in competitive anxiety direction and competition stress. *International Review of Sport and Exercise Psychology, 1*, 45–57.

Hardy, J., Hall, C. R., & Alexander, M. R. (2001). Exploring self-talk and affective states in sport. *Journal of Sports Sciences, 19*, 469–475.

Harris, D. V. (1986). Relaxation and energizing techniques for regulation of arousal. In J. M. Williams (Ed.), *Applied sport psychology: Personal growth to peak performance* (pp. 185–208). Mountain View, CA: Mayfield Publishing Company.

Harris, K. J., & Kacmar, K. M. (2006). Too much of a good thing: The curvilinear effect of leader–member exchange on stress. *The Journal of Social Psychology, 146*, 65–84.

Hatfield, E. Cacioppo, J. T., & Rapson, R. L. (1994). *Emotional contagion*. Cambridge, UK: Cambridge University Press.

Hatzigeorgiadis, A., Zourbanos, N., Mpoumpaki, S., & Theodorakis, Y. (2009). Mechanisms underlying the self-talk–performance relationship: The effects of motivational self-talk on self-confidence and anxiety. *Psychology of Sport and Exercise, 10*, 186–192.

Hohmann, G. W. (1966). Some effects of spinal cord lesions on experiencing emotional feelings. *Psychophysiology, 3*, 143–156.

Iacoboni, M. (2009). Imitation, empathy, and mirror neurons. *Annual Review of Psychology, 60*, 653–670.

Jackson, S. A. (2000). Joy, fun and flow state in sport. In Y. L. Hanin (Ed.), *Emotions in sport* (pp. 135–155). Champaign, IL: Human Kinetics.

Jackson, S. A., Mayocchi, L., & Dover, J. (1998). Life after winning gold: II. Coping with the change as an Olympic gold medalist. *The Sport Psychologist, 12*, 137–155.

Jamieson, J. P., Mendes, W. B., Blackstock, E., & Schmader, T. (2010). Turning the knots in your stomach into bows: Reappraising arousal improves performance on the GRE. *Journal of Experimental Social Psychology, 46*, 208–212.

Jensen-Campbell, L. A., Knack, J. M., Waldrip, A. M., & Campbell, S. D. (2007). Do Big Five personality traits associated with self-control influence the regulation of anger and aggression? *Journal of Research in Personality, 41*, 403–424.

Jones, G. (1995). More than just a game: Research developments and issues in competitive anxiety in sport. *British Journal of Psychology, 86*, 449–478.

Jones, M. V. (2003). Controlling emotions in sport. *The Sport Psychologist, 17*, 471–486.

Jones, M. V., Lane, A. M., Bray, S., Uphill, M., & Catlin, J. (2005). Development and validation of the Sport Emotion Questionnaire (SEQ). *Journal of Sport and Exercise Psychology, 27*, 407–431.

Jones, M. V., Lavallee, D., & Thatcher, J. (2004). Coping and emotion in sport: Future directions. In D. Lavallee, J. Thatcher, & M. V. Jones (Eds.), *Coping and Emotion in Sport* (pp. 273–280). Hauppauge, NY: Nova Science Publishers.

Jones, M. V., Mace, R. D., Bray, S. R., MacRae, A., & Stockbridge, C. (2002). The impact of motivational imagery on the emotional state and self-efficacy levels of novice climbers. *Journal of Sport Behavior, 25*, 57–73.

Jones, M. V., Mace, R. D., & Williams, S. (2000). Relationship between emotional state and performance during international field hockey matches. *Perceptual and Motor Skills, 90*, 691–701.

Jones, M. V., Meijen, C., McCarthy, P. J., & Sheffield, D. (2009). A theory of challenge and threat states in athletes. *International Review of Sport and Exercise Psychology, 2*, 161–180.

Jones, M. V., & Uphill, M. (2004). Antecedents and consequences of emotion in sport. In D. Lavallee, J. Thatcher, & M. V. Jones (Eds.), *Coping and emotion in sport* (pp. 9–28). Hauppauge, NY: Nova Science Publishers.

Kerr, J. H. (1997). Motivation and emotion in sport. East Sussex, UK: Psychology Press Ltd.

Lane, A. M., & Terry, P. C. (2000). The nature of mood: Development of a conceptual model with a focus on depression. *Journal of Applied Sport Psychology, 12*, 16–33.

Lang, P. J. (1979). A bio-informational theory of emotional imagery. *Psychophysiology, 16*, 495–512.

Laughlin, S. B. (2004). The implications of metabolic energy requirements for the representation of information in neurons. In M. S. Gazzinga (Ed.), *The cognitive neurosciences* (pp. 187–196). Cambridge, MA: MIT Press.

Lazarus, R. S. (1991). *Emotion and adaptation*. Oxford, UK: Oxford University Press.

Lazarus, R. S. (1999). *Stress and emotion: A new synthesis*. London: Free Association Books.

Lazarus, R. S. (2000a). Cognitive-motivational-relational theory of emotion. In Y. L. Hanin (Ed.), *Emotions in sport* (pp. 39–63). Champaign, IL: Human Kinetics.

Lazarus, R. S. (2000b). How emotions influence performance in competitive sports. *The Sport Psychologist, 14*, 229–252.

Lazarus, R. S., & Folkman, S. (1984). *Stress, appraisal, and coping.* New York: Springer Publishing Company.

Lerner, J. S., & Keltner, D. (2001). Fear, anger, and risk. *Journal of Personality and Social Psychology, 81*, 146–159.

Lundqvist, C., Kentta, G., & Raglin, J. S. (2010). Directional anxiety responses in elite and sub-elite young athletes: Intensity of anxiety symptoms matters. *Scandinavian Journal of Medicine and Science in Sports.* doi: SMS1102 [pii] 10.1111/j.1600-0838.2010.01102.x

Lyubomirsky, S., King, L., & Diener, E. (2005). The benefits of frequent positive affect: Does happiness lead to success? *Psychological Bulletin, 131*, 803–855.

Malmo, R. B. (1959). Activation: A neuropsychological dimension. *Psychological Review, 66*, 367–386.

Martin, K. A., Moritz, S. E., & Hall, C. R. (1999). Imagery use in sport: A literature review and applied model. *The Sport Psychologist, 13*, 245–268.

Masters, R., & Maxwell, J. (2008).The theory of reinvestment. *International Review of Sport and Exercise Psychology, 1*, 160–183.

Maynard, I. W., & Cotton, P. C. J. (1993). An investigation of two stress management techniques in field setting. *The Sport Psychologist, 7*, 375–387.

Maynard, I. W., Hemmings, B., & Warwick-Evans, L. (1995). The effects of a somatic intervention strategy on competitive state anxiety and performance in semiprofessional soccer players. *The Sport Psychologist, 9*, 51–64.

McCarthy, P. J., Jones, M. V., Harwood, C. G., & Davenport, L. (2010). Using goal setting to enhance positive affect among junior multievent athletes. *Journal of Clinical Sport Psychology, 4*, 53–68.

McGraw, A. P., Mellers, B. A., & Tetlock, P. E. (2005). Expectations and emotions of Olympic athletes. *Journal of Experimental Social Psychology, 41*, 438–446.

Mendes, W. B., Major, B., McCoy, S., & Blascovich, J. (2008). How attributional ambiguity shapes physiological and emotional responses to social rejection and acceptance. *Journal of Personality and Social Psychology, 94*, 278–291.

Moran, A., Byrne, A., & McGlade, N. (2002). The effects of anxiety and strategic planning on visual search behavior. *Journal of Sports Sciences, 20*, 225–236.

Morgan, W. P. (1985). Selected psychological factors limiting performance: A mental health model. In D. H. Clarke & H. M. Eckert (Eds.), *Limits of human performance* (pp. 70–80). Champaign, IL: Human Kinetics.

Munroe, K. J., Giacobbi, P. R., Hall, C., & Weinberg, R. (2000). The four Ws of imagery use: Where, when, why, and what. *The Sport Psychologist, 14*, 119–137.

Muraven, M. (2010). Building self-control strength: Practicing self-control leads to improved self-control performance. *Journal of Experimental Social Psychology, 46*, 465–468.

Murphy, S. M., Woolfolk, R. L., & Budney, A. J. (1988). The effects of emotive imagery on strength performance. *Journal of Sport and Exercise Psychology, 10*, 334–345.

Neave, N., & Wolfson, S. (2003). Testosterone, territoriality, and the 'home advantage'. *Physiology and Behavior, 78*, 269–275.

Nicholls, A. R., & Polman, R. C. J. (2007). Coping in sport: A systematic review. *Journal of Sports Sciences, 25*, 11–31.

Noteboom, J. T., Barnholt, K, R., & Enoka, R. M. (2001). Activation of the arousal response and impairment of performance increase with anxiety and stressor intensity. *Journal of Applied Physiology, 91*, 2093–2101.

Noteboom, J. T., Fleshner, M., & Enoka, R. M. (2001). Activation of the arousal response can impair performance on a simple motor task. *Journal of Applied Physiology, 91*, 821–831.

Ochsner, K. N., & Gross, J. J. (2005). The cognitive control of emotion. *Trends in Cognitive Sciences, 9*, 242–249.

Oxendine, J. B. (1970). Emotional arousal and motor performance. *Quest, 13*, 23–32.

Parfitt, G., Hardy, L., & Pates, J. (1995). Somatic anxiety and physiological arousal: Their effects upon a high anaerobic, low memory demand task. *International Journal of Sport Psychology, 26*, 196–213.

Parfitt, G., & Pates, J. (1999). The effects of cognitive and somatic anxiety and self-confidence on components of performance during competition. *Journal of Sports Sciences, 17*, 351–356.

Parkinson, B., Totterdell, P., Briner, R. B., & Reynolds, S. (1996). *Changing moods: The psychology of mood and mood regulation.* London: Longman.

Perkins, D., Wilson, G. V., & Kerr, J. H. (2001). The effects of elevated arousal and mood on maximal strength performance in athletes. *Journal of Applied Sport Psychology, 13*, 239–259.

Piaget, J. (1969). *The child's conception of time.* London: Routledge & Keegan Paul.

Platow, M. J., Durante, M., Williams, N., Garrett, M., Walshe, J., Cincotta, S., et al. (1999). The contribution of sport fan social identity to the production of prosocial behavior. *Group Dynamics: Theory, Research, and Practice, 3*, 161–169.

Richards, J. M., & Gross, J. J. (2000).Emotion regulation and memory: The cognitive costs of keeping one's cool. *Journal of Personality and Social Psychology, 79*, 410–424.

Robazza, C., Bortoli, L., & Hanin, Y. (2004). Precompetition emotions, bodily symptoms, and task-specific qualities as predictors of performance in high-level karate athletes. *Journal of Applied Sport Psychology, 16*, 151–165.

Robazza, C., Pellizzari, M., Bertollo, M., & Hanin, Y. L. (2008). Functional impact of emotions on athletic performance: Comparing the IZOF model and the directional perception approach. *Journal of Sports Sciences, 26*, 1033–1047.

Roese, N. J. (1997). Counterfactual thinking. *Psychological Bulletin, 121*, 133–148.

Roese, N. J., & Olson, J. M. (1993). Self-esteem and counterfactual thinking. *Journal of Personality and Social Psychology, 65*, 199–206.

Rolls, E. T. (2005). *Emotion explained.* Oxford, UK: Oxford University Press.

Rosenberg, E. L. (1998). Levels of analysis and organisation of affect. *Review of General Psychology, 2*, 247–270.

Salvador, A., & Costa, R. (2009). Coping with competition: Neuroendocrine responses and cognitive variables. *Neuroscience and Biobehavioral Reviews, 33*, 160–170.

Scanlan, T. K., Russell, D. G., Beals, K. P., & Scanlan, L. A. (2003). Project on elite athlete commitment (PEAK): II. A direct test and expansion of the Sport Commitment Model with elite amateur sportsmen. *Journal of Sport and Exercise Psychology, 25*, 377–401.

Schmeichel, B. J. (2007). Attention control, memory updating, and emotion regulation temporarily reduce the capacity for executive control. *Journal of Experimental Psychology: General, 136*, 241–255.

Schmeichel, B. J., Volokhov, R. N., & Demaree, H. A. (2008). Working memory capacity and the self-regulation of emotional expression and experience. *Journal of Personality and Social Psychology, 95*, 1526–1540.

Schweiger Gallo, I., & Gollwitzer, P. M. (2007). Implementation intentions: Control of fear despite cognitive load. *Psicothema, 19*, 280–285.

Schweiger Gallo, I., Keil, A., McCulloch, K. C., Rockstrock, B., & Gollwitzer, P. M. (2009). Strategic automation of emotion regulation. *Journal of Personality and Social Psychology, 96*, 11–31.

Seery, M. D., Weisbuch, M., & Blascovich, J. (2009). Something to gain, something to lose: The cardiovascular consequences of outcome framing. *International Journal of Psychophysiology, 73*, 308–312.

Seligman, M. E. P., Steen, T. A., Park, N., & Peterson, C. (2005). Positive psychology progress: Empirical validation of interventions. *American Psychologist, 60*, 410–421.

Skinner, N., & Brewer, N. (2004). Adaptive approaches to competition: Challenge appraisals and positive emotion. *Journal of Sport and Exercise Psychology, 26*, 283–305.

Tamir, M., & Ford, B. Q. (2009). Choosing to be afraid: Preferences for fear as a function of goal pursuit. *Emotion, 9*, 488–497.

Tice, D. M., Baumeister, R. F., Shmueli, D., & Muraven, M. (2007). Restoring the self: Positive affect helps improve self-regulation following ego depletion. *Journal of Experimental Social Psychology, 43*, 379–384.

Tod, D., & McGuigan, M. (2001). Maximizing strength training through goal setting. *Strength and Conditioning Journal, 23*, 22–27.

Totterdell, P. (2000). Catching moods and hitting runs: Mood linkage and subjective performance in professional sport teams. *Journal of Applied Psychology, 85*, 848–859.

Tugade, M. M., & Fredrickson, B. L. (2004). Resilient individuals use positive emotions to bounce back from negative emotional experiences. *Journal of Personality and Social Psychology, 86*, 320–333.

Uphill, M., & Jones, M. V. (2004). Cognitive-Motivational-Relational-Theory as a framework for coping with emotions in sport. In D. Lavallee, J. Thatcher, & M. V. Jones (Eds.), *Coping and emotion in sport* (pp. 75–89). Hauppauge, NY: Nova Science Publishers.

Uphill, M. A., & Jones, M. V. (2007). Antecedents of emotions in elite athletes: A cognitive motivational relational theory perspective. *Research Quarterly for Exercise and Sport, 78*, 79–89.

Uphill, M. A., McCarthy, P. J., & Jones, M. V. (2009). Getting a grip on emotion regulation in sport: Conceptual foundations and practical application. In S. Mellalieu & S. Hanton (Eds.), *Advances in applied sport psychology* (pp. 162–194). London: Routledge.

Vallerand, R. J., & Blanchard, C. M. (2000). The study of emotion in sport and exercise: Historical, definitional, and conceptual perspectives. In Y. L. Hanin (Ed.), *Emotions in sport* (pp. 3–37). Champaign, IL: Human Kinetics.

Vargas-Tonsing, T. M. (2009). An exploratory examination of the effects of coaches' pre-game speeches on athletes' perceptions of self-efficacy and emotion. *Journal of Sport Behavior, 32*, 92–111.

Vargas-Tonsing, T. M., & Guan, J. (2007). Athletes' preferences for informational and emotional pre-game speech content. *International Journal of Sports Sciences and Coaching, 2*, 171–180.

Watson, D., & Tellegen, A. (1985). Toward a consensual structure of mood. *Psychological Bulletin, 98*, 219–235.

Wegner, D. M. (1994). Ironic processes of mental control. *Psychological Review, 101*, 34–52.

Weiner, B. (1986). *An attributional theory of motivation and emotion.* New York: Springer-Verlag.

Williams, S. E., Cumming, J., & Balanos, G. M. (2010). The use of imagery to manipulate challenge and threat appraisal states in athletes. *Journal of Sport and Exercise Psychology, 32*, 339–358.

Wilson, M. R., Wood, G., Vine, S. J. (2009). Anxiety, attentional control, and performance impairment in penalty kicks. *Journal of Sport Exercise Psychology, 31*, 761–775.

Wood, J. V., Heimpel, S. A., & Michela, J. L. (2003). Savoring versus dampening: Self-esteem differences in regulating positive affect. *Journal of Personality and Social Psychology, 85*, 566–580.

Woodman, T., Davis, P. A., Hardy, L., Callow, N., Glasscock, I., & Yuill-Proctor, J. (2009). Emotions and sport performance: An exploration of happiness, hope, and anger. *Journal of Sport and Exercise Psychology, 31*, 169–188.

Woodman, T., & Hardy, L. (2001). Stress and anxiety. In R. N. Singer, H. A. Hausenblas, & C. M. Janelle (Eds.), *Handbook of research on sport psychology* (pp. 290–318.) New York: John Wiley and Sons.

Zillmann, D., Katcher, A. H., & Milavsky, B. (1972). Excitation transfer from physical exercise to subsequent aggressive behavior. *Journal of Experimental Social Psychology, 8*, 247–259.

Anxiety: Attention, the Brain, the Body, and Performance

Mark R. Wilson

Abstract

In sport psychology, the relationship between competitive anxiety and performance has been one of the most debated and researched topics of enquiry. However, the mechanisms underlying this relationship are still unclear, as are the reasons why performance can sometimes be optimal ("clutch" performance) and sometimes far below what should be achieved ("choking"). The current chapter integrates research findings and models from the neuroscience, cognitive psychology, human movement science, and sport performance literature to offer a potential explanatory framework, especially with respect to self-paced, visually guided skills. The mediating role of visual attention is implicated, as it has been proposed to be central to both the top-down control of motor planning and the effects of anxiety on cognitive performance. Contemporary research testing the effects of anxiety on visual attention (particularly the quiet eye) in performance environments, and the efficacy of attentional training programs, are discussed.

Key Words: Attention, gaze, quiet eye, pressure, choking, competition

> Some people think football is a matter of life and death.
> I don't like that attitude. I can assure them it is much
> more serious than that.
> —*Bill Shankly* (then manager of Liverpool FC), *In
> Sunday Times (UK)* October 4, 1981

Performing in professional competitive sport requires athletes to make split-second decisions, coordinate their limbs within multiple degrees of freedom, and maintain fine motor control under physical and mental fatigue—all while operating under the stress imposed by perceptions of the consequences of victory or defeat. Although other settings (e.g., military and emergency services) are true proving grounds for the pressures Shankly alludes to (see Janelle & Hatfield, 2008), there is no doubt that to succeed in sport, athletes must excel in evaluative conditions. However, sporting history is replete with examples of highly skilled athletes who failed to cope with this pressure and performed below their best just when optimal performance was most important (e.g., Syed, 2010).

It is therefore perhaps not surprising that the relationship between competitive anxiety and sports performance has been one of the most debated and investigated topics in the sport psychology literature

(Beilock & Gray, 2007; Hanton, Neil, & Mellalieu, 2008; Wilson, 2008; Woodman & Hardy, 2001). Although advances have been made by sport psychologists over the last 30 years in terms of the measurement, interpretation, and categorization of constructs related to anxiety, less systematic examination has been made of the mechanisms underlying the influence of anxiety on sporting performance (Janelle, 2002). The aim of this chapter is to integrate knowledge from the neuroscience, cognitive psychology, human movement science, and sport performance literature, in order to offer a mechanistic account of this relationship. Specifically, the mediating role of visual attention is implicated, as it has been proposed to be central to both the top-down control of motor planning and the effects of anxiety on cognitive performance.

Although some of the research reviewed may be of a fundamental motor control or cognitive psychology nature, the relevance to sport psychology and sporting performance should be evident. It has been suggested that of all the psychological constructs deemed important to quality sporting performance, the most critical factor is attention to the right *things* at the right *time* (Janelle, 2002; Vickers, 2007; see also Chapter 6, this volume). This chapter reviews contemporary research that has examined *how* anxiety might disrupt the optimal allocation of attention (location and timing) for sport skills. From an applied perspective, training regimes that may help performers maintain effective visual attention under pressure are also discussed. First, though, a brief introduction and historical perspective to competitive sport anxiety research will be provided.

Competitive Sport Anxiety

As this topic is one of the largest and most diverse research areas in sport psychology, it is not possible to adequately review all the relevant research in this chapter (see Hanton, et al., 2008; Jones, 1995; Raglin & Hanin, 2000; Wilson, 2008; Woodman & Hardy, 2001). However, the following sections provide a brief summary of what anxiety may mean in a sport/performance context and outline some of the most relevant theories. Generally, anxiety is postulated to occur as a result of threat and is related to the subjective evaluation of a situation with regard to one's self-esteem (Eysenck, 1992). It is considered a negative emotional state characterized by nervousness, worry, and apprehension and is associated with increased physiological arousal. Anxiety can be classified as a changing mood state and situation dependent (state anxiety), or an aspect of

personality that generally influences behavior (trait anxiety; Spielberger, 1983).

In sport settings, anxiety is usually related to the ego-threatening nature of the competitive environment and, "refers to an unpleasant psychological state in reaction to perceived threat concerning the performance of a task under pressure" (Cheng, Hardy, & Markland, 2009, p. 271). Baumeister (1984) defined pressure as "any factor or combination of factors that increases the importance of performing well" (p. 610). Alongside uncertainty regarding the outcome, pressure is considered to be the most common source of situational stress in sport (Weinberg & Gould, 2007). The relationship between anxiety and performance has most frequently been considered in terms of the consequences of poor performance under pressure—the dreaded choke!

Choking Under Pressure

Choking under pressure is a pejorative colloquial term used to describe suboptimal sporting performance under stressful conditions (Hill, Hanton, Matthews, & Fleming, 2010). Choking is defined as, "the occurrence of inferior performance despite striving and incentives for superior performance" (Baumeister & Showers, 1986, p. 361). The choking phenomenon, which can involve acute or chronic bouts of suboptimal performance, is a complex process involving the interplay of several cognitive, attentional, emotional, and situational factors (Gucciardi, Longbottom, Jackson, & Dimmock, 2010). Clark, Tofler, and Lardon (2005) suggest that while choking, the athlete is able to make rational decisions and select the correct "plan of action" under pressure, but cannot *execute* it because of intervening psychological factors. Several theories have emerged that have attempted to explain the mechanisms underlying choking; however, self-focus and distraction theories have received the most attention (e.g., Beilock & Carr, 2001; Gucciardi & Dimmock, 2008; Masters, 1992; Mullen & Hardy, 2000; Wilson, Chattington, Marple-Horvat, & Smith, 2007).

SELF-FOCUS THEORIES

Self-focus theories predict that pressure situations raise anxiety and self-consciousness about performing successfully, which in turn increase the attention paid to skill processes and their step-by-step control. The proposed mechanism of disruption is therefore the effortful allocation of attention to previously automated processes (Lewis & Linder,

1997). The most acknowledged self-focus theories are the *explicit monitoring hypothesis* (EMH; Beilock & Carr, 2001) and the *theory of reinvestment* (or the conscious processing hypothesis; Masters, 1992; see Chapter 7, this volume). Although the theories possess a number of similarities (e.g., that self-focus is particularly disruptive to expert performers), there are important differences regarding the mechanisms underlying choking. Reinvestment theory implicates conscious *control* of skill execution, whereas the EMH states that performance is disrupted by the athlete *monitoring* the step-by-step execution of the skill. Both theories have received considerable support in the sport psychology literature (see Beilock & Gray, 2007; Masters & Maxwell, 2008, for reviews).

DISTRACTION THEORIES

Distraction theories (e.g., cognitive interference theory; Sarason, 1988) propose that cognitive anxiety, in the form of worry, is resource intensive and causes a diversion of attention from task-relevant cues. This diversion of resources effectively changes single-task performance into a dual-task situation in which controlling the task at hand and attending to worrisome thoughts compete for attention (Beilock & Carr, 2001). These thoughts therefore interfere with the mental processes that support performance as adequate attention cannot be directed to task-relevant information (Wilson, 2008).

It is noteworthy that self-focus and distraction accounts of choking make essentially opposite predictions regarding how pressure exerts its impact, although both implicate attentional mechanisms. Distraction theories suggest that anxiety shifts necessary attention away from task execution, whereas self-focus theories suggest that anxiety shifts too much attention to skill execution processes. As both accounts have received empirical support, it is clear that there are (at least) two ways in which increased pressure can induce skill failure, what Beilock and Gray (2007) term "Pressure's double whammy."

Clutch Performance

Notwithstanding the support for attentional explanations of choking, the predicted negative influence of anxiety on sporting performance is less than would be expected (Wilson, 2008). Indeed, it is notable that some athletes not only do not choke, but actually tend to perform better than usual under pressure (Otten, 2009). Otten defines such "clutch: performance as, "any performance increment or superior performance that occurs under

pressure circumstances" (p. 584). Support for clutch performance is provided by at least five theoretical frameworks that have been tested in the sporting domain: the directional perspective (Jones, 1991), the transactional perspective of stress (Lazarus & Folkman, 1984), processing efficiency theory (PET; Eysenck & Calvo, 1992), the cusp catastrophe model (Hardy, 1996), and Cheng et al.'s (2009) three-dimensional model.

THE DIRECTIONAL PERSPECTIVE

Jones (1991) suggested that performers may not always interpret their anxiety symptoms as being debilitative toward performance but may in fact feel that they are necessary for mental preparation and performance (i.e., facilitative). Jones and colleagues therefore questioned the utility of solely measuring anxiety in terms of intensity (how anxious one feels) and suggested that it was more important to consider whether the intensity of symptoms experienced were interpreted as positive or negative toward upcoming performance (see Jones, 1995, for an early review). Jones (1995) further explained his notion of facilitative and debilitative interpretations of anxiety symptoms using a control model based on Carver and Scheier's (1988) work. Performers who appraise that they possess a degree of control over a potentially threatening situation and can cope with their anxiety symptoms—thus achieving their goals—are predicted to interpret symptoms as facilitative to performance. In contrast, performers who appraise that they are not in control, cannot cope with the situation, and possess negative expectancies regarding goal attainment are predicted to interpret such symptoms in a negative (debilitative) manner.

There has been a great deal of support for the directional perspective, and a range of personal and situational variables have been investigated to further our understanding of the directional response (see Hanton et al., 2008, for a recent review). Furthermore, Hanton and colleagues have started to examine how performers might be trained in the psychological skills required to effectively use their anxiety symptoms in a productive way and to develop a rational appraisal process in relation to their experiences during competition (see Hanton, Thomas, & Mellalieu, 2009). There are, therefore, clear links between this directional perspective to competitive anxiety and the more general, transactional perspective of stress espoused by Lazarus (Lazarus, 2000, Lazarus & Folkman, 1984).

THE TRANSACTIONAL PERSPECTIVE OF STRESS

Stress can be conceived as an ongoing transactional process between the environmental demands and the individual's resources, with anxiety resulting from an imbalance between these demands and coping resources (Lazarus & Folkman, 1984). The primary emphasis of this transactional or process approach is, therefore, on how individuals *cope* with stress. Coping is defined as, "constantly changing cognitive and behavioural efforts to manage specific external and/or internal demands that are appraised as taxing or exceeding the resources of a person" (Lazarus & Folkman, 1984, pp.141). Lazarus further distinguished between *primary* and *secondary* appraisals in the coping process (Lazarus, 2000). Primary appraisal is related to an evaluation of how important the situation is to an individual and whether or not it might endanger his or her well-being (in terms of harm/loss, threat, challenge, benefit). Secondary appraisal is the cognitive-evaluative process of the coping options available to the individual. Through the effective development of coping resources and productive appraisals, performers can therefore cope with the pressures inherent in competitive environments (e.g., Woodman & Hardy, 2001).

PROCESSING EFFICIENCY THEORY

Processing efficiency theory (PET) postulates that cognitive anxiety in the form of worry influences performance in two ways. First, as outlined for distraction theories, worry is assumed to pre-empt storage and processing resources from working memory, producing performance decrements in tasks that impose high levels of mental demand (Eysenck, 1992). Second, worry is also proposed to serve a motivational function. Concern over suboptimal performance leads to the allocation of additional processing resources (i.e., effort) to tasks or to the initiation of alternative processing strategies designed to maintain performance (Eysenck & Calvo, 1992). Although self-focus theories provide a potential explanation of how increased effort may be directed inappropriately to task control, PET explains how increased effort might aid performance (e.g., Edwards, Kingston, Hardy, & Gould, 2002). A particular strength of PET is, therefore, its ability to account for occasions when performance is not significantly impaired despite heightened anxiety (see Wilson, 2008, for a review of tests of PET in the sporting domain).

CATASTROPHE MODEL

Hardy (1996) proposed the cusp catastrophe model of anxiety and performance as a means of explaining the mixed findings that had previously been reported regarding the effects of anxiety upon performance. The model is based on the view that performance anxiety is a multidimensional construct combining a cognitive component (worry) and a physiological arousal component. According to the catastrophe model, performance depends on a complex interaction between these components. This interaction is used to explain how best and worst performance levels will occur when cognitive anxiety is high, depending on the level of physiological arousal experienced (Hardy, 1996). Although the model is difficult to test empirically and has received criticism (see Tenenbaum & Becker, 2005), it does provide an elegant framework to explain how clutch performance and choking can occur under high pressure. Furthermore, one of the strengths of the model is that different control parameters can be selected to examine other potential interactions in performance disruption (e.g., Beattie & Davies, 2010; Hardy, Beattie, & Woodman, 2007).

THREE-DIMENSIONAL CONCEPTUALIZATION OF PERFORMANCE ANXIETY

Cheng et al.'s (2009) framework is a recent attempt at reconceptualizing performance anxiety, due in part to a concern that the adaptive nature of anxiety had been under-represented in the sport psychology literature. This conceptual framework contains three main dimension of anxiety, characterized by five subcomponents: a cognitive dimension composed of worry and self-focused attention, a physiological dimension composed of autonomous hyperactivity and somatic tension, and a regulatory dimension indicated by perceived control.

Perceived control reflects the adaptive possibilities of anxiety within the framework and is defined as, "the perception of one's capacities to be able to cope and attain goals under stress" (Cheng et al., 2009, p. 273). Perceived control was also highlighted as a key mediator of clutch performance by Otten (2009) and is an important element of both PET (Eysenck & Calvo, 1992) and Carver and Scheier's (1988) control-process model of anxiety. Carver and Scheier proposed that expectancies regarding success in a task were critical in determining responses to and effects of anxiety. Cheng et al.'s new three-dimensional model of performance anxiety represents a promising step toward providing a detailed explanation for the sometimes conflicting results found in the sport anxiety literature. However, more research is required to develop its factorial structure and measures by which to test it.

Anxiety, Attention, and Cognitive Performance

As the brief summary of the competitive anxiety and choking under pressure literature has highlighted, attentional mechanisms are critical in understanding the relationship between increased anxiety and sporting performance. The remainder of the chapter will now examine these attentional mechanisms in more detail using a cognitive neuropsychology perspective (Moran, 2009). As the title of the chapter suggests, this review will focus on a cognitive approach to threat-related attentional bias ("anxiety"), the neural substrates underlying attention and anxiety ("the brain"), the planning and control of visually guided movements ("the body"), and the effect of all of these on sport ("performance").

Anxiety: A Cognitive Psychology Perspective

The preceding section outlined some of the cognitive models of anxiety that have been most frequently examined in sport. However, the influence of anxiety on performance has had a long history of research interest in applied environments, originally in relation to test anxiety (see Stöber & Pekrun, 2004). For school students, individual differences in test anxiety play a major role not only for their academic achievement, but also for more wide-ranging outcomes, such as their career advancement and their personality development and health (Stöber & Pekrun, 2004). Research has tended to support an attentional resource explanation, with increased worry being related to lower examination performance (Keogh & French, 2001; Wine, 1971). The following section discusses some of the main concepts underpinning the influence of anxiety on attention.

Anxiety and Attentional Bias

From an evolutionary perspective, anxiety (like other emotions) evolved to quickly organize our cognitive functions when necessary and should therefore not just be considered as "negative" (Cheng et al., 2009). Anxiety has/had a functional role, acting as a defence mechanism that sends out warning signals that protect and prepare an individual to respond more effectively to perceived threat (Ohman, 2000). Additionally, another evolutionary advantage of anxiety could be that worrying about danger forces people to take fewer risks, seek safety, and focus on doing things well (to avoid the consequences of poor performance). However, these same threat bias processes have also been linked to less functional behaviors in our "modern" world, as evidenced in a diverse range of anxiety disorders (e.g., generalized anxiety, social phobias, physical phobias, etc.).

Anxiety disorders and generalized heightened anxiety can be hugely disruptive to everyday life. Consequently, there is a great deal of interest in "mainstream" cognitive psychology in advancing our understanding of the mechanisms underlying anxiety. Most theoretical models of anxiety disorders implicate attention to threat-relevant information in their etiology and maintenance (Weierich, Treat, & Hollingworth, 2008). For example, an enhanced tendency to select threatening items for processing is likely to lead to an artificially increased perception of the extent of threat in the environment, thereby influencing subsequent cognitive and emotional processes related to anxiety (Yiend, 2008).

A strong body of evidence now shows that anxiety is indeed associated with an attentional bias toward and an inability to "disengage" from the processing of threat-related distracters, and/or an enhanced distractibility in the presence of task-irrelevant threatening stimuli (see Bar-Haim, Lamy, Pergamin, Bakermans-Kranenburg, & van IJzendoorn, 2007; Weierich et al., 2008, for reviews and discussion). These cognitive models of anxiety extend biased competition models of selective attention, which implicate the interplay between "bottom-up" sensory mechanisms and "top-down" control processes (see Duncan, 2006, for a review). Selective attention to threat is therefore argued to be determined by the relative signal strength from a preattentive threat evaluation mechanism versus that from top-down control mechanisms (Pachego-Unguettit, Acosta, Callejas, & Lapianez, 2010). Anxiety alters the strength of output from the preattentive threat evaluation system, increasing the likelihood that threat-related stimuli will capture attention (Mogg & Bradley, 1999).

REGULATORY ATTENTIONAL CONTROL

Derryberry and Reed (2002) provide an interesting adjunct to the typical finding that attentional biases are central to both processing and structural aspects of the experience of anxiety. These authors suggest that although individuals may differ in the way in which attention (relatively automatically) amplifies threat and exacerbates anxiety, they may also differ in the extent to which they use *voluntary* attention to control orienting. In effect, it is voluntary attention that is recruited in the coping strategies that people use to regulate their anxiety. Anxious individuals who have poorer attentional control find it more difficult to disengage from threatening stimuli than anxious individuals with better attentional control.

Derryberry and Reed adopted Posner and Raichle's (1994) cognitive neuroscience model of attention, which considers both involuntary and voluntary processes. The *posterior* attentional system is a relatively reactive system that orients the attentional "spotlight" from one location to another. Once information is engaged, it is transmitted to the *anterior* attentional system, which acts as an executive system that carries out more voluntary attentional functions. The anterior system can regulate the posterior system, thereby providing voluntary control (guided by expectations or motives) over the allocation of attention in space (see also Rothbart, Sheese, & Posner, 2007). Derryberry and Reed (2002) argue that the anterior system might help reduce anxiety (and improve performance) by enabling an individual to disengage from threat and engage effective attentional control on productive cues.

We will return to these ideas later in the chapter, as the concept of directing attention to productive (or task-relevant) cues is a critical component of *quiet eye* training interventions.

The Brain: Neural Mechanisms

The advent of neuroimaging has provided a route for examining the neural substrate of associative and attentional processes in humans. Although this chapter focuses mainly on the cognitive and attentional mechanisms underpinning the influence of anxiety on performance, other neural pathways have been implicated in the stress response associated with anxiety. For example, it is known that stress causes various physiological alterations, including homeostatic imbalances and activation of the hypothalamic-pituitary-adrenal (HPA) axis. During a stress response, corticotropin-releasing factor (CRF) activates the HPA axis, to stimulate the release of adrenocorticotropic hormone (ACTH). Corticotropin-releasing factor has also been proposed to have an involvement in the development of anxiety-related and mood disorders (Bale & Vale, 2004). As a detailed discussion of all arousal-related

mechanisms is beyond the scope of this chapter, the remainder of this section will return to our focus on attentional processes underlying anxiety.

Attention and the Dorsal Lateral Prefrontal Cortex

Recent work by Bishop and colleagues has revealed that anxiety is associated with both enhanced amygdala activation and reduced recruitment of prefrontal cortical areas, primarily the dorsal lateral prefrontal cortex (DLPFC; see Bishop, 2007, 2008, 2009). The amygdala is part of the limbic system, a set of brain structures supporting a variety of functions including emotion, behavior, long-term memory, and olfaction (Swanson & Petrovich, 1998). The amygdala performs a primary role in the processing and memory of emotional reactions and is a key structure in the processing of threat-related stimuli (Bishop, Duncan, & Lawrence, 2004; Phelps, 2006).

The DLPFC is located on the middle frontal gyrus and superior frontal gyrus (Petrides, 2005) and is thought to support cognitive control processes that enable voluntarily control of actions (MacDonald, Cohen, Stenger, & Carter, 2000; Weissman, Perkins, & Woldorff, 2004). The DLPFC has been implicated in sustained and flexible control of attention, particularly for visuospatial working memory tasks (Knudsen, 2007). Importantly, in relation to the current chapter, this structure is thought to support the establishment and maintenance of representations for current goals and rules to facilitate task-related performance (Bishop, 2009; Corbetta & Schulman, 2002).

Bishop's research suggests that anxiety disrupts the amygdala–prefrontal circuitry, with deficient recruitment of prefrontal control mechanisms and amygdaloid hyperresponsivity to threat leading to a threat-related processing bias in anxious individuals (Bishop, 2007). In broad terms, these neuroscience findings provide support for the theories from the cognitive psychology literature referred to earlier (e.g., Bar-Haim et al., 2007; Weierich et al., 2008). Of particular interest to the current chapter is the impact that anxiety has been shown to exert on conscious, attentional control. A recent functional magnetic resonance imaging (fMRI) study by Bishop (2009) utilizing a response-conflict task revealed that anxious participants were slower to identify targets in the presence of incongruent distracters. Anxiety was also associated with deficient recruitment of DLPFC mechanisms used to augment attentional control in response to processing conflict.

A Theoretical Framework: Attentional Control Theory

A recent theoretical development from cognitive psychology, *attentional control theory* (ACT; Eysenck, Derakshan, Santos, & Calvo, 2007), aims to provide a framework by which to understand the influence of anxiety on attentional control and cognitive performance. Attentional control theory is an extension and development of processing efficiency theory (PET; Eysenck & Calvo, 1992), which has previously received empirical support in the cognitive psychology (see Eysenck et al., 2007, for a review) and sport psychology (see Wilson, 2008, for a review) literature. The primary hypothesis of PET is that anxiety impairs the efficiency of the central executive, an attention-like, limited capacity component of working memory (see Baddeley, 1986, 2001). When anxious, the efficiency with which individuals process and act upon information decreases, potentially resulting in performance degradation. Whereas PET makes predictions about the effect of anxiety on the general efficiency by which information is processed, ACT is more explicit about the specific attentional processes involved, as discussed below.

TOP-DOWN VERSUS STIMULUS-DRIVEN ATTENTIONAL CONTROL

Attentional control theory shares similarities with other theoretical models of anxiety disorders that propose that anxious individuals both orient more rapidly to anxiety-inducing stimuli and disengage from them more slowly (see Weierich et al., 2008, for a review). Eysenck et al. (2007) suggest that anxiety is likely to cause a diversion of processing resources from task-relevant stimuli toward task-irrelevant (and particularly threatening) stimuli. This impairment in attentional control is proposed to occur irrespective of whether these stimuli are external (e.g., environmental distractors) or internal (e.g., worrying thoughts). The authors explicitly relate this impairment of attentional control to a disruption in the balance of two attentional systems first outlined by Corbetta and colleagues: the goal-directed and the stimulus-driven systems (Corbetta & Schulman, 2002; Corbetta, Patel, & Shulman, 2008).[1] According to ACT, anxiety disrupts the balance between these two attentional systems by increasing the influence of the stimulus-driven attentional system at the expense of the more efficient goal-directed system (Eysenck et al., 2007).

The top-down (goal-directed) control system is centered on the dorsal posterior parietal and frontal cortex and is involved in preparing and applying goal-directed selection of stimuli and action responses. The stimulus-driven control system includes the temporoparietal cortex and inferior frontal cortex and is largely lateralized to the right hemisphere (Corbetta & Schulman, 2002). Corbetta and Schulman suggest that this ventral frontoparietal network works as a "circuit breaker" (2000, p. 201) for the dorsal system. This circuit breaking effect can be an adaptive process, directing attention to potentially important or salient events. However, as anxiety alters the strength of output from the preattentive threat evaluation system, the likelihood that threat-related stimuli will capture attention is increased. If top-down attentional control is required to effectively complete a task, such stimulus-driven (ventral) processing will likely impair effective attentional control and potentially task performance (see Pachego-Unguettit et al., 2010, for a discussion of how trait and state anxiety may modulate attention through different effects on top-down and stimulus-driven attentional control).

CENTRAL EXECUTIVE FUNCTIONS: INHIBITION AND SHIFTING

Attentional control theory also makes predictions regarding those specific functions of the central executive that are most adversely affected by anxiety; namely, the "inhibition" and "shifting" functions (based on Miyake et al., 2000). The inhibition function involves using attentional control to resist disruption or interference from task-irrelevant stimuli (negative control). The shifting function involves using attentional control to shift the allocation of attention in a flexible and optimal way to remain focused on the task stimulus or stimuli that are currently most relevant (positive control). It is the impaired functioning of these elements of attentional control (i.e., inhibition and shifting) that is proposed to disrupt the balance between the goal-directed and stimulus-driven attentional systems (Eysenck & Derakshan, 2011; Eysenck et al., 2007).

As different sports make varying demands on inhibition and switching functions, anxiety is likely to impair attentional control (and potentially performance) via different mechanisms. For example, attentional control is likely to be impaired in target sports (e.g., shooting and archery) via less efficient inhibition of internal and external distracting stimuli. On the other hand, in invasion sports (e.g., football, basketball, etc.), it is the inability to effectively scan for appropriate cues that may impair performance (e.g., "ball watching").

There is considerable evidence that anxiety is associated with increased susceptibility to distraction and thus impaired efficiency of the inhibition function (Eysenck & Derakshan, 2011). This research has typically involved paradigms in which conditions vary in terms of the presence and/or nature of distracting stimuli (see Derakshan & Eysenck, 2009, for a review). Research testing the prediction that anxiety impairs the efficiency of the shifting function typically adopts the task-switching paradigm (Derakshan & Eysenck, 2009). These sorts of "process pure" tasks that isolate inhibition or switching functions are difficult to replicate in sport settings. However, Eysenck and Derakshan (2011) suggest that by tracking eye movements on tasks in which it is possible to specify *where* visual attention should be and *how* it might switch over time, optimal top-down attentional control (whether it is negative or positive) can be assessed.

The following section examines how this form of inquiry has been successfully adopted by researchers aiming to understand how vision provides the information needed to support goal-directed action (e.g., Land, 2009; Vickers, 2007).

The Body: Visual Attention and Visuomotor Control

Most of the research implicating attention in anxiety-induced performance disruptions has used cognitive tasks, which raises the question of whether the same principles can be applied to visuomotor (sport) tasks. By emphasizing mental processes only, cognitive psychology research has tended to ignore the planning and control of motor outputs. However, in order to behave adaptively in a complex environment, an individual must select the information that is most relevant at any point in time, so that effective plans for action can be developed (Knudsen, 2007). Indeed, the principal function of vision for our Neolithic ancestors was to provide the information required to support the actions of everyday life—hunting, foraging, lighting fires, etc. (Land, 2009). Attention and preparation for action are therefore closely linked, as is eloquently illustrated by William James' quote; "My thinking is first and last and always for the sake of my doing" (1890, p. 333).

So, how important is visual attention in the control of motor tasks? Does anxiety affect attentional control in motor tasks in the same way that it does in cognitive tasks? The following sections address these questions.

Neuroscience and Visually Guided Movement

A great deal of cognitive neuroscience research supports the use of gaze measures as correlates of visual attention (e.g., Corbetta, 1998; Henderson, 2003; Shipp, 2004). It is generally accepted that a change in gaze requires the activation of covert and then overt attention, and it is difficult to shift the point of gaze without shifting covert attention (Shinoda, Hayhoe, & Shrivastava, 2001). The close linkage between gaze and visual attention is especially apparent in visually guided manual tasks. Individuals learn to program spatially congruent eye and hand motor commands, so that fixations on objects precede manual reaching and pass visually acquired goal position information to the arm and hand control systems (Land, 2009; Neggers & Bekkering, 2000; Sailer, Flanagan, & Johansson, 2005). Task-specific (goal-directed) eye movements that support the planning and control of manual action are therefore under top-down attentional control and are present throughout action sequences for more complex tasks (Land, 2009).

The development of lightweight head-mounted eyetrackers has meant that the planning and control of visually guided actions can now be undertaken in more natural environments (see Land, 2006, 2009). This research has shown that fixations extract very specific information needed by an ongoing task (Ballard & Hayhoe, 2009). Indeed, there is now general agreement that top-down instructions dominate gaze behavior during the performance of visually guided actions; very little visual information is taken up that is not of immediate use to the task (see Land, 2009, for examples).

For example, driving is a classic example of visually guided behavior in which the eyes move in relation to and just before another action. When driving along a winding road, eye movements and steering are tightly linked; when approaching a bend, the driver looks across to the inside curb (the tangent point) some time before turning the steering wheel (Land & Lee, 1994; Wilson, Stephenson, Chattington, & Marple-Horvat, 2007). Indeed, the degree of coordination and relative timing of the eye movements has been shown to be strongly linked to driving performance in simulated racing (Marple-Horvat et al., 2005; Wilson, Stephenson et al., 2007; Wilson, Chattington, & Marple-Horvat, 2008).

Recent research in laparoscopic surgery environments has also revealed differences in the gaze strategies of experienced and novice operators (Wilson, McGrath, Vine, Brewer, Defriend, & Masters, 2010, 2011). While novices switch their gaze between the tools they are controlling and the target they are aiming for, experienced performers adopt a "target locking" strategy in which they locate tool position using peripheral vision. This is a more skilled visuomotor strategy as it involves the ability to predict the consequences of one's actions and implement mapping rules relating motor and sensory signals (see Sailer et al., 2005).

In sport tasks, it has also been demonstrated that experts tend to use more efficient gaze strategies than nonexperts, focusing on only the information that is most useful to complete the task at hand (see Mann, Williams, Ward, & Janelle, 2007, for a recent meta-analysis on perceptual-cognitive expertise in sport). For example, recent research examining the cues used by cricket batsmen has revealed that, in addition to a capability to pick up advance information from the same cues used by intermediate and low-skilled players, highly skilled players demonstrated the additional, unique capability of picking up advance information from some specific early cues (especially bowling hand and arm cues) to which the less skilled players were not attuned. (e.g., Müller, Abernethy, & Farrow, 2006).

The preceding discussion has identified that gaze strategies are not random and appear to develop in accord with task demands to simplify the planning and control of movement. In outlining how the visual control of action unfolds, Land (2009) has described the role of several distinct but interacting brain systems. First, the gaze system is responsible for locating and fixating (targeting) task-relevant objects. Second, the motor system that controls the limbs carries out the task at hand. Third, the visual system supplies information to the other two systems, providing feedback as to what is being fixated and directional guidance to the motor system. These three systems are subject to joint programming by the *schema system*, a supervisory system mainly located in the DLPFC, which specifies the goals of the current task and then determines the sequence of actions that will achieve these (via attentional pathways). Land (2009) describes the schema as a basic unit of top-down control of action, "a set of instructions that determines where gaze will be directed, what information the visual system will be called upon to provide, and what action will be taken" (p. 53–54).

Land (2009) suggests that the temporal and spatial relationships between gaze fixations and the action they facilitate are of particular interest because they indicate the sequence in which the top-down schema instructions are obeyed and the precision required for their execution. Generally, fixation is close to the site of the action and precedes action by a short interval—approximately 1 second for many tasks (Land, 2009). In the sport-based literature, a particular measure of efficient visual attentional control, the quiet eye (QE; Vickers, 1996) relates explicitly to the spatial and temporal coordination of gaze and motor control. Indeed, the QE offers great potential in answering Land's concluding call to action for future research: "The challenge is now to find out how descending attentional mechanisms control gaze during purposeful action" (p. 61).

The Quiet Eye

The QE has been defined as the final fixation toward a relevant target prior to the execution of the critical phase of movement and has been adopted as a measure of optimal visual attentional control in visuomotor tasks (Vickers, 2007). Seminal work by Vickers (1996) highlighted the importance of the QE fixation in the basketball free throw. Vickers highlighted that expert performers displayed an optimal timing and duration of their final fixation toward the target, prior to the execution of the critical movement. The QE has since been shown to underlie higher levels of skill and performance in a wide range of aiming and interceptive skills, with experts having longer QE durations than nonexperts and successful attempts having longer QE durations than unsuccessful attempts (see Mann et al., 2007; Vickers, 2009, for reviews). The neural mechanisms by which the QE works are yet to be fully understood; however, the QE has been proposed to reflect a critical period of cognitive processing during which the parameters of the movement, such as force, direction, and velocity, are fine-tuned and programmed (Vickers, 1996).

Vickers (1996) used Posner and Raichle's (1994) conceptualization of posterior orienting, anterior executive networks to provide support for her postulations of how the QE may provide optimal attentional control. However, the explanation perhaps resonates more closely with Corbetta and Shulman's (2002) top-down, goal-directed attentional system (or "dorsal attention"; Corbetta et al., 2008). As previously highlighted, this system is important for response or action selection and is involved in linking relevant stimuli to motor planning (Corbetta et al., 2008; Jeannerod, 1997; MacDonald et al., 2000). Theoretically, longer QE periods therefore allow performers an extended duration of response programming, while minimizing distraction from other environmental cues (Vickers, 1996). In the language of Corbetta and colleagues, the QE may help maintain effective goal-driven attentional control, while reducing the impact of the stimulus-driven attentional system. If the predictions of ACT are to be upheld for visuomotor skills, anxiety should disrupt the QE, as the relative emphasis between goal-directed and stimulus-driven attentional control is shifted. The following section discusses contemporary research that has examined the influence of anxiety on the QE.

Performance: The Effect of Competitive Anxiety on the Quiet Eye

Recent research has demonstrated that goal-directed attentional control, as indexed by QE, may be impaired (shorter QE durations) under heightened levels of state anxiety (Behan & Wilson, 2008; Causer, Holmes, Smith, & Williams, 2011a; Vickers & Williams, 2007; Wilson & Vine, 2009; Wilson, Vine, & Wood, 2009; Wilson, Wood, & Vine, 2009; Wood & Wilson, 2010). Both Behan and Wilson (2008) in an archery task, and Wilson, Vine, et al. (2009) in basketball shooting, found that anxiety impaired the ability of participants to maintain goal-directed attention on the relevant target location for long enough to process the critical direction and force information required for successful performance. Quiet eye durations were reduced in the threatening condition as participants made more, shorter duration fixations to locations around the target area. A subsequent drop in performance effectiveness in pressure conditions was evident in both studies. These findings can be explained in terms of the circuit-breaking effect outlined by Corbetta and colleagues and subsequently applied to the influence of anxiety on attentional control by Eysenck et al. (2007). The increased emphasis of the ventral system appears to have disrupted the efficient and quiet focus created by the QE (dorsal attention), making the performers more distractible (see also Causer et al., 2011a).

Although it might be difficult to unpick how internal distractions (worry and negative rumination) influence visual attentional control in these studies, a more explicit test of the predictions of ACT is possible in tasks in which visual distractions are present. For example, Coombes, Higgins, Gamble, Cauraugh, and Janelle (2009) have recently demonstrated that the presence of distracting negative emotional images impairs the attentional control of individuals carrying out a motor task involving goal-directed force contractions. Wilson and Vine (2009), in an extension of their earlier basketball study (Wilson, Vine, et al., 2009) found that anxious participants were more likely to fixate on the ball in their hands during the lift stage of the throw, thus shortening their optimal QE durations.

An aiming task that has been the subject of recent investigation and involves a task-relevant visual distracter is the football (soccer) penalty. This is an interesting task to study from an ACT perspective for a number of reasons. First, anxiety has been shown to be *the* major contributing factor that influences performance failure in soccer penalty shoot-outs (Jordet, 2009; Jordet, Hartman, Visscher, & Lemmink, 2007). Second, the goalkeeper's actions are the principal source of uncertainty bearing on the shooter's success in achieving his or her goal, in what would otherwise be a straightforward aiming task. Given that the goalkeeper is therefore a threatening external stimulus in this evaluative situation, it is interesting to determine what effect the goalkeeper might have on the penalty taker's attentional control and performance.

Wilson, Wood et al. (2009) attempted to determine how anxiety affected the gaze and aiming behaviors of penalty takers. The results indicated that when anxious, participants were significantly quicker to fixate on the (centrally located) goalkeeper and fixated upon him for longer periods. This anxiety-induced change in gaze behavior led to disruption in aiming behavior, resulting in more centrally hit kicks and more saved shots. These findings are consistent with the predictions of ACT, as anxious individuals showed an attentional bias toward the salient and threatening stimulus (the goalkeeper) at the expense of goal-driven, task-relevant stimuli (the optimal scoring zones just inside the post of the goal).

Wood and Wilson (2010) then further manipulated the saliency of the goalkeeper by asking him to attempt to distract the penalty taker (by waving his arms) under counterbalanced conditions of threat. Results suggested that participants were more distracted by a moving goalkeeper than a stationary one and struggled to disengage from a moving goalkeeper under situations of high threat. Significantly more penalties were saved when the goalkeeper was distracting, and shots were also hit closer to the goalkeeper on these trials. The authors concluded that this shift in attentional control toward the "threatening" and distracting goalkeeper was again supportive of the predictions of ACT.

The results from the highlighted research in sport settings suggest that the QE is sensitive to increases in anxiety and may be a useful index of the efficiency of visual attentional control in aiming tasks. Interestingly, Vickers and Williams (2007) found that elite biathletes who increased their QE duration during high-pressure competition, compared to low-pressure practice, were less susceptible to sudden performance disruption or "choking." Vickers and Williams suggested that the act of allocating attention externally to critical task information (via the QE) appeared to insulate athletes from the normally debilitating effects of anxiety. Wilson and colleagues have therefore suggested that QE training programs may be a useful intervention to enhance attentional control in stressful environments (Wilson, 2010). By actively maintaining effective gaze behavior, the negative effects of anxiety on visual attentional control and subsequent performance may be alleviated (Behan & Wilson, 2008).

Implications for Sport Psychologists

A key goal of a consultant sport psychologist is to help performers deal with the emotional and cognitive factors inherent in performing in ego-threatening situations (e.g., Hardy, Jones, & Gould, 1996; Zinsser, Bunker, & Williams, 2006). Eysenck et al. (2007) suggest that the adverse effects of stimulus-driven attentional control can be reduced or eliminated by adopting compensatory strategies. The authors suggest the use of increased task-based effort and processing resources, but don't provide guidance as to how this may work in practice. Applied sport psychology research has outlined the benefit of focusing effort on "controlling the controllables" and maintaining present/process-focused attention in order to cope with the distracting nature of cognitive intrusions (e.g., Mullen & Hardy, 2010; Wilson & Smith, 2007).

Pre-performance routines, consisting of behavioral and cognitive elements, have been proposed as a useful strategy for maintaining concentration and perceptions of control in pressurized environments (Moran, 1996). Singer's five-step strategy, a particular example of a pre-performance routine, has been shown to facilitate learning and performance in a number of laboratory and field studies (see Singer, 2000, 2002). It focuses on creating the conditions for a "just do it" performance state and emphasizes that optimally focused attention is best achieved by selecting one, appropriate external cue. The QE may be seen as part of such a pre-performance routine, helping the performer focus on what he or she can control (an external, process-related cue) rather than on nonproductive (internal) thoughts and emotions (see Wilson & Richards, 2010, for a discussion of how this pre-performance routine might be developed).

Quiet Eye Training

The aim of QE training is to better prepare individuals for dealing with pressure by guiding them to focus on their optimal visual cues for accurate performance. It is therefore important to know what these cues are, and when and how long they should be fixated during the planning and execution of a sport skill. To date, the research examining QE training as a means of dealing with the evaluative threat inherent in sporting competition has focused on aiming tasks, in which there has already been much QE research (e.g., golf, basketball free-throw shooting, and shotgun shooting). This is important as the characteristics of optimal visual attention are well known in these tasks and can be incorporated easily into a pre-shot routine (see Wilson & Richards, 2010).

For example, in golf putting, training would first focus on providing golfers with video feedback of the gaze strategy they currently adopt (using a mobile gaze registration system). Second, they are asked to compare their own strategy to that of an expert video model, adopting effective QE attentional control. Third, the importance of this gaze strategy is reinforced by discussing some of the key elements of effective visuomotor control with the golfer. Finally, the golfer continues to practice the gaze strategy with video feedback and works the process into his or her "normal" pre-putt routine. The important elements to include are that, after they have lined up the putt and imagined a successful outcome, they should direct a final fixation to the back of the ball and maintain this for about a second (for example by saying, "clean contact") before initiating the backswing of the putter head. The golfer is reminded to maintain this fixation during the putting stroke and to keep it on the green (where the ball was) for half a second after contact (to ensure attention is totally focused on the process of contact and not on the outcome of where the ball goes).

WHAT MECHANISMS UNDERPIN QUIET EYE TRAINING?

There are at least four mechanisms through which QE training helps maintain performance under pressure, consisting of both visuomotor control and psychological control elements (see also Vine, Moore, & Wilson, 2011). First, as discussed already, the motor system tends to be more accurate when provided with timely information about targets from the gaze system. Quiet eye training provides "technical" guidance to performers to ensure that their attentional control, gaze control, and motor control are effectively coordinated (see section on Action-Focused Coping). So, for example, in golf putting, by holding a ball-focused QE throughout a putting stroke and through impact, golfers are able to replicate a more accurate contact with the sweet spot of the putter, thus ensuring more consistent ball strike.

Second, the QE may provide the "external focus of attention" described by Wulf and colleagues (see Wulf, 2007) or the "external cue" described in Singer's (2000, 2002) five-step pre-performance routine. Singer advocates focusing on an external cue to prevent athletes from focusing on internal or external distracters, negative thoughts, or the mechanics of skill execution (Singer, 2002). As the stimulus-driven attentional system is more active when performers are anxious (Eysenck et al., 2007), such internal and external distracters are more likely to influence performance under pressure. A further advantage of QE training is that not only is the external *target* of the focus of attention considered, but also its optimal *duration* and *timing* relative to the key movement components of the task (Vine & Wilson, 2010). Linked to this second explanation is the idea that QE training might also act as a form of implicit motor learning (Masters, 1992) when applied to novices. By preventing the generation of explicit rules related to movement control and freeing up attentional resources, QE trained performers are unable to choke via mechanisms related to reinvestment (Wilson, McGrath, & Coleman, 2010). In this way, QE training appears to be supportive of William James' famous quote relating to attentional control: "Keep your eye at the place aimed at, and your hand will fetch [the target]; think of your hand, and you will likely miss your aim" (James, 1890, p. 520).

Third, the QE may also help provide a focus on what is controllable (e.g., maintaining a steady fixation and good contact) rather than what is not (a successful outcome) when performers are under pressure. As competitive anxiety is associated with the outcome uncertainty of a task, it is easy for attention to be involuntarily "attracted" toward such future-related thoughts. However, as highlighted by Derryberry and Reed (2002), individuals can utilize voluntary (anterior system) control of their attention to facilitate the posterior system's capacity to disengage from threatening stimuli. Quiet eye training provides a task-relevant location for attention to engage and can include cue word phrases to reinforce the "in control" nature of the process.

Fourth, QE training may simply help the performer achieve general quiescence of the psychomotor system (i.e., create a more relaxed pre-performance state). Previous research has demonstrated that superior visuomotor performance is reflected in increased psychomotor and neural efficiency (e.g., Janelle & Hatfield 2008; Yarrow, Brown, & Krakauer, 2009). The quiet focus provided by the QE fixation might help pressure performance by providing a moment of calm just prior to and during the performance of motor skills. For example, Singer (2002) also suggested that an external (target) fixation period serves as a means of self-regulation to enter and sustain an optimal attentional state for performing.

Although some areas of overlap exist between the mechanisms highlighted above, subsequent research should attempt to untangle *how* the QE exerts its influence on pressurized performance through these various pathways. Although this has not been achieved to date, there has been growing support for the efficacy of QE training for both novices and experienced performers in evaluative conditions.

QUIET EYE TRAINING: RESEARCH SUPPORT

Recent research has demonstrated that novices taught basketball free-throw shooting (Vine & Wilson, 2011) and golf-putting (Vine & Wilson, 2010) via a QE training program learn more quickly and have more robust performance under stress than those trained using a traditional "movement-focused" training program. In both these studies, QE-trained novices maintained their QE periods at above optimal threshold levels in a condition designed to increase ego threat. Importantly, these performers also maintained performance at low pressure levels, whereas the movement-trained group performed significantly worse under pressure. The movement-trained group also displayed impaired QE fixations that were below optimal thresholds and significantly lower than their QE-trained counterparts.

Quiet eye training has also recently been shown to protect against stress-related performance effects in more experienced performers who have already developed their idiosyncratic gaze strategies (Causer, Holmes, & Williams, 2011b). For example, a recent study by Vine, Moore, and Wilson (2011) sought to demonstrate if a brief QE training intervention might help to protect low-handicap golfers from the impact of competition pressure. The golfers (average handicap 2.5) were split into two groups and recorded their putting performance over ten rounds before and after coming to the laboratory. One group received an individual 2-hour QE training intervention during this period, whereas the other group only received the gaze feedback of their own gaze behavior. The QE-trained group performed significantly better in a subsequent laboratory-based pressure competition; holing 17% more putts than their competitors. The performance improvements also transferred to the course, with the QE-trained group holing 6% more putts from 6–10 ft and reducing their average number of putts by two per round following training.

A 3-week QE training program has also recently been developed for soccer players to train the penalty kick and was tested by means of an experimental penalty shootout (Wood & Wilson, 2011). The aim of the study was to explore if, by aligning gaze with aiming intention, penalty takers could increase their shooting accuracy. Although other aspects of the penalty shootout scenario are outside the kicker's control, penalties that are struck to the corners of the goal are more likely to score, irrespective of the behaviors and ability of the goalkeeper (Bar-Eli & Azar, 2009). The training did help the QE-trained participants to shoot more accurately than their control group counterparts in a retention test and to maintain their performance under the pressure of a shootout. However, the results were somewhat equivocal as to the benefit of maintaining long, distal aiming fixations, as the control group also maintained performance under pressure, despite having poorer attentional control (Wood & Wilson, 2011).

ACTION-FOCUSED COPING

The intention of QE training is, therefore, to (re)direct the performer to the critical cues required for successful performance, rather than to focus on dealing with either the emotions or cognitions surrounding the pressure environment (Wilson, 2010). In this way, the approach is mechanisms-driven and focuses on what the performers know

they can control. Hanin and Hanina (2009) have also recently suggested that interventions for "performance problems" do not always have to be emotion-focused; that is, designed to help the athlete find (and/or maintain) an optimal performance state in stressful conditions. Instead, action-focused coping is related to technical execution and requires the performer to understand more about how he or she performs well and why things may go wrong under pressure. Specifically, performers self-generate a chain of interrelated task components that they can then rate to determine individual zones for optimal performance. The authors argue that whereas emotion-focused coping directly affects the performer's emotional state, action-focused coping aims to directly optimize the performance process (through technical excellence).

The strength of such an approach is that athletes are tuned into the language of performance data feedback and tend to find the objective nature of such feedback intuitive. Furthermore, some performers will find the technical focus to be less negatively charged and threatening than discussing emotional concerns underlying their choking experiences. A concern with the technique-focused nature of action-focused coping is that by building the athlete's knowledge base of the movements underlying performance, the propensity to reinvest in this knowledge under pressure is increased (Masters, 1992; Masters & Maxwell, 2008). A specific advantage of gaze-related action-focused coping is that it may actually prevent reinvestment and act as a form of implicit motor learning (Wilson, McGrath, & Coleman, 2010).

Training with Anxiety

Another interesting approach to dealing with the attentional disruptions caused by increased anxiety has been outlined by Raul Oudejans and colleagues (Nieuwenhuys & Oudejans, 2010; Oudejans, 2008; Oudejans & Nieuwenhuys, 2009; Oudejans & Pijpers, 2009, 2010). These authors have demonstrated that training *with* anxiety can lead to improved performance under future stressful circumstances (see also Baumeister, 1984; Beilock & Carr, 2001, for discussions of *acclimatization training*). For example, in Oudejans and Pijpers' (2009) study, performers practiced perceptual-motor tasks (basketball free-throw shooting and dart throwing) with or without induced anxiety. Only after training with anxiety did performance no longer deteriorate during a pressurized transfer test, despite these performers experiencing similar elevated levels of anxiety, heart rate, and perceived effort to their control group counterparts. The authors concluded that practising under anxiety can prevent choking in expert perceptual-motor performance, as one acclimatizes to the specific processes accompanying anxiety.

Oudejans and colleagues have also applied this training protocol outside of sport, to police officers using firearms (Oudejans, 2008; Nieuwenhuys & Oudejans, 2010). For example, Oudejans (2008) found that police officers' shooting accuracy decreased significantly when they performed in stressful conditions, in which opponents shot back using colored soap cartridges. However, police officers who practiced handgun shooting with high levels of anxiety (against the opponent) performed better at this task after training compared to a control group who practiced with low anxiety (on cardboard targets).

In explaining these effects, Oudejans and Nieuwenhuys (2009) suggested that performers who train with anxiety may invest their increased mental effort more efficiently and effectively (as hypothesized by Eysenck and colleagues' processing efficiency theory and attentional control theory). Individuals who have not trained with anxiety still invest increased effort when anxious, but this is done less effectively and may not be directed to the right (goal-directed) targets or processes. The benefit of training with anxiety is, therefore, explicitly related to attentional control and a more effective and efficient use of limited visual attentional resources.

Conclusion

Research from cognitive psychology and neuroscience has implicated attentional mechanisms as mediating the anxiety–performance relationship. Although much of this research has examined the impact of trait (dispositional) anxiety on visual attention and cognitive task performance (see Pachego-Unguettit et al., 2010, for a discussion), there are still clear implications for sport, where the impact of state anxiety appears to be more relevant. As Janelle (2002) highlights, "Given the heavy reliance on visual input for decision making and response planning in sport tasks, logical questions concern whether and how visual attention is modified under increased anxiety" (p. 237). However, little research has tried to answer these questions. The chapter discussed contemporary research examining sport skills that has examined how the QE (an objective measure of visual attention) might be impaired when performers are anxious. It finished with a discussion of training programs that may help performers maintain this optimal attentional control even when they are anxious.

The approach of intervening by focusing upon the athlete's ability to control certain aspects of his or her active motor preparation (e.g., QE) in order to limit the disruptive effects of anxiety is a new one in sport psychology. Traditional anxiety-reduction interventions have typically focused on arousal reduction (e.g., relaxation) and cognitive control (e.g., positive self-talk) strategies. This attentional approach to anxiety coping may represent a major breakthrough in the applied sport psychology area, and certainly this paradigm-changing approach is deserving of greater applied and outcome-based research.

Future Directions

• More research is required to understand the mechanisms of effective visuomotor control and how these may be impaired under pressure for a variety of sport tasks. How exactly does maintaining a longer QE help performance under pressure?

• Whereas aiming skills are the easiest to assess from a gaze control perspective, other sport skills requiring decision-making would potentially be a useful avenue for inquiry (e.g., Raab & Johnson, 2007).

• Other performance arenas where visuomotor control is required under pressure are also ripe for examination. Experts from movement science have already started to apply knowledge gained in sport settings to military (Janelle & Hatfield, 2008), police (Oudejans, 2008), and surgical (Wilson, McGrath, & Coleman, 2010) environments, as alluded to in previous sections. For example, Wilson and colleagues have recently demonstrated that novice surgeons following a gaze training intervention were better able to perform a laparoscopic task under stressful, multitasking conditions than were surgeons trained using a technical (explicit motor learning) or discovery learning approach (Wilson et al., 2011).

• Dispositional mediators of the anxiety–performance relationship have probably been under-represented in the sport/performance literature (whereas in most other domains these trait differences in attentional control have received most attention). Individual differences in executive processes may be important for an understanding of the development and maintenance of negative emotional states (Eysenck & Derakshan, 2011). In the sport-based literature Masters and colleagues have examined the influence of trait reinvestment on performance under pressure (see Masters, this book). However, do some individuals have genetic advantages in terms of executive attentional control (see Emes, Vickers, & Livingston, 1994; Rothbart et al., 2007)? Might these advantages be determined early through measures of visual attentional control (e.g., QE)?

• Both QE-based training and acclimatization training have been shown to be effective in protecting performance against choking by changing the effectiveness of attentional control. More research is required testing these interventions, and perhaps a combined approach might lead to even stronger effects.

Acknowledgments

I would like to acknowledge the major contribution of my two (recently qualified) Ph.D. students, Dr. Sam Vine and Dr. Greg Wood, in the completion of the original research outlined in this chapter. This chapter was written while I was on a research fellowship at the Institute of Human Performance, University of Hong Kong, funded by the Department of Business, Innovation, and Skills (UK).

Note

1. Note the similarity to the anterior/executive (voluntary) and posterior (involuntary) attentional systems described in Posner and Raichle's (1994) model, discussed earlier.

References

Baddeley, A. D. (1986). *Working memory*. Oxford, UK: Clarendon Press.

Baddeley, A. D. (2001). Is working memory still working? *American Psychologist, 56*, 851–864.

Bale, T. L., & Vale, W. W. (2004). CRF and CRF receptors: Role in stress responsivity and other behaviours. *Annual Review of Pharmacological Toxicology, 44*, 525–557.

Ballard, D. H., & Hayhoe, M. M. (2009). Modelling the role of task in the control of gaze. *Visual Cognition, 17*, 1185–1204.

Bar-Eli, M., & Azar, O. H. (2009). Penalty kicks in soccer: An empirical analysis of shooting strategies and goalkeepers' preferences. *Soccer and Society, 10*, 183–191.

Bar-Haim, Y., Lamy, D., Pergamin, L., Bakermans-Kranenburg, M. J., & van IJzendoorn, M. H. (2007). Threat-related attentional bias in anxious and nonanxious individuals: A meta-analytic study. *Psychological Bulletin, 133*, 1–24.

Baumeister, R. F. (1984). Choking under pressure: Self-consciousness and paradoxical effects of incentives on skillful performance. *Journal of Personality and Social Psychology, 46*, 610–620.

Baumeister, R. F., & Showers, C. J. (1986). A review of paradoxical performance effects: Choking under pressure in sports and mental tests. *European Journal of Social Psychology, 16*, 361–383.

Beattie, S., & Davies, M. (2010). A test of engagement versus disengagement in catastrophe models. *British Journal of Psychology, 101*, 361–371.

Behan, M., & Wilson, M. (2008). State anxiety and visual attention: The role of the quiet eye period in aiming to a far target. *Journal of Sports Sciences, 26*, 207–215.

Beilock, S. L., & Carr, T. H. (2001). On the fragility of skilled performance: What governs choking under pressure? *Journal of Experimental Psychology, 130*, 701–725.

Beilock, S. L., & Gray, R. (2007). Why do athletes choke under pressure? In G. Tenenbaum & R. C. Eklund. (Eds.), *Handbook of sports psychology* (3rd ed., pp. 425–444). Hoboken, NJ: Wiley & Sons.

Bishop S. J. (2007). Neurocognitive mechanisms of anxiety: An integrative account. *Trends in Cognitive Sciences, 11*, 307–316.

Bishop, S. J. (2008). Neural mechanisms underlying selective attention to threat. *Annals of New York Academy of Sciences, 1129*, 141–152.

Bishop, S. J. (2009). Trait anxiety and impoverished prefrontal control of attention. *Nature Neuroscience, 12*, 92–98.

Bishop, S. J., Duncan, J., & Lawrence, A. D. (2004). State anxiety modulation of the amygdala response to unattended threat-related stimuli. *Journal of Neuroscience, 24*, 10364–10368.

Carver, C. S., & Scheier, M. F. (1988). A control-process perspective on anxiety. *Anxiety Research, 1*, 17–22.

Causer, J., Holmes, P. S., Smith, N. C., & Williams, A. M. (2011a). Anxiety, movement kinematics, and visual attention in elite-level performers. *Emotion, 11*, 595–602.

Causer, J., Holmes, P. S., & Williams, A. M. (2011b). Quiet eye training in a visuomotor control task. *Medicine and Science in Sports and Exercise, 43*, 1042–1049.

Cheng, W. -N. K., Hardy, L., & Markland, D. (2009). Toward a three-dimensional conceptualization of performance anxiety: Rational and initial measurement development. *Psychology of Sport and Exercise, 10*, 271–278.

Clark, T. P., Tofler, I. R., & Lardon, M. T. (2005). The sport psychiatrist and golf. *Clinics in Sports Medicine, 24*, 959–971.

Coombes, S. A., Higgins, T., Gamble, K. M., Cauraugh, J. H., & Janelle, C. M. (2009). Attentional control theory: Anxiety, emotion, and motor planning. *Journal of Anxiety Disorders, 23*, 1072–1079.

Corbetta, M. (1998). Frontoparietal cortical networks for directing attention and the eye to visual locations: Identical, independent, or overlapping. *Proceedings of the National Academy of Sciences, 95*, 831–838.

Corbetta, M., Patel, G., & Schulman, G. L. (2008). The reorienting system of the human brain: From environment to theory of mind. *Neuron, 58*, 306–324.

Corbetta, M., & Shulman, G. L. (2002). Control of goal-directed and stimulus-driven attention in the brain. *Nature Reviews Neuroscience, 3*, 201–215.

Derakshan, N., & Eysenck, M. W. (2009). Anxiety, processing efficiency, and cognitive performance: New developments from attentional control theory. *European Psychologist, 14*, 168–176.

Derryberry, D., & Reed, M. A. (2002). Anxiety-related attentional biases and their regulation by attentional control. *Journal of Abnormal Psychology, 111*, 225–236.

Duncan, J. (2006). EPS mid-career award 2004: Brain mechanisms of attention. *Quarterly Journal of Experimental Psychology, 59*, 2–27.

Edwards, T., Kingston, K., Hardy, L., & Gould, D. (2002). A qualitative analysis of catastrophic performances and the associated thoughts, feelings and emotions. *The Sport Psychologist, 16*, 1–19.

Emes, C., Vickers, J. N., & Livingston, L. (1994). Gaze control of children with high versus low motor proficiency. *Adapted physical activity* (pp. 147–154). Tokyo: Springer-Verlag.

Eysenck, M. W. (1992). *Anxiety: The cognitive perspective*. Hove, UK: Lawrence Erlbaum.

Eysenck, M. W., & Calvo, M. G. (1992). Anxiety and performance: The processing efficiency theory. *Cognition and Emotion, 6*, 409–434.

Eysenck, M. W., & Derakshan, N. (2011). New perspectives on attentional control theory. *Personality and Individual Differences, 50*, 955–960.

Eysenck, M. W., Derakshan, N., Santos, R., & Calvo, M. G. (2007). Anxiety and cognitive performance: Attentional control theory. *Emotion, 7*, 336–353.

Gucciardi, D. F., & Dimmock, J. A. (2008). Choking under pressure in sensorimotor skills: Conscious processing or depleted attentional resources? *Psychology of Sport and Exercise, 9*, 45–59.

Gucciardi, D. F., Longbottom, J. L., Jackson, B., & Dimmock, J. A. (2010). Experienced golfers' perspectives on choking under pressure. *Journal of Sport and Exercise Psychology, 32*, 61–83.

Hanin, Y., & Hanina, M. (2009). Optimization of performance in top-level athletes: An action-focused coping approach. *International Journal of Sports Science and Coaching, 4*, 47–58.

Hanton, S., Neil, R., & Mellalieu, S. D. (2008). Recent developments in competitive anxiety direction and competition stress research. *International Review of Sport and Exercise Psychology, 1*, 45–57.

Hanton, S., Thomas, O., & Mellalieu, S. D. (2009). Management of competitive stress in elite sport. In B.W. Brewer (Ed.) *The Olympic handbook of sports medicine and science: Sport psychology* (pp. 30–42). Oxford, UK: Wiley-Blackwell.

Hardy, L. (1996). A test of catastrophe models of anxiety and sport performance against multidimensional anxiety theory models using the method of dynamic differences. *Anxiety, Stress, and Coping, 9*, 69–86.

Hardy, L., Beattie, S., & Woodman, T. (2007). Anxiety-induced performance catastrophes: Investigating effort required as an asymmetry factor. *British Journal of Psychology, 98*, 15–31.

Hardy, L., Jones, G. & Gould, D. (1996). *Understanding psychological preparation for sport*. Chichester, UK: Wiley.

Henderson, J. M. (2003). Human gaze control during real-world scene perception. *Trends in Cognitive Science, 7*, 498–504.

Hill, D. M., Hanton, S., Matthews, N., & Fleming, S. (2010). Choking in sport: A review. *International Review of Sport and Exercise Psychology, 3*, 24–39.

James, W. (1890). *Principles of psychology*. New York: Holt.

Janelle, C. M. (2002). Anxiety, arousal and visual attention: A mechanistic account of performance variability. *Journal of Sports Sciences, 20*, 237–251.

Janelle, C. M., & Hatfield, B. (2008). Visual attention and brain processes that underlie expert performance: Implications for sport and military psychology. *Military Psychology, 20*, 117–134.

Jeannerod, M. (1997). *The cognitive neuroscience of action*. Cambridge, MA: Blackwell.

Jones, G. (1991). Recent issues in competitive state anxiety research. *The Psychologist, 4*, 152–155.

Jones, G. (1995). More than just a game: Research developments and issues in competitive anxiety in sport. *British Journal of Psychology, 86*, 449–478.

Jordet, G. (2009). Why do English players fail in soccer penalty shootouts? A study of team status, self-regulation, and choking under pressure. *Journal of Sports Sciences, 27*, 97–106.

Jordet, G., Hartman, E., Visscher, C., & Lemmink, K. A. P. M. (2007). Kicks from the penalty mark in soccer: The roles of stress, skill, and fatigue for kick outcomes. *Journal of Sports Sciences, 25*, 121–129.

Keogh, E., & French, C. C. (2001). Test anxiety, evaluative stress, and susceptibility to distraction from threat. *European Journal of Personality, 15*, 123–141.

Knudsen, E. I. (2007). Fundamental components of attention. *Annual Review of Neuroscience, 30*, 57–78.

Land, M. F. (2006). Eye movements and the control of actions in everyday life. *Progress in Retinal and Eye Research, 25*, 296–324.

Land, M. F. (2009). Vision, eye movements, and natural behavior. *Visual Neuroscience, 26*, 51–62.

Land, M. F., & Lee, D. N. (1994). Where we look when we steer. *Nature, 369*, 742–744.

Lazarus, R. S. (2000). Cognitive-motivational-relational theory of emotion. In Y. Hanin (Ed.), *Emotions in sport* (pp. 39–63). Champaign, IL: Human Kinetics.

Lazarus, R. S., & Folkman, S. (1984). *Stress, appraisal, and coping*. New York: Springer.

Lewis, B. P., & Linder, D. E. (1997). Thinking about choking? Attentional processes and paradoxical performance. *Personality and Social Psychology Bulletin, 23*, 937–944.

MacDonald, A. W., III, Cohen, J. D., Stenger, V. A., & Carter, C. S. (2000). Dissociating the role of the dorsolateral prefrontal and anterior cingulate cortex in cognitive control. *Science, 288*, 1835–1838.

Mann, D. T. Y., Williams, A. M., Ward, P., & Janelle, C. M. (2007). Perceptual-cognitive expertise in sport: A meta analysis. *Journal of Sport and Exercise Psychology, 29*, 457–478.

Marple-Horvat, D. E., Chattington, M., Anglesea, M., Ashford, D. G., Wilson, M., & Keil, D. (2005). Prevention of coordinated eye movements and steering impairs driving performance. *Experimental Brain Research, 163*, 411–420.

Masters, R. S. W. (1992). Knowledge, knerves and know-how: The role of explicit versus implicit knowledge in the breakdown of a complex motor skill under pressure. *British Journal of Psychology, 83*, 343–358.

Masters, R. S. W., & Maxwell, J. P. (2008). The theory of reinvestment. *International Review of Sport and Exercise Psychology, 1*, 160–183.

Miyake, A., Friedman, N. P., Emerson, M. J., Witzki, A. H., Howerter, A., & Wager, T. D. (2000). The unity and diversity of executive functions and their contributions to complex "frontal lobe" tasks: A latent variable analysis. *Cognitive Psychology, 41*, 49–100.

Mogg, K., & Bradley, B. P. (1999). A cognitive-motivational analysis of anxiety. *Behaviour Research and Therapy, 36*, 809–848.

Moran, A. P. (1996). T*he psychology of concentration in sports performers: A cognitive analysis*. Hove, UK: Psychology Press.

Moran, A. P. (2009). Cognitive psychology in sport: Progress and prospects. *Psychology of Sport and Exercise, 10,* 420–426.

Mullen, R., & Hardy, L. (2000). State anxiety and motor performance: Testing the conscious processing hypothesis. *Journal of Sports Sciences, 18,* 785–799.

Mullen, R., & Hardy, L. (2010). Conscious processing and the process goal paradox. *Journal of Sport and Exercise Psychology, 32,* 275–297.

Müller, S., Abernethy, B., & Farrow, D. (2006). How do world-class cricket batsmen anticipate a bowler's intention? *The Quarterly Journal of Experimental Psychology, 59,* 2162–2186.

Neggers, S. F., & Bekkering, H. (2000). Coordinated control of eye and hand movements in dynamic reaching. *Human Movement Science, 21,* 349–376.

Nieuwenhuys, A., & Oudejans, R. R. D. (2010). Effects of anxiety on handgun shooting behavior of police officers: A pilot study. *Anxiety, Stress and Coping, 23,* 225–233.

Ohman, A. (2000). Fear and anxiety: Evolutionary, cognitive and clinical perspectives. In M. Lewis & J. M. Haviland-Jones (Eds.), *Handbook of emotions* (2nd ed., pp. 573–593). New York: Guilford Press.

Otten, M. (2009). Choking vs. clutch performance: A study of sport performance under pressure. *Journal of Sport and Exercise Psychology,* 31, 583–601.

Oudejans, R. R. D. (2008). Reality based practice under pressure improves handgun shooting performance of police officers. *Ergonomics, 51,* 261–273.

Oudejans, R. R. D., & Nieuwenhuys, A. (2009). Perceiving and moving in sports and other high pressure contexts. *Progress in Brain Research, 174,* 35–48.

Oudejans, R. R. D., & Pijpers, J. R. (2009). Training with anxiety has a positive effect on expert perceptual-motor performance under pressure. *Quarterly Journal of Experimental Psychology, 62,* 1631–1647.

Oudejans, R. R. D., & Pijpers, J. R. (2010). Training with mild anxiety may prevent choking under higher levels of anxiety. *Psychology of Sport and Exercise, 11,* 44–50.

Pachego-Unguettit, A. P., Acosta, A., Callejas, A., &, Lapianez, J. (2010). Attention and anxiety: Different attentional functioning under state and trait anxiety. *Psychological Science, 21,* 298–304.

Petrides, M. (2005). Lateral prefrontal cortex: Architectonic and functional organization. *Philosophical Transactions of the Royal Society B, 360,* 781–795.

Phelps, E. (2006). Emotion and cognition: Insights from studies of human amygdala. *Annual Review of Psychology, 57,* 27–53.

Posner, M. I., & Raichle, M. E. (1994). *Images of mind.* New York: Scientific American Library.

Raab, M., & Johnson, J. (2007). Option-generation and resulting choices. *Journal of Experimental Psychology: Applied, 13,* 158–170.

Raglin, J. S., & Hanin, Y. L. (2000). Competitive anxiety. In Y. Hanin (Ed.), *Emotions in sport* (pp. 93–112). Champaign, IL: Human Kinetics.

Rothbart, M. K., Sheese, B. E., & Posner, M. I. (2007). Executive attention and effortful control: Linking temperament, brain networks and genes. *Child Development Perspectives, 1,* 2–7.

Sailer, U., Flanagan, J. R., & Johansson, R. S. (2005). Eye-hand coordination during learning of a novel visuomotor task. *Journal of Neuroscience, 25,* 8833–8842.

Sarason, I. G. (1988). Anxiety, self-preoccupation and attention. *Anxiety Research, 1,* 3–7.

Shinoda, H., Hayhoe, M. M., & Shrivastava, A. (2001). What controls attention in natural environments? *Vision Research, 41,* 3535–3545.

Shipp, S. (2004). The brain circuitry of attention. *Trends in Cognitive Science, 8,* 223–230.

Singer, R. N. (2000). Performance and human factors: Considerations about cognition and attention for self-paced and externally-paced events. *Ergonomics, 43,* 1661–1680.

Singer, R. N. (2002). Preperformance state, Routines and automaticity: What does it take to realise expertise in self paced events? *Journal of Sport and Exercise Psychology, 24,* 359–375.

Spielberger, C. D. (1983). *Manual for the State Trait Anxiety Inventory.* Palo Alto, CA: Consulting Psychologists Press.

Stöber, J., & Pekrun, R. (2004). Advances in test anxiety research (Editorial). *Anxiety, Stress, and Coping, 17,* 205–211.

Swanson, L. W., & Petrovich, G. D. (1998). What is the amygdala? *Trends in Neuroscience, 21,* 323–331.

Syed, M. (2010). *Bounce: How champions are made.* London: Fourth Estate.

Tenenbaum, G., & Becker, B. (2005). Is self-confidence a bias factor in higher-order catastrophe models? An exploratory analysis—A critique. *Journal of Sport and Exercise Psychology, 27,* 375–381.

Vickers, J. N. (1996). Visual control when aiming at a far target. *Journal of Experimental Psychology: Human Perception and Performance, 2,* 324–354.

Vickers, J. N. (2007). *Perception, cognition and decision training: The quiet eye in action.* Champaign IL: Human Kinetics.

Vickers, J. N. (2009). Advances in coupling perception and action: The quiet eye as a bidirectional link between gaze, attention, and action. *Progress in Brain Research, 174,* 279–288.

Vickers, J. N., & Williams, A. M. (2007). Performing under pressure: The effects of physiological arousal, cognitive anxiety, and gaze control in biathlon. *Journal of Motor Behavior, 39,* 381–394.

Vine, S. J., & Wilson, M. R. (2010). Quiet eye training: Effects on learning and performance under pressure. *Journal of Applied Sport Psychology, 22,* 361–376.

Vine, S. J., & Wilson, M. R. (2011). The influence of Quiet Eye training and pressure on attentional control in a visuo-motor task. *Acta Psychologica, 136,* 340–346.

Vine, S. J., Moore, L. J., & Wilson, M. R. (2011). Quiet eye training facilitates competitive putting performance in elite golfers. *Frontiers in Movement Science and Sport Psychology, 2,* 8. doi: 10.3389/fpsyg.2011.00008

Weierich, M. R., Treat, T. A., & Hollingworth, A. (2008). Theories and measurement of visual attentional processing in anxiety. *Cognition and Emotion, 22,* 985–1018.

Weinberg, R. S., & Gould, D. (2007). *Foundations of sport and exercise psychology* (4th ed.). Champaign, IL: Human Kinetics.

Weissman, D. H., Perkins, A. S., & Woldorff, M. G. (2008). Cognitive control in social situations: A role for the dorsolateral prefrontal cortex. *Neuroimage, 40,* 955–962.

Wilson, M. (2008). From processing efficiency to attentional control: A mechanistic account of the anxiety-performance relationship. *International Review of Sport and Exercise Psychology, 1,* 184–201.

Wilson, M. (2010). Gaze and cognitive control in motor performance: Implications for skill training. *The Sport and Exercise Scientist, 23,* 29–30.

Wilson, M., Chattington, M., & Marple-Horvat, D. E. (2008). Eye movements drive steering: The effect of reduced eye movement distribution on steering and driving performance. *Journal of Motor Behavior, 40,* 190–202.

Wilson, M., Chattington, M., Marple-Horvat, D. E., & Smith, N. C. (2007). A comparison of self-focus versus attentional explanations of choking. *Journal of Sport and Exercise Psychology, 29,* 439–456.

Wilson, M., McGrath, J., & Coleman, M. (2010). Developing basic eye-hand coordination skills for laparoscopic surgery using gaze training. *British Journal of Urology—International, 105,* 1356–1358.

Wilson, M., & Smith, N. C. (2007). A test of the predictions of processing efficiency theory during elite team competition using the Thought Occurrence Questionnaire for Sport. *International Journal of Sport Psychology, 38,* 245–262.

Wilson, M., Stephenson, S., Chattington, M., & Marple-Horvat, D. E. (2007). Eye movements coordinated with steering benefit performance even when vision is denied. *Experimental Brain Research, 176,* 397–412.

Wilson, M. R., McGrath, J., Vine, S. J., Brewer, J., Defriend, D., & Masters, R. S. W. (2010). Psychomotor control in a virtual laparoscopic surgery training environment: Gaze control parameters differentiate novices from experts. *Surgical Endoscopy, 24,* 2458–2464.

Wilson, M. R., McGrath, J. S., Vine, S. J., Brewer, J., Defriend, D., & Masters, R. S. W. (2011). Perceptual impairment and visuomotor control in virtual laparoscopic surgery. *Surgical Endoscopy, 25,* 2268–2274.

Wilson, M. R., & Richards, H. (2010). Putting it together: Skills for pressure performance. In D. Collins, A. Button, & H. Richards (Eds.), *Performance psychology* (pp. 333–356). Edinburgh, UK: Elsevier.

Wilson, M. R., & Vine, S. J. (2009). Performing under pressure: Attentional control and the suppression of vision in basketball free-throw shooting. In C. H. Chang (Ed.), *Handbook of sports psychology* (pp. 277–296). Hauppauge, NY: Nova Science.

Wilson, M. R., Vine, S. J., Bright, E., Defriend, D., Masters, R. S. W., & McGrath, J. S. (2011). Gaze training enhances laparoscopic technical skill acquisition and multi-tasking performance: A randomized controlled study. *Surgical Endoscopy. 25,* 3731–3739.

Wilson, M. R., Vine, S. J., & Wood, G. (2009). The influence of anxiety on visual attentional control in basketball free throw shooting. *Journal of Sport and Exercise Psychology, 31,* 152–168.

Wilson, M. R., Wood, G., &, Vine, S. J. (2009). Anxiety, attentional control and performance impairment in penalty kicks. *Journal of Sport and Exercise Psychology, 31,* 761–775.

Wine, J. (1971). Test anxiety and direction of attention. *Psychological Bulletin, 76,* 92–104.

Wood, G., & Wilson, M. R. (2010). Goalkeeper distractions increase the likelihood of missing a penalty kick. *Journal of Sports Sciences, 28,* 937–946.

Wood, G., & Wilson, M. R. (2011). Quiet Eye training for soccer penalty kicks. *Cognitive Processing, 12,* 257–266.

Woodman, T., & Hardy, L. (2001). Stress and anxiety. In R. N. Singer, H. A. Hausenblas, & C. M. Janelle (Eds.), *Handbook of sport psychology* (pp. 127–170). New York: Wiley.

Wulf, G. (2007). *Attention and motor skill learning.* Champaign, IL: Human Kinematics.

Yarrow, K., Brown, P., & Krakauer, J. W. (2009). Inside the brain of an elite athlete: The neural processes that support high achievement in sports. *Nature Reviews Neuroscience, 10,* 585–596.

Yiend, J. (2008). The effects of emotion on attention: A review of attentional processing of emotional information. *Cognition and Emotion, 24,* 3–47.

Zinsser, N., Bunker, L. K., & Williams, J. M. (2006). Cognitive techniques for improving performance and building confidence. In J. M. Williams (Ed.), *Applied sport psychology: Personal growth to peak performance* (5th ed., pp. 349–381). Mountain View, CA: Mayfield.

Cognitions: Self-Talk and Performance

Yannis Theodorakis, Antonis Hatzigeorgiadis, *and* Nikos Zourbanos

Abstract

The main objective of this chapter is to provide an overview of the self-talk literature in sport psychology, in particular with regard to the links between self-talk and performance. Definitions and conceptualizations are discussed, and measurement issues are presented. The main research questions that have been addressed and the research paradigms that have been adopted to address these questions are then outlined. The content of athletes' self-talk and the use of self-talk strategies are then described, and the factors shaping and influencing self-talk are discussed. The main body of the chapter focuses on the relationship between self-talk and performance, with particular emphasis placed on research advances regarding the mechanisms that may explain the facilitating effects of self-talk on performance. A brief look at performance-related self-talk research within other psychology domains is then presented. Finally, applied recommendations and future research directions are discussed.

Key Words: Thought and action, cognition and behavior, self-statements, self-instructions, research paradigms, antecedents, functions, mechanisms, applications

The study of human thought dates back to the beginning of scientific inquiry. Plato, in his discourse "Theaetetus or about science," defined thoughts as "the conversation, which the soul holds with itself" (Plato, trans. 1993). Even before Plato, Stoic philosophers argued that thoughts play a critical role in the formulation of behavior and emotions (Reardon, 1993). The inquiry on the role of thoughts in human behavior is evident in the works of philosophers, theorists, and researchers (Wiley, 2006). Despite its apparent importance, and despite the recent growth of cognitive sport psychology (Moran, 2009), the study of thoughts has not received particular attention in the sport psychology literature. It is only in the last two decades that researchers have become interested in exploring the role of thoughts in relation to the sport context; nonetheless, a recent sustained growth in the sport self-talk literature can be detected.

The present chapter reviews the broader self-talk literature and focuses on the links between self-talk and performance. The purpose is to summarize the relevant literature, address issues and controversies, and provide direction and inspiration for future research and applications. First, definitions and conceptualizations of self-talk will be presented; research questions and research approaches will be outlined along with measurement issues. Descriptive studies and research examining self-talk antecedents will be reviewed. The relationship between self-talk and performance will be thoroughly explored, with particular emphasis placed on recent developments involving the mechanisms through which self-talk operates. A broader performance psychology perspective will then be attempted through an overview of relevant literature in other performance settings. The chapter will close with a discussion of practical applications and future research directions.

Defining Self-Talk in Sport

Various terms have been used in the psychology literature to describe the same or similar constructs related to thoughts: automatic thoughts, internal dialogue, inner conversation, subvocal speech, self-verbalizations, self-instructions, and self-statements. In the sport psychology literature, the term *self-talk* has prevailed. Several descriptions or definitions have been suggested in the sport self-talk literature, from general and simplistic to more detailed and sophisticated. Hardy (2006), attempting to "speak clearly," presented an elaborate analysis regarding the conceptualization of self-talk. He discriminated between the more general, thought-oriented or "global" definitions of self-talk, and the more precise, dialogue-oriented or "self-statements" definitions of self-talk. He argued that the latter are the more appropriate to describe the sport self-talk approach and literature, and subsequently suggested a comprehensive definition of self-talk, suggesting that self-talk should be viewed as: "(a) verbalizations or statements addressed to the self; (b) multidimensional in nature; (c) having interpretive elements associated with the content of statements employed; (d) is somewhat dynamic; and (e) serving at least two functions; instructional and motivational for the athlete" (p. 84). In concluding, Hardy added that the progress of research will probably allow further refinement of this definition. Indeed, Zourbanos, Hatzigeorgiadis, Tsiakaras, Chroni, and Theodorakis (2010, p. 782), taking into consideration the social influences on self-talk, noted that it can be "malleable to perceptions and interpretations of stimuli from the social environment."

A final note with respect to what constitutes self-talk in the sport psychology literature is essential. Hatzigeorgiadis and Biddle (2008) discriminated between two different approaches to the study of self-talk: self-talk as spontaneous thoughts that individuals experience and self-talk as a mental strategy with the use of specific cues. Hardy, Oliver, and Tod (2009) further clarified that self-talk can either refer to automatic thoughts that may occur spontaneously, or to deliberate statements addressed to oneself, and also to the strategic use of cues and self-talk plans. This distinction will be more elaborately addressed below.

Several attempts to describe the underlying dimensions of self-talk reveal some confusion over definitions. First, a distinction between positive and negative self-talk has been proposed. Self-talk has been described as positive or negative depending on the content, but also depending on the impact it may have. In certain instances, the two have been used without differentiation. Such an approach is misleading, as it is possible that positive statements can have negative effects and negative statements can have positive effects, based on individual and situational characteristics. Therefore, we suggest that a distinction between positive and negative self-talk should be based solely on the content of the statements and not the impact. With regard to the impact self-talk can have on outcome variables, such as performance, the terms *facilitative effects* and *debilitative effects* should be preferred. A second distinction described has been that between motivational and instructional self-talk. Motivational self-talk refer to "psyching-up" and confidence building cues, whereas instructional self-talk refers to focusing or directing attention cues, and cues providing instruction with regard to technique, strategy, or kinesthetic attributes of a skill. The description of self-talk as instructional or motivational is generally based on the content but has also been based on the function of self-talk. As there is evidence that self-talk cues can serve several functions irrespective of their content, researchers should be clear when using the terms *instructional* and *motivational* as to whether this refers to the content or the function. As with the positive–negative self-talk distinction, our suggestion is to describe cues as instructional or motivational based on the content rather than the function they serve. The issue of self-talk functions is discussed in more details in a later section of the chapter.

Research Questions and Paradigms

There are three key research questions with regard to understanding self-talk and performance. The first involves the description and the content of athletes' self-talk. The second involves the antecedents—those factors that determine, shape, or influence self-talk. The third involves the consequences—the impact self-talk has on outcome variables, and, most importantly, performance. To date, the research on the effects of self-talk on performance has dominated sport psychology literature. Following the trend of the literature, and also following the orientations of this Handbook, the present chapter will focus on research examining the relationship between self-talk and performance. Nonetheless, the literature concerning the description and the antecedents of self-talk is briefly reviewed below.

Before proceeding to the examination of the literature, it is important to identify and distinguish the paradigms that researchers have used for the study of self-talk. Two different research paradigms are evident in the self-talk literature. The first refers to self-talk as inherent thoughts and self-statements that athletes address to themselves, mostly during sport performance. This paradigm mainly focuses on the occurrence and the frequency of such statements or automatic thoughts, which may occur with or without conscious awareness, inherently or deliberately. The second paradigm refers to the use of self-talk as a mental strategy, in which self-talk cues or self-talk plans are used with the aim of enhancing performance or achieving other related outcomes. The first paradigm has been mostly used in field studies, descriptive or correlational, to describe the content of athletes' self-talk, to explore self-talk antecedents, and to examine the relationship between self-talk and performance. The second paradigm has been used for both the descriptive study of self-talk, with regard to the use of self-talk as a strategy, and mostly for the study of the impact of self-talk strategies on performance through experimental research. The characteristics of research using the two paradigms will be discussed after the presentation of the measurements that have been developed to facilitate this research.

Measurement of Self-Talk in the Sport Literature

Vygotsky (1962) suggested that the study of inner speech is among the most difficult of research fields. Several methodological approaches have been applied in the cognitive assessment literature, varying from concurrent to retrospective and from unstructured to fully structured assessments. These include think-aloud procedures, free association, recording of private speech, random sampling, self-monitoring, videotape thought reconstruction, self-statement inventories, interviews, and thought listing (Guerrero, 2005). Nisbett and Wilson (1977) stressed that assessment relies on individuals' reports and is therefore dependent on memory, perceptions, desires, consciousness, and will to share. Along the same lines, Dobson and Dozois (2003) argued that we cannot have perfect access to cognition, as individuals report cognitions on the basis of their likelihood of occurrence rather than their actual occurrence. Despite these limitations, as the content of human thought cannot be assessed through external observation or by any objective method, self-reports provide us metacognitive knowledge that can be used to help us understand individuals' perceptions, motives, and cognitions (Guerrero,

2005). In the sport psychology literature, interviews have been used for exploratory purposes and in-depth studies, whereas questionnaires have been used for the purposes of qualitative research; these questionnaires are outlined below.

In accordance with the two research paradigms just described, two broader types of measures have been developed and used: first, instruments aiming to describe the use and the purpose of self-talk; and second, instruments that assess the content and structure of self-talk. Concerning the former, one of the first inventories investigating self-talk in sport was the Test of Performance Strategies (TOPS; Thomas, Murphy, & Hardy, 1999), which has proved valuable in advancing applied research. The TOPS has been recently refined (Hardy, Roberts, Thomas, & Murphy, 2010); the latest version assesses, among others strategies, the use of self-talk strategy in training and competition, but also the frequency of negative thoughts during competition. Attempting to provide a more elaborate measure for the description of self-talk, Hardy, Hall, and Hardy (2005) developed, based on descriptive evidence, the Self-Talk Use Questionnaire (STUQ). The STUQ explores four descriptive dimensions of self-talk: where, when, what, and why athletes use self-talk. Based on Hardy et al.'s findings, Zervas, Stavrou, and Psychountaki (2007) developed the Self-Talk Questionnaire (S-TQ), an instrument assessing the two key self-talk functions of instruction and motivation. In a similar line of research, but using more elaborate methods, Theodorakis, Hatzigeorgiadis, and Chroni (2008) utilized existing empirical evidence and raw data from a large number of athletes to develop the Functions of Self-Talk Questionnaire (FSTQ), an instrument that identifies the likely mechanisms through which self-talk facilitates performance. According to the FSTQ dimensions, self-talk can serve to enhance attentional focus, increase confidence, regulate effort, control cognitive and emotional reactions, and trigger automatic execution.

Regarding the second type of self-talk measures, instruments have been developed to investigate those things that athletes say to themselves or the thoughts they inherently experience. Hatzigeorgiadis and Biddle (2000) developed the Thought Occurrence Questionnaire for Sport (TOQS) based on the structure of a previously developed instrument in psychology (Thoughts Occurrence Questionnaire; Sarason, Sarason, Keefe, Hayes, & Shearin, 1986) and interviews conducted with athletes. The TOQS assesses three dimensions of cognitive interference: performance worries, irrelevant thoughts, and thoughts of escape, and has shown good psychometric properties (Hatzigeorgiadis & Biddle, 2000; Lane, Harwood, & Nevill, 2005). The same year, Krohne and Hindel (2000) developed the Cognitive Interference Test—Table Tennis, an instrument similar to the TOQS, which assesses worry and self-doubt thoughts, irrelevant thoughts, and emotional tension with respect to the sport of table tennis. As is apparent from the description of these instruments, none has examined positive dimensions of athletes' self-talk. To address this limitation and further advance self-talk measurement in sport, Zourbanos, Hatzigeorgiadis, Chroni, Theodorakis, and Papaioannou (2009) developed the Automatic Self-Talk Questionnaire for Sport (ASTQS), a comprehensive instrument for the evaluation of athletes' self-talk content. Their investigation supported the multidimensionality of athletes' self-talk and revealed an extra dimension of intrusive self-talk, as well as dimensions of positive self-talk. In particular, eight distinct self-talk dimensions were identified, four of which were labeled as positive (psych-up, confidence, anxiety control, and instruction), and four as negative (worry, disengagement, somatic fatigue, and irrelevant thoughts).

An alternative assessment approach has been developed by Van Raalte, Brewer, Rivera, and Petitpas (1994). Attempting to provide a more objective look at athletes' self-talk, they developed the Self-Talk and Gestures Rating Scale (STAGRS). This observational tool was developed through observations of tennis matches, during which various self-talk and gestures were recorded. Three broad self-talk dimensions were identified, positive, negative, and instruction. This instrument can be used to assess only what the authors called "public self-talk"; that is, self-talk visible to the observer and not what may be happening in athletes' mind. Nevertheless, the STAGRS has provided a useful perspective to the assessment of self-talk.

To summarize, the development of assessment inventories in the self-talk area has progressed from simple to more comprehensive, with the recently developed ASTQS providing the means to exploring mainly the content but also the antecedents and the outcomes related to different self-talk patterns. We suggest that the concurrent use of alternative assessment methodologies, such as observation and video recall, be employed to further enhance the assessment of athletes' self-talk.

Description of Self-Talk

Descriptive studies on self-talk can be divided into two basic categories: studies describing the content and frequency of self-talk, and studies describing the use of self-talk and relevant group differences based on personal characteristics. Research on the content of self-talk has primarily used the field-descriptive approach. Studies have investigated the nature of athletes' self-talk in competitive settings, and also the use and frequency of self-talk as a mental strategy. Hatzigeorgiadis and Biddle (2000), in developing the TOQS, identified that athletes' interfering thoughts mostly involved worries about performance and competition, and, to a lesser degree, disengagement thoughts and thoughts irrelevant to the context of the competition. Similarly, in developing the ASTQS, Zourbanos et al. (2009) reported that self-talk related to psych-up and confidence is the most frequent positive self-talk in athletes, whereas in support of previous findings (Hatzigeorgiadis & Biddle, 2000; Lane et al., 2005), worrying thoughts are the most common type of negative self-talk in athletes.

Van Raalte et al. (1994) assessed observable self-talk and gestures in tennis players during competitive performance. They reported that some sort of self-talk or gesture was evident in approximately 30% of points played. The majority of this "self-talk" was negative. Most of the positive "self-talk" followed won points. Finally, instructional "self-talk" was also evident through the use of movements that were performed when the ball was not in play, followed by relevant instruction. In a similar study with adults, Van Raalte, Cornelius, Hatten, and Brewer (2000) reported similar results. Positive, negative, and instructional self-talk was observed, with negative self-talk prevailing in frequency. In addition, they reported that players using more positive self-talk were those also using more negative self-talk, which suggests that some individuals are more prone to expressing themselves through self-talk, or that, for some individuals, such expression is more observable than for others.

Hardy, Gammage, and Hall (2001) explored the use of athletes' self-talk by examining the "four W's" related to self-talk: what, where, when, and why. With regard to *where*, it was reported that, as expected, athletes mostly used self-talk within the sporting environment. With regard to *when*, they identified that the most frequently reported times for using self-talk were before and during competition and also during practice. With regard to *what*, the results showed that athletes mostly reported positive compared to negative and irrelevant self-talk, through the use of phrases rather than smaller cues, and specific instructions. Finally, with regard to the *why*, it was revealed that athletes used self-talk mostly for focusing, but also for purposes of skill development and strategy, psyching-up and confidence, and regulating drive and effort.

Hardy, Hall, and Hardy (2005) examined what athletes say to themselves as a function of sex, sport type, skill level, and competitive setting. They reported that positive self-talk was more frequent than negative and neutral self-talk. Furthermore, their results showed that individual sport athletes used more self-talk than team sport athletes, and that athletes used self-talk more in competition compared to training. They also reported that the majority of self-talk was internal (silent) rather than external (vocalized). Similar results were also reported by Hardy, Hall, and Hardy (2004). Athletes competing in individual sports and more skilled athletes reported more use of self-talk compared to athletes competing in team sports and less skilled athletes. In addition, athletes reported greater use of self-talk as the competitive season progressed. Overall, the descriptive evidence on the content and use of self-talk has provided the basis for understanding what athletes say to themselves and helps guide research with regard to the causes and the consequences of athletes' self-talk.

Antecedents of Self-Talk

Studying the antecedents of self-talk is an important research direction. Understanding the factors that shape or influence self-talk can facilitate attempts to intervene and change such factors, thus regulating self-talk according to individual needs. Despite the limited number of studies investigating factors that may influence athletes' self-talk, Hardy et al. (2009) attempted to provide a working framework for the study of self-talk, and, based on the existing research evidence, suggested two classes of antecedents: personal and situational. In their presentation of the model, coaching-related factors were included in the situational factors. In our approach, we will treat coaching factors as the base of a new dimension that should be added: social and environmental factors.

Personal Factors

Considering the overall lack of research on self-talk antecedents, research on personal factors has been limited to the examination of achievement goals. In one of the first studies examining factors related to the cognitive activation of athletes, Hatzigeorgiadis and Biddle (1999) tested the relationship between goal orientations and negative self-talk as a function of perceived competence during sport performance. The results revealed that task orientation was negatively related to disengagement thoughts irrespective of perceptions of competence. Furthermore, it was reported that for athletes with lower perceived competence, ego orientation was positively related to experiencing disengagement thoughts, whereas for athletes with higher perceived competence, no relationship between ego orientations and disengagement thoughts emerged. Nevertheless, the instrument that was used proved psychometrically inappropriate for the evaluation of worrying (negative) self-talk, thus only disengagement thoughts were analyzed.

Having developed a sport-suitable instrument for the assessment of interfering thoughts (TOQS; Hatzigeorgiadis & Biddle, 2000), the relationship between goal orientations and negative thoughts was reassessed. Hatzigeorgiadis and Biddle (2002) found that athletes with high ego and low task orientations were more vulnerable to disengagement thoughts than were athletes with different goal profiles, whereas no consistent differences emerged for worrying thoughts. Hatzigeorgiadis (2002), in another study involving goal orientation, reported that self-consciousness was related to disengagement thoughts and mediated the relationship between ego orientations and disengagement thoughts. A common characteristic of the studies reported above is that they focused on negative content types of thoughts. In a study examining the relationship between goal orientations and self-talk, this time including positive self-talk, Harwood, Cumming, and Fletcher (2004) used cluster analysis to classify athletes into motivational profiles and reported that athletes with higher task and moderate ego orientations reported more positive thinking that did athletes with lower task and moderate ego orientations and athletes with moderate task and lower ego goal orientations. Overall, the results seem to suggest that task orientation shows more "adaptive" (at least in terms of content) relationships with thought patterns, whereas for ego orientation, self-talk relationships may depend on other personal or situational factors.

Situational Factors

Van Raalte et al. (2000) first investigated the role of situational variables in shaping self-talk. In particular, they examined march circumstances as a predictor of positive and negative self-talk in tennis players. They reported that negative self-talk was evident following lost points or fault serving, whereas, for some participants, positive or instructional self-talk was observed after losing a point. Even though observational measures were used to assess self-talk, the results of this study provided initial evidence that the progress of the competition could be central in determining athletes' self-talk. Further support for this proposition was provided by Hatzigeorgiadis and Biddle (2008), who, following the assumptions of Carver and Scheier's (1988) control process model, examined discrepancies between goals and performance as predictors of negative self-talk in runners. The results revealed a strong relationship between such discrepancies and negative self-talk, suggesting that what is going on during competition to a large degree determines athletes' self-talk, at least negative self-talk. In the same study, Hatzigeorgiadis and Biddle also reported that pre-competition cognitive anxiety intensity was positively related to negative self-talk, whereas pre-competition cognitive anxiety direction was negatively related to negative self-talk. The role of discrepancies between goal and performance in generating negative self-talk received further experimental support from Hatzigeorgiadis (2006). After creating conditions of smaller-recoverable discrepancies and larger-unrecoverable discrepancies in a rowing task through manipulation of time goals, it was revealed that participants in the large discrepancies condition reported more negative disengagement thoughts.

Social-Environmental Factors

A final line of research with regard to factors influencing the content of self-talk has been initiated by Zourbanos (2008). Based on the work of Burnett (1996, 1999) in educational settings, Zourbanos considered the role of significant others in shaping athletes' self-talk, and in particular the role of the admittedly most crucial *significant other* for athletes, the coach. In two pilot studies, Zourbanos, Theodorakis, and Hatzigeorgiadis (2006) and Zourbanos, Hatzigeorgiadis, and Theodorakis (2007) reported that coaching behavior, support, and statements by coaches addressed to athletes are related to athletes' positive and negative self-talk. The development of the ASTQS (Zourbanos et al., 2009) helped further extend this research. First, in a multimethod investigation, the impact of coaching behavior, as conceptualized by Williams et al. (2003)

through the Coaching Behavior Questionnaire, was examined (Zourbanos et al., 2010). Field correlational evidence showed that supportive and negative coaching behavior is linked to different patterns of thought content, with particular effects for negative self-talk. Support for causal inferences were provided through experimental evidence that showed that coaching behavior can influence athletes' positive and negative self-talk. In a second investigation (Zourbanos et al., 2011), the role of received social support provided by the coach was examined. The significant role of the coach in relation to athletes' self-talk was further supported. In particular, stronger relationships were found between emotional and esteem support and negative dimensions of self-talk. Considering that these are the first studies to explore the role and the impact of the coach on athletes' self-talk, further research is warranted to enhance our understanding. Nevertheless, the thorough investigations that have been carried out suggest that the coach is an important factor in shaping athletes' self-talk, and encourages the investigation of further social-environmental parameters.

Hardy et al. (2009), in their framework for the study of self-talk, suggested two categories of self-talk antecedents: personal and situational. Our research, led by Zourbanos (Zourbanos et al., 2006, 2007, 2010, 2011) leads us to suggest that the influence of the coach and broader social and environmental factors should be considered as a separate class of self-talk antecedents.

Summarizing the findings in self-talk antecedents research, it is apparent that situational factors, and in particular factors related to the progress of a competition or performance, seem to be the most influential determinants of athletes' self-talk; yet, much remains to be explored. Further examination of the factors that shape athletes' self-talk will greatly enhance our understanding and our potential to intervene and change self-talk in effective directions. As most of these studies are field-correlational studies, we cannot ascertain causality between antecedents and self-talk. Even though such causal interpretation can be partly justified through reason or theories, the lack of methodologically sound evidence highlights the need for further experimental research investigating antecedents of athletes' self-talk.

Self-Talk and Performance
Field Studies

It is entirely reasonable that self-talk research in sport has mostly focused on the relationship between self-talk and performance. Early attempts to approach this relationship date back to the 1970s, the early years of self-talk research. Mahoney and Avener (1977) explored psychological factors in gymnasts competing to qualify for the Olympic Games. Their findings showed that those who qualified reported more frequent self-talk in training and in competition, and a similar trend emerged for instructional self-talk. Highlen and Bennett (1979), in an exploratory study examining differences in psychological skills and attributes in wrestlers competing to qualify for the Pan-American championship, found that those who qualified reported less negative self-talk prior to competition than did those who did not qualify. In a similar study with divers and wrestlers, Highlen and Bennett (1983) found that, for divers, qualifiers reported more self-instruction, less negative, but also less positive self-talk (praise); for wrestlers, qualifiers reported more critical self-talk and less negative self-talk than non-qualifiers. Rotella, Gansneder, Ojala, and Billings (1980), in another comparative study, reported that more and less successful skiers did not differ in their self-talk. Similarly, using a within-subjects design, Dagrou, Gauvin, and Halliwell (1991) found that athletes reported similar self-talk during their best and worst performances.

Two other field studies using a different approach than retrospective assessment have attempted to relate self-talk with performance. Van Raalte et al. (1994), through systematic observation of observable self-talk in young tennis players, reported that positive self-talk was not related to better performance, but negative self-talk was associated with worse performance. In a similar study with adults, Van Raalte et al. (2000) found that positive and negative self-talk could not significantly predict the outcome of the following point, suggesting that self-talk was not related to performance.

Overall, the field studies have not provided consistent results regarding the relationship between athletes' self-talk and performance. Several explanations are likely to account for this inconsistency. First, a variety of conceptual issues have confused the findings: different approaches in the conceptualization of self-talk; unclear descriptions of how self-talk was assessed; use of single-item measures; and, most importantly, the lack of clarity with regard to assessing self-talk as a strategy or as spontaneous self-talk. Second, the assessment of performance, or more accurately the performance criterion that was used, ranging from qualifying versus not qualifying athletes, more successful versus less successful

athletes, best and worst performances, and game or situational outcomes, may also account for much of the variability in results, especially when considering the large and more decisive number of factors that may influence or determine such performance dimensions. A final point regarding this line of research is the inability to argue for the causality of the relationship. It is plausible and perhaps likely that self-talk influences performance or components of performance; however, it is equally likely that the quality of performance determines athletes' self-talk; you think positively when you are doing well and negatively when not. Nevertheless, this research approach has been useful in advancing self-talk research and can help provide inspiration and ideas for further research development.

Experimental Studies

The large majority of experimental studies in the sport self-talk literature have focused on the effectiveness of self-talk interventions on task performance. The quest for demonstrating the beneficial effects of self-talk strategies on performance started through researchers' attempts to explore the use of cues aiming to provide instruction and reinforcement to athletes. In some of the first studies to explore the effectiveness of self-talk strategies, Weinberg, Smith, Jackson, and Gould (1984) and Hamilton and Fremouw (1985) reported that positive self-talk improved endurance and basketball performance, respectively. Ziegler (1987) examined the effect of a four-step self-talk instruction strategy on tennis forehand and backhand strokes and reported significant performance improvement for both strokes. Finally, Rushall, Hall, Roux, Sasseville, and Rushall (1988) examined the impact of three different types of self-talk: instruction, mood, and positive self-talk, on skiing performance. Their results showed that all types of self-talk cues resulted in improved performance.

The self-talk intervention literature has expanded considerably since then. Self-talk has proven effective in facilitating learning and enhancing performance in a variety of tasks and skills, varying from fine motor skills (Van Raalte et al., 1995) to gross motor skills (Edwards, Tod, & McGuigan, 2008) and from novel tasks (Hatzigeorgiadis, Theodorakis, & Zourbanos, 2004) to learned tasks (Malouff & Murphy, 2006), and in different populations varying from students (Theodorakis, Chroni, Laparidis, Bebetsos, & Douma, 2001) to young and beginner athletes (Goudas, Hatzidimitriou, & Kikidi, 2006; Perkos, Theodorakis, & Chroni, 2002), to more experienced (Landin & Hebert, 1999) and elite athletes (Mallett & Hanrahan, 1997).

MATCHING HYPOTHESIS

Contemporary research has attempted to examine and compare the effectiveness of different types of self-talk with different tasks. Theodorakis, Weinberg, Natsis, Douma, and Kazakas (2000) suggested that different self-talk cues should be appropriate for different tasks and proposed the matching hypothesis, assuming that instructional cues should be more beneficial for finer motor skill tasks, whereas motivational cues should be more beneficial for grosser motor tasks. In a series of experiments that followed, their hypotheses received partial support. In particular, for two accuracy tasks, a football (soccer) passing task and a badminton serve task, only instructional self-talk was effective; for a sit-up endurance task no effects were identified, whereas for an isokinetic strength task, instructional and motivational self-talk were both effective. In a similar study, Hatzigeorgiadis et al. (2004) compared the effectiveness of instructional and motivational self-talk on a precision and a power water polo task. Their results were somewhat different from those of Theodorakis et al. (2000), but also provided support for the matching hypothesis. They found that for the precision task, both types of self-talk improved performance, with the instructional self-talk having a greater effect, whereas for the power task, only motivational self-talk was effective. Tod, Thatcher, McGuigan, and Thatcher (2008) and Edwards et al. (2008) compared the effectiveness of instructional and motivational cues on vertical jump performance using within-subjects designs. In the first study, only motivational self-talk improved performance, whereas in the second, both instructional and motivational cues were effective. Finally, Kolovelonis, Goudas, and Dermitzaki (2011) reported that instructional and motivational self-talk cues were equally effective at a basketball chest pass, whereas for a push-ups test both types of self-talk were effective, with motivational self-talk having a significantly greater effect than instructional self-talk. Overall, despite the differences identified in the findings above, the assumptions of the matching hypothesis have received reasonable support from the studies that attempted to compare the use of instructional and motivational self-talk on different tasks.

SELF-TALK CHARACTERISTICS

Two more issues with regard to the characteristics of the self-talk cues that are used by athletes

should be reported. First is the use of internal (silent) and external (audible) self-talk. In most of the early studies, external self-talk was used, possibly for two reasons: a methodological one, to make sure that self-talk was indeed used by participants (Hatzigeorgiadis et al., 2004); and a practical one, that self-talk may be more effective when participants can actually hear their self-talk (Hardy, 2006). Eventually, reports from participants showed that, for some individuals, it felt awkward and distracting to use external self-talk and this might have hindered the effectiveness of the strategy (Masciana, Van Raalte, Brewer, Brandon, & Coughlin, 2001). Therefore, internal self-talk was used in many of the studies that followed. The problem of whether cues are actually used by participants, which raised concerns regarding the methodological integrity of the research, was dealt with by the use of manipulation checks.

The second issue concerns the selection of the cues that are being used. Initially, studies were designed using specific cues (e.g., Van Raalte et al., 1995), mostly based on the expertise of coaches when self-talk involved technical instruction or the expertise of the researcher (or common sense) when self-talk involved reinforcement and psyching-up. Eventually, in certain studies, the use of self-talk lists was adopted, from which participants were asked to choose the cues they thought were more suitable for them (Schüler & Langens, 2007). With regard to both the above issues, more recent studies have adopted a more self-determined approach to the selection and use of self-talk by allowing participants to choose the cues to be used, as well as the way they will use them (Malouff & Murphy, 2006). Even though this approach is less controlled, it could be expected to be more effective, considering that the use of self-talk should be adjusted according to not only the needs but also the preferences of the individuals. Nevertheless, no direct comparisons have been made with regard to the use of self-selected or assigned forms of self-talk and therefore no firm conclusions can be drawn.

TYPE OF INTERVENTION

A final issue that requires consideration is the type of intervention that studies have employed. Interestingly, the majority of studies have used cross-sectional interventions. Few studies have used short training interventions, and even fewer longer interventions. Hatzigeorgiadis and colleagues have used on two occasions short training programs that have proven effective with young tennis players. In particular, Hatzigeorgiadis, Zourbanos, Goltsios, and Theodorakis (2008) and Hatzigeorgiadis, Zourbanos, Mpoumpaki, and Theodorakis (2009) tested the effectiveness of a 3-day self-talk training program on forehand accuracy performance. During training, participants practiced different types of self-talk on a backhand task, so that they became familiar with the use of self-talk with a variety of cues, but also while attempting to minimize learning effects. The results in both studies showed that performance of the intervention groups improved significantly over that of the control group. Similar short training interventions have been also conducted with student samples by Cornspan, Overby, and Lerner (2004) in a golf putting task; Cutton and Landin (2007) in a tennis forehand task; and Hatzigeorgiadis, Zourbanos, and Theodorakis (2007) in a water polo task.

Two studies have implemented extensive interventions with athletes. In the first, Perkos et al. (2002) applied a 12-week intervention, including one self-talk training session per week, with young basketball players. They reported that the intervention group performed better than the control group in passing and dribbling, but not in shooting. Similar procedures were followed by Harbalis, Hatzigeorgiadis, and Theodorakis (2008) with a sample of adult wheelchair basketball players. They included 24 self-talk training sessions within a 12-week period and reported that passing and dribbling performance of the intervention group improved significantly, whereas performance of the control group remained stable. Finally, in a school-based intervention, Anderson, Vogel, and Albrecht (1999) applied a nine-session self-talk training program during physical education classes over a 3-week period, to test learning effects on an overhand throw. They reported that the self-talk training group performed better than a traditional learning and a demonstration-only group. Self-talk intervention programs have also been applied to athletes using single-subject multiple baseline designs; these are described in the following section.

RESEARCH DESIGNS

Various research designs have been used to explore the effectiveness of self-talk: true experimental designs, which include pre- and post-intervention measures in intervention and control groups; but also quasi-experimental designs that include only post-intervention measures in experimental and control groups; or pre- and post-intervention measures for intervention groups only. Finally, studies using single-subject multiple-baseline designs have been also used. Even though the true experimental designs provide the stronger support for the effectiveness of self-talk, the use of alternative designs has contributed to advancing the self-talk literature. The use of single-subject multiple-baseline designs has provided valuable evidence because, in certain instances, these studies have used higher level athletes and performance measurements resembling more competitive sport performance (e.g., 100 m sprinting) than in other experimental studies, in which sport task performance (e.g., vertical jump) has been mostly used. In particular, single-subject multiple-baseline designs have demonstrated self-talk effectiveness in enhancing performance in figure skating routines (Ming & Martin, 1996), sprinting performance (Mallett & Hanrahan, 1997), a tennis sequential shots task (Landin & Hebert, 1999), and a football (soccer) shooting task (Johnson, Hrycaiko, Johnson, & Halas, 2004). The marked effectiveness of these studies should be attributed to the extended intervention periods characterizing this research design.

MENTAL PACKAGES

The self-talk technique has also been included in several interventions implementing mental skills packages for performance improvement (e.g., Patrick & Hrycaiko, 1998; Thelwell & Maynard, 2003). Various strategies have been combined with self-talk, such as relaxation (Rogerson & Hrycaiko, 2002), imagery (Cumming, Nordin, Horton, & Reynolds, 2006), goal setting (Papaioannou, Ballon, Theodorakis, & Auwelle, 2004), and combined goal setting, imagery, and relaxation (e.g., Blakeslee & Goff, 2007; Patrick & Hrycaiko, 1998; Thelwell & Greenlees, 2003). Finally, two recent studies have examined the combined effects of self-talk and performance feedback (Cutton & Landin, 2007; Latinjak, Torregrosa, & Renom, 2011). These packages, most of which have been tested through single-subject multiple-baseline designs, have also proved particularly effective in enhancing performance. As Hardy et al. (2009) indicate, in most of these studies, it is not possible to identify the unique impact of any of the strategies used. However, experimental studies, including pure self-talk groups in addition to combined strategies groups have allowed the identification of such effects (e.g., Cutton & Landin, 2007; Latinjak et al., 2011; Papaioannou et al., 2004).

EFFECTIVENESS OF SELF-TALK INTERVENTIONS

Hatzigeorgiadis, Zourbanos, Galanis, and Theodorakis (2011) have recently attempted a research synthesis on the self-talk–performance relationship through meta-analysis. Overall, they found a moderate positive effect size (d = .48). Furthermore, based on the existing self-talk literature, they examined a number of moderators that may regulate the impact of self-talk on performance. They reported that the most pertinent moderator was the implementation of training in the self-talk technique, as they found that interventions including training were more effective (d = .80) compared to those not including training (d = .37). They also found that self-talk was more effective for novel (d = .73) rather than learned tasks (d = .41), and for tasks characterized by precision, coordination, or fine execution (d = .67), rather than gross tasks requiring strength and endurance (d = .26). Finally, the matching hypothesis was partly supported as instructional self-talk proved more effective than motivational self-talk for fine tasks; and moreover, instructional self-talk was more effective for fine tasks compared to gross tasks. In summary, their results provided robust evidence for the effectiveness of self-talk interventions.

In a number of studies, the effectiveness of self-talk interventions has not been fully supported. In addition, it is likely that studies that have not been successful in enhancing performance have not been published. Examples of such findings can be found in studies where not all treatments were effective. Hatzigeorgiadis et al. (2004) found that instructional self-talk did not improve performance on a power water polo task; Theodorakis et al. (2000) reported that the motivational self-talk group did not improve on a football shooting task, whereas neither instructional nor motivational self-talk resulted in better sit-up performance compared to the control group; Perkos et al. (2002) found that a 12-week intervention did not improve performance on a shooting task; Harvey, Van Raalte, and Brewer (2002) found no differences in accuracy for a golf putt task between self-talk and control groups. The effectiveness of a technique depends on several parameters. A combination of choices and circumstances is likely to make an intervention ineffective. The testing of alternative types of self-talk, the choice of the tasks, the lack of self-talk training (especially when well-learned tasks are used), and in some cases the choice of statistical criteria may be some of the reasons that may explain such findings. Finally, Hardy, Hall, Gibbs, and Greenslade (2005) raised the issue of appropriate manipulation checks, after identifying that the a priori conditions were contaminated mostly due to the use of self-talk from participants in the control group. The lack of support in these instances indicates the need for robust methodologies and appropriate self-talk plans in relation to the context.

Overall, self-talk interventions have proven effective in facilitating learning and enhancing sport task performance. Nevertheless, several issues require consideration with regard to the characteristics of the studies that have been reviewed thus far. First, with regard to participants, the majority of studies have used students, student-athletes, or young and beginner athletes to test the effectiveness of self-talk interventions. Access to higher level or elite athletes is not easily granted, especially when interventions that may require extensive involvement for research purposes are attempted. Still, such studies are needed to further establish self-talk as an effective mental strategy in sport. Most importantly, if there is one key research question that requires more persistent consideration, it is the examination of self-talk as a strategy for the enhancement of competitive performance. Studies have focused on motor tasks, sport tasks, or performance components, but research on global competitive sport performance is lacking. Two relevant examples can be cited: first, the study of Mallet and Hanrahan (1997), who tested sprinting performance over a 100 m race, a real and complete sprinting event that, however, took place under experimental conditions (not real competition); and the study by Schuler and Langens (2007) who examined the buffering effects of self-talk on "psychological crisis" and on performance during an actual marathon competition. Access to competitive sport settings is not always easy to achieve. Most importantly, the field experimental designs that are required in such situations often have methodological shortcomings, such as difficulty controlling conditions and the complexity of assessing performance in certain sports. These factors probably deter researchers from attempting such designs, especially considering the methodological problems that should be addressed when attempting to publish such studies. Nevertheless, to develop the self-talk knowledge base this type of research needs to be pursued.

Functions/Mechanisms of Self-Talk

Studying the evidence regarding the effectiveness of self-talk and the use of different cues on task performance, Hatzigeorgiadis et al. (2007, p. 241) noticed that "certain self-talk cues can be more effective for some tasks than for others...in addition, some self-talk cues can be more effective than other self-talk cues in certain tasks." Based on that observation, they suggested that different cues may operate through different functions, and this may explain some of the variation in results in the literature. Now that robust evidence regarding the effectiveness of self-talk has been established, the issue of functions (i.e., the mechanisms through which self-talk facilitates performance) is currently receiving increasing research attention.

Meichenbaum (1977) presented a self-instructional approach to cognitive behavior modification. He particularly stressed the importance of investigating the functions through which thoughts affect behavioral processes. He suggested that "the goal of a cognitive functional assessment is to describe...the functional significance of engaging in self-statements of a particular sort followed by an individual's particular behavior" (p. 202). Meichenbaum regarded self-statements as indices of individuals' beliefs that may mediate behavioral performance. He proposed that self-instructions can direct individuals' attention to task-relevant stimuli, maintain useful information in the short-term memory, and protect individuals from experiencing disturbing thoughts. Furthermore, he claimed that self-statements may have an impact on individuals' expectations regarding their capacity to cope with a situation, and can be used for reassuring oneself and identifying behaviors that could become cues for action. Meichenbaum concluded that internal dialogue influences individuals' attentional and appraisal processes.

In one of the early studies in sport psychology, Rushall et al. (1988), based on earlier pain research (e.g., Jaremko, 1987), claimed that the use of specific cues by athletes could block thoughts related to or stemming from performance fatigue. Subsequently, they developed an intervention based on three assumptions regarding the way self-talk may facilitate performance. In particular, they suggested that different cues may be effective in enhancing performance but through different means; they hypothesized that task instruction cues would increase mechanical efficacy of skills, cues involving mood words would increase the mechanical capacities of athletes, and cues involving positive words would increase the physiological efficiency of athletes.

In the contemporary sport self-talk literature, Landin (1994) first overviewed the issue of the mechanisms underpinning the self-talk–performance relationship. Landin stressed the relevance of attention

and information processing approaches, as related to the effectiveness of self-talk. With regard to attention, he considered the relevance of Nideffer's attentional framework and suggested that verbal cues can facilitate performance through enhancing appropriate attentional focus, but also through helping transition from one attentional style to another. With regard to information processing, Wrisberg's (1993) theoretical propositions were utilized to suggest that the use of self-talk cues can help: perceptual processing, directing individuals' attention to task-relevant stimuli; decision processing, facilitating the selection of appropriate responses; and effector processing, initiating movement sequences. Hardy (2006), in appraising relevant theories, considered in addition the relevance of Bandura's self-efficacy theory. He suggested that self-talk may facilitate performance through increasing self-efficacy beliefs as a source of internal verbal persuasion.

Two more approaches to understanding the mechanisms through which self-talk may influence performance have emerged from the study of the relationship between anxiety and performance: Eysenck's *processing efficiency theory* (recently reformed into *attentional control theory*; Eysenck, Derakshan, Santos, & Calvo, 2007) and Carver's (1979) cybernetic model of self-attention processes (later developed into *control process theory*; Carver, 1996; Carver & Scheier, 1988). Eysenck (1992), based on an observation of inconsistent findings regarding the anxiety–performance relationship, suggested that anxiety is not always detrimental to performance because it may serve a motivational function. According to the processing efficiency model, anxiety, and mostly its cognitive component (i.e., worry) reduces processing efficiency but not necessarily performance. This is because, to cope with the source of anxiety, performers may allocate resources to additional strategies, such as effort, which may compensate for performance losses stemming from reduced processing. Carver and Scheier (1988) suggested that individuals experiencing worries during task performance monitor their progress toward goal attainment. Subsequently, those believing they are in a position to attain the goal will renew efforts toward the goal, whereas those not believing they can attain their goal will withdraw either mentally or behaviorally.

Hatzigeorgiadis and Biddle (2001) attempted to test the predictions of Eysenck's processing efficiency theory (1992) and Carver and Scheier's control process model (1988) in a sport setting. They examined relationships between negative self-talk, in the form of worry, and performance components, in the form of effort and concentration, as a function of athletes' expectancies to attain their goals. They reported that negative self-talk was negatively related to concentration regardless of goal attainment expectancies, whereas for effort a moderating role was identified for goal attainment expectancies. In particular, for athletes holding lower goal attainment expectancies, negative self-talk was negatively related to effort, whereas for athletes holding higher goal attainment expectancies, negative self-talk was positively related to effort. Despite the limitations involving the self-reported assessment of effort and concentration and the retrospective design of the study, the findings provided useful insights into the relationships between negative self-talk and performance. Experimental evidence for the role of expectancies in regulating effort were provided by Hatzigeorgiadis (2006); however, in this study, expectancies were manipulated and self-talk was not assessed. Overall, the above findings support the relevance of Eysenck's and Carver and Scheier's assumptions with regard to sport performance and show that effort and concentration are among the mechanisms that may explain the effects of self-talk on performance.

In their framework for the study of self-talk in sport, Hardy et al. (2009) proposed four dimensions of mechanisms that may explain the relationship between self-talk and performance. They discriminated between cognitive, motivational, behavioral, and affective mechanisms. Cognitive mechanisms refer to the attentional control and information processing mechanisms identified by Landin (1994). Motivational mechanisms were based on self-efficacy theory and mostly involved the role of effort and persistence. Behavioral mechanisms related to the effects self-talk can have on movement patterns and technique as a possible explanation for performance enhancement. Finally, affective mechanisms referred to the regulation of affective states, in particular anxiety, through the use of self-talk.

In an attempt to empirically examine these propositions, Theodorakis et al. (2008) progressed from gathering raw field data to the development and validation of an instrument assessing the various mechanisms of self-talk. Their investigation developed over three stages. In the first stage, raw data themes were collected from athletes through open-ended questionnaires, and additional themes were developed based on empirical evidence (e.g. Hardy et al., 2001; Van Raalte et al., 1994). In the second stage, the factorial structure of these themes was

examined by means of exploratory factor analyses, whereas in the third stage the results of the exploratory analyses were replicated through confirmatory factor analysis. The investigation supported the psychometric integrity of the Functions of Self-Talk Questionnaire (FSTQ; Theodorakis et al., 2008) and suggested that self-talk may function through five potential mechanisms: enhancing attentional focus, increasing confidence, regulating effort, controlling cognitive and emotional reactions, and triggering automatic execution.

Preliminary evidence regarding the mechanisms through which self-talk facilitates performance has been provided through intervention studies in which participants were asked to report (through open-ended questions or small lists) their perceptions regarding the effectiveness of self-talk. Landin and Hebert (1999) interviewed young female tennis players after implementing a single-subject multiple-baseline self-talk intervention. Participants reported that the use of self-talk helped them maintain an appropriate attentional focus, increase their confidence, and triggered automatic performance. Johnson et al. (2004) used a similar design and procedures in a study with young female football players and reported that the use of self-talk increased participants' confidence and enhanced their focus on task-relevant cues. Perkos et al. (2002) asked young novice basketball players who participated in a 12-week self-talk intervention to rate the effects of self-talk using a short questionnaire. Participants scored highest on concentration, followed by confidence and relaxation. Finally, Thelwell and Greenlees (2003) implemented a mental skills training program on recreational athletes, who reported that self-talk helped them increase motivation, concentration, and confidence. Overall, this preliminary evidence centers around two potential mechanisms involving concentration and confidence.

More systematic evidence has been added through Wayde and Hanton's (2008) qualitative examination of the mechanisms by which the use of psychological skills influence sport performance. In a study with 15 elite athletes representing a variety of individual and team sports, the authors investigated through semi-structured interviews the mechanisms underlying the effectiveness of self-talk (among other strategies). The results showed that self-talk was linked to enhancing motivation and effort, increasing concentration, controlling anxiety, and raising self-confidence, thus providing support for the key propositions regarding the mechanisms explaining the effectiveness of self-talk.

Empirical evidence regarding the functions of self-talk through the use of the FSTQ has been provided by two studies. Hatzigeorgiadis (2006), using a within-subjects design, investigated the functions of a motivational and an instructional self-talk cue on students performing a swimming task. The results revealed that participants scored higher on the concentration function regardless of the self-talk cue that was used, but also that scores for the effort function were higher when using the motivational cue compared to when using the instructional cue. No cue-related differences were identified for the functions of concentration, confidence, cognitive and emotional control, and automaticity. In a similar experiment, Hatzigeorgiadis et al. (2007) compared the functions of an anxiety control cue and an instructional cue in students performing a precision water polo task. The results showed that, again, participants scored higher on the concentration function irrespective of the cue used. Furthermore, participants scored higher on cognitive and emotional control when using the anxiety control cue than when using the instructional self-talk cue. Scores for the remaining FSTQ dimensions did not differ when using instructional or anxiety control cues.

Collectively, the results of these experiments suggest that, according to participants' perceptions, the principal mechanism through which self-talk facilitates performance is the attentional mechanism, at least for the case of novel tasks. Furthermore, the results support the proposition that different types of self-talk serve different functions depending on the content of the cues. On one hand, it was reported that motivational and anxiety control cues had greater reported impact on effort and anxiety control, compared to an instructional cue. On the other hand, the cues were reported to have similar effects for the nontargeted functions; that is, automaticity, confidence, and anxiety in the first experiment, and automaticity, confidence, and effort in the second experiment. Overall, these findings suggest that different self-talk cues may have different effects through the operation of different mechanisms, which may, however, operate concurrently. The above findings encourage further experimental investigations regarding the way self-talk facilitates performance.

Experimental Evidence

More direct evidence regarding the mechanisms through which self-talk operates has been provided by experimental studies. In the first study addressing the issue of self-talk mechanisms, Hatzigeorgiadis et al. (2004) tested the effectiveness of self-talk on a precision and a power water polo task according to the matching hypothesis, and, at the same time, examined the impact of self-talk on interfering thoughts during task performance. The results revealed that, for both tasks, the use of both instructional and motivational self-talk reduced the occurrence of interfering thoughts, thus implying enhanced concentration. Similar findings have been reported by Latinjak, Torregrosa, and Renom (2010) in a study with adult tennis players. They reported that for players in a self-talk intervention group, execution-related thoughts increased and outcome-related thoughts decreased compared to baseline measures, whereas no changes were found for the control group. They subsequently argued that their results supported the idea that self-talk could help athletes to focus on task relevant information.

In the Hatzigeorgiadis et al. (2007) experiment mentioned above, apart from the FSTQ, direct measures of anxiety, cognitive interference, confidence, effort, and automaticity were used to test the effects of self-talk on these constructs. The results showed that, overall, the use of self-talk increased effort and reduced interfering thoughts, anxiety, and automaticity. When comparing the anxiety control and instruction self-talk cues, differences in the examined constructs emerged only for cognitive and somatic anxiety, with the anxiety control cue producing greater reduction than the instructional cue.

Two more studies, with young athletes this time, have been conducted with regard to the potential mechanisms of anxiety and self-efficacy. Hatzigeorgiadis et al. (2008) examined the effectiveness of a self-talk intervention on improving forehand drive performance, but also self-efficacy in young tennis players. The results showed that the use of motivational self-talk improved self-efficacy and performance, and, moreover, that increases in self-efficacy were related to increases in performance, thus suggesting that self-efficacy may be a viable mediator (i.e., a mechanism explaining the facilitating effects of self-talk). In a similar experiment, also with young tennis players, Hatzigeorgiadis et al. (2009) tested the impact of a self-talk intervention on performance and anxiety. The results showed that the use of motivational self-talk increased self-confidence and decreased cognitive and somatic anxiety. Increases in self-confidence were related to increases in performance, whereas decreases in anxiety were not related to performance improvement.

Interestingly, such correlational patterns have emerged between anxiety components and performance from meta-analyses (Craft, Magyar, Becker, & Feltz, 2003; Woodman & Hardy, 2003).

The study of the mechanisms through which self-talk operates has the potential to enhance our understanding of the self-talk process. Summarizing the evidence so far, it can be argued that, according to the preliminary findings, self-talk mainly facilitates performance through attentional mechanisms, at least in the case of novel tasks or young and beginner athletes. Moreover, as self-talk may serve different functions, the type of self-talk and the particular content of the cues may be crucial in regulating the effectiveness of self-talk strategies. Research into the mechanisms of self-talk is a rather new and unexplored area, which provides a challenging ground to expand self-talk research.

Implications

Two sets of practical applications can be discussed based on the findings that have been presented in this chapter: one concerning the control and regulation of inherent self-talk, and one concerning the use of self-talk strategies to enhance performance. The former involves preventing unwanted self-talk and fostering facilitative self-talk, whereas the latter involves developing effective self-talk plans to address athletes' specific needs.

Regulation of Inherent Self-Talk

From the perspective of personal and situational factors, goal orientations/involvement and anxiety can help control inherent self-talk. The philosophy, but also the achievability, of the goals that are pursued seems an important issue. The findings suggest that task- and ego-oriented athletes are likely to experience similar levels of performance-related worries; nevertheless, the adoption of self-referenced goals will prevent impulses of disengagement due to the control athletes have over their goals. The progress of a game or a competition and the quality of performance in relation to the goal is probably the most decisive factor in shaping athletes' self-talk. Therefore, goals should be personal, self-referenced, and controllable. Such goals will reduce the likelihood of large discrepancies between goals and performance, therefore preventing unwanted and disengagement thoughts.

Anxiety is another personal factor that should be considered. Intensity and direction of competitive anxiety has been linked to experiencing negative self-talk. Even though such negative thoughts may not necessarily harm performance, it is preferred that they do not occur. With regard to the intensity of anxiety, regulation strategies can help reduce anxiety symptoms and subsequently reduce negative thoughts, whereas with regard to anxiety direction, athletes should be trained to accept anxiety symptoms as a normal reaction to competition and interpret it as a sign of readiness. Lowering the intensity and controlling the interpretation of anxiety can help regulate inherent self-talk.

From the perspective of social factors, the role of the coach seems of particular importance. The findings so far suggest that athletes' negative self-talk is more vulnerable to social influences. Supportive coaching behavior has been linked to reduced negative self-talk, whereas coaching behavior endorsing negative approaches is related to athletes' negative self-talk. Coaches can therefore assist the regulation of self-talk through the adoption of a positive stance, reinforcing, giving contingent feedback, providing social support—especially support related to athletes' self-esteem—but mostly avoiding becoming negative and using negative statements and irrational criticism when addressing to their athletes.

Finally, using self-talk plans has been found to reduce the occurrence of intrusive thoughts. Therefore, apart from facilitating performance, an issue addressed more thoroughly in the following section, the use of facilitative self-talk can also be useful in preventing unwanted self-talk.

Self-talk Strategies

The findings emphatically support the effectiveness of self-talk on facilitating learning and enhancing task performance. Therefore, the development of self-talk strategies and plans should be strongly encouraged. Apart from the two purposes identified above, several other effects are likely to be achieved. Even though research has not yet supported all of the possible functions self-talk serves, it is possible that self-talk, when designed carefully and in accordance with an individual's needs, can serve to enhance attention, regulate cognitive and emotional reactions, boost confidence, trigger automatic performance, and increase motivation, drive, and effort.

With regard to the characteristics of the task, self-talk seems to be more effective for novel compared to learned tasks. This is a reasonable finding, because improving on novel tasks is generally easier than improving on learned tasks. Nevertheless, self-talk has also proven effective for learned tasks, for which even small improvements may be very meaningful and important for athletes. Also, in relation to the characteristics of the task, fine motor tasks seem to benefit more from self-talk strategies. Research into self-talk functions has revealed that the key mechanism explaining the effectiveness of self-talk seems to be the enhancement of attention to the task. Considering that fine motor tasks may benefit more from increases in attention, compared to gross motor tasks, it makes sense that the use of self-talk can be more effective for such tasks.

Considering age and experience of participants, the guidelines coincide with those concerning novel and learned tasks. The use of self-talk can have an immediate impact for learning; therefore, it should be particularly effective for youngsters and beginner athletes, for learning skills, improving technique, and correcting mistakes. The use of instructional self-talk would seem more suitable for these purposes. In contrast, for more experienced and higher level athletes, for whom skills are well mastered, it may be more appropriate to use plans aimed at developing performance routines, psyching-up, and triggering automatic, unconscious performance.

Of particular significance is the selection of appropriate self-talk type and cues. Considering that the matching hypothesis has received considerable support, it is very important that self-talk cues, plans, and strategies are developed on the basis of individual needs and task characteristics, thus only general recommendation can be made. Instructional cues should be more appropriate for learning or improving technique, particularly in finer tasks characterized by precision and accuracy. In contrast, for tasks involving gross skills (power, strength, and endurance), the use of motivational self-talk can be more effective because physical effort, drive, and confidence may be more critical for performance. Having made this suggestion, it is necessary to stress again that different types of self-talk may operate and be effective through different mechanisms and therefore the selection of self-talk should be based on the mechanisms that need to be activated according to the specific situation.

The decision regarding the choice of the particular cues, and the way these cues will be expressed, is recommended to be made collectively by athlete and coach or sport psychologist because athletes' preferences should be seriously taken into account. In addition, going through the process of trial and error may give even better results for finalizing the selection of cues and self-talk plans.

Most importantly, athletes should encompass self-talk in their training routines. Practicing will maximize gains, especially in the case of more experienced and higher level athletes. At that level, improvement is hard to achieve and even small performance gains can make a big difference; therefore, training self-talk is imperative. As mentioned before, for younger and beginner athletes, self-talk can have more immediate effects. Observing such performance changes will foster the belief in self-talk and encourage its use in practice, which in turn should enhance the effectiveness of self-talk strategies. As for every performance, so for self-talk, practice will make perfect.

Self-talk in Other Performance Domains

Cognitive interventions involving self-talk strategies have a relatively long research history in other areas of psychology. Psychologists became interested following Vygotsky's (1962) speculations that inner speech can have a self-regulating role in children in communication and situational appraisals. On a similar note, Luria (1962/1980) suggested that children gradually develop the ability to regulate elementary forms of action through spoken instructions. Based on these assumptions, Meichenbaum and Goodman (1971) tested the effectiveness of a self-talk intervention with impulsive children. They reported that self-talk training improved performance in tasks requiring caution, precision, planning, and attention. Since these initial research attempts and the seminal work of Meichenbaum (1977) on cognitive-behavioral modification, and Ellis (1976) on rational emotive theory, the implementation of self-talk interventions has expanded in several fields.

Following the original research paths, self-talk strategies were tested in children with learning difficulties. Wong, Harris, and Graham (1991) reported that self-instruction training improved reading comprehension and performance in writing, spelling, and mathematics in children with learning disabilities. Similarly, Kamann and Wong (1993) found that the use of coping self-statements increased positive self-talk and reduced negative self-talk during mathematical problem-solving and increased performance in children with learning disabilities. Swanson and Kozleski (1985) reported that self-talk training had a positive impact on academic and communication performance in handicapped children. In a more clinical context, O'Callaghan and Couvadelli (1998) implemented a self-instruction training program on brain injured neurologically impaired adults and reported performance improvements on cognitive task performance. Callicott and

Park (2003) found a self-instructional intervention resulted in a small but meaningful effect for academic performance on students with emotional and behavioral disorders. The effectiveness of self-instructional strategies on cognitive performance has also been tested in the rational-emotive context. Schill, Monroe, Evans, and Ramanaiah (1978) and Bonadies and Bass (1984) reported that individuals in a rational self-statements group performed better on cognitive tasks than did individuals in an irrational self-statements group and a neutral group.

Also with regard to cognitive performance, a significant amount of research has examined the role of self-instructions in the context of the task-switching paradigm. Emerson and Miyake (2003) supported the facilitating effects of self-instructional cues on performance when switching between tasks and suggested that self-directed speech can serve to retrieve and activate phonological representations of the upcoming task. From a developmental perspective, self-instructional strategies in task switching have proven useful in children and younger adults, but seem particularly beneficial for older adults (Kray, 2006; Kray, Eber, & Karbach, 2008).

Organizational psychology is another field in which self-talk has been tested. In some of the early relevant studies, Richardson and Stone (1981) found that the use of facilitative self-talk by trainee counselors led to higher levels of reflection, confrontation, and empathy. Kurpius, Benjamin, and Morran (1985) reported that increased positive self-talk was associated with the formulation of better clinical hypotheses. Finally, Latham and Budworth (2006) reported that individuals receiving training in verbal self-instruction performed better in a job selection interview than did a control group.

In addition, self-talk has been used in studies implementing cognitive strategies in various fields. First, self-regulated strategies development (Harris & Graham, 1996) has been widely used in educational contexts (e.g., Graham, Harris, & Mason, 2005). Self-regulated strategies development is a program aiming at enhancing academic performance through the teaching of cognitive strategies involving instructional procedures. The application of the program has proven particularly effective especially for students with learning difficulties (Graham & Harris, 2003).

Thought self-leadership (Manz & Neck, 1991) is a cognitive model that has become popular in organizational psychology. Based on the principle of self-leadership, described as the process of influencing oneself, the model of thought self-leadership involves the use of cognitive strategies, such as self-talk, aimed at enhancing individual and organizational performance in the entrepreneurship context. Evidence has supported the beneficial effects of these strategies on employees' behavior and emotion (Neck & Manz, 1996), self-efficacy (Prussia, Anderson, & Manz, 1998), and goal performance (Godwin, Neck, & Houghton, 1999).

The development of life skills, described by Danish and Donahue (1995) as those physical, behavioral, interpersonal, intrapersonal, and cognitive abilities that enable young people to succeed in the different environments in which they live, has also involved the training and use of self-talk strategies. Such interventions aim to develop skills for resolving problems, performing under pressure, meeting challenges, communicating, and working with a team (Danish & Nellen, 1997), and they have received considerable attention in physical education and youth sport development programs (e.g., Goudas, Dermitzaki, Leondari, & Danish, 2006; Goudas & Giannoudis, 2008).

Finally, self-talk has been part of multistrategy non–performance targeted interventions in health psychology involving self-concepts and self-esteem (Burnett, 1999; Burnett & McCrindle, 1999), smoking cessation (Steffy, Meichenbaum, & Best 1970), coping with pain (Sanders, Shepherd, Cleghorn, & Woolford, 1994), hospitalization distress (Zastowny, Kirschenbaum, & Meng, 1986), anxiety disorders and depression (Kendall, 2006; Treadwell & Kendall, 1996), and injury rehabilitation (Theodorakis, Beneca, Goudas, Antoniou, & Malliou, 1998).

Summarizing the relevant literature, it becomes apparent that self-talk is a strategy that has been considered in various fields. However, it can be argued that the investigation of self-talk has been limited and nonsystematic in achievement performance contexts and that self-talk has been mostly used as part of wider cognitive interventions. The effectiveness of self-talk in sport suggests that evidence from the sport context should be better disseminated, so that the knowledge base regarding self-talk interventions developed with athletes become more widely known and used in other achievement settings.

Conclusion

The research directions described below focus mostly on the issues that have been touched upon in this chapter, and are presented with respect to the main research paradigms that are used in the sport self-talk literature. However, before proceeding with the research questions it is useful to present some methodological considerations with regard to the two principle research paradigms.

With regard to the examination of the antecedents and consequences of inherent self-talk, the limited research to date has relied on field studies. It is important to stress once again that field studies can only provide correlational evidence; thus, the examination of antecedents and consequences needs to advance to experimental research. Nonetheless, field findings are always important and play a significant role in identifying key factors related to athletes' self-talk; considering the general lack of research, more field studies should be also conducted.

With regard to the effectiveness of self-talk interventions, where experimental research has been conducted, experimental field research is lacking. Having mentioned that, there are some important reasons justifying this absence of studies. Experimental field research has limited experimental integrity. Controlling extraneous variables in the field is not possible, and sport performance depends on many such variables, thus weakening considerably the strength of the designs. As a result, such research attempts have limited publication chances, which obviously discourages the implementation of such studies. Also, the controversy over the assessment of performance that is also evident in other parts of the sport psychology literature further deters researchers. Nevertheless, until more attempts are made to carry out such studies, we will not be able to develop strong arguments for the effects of self-talk on competitive sport performance. Therefore, researchers should be encouraged to attempt and support such experiments. The contribution of editors in encouraging the publication of such studies, given their limitations, may also be valuable in helping generate such research.

Future Directions
INHERENT SELF-TALK

Self-talk as the content of thoughts athletes experience and the self-statements they intuitively use has received very limited research attention. Despite the importance of identifying what is going on in athletes' minds during sport performance, until recently few studies examined the content of athletes self-talk, the factors that shape and influence athletes' self-talk, and the consequences this self-talk has on athletes' affect and behavior, and most importantly, performance.

First, with regard to the content and the structure of athletes' self-talk, the development of the ASTQS clearly facilitates advances in this line of research. Nonetheless, the ASTQS is a newly developed instrument. Further validation will enhance our confidence in using the ASTQS, but could also identify how the instrument could be further developed to better describe and explore athletes' self-talk. Studies extending the psychometric integrity of the instrument and studies employing combinations of assessment methods will help enhance our understanding of athletes' self-talk. The use of observation and retrospective video-recall in addition to self-report questionnaires is deserving of more widespread implementation, as each of these methods (a) can be applied in field studies (in contrast to methods that cannot be applied, such as thinking aloud and thought listing) and (b) can complement each other.

Second, with regard to antecedents, a broad range of personal, situational, and social-environmental factors influencing self-talk can be explored. The highest priority should probably be given to factors for which interventions (a) are possible and (b) can have an important chance of changing behavior. Therefore, investigating issues like the role of motivational climate in relation to achievement goals and self-determination, coaching behaviors, and athletes' perceptions and interpretation of competitive situations, could further enhance our understanding regarding the generation and the determinants of athletes' self-talk. Furthermore, research on personal factors can facilitate our understanding of individual differences in self-talk experiences.

Finally, with regard to the consequences research, the effects of self-talk on performance and performance components, along with research on the underlying mechanisms derived from the theoretical approaches identified in earlier parts of the chapter, is clearly lacking and should be further developed. The theoretical framework of Eysenck (1992), identifying the attentional and motivational impact of self-referent thoughts, may be the most appropriate framework for the advancement of this research line. Furthermore, the framework suggested by Hardy et al. (2009) and also the empirical findings of Theodorakis et al. (2008) with regard to the mechanisms of self-talk, in particular for the sport context, should be further explored and advanced.

SELF-TALK AS MENTAL STRATEGY

One particular line of research warrants consideration with regard to the effectiveness of self-talk strategies: the examination of the impact of self-talk on global sport performance and in competitive settings. With regard to the former, research has focused on motor or sport task performance, rather than sport performance, whereas with regard to the latter, very few studies have attempted to test the effectiveness of self-talk on competitive performance (Schüler & Langens, 2007). We now know that self-talk is effective in enhancing task performance, and this is, by itself, an important finding. However, exploring whether self-talk influences competitive performance outcomes may provide new avenues for research. Hardy et al. (2009) rightly argue it may not be possible (at least in certain sports) to produce such evidence. Nor, perhaps, is it necessary before arguing for the value of self-talk in enhancing competitive performance. Although we agree, especially given the methodological considerations provided above, we believe that now is the appropriate time to attempt such challenging research.

Research on self-talk interventions still has a long way to go. Examination of the mechanisms that explain the facilitating effects of self-talk on performance is a priority. Identifying the mechanisms underlying the effectiveness of self-talk will allow us to develop and implement more effective self-talk strategies. Our work (Hatzigeorgiadis et al., 2004, 2007, 2008, 2009) has provided valuable evidence that can guide further developments in this direction. Extending this research would involve further testing the mechanisms identified by Hardy et al. (2009) and Theodorakis et al. (2008), but also forwarding research beyond that, to the examination of physiological and biomechanical factors. Gibson and Foster (2007), in a review examining self-talk from a physiological perspective, noticed that although a large number of brain regions are involved in the generation and control of overt and covert speech (Blank et al., 2002), and despite identification of anatomical and physiological correlates to self-talk (Shergill et al., 2002), no studies examine the neural correlates of self-talk in physical activity and sport contexts. Future cross-disciplinary research could examine self-talk during physical activity using brain scanning and signal processing techniques.

We believe that self-talk is a very fertile research area; it is a field in which theory can be tested but also developed, and, at the same time, it is a field in which applied research can provide valuable evidence for athletes and practitioners. Considering the literature reviewed in this chapter and the directions that are available for further scientific endeavors, the broader study of athletes' performance-related cognitions provides exciting opportunities for sport and performance psychology researchers.

References

Anderson, A., Vogel, P., & Albrecht, R. (1999). The effect of instructional self-talk on the overhand throw. *Physical Educator, 56*, 215–221.

Blakeslee, M. L., & Goff, D. M. (2007). The effects of a mental skills training package on equestrians. *The Sport Psychologist, 21*, 288–301.

Blank, S. C., Scott, S. K., Murphy, K., et al. (2002). Speech production: Wernicke, Broca and beyond. *Brain, 125*, 1829–1838.

Bonadies, G. A., & Bass, B. A. (1984). Effects of self-verbalizations upon emotional arousal and performance: A test of rational-emotive theory. *Perceptual and Motor Skills, 59*, 939–948.

Burnett, P. C. (1996). Children's self-talk and significant others' positive and negative statements. *Educational Psychology, 16*, 57–67.

Burnett, P. C. (1999). Children's self-talk and academic self-concepts. The impact of teachers' statements. *Educational Psychology in Practice, 15*, 195–200.

Burnett, P. C., & McCrindle, A. R. (1999). The relationship between significant others' positive and negative statements, self-talk and self-esteem. *Child Study Journal, 29*, 39–48.

Callicott, K. J., & Park, H. (2003). Effects of self-talk on academic engagement and academic responding. *Behavioral Disorders, 29*, 48–64.

Carver, C. S. (1979). A cybernetic model of self-attention processes. *Journal of Personality and Social Psychology, 37*, 1251–1280.

Carver, C. S. (1996). Cognitive interference and the structure of behaviour. In I. G. Sarason, G. R. Pierce, & B. R. Sarason (Eds.), *Cognitive interference: Theories, methods, and findings* (pp. 25–45). Mahwah, NJ: Lawrence Erlbaum Associates.

Carver, C. S., & Scheier, M. F. (1988). A control-process perspective on anxiety. *Anxiety Research, 1*, 17–22.

Cornspan, A. S., Overby, L. Y., & Lerner, B. S. (2004). Analysis and performance of pre-performance imagery and other strategies on a golf putting task. *Journal of Mental Imagery, 28*, 59–74.

Craft, L. L., Magyar, T. M., Becker, B. J., & Feltz, D. L. (2003). The relationship between the Competitive State Anxiety Inventory-2 and sport performance: A meta-analysis. *Journal of Sport and Exercise Psychology, 25*, 44–65.

Cumming, J., Nordin, S. M., Horton, R., & Reynolds, S. (2006). Examining the direction of imagery and self-talk on dart-throwing performance and self-efficacy. *The Sport Psychologist, 20*, 257–274.

Cutton, D. M., & Landin, D. (2007). The effects of self-talk and augmented feedback on learning the tennis forehand. *Journal of Applied Sport Psychology, 19*, 288–303.

Dagrou, E., Gauvin, L., & Halliwell, W. (1991). La preparation mentale des athletes Ivoiriens: Pratiques courantes de perspectives de recherche. (Mental preparation of Ivory Coast athletes: Current practice and research perspective). *International Journal of Sport Psychology, 22*, 15–34.

Danish, S. J., & Donohue, T. (1995). Understanding media's influence on the development of antisocial and prosocial behavior. In R. Hampton, P. Jenkins, & T. Gullota (Eds.),

Preventing violence in America (pp. 133–156). Thousand Oaks, CA: Sage.

Danish, S. J., & Nellen, V. C. (1997). New roles for sport psychologists: Teaching life skills through sport to at risk youth. *Quest, 49,* 100–113.

Dobson, K. S., & Dozois, D. J. A. (2003). Historical and philosophical bases of the cognitive- behavioral therapies. In K. S. Dobson (Ed.), *Handbook of cognitive-behavioral therapies* (2nd ed., pp. 4–39). New York: The Guilford Press.

Edwards, C., Tod, D., & McGuigan, M. (2008). Self-talk influences vertical jump performance and kinematics in male rugby union players. *Journal of Sports Sciences, 26,* 1459–1465.

Ellis, A. (1976). *Reason and emotion in psychotherapy.* New York: Lyle Stuart.

Emerson, M. J., & Miyake, A. (2003). The role of inner speech in task switching: A dual-task investigation. *Journal of Memory and Language, 48,* 148–168.

Eysenck, M. W. (1992). *Anxiety: The cognitive perspective.* Hove, UK: Lawrence Erlbaum.

Eysenck, M. W., Derakshan, N., Santos, R., & Calvo, M.G. (2007). Anxiety and cognitive performance: Attentional control theory. *Emotions, 7,* 336–353.

Godwin, J. L., Neck, C. P., & Houghton, J. D. (1999). The impact of thought self-leadership on individual goal performance: A cognitive perspective. *Journal of Management Development, 18,* 153–169.

Goudas, M., Dermitzaki, E., Leondari, A., & Danish, S. (2006). The effectiveness of teaching a life-skills program in a physical education context. *European Journal of Psychology of Education, 21,* 429–438.

Goudas, M., & Giannoudis, G. (2008). A team-sports-based life-skills program in a physical education context. *Learning and Instruction, 18,* 528–536.

Goudas, M., Hatzidimitriou, V., & Kikidi, M. (2006). The effects of self-talk on throwing- and jumping-events performance. *Hellenic Journal of Psychology, 3,* 105–116.

Graham, S., & Harris, K. R. (2003). Students with learning disabilities and the process of writing: A meta-analysis of SRSD studies. In L. Swanson, K. Harris, & S. Graham (Eds.), *Handbook of learning disabilities* (pp. 323–344). New York: Guilford.

Graham, S., Harris, K. R., & Mason, L. (2005). Improving the writing performance, knowledge and motivation of young struggling writers. The effects of self-regulated strategy development. *Contemporary Educational Psychology, 30,* 207–241.

Guerrero, M. C. M. (2005). *Inner speech-L2: Thinking words in a second language.* New York: Springer.

Hamilton, S. A., & Fremouw, W. J. (1985). Cognitive behavioral training for college basket-ball free-throw performance. *Cognitive Therapy and Research, 9,* 479–483.

Harbalis, T., Hatzigeorgiadis, A., & Theodorakis, Y. (2008). Self-talk in wheel chair basketball: The effects of an intervention program on dribbling and passing performance. *International Journal of Special Education, 23,* 62–69.

Hardy, J. (2006). Speaking clearly: A critical review of the self-talk literature. *Psychology of Sport and Exercise, 7,* 81–97.

Hardy, J., Gammage, K., & Hall, C. R. (2001). A description of athlete self-talk. *The Sport Psychologist, 15,* 306–318.

Hardy, J., Hall, C. R., Gibbs, C., & Greenslade, C. (2005). Self-talk and gross motor skill performance. *Athletic Insight: The Online Journal of Sport Psychology.* Retrieved from http://www.athleticinsight.com/Vol7Iss2/SelfTalkPerformance.htm

Hardy, J., Hall, C. R., & Hardy, L. (2004). A note on athletes' use of self-talk. *Journal of Applied Sport Psychology, 16,* 251–257.

Hardy, J., Hall, C. R., & Hardy, L. (2005). Quantifying athlete self-talk. *Journal of Sports Sciences, 23,* 905–917.

Hardy, J. Oliver, E., & Tod, D. (2009). A framework for the study and application of self-talk in sport. In S. D. Mellalieu & S. Hanton (Eds.), *Advances in applied sport psychology: A review* (pp. 37–74). London: Routledge.

Hardy, L., Roberts, R., Thomas, P. R., & Murphy, S. M. (2010). Test of Performance Strategies (TOPS): Instrument refinement using confirmatory factor analysis. *Psychology of Sport and Exercise, 11,* 27–35.

Harris, K. R., & Graham, S. (1996). *Making the writing process work: Strategies for composition and self-regulation.* Cambridge, MA: Brookline.

Harvey, D. T., Van Raalte, J. L., & Brewer, B. W. (2002). Relationship between self talk and golf performance. *International Sports Journal, 6,* 84–91.

Harwood, C., Cumming, J., & Fletcher, D. (2004). Motivational profiles and psychological skills use within elite youth sport. *Journal of Applied Sport Psychology, 16,* 318–332.

Hatzigeorgiadis, A. (2002). Thoughts of escape during competition: The role of goal orientation and self-consciousness. *Psychology of Sport and Exercise, 3,* 195–207.

Hatzigeorgiadis, A. (2006). Approach and avoidance coping during task performance in young men: The role of goal attainment expectancies. *Journal of Sports Sciences, 24,* 299–307.

Hatzigeorgiadis, A. (2006). Instructional and motivational self-talk: An investigation on perceived self-talk functions. *Hellenic Journal of Psychology, 3,* 164–175.

Hatzigeorgiadis, A., & Biddle, S. J. H. (1999). The effects of goal orientation and perceived competence on cognitive interference during tennis and snooker performance. *Journal of Sport Behavior, 22,* 479–501.

Hatzigeorgiadis, A., & Biddle, S. J. H. (2000). Assessing cognitive interference in sports: The development of the Thought Occurrence Questionnaire for Sport (TOQS). *Anxiety, Stress, and Coping, 13,* 65–86.

Hatzigeorgiadis, A., & Biddle, S. J. H. (2001). Athletes' perceptions of how cognitive interference during competition influences concentration and effort. *Anxiety, Stress and Coping, 14,* 411–429.

Hatzigeorgiadis, A., & Biddle, S. J. H. (2002). Cognitive interference during competition among athletes with different goal orientation profiles. *Journal of Sports Sciences, 20,* 707–715.

Hatzigeorgiadis, A., & Biddle, S. J. H. (2008). Negative thoughts during sport performance: Relationships with pre-competition anxiety and goal-performance discrepancies. *Journal of Sport Behavior, 31,* 237–253.

Hatzigeorgiadis, A., Theodorakis, Y., & Zourbanos, N. (2004). Self-talk in the swimming pool: The effects of self-talk on thought content and performance on water polo tasks. *Journal of Applied Sport Psychology, 16,* 138–150.

Hatzigeorgiadis, A., Zourbanos, N., Galanis, E., & Theodorakis, Y. (2011). Self-talk and sports performance: A meta-analysis. *Perspectives on Psychological Science, 6,* 348–356.

Hatzigeorgiadis, A., Zourbanos, N., Goltsios, C., & Theodorakis, Y. (2008). Investigating the functions of self-talk: The effects of motivational self-talk on self-efficacy and performance in young tennis players. *The Sport Psychologist, 22,* 458–471.

Hatzigeorgiadis, A., Zourbanos, N., Mpoumpaki, S., & Theodorakis, Y. (2009). Mechanisms underlying the self-talk-performance relationship: The effects of motivational self-talk on self-confidence and anxiety. *Psychology of Sport and Exercise, 10*, 185–192.

Hatzigeorgiadis, A., Zourbanos, N., & Theodorakis, Y. (2007). The moderating effects of self-talk content on self-talk functions. *Journal of Applied Sport Psychology, 19*, 240–251.

Highlen, P. S., & Bennett, B. B. (1979). Psychological characteristics of successful and nonsuccessful elite wrestlers: An exploratory study. *Journal of Sport Psychology, 1*, 123–137.

Highlen, P. S., & Bennett, B. B. (1983). Elite divers and wrestlers: A comparison between open and closed skill athletes. *Journal of Sport Psychology, 1*, 390–409.

Jaremko, M. E. (1987). Cognitive strategies in the control of pain tolerance. *Journal of Behavior Therapy and Experimental Psychiatry, 9*, 239–244.

Johnson, J., Hrycaiko, D. W., Johnson, G. V., & Halas, J. M. (2004). Self-talk and female youth soccer performance. *The Sport Psychologist, 18*, 44–59.

Kamann, M. P., & Wong, B. Y. L. (1993). Inducing adaptive coping self-statements in children with learning disabilities through self-instruction training. *Journal of Learning Disabilities, 26*, 630–638.

Kendall, P. C. (2006). Guiding theory for therapy with children and adolescents. In P. C. Kendall (Ed.), *Child and adolescent therapy: Cognitive-behavioral procedures* (3rd ed., pp. 3–32). New York: Guilford Press.

Kray, J. (2006). Task-set switching under cue-based and memory-based switching conditions in younger and older adults. *Brain Research, 1105*, 83–92.

Kray, J., Eber, J., & Karbach, J. (2008). Verbal self-instructions in task-switching: A compensatory tool for action control deficits in childhood and old age? *Developmental Science, 11*, 223–236.

Kolovelonis, A., Goudas, M., & Dermitzaki, I. (2011). The effects of instructional and motivational self-talk on students' performance in physical education. *Psychology of Sport and Exercise, 12*, 153–158.

Krohne, H. W., & Hindel, C. (2000). Anxiety, cognitive interference, and sports performance: The Cognitive Interference Test—table tennis. *Anxiety, Stress & Coping, 13*, 27–52.

Kurpius, D. J., Benjamin, D., & Morran, D. K. (1985). Effects of teaching a cognitive strategy on counselor trainee internal dialogue and clinical hypothesis formulation. *Journal of Counseling Psychology, 32*, 263–271.

Landin, D. (1994). The role of verbal cues in skill learning. *Quest, 46*, 299–313.

Landin, D., & Hebert, E. P. (1999). The influence of self-talk on the performance of skilled female tennis players. *Journal of Applied Sport Psychology, 11*, 263–282.

Lane, A. M., Harwood, C., & Nevill, A. M. (2005). Confirmatory factor analysis of the Thought Occurrence Questionnaire for Sport (TOQS) among adolescent athletes. *Anxiety, Stress, and Coping, 18*, 245–254.

Latham, G. P., & Budworth, M. H. (2006). The effect of training in verbal self-guidance on the self-efficacy and performance of native North Americans in the selection interview. *Journal of Vocational Behavior, 68*, 516–523.

Latinjak, A. T., Torregrosa, M., & Renom, J. (2010). Studying the effects of self-talk on thought content with male adult tennis players. *Perceptual and Motor Skills, 111*, 249–260.

Latinjak, A. T., Torregrosa, M., & Renom, J. (2011). Combining self-talk and performance feedback: Their effectiveness with adult tennis players. *The Sport Psychologist, 25*, 18–31.

Luria, A. R. (1962/1980). *Higher cortical functions in man* New York: Basic Books.

Mahoney, M. J., & Avener, M. (1977). Psychology of the elite athlete: An exploratory study. *Cognitive Therapy and Research, 1*, 135–141.

Mallett, C. J., & Hanrahan, S. J. (1997). Race modeling: An effective cognitive strategy for the 100 m sprinter? *The Sport Psychologist, 11*, 72–85.

Malouff, J. M., & Murphy, C. (2006). Effects of self-instructions on sport performance. *Journal of Sport Behavior, 29*, 159–168.

Manz, C. C., & Neck, C. P. (1991). Inner leadership: Creating productive thought patterns. *The Executive, 5*, 87–95.

Masciana, R. C., Van Raalte, J. L., Brewer, B. W., Brandon, M. G., &Coughlin, M. A. (2001). Effects of cognitive strategies on dart throwing performance. *International Sports Journal, 5*, 31–39.

Meichenbaum, D. H. (1977). *Cognitive behavior modification: An integrative approach*. New York: Plenum.

Meichenbaum, D. H., & Goodman, J. (1971). Training impulsive children to talk to themselves: A means of developing self-control. *Journal of Abnormal Psychology, 77*, 115–126.

Ming, S., & Martin, G. L. (1996). Single-subject evaluation of a self-talk package for improving figure skating performance. *The Sport Psychologist, 10*, 227–238.

Moran, A. (2009). Cognitive psychology in sport: Progress and prospects. *Psychology of Sport and Exercise, 10*, 420–426.

Neck, C. P., & Manz, C. C. (1996). Thought self-leadership: The impact of mental strategies training on employee behavior, cognition, and emotion. *Journal of Organizational Behavior, 17*, 445–467.

Nisbett, R., & Wilson, T. (1977). Telling more than we can know: Verbal reports on mental processes. *Psychological Review, 84*, 231–259.

O'Callaghan, M. E., & Couvadelli, B. (1998). Use of self-instructional strategies with three neurologically impaired adults. *Cognitive Therapy and Research, 22*, 91–107.

Papaioannou, A., Ballon, F., Theodorakis, Y., & Auwelle, Y. (2004). Combined effect of goal-setting and self-talk in performance of a soccer shooting task. *Perceptual and Motor Skills, 98*, 89–99.

Patrick, T. D., & Hrycaiko, D.W. (1998). Effects of a mental training package on an endurance performance. *The Sport Psychologist, 12*, 283–299.

Perkos, S., Theodorakis, Y., & Chroni, S. (2002). Enhancing performance and skill acquisition in novice basketball players with instructional self-talk. *The Sport Psychologist, 16*, 368–383.

Prussia, G. E., Anderson, J. S., & Manz, C. C. (1998). Self-leadership and performance outcomes: The mediating influence of self-efficacy. *Journal of Organizational Behavior, 19*, 523–538.

Reardon, J. P. (1993). Handling the self-talk of athletes. In K. P. Henschen & W. F. Straub (Eds.), *Sport psychology: An analysis of athlete behavior* (3rd ed., pp. 203–211). Forest Glen, MI: Mouvement Publications.

Richardson, B., & Stone, G. L. (1981). Effects of cognitive adjustment procedure within a micro counseling situation. *Journal of Counseling Psychology, 26*, 168–175.

Rogerson, L. J., & Hrycaiko, D. W. (2002). Enhancing competitive performance of ice hockey goaltenders using centering and self-talk. *Journal of Applied Sport Psychology, 14*, 14–26.

Rotella, R. J., Gansneder, B., Ojala, D., & Billings, J. (1980). Cognitions and coping strategies of elite skiers: An exploratory study on young developing athletes. *Journal of Sport Psychology, 2*, 350–354.

Rushall, B., Hall, M., Roux, L., Sasseville, J., & Rushall, A. C. (1988). Effects of three types of thought content instructions on skiing performance. *The Sport Psychologist, 2*, 283–297.

Sanders, M. R., Shepherd, R. W., Cleghorn, G., & Woolford, H. (1994). The treatment of recurrent abdominal pain in children: A controlled comparison of cognitive-behavioral family intervention and standard pediatric care. *Journal of Consulting and Clinical Psychology, 62*, 306–314.

Sarason, I. G., Sarason, B. R., Keefe, D. E., Hayes, B. E., & Shearin, E. N. (1986). Cognitive interference: Situational determinants and traitlike characteristics. *Journal of Personality and Social Psychology, 51*, 215–226.

Schill, T., Monroe, S., Evans, R., & Ramanaiah, N. (1978). The effect of self-verbalizations on performance: Test of the rational-emotive position. *Psychotherapy: Theory, Research, and Practice, 15*, 2–7.

Schüler, J., & Langens, T. A. (2007). Psychological crisis in a marathon and the buffering effects of self-verbalizations. *Journal of Applied Social Psychology, 37*, 2319–2344.

Shergill, S. S., Brammer, M. J., Fukuda, R., et al. (2002). Modulation of activity in temporal cortex during generation of inner speech. *Human Brain Map, 16*, 219–227.

St. Clair Gibson, A., & Foster, C. (2007). The role of self-talk in the awareness of physiological state and physical performance. *Sports Medicine, 37*, 1029–1044.

Steffy, R. A., Meichenbaum, D., & Best, J. A. (1970). Aversive and cognitive factors in the modification of smoking behavior. *Behavioral Research and Therapy, 8*, 115–125.

Swanson, H. L., & Kozleski, E. B.(1985). Self-talk and handicapped children's academic needs: Applications of cognitive behavior modification. *Techniques: A Journal for Remedial Education and Counseling, 1*, 367–379.

Thelwell, R. C., & Greenlees, I. A. (2003). Developing competitive endurance performance using mental skills training. *The Sport Psychologist, 17*, 318–337.

Thelwell, R. C., & Maynard, I. W. (2003). The effects of a mental skills package on 'repeatable good performance' in cricketers. *Psychology of Sport and Exercise, 4*, 377–396.

Theodorakis, Y., Beneca, A., Goudas, M., Antoniou, P., & Malliou, P. (1998). The effect of self-talk on injury rehabilitation. *European Yearbook of Sport Psychology, 2*, 124–135.

Theodorakis, Y., Chroni, S., Laparidis, K., Bebestos, V., & Douma, I. (2001). Self-talk in a basketball shooting task. *Perceptual and Motor Skills, 92*, 309–315.

Theodorakis, Y., Hatzigeorgiadis, A., & Chroni, S. (2008). The Functions of Self-Talk Questionnaire: Investigating how self-talk strategies operate. *Measurement in Physical Education and Exercise Science, 12*, 10–30.

Theodorakis, Y., Weinberg, R., Natsis, P., Douma, I., & Kazakas, P. (2000). The effects of motivational versus instructional self-talk on improving motor performance. *The Sport Psychologist, 14*, 253–272.

Thomas, P. R., Murphy, S. M., & Hardy, L. (1999). Test of performance strategies: Development and preliminary validation of a comprehensive measure of athletes' psychological skills. *Journal of Sports Sciences, 17*, 697–711.

Tod, D. A., Thatcher, R., McGuigan, M., & Thatcher, J. (2008). Effects of instructional and motivational self-talk on the vertical jump. *National Strength and Conditioning Association, 23*, 196–202.

Treadwell, K. R. H., & Kendall, P. C. (1996). Self-talk in youth with anxiety disorders: States of mind, content specificity, and treatment outcome. *Journal of Consulting and Clinical Psychology, 64*, 941–950.

Van Raalte, J. L., Brewer, B. W., Lewis, B. P., Linder, D. E., Wildman, G., & Kozimor, J. (1995). Cork! The effects of positive and negative self-talk on dart performance. *Journal of Sport Behavior, 3*, 50–57.

Van Raalte, J. L., Brewer, B. W., Rivera, P. M., & Petitpas, A. J. (1994). The relationship between observable self-talk and competitive junior tennis players' performances. *Journal of Sport and Exercise Psychology, 16*, 400–415.

Van Raalte, J. L., Cornelius, A. E., Hatten, S. J., & Brewer, B. W. (2000). The antecedents and consequences of self-talk in competitive tennis. *Journal of Sport and Exercise Psychology, 22*, 345–356.

Vygotsky, L. (1962). *Thought and language*. (A. Kozulin, Trans. & Ed.). Cambridge, MA: MIT Press.

Wayde, R., & Hanton, S. (2008). Basic psychological skills usage and competitive anxiety responses: Perceived underlying mechanisms. *Research Quarterly for Exercise and Sport, 79*, 363–373.

Weinberg, R. S., Smith, J., Jackson, A., & Gould, D. (1984). Effect of association, dissociation, and positive self-talk on endurance performance. *Canadian Journal of Applied Sport Sciences, 9*, 25–32.

Wiley, N. (2006). Pragmatism and the dialogical self. *International Journal for Dialogical Science, 1*, 5–21.

Williams, J. M., Jerome, G. J., Kenow, L. J., Rogers, T., Sartain, T. A., & Darland, G. (2003). Factor structure of the coaching behavior questionnaire and its relationship to athlete variables. *The Sport Psychologist, 17*, 16–34.

Wong, B. Y. L., Harris, K., & Graham, S. (1991). Academic applications of cognitive-behavioral programs with learning disabled students. In P. C. Kendall (Ed.), *Child and adolescent therapy* (pp. 245–275). New York: Guilford.

Woodman, T., & Hardy, L. (2003). The relative impact of cognitive anxiety and self-confidence upon sports performance: A meta-analysis. *Journal of Sports Sciences, 21*, 443–457.

Wrisberg, C. A. (1993). Levels of performance skill. In R. N. Singer, M. Murphey, & L. K. Tennant (Eds.), *Handbook of research on sport psychology* (pp. 61–71), New York: Macmillan.

Zastowny, T. R., Kirschenbaum D. S., & Meng, A. L. (1986). Coping skills training for children: Effects on distress before, during, and after hospitalization for surgery. *Health Psychology, 5*, 231–247.

Zervas, Y., Stavrou, N. A., & Psychountaki, M. (2007). Development and validation of the Self-Talk Questionnaire (S-TQ) for Sports. *Journal of Applied Sport Psychology, 19*, 142–159.

Ziegler, S. G. (1987). Effects of stimulus cueing on the acquisition of ground strokes by beginning tennis players. *Journal of Applied Behavior Analysis, 20*, 405–411.

Zourbanos, N. (2008). *The influence of coaching behavior and social support on the formulation of athletes' self-talk*. Unpublished doctoral dissertation, University of Thessaly, Greece.

Zourbanos, N., Hatzigeorgiadis, A., Chroni, S., Theodorakis, Y., & Papaioannou, A. (2009). Automatic Self-Talk Questionnaire for Sports (ASTQS): Development and preliminary validity of a measure identifying the structure of athletes' self-talk. *The Sport Psychologist, 23*, 233–251.

Zourbanos, N., Hatzigeorgiadis, A., Goudas, M., Papaioannou, A., Chroni, S., & Theodorakis, Y. (2011). The social side of self-talk: Relationships between perceptions of support received from the coach and athletes' self-talk. *Psychology of Sport and Exercise, 12*, 407–414.

Zourbanos, N., Hatzigeorgiadis, A., & Theodorakis, Y. (2007). A preliminary investigation of the relationship between athletes' self-talk and coaches' behavior and statements. *International Journal of Sports Science and Coaching, 2*, 57–66.

Zourbanos, N., Hatzigeorgiadis, A., Tsiakaras, N., Chroni, S., & Theodorakis, Y. (2010). A multi-method examination of the relationship between coaching behavior and athletes' inherent self-talk. *Journal of Sport and Exercise Psychology, 32*, 764–785.

Zourbanos, N., Theodorakis, Y., & Hatzigeoriadis, A. (2006). Coaches' behavior, social support and athletes' self-talk. *Hellenic Journal of Psychology, 3*, 150–163.

The Role of Imagery in Performance

Jennifer Cumming *and* Sarah E. Williams

Abstract

Imagery is both a fundamental cognitive process for producing motor actions and a performance-enhancing technique widely used by athletes and dancers. In this chapter, we review findings from basic and applied research to comprehensively define imagery and describe its key characteristics. Using a cognitive neuroscience explanation, we discuss how imagery is involved with motor skill performance and the practical implications for this explanation in planning more effective interventions through application of the PETTLEP model (Holmes & Collins, 2001). We also focus on the development of imagery ability, an important individual difference variable impacting the value of imagery, and discuss how certain aspects of this characteristic can be improved. We then describe other imagery outcomes and offer a revised model based on our review to guide further research and application. We conclude with future directions for imagery research and its practical use for performers, including contemporary issues to be addressed by researchers in the field.

Key Words: Functional equivalence, modality, perspective, agency, angle, deliberation, learning, performance, application, PETTLEP, applied model of imagery use

Imagery is a cognitive process fundamental to motor learning and performance. When we consciously internally represent an action through imagery, the same brain areas involved in the unconscious planning and execution of movements are activated (Lotze & Halsband, 2006; Munzert, Lorey, & Zentgraf, 2009). Importantly, imagery shares neural and behavioral similarity to the genuine experience. This functional relationship provides researchers with a direct approach to studying covert motor processes important in everyday life, such as anticipating the effects of an action, preparing or intending to move, learning or relearning motor skills (e.g., recovery after stoke), or remembering an action (Jeannerod, 1995). Due to this wide application and ability to gain insights into underlying mechanisms, imagery is of interest to a range of fields including cognitive psychology, neuropsychology, neurophysiology, neurorehabilitation, motor learning, motor control, and physiotherapy (Lotze & Halsband, 2006; Munzert et al., 2009; Murphy & Martin, 2002).

Imagery is also a mental technique that can be refined with practice and utilized in many ways. It is a well-known performance-enhancing strategy and extensively used in applied fields, particularly sport, dance, and exercise psychology (for a review, see Cumming & Ramsey, 2009; Murphy, Nordin, & Cumming, 2008; Weinberg, 2008). A main function of imagery is to aid self-regulation of thoughts, feelings, and behaviors, and it is a characteristic of successful performers (e.g., Cumming & Hall, 2002; Orlick & Partington, 1988; Salmon, Hall, & Haslam, 1994). Many anecdotal reports exist from elite athletes and dancers describing the significant role played by imagery in their preparation for top performances. For example, sprinter John Regis described training for a major championship by, "imaging the perfect race and the feeling I got when I was running the perfect race. When that happens it's called being in the zone, because you just don't seem able to lose or run badly" (Grout & Perrin, 2004, p. 103).

In this chapter, we pull from varied research areas to offer different perspectives on imagery and more fully describe this dynamic, complex, and ubiquitous construct. We begin by providing a definition to explain five key characteristics of the imagery process. Using a cognitive neuroscience explanation, we discuss how imagery is involved with motor skill performance and the practical implications for creating more effective imagery. Our discussion then broadens to include other imagery outcomes, and we offer a revised model to guide further research and application. We conclude with several contemporary issues to provide direction for future investigations in the field.

Defining Imagery and Its Characteristics

Defining the term "imagery" has not proved to be a simple or easy task. Many definitions offer different descriptions of what imagery entails and explanations about its many functions. Morris, Spittle, and Watt (2005) explain "the focus of each definition varies depending on the purpose for which the imagery description is used" (p. 14), which makes it difficult for authors to select a single conceptualization of the construct. A consistent theme is to consider imagery as a mental activity involving the internal representations of information without the stimulus present (Moran, 2009). Recently, Holmes and Calmels (2008) adapted Morris et al.'s working definition to account for neuroscientific evidence of the shared neural activation between imagery and physically executed behavior:

> Imagery, in the context of sport, may be considered as the neural generation or regeneration of parts of a brain representation/neural network involving primarily top-down sensorial, perceptual and affective characteristics, that are primarily under the conscious control of the imager and which may occur in the absence of perceptual afference functionally equivalent to the actual sporting experience.
> (*Holmes & Calmels*, 2008, p. 433)

We will use this definition as the starting point for describing five key characteristics of the imagery process: modality, perspective, angle, agency, and deliberation (see Table 11.1 for a summary). Although a sport setting is specified, this definition applies to the range of performance circumstances discussed in this chapter.

Table 11.1 Key characteristics of the imagery process

Characteristic	Definition	Components
Modality	The sensory modality (or modalities) involved.	Auditory Gustatory Kinesthetic Olfactory Tactile Visual
Perspective	The visual perspective adopted.	1PP (internal visual imagery) 3PP (external visual imagery)
Angle	The viewing angle when imaging in 3PP.	Above Front Behind Side on (from right or left)*
Agency	The author or agent of the behavior being imaged.	Self Other
Deliberation	The degree to which imagery is consciously and purposefully employed.	Spontaneous or triggered Deliberate mental practice

For a more extensive list of viewing angles, see Callow, N. & Roberts, R. (2010). Imagery research: An investigation of three issues. *Psychology of Sport and Exercise, 11,* 325–329.

At its most basic level, Holmes and Calmels (2008) describe imagery as a top-down, knowledge-driven process. The starting point for image generation is typically, but not necessarily, when individuals close their eyes. Information is then retrieved from long-term memory to use within working memory to create or recreate an experience (Morris et al., 2005). It is here where other imagery subprocesses occur, namely image transformation (i.e., rotate or modify the characteristics of an image), image scanning (e.g., detect details in the image), and image maintenance (e.g., sustain images for a period of time). Imagery is therefore dynamic in nature, involving other cognitive processes such as memory. It is also not limited to recalling information from the past, but also allows individuals to create new experiences that have not yet occurred (Denis, 1985).

Another element of Holmes and Calmels' (2008) definition is the idea that imagery is a quasi-sensory or perception-like process happening in the absence of any external stimulus input (also see Kosslyn, Thompson, & Ganis, 2006; Richardson, 1969). The imagined perceptual experience can occur in different sensory modalities; namely, auditory, gustatory, kinesthetic, olfactory, tactile, and visual. Visual imagery is experienced as seeing with the "mind's eye," auditory imagery is experienced as hearing with the "mind's ear," tactile imagery is experienced as feeling with the "mind's skin," and so on (Kosslyn et al., 2006). Further, defining imagery as a multisensory construct is also consistent with how athletes, dancers, and exercisers describe their imagery experiences (Driediger, Hall, & Callow, 2006; Munroe, Giacobbi, Hall, & Weinberg, 2000; Nordin & Cumming, 2005b; Short, Hall, Engel, & Nigg, 2004).

When imagery pertains to simulating an action or movement, the focus is typically on visual and kinesthetic modalities. The visual representation contains information about what the individual "sees" in the image (e.g., your club head making contact with the ball when playing golf), and this can be viewed from either a first-person (1PP) or third-person perspective (3PP). In 1PP, also known as *internal visual imagery*, the movement is imaged as if the individual is taking part in the actual action; that is, through their own eyes. By comparison, the individual would occupy the position of an observer in the 3PP and image the action from outside of his or her own body; that is, as if watching themselves performing on television or on a stage. For this reason, 3PP is also known as *external visual imagery*.

Particularly in the case of the 3PP, single or multiple angles can be adopted to provide individuals with additional visual information about the movement to be performed (Holmes & Calmels, 2008). Professional dancers interviewed by Nordin and Cumming (2005b) described seeing themselves from above and/or diagonally, as well as experiencing both visual perspectives simultaneously. More recently, Callow and Roberts (2010) reported ten different viewing angles employed by participants when they completed the external visual imagery subscale of the Vividness of Movement Imagery Questionnaire-2 (VMIQ-2; Roberts, Callow, Hardy, Markland, & Bringer, 2008). The four most reported angles were behind, in front, side on from the left, and side on from the right. From this research and anecdotal reports (e.g., Holmes & Calmels, 2008), it is evident that performers transform or rotate images to take advantage of different viewing angles. They also alternate between viewing perspectives as it suits the nature of the task and/or their stage of learning.

Although hypotheses are less advanced for viewing angle, 1PP has been found to benefit simple, well-learned tasks and those depending on perceptual information (e.g., anticipating the direction of the ball when receiving a serve in tennis) whereas 3PP is more useful for tasks emphasizing technical form or body shape (e.g., the precise body movements involved in performing a spiral sequence in figure skating) (Hardy, 1997). It is plausible that specific or multiple angles may further enhance the effects of 3PP for form-based tasks by providing the imager with visual information not otherwise accessible to them in 1PP. For example, a ballet dancer may image herself from behind, the front, and the side to analyze her body position when performing an attitude or développé. Further, utilizing different viewing angles might aid in the learning and memorization of tactics and strategies. As another example, viewing the football pitch from above may help a player to understand where his needs to be positioned in relation to his teammates.

In addition to viewing perspective and angle, it is also important to clarify the behavioral agency or authorship of the visual image. Individuals can image their own performance or that of another person (Holmes & Calmels, 2008; Ruby & Decety, 2001). 1PP is typically associated with the self being the agent of one's behavior, but this can also refer to adopting the perspective of someone else. The latter allows the individual to put him- or herself in the place of another person (e.g., "put yourself in their shoes") to predict and understand the actions of others (Jeannerod, 2006). In 3PP, either the self or another person can be seen as the agent of the behavior. For example, a basketball player might mentally create a scene involving his or her team member successfully performing a foul shot and view it from the position he or she normally occupies on the court. Imagery research can sometimes be ambiguous as to whether 3PP is referring to the self or other performing the action, and this lack of distinction may potentially confound study results. At a neural level, behavioral agency can be distinguished with brain imaging techniques such as functional magnetic resonance imaging (fMRI), positron emission tomography (PET), or transcranial magnetic stimulation (TMS). Using PET, Ruby and Decety (2001) asked participants to image either themselves or the experimenter performing a given action, in this case, acting with a particular object (e.g., a razor, shovel, or ball). Although an overlap in neural networks was found, distinctive areas were activated during the internal representation of self-produced actions compared to when simulating the actions generated by others. Imaging oneself making the action mirrored the pattern found during actual execution of the movement, whereas imaging others generating the action was akin to activation occurring when individuals watch the movements of others.

The kinesthetic modality of movement imagery involves representing the sensations of how it "feels" to perform an action, such as the tension in your muscles when they contract as you run up a flight of stairs. This internal feel involves an awareness of the position and movements of the parts of the body, known as *proprioception* or *kinesthesia*, as well as the force and effort perceived during movement and effort (Callow & Waters, 2005). It may also consist of other types of feelings relevant to the performer or nature of the task. Qualitative research suggests that imaged feelings also include physiological responses (e.g., changes in heart rate or body temperature), pain and healing (e.g., imaging how a ligament tear feels and how it heals during the rehabilitation process), emotions (e.g., feeling happy), rhythm and timing (e.g., imaging in slow or fast motion), weight (e.g., feeling light or heavy), and spatial awareness (e.g., bodily position and/or position in relation to other objects) (Callow & Waters, 2005; Driediger et al., 2006; Nordin & Cumming, 2005b). Thus, many interpretations may result when performers are asked to rate how easy or difficult it is for them to feel an image, such as when asked to complete manipulation checks about

their imagery experiences. For the sake of clarity in research, as well as applied settings, what is meant by "feel" should be specifically defined for, or by, participants.

A conceptual distinction between imagery modality and perspective is also needed because the term "internal imagery" has historically been equated with kinesthetic imagery. The confusion likely stems from Mahoney and Avener's (1977) seminal paper highlighting imagery as an internal characteristic of successful gymnasts at the 1976 U.S. Olympic trials. Although Mahoney and Avener defined internal imagery as "being inside his/her body and experiencing those sensations which might be expected in the real life situation" (p. 137), the gymnasts were asked whether they experienced what the image would feel like in their muscles (i.e., kinesthetic imagery). Subsequent research has not always found internal imagery to be favored by successful performers (Ungerleider & Golding, 1991). It is also now well established that individuals are capable of experiencing kinesthetic sensations when imaging from an external visual perspective (e.g., Cumming & Ste-Marie, 2001). For these reasons, imagery perspective is now more appropriately considered the viewpoint that an individual takes during imagery rather than the sensory modality involved (Hardy, 1997; Morris et al., 2005).

Importantly, individuals can detect a difference between visual and kinesthetic imagery, but these modalities do not occur in isolation. It is possible to experience more than one modality simultaneously and shift attention between modalities as instructed (Munzert et al., 2009). When completing the Movement Imagery Questionnaire-Revised (MIQ-R; Hall & Martin, 1997), participants are asked to rate their ease of "seeing" and "feeling" four movements (knee raise, arm movement, waist bend, and jump). Although scores for visual and kinesthetic imagery ability tend to be positively correlated with each other, the strength of this relationship is only moderate in nature ($r = .44$; Hall & Martin, 1997). From a psychometric point of view, visual and kinesthetic imagery of movement appear to be separate but related constructs.

Further, there is evidence that visual and kinesthetic imagery are neurally discernible (e.g., Guillot et al., 2009). Using fMRI, Guillot et al. revealed a divergent pattern of increased brain activation in skilled imagers following instructions to first-person visually or kinesthetically image a finger sequence consisting of eight moves. Both types of imagery shared common activations related to movement (i.e., lateral premotor cortex), but areas involved with visual perception (i.e., the occipital regions and the superior parietal lobules) yielded more activity during visual imagery, whereas kinesthetic imagery resulted in greater activity in structures associated with motor processes (i.e., the inferior parietal lobule). The authors concluded that individuals are able to selectively attend to one sensory modality when generating an image, but will still have a general mental representation of the movement regardless of whether the sensory modality is visual or kinesthetic. This finding also helps clarify the concept of motor imagery, which Moran (2009) argues has been too narrowly defined by cognitive neuroscientists. It is a commonly used term, but there is no definite agreement on how it should be defined. For example, Decety (1996) describes motor imagery as being comparable, "to the so-called internal imagery (or first person perspective) of sport psychologists" (p. 87). Jeannerod (1994) takes a more general approach by explaining motor imagery as the mental representation of an overt action without associated movement. The extant fMRI evidence makes it clear that motor images do consist of both visual and kinesthetic representations. Thus, motor imagery is probably most appropriately defined by describing content rather than the modality, perspective, or agency involved. However, to avoid confusion, these latter characteristics should be specified when providing instructions to research participants or performers in applied settings.

The final characteristic of imagery discussed here is that it differs from dreaming because individuals are awake and conscious when generating images (White & Hardy, 1998). How aware and purposeful individuals are about this process ranges on a continuum of deliberation (Nordin, Cumming, Vincent, & McGrory, 2006). At one end of the continuum, images are spontaneously generated in response to a trigger and not necessarily experienced at a high level of awareness (Nordin & Cumming, 2005b). Triggers can be internal, including performing actions, talking to oneself, a particular sensation (e.g., hearing a piece of music), or physiological responses (e.g., heart beating). External cues might involve watching others live or on videotape, as well as writing, reading, watching television, or a viewing a photograph. Most images that people experience on an everyday basis are spontaneous in nature and not generated with any particular purpose in mind (e.g., Vecchio & Bonifacio, 1997). In contrast, at the other end of the continuum is deliberate and systematic imagery practice. This type of mental activity is under voluntary control and requires skill, effort, and concentration on the part of the individual to generate, transform, inspect, and maintain images (Cumming & Hall, 2002; Cumming, Hall, & Starkes, 2005). Performers, particularly those at an elite level, will engage in regular imagery sessions that are planned in advance (e.g., what they will image and for how long) (e.g., Nordin et al., 2006; Orlick & Partington, 1988). These variations in deliberation led Cumming and Ramsey (2009) to caution researchers in their employment of "use" when describing performers' imagery. This term implies that deliberate intention was involved in the imagery process, when the images may have been unexpectedly generated.

In conclusion, the many definitions and conceptualizations of imagery have enabled us to describe this complex and multifaceted cognitive process, with particular attention paid to five key characteristics to consider in research and applied settings (i.e., modality, perspective, angle, agency, and deliberation). In the next section, we turn our attention to explaining how imagery is involved with performance by further expanding on the neuroscientific evidence introduced earlier.

How Imagery Is Involved with Performance

To elucidate how imagery can enhance performance, in this next section we introduce its hypothesized functional equivalence to motor behavior and describe the different brain processes involved. We define neural plasticity and explain how the brain changes when we learn a skill. The role played by imagery during the acquisition and execution of physical skills is discussed with specific mention to the use of pre-performance imagery to prime or stimulate subsequent movement. Finally, we explain how the degree of functional equivalence between imagery and physical performance affects imagery effectiveness.

Functional Equivalence

Imagery has long been acknowledged to benefit motor learning and performance, but few theories have satisfactorily accounted for how it works (Murphy et al., 2008). As neuroimaging techniques (e.g., PET and fMRI) have become more widely available, advancement into the underlying mechanism has been made by the detection of a degree of neural overlap between imagery and the preparation and production of actual movements. This similarity is known as *functional equivalence* because imagery is in some ways equivalent to motor behavior (Johnson, 1982). Both share common brain areas and many of the same properties (Lotze & Halsband, 2006; Lotze & Zentgraf, 2010; MacIntyre & Moran, 2010; Munzert et al., 2009). Applying also to observation of movement (see Chapter 13 this volume), when we image movement, the motor and motor-related areas of the cerebral cortex are activated, including the primary motor cortex (M1), premotor areas (e.g., supplementary motor area, premotor cortex), primary somatosensory cortex, parts of the parietal lobe, and subcortical areas of the cerebellum and basal ganglia. There is some dispute over whether activation in the primary motor cortex is due to imagery or caused by inhibition of movement execution (Lotze & Halsband, 2006). It is also notable that distinctions can be made between imagery and execution in specific brain areas. For example, Gerardin et al. (2000) observed different parts of the striatum active. Even though imagery and execution share many anatomical substrates, it would therefore be misleading to suggest these were identical or to claim complete functional equivalence (Holmes & Calmels, 2008).

Functional equivalence is also evident by the physiological responses elicited during imagery mirroring actual behavior. Electromyographic (EMG) activity recorded during imagery of sporting scenarios is reflective of the muscle activity expected in the actual situation (e.g., Bird, 1984). During mental imagery of lifting a dumbbell, Guillot et al. (2007) found EMG activation in the nine upper arm muscles to correlate with actual physical movement. Further, responses generated in the muscle cells during imagery were reflective of task demands. When participants imaged lifting a heavier weight, they experienced a greater increase in EMG activity compared to imagery of a lighter weight. Imagery also produces cardiovascular and respiratory responses. Again reflecting the imaged content, Wuyam et al. (1995) reported individual's breathing frequency during imagery of themselves exercising to correlate with the imaged exercise intensity.

Further support for the functional equivalence hypothesis is by the preservation of the temporal characteristics of movements during imagery. Mental chronometric studies have showed that movement imagery duration is similar to the time it takes to execute that same movement (Guillot & Collet, 2005). A classic example involved blindfolded participants either walking or imaging walking a variety of distances. Results revealed both actual and imaged movement times increased with greater walking distance (Decety, Jeannerod, & Prablanc, 1989). This speed–accuracy tradeoff, described as *Fitt's Law*, demonstrates how imaged movement adheres to the same biomechanical rules as actual movement.

A perceptual functional equivalence also exists with imagery and like-sensory modalities (e.g., vision and visual imagery). An overlap in neural activity has been demonstrated for imagery of specific senses, including visual imagery (Kosslyn, Thompson, & Alpert, 1997), auditory imagery (Halpern & Zatorre, 1999), and olfactory imagery (Djordjevic, Zatorre, Petrides, Boyle, & Jones-Gotman, 2005). Therefore, to see with the "mind's eye," hear with the "mind's ear," and so on, the same neural processes involved in actual perception are drawn upon to recreate these experiences (Murphy et al., 2008). These findings led Kosslyn et al. to conclude that "imagery, in many ways, can stand in for a perceptual stimulus or situation" (p. 641).

Effect of Imagery on Physical Performance

After establishing the many similarities between movement imagery and actual movement, we will next consider how this co-activation leads to improvements in movement execution and sporting performance. When learning a new motor skill, various changes are thought to occur in the brain, including a strengthening of neuronal connections, the addition or removal of connections, and new cell formation. This reorganization is often termed *plasticity* and includes both short- and long-term changes (for a review, see Holmes, Cumming, & Edwards, 2010). Short-term changes appear to be a result of the strengthening in neural connections leading to changes in the borders of motor maps. For example, participants who physically performed repetitive synchronized thumb abductions and foot extensions experienced a shift in the thumb motor map toward the foot motor map (Liepert, Terborg, & Weiller, 1999). Liepert et al. explained the change, which occurred after only 120 synchronized movements, as being due to the interactions between the areas of hand and foot representation in the motor cortex. Long-term changes are thought to occur from the development and formation of synapses (Holmes et al., 2010). There also appears to be more economic neural activity following extended skill learning. Hatfield, Haufler, and Spalding (2006) proposed that skilled performers eliminate task-irrelevant cerebral cortical and subcortical connections to experience a reduction in the complexity of motor control processes organization. Thus, brain activation of a skilled performer will appear different when performing a motor skill from their set of expert skills compared to a novice performer.

All these changes in neural plasticity, both short- and long-term, are due to activation of the relevant neural areas through execution of the movement. Imagery may also contribute to brain reorganization, as suggested by Kosslyn, Ganis, and Thompson (2001), "imaging, making movements might exercise the relevant brain areas...which in turn facilitate performance" (p. 639). Only a few studies have investigated whether imaging movements leads to permanent neural plastic changes (e.g., Nyberg, Eriksson, Larsson, & Marklund, 2006). For example, Nyberg et al. (2006) found imagery of a novel finger tapping sequence to produce neuroplastic changes in the absence of physical practice, demonstrating perhaps why imagery is an effective method for the learning of skills. These important findings have also led to imagery being more commonly employed in the rehabilitation setting, particularly for helping stroke patients relearn basic movements (for review, see Page, 2010). After a stroke, individuals experience a reduction in motor cortex excitability and decreases in the size of cortical representations of paretic muscles (Liepert et al., 1998). Through repetitive, task-specific, affected-limb practice, the size of the brain regions representing that particular limb increase and functional changes occur (Dean & Shephard, 1997). Imagery is used as a supplement to this physical practice to facilitate the neuroplasticity alterations obtained by further activating the brain areas involved (Jackson, Doyon, Richards, & Malouin, 2004).

As well as leading to long-term changes in performance, the co-activation between movement imagery and execution allows imagery to provide more immediate effects to subsequent performance through its ability to "prime" the movement execution. Imagery is thought to activate and strengthen the mental representations responsible for actual performance of the movement (Murphy et al., 2008). Through this activation, the neurons responsible for movement are likely to be more prepared to correctly activate during movement execution. This type of priming has been found for the neurally similar cognitive activity of action observation; that is, observation of an action subsequently produced quicker and more accurate movements of the same action (e.g., Craighero, Fadiga, Umilta, & Rizzolatti, 1996). Less motor control research has investigated the "priming" effects imagery has on movement execution. But, within the sport setting,

studies have consistently demonstrated the benefits of using imagery immediately prior to movement execution for different sport skills, including golf putting (Short et al., 2002), dart throwing (Nordin & Cumming, 2005a), table tennis (e.g., Li-Wei, Qi-Wei, Orlick, & Zitzelsberger, 1992), and tennis (e.g., Robin et al., 2007). It should be noted that, as well as facilitating performance, Nordin and Cumming (2005a) demonstrated how imagery can also prime a debilitation to performance. In their study, when participants imaged incorrectly performing a dart throwing task, they experienced a subsequent reduction in performance.

When considering together the immediate effects imagery can have on performance and those benefits occurring from changes in neural plasticity over time, this research tells us that the areas of brain activation during imagery should be as similar as possible to those active during execution of the desired outcome. In the case of observation to prime movement, a greater congruency between the prime (observed action) and subsequent execution of the action leads to better execution (e.g., Brass, Bekkering, & Prinz, 2001). The effectiveness of the observation prime is attributed to the greater overlap in areas of brain activity during the prime and the movement execution. A similar principle also applies to imagery when it serves to prime movement execution. Put another way, functional equivalence can be increased at the representational level by having images as congruent as possible to the movement to be performed. By creating greater neural overlap during movement imagery, more of the neural processes involved in movement execution will be activated and subsequently strengthened. We will explore how this may be done in the subsequent section focusing on how to maximize the effectiveness of imagery interventions.

How and What to Image: Maximizing Effectiveness of Imagery Interventions

Having a better understanding of the mechanism underlying imagery's beneficial effects on performance enables researchers and practitioners to more adequately apply imagery in a variety of settings. In the following section, we discuss the practical implications of the neuroscientific explanation presented above by reviewing the evidence for a model based upon it. The model, termed PETTLEP (Holmes & Collins, 2001, 2002), aims to improve imagery interventions by maximizing the overlap in brain activation between imaged and genuine behaviors. Our main focus is how this model informs performance enhancement, but we also consider PETTLEP with regards to the important role played by imagery as a rehabilitation strategy.

Further capitalizing on the neuroscientific explanation, we also examine how individual differences in imagery ability influence the impact of imagery interventions. It is apparent that high imagery ability is an advantageous attribute for performers but less clear is how this quality can be systematically improved. We propose methods for enhancing imagery ability based on cognitive neuroscience evidence and outline the burgeoning evidence for this research direction.

PETTLEP Model

To maximize the potential for overlap in neural activation between real and imaged behaviors, the PETTLEP model encourages individuals to create conditions for imagery rehearsal that mimics as closely as possibly the circumstances of physical practice or performance (Holmes & Collins, 2001, 2002). The model outlines seven elements to amplify the equivalence at the representational level between imagery and actual performance, with every element represented by a different letter of the PETTLEP acronym: *P*hysical, *E*nvironment, *T*ask, *T*iming, *L*earning, *E*motion, and *P*erspective. A definition of each element is provided in Table 11.2 and illustrated with the example of a tennis player attempting to improve return of serve via imagery (for further description elsewhere, see also Cumming

& Ramsey, 2009; Holmes & Collins, 2001, 2002). The model also incorporates Lang's (1977, 1979) bioinformational theory by encouraging the elements to contain propositional information about the *stimulus* (i.e., specific details concerning the stimuli in the environment including multisensory information), *response* (i.e., the cognitive and behavioral response of the individual to this stimulus), and *meaning* (i.e., the subjective interpretation of the response) of the imaged scene. To continue with the tennis example, the player might use imagery to compare how he or she responds to easy and difficult serves and the resulting positive and/or negative feelings.

Evidence broadly supports the PETTLEP model and indicates its importance within sport settings. The physical and environment elements have been manipulated, either individually or in combination, to produce marked benefits compared to no imagery placebo controls or traditional imagery conditions (Callow, Roberts, & Fawkes, 2006; Guillot, Collet, & Dittmar, 2005; Smith, Wright, Allsopp, & Westhead, 2007; Smith, Wright, & Cantwell, 2008). Less conclusive are the findings from studies with a focus on the timing or emotion elements (Forlenza, 2010; O & Munroe-Chandler, 2008; Ramsey, Cumming, Edwards, Williams, & Brunning, 2010). The PETTLEP model explains that imaging in real time is desirable because it closely mimics actual task demands. Yet, O and Munroe-Chandler found improvements on a soccer

Table 11.2 Elements of the PETTLEP model

Element	Definition	Example
Physical	Physical nature of imagery, including body position, clothing, and sport equipment specific to task/situation.	Occupy position to receive serve while wearing tennis clothes and holding his/her racquet.
Environment	Physical environment where imagery is performed.	Perform imagery on the tennis court where match will occur.
Task	Characteristics of the task and expertise level.	Preview shots typically made in response to serve.
Timing	Temporal nature of imagery.	Perform imagery in real-time.
Learning	Imagery content evolves with learning and refinement of behavior.	Makes technical correction to shots in response to feedback.
Emotion	Affective and emotional response to situation.	Feel positive, confident, and in control of the situation.
Perspective	Visual perspective adopted (1PP vs. 3PP).	View images through 3PP analyze body position then switch to 1PP to anticipate service reception.

dribbling task regardless of whether participants imaged in real-time, slow-motion, or beginning in slow motion and concluding with real-time imagery. Because the task was novel for the performers, slow motion imagery may have benefited their learning to the same extent as the other timing conditions (Holmes & Collins, 2001). Whether imaging in slow motion similarly affects performance of well-learned tasks still remains to be investigated, but Calmels and Fournier (2001) have shown that experienced gymnasts will vary their imagery speed depending on the situation (e.g., training vs. competition) and the function of the imagery (e.g., learning vs. managing pre-performance anxiety). Their finding suggests that the timing element likely needs to be considered in conjunction with other PETTLEP elements, particularly task and learning.

The emotions experienced in response to a performance situation are part of the network of response propositions that individuals access for more vivid and meaningful imagery (Lang, 1977, 1979). The PETTLEP model advocates the inclusion of equivalent emotions to those felt during the real-life situation. This premise was tested by Ramsey et al. (2010) by comparing soccer players who received imagery scripts describing the same stimulus information but differing in emotional content only. Both groups performed their imagery four times a week for 6 weeks and significantly improved their penalty kick performance compared to the control group who did stretching exercises. No beneficial effects were found for self-efficacy or interpretations of anxiety symptoms, but the authors recognized limitations in their choice of testing environment (i.e., a regular training session rather than a real-life match). Although there is experimental evidence indicating that individuals can elicit feelings during imagery of hypothetical competitive situations mirroring those experienced pre-competition (Cumming, Olphin, & Law, 2007; Williams, Cumming, & Balanos, 2010), interventions are still needed to substantiate whether imaging equivalent emotions benefits actual emotional self-regulation.

Because the elements interact, the value of a PETTLEP approach also increases when more elements are included in the intervention (Smith et al., 2007). For example, a full PETTLEP intervention with all seven elements was more effective for improving performance of a difficult gymnastic skill (i.e., turning straight jump on the beam) than less functionally equivalent imagery containing only the timing and perspective elements (Smith et al., 2007). As proposed by the model, incorporating all

elements serves to closely approximate the real-life situation. However, Cumming and Ramsey (2009) pointed out certain circumstances, such as when ill, injured, traveling, or unable to access facilities, when it may not be practical for performers to image in the environment or be physically involved with the movement. In these situations, imagery has been advocated as a flexible substitute to physical practice for maintaining skill level, motivation, and self-confidence (Hall, 2001). To optimize functional equivalence, performers could alternatively use pictures, sounds, video clips, and sport accessories (e.g., clothing, equipment) to provide stimulus and response information for their imagery.

The amount of PETTLEP imagery also seems to matter. Wakefield and Smith (2009) found that imaging 20 netball shots three times a week was more effective than once or twice a week. Further, PETTLEP imagery is more effective when combined with physical practice (Smith et al., 2008). Experienced golfers practiced 15 shots twice per week for 6 weeks either by engaging in PETTLEP imagery only, physical practice only, or alternating between PETTLEP imagery once per week and physical practice once per week. The combined PETTLEP imagery and physical practice group significantly outperformed the other two groups at post test, with no differences found between PETTLEP imagery only and physical practice only groups. Both studies reinforce imagery as a form of deliberate practice and its value as a supplement to regular physical practice (Cumming & Hall, 2002; Hall, 2001).

An issue not yet extensively explored with PETTELP is what effect manipulating the elements has on imagery ability. As we will see in the next section, individuals vary in their ability to generate and manipulate images, and these differences will impact the magnitude of intervention effects (Hall, 1998). In the same way that PETTLEP imagery can manifest greater performance improvements, it is also likely that greater functional equivalence will also aid individuals in creating more vivid images. Gould and Damarjian (1996) suggested that holding a piece of equipment relevant to one's sport and replicating the physical movements made during actual performance (i.e., physical element) might increase imagery vividness by enabling performers to more easily recall appropriate kinesthetic sensations. Using Schwartz and Holton's (2000) concept of representational updating, Callow et al. (2006) argued further that this type of dynamic imagery will help individuals to image how one movement (e.g., the starting position) causes a second movement, thereby updating the representation held in working memory. Because imagery vividness is reflected in the richness of the representation displayed, the increased vividness resulting from the representational updating might therefore lead to performance benefits. In other words, Callow et al. suggest that imagery ability may mediate the effects of PETTLEP imagery on performance. In support, skiers in their study gave higher vividness ratings when their imagery incorporated physical and environmental elements of the PETTLEP model. Whether imagery ability does explain PETTLEP effectiveness and what role is played by elements other than physical and environmental is still to be determined by future research. However, the model does help fill a void in the literature by providing specific strategies to researchers and practitioners for enhancing imagery ability.

Research on the PETTLEP model has mainly focused on sport settings to date. Model testing is still needed with samples diverse in age (e.g., young athletes) and across a variety of performance situations (e.g., dance, music, exercise). Also warranted is the exploration of PETTLEP imagery within clinical populations for rehabilitation purposes. It is likely that enhancing the impact of imagery interventions by manipulating the seven elements will also benefit motor problems in individuals with cerebral palsy, developmental coordination disorder, and Parkinson disease; recovery of lost function and motor skill relearning following stroke or spinal cord injury; and pain management and increased strength and flexibility following athletic injury. Another critical development would be to examine what changes occur in the brain following PETTLEP imagery and to provide evidence for increased functional equivalence at the representation level.

Imagery Ability

The ability to generate and control images is present in all individuals but to varying degrees. More successful athletes, for example, report greater vividness of movement images (Roberts et al., 2008). Although frequently termed "imagery ability" in many books and journal articles, as we discuss in this chapter, imagery is also a collection of skills that are modifiable with training and experience rather than simply a general, undifferentiated fixed ability (Hall, 2001; Kosslyn, Brunn, Cave, & Wallach, 1984). We propose that although some individuals inherently find it easier to image than others, characteristics/elements associated with imaging can be honed and improved. In other words, it is possible

to become more proficient in imaging. Thus, a person's capability to generate and control images is partly fixed and partly modifiable, with the former reflected by the developmental changes occurring as a result of maturation. Through the use of mental rotation tasks, it is apparent that children from as young as 5 or 6 years of age can perform movement imagery (e.g., Kosslyn, Margolis, Barrett, Goldknopf, & Daly, 1990; Marmor, 1975). But, compared to adults, young children have a tighter link between their perceptual and sensorimotor processes (Piaget, 1954). As a result, motor processes contribute to children's imagery even more so than they do to adults' movement imagery (Funk, Brugger, & Wilkening, 2005). This may be why visual and kinesthetic imagery develops in children at different rates (Livesey, 2002), with children 6 years and younger being kinesthetically poor (e.g., Ashby, 1983). An individual's capability to image does not fully develop until 14 years of age (Kosslyn et al., 1990), but it can have a substantial impact on the development of movement capabilities. Children with developmental coordination disorder have an impaired ability to generate and monitor internal models of action compared to their typically developing peers. This deficit is thought to contribute to why these children find it difficult to execute various everyday tasks such as tying a shoe lace, pouring a glass of water, or catching a ball (Wilson et al., 2004). The ability to image continues to develop across the lifespan, but from age 50 onward there is an apparent reduction in an individual's capability to image (Isaac & Marks, 1994).

COMPONENTS OF IMAGERY ABILITY

An individual's ability to image is represented by an amalgamation of components and characteristics (Morris et al., 2005). Two of the most commonly discussed are vividness and controllability (e.g., Denis, 1985; Moran, 1993; Murphy & Martin, 2002). Moran described vividness of an image as "its clarity and 'sharpness' or sensory richness," and controllability as the "ease and accuracy with which an image can be transformed or manipulated in one's mind" (p. 158). Vividness is an aspect of imagery concerned with the actual generation of the imagery, whereas controllability refers to the transformation and maintenance of the image once it has been generated. Other components include the ease with which individuals are able to generate a scenario (Hall & Martin, 1997; Williams & Cumming, 2011) and the level of emotion associated with it (Gregg & Hall, 2006). To maximize what can be viewed during imagery, we would also like to suggest the aptitude for switching between visual perspectives (1PP, 3PP) and viewing angle as another form of imagery ability. Few studies have considered this component, but a dancer interviewed by Nordin and Cumming (2005b) described her ability to switch visual imagery perspectives to meet task demands.

Another aspect of performers' imagery ability is the capacity to generate different imagery content. Williams and Cumming (2011) recently demonstrated that athletes' ease of imaging will vary depending on the content of the imagery scenarios. The athletes in their study found it significantly easier to image scenes describing the feelings associated with performing (affect imagery ability), compared to images associated with performing skills (skill imagery ability). In turn, these images were significantly easier to generate compared to images associated with performing strategies (strategy imagery ability), achieving specific goals (goal imagery ability), and mastery-type images describing remaining in control in the face of adversity or in tough situations (mastery imagery ability). Consequently, information about a performer's ability to image particular imagery content will not likely generalize to all types of imagery content that might constitute an intervention. A similarly overlooked characteristic is performers' "meta-imagery" processes, which refers to their knowledge of their imagery skills and experiences and the control they have over it (for a review, see MacIntyre & Moran, 2010). An athlete who is more aware of his imagery capabilities is likely to have a greater understanding of not only the type of imagery he finds to be most beneficial, but also self-regulate when and how he is able to maximize his imagery experiences (e.g., use the viewing perspective and angle most suitable for the task demands) to achieve desired outcomes. When asking athletes about the effectiveness of their imagery, for example, those who imaged more frequently also found it more effective for a variety of functions and easier to image (Nordin & Cumming, 2008).

THE IMPORTANCE OF IMAGERY ABILITY AND ITS ASSESSMENT

An individual's ability to create and control vivid images will influence his or her effectiveness at achieving intended outcomes (Martin, Moritz, & Hall, 1999). Interventions have been found to be more effective for individual's displaying a higher level of imagery ability when using imagery to improve motor performance (Goss, Hall, Buckolz, & Fishburne, 1986) and motivational outcomes, including self-efficacy (McKenzie & Howe, 1997). In a study to improve service return accuracy in tennis, for example, Robin et al. (2007) found imagery use in conjunction with physical practice improved performance for both good and poor imagers, but the better imagers improved more.

Because individual differences in imagery ability are important to consider, it has become common practice to screen performers prior to interventions (Cumming & Ramsey, 2009). Athletes who display poor imagery ability are usually either excluded (e.g., Callow, Hardy, & Hall, 2001) or provided with training exercises to facilitate their imagery generation (e.g., Cumming et al., 2007; Williams et al., 2010). To accomplish this task, however, researchers must have access to valid and reliable means to assess imagery ability. As Lang (1977) indicated, because imagery can only be observed by the person performing it and not by others, measuring an individual's imagery ability is not a simple process. The most common method is to use self-report questionnaires, with the two most popular and well-established being the VMIQ2 (Roberts et al., 2008) and the MIQ-R (Hall & Martin, 1997) to measure visual and kinesthetic ability to image simple movements and actions. A recent development in imagery ability measurement has resulted in the Sport Imagery Ability Questionnaire (SIAQ; Williams & Cumming, 2011). The SIAQ assesses athletes' ability to image five different sport-specific imagery types: skill, strategy, goal, affect, and mastery. Consequently, a range of measurement tools are available to meet researchers' needs.

IMPROVING IMAGERY ABILITY

Improvements in imagery ability have typically been assessed by administering questionnaires prior to and following an intervention. For example, Rodgers, Hall, and Buckolz (1991) reported significant improvements in figure skaters' visual ease of imaging after 16 weeks of imagery training. However, current imagery ability measures are not able to fully capture all the various dimensions that constitute an individual's ability to image (Cumming & Ste-Marie, 2001; Murphy & Martin, 2002). Furthermore, these different components may vary in how susceptible they are to improvement. It would appear that whereas some characteristics of the imagery process are innate and emerge through childhood and adolescence (i.e., an ability), certain aspects are more suitably classified as a skill that can be modified through various training exercises.

Greater knowledge and understanding of imagery ability components and how these can be measured will aid our understanding of which components can be improved and how this can be achieved. Despite research and various models highlighting the importance of imagery ability (e.g., Holmes & Collins, 2001; Martin et al., 1999), surprisingly little attention has been paid to how imagery ability is effectively developed. Stimulus and response training, based on bioinformational theory (Lang, 1977, 1979; Lang, Kozak, Miller, Levin, & McLean, 1980), and creating imagery in layers are approaches becoming more popular in the literature (e.g., Cumming et al., 2007; Evans, Jones, & Mullen, 2004; Williams et al., 2010). We have already suggested using the PETTLEP model as a way to enhance imagery by increasing the overlap in neural activity between movement imagery and execution.

Due to common areas of brain activation, imagery ability can also be enhanced through observation (Williams, Cumming, & Edwards, 2011). Studies have described imagery and observation as similar but distinct processes (McCullagh & Weiss, 2001), and similarly to imagery, observation is used by athletes to enhance skills, strategies, and motivational aspects of performance (Cumming, Clark, Ste-Marie, McCullagh, & Hall 2005). Video modeling has been commonly employed to aid image generation in applied settings, but research investigating the interaction between these two cognitive activities is less frequent (Morris et al., 2005). Even less attention has been paid to the potential benefits of observation on imagery's effectiveness, but evidence suggests a combination of imagery and observation in the absence of physical practice also appears to produce greater performance enhancements compared to imagery on its own (e.g., Atienza, Balaguer, & Garcia-Merita, 1998). By observing a model, an individual receives a clear and vivid instruction of what he or she is required to image (Lang, 1979). Videos of the self or others performing also include specific sensory information to incorporate into an image to improve its quality (Gould & Damarjian, 1996).

Investigating whether observation could serve as a prime to imagery ability, Williams et al. (2011) asked individuals to complete the MIQ-3 (the MIQ-R was revised by these authors to separate visual imagery into 1PP and 3PP, resulting in three subscales including kinesthetic imagery) under four different conditions: (1) *movement prime* (the MIQ-3 was completed in its usual format, in which participants physically perform the movement before imagining the scenario and then rate the ease with which they are able to image the movement); (2) *external observation condition* (same format as the movement prime condition but movement execution was replaced by observation of the movement from an external observation perspective); (3) *internal observation condition* (same format as the external observation condition but the observation was from an internal perspective); and (4) *image-only condition* (the MIQ-3 was completed without prior movement or prior observation; participants simply imaged the scenario and rated the ease with which they were able to do this). Results revealed that MIQ-3 scores were significantly higher during all three prime conditions compared to the image-only condition. Observation was successful in priming and enhancing imagery ability, but for visual imagery, the imagery perspective needed to be congruent with the observation perspective adopted. That is, both the imagery and observation needed to be done from the same perspective for maximum benefit (i.e., 3PP observation and 3PP imagery or 1PP observation and 1PP imagery).

Beyond Skill Performance: Other Outcomes of Imagery

Most of this chapter has been concerned with the effects of imagery on motor skill performance, but many other beneficial effects can be achieved from imagery relating to motivation, attention, arousal and emotional control, confidence and self-efficacy, problem-solving, memorization, planning and creative thought, reviewing and evaluation, strength, flexibility, and healing (Bernier & Fournier, 2010; Munroe et al., 2000; Murphy et al., 2008; Nordin & Cumming, 2005b, 2008; Ranganathan, Sieminow, Liu, Sahgal, & Yue, 2004). Within the applied model of imagery use (see Figure 11.1; Martin et al., 1999), these outcomes mainly fall under three major categories: facilitating the learning and performance of skills and strategies; modifying cognitions; and regulating arousal and competitive anxiety.

This model explains that, as governed by the situation, athletes should image the affective, behavioral, and cognitive changes they desire to achieve. In other words, "what you see is what you get." A number of theoretically and conceptually meaningful relationships have emerged between types of imagery and the outcomes achieved (for a review,

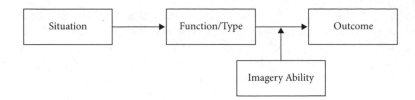

Figure 11.1 Applied model of imagery use.

see Cumming & Ramsey, 2009). For example, skill-based images have led to skill learning (e.g., Nordin & Cumming, 2005a), goal-based images have increased motivation (e.g., Martin & Hall, 1995), and confidence-based images have enhanced beliefs about one's abilities (e.g., Callow et al., 2001). Thus, it appears beneficial to match imagery content to anticipated outcomes.

Growing evidence also suggests that imagery will bring about other unintentional results. That is, there is more to imagery content that what meets the eye (Nordin & Cumming, 2005a; Short, Monsma, & Short, 2004). Indeed, numerous investigations have found more than one outcome resulting from using a type of imagery (e.g., Callow & Hardy, 2001; Callow et al., 2006; Callow & Waters, 2005; Evans et al., 2004; Nordin & Cumming, 2005a, 2008). For example, skill-based imagery can also serve as a source of performance accomplishment to increase self-efficacy beliefs (Nordin & Cumming, 2005a), and both goal-based and confidence-based images can improve skill learning (Martin & Hall, 1995; Nordin & Cumming, 2005a).

Rather than content determining what outcomes are achieved, the benefits of an imagery intervention depend instead on the function of this content for the individual (Callow & Hardy, 2001). For example, a dancer might use imagery to feel more confident (function), and the result of this imagery might be increased confidence (outcome). Paivio (1985) proposed that imagery has both cognitive and motivational functions, and each operates at specific and general levels. The resulting 2 × 2 framework (cognitive specific, cognitive general, motivational specific, and motivational general) formed the basis of early explorations into why athletes image (Salmon et al., 1994) and led to the Sport Imagery Questionnaire (SIQ; Hall, Mack, Paivio, & Hausenblas, 1998). As part of the questionnaire's validation, motivational general was further divided into arousal and mastery function, and all five measured functions represented by different subscales. What has led to subsequent confusion was the decision to define the imagery functions by their closely related content, with "what" athletes are

imaging considered interchangeable with "why" (for discussions on this issue, see Cumming & Ramsey, 2009; Murphy et al., 2008). Hall (2001) has since argued that function should not be presumed by the content of athletes' imagery. For example, the SIQ item "Before attempting a particular skill, I imagine myself performing it perfectly" may be done for its intended cognitive specific function (e.g., to develop the skill), but also can serve motivational specific (e.g., to preview goal achievement), motivational general-arousal (e.g., to ease worries and tension about progress), and motivational general-mastery (e.g., to build confidence) functions for the performer. Alternatively, it is possible that the respondent does not consciously generate this image for any specific purpose. Instead, the image might occur spontaneously in response to a cue (Murphy et al., 2008; Nordin et al., 2006).

Noting the potential ambiguity caused by equating content with function, Short et al. (2004) modified the SIQ to ask athletes to indicate why they used each type of imagery listed on the questionnaire by choosing from five functions: to assist the learning and performance of new skills or strategies, or to effect motivation, arousal/anxiety, or confidence. All imagery types were found to serve their designated functions, but five of the 30 items were perceived as serving an unintended function, and all items were perceived as serving several functions to some extent. Other investigations have also confirmed that performers employ the same image for different reasons, thus a conceptual distinction is now made between the terms "type" and "function" (Bernier & Fournier, 2010; Cumming & Ramsey, 2009; MacIntyre & Moran, 2010; Murphy et al., 2008; Nordin & Cumming, 2005b, 2008). The consensus is that *type* denotes what performers' image and *function* explains why. With this difference in mind, the subscales of the SIQ are likely best considered imagery types rather than functions.

Revised Applied Model of Deliberate Imagery Use

With clarification made to type and function, we now need to separate them in the applied model of imagery use (Martin et al., 1999). We agree with Fournier, Deremaux, and Bernier (2008) that function rather than type should form the central feature and propose a revised model (Figure 11.2) to build on their thinking and those of others (e.g., MacIntyre & Moran, 2010; Murphy et al., 2008). Since its inception, the applied model has been embraced by researchers and practitioners alike as a simple, practical, and testable framework. It provides specific predictions and guidance for the selection of variables to include in experiments. The model also ensures that interventions are designed with specific goals or outcomes in mind. There is also diverse evidence favoring its basic tenets (Cumming & Ramsey, 2009).

The revised model embraces these strengths and remains true to its original by representing "where," "when," and "why" performers use imagery to achieve desired outcomes. It also demonstrates how this is influenced by the performers' capability to image. Additionally, we have answered Martin et al.'s call to elaborate on the model by adding "who," "what," and "how" to its components. But probably the most important refinement we have made is to acknowledge personal meaning as the link between imagery function and type. Although we refer to performers (e.g., athletes, dancers, musicians), this model has broader application to the same clinical populations mentioned in the PETTLEP imagery section. We thus encourage testing of the revised applied model in a range of settings, including exercise, dance, and rehabilitation, and with different populations. For several model components, we also discuss how these can be informed by elements of the PETTLEP model to maximize imagery effectiveness further. An intervention combining both models will enable individuals to perform functionally equivalent imagery that is personally meaningful to their goal achievement (Cumming & Ramsey, 2009).

WHY, WHAT, AND PERSONAL MEANING

Our model specifies that the function (rather than type) of performers' imagery will determine affective, cognitive, and behavioral outcomes via the content generated. Consistent with Martin et al.'s conceptualization, these relationships will be theoretically and conceptually meaningful, thus allowing for specific predictions and testing. A key difference in our thinking is that the function will be served mainly, but is not restricted to, content reflecting this function. This allows for imagery types that do not fit within Paivio's cognitive and motivational imagery framework to be included, as well as the combination of imagery types (e.g., skill-based and confidence-based imagery might be combined to serve the function of feeling more confident of performing a certain skill consistently well). We also presume that performers' are imaging with some degree of conscious intent or deliberation in order for the imagery to serve a function. Spontaneous imagery will generate content and achieve outcomes but will be experienced with no particular function in mind.

In many circumstances, the performers' imagery function will match the type of imagery used to achieve the desired outcome. However, as already pointed out, these relationships are not always straightforward as predicted in the original applied model. Imagery is a highly personal experience, and what is imaged can carry different meanings to different individuals, as has been emphasized in some imagery models, notably Ahsen's triple-code model

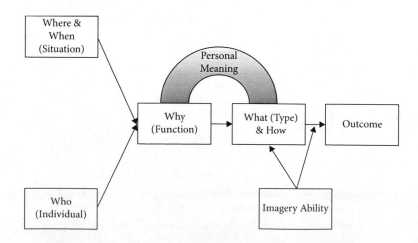

Figure 11.2 Revised applied model of deliberate imagery use.

(Ahsen, 1984) and Lang's bioinformational theory (Lang, 1979). Although mentioned by Martin et al. (1999) in their development of the original applied model, this concept is absent from the framework. We consider the personal meaning attached to the imagery experience as the key for determining what content corresponds to function. Thus, in our revised model, we portray personal meaning as a bridge between function and content. To illustrate why, in their case study of an elite rugby union player, Evans et al. (2004) describe his preference for technical and tactical images to increase his confidence, control anxiety levels, and prepare effectively for matches rather than the affective- or mastery-based content prescribed by the "what you see is what you get" principle.

Consequently, a key consideration when developing imagery interventions is not only the desired outcome, but what type(s) of imagery will serve the function for the intended person. For this reason, Short and Short (2005) advocate deciding on the imagery function first, before determining with the performer what content will facilitate it. Although more time-consuming for the researcher/practitioners, the pros of finding out this information will likely outweigh the cons. When an intervention is personalized to the specific needs of the performer, it will carry greater weight and he or she will likely find it more enjoyable and easier to perform (Cumming & Ramsey, 2009). In doing so, the imagery function will not only correspond theoretically to intervention goals, but the content will also be meaningful for the individual.

WHERE, WHEN AND WHO: IMAGERY ANTECEDENTS

The situation is retained in the revised applied model as having a direct influence on the reasons that performers image (Martin et al., 1999). This component encourages consideration for where and when imagery takes place when planning an intervention, and performers report doing so at diverse times and locations (Munroe et al., 2000; Nordin & Cumming, 2005b). From PETTLEP imagery research, it is already established that being in the environment where the actual or intended behavior will occur maximizes imagery effectiveness (Callow et al., 2006; Guillot et al., 2005; Smith et al., 2007). We also include the individual (i.e., who) as another antecedent composed of factors such as the person's age, gender, experience, disposition (e.g., achievement goal orientation, self-determination, perfectionism), and general ability to image. This is not

an exhaustive list but provided as a starting point for researchers to develop testable predictions. For example, knowing that an athlete is high in ego orientation might explain why she perceives images of herself outperforming others to be motivational (Harwood, Cumming, & Fletcher, 2004).

HOW TO IMAGE

When planning an imagery intervention or experiment, it is also important to think about how the performers will image. Because this concept is so closely related to what performers' image, they are represented together in Figure 11.2. As discussed at the outset of the chapter, the imagery process will be characterized by modality, perspective, angle, agency, and deliberation. Qualitative research (Munroe et al, 2000; Nordin & Cumming, 2005b) also informs us of other characteristics, such as the amount, duration, speed, vividness, and color of the imagery. The PETTLEP model elaborates on how external or internal cues can provide individuals with a starting point for image generation. These triggers can serve a reminder to prompt greater image use and adherence to the intervention. Also necessary to consider is how performers can develop their images by adding clarity and layers of detail to make fuzzy or simple images more vivid or complex (Calmels, Berthoumieux, & d'Arripe-Longueville, 2004; Evans et al., 2004; Nordin & Cumming, 2005b). Finally, the degree to which performers approach their imagery in a deliberate, structured, and planned way (e.g., what they will image and for how long) constitutes another aspect of this component of the revised applied model.

IMAGERY ABILITY

The last component of the model is imagery ability, which we propose will directly influence what and how a person images. Individuals vary in their ability to image different types of cognitive and motivational content (Williams & Cumming, 2011). For example, some people might find it easier to image emotions than skill execution. When it comes to selecting content to serve a particular function, it is likely that people will choose imagery content they find easier to generate. In support, Williams and Cumming (2012) found that the ability to image certain content significantly predicted how frequently individuals use imagery of that content. Imagery ability may also similarly influence the modality, perspective, angle, or agent of behavior imaged, as well as other characteristics such as the amount, duration, speed, and color of the imagery. This is because individuals who find it easier to image in a certain way (e.g., in real time from a first-person perspective) may also be more likely to use this preference to determine how they image.

Because imagery ability will influence what and how individuals image, it will also indirectly affect what outcomes are achieved (i.e., mediation). Take, for instance, the visual imagery perspective adopted. Individuals who are unable to form images from a certain viewpoint (e.g., 3PP) will correspondingly be unable to generate certain types of content (e.g., viewing what one looks like performing a movement from behind or the side). If a certain visual perspective is more desirable for the task (e.g., form-based movement), the outcome achieved by the imagery might therefore be hampered by the individual's lack of ability to image from that perspective.

In keeping with Martin et al.'s (1999) original conceptualization, imagery ability is also considered to moderate the relationship between what performers' image and the outcomes achieved (as reflected by the dashed line in Figure 11.2). Whether imagery ability is best considered a mediator, a moderator, or both, requires further testing. When the applied model was published, only movement imagery ability had been tested as a moderator between skill-based imagery and performance outcomes. Mainly due to limitations in imagery ability measurement (Hall, 1998), research has been slow to test whether this relationship also holds true for other types of imagery and other outcomes (e.g., Cumming, 2008; Nordin & Cumming, 2008). However, the available data strongly point to individual differences confounding imagery interventions, thus indicating a need to measure imagery ability as part of screening procedures and to assess changes occurring throughout. Also to be considered are other components to imagery ability mentioned earlier in this chapter, including imagery perspective and angle switching, as well as meta-imagery processes. Finally, we encourage researchers to include measurements of imagery ability before, during, and after interventions to measure any improvements made.

Conclusion

In this chapter, we have described imagery as both a fundamental cognitive process for producing motor actions and a performance-enhancing technique widely used by athletes and dancers. Using Holmes and Calmels' (2008) definition as the basis, we focused on key characteristics of the imagery and the imagery process. Research from the field of cognitive neuroscience helps explain how imagery is involved with motor skill performance, including the concepts of functional equivalence and neural plasticity, and helps guide the planning of more effective interventions through application of the PETTLEP model (Holmes & Collins, 2001). We also discussed the role played by imagery ability and made suggestions for how this skill can be trained. Finally, we described other imagery outcomes and offered a revised applied model of imagery use. Although our chapter has discussed on many contemporary issues, challenges still remain for imagery researchers, and we touch on these in the final section.

Future Directions
HOW PERSONALIZED DO IMAGERY INTERVENTIONS NEED TO BE?

Applied sport psychologists recommend the need to plan the content of imagery interventions with the individual needs of the performers in mind. Particularly within consulting sessions, the function and content of imagery are elicited through discussions about personally meaningful stimulus and response propositions. This information provides material for writing imagery scripts or developing cues to trigger the imagery process. Not to be overlooked is also the performers' preferences for how to image, which could form part of the intervention goals (e.g., developing greater vividness or the ability switch perspectives). In other words, it is possible to individualize every aspect of the intervention from content to delivery (Cumming & Ramsey, 2009). However, it is not always feasible or appropriate to do so. For example, in experimentally designed studies, researchers may choose to test theoretical hypotheses by providing different sets of instructions to participants. Currently unknown is what effect these research-driven instructions have on imagery compared to the more participant-driven scripts characteristic of consulting work or field-based interventions. A solution to this problem may fall in the middle of these two extremes, using procedures for partially individualizing imagery by asking participants to provide stimulus information based on their past experiences combined with researcher-driven response information (e.g., Cumming et al., 2007; Williams et al., 2010).

HOW DO WE KNOW SOMEONE IS IMAGING?

Due to imagery being a covert and subjective experience, imagery researchers have long been troubled by the problem of knowing whether a person is actually imaging, and, if they are imaging, whether their accounts about their imagery experiences are accurate. These limitations have created doubts about explicit forms of imagery (i.e., conscious internal representations of behavior) and the use of self-report measures (e.g., questionnaires, mental chronometry). It may also be difficult for participants to provide precise verbal reports of a primarily nonverbal experience. An alternative approach has been to examine implicit forms of imagery (i.e., nonconscious internal representations of behavior) using paradigms such as mental rotation tasks. Different types of stimuli are presented on a computer screen (e.g., pictures of hands and feet in different views and angular orientations) and participants are asked to make laterality judgments (e.g., Is it a right or left foot?). The assumption is that participants will use imagery to mentally rotate the body part to determine what judgment to make. Although this approach provides a more objective measure, it does not appear to tap the same type of imagery ability as measured through self-report methods (Lequerica, Rapport, Axelrod, Telmet, & Whitman, 2002). It is also possible that participants are using a strategy other than imagery to form their decisions. A growing trend is to combine self-report with other indices of the imagery experience, including physiological and neurophysiological measures (Guillot & Collet, 2005). For example, changes in the physiological state of the imager can be assessed by recording heart rate and stroke volume to indicate that response information is being included in the imagery (Cumming et al., 2007; Williams et al., 2010).

ESTABLISHING THE MOST EFFECTIVE METHODS FOR IMPROVING IMAGERY ABILITY

As we emphasized throughout the chapter, imagery ability is considered very much modifiable through training and experience, rather than being a solely fixed attribute. Research is starting to establish various methods that are capable of facilitating and improving an individual's proficiency at imaging imagery, and the next logical step would be to compare these methods to determine which is most effective for developing different imagery ability components. For example, observation may serve as a better method to improve movement imagery ability when the focus is on the correct execution of the movement, whereas layering exercises may be more beneficial when the imagery is more focused on specific feelings and emotions associated with the image. Another important point to consider is whether these techniques can bring about any retention effects or whether they simply act as a prime by facilitating neural activation during the imagery process.

References

Ahsen, A. (1984). ISM: The triple code model for imagery and psychophysiology. *Journal of Mental Imagery, 8,* 15–42.

Ashby, A. A. (1983). Developmental study of short-term characteristics for kinaesthetic movement information. *Perceptual and Motor Skills, 57,* 649–650.

Atienza, F. L., Balaguer, I., & Garcia-Merita, M. L. (1998). Video modelling and imaging training on performance of tennis service of 9- to 12- year-old children. *Perceptual and motor skills, 87,* 519–529

Bernier, M., & Fournier, J. F. (2010). Functions of mental imagery in expert golfers. *Psychology of Sport and Exercise, 11,* 444–452.

Bird, E. I. (1984). EMG quantification of mental rehearsal. *Perceptual and Motor Skills, 59,* 899–906.

Brass, M., Bekkering, H., & Prinz, W. (2001). Movement observation affects movement execution in a simple response task. *Acta Psychologica, 106,* 3–22.

Callow, N., & Hardy, L. (2001). Types of imagery associated with sport confidence in netball players of varying skill levels. *Journal of Applied Sport Psychology, 13,* 1–17.

Callow, N., Hardy, L., & Hall, C. (2001). The effects of a motivational general-mastery imagery intervention on the sport confidence of high-level badminton players. *Research Quarterly for Exercise and Sport, 72,* 389–400.

Callow, N., & Roberts, R. (2010). Imagery research: An investigation of three issues. *Psychology of Sport and Exercise, 11,* 325–329.

Callow, N., Roberts, R., & Fawkes, J. Z. (2006). Effects of dynamic and static imagery on vividness of imagery, skiing performance, and confidence. *Journal of Imagery Research and Physical Activity, 1,* 1–13.

Callow, N., & Waters, A. (2005). The effect of kinesthetic imagery on the sport confidence of flat-race horse jockeys. *Psychology of Sport and Exercise, 6,* 443–459.

Calmels, C., Berthoumieux, C., & d'Arripe-Longueville, F. (2004). Effects of an imagery training program on selective attention of national softball players. *The Sport Psychologist, 18,* 272–296.

Calmels, C., & Fournier, J. F. (2001). Duration of physical and mental execution of gymnastics routines. *The Sport Psychologist, 15,* 142–150.

Craighero, L., Fadiga, L., Umilta, C. A., & Rizzolatti, G. (1996). Evidence for visuomotor priming effect. *Neuroreport, 8,* 347–349.

Cumming, J. (2008). Investigating the relationship between exercise imagery, leisure time exercise behaviour, and exercise self-efficacy. *Journal of Applied Sport Psychology, 20,* 184–198.

Cumming, J., Clark, S. E., Ste-Marie, D. M., McCullagh, P., & Hall, C. (2005). The functions of observational learning questionnaire (FOLQ). *Psychology of Sport and Exercise, 6,* 517–537.

Cumming, J., & Hall, C. (2002). Deliberate imagery practice: The development of imagery skills in competitive athletes. *Journal of Sport Sciences, 20,* 137–145.

Cumming, J., Hall, C., & Starkes, J. (2005). Deliberate imagery practice: The reliability of using a retrospective recall methodology. *Research Quarterly for Exercise and Sport, 76*(3), 306–314.

Cumming, J., Olphin, T., & Law, M. (2007). Self-reported psychological states and physiological responses to different types of motivational general imagery. *Journal of Sport and Exercise Psychology, 29,* 629–644.

Cumming, J., & Ramsey, R. (2009). Imagery interventions in sport. In S. D. Mellalieu & S. Hanton (Eds.), *Advances in applied sport psychology: A review* (pp. 5–36). London: Routledge.

Cumming, J. L., & Ste-Marie, D. M. (2001). The cognitive and motivational effects of imagery training: A matter of perspective. *The Sport Psychologist, 15,* 276–287.

Dean, C. M., & Shephard, R. B. (1997). Task-related training improves performance of seated reaching tasks after stroke. A randomized control. *Stroke, 28,* 722–728.

Decety, J. (1996). Do imagined and executed actions share the same neural substrate? *Cognitive Brain Research, 3,* 87–93.

Decety, J., Jeannerod, M., & Prablanc, C. (1989). The timing of mentally represented actions. *Behavioral Brain Research, 34,* 35–42.

Denis, M. (1985). Visual imagery and the use of mental practice in the development of motor skills. *Canadian Journal of Applied Sport Science, 10,* 4S–16S.

Djordjevic, J., Zatorre, R. J., Petrides, M., Boyle, J. A., & Jones-Gotman, M. (2005). Functional neuroimaging of odor imagery. *Neuroimage, 24,* 791–801.

Driediger, M., Hall, C., & Callow, N. (2006). Imagery used by injured athletes: A qualitative analysis. *Journal of Sport Sciences, 24,* 261–272

Evans, L., Jones, L., & Mullen, R. (2004). An imagery intervention during the competitive season with an elite rugby union player. *The Sport Psychologist, 18,* 252–271.

Forlenza, S. T. (2010). *Imagery speed, task difficulty, and self-efficacy: How fast (or slow) to go?* Unpublished masters thesis, Miami University.

Fournier, J. F., Deremaux, S., & Bernier, M. (2008). Content, characteristics and function of mental images. *Psychology of Sport and Exercise, 9,* 734–748.

Funk, M., Brugger, P., & Wilkening, F. (2005). Motor processes in children's imagery: The case of mental rotation of hands. *Developmental Science, 8,* 402–408.

Gerardin, E., Sirigu, A., Lehéricy, S., Poline, J. B, Gaymard, B., & Marsault, C. (2000). Partially overlapping neural networks for real and imagined hand movements. *Cerebral Cortex, 10,* 1093–1104.

Goss, S., Hall, C., Buckolz, E., & Fishburne, G. (1986). Imagery ability and the acquisition and retention of movements, *Memory and Cognition, 14,* 469–477.

Gould, D., & Damarjian, N. (1996). Imagery training for peak performance. In J. L. Van Raalte & B. W. Brewer (Eds.), *Exploring sport and exercise psychology* (1st ed., pp. 25–50). Washington, DC: American Psychological Association.

Gregg, M., & Hall, C. (2006). Measurement of motivational imagery abilities in sport. *Journal of Sports Sciences, 24,* 961–971.

Grout, J., & Perrin, S. (2004). *Mind games: Inspirational lessons from the world's finest sports stars.* Chichester, UK: John Wiley & Sons.

Guillot, A., & Collet, C. (2005). Duration of mentally simulated movement: A review. *Journal of Motor Behavior, 37,* 10–20.

Guillot, A., Collet, C., & Dittmar, A. (2005). Influence of environmental context on motor imagery quality. *Biology of Sport, 22,* 215–226.

Guillot, A., Collet, C., Nguyen, V. A., Malouin, F., Richards, C., & Doyon, J. (2009). Brain activity during visual versus kinesthetic imagery: An fMRI study. *Human Brain Mapping, 30,* 2157–2172.

Guillot, A., Lebon, F., Rouffet, D., Champely, S., Doyon, J., & Collet, C. (2007). Muscular responses during motor imagery as a function of muscle contraction types. *International Journal of Psychophysiology, 66,* 18–27.

Hall, C. R. (1998). Measuring imagery abilities and imagery use. In J. L. Duda (Ed.), *Advances in sport and exercise psychology measurement* (pp. 165–172). Morgantown, WV: Fitness Information Technology.

Hall, C. (2001). Imagery in sport and exercise. In R. N. Singer, H. Hausenblas, & C. M. Janelle (Eds.), *Handbook of sport psychology* (2nd ed., pp. 529–549). New York, NY: John Wiley & Sons.

Hall, C., Mack, D., Paivio, A., & Hausenblas, H. (1998). Imagery use by athletes: Development of the sport imagery questionnaire. *International Journal of Sport Psychology, 29,* 73–89.

Hall, C., & Martin, K. A. (1997). Measuring movement imagery abilities: A revision of the Movement Imagery Questionnaire. *Journal of Mental Imagery, 21,* 143–154.

Halpern, A. R., & Zatorre, R. J. (1999). When that tune runs through your head: A PET investigation of auditory imagery for familiar melodies. *Cerebral Cortex, 9,* 697–704.

Hardy, L. (1997). The Coleman Roberts Griffith address: Three myths about applied consultancy work. *Journal of Applied Sport Psychology, 9,* 277–294.

Harwood, C., Cumming, J., & Fletcher, D. (2004). Motivational profiles and psychological skills use within elite youth sport. *Journal of Applied Sport Psychology, 16,* 318–332.

Hatfield, B. D., Haufler, A. J., & Spalding, T. W. (2006). A cognitive neuroscience perspective on sport performance. In E.O. Acevedo & P. Ekkekakis (Eds.), *Psychobiology of physical activity* (pp. 221–241). Champaign, IL: Human Kinestics.

Holmes, P. S., & Calmels, C. (2008). A neuroscientific review of imagery and observation use in sport. *Journal of Motor Behavior, 40,* 433–445.

Holmes, P. S., & Collins, D. J. (2001). The PETTLEP approach to motor imagery: A functional equivalence model for sport psychologists. *Journal of Applied Sport Psychology, 13,* 60–83.

Holmes, P., & Collins, D. (2002). Functional equivalence solutions for problems with motor imagery. In I. Cockerill (Ed.), *Solutions in sport psychology* (1st ed., pp. 120–140). London: Thomson.

Holmes, P. S., Cumming, J., & Edwards, M. G. (2010). Movement imagery, observation, and skill. In A. Guillot & C. Collet (Eds.), *The neurophysiological foundations of mental and motor imagery* (pp. 245–269). Oxford, UK: Oxford University Press.

Isaac, A. R., & Marks, D. M. (1994). Individual differences in mental imagery experience: Developmental changes and specialization. *British Journal of Psychology, 85,* 479–500.

Jackson, P. L., Doyon, J., Richards, C. L., & Malouin, F. (2004). The efficacy of combined physical and mental practice in the learning of a foot-sequence task after stroke: A case report. *Neurorehabilitation and Neural Repair, 18,* 106–111.

Jeannerod, M. (1994). The representing brain- neural correlates of motor intention and imagery. *Behavioral Brain Sciences, 17,* 187–202.

Jeannerod, M. (1995). Mental imagery in the motor context. *Neuropsychology, 33,* 1419–1432.

Jeannerod, M. (2006). *Motor cognition: What actions tell to the self*. New York: Oxford University Press.

Johnson, P. (1982). The functional equivalence of imagery and movement, *The Quarterly Journal of Experimental Psychology, 34*, 349–365.

Kosslyn, S. M., Brunn, J., Cave, K. R., & Wallach, R. W. (1984). Individual differences in mental imagery ability: A computational analysis. *Cognition, 18*, 195–243.

Kosslyn, S. M., Ganis, G., & Thompson, W. L. (2001). Neural foundations of imagery. *Nature Reviews Neuroscience, 2*, 635–739.

Kosslyn, S. M., Margolis, J. A., Barrett, A. M., Goldknopf, E. J., & Daly, P. F. (1990). Age differences in imagery ability. *Child Development, 61*, 995–1010.

Kosslyn, S. M., Thompson, W. L., & Alpert, N. M. (1997). Neural systems shared by visual imagery and visual perception: A positron emission tomography study. *NeuroImage, 6*, 320–334.

Kosslyn, S. M., Thompson, W. L., & Ganis, G. (2006). *The case for mental imagery*. New York: Oxford University Press.

Lang, P. J. (1977). Imagery in therapy: An Information-processing analysis of fear. *Behavior Therapy, 8*, 862–886.

Lang, P. J. (1979). A bio-informational theory of emotional imagery. *Psychophysiology, 16*, 495–512.

Lang, P. J., Kozak, M. J., Miller, G. A., Levin, D. N., & McLean, A., Jr. (1980). Emotional imagery: Conceptual structure and pattern of somato-visceral response. *Psychophysiology, 17*, 179–192.

Lequerica, A., Rapport, L., Axelrod, B. N., Telmet, K., & Whitman, R. D. (2002). Subjective and objective assessment methods of mental imagery control: Construct validation of self-report measures. *Journal of Clinical and Experimental Neuropsychology, 24*, 1103–1116.

Liepert, J., Bauder, H., Sommer, M., Dettmers, C., Taub, E., & Weiller, C. (1998). Motor cortex plasticity during constrained-induced movement therapy in chronic stroke patients. *Neuroscience Letters, 250*, 5–8.

Liepert, J., Terborg, C., & Weiller, C. (1999). Motor plasticity induced by synchronized thumb and foot movements. *Experimental Brain Research, 125*, 435–439.

Livesey, D. J. (2002). Age differences in the relationship between visual movement imagery and performance on kinesthetic acuity tests. *Developmental Psychology, 38*, 279–287.

Li-Wei, A., Qi-Wei, M., Orlick, T., & Zitzelsberger, L. (1992). The effect of mental-imagery training on performance enhancement with 7–10 year old children. *The Sport Psychologist, 6*, 230–241.

Lotze, M., & Halsband, U. (2006). Motor imagery. *Journal of Physiology Paris, 99*, 386–395.

Lotze, M., & Zentgraf, K. (2010). Contribution of the primary motor cortex to motor imagery. In A. Guillot & C. Collet (Eds.), *The neurophysiological foundations of mental and motor imagery* (pp. 31–45). Oxford, UK: Oxford University Press.

MacIntyre, T., & Moran, A. (2010). Meta-imagery processes among elite sports performers. In A. Guillot & C. Collet (Eds.), *The neurophysiological foundations of mental and motor imagery* (pp. 227–244). Oxford, UK: Oxford University Press.

Mahoney, M. J., & Avener, M. (1977). Psychology of the elite athlete: An exploratory study. *Cognitive Therapy and Research, 1*, 135–141.

Marmor, G. S. (1975). Development of kinetic images: When does the child first represent movement in mental images? *Cognitive Psychology, 7*, 548–559.

Martin, K. A., & Hall, C. (1995). Using mental imagery to enhance intrinsic motivation. *Journal of Sport and Exercise Psychology, 17*, 54–69.

Martin, K. A., Moritz, S. E., & Hall, C. (1999). Imagery use in sport: A literature review and applied model. *The Sport Psychologist, 13*, 245–268.

McCullagh, P., & Weiss, M. R. (2001). Modeling: Considerations for motor skill performance and psychological responses. In R. N. Singer, H. A. Hausenblas, & C. M. Janelle (Eds.), *The handbook of sport psychology* (2nd ed., pp. 205–238). New York: John Wiley & Sons Inc.

McKenzie, A. D., & Howe, B. L. (1997). The effect of imagery on self-efficacy for a motor skill. *International Journal of Sport Psychology, 28*, 196–210.

Moran, A. (1993). Conceptual and methodological issues in the measurement of mental imagery skills in athletes. *Journal of Sport Behavior, 16*, 156–170.

Moran, A. P. (2009). Cognitive psychology in sport: Progress and prospects. *Psychology of Sport and Exercise, 10*, 420–426.

Morris, T., Spittle, M., & Watt, A. P. (2005). *Imagery in sport*. Champaign, IL: Human Kinetics.

Munroe, K., Giacobbi, P. R., Hall, C., & Weinberg, R. (2000). The four Ws of imagery use: Where, when, why, and what. *The Sport Psychologist, 14*, 119–137.

Munzert, J., Lorey, B., & Zentgraf, K. (2009). Cognitive motor processes: The role of motor imagery in the study of motor representations. *Brain Research Reviews, 60*, 306–326.

Murphy, S., & Martin, K. A. (2002). The use of imagery in sport. In T. Horn (Ed.), *Advances in sport psychology* (2nd ed., pp. 405–439). Champaign, IL: Human Kinetics.

Murphy, S., Nordin, S. M., & Cumming, J. (2008). Imagery in sport, exercise and dance. In T. Horn (Ed.), *Advances in sport and exercise psychology* (3rd ed., pp. 297–324). Champaign, IL: Human Kinetics.

Nordin, S. M., & Cumming, J. (2005a). More than meets the eye: Investigating imagery type, direction, and outcome. *The Sport Psychologist, 19*, 1–17.

Nordin, S. M., & Cumming, J. (2005b). Professional dancers describe their imagery: Where, when, what, why, and how. *The Sport Psychologist, 19*, 395–416.

Nordin, S. M., & Cumming, J. (2008). Types and functions of athletes' imagery: Testing predictions from the applied model of imagery use by examining effectiveness. *International Journal of Sport and Exercise Psychology, 6*, 189–206.

Nordin, S. M., Cumming, J., Vincent, J., & McGrory, S. (2006). Mental training or spontaneous play? Examining which types of imagery constitute deliberate practice in sport. *Journal of Applied Sport Psychology, 18*, 345–362.

Nyberg, L., Eriksson, J., Larsson, A., & Marklund, P. (2006). Learning by doing verses learning by thinking: An fMRI study of motor and mental training. *Neuropsychologia, 44*, 711–717.

O, J., & Munroe-Chandler, K. (2008). The effects of image speed on the performance of a soccer task. *The Sport Psychologist, 22*, 1–17.

Orlick, T., & Partington, J. (1988). Mental links to excellence. *Sport Psychologist, 2*, 105–130.

Page, S. J. (2010). An overview of the effectiveness of motor imagery after a stroke: A neuroimaging approach. In A. Guillot & C. Collet (Eds.), *The neurophysiological foundations of mental and motor imagery* (pp. 145–160). Oxford, UK: Oxford University Press.

Paivio, A. (1985). Cognitive and motivational functions of imagery in human performance. *Canadian Journal of Applied Sport Sciences, 10,* 22S–28S.

Piaget, J. (1954). *The construction of reality in the child.* New York: Basic Books.

Ramsey, R., Cumming, J., Edwards, M. G., Williams, S., & Brunning, C. (2010). Examining the emotion aspect of PETTLEP-based imagery with penalty taking in soccer. *Journal of Sport Behavior, 33,* 295–315.

Ranganathan, V. K., Siemionow, V., Liu, J. Z., Sahgal, V., & Yue, G. H. (2004). From mental power to muscle power: Gaining strength by using the mind. *Neuropsychologia, 42,* 944–956.

Richardson, A. (1969). *Mental imagery.* New York: Springer.

Roberts, R., Callow, N., Hardy, L., Markland, D., & Bringer, J. (2008). Movement imagery ability: Development and assessment of a revised version of the vividness of movement imagery questionnaire. *Journal of Sport and Exercise Psychology, 30,* 200–221.

Robin, N., Dominique, L., Toussaint, L., Blandin, Y., Guillot, A., & Le Her, M. (2007). Effects of motor imagery training on service return accuracy in tennis: The role of imagery ability. *International Journal of Sport and Exercise Psychology, 2,* 175–186.

Rodgers, W., Hall, C., & Buckolz, E. (1991). The effect of an imagery training program on imagery ability, imagery use, and figure skating performance. *Journal of Applied Sport Psychology, 3,* 109–125.

Ruby, P., & Decety, J. (2001). Effect of subjective perspective taking during simulation of action: A PET investigation of agency. *Nature Neuroscience, 4,* 546–550.

Salmon, J., Hall, C., & Haslam, I. R. (1994). The use of imagery by soccer players. *Journal of Applied Sport Psychology, 6,* 116–133.

Schwartz, D. L., & Holton, D. L. (2000). Tool use and the effect of action on the imagination. *Journal of Experimental Psychology: Learning, Memory, and Cognition, 26,* 1655–1665.

Short, S. E., Bruggeman, J. M., Engel, S. G., Marback, T. L., Wang, L. J., Willadsen, A., et al. (2002). The effect of imagery function and imagery direction on self-efficacy and performance on a golf-putting task. *The Sport Psychologist, 16,* 48–67.

Short, S. E., Hall, C. R., Engel, S. R., & Nigg, C. R. (2004). Exercise imagery and the stages of change. *Journal of Mental Imagery, 28,* 61–78.

Short, S. E., Monsma, E. V., & Short, M. (2004). Is what you see really what you get? Athletes' perceptions of imagery functions. *The Sport Psychologist, 18,* 341–349.

Short, S. E., & Short, M. W. (2005). Differences between high- and low-confident football players on imagery functions: A consideration of the athletes' perceptions. *Journal of Applied Sport Psychology, 17,* 197–208.

Smith, D., Wright, C. J., Allsopp, A., & Westhead, H. (2007). It's all in the mind: PETTLEP-based imagery and sports performance. *Journal of Applied Sport Psychology, 19,* 80–92.

Smith, D., Wright, C. J., & Cantwell, C. (2008). Beating the bunker: The effect of PETTLEP imagery on golf bunker shot performance. *Research Quarterly for Exercise and Sport, 79,* 385–391.

Ungerleider, S., & Golding, J. M. (1991). Mental practice among Olympic athletes. *Perceptual and Motor Skills, 72,* 1007–1017.

Vecchio, L., & Bonifacio, M. (1997). Different images in different situations: A diary study of the spontaneous use of imagery. *Journal of Mental Imagery, 21,* 147–170.

Wakefield, C., & Smith, D. (2009). Impact of differing frequencies of PETTLEP imagery on netball shooting performance. *Journal of Imagery Research in Sport and Physical Activity, 4,* 1–12.

Weinberg, R. (2008). Does imagery work? Effects on performance and mental skills. *Journal of Imagery Research in Sport and Physical Activity, 3,* 1–21.

White, A., & Hardy, L. (1998). An in-depth analysis of the uses of imagery by high-level slalom canoeists and artistic gymnasts. *The Sport Psychologist, 12,* 387–403.

Williams, S. E., & Cumming, J. (2011). Measuring athlete imagery ability: The Sport Imagery Ability Questionnaire. *Journal of Sport and Exercise Psychology, 33,* 416–440.

Williams, S. E., & Cumming, J. (2012). Athletes' ease of imaging predicts their imagery and observational learning use. *Psychology of Sport and Exercise, 13,* 363–370.

Williams, S. E., Cumming, J., & Balanos, G. M. (2010). The use of imagery to manipulate challenge and threat appraisal states in athletes. *Journal of Sport and Exercise Psychology, 32,* 339–358.

Williams, S. E., Cumming, J., & Edwards, M. G. (2011). The functional equivalence between movement imagery, observation, and execution influences imagery ability. *Research Quarterly for Exercise and Sport, 82,* 555–564.

Wilson, P. H., Maruff, P., Butson, M., Wiliams, J., Lum, J., & Thomas, P. R. (2004). Internal representation of movement in children with developmental coordination disorder: A mental rotation task. *Developmental Medicine and Child Neurology, 46,* 754–759.

Wuyam, B., Moosavi, S. H., Decety, J., Adams, L., Lansing, R. W., & Guz, A. (1995). Mental simulation of dynamic exercise produces respiratory responses which are more apparent in competitive sportsmen. *Journal of Physiology (Cambridge), 482,* 713–724.

Motivation: Self-Determination
Theory and Performance in Sport

Martyn Standage

Abstract

Performance, by its very nature, epitomizes the construct of human motivation (i.e., individuals being moved to act). Motivation research therefore plays a vital role in providing a better understanding of the conditions and processes that support optimal performance, as well as a performer's well-being, development, functioning, and persistence. In this chapter, the central components and phenomena addressed within the meta-theory of self-determination theory (SDT; Ryan & Deci, 2000, 2008) are outlined. A critique of empirical work related to performance and achievement is then provided before the focus shifts to an appraisal of a number of key issues related to sport performance and measurement. In the penultimate section, a number of applications aimed at supporting optimal performance and engagement are presented in the form of supports for basic psychological needs (i.e., for autonomy, competence, and relatedness). Last, a number of future research directions are presented and discussed.

Key Words: Self-determination theory, motivation, autonomy support, need-satisfaction, goals, sport psychology, performance psychology

The topic of motivation addresses the *energizing, direction, regulation,* and *persistence* of human behavior and is evidenced in all aspects of activation and intention (Ryan & Deci, 2000). In addressing "why" and "what" moves individuals to act (cf. Deci & Ryan, 2000), few contexts exemplify the topic of motivation as acutely as the sport domain. The ongoing energy required for an athlete to persist in high-quality training sessions, both across long grueling seasons and in the face of competitive failure, reveals why motivation is considered a foundation to sport achievement and performance. It is also not surprising therefore that researchers, coaches, and sporting associations have all shown a vested interest in better understanding the factors and processes that support, as opposed to forestall, high-quality forms of motivation (Standage & Ryan, 2012).

To better understand the role of motivation in sport, it is essential to consider the conditions and processes that move an athlete to act, think, and develop. That is, some athletes may play their sport simply for the pleasure and satisfaction that they gain from learning new skills, others may be urged into action for external factors (e.g., rewards, awards, etc), others may engage for internal sanctions (e.g., they would feel guilty for letting people down if they were not to play), whereas some may be moved to act via the value that they have developed for their sport as an activity. The reasons underpinning the activation and intentionality of behavior can be very diverse, and the presence of such multiple motives substantiates the view that motivation is a more complex entity than often viewed (e.g., a unitary phenomenon, varying mainly in *quantity*; Bandura, 1997). Indeed, researchers and practitioners within and across many life contexts are coming to realize that fostering optimal, sustained, and adaptive engagement in sport (and other life contexts) is also dependent on the *quality* of one's motivation (e.g., Deci & Ryan, 2008; Standage & Ryan, 2012). Much can be gleaned from distinguishing between distinct types (or kinds) of motivation that vary in their inherent qualities and regulatory processes. Corroboration for this approach has been provided by a vast body of empirical work that documents that differential responses to important outcomes (e.g., performance, behavioral persistence, and well-being) are associated with the quality of the participants' reported motivation (see Ntoumanis, 2012; and Standage & Ryan, 2012, for reviews).

A meta-theory of human motivation, personality, and emotion that addresses the quality of motivation, as well as the conditions that promote, as oppose to forestall, optimal engagement, growth, and development is *self-determination theory* (SDT; Deci & Ryan, 2000; Ryan & Deci, 2000, 2008). There has been a burgeoning growth in sport and exercise psychology research grounded within SDT (see Hagger & Chatzisarantis, 2007). This increase in research attention appears to be commensurate with the need for motivation theories within sport, exercise, and health contexts to address a greater breadth of motivational phenomena than social cognitive perspectives (e.g., achievement goal theories, self-efficacy theory) that center largely on competence-related issues (Standage & Ryan, 2012).

The purpose of this chapter is to present the central components and motivational phenomena addressed within SDT, critiquing extant findings pertinent to performance and achievement within the sport domain. Although the primary focus will be on the sport-related literature, evidence will also be presented from other achievement domains as and when appropriate (e.g., academia, business). After presenting the theoretical tenets of SDT and reviewing pertinent literature, the focus will shift to issues of measurement (i.e., of performance) and translation of basic research to practice. In the penultimate section, suggestions for applications aimed at supporting the processes and social conditions conducive to fostering optimal performance and achievement are made. Last, a number of future research directions are presented and discussed.

Self-Determination Theory

Stemming from the seminal work of Edward Deci and Richard Ryan, SDT has evolved over the past five decades via a comprehensive and systematic program of inductive research to form a sophisticated meta-theory (see Vansteenkiste, Niemiec, & Soenens, 2010, for a detailed historical overview).

The overall SDT framework is made up of five interrelated mini-theories that were developed to address specific motivational phenomena: *cognitive evaluation theory, organismic integration theory, causality orientations theory, basic psychological needs theory*, and *goal contents theory* (see Ryan & Deci, 2008; Vansteenkiste et al., 2010, for a more detailed discussion of each mini-theory). Although each mini-theory was developed to explain specific phenomena, they are coherently linked, integrable, and organized within the broader SDT framework by organismic and dialectical propositions, and by the unifying concept of basic psychological needs (i.e., for autonomy, competence, and relatedness) (cf. Ryan & Deci, 2002).

Building Blocks of Self-Determination Theory and Mapping of Mini-Theories

Self-determination theory encompasses organismic and dialectical elements to explain human motivation. The organismic proposition within SDT holds that humans are active, growth-oriented organisms, who are self-motivated to seek optimal challenges and new experiences to master and integrate within a coherent sense of self (Ryan & Deci, 2002). *Intrinsic motivation* is the prototype of active human growth tendencies within SDT, reflecting the spontaneous (i.e., action emanates from within) and autotelic propensity (i.e., engagement in the activity is experienced as an end in and of itself) to apply and extend one's existing capabilities (Ryan & Stiller, 1991).

Cognitive Evaluation Theory

It was the study of intrinsic motivation that led to the now well-articulated mini-theory called *cognitive evaluation theory* (CET; Deci, 1975; Deci & Ryan, 1980). Specifically, CET provided an organizing structure and theoretical lens to consider the effects of differing aspects of the social context (e.g., rewards, feedback, and evaluations) and their impact on an individuals' interest, enjoyment, and free-choice persistence in activities (see Deci & Ryan, 1985). Briefly, CET posits that any event that satisfies an individual's innate need for *competence* (i.e., the need to interact effectively within the environment) and *autonomy* (i.e., the need to experience activities as self-endorsed and enacted by choice) will enhance a person's intrinsic motivation. In contrast, conditions that are not conducive to the promotion of competence and/or are deemed controlling are conjectured to impede or undermine an individuals' intrinsic motivation. Laboratory and field research has supported the tenets of CET, with events supportive of autonomy (e.g., provision of choice) and competence (e.g., optimal challenge) being shown to enhance intrinsic motivation. In contrast, factors considered by the actor to be controlling (e.g., rewards) or impeding their competence (e.g., negative feedback) have been shown to undermine a person's level of intrinsic motivation (see Deci & Ryan, 1985, for a review of CET; for a sport-specific review, see Vallerand, 2007). Last, it is important to note that, within CET, competence is not theorized to support intrinsic motivation unless accompanied by feelings of autonomy (Ryan & Deci, 2000).

Organismic Integration Theory

Although intrinsic motivation is the prototype of human growth tendencies, according to SDT people hold multiple motives for activities and collectively these determine their overall quality of motivation (Ryan & Connell, 1989). Intentional action within sport, and indeed across all life domains, can be intrinsically or extrinsically driven. Extrinsic motivation embraces a broad variety of behaviors that are characterized by an individual's goal of action being governed by outcomes that are extrinsic to the behavior itself (e.g., obtaining a tangible reward or outcome, avoidance of punishment). Rather than considering extrinsic motivation to be antithetical to intrinsic motivation (e.g., deCharms, 1968), within SDT a differentiated perspective on extrinsic motivation is adopted, the tenets of which are specified within a second mini-theory labeled *organismic integration theory* (OIT; Deci & Ryan, 1985). This mini-theory was developed to describe a continuum of autonomy underpinning unique types of extrinsic motivation ranging from those that are controlled via external contingencies (i.e., highly controlled) to those personally valued and self-endorsed (Ryan & Deci, 2008). Put simply, people can feel autonomous when acting through extrinsic motivation. The different types of extrinsic motivation outlined in OIT are, from most to least autonomous, labeled *integrated regulation, identified regulation, introjected regulation*, and *external regulation* (see Deci & Ryan, 1985; Ryan & Deci, 2002).

The different types of motivation embraced within SDT, their regulatory processes, and the defining features of each unique regulation appear in Figure 12.1. The four regulations pertinent to SDT's multidimensional perspective of extrinsic motivation are located between the extremities of inaction and action. These unique types of extrinsic

MOTIVATION TYPE	AMOTIVATION	EXTRINSIC MOTIVATION				INTRINSIC MOTIVATION
REGULATION STYLE	Non-regulation	External	Introjection	Identified	Integration	Intrinsic
INTERNALIZATION	No	No	Partial	Almost full	Full	Not required
DEFINING FEATURES	Lack of -competence -contingency -intention -activity value	Presence of external -constraints -rewards -compliance -punishments	Focus on approval (i.e. self or others) -ego involvement -internal rewards and punishment	-Activity valued -Personally important -Consciously pursued	-Synthesis of identified regulations to self -Awareness -Congruence	Action is based in interest and inherent satisfaction
LOCATION ON THE AUTONOMY CONTINUUM		Controlled Motivation		Autonomous Motivation		
PERCEIVED LOCUS OF CAUSALITY	Impersonal	External	Somewhat external	Somewhat internal	Internal	Internal

Figure 12.1 Schematic overview of the self-determination continuum outlining the types of motivation advanced within self-determination theory and related processes. Adapted from Standage & Ryan, 2012.

motivation are anchored between amotivation (a state of lacking intention to act) and intrinsic motivation (the prototype of autonomous regulation). The most controlling (or least autonomous) form of extrinsic motivation is termed *external regulation*, which is the classical case of extrinsic motivation in which actions, although intentional, are controlled by external contingencies such as tangible rewards and punishments (Deci & Ryan, 2000). For example, a young swimmer who attends practice because he wishes to please (or appease) his parents is acting out of external regulation.

The next three types of extrinsic motivation are characterized by differing levels of autonomous functioning. That is, within SDT these three types of motivation are distinguished based on the manner in which people internalize and integrate values, belief systems, and practices (Ryan & Deci, 2002).

The first and least autonomous of these regulations is labeled *introjected regulation*, which occurs when an individual partially internalizes an external regulation (Deci & Ryan, 1985). Introjected regulation is still a controlling motivation type that is underpinned by self-esteem–related contingencies. That is, when acting via introjected regulation, the person is controlled by internal as opposed to external pressures and contingencies, with the basis for behavior deriving from intrapersonal sanctions (e.g., shame, guilt) or internal rewards (e.g., ego-involvement, pride). For example, a gymnast who feels pride when achieving a predefined standard yet reproves herself with shame if this standard is not attained would be acting out of introjected regulation.

Next on the internalization continuum is a relatively autonomous form of motivation termed *identified regulation*. Here, the behavior is fueled by the purpose, benefits, or values offered by an activity to a person's goals, values, or aspirations (Ryan & Deci, 2008). However, despite being autonomously enacted, it is the instrumental usefulness of the activity that guides behavior as opposed to inherent interest. For example, a football player who goes running, not for the reason that he likes the activity per se, but because he recognizes the benefits of the activity (e.g., increased stamina, endurance) for his performance would be acting via identified regulation. The final form of motivation rivals intrinsic motivation in terms of relative autonomy and self-endorsement and is termed *integrated regulation* (Ryan, Williams, Patrick, & Deci, 2009). Integrated regulation is the most autonomous form of extrinsic motivation, reflecting the stage at which identified regulations have been coordinated and

made concordant with other well-internalized life goals so that they are brought into congruence with the person's other values and needs (Ryan & Deci, 2000). Although sharing numerous attributes with intrinsic motivation (e.g., it is autonomous and self-endorsed), integrated regulation is still considered extrinsic as the action is performed to obtain personally important outcomes as opposed to for the interest and enjoyment inherent within activities (Ryan & Deci, 2002). For example, a basketball player who takes part in the sport as it is part of his identity and akin within his other values, goals, and needs would be acting through integrated regulation (i.e., he has integrated and coordinated the identification of basketball with other aspects of himself).

AMOTIVATION

Although intentional behavior can be intrinsically or extrinsically driven, a construct termed *amotivation* is also included within SDT. Amotivation concerns nonintentional actions or behaviors that lack energy (i.e., the person passively performs activities) and are regulated by factors that are completely beyond an individual's control (Ryan & Deci, 2000). A state of amotivation may arise from a lack of competence, the belief that an activity is unimportant, and/or when a person does not perceive contingencies between his or her behavior and the desired outcome(s) (Ryan & Deci, 2000; Vallerand, 1997). An individual may also be volitionally amotivated because she does not consider an activity to be of interest or value (Ryan et al., 2009).

It is worth noting that, in recent years, SDT researchers have moved to distinguish motivation on the basis of it being autonomous or controlled (Deci & Ryan, 2008). To this end, within SDT it is held that autonomous motivation (relative to controlled motivation) will lead to or correlate with more adaptive consequences (cf. Standage & Ryan, 2012; Vansteenkiste et al., 2010).

Basic Psychological Needs Theory

The organismic assumption within OIT holds that people have a natural inclination to actively internalize and integrate values and regulations as they attempt to actualize their capacities and skills (Ryan & Deci, 2008). However, individuals do not reside in a social void; rather, they exist within social contexts that serve to support or impede their organismic natural tendencies toward active engagement, development, and psychological growth (Deci & Ryan, 1991). That is, it is this dialectical component embraced within SDT that addresses the interplay between the active self and various forces (external and internal) that support or impede this natural process. The supports for psychological health and well-being are elaborated within a third mini-theory labeled *basic psychological needs theory* (BPNT; Ryan & Deci, 2000).

The central premise of BPNT is that people must satisfy three basic psychological needs to experience positive outcomes (e.g., autonomous forms of motivation, optimal development, psychological well-being; Deci & Vansteenkiste, 2004). These three psychological needs are for *autonomy,* the need to experience activities as self-endorsed and choicefully enacted, *competence,* the need to interact effectively within the environment, and *relatedness,* the need to feel close to, connected to, and cared for with important others (Ryan & Deci, 2002). As these psychological needs are considered the essential foundations of psychological health and wellness, if the social context impedes or undermines these needs then ill-being, alienated functioning, and passivity are expected (Deci & Vansteenkiste, 2004). Research across several life domains including sport, exercise, education, and business has provided empirical support for the veracity of the basic needs approach within SDT. Indeed, results from dozens of studies employing a range of methodologies have shown need-satisfaction to predict a wide range of positive consequences, including performance (cf. Ryan & Deci, 2008).

Goal Contents Theory

The most recently added mini-theory to the broader SDT framework is called *goal contents theory* (GCT; Ryan et al., 2009; Vansteenkiste et al., 2010). The tenets within GCT were originally addressed under the banner of BPNT (e.g., see Ryan & Deci, 2002) and concern the goals that people pursue (i.e., intrinsic vs. extrinsic) and how holding different goals differentially impacts on motivation and wellness. The distinction between intrinsic and extrinsic goals derives from the work of Kasser and Ryan (1993, 1996), who labeled goals with an internal foci as being *intrinsic* (e.g., growth, affiliation, community contribution, and maintenance of physical health) and those with an outward orientation as being *extrinsic* (e.g., financial success, social recognition, and image/attractiveness). As intrinsic goals are those focused toward developing one's personal interests, values, and potentials and are inherently satisfying to pursue, they are assumed to be directly supportive of basic psychological need

satisfaction. On the other hand, extrinsic goals are characterized by a focus on external indicators of worth (e.g., fame, wealth; Kasser & Ryan, 1996; Vansteenkiste, Lens, & Deci, 2006) and are therefore less supportive, or even undermining, of basic psychological needs (Deci & Ryan, 2000; Kasser, 2002). A growing body of empirical evidence has provided support for the notion that intrinsic (relative to extrinsic) life goals are associated with positive indicators of well-being and adjustment (e.g., see Vansteenkiste et al., 2010).

Causality Orientations Theory

A further mini-theory within SDT is labeled *causality orientations theory* (COT; Deci & Ryan, 1985). Causality orientations theory is concerned with peoples' inner resources and holds that all individuals, to some degree, have varying levels of *autonomy orientation* (i.e., a disposition to orient toward intrinsic motivation and well-integrated extrinsic motivation), *controlled orientation* (i.e., an orientation toward being motivated by internal and/or external controls, constraints, and directives), and *impersonal orientation* (i.e., a tendency for people to consider themselves as incompetent and to act without intentionality) (cf. Deci & Ryan, 1985). Viewed as developmental outcomes, causality orientations stem from repeated interactions between the active, developing individual and their social world. Rather than operating at the domain-specific or activity level (i.e., as the motives and/or social contexts discussed thus far), causality orientations operate at a more global level and concern an individual's consistent and stable pattern of thinking pertaining to seeking out, selecting, and interpreting the initiation and regulation of their behavior (Deci & Ryan, 1985). Past work has shown that the endorsement of an autonomous orientation is predictive of effective functioning, adaptive behavior, and psychological health (cf. Vansteenkiste et al., 2010). In contrast, control and impersonal orientations have shown distinct associations with various indicators that are not indicative of general well-being and optimal functioning (e.g., various forms of pressured compliance, higher social anxiety, a tendency to dehumanize others, and increased levels of aggression) (Deci & Ryan, 1985; Vansteenkiste et al., 2010).[1]

Self-Determination Theory and Sport Performance
Motivation Quality and Performance

The organization of the motivational types along a continuum of internalization as specified within

OIT is particularly helpful when investigating associations among motivational styles and outcome variables of interest (Ryan & Connell 1989). In relation to performance, SDT specifies that when individuals are autonomously motivated in their actions, rather than being controlled to act, they experience more interest, excitement, and confidence that manifests in enhanced performance and persistence (Ryan & Deci, 2000). Thus, commensurate with the tenets of SDT—intrinsic motivation and integrated regulation—will be most positively associated with performance, followed by identified regulation. Conversely, external regulation and amotivation are hypothesized to be negatively associated with indicators of performance. Introjected regulation lies between external regulation and identified regulation, and, although past work has shown this form of motivation to be related to the short-term performance of a behavior (e.g., Gillison, Standage, & Skevington, 2011), research shows that acting out of introjected regulation does not to lead to long-term persistence in a behavior; that is, introjects are fragile as the individual does not feel ownership (e.g., Pelletier, Fortier, Vallerand, & Brière, 2001).

Initial lab-based experiments generally showed that individuals who were induced to participate in tasks for internal (or autonomous) reasons persisted longer in free-choice behavior than did those motivated by extrinsic factors (cf. Deci, Koestner, & Ryan, 1999; Deci & Ryan, 1985). Extending such exploration to various life domains, dozens of studies encompassing a range of methodologies have supported the tenets of OIT by documenting the advantages that autonomous motivation has for positive motivational consequences, such as persistence, enhanced psychological well-being, better performance, and the like (cf. Deci & Ryan, 2008). For example, in sport settings autonomous motivation has been shown to predict adaptive outcomes, such as better well-being and vitality (Gagné, Ryan, & Bargmann, 2003); higher levels of flow (Kowal & Fortier, 1999); greater reported effort, interest, and persistence (Pelletier et al., 1995; 2001); and positive sportsmanship orientations (Ntoumanis & Standage, 2009). In contrast, controlling types of extrinsic motivation and/or amotivation have been shown to be linked with maladaptive consequences, such as athlete burnout (e.g., Lonsdale, Hodge, & Rose, 2008, 2009), low levels of dispositional flow (Lonsdale et al., 2008), sport dropout (Pelletier et al., 2001), reported aggression (Chantal, Robin, Vernat, & Bernache-Assollant, 2005), and an acceptance

of cheating (Ntoumanis & Standage, 2009) (see Ntoumanis, 2012 for a review).

Research examining the relationship between the types of motivation described within SDT and performance is scarce. In sport, and particularly at the higher levels, this is somewhat surprising as performance is the variable of central interest (Treasure, Lemyre, Kuczka, & Standage, 2007). Akin to research in other domains, such as education (e.g., Burton, Lydon, D'Alessandro, & Koestner, 2006; Fortier, Vallerand, & Guay, 1995), research that has been conducted in sport has supported the tenets of SDT by showing autonomous (or high quality) forms of motivation to positively predict performance—that is, objective performance data or coach ratings of performance (e.g., Blanchard, Mask, Vallerand, de la Sablonnière, & Provencher, 2007; Charbonneau, Barling, & Kelloway, 2001; Gillet, Berjot, & Gobancé, 2009; Gillet, Vallerand, Amoura, & Baldes, 2010). For example, in a longitudinal study with a sample of 90 young tennis players across three competitive seasons, Gillet et al. (2009) found autonomous motivation, as measured by a self-determination index (SDI) to positively predict better objective performance data as provided by the French Tennis Federation. Specifically, autonomous motivation at the beginning of a season was predictive of tennis performance during the following 2 years, and autonomous motivation at Time 2 (assessed at the end of the second season) positively predicted performance during the third season. Similarly, Gillet et al. (2010) reported that situational autonomous motivation (i.e., an SDI index at the situational level—or state level) as assessed 1–2 hours before a judo competition positively predicted objective performance during competition, using data obtained from the French Judo Federation.

In the school physical education (PE) context, recent work by Standage, Sebire, and Stokes (2011) examined the relationship between autonomous and controlled motivation and students' performance on a physical fitness test (the Multistage Fitness Test). Data pertaining to students' motivation toward PE were collected from 519 students 1 week prior to performing the multistage fitness test in their normal PE class. After controlling for gender, results showed autonomous motivation to positively predict performance. Controlled motivation was unrelated to performance.

Although, for the most part, extant findings support the tenets of SDT, one study yielded results that did not support the predictions of OIT. Specifically,

Chantal, Guay, Dobreva-Martinova, and Vallerand (1996) examined the motivational profiles of 98 elite Bulgarian athletes from a variety of different sports (e.g., figure skating, canoeing, biathlon, skiing, tennis, and boxing). Participants' motivation responses were linked with their performance as quantified by titles and medals won over 2 years at National, World, and Olympic Championships. Analyses revealed that less autonomous forms of extrinsic motivation were associated with better performances within the controlling culture of post-communist Bulgaria. That is, when compared to less successful athletes, the best performing athletes displayed higher levels of nonautonomous extrinsic motivation (indexed by a composite score of introjected regulation and external regulation) as well as higher levels of amotivation. Thus, title holders and medal winners reported, with more frequency, that external rewards, feelings of obligation, and pressure were their primary sources of motivation. Commenting on these unexpected findings, the authors surmised that the highly competitive sport structure that prevailed in Bulgaria at the time influenced the athletes' motivation, in that the sport structure strongly emphasized winning, regardless of the costs.

Although performance has not received extensive attention in the sport literature, some dependent variables proximal to performance have been examined. For example, Pelletier and colleagues (2001) conducted a prospective study with competitive swimmers to examine the relationships between the coaches' interpersonal behavior (autonomy support versus control), the types of motivational regulation, and behavioral persistence (i.e., persistence versus dropout). Structural equation modeling analyses revealed that perceiving the coach to be autonomy-supportive positively predicted autonomous forms of motivation (viz., intrinsic motivation and identified regulation) and negatively predicted reported amotivation. To a lesser extent, autonomy support positively predicted introjected regulation. In contrast, perceiving the coach to be controlling positively predicted amotivation and controlling forms of extrinsic motivation (i.e., external regulation and introjected regulation). Swimmers who reported autonomous forms of motivation at the first time point showed greater persistence as assessed 10 and 22 months later. Additionally, swimmers who exhibited amotivation at the first time point had the highest dropout rate at both 10 and 22 months. Interestingly, introjected regulation was a significant and positive predictor of persistence at 10 months,

but not at 22 months. External regulation negatively predicted persistence at 22 months. Further, autonomous motivation was found to be negatively related to intentions to discontinue involvement in one's sport. Similarly, Sarrazin, Vallerand, Guillet, Pelletier, and Cury (2002) found that female handball players who dropped out of the sport had lower levels of intrinsic motivation and higher levels of amotivation than did players who persisted.

A final illustrative study was conducted in the exercise domain by Standage, Sebire, and Loney (2008), who examined whether a positive relationship existed between autonomous exercise motivation and objectively assessed exercise behavior, as assessed by persistence, intensity, and frequency. The authors assessed moderate-intensity exercise of durations greater (or equal) to 10 minutes, 20 minutes, and an accumulation of activity needed to meet the American College of Sport Medicine/American Heart Association (ACSM/AHA) guidelines, using a unit (the Actiheart; Cambridge Neurotechnology, United Kingdom) that employs a synchronized branched equation to predict energy expenditure above rest from simultaneously recorded heart rate and accelerometry data. After controlling for the potential confounding effects of gender and a marker of body composition (i.e., a combined index of body mass [BMI] and waist circumference), results showed that autonomous motivation positively predicted the amount of time spent in moderate bouts of exercise behavior for bouts of 10 or more and 20 or more minutes over a 7-day period, and an accumulation of activity needed to meet the ACSM/AHA guidelines. In this work, controlled motivation was unrelated to time spent in bouts of exercise behavior. Such findings show the autonomous versus controlled motivation distinction to be useful in predicting objectively assessed engagement in exercise at levels that are deemed to be health-enhancing (cf. Haskell et al., 2007).

Sport Performance Research and Assessment Issues

Researchers in sport and exercise psychology have studied numerous cognitive, affective, and behavioral outcomes in relationship to the motivational variables of SDT (for reviews see Ntoumanis, 2012; Standage & Ryan, 2012; Vallerand, 2007), but little research attention has been paid to sport performance as a dependent variable. This lack of attention has been noted in previous reviews of the literature (e.g., Vallerand & Losier, 1999; Vallerand, 2001), but despite some increase in research in this area, still relatively few attempts have been made to incorporate indices of objective performance in motivational research. As an immensely important outcome variable within the sport domain, this void is somewhat surprising, and more work incorporating performance is certainly needed.

Assessment methods used in the existing research in this area have relied heavily on subjective ratings of performance. For example, a number of studies have examined how motivation relates to participants' own ratings of their performance (e.g., Blanchard et al., 2007; Halvari, Ulstad, Bagøien, & Skjesol, 2009), coaches' ratings of performance (e.g., Blanchard et al., 2007; Mouratidis, Vansteenkiste, Lens, & Sideridis, 2008, study 2), and in school settings—graded performance (e.g., Fortier et al., 1995). Although the latter two approaches somewhat address issues related to common-method variance (i.e., a source of systematic error in which an observed relationship between scores may be influenced by the similarity of measurement methods rather than the constructs represented by the measures; Podsakoff, MacKenzie, Lee, & Podsakoff, 2003), it is clear that objective indices of performance would be preferable to subjective reporting/ratings (e.g., Gillet et al., 2010). Research in organizational psychology provides support for a move toward more objective indices of performance. Specifically, results from a meta-analysis (n of studies = 50; sample size = 8,341) comparing objective and subjective ratings of employee performance provided support for the notion that the methods should not be used interchangeably; there was a corrected mean correlation of = .389 between the two methods (Bommer, Johnson, Rich, Podsakoff, & Mackenzie, 1995).

Objective measures of sport performance are less prone to a number of well-documented sources of systematic bias and random error that plague subjective assessments/ratings. Yet researchers need to carefully choose the objective methods, focus, and approach used in their work (see Atkinson & Nevill, 2001; Hopkins, Hawley, & Burke, 1999, for issues related to design and analysis). Indeed, a number of important issues warrant careful consideration for researchers including; (i) Regardless of what objective marker of performance is being employed, it is important that it has adequate internal and external validity. Thus, the indicator of performance utilized should have high validity with the target activity or with the skills comprising the activity. (ii) Motivation has been explored in relation to objective performance in laboratory settings (e.g.,

Hulleman, De Koning, Hettinga, & Foster, 2007), but such settings are often void of external validity. Thus, researchers need to be extremely wary as to whether observed effects within lab settings would occur in real sport events (Hopkins et al., 1999). Examples include that skilled movement is required in on-water rowing and this would not be captured by a rowing ergometer, anxiety would be expected to be higher in competitive situations, proximal assessments of motivation would be aimed at the task at hand as opposed to the sport event itself, and lab setting are devoid of some important external environmental factors (e.g., in cycling time trials in the lab would not be exposed to hills and wind as experienced during real cycling) (Atkinson & Nevill, 2001; Hopkins et al., 1999). Not withstanding the fact that laboratory trials would provide valuable insight into the relationships between SDT variables and performance, no performance-based research is more valid than utilizing actual competitive events (cf. Hopkins et al., 1999). (iii) When attempting to examine performance in competitive settings, it would be useful for researchers to consider an estimation of the "size of worthwhile effects" as they relate to different types of sport (e.g., within the 100 m sprint, this effect would be very small—i.e., as low as .3% at the elite level; Hopkins et al., 1999). Such an approach would provide insight into the contribution of motivation variables to meaningful indicators of performance and/or performance enhancement. (iv) Although objective assessments of actual event performance are highly desirable, within top-level athletes numerous logistical issues arise that may preclude active research involvement. Regardless of being difficult, it is possible to use competitive performance as the dependent variable of interest. This may be best achieved through quasi-experimental designs, in which athletes are exposed to treatment and control periods slotted in between multiple observations of performance over time (Atkinson & Nevill, 2001; see Hopkins et al., 1999, for a discussion). Despite overcoming a number of external validity issues, such an approach would decrease internal validity in research involving competitive athletes as one could not ethically restrict a particular treatment (i.e., there would be no control group for comparison). (v) Research should also distinguish between performance that reflects a collection of performances (i.e., at a contextual level, such as performance over a season) or situational (or "state"; i.e., an instance of performance that is currently occurring or has just occurred) (Vallerand, 2001). (vi) Researchers undertaking longitudinal work should also consider that objective markers of performance—those assessed via performance outcomes—may not be strongly associated with each other; that is, they may lack temporal stability (e.g., Gillet et al., 2009). (vii) Future work, it would be valuable for researchers to consider various dimensions of sport performance, as well as the proximity of the motivational variables being assessed within that particular investigation—for example, situational motivation should be a better predictor of immediately impending performance than one's contextual motivation (cf. Vallerand, 1997).

Promoting High-Quality Motivation and Performance

Empirical research has shown autonomous forms of motivation to generally yield better well-being, as well as more effective performance than controlled motivation. Thus, an important strand of work within SDT has been to identify and test the social conditions and processes that support optimal motivation, well-being, and performance. According to the theoretical tenets within SDT, social contexts that provide the necessary supports for peoples' basic psychological needs for autonomy, competence, and relatedness are conducive to high-quality forms of motivation, support well-being, and facilitate better performance. I will now examine research pertaining to a number of these social factors (see Vallerand, 2007, for a more detailed sport-related review).

AUTONOMY SUPPORT AND PERFORMANCE

Self-determination theory-related research has shown that the social contexts promoted by significant others (e.g., coaches, managers, teachers, and peers) play an important role in facilitating or impeding the motivational strivings, well-being, and development of individuals—and, in turn, the quality of their performance. An interpersonal context that has received attention from SDT researchers is that of *autonomy support*, social contexts that support choice, initiation, and understanding, while minimizing the need to perform and act in a prescribed manner (cf. Deci & Ryan, 2008). Although labeled "autonomy-supportive" contexts, such environments actually enhance the likelihood of an individual satisfying all three needs, including competence and relatedness (Baard, Deci, & Ryan, 2004; Ryan & Deci, 2000). When a person's autonomy is supported, not only is the supporter likely to be attuned to other needs, but the individual will be more empowered and free to actively fulfill other needs. In a sample of law students, Sheldon and

Krieger (2007) found that students' perceptions of autonomy support positively predicted law school grade point average (GPA) as a function of supporting levels of need satisfaction.

Research in school and higher education settings has shown that perceptions of autonomy support are positively associated with indices of performance such as GPA, course grades, teacher-rated performance, and solution of puzzles (e.g., Patall, Cooper, & Wynn, 2010; Reeve & Jang, 2006; Sheldon & Krieger, 2007; Vansteenkiste, Simons, Lens, Sheldon, & Deci, 2004). Also supportive of SDT is research in educational settings showing that performance and achievement are impaired when students are exposed to teachers employing controlling strategies (e.g., Flink, Boggiano, & Barrett, 1990). Some experimental support also exists regarding the positive impact that autonomy-supportive contexts have on motivation-related outcomes. For example, in a study with students who were introduced to a new exercise activity, tai-bo, Vansteenkiste et al. (2004) found that the provision of an autonomy-supportive context was linked to increased effort, more autonomous forms of motivation, greater persistence (of up to 4 months), and future enrollment in a tai-bo club.

FEEDBACK AND PERFORMANCE

By their very nature, competitive sport situations make the outcomes of winning and losing inevitable. Guided by CET, research has shown that the provision of positive, competence-affirmative feedback (communicated in an autonomy supportive way; Ryan, 1982) enhances intrinsic motivation and free-choice behavior in activities (Deci et al., 1999). Although performance has been examined as an outcome of motivation, it is important to recognize that the dynamic interplay between key SDT constructs (e.g., goal contents, need satisfaction, and behavioral regulations) at various levels (person-level and day-level) means that performance feedback or subjective perceptions of personal success can reflect important antecedents of need satisfaction and motivation (e.g., Blanchard et al., 2007; Gillet et al., 2009). In addition to being predicted by autonomous motivation, past longitudinal work has shown personal and team performance to positively predict situational autonomous motivation and perceptions of autonomy, competence, and relatedness (Blanchard et al., 2007; Gillet et al., 2009).

COOPERATION AND PERFORMANCE

There are many situations within sport in which athletes are asked to cooperate toward a common objective. To this end, Tauer and Harackiewicz (2004) conducted a series of four studies to assess the effects of competition, cooperation, and intergroup competition on the performance and task enjoyment of children partaking in a basketball free-throw task. Three findings of interest emerged. First, the results replicated the findings of competitive success and failure feedback—that is, empirical work has shown winning to increase competence perceptions and intrinsic interest, whereas losing has been negatively linked to perceptions of competence and intrinsic motivation (e.g., Reeve & Deci, 1996). Second, in comparing pure competition and pure cooperation, the authors found no differences on task enjoyment or performance. Third, in the two out of three studies in which performance was assessed, intergroup competition was found to consistently lead to the highest levels of task enjoyment and performance. Tauer and Harackiewicz argued that engaging in intergroup competition leads individuals to be provided with the best overall experience as they derive the benefits available from competition and cooperation. That is, they experience the excitement and challenge of competition, as well as the interpersonal enthusiasm and relatedness that come from having a teammate.

Facilitating Motivation and Performance: The Role of Basic Psychological Needs

As already discussed, a fundamental premise within SDT is that for people to be optimally motivated, experience psychological well-being, and function and perform effectively within and across life domains (including sport), they must satisfy three basic psychological needs (for autonomy, competence, and relatedness; Ryan & Deci, 2008). In sport settings, the satisfaction of the basic needs has been shown to positively predict autonomous forms of motivation (both independently and when combined; e.g., Blanchard et al., 2007; Gillet et al., 2009; McDonough & Crocker, 2007), well-being (Gagné et al., 2003; Smith, Ntoumanis, Duda, & Vansteenkiste, 2011), and vitality (Adie, Duda, & Ntoumanis, 2008; Gagné et al., 2003). Similarly, need-satisfaction measures have been shown to be negatively linked with athlete burnout and negative affect (e.g., Bartholomew, Ntoumanis, Ryan, Bosch, & Thøgersen-Ntoumani, 2011; Lonsdale et al., 2008). Recently, Bartholomew and her colleagues (Bartholomew, Ntoumanis, Ryan, & Thøgersen-Ntoumani, 2011) argued that low scores on measures of psychological need satisfaction do not adequately align to assess the intensity of frustration

from need thwarting as described within SDT (e.g., Deci & Ryan, 2000). Having developed a measure of need-thwarting in the sport context (see Bartholomew, Ntoumanis, & Thøgersen-Ntoumani, 2010), research using this new inventory has shown need-thwarting to be a positive predictor of exhaustion, disordered eating, depression, negative affect, burnout, and perturbed physiological arousal (as indexed by elevated levels of secretory immunoglobulin A prior to training; Bartholomew et al., 2011; Bartholomew et al., 2011).

Existing sport-related research examining the motivational predictors of performance have specified and tested models that consider performance to be a determinant of the need-satisfaction constructs. Although such models are appropriate, as mentioned previously in the chapter, the variables within SDT are dynamic at contextual and especially situational levels, thus it is possible to also consider the energizing basic need constructs to predict performance (or performance to be a consequence of need-satisfaction). Insight into such relationships can be gleaned from work in other contexts. For example, Baard, Deci, and Ryan (2004) reported basic need satisfaction to positively predict performance evaluations and psychological adjustment in employees at a banking firm. Similarly, and in the context of law education, Sheldon and Krieger (2007) found that the satisfaction of autonomy and competence positively predicted graded performance of students after controlling for undergraduate GPA. Extending this work into the sports domain, future work examining the dynamic interplay among the needs when predicting sport performance seems warranted.

Goal Contents and Performance

Research has shown the intrinsic versus extrinsic goal distinction outlined within GCT to offer valuable insight into a person's well-being, adjustment, and performance (cf. Vansteenkiste et al., 2006). For example, in their goal promotion work with a sample of high school participants, Vansteenkiste et al. (2004, Study 3) used written scripts to frame tai-bo exercises as being for either the attainment of intrinsic (i.e., physical health) or extrinsic (i.e., appearing attractive to others) goals. Results showed that participants randomly assigned to the intrinsic goal framing group displayed greater behavioral persistence and performance on the tai-bo exercise.

Within an exercise setting, Sebire, Standage, and Vansteenkiste (2011) examined the effects of the content and regulation of adults' exercise goals on performing objectively assessed bouts of exercise behavior. Results showed that relative intrinsic exercise goals had a positive indirect effect on physical activity through autonomous motivation. No direct independent effect of goal content on behavior was found, but support was provided for a motivational sequence in which intrinsic goal content supports autonomous motivation, which in turn positively predicts physical activity and bouts of exercise behavior.

To date, the lack of a valid and reliable assessment of sport-based goal content has precluded a detailed exploration of the concomitants of individuals' reported goals for sport and their relationship with performance. Future work in this area seems warranted. In developing such a measure, it is important to note that although participation in sport may stand in the service of various goals (e.g., skill improvement, fitness, fame, image, financial success, etc.), not all goals are considered to be either intrinsic or extrinsic in nature, as the distinction within SDT is not meant to be exhaustive in encompassing all possible goals (e.g., Ryan, Huta, & Deci, 2008; see Sebire, Standage, & Vansteenkiste, 2008, regarding the development of such a measure for the exercise context).

Applications

Empirical research utilizing the SDT framework has demonstrated that social conditions that are supportive of an individual's basic needs provide the basis for optimal motivation, enhanced wellness, improved adjustment, and better performance (Standage & Ryan, 2012). The situational components that may provide supports for each basic need and in turn catalyze the appropriate environment for better (or improved) performance will now be examined (see Mageau & Vallerand, 2003, for a more detailed discussion; see Vansteenkiste, Soenens, & Lens, 2007, for a review regarding applications from a GCT perspective).

Basic Needs and Supports
Supports for Autonomy

A number of empirically supported techniques provide insight into how coaches may provide support for athletes' perceptions of autonomy. These components include maximizing opportunity for choice (e.g., Zuckerman, Porac, Lathin, Smith, & Deci, 1978), providing meaningful rationales (e.g., Deci et al., 1994), acknowledging people's feelings (e.g., Koestner, Ryan, Bernieri, & Holt, 1984), minimizing ego-involvement (i.e., a means–ends orientation that entails putting one's self-esteem "on the

line" based upon attaining a specified performance outcome; e.g., Ryan, 1982), reducing controlling self-talk (Oliver, Markland, Hardy, & Petherick, 2008), and communicating in an autonomy-supportive manner (e.g., Ryan, Mims, & Koestner, 1983).

Improvements in sport performance inevitably rely on increasing an athlete's awareness and involvement in his or her sport and training activities. However, sport encompasses activities that are desirable but not always intrinsically interesting (e.g., training and practice). Self-determination theory sheds light on how a coach may deal with this issue via the process of internalization. Central to such an endeavor is the provision of meaningful rationales that provide a basis for athletes to understand why a target behavior is important. For example, a soccer coach may convey the benefits that circuit training and endurance work will offer to her athletes' stamina and their ability to play for the full 90 minutes (e.g., "Circuit training will improve your fitness, strength, and overall health for soccer"). Lab-based work conducted by Deci et al. (1994) showed that the provision of a meaningful rationale for an uninteresting activity (along with acknowledgment of feelings and the conveyance of choice) promoted internalization and integration. To be effective, however, meaningful rationales within the sport domain should be presented in a noncontrolling way, while providing some form of choice and acknowledgment of the athletes' feelings (Deci et al., 1994). Communicating choice and support (e.g., "You may want to," "You can try to") is more likely to support autonomy (cf. Deci et al., 1994; Ryan et al., 1983). Empirical support for the latter suggestion has been provided in work by Hodgins, Yacko, and Gottlieb (2006, Study 3), who showed that priming members of a university rowing team with autonomous words (e.g., choose, freedom) led to faster times on a rowing machine than priming members with controlling (e.g., must, should) and amotivational words (e.g., passive, uncontrollable).

Supporting choice has been shown to enhance reported and behavioral markers of intrinsic motivation (Zuckerman et al., 1978), and, in turn, intrinsic motivation has been shown to support better reported performance and percentage of performance improvement (e.g., Charbonneau et al., 2001). Within the sport context, a coach would therefore do well to facilitate choice by maximizing the options available to athletes by listening to them, rather than imposing his or her view, and involving them in the decision-making as it pertains to their training, as opposed to simply prescribing activities. He or she may also need to express empathy or acknowledgment of athlete concerns during the season. A coach who is receptive to feedback (or even criticism) may allow athletes to perceive that their voices are respected and taken into consideration (e.g., Reeve, 2009). Such feedback may result in better, more convincing rationales being provided or in structural changes (e.g., more choices) that are more authentic in nature (Ntoumanis, 2012).

Research couched within CET has shown that when people are ego-involved (i.e., their motivational orientation is pressured on proving their self-worth), they report their intrinsic motivation toward the task at hand to decrease in comparison with participants given a task-involved induction (e.g., drawing attention to the activity itself so as to operate in an internally referenced and informational manner) (e.g., Ryan, 1982). In attempts to improve the skills and abilities underpinning improved athlete performance, sport coaches would do well to promote a task-involved orientation in their athletes. Such an endeavor may be best facilitated by focusing on mastering the inherent qualities of tasks and helping individuals to focus on self-referenced and progressive improvement, and by supporting ongoing effortful and autonomous engagement with their sporting endeavors. Sport coaches could also be attuned to, and intervene in, the controlling self-talk that so often accompanies ego-involvement (see Oliver et al., 2008).

Supports for Competence

Self-determination theory-based research has also provided evidence for a number of competence supports that can be readily applied to sport to improve the quality of engagement and performance. These social inputs include provision for optimal challenge (e.g., Deci, 1975), appropriate administration of positive feedback (e.g., Ryan, 1982; Vallerand & Reid, 1984), and fostering task involvement (e.g., Ryan, 1982; Ryan, Mims, & Koestner, 1991).

Within SDT, the *provision of structure* is essential to the development of competence (Grolnick & Seal, 2008; Markland, Ryan, Tobin, & Rollnick, 2005). For example, coaches should provide clear guidance and communicate well defined expectations as to what their athletes need to do to achieve their goals (e.g., plans, goals, standards, rules, schedules as they relate to improvements and better performance). It is important to note that the provision of structure aids motivation insofar as it is implemented in an autonomy-supportive way (Standage & Ryan,

2012). A lack of structure may promote training and performance environments that are indulgent, permissive, or laissez-faire due to lack of autonomy support (e.g., Reeve, 2006).

Research organized by SDT also suggests that sport coaches should work in a collaborative manner with their athletes to ensure that they are engaged in tasks and activities that are optimally challenging; that is, those that are defined and well-suited to the competencies of the athletes (cf. Deci & Ryan, 1985). Optimally challenging tasks and activities permit athletes to test and expand their capabilities and, with concerted effort, to achieve performance improvements. Tasks and activities perceived to be too easy may foster feelings of boredom, whereas tasks and activities that are too difficult are likely to be anxiety provoking (Csikszentimihalyi, 1975; Deci & Ryan, 2002). To provide the progression required to improve performance, realistic goal setting should be promoted by coaches and careful monitoring of progress undertaken. This should be done in a challenging yet attainable way, and more challenging tasks and activities should be provided on an ongoing basis. Such objectives would be best achieved via providing support for structure, so that the athlete understands the behavior–outcome contingencies, has well defined expectations, and is provided clear feedback (Standage & Ryan, 2012).

A basic principle within CET is that for individuals to experience and maintain intrinsic motivation, they must satisfy their competence within the context of autonomy. Research has shown positive feedback to support perceptions of competence when provided in an autonomy-supportive way (informational; Deci & Ryan, 1985), but not when conveyed in a controlling manner (Ryan, 1982). Moreover, recent work has also shown that corrective performance-related feedback can support autonomous forms of motivation and well-being if provided in an autonomy-supportive manner and perceived as being legitimate (Mouratidis, Lens, & Vansteenkiste, 2010). This research suggests that sport coaches should use positive, task-related, and personally relevant feedback in their endeavors to enhance perceptions of competence, autonomy, and, subsequently, autonomous engagement and performance. Likewise, as corrective information is central to improvements in performance, the findings of Mouratidis et al.'s work suggest that coaches would do well to convey such information in an autonomy-supportive way and by explaining why such feedback is pertinent to performance enhancements (i.e., why it is justified). In such communications, coaches should engage with their athletes, so that they take the athletes' perspective, offer choice about overcoming faults, and provide a meaningful rationale for the target behavior (Mouratidis et al., 2010). Last, drawing attention to the inherent qualities of the activity, conveying informational feedback, and focusing on internally referenced learning should be employed to foster a task-involved orientation in athletes.

Supports for Relatedness

Drawing from SDT and research involving children in educational settings (Grolnick & Ryan, 1989; Roth, Assor, Niemiec, Ryan, & Deci, 2009), it would be expected that athletes are more likely to accept and internalize the values, norms, and guidelines espoused by their coaches if they feel a sense of connection and belonging. To support secure attachments and perceptions of belonging, coaches would do well to express an authentic interest and interact with them in a caring and warm manner (see also Chapter 21, this volume). Coaches who express empathy, avoid blame and/or being judgmental, and acknowledge the perspective, feelings, and values of their athletes are more likely to foster a sense of relatedness in coach–athlete interactions (cf. Mageau & Vallerand, 2003).

As relatedness entails a sense of being significant and cared for by others, one element of sport settings that can foster relatedness is involvement. From the SDT perspective, involvement has been defined as the degree to which significant others devote time, energy, and interest to the other (Grolnick & Ryan, 1989). When parents, coaches, and trainers show interest and dedication, their involvement is more likely to facilitate relatedness and, in turn, the internalization of values and motives. As with structure, involvement must be characterized by autonomy support, rather than pressure and control, to effectively promote integration and true self-regulation (Standage & Ryan, 2012). Another means of attempting to develop a sense of connection and belonging with others could be by pairing athletes with similar aims, objectives, and ability. Such an approach may provide provision for cooperation and relational support, as well as supporting mutually beneficial training schedules and goals.

Conclusion

The meta-theory of SDT views motivation as a complex phenomenon fed by numerous sources. Although some sources are experienced as controlling and acting on the self, others stem from within the self and represent volition and growth. This chapter has described research demonstrating multiple advantages of more autonomous motivations in facilitating and supporting achievement and performance. A number of social conditions that support rather than undermine autonomous engagement, growth, development, and performance have been discussed, and practical steps that coaches can take to set the stage for these gains have been identified. Drawing and extending on existing work, the next section makes suggestions for future work related to motivational processes and performance. To this effect, it is hoped that this chapter will stimulate thoughtful contemplation of the utility of SDT in the performance area and encourage future SDT research to further examine the processes underpinning performance and achievement.

Future Directions

Many potential directions for future motivation research from the SDT tradition can be taken pertaining to performance in sport and other domains. This section is not a comprehensive review for directing future research; rather, the directions highlighted here illustrate just a few interesting avenues of inquiry based on the tenets of SDT.

Research designed to better understand the dynamic interplay between key sport-related SDT constructs (e.g., autonomy support, need satisfaction, need-thwarting, and behavioral regulations) represents an intriguing direction for sport-related research. Such research could draw upon and extend the methods used to examine the relationships among basic need satisfaction and indices of well-being using within- and between-person designs (e.g., Reis, Sheldon, Gable, Roscoe, & Ryan, 2000). That is, by obtaining multiple datapoints at various levels (e.g., person-level and day-level) alongside ongoing assessments of actual, objectively assessed sports performance, valuable insights into how fluctuations in motives and goals interact with need-satisfaction to support changes in performance might be gained. In addition to being important from an applied research perspective, data from such work would also be interesting and theoretically informative.

Staying with the idea of examining the dynamic nature of motivational processes within SDT at various levels (e.g., person-level and day-level) and relating this to objective performance, an important question relates to the level at which one assesses performance. To this end, Vallerand (2001) called for research to distinguish performance in terms of a collection of performances (i.e., at a contextual level) or situational (or "state"; i.e., an instance of performance that is currently occurring or has just occurred). As such, in the aforementioned suggestion for longitudinal work, it would seem appropriate to employ a mixed modeling approach that would allow for possible issues such as performance being more variable in training (i.e., if the research question was looking at motivation and performance in training and competitive environs; e.g., see Vandenbogaerde & Hopkins, 2010).

As already mentioned, few attempts have been made to examine the motivational factors and processes that support sport performance. Future research designed to help overcome this void in the literature would do well to incorporate actual performance data or objective and meaningful indices of performance; for example, measures that have high validity with the target activity and comprise an estimation of worthwhile effect for the sport at hand.

As with most avenues of psychological inquiry, the development and/or refinement of measurement tools is warranted as researchers attempt to better understand the motivational basis for performance. Although a number of valid and reliable assessments exist to measure motivation, need-satisfaction, and need-thwarting in sport, similar context-specific measures of other SDT constructs are needed (e.g., perceptions of an autonomy-supportive climate, structure, involvement, and goal content). It would be extremely beneficial to involve members of the proposed target sample in all stages of the questionnaire development process (e.g., focus groups, item development, item meaning, etc.) to ensure that measurement items adequately capture accurate accounts of the processes that operate in sport settings (Standage & Vallerand, 2008). Last, researchers should be careful to ensure that new measures or refinements to existing scales are based on theory rather than being data driven (cf. Mulaik, 1987).

As should be evident from the applications section of this chapter, as well as from reviews published elsewhere (e.g., Ntoumanis, 2012; Standage & Ryan, 2012; Standage & Vallerand 2008; cf. Hagger & Chatzisarantis, 2007), many potential strategies based on the tenets of SDT can be implemented and evaluated in sport and other performance domains. As with work in other contexts (e.g., health care), researchers should systematically develop key elements (or intended "active ingredients") prior to testing their effects in large-scale projects (e.g., via randomized controlled trials). Indeed, several smaller (or pilot) studies may be required to progressively refine the design and procedures prior to empirically testing the effectiveness of such methods in sport settings, as well as to evaluate how these techniques may best serve to enhance performance and athlete well-being. Interventions may work best if they are tailored to specific contexts, so process and outcome evaluations should be nested in the work to help identify why certain interventions were successful or failed (e.g., assessments of fidelity, quality of implementation, contextual variables related to outcomes, etc.; see Craig et al., 2008, for a review). Last, Standage and Ryan (2012) recently suggested the use of simultaneous mixed-method approaches as being an effective addition to intervention trials couched in SDT. Indeed, extending this approach to sport-related research would glean in-depth accounts of the differing motivational experiences of particular groupings (i.e., those for whom an intervention was effective, those who changed little, if at all, and those for whom an intervention had unintended or negative effects).

Note

1. Very little attention has been given to the study of COT within sport settings, either in terms of general empirical investigation or when predicting performance. This lack of attention is most likely due to the conceptualization of causality orientations as residing and operating across domains (i.e., a general level) as opposed to being domain-specific (e.g., toward exercise, sport, education, etc). Due to this reason, COT is not reviewed further in the *Self-Determination Theory and Sport Performance* section of this chapter, although a link is offered for COT tenets within the *Applications* section.

References

Adie, J. W., Duda, J. L., & Ntoumanis, N. (2008). Autonomy support, basic need satisfaction and the optimal functioning of adult male and female sport participants: A test of basic needs theory. *Motivation and Emotion, 32*, 189–199.

Atkinson, G., & Nevill, A.M. (2001). Selected issues in the design and analysis of sport performance research. *Journal of Sports Sciences, 19*, 811–827.

Baard, P. P., Deci, E. L., & Ryan, R. M. (2004). Intrinsic need satisfaction: A motivational basis of performance and well-being in two work settings. *Journal of Applied Social Psychology, 34*, 2045–2068.

Bandura, A. (1997). *Self-efficacy: The exercise of control.* New York: Freeman.

Bartholomew, K., Ntoumanis, N., & Ryan, R., & Thøgersen-Ntoumani, C. (2011). Psychological need thwarting in the sport context: Development and initial validation of a psychometric scale. *Journal of Sport and Exercise Psychology, 33*, 75–102.

Bartholomew, K. J., Ntoumanis, N., & Thøgersen-Ntoumani, C. (2010). The controlling interpersonal style in a coaching context: Development and initial validation of a psychometric scale. *Journal of Sport and Exercise Psychology, 32*, 193–216.

Bartholomew, K. J., Ntoumanis, N., Bosch, J. A., Ryan, R. M., & Thøgersen-Ntoumani, C. (2011). Self-determination theory and diminished human functioning: The role of interpersonal control and psychological need thwarting. *Personality and Social Psychology Bulletin, 37,* 1459–1473.

Blanchard, C. M., Mask, L., Vallerand, R. J., de la Sablonnière, R., & Provencher, P. (2007). Reciprocal relationships between contextual and situational motivation in a sport setting. *Psychology of Sport and Exercise, 8,* 854–873.

Bommer, W. H., Johnson, J. J., Rich, G. A., Podsakoff, P. M., Mackenzie, S. B. (1995). On the interchangeability of objective and subjective measures of employee performance: A meta-analysis. *Personnel Psychology,* 48, 587–605.

Burton, K. D., Lydon, J. E., D'Alessandro, D. U., & Koestner, R. (2006). The differential effects of intrinsic and identified motivation on well-being and performance: Prospective, experimental and implicit approaches to self-determination theory. *Journal of Personality and Social Psychology, 91,* 750–762.

Chantal, Y., Guay, F., Dobreva-Martinova, T., & Vallerand, R. J. (1996). Motivation and elite performance: An exploratory investigation with Bulgarian athletes. *International Journal of Sport Psychology, 27,* 173–182.

Chantal, Y., Robin, P., Vernat, J. P., & Bernache-Assollant, I. (2005). Motivation, sportpersonship, and athletic aggression: A meditational analysis. *Psychology of Sport and Exercise, 6,* 233–249.

Charbonneau, D., Barling, J., & Kelloway, E. K. (2001). Transformational leadership and sports performance: The mediating role of intrinsic motivation. *Journal of Applied Social Psychology, 31,* 1521–1534.

Craig, P., Dieppe, P., Macintyre. S., Mitchie, S., Nazareth, I., & Petticrew, M. (2008). Developing and evaluating complex interventions: the new Medical Research Council guidance, *BMJ, 337,* 979–983.

Csikszentimihalyi, M. (1975). *Beyond boredom and anxiety: Experiencing flow in work and play.* San Francisco, CA: Jossey-Bass.

deCharms, R. (1968). Personal causation: The internal affective determinants of behavior. New York: Academic Press.

Deci, E. L. (1975). *Intrinsic motivation.* New York: Plenum.

Deci, E. L., Eghrari, H., Patrick, B. C., & Leone, D. (1994). Facilitating internalization: The self-determination theory perspective. *Journal of Personality, 62,* 119–142.

Deci, E. L., Koestner, R., & Ryan, R. M. (1999). A meta-analytic review of experiments examining the effects of extrinsic rewards on intrinsic motivation. *Psychological Bulletin, 125,* 627–668.

Deci, E. L., & Ryan, R. M. (1980). The empirical exploration of intrinsic motivational processes. In L. Berkowitz (Ed.), *Advances in experimental social psychology* (pp. 39–80). New York: Academic Press.

Deci, E. L., & Ryan, R. M. (1985). *Intrinsic motivation and self-determination in human behavior.* New York: Plenum.

Deci, E. L., & Ryan, R. M. (1991). A motivational approach to self: Integration in personality. In R. A. Dienstbier (Ed.), *Nebraska symposium on motivation: Perspectives on motivation, Vol. 38* (pp. 237–288). Lincoln, NE: University of Nebraska.

Deci, E. L., & Ryan, R. M. (2000). The 'what' and 'why' of goal pursuits: Human needs and the self-determination of behavior. *Psychological Inquiry, 11,* 227–268.

Deci, E. L., & Ryan, R. M. (2002). The paradox of achievement: The harder you push, the worse it gets. In J. Aronson (Ed.), *Improving academic achievement: Contributions of social psychology* (pp. 59–85). New York: Academic Press.

Deci, E. L., & Ryan, R. M. (2008). Facilitating optimal motivation and psychological well-being across life's domains. *Canadian Psychology, 49,* 14–23.

Deci, E. L., & Vansteenkiste, M. (2004). Self-determination theory and basic need satisfaction: Understanding human development in positive psychology. *Ricerche di Psicologia, 27,* 17–34.

Flink, C., Boggiano, A. K., & Barrett, M. (1990). Controlling teaching strategies: Undermining children's self-determination and performance. *Journal of Personality and Social Psychology, 59,* 916–924.

Fortier, M. S., Vallerand, R. J., & Guay, F. (1995). Academic motivation and school performance: Toward a structural model. *Contemporary Educational Psychology, 20,* 257–274.

Gagné, M., Ryan, R. M., & Bargmann, K. (2003). Autonomy support and need satisfaction in the motivation and well-being of gymnasts. *Journal of Applied Sport Psychology, 15,* 372–390.

Gillet, N., Berjot, S., & Gobancé, L. (2009). A motivational model of performance in the sport domain. *European Journal of Sport Science, 9,* 151–158.

Gillet, N., Vallerand, R. J., Amoura, S., & Baldes, B. (2010). Influence of coaches' autonomy support on athletes' motivation and sport performance: A test of the hierarchical model of intrinsic and extrinsic motivation. *Psychology of Sport and Exercise, 11,* 155–161.

Gillison, F. B., Standage, M., & Skevington, S. M. (2011). Motivation and body-related factors as discriminators of change in adolescents' exercise behavior profiles. *Journal of Adolescent Health, 48,* 44–51.

Grolnick, W. S., & Ryan, R. M. (1989). Parent styles associated with children's self-regulation and competence in school. *Journal of Educational Psychology, 81,* 143–154.

Grolnick, W. S., & Seal, K. (2008). *Pressured parents, stressed-out kids: Dealing with competition while raising a successful child.* Amherst, NY: Prometheus Press.

Hagger, M. S., & Chatzisarantis, N. L. D. (2007). *Intrinsic motivation and self-determination in exercise and sport.* Champaign, IL: Human Kinetics.

Halvari, H., Ulstad S. O., Bagøien, T. E., & Skjesol, K. (2009). Autonomy support and its links to physical activity and competitive performance: Mediations through motivation, competence, action orientation and harmonious passion, and the moderator role of autonomy support by perceived competence. *Scandinavian Journal of Educational Research, 53,* 533–555.

Haskell, W. L., Lee, I. M., Pate, R. R., Powell, K. E., Blair, S. N., Franklin, B. A., et al. (2007). Physical activity and public health: Updated recommendation for adults from the American College of Sports Medicine and the American Heart Association. *Medicine and Science in Sports and Exercise, 39,* 1423–1434.

Hodgins, H. S., Yacko, H. A., & Gottlieb, E. (2006). Autonomy and nondefensiveness. *Motivation and Emotion, 30,* 283–293.

Hopkins, W. G., Hawley, W. G., & Burke, L. M. (1999). Design and analysis of research on sport performance enhancement. *Medicine and Science in Sports and Exercise, 31,* 472–485.

Hulleman, M., De Koning, J. J., Hettinga, F. J., & Foster, C. (2007). The effect of extrinsic motivation on cycle time trial performance. *Medicine and Science in Sports and Exercise, 39,* 709–715.

Kasser, T. (2002). *The high price of materialism*. Cambridge, MA: MIT Press.

Kasser, T., & Ryan, R. M. (1993). A dark side of the American dream: Correlates of financial success as a central life aspiration. *Journal of Personality and Social Psychology, 65*, 410–422.

Kasser, T., & Ryan, R. M. (1996). Further examining the American dream: Differential correlates of intrinsic and extrinsic goals. *Personality and Social Psychology Bulletin, 22*, 280–287.

Koestner, R., Ryan, R. M., Bernieri, F., & Holt, K. (1984). Setting limits on children's behavior: The differential effects of controlling versus informational styles on children's intrinsic motivation and creativity. *Journal of Personality, 52*, 233–248.

Kowal, J., & Fortier, M. S. (1999). Motivational determinants of flow: Contributions from self-determination theory. *The Journal of Social Psychology, 139*, 355–368.

Lonsdale, C., Hodge, K., & Rose, E. A. (2009). The Behavioral Regulation in Sport Questionnaire (BRSQ): Instrument development and initial validity evidence. *Journal of Sport and Exercise Psychology, 30*, 323–355.

Lonsdale, C., Hodge, K., & Rose, E. (2009). Athlete burnout in elite sport: A self-determination perspective. *Journal of Sports Sciences, 27*, 785–795.

Mageau, G. A., & Vallerand, R. J. (2003). The coach-athlete relationship: A motivational model. *Journal of Sports Sciences, 21*, 883–904.

Markland, D., Ryan, R. M., Tobin, V. J., & Rollnick, S. (2005). Motivational interviewing and self-determination theory. *Journal of Social and Clinical Psychology, 24*, 811–831.

McDonough, M. H., & Crocker, P. R. E. (2007). Testing self-determined motivation as a mediator of the relationship between psychological needs and affective and behavioral outcomes. *Journal of Sport and Exercise Psychology, 29*, 645–663.

Mouratidis, A., Lens, W., & Vansteenkiste, M. (2010). How you provide corrective feedback makes a difference: The motivating role of communicating in an autonomy-supportive way. *Journal of Sport and Exercise Psychology, 32*, 619–637.

Mouratidis, A., Vansteenkiste, M., Lens, W., & Sideridis, G. (2008). The motivating role of positive feedback in sport and physical education: evidence for a motivational model. *Journal of Sport and Exercise Psychology, 30*, 240–258.

Mulaik, S.A. (1987). A brief history of philosophical foundations of exploratory factor analysis. *Multivariate Behavioural Research, 22*, 267–305.

Ntoumanis, N. (2012). A self-determination theory perspective on motivation in sport and physical education: Current trends and possible future research directions. In G.C. Roberts & D. C. Treasure (Eds). *Advances in motivation in sport and exercise* (3rd ed., pp. 91–128). Champaign, IL: Human Kinetics.

Ntoumanis, N., & Standage, M. (2009). Morality in sport: A self-determination theory perspective. *Journal of Applied Sport Psychology, 21*, 365–380.

Oliver, E. J., Markland, D., Hardy, J., & Petherick, C. M. (2008). The effects of autonomy-supportive versus controlling environments on self-talk. *Motivation and Emotion, 32*, 200–212.

Patall, E. A., Cooper, H., & Wynn, S. R. (2010). The effectiveness and relative importance of choice in the classroom. *Journal of Educational Psychology, 102*, 896–915.

Pelletier, L. G., Fortier, M. S., Vallerand, R. J., & Brière, N. M. (2001). Associations among perceived autonomy support, forms of self-regulation, and persistence: A prospective study. *Motivation and Emotion, 25*, 279–306.

Pelletier, L.G., Fortier, M., Vallerand, R.J., Tuson, K.M., Briere, N.M., & Blais, M.R. (1995). The Sports Motivation Scale (SMS): A measure of intrinsic motivation, extrinsic motivation and amotivation in sports. *Journal of Sport and Exercise Psychology, 17*, 35–53.

Podsakoff, P. M., MacKenzie, S. B., Lee, J. Y., & Podsakoff, N. P. (2003). Common method biases in behavioral research: A critical review of the literature and recommended remedies. *Journal of Applied Psychology, 88*, 879–903.

Reeve, J. (2006). Extrinsic rewards and inner motivation. In C. M. Evertson & C. S. Weinstein (Eds.), *Handbook of classroom management: Research, practice, and contemporary issues* (pp. 645–664). Mahwah, NJ: Lawrence Erlbaum Associates Publishers.

Reeve, J. (2009). Why teachers adopt a controlling motivating style toward students and how they can become more autonomy supportive. *Educational Psychologist, 44*, 159–175

Reeve, J., & Deci, E. L. (1996). Elements of the competitive situation that affect intrinsic motivation. *Personality and Social Psychology Bulletin, 22*, 24–33.

Reeve, J., & Jang, H. (2006). What teachers say and do to support students' autonomy during a learning activity. *Journal of Educational Psychology, 98*, 209–218.

Reis, H. T, Sheldon, K. M., Gable, S. L., Roscoe, J., & Ryan, R. M. (2000). Daily well-being: The role of autonomy, competence, and relatedness. *Personality and Social Psychology Bulletin, 26*, 419–435.

Roth, G., Assor, A., Niemiec, C. P., Ryan, R. M., & Deci, E. L. (2009). The emotional and academic consequences of parental conditional regard: Comparing conditional positive regard, conditional negative regard, and autonomy support as parenting practices. *Developmental Psychology, 45*, 1119–1142.

Ryan, R. M. (1982). Control and information in the intrapersonal sphere: An extension of cognitive evaluation theory. *Journal of Personality and Social Psychology, 43*, 450–461.

Ryan, R. M., & Connell, J. P. (1989). Perceived locus of causality and internalization: Examining reasons for acting in two domains. *Journal of Personality and Social Psychology, 57*, 749–761.

Ryan, R. M., & Deci, E. L. (2000). Self-determination theory and the facilitation of intrinsic motivation, social development, and well-being. *American Psychologist, 55*, 68–78.

Ryan, R. M., & Deci, E. L. (2002). An overview of self-determination theory: An organismic-dialectical perspective. In E. L. Deci & R. M. Ryan (Eds.), *Handbook of self-determination theory research* (pp. 3–33). Rochester NY: University of Rochester Press.

Ryan, R. M., & Deci, E. L. (2008). Self-determination theory and the role of basic psychological needs in personality and the organization of behavior. In O. P. John, R. W. Robbins, & L. A. Pervin (Eds.), *Handbook of personality: Theory and research* (pp. 654–678). New York: The Guilford Press.

Ryan, R. M., Huta, V., & Deci, E. L. (2008). Living well: A self-determination theory perspective on eudaimonia. *Journal of Happiness Studies, 9*, 139–170.

Ryan, R. M., Mims, V., & Koestner, R. (1983). Relation of reward contingency and interpersonal context to intrinsic motivation: A review and test using cognitive evaluation theory. *Journal of Personality and Social Psychology, 45*, 736–750.

Ryan, R. M., Koestner, R., & Deci, E. L. (1991). Ego-involved persistence: When free-choice behavior is not intrinsically motivated. *Motivation and Emotion, 15*, 185–205.

Ryan, R. M., & Stiller, J. (1991). The social contexts of internalization: Parent and teacher influences on autonomy, motivation and learning. In P. R. Pintrich & M. L. Maehr (Eds.), *Advances in motivation and achievement* (Vol. 7, pp. 115–149). Greenwich, CT: JAI Press.

Ryan, R. M., Williams, G. C., Patrick, H., & Deci, E. L. (2009). Self-determination theory and physical activity: The dynamics of motivation in development and wellness. *Hellenic Journal of Psychology, 6*, 107–124.

Sarrazin, P., Vallerand, R. J., Guillet, E., Pelletier, L. G., & Cury, F. (2002). Motivation and dropout in female handballers: A 21-month prospective study. *European Journal of Social Psychology, 32*, 395–418.

Sebire, S. J., Standage, M., & Vansteenkiste, M. (2008). Development and validation of the Goal Content for Exercise Questionnaire. *Journal of Sport and Exercise Psychology, 30*, 353–377.

Sebire, S. J., Standage, M., & Vansteenkiste, M. (2011). Predicting objectively assessed exercise behavior from the content and regulation of exercise goals: Evidence for a mediational model. *Journal of Sport and Exercise Psychology, 33*, 175–197.

Sheldon, K. M. & Krieger, L. K. (2007). Understanding the negative effects of legal education on law students: A longitudinal test and extension of self-determination theory. *Personality and Social Psychology Bulletin, 33*, 883–897.

Smith, A., Ntoumanis, N., Duda, J. L., & Vansteenkiste, M. (2011). Goal striving, coping, and well-being in sport: A prospective investigation of the self-concordance model. *Journal of Sport and Exercise Psychology, 33*, 124–145.

Standage, M., & Ryan, R.M. (2012). Self-determination theory and exercise motivation: Facilitating self-regulatory processes to support and maintain health and well-being. In G.C. Roberts & D.C. Treasure (Eds.), *Advances in motivation in sport and exercise* (3rd ed., pp. 233–270). Champaign, IL: Human Kinetics.

Standage, M., Sebire, S. J., & Loney, T. (2008). Does exercise motivation predict engagement in objectively assessed bouts of moderate-intensity exercise behavior? A self-determination theory perspective. *Journal of Sport and Exercise Psychology, 30*, 337–352.

Standage, M., Sebire, S.J., & Stokes, K.A. (2011). *The relationship between autonomous and controlled motivation with 20-metre shuttle run performance in a naturally occurring school PE setting.* Manuscript submitted for publication.

Standage, M., & Vallerand, R. J. (2008). Self-determined motivation in sport and exercise groups. In M. R. Beauchamp & M. A. Eys (Eds.), *Group dynamics advances in sport and exercise psychology: Contemporary themes* (pp. 179–199). New York: Routledge.

Tauer, J.M., & Harackiewicz, J.M. (2004). The effects of cooperation and competition on intrinsic motivation and performance. *Journal of Personality and Social Psychology, 86*, 849–861.

Treasure, D.C., Lemyre, N., Kuczka, K.K., & Standage, M. (2007). Motivation in elite sport: A self-determination perspective. In M.S. Hagger & N.L.D. Chatzisarantis (Eds.), *Intrinsic motivation and self-determination in exercise and sport* (pp. 153–165). Champaign, IL: Human Kinetics.

Vallerand, R. J. (1997). Toward a hierarchical model of intrinsic and extrinsic motivation. In M. P. Zanna (Ed.), *Advances in experimental social psychology* (pp. 271–360). San Diego, CA: Academic Press.

Vallerand, R.J. (2001). A Hierarchical Model of Intrinsic and Extrinsic Motivation in sport and exercise. In G. Roberts (Ed.) *Advances in motivation in sport and exercise* (pp. 263–319). Champaign, IL: Human Kinetics.

Vallerand, R. J. (2007). Intrinsic and extrinsic motivation in sport and physical activity: A review and a look at the future. In G. Tenenbaum, & E. Eklund (Eds.), *Handbook of sport psychology* (3 ed., pp. 59–84). New York: John Wiley.

Vallerand, R. J., & Losier G F. (1999). An integrative analysis of intrinsic and extrinsic motivation in sport. *Journal of Applied Sport Psychology, 11*, 142–169.

Vallerand, R. J., & Reid, G. (1984). On the causal effects of perceived competence on intrinsic motivation: A test of cognitive evaluation theory. *Journal of Sport Psychology, 6*, 94–102.

Vandenbogaerde, T. J., & Hopkins, W. G. (2010). Monitoring acute effects on athletic performance with mixed linear modeling. *Medicine and Science in Sports and Exercise, 42*, 1339–1344.

Vansteenkiste, M., Lens, W., & Deci, E. L. (2006). Intrinsic versus extrinsic goal contents in self-determination theory: Another look at the quality of academic motivation. *Educational Psychologist, 41*, 19–31.

Vansteenkiste, M., Niemiec, C. P., & Soenens, B. (2010). The development of the five mini theories of self-determination theory: An historical overview, emerging trends, and future directions. In T. Urdan, & S. Karabenick (Eds.). *Advances in motivation and achievement, vol. 16A: The decade ahead* (pp. 105–165). Bingley, UK: Emerald Group Publishing Limited.

Vansteenkiste, M., Simons, J., Lens, W., Sheldon, K. M., & Deci, E. L. (2004). Motivating learning, performance, and persistence: The synergistic effects of intrinsic goal contents and autonomy supportive contexts. *Journal of Personality and Social Psychology, 87*, 246–260.

Vansteenkiste, M., Soenens, B., & Lens, W. (2007). Intrinsic versus extrinsic goal promotion in exercise and sport: Understanding the differential impacts on performance and persistence (pp. 167–180). In M. S. Hagger and N. L. D. Chatzisarantis (Eds.), *Intrinsic motivation and self-determination in exercise and sport.* Champaign, IL: Human Kinetics.

Zuckerman, M., Porac, J., Lathin, D., Smith, R., & Deci, E. L. (1978). On the importance of self-determination for intrinsically-motivated behavior. *Personality and Social Psychology Bulletin, 4*, 443–446.

Modeling and Performance

Penny McCullagh, Barbi Law, *and* Diane Ste-Marie

Abstract

In this chapter we review theoretical and conceptual approaches in the sport and exercise psychology literature, as well as recognizing research in other domains (performing arts, education, medicine, health) to determine the influence that watching oneself or others can have on one's own performance, as well as on psychological variables such as self-efficacy, anxiety, and self-regulation. We recognize that various terms have been used to describe this phenomenon, including observational learning, modeling, and self-modeling, and we also review recent research that shows how athletes use observation in realistic sport settings. Finally, a brief discussion of role models and the influence that technology has had, including the influence of virtual models, is highlighted. Suggestions for future research are included throughout the chapter.

Key Words: Observational learning, self-modeling, modeling, video, virtual model, role models, dyad learning, self-efficacy, self-regulation

The adage "a picture is worth a thousand words", is a popular phrase that we hear in a variety of settings. There is controversy, not necessarily over the claim, but rather over its origin. Some suggest the phrase came from an early Chinese proverb translated as "a picture's meaning can express ten thousand words" although this claim cannot be verified. Reference in *The Yale Book of Quotations* (Shapiro, 2006) suggests that Frederick Barnard used the phrase in 1927, in the *Printer's Ink*. Despite the origin of the phrase, there seems to be a natural belief that pictures convey an abundant amount of information.

Among coaches, trainers, and teachers, the positive value of demonstrations is widely accepted, and researchers investigate this issue under the realm of observational learning. Over the years, numerous labels have been used to describe this phenomenon, including imitation, vicarious learning, identification learning, and modeling, to name a few. In a review, Greer, Dudek-Singer, and Gautreaux (2006)

suggested that the variety of terms used has actually impeded the progress of studies across a number of domains, primarily because the terms actually refer to different types of behaviors. In the context of this chapter, we will use the terms *observational learning* and *modeling* interchangeably and consider any situation in which an individual can observe the self or others engaging in a behavior as a modeling/observational learning experience.

Within the field of sport psychology, an area concerned with theoretical approaches and practical applications for performance enhancement, it is surprising that more attention has not been paid to this topic. McCullagh and Weiss (2002) reviewed some of the research in this area and labeled observational learning "the forgotten psychological method in sport psychology." They suggested that numerous other performance interventions were advocated in the literature despite the important theoretical underpinning and empirical research that documented the effectiveness of observational learning for performance modification. In fact, verification of the absence of attention to modeling was seen in McCullagh and Wilson's (2007) content analysis of the top ten sport psychology textbooks and 27 sport psychology course syllabi, an analysis that showed that only .88% of the textbook pages and .94% of the syllabi were dedicated to the topic of observational learning. Thus, we are pleased to contribute this chapter on the topic of observational learning.

Perhaps the contributions of modeling have often been overlooked as a result of being embedded within other interventions. The most common occurrence is within imagery research. In reviewing the literature, Martin, Moritz, and Hall (1999) noted that many imagery studies were confounded with other treatments and reported that demonstrations were often used in imagery studies to provide the stimulus, but were not recognized as part of the intervention. Similarly, McCullagh and Ram (2000) reviewed imagery studies published in three popular sport psychology journals over a 10-year period and found that over half the imagery studies used demonstrations, videos, or pictures as stimuli for the imagery intervention. Thus, many of the effects attributed to imagery may actually be a result of modeling plus imagery. As you move forward in the chapter, you will come across other examples of modeling being part of a larger intervention. We encourage you to find those examples and question how researchers can better tease apart the contributions of modeling in multilayered interventions.

In this chapter, we review conceptual and theoretical approaches to observational learning/modeling, examine current research on modifications of both physical and psychological behaviors, and present how athletes use modeling in real-life settings. We then move beyond the field of sport psychology and examine some of the varied domains and settings that employ demonstrations as a training technique, and discuss the widespread interest in role models in sport and beyond. Practical recommendations for using modeling as a skill-learning and performance enhancement technique, in addition to directions for future research, are provided throughout.

Conceptual and Theoretical Approaches to Modeling

Over the last 100 years, a variety of approaches have tried to explain how behaviors are modified as a function of observation. Many of the psychological explanations are reflective of the orientations or paradigms of research in vogue at the time. Although early explanations for imitation relied on instinctual approaches (e.g., Ellwood, 1917; Tarde, 1903; Woodworth, 1922), other explanations went beyond instinct and included the importance of higher order responses such as affect (Morgan, 1896), voluntary control (McDougall, 1908), associative behavior (Allport, 1924; Holt, 1931), and reinforcement (Gerwitz & Stingle, 1968; Miller & Dollard, 1941). These early explanations, however, had some shortcomings because they tried to explain how behaviors already in one's repertoire were modeled, but failed to explain how new behaviors were learned.

Building on ideas proposed by Miller and Dollard (1941) and then Sheffield (1961), Bandura moved the field of observational learning forward through his progressive conceptual reformulations (1965, 1969, 1971, 1986, 1997). In his early explanations, Bandura suggested that four subprocesses were important for the observational learning process—attention, retention, motor reproduction, and motivation. In his later writings, he couched the observational learning process within social cognitive theory. Within this framework, self-efficacy (i.e., one's belief in his or her ability to produce a specific behavioral response in a particular situation) serves as a major impetus for action. Four sources of information are predicted to influence self-efficacy: performance accomplishments, vicarious experiences, verbal persuasion, and affective and physiological states. Modeling is directly related to the two strongest sources of efficacy: performance accomplishments and vicarious experience. Performance accomplishments, or mastery experiences, are extremely robust since they are a direct reflection of one's capabilities. If you already accomplished a particular task, then get to see that performance at a later time, you are likely to think you can accomplish the task in the future.

The second strongest source of self-efficacy is argued to be vicarious experience, which, by definition, includes not only modeling, but imagery as well. If one has not already accomplished a task, then it is possible to watch others perform the task (or image oneself performing the task) with the notion that self-efficacy will be enhanced, especially if one perceives the model to be similar to oneself (Bandura, 1986). Bandura's conceptualizations of the observational learning process have had a profound influence on subsequent research.

Recent work on observational learning has placed this process within the cognitive-motivational framework of self-regulation. Self-regulation as a cognitive strategy for goal-directed behavior has been discussed in the psychological literature for quite some time. Self-regulation has been defined as underlying meta-cognitive, behavioral, and motivational processes that learners engage in to attain any given task (Zimmerman, 1996). Researchers who have promoted the study of modeling within a theoretical framework of self-regulation include Bandura (1986, 1991), Kirschenbaum (1984), Schunk (1991), and Zimmerman (1989, 2000). For example, within Kirschenbaum's five-stage model of self-regulation, the fact that a standard of comparison is needed to move through the stages of self-regulation is evidence of the interplay between modeling and self-regulation. A further example involves Zimmerman's work. Zimmerman frames his notions of self-regulation within the person-behavior-environment triadic cycle forwarded by Bandura (1986, 1991) in social cognitive theory. Thus, a person's attitudes, behaviors, and thoughts are influenced by what surrounds them in the environment and this, in turn, affects behavior or performance. According to his ideas, self-regulation includes cognitive processes that occur before (forethought), during (performance control), and after (self-reflection) action. Similar to Kirschenbaum, the comparison of performance to a standard is critical in this model, further reinforcing the notion that the influences of observing another or oneself can be conceptualized within a self-regulation framework.

An even stronger theoretical linkage concerning modeling and self-regulation has been advanced in Zimmerman and colleagues' social cognitive model of sequential skill acquisition (e.g., Schunk & Zimmerman, 1996, 1997; Zimmerman & Kitsantas, 1997, 1999). In that model, it is argued that the acquisition of new skills becomes self-regulated by progressing through four stages: observation, emulation, self-control, and finally, self-regulation. Modeling, or observation, is the first stage, and this is where the observer picks up necessary task information. Emulation occurs when the learner attempts the skill and receives feedback that helps develop the standards for correct performance. Self-control comes when learners can automatically execute the skill and compare their performance to their own internal standards. The final stage of self-regulation occurs when learners can adapt their behaviors to changing conditions. Here, the learner can focus on performance and determine which process produces the best outcome.

A different perspective on modeling is offered by Scully and Newell (1985), who built upon ideas expressed by Gibson (1979) and suggested a more dynamic approach to modeling than the previous cognitive interpretations. They suggested that the visual system automatically picks up relevant information that provides for the control and coordination needed for movement and that there is no need for a cognitive code. Instead, the important features are the invariant coordination relationships among the movement of body parts (i.e., relative motion information).

The hypothesis that people pick up the invariant features of movement was espoused by Johansson (1973) and has been tested using a technique called *point-light display*, where reflective joint markers are used to create small lights at key joints during movement. Individuals then watch these lights in motion without viewing the actual body parts. Hodges, Hayes, Breslin, and Williams (2005) conducted a series of experiments using point-light displays to examine if relative motion was the key to observational learning. They reported that learners could get sufficient information from point-light displays to execute the required movement even when relative motion information was not provided (see also Hodges, Williams, Hayes, & Breslin, 2007). They went on to increase the complexity of the types of tasks used (Breslin, Hodges, Williams, Kremer, & Curran, 2005, 2006; Hayes, Hodges, Horn, & Williams, 2007) and found that the outcome motion required of the learner and whether they received feedback were more important than the coordination displayed by the model. In addition, they found that observers tended to learn from the end of motion information more than from whole-body displays; for example, the release point of a bowling action. Thus, although the importance of visual display has provided an interesting view on the observational learning process, it does not seem to hold sufficient evidence to eliminate the importance of cognitions.

A final approach to observational learning research comes from the neurophysiological perspective. The key discovery of mirror neurons by an Italian team of researchers in the early 1990s (di Pellegrino, Fadiga, Fogassi, Gallese, & Rizzolatti, 1992) created much excitement in the field. This group found that when monkeys watched other monkeys reach and grasp, neurons in the F5 area of the motor cortex became active. Since this early research, many studies have examined this phenomenon in humans. For example, Vogt and Thomaschke (2007) specifically reviewed monkey and human research from both a behavioral and neurophysiological perspective. They concluded that the mirror neuron system (MNS) in monkeys appeared to be sensitive to high-level strategic aspects of the observed action; in other words, the ability to understand the observed action. The human MNS indicated an enhanced capacity for representing and imitating several aspects of observed action, such as motor planning and coding certain kinematic details of the movement.

Other recent review papers link mirror neurons with observational learning across a variety of disciplines including, but not limited to, education (van Gog, Paas, Marcus, Ayres, & Sweller, 2009), cognitive science (Obhi & Hogeveen, 2010), and neuroscience (Buccino & Riggio, 2006). Although there is widespread agreement that brain activity occurs when individuals watch others move, there is still debate about how this is turned into learned behavior. Readers are referred to a recent edited edition on the neurocognition of dance that highlights some the recent trends in this research (Bläsing, Puttke, & Schack, 2010).

The Impact of Modeling in Sport and Physical Activity Domains

By now, it must be evident that research on observational learning has taken giant leaps over the last three decades, and it would thus be impossible to provide a comprehensive review of all research in this area (for a sampling of previous reviews see Hodges et al., 2007; Lysklett, Whiting, & Hoff, 2001; McCullagh, 1983; McCullagh & Weiss, 2001; McCullagh, Weiss, & Ross, 1989; Weiss, Ebbeck, & Wiese-Bjornstal, 1993; Vogt & Thomaschke, 2007). Therefore, here, we focus on a few topics that we think are most important for sport and performance psychology. Specifically, we examine how effective demonstrations are compared to more traditional learning techniques that incorporate feedback and practice, appraise some literature that examines the skill level of the model, consider what happens when you watch yourself, and, finally, see what happens when you learn alongside others.

Modeling Compared to Practice and Verbal Instructions

Researchers have long recognized the importance of providing information to learners. Generally three types of information have been deemed important

(Newell, 1981): information before action, such as verbal instructions or demonstrations; information during action, such as concurrent augmented feedback or intrinsic feedback (e.g., visual, kinesthetic); and information after action, such as knowledge of results (KR) or knowledge of performance (KP). Within the motor learning literature, the majority of research has focused on the latter form of information (i.e., the role of feedback), but mainly as verbal information supplied as KR (e.g., Adams, 1971; Schmidt, 1975). Only recently have motor learning researchers moved to focus on observational learning.

The primary difference between physical and observational practice is that, in the latter situation, the observer does not execute a physical response and thus does not prepare for the movement nor receive sensory feedback. Research has shown that observational practice is better than no practice at all, but is not as effective as physical practice (e.g., Blandin, Proteau, & Alain, 1994; Kohl & Shea, 1992). Shea, Wright, Wulf and Whitacre (2000) wanted to further test the power of observational learning compared to physical practice and no practice. They compared these three conditions on the learning of a video game, then followed the learners through delayed retention and transfer tests. They hypothesized that the physical practice group would perform better on the retention test than the observational practice group. However, they argued that the observational practice group would fare well on a transfer test when there were new task requirements, and that the physical practice group would only have learned the general coordination pattern of the task but not be able to transfer this knowledge to different specific task characteristics. The predictions were upheld, suggesting that observational learners can pick up general task requirements that can help them during transfer, but do not do as well during a straight retention test because they have not learned the specific task requirements. In a second experiment, they found that combining physical and observational learning led to the best transfer of performance. Other research also highlights the transfer and retention benefits of observational learning, further noting that providing verbal cues in addition to the modeled information is useful (Janelle, Champenoy, Coombes, & Mousseau, 2003; Meaney & Edwards, 1996; Weiss, 1983; Weiss & Klint, 1987).

Horn, Williams, Hayes, Hodges, and Scott (2007) suggested that too much attention had been paid to the influence of observational learning on retention and transfer at the expense of ignoring early acquisition effects. They proposed that if observational learning did indeed provide initial success for learners, this might have applied implications, especially in practical situations in which enhanced immediate performance would be noticed by the coach or teacher. They compared intra-limb coordination of those who observed a model compared to those who practiced a novel ball throwing skill through discovery learning and reported that observational learning was a rate enhancer—it impacted coordinated behavior immediately.

This research might provide some guidelines for practitioners who want to use video for the acquisition of sport skills. It appears that combining observational learning with physical practice and verbal information is an excellent means for enhancing not only early acquisition, but also the retention and transfer of skills. Importantly, however, a host of factors may influence observational learning; just a few of these include the characteristics of the model, the type of task, and the skill level of the learner. Four of these issues are addressed next.

Learning Versus Expert Models

Imagine that you are the coach of a group and are about to teach a new skill. You may well choose to give a demonstration, since you want to provide your learners with the best possible information, so you decide you will have the most skilled person in your group show the others how to do it. Such a choice is intuitively appealing and probably the most popular choice. But is it the best choice?

Early research by Martens, Burwitz, and Zuckerman (1976) tested the notion of watching a correct model versus watching others who were in the process of learning the motor skill, with the idea that learners who watched others learning would be better able to discern important task aspects and subsequently learn more from a learning model than from a correct model. Results from three experiments, however, failed to support this hypothesis, and thus the correct model was deemed the best one to use. Little research on learning models occurred after this until Adams (1986) examined the role of learning models along with the provision of KR. He reasoned that learners who also received the model's KR would become more actively involved in the learning process than would those who merely observed. In his research, participants physically practiced the skill and received KR, watched a model and received model KR, or watched a model with no model KR. A slight advantage was shown

for those who watched a model and also heard the model's KR. McCullagh and Caird (1990) extended Adam's work by adding modeling groups that were yoked to the physical practice group. Additionally, participants did not receive KR about their own movement and were only provided with the KR of the observed model. Again, it was demonstrated that a learning model assisted in motor learning, despite the fact learners did not receive their own KR. In fact, the learning model group without KR performed as well as the physical practice group that received KR, thus doing as well as the group that is typically considered the gold standard for acquisition.

Although subsequent research (e.g., Herbert & Landin, 1994; McCullagh & Myers, 1997; Pollock & Lee, 1992; Weir & Leavitt, 1990) has not provided the same clarity of results, the findings still bring into question the idea that only correct performance models can be of value. Lee, Swinnen, and Serrien (1994) suggested that watching a learning model may in fact require more cognitive effort, and thus lead to better performance. An interesting notion would be to cross the learning models and correct models with learner level of expertise to provide a clear answer as to when learning models are most effective. It may be that learning models are good for learners, whereas expert models are good for experts. Indeed, the similarity of the model to the learner has been proposed as an important factor to consider in modeling research (e.g., Gould & Weiss, 1981; Schunk, Hanson, & Cox, 1987) and may provide further insight into these modeling effects.

Mastery Versus Coping Models

Mastery and coping models are similar to correct and learning models. Mastery models demonstrate correct performance; in addition, they also verbalize confidence and show positive affect. Coping models show skill progression over trials (similar to a learning model), show increasing self-efficacy over time, and show strategies for learning the skill (Schunk et al., 1987). Coping models have been used extensively to examine a wide variety of behaviors in therapeutic settings (e.g., Meichenbaum, 1971), and most studies suggest that using a coping model leads to the greatest behavior change. Coping models have also received some attention in rehabilitation settings (e.g., Flint, 1993). In the area of motor skill learning, studies have yielded varied results. For example, extending some early findings by Lewis (1974), Weiss, McCullagh, Smith, and Berlant

(1998) examined the influence of peer coping and mastery models in children identified as fearful of swimming. Both modeling conditions produced better performance than a nondemonstration control, suggesting equal benefits for the mastery and coping models, although the effect sizes were larger for coping models. Similarly, research by Clark and Ste-Marie (2002) did not show significant differences between mastery and coping models. A strong noted trend, however, was that the mastery model assisted with physical performance scores more than the coping model, whereas the coping model assisted more with modifying psychological variables, such as raising self-efficacy.

Other research, however, has shown clear differences between the model types. For example, Kitsantas, Zimmerman, and Cleary (2000) examined the influence of mastery and coping models on skill acquisition, within Zimmerman and colleagues' four-stage model of sequential self-regulation (e.g., Schunk & Zimmerman, 1996, 1997; Zimmerman & Kitsantas, 1997, 1999). Kitsantas et al. attempted to determine if coping and mastery models produced different effects on the observation and emulation states of learning. It was expected that watching coping models would help learners discriminate errors, whereas those who watched a mastery model would not learn about error detection. In turn, coping models would then lead to better performance and higher self-efficacy. Data indicated that the best performance and higher levels of self-efficacy were attained by those who watched a coping model, followed by those who watched a mastery model, and finally by the control group who received no modeling. The varied findings on this topic suggest that continued research is needed on mastery and coping models that seeks to identify the defining characteristics that lead to the success of the model for learning.

Self-Modeling

A relatively new area within observational learning of physical skills is that of self-as-a-model interventions, in the form of either self-modeling or self-observation. According to Dowrick (1999), self-modeling involves seeing "images of oneself engaged in adaptive behavior" (p. 23). Typically, these videos go beyond mere observation of what a learner performed and are actually edited video tapes that show only the best behaviors. This is accomplished by removing error performances; this type of self-modeling is known as *positive self-review*. Another type of self-modeling identified

by Dowrick, called *feedforward*, involves viewing videos that show behaviors not yet achieved by the learner, but that are possible based on their current repertoire. Special editing of the videos is necessary to produce these feedforward models. In contrast, self-observation is the basic video replay of a person's current performance level.

As revealed in a review by Dowrick (1999), research on self-modeling is by no means new in the therapeutic and training literature. He identified over 150 studies and found positive effects for self-modeling in a number of settings, including selective mutism, academics, and social behaviors. Dowrick noted, however, that only a few studies on self-modeling had been completed in the physical domain at the time of his review (Boyer, 1987; Bradley, 1993; Melody, 1990; Scraba, 1989; Winfrey & Weeks, 1993), and some had shown positive effects for the use of self-modeling. Since 1999, a number of self-modeling studies have been completed in the physical domain. The logic behind the majority of this research was that a self-modeling video involved seeing oneself performing the skill at a near mastery level, and this would be a performance accomplishment—the strongest source of self-efficacy. Moreover, in combination with the increased benefits of model similarity (e.g., Schunk et al., 1987), self-modeling should produce greater performance benefits than no model and may even be superior to other model types.

Although these theoretical implications seem sound, the results of studies examining this issue are less clear. For example, performance benefits of self-modeling for motor skill acquisition have been seen for such skills as swimming (Clark & Ste-Marie, 2007; Dowrick & Dove, 1980; Starek & McCullagh, 1999) and basketball throwing (Bradley, 1993; Melody, 1990). Moreover, Starek and McCullagh's research showed the self-modeling intervention to be superior to peer modeling. Similarly, self-modeling was also shown to enhance physical performance more than self-observation in Clark and Ste-Marie's research. In contrast, research testing self-modeling for volleyball skills (Ram & McCullagh, 2003), figure skating skills (Law & Ste-Marie, 2005), and beam skills (Winfrey & Weeks, 1993) have not yielded physical performance benefits. These equivocal results suggest that other determining factors need to be uncovered to understand how to optimize self-modeling for motor skill acquisition. Such characteristics could include the learner, the stage of learning, or the type of task. Indeed, a meta-analysis by Ashford, Bennett, and

Davids (2006) has shown that skill classification in terms of discrete, serial, and continuous tasks is an important consideration for modeling benefits.

Moving from the learning of motor skills to competitive performance, reports of using self-modeling with competitive athletes appeared in the popular literature (see Balf, 1996; Livermore, 1996) more than a decade ago, but limited research data are available. Examples of self-modeling use has been seen with basketball players (Templin & Vernacchia, 1995), hockey players (Halliwell, 1990), and a weight lifter (Maille, 1985, as cited in Franks & Maile, 1991), with each reporting positive performance benefits, whereas its use with divers did not show benefits (Rymal, Martini, & Ste-Marie, 2010).

Our belief is that the use of self-modeling in real-life situations will continue to grow along with the development of enhanced technology. A look at professional sport shows clear evidence of this. For example, a report in the *San Francisco Chronicle* (2000) revealed that the San Francisco Giants have been watching themselves on video in the dugout for years. Major league pitcher Jason Jennings of the Colorado Rockies uses his iPod to watch edited versions of his pitches and their outcomes before his games (Associated Press, 2006). A further example is McCullagh's use of self-modeling videos with Olympic archers to modify psychological skills (as cited in Balf, 1996; Livermore, 1996). Therefore, continued research that determines best practices for self-modeling is warranted.

Learning in Dyads

A final area that typically falls outside the observational learning radar, but certainly is related, is the literature on learning in dyads. Labeled *peer modeling, peer tutoring,* or *collaborative learning* in the education literature (Topping & Ehly, 1998), this paradigm refers to how people learn when paired with others. Attempting to extend the educational literature to the physical domain, d'Arripe-Longueville, Gernigon, Huet, Winnykamen, and Cadopi (2002a) examined the influence of skill level on motivation and performance in swimming. Students were assigned to learn with either a novice, intermediate, or skilled peer. They found that for girls, skilled or intermediate tutors produced the best results, yet for boys, the skilled tutor was best. In a subsequent study on peer-assisted learning in swimming (d'Arripe-Longueville Gernigon, Huet, Cadopi, & Winnykamen, 2002b), the researchers analyzed the peer interactions when individuals were in pairs of equal ability (symmetrical pairs—both

novice) or in pairs of different abilities (asymmetrical pairs—one novice, one skilled). For males, the asymmetrical condition proved better for performance. These findings may provide some ideas on grouping students for learning, with the suggestion that pair groupings work best when the novice is paired with an individual who is at a higher level of performance. Interestingly, this contradicts some of the literature previously addressing mastery and coping models, and thus the differences between dyad learning and other observational situations should be further explored. The findings also suggest that gender should be a factor studied more within observational learning.

Other research examining learning in dyads has taken an efficiency approach (Granado & Wulf, 2007; Shea, Wulf, & Whitacre, 1999). In a first experiment, Shea et al. found that practicing in dyads in which one person performed one trial while the partner watched, then both switched positions to allow the partner to talk about strategies employed, led to the most efficient and effective practice and better retention than learning the task alone. Given that the first experiment allowed partners to dialog between trials, it was not clear whether the performance benefits were due primarily to the dialog or primarily due to observation. The follow-up study by Granado and Wulf (2007) set out to examine the individual effects of each, as well as the additive effect. They crossed observation and dialog in four experimental conditions and found that the conditions that included observation produced better performance than the dialog condition alone, and this advantage transferred to a retention phase when each member of the dyad practiced alone.

Other work has examined whether working in dyads can also have an influence on inhibitory responses. Inhibition of return (IOR) is a phenomenon that occurs to bias a person from responding to the same location to which they have just responded. Within an experimental paradigm, it refers to the slowing of responses to a target that appears in the same location as an event that occurred previously. Most of the work examining IOR has used a single-person paradigm, but Welsh, Elliot, Anson, Dhillon, Weeks, Lyons, and Chua (2005) investigated whether this same phenomenon would occur in social situations in which one person watched another. In this context, they found the IOR effect was similar whether the person responded him- or herself or watched another individual's reach to a target. In a follow-up experiment that examined the underlying mechanisms that caused the IOR effects in dyads, Welsh, McDougall, and Weeks (2009) suggested that the underlying cognitive mechanisms were the same whether persons generated the response themselves or whether they watched another individual generate the response.

This section focused on the varied types of models that can be used in observational learning, as well as the effectiveness of such models, and other influences that action observation can have on an observer. The emphasis, however, has been on the physical performance benefits in the motor skill domain as a result of observation. In the next sections, we turn to its broader influences for varied psychological skills, as well as other domains of impact.

The Impact of Modeling on Psychological Behaviors

When compared to the extensive research examining behavioral effects of modeling, there is markedly less research examining the psychological effects of modeling. Not surprisingly, the majority of modeling research conducted from a psychological perspective has taken a social cognitive (Bandura, 1986) approach and has focused on self-efficacy. Within the last decade, Zimmerman's (2000) self-regulation of learning framework has also become a popular model for examining psychological effects of modeling. As modeling research becomes more interdisciplinary, it is likely we will witness large steps forward in our understanding of the psychological impact of modeling. In this section, we provide an overview of the effects of modeling on self-efficacy, and we highlight other psychological responses that may be influenced by modeling in sport and physical activity settings.

Self-Efficacy

Self-efficacy is a central concept in Bandura's (1997) more recent conceptualizations of how modeling influences behavioral responses. Self-efficacy is viewed as a mediator of the modeling–performance relationship. Although the role of self-efficacy as a true mediator has not always been supported (e.g., Maddison, Prapavessis, & Clatworthy, 2006; McAuley, 1985), studies using a wide array of model types have found that modeling does have a positive impact on self-efficacy. In fact, the question "which model type is effective for building self-efficacy?" appears to have many answers.

One model type that appears to be particularly powerful for fostering self-efficacy beliefs is a *coping model*. Studies examining both children (Clark

& Ste-Marie, 2002) and female university students (Kitsantas et al., 2000) learning novel tasks have found that a coping model produced greater improvements in self-efficacy than both a mastery model and a control condition. It also appears that mastery or expert models can produce positive changes in self-efficacy, particularly if the learner is able to interact with the model. Feltz, Landers, and Raeder (1979) demonstrated that participant modeling, a form of modeling whereby an expert model demonstrates the skill and then instructs the learner on how to perform the skill, can be used with high-avoidance tasks (e.g., back dive) to produce greater increases in self-efficacy than simply providing a live or video model alone. McAuley's (1985) research with females learning a new gymnastics skill also found that both aided and unaided participant modeling produced higher self-efficacy and lower anxiety than a control condition, with self-efficacy being a strong predictor of performance.

The benefit of model–observer interactions has also been observed in research examining the effect of practicing in dyads. Legrain, d'Arripe-Longueville, and Gernigon's (2003a,b) research examining the use of peer tutors for teaching boxing among college students demonstrated that practicing with a peer tutor produces greater changes in self-efficacy than does physical practice alone, for both the participants and the tutors. Additionally, untrained peer tutors were more effective than trained peer tutors for enhancing self-efficacy, although practicing with a trained peer tutor led to greater improvements in outcome scores. Conversely, d'Arripe-Longueville et al. (2002a) found that among novice high school swimmers, skilled tutors led to higher self-efficacy and performance.

One key model characteristic that has been related to producing changes in self-efficacy is model–observer similarity. The assertion that models who are perceived as more similar to the learner will increase self-efficacy beliefs has been supported in research (e.g., George, Feltz, & Chase, 1992). However, the assumption that the self would be the most similar model, and thus, self-modeling would produce strong changes in self-efficacy has not been strongly supported. Some researchers have found self-modeling to produce equivalent improvements in self-efficacy as self-observation (Clark & Ste-Marie, 2007) and peer modeling (Starek & McCullagh, 1999), and that self-modeling paired with other psychological techniques improves self-efficacy (Barker & Jones, 2006). However, an approximately equal number of studies have found self-modeling to have no effect on self-efficacy (Ram & McCullagh, 2003), even when compared with a practice-only control group (Law & Ste-Marie, 2005; Winfrey & Weeks, 1993). It should also be noted that these studies have examined various tasks and competitive levels, making it difficult to draw decisive conclusions regarding self-modeling and self-efficacy. Further studies are needed to separate the effects of different model types on self-efficacy for performers at varying skill levels and with different task demands.

All of the modeling studies to date that explore changes in self-efficacy have focused on self-efficacy for specific tasks. However, as Bandura (1997) stated, self-efficacy is specific to the situation at hand. Therefore, it is likely that performers may demonstrate self-efficacy not only for specific tasks, but for other aspects of performance. In fact, the distinction between different forms of self-efficacy is often made within the exercise psychology literature (e.g., task and coping efficacy; Rodgers & Sullivan, 2001), but has rarely been made within the observational learning literature. Law and Hall's (2009b) study, however, is one example of how different forms of self-efficacy have been examined. Specifically, they explored the relationship between use of the skill, strategy, and performance functions of observational learning (see Uses of Modeling section in this chapter for further information on the functions of observational learning) and three forms of self-efficacy beliefs: self-efficacy for skills, self-efficacy for strategies, and self-efficacy to regulate mental states. Among adults who were learning a new interactive sport (e.g., tennis, football), use of the performance function of observational learning was the only significant predictor of self-efficacy to regulate mental states. However, among adults who were learning a new independent sport (e.g., rowing, running), use of the skill function of observational learning predicted both self-efficacy to learn skills and strategies. This illustrates the multidimensional nature of modeling and its potential for influencing beliefs for more than skill performance alone.

Motivation

Understanding and enhancing a performer's motivation is a topic of interest to researchers, parents, and coaches alike. Research has examined the role of motivation as both a consequence of modeling and an antecedent. Studies examining the effect of modeling on motivation have produced equivocal findings to date. In a sample of young swimmers, Clark and Ste-Marie (2007) found that children receiving a self-modeling intervention reported significantly higher scores on the challenge subscale of the revised Motivation Orientation in Sport questionnaire (Weiss, Bredemeier, & Shewchuk, 1985) compared to children receiving a self-observation or control treatment, indicating that self-modeling enhanced children's preference for pursuing challenging activities (i.e., a form of intrinsic motivation). However, among high school–aged performers, other studies have found no such effects for self-modeling (Law & Ste-Marie, 2005) or untrained versus trained peer tutors (Legrain et al., 2003b).

Examining motivation from an achievement goal perspective (Nicholls, 1984), d'Arripe-Longueville et al. (2002a) found that, among high school swimmers, males practicing with a same-sex tutor adopted more ego-oriented goals whereas females adopted more task-oriented goals. In contrast, other researchers have examined how motivational orientations influence the benefits gained from modeling. Little and McCullagh (1989) examined the relationship between goal orientation and instructional strategies on motor skill performance. Their findings tentatively suggest that for improving movement form, intrinsically motivated children may benefit more from receiving KP, whereas extrinsically motivated children benefit from KR as well as KP information. In a follow-up to Little and McCullagh's research, Berlant and Weiss (1997) examined the role of achievement goal orientation on learners' focus during the modeling process. They hypothesized that learners with a task orientation would be more likely to focus on skill mastery, whereas those with an ego orientation would focus on performance outcomes. However, their results did not support these hypotheses. The researchers suggested that this may be partially due to the nature of how modeled information is perceived by the learner, as well as the relationship between perceived competence and achievement goals. The learners in this study had low levels of perceived competence; thus, the findings may have been different given a more experienced and confident sample. Taken together, these findings tentatively suggest that modeling interacts with the most salient observer characteristics in a given situation to produce a task-specific goal orientation. Clearly, further research is needed to explain the relationship between motivation and modeling experiences.

Anxiety

According to Bandura's (1977) conceptualization of self-efficacy and anxiety reduction, state anxiety is another psychological construct that may be reduced via observation and may produce improvements in performance. Certainly, it would make intuitive sense that seeing someone like you succeed at a task that you have high anxiety for would help to alleviate feelings of anxiety about being able to succeed yourself. Unfortunately, modeling research within the motor skill domain has not found consistent support for this assertion. McAuley (1985) performed a test of this hypothesis by assigning novice female gymnasts with high avoidance/anxiety for the task to one of three conditions: unaided participant modeling, aided participant modeling, and a control group. Participants in both participant modeling groups reported decreased state anxiety compared to participants in the control group; however, self-efficacy, not anxiety, was a significant predictor of performance. Other studies examining self-modeling and its influences on state anxiety, however, have found no difference when compared to a peer model (Starek & McCullagh, 1999) and a control group (Law & Ste-Marie, 2005). It may be that the initial level of anxiety with the task is an important factor to consider when evaluating the role of modeling on anxiety.

Self-Regulatory Processes

Research examining the influence of modeling on self-regulatory processes has not received much attention until fairly recently. Much of the recent research examining the impact of modeling on self-regulatory processes has been conducted using Zimmerman's (2000) model of self-regulation. Using this model, it appears as though providing a modeling intervention during the forethought phase has a positive impact on several self-regulatory processes. Rymal et al. (2010) took a qualitative approach by interviewing competitive divers following an intervention that involved the viewing of self-modeling videos immediately prior to competing. Divers reported engaging in mainly self-motivational belief and strategic planning processes during the forethought phase and making self-judgments and self-reactions during the self-reflection phase as a result of the video.

Using quantitative methods, researchers have shown that various types of models were linked to enhanced self-regulatory functioning, particularly within the self-reflection phase of Zimmerman's (2000) model. Kitsantas et al. (2000) examined the effect of coping versus mastery models on the dart throwing skill and self-regulation of high school girls. Girls in the coping model group showed

higher levels of self-satisfaction than did girls in the mastery model group, with both modeling groups scoring higher than the control group. Clark and Ste-Marie (2007) also reported that self-modeling produced greater improvements in self-satisfaction beliefs than both self-observation and a control condition in children learning to swim. Kitsantas et al. also found that viewing a coping model led to greater intrinsic interest and more adaptive attributions for performance compared to the other groups. Finally, Legrain et al. (2003b) reported that students who practiced with peer tutors made more adaptive attributions for their performance compared to students in a physical practice only control group. Although these findings are encouraging, more research is needed to explain the mechanisms by which modeling influences self-regulation.

This section reviewed the varied psychological influences that can arise through observation. Certainly, processes and beliefs, such as self-efficacy, motivation, anxiety, and self-regulation, have all been shown to have important influences on skill acquisition and performance alone. Thus, any one intervention that can affect a number of these processes and beliefs is a powerful one. Interestingly, the next section highlights the fact that although research on the uses of modeling by athletes shows they do use it for physical performance benefits, they may need to be persuaded to use it for other functions related to the psychological benefits outlined here.

Use of Modeling by Athletes

Notably, the vast majority of the modeling research to date has been conducted in laboratory-based settings, using experimenter-driven designs. Several researchers have highlighted the need to understand how modeling is used in naturalistic sport settings and how it is employed by the athletes themselves (e.g., Cumming, Clark, Ste-Marie, McCullagh, & Hall, 2005; Hars & Calmels, 2007). Considering how much of their training time athletes spend on their own, and the importance of being able to self-regulate the strategies they use to optimize practice, it is essential that we understand modeling from the athlete's perspective. In fact, recent studies have sought to do just that.

Cumming et al. (2005) conducted the first study aimed at explaining why athletes use modeling. In that series of studies, they created and tested the psychometrics of the Functions of Observational Learning Questionnaire (FOLQ). They found that athletes reported using observational learning for three functions: to learn and improve skills (skill function), to learn and improve strategies (strategy function), and to control arousal levels and psychological states for performance (performance function). Athletes consistently reported using the skill function most frequently, followed by the strategy and performance functions (Cumming et al., 2005; Hall et al., 2009; Law & Hall, 2009a,b; Wesch, Law, & Hall, 2007). As mentioned earlier, the performance functions were used rather rarely by the athletes, thus research concerning why this is the case may be fruitful.

Since the publication of the FOLQ (Cumming et al., 2005), several studies have used this tool to explore how modeling use may differ across different groups of athletes. The majority of these studies have found no gender differences in modeling use (Cumming et al., 2005; Hall et al., 2009; Law & Hall, 2009a,b), with the exception of Wesch et al. (2007) who found that males employ more of the performance function than do females. This should be interpreted with caution, however, as the effect size was quite small. Similarly, Wesch et al. (2007) found varsity athletes use modeling to a greater extent than recreational level athletes, yet other studies have found no such differences according to skill level (Cumming et al., 2005; Hall et al., 2009).

When examining how athletes use modeling according to sport type, it appears that team sport athletes make greater use of the strategy function, whereas individual sport athletes make greater use of the skill function (Wesch et al., 2007). As well, the differences in strategy use between sport types are apparent in both practice and competition (Hall et al., 2009). Research using a different classification system found that independent sport athletes also use more of the skill and performance functions than do interactive sport athletes (Cumming et al., 2005; Law & Hall, 2009b). These differences may be partly related to the availability of different models within each of these training environments, as well as to sport demands. That is, athletes who compete independently and train alone may have less access to a wide variety of models, whereas athletes training in a team sport environment or in interactive sports may have greater opportunity to watch not only the coach, but other athletes at their level, and thus the opportunity to observe a wide variety of skill, strategy, and psychological performance-related situations. As well, interactive and team sport athletes may have a greater focus on acquiring strategies, while independent and individual sport athletes may have a greater focus on

skills and managing cognitions to help them perform independently.

Law and Hall (2009a) have extended work with the FOLQ to examine modeling use in specific groups of athletes. They found that older golfers used less of all functions of modeling compared to younger golfers, regardless of skill level. This suggests that there may be generational differences in the use of modeling. Perhaps this is tied to the enhanced availability of video feedback for younger generations of golfers throughout their development.

It is important to note that the development of the FOLQ was based upon Paivio's (1985) conceptualization of the functions of imagery and the Sport Imagery Questionnaire (SIQ; a questionnaire measuring the functions of imagery in sport; Hall, Mack, Paivio, & Hausenblaus, 1998), and, as such, the items were aligned with functions already identified by athletes as reasons why they use imagery in sport (see Chapter 11, this volume). Thus, there is the potential that athletes may use modeling for functions unique from those identified in the FOLQ. This possibility was explored by Hars and Calmels (2007), who took a qualitative approach to examining how competitive gymnasts use self-observation in practice. Gymnasts were videotaped practicing their uneven bar routines and were then asked to review the video following each attempt and to use a think-aloud protocol to describe why and what they were watching on the video. Findings show that gymnasts attended to mainly spatial information about their performance and that they used the self-observation for self-assessment, enhancing technical execution, and increasing visual perception and imagery use.

These studies take the first few steps toward extending our understanding of the power of modeling in sport and shed light upon how it is used from the learner's perspective. Research on modeling in sport from an applied psychology perspective, however, is still in its infancy and there are many ways in which it can be advanced. We do not fully understand the range of psychological effects produced by modeling or how they may contribute to changes in physical performance. Perhaps the least understood areas are how modeling is used by learners and how to best encourage the effective use of modeling among athletes of various developmental levels.

Current Modeling Research in Other Domains

To date, there has not been a review of modeling across performance domains, and perhaps for good reason: modeling is omnipresent! If you consider all of the situations you encounter in your daily life, it is likely that you engage in some form of modeling for many of them. Given the space limitations, we cannot provide a complete review of modeling in all domains. Rather, we will highlight current findings in several domains to illustrate the diverse ways in which modeling has been used to produce changes in cognitions and behavior, but, unfortunately, will have to refer readers to references of interest in domains such as business (Ellis, Ganzach, Castle, & Sekely, 2010; Kempster, 2009; Nadler, Thompson & Van Boven, 2003), counseling and therapy (Fukkink, 2008; King, 2009; Meharg & Woltersdorf, 1990; Wade, Oberjohn, Burkhardt, & Greenberg, 2009), training (Rosen, Salas, Pavlas, Jensen, Fu, & Lampton, 2010), and rehabilitation (Flint, 1993; Maddison et al., 2006; McCullagh, Ste-Marie, & Law, in press).

Education

Compared to other domains, a much larger portion of the research on modeling has been conducted within the field of education and has targeted a wide range of behavioral and cognitive outcomes. In fact, it is within this domain that the majority of self-as-a-model research has been conducted (for reviews, see Dowrick, 1999; Hitchcock, Dowrick, & Prater, 2003).

A large proportion of modeling studies focus on enhancing student performance in mathematics and science. Schunk et al.'s work (Schunk, 1981; Schunk & Hanson, 1985, 1989; Schunk et al., 1987) has demonstrated the effectiveness of several model types for improving students' self-efficacy and math performance. Their work has shown that modeling is superior to didactic instruction for improving students' efficacy beliefs and performance. Moreover, it encouraged children to make effort-related attributions and increased the congruence between their personal judgments of efficacy and their performance. Such findings certainly have implications for how teachers provide math instruction, particularly for students who struggle with this subject area.

Modeling has also been used as part of an attributional retraining program to encourage girls in the sciences. Ziegler and Stoeger (2004) created a video intervention that combined an expert model (i.e., a female with a doctorate in chemistry) with peer models (i.e., a male and a female student who had completed chemistry courses) discussing their experiences in chemistry, strategies for learning chemistry concepts, and reinforcing effort-related attributions as the reason for their success. Girls who viewed the video reported more adaptive attributional styles, as well as perceptions of control and ability as compared to girls in the control condition and boys in both conditions. These findings demonstrate the opportunity to employ modeling not just for skill learning but to modify psychological responses that foster achievement.

Modeling, and self-modeling in particular, has been employed extensively to help children with exceptionalities perform in the educational setting. As examples, Kehle and colleagues have successfully used self-modeling to target behaviors associated with selective mutism (Kehle, Madaus, Baratta, & Bray, 1998), stuttering (Bray & Kehle, 1996), and on-task behavior in the classroom (Clare, Jenson, Kehle, & Bray, 2000; Kehle, Clark, Jenson, & Wampold, 1986). Modeling has also been advocated as a potential treatment for children with autism and other developmental disabilities (e.g., Buggey, 2009). Using a multiple baseline design, Gena, Couloura, and Kymissis (2005) provided preschoolers with autism with either a series of live therapist demonstrations or videotaped peer modeling demonstrations showing appropriate affective responses in various situations. They found that all forms of modeling increased children's appropriate affective responses.

Modeling is not only used to influence student behavior, but also to modify preservice teachers' behaviors. Allison's (1987) qualitative examination of what preservice teachers observe during their early field experiences revealed that they observed both relevant and irrelevant aspects of the environment. This highlights the need to ensure that preservice teachers' attention is directed to the key elements for fostering their teaching and evaluative skills. Moreno and Ortegano-Layne (2008) found that teacher candidates provided with video and animated models of classroom exemplars demonstrated both more positive attitudes toward learning and superior ability to apply the demonstrated teaching principles compared to candidates provided with textual exemplars. A follow-up study to this highlighted that, for animated exemplars to be most effective, they should be paired with metacognitive prompts to remind the teacher candidate of the specific teaching principles being demonstrated and to cue his or her attention to relevant features of the demonstration (Moreno, 2009).

Performing Arts

Modeling has long been a topic of interest within the performing arts (see Chapter 5, this volume). Surprisingly, though, most of this research has focused on the pedagogical applications of modeling as opposed to how it can be used for performance enhancement. Research within music education classes has found, as with research with sport skills, that modeling creates greater performance improvements than does verbal instructions alone (e.g., Dickey, 1991). In addition, self-observation videos, with or without instructor feedback, have been used to improve technical skills of beginning conductors (e.g., Yarbrough, Wapnick, & Kelly, 1979). Expert models are also advocated as a method for increasing prospective music teachers' knowledge and interest in becoming music educators (Gonzo & Forsythe, 1976). Readers are directed to Haston's (2007) paper, wherein he offers several practical guidelines for using modeling within music education.

Similarly, modeling research within dance has focused on how best to provide modeling experiences in a teaching context. Radell, Adame, and Cole (2003) found that college students who were beginners in a ballet class showed greater skill acquisition when they were in a room without mirrors than with mirrors. Qualitative research exploring how girls in a dance school perceived modeling revealed that they experienced both positive and negative feelings from observing themselves and others, and indicated that often viewing their performances on video exacerbated any negative feelings they had about their performance. The girls in this study indicated a preference for completing evaluations of their dance on a one-to-one basis or by conducting self-evaluations from video privately (Cassady, Clarke, & Latham, 2004). It must certainly be recognized that it takes many individuals some adaptation time to get used to watching themselves and to focus on the appropriate cues as opposed to clothing, hair, and other personal attributes. It certainly appears as though the performing arts are one context in which the cognitive, affective, and behavioral responses to modeling could be further explored, given the counterintuitive findings presented here.

Medicine

Wulf, Shea, and Lewthwaite (2010) cite observational learning as one of four factors that are proven to improve motor learning and that have applications to the field of medicine. Indeed, modeling techniques appear to be quite prevalent within the medical literature and target skill development for students and certified practitioners, as well as being advocated as a method for improving patient education.

Several studies promote the use of role modeling, mentorship, preceptorship, and job shadowing as part of the learning process for nursing and medical students. Although a variety of terms are used to describe these experiences, they all involve some aspect of modeling, typically of an established professional (i.e., expert model). Studies have demonstrated that nursing students develop improved communication and negotiation skills through preceptor relationships (Clayton, Broome, & Ellis, 1989) and shadowing experiences (Eddy & Schermer, 1999). Medical students report similar benefits. For example, pediatric residents report learning "how to talk" and "how to think things through" from observing their preceptors (Balmer, Serwint, Ruzek, Ludwig, & Giardino, 2007).

Modeling has also been used within the medical field to enhance professional development opportunities for practicing clinicians. Interviews with both established and aspiring physician-leaders within medical centers reveal that role modeling is perceived as a key element in helping them to progress in their careers, particularly when it is available as a series of short, focused observations with various skilled physician-leaders (Taylor, Taylor, & Stoller, 2009). As well, video posting sites, such as YouTube, contain videos demonstrating treatment skills that practicing physiotherapists can use as a reference (PT in Motion, 2010). Although some of these videos may be posted by instructors or associations for ongoing skill training, others have not necessarily been evaluated in terms of their accuracy. As mentioned previously, technological advances create a need for research related to how learners will access modeled information and program evaluation for its effectiveness, a point we will shortly return to in more depth.

Video-based modeling is also used to develop specific surgical skills and provide additional exposure to techniques, as the opportunity for physically practicing many techniques is often limited in medical programs. Research examining the effect of expert models has found that modeling plus physical practice is superior to a control condition for teaching suture skills (Custers, Regehr, McCulloch, Peniston, & Reznick, 1999). Web-based modeling has also shown promise as a method of increasing residents' technical skills and confidence (Woo et al.,

2009). Further, Hamad, Brown, and Clavijo-Alvarez (2007) found that surgical residents who experienced self-observation via video debriefing with an experienced surgeon after completing laparoscopic surgery were less likely to commit technical errors resulting in adverse events. Clearly, modeling experiences have great potential for enhancing learning among this population.

Health Behavior Change

Although not explicitly referred to as modeling, many mass media campaigns use models to deliver their messages. Often, these are celebrities designed to act as a role model or someone viewers will consider to be similar to them (i.e., a coping model). For example, Canada's recent ParticipACTION campaign includes a series of public service announcements featuring popular media figures and "ordinary Canadians" sharing their strategies for engaging in regular physical activity (ParticipACTION, n.d.). Aside from physical activity promotion, modeling has been used as a strategy to promote a wide range of personal safety and health behaviors. For example, researchers have found that viewing a videotape of multiple models using personal protective equipment had a positive influence on new worker's use of the same protective equipment (Olson, Grosshuesch, Schmidt, Gray, & Wipfli, 2009).

Other studies have examined the effect of models, presented via mass media campaigns, on social physique anxiety. Berry and Howe (2004) found that undergraduate students exposed to health-based advertising showed decreases in their level of social physique anxiety, while, contrary to their hypotheses, students exposed to appearance-based advertising showed no significant increase in social physique anxiety. The influence of modeling on perceptions of the physique is also apparent among young men. Blond's (2008) literature review, based on a sample of 15 studies on this topic, found that exposure to images of the "ideal body" had a small and significant negative impact on men's body dissatisfaction. These findings certainly have implications for the use of modeling within advertising, as well as in health promotional material, particularly for children and adolescents. Taken together, the exercise psychology literature that may be linked to "modeling" experiences demonstrates the key role of both model and learner (or exerciser) characteristics in the success of the intervention for producing change in cognitions, affect, and behavior. Again, this draws a clear parallel to findings within

the motor learning domain and suggests that greater cross-discipline considerations between exercise and sport psychology may be helpful for advancing research in both areas.

Considerable research has also examined the influence of modeling on eating behaviors. As part of an eating disorders prevention program, Withers and Wertheim (2004) provided adolescent girls with a video of a female who was considered a recovering anorexic and was a spokesperson for a national Anorexia and Bulimia Foundation (i.e., a peer-expert model). The model provided information on determinants of body size, media influences on perceptions of the ideal body, the negative effects of extreme dieting, and suggestions for maintaining a positive body image. Girls who watched the video reported more positive body image and higher levels of knowledge compared to a control group. Research examining eating behavior has found that young females have a tendency to eat more when exposed to a high food-intake peer compared to a low food-intake peer (Hermans, Engels, Larsen, & Herman, 2009). Surprisingly, these findings were apparent only when the model and observer did not interact; there were no differences in food intake when the model and observer were engaged in social interaction.

Another example of a unique use of modeling involves the use of radio role models for prevention of mother–child transmission of HIV (Sebert Kuhlmann et al., 2008). Sebert Kuhlmann et al. examined the effects of the MARCH strategy drama, which is a radio serial drama that airs in a series of 250 episodes, each lasting 15 minutes. Episodes were written by citizens of Botswana and aimed to reinforce methods for avoiding HIV infection and transmission. Using survey data, they found that pregnant women who identified with women in the serial drama (i.e., named one as their favorite character) were almost twice as likely to be testing for HIV as those who did not. This illustrates the potential power of other forms of models, aside from purely video-based modeling. In fact, in our next section, we highlight the idea of other role model influences.

The emphasis of this section of the chapter related to the many domains in which modeling have been used. The use of the modeling was not always the main emphasis of the research, but rather was often embedded within a larger intervention. This fact is important to highlight as our understanding of the efficacy of modeling will only emerge when we can isolate its contributions within these varied research paradigms. This point is also evident in the next section, which explores the use of role models.

Role Models in Sport and Other Domains

The impact of role models on medical students, music performers, or in relation to entrepreneurial skills, negotiation skills, and career aspirations, to name a few, can be found in the psychology literature. Within the sport domain there are numerous writings about the influence of sport role models, but empirical research is far less available. The idea that role models can have a positive impact on behavior is widespread, and many programs use role modeling as a basis for interventions or programs (Payne, Reynolds, Brown, & Fleming, 2002). Further, Payne et al. also noted that many of these programs lack an assessment component and therefore have little data to support the assumed claims; this leaves an obvious area for empirical research related to the influences of role models on behavior. Regardless, in this section, we will review studies related to who can act as role models and possible theoretical approaches to understand potential influences of these role models on behavior change, with an emphasis on sport and physical activity.

Many individuals may serve as role models. Family members and teachers are a prime source, especially during the early years, and then peers also become important. Research (e.g., Babkes & Weiss, 1999; Brustad, 1983) has shown that parents who are positive exercise role models and are more positive about their child's competency are more likely to have children who have higher perceived competence, enjoyment, and satisfaction. Teachers can also be important role models. Thomson (1996) showed students a video of an apparently fit teacher delivering fitness and diet guidelines. A different group was shown the same information in a video, but this time the same person was wearing a body suit beneath his clothing, making him look heavier. Students scored significantly higher on a knowledge test after viewing the fit instructor, suggesting that a fit instructor acted as a more appropriate role model. In other research (e.g., Cardinal & Cardinal, 2002), physical education majors had more positive attitudes toward the importance of role modeling behaviors for physical activity than did other students.

An area with more empirical research on the influence of modeling and role models is that of aggressive behavior. According to Bandura (1973), aggressive behaviors are primarily acquired through modeling and vicarious processes. Smith (1978)

conducted studies on aggressive behaviors in ice hockey over a numbers of years and found that most youth learned their aggressive behaviors from watching professionals. Mugno and Feltz (1985) found similar results in youth football players. Along similar lines, Weiss, Kipp, and Goodman (2010) recently determined that youth hockey player role models from the National Hockey League (NHL) could be classified as aggressive/hard-working or gentlemanly/skilled. Those youth players who perceived aggressive acts to be more legitimate were more likely to have aggressive role models than were those who perceived these unsportsmanlike behaviors as less legitimate.

In terms of theoretical frameworks, Payne et al. (2002) identified a number of theoretical perspectives that might have an impact on the role model question. They, of course, noted the primary importance of Bandura's (1986) social cognitive theory, as well as self-efficacy theory. They also suggested frameworks such as Haney's (1997) work on mentorship, in addition to the transtheoretical model of behavior change (Prochaska & Marcus, 1994), and the theory of planned behavior (Azjen, 1985) with regard to the impact of role models on physical activity behaviors. There is no doubt that some of the conceptual or theoretical approaches to observational learning are directly related to role modeling. We suggest that it may be useful to try to bring these literatures under one theoretical umbrella in an attempt to provide a parsimonious approach to similar behaviors. In terms of role modeling, it might well be a cautious interpretation to suggest "what they see, may be what you get" and to recognize that role models may not always be positive.

Technology and Advances in Observing

As with other techniques for teaching skills and conveying information, the "face" of modeling has been greatly influenced by advances in technology. In this section, we review how technology has shaped the use of modeling, as well as its impact on our understanding of "what" we learn through modeling. We also highlight some of the ways in which modeling is paired with other technologies to create learning experiences. Finally, we provide some cautionary notes regarding the use of video modeling.

Early modeling studies that strived to manipulate film-based demonstrations were largely limited by the cost and availability of technology and relied mainly on manually cutting and pasting film loops and modifying the projector speed to create slow-motion demonstrations (e.g., Priebe & Burton, 1939). This also limited the model types used to those categories of "other" models and made self-as-a-model techniques impractical. With advances in video technology and the inclusion of video editing programs, such as Windows Movie Maker and iDVD, preinstalled on laptops and desktop computers, modeling has progressed to a point at which it is quick and easy for researchers, coaches, mental training consultants, or the athletes themselves to create, edit, and manipulate modeling displays.

With this widespread availability of digital videotaping, editing technology, and ease of transporting this technology into the field, the use of video feedback is now advocated within both coaching (Chighisola, 1989; Sawicki, 2009) and sport psychology consulting (Halliwell, 1990; Ives, Straub, & Shelley, 2002) practices. Indeed, highlight videos are promoted as a way of enhancing athletes' competitive performance (Halliwell, 1990; Leavitt, Young, & Connelly, 1989; Templin & Vernacchia, 1995). Walsh (1997) provided a unique example of video-based modeling by filming the athlete's performance through a camera mounted on the athlete and then having the coach and athlete collaboratively review the video to assess performance and decision-making. This results in a unique self-observation experience for the athlete, as well as a means for fostering communication within the coach–athlete relationship.

Research examining the use of video-based modeling has moved beyond being used solely to teach and refine sport skills and is also employed to modify coaching behaviors (More & Franks, 1996). Coaching education has also been influenced by the easy availability of the internet. One example of this is an online training course to educate youth sport coaches about concussion prevention and management. Coaches who received an interactive online format for the course, with information provided by high-status models, showed greater increases in their knowledge about concussions and self-efficacy for preventing and managing concussions among their athletes compared to a control group who received no concussion training (Glang, Koester, Beaver, Clay, & McLaughlin, 2010). The effectiveness of this program, however, was not evaluated in terms of whether coaches changed their behavior following the program or its effectiveness in relation to a traditional classroom-based program. Other modeling approaches using the internet include having business students interact with professional role models in an online video and videoconferencing forum (Robertson & Collins, 2003) and having students seek out online media clips (i.e., online models) to illustrate management concepts discussed in class (Tyler, Anderson, & Tyler, 2009).

Aside from its extensive use in applied sport settings, advances in technology have also helped to shed light upon the attentional, perceptual, and neurophysiological processes involved in modeling. As examples, functional magnetic resonance imaging (fMRI) technology can be used to examine which areas of the brain are activated during observation and action, and the use of point-light displays have been instrumental in helping researchers to uncover what we attend to when observing a demonstration. Researchers using this technology have demonstrated that we can acquire novel motor skills from observing biological motion, and it has helped to identify the specific aspects of movement to which the learner attends (Hodges et al., 2007).

Technology has also advanced how demonstrations are presented and manipulated, specifically through the addition of animated and interactive models and online observational learning opportunities. Wouters and colleagues (2007, 2009, 2010) have examined how creating an interactive modeling experience using animated models influences learning of problem-solving skills. Drawing upon social cognitive theory (Bandura, 1986), Zimmerman's framework for self-regulation (Schunk & Zimmerman, 1997; Zimmerman & Kitsantas, 2002), and Kennedy's model of interactivity (2004), Wouters et al. (2007, 2009, 2010) created a video-based modeling experience wherein the learner interacted with an animated character giving the demonstration. The character provided feedback and learning prompts to the learner, and the choices the learner made influenced the way in which the demonstration continued. Although research in this area is in its infancy, early studies show that animated models can be effective for learning; however, the modality of instructions (verbal vs. written; Wouters et al., 2009) and observer's illusion of control over the stimuli (Wouters et al., 2010) influenced performance on transfer tasks.

Modeling has also moved into the virtual reality world. In a recent set of three experiments, Fox and Bailenson (2009) relied on previous work that determined the importance of model similarity for maximal modeling effects. Using a technique they labeled *immersive virtual environment technology*, they used an individual's own photograph to create a model remarkably similar to the person that could be rewarded and punished for various behaviors. They found that watching one's virtual self led to more exercise behavior than did watching virtual others. With such advanced techniques, it is relatively easy to create feedforward conditions, wherein individuals can see themselves performing behaviors they have not yet achieved.

It is clear that advances in technology are reflected in innovative methods for studying modeling. Murphy (2009) suggests that video and computer games provide a new arena for examining sport and exercise psychology theories and interventions. For example, within the online realm, adults who engage in online gaming and whose self-identity is strongly tied to their online video game avatars make judgments about their own bodies based upon the physique of their avatars, suggesting that there is some assimilation in self-identity between the individual and his or her avatar (Chandler, Konrath, & Schwarz, 2009). There are certainly possibilities for applied research with the development of interactive game technologies such as the Nintendo Wii, Playstation MOVE, and Xbox Kinect. All of these game systems offer new forms of physical feedback to the players, often in combination with onscreen avatar activity. These new modes of feedback could certainly influence new questions regarding KR and KP. As Murphy points out, however, researchers in other fields who study serious games (i.e., video and computer games, or digital game-based learning) examine the same topics as those studied by sport and exercise psychologists, including motivation, teamwork, leadership, psychological skills, and skill transfer (Lieberman, 2006). As we have suggested for other topics related to observational learning, enhanced communication between these fields may lead to a greater understanding of digital game-based learning methods, as well as psychological concepts.

Although the technology for recording, editing, and viewing the performances of ourselves and others is constantly evolving and can be used to facilitate a plethora of positive outcomes, the use of this technology does not come without concerns that researchers, coaches, and consultants should consider. In their review of digital video uses in consulting, Ives et al. (2002) remind coaches and consultants to be cognizant of the privacy and ethical concerns related to the use of videotaping athletes. Specifically, they highlight the need to ensure privacy of athlete videos and to protect against videos being used for other purposes (i.e., video can be edited to misrepresent a situation). Given the ease with which video can be edited, a situation captured for consulting purposes could be taken out of context. Certainly, access to and ownership of the videotaped footage must be clear so that it does not become a concern for athletes or parents of young athletes.

In addition to protecting the trust and rights of the athletes, researchers and practitioners should also consider the potential psychological effects on the learner, particularly unintended effects. This may be of particular concern when developing and evaluating the efficacy of interventions based upon modeling. Children and adults who show strong connections to television and online media may interpret the information presented differently than would those with a weaker affiliation. Research examining college students' attitudes and beliefs regarding their peers' sexual behavior has shown that students who perceive television content as realistic are more likely to report more permissive attitudes toward sexual behavior after viewing sexual television content than do college students who rated television as unrealistic (Taylor, 2005).

Taken together, these above studies suggest that not only is model–observer similarity an important determinant of modeling effects, but that the observer's perceptions of the accuracy of the situation portrayed may also be a powerful influence. Thus, researchers should be aware of the importance of not only the words and actions shown in video, but also the entire set of model and situation characteristics and how much the viewer can relate to them. In fact, qualitative research examining observers' perceptions of the effectiveness of television mass media campaigns targeting healthy eating identified role modeling as one of the least often used strategies in the selected ad campaigns, yet participants reported that being able to relate to the model was one of the most important factors influencing the effectiveness of these campaigns (Dale & Hanbury, 2010).

The findings summarized highlight the need for researchers to consider what is being modeled (intentionally or unintentionally) and to gain insight into the athletes' perceptions of the demonstration in order to ensure that technology is being used to benefit the athlete and to reduce unintended negative consequences. Although this chapter has focused primarily on positive behavior change, there is no doubt that seeing the wrong thing may lead to doing the wrong thing.

Conclusion

The variety, quality, and depth of research described in this chapter establishes the critical importance of modeling on the acquisition and performance of skills. Moreover, we hope we have opened the reader's eyes to the varied situations in which observational learning or modeling plays a role. Certainly, one of the messages of this chapter has been to highlight how observational learning is often overlooked and not given credit in experimental paradigms that actually include modeling as a component (e.g., a recent study by Tracey [2011] examined the influence of a personal motivation video on a variety of psychological skills but did not cite the self-modeling research). Readers of the applied sport psychology literature are encouraged to closely examine the possible contributions of modeling in all intervention research.

A further implication of this work is for practitioners who come from a wide array of settings. We encourage them to be aware of the various factors that influence the efficacy of observational practice and to understand that a variety of approaches are available to use when implementing this form of practice. Practitioners do not only need to use skilled models, but can also rely on peer learning models, coping models, and self-as-a-model techniques, to name a few. They should also consider the characteristics of the learner, understanding such factors as the learner's perspective and stage of learning. In addition, although practitioners readily consider the use of modeling for the modification of physical performance, its use for strategy, regulation of arousal states, and other psychological influences should also be considered. The functions of observational learning are broader than what seems to be currently put into practice.

The final set of implications applies to those interested in pursuing research on observational learning. It is evident that a large number of research questions remain unanswered. A better understanding of the factors associated with the equivocal findings in research related to model type is one such example. Also necessary are research paradigms that allow researchers to disentangle the contributions of observation versus other aspects of the research design; such examples include video-based interventions that combine both factual information and modeling, or imagery interventions that include modeling as a component, in addition to the research related to role models. In fact, a number of studies were not included in this review due to the difficulty associated with clearly identifying the contributions of modeling in the intervention. Continued research in the domain of observational learning is necessary to provide a clearer picture to practitioners. After all, we know "that a picture is worth a thousand words".

Acknowledgments

We would like to acknowledge the assistance of Angelica M. Villalpando from CSU East Bay and Nadine Steenhoek from Nipissing University for their assistance in gathering references for this chapter.

References

Adams, J. A. (1971). A closed loop theory of motor learning. *Journal of Motor Behavior, 3,* 111–150.

Adams, J. A. (1986). The use of the model's knowledge of results to increase the observer's performance. *Journal of Human Movement Studies, 12,* 89–98.

Allison, P. C. (1987). What and how preservice physical education teachers observe during an early field experience. *Research Quarterly for Exercise and Sport, 58*(3), 242–249.

Allport, F. H. (1924). *Social psychology.* Boston: Houghton Mifflin Company.

Ashford, D., Bennett, S. J., & Davids, K. (2006). Observational modeling effects for movement dynamics and movement outcome measures across differing task constraints: A meta-analysis. *Journal of Motor Behavior, 38*(3), 185–205.

Associated Press. (2006, June 16). *Rockies using video Ipods to study swings, hitters.* Retrieved from http://espn.go.com/mlb/news/story?id+2486924

Azjen, I. (1985). From intentions to actions: A theory of planned behavior. In J. Kuhl & J. Beckmann (Eds.), *Springer series in social psychology* (pp. 11–39). Berlin: Springer.

Babkes, M. L., & Weiss, M. R. (1999). Parental influence on children's cognitive and affective responses to competitive soccer participation. *Pediatric Exercise Science, 11,* 44–62

Balf, T. (1996). Think like a winner. *Self, 18,* 116–119.

Balmer, D., Serwint, J. R., Ruzek, S. B., Ludwig, S., & Giardino, A. P. (2007). Learning behind the scenes: Perceptions and observations of role modeling in pediatric residents' continuity experience. *Ambulatory Pediatrics, 7*(2), 176–181.

Bandura, A. (1965). Vicarious processes: A case of no-trial learning. *Advances in Experimental Social Psychology, 2,* 1–55.

Bandura, A. (1969). *Principles of behavior modification.* New York: Holt, Reinhart, & Winston.

Bandura, A. (1971). Analysis of modeling processes. In A. Bandura (Ed.), *Psychological modeling: Conflicting theories* (pp.1–62). Chicago: Adline-Atherton.

Bandura, A. (1973). *Aggression: A social learning analysis.* Englewood Cliffs, NJ: Prentice Hall.

Bandura, A. (1977). Self-efficacy: Toward a unifying theory of behavioral change. *Psychological Review, 84,* 191–215.

Bandura, A. (1986). *Social foundations of thought and action: A social cognitive theory.* Englewood Cliffs, NJ: Prentice-Hall.

Bandura, A. (1991). Human agency: The rhetoric and the reality. *American Psychologist, 46*(2), 157–162.

Bandura, A. (1997). *Self-efficacy: The exercise of control.* New York: Freeman.

Barker, J. B., & Jones, M. V. (2006). Using hypnosis, technique refinement, and self modeling to enhance self-efficacy: A case study in cricket. *The Sport Psychologist, 20,* 94–110.

Barry, T.R., & Howe, B.L. (2004). Effects of health-based and appearance-based exercise advertising on exercise attitudes, social physique anxiety and self-presentation in and exercise setting. *Social Behavior and Personality, 32,* 1–12.

Berlant, A. R., & Weiss, M. R. (1997). Goal orientation and the modeling process: An individual's focus on form and outcome. *Research Quarterly for Exercise and Sport, 68*(4), 317–330.

Blandin, Y., Proteau, L., & Alain, C. (1994). On the cognitive processes underlying contextual interference and observational learning. *Journal of Motor Behavior, 26*(1), 18–26.

Bläsing, B., Puttke, M., & Schack, T. (2010). *The neurocognition of dance: Mind, movement and motor skills.* New York: Psychology Press.

Blond, A. (2008). Impact of exposure to images of ideal bodies on male body dissatisfaction: A review. *Body Image, 5*(3), 244–250.

Boyer, B. L. (1987). *Using the self-as-a-model with video editing in athletic performance.* Unpublished master's thesis, University of the Pacific, Stockton, CA.

Bradley, R. D. (1993). *The use of goal-setting and positive self-modeling to enhance self-efficacy and performance for the basketball free throw.* Unpublished doctoral dissertation, University of Maryland, College Park.

Bray, M. A., & Kehle, T. J. (1996). Self-modeling as an intervention of stuttering. *School Psychology Review, 25,* 358–369.

Breslin, G., Hodges, N. J., Williams, A. M, Kremer, J., & Curran, W. (2005). Modelling relative motion to facilitate intra-limb coordination. *Human Movement Science, 24,* 446–463.

Breslin, G., Hodges, N. J., Williams, A. M, Kremer, J., & Curran, W. (2006). A comparison of intra- and inter-limb relative motion information in modeling a novel motor skill. *Human Movement Science, 25,* 753–766.

Brustad, R. J. (1983). Who will go out and play? Parental and psychological influences on children's attraction to physical activity. *Journal of Sport and Exercise Psychology, 14,* 59–77.

Buccino, G., & Riggio, L. (2006). The role of the mirror neuron system in motor learning. *Kinesiology, 38,* 5–15.

Buggey, T. (2009). *Seeing is believing: Video self-modeling for people with autism and developmental disabilities.* Downsview, ON: Woodbine House via Monarch Books of Canada.

Cardinal, B. J., & Cardinal, M. K. (2002). Role modeling attitudes and physical activity and fitness promoting behaviors of prospective physical education specialists and non specialists. *Journal of the International Council for Health, 38*(3), 22–26.

Cassady, H., Clarke, G., & Latham, A. M. (2004). Experiencing evaluation: A case of study of girls' dance. *Physical Education and Sport Pedagogy, 9*(1), 23–36.

Chandler, J., Konrath, S., & Schwarz, N. (2009). Online and on my mind: Temporary and chronic accessibility moderate the influence of media figures. *Media Psychology, 12,* 210–226.

Chighisola, D. A. (1989). Coaching with video tape. *Scholastic Coach, 58*(8), 76–77, 110.

Clare, S. K., Jenson, W. R., Kehle, T. J., & Bray, M. A. (2000). Self-modeling as a treatment for increasing on-task behavior. *Psychology in the Schools, 37*(6), 517–522.

Clark, S. E., & Ste-Marie, D. M. (2002). Peer mastery versus peer coping models: Model type has different effects on psychological and physical performance measures. *Journal of Human Movement Studies, 43,* 179–186.

Clark, S. E., & Ste-Marie, D. M. (2007). The impact of self-as-a-model interventions on children's self regulation of learning and swimming performance. *Journal of Sports Sciences, 25*(5), 557–586.

Clayton, G., Broome, M., & Ellis, L. (1989). Relationship between a preceptorship experience and role socialization of graduate nurses. *Journal of Nursing Education, 28,* 72–75.

Cumming, J., Clark, S. E., Ste-Marie, D. M., McCullagh, P., & Hall, C. (2005). The functions of observational learning questionnaire (FOLQ). *Psychology of Sport and Exercise, 6,* 517–537.

Custers, E. J. F. M., Regehr, G., McCulloch, W., Peniston, C., & Reznick, R. (1999). The effects of modeling on learning a simple surgical procedure: See one, do one or see many, do one? *Advances in Health Science Education, 4,* 123–143.

Dale, R., & Hanbury, A. (2010). A simple methodology for piloting and evaluating mass media interventions: An exploratory study. *Psychology, Health and Medicine, 15*(2), 231–242.

d'Arripe-Longueville, F., Gernigon, C., Huet, M., Cadopi, M., & Winnykamen, F. (2002a). Peer tutoring in a physical education setting: Influence of tutor skill level on novice learners' motivation and performance. *Journal of Teaching in Physical Education, 22,* 105–123.

d'Arripe-Longueville, F., Gernigon, C., Huet, M., Winnykamen, & Cadopi, M. (2002b). Peer-assisted learning in the physical activity domain: Dyad type and gender differences. *Journal of Sport and Exercise Psychology, 24,* 219–238.

Dickey, M. R. (1991). A comparison of verbal instruction and nonverbal teacher-student modeling in instrumental ensembles. *Journal of Research in Music Education, 39*(2), 132–142.

di Pellegrino, G., Fadiga, L., Fogassi, L., Gallese, V., & Rizzolatti, G. (1992). Understanding motor events: A neurophysiological study. *Experimental Brain Research, 91,* 176–180.

Dowrick, P. W. (1999). A review of self modeling and related inventions. *Applied and Preventive Psychology, 8,* 23–39.

Dowrick, P. W., & Dove, C. (1980). The use of self-modeling to improve the performance of spina bifida children. *Journal of Applied Behavior Analysis, 13,* 51–56.

Eddy, M. E., & Schermer, J. (1999). Shadowing: A strategy to strengthen the negotiating style of baccalaureate nursing students. *Journal of Nursing Education, 38*(8), 364–367.

Ellis, S., Ganzach, Y., Castle, E., & Sekely, G. (2010). The effect of filmed versus personal after-event reviews on task performances: The mediating and moderating role of self-efficacy. *Journal of Applied Psychology, 95*(1), 122–131.

Ellwood, C. A. (1917). *An introduction to social psychology.* New York: D. Appleton & Company.

Feltz, D. L., Landers, D. M., & Raeder, U. (1979). Enhancing self-efficacy in high avoidance motor tasks: A comparison of modeling techniques. *Journal of Sport Psychology, 1,* 112–122.

Flint, F. A. (1993). The psychological effects of modeling in athletic injury rehabilitation. In D. Pargman (Ed.), *Psychological bases of sport injuries* (pp. 221–234). Morgantown, WV: Fitness Information Technology.

Fox, H., & Bailenson, J. N. (2009). Virtual self-modeling: The effects of vicarious reinforcement and identification on exercise behaviors. *Media Psychology, 12,* 1–25.

Franks, J. M., & Maile, L. J. (1991). The use of video in sport skill acquisition. In P. W. Dowrick (Ed.), *Practical guide to using video in the behavioral sciences* (pp. 231–243). Toronto, ON: John Wiley & Sons.

Fukkink, R. G. (2008). Video feedback in widescreen: A meta-analysis of family programs. *Clinical Psychology Review, 28*, 904–916.

Gena, A., Couloura, S., & Kymissis, E. (2005). Modifying the affective behavior of preschoolers with autism using in-vivo or video modeling and reinforcement contingencies. *Journal of Autism and Developmental Disorders, 35*(5). doi:10.1007/s10303-005-0014-9

George, T. R., Feltz, D. L., & Chase, M. A. (1992). Effects of model similarity on self efficacy and muscular endurance: A second look. *Journal of Sport and Exercise Psychology, 14*, 237–248.

Gerwitz, J. L., & Stingle, K. C. (1968). The learning of generalized imitation as the basis for identification. *Psychological Review, 75*, 374–397.

Gibson, J. J. (1979). *The Ecological approach to visual perception.* Boston: Houghton Mifflin.

Glang, A., Koester, M. C., Beaver, S., Clay, J., & McLaughlin, K. (2010). Online training in sports concussion for youth sport coaches. *International Journal of Sports Science and Coaching, 5*(1), 1–12.

Gonzo, C., & Forsythe, J. (1976). Developing and using videotapes to teach rehearsal techniques and principles. *Journal of Research in Music Education, 24*(1), 23–41.

Gould, D. R., & Weiss, M. R. (1981). The effects of model similarity and model talk on self-efficacy and muscular endurance. *Journal of Sport Psychology, 3*, 17–29.

Granado, C., & Wulf, G. (2007). Enhancing motor learning through dyad practice contributions of observation and dialogue. *Research Quarterly for Exercise and Sport, 78*(3), 197–203.

Greer, R. D., Dudek-Singer, J., & Gautreaux, G. (2006). Observational learning. *International Journal of Psychology, 41*(6), 486–499.

Hall, C. R., Mack, D., Paivio, A., & Hausenblas, H. A. (1998). Imagery use by athletes: Development of the sport imagery questionnaire. *International Journal of Sport Psychology, 29*(1), 73–89.

Hall, C. R., Munroe-Chandler, K. J., Cumming, J., Law, B., Ramsey, R., & Murphy, L. (2009). Imagery and observational learning and their relationship to sport confidence. *Journal of Sports Sciences, 27*(4), 327–337.

Halliwell, W. (1990). Providing sport psychology consulting services in professional hockey. *The Sport Psychologist, 4*, 369–377.

Hamad, G. G., Brown, M. T., & Clavijo-Alvarez, J. O. (2007). Postoperative video debriefing reduces technical errors in laparoscopic surgery. *The American Journal of Surgery, 194*, 110–114.

Haney, A. (1997). The role of mentorship in the workplace. In M. C. Taylor (Ed.), *Workplace education* (pp. 211–228). Toronto, ON: Culture Concepts.

Hars, M., & Calmels, C. (2007). Observation of elite gymnastic performance: Processes and perceived functions of observation. *Psychology of Sport and Exercise, 8*, 337–354.

Haston, W. (2007). Teacher modeling as an effective teaching strategy. *Music Educators Journal, 93*(1), 26–30.

Hayes, S. J., Hodges, N. J., Horn, R. R., & Williams, A. (2007). The efficacy of demonstrations in teaching children and unfamiliar movement skill: The effects of object-oriented actions and point light demonstrations. *Journal of Sports Sciences, 25*(5), 559–575.

Herbert, E. P., & Landin, D. (1994). Effects of a learning model and augmented feedback in tennis skill acquisition. *Research Quarterly for Exercise and Sport, 55*, 24–31.

Hermans, R. C. J., Engels, R. C. M. E., Larsen, J. K., & Herman, C. P. (2009). Modeling of palatable food intake. The influence of quality of social interaction. *Appetite, 52*, 801–804.

Hitchcock, C. H., Dowrick, P. W., & Prater, M. A. (2003). Video self-modeling intervention in school-based settings: A review. *Remedial and Special Education, 24*(1), 36–45, 56.

Hodges, N. J., Hayes, S. J., Breslin, G., & Williams, A. M. (2005). An evaluation of the minimal constraining information during movement observation and reproduction. *Acta Psychologica, 119*, 264–282.

Hodges, N. J., Williams, A. M., Hayes, S. J., & Breslin, G. (2007). What is modelled during observational learning? *Journal of Sports Sciences, 25*(5), 531–545.

Holt, E. B. (1931). *Animal drive and the learning process.* New York: Holt.

Horn, R. R., Williams, A. M., Hayes, S. J., Hodges, N. J., & Scott, M. A. (2007). Demonstration as a rate enhancer to changes in coordination during early skill acquisition. *Journal of Sports Sciences, 25*, 559–575.

Ives, J. C., Straub, W. F., & Shelley, G. A. (2002). Enhancing athletic performance using digital video in consulting. *Journal of Applied Sport Psychology, 14*, 237–245.

Janelle, C. M., Champenoy, J. D., Coombes, S. A., & Mousseau, M. B. (2003). Mechanisms of attentional cueing during observational learning to facilitate motor skill acquisition. *Journal of Sports Science, 21*, 825–838.

Johansson, G. (1973). Visual perception of biological motion and a model for its analysis. *Perception and Psychophysics, 14*, 201–211.

Kehle, T. J., Clark, E., Jenson, W. R., & Wampold, B. E. (1986). Effectiveness of self observation with behavior disordered elementary school children. *School Psychology Review, 19*, 115–122.

Kehle, T. J., Madaus, M. M., Baratta, V. S., & Bray, M. A. (1998). Augmented self modeling as a treatment for children with selective mutism. *Journal of School Psychology, 36*, 377–399.

Kempster, S. (2009). Observing the invisible: Examining the role of observational learning in the development of leadership practice. *Journal of Management Development, 28*(5), 439–456.

Kennedy, G. E. (2004). Promoting cognition in multimedia interactivity research. *Journal of Interactive Learning Research, 15*, 43–61.

King, G. (2009). A framework of personal and environmental learning-based strategies to foster therapist expertise. *Learning in Health and Social Care, 8*(3), 185–199. doi:10.1111/j.1473-6861.2008.00210.x

Kirschenbaum, D. S. (1984). Self-regulation and sport psychology: Nurturing an emerging symbiosis. *Journal of Sport Psychology, 6*, 159–183.

Kitsantas, A., Zimmerman, B. J., & Cleary, T. (2000). The role of observation and emulation in the development of athletic self-regulation. *Journal of Educational Psychology, 92*(4), 811–817.

Kohl, R. M., & Shea, C. H. (1992). Observational learning: Influences on temporal response organization. *Human Performances, 5*(3), 235–244.

Law, B., & Hall, C. (2009a). The relationships among skill level, age, and golfers' observational learning use. *The Sport Psychologist, 23,* 42–58.

Law, B., & Hall, C. (2009b). Observational learning use and self-efficacy beliefs in adult sport novices. *Psychology of Sport and Exercise, 10,* 263–270.

Law, B., & Ste-Marie, D. M. (2005). Effects of self-modeling on figure skating jump performance and psychological variables. *European Journal of Sport Science, 5*(3), 143–152.

Leavitt, J., Young, J., & Connelly, D. (1989). The effects of videotape highlights on state self-confidence. *Journal of Applied Research in Coaching and Athletics, 4,* 225–232.

Lee, T. D., Swinnen, S. P., & Serrien, D. J. (1994). Cognitive effort and motor learning. *Quest, 46,* 328–344.

Legrain, P., d'Arripe-Longueville, F., & Gernigon, C. (2003a). Peer tutoring in a sport setting: Are there any benefits for tutors? *The Sport Psychologist, 17,* 77–94.

Legrain, P., d'Arripe-Longueville, F., & Gernigon, C. (2003b). The influence of trained peer tutoring on tutors' motivation and performance in a French boxing setting. *Journal of Sports Sciences, 21,* 539–550.

Lewis, S. (1974). A comparison of behavior therapy techniques in the reduction of fearful avoidance behavior. *Behavior Therapy, 5,* 648–655.

Lieberman, D. A. (2006). What can we learn from playing interactive video games? In P. Vorderer & J. Bryant (Eds.), *Playing video games: Motives, responses, and consequences* (pp. 379–397). Mahwah, NJ: Lawrence Erlbaum Associates.

Little, W. S., & McCullagh, P. (1989). Motivation orientation and modeled instruction strategies: The effects on form and accuracy. *Journal of Sport and Exercise Psychology, 11,* 41–53.

Livermore, B. (1996 July/August). Mind games. *Women's Sport and Fitness, 18,* 77–78.

Lysklett, O. B., Whiting, J., & Hoff, I. (2001). Observational learning of motor skills. *Corpus, Psyche Et Ecoietas, 8*(1–2), 1–22.

Maddison, R., Prapavessis, H., & Clatworthy, M. (2006). Modeling and rehabilitation following anterior cruciate ligament reconstruction. *Annals of Behavioral Medicine, 31*(1), 89–98.

Maile, L. (1985). *Self-modeling and power lifting: A new look at peak performance.* Unpublished master's thesis. University of Alaska, Anchorage.

Martens, R., Burwitz, L., & Zuckerman, J. (1976). Modeling effects on motor performance. *Research Quarterly, 47,* 277–291.

Martin, K. A., Moritz, S. E., & Hall, C. R. (1999). Imagery use in sport: A literature review and applied model. *The Sport Psychologist, 13,* 245–268.

McAuley, E. (1985). Modeling and self-efficacy: A test of Bandura's model. *Journal of Sport Psychology, 7,* 283–295.

McCullagh, P. (1983). Modeling: Learning, developmental and social-psychological considerations. In R. N. Singer, M. Murphey, & L. K. Tennant (Eds.), *Handbook of research on sport psychology* (pp. 106–125). New York: Macmillan.

McCullagh, P., & Caird, J. K. (1990). Correct and learning models and the use of model knowledge of results in the acquisition and retention of a motor skill. *Journal of Human Movement Studies, 18,* 107–116.

McCullagh, P., & Meyers, K. N. (1997). Learning versus correct models: Influence of model type on the learning of a free-weight squat lift. *Research Quarterly for Exercise and Sport, 68,* 56–61.

McCullagh, P., & Ram, N. (2000). A comparison of imagery and modeling. *Journal of Sport and Exercise Psychology, 22,* S9.

McCullagh, P., Ste-Marie, D. M., & Law, B. (in press). Modeling: Is what you see what you get? In J. L. Van Raalte & B. W. Brewer (Eds.), *Exploring sport and exercise psychology* (3rd ed.). Washington, DC: American Psychological Association.

McCullagh, P., & Weiss, M. R. (2001). Modeling: Considerations for motor skill performance and psychological responses. In R. N. Singer, H. A. Hausenblaus, & C. M. Janelle (Eds.). *Handbook of sport psychology* (2nd ed., pp. 205–238). New York: Wiley.

McCullagh, P., & Weiss, M. R. (2002). Observational learning: The forgotten psychological method in sport psychology. In J. L. Van Raalte & B. W. Brewer (Eds.), *Exploring sport and exercise psychology* (2nd ed., pp. 131–150). Washington, DC: American Psychological Association.

McCullagh P., Weiss, M. R., & Ross, D. (1989). Modeling considerations in motor skill acquisition and performance: An integrated approach. In K. B. Pandolf (Ed.), *Exercise and sport sciences reviews* (Vol. 17, pp. 475–513). Baltimore: Williams & Wilkins.

McCullagh, P., & Wilson, G. (2007). Psychology of physical activity: What should students know? *Quest, 59,* 42–54.

McDougall, W. (1908). *An introduction to social psychology.* London: Methuen.

Meaney, K. S., & Edwards, R.(1996). Exsenanzas en un gimnasio: An investigation of modeling and verbal rehearsal on the motor performance of Hispanic limited English proficient children. *Research Quarterly for Exercise and Sport, 68,* 203–214.

Meharg, S. S., & Woltersdorf, M. A. (1990). Therapeutic use of videotape self-modeling: A review. *Advanced Behavioral Research Therapy, 12,* 85–99.

Meichenbaum, D. H. (1971). Examination of model characteristics in reducing avoidance behavior. *Journal of Personality and Social Psychology, 17*(3), 298–307.

Melody, D. W. (1990). The influence of self-modeling upon free-throw shooting. *Dissertation Abstracts International, 52–02*(A), 478.

Miller, N. E., & Dollard, J. (1941). *Social learning and imitation.* New Haven, CT: Yale University Press.

More, K. G., & Franks, I. M. (1996). Analysis and modification of verbal coaching behavior: The usefulness of a data-driven intervention strategy. *Journal of Sports Sciences, 14,* 523–543.

Moreno, R. (2009). Learning from animated classroom exemplars: The case for guiding student teachers' observations with metacognitive prompts. *Educational Research and Evaluation, 15*(5), 487–501.

Moreno, R., & Ortegano-Layne, L. (2008). Do classroom exemplars promote the application of principles in teacher education? A comparison of videos, animations, and narratives. *Educational Technology Research and Development, 56,* 449–465.

Morgan, C. L. (1896). *Habitat and instinct.* London: E. Arnold Press.

Mugno, D. A., & Feltz, D. L. (1985). The social learning of aggression in youth football in the United States. *Canadian Journal of Applied Sport Sciences, 10,* 26–35.

Murphy, S. (2009). Video games, competition and exercise: A new opportunity for sport psychologists? *The Sport Psychologist, 23,* 487–503.

Nadler, J., Thompson, L., & Van Boven, L. (2003). Learning negotiation skills: Four models of knowledge creation and transfer. *Management Science, 49*(4), 529–540.

Newell, K. M. (1981). Skill learning. In D. H. Holding (Ed.), *Human skills* (pp. 203–226). New York: Wiley.

Nicholls, J. G. (1984). Achievement motivation: Conceptions of ability, subjective experience, task choice, and performance. *Psychological Review, 91*, 328–346.

Obhi, S. S., & Hogeveen, J. (2010). Incidental action observation modulates muscle activity. *Experimental Brain Research, 203*(2), 427–235.

Olson, R., Grosshuesch, A., Schmidt, S., Gray, M., & Wipfli, B. (2009). Observational learning and workplace safety: The effects of viewing the collective behavior of multiple social models on the use of personal protective equipment. *Journal of Safety Research, 40*, 383–387.

Paivio, A. (1985). Cognitive and motivational functions of imagery in human performance. *Canadian Journal of Applied Sports Sciences, 10*, 22S–28S.

ParticipACTION. (n.d.). *Stories.* Retrieved from http://www.participaction.com/en-us/Stories/ViewStories.aspx

Payne W. R., Reynolds M., Brown S., & Fleming A. (2002). *Sports role models and their impact on participation on physical activity: A literature review.* Victorian Health Promotion Foundation. http://fulltext.ausport.gov.au/fulltext/2002/vic/Role_Model.pdf

Pollock, B. J., & Lee, T. D. (1992). Effects of the model's skill level on observational learning. *Research Quarterly for Exercise and Sport, 63*, 25–29.

Priebe, R. E., & Burton, W. H. (1939). The slow-motion picture as a coaching device. *The School Review, 47*(3), 192–198.

Prochaska, J. O., & Marcus, B. H. (1994). The transtheoretical model: Applications to exercise. In R. K. Dishman (Ed.), *Advances in exercise adherence* (pp. 161–180). Champaign, IL: Human Kinetics.

PT in Motion. (2010). Health care technology today. *PT in Motion, 2*(2), 34.

Radell, S. A., Adame, D. D., & Cole, S. P. (2003). Effect of teaching with mirrors on ballet dance performance. *Perceptual and Motor Skills, 97*(3), 960–964.

Ram, N., & McCullagh, P. (2003). Self-modeling: Influence on psychological responses and physical performance. *The Sport Psychologist, 17*, 220–241.

Robertson, M., & Collins, A. (2003). The video role model as an enterprise teaching aid. *Education and Training, 45*(6), 331–340.

Rodgers, W. M., & Sullivan, M. J. L. (2001). Task, coping, and scheduling self-efficacy in relation to frequency of physical activity. *Journal of Applied Social Psychology, 31*(4), 741–753.

Rosen, M. A., Salas, E., Pavlas, D., Jensen, R., Fu, D., & Lampton, D. (2010). Demonstration-based training: A review of instructional features. *Human Factors, 52*, 596–609.

Rymal, A. M., Martini, R., & Ste-Marie, D. M. (2010). Self-regulatory processes employed during self-modeling: A qualitative analysis, *The Sport Psychologist, 24*, 1–15.

Sawicki, O. (2009). The interaction of sport and technology: The broad versus detailed perspective. *Coaches Plan/Plan du Coach, 16*(2), 15–17.

San Francisco Chronicle. (2000, March 30). Instant replay: Giants see an edge with digitized video system. B1.

Schmidt, R. A. (1975). A schema theory of discrete motor skill learning. *Psychological Review, 82*, 225–260.

Schunk, D. H. (1981). Modeling and attributional effects on children's achievement: A self-efficacy analysis. *Journal of Educational Psychology, 73*(1), 93–105.

Schunk, D. H. (1991). Self-efficacy and academic motivation. *Educational Psychologist, 26*, 207–231.

Schunk, D. H., & Hanson, A. R. (1985). Peer models: Influence on children's self efficacy and achievement. *Journal of Educational Psychology, 77*, 54–61.

Schunk, D. H., & Hanson, A. R. (1989). Self-modeling and children's cognitive skill learning. *Journal of Educational Psychology, 81*(2), 155–163.

Schunk, D. H., Hanson, A. R., & Cox, P. D. (1987). Peer-model attributes and children's achievement behaviors. *Journal of Educational Psychology, 79*(1), 54–61.

Schunk, D. H., & Zimmerman, B.J. (1997). Social origins of self-regulatory competence. *Educational Psychologist, 32*(4), 195–208.

Schunk, D. H., & Zimmerman, B. J. (1996). Modeling and self-efficacy influences on children's development of self-regulation. In J. Juvonen & K. R. Wentzel (Eds.), *Social motivation: Understanding children's school adjustment* (pp. 154–180). Cambridge, UK: Cambridge University Press.

Scraba, P. (1989). *Self-modeling for teaching swimming to children with physical disabilities.* Unpublished doctoral dissertation, University of Connecticut, Storrs.

Scully, D. M., & Newell, K. M. (1985). Observational Learning and the acquisition of motor skills: Toward a visual perception perspective. *Journal of Human Movement Studies, 11*, 169–186.

Sebert Kuhlmann, A. K., Kraft, J. M., Galavotti, C., Creek, T. L., Mooki, M., & Ntumy, R. (2008). Radio role models for the prevention of mother-to-child transmission of HIV and HIV testing among pregnant women in Botswana. *Health Promotion International, 23*(3). doi: 10.1093/heapro/dan011

Shapiro, F. R. (2006). *The Yale book of quotations.* New Haven, CT: Yale University Press.

Shea, C. H., Wright, D. L., Wulf, G., & Whitacre, C. (2000). Physical and observational practice afford unique learning opportunities. *Journal of Motor Behavior, 32*(1), 27–36.

Shea, C. H., Wulf, G., & Whitacre, C. (1999). Enhancing training efficiency and effectiveness through the use of dyad training. *Journal of Motor Behavior, 31*(2), 119–125.

Sheffield, F. D. (1961). Theoretical considerations in the learning of complex sequential tasks from demonstration and practice. In A. A. Lumsdaine (Ed.), *Student response in programmed instruction: A symposium* (pp. 13–32). Washington, DC: National Academy of Sciences-National Research Council.

Smith, M. D. (1978). Social learning of violence in minor hockey. In F. L. Smoll & R. E. Smith (Eds.), *Psychological perspectives in youth sports* (pp. 91–106). Washington, DC: Hemisphere Publishing.

Starek, J., & McCullagh, P. (1999). The effect of self-modeling on the performance of beginning swimmers. *The Sport Psychologist, 13*, 269–287.

Tarde, G. (1903). *The laws of imitation* (E. Clews Parsons, Trans.). New York: Henry Holt and Company.

Taylor, C. A., Taylor, J. C., & Stoller, J. K. (2009). The influence of mentorship and role modeling on developing physician-leaders: Views of aspiring and established physician-leaders. *Journal of General Internal Medicine, 24*(10), 1130–1134.

Taylor, L. D. (2005). Effects of visual and verbal sexual television content and perceived realism on attitudes and beliefs. *The Journal of Sex Research, 42*(2), 130–137.

Templin, D. P., & Vernacchia, R. A. (1995). The effect of highlight music videotapes upon the game performance of intercollegiate basketball players. *The Sport Psychologist, 9*, 41–50.

Thomson, C. W. (1996). Apparent teacher fitness level and its effect on student test scores. *Indiana Association for Health, Physical Education, Recreation, and Dance, 25*, 17–20.

Topping, K., & Ehly, S. (Eds.). (1998). *Peer-assisted learning.* Mahwah, NJ: L. Erlbaum Associates, Inc.

Tracey, J. (2011). Benefits and usefulness of a personal motivation video: A case study of a professional mountain bike racer. *Journal of Applied Sport Psychology, 23*, 308–325. doi: 10.1080/10413200.2011.558364

Tyler, C. L., Anderson, M. H., & Tyler, J. M. (2009). Giving students new eyes: The benefit of having students find media clips to illustrate management concepts. *Journal of Management Education, 33*(4), 444–461.

van Gog, T., Paas, F., Marcus, N., Ayres, P., & Sweller, J. (2009). The mirror neuron system and observational learning: Implications for the effectiveness of dynamic visualizations. *Educational Psychology Review, 21*, 21–30.

Vogt, S., & Thomaschke, R. (2007). From visuo-moto interactions to imitation learning: Behavioural and brain imaging studies. *Journal of Sports Sciences, 25*(5), 497–517.

Wade, S. L., Oberjohn, K., Burkhardt, A., & Greenberg, I. (2009). Feasibility and preliminary efficacy of a web-based parenting skills program for young children with traumatic brain injury. *Journal of Head Trauma Rehabilitation, 24*(4), 239–247.

Walsh, S. E. (1997). The development of a protocol to provide real-time information to enhance coach-performer interactions. *Scientific Journal of Orienteering, 13*, 47–53.

Weir, P. L., & Leavitt, J. L. (1990). Effects of model's skill level and model's knowledge of results on the performance of a dart throwing task. *Human Movement Science, 9*, 369–383.

Weiss, M. R. (1983). Modeling and motor performance: A developmental perspective. *Research Quarterly for Exercise and Sport, 54*, 190–197.

Weiss, M. R., Bredemeier, B. J., & Shewchuk, R. M. (1985). An intrinsic/extrinsic motivation scale for the youth sport setting: A confirmatory factor analysis. *Journal of Sports Psychology, 7*, 75–91.

Weiss, M. R., Ebbeck, V., & Wiese-Bjornstal, D. M. (1993). Developmental and psychological skills related to children's observational learning of physical skills. *Pediatric Exercise Science, 5*, 301–317.

Weiss, M. R., Kipp, L. E., & Goodman, D. (2010). Youth hockey players' attitudes, perceived social approval, situational temptation, and role models. *Journal of Sport and Exercise Psychology, 32*, S228–S229.

Weiss, M. R., & Klint, K. A. (1987). Show and tell in the gymnasium: An investigation of developmental differences in modeling and verbal rehearsal of motor skills. *Research Quarterly for Exercise and Sport, 58*(3), 234–241.

Weiss, M. R., McCullagh, P., Smith, A. L., & Berlant, A. R. (1998). Observational learning and the fearful child: Influence of peer models on swimming skill performance and psychological responses. *Research Quarterly for Exercise and Sport, 69*, 380–394.

Welsh, T. N., Elliott, D., Anson, J. G., Dhillon, V., Weeks, D. J., Lyons, J. L., & Chua, R. (2005). Does Joe influence Fred's action? Inhibition of return across different nervous systems. *Neuroscience Letters, 385*, 99–104.

Welsh, T. N., McDougall, L. M., & Weeks, D. J. (2009). The performance and observation of action shape future behaviour. *Brain and Cognition, 71*, 64–71.

Wesch, N. N., Law, B., & Hall, C. R. (2007). The use of observational learning by athletes. *Journal of Sports Behavior, 30*(2), 219–229.

Winfrey, M. L., & Weeks, D. L. (1993). Effects of self-modeling on self-efficacy and balance beam performance. *Perceptual and Motor Skills, 77*, 907–913.

Withers, G. F., & Wertheim, E. H. (2004). Applying the elaboration likelihood model of persuasion to a videotape-based eating disorders primary prevention program for adolescent girls. *Eating Disorders, 12*, 103–124.

Woo, M. Y., Frank, J., Lee, A. C., Thompson, C., Cardinal, P., Yeung, M., & Beeker, J. (2009). Effectiveness of a novel training program for emergency medicine residents in ultrasound-guided insertion of central venous catheters. *Canadian Journal of Emergency Medicine, 11*(4), 343–348.

Woodworth, R. S. (1922). *Dynamic psychology.* New York: Columbia University Press.

Wouters, P., Paas, F., & van Merriënboer, J. J. G. (2009). Observational learning from animated models: Effects of modality and reflection on transfer. *Contemporary Educational Psychology, 34*, 1–8.

Wouters, P., Paas, F., & van Merriënboer, J. J. G. (2010). Observational learning from animated models: Effects of studying-practicing alternation and illusion of control on transfer. *Instructional Science, 38*, 89–104.

Wouters, P., Tabbers, H. K., & Paas, F. (2007). Interactivity in video-based models. *Educational Psychology Review, 19*, 327–342.

Wulf, G., Shea, C., & Lewthwaite, R. (2010). Motor skill learning and performance: A review of influential factors. *Medical Education, 44*, 75–84. doi:10.1111/j.1365-2923.2009.03421.x

Yarbrough, C., Wapnick, J., & Kelly, R. (1979). Effect of videotape feedback techniques on performance, verbalization, and attitude of beginning conductors. *Journal of Research in Music Education, 27*(2), 103–112.

Ziegler, A., & Stoeger, H. (2004). Evaluation of an attributional retraining (modeling technique) to reduce gender differences in chemistry instruction. *High Ability Studies, 15*(1). doi: 10.1080/135981304200002253-48

Zimmerman, B. J. (1989). A social cognitive view of self-regulated academic learning. *Journal of Educational Psychology, 81*(3), 329–339.

Zimmerman, B. J. (1996). Enhancing student academic and health functioning: A self-regulatory perspective. *School Psychology Quarterly, 11*, 47–66.

Zimmerman, B. J. (2000). Attaining self-regulation: A social cognitive perspective. In M. Boekaerts, P. R. Pintrich, & M. Zeidner (Eds.), *Handbook of self-regulation* (pp. 13–39). San Diego, CA: Academic Press.

Zimmerman, B. J., & Kitsantas, A. (1997). Developmental phases in self-regulation: Shifting from process goals to outcome goals. *Journal of Educational Psychology, 89*, 29–36.

Zimmerman, B. J., & Kitsantas, A. (1999). Acquiring writing revision and self-regulatory skill, through observation and emulation. *Journal of Educational Psychology, 94*(4), 660–668.

Zimmerman, B. J. & Kitsantas A. (2002). Acquiring writing revision and self-regulatory skill through observation and emulation. *Journal of Educational Psychology, 94*(4), 660–668.

Efficacy Beliefs and Human Performance: From Independent Action to Interpersonal Functioning

Mark R. Beauchamp, Ben Jackson, *and* Katie L. Morton

Abstract

The beliefs that people have in their own, others', and their teams' capabilities have been extensively studied in the fields of sport and performance psychology. This is perhaps unsurprising, given that these *efficacy beliefs* have consistently been found to predict a variety of indicators of improved performance, and, importantly, have also been shown to be malleable and thus enhanced through intervention. In this chapter, we provide a conceptual overview of the distinct types of efficacy belief that exist when people 'perform' specific tasks within individual, relational, and group settings. In addition, we discuss the sources of these efficacy cognitions, as well as the direct and indirect implications for personal, relational, and group/team performance. We also provide a brief discussion of implications for applied practice, and highlight some important questions for future research in sport and performance psychology.

Key Words: Self-efficacy theory, relational efficacy, role efficacy, tripartite model, collective efficacy, coaching efficacy, sport psychology, performance psychology

Reflecting on his 1953 ascent of Mount Everest, Sir Edmund Hillary was once reported to remark "it is not the mountain we conquer but ourselves" (Kuchler, 2003, p. 20). In recent years, climbing Everest has often been used as a metaphor to represent the ultimate achievement in any given field. However, what is certainly as true as it was almost 60 years ago when Hillary accomplished this feat is that the successful pursuit of any challenging task is often influenced by the *beliefs* that we hold about what we are capable of achieving in a given situation. Such beliefs have been studied in a diverse range of contexts in the fields of sport and performance psychology and, in particular, through the conceptual framework offered by *self-efficacy theory* (Bandura, 1977, 1997). Self-efficacy theory is grounded within the broader conceptual framework provided by social cognitive theory (Bandura, 1986), with self-efficacy defined as an individual's

"belief in one's capabilities to organize and execute the courses of action required to produce given attainments" (Bandura, 1997, p. 3).

Self-efficacy beliefs can vary in terms of their level, strength, and generality (Bandura 1977, 1997). The *level* at which efficacy beliefs exist can range from relatively straightforward situational demands to challenging requirements, and indeed it is often under particularly demanding conditions, or levels, that efficacy beliefs become particularly salient (Bandura, 1997). The *strength* of a person's efficacy beliefs correspond to the degree of confidence that a person has in his or her capabilities. For example, an athlete may be 100% confident (efficacy strength) of her capabilities to perform a given skill at the regional level (efficacy level), but only 50% confident (efficacy strength) in her capabilities to perform that same skill on the international stage (efficacy level). Finally, *generality* refers to the extent to which a set of efficacy beliefs may generalize across a range of activities. For example, a person may be highly confident in his or her capability to perform multiple types of racquet sports. However, another person may be highly confident while playing tennis, but not badminton. In the former case, the person's efficacy beliefs would be said to generalize across (racquet sport) contexts, but in the latter case they would not. In this chapter, we provide a review of the extant literature linking self-efficacy appraisals to personal functioning and human performance, and we identify how such beliefs emerge in the first place. However, in recognition of the fact that individuals often perform with others in relational (e.g., coach–athlete, supervisor–employee) and group (e.g., sport teams, project groups) settings, we also consider the application of other forms of efficacy belief that emerge within interpersonal contexts and explain how these beliefs influence human functioning. In this chapter, we consider "performance" in its broadest sense to reflect the pursuit of accomplishment in relation to some predetermined standard, and we draw from diverse domains of human endeavor to address these issues.

Self-Efficacy Beliefs and Personal Performance: Explanatory Mechanisms and Empirical Evidence

Across various life contexts, the beliefs that people have in their own capabilities have consistently been found to predict improved personal performance and accomplishment. Such contexts include sports (Feltz, Chow, & Hepler, 2008; Moritz, Feltz, Fahrbach, & Mack, 2000), education (Carmona, Buunk, Dijkstra, & Pieró, 2008; Multon, Brown,

& Lent, 1991; Pajares, 1996), and the workplace (Judge, Jackson, Shaw, Scott, & Rich, 2007; Sadri & Robertson, 1993; Stajkovic & Luthans, 1998). To better understand *how* self-efficacy beliefs foster improved performance, it is important to consider the *mechanisms* through which the former psychological construct impacts on the latter behavioral outcome.

Although self-efficacy is most often operationalized as having a *direct* impact on performance (cf. Moritz et al., 2000), a number of processes operate through which these conceptions of personal agency influence performance. That is, alongside direct effects, self-efficacy beliefs also play an *indirect* role in performance enhancement via positive effects on a number of mediating factors (see Figure 14.1). For example, according to Bandura (1982), self-efficacy judgments shape both one's choice of activities and also the settings in which those activities are performed. Thus, if a person lacks the belief to complete a task or perform in a specific context, he may simply decide to avoid that task, even if, in objective/rational terms, he is capable or has the resources to complete it (e.g., Chase, 2001; Escartí & Guzmán, 1999). When people perceive themselves to be efficacious, they also tend to exert greater effort (e.g., Hutchinson, Sherman, Martinovic, & Tenenbaum, 2008) and persistence (e.g., Bouffard-Bouchard, Parent, & Larivée, 1991; Gao, Xiang, Harrison, Guan, & Rao, 2008) in performing the requisite tasks than do those crippled with self-doubt. Directly related to this, results from both experimental and longitudinal studies have consistently demonstrated that improved perceptions of personal efficacy are related to the selection of more challenging goals (Boyce & Bingham,

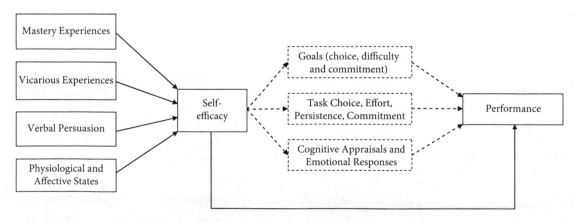

Figure 14.1 Sources of self-efficacy as well as mediators of the self-efficacy–performance relationship.

1997; Kane, Marks, Zaccaro, & Blair, 1996; Tolli & Schmidt, 2008; Vrugt & Koenis, 2002), as well as greater commitment to those goals (Lerner & Locke, 1995). In one interesting investigation with a sample of 123 university academics, Vrugt and Koenis (2002) reported that greater self-efficacy relating to one's research capabilities predicted elevated career goals (related to research output), and that these goals predicted productivity 2 years later. Taken together, individuals who believe in their abilities tend to display a greater willingness to tackle difficult tasks, and their efforts are often sustained in order to reach those higher performance standards.

Evidence also suggests that when people perceive themselves to be efficacious, they tend to appraise environmental cues and performance conditions (cf. Bandura, 1997; 2001) rather differently to those lacking confidence in what they can accomplish. In particular, efficacious individuals construe tasks as challenging rather than threatening (e.g., Karademas & Kalantzi-Azizi, 2004; Skinner & Brewer, 2002), are more optimistic (e.g., Chemers, Hu, & Garcia, 2001; Kavussanu & McAuley, 1995), are less likely to anticipate negative outcomes (e.g., Cartoni, Minganti, & Zelli, 2005), and report reductions in undesirable emotions (e.g., debilitative anxiety, fear) that may accompany task execution (e.g., Caprara et al., 2008; Hanton, Mellalieu, & Hall, 2004; Martin, 2002; Rudolph & Butki, 1998). In sum, although self-efficacy has been shown to directly underpin task functioning, the relations between self-efficacy and performance in sport and other contexts appear to be mediated via a series of other cognitive mechanisms, including improved effort, persistence, positive appraisals, goal selection and commitment.

Self-Efficacy and Resilience: Dealing with Adversity

Although self-efficacy invariably acts as a consistent antecedent of task performance (as highlighted in the previous section), compelling evidence also suggests that self-efficacy moderates how individuals react following disappointing or substandard performances. Specifically, Bandura (1997, 2001) posited that a high degree of confidence in one's ability serves as an important cognitive buffer, limiting the damaging effects that may arise due to suboptimal performance experiences. For instance, individuals who are highly efficacious tend to ascribe their failures to a lack of effort, which represents a factor that they can rectify, rather than a shortcoming in their ability (Chase, 2001; Coffee & Rees, 2008;

Coffee, Rees, & Haslam, 2009). Following poor performances, a strong sense of self-efficacy has also been shown to protect against reductions in positive affect (Brown, Malouff, & Schutte, 2005) and promote resilience to negative performance feedback (Nease, Mudgett, & Quiñones, 1999). Interestingly, under lab-based experimental conditions in which negative feedback was repeatedly provided following task completion, Nease and colleagues (1999) reported that higher levels of self-efficacy among study participants led to reduced acceptance of negative evaluations. Taken together, not only do efficacious individuals outperform their self-doubting counterparts, their confidence may also allow them to overcome adverse experiences without any lasting damage to their sense of self.

Sources of Self-Efficacy Beliefs Across Diverse Contexts

According to Bandura (1977, 1997), self-efficacy beliefs derive primarily from a person's enactive *mastery experiences* (past accomplishments), *vicarious experiences* (modeling), *verbal persuasion,* and *physiological and affective states*. Enactive mastery experiences correspond to a person's perceptions of what he or she has accomplished in the past and are theorized to represent the strongest source of efficacy information (Bandura, 1997). Vicarious experiences involve observing the behaviors of others through observational/social learning, or what is more commonly referred to as *social modeling* ("If Johnny can do it, then I can too!"). In addition to social (live) modeling, a specific form of modeling that has received considerable attention within the field of sport and performance psychology is what Bandura refers to as *cognitive self-modeling* (1997, p. 95), or what others typically refer to as *mental imagery*. Research suggests that when people invoke images that are mastery-laden and reflective of a person feeling confident, this can translate into elevated levels of personal efficacy (see Chapter 11, this volume). Verbal persuasion occurs when people express their belief in others through the provision of competence-based verbal feedback. Finally, physiological and affective states are theorized to influence self-efficacy when those states (e.g., elevated somatic responses) are cognitively processed and are associated with or attributed to greater perceptions of capacity or competence (see Figure 14.1). A considerable amount of empirical evidence has accumulated in support of Bandura's theoretical assertions. Furthermore, extensive narrative reviews have been conducted in the sport and performance psychology literatures with regard to the sources of self-efficacy; thus, we restrict our discussion of the sources of self-efficacy in this section to a brief synopsis (for excellent overviews, interested readers are encouraged to see Feltz, Short, & Sullivan, 2008; Pajares & Urdan, 2006).

As for the most influential source of self-efficacy appraisals, research in sport (Wise & Trunnell, 2001), educational (Lent et al., 2009), and occupational settings (Tay, Ang, & Van Dyne, 2006) has consistently demonstrated that people's self-efficacy beliefs are elevated when they experience success in a given task. As Bandura (1997) noted, *mastery experiences* provide critical diagnostic information to the focal person about his or her capabilities when performing the same or a similar task again in the future. To a similar extent, the study of social and observational learning (i.e., *vicarious experiences*) has been extensive across domains of human functioning, with observations of others providing important directives about what people are capable of achieving. To highlight the pervasiveness of this relationship between live modeling and self-efficacy, it is noteworthy that these relations have not only been established by trainees/students (Escartí & Guzmán, 1999; see also Chapter 13, this volume), but also among those responsible for their training, in particular among teachers, counselors, and consultants (Johnson & Stewart, 2008).

With regard to cognitive-self-modeling, an extensive body of evidence has provided support for the link between *imaginal experiences* and elevated self-efficacy beliefs. In particular, when people make use of mastery-oriented imagery (i.e., images imbuing control and confidence), they tend to feel more efficacious and indeed perform better (Beauchamp, Bray, & Albinson, 2002; Ross-Stewart & Short, 2009). While mental imagery has certainly been used extensively as a psychological skill to enhance self-efficacy beliefs among elite athletes and performing artists (see Chapter 11, this volume), it is also noteworthy that mental imagery has been used to good effect as a means of intervention to facilitate the self-efficacy beliefs among rather different populations, such as older adults suffering from memory loss (West, Bagwell, & Dark-Freudeman, 2008).

Although a less powerful source of efficacy information, information conveyed by *verbal persuasion* has also been found to influence a person's self-efficacy beliefs. Of direct relevance to this chapter, a growing body of observational and experimental research conducted within organizational (Avolio, Zhu, Koh, & Bhatia, 2004; Kark, Shamir, & Chen,

2003), military (Dvir, Eden, Avolio, & Shamir, 2002), and educational (Beauchamp, Barling, & Morton, 2011) settings has provided evidence that transformational leadership elevates the self-efficacy beliefs of employees, soldiers, and students, respectively. Transformational leadership (see also Chapter 17, this volume) involves actions that transcend one's own self-interests with the purpose of empowering, inspiring, and challenging others to achieve higher levels of functioning (Bass & Riggio, 2006). One of the central theoretical tenets of transformational leadership theory is that when leaders communicate (through verbal persuasion) with others through the demonstration of transformational principles, they elevate followers' confidence to exceed expected standards (Bass, 1998). Recent research has extended transformational leadership to the field of sport psychology (Tucker, Turner, Barling, & McEvoy, 2010) but has yet to test the transformational leadership–athlete self-efficacy relationship within this context.

In addition, perceptions of one's *physiological condition* (e.g., fatigue, illness) have also been found to play a role in influencing a person's self-efficacy beliefs, in particular when the task being performed requires some degree of physical exertion. For example, Jackson, Knapp, and Beauchamp (2008) found that when international-level athletes reported decrements in strength, as well as the prevalence of injury, fatigue, and pain, their conceptions of self-efficacy were impaired. Interestingly, when intervention programs (typically with older adult and patient populations) have focused on improving people's physical condition through aerobic/ strength training, their self-efficacy beliefs have been found to improve (Gowans, de Hueck, Voss, Silaj, & Abbey 2004; Tsutsumi, Don, Zaichkowsky, & Delizonna, 1997). In a similar regard, when a person's *affective and emotional states* are positive, he or she tends to report improved self-efficacy to accomplish the task at hand, and conversely, when people report debilitated emotional states, their efficacy beliefs tend to diminish (Thelwell, Lane, & Weston, 2007; Welch, Hulley, & Beauchamp, 2010).

Although extensive research has sought to examine the unique predictive effects of the above six sources, some studies have taken a multimodal approach and incorporated some combination (i.e., two or more) of the aforementioned sources. In sport and educational domains, this is particularly illustrated by studies that have sought to investigate the influence of distinct types of motivational climate in relation to group members' self-efficacy beliefs. Grounded within the achievement goal theory literature (cf. Nicholls, 1984), motivational climates have been typically conceptualized as the extent to which the environment created within a class or team tends to endorse task-involving or ego-involving goals (Ames & Archer, 1988). Task-involving climates tend to promote self-referent improvement, skill development, and task accomplishment, whereas ego-involved climates tend to focus on demonstrating superiority over opponents (and team/class-mates) and intra-team rivalry. In deconstructing the specific components of these two types of motivational climate, it is evident that multiple sources of self-efficacy information will likely be communicated to group members, especially by the respective teacher (in education settings) or team coach (in sport). For example, task-involving climates are more likely to create enriched opportunities for self-referent improvement (i.e., mastery), as well as modeling opportunities (vicarious learning) that focus on skill development, than ego-involved climates. In support of this, research within sport team settings suggests that when coaches develop climates that are task-involving, the players tend to report elevated levels of self-efficacy (Kavussanu & Roberts, 1996; Magyar & Feltz, 2003).

Self-Efficacy and Performance: Recursive Spirals

To the extent that individuals' performance attainments both stem from and contribute to their efficacy judgments, it is unsurprising that a number of authors have devoted attention to understanding the reciprocal (i.e., bidirectional) nature of the relationship between self-efficacy and performance. Elaborating on Bandura's (1977) original writing, Lindsley, Brass, and Thomas (1995) detailed the temporally recursive link between efficacy beliefs and performance. They described that the "deviation-amplifying" (or reciprocal) nature of the relationship between these variables may result in either upward spirals, in which performance attainments lead to enhanced self-efficacy and then further increases in performance, or downward spirals, in which case poor performance and increased self-doubt occur in a cyclical fashion. Research within sport (Feltz, Chow, et al., 2008), and education (Heggestad & Kanfer, 2005; Williams & Williams, 2010) contexts has provided evidence for this phenomenon; in sport, these patterns are often described when athletes are said to experience

"momentum" or a "hot streak" (i.e., upward spirals), or conversely are in a "slump" (i.e., downward spirals). As one example, golfer Ernie Els alluded to the positive nature of this feedback mechanism following two early-season victories in 2010 by remarking, "The win in Miami was big for me as it got [me] a lot of confidence back and then obviously [the second victory at] Bay Hill was a run on from that" ("Els aiming to maintain hot streak," 2010).

Clearly, we do not perpetually find ourselves in a state of either upward or downward momentum, and Lindsley et al. (1995) theorized that the likelihood of spirals forming may depend upon a number of precipitating conditions (e.g., task feedback, complexity, experience, attributions). Moreover, they noted several volitional (i.e., self-correcting) as well as inadvertent methods by which these cycles may be broken. For instance, individuals may find themselves able to reverse downward patterns by attributional reframing (i.e., searching for controllable causes that can be rectified, such as effort), redefining perceptions of success and failure (from norm- to self-referenced), and focusing on each of the constituent parts involved in performance in isolation (rather than solely focused on the outcome). On the other hand, with repeated successes, people may insufficiently process and evaluate the reasons for their good performance, and this complacency may ultimately break the spiral (Lindsley et al., 1995). Furthermore, in many performance contexts, such as sports, a number of unique factors that are beyond one's personal control (or sense of agency) may bring an abrupt halt to upward as well as downward spirals, such as decisions from officials, an opponent's skill level, or injury.

Considering the Diverse Forms of Personal Efficacy Required to Maximize Human Functioning

In seeking to explore the performance-related outcomes associated with efficacy beliefs, researchers have often focused their attention squarely on how confident an individual is in his or her ability to complete the primary task in question (i.e., *task self-efficacy*). Nevertheless, in seeking to overcome the various challenges and obstacles that exist in real-world pursuits, we invariably develop conceptions about aspects of our capabilities that extend beyond simply how well we can perform that primary task and involve factors such as coping with setbacks, learning new skills, and making effective decisions. In this section, we consider a number of salient personal efficacy constructs that exist alongside, and indeed complement, task-related efficacy perceptions.

In many achievement contexts—such as sports—*competitive* (or *comparative*) *efficacy* beliefs (Feltz & Lirgg, 1998) become highly salient and involve an individual's confidence in his or her ability to outperform a competitor (e.g., "I am confident I can beat my opponent"). Although the frame of reference (i.e., a normative evaluation) used in forming these judgments distinguishes this construct from task self-efficacy, it has been shown that competitive efficacy and task self-efficacy may be determined by comparable factors (e.g., performance accomplishments, vicarious influences, imaginal experiences; Feltz & Reissinger, 1990). That said, the nature and strength of the relationship between competitive and task efficacy perceptions is presently unclear, and the unique consequences that align with competitive efficacy beliefs have yet to receive systematic empirical investigation. Drawing from the literature on achievement goal theory (cf. Nicholls, 1984), however, it seems reasonable to caution that developing strategies to bolster comparative efficacy beliefs may, in the long run, be debilitative. That is, although an emphasis on self-referent competence enhancement (such as those used in task self-efficacy interventions) may certainly represent an adaptive developmental strategy, seeking to promote norm-referent perceptions of competence ("You're better than X") might lead to stifling and maladaptive development.

Several additional efficacy constructs also play a role in shaping individual functioning within achievement pursuits. For instance, *learning efficacy* focuses on individuals' beliefs in their capability to learn a new skill ("I'm good at learning new skills") and may be a critical factor in skill acquisition contexts (see also Chapter 23, this volume). Although research on this form of efficacy in sport and performance contexts is sparse, it is likely that, particularly under challenging conditions, those who are confident in their learning ability may devote greater time to practicing and refining their skills (Bandura, 1997). It has also been documented that those who view themselves as highly competent decision-makers (i.e., high *decision-making efficacy*) display enhanced performance on athletic tasks (e.g., Hepler & Chase, 2008), as well as in simulated business settings (Bandura & Wood, 1989; Wood & Bandura, 1989). Moreover, by manipulating participants' decision-making efficacy perceptions using bogus feedback on a decision-based task, Krueger and Dickson (1994) revealed that individuals who were highly confident in their decision-making capabilities perceived greater task-related opportunity, reduced threat, and were more likely to take risks than those who doubted their ability. In a similar vein, *problem-solving efficacy* relates to individuals' beliefs in their problem-solving capacities and has been found to predict improved performance in academic settings (Pajares & Miller, 1994), as well as the more productive use of coping strategies (Frydenberg & Lewis, 2009). Although problem-solving efficacy has yet to receive systematic attention within the sport domain, we would expect that problem-solving efficacy would be particularly important in activities requiring complex challenges (e.g., climbing expeditions, motor racing).

Although most performance-related activities require the effective execution of *proactive* competencies (e.g., problem-solving, decision-making, learning capabilities), successful task pursuit often requires the exhibition of *reactive* competencies, such as dealing with various stressors and threats. In such instances, one's ability to demonstrate *coping efficacy* (Bandura, 1986) becomes particularly salient and involves a person's confidence to cope in the face of perceived threats. In academic settings, students tend to report higher coping efficacy perceptions when they perceive strong family support (e.g., Klink, Byars-Winston, & Bakken, 2008); coping efficacy has in turn been shown to predict reduced levels of anxiety (see Bandura, 1993) and persistence in the face of academic barriers (e.g., Lent et al., 2001; Luzzo & McWhirter, 2001). Moreover, teachers who believe they can cope effectively with occupational threats may be less susceptible to burnout via the use of more adaptive (i.e., task-focused) methods for overcoming stressors (Chwalisz, Altmaier, & Russell, 1992). Coping efficacy beliefs have also received some research attention in sport and exercise settings. For instance, athletes who believe more strongly in their coping abilities prior to competition have been shown to report reduced perceptions of pre-competitive somatic and cognitive anxiety, as well as more favorable post-competition ratings of their performance (Nicholls, Polman, & Levy, 2010).

An area of research that has received considerable attention within the field of health psychology, but that also has considerable potential within performance contexts, corresponds to the study of *self-regulatory efficacy* (Maddux, Norton, & Leary, 1988). For successful behavior change, especially with regard to implementing health-enhancing strategies, a number of scholars have argued that self-regulatory efficacy (individuals' judgments about their abilities to effectively self-regulate) is more important than task self-efficacy (Anderson, Winett, & Wojcik, 2007). Specifically, the main issue is not whether a person can perform an activity or task occasionally, but whether he or she believes that potential barriers can be overcome in order to regularly perform that task or activity. In the field of behavioral medicine, factors such as one's confidence to manage one's own schedule (scheduling self-efficacy), overcome obstacles such as cost or travel (barriers self-efficacy), sustain behavior change over time (maintenance self-efficacy), and resume action/physical activity following a lapse (recovery self-efficacy) have been conceptualized as subcomponents of self-regulatory efficacy and found to independently predict factors such as improved program adherence, intentions, and involvement (e.g., Bray, Gyurcsik, Culos-Reed, Dawson, & Martin, 2001; Cramp & Brawley, 2009; Luszczynska & Sutton, 2006; Rodgers, Wilson, Hall, Fraser, & Murray, 2008; Spink & Nickel, 2010; Woodgate, Brawley, & Weston, 2005). In essence, self-regulation is a goal guidance process that involves personal monitoring and implementation of change and maintenance mechanisms, aimed at task-specific outcomes (Maes & Karoly, 2005). Self-regulatory efficacy beliefs, especially with regard to overcoming barriers to learning, have been identified as being particularly important within educational contexts (Usher & Pajares, 2006). In a similar regard, we would anticipate that self-regulatory efficacy is equally salient in other performance-based contexts such as sports, whereby athletes are required to overcome (training, injury rehabilitation) barriers and sustain behavioral change (e.g., implement new training approaches) over time.

The concepts covered in this section focus primarily on various aspects of one's ability to learn, manage, execute, and maintain a behavior or course of action. However, the final efficacy construct that we describe is rooted in perceptions about one's impression management (or self-presentational) capabilities. Specifically, *self-presentational efficacy* (Leary & Kowalski, 1995) describes one's confidence in conveying a desired impression to others (e.g., appearing strong, fit, coordinated, physically attractive). A prominent line of inquiry in this area has focused on the situational conditions that influence exercise-related self-presentational efficacy beliefs, and research has shown that a variety of factors (e.g., being observed, being videotaped,

watching a "perfect-looking" model, mirrored environments) evoke doubts regarding one's impression management ability (e.g., Fleming & Martin Ginis, 2004; Gammage, Martin-Ginis, & Hall, 2004; McAuley, Bane, & Mihalko, 1995). Although self-presentational efficacy has primarily been studied in physical activity contexts, we would expect that any context in which effective self-presentation is necessary (e.g., public speaking, theater, aesthetic sports) would require elevated conceptions of personal efficacy. This remains a promising topic to be addressed within future research.

Self-Efficacy's Achilles Heel: When the Predictive Effects Are Lost or Reversed

Balanced against the considerable evidence that emphasizes the virtues of believing in one's capabilities, being highly efficacious is not without its downsides. The potential dangers that may exist for highly efficacious performers is perhaps best illustrated by the old proverb "good swimmers are oftenest drowned," which suggests that overconfidence (or complacency) about what one can accomplish may undermine one's capacity to achieve the desired set of outcomes. While acknowledging the widely supported notion that self-efficacy can act as an empowering and adaptive cognition, in this section, we consider some of the caveats to this rule by examining the situations in which a high level of confidence in oneself may fail to promote desirable outcomes and predict performance. First, on a general level, Bandura (1997) outlined a number of factors that may disrupt the positive efficacy–performance relationship, such as when self-efficacy and performance measures are highly discordant, self-efficacy measures do not tap into an adequate range of capabilities, and the individual possesses insufficient performance-related information or the task demands are ambiguous. The former two instances clearly reflect methodological artifacts, which can be appropriately remedied by ensuring direct concordance between the frame of reference for the independent and dependent measures in any given study, and also the need to ensure that efficacy instruments tap into the diverse range of competencies required for successful task execution. The latter instance, however, reflects a conceptual and interpretive caveat, which has important applied implications. Specifically, if an individual has a strong sense of confidence in his or her capabilities, but the bases for those judgments are based on inadequate knowledge of the task at hand, such conceptions of agency may not only fail to predict adaptive task-related accomplishment, but may result in seriously compromised behavioral choice (such as the swimmer who believes that his capabilities are greater than they actually are).

On a different note, Bandura (1982) also stressed that a high sense of self-efficacy about an upcoming task or competition during the period leading up to executing the task (preparatory phase) may account for complacent behaviors characterized by reduced practice, effort, and investment in preparation. For instance, an athlete who is supremely confident about a forthcoming competition may feel little need to devote time to skill and strategy rehearsal in the weeks leading up to the event. In a recent qualitative study, members of elite athlete dyads described this debilitating effect, noting that complacency may arise as a result of high self-efficacy (Jackson et al., 2008). In academic settings, Moores and Chang (2008) also showed that in a group of overconfident students (i.e., whose stated expectations 1 week prior to performing exceeded their subsequent test performance level), their preparatory self-efficacy beliefs were negatively associated with test performance scores (see also Mann & Eland, 2005).

A series of studies presented by Vancouver and colleagues (Vancouver & Kendall, 2006; Vancouver, Thompson, Tischner, & Putka, 2002; Vancouver, Thompson, & Williams, 2001) have also sought to provide evidence that the relationship between task self-efficacy and performance attainment at the within-person level might be inverse (i.e., negative) in nature (see also Yeo & Neal, 2006). Contradicting the wealth of literature documenting a positive relationship between self-efficacy and performance (discussed previously), Vancouver and colleagues argue that a high degree of confidence in one's ability actually plays an incapacitating role with respect to motivation and task execution. Their work draws broadly from Powers' (1978, 1991) perceptual control theory (PCT), in claiming that self-efficacy occupies a central role in the cyclical relationship between goal striving and performance attainment. At the most basic level, PCT contends that individuals seek to reduce the discrepancy between what they desire to achieve (i.e., their goal aspirations) and what they actually achieve (i.e., their performance outcomes), proposing that motivation is greatest when this discrepancy is large (i.e., when performance attainments fall well short of desired levels). Accordingly, when the discrepancy is reduced (i.e., their performance level meets their goal), individuals become complacent and their motivational drive is diminished (Vancouver & Kendall, 2006). Presenting data from laboratory and field-based settings, Vancouver theorizes that highly confident individuals may more optimistically appraise the extent to which they are meeting their goals, thus helping to artificially reduce the goal–performance discrepancy. Thus, efficacious individuals devote fewer motivational resources to meeting subsequent goals and therefore experience reductions in future performance.

Support for the notion that confidence and task execution may not be related in a positive and linear fashion has also been documented with respect to shooting (Gould, Petlichkoff, Simons, & Vevera, 1987) and golf (Hardy, Woodman, & Carrington, 2004) performance. More recently, Woodman and colleagues (Woodman, Akehurst, Hardy, & Beattie, 2010) also illustrated that performance benefits on physical tasks may arise from reductions in one's confidence beliefs. Following a practice trial in which all subjects were asked to skip with a rope continuously for 1 minute, half the participants in Woodman et al.'s (2010) study were informed that the rope they would use on their second trial was "harder" to skip with (i.e., to reduce their confidence). Although confidence was significantly reduced for those who received bogus instructions prior to the second trial, these individuals actually increased their performance on the repeat task. In line with Vancouver and colleagues' interpretation, Woodman et al. contended that reductions in confidence may account for increases in one's perceived discrepancy (between current and desired performance), thus promoting greater effort and subsequent performance.

This literature clearly contradicts the fundamental tenets offered by self-efficacy theory by proposing that an inverse relationship exists between efficacy beliefs and performance attainments over time. In response, Bandura and Locke (2003) highlighted a series of theoretical and methodological issues with Vancouver and colleagues' assertions. First, they noted that positioning the self-efficacy construct within PCT is conceptually inappropriate. The notion of personal agency within self-efficacy theory states that successful performance (in personally meaningful scenarios) is followed by a host of evaluative responses, often including the revision of one's future goals, which ensures that a *new* discrepancy is formed and effort/motivation sustained. Methodologically speaking, Bandura and Locke also criticized Vancouver and colleagues' studies on the grounds that the laboratory tasks used lacked generalizability to meaningful real-world contexts, such as those that take place within sport and many performance settings. Accordingly, these tasks may do little to elicit the various self-reactive and reflective processes (e.g., modifying one's aspirations) that are central within self-efficacy theory. Nonetheless, at a minimum, the studies by Vancouver and colleagues (see also Vancouver, More, & Yoder, 2008) suggest the possibility of moderator variables (e.g., task meaningfulness) that may affect the self-efficacy–performance relationship, and potentially provide an alternative perspective with regard to the role of efficacy beliefs in performance settings.

Personal Efficacy Beliefs to Perform Interpersonal Tasks

In sport, and indeed across many performance contexts, whether in business, education, or the performing arts, people often operate in a social context in which they both influence and are influenced by others (cf. Bandura 1986, 1997). In addition to research that has centered on people's beliefs in their personal capabilities to perform *independent* (or individual) tasks, a growing body of research has also sought to consider the efficacy beliefs that people form in relation to the performance of *interdependent* tasks; that is, those that are performed in association with or in support of others. We recognize that the performance of individual tasks, such as hitting a ball, driving a car, or making a public speech, and the efficacy beliefs to perform those tasks, will invariably be influenced by other people through modeling, verbal persuasion, and so forth. However, in each of these cases, the tasks in question are not performed with *interpersonal action* in mind, whereby the focal person interacts with another person to help that other person "perform" more effectively. Contrast this with a teacher or coach whose primary objective is to support the learning and development of her students, or an athlete whose role on his team is to facilitate the performance of other players on the team (e.g., setter in volleyball). In these examples, personal efficacy beliefs are certainly critical, but in each of these cases, the types of tasks involved are interdependent in nature. It is to these types of tasks—and the personal efficacy beliefs that underpin these interdependent processes—that we now turn our attention. In particular, we focus on teacher efficacy, coaching efficacy, and role efficacy as forms of efficacy belief that that are characterized by interpersonal interaction.

Teacher Efficacy

Teacher efficacy is concerned with the beliefs that teachers have in their capabilities to influence the learning and development of their students (Bandura, 1997; Tschannen-Moran & Woolfolk Hoy, 2001). The study of teacher efficacy (or teacher self-efficacy) has been extensive in a range of educational contexts, including elementary (Gresham, 2008) and high schools (Caprara, Barbaranelli, Steca, & Malone, 2006) through to universities (Bailey, 1999). From a conceptual perspective, teacher efficacy is grounded within Bandura's (1977, 1997) broader conceptual model of self-efficacy theory. Thus, the sources of teacher efficacy beliefs are theorized to directly align with other forms of personal efficacy. Consistent with this conceptual perspective, studies have demonstrated that teaching practice and experience (cf. mastery experiences) are among the most potent sources of teacher efficacy (Mulholland & Wallace, 2001; Poulou, 2007). In addition, verbal/social persuasion has been shown to influence teachers' self-efficacy beliefs. For example, teacher perceptions of student responses during class (in particular, displays of student enthusiasm) have been shown to be an important source of teachers' self-efficacy beliefs (Milner & Hoy, 2003; Poulou, 2007).

A host of research supports the critical influence of a teacher's self-efficacy beliefs on their own performance and behaviors. For example, teaching efficacy predicts the effort that teachers invest in teaching and their resilience in the face of setbacks and challenges (Tschannen-Moran, Woolfolk Hoy, & Hoy, 1998). Teacher self-efficacy is also related to the use of improved instructional and teaching strategies, such as the fostering of a mastery goal structure in class (Wolters & Daugherty, 2007) and a greater willingness to be more open to new teaching ideas and methods (Ross, 1992). In addition, teachers with elevated self-efficacy beliefs tend to be less critical and judgmental of students (Ashton & Webb, 1986) and be more willing to support and cope with students with behavioral and emotional difficulties (Poulou & Norwich, 2002).

In addition to these intra-individual outcomes for teachers associated with elevated teacher efficacy, elevated teacher efficacy beliefs have also been found to transfer on to their students and result in a series of adaptive inter-individual outcomes. These outcomes include improved student motivation (Midgley, Feldlaufer, & Eccles, 1989), self-efficacy (Anderson, Greene, & Loewen, 1988), and ultimately academic achievement (Ashton & Webb,

1986, Ross, 1992; Caprara et al., 2006). Although the majority of research on teacher efficacy has made use of correlational designs (cf. Henson, 2001), there is some experimental evidence to suggest that teacher efficacy can be developed and fostered through professional development programs (Haney, Wang, Keil, & Zoffel, 2007; Ross & Bruce, 2007) that specifically target the major theoretical sources of self-efficacy (cf. Bandura 1997).

Coaching Efficacy

In the same way that teachers play a major role in shaping the development of their students, coaches also play an important role in facilitating the effective learning and performance of their athletes. In recognition of this, Feltz and her colleagues (Feltz, Chase, Moritz, & Sullivan, 1999) developed a conceptual model of coaching efficacy for use within sport contexts that drew directly from the work of Denham and Michael (1981) on teaching efficacy. In recognition of the similarity between teaching and coaching as concepts, Feltz and colleagues (1999) conceptualized coaching efficacy in terms of coaches' beliefs in their capabilities to affect the learning and development of their athletes. However, in recognition of the distinct social context (i.e., sport) in which coaches operate, Feltz et al. also conceptualized coaching efficacy in relation to their game strategy, motivational, technique, and character-building capabilities. Although initial research provided empirical support for this multidimensional (i.e., four lower order dimensions contributing toward a single higher order factor) conceptualization of coaching efficacy (Feltz et al., 1999), recent research by Myers, Feltz, Chase, Reckase, and Hancock (2008) has extended this framework to also include a dimension related to coaches' physical conditioning capabilities (i.e., coaches' confidence in their abilities to prepare their athletes physically for participation in their sport).

In addition to various conceptual and measurement refinements that have taken place in this area, research has also focused on identifying factors that predict (i.e., antecedents) and are predicted by (i.e., consequences) coaches' efficacy beliefs. Rooted in Bandura's (1997) proposals about the origins of self-efficacy perceptions, Feltz et al. (1999) theorized that coaches would be highly confident in their ability when they had mastery experiences as a coach (i.e., their coaching experience, previous win–loss record, preparation), perceived their athletes as being highly skilled, and perceived a high degree of social support from relevant individuals/groups, such as parents, the community, school, and administrators. Empirical examination has not only revealed support for each of these coaching efficacy antecedents (Feltz et al., 1999; Kavussanu, Boardley, Jutkiewicz, Vincent, & Ring, 2008; Marback, Short, Short, & Sullivan, 2005; Myers, Vargas-Tonsing, & Feltz, 2005) but has also begun to extend the network of variables that shape coaches' confidence levels. For instance, coaches have been shown to be more confident in their abilities as a result of their own extensive playing experience (Chase, Feltz, Hayashi, & Hepler, 2005; Feltz, Hepler, Roman, & Paiement, 2009; Sullivan, Gee, & Feltz, 2006), perceptions of player improvement (Chase et al., 2005; Feltz et al., 2009), participation in coach education programs (Campbell & Sullivan, 2005; Malete & Feltz, 2000), as well as through the use of mental imagery techniques (Short, Smiley, & Ross-Stewart, 2005).

Feltz and colleagues (1999) also drew from the key tenets of self-efficacy theory (Bandura, 1997) in proposing that coaches' efficacy beliefs would predict various personal outcomes, including instructional behaviors (e.g., use of motivational and corrective feedback, coaching style) and coaches' commitment to coaching. Consistent with this theorizing, coaching efficacy has been shown to be related to greater use of praise, encouragement, instruction, and positive feedback (Feltz et al., 1999; Sullivan & Kent, 2003), and it also positively predicts coaches' commitment to their role (Kent & Sullivan, 2003). Although these findings emphasize the personal consequences associated with coaches' efficacy beliefs (e.g., a coach's own commitment), conceptualizations of coaching efficacy (Feltz et al., 1999) and coach effectiveness (Horn, 2002) also predict that coaches' efficacy beliefs represent important antecedents of athlete and team (as well as coach) functioning (e.g., athlete/team performance). Specifically, recent investigations have provided evidence for the interpersonal effects associated with coaching efficacy, whereby athletes working under highly efficacious coaches have been shown to display increased perceptions of team efficacy (Vargas-Tonsing, Warners, & Feltz, 2003), as well as improved team performance as measured by win–loss records (Myers et al., 2005). In short, although athletes' perceptions and actions are shaped in no small part by their own self-efficacy beliefs, the beliefs of the person upon whom they depend for direction and development (i.e., their coach) represent an important source of favorable athlete/team outcomes.

Role Efficacy

Each of the above forms of efficacy are concerned with the beliefs of those responsible for the teaching and training of others. We now turn our attention to the personal efficacy beliefs of group members who are required to perform their various role responsibilities within an integrated and interdependent team system. In team environments, members' efficacy beliefs to perform these interdependent responsibilities can have a major bearing on their own and others' successful pursuit of role performance effectiveness. As Bandura (1999) noted "if people are to work together successfully, the members of a group have to perform their roles with a high sense of efficacy" (p. 227). Roles can be both formal and informal (Mabry & Barnes, 1980). Formal roles are those that are typically prescribed with the express purpose of meeting the team's instrumental objectives, whereas informal roles are those that typically emerge through intra-group interactions and include those such as the social convener, comedian, or mentor (Cope, Eys, Beauchamp, Schinke, & Bosselut, 2011). Research on role efficacy has primarily focused on formal role responsibilities, and in the sport domain can be traced to the work of Bray and his colleagues (Bray & Brawley, 2002; Bray, Brawley, & Carron, 2002), who conceptualized role efficacy as team members' perceived capabilities to perform their formal interdependent role responsibilities.

Of particular note, Bray et al. (2002) provided evidence for the discriminant validity of the role efficacy construct, insofar as role efficacy was related to but also found to be empirically distinct from athletes' self-efficacy beliefs. To illustrate how the two concepts differ, using the example of soccer, it is worth considering a player who might be highly efficacious in his capabilities to perform the different technical skills required to play the sport (e.g., dribbling, shooting) but lack the necessary efficacy to perform a given role as specified by the coach, such as a defensive midfield player. A prominent source of team members' role efficacy beliefs corresponds to the extent to which they are clear about the roles they have been assigned. Conversely, when team members lack such role clarity (and thus, experience role ambiguity), their efficacy beliefs to perform their role responsibilities suffer (Beauchamp, Bray, Eys, & Carron, 2002; Beauchamp, Bray, Fielding, & Eys, 2005). In one study that tested this proposition, Beauchamp, Bray, Eys, et al. (2002) examined the relationships between role ambiguity and role efficacy, as well as the relations between role efficacy

and role performance effectiveness. The study used a sample of youth rugby players and found that when players reported themselves to be clear in terms of their scope of responsibilities, they also rated themselves as being more efficacious in their capabilities to perform these duties. Furthermore, these role efficacy judgments subsequently predicted indices of players' role performance effectiveness, as rated by their coaches. That is, role clarity predicted role performance, and role efficacy beliefs mediated that relationship.

In line with the theoretical tenets of self-efficacy theory, another major source of members' role-related efficacy corresponds to the opportunities and experiences (or lack thereof) that team members are provided to master their roles. In their study with university basketball players, Bray et al. (2002) examined the self- and role-related efficacy beliefs of starters and nonstarters, and, although no differences were found with respect to their self-efficacy beliefs, nonstarters reported significantly lower levels of role efficacy than did starters. As an explanation for this, Bray et al. noted that bench players were given less playing time and thus experienced fewer opportunities to develop mastery of their diverse duties. This finding has important implications for practice. That is, if coaches or team leaders sideline various members of a team and provide limited opportunities to master their role-related tasks (whether in sports, business, or other performance contexts), one shouldn't be particularly surprised if those same members lack confidence when they are asked to step up to perform those responsibilities at short notice.

Efficacy Beliefs and Performance in Close Relational Settings: Shifting the Referent from Self to Another

In the case of each of the forms of efficacy described thus far, the frame of reference for those beliefs is the same as the person holding those beliefs ("I am confident in *my own* capabilities to do *x*"). However, within many interdependent settings, such as coach–athlete relationships, a person will often develop some level of confidence in a significant *other's* capabilities; in which case, the frame of reference shifts from oneself to the significant other ("I am confident in *my coach's* capabilities to do *y*"). Lent and Lopez (2002) termed one's confidence in another's capabilities as *other-efficacy,* and theorized that this construct may in fact both bolster one's own sense of personal efficacy or compensate for personal inefficacy when performing particular tasks. From a theoretical perspective, Lent and Lopez conceptualized other-efficacy as constituting one of three complementary efficacy cognitions that exist within close relationships. Specifically, they developed a tripartite model of relational efficacy that included other-efficacy, self-efficacy (as described earlier), and lastly, *relation-inferred self-efficacy* (*RISE*). RISE is a meta-perception that constitutes an appraisal (or estimation) of how confident one's partner is in one's own capabilities. Although the detailed tenets of the tripartite model have been discussed elsewhere (see Lent & Lopez, 2002), of direct relevance to this chapter is the theoretical position that the three tripartite constructs are causally inter-related and independently associated with a series of performance-related outcomes within interdependent/dyadic settings.

Although initial research on the tripartite model focused on romantic relationships (Lopez & Lent, 1991), a series of studies have accumulated in the sport domain that emphasize the utility of considering other-efficacy and RISE alongside self-efficacy beliefs. The impetus for this work can be traced to a study of relational efficacy in the sport of eventing (horse–athlete) by Beauchamp and Whinton (2005). In that study, riders were asked to rate their confidence in their own (self-efficacy) and their horse's capabilities (other-efficacy) immediately before competition, and objective measures of performance were subsequently derived from each phase of competition. Although the "partnership" assessed in this study would be considered fairly unusual, it is noteworthy that in this study athletes' self- *and* other-efficacy beliefs were each able to explain unique variance in riding performance scores. That is, athletes' confidence in their horses' capabilities was able to explain additional variance in performance scores above that explained by self-efficacy alone.

Building upon this initial investigation, Jackson and colleagues conducted a series of qualitative (Jackson, Knapp, & Beauchamp, 2008, 2009) and observational (Jackson & Beauchamp, 2010a; Jackson, Beauchamp, & Knapp, 2007; Jackson, Grove, & Beauchamp, 2010) studies that emphasized the value of developing a strong sense of relational efficacy in both coach–athlete and athlete–athlete dyads. The results of these studies suggest that the tripartite efficacy beliefs embedded within Lent and Lopez's (2002) model may display both *actor* and *partner* effects in relation to key indices of relationship functioning. An actor effect occurs when a predictor variable is related to an outcome

for the same person, whereas a partner effect exists when a predictor variable is related to an outcome for the partner (Kenny, Kashy, & Cook, 2006). As one example, among both coaches and athletes within coach–athlete dyads, other-efficacy beliefs have been found to display both actor *and* partner effects in relation to indices of relationship commitment and effort (Jackson & Beauchamp, 2010a). That is, when coaches felt confident in their athletes' capabilities, not only did this serve to predict greater effort and commitment on behalf of the coaches, but this also appeared to transfer onto the athletes, whereby athletes were more committed and displayed greater effort (Jackson & Beauchamp, 2010a). The same effects were also evident for athletes' other-efficacy beliefs in relation to their own effort/commitment, as well as those same outcomes among their coaches.

According to Lent and Lopez (2002), positive RISE beliefs are theorized to represent a source of self-validation and a key support mechanism for members of close relationships. That is, believing that a partner is confident in one's own ability (high RISE) fosters appreciation of the partner, as well as greater commitment to and desire to interact with that person. There is some support for this proposition. For example, Jackson and Beauchamp (2010a) found that coach RISE beliefs resulted in positive actor and partner effects for commitment. Specifically, when coaches believed that their athletes were confident in the coaches' capabilities, this resulted in both the coach and athlete being more committed. Nevertheless, some evidence also suggests high RISE beliefs among athletes (i.e., the low-status member in the coach–athlete relationship) is related to reduced commitment among both athletes themselves and their coaches (Jackson & Beauchamp, 2010a; Jackson et al., 2010). As one potential explanation for this, Jackson and Beauchamp suggested that athletes may become complacent when they believe that their coach is highly confident in their abilities, which in turn may generate a form of social loafing (i.e., reduced relationship commitment). Given the contradictory findings for RISE, research is clearly still required to ascertain the function of this efficacy-based meta-perception.

Group Conceptions of Agency: Collective Efficacy and Team Performance

In the final form of efficacy belief to be covered within this chapter, we now shift attention to *collective efficacy*. In team settings, the groups' belief about how they can perform as a unit is theorized to be an important predictor of subsequent team performance (Bandura, 2000). Often seen as the group counterpart to self-efficacy, Bandura conceptualized collective efficacy as a group's shared belief in their conjoint capabilities to produce desired results. Although collective efficacy represents a group's shared belief, it is conceptualized as individuals' perceptions regarding the team or groups' capabilities (Bandura, 1997). From a measurement perspective, group/team members are typically queried about their personal confidence in their team's capabilities (e.g., "Rate your confidence in your team's ability....") to perform particular tasks, and these individual responses are aggregated to the group level (see Myers & Feltz, 2007, for an excellent discussion on the measurement of collective efficacy in sport/team settings).

Although the sources of collective efficacy are theorized to reflect those found at the individual level with *self*-efficacy (e.g., mastery experiences, vicarious experiences, verbal/social persuasion), in this case they operate at the group level. For example, previous experiences of group success are once again purported to be a primary source of collective efficacy information (Bandura, 1997), and, in the sport domain, this has been demonstrated in a number of studies (Feltz & Lirgg, 1998; Myers, Payment, & Feltz, 2004). A growing body of research also suggests that leadership behaviors are an important determinant of collective efficacy beliefs (Chen & Bliese, 2002; Jung & Sosik, 2002). For example, Jung and Sosik (2002) demonstrated that transformational leadership was positively related to the extent to which members felt personally empowered, which in turn was positively associated with improved collective efficacy. Although leadership behaviors closely align with Bandura's (1997) notion of verbal and social persuasion, it should also be noted that leaders go beyond just providing verbal persuasion and direct members' goal-oriented actions in an attempt to enhance group processes (Chen & Bliese, 2002). To highlight the manner in which leaders and coaches can potentially elevate team members' efficacy beliefs, as well as the *transferable* nature of efficacy "information," the laboratory study by Hoyt, Murphy, Halverson, and Watson (2003) is particularly noteworthy. Specifically, Hoyt et al. found that when leaders believed in their team members' capabilities, their team members subsequently adopted their leaders' beliefs and thus believed in their team (i.e., demonstrated greater collective efficacy) to a greater extent.

A growing body of research also suggests that other factors are important in the development of collective efficacy, such as a task-involving motivational climate (Heuzé, Sarrazin, Masiero, Raimbault, & Thomas, 2006; Magyar, Feltz, & Simpson, 2004), and group cohesion (Lent, Schmidt, & Schmidt, 2006; Paskevich, Brawley, Dorsch, & Widmeyer, 1999; see also Chapter 16, this volume). Interestingly, the task-related dimensions of cohesion, rather than the social dimensions, have been found to be more closely associated with collective efficacy (Paskevich et al., 1999). Although cohesion has most typically been operationalized as an antecedent of collective efficacy (Lent et al., 2006; Paskevich et al., 1999), it is also conceivable that cohesion may in fact derive (as an outcome) from greater collective efficacy. Experimental research is still required to determine the precise causal relations between cohesion and members' team-based efficacy judgments.

A likely reason for the considerable interest in the collective efficacy construct relates to the growing body of evidence supporting the positive associations between collective efficacy and team attainment. Most notably, beliefs of collective efficacy have been found to be a better predictor of team-level performance-related outcomes than the summation of individuals' self-efficacy beliefs (Gully, Incalcaterra, Joshi, & Beaubien, 2002). The predictive effects of collective efficacy beliefs in relation to improved group functioning have been demonstrated across a variety of settings, most notably in sport teams (Myers, Feltz, & Short, 2004; Myers, Payment, et al., 2004), neighborhood communities (Cohen, Finch, Bower, & Sastry, 2006), education classes (Ware & Kitsantas, 2007), and even music ensembles (Matthews & Kitsantas, 2007). Of particular relevance, Myers, Payment et al. (2004) found, using a prospective observational design with collegiate ice hockey teams, that the collective efficacy beliefs held by team members consistently predicted subsequent team performance even after past performances were controlled. In sum, and to highlight the relationship between collective efficacy and group functioning across diverse performance contexts, Stajkovic, Lee, and Nyberg (2009) conducted a comprehensive meta-analysis and found that, after controlling for sample-adjusted meta-analytic deviancy outliers, the weighted average correlation between collective efficacy and performance was .35. Collectively, this suggests that members' beliefs about what the team can accomplish do in fact predict objective measures of team accomplishment.

As with self-efficacy, the relations between collective efficacy and performance are theorized to have both direct and indirect effects in relation to performance. Although direct effects models have most often been tested within the extant sport and performance psychology literature, a growing body of evidence points to potential mediating mechanisms linking collective efficacy to performance outcomes. One such mechanism that has been found to mediate the relations between collective efficacy and performance corresponds to members' group goals (Bray, 2004). Specifically, when members are more efficacious about what they can collectively achieve, they tend to set higher group goals, which in turn predicts improved group performance (Bray, 2004). Interestingly, elevated perceptions of collective efficacy have also been found to be related to factors such as reduced task anxiety (Greenlees, Nunn, Graydon, & Maynard, 1999), improved task engagement (Salanova, Llorens, Cifre, Martínez, & Schaufeli, 2003), and greater job satisfaction (Klassen, Usher, & Bong, 2010); these may also act as individual-level mediating mechanisms in relation to personal performance improvements within team/group environments.

Parenthetically, the promotion of collective efficacy appears to come with a caveat. That is, although elevated levels of collective efficacy have overwhelmingly been found to be advantageous, some recent work by Goncalo, Polman, and Maslach (2010) suggests that while it may be beneficial for collective efficacy to develop over time, premature conceptions of elevated collective efficacy may in fact impede the group in achieving its desired outcomes. Specifically, Goncalo et al. found that if groups had elevated confidence early on in their respective development, they failed to engage in a beneficial form of process conflict and thereby failed to consider strategies that could be advantageous to the group. In summary, the authors concluded that if high levels of collective efficacy come too soon in a group's respective development, this might be problematic, whereas if collective efficacy is established over time, this may indeed may facilitate team performance.

Conclusion
Efficacy Beliefs and Performance Enhancement: From Theory and Research to Practical Recommendations

One of the great strengths of self-efficacy theory (Bandura, 1997) is that it provides practitioners (e.g., coaches, consultants, clinicians, teachers) with a highly practical, evidence-based framework from which they can develop interventions centered on enhancing people's efficacy beliefs. Specifically, each of the sources of efficacy, discussed earlier in this chapter (see also Figure 14.1) offer viable means through which to bolster people's personal conceptions about what they can accomplish and, in essence, build their confidence. For example, in the pursuit of bolstering people's self-efficacy beliefs, practitioners can be encouraged to target each of the primary sources outlined by Bandura (1997), such as providing clients with greater opportunities to experience personal mastery, observe similar others completing the task, envision themselves through guided imagery mastering specific challenges, and so forth. That said, although Bandura offers a series of sources through which to bolster personal efficacy beliefs, it is also pertinent to note that mastery experiences represent the most powerful resource through which to build these personal conceptions of agency. With this in mind, practitioners should give specific consideration to the *type* of efficacy that they wish to bolster and then provide ongoing experiences for mastery enactment that align with that specific efficacy cognition. Note that the more specific practitioners can be the better; for example, if a basketball player lacks confidence to perform his or her role on a team (i.e., low role efficacy), practices should not simply be constructed to provide greater opportunities to master the independent skills involved in basketball (e.g., dribbling, shooting), but should be constructed to provide the focal athlete with greater opportunities to practice his or her role within the context of the larger group system.

For efficacy-based interventions to be effective, it is also imperative that they are implemented at the appropriate level. For example, if an objective is to improve a team's sense of collective efficacy, it would not be sufficient to simply work with one or two key members of a given team, and then expect the team as a whole to feel more efficacious about its conjoint capabilities. In such an instance, the intervention should involve all team members to ensure that that they all feel collectively confident about what they can collectively accomplish. As another example, given the transference effects that have been found with regard to other-efficacy beliefs (vis à vis partner effects; Jackson & Beauchamp, 2010a), any interventions designed to maximize coach–athlete relationship functioning would be encouraged to include both the coach and athlete and not just one member of the dyad.

Within the fields of sport and performance psychology, an extensive number of experimental studies have been published that provide empirical support for the utility of efficacy-based interventions. For example, intervention programs have been developed to increase self-efficacy in contexts as diverse as addiction behaviors (Hyde, Hankins, Deale, & Marteau, 2008), physical activity enhancement (Ashford, Edmunds, & French, 2010), military personnel development (Dvir et al., 2002), coach education (Malete & Feltz, 2000), and chronic disease management (Marks & Allegrante, 2005), to name but a few. Given the consistent predictive capability of efficacy beliefs for improved performance and functioning across diverse life contexts, allied with people's innate need to feel personally competent (Deci & Ryan, 2000), we would anticipate that interventions guided by self-efficacy theory will continue to develop within the field of applied psychology, and efficacy-based cognitions will continue to represent critical constructs within the realm of positive psychology (cf. Seligman & Csikszentmihalyi, 2000).

Future Directions

Self-efficacy theory represents one of the most studied and widely endorsed social cognitive models of human functioning. Indeed, the accumulated evidence over the past three decades gives some credence to Bandura's assertion that "beliefs of personal efficacy constitute *the key factor* of human agency" (p. 3, *emphasis added*). Nevertheless, and in spite of the burgeoning interest in this area, a number of lines of enquiry have yet to receive sustained research attention. In Chapter 9 of their recent book, Feltz, Short, et al. (2008) highlighted a series of promising directions for future research involving self-efficacy theory, and interested readers are encouraged to read that excellent text. Here, we highlight a series of additional avenues for future enquiry that we believe have considerable theoretical and applied implications for those interested in sport and performance psychology:

• *Investigate the role of learning efficacy in sport and other performance contexts.* At the outset of this chapter, we highlighted a number of forms of personal efficacy that we believe have particular relevance for the pursuit of human achievement (e.g., self-regulatory efficacy, self-presentational efficacy, coping self-efficacy). However, it is the study of learning efficacy that we believe has especial relevance for sport and performance

contexts. Perhaps unsurprisingly, learning self-efficacy has most commonly been studied within school-based and academic settings (see Zimmerman, 2000). However, although interest in this construct within other performance contexts has been somewhat limited, we believe that its utility is highly salient in training scenarios that include (but are not limited to) military, musical, surgical, and athletic apprentices. Indeed, drawing from the tenets of self-efficacy theory (Bandura, 1997; Zimmerman, 2000), one would expect under challenging conditions that those who are confident in their ability to learn will expend greater energy in practicing and seeking to improve their skills, and interventions designed to foster improved perceptions about people's abilities to learn (especially among those who *perceive* they have limited capacities to learn) will result in improved training outcomes.

• *Examine the causal pathways between each of the tripartite efficacy constructs.* In mapping out their tripartite model, Lent and Lopez (2002) theorized that each of the tripartite efficacy constructs would be causally inter-related within relationship settings. To date, however, evidence for these triadic reciprocal pathways (self-efficacy, other-efficacy, and RISE) has been restricted to use of observational designs. In future, it would be theoretically interesting and practically useful to examine the causal interconnections between these constructs through the use of experimental protocols. For example, issues that could be addressed might include: (a) if other-efficacy is boosted through intervention, does this in fact act to bolster a person's sense of self-efficacy, and can a person's inefficacy be compensated for by other-efficacy? Furthermore (b) to what extent do RISE beliefs act as a cognitive filter through which self-efficacy beliefs can be enhanced?

• *Extend knowledge of the sources of role efficacy and test these through experimental designs.* Although the study of role efficacy has not been as extensive as the study of self-efficacy, the research evidence accumulated to date suggests that role-related conceptions of personal agency are an important predictor of role performance effectiveness (Beauchamp, Bray, Eys, et al., 2002; Bray et al., 2002). However, as with the study of relational efficacy, research in this area has primarily been cross-sectional or prospective in nature and has yet to make use of experimental designs. With this in mind, very few studies have examined the sources of role efficacy, and those that have done so have again primarily made use of observational protocols. Thus, drawing from the extant literature in this area, it would be interesting to extend findings from Beauchamp, Bray, Eys, et al. (2002) and Bray et al. (2002) to examine the extent to which role ambiguity and personal mastery experiences can be manipulated through intervention and thereafter influence role efficacy, and, indeed, role performance effectiveness. Furthermore, it would be fascinating and useful to understand what other factors may act as antecedents of role efficacy in sports and other performance domains (e.g., transformational leadership).

• *Extend meta-perception theory to the self-efficacy construct.* Self-efficacy is a *direct perception* (cf. Kenny & Acitelli, 2001) involving a person's beliefs about his or her own capabilities. However, in a recent theoretical paper, Jackson and Beauchamp (2010b) provided an extended discussion regarding the role of self-efficacy when conceptualized as a meta-perception and presented qualitative evidence from elite coach–athlete and athlete–athlete dyads in support of their conceptualization. That is, what happens when a person appraises the self-efficacy beliefs of a significant other, such as coach or teammate? The study of meta-perceptions has been the subject of much research attention within social psychology (see Kenny, 1994; Kenny & DePaulo, 1993), and in the context of sport, Jackson and Beauchamp provided evidence that *estimations of the other person's self-efficacy* (EOSE) beliefs are related to a series of intrapersonal (e.g., personal motivation) and interpersonal (e.g., relationship persistence intentions) outcomes. In future, it would be interesting to examine the extent to which EOSE beliefs can be manipulated through experimentation and the extent to which this metaperception might causally predict salient intrapersonal and interpersonal outcomes.

• *Establish causal pathways between collective efficacy and group cohesion.* In the group dynamics literature, task cohesion has been positioned as a theoretical antecedent of collective efficacy (Paskevich et al., 1999). Although the results of (prospective and cross-sectional) observational research has provided some evidence for this directionality, establishing the causal pathways between these two constructs would have both theoretical and practical relevance. That is, if task cohesion can be established as a causal antecedent through experimental designs, then from an applied perspective, this would provide stronger evidence to suggest that processes designed to foster group unity around its task-related objectives (i.e., team building strategies) can be used to build a team's sense of collective agency.

In his seminal paper, self-efficacy theory was conceptualized by Bandura (1977) as "a unifying theory of behavioral change" (and was described as such within the title to his paper). In the three decades since this paper was published, self-efficacy theory has been applied extensively in diverse domains of human functioning, with sport and performance psychology being one of the major beneficiaries. In this chapter, we presented a synopsis of some of the salient types of efficacy belief that have particular relevance for achievement settings, and provided a summary of their distinct sources and performance-related consequences. We also highlighted some extensions to self-efficacy theory (such as the tripartite model of relational efficacy presented by Lent and Lopez), revealed some challenging perspectives to self-efficacy theory (such as those offered by Vancouver and his colleagues), and articulated some pressing considerations for those concerned with intervention. We also highlighted a series of avenues that might be pursued by those interested in conducting research within this area. In sum, in spite of the voluminous amount of research done in this area, the study of self-efficacy theory and performance remains as vibrant now as it was following its initial conception.

References

Ames, C., & Archer, J. (1988). Achievement goals in the classroom: Students' learning strategies and motivation processes. *Journal of Educational Psychology, 80*, 260–267.

Anderson, E. S., Winett, R. A., & Wojcik, J. R. (2007). Self-regulation, self-efficacy, outcome expectations, and social support: Social cognitive theory and nutrition behavior. *Annals of Behavioral Medicine, 34*, 304–312.

Anderson, R., Greene, M., & Loewen, P. (1988). Relationships among teachers' and students' thinking skills, sense of efficacy, and student achievement. *Alberta Journal of Educational Research, 34*, 148–165.

Ashford, S., Edmunds, J., & French, D. P. (2010). What is the best way to change self-efficacy to promote lifestyle and recreational physical activity? A systematic review with meta-analysis. *British Journal of Health Psychology, 15*, 265–288.

Ashton, P., & Webb, R. (1986). *Making a difference: Teachers' sense of efficacy and student achievement.* New York: Longman.

Avolio, B., Zhu, W., Koh, W., & Bhatia, P. (2004). Transformational leadership and organizational commitment: Mediating role of psychological empowerment and moderating role of structural distance. *Journal of Organizational Behavior, 25*, 951–968

Bailey, J. G. (1999). Academics' motivation and self-efficacy for teaching and research. *Higher Education Research and Development, 18*, 343–359.

Bandura, A. (1977). Self-efficacy: Toward a unifying theory of behavioral change. *Psychological Review, 84*, 191–215.

Bandura, A. (1982). Self-efficacy mechanism in human agency. *The American Psychologist, 37*, 122–147.

Bandura, A. (1986). *Social foundations of thought and action: A social cognitive theory.* Englewood Cliffs, NJ: Prentice-Hall.

Bandura, A. (1993). Perceived self-efficacy and cognitive development and functioning. *Educational Psychologist, 28*, 117–148.

Bandura, A. (1997). *Self-efficacy: The exercise of control.* New York: W. H. Freeman & Company.

Bandura, A. (1999). Social cognitive theory of personality. In D. Cervone & Y. Shoda (Eds.), *The coherence of personality: Social-cognitive bases of consistency, variability, and organization* (pp. 105–241). New York: Guilford.

Bandura, A. (2000). Exercise of human agency through collective efficacy. *Current Directions in Psychological Science, 9*, 75–78.

Bandura, A. (2001). Social cognitive theory: An agentive perspective. *Annual Review of Psychology, 52*, 1–26.

Bandura, A., & Locke, E. A. (2003). Negative self-efficacy and goal effects revisited. *Journal of Applied Psychology, 88*, 87–99.

Bandura, A., & Wood, R. E. (1989). Effect of perceived controllability and performance standards on self-regulation of complex decision-making. *Journal of Personality and Social Psychology, 56*, 805–814.

Bass, B. M. (1998). *Transformational leadership: Industry, military, and educational impact.* Mahwah, NJ: Erlbaum.

Bass, B. M., & Riggio, R. E. (2006). *Transformational leadership* (2nd ed.). Mahwah, NJ: Erlbaum.

Beauchamp, M. R., Barling, J., & Morton, K. L. (2011). Transformational teaching and adolescent self-determined motivation, self-efficacy, and intentions to engage in leisure time physically activity: A randomized controlled pilot trial. *Applied Psychology: Health and Well-Being, 3*(2), 127–150.

Beauchamp, M. R., Bray, S. R., & Albinson, J. G. (2002). Pre-competition imagery, self-efficacy and performance in collegiate golfers. *Journal of Sports Sciences, 20*, 697–705.

Beauchamp, M. R., Bray, S. R., Eys, M. A., & Carron, A. V. (2002). Role ambiguity, role efficacy, and role performance: Multidimensional and mediational relationships within interdependent sport teams. *Group Dynamics: Theory, Research, and Practice, 6*, 229–242.

Beauchamp, M. R., Bray, S. R., Fielding, A., Eys, M. A. (2005). A multilevel investigation of the relationship between role ambiguity and role efficacy in sport. *Psychology of Sport and Exercise, 6*, 289–302.

Beauchamp, M. R., & Whinton, L. C. (2005). Self-efficacy and other-efficacy in dyadic performance: Riding as one in equestrian eventing. *Journal of Sport and Exercise Psychology, 27*, 245–252.

Bouffard-Bouchard, T., Parent, S., & Larivée, S. (1991). Influence of self-efficacy on self-regulation and performance among junior and senior high-school age students. *International Journal of Behavioral Development, 14*, 153–164.

Boyce, B. A., & Bingham, S. M. (1997). The effects of self-efficacy and goal setting on bowling performance. *Journal of Teaching in Physical Education, 16*, 312–323.

Bray, S. R. (2004). Collective efficacy, group goals, and group performance of a muscular endurance task. *Small Group Research, 35*, 230–238.

Bray, S. R., & Brawley, L. R. (2002). Role efficacy, role clarity, and role performance effectiveness. *Small Group Research, 33*, 233–253.

Bray, S. R., Brawley, L. R., & Carron, A. V. (2002). Efficacy for interdependent role functions: Evidence from the sport domain. *Small Group Research, 33*, 644–666.

Bray, S. R., Gyurcsik, N. C., Culos-Reed, S. N., Dawson, K. A., & Martin, K. A. (2001). An exploratory investigation of the relationship between proxy efficacy, self-efficacy and exercise attendance. *Journal of Health Psychology, 6*, 425–434.

Brown, L. J., Malouff, J. M., & Schutte, N. S. (2005). The effectiveness of a self-efficacy intervention for helping adolescents cope with sport-competition loss. *Journal of Sport Behavior, 28*, 136–150.

Campbell, T., & Sullivan, P. J. (2005). The effect of a standardized coaching education program on the efficacy of novice coaches. *Avante, 11*, 56–68.

Carmona, C., Buunk, A. P., Dijkstra, A., & Pieró, J. M. (2008). The relationship between goal orientation, social comparison responses, self-efficacy, and performance. *European Psychologist, 13*, 188–196.

Caprara, G. V., Barbaranelli, C., Steca, P., & Malone, P. S. (2006). Teachers' self efficacy beliefs as determinants of jobs satisfaction and students' academic achievement: A study at the school level. *Journal of School Psychology, 44*, 473–490.

Caprara, G. V., Di Giunta, L., Eisenberg, N., Gerbino, M., Pastorelli, C., & Tramontano, C. (2008). Assessing regulatory emotional self-efficacy in three countries. *Psychological Assessment, 20*, 227–237.

Cartoni, A. C., Minganti, C., & Zelli, A. (2005). Gender, age, and professional-level differences in the psychological correlates of fear of injury in Italian gymnasts. *Journal of Sport Behavior, 28*, 3–17.

Chase, M. A. (2001). Children's self-efficacy, motivational intentions, and attributions in physical education and sport. *Research Quarterly for Exercise and Sport, 72*, 47–54.

Chase, M. A., Feltz, D. L., Hayashi, S. W., & Hepler, T. J. (2005). Sources of coaching efficacy: The coaches' perspective. *International Journal of Sport and Exercise Psychology, 3*, 27–40.

Chemers, M. M., Hu, L., & Garcia, B. F. (2001). Academic self-efficacy and first year college student performance and adjustment. *Journal of Educational Psychology, 93*, 55–64.

Chen, G., & Bliese, P. D. (2002). The role of different levels of leadership in predicting self- and collective efficacy: Evidence for discontinuity. *Journal of Applied Psychology, 87*, 549–556.

Chwalisz, K. D., Altmaier, E. M., & Russell, D. W. (1992). Causal attributions, self-efficacy cognitions, and coping with stress. *Journal of Social and Clinical Psychology, 11*, 377–400.

Coffee, P., & Rees, T. (2008). The CSGU: A measure of controllability, stability, globality, and universality attributions. *Journal of Sport and Exercise Psychology, 30*, 611–641.

Coffee, P., & Rees, T., & Haslam, S. A. (2009). Bouncing back from failure: The interactive impact of perceived controllability and stability on self-efficacy beliefs and future task performance. *Journal of Sports Sciences, 27*, 1117–1124.

Cohen, D., Finch, B., Bower, A., & Sastry, N. (2006). Collective efficacy and obesity: The potential influence of social factors on health. *Social Science and Medicine, 62*, 769–778.

Cope, C. J., Eys, M. A., Beauchamp, M. R., Schinke, R. J., & Bosselut, G. (2011). Informal roles on sport teams. *International Journal of Sport and Exercise Psychology, 9*(1), 19–30.

Cramp, A. G., & Brawley, L. R. (2009). Sustaining self-regulatory efficacy and psychological outcome expectations for postnatal exercise: Effects of a group-mediated cognitive behavioural intervention. *British Journal of Health Psychology,* *14*, 595–611.

Deci, E. L., & Ryan, R. M. (2000). The "what" and "why" of goal pursuits: Human needs and the self-determination of behavior. *Psychological Inquiry, 11*, 227–268.

Denham, C. H., & Michael, J. J. (1981). Teacher sense of efficacy: A definition of the construct and a model for further research. *Educational Research Quarterly, 5*, 39–63.

Dvir, T., Eden, D., Avolio, B. J., & Shamir, B. (2002). Impact of transformational leadership on follower development and performance: A field experiment. *Academy of Management Journal, 45*, 735–744.

Els aiming to maintain hot streak. (2010, April 22nd). *The Irish Times.* Retrieved June 4, 2010, from http://www.irishtimes.com/newspaper/sport/2010/0422/1224268875914.html

Escartí, A., & Guzmán, J. F. (1999). Effects of feedback on self-efficacy, performance, and choice on an athletic task. *Journal of Applied Sport Psychology, 11*, 83–96.

Feltz, D. L., Chase, M. A., Moritz, S. E., & Sullivan, P. J. (1999). A conceptual model of coaching efficacy: Preliminary investigation and instrument development. *Journal of Educational Psychology, 91*, 765–776.

Feltz, D. L., Chow, G. M., & Hepler, T. L. (2008). Path analysis of self-efficacy and diving performance revisited. *Journal of Sport and Exercise Psychology, 30*, 401–411.

Feltz, D. L., Hepler, T. L., Roman, N., & Paiement, C. (2009). Coaching efficacy and volunteer youth sport coaches. *The Sport Psychologist, 23*, 24–41.

Feltz, D. L., & Lirgg, C. D. (1998). Perceived team and player efficacy in hockey. *Journal of Applied Psychology, 83*, 557–564.

Feltz, D. L., & Reissinger, C. A. (1990). Effects of in vivo emotive imagery and performance feedback on self-efficacy and muscular endurance. *Journal of Sport and Exercise Psychology, 12*, 132–143.

Feltz, D. L., Short, S. E., & Sullivan P. J. (2008). *Self-efficacy in sport.* Champaign, IL: Human Kinetics.

Fleming, J. C., & Martin Ginis, K. A. (2004). The effects of commercial exercise video models on women's self-presentational efficacy and exercise task self-efficacy. *Journal of Applied Sport Psychology, 16*, 92–102.

Frydenberg, E., & Lewis, R. (2009). Relations among well-being, avoidant coping, and active coping in a large sample of Australian adolescents. *Psychological Reports, 104*, 745–758.

Gammage, K. L., Martin-Ginis, K. A., & Hall, C. R. (2004). Self-presentational efficacy: Its influence on social anxiety in an exercise context. *Journal of Sport and Exercise Psychology, 26*, 179–190.

Gao, Z., Xiang, P., Harrison, L., Jr., Guan, J., & Rao, Y. (2008). A cross-cultural analysis of self-efficacy and achievement goals between American and Chinese college students in physical education. *International Journal of Sport Psychology, 39*, 312–328.

Goncalo, J. A., Polman, E., & Maslach, C. (2010). Can confidence come too soon? Collective efficacy, conflict and group performance over time. *Organizational Behavior and Human Decision Processes, 113*, 13–24.

Gould, D., Petlichkoff, L., Simons, J., & Vevera, M. (1987). Relationship between competitive state anxiety inventory-2 subscale scores and pistol shooting performance. *Journal of Sport Psychology, 9*, 33–42.

Gowans, S. E., de Hueck, A., Voss, S., Silaj, A., & Abbey, S. E. (2004). Six-month and one-year follow-up of 23 weeks of aerobic exercise for individuals with fibromyalgia. *Arthritis and Rheumatism, 51*, 890–898.

Greenlees, I. A., Nunn, R. L., Graydon, J. K., & Maynard, I. W. (1999). The relationship between collective efficacy and precompetitive affect in rugby players: Testing Bandura's model of collective efficacy. *Perceptual and Motor Skills, 89*, 431–440.

Gresham, G. (2008). Mathematics anxiety and mathematics teacher efficacy in elementary pre-service teachers. *Teaching Education, 19*, 171–184.

Gully, S. M., Incalcaterra, K. A., Joshi, A., & Beaubien, J. M. (2002). A meta-analysis of team-efficacy, potency, and performance: Interdependence and level of analysis as moderators of observed relationships. *Journal of Applied Psychology, 87*, 819–832.

Haney, J. J., Wang, J., Keil, C., & Zoffel, J. (2007). Enhancing teachers' beliefs and practices through problem-based learning focused on pertinent issues of environmental health science. *Journal of Environmental Education, 38*, 25–33.

Hanton, S., Mellalieu, S. D., & Hall, R. (2004). Self-confidence and anxiety interpretation: A qualitative investigation. *Psychology of Sport and Exercise, 5*, 477–495.

Hardy, L., Woodman, T., & Carrington, S. (2004). Is self-confidence a bias factor in higher order catastrophe models? An explanatory analysis. *Journal of Sport and Exercise Psychology, 26*, 359–368.

Heggestad, E. D., & Kanfer, R. (2005). The predictive validity of self-efficacy in training performance: Little more than past performance. *Journal of Experimental Psychology: Applied, 11*, 84–97.

Henson, R. K. (2001). The effects of participation in teacher research on teacher efficacy. *Teaching and Teacher Education, 17*, 819–836.

Hepler, T. J., & Chase, M. A. (2008). Relationship between decision-making self-efficacy, task self-efficacy, and the performance of a sport skill. *Journal of Sports Sciences, 26*, 603–610.

Heuzé, J. P., Sarrazin, P., Masiero, M., Raimbault, N., & Thomas, J. P. (2006). The relationships of perceived motivational climate to cohesion and collective efficacy in elite female teams. *Journal of Applied Sport Psychology, 18*, 201–218.

Horn, T. S. (2002). Coaching effectiveness in the sports domain. In T. S. Horn (Ed.), *Advances in sport psychology* (pp. 309–354). Champaign, IL: Human Kinetics.

Hoyt, C. L., Murphy, S. E., Halverson, S. K., & Watson, C. B. (2003). Group leadership: Efficacy and effectiveness. *Group Dynamics: Theory, Research, and Practice, 7*, 259–274.

Hutchinson, J. C., Sherman, T., Martinovic, N., & Tenenbaum, G. (2008). The effect of manipulated self-efficacy on perceived and sustained effort. *Journal of Applied Sport Psychology, 20*, 457–472.

Hyde, J., Hankins, M., Deale, A., & Marteau, T. M. (2008). Interventions to increase self-efficacy in the context of addiction behavior. *Journal of Health Psychology, 13*, 607–623.

Jackson, B., & Beauchamp, M. R. (2010a). Efficacy beliefs in athlete-coach dyads: Prospective relationships using actor-partner interdependence models. *Applied Psychology: An International Review, 59*, 220–242.

Jackson, B., & Beauchamp, M. R. (2010b). Self-efficacy as a metaperception within coach-athlete and athlete-athlete relationships. *Psychology of Sport and Exercise, 11*, 188–196.

Jackson, B., Beauchamp, M. R., & Knapp, P. (2007). Relational efficacy beliefs in athlete dyads: An investigation using actor-partner interdependence models. *Journal of Sport and Exercise Psychology, 29*, 170–189.

Jackson, B., Grove, R., & Beauchamp, M. R. (2010). Relational efficacy beliefs and relationship quality within coach-athlete dyads. *Journal of Social and Personal Relationships, 27*, 1035–1050.

Jackson, B., Knapp, P., & Beauchamp, M. R. (2008). Origins and consequences of tripartite efficacy beliefs within elite athlete dyads. *Journal of Sport and Exercise Psychology, 30*, 512–540.

Jackson, B., Knapp, P., & Beauchamp, M. R. (2009). The coach-athlete relationship: A tripartite efficacy perspective. *The Sport Psychologist, 23*, 203–232.

Johnson, E. A., & Stewart, D. W. (2008). Perceived competence in supervisory roles: A social cognitive analysis. *Training and Education in Professional Psychology, 2*, 229–236.

Judge, T. A., Jackson, C. L., Shaw, J. C., Scott, B. A., & Rich, B. L. (2007). Self-efficacy and work-related performance: The integral role of individual differences. *Journal of Applied Psychology, 92*, 107–127.

Jung, D. I., & Sosik, J. J. (2002). Transformational leadership in work groups: The role of empowerment, cohesiveness, and collective efficacy on perceived group performance. *Small Group Research, 33*, 313–336.

Kane, T. D., Marks, M. A., Zaccaro, S. J., & Blair, V. (1996). Self-efficacy, personal goals, and wrestlers' self-regulation. *Journal of Sport and Exercise Psychology, 18*, 36–48.

Karademas, E. C., & Kalantzi-Azizi, A. (2004). The stress process, self-efficacy expectations, and psychological health. *Personality and Individual Differences, 37*, 1033–1043.

Kark, R., Shamir, B., & Chen, G. (2003). The two faces of transformational leadership: Empowerment and dependency. *Journal of Applied Psychology, 88*, 246–255.

Kavussanu, M., Boardley, I. D., Jutkiewicz, N., Vincent, S., & Ring, C. (2008). Coaching efficacy and coaching effectiveness: Examining their predictors and comparing coaches' and athletes' reports. *The Sport Psychologist, 22*, 383–404.

Kavussanu, M., & McAuley, E. M. (1995). Exercise and optimism: Are highly active individuals more optimistic? *Journal of Sport and Exercise Psychology, 17*, 246–258.

Kavussanu, M., & Roberts, G. C. (1996). Motivation in physical activity contexts: The relationship of perceived motivational climate to intrinsic motivation and self-efficacy. *Journal of Sport and Exercise Psychology, 18*, 264–280.

Kenny, D. A. (1994). *Interpersonal perception: A social relations analysis.* New York: Guilford.

Kenny, D. A., & Acitelli, L. K. (2001). Accuracy and bias in perceptions of the partner in close relationships. *Journal of Personality and Social Psychology, 80*, 439–448.

Kenny, D. A., & DePaulo, B. M. (1993). Do people know how others view them? An empirical and theoretical account. *Psychological Bulletin, 114*, 145–161.

Kenny, D. A., Kashy, D. A., & Cook, W. L. (2006). *Dyadic data analysis.* New York: Guilford.

Kent, A., & Sullivan, P. J. (2003). Coaching efficacy as a predictor of university coaches' commitment. *International Sports Journal, 7*, 78–88.

Klassen, R. M., Usher, E. L., & Bong, M. (2010). Teachers' collective efficacy, job satisfaction, and job stress in cross-cultural context. *Journal of Experimental Education, 78*, 464–486.

Klink, J. L., Byars-Winston, A., & Bakken, L. L. (2008). Coping efficacy and perceived family support: Potential factors for reducing stress in premedical students. *Medical Education, 42*, 572–579.

Krueger, N., & Dickson, P. R. (1994). How believing in ourselves increases risk taking: Perceived self-efficacy and opportunity recognition. *Decision Sciences, 25*, 385–400.

Kuchler, B. L. (2003). *That's life: Wild wit and wisdom.* Minocqua, WI: Willow Creek Press.

Leary, M. R., & Kowalski, R. M. (1995). *Social anxiety.* New York: Guilford Press.

Lent, R. W., Brown, S. D., Brenner, B., Chopra, S. B., Davis, T., Talleyrand, R., & Suthakaran, V. (2001). The role of contextual supports and barriers in the choice of math/science educational options: A test of social cognitive hypotheses. *Journal of Counselling Psychology, 48*, 474–483.

Lent, R. W., Cinamon, R. G., Bryan, N. A., Jezzi, M. M., Martin, H. M., & Lim, R. (2009). Perceived sources of change in trainees' self-efficacy beliefs. *Psychotherapy: Theory, Research, Practice, Training, 46*, 317–327.

Lent, R. W., & Lopez, F. G. (2002). Cognitive ties that bind: A tripartite view of efficacy beliefs in growth-promoting relationships. *Journal of Social and Clinical Psychology, 21*, 256–286.

Lent, R. W., Schmidt, J., & Schmidt, L. (2006). Collective efficacy beliefs in student work teams: Relation to self-efficacy, cohesion, and performance. *Journal of Vocational Behavior, 68*, 73–84.

Lerner, B. S., & Locke, E. A. (1995). The effects of goal setting, self-efficacy, competition, and personal traits on the performance of an endurance task. *Journal of Sport and Exercise Psychology, 17*, 138–152.

Lindsley, D. H., Brass, D. J., & Thomas, J. B. (1995). Efficacy-performance spirals: A multilevel perspective. *Academy of Management Review, 20*, 645–678.

Lopez, F. G., & Lent, R. W. (1991). Efficacy-based predictors of relationship adjustment and persistence among college students. *Journal of College Student Development, 32*, 223–229.

Luszczynska, A., & Sutton, S. (2006). Physical activity after cardiac rehabilitation: Evidence that different types of self-efficacy are important in maintainers and relapsers. *Rehabilitation Psychology, 51*, 314–321.

Luzzo, D. A., & McWhirter, E. H. (2001). Sex and ethnic differences in the perception of educational and career-related barriers and levels of coping efficacy. *Journal of Counseling and Development, 79*, 61–67.

Mabry, E. A., & Barnes, R. E. (1980). *The dynamics of small group communication.* Englewood Cliffs, NJ: Prentice-Hall.

Maddux, J. E., Norton, L. W., & Leary, M. R. (1988). Cognitive components of social anxiety: An investigation into the integration of self-presentation theory and self-efficacy theory. *Journal of Social and Clinical Psychology, 6*, 180–190.

Maes, S., & Karoly, P. (2005). Self-regulation assessment and intervention in physical health and illness: A review. *Applied Psychology: An International Review, 54*, 245–277.

Magyar, T. M., & Feltz, D. L. (2003). The influence of dispositional and situational tendencies on adolescent girls' sport confidence sources. *Psychology of Sport and Exercise, 4*, 175–190.

Magyar, T. M., Feltz, D. L., & Simpson, I. P. (2004). Individual and crew level determinants of collective efficacy in rowing. *Journal of Sport and Exercise Psychology, 26*, 136–153.

Malete, L., & Feltz, D. L. (2000). The effect of a coaching education program on coaching efficacy. *The Sport Psychologist, 14*, 410–417.

Mann, D. D., & Eland, D. C. (2005). Self-efficacy in mastery learning. *Perceptual and Motor Skills, 100*, 77–84.

Marback, T. L., Short, S. E., Short, M. W., & Sullivan, P. J. (2005). Coaching confidence: An examination of sources and gender differences. *Journal of Sport Behavior, 28*, 18–34.

Marks, R., & Allegrante, J. P. (2005). A review and synthesis of research evidence for self-efficacy-enhancing interventions for reducing chronic disability: Implications for health education (Part II). *Health Promotion Practice, 6*, 148–156.

Martin, J. J. (2002). Training and performance self-efficacy, affect, and performance in wheelchair road racers. *The Sport Psychologist, 16*, 384–395.

Matthews, W. K., & Kitsantas, A. (2007). Group cohesion, collective efficacy, and motivational climate as predictors of conductor support in music ensembles. *Journal of Research in Music Education, 55*, 6–17.

McAuley, E., Bane, S. M., & Mihalko, S. L. (1995). Exercise in middle-aged adults: Self-efficacy and self-presentational outcomes. *Preventive Medicine, 24*, 319–328.

Midgley, D., Feldlaufer, H., & Eccles, J. (1989). Change in teacher efficacy and student self and task-related beliefs in mathematics during the transition to junior high school. *Journal of Educational Psychology, 81*, 247–258.

Milner, H., & Hoy, A. (2003). A case study of an African American teacher's self-efficacy, stereotype threat and persistence. *Teaching and Teacher Education, 19*, 263–276.

Moores, T. T., & Chang, J. C-J. (2008). Self-efficacy, overconfidence, and the negative effect on subsequent performance: A field study. *Information and Management, 46*, 69–76.

Moritz, S. E., Feltz, D. L., Fahrbach, K. R., & Mack, D. E. (2000). The relation of self efficacy measures to sport performance: A meta-analytic review. *Research Quarterly for Exercise and Sport, 71*, 280–294.

Mulholland, J., & Wallace, J. (2001). Teacher induction and elementary science teaching: Enhancing self-efficacy. *Teaching and Teacher Education, 17*, 243–261.

Multon, K. D., Brown, S. D., & Lent, R. W. (1991). Relation of self-efficacy beliefs to academic outcomes: A meta-analytic investigation. *Journal of Counseling Psychology, 38*, 30–38.

Myers, N. D. & Feltz, D. L. (2007). From self-efficacy to collective efficacy in sport: Transitional methodological issues. In G. Tenenbaum & R. C. Eklund (Eds.), Handbook of sport psychology (3rd ed., pp. 799–819). Hoboken, NJ: Wiley.

Myers, N. D., Feltz, D. L., Chase, M. A., Reckase, M. D., & Hancock, D. R. (2008). The Coaching Efficacy Scale II—high school teams. *Educational and Psychological Measurement, 68*, 1059–1076.

Myers, N. D., Feltz, D. L., & Short, S. E. (2004). Collective efficacy and team performance: A longitudinal study of collegiate football teams. *Group Dynamics: Theory, Research, and Practice, 8*, 126–138.

Myers, N. D., Payment, C. A., & Feltz, D. L. (2004). Reciprocal relationships between collective efficacy and team performance in women's ice hockey. *Group Dynamics: Theory, Research, and Practice, 8*, 182–195.

Myers, N. D., Vargas-Tonsing, T. M., & Feltz, D. L. (2005). Coaching efficacy in intercollegiate coaches: Sources, coaching behavior, and team variables. *Psychology of Sport and Exercise, 6*, 129–143.

Nease, A. A., Mudgett, B. O., & Quiñones, M. A. (1999). Relationships among feedback sign, self-efficacy, and acceptance of performance feedback. *Journal of Applied Psychology, 84*, 806–814.

Nicholls, A. R., Polman, R., & Levy, A. R. (2010). Coping self-efficacy, pre-competitive anxiety, and subjective performance among athletes. *European Journal of Sport Science, 10*, 97–102.

Nicholls, J. G. (1984). Achievement motivation: Conceptions of ability, subjective experience, task choice, and performance. *Psychological Review, 91*, 328–346.

Pajares, F. (1996). Self-efficacy beliefs in academic settings. *Review of Educational Research, 66*, 543–578.

Pajares, F., & Miller, M. D. (1994). The role of self-efficacy and self-concept beliefs in mathematical problem-solving: A path analysis. *Journal of Educational Psychology, 86*, 193–203.

Pajares, F., & Urdan, T. (2006). *Adolescent self-efficacy.* Volume 5 in the Adolescence and Education series. Greenwich, CT: Information Age Publishing.

Paskevich, D. M., Brawley, L. R., Dorsch, K. D., & Widmeyer, W. N. (1999). Relationship between collective efficacy and team cohesion: Conceptual and measurement issues. *Group Dynamics: Theory, Research, and Practice, 3*, 210–222.

Poulou, M. (2007). Personal teaching efficacy and its sources: Student teachers' perceptions. *Educational Psychology, 27*, 191–218.

Poulou, M., & Norwich, B. (2002). Teachers' cognitive, affective and behavioural responses to children with emotional and behavioural difficulties: A model of decision making. *British Educational Research Journal, 28*, 111–138.

Powers, W. T. (1978). Quantitative analysis of purposive systems: Some spadework at the foundations of scientific psychology. *Psychological Review, 85*, 417–435.

Powers, W. T. (1991). Commentary on Bandura's "human agency." *American Psychologist, 46*, 151–153.

Rodgers, W. M., Wilson, P. M., Hall, C. R., Fraser, S. N., & Murray, T. C. (2008). Evidence for a multidimensional self-efficacy for exercise scale. *Research Quarterly in Exercise and Sport, 79*, 222–234.

Ross, J. (1992). Teacher efficacy and the effects of coaching on student achievement. *Canadian Journal of Education, 17*, 51–65.

Ross, J., & Bruce, C. (2007). Professional development effects on teacher efficacy: Results of a randomized field trial. *Journal of Educational Research, 101*, 50–60.

Ross-Stewart, L., & Short, S. E. (2009). The frequency and perceived effectiveness of images used to build, maintain, and regain Confidence. *Journal of Applied Sport Psychology, 21*, S34–S47.

Rudolph, D. L., & Butki, B. D. (1998). Self-efficacy and affective responses to short bouts of exercise. *Journal of Applied Sport Psychology, 10*, 268–280.

Sadri, G., & Robertson, I. T. (1993). Self-efficacy and work-related behavior: A review and meta-analysis. *Applied Psychology: An International Review, 42*, 139–152.

Salanova, M., Llorens, S., Cifre, E., Martínez, I., & Schaufeli, W. B. (2003). Perceived collective efficacy, subjective well-being and task performance among electronic work groups: An experimental study. *Small Group Research, 34*, 43–73.

Seligman, M., & Csikszentmihalyi, M. (2000). Positive psychology: An introduction. *American Psychologist, 55*, 5–14.

Short, S. E., Smiley, M., & Ross-Stewart, L. (2005). The relationships among imagery use and efficacy beliefs in coaches. *The Sport Psychologist, 19*, 380–394.

Skinner, N., & Brewer, N. (2002). The dynamics of threat and challenge appraisals prior to a stressful achievement event. *Journal of Personality and Social Psychology, 83*, 678–692.

Spink, K. S., & Nickel, D. (2010). Self-regulatory efficacy as a mediator between attributions and intention for health-related physical activity. *Journal of Health Psychology, 15*, 75–84.

Stajkovic, A. D., Lee, D., & Nyberg, A.J. (2009). Collective efficacy, group potency, and group performance: Meta-analyses of their relationships, and test of mediation model. *Journal of Applied Psychology, 94*, 814–828.

Stajkovic, A. D., & Luthans, F. (1998). Self-efficacy and work-related performance: A meta-analysis. *Psychological Bulletin, 124*, 240–261.

Sullivan, P. J., Gee, C. J., & Feltz, D. L. (2006). Playing experience: The content knowledge source of coaching efficacy beliefs. In A.V. Mitel (Ed.), *Trends in educational psychology*. New York: Nova Publishers.

Sullivan, P. J., & Kent, A. (2003). Coaching efficacy as a predictor of leadership style in intercollegiate athletics. *Journal of Applied Sport Psychology, 15*, 1–11.

Tay, C., Ang, S., & Van Dyne, L. (2006). Personality, biographical characteristics, and job interview success: Longitudinal study of the mediating effects of interviewing self-efficacy and the moderating effects of internal locus of causality. *Journal of Applied Psychology, 91*, 446–454.

Thelwell, R. C., Lane, A. M., & Weston, N. J. V. (2007). Mood states, self-set goals, self-efficacy and performance in academic examinations. *Personality and Individual Differences, 42*, 573–583.

Tolli, A. P., & Schmidt, A. M. (2008). The role of feedback, causal attributions, and self-efficacy in goal revision. *Journal of Applied Psychology, 93*, 692–701.

Tschannen-Moran, M., & Woolfolk Hoy, A. (2001). Teacher efficacy: Capturing an elusive concept. *Teaching and Teacher Education, 17*, 783–805.

Tschannen-Moran, M., Woolfolk Hoy, A., & Hoy, W. K. (1998). Teacher efficacy: Its meaning and measure. *Review of Educational Research, 68*, 202–248.

Tsutsumi, T., Don, B. M., Zaichkowsky, L. D., & Delizonna, L. L. (1997). Physical fitness and psychological benefits of strength training in community dwelling older adults. *Applied Human Science, 16*, 257–266.

Tucker, S., Turner, N., Barling, J., & McEvoy, M. (2010). Transformational leadership and children's aggression in team settings: A short-term longitudinal study. *Leadership Quarterly, 21*, 389–399.

Usher, E. L., & Pajares, F. (2006). Sources of academic and self-regulatory efficacy beliefs of entering middle school students. *Contemporary Educational Psychology, 31*, 125–141.

Vancouver, J. B., & Kendall, L. (2006). When self-efficacy negatively relates to motivation and performance in a learning context. *Journal of Applied Psychology, 91*, 1146–1153.

Vancouver, J. B., More, K. M., & Yoder, R. J. (2008). Self-efficacy and resource allocation: Support for a nonmonotonic, discontinuous model. *Journal of Applied Psychology, 93*, 35–47.

Vancouver, J. B., Thompson, C. M., Tischner, E. C., & Putka, D. J. (2002). Two studies examining the negative effect of self-efficacy on performance. *Journal of Applied Psychology, 87*, 506–516.

Vancouver, J. B., Thompson, C. M., & Williams, A. A. (2001). The changing signs in the relationships between self-efficacy, personal goals, and performance. *Journal of Applied Psychology, 86*, 605–620.

Vargas-Tonsing, T. M., Warners, A. L., & Feltz, D. L. (2003). The predictability of coaching efficacy on team efficacy and player efficacy in volleyball. *Journal of Sport Behavior, 26*, 396–407.

Vrugt, A., & Koenis, S. (2002). Perceived self-efficacy, personal goals, social comparison, scientific productivity. *Applied Psychology: An International Review, 51*, 593–607.

Ware, H., & Kitsantas, A. (2007). Teacher and collective efficacy beliefs as predictors of professional commitment. *Journal of Educational Research, 100*, 303–310.

Welch, A. S., Hulley, A., & Beauchamp, M. R. (2010). Affect and self-efficacy responses during moderate-intensity exercise among low-active women: The effect of cognitive appraisal. *Journal of Sport and Exercise Psychology, 32*, 154–175.

West, R. L., Bagwell, D. K., & Dark-Freudeman, A. (2008). Self-efficacy and memory aging: The impact of a memory intervention based on self-efficacy. *Aging, Neuropsychology, and Cognition, 15*, 302–329.

Williams, T., & Williams, K. (2010). Self-efficacy and performance in mathematics: Reciprocal determinism in 33 nations. *Journal of Educational Psychology, 102*, 453–466.

Wise, J. B., & Trunnell, E. P. (2001). The influence of sources of self-efficacy upon efficacy strength. *Journal of Sport and Exercise Psychology, 2*, 268–280.

Wolters, C. A., & Daugherty, S. G. (2007). Goal structures and teachers' sense of efficacy: Their relation and association to teaching experience and academic level. *Journal of Educational Psychology, 99*, 181–193.

Wood, R. E., & Bandura, A. (1989). Impact of conceptions of ability on self-regulatory mechanisms and complex decision-making. *Journal of Personality and Social Psychology, 56*, 407–415.

Woodgate, J., Brawley, L. R., & Weston, Z. J. (2005). Maintenance cardiac rehabilitation exercise adherence: Effects of task and self-regulatory self-efficacy. *Journal of Applied Social Psychology, 35*, 183–197.

Woodman, T., Akehurst, S., Hardy, L., & Beattie, S. (2010). Self-confidence and performance: A little self-doubt helps. *Psychology of Sport and Exercise, 11*, 467–470.

Yeo, G. B., & Neal, A. (2006). An examination of the dynamic relationship between self-efficacy and performance across levels of analysis and levels of specificity. *Journal of Applied Psychology, 91*, 1088–1101.

Zimmerman, B. J. (2000). Self-efficacy: An essential motive to learn. *Contemporary Educational Psychology, 25*, 82–91.

Perfectionism and Performance

Joachim Stoeber

Abstract

Perfectionism is a personality disposition related to individual differences in performance in sport, school, and other areas of life where performance, tests, and competition play a major role. This chapter discusses the importance of differentiating two main dimensions of perfectionism—perfectionistic strivings and perfectionistic concerns—when examining the relationships between perfectionism and performance in sport, education, music competitions, aptitude tests, and laboratory tasks. The chapter presents studies showing that perfectionistic strivings are positively associated with performance and predict higher performance beyond people's general aptitude and previous performance level. In contrast, perfectionistic concerns are not consistently negatively associated with performance. To conclude the chapter, implications for applied psychology are discussed, as are open questions for future research regarding issues such as the development of perfectionism, performance and efficiency, and gender differences.

Key Words: Perfectionism, performance, sport, training, competition, students, grade point average, achievement, effort, general aptitude

Perfectionism
Perfectionistic Strivings and Perfectionistic Concerns

Perfectionism is a personality disposition characterized by striving for flawlessness and setting exceedingly high standards for performance, accompanied by tendencies for overly critical evaluations (Flett & Hewitt, 2002; Frost, Marten, Lahart, & Rosenblate, 1990). It is a disposition that pervades all areas of life, particularly work and school, and may also affect one's personal appearance and social relationships (Stoeber & Stoeber, 2009). Moreover, perfectionism is a common characteristic in competitive athletes (Dunn, Gotwals, & Causgrove Dunn, 2005).

Traditionally, perfectionism has been regarded as a sign of psychological maladjustment and disorder (e.g., Burns, 1980; Pacht, 1984) because

people seeking psychological help for anxiety and depression often show elevated levels of perfectionism. These early psychological conceptions regarded perfectionism as a one-dimensional personality disposition (e.g., Burns, 1980). In the 1990s, however, a more differentiated view emerged conceptualizing perfectionism as multidimensional and multifaceted (Frost et al., 1990; Hewitt & Flett, 1991; see Enns & Cox, 2002, for a review). A consensus has emerged from this research that two main dimensions of perfectionism should be differentiated (Frost, Heimberg, Holt, Mattia, & Neubauer, 1993; Stoeber & Otto, 2006): perfectionistic strivings and perfectionistic concerns. The first dimension—perfectionistic strivings—captures those aspects of perfectionism associated with striving for perfection and setting exceedingly high standards of performance. The second dimension—perfectionistic concerns—captures those aspects associated with concerns over making mistakes, fear of negative evaluation by others, and feelings of discrepancy between one's expectations and performance.

The differentiation between the two dimensions is of central importance to the understanding of perfectionism. Whereas the two dimensions are often highly correlated—most people who show elevated levels of perfectionistic strivings also show elevated levels of perfectionistic concerns—they show differential, and often contrasting, patterns of relationships. Perfectionistic concerns show strong and consistent negative relationships—that is, positive associations with negative characteristics, processes, and outcomes (e.g., neuroticism, maladaptive coping, negative affect) and indicators of psychological maladjustment and mental disorder (e.g., depression). In contrast, perfectionistic strivings often show positive relationships—that is, positive associations with positive characteristics, processes, and outcomes (e.g., conscientiousness, adaptive coping, positive affect) and indicators of subjective well-being and good psychological adjustment (e.g., satisfaction with life) (see Stoeber & Otto, 2006, for a comprehensive review). Moreover, and in the present context more importantly, perfectionistic strivings and perfectionistic concerns also show differential relationships with performance.

However, it is important to note that the positive associations of perfectionistic strivings are often "masked" by the negative associations of perfectionistic concerns, and therefore may show only when the overlap of perfectionistic strivings with perfectionistic concerns is controlled for (R. W. Hill, Huelsman, & Araujo, 2010; Stoeber & Otto, 2006). Consequently, some researchers prefer to examine the differential relationships of perfectionistic strivings and perfectionistic concerns by adopting a group-based approach differentiating three groups of perfectionists (see Figure 15.1): healthy perfectionists (also called adaptive perfectionists), who are defined as people with high levels of perfectionistic strivings and low levels of perfectionistic concerns; unhealthy perfectionists (also called maladaptive perfectionists), who are defined as people with both high levels of perfectionistic strivings and high levels of perfectionistic concerns; and nonperfectionists, who are defined as people with low levels of perfectionistic strivings (Rice & Ashby, 2007; Stoeber & Otto, 2006).

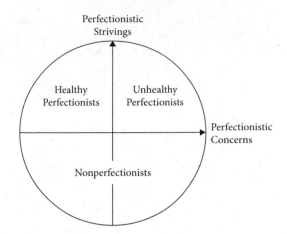

Figure 15.1 Across multidimensional models of perfectionism, two main dimensions of perfectionism can be distinguished (perfectionistic strivings, perfectionistic concerns), which can be used to differentiate between three groups of perfectionists (healthy perfectionists, unhealthy perfectionists, nonperfectionists). Adapted from Stoeber, J., & Otto, K. (2006). Positive conceptions of perfectionism: Approaches, evidence, challenges. *Personality and Social Psychology Review, 10,* 295–319, with permission of the publisher, Lawrence Erlbaum Associates, Inc.

Measures

To measure individual differences in perfectionistic strivings and perfectionistic concerns, a number of multidimensional measures of perfectionism are available that have demonstrated reliability and validity. Measures of general perfectionism include the Frost Multidimensional Perfectionism Scale (FMPS; Frost et al., 1990), the Multidimensional Perfectionism Scale (MPS; Hewitt & Flett, 1991, 2004), the Almost Perfect Scale-Revised (APS-R; Slaney, Rice, Mobley, Trippi, & Ashby, 2001), and the Perfectionism Inventory (PI; R. W. Hill et al., 2004). Measures of perfectionism in sport include the Sport Multidimensional Perfectionism Scale (Sport-MPS; Dunn, Causgrove Dunn, & Syrotuik, 2002; revised version: Gotwals & Dunn, 2009) and the Multidimensional Inventory of Perfectionism in Sport (MIPS; Stöber, Otto, & Stoll, 2004; English version: Stoeber, Otto, & Stoll, 2006). Finally, there is the Multidimensional Perfectionism Cognitions Inventory (MPCI; Kobori & Tanno, 2004; English version: Stoeber, Kobori, & Tanno, 2010), which measures individual differences in cognitions associated with multidimensional perfectionism that are more fleeting than those captured by the other measures which largely capture stable individual differences.

The two dimensions—perfectionistic strivings and perfectionistic concerns—are best captured when each dimension is measured with multiple scales (Frost et al., 1993; Stoeber & Otto, 2006; for a sport example, see Stoeber, Stoll, Salmi, & Tiikkaja, 2009). However, there are single scales that represent proxy measures of the two dimensions. Regarding the perfectionistic strivings dimension, proxy measures are the FMPS Personal Standards scale, particularly when only the items capturing pure personal standards are regarded (DiBartolo, Frost, Chang, LaSota, & Grills, 2004); the MPS Self-Oriented Perfectionism scale, particularly when only the items capturing perfectionistic striving are regarded (Campbell & Di Paula, 2002; Stoeber & Childs, 2010); the APS-R High Standards scale; the PI Striving for Excellence scale; the Sport-MPS Personal Standards scale; the MIPS Striving for Perfection scale; and the MPCI Personal Standards scale. Regarding the perfectionistic concerns dimension, proxy measures are the FMPS Concern over Mistakes scale or the combination of the FMPS Concern over Mistakes and Doubts about Action scales (Stöber, 1998; Stumpf & Parker, 2000); the MPS Socially Prescribed Perfectionism scale, particularly when the items capturing conditional acceptance are regarded (Campbell & Di Paula, 2002; Stoeber & Childs, 2010); the APS-R Discrepancy scale; the PI Concern over Mistakes scale; the Sport-MPS Concern over Mistakes scale; the MIPS Negative Reactions to Imperfection scale; and the MPCI Concern over Mistakes scale.

To know which scales represent proxy measures of the two dimensions of perfectionism helps to understand the findings of studies that do not use multiple scales to measure the two dimensions shown in Figure 15.1. Moreover, it helps to understand the findings of studies that follow the group-based approach to differentiate between healthy perfectionists, unhealthy perfectionists, and nonperfectionists (see again Figure 15.1) which do not use multiple scales and cluster analytic methods to arrive at the three perfectionist groups (see Stoeber & Otto, 2006), but instead use single scales to measure each of the two dimensions—mostly the APS-R High Standards scale to measure perfectionistic strivings, and the APS-R Discrepancy scale to measure perfectionistic concern—to form the three groups of perfectionists (e.g., Rice & Ashby, 2007).

Perfectionism and Performance

Considering the conceptualization of perfectionism and the importance that perfectionists put on high standards of performance (Flett & Hewitt, 2002; Frost et al., 1990), it comes as a surprise that until recently perfectionism research has largely ignored how perfectionism relates to performance. Instead, the vast majority of research—following the traditional view prominent in clinical psychology and psychiatry that perfectionism is a pathological personality characteristic requiring treatment (e.g., Burns, 1980; Pacht, 1984)—focused on investigating how perfectionism is related to indicators of psychological maladjustment, clinical symptoms, and mental disorder (e.g., Flett & Hewitt, 2002, 2007). The one exception is academic performance, in which numerous studies—following a view prominent in personality and individual differences and counseling psychology that perfectionism is a "normal" personality characteristic that has positive and negative aspects—have investigated how perfectionism is related to students' exam performance, grades, and grade point average (GPA).

Academic Performance

Regarding the studies on perfectionism and academic performance, the overwhelming majority shows that perfectionistic strivings are positively associated with academic performance: Students with higher levels of perfectionistic strivings show higher exam performance, higher individual grades, and a higher GPA than do students with lower levels of perfectionistic strivings (Accordino, Accordino, & Slaney, 2000; Bieling, Israeli, Smith, & Antony, 2003; Blankstein, Dunkley, & Wilson, 2008; Blankstein & Winkworth, 2004; Brown et al., 1999; Castro & Rice, 2003; Enns, Cox, Sareen, & Freeman, 2001; Grzegorek, Slaney, Franze, & Rice, 2004; Kawamura, Frost, & Harmatz, 2002; Leenaars & Lester, 2006; Nounopoulos, Ashby, & Gilman, 2006; Rice & Ashby, 2007; Sevlever & Rice, 2010; Stoeber & Eismann, 2007; Stoeber & Rambow, 2007; Vandiver & Worrell, 2002; Verner-Filion & Gaudreau, 2010; Witcher, Alexander, Onwuegbuzie, Collins, & Witcher, 2007). In contrast, the relationship of perfectionistic concerns with academic performance is less clear. Whereas most studies did not find significant negative correlations of perfectionistic concerns with academic performance (Stoeber & Otto, 2006), some studies report small negative correlations (Blankstein et al., 2008; Flett, Blankstein, & Hewitt, 2009; Leenaars & Lester, 2006; Mobley, Slaney, & Rice, 2005; Nounopoulos et al., 2006; Rice & Ashby, 2007; Sevlever & Rice, 2010; Vandiver & Worrell, 2002). However, the majority of these findings are from studies that measured perfectionistic concerns with the APS-R Discrepancy scale (Slaney et al., 2001), which mainly captures perfectionistic concerns about the discrepancy between one's expectations and performance. Consequently, the findings of perfectionistic concerns' negative associations with academic performance may be specific to the APS-R Discrepancy scale and may not generalize to other measures of perfectionistic concerns.

Further evidence that perfectionistic strivings are associated with higher academic performance (and perfectionistic concerns not necessarily with lower academic performance) comes from three studies that followed the group-based approach differentiating healthy perfectionists, unhealthy perfectionists, and nonperfectionists (cf. Figure 15.1) and found significant GPA differences among the three groups (Grzegorek et al., 2004; Rice & Slaney, 2002, Studies 1 and 2). In all three studies, healthy perfectionists had a higher GPA than did nonperfectionists. Moreover, in two studies (Rice & Slaney, 2002, Studies 1 and 2), healthy perfectionists also had a higher GPA than did unhealthy perfectionists, whereas in one study (Grzegorek et al., 2004) healthy perfectionists did not. Instead, healthy and unhealthy perfectionists both had a higher GPA than did nonperfectionists.

Performance in Music Competitions, Aptitude Tests, and Simple Laboratory Tasks

In comparison to the numerous studies that investigated the relationships between perfectionism and academic performance, studies investigating the relationships between perfectionism and performance in other areas are few. Disregarding the studies on sport performance (which are discussed in the following section), there are so far only four studies differentiating perfectionistic strivings and perfectionistic concerns that investigated nonacademic indicators of performance and found significant relationships between perfectionism and performance: one investigating performance in music competitions (Stoeber & Eismann, 2007), one investigating performance in aptitude tests (Stoeber & Kersting, 2007), and two investigating performance in simple laboratory tasks (Kobori & Tanno, 2005; Stoeber, Chesterman, & Tarn, 2010).

Stoeber and Eismann (2007) investigated a sample of young talented musicians examining whether perfectionism was related to the number of awards that the musicians had won in music competitions on local, state, and national levels (coming in first, second, or third place). Results showed that,

whereas perfectionistic concerns were unrelated to the number of awards musicians had won, perfectionistic strivings were positively related to the number of awards: Musicians with higher levels of perfectionistic strivings in their music studies had on average won more awards than musicians with lower levels of perfectionistic strivings, suggesting that perfectionistic strivings show a positive relationship with how well young aspiring musicians perform in competitions.

Stoeber and Kersting (2007) investigated a diverse sample of young people (university students, people recruited at job centers) to examine whether perfectionistic strivings predicted how people performed in aptitude tests typically used in personnel selection, such as reasoning tests, speed tests, and work sample tests (sorting letters, processing e-mails). Results showed that perfectionistic strivings predicted higher test scores in the reasoning tests and the work sample tests, but not in the speed tests (with the exception of the verbal speed tests). Furthermore, perfectionistic strivings predicted performance in the work sample tests beyond what was predicted by young people's performance in the reasoning and speed tests—tests that are usually administered to measure people's general aptitude or "intelligence"—indicating that perfectionistic strivings explain variance in performance in work-relevant tasks beyond what can be explained by individual differences in general aptitude. Moreover, the study included a measure of conscientious achievement striving, which is the facet of trait conscientiousness (Costa & McCrae, 1995) that has shown the highest correlations with both perfectionistic strivings and performance, to examine how individual differences in the achievement striving facet of trait conscientiousness contributed to the results. As expected, conscientious achievement striving showed a substantial positive correlation with perfectionistic strivings. However, only perfectionistic strivings (but not conscientious achievement striving) predicted higher performance in the reasoning and work sample tests, and also explained variance in the work sample tests beyond reasoning and speed, suggesting that perfectionistic strivings have positive effects on performance that go beyond the established findings of trait conscientiousness on performance.

Regarding performance in simple laboratory tasks, a first study (Kobori & Tanno, 2005) investigated performance in a computerized version of the Stroop color-naming task (Stroop, 1935), in which the names of colors were presented in differently colored text (e.g., the word "GREEN" was presented in red letters) and participants had to press a key representing the color of the word's letters, ignoring the word's meaning. The task was paced by the computer program (participants had 800 ms to respond to each word). Results showed that, whereas perfectionistic concerns did not show any significant correlations with task performance, perfectionistic strivings showed a positive correlation with task performance: Participants high in perfectionistic strivings achieved a higher number of correct answers in the task than did participants low in perfectionistic strivings.

A second study (Stoeber et al., 2010) investigated performance in a modified version of the letter detection task used by Tallis, Eysenck, and Mathews (1991). On a computer screen, participants were presented 100 slides with 25 letters and numbers ordered in a 5 × 5 array. Half of the slides contained the letter "E," and the other half did not. The task was to detect the letter "E," and participants had two response keys: one key for "E present" responses, and one for "E absent" responses. In contrast to Kobori and Tanno's (2005) study, the task was self-paced because the authors wanted to measure time-on-task (i.e., the time participants took to complete the task) as an objective measure of effort that participants put into the task. Results showed that perfectionistic concerns showed no significant correlations with either task performance or time-on-task. In contrast, perfectionistic strivings showed a positive correlation with the number of correct responses. Moreover, they showed a positive correlation with time-on-task, suggesting that participants high in perfectionistic strivings put more effort in the task than did participants low in perfectionistic strivings, and that this increased effort was responsible for their higher task performance. This was confirmed when mediation analyses were conducted showing that time on task fully mediated the relationship between perfectionistic strivings and task performance.

Mediation is a key concept in psychological research (Baron & Kenny, 1986) because a mediator represents a "mechanism of action, a vehicle whereby a putative cause has its putative effect" (Cole & Maxwell, 2003, p. 558). Consequently, Stoeber et al.'s (2010) findings have important implications for research on perfectionism and performance because they suggest that invested effort is one mechanism that may explain how perfectionistic strivings lead to higher performance. Previous studies had already suggested that perfectionistic strivings may be associated with higher effort. For example, students high in perfectionistic strivings intend to study more (i.e., invest more hours studying) than do students low in perfectionistic strivings (Bieling et al., 2003; Brown et al., 1999), and young musicians high in perfectionistic strivings spend more time practicing than do young musicians low in perfectionistic strivings (Stoeber & Eismann, 2007). Stoeber et al.'s (2010) findings, however, were the first to demonstrate that people high in perfectionistic strivings actually invest more effort in task performance and that the additional effort they invest is responsible for their higher task performance.

Sport Performance

Finally, four studies investigated the relationships of perfectionism and sport-related performance. Unfortunately, their findings are not as straightforward as those discussed so far. Whereas three of the four studies found perfectionistic strivings to predict higher performance (Stoeber, Uphill, & Hotham, 2009, Studies 1 and 2; Stoll, Lau, & Stoeber, 2008), one study found perfectionistic strivings to predict lower performance after failure (Anshel & Mansouri, 2005), and one study found that athletes high in perfectionistic strivings and high in perfectionistic concerns—that is, athletes who would be considered "unhealthy" perfectionists according to the model in Figure 15.1—showed the largest performance increments over a series of trials (Stoll et al., 2008). Therefore, I will discuss these studies in greater detail than the previous studies.

Anshel and Mansouri (2005) conducted a laboratory study investigating the performance of 30 male undergraduate athletes in a body-balancing task. Athletes completed a multidimensional measure of perfectionism, including scales that measured perfectionistic strivings (the FMPS Personal Standards scale) and perfectionistic concerns (the FMPS Concern over Mistakes scale). Following this, they were asked to perform a body-balancing task on a stabilometer for 20 trials. In half of the trials, athletes received no feedback on their performance. In the other half, they received false negative feedback that they were failing to reach their previous best. Results showed that perfectionistic strivings and perfectionistic concerns were unrelated to performance when athletes received no feedback, but both were associated with impaired performance when athletes received false negative feedback on their performance, suggesting that perfectionism may undermine sport performance when athletes are made to believe that they are underperforming.

The study's findings need to be interpreted with caution, however. First, with 30 athletes, the sample was rather small. Therefore, the findings may not be as reliable as they would have been if a larger sample had been used (cf. Maxwell, 2004). Second, the study measured athletes' general perfectionism (using the FMPS), not their perfectionism in sport (using a sport-specific measure like the Sport-MPS or the MIPS). This is important because research comparing athletes' levels of perfectionism across different domains (sport, school, general life) found that athletes show significantly higher levels of perfectionism in sport than at school and in general life (Dunn et al., 2005). Consequently, measures of general perfectionism may not capture the degree of athletes' perfectionism in sport (Dunn, Craft, Causgrove Dunn, & Gotwals, 2011). Finally, and most importantly, the study was conducted in a laboratory setting using a measure of sport performance (body-balancing performance on a stabilometer) that may have limited predictive validity for athletes' sport performance in "real-life" settings because body-balancing may be a key requirement in some disciplines (e.g., gymnastics), but not in others. Consequently, it can be expected that findings are different when studies investigate the relationships of perfectionism and sport performance out in the field—in training and in competitions—using sport-specific measures of perfectionism and examining larger samples of athletes.

Stoll and colleagues (2008) conducted a field study on perfectionism and training performance in 122 undergraduate student athletes. First, athletes completed a questionnaire assessing perfectionistic strivings (using the MIPS Striving for Perfection scale) and perfectionistic concerns (using the MIPS Negative Reactions to Imperfection scale) during training. Afterward, they performed a series of four trials with a new basketball training task that required scoring baskets from a nonstandard position. Results showed that perfectionistic strivings were associated with higher overall performance when performance was averaged across trials. Perfectionistic strivings, however, were unrelated to performance increments; that is, how much athletes improved their performance over the four trials. Instead, the interaction of perfectionistic strivings and perfectionistic concerns predicted performance increments: Athletes who were high in both perfectionistic strivings and perfectionistic concerns showed the largest performance increments over the four trials.

Although the finding of perfectionistic strivings associated with higher performance was as expected (and in line with the findings from the studies on perfectionism and performance outside sports discussed in the previous sections), the findings that athletes high in both perfectionistic strivings and perfectionistic concerns showed the largest performance increments was unexpected. Speculating on why this was the case, Stoll et al. (2008) noted that the scale they used to measure perfectionistic concerns (the MIPS Negative Reactions to Imperfection scale) contains items that capture anger, dissatisfaction, and frustration after mistakes and unsatisfactory performance (e.g., "I get completely furious when I make a mistake"). Thus, athletes who were high in both dimensions of perfectionism—high in perfectionistic strivings and high in negative reactions to imperfection—may have wanted to show a perfect training performance but experienced more anger, frustration, and dissatisfaction with their imperfect performance. As a result, they may have been more motivated to improve their performance (which at the beginning of the trials was no better than that of the other athletes) over the consecutive trials to avoid further anger, frustration, and dissatisfaction (cf. Frost & Henderson, 1991; Vallance, Dunn, & Causgrove Dunn, 2006). In comparison, athletes who were high in perfectionistic strivings (but not high in negative reactions to imperfection) may not have experienced strong negative affective reactions when their performance was imperfect and thus were less motivated to improve their performance, especially as their performance was higher than those of the other athletes across all four trials anyway. However, Stoll and colleagues' explanation, although plausible, faces the challenge that negative affective reactions usually lead to impaired performance, not improved performance. Consequently, future studies need to replicate the findings and include additional variables that may explain how athletes high in both dimensions of perfectionism may have "channeled" their negative affective reactions to improve their performance.

Finally, Stoeber, Uphill, and Hotham (2009) conducted two field studies investigating the relationships of perfectionism and competitive performance in triathletes and how perfectionistic strivings influence triathletes' race performance. The first study investigated race performance in 112 triathletes competing over the half-Ironman distance (1.9 km swimming, 90 km cycling, 21 km running), and the second study 321 triathletes competing over the Olympic distance (1.5 km swimming, 40 km cycling, 10 km running). Both studies employed a prospective correlational design. Athletes completed measures of perfectionistic strivings (the Sport-MPS Personal Standards scale) and perfectionistic concerns (the Sport-MPS Concern over Mistakes scale)—all of which were adapted to specifically refer to triathlon—the day before the race they had registered for. In addition, they indicated their previous performance level (seasonal best) and completed a questionnaire on the achievement goals they pursued in the upcoming race regarding four goals: performance approach goals (e.g., "It is important to me to perform better than others"), performance avoidance goals ("I just want to avoid performing worse than others"), mastery approach goals (e.g., "It is important to me to perform as well as I possibly can"), and mastery avoidance goals (e.g., "I worry that I may not perform as well as I possibly can") (Conroy, Elliot, & Hofer, 2003). In both studies, only perfectionistic strivings predicted triathletes' performance, whereas perfectionistic concerns were unrelated to performance. What is more, perfectionistic strivings predicted triathletes' performance beyond what was expected from their seasonal best (also controlling for gender and age). Furthermore, mediation analyses showed that the contrast between performance approach goals and performance avoidance goals fully mediated the effects of perfectionistic strivings on race performance. Triathletes high in perfectionistic strivings pursued performance approach goals rather than performance avoidance goals, and the greater the difference between the two goals, the better was their race performance. In short, triathletes high in perfectionistic strivings set more approach-oriented performance goals for the race and thus achieved a race performance that was higher than that of athletes low in perfectionistic strivings.

The findings from basketball training (Stoll et al., 2008) and triathlon competitions (Stoeber, Uphill, & Hotham, 2009) have important implications for research on perfectionism and sport performance because they indicate that, in real-life settings and in the absence of false-failure feedback on performance, athletes high in perfectionistic strivings achieve higher levels of sport performance than do athletes low in perfectionistic strivings. What is more, perfectionistic strivings predict competitive performance beyond what is expected from athletes' previous performance level (Stoeber, Uphill, & Hotham, 2009). Finally, the results of Stoeber and colleagues' mediation analyses suggest that the kind and combination of achievement goals that athletes pursue represent another "mechanism" that may explain how perfectionistic strivings lead to higher performance; namely, by more strongly endorsing performance approach goals (i.e., perform better than other competitors) than performance avoidance goals (i.e., avoid performing worse than other competitors) when athletes set goals for their performance in an upcoming competition (see also Stoeber & Crombie, 2010).

Implications for Applied Psychology

The findings that perfectionistic strivings are associated with higher performance—higher academic performance at school and university; higher performance in music competitions, aptitude tests, and simple laboratory tasks; and higher sport performance in training and competitions—have important implications for our understanding and our evaluation of perfectionism. Perfectionism does not necessarily lead to impaired performance. On the contrary, with perfectionistic strivings, there is a dimension to perfectionism that motivates individuals to strive for the best possible outcome, making them set higher standards than others and give their best effort. As a consequence, individuals high in perfectionistic strivings can achieve a higher performance than can individuals low in perfectionistic strivings. Therefore, perfectionistic strivings represent an aspect of perfectionism that has implications for all areas of psychology in which performance plays a key role. Particularly, the findings that perfectionistic strivings predict higher performance beyond what is expected from people's general aptitude and previous performance level are noteworthy. For example, given that perfectionistic strivings predict higher performance in tests that are used in personnel selection (Stoeber & Kersting, 2007), industrial and organizational psychologists should investigate the role of perfectionism in recruitment and selection.

Moreover, regarding applied sport psychology, the findings that perfectionistic strivings show positive associations with training performance (Stoll et al., 2008) and predict competitive performance beyond athletes' previous performance level (Stoeber, Uphill, & Hotham, 2009) have important implications for athletes, coaches, and personal trainers and advisors, as they show that perfectionism is not necessarily a debilitating characteristic that is certain to undermine sport performance and prevent athletic development (Flett & Hewitt, 2005; Hall, 2006). Instead, perfectionistic strivings may help motivate athletes to achieve their best and boost their performance in training and competitions. Consequently, perfectionistic strivings may form part of the kind of "adaptive perfectionism" that was found to be a typical characteristic of Olympic champions (see Gould, Dieffenbach, & Moffett, 2002).

However, there is one important caveat. As mentioned earlier, most people who show elevated levels of perfectionistic strivings also show elevated levels of perfectionistic concerns, as indicated by the significant (and often large) positive correlations between perfectionistic strivings and concerns found in terms of general perfectionism (Stoeber & Otto, 2006) and perfectionism in sport (e.g., Stoeber, Otto, Pescheck, Becker, & Stoll, 2007; Stoeber, Stoll, et al., 2009). This represents a problem because perfectionistic concerns—although not necessarily leading to impaired performance—have shown close links with characteristics and processes that may impair performance: Whereas perfectionistic strivings in athletes are associated with characteristics and processes that are likely to have positive effects on athletes' performance: such as hope of success, competitive self-confidence, approach goal orientations, and self-serving attributions of success and failure (Stoeber & Becker, 2008; Stoeber et al., 2007; Stoeber, Stoll, Pescheck, & Otto, 2008), perfectionistic concerns in athletes are associated with characteristics and processes that are likely to have negative effects, such as fear of failure, competitive anxiety, avoidance goal orientations, and self-depreciating attributions of success and failure (Sagar & Stoeber, 2009; Stoeber & Becker, 2008; Stoeber et al., 2007, 2008). Moreover, perfectionistic concerns are associated with athlete burnout not only in adult athletes, but already in adolescent athletes (Gould, Udry, Tuffey, & Loehr, 1996; A. P. Hill, Hall, Appleton, & Kozub, 2008). Consequently, perfectionistic concerns represent an aspect of perfectionism that clearly is maladaptive and poses a serious risk to athletes' motivation, self-esteem, health, and athletic development (Hall, 2006).

But how can coaches help athletes who suffer from perfectionistic concerns, and how can such athletes help themselves? Fortunately, two excellent self-help guides are available to everyone who wants to curb the negative aspects of perfectionism. First, there is Antony and Swinson's (1998) guide, which contains procedures and techniques (e.g., identifying and challenging maladaptive perfectionistic thoughts and behaviors) that have shown to be effective in helping perfectionists to cope with the negative aspects of perfectionism (Pleva & Wade,

2007). Second, there is Shafran, Egan, and Wade's (2010) guide, which contains further tried and tested techniques, based on cognitive-behavioral methods, to help people suffering from perfectionistic concerns to overcome their concerns (and the associated negative thoughts, feelings, and behaviors) and learn to be less concerned over making mistakes, less afraid of negative evaluation by others, and less afflicted by feelings of discrepancy between one's expectations and performance. The techniques from both self-help guides can be easily applied— and easily adapted to the sport context—and thus may represent a helpful toolkit for anybody suffering from perfectionistic concerns or working with people who suffer from such concerns. However, more applied research is needed including athletes and other nonclinical populations to confirm that the techniques are widely applicable and generally effective in reducing perfectionistic concerns.

Conclusion

Little evidence suggests that perfectionistic strivings are detrimental to performance. On the contrary, across different domains and different indicators of performance, the evidence suggests that perfectionistic strivings are associated with higher performance and predict higher performance beyond what is expected from individuals' general aptitude or previous performance level. Perfectionistic strivings appear to have a motivational quality that give individuals an extra "boost" to do their best, make an additional effort, and achieve the best possible results. Even some clinical psychologists are beginning to recognize that there is nothing unhealthy or maladaptive about perfectionistic strivings as such (e.g., Lundh, 2004). On the contrary, perfectionistic strivings may form part of a "healthy pursuit of excellence" (Shafran, Cooper, & Fairburn, 2002, p. 778). However, this may only be the case when perfectionistic strivings are not accompanied by elevated levels of perfectionistic concerns (cf. Figure 15.1) because research has shown that perfectionistic concerns are unhealthy and maladaptive and—although they may not be immediately detrimental to performance—represent a serious risk to people's happiness, well-being, and mental health.

Future Directions

Over the last 20 years, research on perfectionism has made tremendous progress in providing many important insights that have broadened and deepened our knowledge about what perfectionism is and what it does. For example, we now know that perfectionism is best conceptualized as a multidimensional characteristic, and we know about the importance of differentiating perfectionistic strivings and perfectionistic concerns. Moreover, an increasing number of studies demonstrates that perfectionistic strivings are associated with and predictive of higher performance across different areas of life and in various achievement situations.

Nevertheless, there are still many open questions regarding perfectionism in general and the relationships of perfectionism and performance in particular. First, we still know little about how individual differences in perfectionism develop over a person's life. There is general agreement that perfectionism has its roots in childhood development and that parents play a key role in the development of general perfectionism (for reviews, see Flett, Hewitt, Oliver, & Macdonald, 2002; Stoeber & Childs, 2011) and perfectionism in sport (Appleton, Hall, & Hill, 2010; Sapieja, Dunn, & Holt, 2011). However, it is unclear what parental factors are responsible for the *differential* development of perfectionistic strivings compared to perfectionistic concerns; that is, what factors contribute to the development of perfectionistic strivings and what factors contribute to the development of perfectionistic concerns. Unfortunately, there is a dearth of longitudinal studies investigating how parental factors influence the development of perfectionism. Although the few longitudinal studies available indicate that harsh parenting and psychologically controlling parenting are factors that contribute to the development of perfectionistic concerns (e.g., Soenens et al., 2008), it is unclear how parents contribute to the development of perfectionistic strivings. Findings from a study by Rice, Lopez, and Vergara (2005) suggest that parental expectations (parents expecting their children to be perfect) lead to perfectionistic strivings, whereas parental criticism (parents criticizing their children if they are not perfect) leads to perfectionistic concerns (see also McArdle & Duda, 2008). However, the study did not employ a longitudinal design. Moreover, other factors than parental factors need to be taken into account; for example, differences in children's broad personality traits. As was shown in a recent longitudinal study, adolescents who were high in the personality trait of conscientiousness (i.e., the personality trait capturing individual differences in organization, persistence, and motivation in goal-directed behavior) were found to show increases in perfectionistic strivings over time (Stoeber, Otto, & Dalbert,

2009), indicating that individual differences in trait conscientiousness are a factor in the development of perfectionistic strivings.

Another open question concerns gender differences. So far, little is known about gender differences in perfectionism because most studies on perfectionism do not report gender differences, and the studies that do have produced inconclusive or inconsistent findings. Regarding absolute levels of perfectionism, there are findings suggesting that female athletes have higher levels of perfectionistic concerns than do male athletes (Anshel, Kim, & Henry, 2009). However, the majority of studies reporting gender differences did not find that females show any higher (or lower) levels of perfectionistic strivings and perfectionistic concerns, neither regarding general perfectionism (e.g., Blankstein et al., 2008; Hewitt & Flett, 2004; Stoeber & Stoeber, 2009) nor perfectionism in sport (e.g., Anshel & Eom, 2003). As concerns gender differences in the relationships between perfectionism and performance, the findings are unclear, too. Whereas the majority of studies on perfectionism and performance that analyzed gender differences did not find evidence that the relationships were different for males and females, two studies that found such evidence show inconsistent findings. Both studies investigated academic performance, as indicated by GPA. In one study (Blankstein & Winkworth, 2004), perfectionistic strivings predicted GPA only in men, but not in women. In the other study (Kawamura et al., 2002), perfectionistic strivings showed a significantly higher positive correlation with GPA in females than in males. Consequently, more research on gender differences in perfectionism is needed to confirm that there are significant and consistent gender differences in perfectionism and its relationships with performance—or to confirm that the "gender similarities hypothesis" (Hyde, 2005) also holds for perfectionism; that is, that perfectionism is another characteristic in which males and females do not show meaningful differences.

Moreover, more research is needed to find further mediators of the perfectionism–performance relationship that explain how perfectionistic strivings lead to higher performance. Whereas invested effort indicated by the time invested in task performance (Stoeber et al., 2010) and stronger approach than avoidance orientations in performance goals (Stoeber, Uphill, & Hotham, 2009) are important explanatory mechanisms, they may be limited to certain tasks and contexts (e.g., self-paced tasks, athletic competitions). Consequently, future research needs to look at other factors such as aspiration level and goal setting, considering that perfectionistic strivings have been associated with higher aspiration levels and with raising one's aspiration levels after success (Kobori, Hayakawa, & Tanno, 2009; Stoeber, Hutchfield, & Wood, 2008). Another important issue for future research is how perfectionism is related to efficiency of performance. Theory and research on anxiety and performance have long made the distinction between absolute performance and relative performance (or efficiency), taking into account the effort invested to achieve a specific level of performance (Eysenck & Calvo, 1992). Because perfectionistic strivings are associated with both higher absolute performance and higher effort, it is important to consider effort when investigating perfectionism and task performance, because when effort is taken into account and performance is regarded relative to invested effort (e.g., dividing absolute performance by invested effort), it may well be that perfectionistic strivings are associated with higher absolute performance, but lower efficiency—as was demonstrated in two recent studies on perfectionism and proof-reading performance (Stoeber, 2011; Stoeber & Eysenck, 2008).

Furthermore, future research has to take note that perfectionism can be highly domain-specific (e.g., Dunn et al., 2005; Stoeber & Stoeber, 2009). Consequently, some of the central studies discussed in this chapter either used domain-specific measures of perfectionism (particularly the studies regarding sport performance) or presented participants the perfectionism measures together with instructions emphasizing the specific domain that the researchers were interested in. For example, in Stoeber and Kersting's (2007) study, instructions were modified to specifically measure perfectionistic strivings in test situations by asking participants to indicate how they usually approached test situations (e.g., tests, written exams, oral exams). And in Stoeber and Eismann's (2007) study, participants were instructed to answer all items with respect to their main music subject (e.g., piano, violin, singing lessons). Although it is unclear to what the degree the relationships between perfectionistic strivings and performance were influenced by the instructions' intentions to make the perfectionism measures more domain-specific, it is conceivable that the relationships the studies report are stronger than if the perfectionism measures had been used with standard instructions not stressing certain domains.

Finally, and most importantly, prospective and longitudinal studies using cross-lagged designs are needed to clarify the causal direction of the relationships between perfectionism and performance (i.e., perfectionistic strivings "causing" higher performance, not vice versa) because some researchers have argued that higher academic performance may be a factor contributing to the development of perfectionism in children and adolescents (e.g., Flett et al., 2002). Moreover, we need to know more about the long-term consequences of perfectionistic strivings on performance because other researchers have argued that perfectionistic strivings—although boosting performance in the short run—may have negative consequences in the long run, such as burnout (e.g., Hall, 2006), and thus may be detrimental to sustained performance.

References

Accordino, D. B., Accordino, M. P., & Slaney, R. B. (2000). An investigation of perfectionism, mental health, achievement, and achievement motivation in adolescents. *Psychology in the Schools, 37*, 535–545.

Anshel, M. H., & Eom, H. J. (2003). Exploring the dimensions of perfectionism in sport. *International Journal of Sport Psychology, 34*, 255–271.

Anshel, M. H., Kim, J. K., & Henry, R. (2009). Reconceptualizing indicants of sport perfectionism as a function of gender. *Journal of Sport Behavior, 32*, 395–418.

Anshel, M. H., & Mansouri, H. (2005). Influences of perfectionism on motor performance, affect, and causal attributions in response to critical information feedback. *Journal of Sport Behavior, 28*, 99–124.

Antony, M. M., & Swinson, R. P. (1998). *When perfect isn't good enough: Strategies for coping with perfectionism*. Oakland, CA: New Harbinger.

Appleton, P. R., Hall, H. K., & Hill, A. P. (2010). Family patterns of perfectionism: An examination of elite junior athletes and their parents. *Psychology of Sport and Exercise, 11*, 363–371.

Baron, R. M., & Kenny, D. A. (1986). The moderator-mediator variable distinction in social psychological research: Conceptual, strategic, and statistical considerations. *Journal of Personality and Social Psychology, 51*, 1173–1182.

Bieling, P. J., Israeli, A., Smith, J., & Antony, M. M. (2003). Making the grade: The behavioral consequences of perfectionism in the classroom. *Personality and Individual Differences, 35*, 163–178.

Blankstein, K. R., Dunkley, D. M., & Wilson, J. (2008). Evaluative concerns and personal standards perfectionism: Self-esteem as a mediator and moderator of relations with personal and academic needs and estimated GPA. *Current Psychology, 27*, 29–61.

Blankstein, K. R., & Winkworth, G. R. (2004). Dimensions of perfectionism and levels of attributions for grades: Relations with dysphoria and academic performance. *Journal of Rational-Emotive and Cognitive-Behavior Therapy, 22*, 267–295.

Brown, E. J., Heimberg, R. G., Frost, R. O., Makris, G. S., Juster, H. R., & Leung, A. W. (1999). Relationship of perfectionism to affect, expectations, attributions, and performance in the classroom. *Journal of Social and Clinical Psychology, 18,* 98–120.

Burns, D. D. (1980). The perfectionist's script for self-defeat. *Psychology Today, 14*(6), 34–52.

Campbell, J. D., & Di Paula, A. (2002). Perfectionistic self-beliefs: Their relation to personality and goal pursuit. In G. L. Flett & P. L. Hewitt (Eds.), *Perfectionism: Theory, research, and treatment* (pp. 181–198). Washington, DC: American Psychological Association.

Castro, J. R., & Rice, K. G. (2003). Perfectionism and ethnicity: Implications for depressive symptoms and self-reported academic achievement. *Cultural Diversity and Ethnic Minority Psychology, 9,* 64–78.

Cole, D. A., & Maxwell, S. E. (2003). Testing mediational models with longitudinal data: Questions and tips in the use of structural equation modeling. *Journal of Abnormal Psychology, 112,* 558–577.

Conroy, D. E., Elliot, A. J., & Hofer, S. M. (2003). A 2 × 2 achievement goals questionnaire for sport: Evidence for factorial invariance, temporal stability, and external validity. *Journal of Sport and Exercise Psychology, 25,* 456–476.

Costa, P. T., Jr., & McCrae, R. R. (1995). Domains and facets: Hierarchical personality assessment using the Revised NEO Personality Inventory. *Journal of Personality Assessment, 64,* 21–50.

DiBartolo, P. M., Frost, R. O., Chang, P., LaSota, M., & Grills, A. E. (2004). Shedding light on the relationship between personal standards and psychopathology: The case for contingent self-worth. *Journal of Rational-Emotive and Cognitive-Behavior Therapy, 22,* 241–254.

Dunn, J. G. H., Causgrove Dunn, J., & Syrotuik, D. G. (2002). Relationship between multidimensional perfectionism and goal orientations in sport. *Journal of Sport and Exercise Psychology, 24,* 376–395.

Dunn, J. G. H., Craft, J. M., Causgrove Dunn, J., & Gotwals, J. K. (2011). Comparing a domain-specific and global measure of perfectionism in competitive female figure skaters. *Journal of Sport Behavior, 34,* 25–46.

Dunn, J. G. H., Gotwals, J. K., & Causgrove Dunn, J. (2005). An examination of the domain specificity of perfectionism among intercollegiate student-athletes. *Personality and Individual Differences, 38,* 1439–1448.

Enns, M. W., & Cox, B. J. (2002). The nature and assessment of perfectionism: A critical analysis. In G. L. Flett & P. L. Hewitt (Eds.), *Perfectionism: Theory, research, and treatment* (pp. 33–62). Washington, DC: American Psychological Association.

Enns, M. W., Cox, B. J., Sareen, J., & Freeman, P. (2001). Adaptive and maladaptive perfectionism in medical students: A longitudinal investigation. *Medical Education, 35,* 1034–1042.

Eysenck, M. W., & Calvo, M. G. (1992). Anxiety and performance: The processing efficiency theory. *Cognition and Emotion, 6,* 409–434.

Flett, G. L., Blankstein, K. R., & Hewitt, P. L. (2009). Perfectionism, performance, and state positive affect and negative affect after a classroom test. *Canadian Journal of School Psychology, 24,* 4–18.

Flett, G. L., & Hewitt, P. L. (2002). Perfectionism and maladjustment: An overview of theoretical, definitional, and treatment issues. In P. L. Hewitt & G. L. Flett (Eds.), *Perfectionism: Theory, research, and treatment* (pp. 5–31). Washington, DC: American Psychological Association.

Flett, G. L., & Hewitt, P. L. (2005). The perils of perfectionism in sports and exercise. *Current Directions in Psychological Science, 14,* 14–18.

Flett, G. L., & Hewitt, P. L. (2007). Cognitive and self-regulation aspects of perfectionism and their implications for treatment: Introduction to the special issue. *Journal of Cognitive-Emotive and Cognitive-Behavior Therapy, 25,* 227–236.

Flett, G. L., Hewitt, P. L., Oliver, J. M., & Macdonald, S. (2002). Perfectionism in children and their parents: A developmental analysis. In G. L. Flett & P. L. Hewitt (Eds.), *Perfectionism: Theory, research, and treatment* (pp. 89–132). Washington, DC: American Psychological Association.

Frost, R. O., Heimberg, R. G., Holt, C. S., Mattia, J. I., & Neubauer, A. L. (1993). A comparison of two measures of perfectionism. *Personality and Individual Differences, 14,* 119–126.

Frost, R. O., & Henderson, K. J. (1991). Perfectionism and reactions to athletic competition. *Journal of Sport and Exercise Psychology, 13,* 323–335.

Frost, R. O., Marten, P. A., Lahart, C., & Rosenblate, R. (1990). The dimensions of perfectionism. *Cognitive Therapy and Research, 14,* 449–468.

Gotwals, J. K., & Dunn, J. G. H. (2009). A multi-method multi-analytic approach to establish internal construct validity evidence: The Sport Multidimensional Perfectionism Scale 2. *Measurement in Physical Education and Exercise Science, 13,* 71–92.

Gould, D., Dieffenbach, K., & Moffett, A. (2002). Psychological characteristics and their development in Olympic champions. *Journal of Applied Sport Psychology, 14,* 172–204.

Gould, D., Udry, E., Tuffey, S., & Loehr, J. (1996). Burnout in competitive junior tennis players: I. A quantitative psychological assessment. *The Sport Psychologist, 10,* 322–340.

Grzegorek, J. L., Slaney, R. B., Franze, S., & Rice, K. G. (2004). Self-criticism, dependency, self-esteem, and grade point average satisfaction among clusters of perfectionists and nonperfectionists. *Journal of Counseling Psychology, 51,* 192–200.

Hall, H. K. (2006). Perfectionism: A hallmark quality of world class performers, or a psychological impediment to athletic development? In D. Hackfort & G. Tenenbaum (Eds.), *Essential processes for attaining peak performance* (Vol. 1, pp. 178–211). Oxford, UK: Meyer & Meyer.

Hewitt, P. L., & Flett, G. L. (1991). Perfectionism in the self and social contexts: Conceptualization, assessment, and association with psychopathology. *Journal of Personality and Social Psychology, 60,* 456–470.

Hewitt, P. L., & Flett, G. L. (2004). *Multidimensional Perfectionism Scale (MPS): Technical manual.* Toronto, ON: Multi-Health Systems.

Hill, A. P., Hall, H. K., Appleton, P. R., & Kozub, S. A. (2008). Perfectionism and burnout in junior elite soccer players: The mediating influence of unconditional self-acceptance. *Psychology of Sport and Exercise, 9,* 630–644.

Hill, R. W., Huelsman, T. J., & Araujo, G. (2010). Perfectionistic concerns suppress associations between perfectionistic strivings and positive life outcomes. *Personality and Individual Differences, 48,* 584–589.

Hill, R. W., Huelsman, T. J., Furr, R. M., Kibler, J., Vicente, B. B., & Kennedy, C. (2004). A new measure of perfectionism: The Perfectionism Inventory. *Journal of Personality Assessment, 82,* 80–91.

Hyde, J. S. (2005). The gender similarities hypothesis. *American Psychologist, 60,* 561–592.

Kawamura, K. Y., Frost, R. O., & Harmatz, M. G. (2002). The relationship of perceived parenting style to perfectionism. *Personality and Individual Differences, 32*, 317–327.

Kobori, O., Hayakawa, M., & Tanno, Y. (2009). Do perfectionists raise their standards after success? An experimental examination of the revaluation of standard setting in perfectionism. *Journal of Behavior Therapy and Experimental Psychiatry, 40*, 515–521.

Kobori, O., & Tanno, Y. (2004). Development of Multidimensional Perfectionism Cognition Inventory. *Japanese Journal of Personality, 13*, 34–43.

Kobori, O., & Tanno, Y. (2005). Self-oriented perfectionism and its relationship to positive and negative affect: The mediation of positive and negative perfectionism cognitions. *Cognitive Therapy and Research, 29*, 559–571.

Leenaars, L., & Lester, D. (2006). Perfectionism, depression, and academic performance. *Psychological Reports, 99*, 941–942.

Lundh, L. -G. (2004). Perfectionism and acceptance. *Journal of Rational-Emotive and Cognitive-Behavior Therapy, 22*, 255–269.

Maxwell, S. E. (2004). The persistence of underpowered studies in psychological research: Causes, consequences, and remedies. *Psychological Methods, 9*, 147–163.

McArdle, S., & Duda, J. L. (2008). Exploring the etiology of perfectionism and perceptions of self-worth in young athletes. *Social Development, 17*, 980–997.

Mobley, M., Slaney, R. B., & Rice, K. G. (2005). Cultural validity of the Almost Perfect Scale–revised for African American college students. *Journal of Counseling Psychology, 52*, 629–639.

Nounopoulos, A., Ashby, J. S., & Gilman, R. (2006). Coping resources, perfectionism, and academic performance among adolescents. *Psychology in the Schools, 43*, 613–622.

Pacht, A. R. (1984). Reflections on perfection. *American Psychologist, 39*, 386–390.

Pleva, J., & Wade, T. D. (2007). Guided self-help versus pure self-help for perfectionism: A randomised controlled trial. *Behaviour Research and Therapy, 45*, 849–861.

Rice, K. G., & Ashby, J. S. (2007). An efficient method for classifying perfectionists. *Journal of Counseling Psychology, 54*, 72–85.

Rice, K. G., Lopez, F. G., & Vergara, D. (2005). Parental/social influences on perfectionism and adult attachment orientations. *Journal of Social and Clinical Psychology, 24*, 580–605.

Rice, K. G., & Slaney, R. B. (2002). Clusters of perfectionists: Two studies of emotional adjustment and academic achievement. *Measurement and Evaluation in Counseling and Development, 35*, 35–48.

Sagar, S. S., & Stoeber, J. (2009). Perfectionism, fear of failure, and affective responses to success and failure: The central role of fear of experiencing shame and embarrassment. *Journal of Sport and Exercise Psychology, 31*, 602–627.

Sapieja, K. M., Dunn, J. G. H., & Holt, N. L. (2011). Perfectionism and perceptions of parenting styles in male youth soccer. *Journal of Sport and Exercise Psychology, 33*, 20–39.

Sevlever, M., & Rice, K. G. (2010). Perfectionism, depression, anxiety and academic performance in premedical students. *Canadian Medical Education Journal, 1*, e96–e104.

Shafran, R., Cooper, Z., & Fairburn, C. G. (2002). Clinical perfectionism: A cognitive-behavioural analysis. *Behaviour Research and Therapy, 40*, 773–791.

Shafran, R., Egan, S., & Wade, T. (2010). *Overcoming perfectionism: A self-help guide using cognitive behavioral techniques.* London: Robinson.

Slaney, R. B., Rice, K. G., Mobley, M., Trippi, J., & Ashby, J. S. (2001). The revised Almost Perfect Scale. *Measurement and Evaluation in Counseling and Development, 34*, 130–145.

Soenens, B., Luyckx, K., Vansteenkiste, M., Luyten, P., Duriez, B., & Goossens, L. (2008). Maladaptive perfectionism as an intervening variable between psychological control and adolescent depressive symptoms: A three-wave longitudinal study. *Journal of Family Psychology, 22*, 465–474.

Stöber, J. (1998). The Frost Multidimensional Perfectionism Scale: More perfect with four (instead of six) dimensions. *Personality and Individual Differences, 24*, 481–491.

Stöber, J., Otto, K., & Stoll, O. (2004). Mehrdimensionales Inventar zu Perfektionismus im Sport (MIPS) [Multidimensional Inventory of Perfectionism in Sport (MIPS)]. In J. Stöber, K. Otto, E. Pescheck, & O. Stoll, *Skalendokumentation "Perfektionismus im Sport"* (Hallesche Berichte zur Pädagogischen Psychologie, No. 7, pp. 4–13). Halle/Saale, Germany: Department of Educational Psychology, Martin Luther University of Halle-Wittenberg.

Stoeber, J. (2011). Perfectionism, efficiency, and response bias in proof-reading performance: Extension and replication. *Personality and Individual Differences, 50*, 426–429.

Stoeber, J., & Becker, C. (2008). Perfectionism, achievement motives, and attribution of success and failure in female soccer players. *International Journal of Psychology, 43*, 980–987.

Stoeber, J., Chesterman, D., & Tarn, T. -A. (2010). Perfectionism and task performance: Time on task mediates the perfectionistic strivings–performance relationship. *Personality and Individual Differences, 48*, 458–462.

Stoeber, J., & Childs, J. H. (2010). The assessment of self-oriented and socially prescribed perfectionism: Subscales make a difference. *Journal of Personality Assessment, 92*, 577–585.

Stoeber, J., & Childs, J. H. (2011). Perfectionism. In R. J. R. Levesque (Ed.), *Encyclopedia of adolescence* (Vol. 4, Pt. 16, pp. 2053–2059). New York: Springer.

Stoeber, J., & Crombie, R. (2010). Achievement goals and championship performance: Predicting absolute performance and qualification success. *Psychology of Sport and Exercise, 11*, 513–521.

Stoeber, J., & Eismann, U. (2007). Perfectionism in young musicians: Relations with motivation, effort, achievement, and distress. *Personality and Individual Differences, 43*, 2182–2192.

Stoeber, J., & Eysenck, M. W. (2008). Perfectionism and efficiency: Accuracy, response bias, and invested time in proof-reading performance. *Journal of Research in Personality, 42*, 1673–1678.

Stoeber, J., Hutchfield, J., & Wood, K. V. (2008). Perfectionism, self-efficacy, and aspiration level: Differential effects of perfectionistic striving and self-criticism after success and failure. *Personality and Individual Differences, 45*, 323–327.

Stoeber, J., & Kersting, M. (2007). Perfectionism and aptitude test performance: Testees who strive for perfection achieve better test results. *Personality and Individual Differences, 42*, 1093–1103.

Stoeber, J., Kobori, O., & Tanno, Y. (2010). The Multidimensional Perfectionism Cognitions Inventory–English (MPCI-E): Reliability, validity, and relationships with positive and negative affect. *Journal of Personality Assessment, 92*, 16–25.

Stoeber, J., & Otto, K. (2006). Positive conceptions of perfectionism: Approaches, evidence, challenges. *Personality and Social Psychology Review, 10*, 295–319.

Stoeber, J., Otto, K., & Dalbert, C. (2009). Perfectionism and the Big Five: Conscientiousness predicts longitudinal increases in self-oriented perfectionism. *Personality and Individual Differences, 47*, 363–368.

Stoeber, J., Otto, K., Pescheck, E., Becker, C., & Stoll, O. (2007). Perfectionism and competitive anxiety in athletes: Differentiating striving for perfection and negative reactions to imperfection. *Personality and Individual Differences, 42*, 959–969.

Stoeber, J., Otto, K., & Stoll, O. (2006). *Multidimensional Inventory of Perfectionism (MIPS): English version.* Unpublished manuscript, School of Psychology, University of Kent, UK.

Stoeber, J., & Rambow, A. (2007). Perfectionism in adolescent school students: Relations with motivation, achievement, and well-being. *Personality and Individual Differences, 42*, 1379–1389.

Stoeber, J., & Stoeber, F. S. (2009). Domains of perfectionism: Prevalence and relationships with perfectionism, gender, age, and satisfaction with life. *Personality and Individual Differences, 46*, 530–535.

Stoeber, J., Stoll, O., Pescheck, E., & Otto, K. (2008). Perfectionism and achievement goals in athletes: Relations with approach and avoidance orientations in mastery and performance goals. *Psychology of Sport and Exercise, 9*, 102–121.

Stoeber, J., Stoll, O., Salmi, O., & Tiikkaja, J. (2009). Perfectionism and achievement goals in young Finnish ice-hockey players aspiring to make the Under-16 national team. *Journal of Sports Sciences, 27*, 85–94.

Stoeber, J., Uphill, M. A., & Hotham, S. (2009). Predicting race performance in triathlon: The role of perfectionism,

achievement goals, and personal goal setting. *Journal of Sport and Exercise Psychology, 31*, 211–245.

Stoll, O., Lau, A., & Stoeber, J. (2008). Perfectionism and performance in a new basketball training task: Does striving for perfection enhance or undermine performance? *Psychology of Sport and Exercise, 9*, 620–629.

Stroop, J. R. (1935). Studies of interference in serial verbal reactions. *Journal of Experimental Psychology, 18*, 643–662.

Stumpf, H., & Parker, W. D. (2000). A hierarchical structural analysis of perfectionism and its relation to other personality characteristics. *Personality and Individual Differences, 28*, 837–852.

Tallis, F., Eysenck, M. W., & Mathews, A. (1991). Elevated evidence requirements and worry. *Personality and Individual Differences, 12*, 21–27.

Vallance, J. K. H., Dunn, J. G. H., & Causgrove Dunn, J. L. (2006). Perfectionism, anger, and situation criticality in competitive youth ice hockey. *Journal of Sport and Exercise Psychology, 28*, 326–386.

Vandiver, B. J., & Worrell, F. C. (2002). The reliability and validity of scores on the Almost Perfect Scale-Revised with academically talented middle school students. *Journal of Secondary Gifted Education, 13*, 108–119.

Verner-Filion, J., & Gaudreau, P. (2010). From perfectionism to academic adjustment: The mediating role of achievement goals. *Personality and Individual Differences, 49*, 181–186.

Witcher, L. A., Alexander, E. S., Onwuegbuzie, A. J., Collins, K. M. T., & Witcher, A. E. (2007). The relationship between psychology students' levels of perfectionism and achievement in a graduate-level research methodology course. *Personality and Individual Differences, 43*, 1396–1405.

PART 3

Social Psychological Processes in Performance

Teamwork and Performance

Albert V. Carron, Luc J. Martin, *and* Todd M. Loughead

Abstract

This chapter focuses on the nature of teamwork as perceived from the perspective of sport, industrial, and military psychology. First, commonly held definitions for a team in each of these three areas are introduced. This is followed by a discussion of how teamwork is conceptualized. Important correlates of teamwork and performance have been identified within the three areas, including cooperation, role relationships, leadership, and cohesion. We provide a framework to facilitate our discussion of these correlates. Then, research carried out in sport, industry, and the military pertaining to each correlate is reviewed. Because of the perceived importance of teamwork, numerous team building interventions have been undertaken to enhance it. The types of interventions and their relative effectiveness are outlined. Finally, future directions are proposed.

Key Words: Team, teamwork, team performance, conceptualization of teamwork, correlates of teamwork and performance, cooperation, role relationships, leadership, cohesion, team building interventions for teamwork

The value of *teamwork* is intuitively understood in sport. Even Michael Jordan (2010), possibly the most individually skilled basketball player of all time, recognized its importance when he pointed out "talent wins games, but teamwork and intelligence wins championships." Jordan's sentiment is not unique or recent; it also was expressed almost a century ago by one of baseball's best home run hitters, Babe Ruth (2010): "the way a team plays as a whole determines its success. You may have the greatest bunch of individual stars in the world, but if they don't play together, the club won't be worth a dime."

The contributions of teamwork to team success in sport seem self-evident. Increasingly, however, social scientists in a number of other areas, such as business, aviation, health, and the military, have highlighted the need for a more team-oriented approach. In the aviation industry, for example,

Ginnett (1995), after discussing a number of airline disasters, pointed out that:

> It is painfully obvious that some crews do not do as well as they should... If we are to understand effective crew performance, it is essential that we move beyond our focus on the individual to a broader level. We must begin to pay serious attention to the crew as a group if we are to optimize cockpit resources.
> (p. 75)

A similar attitude prevails in the military, where effective teamwork is considered a life-and-death issue—a necessity for survival (Salas, Bowers, & Cannon-Bowers, 1995). As a final example, in business from the late 20th century onward, the enthusiasm for a team-oriented approach has reached such a level that Stevens and Campion (1994) suggested it could be viewed as almost a fad in modern management philosophies.

This chapter considers teamwork from a number of perspectives. In the first section, various approaches taken in defining both teams and teamwork are presented. In the second section, a framework for the presentation of factors considered to be correlates of teamwork are introduced. The third section involves a discussion of research that has focused on those correlates. Across a wide variety of areas, scientists and practitioners have attempted to improve teamwork through team building interventions. The effectiveness of those interventions is examined in the next section. Finally, in the last section, a summary is provided and avenues for future work on teamwork are introduced.

Definitions

In all of the areas in which it seemed important to use the power of teamwork to obtain better individual and collective outcomes, it also became apparent quickly that definitional clarity was essential. Just what is a team? What is teamwork? In sport, the answers always seemed obvious; in other areas, less so. For example, a cockpit crew may be called a team but it may, in reality, be nothing more than a collection of individuals carrying out independent tasks. Therefore, as Salas, Bowers, and Cannon-Bowers (1995) pointed out in their overview of research in the area of military psychology, "the development of…a definition [for what constitutes a team] is critical because we can begin to distinguish teams from other types of groups" (p. 55). What follows here are the definitions advanced in three areas—sport, business, and the military. It should be noted that these three do not represent the only areas where concerns with teamwork are prevalent; for example, medicine and education recognize the importance of teamwork. However, space restrictions forced us to limit our attention to these three.

The Team
SPORT

Carron, Hausenblas, and Eys (2005) noted that "every group is like all other groups, like some other groups, and like no other group" (p. 11). What they meant by this is that every group not only contains characteristics that are common to every other group (e.g., group norm), but they also possess characteristics that are unique to themselves (e.g., the types of norms established). Using the commonality of groups as a basis, Carron and his colleagues combined the characteristics originally included in definitions of a group put forward by social psychology

theoreticians such as Shaw (1981), Fiedler (1967), Bass (1960), Newcomb (1951), and Turner (1982) and defined a sport team as:

> [A] collection of two or more individuals who possess a common identity, have common goals and objectives, share a common fate, exhibit structured patterns of interaction and modes of communication, hold common perceptions about group structure, are personally and instrumentally interdependent, reciprocate interpersonal attraction, and consider themselves to be a group.
> (p. 13)

They also noted that not all of these characteristics necessarily need to be present in all teams all of the time. For example, there are many well-known cases in sport where team members did not ostensibly reciprocate interpersonal attraction.

BUSINESS

In their classic 1993 article, Katzenbach and Smith observed that there are considerable misconceptions about business teams, including the idea that any group that works together is a team. They offered this definition: "a small number of people with complementary skills who are committed to a common purpose, set of performance goals, and approach for which they hold themselves mutually accountable" (Katzenbach & Smith, 1993, p. 69).

Subsequently, Katzenbach and Smith (2005) reemphasized that a business working group is different conceptually and practically from a business team. In the case of the former, performance is simply the sum of what its members do as individuals. Thus, for example, the productivity of a sales force would be the cumulative results of its constituent members, but calling this a team does not make it so. In a team, members work together interdependently, and productivity—both individual and collective—is a result of the joint, collaborative efforts of members. Thus, a recruiting team interviewing applicants in a collective format would be engaged in a joint, collaborative effort—a team task.

MILITARY

The generally accepted definition for a military team was originally advanced by Dyer (1984) in her comprehensive review of the literature. She viewed it as a unit of two or more people who have specific role assignments and interdependence and who possess a common goal. Subsequently, Orasanu and Salas (1993) expanded on this definition to include three additional characteristics they felt were fundamental to a military team. One is the requirement for decisions in the context of a larger task. A second is the presence of team members who have specialized knowledge and skills that are relevant to the task and decision. A third is the presence of task conditions that include time pressure and high workloads. This expanded view of a team is the one typically used today.

Teamwork

Teamwork is a complex multidimensional construct that also has been difficult to define (Rousseau, Aubé, & Savoie, 2006). This complexity provides theoreticians with challenges because—as was pointed out above—definitional clarity is essential for valid measurement.

SPORT

We are unaware of any attempts to define and/or directly measure teamwork in sport. Possibly this void is a result of the perceived simplicity of the construct—that teamwork is quite simply *what teams do*. Also, it is generally assumed that coaches and athletes know when teamwork is or isn't present.

A limitation inherent in this assumption—and the lack of a definition delineating the constituent components of teamwork in sport—is that it's impossible to measure the extent to which any given team does (or doesn't) possess it. We hold to the view expressed by Lord Kelvin (i.e., Sir William Thomson, 2008) over 100 years ago: "If you cannot measure it, you cannot improve it." Developing both a definition for teamwork in sport and a protocol to measure it represents a challenge for the future.

BUSINESS

Rousseau, Aubé, and Savoie (2006) recently reviewed the literature in organizational psychology to determine the definitions, conceptual frameworks, and measurement protocols that have been advanced in regard to teamwork. Initially, they made a distinction between task work behaviors and teamwork behaviors. The former are behaviors necessary to the organization's goals but not necessarily carried out in team tasks. Teamwork behaviors, on the other hand, "represent the overt actions and verbal statements displayed during interactions between team members to ensure a successful collective behavior" (p. 542).

Following their review of 29 frameworks for teamwork behaviors published between 1984 and 2005, Rousseau and his colleagues proposed their own integrated framework. In this framework, teamwork is assumed to have two functions: one is to *regulate task performance,* and the other is to *manage group maintenance*. In turn, the regulation of task performance involves a number of specific behaviors categorized as preparation for work accomplishment (e.g., mission analysis), task-related collaboration (e.g., coordination), work assessment (e.g., performance monitoring), and team adjustment behaviors (e.g., collaborative problem solving). Similarly, the management of team maintenance involves specific behaviors categorized as psychological support (e.g., building and maintaining morale) and conflict management (e.g., resolution of differences).

MILITARY

The predominant approach taken in the definition of teamwork in military psychology has been to define it as what teams do. Thus, for example, Oser, McCallum, Salas, and Morgan (1989), after comprehensive testing of naval units, proposed that teamwork is represented by a team's ability to carry out behaviors that are pertinent to task performance in changing environments. The principal team behaviors identified included the identification and resolution of errors, coordinated intra- and inter-team information exchange, and team reinforcement (i.e., motivational and reinforcing statements).

A Framework for Teamwork

According to Kurt Lewin (1935), the father of group dynamics, the two processes in which all groups are inevitably involved are *locomotion* and *maintenance*. The former is represented by those activities of the group that are directed toward the achievement of its objectives. Thus, locomotion and teamwork are positively correlated; if teamwork is better, locomotion is superior. The second process, maintenance, consists of those activities directed toward keeping the group intact. Groups that are chronically in conflict (or disband) have a reduced likelihood of achieving their objectives. Consequently, maintenance and teamwork are also positively correlated.

In the conceptual framework for teamwork behaviors advanced by Rousseau and his colleagues (2009) for organizational psychology, locomotion (referred to as regulation of team performance) and maintenance (referred to as management of team maintenance) provided the foundation for a hierarchical foundation. For purposes of organization in the present chapter, we have also used locomotion

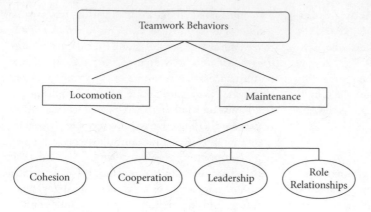

Figure 16.1 Correlates of teamwork.

and maintenance as the foundation for teamwork. Our conceptual framework is illustrated in Figure 16.1. However, in contrast to Rousseau et al., we have not advanced a causal model—research in sport does not support one at this time. Rather, we have chosen to highlight important correlates of effective teamwork. These include cooperation, role relationships, leadership, and cohesion. These are discussed in the sections that follow.

Correlates of Teamwork
Cooperation

One important construct that is related to teamwork is cooperation. In fact, as is pointed out subsequently, cooperation not only contributes to performance through its influence on teamwork, it also contributes to character development, group maintenance, and individual safety in the fields of sport, business, and military (Alonso et al., 2006; Carron et al., 2005; Chatman & Barsade, 1995; Guest, 2008; Jones & George, 1998; Rousseau, Aubé, Savoie, 2006; Weinberg & Gould, 2003)

Guest (2008) highlighted the link between teamwork and cooperation when he stated that "the root meaning of teamwork involves functional cooperation: working together toward a practical purpose" (p. 340). Cooperation itself has been defined as "a social process through which performance is evaluated and rewarded in terms of the collective achievements of a group of people working together to reach a particular goal" (Coakley, 1994, p. 79). These two definitions imply that there is mutual benefit to all members of the group upon completion of a task.

SPORT

The belief that cooperation improves performance is by no means new. As early as 1949, Morton Deutsch used college students to demonstrate the superiority of cooperation over competition. During a period of 5 weeks, students were separated into cooperative or competitive puzzle-solving groups. The competitive group was told that the individual with the most solved puzzles would be rewarded, whereas the cooperative group was told they would receive a team reward. The participants in the competitive group were found to be more self-centered, did not communicate with each other, and did not trust their fellow group members. Conversely, the cooperative group communicated openly, became friends, shared information with one another, and, more importantly, solved more puzzles. Although solving puzzles may not be sport related, the results do agree with the assumption that cooperative teamwork is best for complex and interdependent tasks such as basketball and volleyball (Carron et al., 2005), whereas competition is best for simple reaction time and independent tasks (e.g., archery, sprinting, laboratory tasks) (Carron et al., 2005).

For most professional or competitive amateur sport teams, performance and outcome are the primary objective; however, research in youth sport has provided examples of several other benefits associated with cooperative teamwork. For example, Vazou, Ntoumanis, and Duda (2005) interviewed 30 youth concerning their situational climate. When asked to discuss cooperation, two themes emerged: helping others/each other learn and working together. Both of these responses are process rather than outcome driven.

In 1978, Orlick, McNally, and O'Hara compared special cooperative physical education classes to regular physical education classes. The children in the cooperative classes were characterized as sharing, concerned for others, and willing to help, whereas children in the regular classes were more concerned about themselves.

Marsh and Peart (1988) conducted a similar study. They were interested in the differences between a competitive and cooperative physical fitness program for high school girls. Although physical fitness was improved in both programs, the cooperative group had increased physical and appearance self-concept compared to the competitive group, which was characterized by decreased physical and appearance self-concept.

It appears that cooperative teamwork is beneficial to sport (Carron et al., 2005; Weinberg & Gould, 2003), but also that sport leads to cooperative teamwork (Findlay & Coplan, 2008; Fraser-Thomas & Côté, 2006). For example, Fraser-Thomas and Côté (2006) stated that "youth sport programs have long been considered important to youth's psychosocial development, providing opportunities to learn important life skills such as cooperation, discipline, leadership, and self-control" (p. 12). This sentiment was reinforced by Findlay & Coplan (2008), who found that children involved in sport were more likely to participate in cooperative behavior than were those not involved in sport.

BUSINESS

In business, cooperation is believed to be a collaborative behavior and is grouped with other constructs such as coordination and information exchange (Rousseau et al., 2006). In 1995, Wagner defined it as "the willful contribution of personal effort to the completion of interdependent jobs" (p. 152). Unlike sport, in which cooperation is often discussed as an alternative to competition, business focuses on cooperation as a means of carrying out tasks that are difficult to complete independently (Eby & Dobbins, 1997; Yeatts & Hyten, 1998). Alfie Kohn (1986) proposed that environments that encourage trust and cooperation produce better results in business and also in education, journalism, and the arts.

Jones and George (1998) conceived interpersonal cooperation as an important contributor to organizational performance, as well as a foundation for building trust in the work place. They noted that organizations attempt to create an environment rich in cooperation by re-engineering groups into flatter, more team-based forms, thus giving lower level employees a greater feeling of empowerment. Research supports the view that giving individuals more responsibility and promoting organizational citizenship behavior is possible in a more cooperative environment (Chatman & Barsade, 1995; Katz, 1964; Organ, 1988; Van Dyne, Cummings, & Parks, 1995).

Chatman and Barsade (1995) found that a group-focused culture is extremely important, but that there is also a need for cooperative individuals. One hundred and thirty-nine people with a mean age of 27 participated in their study. Individuals were tested and identified as either cooperative or individualistic using both self-report measures and ratings from coworkers. Once identified, subjects were assigned to one of four groups: cooperative person in a collectivistic setting, cooperative person in an individualistic setting, individualist person in a collectivistic setting, and individualist person in an individualistic setting. Participants were evaluated as cooperative or individualistic by the number of people with whom they interacted, their preference for individual or team rewards, and the degree to which they were oriented toward collectivism or individualism. Results indicated that groups containing cooperative persons in the collective setting were significantly superior to the three other groups and that individualist persons in the individualistic setting were significantly worse than the three other groups. These results highlight the importance of having the right kind of individuals to complement the use of cooperation in the workplace.

MILITARY

In sport and business, a relationship has been found between cooperation, winning, increased production, and profits. In the military, cooperation plays a more important role insofar as it affects member and group safety. In the definition of military teamwork provided earlier, Oser et al. (1989) emphasized the ability of a team to be able to carry out tasks in changing environments. All the team behaviors identified (i.e., identification and resolution of errors, information exchange, and team reinforcement) benefit from cooperation.

In fact, the military health care system emphasizes the importance of cooperation. Alonso et al. (2006) discussed the importance of cooperation among health care workers due to the interdisciplinary nature of the work and their different backgrounds. As an example, physicians are usually asked to make decisions based on the information provided to them, making it imperative that the information be both accurate and properly explained. Healey, Undre, and Vincent (2004) understood the importance of this teamwork and developed the Observational Assessment for Teamwork in Surgery (OTAS) to assess cooperation, leadership, coordination, awareness, and communication.

Another viewpoint highlighting the importance of cooperation comes from Mendel and Bradford (1995), who stated, "mastering interagency cooperation is fundamental to success in military operations" (p. 6). They went on to discuss how the military must cooperate with other nations for missions such as peacekeeping, counterterrorism and insurgency, and disaster relief because at times its independent power is insufficient.

Goette, Huffman, and Meier (2006) examined the tendency for officers in training to cooperate with one another. Members of the Joint Officer Training Program (JOTP) in the Swiss Army were used as their participants. This program places new officers from different branches of the army together for 4 weeks. Half of the individuals were asked questions based on the members in their group, whereas the other half were asked about members not in their group. The participants' willingness to cooperate with certain officers, as well as their beliefs in the willingness of those officers to cooperate with them, were assessed. It was found that 69% of officers indicated a willingness to cooperate with in-group members whereas only 50% were willing to cooperate with out-group members. The beliefs in other group members' tendencies showed a similar trend. A total 57% believed their other group members would cooperate, whereas only 41% believed the out-group members would cooperate.

Role Relationships

Since the 1960s, a significant body of research on role theory has emerged, especially, role ambiguity/role clarity. The proliferation of this research coincided with the introduction of the Kahn, Wolfe, Quinn, Snoek, and Rosenthal (1964) theory of organizational role dynamics. Low role clarity (high role ambiguity) is viewed as ambiguous procedures, goals, criteria, and knowledge of consequences (Rizzo, House, & Lirtzman, 1970). From this perspective, role ambiguity is considered a major stressor since it imposes a high cognitive demand on the individual, who expends energy in an attempt to accomplish the task at hand (Fisher & Gitelson, 1983). This, in turn, negatively impacts the individual's ability to perform effectively (Jackson & Schuler, 1985). In contrast, high role clarity or low role ambiguity is characterized by clear procedures, goals, criteria, and knowledge of consequences (Rizzo et al., 1970). A situation of high role clarity enables individuals to preserve their energy and use it more effectively to accomplish their tasks and objectives (Cohen, 1980).

SPORT

Much of the research concerning role ambiguity in sport has been influenced by the organizational psychology research from Kahn and colleagues (1964) and Rizzo and colleagues (1970). For instance, Grand and Carron (1982) developed items for their Team Climate Questionnaire from Rizzo et al.'s inventory. More recently, Eys and Carron (2001) advanced a conceptual model of role ambiguity in sport heavily influenced by suggestions from Kahn et al. In brief, Eys and Carron suggested that athletes obtain information regarding their role in four areas. That is, athletes need to understand their scope of responsibilities, what behaviors are required to fulfill their roles, how they will be evaluated in regards to role performance, and the consequences of not fulfilling their role responsibilities. Based on this conceptualization of role ambiguity in sport, Beauchamp, Bray, Eys, and Carron (2002) developed the 40-item Role Ambiguity Scale to measure these four dimensions of role ambiguity.

Although the Role Ambiguity Scale is fairly new, a growing body of research has examined role ambiguity in relation to several constructs. This body of research shows that increased role ambiguity is associated with reduced athlete satisfaction (Bebetsos, Theodorakis, & Tsigilis, 2007), reduced task cohesion (Eys & Carron, 2001), increased anxiety (Beauchamp, Bray, Eys, & Carron, 2003), increased role conflict (Beauchamp & Bray, 2001), and inferior performance (Beauchamp et al., 2002). Insofar as the latter is concerned, a significant negative relationship was found between the role ambiguity dimensions of scope of responsibilities and consequences of not fulfilling their role responsibilities and role performance. That is, athletes who were higher in role ambiguity were rated lower in their performance by their coach.

As noted by Eys, Beauchamp, and Bray (2006), role ambiguity is the most extensively researched aspect of role involvement in sport. However, in comparison to business, role ambiguity in sport is in its infancy.

Business

Research concerning organizational roles and role ambiguity/role clarity has a rich history, with research spanning nearly 60 years (Gross, Mason, & McEachern, 1958; Merton, 1949; Parsons, 1951). As a result, an extensive body of research exists on the relationships between role ambiguity/role clarity and a variety of correlates (e.g., absenteeism, job satisfaction, job performance). Katz and Kahn (1978) argued that it is vital to understand the relationship between role ambiguity and job performance since an individual's role (and work behavior) is guided by the social interactions that occur between individuals in the workplace. Not surprisingly, if these interactions are characterized by high role ambiguity, it is anticipated that this will have negative consequences on organizational outcomes (e.g., reduced job performance).

The negative relationship between role ambiguity and job performance can be explained from cognitive and motivational perspectives (Jackson & Schuler, 1985). From a cognitive perspective, role ambiguity should result in lower performance because individuals will have a lack of information on how to perform their roles. From a motivational perspective, role ambiguity will be negatively related to job performance since role ambiguity would weaken the effort-to-performance and performance-to-reward expectancies (Jackson & Schuler, 1985). However, research examining these hypothesized relationships has not consistently found support for this contention. For instance, some studies (e.g., Bedeian, Armenakis, & Curran, 1981; Stumpf & Rabinowitz, 1981) have found no significant relationship between role ambiguity and job performance, whereas others (e.g., Flaherty, Dahlstrom, & Skinner, 1999; Hartenian, Hadaway, & Badovick, 1994) have shown that role ambiguity is negatively related to job performance.

The equivocal findings in this area led to several meta-analytic reviews (e.g., Jackson & Schuler, 1985; Gilboa, Shirom, Fried, & Cooper, 2008). The results from these meta-analyses have demonstrated that role ambiguity is negatively and weakly related to job performance. Although these meta-analytic reviews have consistently found a negative relationship between role ambiguity and job performance, a large amount of the variance in this relationship remains unexplained. This contributes to a suggestion that researchers should try to identify variables that might moderate this relationship. Recently, Shirom, Shechter Gilboa, Fried, and Cooper (2008) examined three potential moderating variables: gender, age, and seniority. Using 30 studies containing 7,700 participants, Shirom et al. found that gender and seniority did not moderate this relationship. However, the mean age of workers had a moderating effect, with negative correlations decreasing with increasing age. The conclusions from these meta-analyses indicate that role ambiguity should not be dismissed as an unimportant variable in the job performance domain.

MILITARY

The military relies on the performance of teams (e.g., platoons, squads, battalions) for many important operational tasks (Salas, Bowers, Cannon-Bowers, 1995). Historically, it was believed that effective teamwork was simply the result of combining appropriately trained individuals. However, several mishaps involving aviation crews, tank crews, and naval surface warfare teams provided evidence that effective team performance was not an automatic occurrence (Salas et al., 1995). As a result, there was a need to examine some of the variables that contribute to effective military team performance to ensure better team performance.

One of the variables believed to impact military team performance is role ambiguity/role clarity. These constructs have been examined primarily in relation to the two outcomes of job strain and organizational commitment, which are believed to be important factors in mission effectiveness (performance) (Witt, 1991). As for the relationship between role ambiguity/role clarity and job performance, some research has examined role ambiguity/role clarity as a moderating variable. In one study, Bliese and Castro (2000) found the relationship between work overload and psychological strain was moderated by role clarity. In a second study, Lang, Thomas, Bliese, and Adler (2007) analyzed the moderating influence of role clarity on Army cadet's job strain. Role clarity was found to be a moderator of the job demands–job strain relationship. In particular, the cadets experiencing high job demands reported less physical and psychological job strain when they reported high role clarity. Taken together, the results from these two studies provide empirical evidence that role clarity is a significant moderator of the job demand–job strain relationship in the military.

Organizational commitment is considered to be important in the military because it reflects an acceptance of the military's goals and values, a desire to exert effort on its behalf, and a willingness to remain in the military (Witt, 1991). Given its importance, Mathieu (1988) advanced a model of organizational commitment in a military context that highlighted the interrelationships among variables believed to influence commitment. One of those variables is role ambiguity. In support of Mathieu's model, Witt (1991) found that role ambiguity was negatively related to organizational commitment ($r = -.26$) for military employees at a research and development laboratory and a military training center.

Leadership

An emerging area within teamwork research is the role that leaders occupy in facilitating effective, well-functioning teams. In particular, it has been suggested that leaders play a vital role in enabling effective performances (Bass, 1990). Recently, research has examined the role that leaders occupy in terms of promoting, developing, and maintaining team effectiveness (e.g., Kozlowski, Gully, Salas, & Cannon-Bowers, 1996; Zaccaro, Rittman, & Marks, 2001).

SPORT

In 1984, Chelladurai noted that leadership was one of the most extensively researched areas in organizational psychology but the study of leadership in sport was sparse and sporadic. In an attempt to encourage research in this area, Chelladurai (1984, 1993) advanced his multidimensional model of leadership—a model accounting for the interaction of traits and situation factors in explaining effective leadership in sports (see Figure 16.2).

The multidimensional model of leadership considers outcomes, such as team performance, athlete satisfaction, and team cohesion as a function of the congruence among three types of leader behaviors: actual coaching behaviors, coaching behaviors preferred by athletes, and behaviors required by the coach to be effective. Characteristics of the situation, coach, and athletes are viewed as antecedents to the three types of coaching behaviors.

To test the hypothesized relationships contained in the multidimensional model of leadership, Chelladurai and Saleh (1980) developed the Leadership Scale for Sports (LSS), which measures five dimensions of coaching behaviors. The first is *autocratic behavior,* which refers to the extent to which the coach makes independent decisions and stresses personal authority. The second, *democratic behavior,* refers to the extent to which the coach allows the athletes to participate in decision-making. Third, *positive feedback* is coaching behaviors that provide reinforcement to an athlete by recognizing and rewarding good performance. Fourth, *social support* is behavior characterized by the coach showing a concern for the welfare of the athletes, developing a positive team atmosphere, and establishing warm interpersonal relations with the athletes. Last, *training and instruction* reflects coaching behaviors aimed at improving athletes' performance by emphasizing hard work and strenuous training.

Research utilizing the LSS has primarily examined coaching behaviors in relation to the outcomes of satisfaction, cohesion, and performance. Chelladurai (1984) was the first to examine the impact of coaching behaviors on the satisfaction of athletes. The results showed that basketball players who preferred higher amounts of training and instruction, democratic behavior, social support, positive feedback, and lower amounts of autocratic behavior from their coach had higher perceptions of satisfaction with the leadership provided by the coach.

Results from research examining the relationship between cohesion and coaching behaviors have been relatively consistent. Specifically, task cohesion has been found to be positively related to coaching democratic behavior, positive feedback, social support, and training and instruction (e.g., Pease & Kozub, 1994; Shields, Gardner, Bredemeier, &

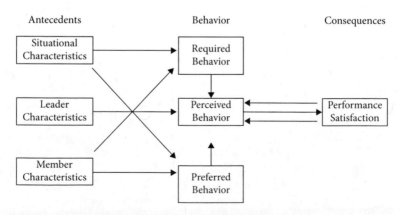

Figure 16.2 Chelladurai's multidimensional model for leadership. Adapted with permission from Chelladurai, P. (1984). Discrepancy between preferences and perceptions of leadership behavior and satisfaction of athletes in varying sports. *Journal of Sport Psychology,* 6(1), 27–41.

Bostrom, 1997; Westre & Weiss, 1991) and negatively related to autocratic behavior (e.g., Shields et al., 1997).

Performance is viewed as an important outcome in the multidimensional model of leadership (Chelladurai, 1984); however, research has found equivocal findings between leadership behaviors and performance. For example, democratic and social support coaching behaviors have demonstrated a negative relationship (e.g., Weiss & Friedrichs, 1986), a positive relationship (e.g., Garland & Barry, 1990), and no relationship (e.g., Turman, 2001) with performance. Similarly, autocratic behavior has also displayed a positive relationship (e.g., Weiss & Friedrichs), a negative relationship (e.g., Garland & Barry; Turman), and no relationship (e.g., Weiss & Friedrichs) with performance. However, it should be noted that the coaching behaviors of positive feedback and training and instruction have consistently displayed a positive relationship with performance in sport (e.g., Alfermann, Lee, & Wurth, 2005; Garland & Barry; Weiss & Friedrichs).

BUSINESS

The study of leadership is widespread in industrial and organizational psychology (Bass, 1990; Yukl, 2002). In fact, leadership research from a behavioral perspective has prospered; Fleishman et al. (1991) identified no fewer than 65 classification systems of leader behavior. Despite the vast number of classification systems, Fleishman and colleagues noted a common trend within nearly every system, in that leader behaviors could be grouped into two main categories: those behaviors dealing with task accomplishment (i.e., task-focused leader behaviors) and those behaviors that enable team interaction and development (i.e., person-focused leader behaviors). Task-focused leader behaviors are those directed toward providing an understanding of the requirements of the task, operating procedures, and the acquisition of task information. Person-focused leader behaviors are those that aid in the attitudes, cognitive structures, and behavioral interactions that must be developed before team members can work effectively as a group (Salas, Dickinson, Converse, & Tannenbaum, 1992).

In a recent meta-analysis, Burke et al. (2006) examined the relationship between leadership behavior (i.e., task- and person-focused) and behaviorally based team performance outcomes (i.e., perceived team effectiveness, team productivity, team learning). The analyses included 50 empirical studies

containing 113 effect sizes. The results showed that task-focused leadership behaviors were significantly related to perceived team effectiveness ($r = .333$) and team productivity ($r = .203$). There were no studies concerning task-focused leadership behaviors and team learning.

Similarly, person-focused leadership behaviors were significantly related to perceived team effectiveness ($r = .360$), team productivity ($r = .284$), and team learning ($r = .560$). These results show that both task- and person-focused leadership behaviors explain a significant amount of variance in team performance outcomes. In particular, task-focused leadership behaviors accounted for 11% of the variance in perceived team effectiveness and 4% of the variance in team productivity. Also, person-focused leadership behaviors explained 13% of the variance in perceived team effectiveness, 8% in team productivity, and 31% in team learning. Taken together, the results suggested that leadership matters in regards to team performance outcomes in the business sector.

MILITARY

Military doctrine (e.g., Department of the Army, 2004) and recent operations in Iraq (Bartone, 2004) have highlighted the importance of leadership as a necessary condition to operational success. In fact, military doctrine has consistently asserted that leadership is a critical core value that includes the development of both mental abilities (e.g., self-discipline) and interpersonal skills (e.g., teamwork; Matthews, Eid, Kelly, Bailey, & Peterson, 2006).

Although military doctrine is clear in stating the importance of leadership in officer development, relatively little empirical research has examined the effectiveness of officer training. Recently, Matthews et al. (2006) examined the development of military leaders by comparing them to a civilian sample. The researchers compared 24 character strengths of leaders identified by Peterson and Seligman (2004) in a sample of West Point cadets between the ages of 18 and 22 years and a civilian sample consisting of U.S. respondents of similar age and education. The West Point cadets rated themselves higher than the U.S. civilians on bravery, prudence, teamwork, curiosity, fairness, honesty, hope, industry, leadership, modesty, self-control, social intelligence, and spirituality.

Despite the fact that (developing) teamwork is a key military interpersonal skill, very little research has examined the influence that leaders have on it. This is surprising, since Fiedler (1955) argued that teamwork is primarily a function of the interpersonal relations among team members, including the relationship between leaders and crew members. Using airplane bomber and tank crews, Fiedler examined the leader's emotional distance between himself and his crew and the crew's effectiveness. A crew was normally comprised of 11 people (i.e., a leader, four officers, and six enlisted personnel). The results indicated two patterns of leadership effectiveness on teamwork. First, leaders who were generally distant toward enlisted personnel—that is reacting to these people in a cold and reserved manner—tempered this distance by having close relationships with their officers. Second, if the leader had close relationships (i.e., warm and accepting) with enlisted personnel, then he compensated for this closeness by maintaining a distant relationship with officers. Taken together, the results indicate that both patterns of relationships foster effective teamwork. The author indicated that when a leader is not close with his subordinates (officers or enlisted personnel), these two groups may look to other members for leadership, which ensures that the team functions effectively.

Cohesion

Groups form and function in several different ways and for many different purposes. Despite these differences, one constant is relative to all groups— each manifests cohesion to some degree. In fact, it has been argued that cohesion is so fundamental to the development and maintenance of groups that, "there can be no such thing as a non-cohesive group; it is a contradiction in terms. If a group exists, it is to some extent cohesive" (Donnelly, Carron, & Chelladurai, 1978, p. 7).

Given the fact that cohesion is, to some degree, present in all groups, it is considered to be the most important small-group variable by some researchers (Golembiewski, 1962; Lott & Lott, 1965). The perceived importance of cohesion is confirmed by the numerous studies since the 1950s, in a wide range of disciplines including sport (e.g., Carron, Brawley, & Widmeyer, 1998), business (e.g., Cota, Evans, Dion, Kilik, & Longman, 1995), and the military (e.g., Oliver, Harman, Hoover, Hayes, & Pandhi, 1999; Siebold, 2007).

SPORT

The area of sport psychology has been the most prevalent provider of cohesion research (Ryska, Yin, Cooley, & Ginn, 1999). Cohesion research in sport psychology has been acknowledged as having advanced theory development in general psychology (Cota et al., 1995), one of the few areas in sport psychology research in which this is the case. There are at least two reasons why sport-related cohesion research has made an impact in the field. First, a definition was advanced that gained acceptance from group dynamic theoreticians. More specifically, initially Carron (1982) and subsequently Carron, Brawley, and Widmeyer (1998) defined cohesion "as a dynamic process that is reflected in the tendency for a group to stick together and remain united in the pursuit of its instrumental objectives and/or for the satisfaction of member affective needs" (p. 213). Prior to this definition, Mudrack (1989) concluded that research on cohesion had "been dominated by confusion, inconsistency, and almost inexcusable sloppiness with regard to defining the construct" (p. 45). The second reason is the development of an inventory that is multidimensional and conceptually driven (Carron, Widmeyer, & Brawley, 1985). The Group Environment Questionnaire (GEQ) is an 18-item inventory that measures four dimensions of cohesion.

Not surprisingly, sport researchers have long been interested in the cohesion–performance relationship in sport. In 2002, Carron, Colman, Wheeler, and Stevens conducted meta-analysis involving 1,044 sport teams and 9,988 athletes. They found a medium to large effect size (ES = .66) in the cohesion–performance relationship. In addition, Carron et al. also examined several potential moderator variables of the cohesion–performance relationship. These analyses showed that cohesion has a stronger relationship with performance in coactive (ES = .77) versus interactive teams (ES = .66); when actual (ES = .69) rather than self-reported performance (ES = .58) is assessed; in female (ES = .95) versus male teams (ES = .56); and across the age/skill spectrum (i.e., ES = .20, .23, .55, .83 for professional, club, intercollegiate, and high school teams, respectively).

BUSINESS

Although research on teamwork and cohesion has a history in business, it is only recently that scholars have advanced theories that attempt to explain how these two concepts relate to one another (LePine, Piccolo, Jackson, Mathieu, & Saul, 2008). Unfortunately, research examining both cohesion and teamwork has been sparse and sporadic and has not accumulated in a consistent manner. One key reason for the dearth of research has been the lack of a definition concerning teamwork (LePine et al.,

2008). On the one hand, cohesion has been viewed as a process contributing to teamwork. On the other hand, teamwork has been viewed as a form of social cohesion (e.g., Kirkman, Tesluk, & Rosen, 2001), whereby cohesion and teamwork are seen as being similar constructs. What does seem to be clear, however, is that cohesion is positively associated with team performance (e.g., Gully, Devine, & Whitney, 1995; Evans & Dion, 1991).

Recognizing these conceptual differences in cohesion and teamwork, using meta-analytic techniques LePine et al. (2008) examined the relationship between cohesion and three types of teamwork processes: *transition processes* (i.e., actions that teams execute between performances), *action processes* (i.e., activities that occur as the team works toward its goals and objectives), and *interpersonal processes* (i.e., team activities that are focused on managing personal relationships). The results showed that cohesion has a strong positive relationship with the transition ($\rho = .60$), action ($\rho = .61$), and interpersonal ($\rho = .53$) processes of teamwork. Taken together, the results suggest that the positive relationship between teamwork and cohesion does not vary as a function of the nature of the teamwork process in question.

MILITARY

Cohesion is a fundamental concept in military psychology, given the need to build and maintain united military units (Siebold, 2006). The importance attached to cohesion was evident when General Peter J. Schoomaker (as cited in Siebold, 2006) noted (after being sworn in as the Chief of Staff for the U.S. Army), "How do we man the Army in a way that provides cohesive, high performing units in this reality of continuous engagement?"

According to Siebold (1999), four situations highlight the need for cohesion in the military. The first situation concerns the intensive lethality of the modern battlefield, with its use of accurate and powerful weapons resulting in an increase in stress casualties. The second situation occurs when armies face adversaries who outnumber them. A third situation is illustrated by the war in Vietnam: During this conflict, the policy was to view military personnel as "spare parts," whereby replacements were readily inserted into established units. Last, military cohesion is of interest since it was essential to the design of a mobile, moderately armed, light infantry unit that could operate using a high degree of teamwork to help offset its limited size and firepower.

As noted above and in the comments made by General Schoomaker (as cited in Siebold, 2006),

a fundamental assumption in military psychology is that cohesion can enhance unit performance. In fact, since the early 1980s, researchers from the U.S. Army Research Institute for the Behavioral and Social Sciences (ARI) have examined what leaders can do to develop their soldiers and build cohesive units that can perform well in combat situations (Siebold, 2007). This program of research followed what the ARI labeled as a training model, whereby they examined how military training was done and the resultant performance. Then, the AIR research group would modify the training and determine if performance improved based on their modifications. The modification made to the training was the development of cohesion among unit members. Given that the modifications were situation specific, it is difficult to provide an all-inclusive list of components that were modified to enhance cohesion. However, elements focused on unit confidence, confidence in leadership, unit teamwork, and development of a sense of pride in the unit. The results indicated that when these elements were modified, there were increases in cohesion that was subsequently related to improved unit performance.

Oliver et al. (1999) conducted a meta-analysis of the cohesion research involving military groups that examined group and individual performance. A total of 39 individual samples were used containing a total of 37,226 participants. The results showed that cohesion was strongly related to performance. Also, cohesion was more strongly correlated with group performance ($r = .40$) than with individual performance ($r = .20$).

Team Building for Teamwork: Strategies and their Effectiveness

> The ideas that come out of most brainstorming sessions are usually superficial, trivial, and not very original. They are rarely useful. The process, however, seems to make uncreative people feel that they are making innovative contributions and that others are listening to them.
> (*Block*, 2010)

This quote by Block (2010) helps to highlight a very important by-product of team building programs: It is not necessarily the outcomes that are important, but the overall effect the process has on the group and its individuals. As an example, prior to the 2009/2010 National Hockey League (NHL) hockey season, the Toronto Maple Leafs spent a few days together in Huntsville, Ontario, at a team building retreat. The experience probably did not improve the team's hockey skills or their performance on the ice (the overall goal of any NHL team). However, it gave the players a chance to form bonds and get to know one another more quickly than if the team had stayed in Toronto. The assumption of any team building retreat is that strengthened bonds will lead to a more efficient and successful group.

This assumption is by no means unique or contemporary. In fact, over a quarter of a century ago, there had been roughly 574 documented cases of team building (Golembiewski, Proehl, & Sink, 1982) from a variety of areas. The overall goal of team building is to remove disruptive barriers and allow a group to function properly while developing processes that will enable more effective solutions for future problems (Beer, 1976). Beer (1980) described team building as a deliberate process to improve both the task and social functioning of a group. More specifically, it has been defined as "a method of helping the group to (a) increase its effectiveness, (b) satisfy the needs of its members, or (c) improve working conditions" (Brawley & Paskevich, 1997, p. 13).

Group dynamics theoreticians have established qualities that should be present for a group to be effective. For example, Woodcock (2010) suggested that clear objectives and agreed goals, openness and confrontation, support and trust, cooperation and conflict resolution, sound working and decision-making procedures, appropriate leadership, regular review, individual development, and sound intergroup relations should all be present in order for teams to be successful.

The achievement of the qualities contained in this list would represent a daunting task for any group leader or manager. Groups by nature are very dynamic, and improving their teamwork and performance is not simple; if it were, every group would succeed. For that reason, researchers have outlined methods used for team building interventions.

In 1976, Beer suggested that when conducting team building interventions, four elements should be targeted, either alone or in combination with each other. The first is *group goal setting*. This allows the group to collectively establish both goals and the means to achieve them. Allowing input from all members of the group provides them with a feeling of entitlement and self-worth. The second is *interpersonal relationships*. This approach focuses on communication between members and is mainly concerned with improving relationships within the group. Third is *individual role involvement*. It is important to effective group functioning for members to understand and accept their respective roles. Finally, the fourth is the *managerial grid approach*, in which the focus is on the leaders. Here, the leaders are provided with strategies to help improve the productivity and subordinate satisfaction in their organizations.

In the sections that follow, the effectiveness of team building in sport, business, and the military is discussed.

SPORT

Effective teamwork is an important goal for sport teams at any level of competition (Stevens & Bloom, 2003). Although the overall effectiveness of team building interventions in sport has shown conflicting findings, teams continue to use them in an attempt to improve intragroup relationships (i.e., cohesion) and performance (i.e., team success). In an attempt to statistically summarize the inconsistent team building findings, Martin, Carron, and Burke (2009) carried out a meta-analysis. They analyzed a variety of outcomes targeted in the literature, including social and task cohesion, individual cognitions, role relationships, anxiety, and performance.

An overall significant positive effect was found. Martin and his colleagues concluded that the most effective team building interventions for sport should use either goal setting or adventure program techniques, be of at least 2 weeks in duration, target independent team sports, and aim at increasing performance.

BUSINESS

Organizational psychology generally uses team building to "try to improve group performance by improving communication, reducing conflict, and generating greater cohesion and commitment among work group members" (Bettenhausen, 1991). Teasing out whether these objectives are successful has been difficult, however, because of a lack of definitional clarity and operationalization of team building, as well as the use of problematic experimental designs. For example, DeMeuse and Liebowitz (1981) analyzed 36 studies and found that none used a true experimental design. Similarly, Woodman and Sherwood (1980) reviewed 30 team building studies and found that only four had acceptable internal validity. As yet another example, Buller (1986), on the basis of his review of nine team building interventions, concluded that the concept and its relationship with performance has not been clearly defined and operationalized.

These results set the stage for a meta-analysis by Neuman, Edwards, and Raju (1989). They located 126 general intervention studies (i.e., not simply team building) used in business and industry settings. The interventions were designed to improve individuals' attitudes toward their jobs, their organizations, and even themselves. The results revealed that of all the interventions used for improving individual satisfaction and changing employee attitudes, team building was the most effective.

A more recent meta-analysis from Salas, Rozell, Mullen, and Driskell (1999) included 11 articles from 1965 to 1990. All studies reported the effects of team building on performance. Overall, the results indicated no significant effect. Four specific types of team building were examined: goal setting, problem-solving, interpersonal relations, and role clarification. The last was the only one found to increase performance.

Although the various reviews have not found that team building is universally effective, recent studies have provided promising results. In 2007, Crown analyzed the use of group and group-centric individual goals for culturally heterogeneous and homogeneous task groups. Her results demonstrated that group goals are most effective in groups composed of both individualists and collectivists. This lends support for the use of group goal setting, a very important aspect of team building. It also suggests that groups do not need to be composed solely of collectivist individuals, but rather of a mix of people who like to work in groups and those who prefer to work alone.

That same year, Rapp and Mathieu (2007) evaluated a generic teamwork skills training program across time and at the individual and group levels. Data were collected from 54 members of eight trained and eight quasi-control master of business administration (MBA) students. The results provided preliminary evidence that generic teamwork skills can indeed be learned. At the individual level, those team members trained in teamwork skills exhibited higher levels of teamwork knowledge and had better teamwork behaviors. At the team level, teams trained in teamwork had higher processes and enhanced levels of performance over time as compared to quasi-control teams. These findings provide support for the belief that teamwork training yields better production, and, eventually, better outcomes.

MILITARY

We are unable to find a meta-analysis that summarizes the existing literature on team building or team training in the military. Therefore, this section provides examples of studies that have explored the effectiveness of these interventions.

In two studies, Eden (1985, 1986) tested the effectiveness of a 3-day team building workshop on organizational functioning in the Israeli army. The experimental units underwent an intensive 3-day team building workshop based on three of the four models described by Beer (1976): goal setting, interpersonal relations, and role clarification. Activities targeted conflict resolution, problem solving, role negotiations, and role clarity. In the first study (Eden, 1985), the results indicated that although most individuals liked the workshops, no significant difference was present for either the functioning of the team or the organizations. In the second (Eden, 1986), however, the results showed that the experimental units significantly improved in teamwork, conflict handling, and understanding about plans compared to the control units.

In an attempt to reduce the number of aircrew-caused aircraft mishaps in U.S. Navy and Marine Corps aviation crews, Alkov and Gaynor (1991) implemented a coordination training course. A total of 58 individuals ranging from chief petty officer, to lieutenant, to commander were involved in the program. The program focused on aircrew decision-making, loss of situation awareness, policy and regulations, command authority, workload performance, use of available resources, operating strategies, and communication skills. After the workshop, significant shifts in participant attitudes toward effective cockpit teamwork were found. In addition, in terms of performance, the aircrew error mishap rate declined in those groups where the program was introduced. Therefore, not only did the coordination training course improve attitudes toward effective cockpit teamwork, it also decreased the amount of errors within the cockpit.

In three studies, Leedom and Simon (1995) examined the effectiveness of team training on performance in military aviation. The first two studies attempted to improve team coordination and performance by using behavior-based training tactics (small-group discussions and exercises), whereas the third study used intra-team familiarity (small-group simulated battles). It was found that behavior-based training was superior for coordination and performance compared to group simulated battles.

Another study demonstrating the effectiveness of team training in the military was reported by Stout, Salas, and Fowlkes (1997). They delivered a 2-day, four-phase (introductory concepts, communication, assertiveness, and situational awareness) intervention to 42 males from a naval aviation community. Results indicated that team training could improve team competencies and effectiveness. More specifically, participants found that training was good for team coordination and that feedback was helpful. It was also found that attitudes from the trained group were significantly more positive than from the control group, and, perhaps most importantly, that performance (percentage of targets hit in training) was significantly greater for the trained groups.

Finally, Salas, Fowlkes, Stout, Milanovich, and Prince (1999) found support for the effectiveness of the crew resource management (CRM) instructional strategy program in two different studies. The CRM program was designed to improve communication, assertiveness, mission analysis, and situational awareness through discussions, class sessions, role-play exercises, and videotapes. Results indicated that participants strongly endorsed the usefulness of the training, had significantly improved attitudes, and also improved performance.

Although there are no reviews for the literature, the previous studies indicate that team building has had a positive impact on performance in the military. A meta-analysis using only studies incorporating team building interventions would contribute greatly to the area and provide stronger evidence for the effectiveness of both team building and team training.

IMPLEMENTING TEAM BUILDING INTERVENTIONS

Research in sport, business, and the military indicates that, overall, team building can be an effective way to increase the effectiveness of most groups. Carron and his colleagues (Carron, Spink, & Prapavessis, 1997; Carron & Spink, 1993) have developed a template that can be used by coaches or consultants interested in using team building interventions. The total process was subdivided into four phases: introductory, conceptual, practical, and intervention. The *introductory phase* informs participants of the research-generated benefits associated with team building interventions. The *conceptual phase* provides a conceptual model to help increase understanding of group dynamics. This phase allows the relationships among the components of the team building intervention to be highlighted for everyone involved.

An assumption that forms the basis for the conceptual model (illustrated in Figure 16.3) is that

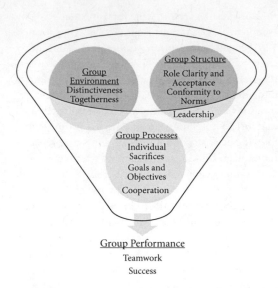

Figure 16.3 Conceptual framework for team building interventions. Based, with permission, from H. Prapavessis and colleagues, 1996, "Team building in sport," *International Journal of Sport Psychology, 27,* 269–285.

performance, the outcome of the team building intervention, can be improved by focusing on the group environment, group structure, and group processes. Insofar as the group environment is concerned, the elements included are togetherness and distinctiveness. As Figure 16.3 shows, the aspects targeted within the group structure category included role clarity and acceptance, conformity to team norms, and team leadership. Finally, the aspects targeted within the group processes category included individual sacrifices, goals and objectives, and cooperation. Examples of each category are provided in Table 16.1.

In the *practical phase*, participants engage in brainstorming to identify behaviors that might be used to increase the likelihood that the aspects illustrated in Figure 16.3 are salient for the group. Some typical behaviors identified are presented in Table 16.1. These team building strategies could be useful for any team or group. Finally, in the *intervention phase*, the behaviors targeted are implemented in the team.

Conclusion

In closing this chapter, some final observations are necessary. First, there is a commonality in the need for definitional clarity insofar as establishing what a team is and what teamwork represents. The magnitude of this challenge is indicated by the

Table 16.1 Examples of specific strategies used to enhance teamwork

Category	Explanation	Strategies
Group Environment		
Distinctiveness	Members feel they are part of an important group	Have identical group attire
Togetherness	Members in close proximity have increased interaction	Reserve a section of lockers in the same section of a locker room
Group Structure		
Role clarity and acceptance	Members understand, accept, and are satisfied with their roles	Schedule weekly meetings to outline and reinforce role responsibilities
Conformity to team norms	Members buy in to norms established by group	Have leaders establish a behavioral code and discuss issues for noncompliance
Team leadership	Members are involved in the decision-making process	Establish an elected member council to bring issues forward to management
Group Processes		
Individual sacrifices	Members are willing to make sacrifices for the benefit of the group	Have leaders assume responsibility for integrating new members into the social network of the group
Goals and objectives	Members have input in group goal setting	Meet to establish process, performance, and outcome goals for the upcoming week
Cooperation	Members of the group are willing to work together	Have older group members provide individual instruction and assistance to members unfamiliar with the system

Source: Adapted from Prapavessis, Carron, & Spink (1996)

amount of theorizing and discussion devoted to these constructs. Although some progress seems to be happening in business and the military, so far the nature of teamwork has not aroused research interest in sport. This could be related to the fact that teamwork is what teams do. Or, perhaps, sport psychologists view the nature of teamwork as a simplistic question, or one already answered, whereas models and theories in other areas suggest that the question is complex and far from resolved.

Second, there is no doubt that the perceived importance of teamwork is universal across areas. Not surprisingly, all groups—marriages, nursing teams, airlines crews, sport teams, business groups, military units, and so on—recognize that their effectiveness is dependent upon teamwork. In the stages associated with scientific progress, however, explanation (i.e., theory development) must be established before application (i.e., interventions)

can be implemented. That is, it is reasonable to conclude that in sport we do not have a rich understanding of what effective teams do. Consequently, sport psychology researchers do not have the knowledge or tools regarding the assessment of teamwork.

Third, it is also apparent that if teamwork is a concern, then practitioners and theoreticians might profit from focusing on the correlates discussed in this chapter (see Figure 16.1). The model presented in this chapter may provide a useful starting point in determining how these correlates influence team effectiveness in sport. A great amount of research in sport, in business, and in the military shows that cooperation, role clarity, cohesion, and leadership are critical factors in teamwork. Space did not provide us with the opportunity to highlight every construct found to be associated with teamwork and team effectiveness. But those we did discuss are important across the areas discussed.

Future Directions

In providing suggestions for future directions for research, it seems wise to limit our focus to the area we know best—sport. In sport, teamwork is generally an unexamined construct from a research perspective. There is currently no definition for teamwork and no means of assessing it directly. Thus, there is a need to determine just what it is: What is the nature of teamwork in sport? Also, what are its antecedents and its consequences? Once there is insight into these questions, attention should be directed toward its assessment. Developing both a definition for teamwork in sport and a protocol to measure it represents a challenge for the future.

References

Alfermann, D., Lee, M. J., & Wurth, S. (2005). Perceived leadership behavior and motivational climate as antecedents of adolescent athletes' skill development. *Athletic Insight: The Online Journal of Sport Psychology, 7*(2), 14–36.

Alkov, R. A., & Gaynor, J. A. (1991). Attitude changes in Navy/Marine flight instructors following an aircrew coordination training course. *The International Journal of Aviation Psychology, 1*, 245–253.

Alonso, A., Baker, D. P., Holtzman, A., Day, R., King, H., Toomey, L., & Salas, E. (2006). Reducing medical error in the Military Health System: How can team training help? *Human Resource Management Review, 16*, 396–415.

Bartone, P. T. (2004). Understanding prisoner abuse at Abu Ghraib: Psychological considerations and leadership implications. *The Military Psychologist, 20*, 12–16.

Bass, B. M. (1960). *Leadership, psychology, and organizational behavior.* New York: Harper.

Bass, B. M. (1990). *Bass and Stogdill's handbook of leadership.* New York: Free Press.

Beauchamp, M. R., & Bray, S. R. (2001). Role ambiguity and role conflict within interdependent teams. *Small Group Research, 32*, 133–157.

Beauchamp, M. R., Bray, S. R., Eys, M. A., & Carron, A. V. (2002). Role ambiguity, role efficacy, and role performance: Multidimensional and mediational relationships within interdependent sport teams. *Group Dynamics: Theory, Research, and Practice, 6*, 229–242.

Beauchamp, M. R., Bray, S. R., Eys, M. A., & Carron, A. V. (2003). The effect of role ambiguity on competitive state anxiety. *Journal of Sport and Exercise Psychology, 25*, 77–92.

Bebetsos, E., Theodorakis, N. D., & Tsigilis, N. (2007). Relations between role ambiguity and athletes' satisfaction among team handball players. *Sport Journal, 10*, 35–45.

Bedeian, A. G., Armenakis, A. A., & Curran, S. M. (1981). The relationship between role stress and job-related, interpersonal, and organizational climate factors. *The Journal of Social Psychology, 11*, 247–260.

Beer, M. (1976). The technology of organization development. In M. D. Dunnette (Ed.), *Handbook of industrial and organizational psychology* (pp. 937–943). Chicago, IL: Rand McNally.

Beer, M. (1980). *Organizational change and development: A systems review.* Glenview, IL: Scott, Foresman.

Bettenhausen, K. L. (1991). Five years of groups research: What we have learned and what needs to be addressed. *Journal of Management, 17*, 345–381.

Bliese, P. D., & Castro, C. A. (2000). Role clarity, work overload and organizational support: Multilevel evidence of the importance of support. *Work and Stress, 14*, 65–73

Block, H. (2010). *Heart quotes center.* Retrieved June 21, 2010, from http://www.heartquotes.net/teamwork-quotes.html

Brawley, L. R., & Paskevich, D. M. (1997). Conducting team building research in context of sport and exercise. *Journal of Applied Sport Psychology, 9*, 11–40.

Buller, P. F. (1986). The team building-task performance relation: Some conceptual and methodological refinements. *Group and Organization Studies, 11*, 147–168.

Buller, P. F., & Bell, C. H. (1986). Effects of team building and goal setting on productivity: A field experiment. *Academy of Management Journal, 29*, 305–328.

Burke, C. S., Stagl, K. C., Klein, C., Goodwin, G. F., Salas, E., & Halpin, S. M. (2006). What type of leadership behaviors are functional in teams? A meta-analysis. *The Leadership Quarterly, 17*, 288–307.

Carron, A. V. (1982). Cohesiveness in sport groups: Interpretations and considerations. *Journal of Sport Psychology, 4*, 123–138.

Carron, A. V., Brawley, L. R., & Widmeyer, W. N. (1998). Measurement of cohesion in sport and exercise. In J. L. Duda (Ed.), *Advances in sport and exercise psychology measurement* (pp. 213–226). Morgantown, WV: Fitness Information Technology.

Carron, A. V., Bray, S. R., & Eys, M. A. (2002). Team cohesion and team success in sport. *Journal of Sports Sciences, 20*, 119–126.

Carron, A. V., Hausenblas, H. A., & Eys, M. A. (2005). *Group dynamics in sport* (3rd ed.). Morgantown, WA: Fitness Information Technology.

Carron, A. V., & Spink, K. S. (1993). Team building in an exercise settings. *The Sport Psychologist, 7*, 8–18.

Carron, A. V., Spink, K. S., & Prapavessis, H. (1997). Team building and cohesiveness in the sport and exercise setting: Use of indirect interventions. *Journal of Applied Sport Psychology, 9*, 61–72.

Carron, A. V., Widmeyer, W. N., & Brawley, L. R. (1985). The development of an instrument to assess cohesion in sport teams: The Group Environment Questionnaire. *Journal of Sport Psychology, 7*, 244–266.

Chatman, J. A., & Barsade, S. G. (1995). Personality, organizational culture, and cooperation: Evidence from a business simulation. *Administrative Science Quarterly, 40*, 423–443.

Chelladurai, P. (1984). Discrepancy between preferences and perceptions of leadership behavior and satisfaction of athletes in varying sports. *Journal of Sport Psychology, 6*, 27–41.

Chelladurai, P. (1993). Leadership. In R. N. Singer, M. Murphey, & L. K. Tennant (Eds.), *Handbook of research on sport psychology* (pp. 647–671). New York: Macmillan. Chelladurai, P., & Saleh, S. D. (1980). Dimensions of leader behavior in sports: Development of a leadership scale. *Journal of Sport Psychology, 2*, 34–45.

Coakley, J. (1994). *Sport in society: Issues and controversies.* St. Louis: Times Mirror/Mosby.

Cohen, C. (1980). After effects of stress on human performance and social behavior: A review of research and theory. *Psychological Bulletin, 88*, 82–108.

Cota, A. A., Evans, C. R., Dion, K. L., Kilik, L., & Longman, R. S. (1995). The structure of group cohesion. *Personality and Social Psychology Bulletin, 21,* 572–580.

DeMeuse, K. P., & Liebowitz, J. S. (1981). An empirical analysis of team building research. *Group and Organization Studies, 6*(3), 357–378.

Department of the Army. (2004). *Field manual—Interim, No. 3-07.22.* Washington, DC: Author.

Deutsch, M. A. (1949). A theory of cooperation and competition. *Human Relations, 2*(2), 129–152.

Donnelly, P., Carron, A. V., & Chelladurai, P. (1978). *Group cohesion and sport.* Ottawa, ON: CAHPER Sociology of Sport Monograph Series.

Dyer, J. (1984). Team research and team training: A state-of-the-art review. In F. A. Muckler (Ed.), *Human factors review: 1984* (pp. 285–323). Santa Monica, CA: Human Factors Society.

Eby, L. T., & Dobbins, G. H. (1997). Collectivistic orientation in teams: An individual and group level analysis. *Journal of Organizational Behavior, 18,* 275–295.

Eden, D. (1985). Team development: A true field experiment at three levels of rigor. *Journal of Applied Psychology, 70,* 94–100.

Eden, D. (1986). Team development: Quasi-experimental confirmation among combat companies. *Group and Organizational Studies, 11,* 133–146.

Evans, C. R., & Dion, K. L. (1991). Group cohesion and performance: A meta-analysis. *Small Group Research, 22,* 175–186.

Eys, M. A., Beauchamp, M. R., & Bray, S. R. (2006). A review of team roles in sport. In S. Hanton & S. Mellalieu (Eds.), *Literature reviews in sport psychology* (pp. 227–255). Hauppauge, NY: Nova Science Publishers.

Eys, M. A., & Carron, A. V. (2001). Role ambiguity, task cohesion, and task self-efficacy. *Small Group Research, 32,* 356–373.

Fiedler, F. E. (1955). The influence of leader-keyman relations on combat crew effectiveness. *The Journal of Abnormal and Social Psychology, 51,* 227–235.

Fiedler, F. E. (1967). *A theory of leadership effectiveness.* New York: McGraw-Hill.

Findlay, L. C., & Coplan, R. J. (2008). Come out and play: Shyness in childhood and the benefits of organized sports participation. *Canadian Journal of Behavioral Sciences, 40,* 153–161.

Fisher, C. D., & Gitelson, R. (1983). A meta-analysis of the correlates of role conflict and role ambiguity. *Journal of Applied Psychology, 68,* 320–333.

Flaherty, T. B., Dahlstrom, R., & Skinner, S. J. (1999). Organizational values and role stress as determinants of customer-oriented selling performance. *The Journal of Personal Selling and Sales Management, 19,* 1–18.

Fleishman, E. A., Mumford, M. D., Zaccaro, S. J., Levin, K. Y., Korotkin, A. L., & Hein, M. B. (1991). Taxonomic efforts in the description of leader behavior: A synthesis and functional interpretation. *The Leadership Quarterly, 4,* 245–287.

Fraser-Thomas, J., & Côté, J. (2006). Youth sports: Implementing findings and moving forward with research. *Athletic Insight, 8,* 12–27.

Garland, D. J., & Barry, J. R. (1990). Personality and leader behaviors in collegiate football: A multidimensional approach to performance. *Journal of Research in Personality, 24,* 355–370.

Gilboa, S., Shirom, A., Fried, Y., & Cooper, C. (2008). A meta-analysis of work demand stressors and job performance: Examining main and moderating effects. *Personnel Psychology, 61,* 227–271.

Ginnett, R. C. (1995). Crews as groups: Their formation and their leadership. In E. L. Wiener, B. G. Kanki, & R. Helmreich (Eds.), *Cockpit resource management* (pp. 71–98). New York: Academic Press.

Goette, L., Huffman, D., & Meier, S. (2006). The impact of group membership on cooperation and norm enforcement: Evidence using random assignment to real social groups. *American Economic Review, 96,* 212–216.

Golembiewski, R. (1962). *The small group.* Chicago: University of Chicago Press.

Golembiewski, R. T., Proehl, C. W., Jr., & Sink, D. (1982). Estimating the success of OD applications. *Training and Development Journal, 72*(10), 86–95.

Grand, R. R., & Carron, A. V. (1982). Development of a team climate questionnaire. *Proceedings of the Annual Conference of the Canadian Society for Psychomotor Learning and Sport Psychology* (pp. 217–229). Edmonton, AB.

Gross, N., Mason, W., & McEachern, A. (1958). *Explorations in role analysis.* New York: Wiley.

Guest, A. M. (2008). Reconsidering teamwork: Popular and local meanings for a common ideal associated with positive youth development. *Youth Society, 39,* 340–361.

Gully, S. M., Devine, D. J., & Whitney, D. J. (1995). A meta-analysis of cohesion and performance: Effects of level of analysis and task interdependence. *Small Group Research, 26,* 497–520.

Hartenian, L. S., Hadaway, F. J., & Badovick, G. J. (1994). Antecedents and consequences of role perceptions: A path analytic approach. *Journal of Applied Business Research, 10,* 40–50.

Healey, A. N., Undre, S., & Vincent, C. A. 2004. Developing observational measures of performance in surgical teams. *Quality and Safety in Health Care, 13,* i33–i40.

Jackson, S. E., & Schuler, R. S. (1985). A meta-analysis and conceptual critique of research on role ambiguity and role conflict in work settings. *Organizational Behavior and Human Decision Processes, 36,* 16–78.

Jones, G. R., & George, J. M. (1998). The experience and evolution of trust: Implications for cooperation and teamwork. *Academy of Management Review, 23,* 531–546.

Jordan, M. (2010). Quotations. Retrieved April 13, 2010, from http://www.boardofwisdom.com/Default.asp?topic=1005&listname=Teamwork

Kahn, R. L., Wolfe, D. M., Quinn, R. P., Snoek, J. D., & Rosenthal, R. A. (1964). *Occupational stress: Studies in role conflict and ambiguity.* New York: Wiley.

Katz, D. (1964). The motivational basis of organizational behaviour. *Behavioral Science, 9,* 131–146.

Katz, D., & Kahn, R. L. (1978). *The social psychology of organizations.* New York: Wiley.

Katzenbach, J. R. & Smith, D. K. (1993). The wisdom of teams. *Small Business Reports, 18,* 68–71.

Katzenbach, J. R., & Smith, D. K. (2005). The discipline of teams. *Harvard Business Review, 83,* 1–9.

Kelvin, L. (Sir William Thomson). (2009). *Quotations.* Retrieved April 13, 2010 from http://zapatopi.net/kelvin/quotes/ meas

Kirkman, B. L., Tesluk, P. E., & Rosen, B. (2001). Assessing the incremental validity of team consensus ratings over aggregation of individual-level data in predicting team effectiveness. *Personnel Psychology, 54*, 645–667.

Kohn, A. (1986). *No contest: The case against competition.* Boston: Houghton Mifflin.

Kozlowski, S. W. J., Gully, S. M., Salas, E., & Cannon-Bowers, J. A. (1996). Team leadership and development: Theory, principles, and guidelines for training leaders and teams. In M. Beyerlein, S. Beyerlein, & D. Johnson (Eds.), *Advances in interdisciplinary studies of work teams* (pp. 253–292). Greenwich, CT: JAI.

Lang, J., Thomas, J. L., Bliese, P. D., & Adler, A. B. (2007). Job demands and job performance: The mediating effect of psychological and physical strain and the moderating effect of role clarity. *Journal of Occupational Health Psychology, 12*, 116–124.

Leedom, D. K., & Simon, R. (1995). Improving team coordination: A case for behaviour based training. *Military Psychology, 7*, 109–122.

LePine, J. A., Piccolo, R. F., Jackson, C. L., Mathieu, J. E., & Saul, J. R. (2008). A meta-analysis of teamwork processes: Tests of a multidimensional model and relationships with team effectiveness criteria. *Personnel Psychology, 61*, 273–307.

Lewin, K. (1935). *A dynamic theory of personality.* New York: McGraw-Hill.

Lott, A. J., & Lott, B. E. (1965). Group cohesiveness as interpersonal attraction: A review of relationships with antecedent and consequent variables. *Psychological Bulletin, 64*, 259–309.

Marsh, H. W., & Peart, N. D. (1988). Competitive and cooperative physical fitness training programs for girls: Effects on physical fitness and multidimensional self-concepts. *Journal of Sport and Exercise Psychology, 10*, 390–407.

Martin, L. J., Carron, A. V., & Burke, S. M. (2009). Team building interventions in sport: A meta-analysis. *Sport and Exercise Psychology Review, 5*, 3–18.

Mathieu, J. E. (1988). A causal model of organizational commitment in a military training environment. *Journal of Vocational Behavior, 32*, 321–335.

Matthews, M. D., Eid, J., Kelly, D., Bailey, J. K. S., & Peterson, C. (2006). Character strengths and virtues of developing military leaders: An international comparison. *Military Psychology, 18*(Suppl.), S57–S68.

Mendel, W. W., & Bradford, D. G. (1995). Interagency cooperation: A regional model for overseas operations. *Institute for National Strategic Studies,* McNair Paper, 37.

Merton, R. (1949). *Social theory and social structure.* Glencoe, IL: Free Press.

Mudrack, P. E. (1989). Defining group cohesiveness: A legacy of confusion. *Small Group Behavior, 20*, 37–49.

Neuman, G. A., Edwards, J. E., & Raju, N. S. (1989). Organizational development interventions: A meta-analysis of their effects on satisfaction and other attitudes. *Personal Psychology, 42*, 461–483.

Newcomb, T. M. (1951). Social psychological theory. In J. H. Rohrer & M. Sherif (Eds.), *Social psychology at the crossroads.* New York: Harper.

Oliver, L. W., Harman, J., Hoover, E., Hayers, S. M., & Pandhi, N. A. (1999). A quantitative integration of the military cohesion literature. *Military psychology, 11*, 57–83.

Orasanu, J., & Salas, E. (1993). Team decision making in complex environments. In G. A. Klein, J. Orasanu, R. Calderwood, & E. E. Zsambok (Eds.), *Decision making in action: Models and methods* (pp. 327–345). Norwood, NJ: Ablex.

Organ, D. W. (1988). *Organizational citizenship behaviour: The good soldier syndrome.* Lexington, MA: Lexington.

Orlick, T. D., McNally, J., & O'Hara, T. (1978). Cooperative games: Systematic analysis and cooperative impact. In F. Smoll & R. Smith (Eds.), *Psychological perspectives in youth sports* (pp. 203–225). Washington, DC: Hemisphere.

Oser, R. L., McCallum, G. A., Salas, E., & Morgan, B. B. (1989). *Toward a definition of teamwork: An analysis of critical team behavior.* Orlando, FL: Naval Training Systems Center. (NTSC Tech, Rep. No. 90-0009)

Parsons, T. (1951). *The social system.* Glencoe, IL: Free Press.

Pease, D. G., & Kozub, S. A. (1994). Perceived coaching behaviors and team cohesion in high school girls basketball teams. *Journal of Sport and Exercise Psychology, 16*, S93.

Peterson, C., & Seligman, M. E. P. (2004). *Character strengths and virtues: A handbook and classification.* New York: Oxford University Press.

Prapavessis, H., Carron, A. V., & Spink, K. S. (1996). Team building in sport. *International Journal of Sport Psychology, 27*, 269–285.

Rapp, T. L., & Mathieu, J. E. (2007). Evaluating an individually self-administered generic teamwork skills training program across time and levels. *Small Group Research, 38*, 532–555.

Rizzo, J. R., House, R. J., & Lirtzman, S. I. (1970). Role conflict and ambiguity in complex organizations. *Administrative Science Quarterly, 15*, 150–163.

Rousseau, V., Aubé, C., & Savoie, A. (2006). Teamwork behaviors: A review and an integration of frameworks. *Small Group Research, 37*, 540–570.

Ruth, B. (2010). *Thinkexist.com.* Retrieved July 15, 2010 from http://thinkexist.com/quotes/babe_ruth/

Ryska, T. A., Yin, Z., Cooley, D., & Ginn, R. (1999). Developing team cohesion: A comparison of cognitive-behavioral strategies of U.S. and Australian sport coaches. *The Journal of Psychology, 133*, 523–539.

Salas, E., Bowers, C. A., & Cannon-Bowers, J. A. (1995). Military team research: 10 years of progress. *Military Psychology, 7*, 55–75.

Salas, E., Dickinson, T. L., Converse, S. A., & Tannenbaum, S. I. (1992). Toward an understanding of team performance and training. In R. W. Swezey & E. Salas (Eds.), *Teams: Their training and performance* (pp. 3–29). Norwood, NJ: ABLEX.

Salas, E., Fowlkes, J. E., Stout, R. J., Milanovich, D. M., & Prince, C. (1999). Does CRM training improve teamwork skills in the cockpit? Two evaluation studies. *Human Factors, 41*, 326–343.

Salas, E., Rozell, D., Mullen, B., & Driskell, J. E. (1999). The effect of team building on performance: An integration. *Small Group Research, 30*, 309–329.

Shaw, M. E. (1981). *Group dynamics: The psychology of small group behavior* (3rd ed.). New York: McGraw-Hill.

Shields, D. L. L., Gardner, D. E., Bredemeier, B. J. L., & Bostrom, A. (1997). The relationship between leadership behaviors and group cohesion in team sports. *The Journal of Psychology, 131*, 196–210.

Shirom, A., Shechter Gilboa, S., Fried, Y., & Cooper, C. L. (2008). Gender, age, and tenure as moderators of work-related stressors' relationships with job performance: A meta-analysis. *Human Relations, 61*, 1371–1398.

Siebold, G. L. (1999). The evolution of the measurement of cohesion. *Military Psychology, 11*, 5–22.

Siebold, G. L. (2006). Military group cohesion. In T. W. Britt, A. B. Adler, & C. A. Castro (Eds.), *Military life: The psychology of serving in peace and combat* (pp. 185–201). Westport, CT: Praeger Security International.

Siebold, G. L. (2007). The essence of military group cohesion. *Armed Forces and Society, 33*, 286–295.

Stevens, D. E., & Bloom, G. A. (2003). The effect of team building on cohesion. *Avante, 9*, 43–54.

Stevens, M. J., & Campion, M. A. (1994). The knowledge, skills, and ability requirements for teamwork: Implications for human resource management. *Journal of management, 20*, 503–530.

Stout, R. J., Salas, E., & Fowlkes, J. E. (1997). Enhancing teamwork in complex environments through team training. *Group Dynamics: Theory, Research, and Practice, 1*, 169–182.

Stumpf, S. A., & Rabinowitz, S. (1981). Career stage as a moderator of performance relationships with facets of job satisfaction and role perceptions. *Journal of Vocational Behavior, 18*, 202–218.

Turman, P. D. (2001). Situational coaching styles: The impact of success and athlete maturity level on coaches' leadership styles over time. *Small Group Research, 32*, 576–594.

Turner, J. C. (1982). Towards a cognitive redefinition of the social group. In H. Tajfel (Ed.), *Social identity and intergroup relations* (pp. 15–39). Cambridge, UK: Cambridge University Press.

Van Dyne, L., Cummings, L. L., & Parks, M. J. (1995). Extrarole behaviours: In pursuit of construct and definitional clarity (a bridge over muddied waters). *Research in Organizational Behavior, 17*, 215–285.

Vazou, S., Ntoumanis, N., & Duda, J. L. (2005). Peer motivational climate in youth sport: A qualitative inquiry. *Psychology of Sport and Exercise, 6*, 497–516.

Wagner, J. A. 1995. Studies of individualism-collectivism: Effects on cooperation in groups. *Academy of Management Journal, 38*, 152–172.

Weinberg, R. S., & Gould, D. (2003). *Foundations of sport and exercise psychology*. Champaign, IL: Human Kinetics.

Weiss, M. R., & Friedrichs, W. D. (1986). The influence of leader behaviors, coach attributes, and institutional variables on performance and satisfaction of collegiate basketball teams. *Journal of Sport Psychology, 8*, 332–346.

Westre, K. R., & Weiss, M. R. (1991). The relationship between perceived coaching behaviors and group cohesion in high school football teams. *The Sport Psychologist, 5*, 41–54.

Witt, L. A. (1991). Negative affect as a moderator of role stressor-commitment relationships. *Military Psychology, 3*, 151–162.

Woodcock, M. (2010). *Team development manual*. Retrieved June 21, 2010, from http://www.oakwoodlearning.com/pdf/book%20summary%20-%20Team%20Dev%20Manual.pdf

Woodman, R. W., & Sherwood, J. J. (1980). The role of team development in organizational effectiveness: A critical review. *Psychological Bulletin, 88*, 166–186.

Yeatts, D. E., & Hyten, C. (1998). *High performing self-managed work teams: A comparison of theory and practice*. Newbury, CA: Sage.

Yukl, G. (2002). *Leadership in organizations* (4th ed.). Englewood Cliffs, NJ: Prentice-Hall.

Zaccaro, S. J., Rittman, A. L., & Marks, M. A. (2001). Team leadership. *The Leadership Quarterly, 12*, 451–483.

Leadership and Manifestations of Sport

Packianathan Chelladurai

Abstract

After summarizing prevalent models of leadership in sport, the chapter identifies the inconsistencies among the guidelines emanating from these models. Based on the three distinct manifestations of sport—*egalitarian sport, elite sport,* and *entertainment sport,* a reconciliation and synthesis is offered based on the different purposes of sport participation—*pursuit of pleasure* and *pursuit of excellence.*

Key Words: Autonomy-support, pursuit of pleasure, pursuit of excellence, deliberate play, deliberate practice, egalitarian sport, elite sport, entertainment sport, mediational model, multidimensional model, ego and task orientations, ego and task climates, decision styles

Leadership

Leadership, defined as "a process that includes influencing the task objectives and strategies of a group or organization, influencing the people in the organization to implement the strategies, and achieve the objectives, influencing group maintenance and identification, and influencing the culture of the organization" (Yukl & Van Fleet, 1992, p. 149), has been a matter of great interest over the centuries and continues to be of great concern in modern times. Many scholars have been engaged in several streams of research investigating leadership in various contexts, its antecedents, and its consequences, and they have advanced different theories of leadership. Several books have been published on the topic and on the exploits of great leaders of business, industry, politics, and, of course, sport. The average person knows more about the exploits of leaders in sport than of leaders in any other contexts. Although many are likely aware of the achievements and styles of great coaches (i.e., leaders in sport) such as Bill Belichick and Vince Lombardi (in football), John Wooden and Pat Summitt (in basketball), Joe Torre and Casey Stengel (in baseball),

Scotty Bowman (in hockey), and Rinus Michels (in soccer), few may know much about what Bill Gates of Microsoft, Jack Welch of General Electric, and Sam Walton of Walmart and Sam's Club have done as leaders.

Although the study of leadership has been intensive and extensive in other performance domains, such is not the case with leadership in sports. Although there are innumerable journalistic accounts of coaches' accomplishments and biographical works, the scientific study of coaching has been rather limited. One of the early attempts at the scientific study of leadership in sports was undertaken by Danielson, Zelhart, and Drake (1975). These researchers administered a modified version of the original Leadership Behavior Description Questionnaire (Halpin & Winer, 1957) to 160 junior and senior high school hockey players, asking the students to indicate the extent to which their coaches modeled the behaviors listed in each questionnaire item. These authors extracted dimensions of leader behavior and found that their respondents perceived their coaches' behaviors to be more communicative and less dominant.

Subsequently, Smith, Smoll, and associates (Smith, Smoll, & Curtis, 1979; Smith, Smoll, & Hunt, 1977), largely focused on youth sports, advanced the mediational model of leadership, and I and my associates (Chelladurai, 1978; Chelladurai & Carron, 1978; Chelladurai & Saleh, 1980) proposed the multidimensional model of leadership. These two streams of research have been dominant in sport psychology for nearly three decades. Recently, two new models of leadership have been advanced. Based on achievement goal theory, Duda and Hall (2001) suggested that the coach is responsible for creating a climate in which either the task or the ego is the predominant driver of performance. A similar approach, autonomy-supportive leadership, has been advanced by Amorose and Horn (2000, 2001), Amorose and Anderson-Butcher (2007), Mageau and Vallerand (2003), and Vallerand (2007).

The following sections review these models and the research attached to them, identify the opposing perspectives of different theories, and offer a synthesis of these perspectives based on the different purposes of sport participation.

Leadership Theories in Sport

In this section, I provide a summary of the principal models of leadership in sport: the *mediational model of leadership*, the *multidimensional model of leadership*, the *model of task- and ego-involving climates*, and *autonomy-supportive leadership*. Readers are encouraged to peruse Chelladurai (2012), Chelladurai (2007), and Chelladurai and Reimer (1998) for more thorough analyses of leadership theories in sport and the measurements thereof.

The Mediational Model of Leadership

Smith and associates (Smith, Smoll, & Hunt, 1977; Smoll & Smith, 1989) advanced the mediational model of leadership to explain leader behavior and its consequences in sport. The model shown in Figure 17.1 consists of coach behaviors, players' perceptions and recollections of those behaviors, players' evaluative reactions, and situational factors.

The dependent variables are the players' perceptions and recall of coach behaviors and their evaluative reactions to those recalled behaviors. This model proposes that the cognitive processes of perceptions, recall, and reactions are as important as player behaviors themselves.

In the mediational model of leadership, coach behaviors are believed to be influenced by the coach's characteristics, including personal goals and/or motives, behavioral intentions, instrumentalities (i.e., perceived link between a valued outcome and a behavior), the perceived norms of the coach's role, inferences regarding player motivation,

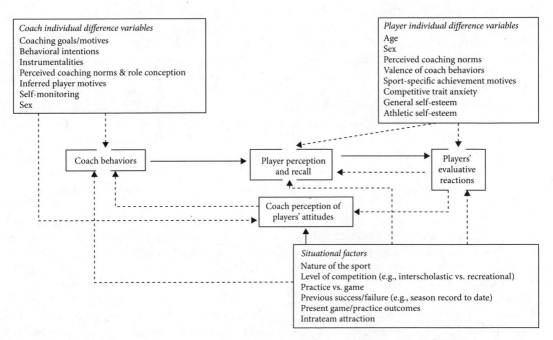

Figure 17.1 Smith and Smoll's mediational model of leadership. From Smoll F. L., & Smith, R. E. (1989). Leadership behaviors in sport: A theoretical model and research paradigm. *Journal of Applied Social Psychology, 19,* 1522–1551.

self-monitoring, and the coach's gender. A coach's behavior is also influenced by his or her perceptions of player attitudes.

Player perceptions, recall, and reactions are also influenced by the individual difference variables of age, gender, perception of coaching norms, the valence attached to coaching behaviors, sport-related achievement motivation, competition anxiety, general self-esteem, and athletic self-esteem. As Smoll and Smith (1989) noted, "a truly comprehensive model of leadership requires that consideration be given not only to situational factors and overt behaviors, but also the cognitive processes and individual difference variables which mediate relationships between antecedents, leader behaviors, and outcomes" (p. 1532). Thus, the central thrust of the model is on player recall and evaluation of the coach's behaviors.

Finally, situational factors—the nature of the sport, practice sessions versus games, previous team success or failure, current status in competitions, level of competition (i.e., recreational versus competitive), and interpersonal attraction within the team—are all believed to have an overarching influence on all the central elements of the model (i.e., coach's behavior, players' perceptions/recollections of those behaviors and their reactions to them).

ASSESSING THE MEDIATIONAL MODEL

Smith, Smoll, and their associates employed several methods to assess the variables just described: the observational method to assess coach behaviors; interviews to seek athletes' perceptions and recollections of leader behaviors and their affective reactions to the sport experience; and a paper-and-pencil test of coaches' perceptions of their own behavior. Coach behaviors are observed with the Coaching Behavior Assessment System (CBAS), which includes 12 categories of leader behaviors (shown in Table 17.1). These behavioral categories include the coach's reactions to immediately preceding player/team behaviors, such as desirable performances, mistakes, or misbehaviors. The other behavior categories are the coach's spontaneous and self-initiated behaviors, including game-related behaviors of technical instruction, encouragement, and organization; and game-irrelevant behavior of general communication (Smith et al., 1977).

The measure of leader behaviors is the frequency with which a coach engages in a given category as observed by one or more observers. To ensure reliability of the observational system, the observers underwent extended study of a training manual

(Smith et al., 1977); group instruction in the use of the scoring system (Smith, Smoll, Hunt, & Clarke, 1976); written tests, wherein the observers defined the 12 categories and scored behavioral examples; scoring of videotaped sequences; and extensive practice and reliability checks in actual field settings (Smith et al., 1977; Smith, Zane, Smoll, & Coppel, 1983). Players' perceptions of a coach's behavior were assessed by providing verbal descriptions and examples of each of the 12 behavioral dimensions to the players, who then indicated how frequently their coach engaged in each of those behaviors on a 7-point scale (1 for "almost never" to 7 for "almost always"). Similarly, coaches were also asked to indicate on 7-point scales (1 for "almost never" to 7 for "almost always") the extent to which they engaged in each of the behaviors. As these are single-item scales, reliability cannot be established. Players' evaluative reactions were assessed by asking them to respond to a number of questions varying from six (Smith, et al., 1983), to eight (Barnett, Smoll, & Smith, 1992; Smoll, Smith, Barnett, & Everett, 1993), to ten (Smoll et al., 1978; Smith & Smoll, 1990), and finally to 11 items (Smith et al., 1979). (See Chelladurai and Riemer [1998] for a further critique of the measures proposed by Smith, Smoll, and associates.)

QUESTIONNAIRE MEASURES OF THE COACHING BEHAVIOR ASSESSMENT SYSTEM
Coaching Feedback Questionnaire

Arguing that the players' interpretation of a coach's behaviors influences their attitude toward the coach and their experiences, and that players' evaluative reactions were not adequately measured in earlier research, Amorose and Horn (2000) developed the Coaching Feedback Questionnaire (CFQ) to measure athletes' perceptions of the types of feedback provided by their coaches. This 16-item scale measures eight categories of feedback, including three categories of responses to players' performance successes (i.e., praise/reinforcement, nonreinforcement, reinforcement combined with technical instruction) and five categories of responses to errors reflected in mistake-contingent encouragement, ignoring mistakes, corrective instruction, punishment, and corrective instruction combined with punishment. The response format is a 5-point scale ranging from "very typical" to "not at all typical," in which the respondents indicate the extent to which their coach provides a given type of feedback. Factor analysis of these 16 categories resulted in three meaningful factors: *positive and informational*

Table 17.1 Response categories of the coaching behavior assessment system

Class I: Reactive Behaviors	
Responses to Desirable Performance	
Reinforcement	A positive, rewarding reaction, verbal or nonverbal, to a good play or good effort
Nonreinforcement	Failure to respond to good performance
Responses to mistakes	
Mistake-contingent encouragement	Encouragement given to a player following a mistake
Mistake-contingent technical instruction	Instructing or demonstrating to a player how to correct a mistake
Punishment	A negative reaction, verbal or nonverbal, following a mistake
Punitive technical instruction	Technical instruction which is given in a punitive or hostile manner following a mistake
Ignoring mistakes	Failure to respond to a player mistake
Response to misbehavior	
Keeping control	Reactions intended to restore or maintain order among team members
Class II: Spontaneous Behaviors	
Game-related	
General technical instruction	Spontaneous instruction in the techniques and strategies of the sport (not following a mistake)
General encouragement	Spontaneous encouragement which does not follow a mistake
Organization	Administrative behavior which sets the stage for play by assigning duties, responsibilities, positions, etc.
Game-irrelevant	
General communication	Interactions with players unrelated to the game.

From Smith, R. E., Smoll, F. L., & Hunt, E. B. (1977). A system for the behavioral assessment of athletic coaches. *Research Quarterly, 48,* 401–407.

feedback, punishment-oriented feedback, and *nonreinforcement/ignoring mistakes.*

Coaching Behavior Questionnaire

In order to measure athletes' perceptions of their coach's ability to communicate, the confidence displayed by their coach, the coach's composure and emotional control, and the effects of the coach's arousal level on athletes as independent factors influencing anxiety and self-confidence, Kenow and Williams (1992) developed their 28-item Coaching Behavior Questionnaire (CBQ) with a response format of a 4-point Likert scale ranging from 1 (strongly disagree) to 4 (strongly agree). Using the composite of the 21 substantive items of the scale, these authors found that higher levels of trait anxiety and state cognitive anxiety and lower self-esteem among athletes were associated with more negative evaluations of a coach's behavior. Further, they also derived five factors from the substantive items, labeling them *cognitive/attentional effects of coach's behavior, supportiveness, emotional control and composure, communication,* and *somatic effects of coach's behavior* (Kenow & Williams, 1992). In a more recent and elaborate study, Williams et al. (2003) proposed a two-factor solution emerging from confirmatory factor analysis; the factors were named *negative activation* (seven items), reflecting the effects of leader behavior on athletes, and *supportiveness/emotional composure* (eight items), measuring athletes' perceptions of coaching behavior. It must be noted that these two factors measure both coach behaviors and the effects of such behaviors.

In summary, the 12-dimensional scheme proposed by Smith, Smoll, and associates encompasses most of the meaningful coaching behaviors in sport. They have also measured leadership from three perspectives—observers, coaches themselves, and the players. Smith, Smoll et al. also found that coaches' behaviors were consistent with their goals and perceived instrumentalities of specific forms of coaching behavior.

The Multidimensional Model of Leadership

The multidimensional model (Chelladurai, 1978, 1993; Chelladurai & Carron, 1978), shown in Figure 17.2, incorporates three states of leader behaviors—*required* (Box 4), *preferred* (Box 6), and *actual* behaviors (Box 5). *Situational characteristics* (Box 1), including the goals of the group, the type of task (e.g., individual vs. team, closed vs. open tasks), and the social and cultural context of the group, are said to influence the required behavior. Such influences may either prescribe certain leader behaviors or proscribe certain forms of leadership.

The preferences of group members for specific forms of leader behavior (e.g., instruction and guidance, social support, and feedback) are largely a function of member characteristics (Box 3), which include personality (e.g., need for achievement, need for affiliation, cognitive structure) as well as task-relevant ability. It is recognized in the model that group members are also attuned to the

situational requirements, and thus their preferences will be shaped both by their personal characteristics and situational contingencies. In a similar manner, the required behavior would also be partly shaped by the nature of the group, as defined by gender, age, skill level, and other variables.

Although the actual behavior (Box 5) is largely a function of the leader's characteristics (Box 2), including personality, expertise, and experience, such behavior will also be strongly influenced by the required behavior as well as by the preferred behavior. That is, the prescriptions and proscriptions imposed by the situation and the preferences of group members have an impact on how the leader behaves.

Finally, the model also incorporates the concept of *transformational leadership*, whereby the leader transforms the aspirations and attitudes of group members (i.e., member characteristics) and subordinate leaders (i.e., leader characteristics) by creating and articulating a new mission for them and convincing them of the viability of that mission (i.e., situational characteristics), and expressing confidence that they can achieve that mission (Bass, 1985).

Congruence Hypothesis

As shown in Figure 17.2, member performance and satisfaction (Box 7) is dependent on how well the leader balances the demands of the situation and member preferences and creates congruence among required, preferred, and actual behaviors. Finally, there are two lines of feedback from performance and member satisfaction to actual behavior. Based on such feedback, a leader may begin to emphasize

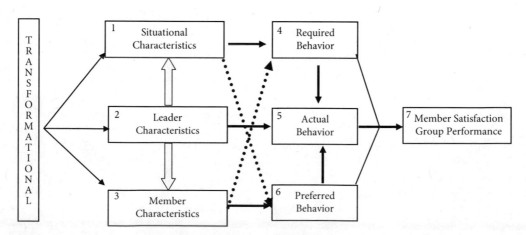

Figure 17.2 Chelladurai's multidimensional model of leadership. From Chelladurai, P. (1993). Leadership. In R. N. Singer, M. Murphy, & K. Tennant (Eds.), *The handbook on research in sport psychology* (pp. 647–671). New York: Macmillan Publishing Company.

the task imperatives if the group fails to achieve desired performance; the leader may engage in those behaviors that would foster warm interpersonal interactions between the leader and members, and among the members, if he or she perceives member morale and satisfaction to be low.

Leadership Scale for Sports

The Leadership Scale for Sport (LSS; Chelladurai & Saleh, 1980) was developed in conjunction with the multidimensional model of leadership and consists of 40 items representing five dimensions of leader behavior—*training and instruction* (13 items), *democratic behavior* (9 items), *autocratic behavior* (5 items), *social support* (8 items), and *positive feedback/rewarding behavior* (5 items). These dimensions of leader behavior are described in Table 17.2. The response format is a 5-point scale ranging from (a) always; (b) often, about 75% of the time; (c) occasionally, about 50% of the time; (d) seldom, about 25% of the time; to (e) never. With different opening stems, the scale can be used to measure athletes' preferences for specific leader behaviors, athletes' perceptions of their coaches' leader behaviors, and/or coaches' perceptions of their own behaviors.

REVISED LEADERSHIP SCALE FOR SPORTS

Zhang, Jensen, and Mann's (1997) modification of the LSS includes the original five dimensions, the instructions, and the response format of the LSS, as well as the same three versions. In addition,

a new dimension of leader behavior, labeled *situational consideration behaviors* and described as behaviors "aimed at considering the situation factors (such as the time, individual, environment, team, and game); setting up individual goals and clarifying ways to reach the goals; differentiating coaching methods at different stages; and assigning an athlete to the right position," is included (pp. 109–110). A criticism of the new scale is that the proposed measurement model should have been subjected to confirmatory factor analysis to verify the model. Furthermore, the only new dimension in the revised scale is subsumed by the five dimensions of the original LSS. Given these issues, parsimony would indicate the use of the shorter, original LSS (Chelladurai, 2007).

Although the psychometric properties of the LSS have been found to be adequate in several studies, the low α values for the subscale of autocratic behavior is a continuing concern. Chelladurai and Riemer (1998) noted that the problem may be due to the items reflecting distinct domains of behavior, such as being aloof, deciding autocratically, and being authoritative. Hence, they suggested developing new subscales to reflect these domains. Furthermore, the LSS does not tap into the dimensions of transformational leadership, which has been recently incorporated into the multidimensional model. It is expected that future research will focus on refining the existing subscales and developing new subscales for transformational leadership.

Table 17.2 Dimensions of leader behavior in sports

Dimension	Description
Training and instruction	Coaching behavior aimed at improving the athletes' performance by emphasizing and facilitating hard and strenuous training; instructing them in the skills, techniques, and tactics of the sport; clarifying the relationship among the members; and by structuring and coordinating the members' activities
Democratic behavior	Coaching behavior which allows greater participation by the athletes in decisions pertaining to group goals, practice methods, and game tactics and strategies
Autocratic behavior	Coaching behavior which involves independent decision-making and stresses personal authority
Social support	Coaching behavior characterized by a concern for the welfare of individual athletes, positive group atmosphere, and warm interpersonal relations with members
Positive feedback	Coaching behavior which reinforces an athlete by recognizing and rewarding good performance

From Chelladurai, P. (1989). *Manual for the Leadership Scale for Sports*. Unpublished manuscript. The University of Western Ontario.

Leadership and Task or Ego Involving Climates

Another line of research that is relevant to leadership and that permeates sport psychology literature is based on achievement goal theory (e.g., Ames, 1992; Duda & Hall, 2001; Nicholls, 1989; Roberts, 1997). Of critical relevance to this chapter is the finding by Nicholls (1984, 1989) that individuals adopt two different achievement goals, *task* goals and *ego* goals. A task goal is self-referenced and is focused on the development of competence and continued improvement as markers of success. Such a goal orientation is also based on the belief that ability or competence is a function of one's effort: "Because perceptions of success and failure tend to be based on self-referenced standards, it is suggested that a focus on task goals will lead to greater absorption in the process of improving and less preoccupation with proving to others how good one is" (Duda & Hall, 2001, p. 418). In contrast, an ego goal is grounded in a concern for demonstrating competence in the presence of others and a desire not to be judged incompetent. Thus, the individual gains a positive sense of competence only if his or her performance is compared favorably with that of others. A person with ego goals tends to view success as a function of possession of high ability rather than a function of effort. In essence, then, personal success is a function of how much better or worse others do. Accordingly, such a person is likely to drop out of those endeavors in which others are expected to do well.

Concomitant with this line of thinking, it has also been shown that the goal orientations of youth can be shaped by the performance context, a significant component of which is leadership. In the context of sport, the coach is said to be responsible for creating a climate that may shape the goal orientations of participants (Duda & Hall, 2001). By treating all members equally and including them all in every activity, and by instilling a sense of communal learning, the coach can create a task-involving climate that emphasizes individual improvements and enjoyment of the processes of enhancing individual team member competence. In such a climate, the coach recognizes and applauds the improvements that individuals make and stresses the importance of effort as its own reward.

In contrast, the coach who compares and contrasts individual performances, criticizes or punishes poor performers, and creates groupings based on performance capabilities is creating an ego-involved climate. In such a climate, "differential structures such as the standards, methods, and criteria underlying evaluation, the nature of recognition and the manner in which it is expressed, the source of authority, the way tasks are structured, and the manner in which individuals are grouped are held to constitute the overriding climate operating in achievement settings" (Duda & Hall, 2001, p. 419).

It must be noted that the two forms of climate form the central thrust of this approach. Leadership is treated as just one of the factors that contribute to the creation of the task- or ego-involving climate. Nevertheless, it has great relevance for this chapter because it refers to two forms of leader behavior: one that creates the task-involving climate and another creating the ego-involving climate. Furthermore, the dependent variable in this model is continued involvement in and enjoyment of the effort in the activity and the improvements made in that activity. Accordingly, the coach behaviors that create the task-involving climate are favored, and the behaviors oriented toward the ego-involving climate are shunned. As will be shown later in the chapter, some elements of ego-involving climate and its associated leader behaviors are functional in the pursuit of excellence in a given activity.

Autonomy-Supportive Leadership

A more recent and novel approach to the study of leadership in sports is that of Amorose and associates (Amorose & Anderson-Butcher, 2007; Amorose & Horn, 2000, 2001) and Vallerand and associates (Mageau & Vallerand, 2003; Vallerand, 2007). This approach is focused on the linkage between a leader's behavior and participant's motivation and continued participation. This new thrust in leadership research is based on Deci and Ryan's (1985; Ryan & Deci, 2000) *self-determination theory* (SDT). The theory specifies that humans are characterized by three needs: autonomy, relatedness, and competence. To the extent that an activity contributes to the satisfaction of these needs, the participant will find the activity motivational and will continue to participate in that activity. Although considerable research has supported the hypotheses of the SDT, much of this research has been carried out in contexts other than sport. Thus, the works of Amorose et al. and Vallerand et al. in this regard are significant contributions to the literature.

The central tenet of this line of research is that the leader, as a significant component of the context of sport participation, can create conditions that foster the sense of competence, autonomy, and relatedness among the participants. The specific form of leader behavior that creates such an impact is labeled *autonomy-support*. In Mageau and Vallerand's (2003) view, autonomy-support involves providing choices within specific rules and boundaries, explaining the tasks and boundaries, recognizing members' feelings and perspectives, allowing individuals to take initiative, providing noncontrolling feedback, avoiding criticisms and rewards to control behavior, and reducing ego-involvement in members.

Mageau and Vallerand's (2003) model of the coach–athlete relationship is presented in Figure 17.3. The central thesis of the model is that a coach's behavior in supporting autonomy among participants, the structure of participation, and his or her interpersonal involvement with the athletes enhance the athletes' sense of being competent, autonomous, and related. These positive feelings then lead to motivation and continued participation. This thesis was largely supported by Amorose and Anderson-Butcher (2007), who found in their study of high school and college athletes that those athletes' perceptions of autonomy-supportive behaviors by their coaches were positively related to their satisfaction of the needs for competence, autonomy, and

relatedness, which were, in turn, related to their beliefs that their participation was self-determined. Although these efforts are laudable, particularly in the articulation of the model, there is a strong need for a valid scale to measure leaders' autonomy-supportive behaviors in the context of sport (Chelladurai, 2007).

Contrasting Approaches to Leadership in Sports

These various models of leadership clearly show that some of the principles or tenets stemming from these theories are inconsistent with each other. It is not uncommon for a field to have several theories on a particular topic, with each emphasizing specific constructs and the interrelationships among them (e.g., consider the extant sport motivational and expertise development theories—see Chapters 23, 25, and 26, this volume). It is also common that such theories identify divergent pathways to a terminal outcome. But it is seldom that any two theories on a topic would advocate opposing (and not simply diverging) perspectives on the topic. But that seems to be the case with reference to the

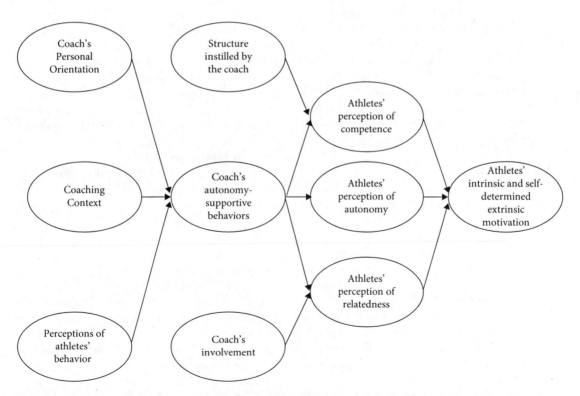

Figure 17.3 Mageau and Vallerand's 2003 model of motivation. From Vallerand, R. J. (2007). Intrinsic and extrinsic motivation in sport and physical activity. In G. Tenenbaum & R. C. Eklund (Eds.), *Handbook of sport psychology* (pp. 59–83). Hoboken, NJ: John Wiley.

theories of leadership in sports outlined in this chapter.

The more demanding and directing type of leadership that I advocated (Chelladurai, 2007), and the studies showing that athletes themselves preferred their coaches to be relatively more autocratic in decision-making (Chelladurai & Arnott, 1985; Chelladurai, Haggerty, & Baxter, 1989; Chelladurai & Quek, 1995) may be labeled *hard leadership*. In contrast, the autonomy-supportive leadership advanced by Amorose and associates (Amorose & Anderson-Butcher, 2007; Amorose & Horn, 2000, 2001) and Vallerand and associates (Mageau & Vallerand, 2003; Vallerand, 2007), and the emphasis on creating and fostering a task-involved climate articulated by Duda and Hall (2001), Nicholls (1989), and Roberts (1997), are all oriented toward cultivating a sense of autonomy and competence in the individual which, in turn, fosters a sense of well-being and intrinsic motivation. This form of leadership may be labeled *soft leadership*, in that it places greater focus on member motivation and commitment to participation.

A general consensus emanating from studies of soft leadership is that (a) creating and maintaining a task-involved climate is beneficial, and the ego-involved climate is detrimental to member satisfaction, enjoyment, and commitment to participation; and (b) a coach's autonomy-supportive behavior is conducive to members' continued motivation and participation, whereas lack of such autonomy support decreases member motivation. The hard leadership approach suggested by my own work (Chelladurai, 2007) and by studies of decision-making styles is more oriented toward individual and team performance excellence.

A Reconciliation Based on Manifestations of Sport

These contrasting approaches to leadership in sports can be reconciled if we consider the purposes of participation in sport and the outcomes that are sought in sport. Although almost everyone has a great interest in sport, either as a participant or as a spectator, the varying manifestations of sport (i.e., subtle differences among the various forms of engagement in sport) are not clearly understood. This is also true to some extent of scholars who study and report on sport and sport participation. But it is important that, when we advance models of leadership and recommendations thereof, we keep in mind the distinctions among these various forms of sport participation.

This section delineates three varieties of engagement in sport.

In distinguishing between "sport" and "athletics," Keating (1964) noted that sport is derived from the French word *desporter*, meaning a diversionary activity from work, the purpose of which is to maximize pleasure for all participants. Sport is characterized by spontaneity (i.e., it does not need any preparation or training), moderation (i.e., it is not practiced in excess), and generosity (i.e., it is tolerant of other participants, particularly opponents). Such participation is a cooperative effort undertaken to maximize the pleasure of all participants. In contrast, *athletics* is derived from the Greek words *athlos* (i.e., a contest), *athlon* (i.e., a prize), and *athlein* (i.e., to contend for a prize). It is a competitive and agonistic activity undertaken to establish the superiority of one over others in seeking a coveted prize. It involves a very high degree of devotion and commitment to the pursuit, extraordinary efforts over a prolonged period of training, and considerable personal sacrifice. As the term "athletics" refers to one form of physical activity in the international context (i.e., track and field), Keating's other labels (*pursuit of pleasure* and *pursuit of excellence*) are used to refer to these two contrasting enterprises (Chelladurai, 2007).

Recently, I (Chelladurai, 2010) have employed the labels *egalitarian sport* to refer to pursuit of pleasure in sport and *elite sport* to refer to pursuit of excellence in sport. In addition, I have highlighted a third form of engagement in sport—*entertainment sport* (also labeled *spectator sport*). These three forms of sport engagement may involve the same sport, but they are distinct enterprises, with different purposes and processes. Egalitarian sport (variously called mass sport or participant sport) is fundamentally a gregarious activity engaged in for the pleasure derived from that activity. It is more closely related to the notion of "play," which Huizinga (1955) defined as a free activity outside of ordinary life that is not serious but that nevertheless absorbs the participant completely. Recently, Côté and his colleagues (Côté, 1999; Côté, Baker, & Abernethy, 2003, 2007) advanced the concept of *deliberate play*, which is akin to the conceptualizations of Huizinga and Keating. Egalitarian sport includes everyone, irrespective of ability. It is an inclusionary process with the motto, "the more, the merrier."

Conversely, elite sport is restricted to persons of high ability who are determined to excel in the activity. It is indeed an exclusionary process whereby those who do not meet the standards are excluded from engaging in elite sport. It is characterized by high dedication, huge sacrifices, and extraordinary effort over a prolonged period of time. Research suggests that it requires 10,000 hours over a 10-year period to excel in any chosen activity (Ericsson, Krampe, & Tesch-Römer, 1993); thus, in contrast to egalitarian sport, elite sport is a serious business characterized by dedication, sacrifice, and intensity. It requires a great deal of planning for deliberate practice and progressively challenging competitions.

As far as entertainment sport is concerned, the more popular a sport is, the more attractive it is to watch it being played. Furthermore, the greater the excellence of the contestants, the more appealing it is to watch the contest. It is not surprising that sport organizations have capitalized on this opportunity to commercialize the entertainment value of their respective sports. The best examples of such commercial ventures in sport are the National Football League and the National Basketball Association in the United States, and the Premier League in England, the Serie A in Italy, the J league in Japan, and the K league in Korea, which provide entertainment in soccer (football). The Indian Premier League in cricket is the latest such venture and is ranked among the strongest and wealthiest leagues in the world. Its brand value was estimated at U.S. $3.98 billion in 2010, and it is the second highest-paid league, trailing only the U.S. National Basketball Association.

The three manifestations (or segments) of sport are illustrated in Figure 17.4. Although the major feature distinguishing these three domains is their differing purposes, a concomitant difference exists in the clients of these segments. They are the general public in egalitarian sport, the few talented individuals in elite sport, and the paying public in entertainment sport. The three segments are also distinguished on the basis of the environments they interact with and the opportunities and threats therein. For egalitarian sport, the environment is localized and consists of the community, local government(s), social clubs, educational institutions, and local media, if any. Although elite sport is still dependent on the local environment to support its existence, it also relies on more distal environmental elements such as regional and national governments; regional, national, and international sport governing bodies; and other competing units in the pursuit of excellence. A unit in entertainment sport (i.e., a franchise) is dependent on both the local and distal environments. For the most part, the paying public hails from the local community; thus, the immediate vicinity constitutes the market. Local governments sanction and, to some extent, sustain the professional franchise. However, its environment extends to sponsors, media, and other agencies that promote the franchise. Furthermore, other franchises in the league and the league that controls the focal franchise are also significant elements in its environment.

In the business lexicon (e.g., Highes & Sweeter, 2009), the terms "farming" and "hunting" refer to two forms of client relationships: the former implies nurturing and retaining existing customers, and the latter refers to recruiting new customers. Borrowing

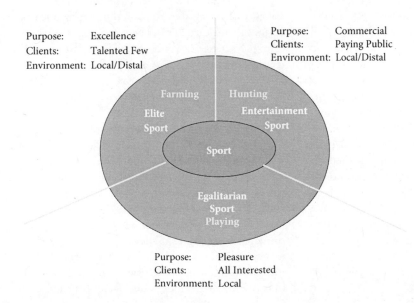

Figure 17.4 Three manifestations of sport.

this analogy, I (Chelladurai, 2010) suggest that the terms *playing*, *farming*, and *hunting* are descriptive of the differences among the three segments of sport. Playing is simply enjoying the kinesthetic sensations experienced while engaging in the sport, and this forms the major attribute of egalitarian sport. Farming is the laborious act of plowing, seeding, watering, and weeding the field, then waiting patiently to reap the harvest. Elite sport resembles farming in that it cultivates excellence in sport over a long time. Entertainment sport resembles *hunting*, in which animals are hunted to be served as food for the family. In this analogy, entertainment sport is involved in recruiting or drafting the excellence produced elsewhere by others and parading such excellence as teams of elite athletes in organized competitions.

The distinction between egalitarian sport and elite sport makes it easier to reconcile the two contrasting approaches to leadership outlined earlier. The present effort to reconcile the contrasting approaches to leadership is confined to egalitarian and elite sport. Entertainment sport is excluded from this discussion for three main reasons. First, the players in entertainment sport are employees of the professional sport franchise, whereas the players in egalitarian and elite sport are clients of the organization. Second, the coach in entertainment sport (in contrast to the leaders in egalitarian and elite sport) has little control over recruiting or dismissing players, nor over the rewards and punishments meted out to players. The third and final reason is that the existing research on leadership in sport has been conducted only in the context of egalitarian and/or elite sport.

The autonomy-supportive leadership approach is oriented toward individual motivation and well-being, and the issue of performance is rarely mentioned in that context. But my idea of leadership in the pursuit of excellence (Chelladurai, 2007) is largely focused on member performance and progressive attainment of excellence. Similarly, the studies on decision-making styles involved competitive basketball teams, in which performance is emphasized. From another perspective, competitive teams in interdependent sports (such as basketball) may not be suited for participative or autonomy-supportive leadership style because of inherent conflicts of interest. For instance, the 12 players on a basketball team vie with each other for a position on the starting five or for a chance to play in competition. Given this intra-team competition, it may not be a good idea to ask the players who should be among the starting five.

I (Chelladurai, 2012) have proposed that a greater focus on task-involving climate is most relevant to the pursuit of pleasure, and that the ego-involved climate is antithetical to the essential thrust of that enterprise. Further, I hold that a task-involved climate is also the bedrock of the pursuit of excellence, in that any person in pursuit of excellence should be constantly striving to cultivate expertise in the activity without reference to other competitors in the field. However, I also believe that the ego-orientation is critical to the pursuit of excellence as excellence can be proved only by performing better than others. Accordingly, the high-performance-focused coach may well create a climate that would foster ego orientation. For example, when a coach expresses disappointment over a mental mistake at a crucial juncture in a competition, it is a punishment (reflecting an ego-involving climate), but it is legitimate and required in the context of the pursuit of excellence. Unequal recognition is certainly problematic in the pursuit of pleasure. However, unequal recognition is part of the process in the pursuit of excellence, as in the distinction between starters and substitutes in basketball. The process of tryouts is to identify and select the best and, by the same token, eliminate those who do not measure up. In essence, pursuit of excellence is an exclusionary process, and therefore, leaders and coaches in pursuit of excellence should not be faulted for not bestowing equal recognition on all.

Intra-team rivalry may also be a necessary condition for pursuit of excellence in team sports. That is, the coach should encourage every athlete to be better than others, including teammates. The striving by everyone to be better than his or her teammates, with a view to getting on the starting line-up, ensures that everyone plays better, so that the whole team plays better. Finally, given that pursuit of excellence consists of practice and performance stages, task involvement needs to be paramount in the practice stage but ego involvement may predominate in the performance stage.

Another way that the discrepancies between the two approaches can be reconciled is to study the contrast between *deliberate play* and *deliberate practice* articulated by Côté and his colleagues (Côté, 1999; Côté, Baker, & Abernethy, 2003, and Côté, Baker, & Abernethy, 2007) . They use the terms *practice* "for organized activities in which the principal focus is on skill development and performance enhancement," and *play* "to describe activities undertaken primarily for intrinsic enjoyment but that may nevertheless ultimately contribute to the acquisition of expertise" (p. 184). The critical characteristics of deliberate play are that it is enjoyable, done for its own sake, flexible, and occurs in various settings without the necessity of adult supervision. In contrast, deliberate practice is a serious and not so enjoyable activity carried out to achieve a future goal, and it is carried out in specialized facilities, often under adult supervision (Côté et al., 2007).

The thrust of the work by Côté and associates is that deliberate play is a precondition for individuals to be continually involved in an activity and thus gain expertise in that activity. It is during deliberate play that one gains an interest in the activity, cultivates different movement patterns, and thereby becomes innovative and creative, which contributes to later expertise in that activity. Readers will recognize that the distinction between deliberate play and deliberate practice parallels Keating's (1964) distinction between pursuit of pleasure and pursuit of excellence. Further, the definition and description of deliberate play approaches Huizinga's (1955) definition of play.

Côté (1999) also noted that the transition from deliberate play to deliberate practice follows three stages: *sampling years*, when one tries out various sports as deliberate play; *specializing years*, when the individual focuses on developing skills in one or two sports; *investment years*, when sport-specific deliberate practice is undertaken. The content and context of deliberate play (or pursuit of pleasure) clearly calls for autonomy-supportive leadership (if and when leadership is present). As the individual gains an abiding interest in a particular activity, gains and appreciates the skills associated with it, and seeks to excel in that activity, he or she steps into the specializing and investment years. Concomitant with this progression through the various stages of gaining expertise, leaders and coaches need to move to a more demanding and commanding type of leadership to help keep the performer focused on increasingly painful and boring work in rigorously planned and deliberate practice. This is not to deny the efficacy or necessity of autonomy-supportive leadership. In fact, one could argue that autonomy-supportive leadership is the foundation on which pursuit of excellence rests. After all, the person has the ultimate autonomy to continue to engage in or drop out of the pursuit of excellence. Further, the coach's demanding and commanding leadership will have the desired effects only if the coach is also attentive to the athlete's needs for autonomy, relatedness, and competence,

and can be accommodative of those needs as much as possible.

In addition, the extent to which the coach who facilitates the pursuit of excellence can support autonomy is largely dependent on both the type of individual and the type of sport. Highly motivated and disciplined individuals are most likely to engage in deliberate practice on their own, without the influence of another. For example, in his early days, Roger Federer won many championships without the services of a coach. In discussing group cohesion in sport, Carron and Chelladurai (1981) suggested that cohesion matters only in interdependent sports because of the need to coordinate the activities of team members. The same argument can be advanced to suggest that a directive and demanding style of leadership is relevant and necessary in interdependent sports, whereas autonomy-supportive leadership is relatively more pertinent to independent sports.

The suggestion that one form of leadership is more germane to one goal of participation and/or one form of sport does not mean that either of the leadership styles is totally absent in either context. Even in pursuit of pleasure or deliberate play, there will likely be some demanding/commanding behaviors by designated leaders. Similarly, high-performance leader may exhibit autonomy-support behavior and cultivate task-orientation in specific instances. The idea that both forms of leadership will be present in both pursuit of pleasure and pursuit of excellence is illustrated in Figure 17.5. It shows that the commanding and demanding leader behaviors will increase as the participant moves from pursuit of pleasure (i.e., deliberate play) toward pursuit of excellence (i.e., deliberate practice). But it also shows that neither form of leadership is totally absent from either of the domains of participation. In summary, either form of leadership can be effective if it matches the purpose of sport participation and whether that activity is individual or team sports.

Conclusion

Several different models of leadership, each supported by research, have been described in this chapter. It is proposed that some of the discrepancies and inconsistencies among them may be reconciled if we take into account the two differing manifestations of sport. The argument here is that pursuit of pleasure and pursuit of excellence are distinct enterprises, with different purposes of participation. The attainment of the different goals of each

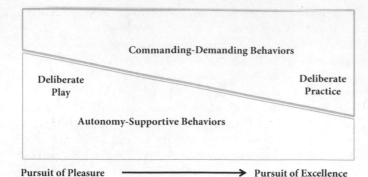

Figure 17.5 Leader behaviors in pursuit of pleasure and excellence.

manifestation is contingent on instituting different structures and processes to achieve them. One of the most significant processes to be considered in this regard is leadership. A distinction is made between soft and hard leadership, and it is suggested that the mix of these leadership approaches should be consistent with the varying purposes of participation in sport.

Future Directions

In this chapter, a critical distinction is made between sport as pursuit of pleasure and sport as pursuit of excellence. Based on this distinction, Chelladurai (2007) has proposed a set of dimensions of leader behaviors appropriate to the pursuit of excellence (see Table 17.3). Further research is necessary to identify which of these behaviors are

Table 17.3 Leader behavior deemed essential in pursuit of excellence

Leader Behavior	Description
Creating a vision	Creating vision with new objectives, instituting new strategies, convincing the athlete of its attainability, and expressing confidence that the athlete can reach that vision
Intellectual stimulation	Challenging existing assumptions and attitudes, encouraging creativity and innovation, and presenting holistic perspectives
Individualized and supportive leadership	Paying individualized and personal attention to the members' needs, treating them individually through frequent contacts, and communicating freely and generously
Personalized recognition	Recognizing and rewarding the hard work, and big and small achievements, particularly during practice sessions
Demanding and directive behavior	Demanding and directing the athletes to persist and carry out the activities of the planned training regimen
Promoting self-efficacy and self-esteem	Extolling the talents and skills of the athlete, expressing confidence in the athlete's capacity to achieve excellence, and encouraging toward even greater efforts
Emphasis on winning	Emphasizing winning in contests as such victories define excellence
Cultivating self-interest	Encouraging athletes to seek the rewards of their own efforts for themselves while being governed by a moral code and a sense of justice to all, including the opponents
Instilling task- and ego orientation	Cultivating and reinforcing progressive improvements in personal performance and focusing on performing better than others
Intra-team rivalry	Encouraging every athlete to be better than his or her own teammates
Training behavior	Training in the *technical aspects* (i.e., in the skills and movement patterns, physical and psychological capabilities); *cognitive aspects* (i.e., the tactics and strategies); and the *emotional aspects* (i.e., recognizing, regulating and exploiting the emotions of self and opponents)

From Chelladurai, P. (2007). Leadership in sports. In G. Tenenbaum & R.C. Eklund (Eds.), *Handbook of sport psychology* (3rd. edition, pp. 113–135). New York: John Wiley.

critical to effective high-performance leadership. Established coaches and former athletes may be interviewed for their views on what leader behaviors are relevant to pursuit of excellence and what behaviors have helped them to achieve excellence. It would be useful if the interviews are held with coaches and players in different types of sport defined by degree of dependence and variability inherent in the sports and the type of participants (e.g., youth vs. adults, females vs. males). Such an effort is most likely to identify the forms of leader behavior most effective for different forms of sport and/or participants.

A fundamental responsibility that goes with proposing a model is the identification and/or development of scales to measure the constructs of that model. Accordingly, the compilation and confirmation of a list of excellence-oriented leader behaviors has to be followed by a serious effort to develop scales to measure those behaviors. In a similar manner, future research should develop appropriate measures to assess the constructs of other models that have not been adequately handled in the past.

References

Ames, C. (1992). Classrooms: Goals, structures, and student motivation. *Journal of Educational Psychology, 84*, 261–271.

Amorose, A. J., & Anderson-Butcher, D. (2007). Autonomy-supportive coaching and self-determined motivation in high school and college athletes: A test of self-determination theory. *Psychology of Sport and Exercise, 8*, 654–670.

Amorose, A. J., & Horn, T. S. (2000). Intrinsic motivation: Relationships with collegiate athletes' gender, scholarship status, and perceptions of their coaches' behavior. *Journal of Sport and Exercise Psychology, 22*, 63–84.

Amorose, A. J., & Horn, T. S. (2001). Pre- to post-season changes in the intrinsic motivation of first year college athletes: Relationships with coaching behavior and scholarship status. *Journal of Applied Sport Psychology, 13*, 355–373.

Barnett, N. P., Smoll, F. L., & Smith, R. E. (1992). Effects of enhancing coach-athlete relationships on youth sport attrition. *The Sport Psychologist, 6*, 111–127.

Bass, B. (1985). *Leadership and performance beyond expectations.* New York: Free Press.

Carron, A. V., & Chelladurai, P. (1981). Cohesiveness as a factor in sport performance. *International Review of Sport Sociology, 2*(16), 21–41.

Chelladurai, P. (1978). *A contingency model of leadership in athletics.* Unpublished doctoral dissertation, Department of Management Sciences, University of Waterloo, Canada.

Chelladurai, P. (1989). *Manual for the Leadership Scale for Sports.* Unpublished manuscript, The University of Western Ontario.

Chelladurai, P. (1993). Leadership. In R. N. Singer, M. Murphy, & K. Tennant (Eds.), *The handbook on research in sport psychology* (pp. 647–671). New York: Macmillan Publishing Company.

Chelladurai, P. (2007). Leadership in sports. In G. Tenenbaum, & R. C. Eklund (Eds.), *Handbook of sport psychology* (3rd ed., pp. 113–135). New York: John Wiley.

Chelladurai, P. (2010, October 13–16). *Human resource management in the sport industry.* Opening keynote paper at the 6th Congress of the Asian Association for Sport Management, Kuala Lumpur, Malaysia.

Chelladurai, P. (2012). Models and measurement of leadership in sports. In G. Tenenbaum, R. Eklund, & A. Kamata (Eds.), *Measurement in sport and exercise psychology* (pp. 433–442). Champaign, IL: Human Kinetics.

Chelladurai, P., & Arnott, M. (1985). Decision styles in coaching: Preferences of basketball players. *Research Quarterly for Exercise and Sport, 56*(1), 15–24.

Chelladurai, P., & Carron, A. V. (1978). *Leadership.* Ottawa: CAHPER, Sociology of Sport Monograph Series.

Chelladurai, P., Haggerty, T. R., & Baxter, P. R. (1989). Decision style choices of university basketball coaches and players. *Journal of Sport and Exercise Psychology, 11*, 201–215.

Chelladurai, P., & Quek, C. B. (1995). Decision style choices of high school basketball coaches: The effects of situational and coach characteristics. *Journal of Sport Behavior, 18*(2), 91–108.

Chelladurai, P., & Riemer, H. (1998). Measurement of leadership in sports. In J. L. Duda (Ed.), *Advancements in sport and exercise psychology measurement* (pp. 227–253). Morgantown, WV: Fitness Information Technology, Inc.

Chelladurai, P., & Saleh, S. D. (1980) Dimensions of leader behavior in sports: Development of a leadership scale. *Journal of Sport Psychology, 2*(1), 34–45.

Côté, J. (1999). The influence of the family in the development of talent in sport. *The Sport Psychologist, 13*, 395–417.

Côté, J., Baker, J., & Abernethy, B. (2003). From play to practice: A developmental framework for the acquisition of expertise in teams sports. In J. Starkes, & K. A. Ericcson (Eds.), *Expert performance in sports: Advances in research on sport expertise* (pp. 89–110). Champaign, IL: Human Kinetics.

Côté, J., Baker, J., & Abernethy, B. (2007). Practice and play in the development of sport expertise. In G. Tenenbaum, & R. C. Eklund (Eds.), *Handbook of sport psychology* (3rd ed., pp. 184–202). New York: John Wiley.

Danielson, R. R., Zelhart, P. F., & Drake, C. J. (1975). Multidimensional scaling and factor analysis of coaching behavior as perceived by high school hockey players. *Research Quarterly, 46*(3), 323–334.

Deci, E. L., & Ryan, R. M. (1985). *Intrinsic motivation and self-determination in human behavior.* New York: Plenum Publishing Corporation.

Duda, J. L., & Hall, H. (2001). Achievement goal theory in sport: Recent extensions and future directions. In R. N. Singer, Hausenbals, H. A., & C. A. Janelle (Eds.), *Handbook of sport psychology* (2nd ed., pp. 417–443). New York: John Wiley & Sons.

Ericsson, K. A., Krampe, R. T., & Tesch-Römer, C. (1993). The role of deliberate practice in the acquisition of expert performance. *Psychological Review, 103*, 363–406.

Halpin, A. W., & Winer, B. J. (1957). A factorial study of the leader behavior description. In R. M. Stogdill, & A. E. Coons (Eds.), *Leader behavior: Its description and measurement.* (pp. 39–51). Columbus: The Ohio State University.

Highes, M., & Sweeter, A. (2009). *Successful e-mail marketing strategies: From hunting to farming.* Chicago: Racom Communications.

Huizinga, J. (1955). *Homo ludens: A study of the play-element in culture*. Boston: Beacon Press.

Keating, J. W. (1964). Sportsmanship as a moral category. *Ethics, 75*, 25–35.

Kenow, L., & Williams, J. M. (1992). Relationship between anxiety, self-confidence, and the evaluation of coaching behaviors. *The Sport Psychologist, 6*, 344–357.

Mageau, G. A., & Vallerand, R. J. (2003). The coach–athlete relationship: A motivational model. *Journal of Sports Sciences, 21*, 883–904.

Nicholls, J. G. (1984). Achievement motivation: Conceptions of ability, subjective experience, task choice, and performance. *Psychological Review, 91*, 328–346.

Nicholls, J. G. (1989). *The competitive ethos and democratic education*. Cambridge, MA: Harvard University Press.

Roberts, G. C. (1997). Future research direction in understanding the motivation of children in sport: A goal orientation perspective. In R. Lidor, & M. Bar Eli (Eds.), *Innovations in sport psychology: Linking theory and practice. Proceedings of the 9th World Congress in Sport Psychology: Part II* (pp. 576–580). Netanya, Israel: Ministry of Education, Culture, and Sport.

Ryan, R. M., & Deci, E. L. (2000). Self determination theory and the facilitation of intrinsic motivation, social development, and well being. *American Psychologist, 55*, 68–78.

Smith, R. E., & Smoll, F. L. (1990). Self-esteem and children's reactions to youth sport coaching behaviors: A field study of self-enhancement processes. *Developmental Psychology, 26*(6), 987–993.

Smith, R. E., Smoll, F. L., & Curtis, B. (1979). Coaching behaviors in little league baseball. In F. L. Smoll, & R. E. Smith (Eds.), *Psychological perspectives in on youth sports* (pp. 173–201). Washington, DC: Hemisphere.

Smith, R. E., Smoll, F. L., & Hunt, E. B. (1977). A system for the behavioral assessment of athletic coaches. *Research Quarterly, 48*, 401–407.

Smith, R. E., Smoll, F. L., Hunt, E. B., Clarke, S. J. (1976). *CBAS audio visual training module* (Video). Seattle: University of Washington.

Smith, R. E., Zane, N. W. S., Smoll, F. L., & Coppel, D. B. (1983). Behavioral assessment in youth sports: Coaching behaviors and children's attitudes. *Medicine and Science in Sport and Exercise, 15*, 208–214.

Smoll F. L., & Smith, R. E. (1989). Leadership behaviors in sport: A theoretical model and research paradigm. *Journal of Applied Social Psychology, 19*, 1522–1551.

Smoll, F. L., Smith, R. E., Barnett, N. P., & Everett, J. J. (1993). Enhancement of children's self-esteem through social support training for youth sport coaches. *Journal of Applied Psychology, 78*(4), 602–610.

Smoll, F. L., Smith, R. E., Curtis, B., & Hunt, E. (1978). Toward a mediational model of coach-player relationships. *Research Quarterly, 49*, 528–541.

Vallerand, R. J. (2007). Intrinsic and extrinsic motivation in sport and physical activity. In G. Tenenbaum, & R. C. Eklund (Eds.), *Handbook of sport psychology* (pp. 59–83). Hoboken, NJ: John Wiley.

Williams, J. M., Jerome, G. J., Kenow, L. J., Rogers, T., Sartain, T. A., & Darland, G. (2003). Factor structure of the coaching behavior questionnaire and its relationship to athlete variables. *The Sport Psychologist, 17*(1), 16–34.

Yukl, G. A., & Van Fleet, D. D. (1992). Theory and research on leadership in organizations. In M. M. Dunnette, & L. M. Hough (Eds.), *Handbook of industrial psychology* (2nd ed., pp. 147–197). Palo Alto, CA: Consulting Psychologists Press.

Zhang, J., Jensen, B. E., & Mann, B. L. (1997). Modification and revision of the Leadership Scale for Sport. *Journal of Sport Behavior, 20*(1), 105–121.

The Psychology of Coaching

Daniel Gould *and* E. Missy Wright

Abstract

The psychology of coaching can be viewed as the scientific study and application of the practice of supporting individuals in achieving specific personal and organizational performance goals, as well as the achievement of nonperformance personal development. Once only associated with sport, coaching psychology is used today to assist individuals of all ages in a wide variety of environments (e.g., military, business, schools). Although the practice of coaching has expanded greatly, research and theory in the area lags. To help rectify this situation, this chapter summarizes the psychology of coaching research, identifies gaps in its knowledge base, and outlines future research directions. This is accomplished first by looking at the traditional context of sport, then expanding to other nonsport areas where coaching is being applied. It is concluded that instead of conducting research in isolated domain-specific silos, researchers should integrate research knowledge across areas.

Key Words: Coaching, psychology of coaching, high performance

Sport psychologists have been long been interested in the psychology of coaching. In outlining the purposes of this field, for example, Coleman Griffith (1925), the father of modern sport psychology in North America, indicated that one of the roles of the sport psychologist was to observe the best coaches, record the principles that they employ, and pass those principles on to less experienced coaches. Griffith (1932) also felt that sport psychologists had an obligation to use the scientific method to inform coaching practice. He did this in writing the *Psychology of Coaching*, one of the first books of its kind.

The psychological aspects of coaching have continued to be of interest to sport psychologists and practitioners alike. Numerous books have been written on the topic and literally hundreds of studies have been conducted. In a comprehensive review of the coaching science literature conducted in 2004 (in which many of the studies focused on

psychological questions), Gilbert and Trudel (2004) identified over 1,100 studies in the area. More recently, sport psychologists have taken what has been known about coaching in the sport context and applied that knowledge to business (Gordon, 2007; Jones, 2002; Murphy, 1996; Loehr & Schwartz, 2001). Accompanying the growth of the positive psychology movement around the world, psychologists at large (e.g., Linley & Harrington, 2005; Palmer, 2005) have taken the metaphor of sport coaching and applied it to other areas of human function (e.g., life coaching, business) under the umbrella of the psychology of coaching (see also Chapter 37, this volume).

However, the sport psychology research literature has not necessarily been used or even recognized in this new "coaching" area. In fact, over the last decade, there has been considerable movement to study coaching in business and general life contexts, which has led to the initiation of new journals like

The Coaching Psychologist in 2005 and *Coaching: An International Journal of Theory, Research and Practice* in 2008.

Given the interest in the psychological aspects of coaching both historically in the field of sport psychology and more recently across disciplines, a need exists to summarize the psychology of coaching research, identify gaps in our knowledge, and outline future research directions. To achieve these purposes, we begin by defining the psychology of coaching. We then review and synthesize the knowledge base on the psychology of coaching, first looking at the traditional context of sport, then expanding to newer areas in which coaching is applied (e.g. business, fitness/health promotion). We conclude by identifying future research directions.

Defining Coaching and the Psychology of Coaching

The derivation of the word *coaching* can be traced to the Hungarian term *koczi* (Hendrickson, 1987, as cited in Stern, 2004). In Hungarian, *koczi* described a carriage that was built to carry passengers over difficult terrain, all the while protecting them from the elements during their journey. The process of guiding and protecting during a journey was applied, metaphorically, to other fields, and today coaching is commonly defined as "the practice of supporting an individual...through the process of achieving a specific personal or professional result" (Coaching, n.d.). Given that sport psychology is defined as the scientific study of human behavior in sport and exercise settings and the application of that knowledge (Weinberg & Gould, 2011), coaching psychology can be viewed as the scientific study and application of this practice of supporting individual athletes and exercisers in achieving specific personal and/or team goals in the sport and in a broader context. Palmer and Whybrow (2005) define it as "a domain of practice for psychologists concerned with the integration of psychological theory and research for promoting individual well-being and performance, as well as group and organizational performance (as adapted from Grant & Palmer, 2002)" (pp. 7–8).

Recently, Grant, Passmore, Cavanagh, and Parker (2010) discussed the utility of thinking about three categories of performance coaching: skills coaching, performance coaching, and developmental coaching. Skills coaching focuses on developing specific skills that a client may need (e.g., the ability to present, negotiate) via instruction, often through modeling and by providing feedback. Performance coaching focuses on the process a client employs to solve some specific workplace problem, often resulting from a performance review. It is often time focused (e.g., improve performance over the next 6 months), with the coach helping the client learn to more effectively set goals and deal with challenges he or she may encounter in achieving specific performance objectives. Finally, developmental coaching takes a broader approach, helping clients develop personal and professional assets often through a reflective process that enhances the ability to understand oneself. This type of coaching is more general and often focuses on helping prepare clients to better deal with future challenges by better understanding themselves. Grant and colleagues suggest that the skills to be effective in each type of coaching situation may be somewhat different.

Research and Theory on the Psychology of Sport Coaching
How Has Coaching Science Been Studied?

Since the 1970s, researchers have paid considerable attention to research on coaching science, which is generally defined as studies of coach-directed processes focused on athlete learning, instruction, and coaching. Coaching science is a comprised of investigations coming from the fields of sport pedagogy, sport psychology, sport biomechanics, and sports medicine. Many of these studies focus on the psychology of coaching.

In 2004, Gilbert and Trudel conducted the most comprehensive review of the coaching science literature by identifying over 1,100 studies, of which 610 met their inclusion criteria. They were interested in examining how much research has been conducted and where it was published, areas of coaching science that have been most examined, the methods most often used, types of participants studied, and the types of sports and sporting contexts examined. Although their results did not examine trends by subdiscipline studied (e.g., coaching psychology), they do provide a useful context for understanding how researchers have approached the study of coaching science in general.

Results of Gilbert and Trudel's (2004) analysis revealed that the studies conducted between 1970 and 2001 could be grouped into four broad categories. These included coaching behavior studies (e.g., coaching effectiveness, coach–athlete relationships, and leadership style employed), studies of coaching thoughts (e.g., coach attitudes, decision-making knowledge, and perceptions), characteristics of coaches studied (e.g., investigations of demographics, gender, and qualifications), and career development investigations (e.g., satisfaction, burn-out, and coach education). The methods employed by the investigators were also identified.

Results from this review also identified a number of important trends in the literature. First, an increase in publication rate occurred between 1970 and 2001, with just under two articles published yearly in the 1970s to over 30 articles published by 2001. Articles were published in over 161 different journals. Second, topics most often examined included articles on coach behavior or what coaches do (51%), followed by career development articles (33%), coaching thought articles (29%), and coaching characteristic articles (26%).[1] Quantitative methods were most often used (80%), with questionnaire studies being most common (69%). However, an increase in qualitative methods was noted over time. Only 14% of the studies employed mixed-method designs. Fourth, head coaches were most often studied. Assistant coaches and other parties (e.g., officials, administrators) who interact or observe coaches were seldom examined. Finally, coaches from team sports were predominately studied, with much less attention given to individual sport coaches.

Based on their review, Gilbert and Trudel (2004) concluded that coaching science has benefited from being studied by researchers representing many subfields of kinesiology. However, because the research was dominated by studies describing behaviors of coaches, more studies that link coaching behaviors with other elements of coaching (such as thoughts and characteristics) are needed. A move to expand beyond quantitative survey methods was noted, with the importance of conducting more qualitative and intervention studies being particularly identified. They also indicated that research needs to move beyond a sole focus on head coaches and include more assistant coaches and other parties that influence coaches, such as officials and parents. A special need to examine female coaches was identified, as less than 5% of the studies reviewed by these researchers have included females. In addition, the research needs to expand beyond studies of team sport coaches and focus more on understanding the coaching process across sports and sport types. Because most of the research conducted to date had been descriptive in nature, a need to use or develop theories specific to coaching was emphasized, with the authors suggesting that the study of coaching practice may lead to theory development and that theory development might better explain coaching practice. Finally, most of the studies conducted in the area have been single, isolated studies with very few lines of research in coaching science being conducted. A need exists to do so.

Other researchers have conducted comprehensive reviews of the literature looking at more specific topics like coaching effectiveness (Horn, 2002, 2007), coaching expertise and effectiveness (Côté & Gilbert, 2009), decision-making processes in coaching (Abraham, Collins, & Martinale; 2006), coaching behaviors (Cushion, 2010), coaching leadership (Vella, Oades, & Crowe, 2010), and coaching behaviors associated with positive youth develop (Conroy & Coatsworth, 2006). Although these specific topics will be discussed later in this chapter, at this point, it is important to note that they all conclude that the psychology of coaching is a complex multivariate process that involves the reciprocal interaction of personal, environmental, and contextual factors. They also call for more research (especially systematic lines of inquiry), the need for theory development, and the use of multiple methods to understand the psychological aspects of coaching.

Psychology of Coaching Theories

Although coaching psychology research parallels that of coaching science in that the vast majority of research has been descriptive in nature, several efforts have been made to develop or apply theories that explain the specific psychological processes involved. Three theories have been most often used in the study of the psychological aspects of coaching. Two of these theories focus on leadership: Smoll and Smith's (1989) *cognitive-mediational coaching leadership model* and Chelladurai's (1978, 2007) *multidimensional model of sport leadership*. The third theory, developed by Mageau and Vallerand (2003), focuses on how the coach–athlete relationship influences motivation. Each of these will be briefly reviewed below.

The cognitive-mediational model of coaching leadership was developed by Smoll and Smith (1989) through their studies of youth sport coaches. It was their contention that to understand coaching leadership, one must consider situational factors and behaviors; individual differences between coaches; and cognitive processes that mediate antecedents, behaviors, and outcomes of coaches. Thus, coaches' behaviors are influenced by the personal makeup of the coach and the situation. However, the effects of a coach's behaviors on his or her athletes are mediated by how the athlete perceives the behaviors initiated by the coach. For example, according to this theory, how the positive or negative feedback given by a coach influence an athletes' performance, motivation, satisfaction, and affective reactions is not only dependent on the behavior exhibited by the coach, but on how the athlete perceives that behavior. A series of studies examining the relationship between youth sport coaches and young athletes' sport participation, motivation, satisfaction, anxiety, and self-esteem has been used as evidence to support this model (see Smoll & Smith, 2002).

The most researched theory in the psychology of coaching is Chelladurai's (1978, 2007) multidimensional model of sport leadership. Consistent with most contemporary theories of leadership, Chelladurai contends that a coach's effectiveness as a leader depends on her or his own characteristics, the characteristics of the athletes being coached, and constraints or situational influences (see also Chapter 17, this volume). In particular, he predicts that a leader is effective when there is a match between the required behavior needed in a situation, the actual behavior emitted by the leader, and the athletes' preferred leadership behaviors. Each of these central tenets are also predicted to be influenced by a variety of antecedent, personal, and situational influences such as age, skill level, organizational norms, and cultural values. Research has generally supported predictions of this model, which suggests that effective coaching is dependent on a match between a coach's preferred style, coach behaviors, the situation, and the preferences of those being coached. For example, when a coach is characterized by a style congruent with the preferences of the athletes, the athletes report more satisfaction and cohesion, better performance, and higher levels of intrinsic motivation. Antecedents of the effectiveness of coaching behaviors have also been identified, such as the age and gender of the athletes being coached. In particular, athletes prefer more autocratic and socially supportive coaches as they get older and more mature, and, in terms of gender, males prefer more autocratic styles of coaching whereas females prefer more democratic and participatory coaching styles (Weinberg & Gould, 2011). The benefits of having a coach lead in a manner consistent with athlete preferences are that athletes perform better, make up teams with increased cohesion, experience higher satisfaction, and have more intrinsic motivation.

Taking a different approach from the leadership theories, Mageau and Vallerand (2003) developed the coach–athlete relationship model of motivation to describe and explain how coaches influence

athletes' motivation. Specifically, this model outlines a sequence of actions explaining how autonomy-supporting styles of coaching influence athletes' intrinsic motivation and self-determined extrinsic motivation (defined to occur when extrinsic reasons for taking part in an activity are accepted and internalized by the person and, therefore, self-determined). Mageau and Vallerand (2003) go on to indicate that autonomy-supportive coaching styles and behaviors imply:

> That coaches provide opportunities for choices, emphasize task relevance, explain reasons underlying rules and limits, acknowledge athletes' feelings and perspective, give athletes opportunities to take initiatives, provide non-controlling competence feedback, avoid controlling motivational strategies, and prevent ego-involvement in their athletes.
> (p. 898)

They further predict that the more coaches adopt such a style and its associated behaviors, the greater the athletes' needs for competence, autonomy, and relatedness are met. This, in turn, results in increased intrinsic motivation and productive self-determined forms of motivation.

Although a wealth of research directly testing Mageau and Vallerand's motivational model is lacking, it is based on three decades of research supporting Deci and Ryan's (1985, 2000) self-determination theory, which holds that it is in an individual's best interest to be intrinsically motivated and that autonomy-supportive instructional behaviors best lead to such behavior (see Chapter 12, this volume). Moreover, a number of sport psychological studies conducted with both coaches and athletes have supported self-determination theory predictions. For example, Scanlan and Lewthwaite (1986) found that young wrestlers who reported lower levels of intrinsic motivation perceived coaches to be more controlling and less supportive. Similarly, studying high school coaches, Amorose and Anderson-Butcher (2007) discovered that an autonomy-supportive coaching leadership style was associated with greater feelings of self-determined behaviors like effort, persistence, and feelings of autonomy in athletes.

Although more research is needed to test the coach–athlete relationship model of motivation (especially tests of the entire model), this theory is based on three decades of research supporting self-determination theory. Not only does it have good explanatory power, but it outlines a number of very specific strategies (e.g., emphasize task relevance, explain reasons underlying rules and limits) that coaches can use to foster intrinsic motivation and self-determined behaviors in their athletes.

Psychology of Coaching Research

Although hundreds of studies have been conducted on the psychological aspects of sport coaching, the vast majority of this research has focused on what makes coaches effective (Côté & Gilbert, 2009; Cushion, 2010; Horn, 2002). Horn (2002) has provided the most comprehensive review of the literature in this area, resulting in a working model of coaching effectiveness. In her model, Horn contends that a coach's behavior "directly" influences athlete motivation, self-perceptions, beliefs, and attitudes, while also indicating that a coach "indirectly" influences his or her athletes as mediated by the athletes' interpretations and perceptions of those behaviors. Personal characteristics of the coach, sociocultural factors, organizational factors, and athlete characteristics are also identified as important antecedents of coaches' behavior. However, the links between these antecedents and a coach's behaviors are mediated by the coach's expectancies, beliefs, values, and behaviors. Hence, based on these antecedent conditions, a coach forms various expectancies and beliefs about his or her athletes, which in turn influence the coach's actual behaviors. These coaching behaviors then directly influence athlete motivation, beliefs, and attitudes and indirectly influence athletes perceptions and interpretations of those coaching actions and behaviors.

Another excellent review of the literature, specifically focusing on coaching effectiveness and expertise, has been conducted by Côté and Gilbert (2009). Côté and Gilbert (2009) define coaching effectiveness as "the consistent application of integrated professional, interpersonal, and intrapersonal knowledge to improve athletes' competence, confidence, connection, and character in specific contexts" (p. 316). Most importantly, they contend that coaching effectiveness is context specific. That is, effectiveness will vary based on whether one is coaching recreational sport, developmental sport, or elite sport. In addition, coaching effectiveness results in changes in four possible athlete outcomes (e.g., competence, confidence, connection, and character), with coaches integrating various sources of knowledge to guide their coaching actions in attempts to influence these outcomes. Côté and Gilbert further contend that expert coaches have complex knowledge structures that include both declarative (content) and procedural (how to deliver or use content) knowledge. Declarative knowledge would include sport-specific, professional (e.g., sport science), and pedagogical knowledge. In addition, effective coaches develop procedural interpersonal knowledge about how to work in complex social systems and intrapersonal knowledge that focuses on an understanding of oneself and consists of both introspection and reflection. Côté and Gilbert (2009), then, have provided a much needed comprehensive definition of coaching effectiveness and a heuristic model that ties the diverse literature together.

Space limitations prevent a more detailed review of the psychology of coaching literature here. Interested readers are referred to the works of Horn (2002), Côté and Gilbert (2009), and Cushion (2010) for more in-depth reviews. However, we will summarize and highlight below some of the major findings resulting from this research.

What Is Known About Effective Coaching Behaviors in Sport?

Cushion (2010) contends that coaching is an ever-changing social process, and, therefore, coaching behaviors must be viewed as a result of a dynamic interaction among coaches, athletes, and environment. However, because of the position of centrality that coaches hold in this process, their behaviors have been of primary interest to researchers. Through their words and actions, coaches have been shown to influence both the performance, cognition, and affective states of their athletes (Horn, 2002).

Some of the initial work in this area focused on the observations of outstanding coaches and the systematic recording of how they coached. For example, Tharp and Gallimore (1976) studied legendary University of California, Los Angeles (UCLA) basketball coach, John Wooden, and found that Wooden's coaching behaviors were characterized by verbal instruction (50%), encouraging players to hustle (13%), scolding and reinstructing (8%), praising and encouraging (7%), and scolding statements of displeasure (7%). More recently, Gallimore and Tharp (2004) reanalyzed their original data and conducted additional interviews with Wooden and his former players. They concluded that Wooden was an excellent and diligent planner, and this planning laid the foundation for the high information load, economy of talk, and practice organization; reserve players received higher incidences of praise than starters; being an exemplary role model was a highly intentional part of Wooden's coaching; and Wooden based his coaching on seven laws of learning that included explanation, demonstration, imitation, and repetition.

Other investigators (e.g., Côté, Salmela, & Russell, 1995) have used qualitative interviews to understand the behaviors coaches report using. Interviews with elite Canadian gymnastic coaches revealed that they most often reported providing supportive environments through the use of positive feedback, gave healthy doses of technical instruction, taught mental skills such as stress management, simulated the mental and physical demands of competition, provided manual training to ensure safety, and stressed physical conditioning. Examining elite-level athletes' perceptions of great coaches, Becker (2009) also used interviews, finding that great coaches exhibit numerous coaching actions that can be broken down into seven categories. These include (1) teach sport skills (tactical, physical, mental, and life skills); (2) communicate effectively; (3) motivate; (4) prepare for competition (tactically, physically, mentally); (5) respond to athletes (through excitement, enjoyment, and displeasure); (6) perform well under pressure; and (7) disregard the irrelevant (focus on big picture).

Looking across these and other studies, reviewers (Cushion, 2010; Gilbert, 2010; Gilbert & Trudel, 2004; Horn, 2002) have generally concluded that top coaches focus on emphasizing instructional behaviors and conveying information. Cushion (2010) also suggests that silence has been identified as a "deliberate" coaching practice of top coaches, in which they intensely focus on the task of observing their athletes. These reviewers of the coaching behavior research have also suggested that these top coaches made efforts to construct positive working environments by providing support and encouragement by praising good performance. However, their feedback is contingent on player performance; they withhold praise unless it is deserved and, at times, scold players for undesirable behaviors. Scolding behaviors and punishment, however, are typically seen least often.

Not all the research has been conducted on elite coaches. Recreational-level youth coaches have also been a primary focus of study (see Conroy & Coatsworth, 2006, for a detailed review). The behaviors and actions of youth sport coaches have been shown to influence young athletes in a number of important ways. In a series of studies spanning several decades Smith, Smoll, and their associates (Smith, Smoll, & Barnett, 1995; Smith, Smoll, & Curtis, 1979; Smoll, Smith, Barnett, & Everett, 1993) found that coaches who were more positive in

their coaching and/or took part in interventions that taught them how to be more positive and encouraging influenced the young athletes they coached in a number of important ways. Specifically, when compared to those coaches who did not undergo the training or were not as positive, these coaches were better liked by their athletes, and their athletes had increased self-esteem, reported lower anxiety and attrition levels, were motivated to participate, and enjoyed playing more.

Coatsworth and Conroy (2006) have also studied coaching behaviors in youth sport coaches. Their findings verified the previous research conducted by Smith, Smoll, and colleagues in that they found that swimming coaches who were trained in psychosocial and behavioral principles had swimmers who exhibited higher levels of self-esteem when compared to swimmers whose coaches did not take part in the intervention. Moreover, this significant relationship was strongest for younger swimmers, as well as for girls who began the program with low self-esteem.

Other researchers have found that when youth coaches create a coaching climate in which the focus is on individual improvement and mastery, young athletes report higher competence, effort, skill improvement, and intrinsic motivation (Halliburton & Weiss, 2002; Smith, Smoll, & Cummings, 2007; Theeboom, De Knoop, & Weiss, 1995; and see also Chapter 24, this volume). For instance, Smith, Smoll, and Cummings (2007) recently found that an intervention in which coaches adopted a mastery approach resulted in decreases in athlete anxiety over the course of a season. Cumming, Smoll, Smith, and Grossbard (2007) also found that young athletes' enjoyment and evaluations of their coach were more strongly related to coaching behaviors and motivational climate than to team win–loss records.

Thoughts, Attitudes, and Opinions of Coaches

A very diverse area of coaching psychology research has focused on the thoughts, attitudes, and opinions of coaches on a wide range of topics. A number of studies have asked coaches to identify the views and opinions about various issues. For example, Gould, Medbery, Damarjian and Lauer (1999) surveyed 153 junior tennis coaches to assess their opinions about the importance of mental skills training, strategies they use to teach mental skills, and recommendations for making mental skills training more effective. The coaches rated reframing pressure, crisis management, self-confidence, and emotional control as the mental skills most difficult to teach. These coaches also listed roadblocks to teaching mental skills, which included a lack of time, difficulty evaluating mental skills training success, a lack of interest, and the lack of availability of model coaches who teach mental skills. In another study, Gould, Greenleaf, Guinan, and Chung (2002) surveyed 65 Olympic coaches for the purpose of identifying variables that influenced both their own performance effectiveness as a coach and their athletes'/teams' performance at the Olympic Games. Most interesting were results that revealed that those variables rated as most influential to coaching performance included marked changes in their coaching behaviors, the inability to establish trust with their athletes, poor crisis management, handling pressure, and making fair but decisive decisions. It was concluded that coaches need to develop psychological skills to handle the pressure of the Olympics, just as their athletes do.

Although studies such as these have been useful in identifying coaches' opinions and attitudes about specific issues in sport, this literature is very difficult to draw general conclusions from because of its idiosyncratic nature, the array of topics addressed (topics explored range from mental training to sportsmanship, and even included areas such as attitudes about what topics to include in coaching education programs), and the lack of any unifying theories that help draw the literature together.

One theoretically based area of study focuses on coaches' efficacy beliefs relative to their ability to coach (Feltz, Short, & Sullivan, 2008). Drawing from the extensive body of research on self-efficacy (Bandura, 1977, 1997), Feltz, Chase, Moritz, and Sullivan (1999) developed a model of coaching efficacy. Coaching efficacy was defined as a coach's belief that he or she has "the capacity to affect the learning and performance of their athletes" (Feltz et al., 2008, p. 153). They contend that coaching efficacy is comprised of four dimensions, all of which have been verified in factor analytic studies. These include game strategy (e.g., ability to coach during competition), motivation (e.g., ability to influence psychological states of athletes), technique (e.g., ability to instruct), and character building (e.g., ability to foster a positive attitude toward sport).

Feltz and her colleagues (1999) contend that the confidence or efficacy that a coach has in his or her own coaching capacities influences important outcomes such as coaching behavior, player and team satisfaction, player and team performance, and player and team self-efficacy. Moreover, one's coaching efficacy has a number of diverse sources such as past experience, prior win–loss record, perceived skill of one's athletes, and social support from the school, parents, community, and administrators.

Initial research testing the coaching efficacy model, although limited, has been encouraging as it has provided support for most of its major predictions (Feltz et al., 2008). For example, the most important sources of coaching efficacy identified have been years of experience and community support, although other sources are being explored (e.g., previous playing experience, imagery). Several studies have also shown that coaching education enhances coaching efficacy (e.g., Campbell & Sullivan, 2005; Lee, Malete, & Feltz, 2002). Finally, coaching efficacy has been found to be linked to coach praise and encouragement (Feltz et al., 1999) and commitment (Kent & Sullivan, 2003), as well as athlete and team outcomes such as satisfaction and performance (Feltz et al., 1999; Myers, Vargas-Tonsing, & Feltz, 2005). Coaching efficacy, then, seems to be an important variable in the psychology of coaching.

Coaching Special Populations
WOMEN AND COACHING

A topic of considerable importance in coaching and coaching psychology is that of women in coaching and differences between coaching male and female athletes. Two central issues characterize this area of study. A primary concern is explaining why women are under-represented in coaching and discovering ways to encourage more women to become and stay involved in coaching. The second area inquires into whether gender-related differences in coaching behaviors and styles are associated with male versus female coaches and in coaching male and female athletes. Each of these will be briefly discussed below.

Acosta and Carpenter (2012) have reported results from a 35-year longitudinal study that provided convincing evidence that women are under-represented in all levels of the coaching profession, despite the enactment of Title IX legislation in the United States in 1972 and the subsequent tremendous growth of participation in women's sports over the last 40 years. For example, only 43% of coaches of women's college sports teams are women, and women hold 57% of the paid assistant coaching positions for women's teams. Also, in 2000, only 11% of the national teams were coached by women in Canada (Marshall, 2001). More disconcerting is the finding that, since 2000, most hires of coaches for women's teams are males. In reviewing the literature explaining the under-representation of women in coaching, Kilty (2006) identified a number of external and internal barriers to women coaching. External barriers included unequal assumptions about competence, in which males are assumed to be more competent; hiring from a principle of similarity, in which most athletic administrators are males and typically hire individuals similar to themselves; homophobia; and a lack of female coaching mentors. Internal barriers included perfectionism, in which women focus on their deficits more than their strengths, lack of assertiveness, inhibition in promotion of their accomplishments, and stress associated with balancing work and personal life. Kilty (2006) concludes by indicating that efforts must be made to recruit and retain more women in coaching by exploring online mentoring program opportunities, developing continuing education classes aimed at promoting connection and voice, identifying best practices for helping female coaches with children stay involved, and identifying effective ways to engage men in advocating for women as coaches.

Finally, after studying Canadian coaches, Reade, Rodgers, and Norman (2009) suggest that proportional hiring practices be implemented. A proportional hiring policy would mandate that more women be hired for higher level coaching positions and more men for lower level positions because their evidence shows that such disproportions currently exist despite women being qualified for higher level positions.

In terms of differences in the psychology of coaching male versus female athletes, very little research has directly examined this issue. However, a number of studies in diverse areas point to the fact that males and females differ in important ways in their psychosocial makeup and, because of this, practitioners have discussed the need for coaches to coach their male and female athletes differently or to better understand the effects of one's coaching behaviors on different genders (Deboer, 2004). For example, after reviewing the literature, Wiese-Bjornstal (2007) indicated that female versus male athletes generally have lower levels of perceived competence (but perhaps more realistic levels), cite emotional support as an important dimension of friendship, are more interested in developing their personal capacities than they are in establishing superiority over others, report more social physique anxiety, are more concerned with coach improprieties, and tend to use higher levels of moral reasoning.

In a qualitative study of cross-country coaches who had coached both male and female athletes, Tuffey (1995) found that these coaches believed that female athletes were coachable, more emotional and sensitive, feel expectations and want to please, are competitive with teammates, and are both academically and weight conscious. In contrast, they described the male athletes they had coached as having more "know it all" attitudes and being more likely to challenge their coach, ego-involved and struggle when not winning, tend to get off track, have more of a team emphasis, and are less emotional than females and/or more likely to hide their emotions. The coaches studied also indicated that they coached their male and female athletes differently—being more blunt and confrontational with their male athletes and more sensitive with their female athletes. The coaches also said that they emphasize winning more with male athletes and doing one's best with female athletes. However, it is important to note that these data were based on interviews with coaches and their perceptions of their effectiveness. Findings were not triangulated through interviews with the coaches' athletes or via observational techniques. Finally, in a study of 38 elite female soccer players from Germany, Norway, Sweden, and the United States, Fasting and Pfister (2000) examined their expectations and evaluations of male versus female coaches. The players reported on strengths and limitations of both male and female coaches that they played for in the past. However, they indicated that male coaches often used a "masculine" style of communication/interaction that involved yelling and being very strict, which was not perceived favorably. These players were also more satisfied with female coaches' communication styles, feeling they were better at understanding them psychologically and demonstrating a more empathic approach.

In addition to the study of gender differences in coaching, in the last few years an increased effort has been made to better understand girls' sport participation and the role that coaches play in this, especially the role that female coaches can play. Specifically, Team Up For Youth (a California-based organization whose mission is to create after-school sports opportunities for youth) dedicated a special initiative to address some of the gender differences that coaches should be aware of and have provided various strategies for coaches to implement when coaching girls across different age groups (2006). These include using lots of praise and fun, cooperative games during the earlier years, and employing peer coaching and team unity development as the girls matured. This initiative not only focused on educating coaches, but also on attracting and training female coaches, as they believe that having "women coaches set off a domino effect" for girls' sport participation (http://www.teamupforyouth. org/ourwork/initiatives/). This approach is consistent with the current research. From her review of the literature, for example, Wiese-Bjornstal (2007) concluded that:

> Girls want coaches to provide good technical instruction and contingent positive feedback; allow them to participate in decision-making about goals, practices, and games; create positive team atmospheres; and develop warm interpersonal relationships with them (Mageau & Vallerand, 2003; Martin, Jackson, Richardson, & Weiller, 1999; Weiss, Ebbeck, & Horn, 1997). These characteristics of social relationships with coaches affect girls' continued participation through increasing their satisfaction with, and confidence in, their sport experiences.
> (p. 11)

In summary, the research conducted thus far suggests that male and female athletes differ in some important ways. Because of these differences, varied psychological approaches to coaching males and females are needed. However, while recognizing gender-related issues, most investigators believe that more differences exist within genders than between them so that, above all else, coaches must treat athletes of all genders as individuals and make efforts to meet their individual needs.

COACHING LIFE SKILLS

In recent years, considerable attention has been focused on studying the development of life skills in physical activity participants, particularly youth (see Gould & Carson, 2008 for a review). Life skills are typically defined as "those internal personal assets, characteristics and skills such as goal setting, emotional control, self-esteem and hard work ethic that can be facilitated or developed in sport and are transferred for use in nonsport settings" (Gould & Carson, 2008, p. 60). Of relevance to this chapter are investigations that have specifically focused on coaching life skills in athletes and the suggestion that coach training should specifically focus on promoting youth social development (Conroy & Coatsworth, 2006; see also Chapter 24, this volume). For example, Gould, Chung, Smith, and White (2006) have examined coaches' attitudes toward

teaching life skills and what life skills they perceive most need development in young athletes. Ratings by coaches showed that taking personal responsibility, developing motivation/work ethic, developing better communication and listening skills, dealing with parents, and achieving better grades were felt to be most in need of development.

In a second study, Jones and Lavelle (2009) conducted qualitative interviews with coaches, sport psychologists, graduate students, and young athletes to identify the life skills that were perceived as most needing development. Findings indicated that two overarching categories of life skills are commonly identified: personal skills (e.g., self-organization, goal setting, motivation) and social skills (e.g., respect, leadership, communication, family interaction). Of the two general categories, social skills were identified as the most in need of development,

Several studies have focused particular attention on the process coaches use to develop life skills in young athletes. For example, Gould and his colleagues (Collins, Gould, Lauer, & Chung, 2009; Gould, Collins, Lauer, & Chung; 2006, 2007) interviewed high school football coaches who were recognized for their effectiveness at developing life skills in their athletes to ascertain their approach toward skill development. These coaches reported using a variety of life skills coaching strategies. Additionally, the coaches were found to have coaching philosophies that placed highest priority on life skills development, were able to foster strong relationships with their athletes, utilized specific life skills strategies that were implemented in both direct and indirect manners, and considered and adapted their life skill teaching strategies to the particular context in which they coached. Finally, and perhaps most importantly, the coaches reported that they did not separate out their life skill coaching, but integrated it in their general coaching strategies.

A season-long case study was used by Holt, Tink, Mandigo, and Fox (2008) to discover how youth learned life skills from their coach and through sport participation. Participants included one Canadian high school soccer team and its coach, with both in-depth interviews and field observations used to collect data. Results revealed that the head coach embraced a philosophy of building relationships with the players and involving them in decisions. Players reported that respect, teamwork, leadership, and initiative were the life outcomes derived from their soccer participation. Little evidence was found that the coach directly taught these life skills, however. In contrast, it was found that this coach created opportunities for his athletes to use life skills and then reinforced players for their use. When asked what life skills transferred beyond sport, only teamwork and leadership were identified by the athletes. Holt and his colleagues (2008) concluded that the athletes created their own life skills learning experiences in the teamwork and leadership areas. They also concluded that it appears that youth with certain life skills are attracted to sport, where they can further develop these skills. Thus, coaching life skills may not be as much about the direct teaching of these skills as about creating conditions in which they can be self-generated, revealed, and reinforced.

Finally, Gould and Carson (2010, 2011) have conducted several empirical studies testing the relationships between perceived coaching actions and behaviors and the development of life skills in young athletes. Findings revealed that high school athletes who reported increased opportunities for the development of emotional regulation, more cognitive skills development, more feedback, pro-social norms, and linkages to community sport experiences also reported experiencing coaching that was characterized by higher levels of facilitating competition strategies, goal setting, talking more about how sport lessons related to life, and positive rapport development. Negative experiences reported from sport participation by the young athletes were associated with greater negative rapport with coaches and fewer coaching efforts to help the athletes work on mental preparation, goal setting, and competition strategies; less modeling of good sportsmanship; and less motivation to work hard on one's own.

These initial studies were recently extended by Gould, Flett, and Lauer (2012) in a study of middle and high school–aged baseball and softball players from an underserved community. The players completed the Youth Experiences Scale (YES-2), a self-report measure of what young people believe they learn from sport (e.g., teamwork, initiative), the Sport Motivational Climate Scale, the Caring Climate Scale, and assessments of the importance their coaches placed on life skills. Although a number of complex multivariate relationships were evident among these variables, the major findings showed that the more coaches created caring, mastery-oriented environments, the more likely that positive YES-2 developmental scores increased. It was also found that ego-oriented climates were associated with negative experiences. This is consistent with earlier research, which has shown that the

motivational (Smith et al., 2007) and caring climates (Fry & Gano-Overway, 2010; Gano-Overway, Newton, Magyar, Fry, Kim, & Guivernau, 2009) created by coaches and adult leaders are correlated to the development of life skills. Thus, if coaches are interested in enhancing the life skills development of their players, the type of coaching climate they create appears to be essential.

Not all the coaching life skills research has focused on young athletes. Flett, Gould, Paule, and Schneider (2010) conducted a study with Canadian university coaches. These coaches described intangible life skills like social character, maturity, resiliency, and work ethic as being important factors facilitating athletic performance. This finding is important because most of the previous life skill coaching research has not linked life skills to enhanced performance, although the coaches identified in the Gould et al. (2006, 2007) high school coaches life skill study were highly successful, winning over 75% of all the games they coached. Those coaches felt that the life skills they helped developed in their athletes not only helped the athletes off the field but on the field as well.

Finally, although these studies show that coaches view life skills as important, and they create environments and act in ways associated with their development, the question remains as to how widespread are these life skills coaching efforts. Several investigators (Boon & Gilbert, 2010; Lacroix, Camire, & Trudel, 2008; McCallister, Blinde, & Weiss, 2000) have found that coaches either are not aware of the life skills objectives of their organization or, although they believe sport participation develops life skills, when probed they can identify few specific strategies for doing so. Boon and Gilbert (2010), in a study focused on teaching citizenship through soccer, summed this up best when they indicated that coaches:

> Despite an average of 10.3 years of youth sport experience and participation in highly structured and well-established youth sport organization (e.g., American Youth Soccer Organization), [coaches] could provide relatively few specific examples of strategies they use to teach citizenship skills. (p. 45)

This has led investigators to conclude that many coaches have been socialized to believe that mere participation in sport fosters the development of life skills and other personal characteristics and are not making the intentional efforts needed to psychologically coach these skills. Indeed, Camire, Forneris,

Trudel, and Bernard (2011) recently outlined specific strategies that coaches should intentionally employ to enhance positive youth development through sport.

Sport sociologist Jay Coakley (2011) has also recently suggested that most people in English-speaking societies have bought into the sport evangelist myth, assuming that sport participation automatically leads to the development of many positive psychosocial outcomes such as leadership, the enhancement of self-esteem, teamwork, and work ethic. However, Coakley suggests that few efforts have been made to support these claims and that little evidence exists to back up and establish the limits of sport for enhancing life skills development. Although we believe that Coakley raises some very important issues, especially concerning the limits of sport for enhancing youth development, he fails to recognize some of the existing sport psychological research linking sport participation to life skills development. Hence, from our review of the literature, we conclude that sport is associated with the development of some life skills, especially when coaches make targeted efforts to develop those skills. What remains unknown, however, is the degree to which coaches take intentional actions to develop these skills, what skills may best be developed in sport, the limits of sport in developing life skills, and the degree to which life skills and character is revealed versus developed via sport participation.

This emerging research on coaching life skills, then, shows that coaches' actions and the participation climates they create are associated with the development of life skills in their athletes. Coaches skilled at teaching life skills use both direct and indirect strategies for teaching life skills and are very intentional in doing so. Athletes appear to develop transferable life skills when their coaches have a philosophy that places primary importance on life skills development, create positive coach–athlete relationships, and create mastery-oriented and caring-motivational participation climates. These conclusions must be tempered, however, by the fact that the majority of research to date has been correlational and descriptive in nature, with the volume of research being limited. More research is needed, especially intervention studies that assess life skills in a prospective fashion. The limits of sport in developing life skills must also be established. Moreover, although many coaches seem to believe that life skills are developed via sport participation, few are making intentional efforts to specifically coach these skills. Hence, a challenge

for sport psychologists and coaching educators is to understand how to persuade coaches that life skills must be intentionally fostered and coached in their programs. These skills will not be "caught" through mere participation.

Coaching Education and Development

One psychology of coaching theme of interest that has emerged over the last two decades has been an examination of the process by which coaches learn to coach. This area of research can be discussed by answering four questions: What experiences lead one to become a coach? What competencies make up coaching expertise? How do coaches learn to develop their competencies? And, how does one's coaching philosophy influence one's coaching? The research focused on each of these questions is discussed here.

WHAT EXPERIENCES LEAD ONE TO COACH?

A number of investigators have been examining what experiences are associated with becoming a coach. Conducting several qualitative interview studies with ice hockey, field hockey, and basketball coaches, Salmela and his colleagues (Salmela, 1995; Salmela, Draper, & Desjardins, 1994) studied the developmental paths they took to become university coaches. Although variability was noted between coaches, consistency was also found and stages of development were identified, such as an early diverse sports involvement, initial coaching experience, and specialist coaching experience. In a more recent quantitative study of 19 Canadian University coaches (10 team, 9 individual sports), Erickson, Côté, and Fraser-Thomas (2007) identified five stages of development for elite sport coaches: (1) early, often diverse, sport participation under the age of 12; (2) competitive sports participation, which could involve multiple or single sport participation with most athlete leadership experiences occurring during this stage (ages 13–18); (3) highly competitive sport participation (ages 19–23); (4) part-time early coaching (ages 24–28); and (5) high-performance elite head coaching.

Based on this research, developing into an expert coach is like developing expertise in other endeavors; it is a long-term process that requires a minimum of 10 years of consistent training and development (Erickson et al., 2007). In addition, those who become expert coaches have previous experiences in the sport they coach, often play multiple sports when they are young, have opportunities to lead as a developing athlete, and often are mentored by more experienced coaches. Missing from this line of research is an in-depth examination of the motives elite coaches have for coaching and a more in-depth examination of the developmental pathways of coaches who are particularly strong in their ability to psychologically coach their athletes.

WHAT COMPETENCIES MAKE UP COACHING EXPERTISE?

Schempp and McCullick (2010) reviewed the literature on coaches' expertise and concluded that expertise in coaching consists of both knowledge and skills, learned through experience. Relative to knowledge, they contend that expert coaches make significant investments in their own learning and, unlike less expert coaches, are never satisfied with their learning. They go on to indicate that their research shows that expert coaches possess extensive knowledge of their sport and are able to synthesize and distill their knowledge into information that athletes can understand and use. Experts also demonstrate greater flexibility in applying knowledge (e.g., the expert coach knows when praise may communicate low expectations whereas the nonexpert coach always provides positive feedback regardless of the individual and context).

In terms of the skills of expert coaches, Schempp and McCullick's (2010) review of the coaching expertise research shows that expert coaches differ from their nonexpert counterparts in their planning, attentional/perceptual, prediction, decision-making, communication, and problem-solving skills. For example, McCullick, Schempp, Hsu et al. (2006) found that expert sport instructors better recognize similarities across situations and time. There also exist working memory differences, as expert coaches have been shown not only to recall greater information about familiar coaching situations, but recall the most relevant information from the situation (McCullick et al., 2006). Finally, expert coaches have the ability to attend to individual players while at the same time monitoring the entire practice or game setting and are better able to distinguish between more versus less relevant information from observations (Schempp & McCullick, 2010). Experts versus nonexperts see past symptoms of performance-based problems and are better at identifying the root causes of poor performance (McCullick, Cummings, & Schempp, 1999).

Although the expert versus nonexpert research literature shows clear differences on a variety of knowledge and skill dimensions, it is somewhat limited in that it has almost exclusively focused on differences related to the teaching of skills. Few studies have examined differences in coaches' ability to communicate, in emotional intelligence, or in use of motivational strategies. Examining differences in these areas is important in light of the coaching leadership research that suggests that emotional intelligence is associated with leader effectiveness (Barling, Slater, & Kelloway, 1999; see also Chapter 4, this volume).

Lyle (2010) reviewed the coach decision-making literature and has suggested a major paradigmatic shift in the way decision-making differences are studied in coaches, arguing that a naturalistic decision-making approach should be adopted. This approach recognizes that coach decision-making is best understood by examining the complex course of decision-making action (the process) versus a set-piece decision-making event. This process involves the coach matching the demands of the situation with the most appropriate action or decisions based on a range of possible solutions learned from a variety of coach training and educational contexts, such as formal education, reflection and discussion, and modeling of significant others. These solutions are also being constantly used and refined via coaching practice. Last, this naturalistic approach relies heavily on intuition, which is argued to be a learned capacity that can be developed and refined through practice. This new approach seems to better address the complexity of coaching, the literature on ways coaches learn, and how coaches must also act on partial information in complex, dynamic environments.

Finally, Abraham, Collins, and Martindale (2006) contend that coaching is largely a decision-making process. They also developed a schematic model explaining the decision-making process in coaching, arguing that decisions are derived from various knowledge sources, including sport-specific, pedagogical, and sport science knowledge sources. These knowledge sources guide coaches' physical, mental, and life skills training efforts that occur in training, preparation, and competition environments and ultimately influence coaching outcomes and goals. Preliminary evidence was also provided for their model from interviews of 16 expert coaches.

HOW DO COACHES LEARN TO COACH?

Many countries around the world have developed formal systems for educating coaches. Most of these systems consist of graded levels or courses and focus attention not only on sport-specific tactics and techniques, but also on more general sport science information about physical training, psychology, and best teaching practices. Historically, coaches have been taught by experts in the various subfields in large-group lecture formats. However, researchers who have interviewed and surveyed coaches have discovered that these formal, lecture-based courses, although often viewed as helpful, are rated much lower in terms of how coaches actually learn when compared to nonformal (e.g., workshop) and informal (e.g., observing other coaches) experiential opportunities housed in the actual contexts that they coach (Trudel, Gilbert, & Werthner, 2010).

These findings have led a number of sport psychologists to the study of how coaches learn and develop. The major finding of this research is that coaches learn to coach much more by doing (coaching) and reflecting on those experiences (Gilbert, Gallimore, & Trudel, 2009) than they do via formal educational programs. Coaches place great value on learning through both experience and via interaction with their peers. This has led researchers to conceptualize coach learning as a social process that is inseparably embedded in specific coaching contexts (Gilbert, 2010). For this reason, contemporary researchers are emphasizing the need to examine the social networks within which coaches learn and how the experiences gained from these social networks impact coach development.

Because researchers now feel that best coaching practices are context-specific, they have begun to better define sport coaching contexts. For example, Trudel and Gilbert (2006) have suggested that coaching practices be studied specific to the recreational sport context, the developmental sport context (programs geared for developing more talented players), and the elite sport context. Other possible contexts to consider are gender of athlete and coach, coach age, and experience. Hence, investigators should study differences across these contexts or qualify their recommendations to the context. In addition to the context, a great deal of attention is being placed on the process of how coaches actually learn in these nonformal and informal settings. Borrowing from general educational research and studying the youth sports environment, for example, Gilbert and Trudel (2004) have discussed the notion of coaching reflection. Based on case studies with six model youth sport coaches, these investigators contend that learning takes place because the coach reflects on his or her experiences in three ways: *reflection in action*, in which a coach reflects on what is happening during a current practice or game; *reflection on action*, in which the coach reflects about what happened after the game or practice is completed; and *retrospective reflection on action*, which occurs at the end of a season. Trudel and Gilbert (2006) also suggest that pedagogical strategies like journaling, creating coaching portfolios, engaging in group discussion, and video analysis are important ways to facilitate coach reflection.

The idea of *learning communities*, in which small groups of coaches with similar goals have regular opportunities to discuss their experiences, share ideas, test solutions, and receive feedback from others, has also been discussed as a way of facilitating coach learning via experience (Gilbert et al., 2009). It is further suggested that keys to implementing such an approach include having regular opportunities to share ideas with other coaches, actually resolving dilemmas with evidence, and making solutions public. Although the idea of coaching learning communities is intuitively appealing in light of what is known about how coaches learn via experience, whether and how they can be implemented given the time demands and competitive nature of sport (i.e., coaches may not want to share ideas with other coaches because they will play their teams later) is a question needing further study.

DOES ONE'S COACHING PHILOSOPHY INFLUENCE ONE'S COACHING?

Only recently have coaching researchers (Jenkins, 2010) called for more scientific research focused on the coaching philosophies that coaches develop and act upon. The lack of research in this area is surprising, given the emphasis placed on developing a coaching philosophy in almost all coaching education programs (e.g., Martens, 2004). Coaching philosophies are thought to focus on coaches' beliefs, values, and priorities, as reflected in the following definitions. One definition of a coaching philosophy is provided by Burton & Raedeke (2008), "a set of beliefs and principles that guide a coach's behavior," (p. 4). Lyle (1999) also provided a more in-depth definition:

> A comprehensive statement about beliefs and behaviors that will characterize the coach's practice. These beliefs and behaviors will either reflect a deeper set of values held by the coach, or will be the recognition of a set of externally imposed expectations to which the coaches feel the need to adhere.
> (p. 28)

Given these definitions, a coach's philosophy is expected to drive coaching actions and, for the purpose of this chapter, the approach and style the coach adopts to psychologically working with their athletes and teams.

The initial research addressing the coaching philosophy–behavior link is mixed. Schempp, McCullick, Busch et al. (2006), in a qualitative study of 31 top golf instructors, reported that these outstanding instructors had definite philosophies of teaching (e.g., beliefs about learner needs, what to teach, purpose, and ways to teach) that guided their teaching. Collins, Gould, Lauer, and Chung (2009) studied award-winning high school coaches, recognized for not only their abilities to be successful on the field but more importantly for their success in developing their athletes as people. Collins et al. found that these individuals had well thought-out philosophies that placed primary importance on developing character in their athletes. Also emphasized were those core values that these coaches indicated drove their coaching actions. In contrast to these studies, McCallister, Blinde, and Weiss (2000), found youth sport coaches espoused core values, such as developing life skills, but found little evidence that the coaches initiated specific strategies to teach these values and skills to their athletes. This might be explained by experience differences in the coaches sampled, as Nash, Sproule, and Horton (2008) found that, as coaches become more experienced and gain knowledge, they are better able to articulate their coaching philosophies and tie that philosophy to the context they coach within. An interesting developmental question, then, is how coaching philosophies are developed in coaches with different levels of experiences and who work in different contexts.

An excellent example of how one's philosophy drives one's coaching practice comes from highly regarded British business coaching expert John Whitmore (2009). Whitmore contends that coaches, in both sport and business, are often ineffective because they spend most of their time telling performers what to do and directing them. He suggests that a much more powerful coaching practice lies in moving away from telling the performer what to do, and instead focuses on asking a series of questions designed to increase performer "self-awareness" while at the same time shifting "responsibility" for performance from the coach to the performer him- or herself. To do this, Whitmore has popularized the GROW model of asking questions, in which the coach focuses on asking her or his athlete a series of "G" or *grow questions* (e.g., "What do you hope to accomplish?" "What would

you like to happen as a result of a coaching session?"); "R" or *reality questions* (e.g., "What have you tried so far?" "What have you seen other people do to accomplish this goal?"); "O" or *option questions* (e.g., "What could you do?" "What options might you try to accomplish your goal?"); and, "W" or *will questions* (e.g., "What will you try to do to accomplish your goal as a result of this discussion?" "What will I see differently over the next 2 weeks as a result of this discussion?"). Although the GROW model is a very popular coaching tool and has had preliminary evidence support its effectiveness (Gant, Curtayne, & Burton, 2009; Spense & Gant, 2005), Whitmore contends that it is just that: a tool or technique. What this model really hinges on is the philosophical approach one adopts when using the GROW model to coach. In particular, Whitmore's approach is grounded in the belief that the best answers to a performance issue or to performing better lie within the performer him- or herself and not necessarily within the coach. The coaches' job is to ask questions using the GROW model and, in so doing, increase performer "awareness" and "generate a feeling of personal responsibility" for one's own performance—versus relying on others to direct performance or solve issues at hand. By doing so, the performer takes more ownership of performance and experiences feelings of autonomy, intrinsic motivation, and pleasure.

More research is needed to examine the correspondence between one's coaching philosophy (beliefs, values) and coaching behaviors. In addition, in reviewing this literature, Jenkins (2010) suggests that self-awareness plays a key role in both developing one's philosophy and understanding the philosophical values–coaching behaviors link, whereas Schempp, McCullick, Busch et al. (2006) emphasize the importance of self-reflection. Moreover, given the increasing emphasis on visionary and transformational leadership in general (Northhouse, 2010) and within sport psychology leadership research (Chelladurai, 2007), it is important for sport psychology researchers to better understand the link between a coaches' philosophy and coaching practice. For example, how does one's philosophy link to relationship skills with athletes, reading athletes' psychological states, allowing athletes to take more ownership of their performance, and the team cohesion–performance relationship? Similarly, how do athlete performance, motivation, and satisfaction change as a result of using a GROW model approach versus more traditional talking at and directive approaches to coaching?

Emerging Research on the Psychology of Coaching

Although mentoring and coaching have surely always existed within high-performance professions, in the last 15 years psychologists, business professionals, military personnel, and scholars from the performing arts have begun to formally employ coaching strategies and terminology in their work with clients. This general coaching movement began in applied settings, in which individuals from these varied backgrounds began to provide individual coaching consultations to improve both client performance and well-being. It has grown considerably; in 2007, for example, it was estimated that 30,000 coaches were working worldwide in an industry generating over $1 billion in revenue annually (Bono, Purvanova, Towler, & Peterson, 2009).

During this period, a number of sport psychologists (Bull, 2006; Gordon, 2007; Jones, 2002; Jones & Morehouse, 2007; Loehr & Schwartz, 2001; Murphy, 1996) have expanded their sport psychology consulting work to business populations, suggesting that parallels exist between high-performance sport and business and that those in business can profit from what has been learned about helping athletes and teams achieve sporting excellence. These individuals have suggested that those in business are elite performers, like athletes, and must manage their physical, mental, emotional, and spiritual energy to achieve peak performance (Loehr & Schwartz, 2001; Murphy, 1996); develop mental toughness skills to cope with the stress and adversity that comes with striving for business excellence (Bull, 2006; Jones & Morehouse, 2007); develop their own leadership skills (Jones, 2002); and create high-performing teams (Gordon, 2007; Jones, 2002). Gordon (2007), however, has noted that not only can sport psychology principles be transferred to help coaches working in the business setting, but also that best business practices, such as creating team visions and missions, can be used by sport coaches to improve performance.

Although applied coaching psychology has exploded in recent years, research and theory on coaching has lagged far behind this applied consulting work. In fact, only in the last decade have researchers become interested in conducting studies on the psychology of coaching in nonsport arenas. Although it is beyond the scope of this chapter to provide a detailed review of this literature, some example studies and trends will be highlighted here. It will also be argued that the scholars from the diverse fields involved in coaching should strive to cross-fertilize their knowledge acquisition efforts by more often reading, integrating, and citing research literature across disciplinary boundaries. This will allow for the identification of general principles that cut across fields, while at the same time helping to identify more context-specific guidelines and highlighting highly idiosyncratic coaching practices.

Although research on the psychology of coaching is in its infancy, a range of topics and issues are beginning to be studied. For example, in the 2009 issue of *Coaching: An International Journal of Theory, Research and Practice,* studies focused on such issues as identifying tools for supporting intuition (Pritchard, 2009), mapping mind complexity as a result of coaching (Berger & Atkins, 2009), the use of a cognitive-behavioral intervention for overcoming procrastination (Karas & Spada, 2009), and the effects coaching has on student examination performance (Passmore & Brown, 2009). A variety of qualitative and quantitative methods have been employed in these studies, and diverse subject populations have been used. Looking across this literature, however, the populations most studied are executive coaches, with life and health coaches and coaching being studied less often (Passmore & Brown, 2009). Research studying coaching in educational settings and coaching with nonadult populations is lacking.

One of the most-studied topics is the effectiveness of coaching. Hernez-Boone (2004, as cited in MacKie, 2007) studied 22 participants from the Center for Creative Leadership leader development program who received follow-up coaching and compared them to noncoached individuals from the program. Interviews revealed that the coached group focused more on leadership and coaching others and reported more often achieving their self-identified objectives. In another study, Karas and Spada (2009) used cognitive-behavioral coaching skills (e.g., decision balance analysis, goal setting, task prioritization, self-talk instruction) using an A-B direct replication across participants design. Participants were seven individuals from the community who were self-identified procrastinators. Results revealed that participants showed declines in procrastination after the intervention, with results only showing slight deteriorations over time. Finally, Hall, Otazo, and Hollenbeck (1999) interviewed 75 executives who were participating in executive coaching at the time of the study. Results revealed that these individuals who were being coached self-reported learning, changes in behaviors, and positive affective changes as a result of their coaching experiences.

As these examples suggest, evidence is starting to be amassed to show that coaching has positive effects in nonsport settings. However, the database is still small, and many studies are descriptive in nature and have not employed rigorous designs. Moreover, given how diverse the field of contemporary coaching is, a need exists to better map out what is happening in the field, who is coaching, and chronicle the current practices these individuals employ. Bono and her colleagues (2009) addressed this issue by surveying over 425 coaches who were either psychologists or nonpsychologists. Results revealed that 282 specific competencies were identified by the sample as skills one needed to coach and were categorized into four categories: *Diagnostic and Planning Capabilities,* which included questioning, listening, communication skills, assessment, analysis, and planning and intervention success assessment; *Intervention and Problem Solving Capabilities,* comprised of a large flexible toolbox, being a motivator, building relationships and achieving rapport, counseling skills, feedback, and holding clients accountable; *Knowledge,* made up of business knowledge, knowledge of human behavior, and knowledge of participant background; and *Personal Qualities,* such as authenticity, honesty and integrity, life and job experience, continuous leaning, self-management and professionalism, and client focus. The ability to build rapport, listen, and counsel were seen as especially critical skills. Given current controversies surrounding what qualifications one needs to be a coach (Gant, Passmore, Cavanagh, & Parker, 2010), Bono et al's. (2009) results indicate that there are as many differences among psychologically trained coaches as there are between psychologically and nonpsychologically trained coaches. Those differences that did exist between the two groups were very small. This led the authors to conclude that the longstanding debate about whether psychological versus nonpsychological training is necessary to prepare one to coach is of limited value. Instead, research should be directed toward answering what specific abilities, knowledge, insights, and skills coaches need to possess in order to be effective and what coaching actions best predict long-term change in clients.

After reviewing the literature on executive coaching research, Feldman and Lankau (2005) concluded that although positive outcomes for clients and organizations have been found, conducting research in this area is very difficult as "coaching is now so diverse that it is more difficult to put boundaries around the construct itself and the appropriate range and scope of its associated outcomes" (p. 845). They also note that coaching is something of a black box because, although we have preliminary evidence of its effectiveness, we cannot explain how and why it works. Establishing a stronger research and theoretical base is essential. Researchers working in this area could also profit greatly from examining the extensive sport psychology–based literature on coaching research and theory.

Conclusion

An explosion of interest in coaching psychology has taken place in recent years, and professionals in a variety of fields are using the psychology of coaching to change the lives of people in all walks of life. However, outside of the sport domain, research into the psychology of coaching is lagging, and few efforts are being made to integrate research across the various domains where it is conducted. In addition, more research, using better designs is needed. There appears to be a great need for theories to help explain when, where, how, and why coaching may or may not be effective, as well as to help identify the key factors that may influence the coaching process. By summarizing the coaching psychology research, and by identifying future directions in the next section, it is hoped that this chapter spurs researchers to systematically examine this important area and helps coaching psychology specialists bridge the research-to-practice and practice-to-research gaps that currently exist.

Future Directions

The practice of psychologically coaching individuals for the purpose of helping them enhance performance is seemingly more popular today than at any other time in history. In addition to psychologically coaching athletes, the field has expanded to coaching individuals in numerous other settings, such as business, medicine, the arts, and the military. Although the growth of coaching psychology is extensive, efforts to conduct research and theory on the topic are lacking, with the exception of four decades of research conducted by sport psychologists on athletic coaching and emerging research in the domain of psychology and business coaching. One thing is clear, more and better research is needed.

After extensively reviewing the coaching effectiveness research in sport, Horn (2002) identified a number of future directions researchers should follow. First, she contends that more effort needs to be placed on developing better measures of coaching behaviors that assess dimensions like nonverbal coach behaviors or the attributions that accompany feedback coaches give to athletes. Second, the importance of examining the antecedents and consequences of coaching behaviors is emphasized. For example, in her own research, Horn and her colleagues (Horn, Lox, & Labrador, 2001) have shown that coaches form expectations of their athletes' capabilities based on personal cues (such as gender and body size) and performance information (such as past accomplishments and skills tests). These expectations in turn influence the coach's behavior (e.g., frequency and quality of coach–athlete interaction, quantity and quality of instruction, types of feedback given), which then influences athletes' performance. Finally, athletes' performance confirms the coach's original expectations. Not only is there a need to further study this coach expectation process in the sport environment, but it would be interesting to see how it works with coaches in other settings, such as business and the arts.

In his review of the coaching behavior research in sport, Cushion (2010) also addresses the need for future research. First, he suggests that instead of focusing simply on assessing the behavior of coaches, researchers should examine how behaviors interact with coaching thoughts. Second, because so much of the existing research has been conducted in North America, studies involving coaching in and/or across cultures would be valuable. Third, researchers need to move beyond studies of head coaches and examine other levels of coaching, such as assistants, or subgroups, such as women or minority coaches. Fourth, because much of the existing coaching behavior research has examined practice environments, there is a need to examine the behaviors and actions of coaches in competitive sport environments. Fifth, because the research shows that few effective coaching behaviors (outside of instruction and reinforcement) are universal, greater efforts must be made to study coaching behaviors in specific contexts. Finally, a need exists to study how instructing individual sport coaches to self-monitor and become aware of their own actions can influence both their coaching and the performance outcomes of those with whom they work.

The review of the literature in this chapter suggests several other potentially fruitful future directions for sport coaching psychology research. First, more research examining gender differences in coaching is needed. In particular, researchers need

to more often employ understudied female coaches as participants. They also need to further explore differences related to how one actually coaches male and female athletes. Interestingly, the coaching psychology research conducted in sport might serve as a good starting point for research on gender differences in coaching in other arenas. The same can be said for research on how coaching can enhance life skills, as this certainly parallels interest in coaching for personal development in nonsport settings.

The theoretically driven work of Mageau and Vallerand (2003) on how coach–athlete relationships influence athlete motivation also points to a number of future research directions. First, a need exists to test the entirety of the model that these researchers have proposed. Only then can possible reciprocal influences be examined. Second, future investigators must identify the obstacles to adopting the suggested autonomy-supportive coaching style predicted to positively enhance self-determined forms of motivation. For example, do coaches believe that controlling behaviors lead to better performance, or are they unaware of their controlling behaviors? Finally, do those athletes who are most vulnerable to controlling behaviors and in most need of them (e.g., athletes with very low intrinsic motivation) frustrate coaches to the degree that the coaches are less likely to use autonomy-supporting behaviors?

Although these suggestions for future research were proposed by investigators focused on coaching in the athletic domain, they could all be easily examined in other coaching domains, such as business, the performing arts, or education. In addition, in both the sport and general coaching psychology literatures, more intervention studies are needed to better establish causal relationships. Longitudinal studies are also needed, allowing investigators to track changes both in coach and client behaviors across phases of the coaching process. Feldman and Lankau (2005) have also outlined a number of important future directions for researchers studying general coaching psychology to consider. These include

• Examining differences between coaching and other helping relationships—career counseling, clinical therapy, business advisement, and mentoring—to determine whether differences are evident between coaches employed by individuals versus organizations
• Identifying the backgrounds and specific skills of coaches and determining if these differences influence their effectiveness

- Learning more about the clients being coached and their specific needs, as well as what client characteristics and dispositions make clients more or less receptive to coaching
- Bettering our understanding of coaching outcomes by looking at both short- and long-term outcomes related to learning, behavior changes, and organizational markers
- Delineating phases of coaching and the best ways to work within those phases
- Better understanding how approaches to coaching (e.g., behaviorist, psychodynamic, systems approach) influence both positive and dysfunctional coaching effectiveness.

Currently, a variety of methods are used to study coaching psychology, and we feel this is a good development as both quantitative and qualitative research can play important roles in advancing knowledge in the area. However, we also feel that regardless of the method used, investigators need to employ more rigorous designs, consider conducting series of interrelated studies, and consider using multiple methods in the same study.

Finally, coaching psychology researchers need to apply or develop more theoretical explanations for why coaching is effective and what factors influence the coaching process. If the psychology of coaching is to advance, it is not only important that the efficacy of coaching be demonstrated, but, given the fact that human behavior results from a reciprocal interaction of personal and environmental factors, knowing why strategies operate will help practitioners more effectively coach in specific contexts.

Acknowledgments

The authors would like to thank Larry Lauer and Shane Murphy for their helpful comments on this manuscript.

Note

1. Percentages in all categories do not add up to 100% because respondents could select more than one response category.

References

Abraham, A., Collins, D., & Martindale, R. (2006). The coaching schematic: Validation through expert coach consensus. *Journal of Sport Sciences, 24*(6), 549–564.

Acosta, R. V., & Carpenter, L. (2012). Women in intercollegiate sport: A longitudinal, national study. Thirdy five year update, 1977–2012. Unpublished manuscript. Available for downloading at www.acostacarpenter.org

Amorose, A. J., & Anderson-Butcher, D. (2007). Autonomy-supportive coaching and self-determined motivation in high school and college athletes: A test of self-determination theory. *Psychology of Sport and Exercise, 8,* 654–670.

Bandura, A. (1977). Self-efficacy: Toward a unifying theory of behavior change. *Psychological Review, 84,* 191–215.

Bandura, A. (1997). *Self-efficacy: The exercise of control.* New York, NY: Freeman.

Barling, J., Slater, F., & Kelloway, E. K. (1999). Transformational leadership and emotional intelligence: An exploratory study. *Leadership and Organization Development Journal, 21,* 157–161.

Becker, A.J. (2009). It's not what they do, it's how they do it: Athlete experiences of great coaching. *International Journal of Sports Science and Coaching, 4*(1), 93–119.

Berger, J. G., & Atkins, P. W.B. (2009). Mapping the complexity of mind: Using the subject-object interview in coaching. *Coaching: An International Journal of Theory, Research and Practice, 2,* 23–36.

Bono, J. E., Purvanova, R. K., Towler, A. J., & Peterson, D. B. (2009). A survey of executive coaching practices. *Personnel Psychology, 62,* 361–404.

Boon, A., & Gilbert, W. (2010). Using the United Nation's Millennium development goals to teach citizenship in youth soccer. *Journal of Coaching Education, 3*(3), 37–55.

Bull, S. J. (2006). *The game plan: Your guide to mental toughness at work.* Chichester, UK: Capstone.

Burton, D., & Raedeke, T. D. (2008). Sport psychology for coaches. *International Journal of Sports Science and Coaching, 3*(2), 291–292.

Camire, M., Forneris, T., Trudel, P., & Bernard, D. (2011). Strategies for helping coaches facilitate positive youth development through sport. *Journal of Sport Psychology in Action, 2*(2), 92–99.

Campbell, T., & Sullivan, P. J. (2005). The effect of a standardized coaching program on the efficacy of novice coaches. *Avante, 11,* 56–68.

Chelladurai, P. (1978). *A contingency model of leadership in athletics.* Unpublished doctoral dissertation, University of Waterloo, Canada.

Chelladurai, P. (2007). Leadership in sports. In G. Tenenbaum & R. C. Eklund (Eds.), *Handbook of sport psychology* (3rd ed., pp. 113–135.). Hoboken, NJ: Wiley.

Coaching. (n.d.). In *Wikipedia.* Retrieved May 25, 2011, from http://en.wikipedia.org/wiki/Coaching.

Coakley, J. (2011). Youth sports: What counts as social development? *Journal of Sport and Social Issues, 35*(3), 1–19.

Collins, K., Gould, D., Lauer, L., & Chung, Y. (2009). Coaching life skills through football: Philosophical beliefs of outstanding high school football coaches. *International Journal of Coaching Science, 3*(1), 1–26.

Conroy, D. E., & Coatsworth, J. D. (2006). Coaching training as a strategy for promoting youth social development. *The Sport Psychologist, 20,* 128–144.

Côté, J. & Gilbert, W. (2009). An integrative definition of coaching effectiveness and expertise. *International Journal of Sports Science and Coaching, 4,* 307–323.

Côté, J., Salmela, J.H., & Russell, S. (1995). The knowledge of high-performance gymnastic coaches: Methodological framework. *The Sport Psychologist, 9*(1), 76–95.

Cumming, S. P., Smoll, F. L., Smith, R. E., & Grossbard, J. R. (2007). Is winning everything? The relative contributions of motivational climate and won-lost percentage in youth sports. *Journal of Applied Sport Psychology, 19,* 322–226.

Cushion, C. (2010). Coach behaviour. In J. Lyle & Chris Cushion (Eds.). *Sports coaching: Professionalisation and practice* (pp. 43–61). Edinburgh, UK: Churchill Livingstone Elsevier.

DeBoer, K. J. (2004). *Gender and Competition: How men and women approach work and play differently.* Monterey, CA: Coaches Choice.

Deci, E. L., & Ryan, R. M. (1985). *Intrinsic motivation and self-determination in human behavior.* New York, NY: Plenum Press.

Deci, E. L., & Ryan, R. M. (2000). The 'what' and 'why' of goal pursuits: Human needs and self-determination of behavior. *Psychological Inquiry, 11,* 227–268.

Erickson, K., Côté, J., & Fraser-Thomas, J. (2007). Sport experiences, milestones, and educational activities associated with performance coaches' development. *The Sport Psychologist, 21,* 302–316.

Fasting, K., & Pfister, G. (2000). Female and male coaches in the eyes of female elite soccer players. *European Physical Education Review, 6,* 91–110.

Feldman, D. C., & Lankau, M. J. (2005). Executive coaching: A review and agenda for future research. *Journal of Management, 31,* 829–848.

Feltz, D. L., Chase, M.A., Motitz, S. A., & Sullivan, P.J. (1999). A conceptual model of coaching efficacy: Preliminary investigation and instrument development. *Journal of Educational Psychology, 91,* 765–776.

Feltz, D.L., Short, S. E., & Sullivan, P. J. (2008). Self-efficacy in sport. Champaign, IL: Human Kinetics.

Flett, M. R., Gould, D. R., Paule, A. L., & Schneider, R. P. (2010). How and why university coaches define, identify, and recruit 'intangibles'. *International Journal of Coaching Science, 4*(2), 15–35.

Fry, M. D., & Gano-Overway, L. A. (2010). Exploring the contributions of the caring climate to the youth sport experience. *Journal of Applied Sport Psychology, 22*(3), 294–304.

Gallimore, R., & Tharp, R. (2004). What a coach can teach a teacher, 1975–2004: Reflection and reanalysis of John Wooden's teaching practices. *The Sport Psychologist, 18,* 119–137.

Gano-Overway, L. A., Newton, M., Magyar, T. M., Fry, M. D., Kim. M., & Guivernau, M. R. (2009). Influence of caring youth sport contexts on efficacy-related beliefs and social behaviors. *Developmental Psychology, 45,* 329–340.

Gant, A. M., Curtayne, L., & Burton, G. (2009). Executive coaching enhances goal attainment, resilience, and workplace well-being: A randomized control study. *The Journal of Positive Psychology, 4*(5), 396–407.

Gant, A. M., Passmore, J., Cavanagh, M. J., & Parker, H. (2010). The state of play in coaching today: A comprehensive review of the field. *International Review of Industrial and Organizational Psychology, 210*(25), 125–167.

Gilbert, W. (2010). Understanding the change process: Valuing what it is that coaches do. *International Journal of Sports Science and Coaching, 5*(2), 173–176.

Gilbert, W., Gallimore, R., & Trudel, P. (2009). A learning community approach to coach development in youth sports. *Journal of Coaching Education, 2*(2), 1–21.

Gilbert, W., & Trudel, P. (2004). Analysis of coaching science research published from 1970–2001. *Research Quarterly for Exercise and Performance, 74*(4), 388–399.

Gordan, S. (2007). Sport and business coaching: Perspectives of a sport psychologist. *Australian Psychologist, 42*(4), 271–282.

Gould, D., & Carson, S. (2008). Personal development through sport. In H. Hebestreit, & O. Barr-Or (Eds.), *The encyclopedia*

of sports medicine – The young athlete (pp. 287–301). Oxford: Blackwell Science.

Gould, D. & Carson, S. (2010). The relationship between perceived coaching behaviors and developmental benefits of high school sports participation. *The Hellenic Journal of Psychology, 7, 298–314.*

Gould, D., & Carson, S. (2011). Young athletes perceptions of the relationship between coaching behaviors and developmental experiences. *International Journal of Coaching Science, 5*(2), 3–29.

Gould, D., Chung, Y., Smith, P., & White, J. (2006). Future directions in coaching life skills: Understanding high school coaches' views and needs, *Athletic Insights: The Online Journal of Sports Psychology, 18*(3). (http://www.athleticinsight.com/Vol8Iss3/CoachingLifeSkills.htm.)

Gould, D., Collins, K., Lauer, L., & Chung, Y. (2006). Coaching life skills: A working model, *Sport and Exercise Psychology Review, 2*(1), 10–18.

Gould, D., Collins, K., Lauer, L., & Chung, Y. (2007). Coaching life skills through football: A study of award winning high school coaches, *Journal of Applied Sport Psychology, 19*(1), 16–37.

Gould, D., Flett, R. M., & Lauer, L. (2012). The relationship between psychosocial developmental and the sports climate experienced by underserved youth. *Psychology of Sport and Exercise, 13*(1), 80–87.

Gould, D., Greenleaf, C., Guinan, D., & Chung, Y. (2002). A survey of U.S. Olympic coaches: Variables perceived to have influenced athlete and performance and coach effectiveness. *The Sport Psychologist, 16,* 229–250.

Gould, D., Medbery, R., Damarjian, N., & Lauer, L. (1999). A survey of mental skills training knowledge, opinions, and practices of junior tennis coaches. *The Sport Psychologist, 11,* 28–50.

Gordon, S. (2007). Sport and business coaching: Perspectives of a sport psychologist. *Australian Psychologist, 42,* 271–282.

Grant, A. M., & Palmer, S. (2002). *Coaching psychology.* Meeting held at the Annual Conference of the Division of Counseling Psychology, British Psychological Society, Torquary, May 18.

Grant, A. M., Passmore, J., Cavanagh, M. J., & Helen, P. (2010). The state of play in coaching today: A comprehensive review of the field. *International Review of Industrial and Organizational Psychology, 25,* 125–167.

Griffith, C. R. (1925). Psychology and its relation to athletic competition. *Physical Education Review, 30,* 193–199.

Griffith, C. R. (1932). *Psychology of coaching.* New York, NY: Charles Scribner's Sons.

Hall, D. T., Otazo, K. L., & Hollenbeck, G. P. (1999). Behind closed doors: What really happens in executive coaching. *Organizational Dynamics, 27,* 39–53.

Halliburton, A. L., & Weiss, M. R. (2002). Sources of competence information and perceived motivational climate among adolescent female gymnasts varying in skill level. *Journal of Sport and Exercise Psychology, 24,* 396–419.

Hernez-Broome, G. (2004). *Impact of coaching following a leadership development program: Coaching is the key to continued development.* Paper presented at the Second ICF Coaching Research Symposium, Quebec, Canada.

Holt, N. L., Tink, L. N., Mandigo, J. L., & Fox, K. R. (2008). Do youth learn life skills through their involvement in high school sport? A case study. *Canadian Journal of Education, 31,* 281–304.

Horn, T. (2002). *Advances in sport psychology* (2nd ed.). Champaign, IL: Human Kinetics.

Horn, T. (2007). *Three decades of research on coaching effectiveness: What do we know and where do we should we go?* Presentation made at the Association of Applied Sport Psychology Conference, Louisville, KY.

Horn, T. S., Lox, C., & Labrador, F. (2001). The self-fulfilling prophecy: When coaches' expectations become a reality. In J. M. Williams (Ed.), *Applied sport psychology: Personal growth to peak performance* (4th ed., pp. 63–81). Mountain View, CA: Mayfield.

Jenkins, S. (2010). Coaching philosophy. In J. Lyle & Chris Cushion (Eds.). *Sports coaching: Professionalisation and practice* (pp. 233–242). Edinburgh, UK: Churchill Livingstone Elsevier.

Jones, G. (2002). Performance excellence: A personal perspective on the link between sport and business, *Journal of Applied Sport Psychology, 14*, 268–281.

Jones, G., & Morehouse, A. (2007). *Developing mental toughness: Gold medal strategies for transforming your business performance.* Oxford, UK: Spring Hill.

Jones, M. I., & Lavallee, D. (2009). Exploring the life skills needs of British adolescent athletes. *Psychology of Sport and Exercise, 10,* 159–167.

Karas, D., & Spada, M. M. B. (2009). Brief cognitive-behavioral coaching for procrastination: A case series. *Coaching: An International Journal of Theory, Research and Practice, 2,* 44–53.

Kent, A., & Sullivan, P. J. (2003). Coaching efficacy as a predictor of university coaches' commitment. *International Sports Journal, 17,* 246–258.

Kilty, K. (2006). Women in coaching. *The Sport Psychologist, 20,* 222–234.

Lacroix, C., Camire, M., & Trudel, P. (2008). High school coaches' characteristics and their perspectives on the purpose of school sports participation. *International Journal of Coaching Science, 2*(2), 23–42.

Lee, K. S., Malete, L., & Feltz, D. L. (2002). The strength of coaching efficacy between certified and noncertified Singapore coaches. *International Journal of Applied Sport Science, 14,* 55–67.

Linley, P. A., & Harrington, S. (2005). Positive psychology and coaching psychology: Perspectives on integration. *The Coaching Psychologist, 1,* 13–14.

Loehr, J., & Schwartz, T. (2001). The making of a corporate athlete. *Harvard Business Review, 79,* 120–128.

Lyle, J. (1999). Coaching philosophy and coaching behavior. In N. Cross, & J. Lyle (Eds.). *The coaching process: Principles and practice of sport* (pp. 15–46). Oxford, UK: Butterworth-Heinemann.

Lyle, J. (2010). Coaches' decision making: A naturalistic decision making analysis. In J. Lyle & C. Cushion (Eds.), *Sports coaching: Professionalisation and practice* (pp. 27–42). Edinburgh, UK: Churchill Livingstone Elsevier.

MacKie, D. (2007). Evaluating the effectiveness of executive coaching: Where are we now and where do we need to be? *Australian Psychologist, 42,* 310–318.

Mageau, G. A., & Vallerand, R. J. (2003). The coach-athlete relationship: A motivational model. *Journal of Sport Sciences, 21,* 883–904.

Marshall, D. (2001). Developing the next generation of women coaches. *Canadian Journal for Women in Coaching Online, 1*(4), 1–8.

Martens, R. (2004). *Successful coaching.* Champaign, IL: Human Kinetics.

Martin, S. B., Jackson, A. W., Richardson, P. A., & Weiller, K. H. (1999). Coaching preferences of adolescent youths and their parents. *Journal of Applied Sport Psychology, 11*(2), 247–262.

McCallister, S. G., Blinde, E. M., & Weiss, W. M. (2000). Teaching values and implementing philosophies: Dilemmas of the youth sport coach. *The Physical Educator, 57,* 34–45.

McCullick, B., Cummings, R. L., & Schempp, P. (1999). The professional orientations of expert golf instructors. *International Journal of Physical Education, 36,* 15–24.

McCullick, B., Schempp, P., Hsu, S. H., Jung, J. H., Vickers, B., & Schuknecht, G. (2006). An analysis of working memories of expert sport instructors. *Journal of Teaching in Physical Education, 25*(2), 149–165.

Murphy, S. (1996). *The achievement zone.* New York, NY: Putnam.

Myers, N. D., Vargas-Tonsing, T. M., & Feltz, D. L. (2005). Coaching efficacy in intercollegiate coaches: Sources, coaching behavior, and team variables. *Psychology of Sport and Exercise, 8,* 182–195.

Nash, C. S., Sproule, J., & Horton, P. (2008). Sport coaches' perceived role frames and philosophies. *International Journal of Sport Science and Coaching, 3*(4), 539–554.

Northhouse, P. G. (2010). *Leadership: Theory and practice* (5th ed.). Thousand Oaks, CA: Sage.

Palmer, S. (2005). The proposal to establish a special group in coaching psychology. *The Coaching Psychologist, 1,* 5–12.

Palmer, S., & Whybrow, A. (2005). The proposal to establish a special group in coaching psychology. *The Coaching Psychologist, 1,* 3–11.

Passmore, J., & Brown, A. (2009). Coaching non-adult students for enhanced examination performance: A longitudinal study. *Coaching: An International Journal of Theory, Research and Practice, 2,* 54–64.

Pritchard, J. (2009). Tools for supporting intuition. *Coaching: An International Journal of Theory, Research and Practice, 2,* 37–43.

Reade, I., Rodgers, W., & Norman, L. (2009). The under-representation of women in coaching: A comparison of male and female Canadian coaches at low and high levels of coaching. *International Journal of Sport Sciences and Coaching, 4,* 505–520.

Salmela, J. H. (1995). Learning from the development of expert coaches. *Coaching and Sport Science Journal, 2*(2), 3–13.

Salmela, J. H., Draper, S. P., & Desjardins, G. (1994). Transitioning phases of expert ice and field hockey coaches' careers. *Access to active living* (pp. 570–575). Victoria, CA: University of Victoria.

Scanlan, T. K., & Lewthwaite, R. (1986). Social psychological aspects of competition for male youth sport participants: Predictors of enjoyment. *Journal of Sport Psychology, 8,* 25–35.

Schempp, P. G., & McCullick, B. (2010). Coaches expertise. In J. Lyle & C. Cushion (Eds.), *Sports coaching: Professionalisation and practice* (pp. 221–232). Edinburgh, UK: Churchill Livingstone Elsevier.

Schempp, P. G., McCullick, B. A., & Busch, C. A., Webster, C., & Shannen, I. S. (2006). The self-monitoring of expert sport instructors. *International Journal of Sports Science and Coaching, 1*(1), 25–35.

Schempp, P. G., McCullick, B., Busch, C. A., Webster, C., & Mason, I. S. (2010). The self-monitoring of expert sport instructors. *International Journal of Sports Science and Coaching, 1*(1), 25–35.

Smith, R. E., & Smoll, F. L. (1989). Leadership behaviors in sport: A theoretical model and research paradigm. *Journal of Applied Social Psychology, 19*(18), 1522–1551.

Smith, R. E., Smoll, F. L., & Barnett, N. P. (1995). Reduction of children's sport performance anxiety through social support and stress-reduction training for coaches. *Journal of Applied Developmental Psychology, 16*, 125–142.

Smith, R. E., Smoll, F. L., & Cummings, S. P. (2007). Effects of a motivational climate intervention for coaches on young athletes' sport performance anxiety. *Journal of Sport and Exercise Psychology, 29*, 39–59.

Smith, R. E., Smoll, F. L., & Curtis, B. (1979). Coach effectiveness training: A cognitive-behavioral approach to enhancing relationship skills in youth sport coaches. *Journal of Sport Psychology, 1*, 59–75.

Smoll, F. L., & Smith, R. E. (2002). Coaching behavior research and intervention in youth sports. In F. L. Smoll & R. E. Smith (Eds.), *Children and youth in sport: A biopsychosocial perspective* (2nd ed., pp. 211–233). Dubuque, IA: Kendall/Hunt.

Smoll, F. L., Smith, R. E., Barnett, N. P., & Everett, J. J. (1993). Enhancement of children's self-esteem through social support training for youth sport coaches. *Journal of Applied Psychology, 78*, 602–610.

Smith, R. E., Smoll, F. L., & Cummings, S. P. (2007). Effects of a motivational climate intervention for coaches on young athletes' sport performance anxiety. *Journal of Sport and Exercise Psychology, 29*(1), 39–59.

Spence, G. B., & Gant, A. (2005). Individual and group life coaching: Initial findings from a randomized controlled trial. In M. Cavanagh, A. M. Gant, & T. Kemp (Eds.), *Coaching: Vol. 1 Theory, research and practice from the behavioural sciences* (pp. 27–42). Brisbane, AU: Australian Academic Press.

Stern, L. R. (2004). Executive coaching: A working definition. *Consulting Psychology Journal: Practice and Research, 56*, 154–162.

Tharp, R. G., & Gallimore, R. (1976). What a coach can teach a teacher. *Psychology Today, 9*, 74–78.

Theeboom, M., De Knoop, P., & Weiss, M. R. (1995). Motivational climate, psychosocial responses, and motor skill development in children's sport: A field-based intervention study. *Journal of Sport and Exercise Psychology, 17*, 294–311.

Trudel, P., & Gilbert, W. D. (2006). Coaching and coaching education. In D. Kirk, M. O'Sullivan, & D. McDonald (Eds.), *Handbook of physical education* (pp. 516–539). London, UK: Sage.

Trudel, P., Gilbert, W., & Werthner, P. (2010). Coaching education effectiveness. In J. Lyle & C. Cushion (Eds.), *Sports coaching: Professionalisation and practice* (pp. 135–152). Edinburgh, UK: Churchill Livingstone Elsevier.

Tuffey, S. (1995). *Coach perceptions of psychological characteristics and behaviors of male and female athletes and their impact on coach behaviors.* Unpublished doctoral dissertation, University of North Carolina, Greensboro.

Vella, S. A., Oades, L. G., & Crowe, T. P. (2010). The application of coach leadership models to coaching practice: Current state and future directions. *International Journal of Sports Science and Coaching, 5*(3), 425–434.

Weinberg R. S., & Gould, D. (2011). Foundations of sport and exercise psychology (5th ed.). Champaign, IL: Human Kinetics.

Wiese-Bjornstal, D. M. (2007). Psychological dimensions of girls' physical activity participation. In M. J. Kane & N. M. LaVoi (Eds.), *The 2007 Tucker Center research report—Developing physically active girls: An evidence based multidisciplinary approach* (pp. 7–28). Minneapolis, MN: The Tucker Center for Research on Girls & Women in Sport, University of Minnesota.

Weiss, M. R., Ebbeck, V., & Horn, T. S. (1997). Children's self-perceptions and sources of physical competence information: A cluster analysis. *Journal of Sport and Exercise Psychology, 19*(1), 52–70.

Whitmore, J. (2009). *Coaching for performance* (4th ed.). Boston, MA: Nicholas Brealey Publishing.

Moral Behavior in Sport

Maria Kavussanu

Abstract

The last decade has seen an important shift of focus in research on sport morality. Researchers have moved from a focus on moral judgment as a moral outcome to the examination of morally relevant behavior. This chapter reflects this shift and reviews research on sport behaviors that could be classified within the moral domain. Different labels have been used to refer to such acts, including prosocial, antisocial, aggressive, and bad/poor behavior. The chapter begins with a discussion of the moral domain and an overview of the main approaches used to measure moral behavior in sport and continues with an extensive review of dispositional and social-environmental factors associated with moral behavior in sport. Next, the effects of demographic and context characteristics on moral action are discussed, followed by a brief review of interventions conducted in physical activity settings. Finally, implications for morality in other performance domains are outlined and directions for future research are provided.

Key Words: Morality, aggression, prosocial behavior, antisocial behavior

In 2008, in a softball game at Central Washington University, an incident occurred that captured national attention in the United States: A player tore her knee ligament while trying to reach first base; as she was unable to move and her teammates were not allowed to touch her, she could not achieve her goal of hitting her first-ever home run. Instead of taking advantage of this injury, two opposition players carried her to touch the second and third bases, and then home plate, thereby helping her achieve her goal. This incident was described by the media as an unbelievable act of sportspersonship and is a shining example of a social act that had positive consequences for its recipient. Unbelievable acts with negative consequences for others also occur in sport. Some notable examples are the rugby player Tom Williams faking an injury to his mouth by biting on a fake blood capsule in a U.K. Premiership rugby-union game and the boxer Mike

Tyson biting off part of Evander Holyfield's ear in response to repeated head butting in a heavyweight world title fight. Although these are extreme acts, other behaviors that could have positive or negative consequences for others' welfare are more common in sport (see Kavussanu, 2006; Kavussanu, Seal, & Phillips, 2006). This chapter focuses on research dealing with such behaviors.

Behaviors that have consequences for others' rights and welfare are the subject of the moral domain. For example, Turiel (1983) found that children and adolescents perceive an act as moral transgression when the behavior has negative consequences for the victim. Moral stimuli used in the research of Turiel and his colleagues (see Turiel, 1983) concern welfare and physical harm (e.g., pushing, shoving, and hitting), psychological harm (e.g., teasing, hurting feelings, ridiculing or name calling), fairness and rights (e.g., breaking a promise or destroying others' property), and positive behaviors (e.g., helping another in need, and sharing).

Others view morality in a broader manner. For example, for Walker (2004), morality refers to voluntary actions that have, at least potentially, social and interpersonal implications and are governed by internal cognitive and emotive mechanisms. Violation of established conventions, which for Turiel (1983) are not part of the moral domain, can also provide moral offense. Also, illegal substance use and abuse, which may be viewed as a personal matter, could have health and behavioral consequences for others in addition to the user.

In both views of morality, the interpersonal consequences of behavior are highlighted as a defining feature of behaviors that are morally relevant . Walker's (2004) definition also highlights the *potential* consequences of actions that are morally relevant. Finally, for Walker (2004) moral functioning is multifaceted, involving the dynamic interplay of thought, emotion, and behavior. Others (e.g., Rest, 1984) have also described multiple components of morality, including moral judgment, moral intention, and implementation of behavior.

In the context of sport, cognitive and behavioral aspects of morality have received much research attention in the past 30 years. Some examples are: moral reasoning (Bredemeier & Shields, 1986); judgments about the legitimacy of injurious acts (Duda, Olson, & Templin, 1991); sportspersonship orientations (Vallerand, Briere, Blanchard, & Provencher, 1997); moral attitudes (Lee, Whitehead, & Ntoumanis, 2007); aggression (Stephens & Bredemeier, 1996); moral judgment, intention, and behavior—collectively referred to as moral functioning—(Kavussanu & Roberts, 2001); and prosocial and antisocial behaviors (Kavussanu, 2006). Although the significance of moral cognition (and emotion) for morality is unquestionable, this chapter focuses on moral *behavior*. In part, this is due to the volume of sport morality research that has been accumulated in the last 10 years. The reader is referred to other reviews of the literature for a comprehensive account of other aspects of morality (e.g., Kavussanu, 2007; Shields & Bredemeier, 2007).

Much of the research conducted in sport has investigated negative social behaviors (see Kavussanu, 2007, 2008), such as trying to injure an opponent, verbally abusing another player, and cheating. The term *antisocial behavior* has been used to refer to such acts. Specifically, antisocial behavior has been defined as voluntary behavior intended to harm or disadvantage another (Kavussanu, 2006;

Sage, Kavussanu, & Duda, 2006). More recently, prosocial behavior has received increased attention by sport researchers (see Kavussanu, 2008). *Prosocial behavior* is voluntary behavior intended to help or benefit another individual or group of individuals (Eisenberg & Fabes, 1998), and examples in sport are lending equipment to an opponent, helping another player off the floor, and encouraging, supporting, or congratulating a teammate. In most sport studies, prosocial and antisocial behaviors have been either inversely associated—with small to medium correlation coefficients—(e.g., Kavussanu, 2006; Boardley & Kavussanu, 2009; Sage & Kavussanu, 2008) or unrelated to each other (e.g., Sage et al., 2006). Consideration of both types of behavior provides a more complete account of the moral conduct that takes place in sport. As Bandura (1999) has put it "people do good things as well as refrain from doing bad things" (p. 194).

Prosocial and antisocial behaviors typically have positive and negative consequences, respectively, for others. Thus, helping an injured player should alleviate his or her distress, and kicking a player should cause him or her to experience pain. However, as Kavussanu and Boardley (2012) point out, if the player does not feel any pain (e.g., because he or she is distracted or has taken analgesic medication), the behaviors will not have the expected consequences. Similarly, encouraging a teammate may not benefit the athlete who does not appreciate such encouragement, verbally abusing a player may not cause psychological harm to the individual who ignores the abuse, and cheating may not have a negative consequence for others if the offender is caught and the situation is rectified. Thus, prosocial and antisocial behaviors have the *potential* to affect others.

The most widely investigated class of antisocial behavior is *aggression*, defined as overt behavior (verbal or physical) that is purposeful (i.e., nonaccidental), chosen with the intent of causing injury, and has the capacity to cause psychological or physical injury to another (Husman & Silva, 1984). The distinction has also been made between *instrumental aggression*, which is behavior directed at the target as a means to an end (e.g., injuring a player to get a competitive advantage), and *hostile aggression*, which is behavior toward another who has angered or provoked the individual and is an end in itself (Husman & Silva, 1984). Aggression has long been investigated as a moral issue and discussed in reviews of moral development and behavior (e.g., Shields & Bredemeier, 1995; Tangney, Stuewig, & Mashek, 2007).

In the psychological literature, the term *moral behavior* has been used to refer to aggression (e.g., Tangney et al., 2007) and prosocial and antisocial behavior (Sage & Kavussanu, 2007a). These behaviors are morally relevant because they can affect others. In this chapter, the term *moral behavior* is used to refer to a broad range of *intentional* acts that could result in positive or negative consequences for others' psychological and physical welfare. The chapter begins by discussing how moral behavior has been typically measured in sport, particularly in the last 10 years, and continues with empirical research examining individual differences and social environmental factors associated with such behavior. Next, demographic and context characteristics are discussed, followed by a review of intervention studies. The chapter ends with potential implications of sport morality research for other performance domains, conclusions, and directions for future research.

The Measurement of Moral Behavior in Sport

In this section, the methods most commonly utilized to measure moral behavior in sport are briefly described. The reader is referred to Kavussanu and Boardley (2012) for a more complete review of these methods. The main methods used to measure moral behavior in sport are self-reports, coach ratings, and behavioral observation and coding. Within each of these categories, only those instruments utilized in most studies reviewed in this chapter are discussed.

Self-Reports

Many researchers, following the lead of Ebbeck and her colleagues (Gibbons, Ebbeck, & Weiss, 1995; Stuart & Ebbeck, 1995), have assessed behavior as one of the four components of morality described by Rest (1984). The other components, which have been typically measured along with behavior, are judgment and intention. However, in line with the focus of this chapter, only the behavior measure is discussed here. Behavior is measured by asking participants to indicate—on a scale ranging from "never" to "very often"—the frequency with which they engaged in the behaviors described in some hypothetical scenarios during a specified period of time. An example of a scenario devised by Kavussanu and Roberts (2001) is:

> Imagine yourself during the last minute of a critical basketball game. A player from the opposite team is going for a fast break, and you are the sole defender.

Because of your position, the only way to stop the player from making the basket may result in an injury. You have to decide whether to risk injuring the player to prevent the basket.
(*Kavussanu & Roberts*, 2001, p. 42)

Three or more scenarios pertaining to different moral issues—for example, pushing an opposing player when the referee is not looking, faking an injury, and risking injury to an opposing player—are utilized. Participants' responses across scenarios are averaged to form a single score for behavior. However, some studies have shown that responses vary depending on the scenario used (e.g., Kavussanu & Spray, 2006). This method is good when one wishes to assess moral judgment and intention because the conditions surrounding the moral issue are clearly delineated. However, it is less than ideal for the assessment of moral behavior. In part, this is because the behaviors described in the scenarios are highly specific. Thus, it is possible that athletes may have not engaged in the specific behaviors described in the scenarios but may have engaged in other harmful behaviors not captured by the measure.

The scenario approach has also been used to measure aggression. Most studies have used a scenario that is part of the Judgments About Moral Behavior in Youth Sport Questionnaire developed by Stephens and colleagues (Stephens & Bredemeier, 1996; Stephens, Bredemeier, & Shields, 1997) to measure players' judgments about what might be done in a game situation that requires a moral decision. Stephens and Bredemeier (1996) operationalized moral behavior as the self-described likelihood to intentionally aggress against an opponent. The aggression scenario is:

> Sue has been caught out of position on defense, and now the opposing team's best player, Wendy, is dribbling toward a one-on-one situation with the goalkeeper. While Sue has no hope of stripping Wendy of the ball, she could tackle from behind, tripping Wendy and preventing the shot. Sue knows that tackling from behind is dangerous, and Wendy will probably get hurt. Sue has to decide whether to tackle from behind.

Participants are asked to imagine being in Wendy's position and identify, out of six situations, the one that represents the most tempting motive to trip Wendy from behind. Then, they are asked to imagine being in the situation they identified as most tempting and indicate—on a scale ranging from "not at all likely" to "very likely"—how likely they would be to trip Wendy (or another protagonist) from behind. Responses to this item measure self-reported *likelihood* to aggress. This variable is a proxy for aggressive behavior because it does not refer to behavior that has occurred, but rather to the likelihood that such behavior will occur in a hypothetical situation. Although the original instrument developed by Stephens et al. (1997) included scenarios referring to lying and cheating, it is the aggression scenario that has been most commonly utilized in sport research. One limitation of this measure is that because it is a single-item measure, its reliability cannot be determined.

Another self-report method used to measure moral behavior in sport asks athletes to think about soccer matches they have played during a competitive season and to indicate—on a scale ranging from "never" to "very often"—the frequency with which they engaged in certain behaviors. Participants are presented with a list of items referring to prosocial (e.g., helping an opponent off the floor, helping an injured opponent) and antisocial (e.g., faking an injury, physically intimidating another player) behaviors (e.g., Kavussanu, 2006; Sage & Kavussanu, 2007a, 2008). Responses are averaged to provide one score for prosocial and one for antisocial behavior. However, in these studies, the prosocial behavior scale had relatively low internal reliability (α range = .64 to .74). Moreover, the instrument was devised to be used with soccer players, thus some items (e.g., diving to fool the referee) are applicable only to soccer.

A more comprehensive attempt to develop a measure of prosocial and antisocial behavior, coupled with the explicit distinction between behavior directed toward teammates and opponents, has been made recently. Based on data from basketball, soccer, hockey, netball, and rugby players recruited from 103 teams, Kavussanu and Boardley (2009) developed the Prosocial and Antisocial Behavior in Sport Scale, which consists of four subscales. Two of them measure prosocial behavior toward teammates (e.g., encouraged a teammate) and opponents (e.g., helped an opponent off the floor), and two measure antisocial behavior toward teammates (e.g., verbally abused a teammate) and opponents (e.g., intentionally distracted an opponent). Behaviors directed toward teammates and opponents are different, which is a reflection of the reality of team sport. For example, it makes sense that a player would intentionally distract his opponent to put him at a disadvantage but not a teammate, as this would conflict with his own goals. This instrument has good to very good reliability (α range = .74 to .86) and is valid for use in a range of team sports. However, its correspondence with behaviors actually occurring in a game is yet to be determined.

Finally, some researchers have adapted instruments created for use in other contexts to the context of sport (e.g., d'Arripe-Longueville, Corrion, Scoffier, Roussel, & Chalabaev, 2010; Rutten et al., 2008). For example, Rutten and colleagues (2008) adapted two questionnaires measuring prosocial and antisocial behavior in nonsport contexts and named their scale the Sports Behavior Inventory. The scale measures antisocial behavior (e.g., "I shout abuse to others during matches") and prosocial behavior (e.g., "When a player bullies my teammate, I say something about it") on the field and includes two other subscales that measure prosocial and antisocial behavior off the field. Respondents indicate the frequency of behavior on a scale ranging from "never" to "always." Rutten and colleagues (2008) reported internal consistency that is very good for antisocial on-field behavior (α = .80) but only marginally acceptable for prosocial on-field behavior (α = .66).

A limitation of self-report measures is that they have not been validated with behavioral observation. Some evidence indicates that self-reported antisocial behavior during the season has been strongly associated with observed behavior during a game at the team level (Kavussanu et al., 2006). However, it is not known whether players' self-reports of their prosocial and antisocial behaviors during a game or a season correspond to their actual behavior during these time frames. This issue could be investigated by obtaining observational and self-report data in a single game to determine the degree of congruency between these two sets of data.

Coach Ratings

Coach ratings are another method used to assess moral behavior. For example, Stuart and Ebbeck (1995) presented coaches with five short "moral dilemmas" describing behaviors such as injuring another player to prevent a basket, pushing an opposing player when the referee is not looking, teasing a teammate, and arguing with an official over a bad call. Coaches were asked to think about practices and games throughout the season and indicate—on a scale ranging from "never" to "always"—how frequently their athletes engaged in the specified behaviors. Coaches' responses to the five dilemmas were averaged to form a single score of behavior. This measure has shown very good internal reliability (α = .82). Coach ratings are a good method of measuring behavior, particularly if ratings from more than one coach are obtained.

Observation

In recent years, behavioral observation and coding has been a fairly popular method to measure moral behavior in sport. Researchers using this method typically videotape games and subsequently code players' behaviors using observational grids that contain operational definitions of the behaviors to be measured. For example, the prosocial behavior of congratulating an opponent has been operationally defined as "Clapping or hand shaking after good performance" (Kavussanu, Stamp, Slade, & Ring, 2009). Then, trained observers code the frequency of behaviors from videotaped games, and the total number of occurrences is used to indicate prosocial behavior, antisocial behavior, or aggression (e.g., Kavussanu et al., 2009; Rascle & Coulomb, 2003; Sage & Kavussanu, 2007b). In studies of instrumental and hostile aggression (e.g., Coulomb-Cabagno & Rascle, 2006; Rascle & Coulomb, 2003), an observational grid has been employed that includes two sets of behavioral categories: one for instrumental behaviors occurring during play (e.g., repelling, retaining, hitting, and cheating; for example, stalling the game) and one for hostile behaviors occurring when the ball is not in play (e.g., insulting, threatening, making obscene gestures or shoving, against opponents, referees, teammates, and others). The rationale for this classification is that if an aggressive behavior does not occur during play, it cannot affect the outcome of the game, thus it cannot be instrumental. Factor analyses have confirmed that these two sets of behaviors represent distinct factors (e.g., Rascle & Coulomb, 2003).

In sum, coach ratings, behavioral observation and coding, and self-report measures have been used to assess moral behavior in sport. Self-report measures include scenarios describing moral issues with accompanying items asking about behavior frequency (or likelihood) and instruments that consist of items referring to a range of behaviors. Although the measures described in this section have been utilized in most studies discussed in this chapter to investigate antecedents of moral behavior in sport, some researchers have used other measures. These measures are briefly described when the findings of the relevant studies are reviewed.

Individual Difference Variables as Antecedents of Moral Behavior

Research in sport morality has proliferated in recent years. Much of this research has centered on dispositional variables as predictors of moral action. In some cases, researchers' primary interest has been in understanding moral behavior, while in others moral behavior has been examined as a potential outcome of motivational constructs. As a result of both sets of efforts, our knowledge of moral action in sport has been considerably enhanced. In this section, empirical research on individual difference variables as antecedents of moral action in sport is reviewed. The constructs that have received research attention—and are discussed below—are achievement and social goals, motivation types, fear of failure, passion, moral identity, moral disengagement, and self-regulatory efficacy.

Achievement Goals

Sport is an achievement context. It is not surprising, therefore, that the link between achievement goals and moral sport behavior has received so much attention. The achievement goal construct is part of achievement goal theory (Nicholls, 1989), which posits that individuals engage in achievement contexts such as sport in order to demonstrate or develop competence. Two major goals operate in such contexts: task and ego orientation. These goals reflect variation in the criteria individuals use to define success and evaluate competence. Task-oriented individuals tend to use self-referenced criteria to judge competence and feel successful when they master a task, whereas ego-oriented people tend to use other-referenced criteria to evaluate competence and feel successful when they do better than others. Due to their focus on normative superiority, ego-oriented individuals may engage in rule violating and cheating behaviors to facilitate this goal (Nicholls, 1989). In contrast, because task-oriented athletes evaluate their competence via self-referenced criteria, cheating and aggressing against another to demonstrate competence in the normative sense is irrelevant. Playing by the rules and experiencing a fair competition should provide a true test of these athletes' competence (Duda et al., 1991).

These proposals have been supported by a number of cross-sectional studies. Specifically, university team sport athletes high in ego orientation were more likely to report low levels of moral functioning as reflected in their judgment, intention, and behavior (Kavussanu & Ntoumanis, 2003). Similarly, adolescent and adult soccer players high in ego orientation reported engaging in antisocial behavior while playing soccer for their team (Kavussanu, 2006; Boardley & Kavussanu, 2010; Sage & Kavussanu, 2007a; Sage et al., 2006); in one study, ego orientation was inversely associated with prosocial behavior (Kavussanu, 2006). In contrast, task orientation has evidenced the reverse pattern of relationships: Highly task-oriented athletes were more likely to engage in prosocial behavior and less likely to engage in antisocial behavior while playing soccer (Kavussanu, 2006; Sage & Kavussanu, 2007a).

To date, only one experiment has manipulated achievement goals to examine their effects on prosocial and antisocial behavior. Specifically, Sage and Kavussanu (2007b) randomly assigned university students to a task, ego, or control group and recorded via a hidden camera (and subsequently coded) their behaviors during two table-soccer games. Examples of coded behaviors are congratulating the opponent and alerting the opponent to missed goal counts for prosocial behavior and breaking the rules and deliberate cheating for antisocial behavior. Participants in the ego-involving group displayed significantly more antisocial behaviors than did those in the task-involving and control groups. Although the three groups did not differ in observed prosocial behavior during game play, the task-involved participants were more likely to allocate bonus goals to their opponent to be added to their final goal total, which led to the award of raffle tickets for use in a £50 cash prize draw.

Overall, the findings of these studies highlight the importance of motivational goal orientation on athletes' moral behavior. Athletes whose primary focus is on demonstrating competence in the normative sense by outperforming others also seem to operate at lower levels of morality. These findings are consistent with Rest's (1984) proposal that motivation is one of the factors that influence one's decision on how to behave, as well as subsequent behavior. The findings also show that the critical goal that may affect antisocial conduct in sport is ego orientation. However, task orientation has a clear link to prosocial behavior. Individuals who tend to focus on self-referenced achievement appear more willing to help others in the athletic context. That task orientation has been primarily associated with prosocial behavior highlights the importance of investigating both prosocial and antisocial behavior in sport. These findings clearly show that the two achievement goals play a role in different aspects of moral behavior.

Social Goals

Although the development or demonstration of competence is a primary motive for engaging in achievement contexts such as sport, sport is also a social context. Thus, individuals may also participate in sport for social reasons. Indeed, Allen (2003) has described three social goals in physical activity contexts: social affiliation, social recognition, and social status. Individuals high in social affiliation seek to develop and maintain mutually satisfying relationships in sport and play sport for the opportunities to socialize with other like-minded people. Those high in social recognition are oriented toward validating themselves through approval or recognition from others, whereas those high in social status seek validation through achieving popularity among peers. To date, only one study has examined Allen's (2003) social goals in relation to moral behavior in sport. Specifically, Sage and Kavussanu (2007a) found that youth soccer players, who pursued social affiliation and social recognition goals, were more likely to behave prosocially toward their teammates and opponents. In contrast, players who were oriented toward achieving social status were less likely to engage in prosocial and more likely to engage in antisocial acts; the effects of social goals on behavior were modest in magnitude. Thus, playing sport for social reasons may have implications for the type of behavior in which athletes engage in that context.

Motivation Types

Self-determination theory has distinguished between intrinsic and extrinsic motivation (Deci & Ryan, 1985). *Intrinsic motivation* refers to doing an activity for its own sake in the absence of extrinsic rewards or incentives, whereas *extrinsic motivation* involves doing an activity for extrinsic reasons. However, different types of extrinsic motivation have also been described, depending on the degree to which behavior is self-determined (or autonomous). Motivation types reflect different reasons for participating in sport, and these reasons have implications for behavior. Athletes who participate in sport for the pure enjoyment they derive from the activity are more likely to be concerned with fair play, whereas those who take part in order to receive external recognition, awards, or prestige are more likely to bend the rules and engage in behaviors that may facilitate extrinsic gains (Donahue et al., 2006).

Donahue and colleagues (2006) examined the link between motivation types and use of performance-enhancing substances in 1,290 national-level adolescent athletes from a variety of individual and team sports. Athletes who participated in their sport for intrinsic reasons (e.g., "I play sport for the satisfaction I experience while I am improving my abilities"), were more likely to report higher sportspersonship, as reflected in respect and concern for the rules and officials and respect for social conventions. The opposite relationship was observed between extrinsic motivation (e.g., "I play sport for the prestige of being an athlete") and these two sportspersonship orientations. Importantly, sportspersonship orientations were inversely associated with athletes' reported use of performance-enhancing substances to specifically improve their performance in the previous 12 months. This finding makes sense as using such drugs is against the rules, which is incompatible with the respect for rules dimension of sportspersonship.

An interesting integration of constructs from achievement goal and self-determination theories has been carried out by Vansteenkiste and his colleagues (Vansteenkiste, Mouratidis, & Lens, 2010). These researchers examined whether pursuing performance approach goals—conceptualized as the *aim* to do better than others (Elliot & McGregor, 2001)—for autonomous or controlling reasons has implications for moral functioning in sport. Participants were asked to indicate whether their aim was to do better than their opponent, and to what extent they pursued this goal for autonomous (e.g., "Because this goal is a challenge to me, because I personally value this goal"), or controlling reasons (e.g., "Because I can only be proud of myself if I do so, because I would feel ashamed if I wouldn't pursue this goal"). They also responded to measures of immoral functioning, such as antisocial behavior, sportspersonship attitude, and aggressiveness. Finally, *objectifying attitude* was measured; this is players' tendency to downgrade their opponents and to perceive them as barriers that need to be overcome at all costs to achieve their aim. Controlling reasons positively predicted objectifying attitude, which in turn was positively associated with immoral functioning. Interestingly, although autonomous reasons and performance approach goals did not predict objectifying attitude or immoral functioning, they were strongly associated with each other.

These findings suggest that trying to win per se is not as important as the reasons why one pursues this goal. Aiming to win for controlling—but not autonomous—reasons is more likely to lead to antisocial conduct when playing sport. It is also worth noting that the null finding for performance approach goals and immoral functioning is not in line with the consistent links between ego orientation—a construct similar to the performance approach goal—and antisocial behavior identified in previous research (e.g., Kavussanu, 2006; Boardley & Kavussanu, 2010; Sage et al., 2006); this suggests that the performance approach goal construct (Elliot & McGregor, 2001) is distinct from the ego goal (Nicholls, 1989). Aiming to outperform one's opponent may not be equivalent to the tendency to evaluate competence using normative criteria and to experience feelings of success when one demonstrates normative competence. In sum, it may not be the aim to win but defining success as the demonstration of superiority over others that leads to unfairness and lack of concern for others.

Fear of Failure

Another construct that is relevant to moral behavior in sport is fear of failure, or the motive to avoid failure in achievement contexts. Individuals high in fear of failure have learned to associate failure with aversive consequences and typically perceive failure in evaluative situations as threatening. To date, only one study has investigated fear of failure in relation to antisocial sport behavior. Specifically, Sagar, Boardley, and Kavussanu (2011) examined fear of failure and antisocial behavior in sport and education in university team sport athletes. Players who reported high fear of failure were more likely to also report engaging in antisocial behavior not only toward their teammates and opponents while playing their sport but also toward their fellow students during the academic year. Thus, fear of failure appears to be a promising construct that could enhance our understanding of antisocial behavior in achievement contexts.

Passion

Passion has been defined as a strong inclination toward an activity that one likes, finds important, and in which one invests a significant amount of time and energy (Vallerand et al., 2003). The distinction has also been made between *harmonious passion*, in which the person is fully engaged in the activity, has control over the activity, and the activity is in harmony with the person's other activities, and *obsessive passion*, in which one feels compelled to engage in the activity, experiences conflict, and the activity takes a lot of space in the person's self (Vallerand et al., 2003). Donahue, Rip, and Vallerand (2009) examined the relationship between passion and reactive aggression (e.g., "At times I cannot control my urge to harm an opponent") in basketball players. Athletes with a predominantly obsessive passion for basketball reported higher levels of reactive aggression than did athletes with a predominantly harmonious passion. This suggests that how athletes approach the activity has implications for their aggressive behavior.

Moral Identity

Moral identity is "the cognitive schema a person holds about his or her moral character" (Aquino, Freeman, Reed, Lim, & Felps, 2009, p. 124) and can function as a self-regulatory mechanism that motivates moral action (Blasi, 1984). This construct originated from the work of Blasi (1984), who proposed that a common set of moral traits are likely to be central to most people's moral self-definitions and that being a moral person may occupy different levels of importance in each person's self-concept. Aquino and Reed (2002) identified nine traits (i.e., caring, compassionate, fair, friendly, generous, helpful, hardworking, honest, and kind) as being characteristic of a moral person and found variation in the degree to which these traits were central to one's self-concept. The extent to which the moral self-schema is experienced as being central to one's self-definition has been referred to as the *internalization dimension* of moral identity (Aquino & Reed, 2002) and has been the main focus of empirical research.

To date, only one study has investigated moral identity in the sport context. Sage et al. (2006) presented adult male soccer players with the nine traits identified as being characteristic of a moral person (Aquino & Reed, 2002) and asked them to respond to five items measuring moral identity centrality. The more central these characteristics were to the players' self-concept, the less likely the players were to report engaging in antisocial behavior while playing soccer. These findings suggest that moral identity is an important variable to consider in sport morality research. However, contrary to research findings in other contexts—that moral identity predicted actual food donations to less well-off groups (Aquino & Reed, 2002)—this construct did not predict prosocial behavior in soccer players. This may be due to the different measures of prosocial behavior employed in the two studies. Nevertheless, it is still unknown whether moral identity is associated with higher prosocial behavior in the sport context. It is possible that the competitive nature of sport buffers the positive effects of moral identity on prosocial behavior, particularly toward opposition players.

Moral Disengagement

Moral disengagement refers to eight mechanisms that individuals use to minimize anticipated negative affect (e.g., guilt, shame) when engaging in transgressive conduct (Bandura, 1991, 1999). These mechanisms act by cognitively reconstruing the harmful behaviors into benign ones, minimizing personal accountability for transgressive acts, misrepresenting the injurious effects that result from harmful conduct, or blaming the character or actions of the victim (Bandura, 1991). The eight mechanisms are euphemistic labeling, moral justification, advantageous comparison, diffusion of responsibility, displacement of responsibility, distortion of consequences, dehumanization, and attribution of blame. A full description can be found in Bandura (1991), and sport-specific examples of each mechanism have been provided by Boardley and Kavussanu (2007).

Moral disengagement in sport has received a lot of research attention in recent years, with abundant evidence attesting to its occurrence (see Boardley & Kavussanu, 2011). Displacement of responsibility, attribution of blame and distortion of consequences are particularly popular mechanisms among basketball and taekwondo athletes (Corrion, Long, Smith, & d'Arripe-Longueville, 2009). In the first study that provided quantitative evidence for the link between moral disengagement and moral behavior in sport, moral disengagement was positively associated with antisocial behavior among team sport athletes (Boardley & Kavussanu, 2007). In line with expectations, its relationship to prosocial behavior was negative. This pattern of relationships has been repeated in other studies (e.g., Boardley & Kavussanu, 2009, 2010). Overall, the findings of these studies show that athletes use mechanisms of moral disengagement which may allow them to engage in antisocial behavior while playing sport.

Self-Regulatory Efficacy

In his social cognitive theory, Bandura (2001) highlights the importance of self-efficacy as a self-regulatory mechanism for behavior. d'Arripe-Longueville et al. (2010) tested self-regulatory mechanisms governing prosocial behavior and the acceptability and likelihood of cheating in adolescent students. Participants responded to scenarios describing hypothetical situations in team sports in which they may be tempted to cheat (i.e., break a rule in basketball) and indicated whether they thought it was okay to cheat (acceptability of cheating) and how likely they would be to cheat if put into the protagonist's position (likelihood of cheating). Affective self-regulatory efficacy (i.e., efficacy to manage mood with opponents) positively predicted resistive self-regulatory efficacy (i.e., efficacy to resist engaging in high-risk activities; for example, peer pressure to cheat in sport), which, in turn, positively predicted prosocial behavior toward teammates through social efficacy (i.e., beliefs in one's capabilities to form and maintain social relationships, work cooperatively with others, and manage different types of interpersonal conflict). Affective self-regulatory efficacy also had a negative effect on moral disengagement, which in turn predicted positively acceptability and likelihood of cheating and negatively prosocial behavior.

This is an interesting study that examined the network of relationships and tested several direct and indirect effects among a number of predictors and outcomes. Given that sport morality is a complex phenomenon, this approach is more likely to enhance our understanding of this phenomenon. However, the sports in which students participated were not reported, thus the suitability of the specific scenarios to the participants' athletic experience is unclear.

Summary

In summary, a number of individual difference variables have been associated with moral behavior in sport. Ego orientation, extrinsic motivation, controlling reasons for pursuing performance approach goals, fear of failure, and obsessive passion have been found to correspond either directly or indirectly to antisocial behavior, aggression, cheating likelihood, and use of performance enhancing substances. An underlying dimension of these variables may be the pressure one puts on the self to perform. Moral identity, moral disengagement, and self-regulatory efficacy have also been associated with moral behavior in sport. Although individual difference variables are important, in sport, a significant role in moral action is also played by the athletes' social environment. Research pertaining to the social context is reviewed next.

Social Antecedents of Moral Behavior

Sport does not occur in a social vacuum. The social context in which sport takes place has the potential to exert a powerful influence on participants' moral action. The social context refers to the people associated with the sport experience: the coach and teammates, who form athletes' immediate team environment; parents, who are part of the wider social sport context; and referees who could affect athletes' behavior during a game. Research pertaining to these individuals is reviewed here. In the vast majority of studies discussed in this section, the constructs were assessed via athlete perceptions. Thus, although they are described as aspects of the social context, in reality they represent *perceived* aspects of that context. The assessment of the social environment via participants' perceptions reflects, in part, the view that it is through the individuals' perceptions that social agents exert their influence (see Ames, 1992).

Coach and Teammates

Athletes train with their coach and teammates and compete with their teammates in the presence of the coach. Given that, for most of their athletic life, athletes come in contact with their coach and teammates, it is not surprising that these individuals have been found to have an important impact on athletes' behavior. Several coach characteristics and behaviors have been investigated and are reviewed in this section. These are character-building efficacy, effectiveness, and competency, attitudes, motivational climate, and moral atmosphere of the team.

CHARACTER-BUILDING EFFICACY, EFFECTIVENESS, AND COMPETENCY

Character-building efficacy, effectiveness, and competency are constructs derived from the coaching efficacy model. This model was proposed by Feltz and colleagues (Feltz, Chase, Moritz, & Sullivan, 1999), who defined coaching efficacy as the extent to which coaches believe that they have the capacity to influence the learning and performance of their athletes. One of its dimensions is character-building efficacy, which refers to coaches' beliefs in their ability to influence their athletes' personal development and positive attitude toward sport. Feltz and her colleagues (1999) proposed that coaches high in character-building efficacy should demonstrate greater frequency of character development behaviors, such as promoting good sportspersonship, respect for others, and fair play, and should have athletes who display more positive attitudes toward sportspersonship and exhibit more fair play behaviors.

The only study that has tested this link to date has not found a relationship between character-building coaching efficacy and reported likelihood to aggress against an opponent in football (Chow, Murray, & Feltz, 2009). However, coaches high in game-strategy efficacy had athletes who reported high likelihood to commit an aggressive act. Game-strategy efficacy refers to coaches' beliefs in their ability to coach and lead their team to successful performance during competition (Feltz et al., 1999) and has been positively associated with coaches' past win–loss record (Feltz et al., 1999). Thus, Chow et al's (2009) finding may suggest that more successful coaches may have more aggressive players. However, research is needed to verify this hypothesis.

Two studies have examined whether character-building coaching effectiveness and competency are associated with players' personal development and positive attitude toward sport. These two constructs, which were proposed independently, were measured by adapting the relevant items from the Coaching Efficacy Scale (Feltz et al., 1999). In the first study (Boardley, Kavussanu, & Ring, 2008), rugby players who perceived that their coach was effective in instilling an attitude of good moral character, fair play, and respect for others, and in promoting good sportspersonship, were more likely to report prosocial behavior toward their opponents while playing rugby. In the second study (Boardley & Kavussanu, 2009), hockey and netball players who perceived that their coach was competent in promoting these attitudes and behaviors were more likely to report more frequent prosocial behavior toward opponents and less frequent antisocial behavior toward both opponents and teammates. The effects of character-building competency on behaviors were mediated by moral disengagement. That is, character-building competency was a negative predictor of moral disengagement, which, in turn, was a negative predictor of prosocial behavior and a positive predictor of antisocial behavior.

FAIR PLAY ATTITUDES AND RELATIONAL SUPPORT

Two other coach variables relevant to moral behavior in sport are coaches' fair play attitudes—for example, whether they respect the opponent and the rules of the game—and the relational support with which they provide their players in terms of acceptance, emotional support, respect for autonomy, quality of communication, and convergence of goals. For instance, a coach who lets athletes solve their problems as much as possible, but also helps them out when they ask, is one who provides high relational support. Rutten and her colleagues (2008) found that adolescent soccer players who perceived their coach as having fair play attitudes were less likely to engage in antisocial behavior while playing soccer. In addition, players who perceived that their coach provided relational support were more

likely to engage in prosocial behavior. Thus, fair play attitudes and relational support appear to have an impact on soccer players' prosocial and antisocial behavior.

MOTIVATIONAL CLIMATE

Motivational climate, a construct of achievement goal theory, refers to the situational goal structure; that is, the achievement goals emphasized and the criteria for success that are conveyed to the participants by significant others, such as coaches, teachers, and parents (Ames, 1992). Those significant others determine important features of the achievement context, such as the evaluation procedures and the distribution of rewards, and, via their behavior, they communicate to the athletes what is valued in that context. Coaches create a performance motivational climate by rewarding only top athletes and valuing normative ability, or a mastery climate by focusing on skill development, valuing effort, and rewarding participants for effort and improvement. Similar to its dispositional counterpart (i.e., ego orientation), performance motivational climate is assumed to lead to antisocial behavior in sport. As in this type of climate the emphasis is on doing better than others, players may be tempted to cheat or engage in other behaviors that could facilitate this goal. In contrast, mastery climate is more likely to promote prosocial sport behavior (see Kavussanu, 2006).

Several studies have investigated the relationship between perceived motivational climate and moral action in sport. These studies have consistently shown that when players perceive a performance motivational climate in their team they are more likely to report higher frequency of antisocial behavior toward their opponents (e.g., Kavussanu & Spray, 2006; Miller, Roberts, & Ommundsen, 2005; Ommundsen, Roberts, Lemyre, & Treasure, 2003), as well as toward their teammates (Boardley & Kavussanu, 2009). Finally, this type of climate has been positively associated with instrumental aggression in male handball players (Rascle, Coulomb-Cabagno, & Delsarte, 2005). With the exception of two studies in which mastery climate positively predicted prosocial behavior toward teammates (Boardley & Kavussanu, 2009) and opponents (Kavussanu, 2006), mastery climate has generally not been associated with moral behavior in sport. A mastery climate, especially if it has a cooperative behavior component, may lead to prosocial behavior, but it will not necessarily deter antisocial conduct. It is the value placed on normative success, communicated to the athletes via the coaches' behavior, that could lead players to cheat, injure, and verbally abuse other players.

MORAL ATMOSPHERE

The construct of moral atmosphere is based on the work of Kohlberg and colleagues (e.g., Power, Higgins, & Kohlberg, 1989). In the sport psychology literature, it has been operationally defined as a set of collective norms regarding morally relevant action on the part of group members (Shields & Bredemeier, 1995). In a sport team, certain philosophies—which are partly the outcome of characteristics of the coach and team members—are developed over time regarding what is appropriate behavior. Teammates' perceptions of their peers' choices in situations that give rise to moral conflict are also part of the moral atmosphere (Shields & Bredemeier, 1995).

Stephens and Bredemeier (1996) were the first to examine moral atmosphere in relation to self-reported likelihood to aggress against an opponent in young female soccer players. They measured athletes' perceptions of the number of teammates willing to tackle an opponent from behind and the degree of importance their coach placed on task and ego goals for the team as dimensions of moral atmosphere. Players who perceived that a large number of their teammates would behave aggressively in a hypothetical situation and that their coach placed importance on ego goals for the team (e.g., it was important to the coach that the team is the best team) also indicated greater likelihood to behave aggressively. Athletes' perceptions of their team's proaggressive norms were the main predictor of reported likelihood to aggress in several other samples of young basketball and soccer players (e.g., Chow et al., 2009; Stephens, 2000).

Moral atmosphere has also been examined in relation to moral judgment, intention, and behavior (collectively referred to as moral functioning). This line of research has typically presented athletes with scenarios describing antisocial behaviors (see Kavussanu, Roberts, & Ntoumanis, 2002) and examined their perceptions of the number of teammates who would engage in these behaviors, as well as their perceptions of their coach as encouraging the behaviors in question. In both items, the qualifier "if it was necessary for the team to win" was used, in line with Shields and colleagues (Shields, Bredemeier, Gardner, & Bostrom, 1995). Basketball and soccer players who thought that their coach encouraged antisocial conduct and that

a large number of their teammates would engage in such conduct, if it was necessary for the team to win, also reported lower levels of moral functioning (Kavussanu et al., 2002; Kavussanu & Spray, 2006; Miller et al., 2005).

An interesting finding revealed in a few studies is the strong link between moral atmosphere and performance motivational climate (e.g., Kavussanu et al., 2002; Kavussanu & Spray, 2006; Ommundsen et al., 2003). Specifically, players who perceive that their coaches create a performance motivational climate in their team also perceive these coaches as encouraging them to push another player, fake an injury, or risk injury to their opponents, if such behaviors are necessary for the team to win. This finding suggests that coaches who create a performance motivational climate in their team may value winning over the players' welfare.

Parents

Parents are not part of the immediate team environment but are important social agents, particularly in childhood and early adolescence. Thus, their attitudes and behaviors should have an influence on young players' moral action in the sport context, particularly when they are actively involved with their child's sport participation. Parental constructs have received much less research attention compared to that received by variables referring to the coach and team members. Parental motivational climate, parental attitudes, and social approval have been examined in relation to moral action in sport and are discussed below.

PARENTAL MOTIVATIONAL CLIMATE

The perceived parent-initiated motivational climate has been described as having three dimensions: learning and enjoyment, success without effort, and worry-conducive (White, Duda, & Hart, 1992). The first dimension is equivalent to a mastery climate, whereas the latter two correspond to a performance motivational climate. To date, only one study has investigated the parent-initiated climate—along with other parental influence variables—in relation to good and bad sport behaviors in male youth ice hockey players (LaVoi & Babkes Stellino, 2008). These behaviors have been defined as positive and negative things, respectively, that players do on and off the ice during games and practices (LaVoi & Babkes Stellino, 2008). Some of the measured behaviors (e.g., helping an opponent off the ice, hurt opponents on purpose) are equivalent to the prosocial and antisocial behaviors examined in other studies (e.g., Kavussanu & Boardley, 2009; Sage et al., 2006); others (e.g., thank the coach, complain about ice time) do not clearly fit the prosocial and antisocial behavior definitions (Eisenberg & Fabes, 1998; Sage et al., 2006); and others (e.g., feel playing outside of rules is part of game) represent attitudes rather than behaviors.

This study reported some interesting findings regarding the link between parental climate—as well as other parental influence variables—and good and bad behaviors. Specifically, players' perceptions of a learning and enjoyment parental climate (e.g., "My parent is most satisfied when I learn something new") and parental involvement (e.g., the extent to which parents were involved in their child's sport participation) were positively associated with good behaviors and inversely linked to bad behaviors in ice hockey. Interestingly, parents' expectations that their children's performance should demonstrate high levels of competence were positively associated with bad behaviors, which were also more likely in players who perceived a worry-conducive parental climate (e.g., "My parent makes me worried about failing"). These findings suggest that children and young adolescents may be sensitive to their parents' expectations regarding their performance in sport, and these perceptions might in turn affect their behavior.

PARENTAL ATTITUDES

Another aspect of parental influence concerns the attitudes parents hold toward their children's behavior. Shields and colleagues referred to bad or poor behaviors as ethically problematic behaviors reflecting cheating, aggression, and disrespect, and examined perceived parental attitudes toward poor sport behaviors in a large sample of athletes drawn from team sports (Shields, LaVoi, Bredemeier, & Power, 2007). Participants were asked to indicate how disappointed their parents would be if they engaged in poor sport behaviors (e.g., cheated, tried to hurt an opponent) and to report their own poor sport behavior during the season (e.g., cheated to help their team win, tried to hurt an opponent to help their team win). Players who thought that their parents would be disappointed if they engaged in poor behaviors were less likely to engage in such behaviors.

SOCIAL APPROVAL

Social approval can be a powerful influence on sport behavior, particularly at a young age. The relationship between perceived social approval and

moral action in youth basketball players was examined by Stuart and Ebbeck (1995). Participants were asked about their perceptions of the approval of five antisocial behaviors (e.g., injuring another player to prevent a basket, pushing an opposing player when the referee is not looking, etc) by their mother, father, coach, and teammates. For example, athletes were asked "Does your dad (mom, coach, teammates) think it is OK for you to push an opposing player when the referee is not looking?"). Players in grades 7 and 8 (but not 4 and 5) who perceived that those significant others approved antisocial behaviors were more likely to be rated by their coaches as engaging in these behaviors. These findings suggest that perceived social approval may influence young adolescents but not children.

Referees

At the outset it must be acknowledged that referees do not have the same status as social agents in the athletic context as do parents, coaches, and teammates because the individuals who act as referees are not the same in every game or match. Nevertheless, referees are important in organized sport, and surprisingly little research has investigated these social agents as part of the sport social environment. Referees can have an impact on athletes' behavior through the decisions they make during a game. In one study, Faccenda, Pantaléon, and Reynes (2009) randomly assigned soccer players to two groups. Half the participants responded to six scenarios describing correct refereeing calls, and the other half responded to six scenarios describing refereeing errors representing just and unjust contexts, respectively. In both cases, all the behaviors described were transgressive regardless of the referee's decision. An example of a scenario used is:

> You are playing a very important match. The score is tied and the game is almost over. You are alone, in a good position to score. The only way that the last defender can stop you is to push you and foul. You do not score. The referee sanctions/does not sanction this player. When you get up, you strike the opponent player.
> (*Faccenda* et al., 2009, p. 405)

Participants indicated how often they really engaged in the described behavior during matches. In addition, they indicated whether or not the described behavior was acceptable (moral judgment) and whether or not they would tend to engage in the described behavior (moral intention). Results showed that players who were presented with an "unjust" refereeing decision reported more frequent engagement in the behaviors than did players who were presented with the just scenario. They also judged transgressive behaviors as acceptable and indicated the intention to engage in such behaviors.

These findings suggest that players may be concerned with seeing justice occur. If the referee does not make a just decision, players feel empowered to punish their opponent, thereby restoring justice. Of course, this could have negative consequences for their own team as, in this particular case, they can be given a red card and removed from the game.

Summary

In summary, athletes' perceptions of several attributes, beliefs, and behaviors of their coaches, teammates, parents, and the referee have implications for their own actions in the sport context. Many desirable coaching variables, such as character-building coaching effectiveness and fair play attitudes, have been positively associated with prosocial behavior, and a learning/enjoyment parental climate has been linked to good behaviors. Conversely, moral atmosphere that condones antisocial conduct, performance coach-initiated, and worry-conducive parent-initiated motivational climates may promote antisocial behavior in the sport context. These constructs are manifested in undesirable behaviors that could put pressure on athletes to perform. Finally, unjust referee decisions may elicit antisocial behavior.

Demographics and Context Characteristics

In addition to identifying individual difference and social-environmental variables associated with moral behavior in sport, researchers have examined participant and context characteristics that do not represent a theoretical construct. These are gender, age, and competitive level. Participation in certain sports has also been associated with sport morality, but this research has been reviewed elsewhere (Kavussanu, 2007). In addition to reporting links between demographics and context characteristics and moral behavior, some attempts have been made to explain why some relationships are observed.

Gender

One of the most consistent findings in sport morality research is differences between males and females. Specifically, males from a variety of team sports have reported higher antisocial behavior toward opponents (Kavussanu & Ntoumanis, 2003;

Kavussanu & Roberts, 2001; Miller et al., 2005) and teammates (Kavussanu & Boardley, 2009), and male soccer and handball players engaged in more aggressive acts than their female counterparts (Coulomb-Cabagno & Rascle, 2006). Male soccer players have also reported lower prosocial behavior toward their opponents but higher prosocial behavior toward their teammates (Kavussanu & Boardley, 2009). These latter findings suggest that the consistent gender differences found in empirical research may be due to the utilization of measures assessing antisocial behavior toward opponents. Although male athletes appear less likely to help their opponents, they may be more willing to encourage, support, and give positive feedback to their teammates. Thus, to further our understanding of gender differences in sport morality, it is important to consider both prosocial and antisocial behavior toward teammates and opponents.

Even though identifying gender differences in moral behavior is important, it is equally important to understand why such differences occur: What leads males to engage in antisocial conduct more often than females while playing sport? This was the main purpose of a study by Kavussanu and her colleagues (2009), who found that male soccer players engaged in a greater number of antisocial behaviors than did their female counterparts during one soccer game. In this study, a diverse number of behaviors were coded from videotaped soccer games. Sport experience, performance motivational climate, and empathy (i.e., the ability to take the perspective of others and experience feelings of sympathy, compassion, and concern for unfortunate others; Davis, 1983) were also examined. All analyses were conducted at the level of the team.

The results showed that male players had played soccer for a longer period of time, perceived a higher performance climate in their team, and reported lower empathy than did female players. Importantly, when the effects of these variables were statistically removed from behavior scores, the significant gender differences in antisocial behavior were substantially reduced. These findings provide preliminary evidence to suggest that males may engage in more antisocial behaviors than females *because* they play their sport for a longer time (possibly because they are used to the occurrence of antisocial behavior in that context), are less empathic, and perceive a performance motivational climate in their team. Indeed, these variables have been consistently linked to antisocial behavior in sport research (e.g., Kavussanu, 2006; Kavussanu & Boardley, 2009;

Sagar et al., 2011). One limitation of this study is that it was cross-sectional, thus the direction of causality cannot be firmly established.

Age

Age is the second demographic variable associated with moral action in sport. However, the literature is limited to adolescents and young adults. Age differences in moral behavior were investigated in two studies, both of which used male soccer players and coded behaviors from videotaped matches. In the first study, prosocial and antisocial behaviors were examined in three age groups (under 13, under 15, and under 17); each group was represented by eight teams, and only one game was coded per team (Kavussanu et al., 2006). The oldest group displayed more frequent antisocial behaviors than the two younger groups and less frequent prosocial behaviors than the youngest group. The three age groups also differed in their perceptions of the motivational climate created by the coach, such that the youngest group perceived a higher mastery climate in their team compared to the other two groups and a lower performance motivational climate than the oldest group. Analysis of covariance showed that age group differences in antisocial and prosocial behavior were substantially reduced when motivational climate was included as a covariate. These findings provide preliminary evidence to suggest that the higher frequency of antisocial and lower frequency of prosocial behaviors observed in older teams may be due to the different types of motivational climate prevalent in these teams.

In the second study (Romand, Pantaléon, & Cabagno, 2009), instrumental and hostile aggression were examined in six teams with members ranging in age from 8 to 25 years, thus representing children, adolescents, and young adults. Each team was observed for three games, and for each player, one score for instrumental and one score for hostile aggression were calculated for the three games. Children displayed less instrumental aggression than adolescents, who in turn were less aggressive than adults; there were no cohort-related differences in hostile aggression. This study offers more consistent evidence for the occurrence of antisocial conduct in soccer: Because their instrumental aggression score was calculated over three games, it should be more representative of players' typical behavior. The findings of this study suggest that athletes may simply learn to use aggression for instrumental purposes but are not necessarily more hostile toward other players at older ages.

These two studies show that antisocial behavior is more frequent in older adolescents and young adults. Both studies are important because they employed observational methods to measure behavior, thereby assessing observed rather than reported behavior. However, both studied only young male soccer players. Thus, the generalizability of their findings to other populations (e.g., females, other team sports, athletes in middle adulthood) is unknown. Finally, both studies were cross-sectional, employing three different age groups; thus, cohort-related factors could provide alternative explanations for the age differences in sport behavior observed in these studies. Longitudinal studies in which the same athletes and teams are studied over a number of years would provide stronger evidence for the causal role of motivational climate on moral behavior in sport.

Competitive Level

Moral behavior also varies as a function of competitive level. Rascle et al. (2005) videotaped young male handball players (aged 13–15) and coded instrumental and hostile aggression. Players competing at a higher competitive level displayed more instrumental aggression than did those competing at a lower level; competitive level had no effect on hostile aggression. Coulomb-Cabagno and Rascle (2006) coded instrumental and hostile aggression from 90 handball and 90 soccer games of French championships equally distributed among three competitive levels. Instrumental aggression increased linearly when competitive level increased in females, but decreased at regional and increased at national level in males. However, males displayed high instrumental aggression across all levels. Hostile aggression decreased linearly in males, but there was no significant difference across competitive levels in females who, overall, displayed very low levels of hostile aggression. It appears that competitive level may affect instrumental but not hostile aggression; this is in line with the age differences in instrumental but not hostile aggression reported by Romand et al. (2009).

Interventions

The studies discussed so far show that a number of variables have been linked to moral behavior in sport. Thus, there would seem to be a sufficient knowledge base to develop interventions in the sport context. Despite the growing evidence pointing to factors associated with moral behavior in sport, to date the only interventions aimed at reducing antisocial and promoting prosocial behavior have been conducted in physical education. The two studies reported in this section developed interventions based on principles from both social learning (Bandura, 1977) and structural-developmental theories (e.g., Kohlberg, 1984).

In the first study, Gibbons et al. (1995) examined the effect of participation in educational activities designed to enhance fair play on prosocial behavior of elementary school children. Intact classrooms were randomly assigned to either a Fair Play for Kids curriculum during physical education only, a Fair Play for Kids curriculum during all school subjects, or a control group. The Fair Play for Kids curriculum includes educational activities that focus on the development of attitudes and behaviors that exemplify the following fair play ideals: respect for rules, the opponent, the officials, and their decisions; providing all individuals with an equal chance to participate; and maintaining self-control at all times (see Gibbons et al., 1995). Teachers rated children on ten behaviors commonly associated with fair play in sports and games (e.g., arguing with teammates, showing off, teasing others). Behavior was measured before and after the intervention, which lasted 7 months. Children in the two intervention groups exhibited significantly higher post-test behavior scores compared to those in the control group, when individual students were used as the unit of analysis.

The second study was conducted by Hassandra and her colleagues (Hassandra, Goudas, Hatzigeorgiadis, & Theodorakis, 2007), who administered a 10-week intervention intended to promote fair play behaviors during games in elementary school students. *Fair play* was defined as respect for rules, teammates, opponent, and officials and their decisions, and consisted of prosocial and antisocial behaviors. The researchers assigned four classes to an experimental group and four classes to a control group. Examples of strategies implemented by the experimental group are demonstration of desirable behaviors, verbal reinforcement of positive social behaviors, rewards (i.e., color cards) when students had shown the target behaviors, and discussion of moral dilemmas. The experimental group showed significant improvement in the fair play behaviors from pre- to post-test, whereas the control group showed no change. Importantly, group differences were maintained after 2 months.

Given that moral behavior intervention studies are rare in physical activity contexts, these investigations make an important contribution to the literature: The studies showed that teachers can promote students' fair play behaviors. However, these findings may not generalize to competitive sport. Although sport and physical education share many features, the social experiences athletes have and the moral issues they face in the two contexts are quite distinct. To date, no studies exist to verify the efficacy of interventions designed to promote prosocial and reduce antisocial behavior in sport. This is a fruitful avenue for future research.

Implications for Morality in Other Performance Domains

Morality is relevant to any interpersonal context. Thus, moral issues can arise in other performance domains that involve interaction among participants, for example, the workplace, education, music, and the arts. Some of the variables that have been examined in the sport domain have also been investigated in other performance domains. In this section, examples of this work are provided and implications of sport morality research for other performance domains are discussed.

A study reviewed in a previous section examined antisocial behavior in sport and education. Specifically, Sagar et al. (2011) investigated whether fear of failure and the extent of participation in team sport predicted antisocial behavior toward one's teammates and opponents in sport and toward one's fellow students in education. Athletes drawn from a variety of team sports who scored high on a general measure of fear of failure and who reported extensive involvement in their team sport, were more likely to behave antisocially toward other players while playing their sport and toward their fellow students during the academic year. Moreover, antisocial behavior in sport was positively related to antisocial behavior in education (Sagar et al., 2011).

Several variables associated with moral behavior in sport have also been empirically linked to moral behavior in education and have implications for morality in the workplace. Specifically, students who are high in ego orientation, focus on extrinsic rewards, experience parental and peer pressure to achieve high grades, and perceive a performance motivational climate in their class are more likely to cheat in their exams (for a review, see Murdock & Anderman, 2006). A performance motivational climate created by one's manager in the workplace should have similar effects on employee behavior. That is, rewarding only the best performers and constantly and explicitly drawing employees' attention to how their performance compares to that of their colleagues may promote antisocial and inhibit prosocial behavior toward one's colleagues.

Many other dispositional variables linked to moral behavior in sport should also have implications for moral behavior in other performance domains. For example, in the performing arts, the individual who views being a moral person as highly central to his self-concept (i.e., moral identity centrality) is less likely to cheat, lie, or try to undermine other performers in order to look better in the eyes of a director, thereby winning an important role in the play. Conversely, these behaviors may be more common in performers who are motivated by prestige and extrinsic rewards, are preoccupied with doing better than others, are motivated to avoid failure, and are obsessively passionate about the activity. These characteristics should have universal application and are relevant to any performance domain.

It is also important to recognize that team sport—where the vast majority of sport morality research has been conducted—is a unique context, in that it is by definition a competitive context in which one has teammates and opponents. Participants unavoidably interact with these individuals during competition. Through this interaction, moral issues are likely to arise, and athletes have opportunities to act both prosocially and antisocially. In contrast, musicians, actors, and other artists typically perform on their own or as part of a team. Some performers, for instance musicians, may take part in competitions, but such competitions are not a defining feature of performance in music, theatre, or art. Thus, normally, these performers are not involved in direct competition with others, and there are no formal rules of "play" by which they need to abide during performance. As a result, performers in other domains do not face the same moral issues as (team) sport performers.

The team dynamics are also different between sport and other performance domains. A theater or orchestra director is concerned with actors or musicians performing the best they can. Although the very act of performing in front of an audience may raise concerns about one's adequacy as a performer, the play or orchestra director cannot possibly encourage antisocial conduct toward opponents because no such opponents exist. Thus, research on character-building effectiveness, moral atmosphere of the team, and performance motivational climate—as these variables have been measured in the sport context—may not have implications for morality in other performance domains. In sum, much—but not all—of the sport morality research findings have implications for moral conduct in other performance domains.

Conclusion

The recent proliferation of sport morality research has led to a substantial increase in our understanding of the factors associated with moral behavior in sport. The manner in which one thinks about moral issues, the centrality of moral identity to one's self, self-efficacy to regulate emotion, and a range of motivational variables appear to influence moral action within the athletic context. However, the most significant effect seems to come from the social environment. When athletes perceive that their coach encourages cheating and aggressive behavior, and that their teammates are willing to cheat and aggress against others, they are more likely to also cheat and aggress against their opponents. Moreover, an emphasis on normative success may be detrimental to fair play. Thus, a range of personal and social variables have been associated with moral behavior in sport.

Directions for Future Research

Although our understanding of sport morality has been considerably enhanced, several issues remain and need to be addressed in future research. First, we know very little about moral behavior in individual sports. Such research does exist (e.g., Donahue et al., 2006), but most studies have used team sport athletes. The limited research in individual sports may, in part, be due to the lack of measures designed specifically for these sports. However, some of the items included in current measures of prosocial (e.g., helped an injured opponent) and antisocial (e.g., verbally abused an opponent) behavior are also relevant to behavior in individual sports. It would be interesting to obtain information on the frequency of moral behavior in these sports. A good first attempt to this end has been recently made by Hodge and Lonsdale (2011).

Second, it is important to keep in mind that most studies are cross-sectional, relying on data collected at a single point in time. Although this is an important step in the research process, particularly when a predictor variable is examined for the first time, this design renders the direction of causality difficult to determine. For instance, the identified relationship between moral disengagement and antisocial behavior does not tell us whether moral disengagement led to antisocial behavior, whether antisocial behavior led to moral disengagement, if these two variables reciprocally influenced each other, or if they were both influenced by a third unmeasured variable. Longitudinal designs, in which both variables are measured at two (or more) time points—sufficiently distant to allow for change to take place—are needed. Researchers can then determine, for example, whether the change in behavior from time 1 to time 2 is predicted by time 1 moral disengagement, or whether the change in moral disengagement from time 1 to time 2 is better predicted by time 1 antisocial behavior. This type of design provides stronger evidence for the direction of causality. However, a better test of this issue can be achieved with experimental designs in which the effects of moral disengagement—or other variables—on antisocial behavior are examined in the laboratory.

Investigating sport morality in the laboratory necessitates the use of suitable tasks to assess moral behavior in that context. One approach is to use—or create—laboratory analogs of the sport context, such as the table soccer task employed by Sage and Kavussanu (2007b) to examine prosocial and antisocial behavior during a motor skill–based competition. It has also been suggested that video sports games can be utilized to study such behavior in an easily observed and measured environment (Murphy, 2009). Alternatively, researchers could investigate athletes' aggression using well-established paradigms, such as the Taylor Aggression Paradigm (1967). This paradigm involves a reaction time competition, in which the participant competes against a fictitious opponent under various levels of provocation. Finally, researchers could use implicit measures of moral attitudes, such as the Implicit Association Test, in which the strength of an attitude can be inferred by the respondents' relative reaction time, to examine judgments and attitudes about moral behavior in sport.

Third, characteristics of the social environment including team and parental variables have nearly always been measured via athletes' perceptions. The rationale for this has been that individuals' perceptions of the same context vary, and it is through these perceptions that social agents exert their influence (see Ames, 1992; Horn, 2002). However, with this methodology, the degree to which athletes project their own thoughts and intentions on others is unknown. For example, in studies assessing moral atmosphere, players who behave antisocially may report that their teammates act in a similar manner, not necessarily because they do so, but because respondents exaggerate these perceptions to justify their own behavior. Studies are needed that incorporate other

methods of measuring moral atmosphere and other dimensions of the team environment. For example, individual athlete reports could be supplemented with observations of the entire team and ratings by the coach(es). Athlete reports can be aggregated and used together with coach reports and team observations to determine the moral atmosphere of the team or other team variables.

Fourth, although most studies have investigated individual predictors of moral behavior, there has been a recent, refreshing shift to examining the *mechanisms* underlying the effects of predictor variables on moral behavior, albeit with a cross-sectional design. For example, it has been found that moral disengagement mediated the effects of perceived character-building competency on prosocial and antisocial behavior (Boardley & Kavussanu, 2009), and objectifying attitude mediated the effects of controlling reasons for pursuing performance approach goals on immoral functioning (Vansteenkiste et al., 2010). Thus, researchers have started to understand why some aspects of the social context or characteristics of the individual may influence moral behavior. Other potential mechanisms could be investigated. For example, performance motivational climate could influence antisocial behavior by reducing players' empathy, while social goals and mastery motivational climate may promote prosocial behavior through their positive effects on social efficacy. Most importantly, researchers need to test the network of relationships among a number of variables, similar to the approach taken by d'Arripe-Longueville et al. (2010), discussed in a previous section. Examining how dispositional and social-environmental predictors of moral behavior are interrelated could enhance our understanding of the processes through which these variables affect moral action.

Fifth, much of the research conducted to date has investigated potential antecedents of antisocial sport behavior. We know very little about the consequences of such behavior, particularly whether it affects performance. The common belief is that, by cheating and acting aggressively, players help their team win. However, an aggressive foul that results in a red card in soccer places the team at a disadvantage, and trying to provoke opposition players to make them react and be penalized by the officials could be distracting for the instigator, as it diverts this player's attention from the game. Moreover, although cheating may help the team when it goes undetected, it could lead to disastrous consequences (for the team) when the cheat is caught. The relationship between antisocial behavior toward opponents and performance in sport is an important one and needs to be explored in future research. Potential consequences of antisocial behavior toward teammates are lower team cohesion, dissatisfaction with being a member of the team, and dropout.

Sixth, a sufficient knowledge base exists, particularly with regard to potential antecedents, to develop a model of moral action in sport. Such an attempt was made by Shields and Bredemeier (1995), who proposed a 12-component model of moral action by integrating elements from Rest's (1984) four-component model of morality, Haan's (1977) model, and the empirical moral psychology literature. Their model is a thoughtful account of research on sport morality and a good attempt to integrate the relevant literature. However, our understanding of moral action in sport has been further enhanced in the last 15 years. A model of moral action that reflects the current state of knowledge, taking into consideration the unique features of the sport context, would make an important contribution to the literature.

Last, but not least, is the issue of intervention. The real challenge for researchers and sport practitioners is to determine whether by intervening to change the variables associated with prosocial and antisocial sport behaviors we can influence the frequency of such behaviors in the field. Evidence that moral behavior can change is available in physical education (e.g., Gibbons et al., 1995; Hassandra et al., 2007), but such evidence does not exist in sport. Interventions in sport can attempt to lower the performance motivational climate of the team, teach coaches to encourage and reward prosocial behavior, and teach parents to emphasize the importance of learning, enjoyment, and fair play in their interactions with their children. The best hope for creating positive and morality-enhancing sports experiences for young athletes may be through implementing such social interventions in their performance environment.

Acknowledgment

The author would like to thank Ian D. Boardley, Christopher Ring, and Luke D. Sage for their helpful suggestions on an earlier draft of this chapter.

References

Allen, J. (2003). Social motivation in youth sport. *Journal of Sport and Exercise Psychology, 25*, 551–567.

Ames, C. (1992). Achievement goals, motivational climate, and motivational processes. In G. C. Roberts (Ed.), *Motivation in sport and exercise* (pp. 161–176). Champaign, IL: Human Kinetics.

Aquino, K., Freeman, D., Reed, A., Lim, V. K. G., & Felps, W. (2009). Testing a social cognitive model of moral behavior: The interactive influence of situations and moral identity centrality. *Journal of Personality and Social Psychology, 97*, 123–141.

Aquino, K., & Reed, A. (2002). The self-importance of moral identity. *Journal of Personality and Social Psychology, 83*, 1423–1440.

Bandura, A. (1977). *Social learning theory*. Englewood Cliffs, NJ: Prentice-Hall.

Bandura, A. (1991). Social cognitive theory of moral thought and action. In W. M. Kurtines & J. L. Gewirtz (Eds.), *Handbook of moral behavior and development: Theory, research, and applications* (Vol. 1, pp. 71–129). Hillsdale, NJ: Lawrence Erlbaum Associates.

Bandura, A. (1999). Moral disengagement in the perpetration of inhumanities. *Personality and Social Psychology Review, 3*, 193–209.

Bandura, A. (2001). Social cognitive theory: An agentic perspective. *Annual Review of Psychology, 52*, 1–26.

Blasi, A. (1984). Moral identity: Its role in moral functioning. In W. Kurtines & J. Gewirtz (Eds.), *Morality, moral behavior and moral development* (pp. 128–139). NY: Wiley.

Boardley, I. D., & Kavussanu, M. (2007). Development and validation of the Moral Disengagement in Sport Scale. *Journal of Sport and Exercise Psychology, 29*, 608–628.

Boardley, I. D., & Kavussanu, M. (2009). The influence of social variables and moral disengagement on prosocial and antisocial behaviours in field hockey and netball. *Journal of Sports Sciences, 27*, 843–854.

Boardley, I. D., & Kavussanu, M. (2010). Effects of goal orientation and perceived value of toughness on antisocial behavior: The mediating role of moral disengagement. *Journal of Sport and Exercise Psychology, 33*, 176–192.

Boardley, I. D., & Kavussanu, M. (2011). Moral disengagement in sport. *International Review of Sport and Exercise Psychology, 4*(2), 93–108.

Boardley, I. D., Kavussanu, M., & Ring, C. (2008). Athletes' perceptions of coaching effectiveness and athlete-related outcomes in rugby union: An investigation based on the coaching efficacy model. *The Sport Psychologist, 22*, 269–287.

Bredemeier, B. J., & Shields, D. L. (1986). Moral growth among athletes and nonathletes: A comparative analysis. *Journal of Genetic Psychology, 147*, 7–18.

Chow, G. M., Murray, K. E., & Feltz, D. L. (2009). Individual, team, and coach predictors of players' likelihood to aggress in youth soccer. *Journal of Sport and Exercise Psychology, 31*, 425–443.

Corrion, K., Long, T., Smith, A. L., & d'Arripe-Longueville, F. (2009). "It's not my fault; it's not serious": Athlete accounts of moral disengagement in competitive sport. *The Sport Psychologist, 23*, 388–404.

Coulomb-Cabagno, G., & Rascle, O. (2006). Team sports players' observed aggression as a function of sex, competitive level, and sport type. *Journal of Applied Social Psychology, 36*, 1980–2000.

Deci, E. L., & Ryan, R. (1985). *Intrinsic motivation and self-determination in human behavior*. New York: Springer.

d'Arripe-Longueville, F., Corrion, K., Scoffier, S., Roussel, P., & Chalabaev, A. (2010). Socio-cognitive self-regulatory mechanisms governing judgments of the acceptability and likelihood of sport cheating. *Journal of Sport and Exercise Psychology*, 32, 595–618.

Davis, M. H. (1983). Measuring individual differences in empathy: Evidence for a multidimensional approach. *Journal of Personality and Social Psychology*, 44, 113–126.

Donahue, E. G., Miquelon, P., Valois, P., Goulet, C., Buist, A., & Vallerand, R. J. (2006). A motivational model of performance-enhancing substance use in elite athletes. *Journal of Sport and Exercise Psychology*, 28, 511–520.

Donahue, E. G., Rip, B., & Vallerand, R. J. (2009). When winning is everything: On passion, identity, and aggression in sport. *Psychology of Sport and Exercise*, 10, 526–534.

Duda, J. L., Olson, L. K., & Templin, T. J. (1991). The relationship of task and ego orientation to sportsmanship attitudes and the perceived legitimacy of injurious acts. *Research Quarterly for Exercise and Sport, 62*, 79–87.

Eisenberg, N., & Fabes, R. A. (1998). Prosocial development. In N. Eisenberg (Ed.), *Handbook of child psychology, Vol. 3*: Social, emotional, and personality development (pp. 701–778). NY: Wiley.

Elliot, A. J., & McGregor, J. A. (2001). A 2 X 2 achievement goal framework. *Journal of Personality and Social Psychology, 80*, 501–519.

Faccenda, L., Pantaleon, N., & Reynes, E. (2009). Significant predictors of soccer players' moral functioning from components of contextual injustice, sensitivity to injustice and moral atmosphere. *Social Justice Research, 22*, 399–415.

Feltz, D. L., Chase, M. A., Moritz, S. E., & Sullivan, P. J. (1999). A conceptual model of coaching efficacy: Preliminary investigation and instrument development. *Journal of Educational Psychology, 91*, 765–776.

Gibbons, S., Ebbeck, V., & Weiss, M. (1995). Fair play for kids: Effects on the moral development of children in physical education. *Research Quarterly for Exercise and Sport, 66*, 245–255.

Haan, N. (1977). *Coping and defending: Processes of self-environment organization*. New York: Academic Press.

Hassandra, M., Goudas, M., Hatzigeorgiadis, A., & Theodorakis, Y. (2007). A fair play intervention program in school Olympic education. *European Journal of Psychology of Education, 22*, 99–114.

Hodge, K., & Lonsdale, C. (2011). Prosocial and antisocial behavior in sport: The role of coaching style, autonomous vs. controlled motivation, and moral disengagement. *Journal of Sport and Exercise Psychology, 33*, 527–547.

Horn, T.S. (2002). Coaching effectiveness in the sports domain. In T.S. Horn (Ed.), *Advances in sport psychology* (pp. 309–354). Champaign, IL: Human Kinetics.

Husman B., & Silva, J. (1984). Aggression: Definitional considerations. In J. M. Silva & R. S. Weinberg (Eds.), *Psychological foundations of sport* (pp. 246–260). Champaign, IL: Human Kinetics.

Kavussanu, M. (2006). Motivational predictors of prosocial and antisocial behaviour in soccer. *Journal of Sports Sciences, 24(6)*, 575–588.

Kavussanu, M. (2007). Morality in sport. In S. Jowett & D. E. Lavallee (Eds.), *Social psychology in sport* (pp. 265–278). Champaign IL: Human Kinetics.

Kavussanu, M. (2008). Moral behaviour in sport: A critical review of the literature. *International Review of Sport and Exercise Psychology, 1*, 124–138.

Kavussanu, M., & Boardley, I. D. (2009). The Prosocial and Antisocial Behavior in Sport Scale. *Journal of Sport and Exercise Psychology, 31*, 1–23.

Kavussanu, M., & Boardley, I. D. (2012). Moral behavior in sport. In G. Tenenbaum, R. J. Eklund & A. Kamata (Eds.), *Handbook of measurement in sport and exercise psychology* (pp. 443–454). Champaign, IL: Human Kinetics.

Kavussanu, M., & Ntoumanis, N. (2003). Participation in sport and moral functioning: Does ego orientation mediate their relationship? *Journal of Sport and Exercise Psychology, 25*, 501–518.

Kavussanu, M., & Roberts, G. C. (2001). Moral functioning in sport: An achievement goal perspective. *Journal of Sport and Exercise Psychology, 23*, 37–54.

Kavussanu, M., Roberts, G. C., & Ntoumanis, N. (2002). Contextual influences on moral functioning of college basketball players. *The Sport Psychologist, 16*, 347–367.

Kavussanu, M., Seal, A. R., & Phillips, D. R. (2006). Observed prosocial and antisocial behaviors in male soccer teams: Age differences across adolescence and the role of motivational variables. *Journal of Applied Sport Psychology, 18*, 326–344.

Kavussanu, M., & Spray, C. M. (2006). Contextual influences on moral functioning of male youth footballers. *The Sport Psychologist, 20*, 1–23.

Kavussanu, M., Stamp, R., Slade, G., & Ring, C. (2009). Observed prosocial and antisocial behaviors in male and female soccer players. *Journal of Applied Sport Psychology, 21*(Supp. 1), S62–S76.

Kohlberg, L. (1984). *Essays on moral development, Vol. 2: The psychology of moral development*. San Francisco: Harper & Row.

LaVoi, N. M., & Babkes Stellino, M. (2008). The relation between perceived parent-created sport climate and competitive male youth hockey players' good and poor sport behaviors. *The Journal of Psychology, 142*, 471–495.

Lee, M. J., Whitehead, J., & Ntoumanis, N. (2007). Development of the Attitudes to Moral Decision-Making in Youth Sport Questionnaire (AMDYSQ). *Psychology of Sport and Exercise, 8*, 369–392.

Miller, B. W., Roberts, G. C., & Ommundsen, Y. (2005). Effect of perceived motivational climate on moral functioning, team moral atmosphere perceptions, and the legitimacy of intentionally injurious acts among competitive youth soccer players. *Psychology of Sport and Exercise, 6*, 461–477.

Murdock, T. B., & Anderman, E. (2006). Motivational perspectives on student cheating: Toward an integrated model of academic dishonesty. *Educational Psychologist, 41*(3), 129–145.

Murphy, S. (2009). Video games, competition and exercise: A new opportunity for sport psychologists? *The Sport Psychologist, 23*, 487–503.

Nicholls, J. G. (1989). *The competitive ethos and democratic education*. Cambridge, MA: Harvard University Press.

Ommundsen, Y., Roberts, G. C., Lemyre, P. N., & Treasure, D. (2003). Perceived motivational climate in male youth soccer: Relations to social-moral functioning, sportspersonship and team norm perceptions. *Psychology of Sport and Exercise, 4*, 397–413.

Power, C., Higgins, A., & Kohlberg, L. A. (1989). *Lawrence Kohlberg's approach to moral education*. New York: Columbia University Press.

Rascle, O., & Coulomb, G. (2003). Aggression in youth handball: Relationships between goal orientations and induced motivational context. *Social Behavior and Personality, 31*(1), 21–34.

Rascle, O., Coulomb-Cabagno, G., & Delsarte, A. (2005). Perceived motivational climate and observed aggression as a function of competitive level in youth male French handball. *Journal of Sport Behavior, 28*(1), 51–67.

Rest, J. R. (1984). The major components of morality. In W. Kurtines & J. Gewirtz (Eds.), *Morality, moral behavior, and moral development* (pp. 556–629). New York: Wiley.

Romand, P., Pantaléon, N., & Cabagno, G. (2009). Age differences in individuals' cognitive and behavioral moral functioning responses in male soccer teams. *Journal of Applied Sport Psychology, 21*, 49–63.

Rutten, E. A., Dekovic, M., Stams, G. J. J. M., Schuengel, C., Hoeksmad, J. B., & Biesta, G. J. J. (2008). On- and off-field antisocial and prosocial behavior in adolescent soccer players: A multilevel study. *Journal of Youth and Adolescence, 31*, 371–387.

Sagar, S., Boardley, I. D., & Kavussanu, M. (2011). Fear of failure and student athletes' inter-personal antisocial behavior in education and sport. *British Journal of Educational Psychology, 81* (3), 391–408.

Sage, L., & Kavussanu, M. (2007a). Multiple goal orientations as predictors of moral behavior in youth soccer. *The Sport Psychologist, 21*, 417–437.

Sage, L., & Kavussanu, M. (2007b). The effects of goal involvement on moral behavior in an experimentally manipulated competitive setting. *Journal of Sport and Exercise Psychology, 29*, 190–207.

Sage, L., & Kavussanu, M. (2008). Goal orientations, motivational climate, and prosocial and antisocial behavior in youth football: Exploring their temporal stability and reciprocal relationships. *Journal of Sports Sciences, 26*, 717–732.

Sage, L., Kavussanu, M., & Duda, J. L. (2006). Goal orientations and moral identity as predictors of prosocial and antisocial functioning in male association football players. *Journal of Sports Sciences, 24*(5), 455–466.

Shields, D. L., & Bredemeier, B. J. L. (1995). *Character development and physical activity.* Champaign IL: Human Kinetics.

Shields, D. L., & Bredemeier, J. L. (2007). Advances in sport morality research. In G. Tenenbaum & R. G. Eklund (Eds.) *Handbook of sport psychology* (3rd ed., pp. 645–661). Hoboken, NJ: John Wiley & Sons.

Shields, D. L. L., Bredemeier, J. L., Gardner, D. E., & Bostrom, A. (1995). Leadership, cohesion, and team norms regarding cheating and aggression. *Sociology of Sport Journal, 12*, 324–336.

Shields, D. L., LaVoi, N. M., Bredemeier, B. L., & Power, F. C. (2007). Predictors of poor sportspersonship in youth sports: Personal attitudes and social influences. *Journal of Sport and Exercise Psychology, 29*, 747–762.

Stephens, D. E. (2000). Predictors of likelihood to aggress in youth soccer: An examination of coed and all-girls teams. *Journal of Sport Behavior, 23*, 311–325.

Stephens, D. E., & Bredemeier, B. J. L. (1996). Moral atmosphere and judgments about aggression in girls' soccer: Relationships among moral and motivational variables. *Journal of Sport and Exercise Psychology, 18*, 158–173.

Stephens, D. E., Bredemeier, B. J. L., & Shields, D. L. L. (1997). Construction of a measure designed to assess players' descriptions and prescriptions for moral behavior in youth sport soccer. *International Journal of Sport Psychology, 28*, 370–390.

Stuart, M., & Ebbeck, V. (1995). The influence of perceived social approval on moral development in youth sport. *Pediatric Exercise Science, 7*, 270–280.

Tangney, J. P., Stuewig, J., & Mashek, D. J. (2007). Moral emotions and moral behavior. *Annual Review of Psychology, 58*, 345–372.

Taylor, S. (1967). Aggressive behavior and physiological arousal as a function of provocation and the tendency to inhibit aggression. *Journal of Personality, 35*, 297–310.

Turiel, E. (1983). *The development of social knowledge: Morality and convention.* Cambridge, UK: Cambridge University Press.

Vallerand, R. J., Blanchard, C., Mageau, G. A., Koestner, R., Ratelle, C., Leonard, M., & Gagne, M. (2003). Les Passions de l'Aime: On obsessive and harmonious passion. *Journal of Personality and Social Psychology, 85*, 756–767.

Vallerand, R. J., Briere, N. M., Blanchard, C., & Provencher, P. (1997). Development and validation of the Multidimensional Sportspersonship Orientations Scale. *Journal of Sport and Exercise Psychology, 19*(2), 197–206.

Vansteenkiste, M., Mouratidis, A., & Lens, W. (2010). Detaching reasons from aims: Fair play and well-being in soccer as a function of pursuing performance-approach goals for autonomous or controlling reasons. *Journal of Sport and Exercise Psychology, 32*, 217–242.

Walker, L. J. (2004). What does moral functioning entail? In T. A. Thorkildsen & H. J. Walberg (Eds.), *Nurturing morality* (pp. 3–18). New York: Springer.

White, S. A., Duda, J. L., & Hart, S. (1992). An exploratory examination of the parent-initiated motivational climate questionnaire. *Perceptual and Motor Skills, 75*, 875–880.

Gender, Identity, and Sport

Emily A. Roper

Abstract

This chapter begins with an introduction to the important terms and concepts specific to understanding the body of work in gender and identity in sport. A brief review of women's history in sport and physical activity is provided, including discussion of Title IX, women and girls' physical activity/sport participation patterns, barriers to gender equity in sport, and why an understanding of the social context is critical for sport and performance professionals. The ways in which females experience, perceive, and physically use their bodies is also addressed. The extensive body of work devoted to the homonegative and heterosexist climate of sport is outlined, with specific attention devoted to the bias and discrimination that lesbian, gay, bisexual, and transgender (LGBT) individuals face within sport and the role that sport and performance professionals play in working toward an inclusive and safe sport environment for all participants. The emergence and growth of feminist sport psychology is addressed with an overview and examples of feminist practice and research in the field. Suggestions for future work in the field are provided throughout the chapter and, in particular, how some of the approaches and research frameworks presented could be used to enhance our understanding of sport and performance psychology.

Key Words: Gender, identity, feminist sport, LGBT and sport, and homonegative

Understanding the complexities of gender and identity in sport and performance settings is critical of sport and performance psychology professionals. Studying sport requires that we consider how gender and identity affects our attitudes, interpretations, responses, and strategies, both in research and practice. As Gill and Kamphoff (2010) suggested, "Our world is shaped by gender and culture. Gender influence is particularly powerful in sport, with some unique features" (p. 419). It is these unique features that will be addressed in this chapter.

Important Terms and Concepts

As many in sport and performance psychology have only a limited academic background in issues pertaining to gender and identity, it is important to begin with a brief review of critical terms and concepts. Whereas *sex* is defined as biological differences between males and females, *gender* is defined as characteristics that a society or culture delineates as masculine or feminine. One's *gender identity* refers to the gender that an individual identifies. *Sexual identity* refers to how an individual defines him- or herself in terms of whom he or she is romantically and sexually attracted to (gay, lesbian, bisexual, heterosexual). This attraction is comprised of not only sexual desire, but emotional and intimate love and support. Sexual identity is often used interchangeably with *sexual orientation*.

Gender ideology differs from culture to culture. Each culture teaches its children the expected social roles for males and females, as well as what is considered masculine or feminine. Through a variety of socializing agents—parents, mass media, peers, teachers, coaches, and religion—children begin learning at a very young age how to "perform" gender (Blackmore, 2003). Socialization is a process that involves a relatively complex dynamic between psychological, social, and cultural considerations of learning and development (Blackmore, 2003; Greendorfer, 2001). As Greendorfer (2001) stated, the "process of socialization plays a key role in integrating individuals into society by transmitting cultural values and traditions from one generation to the next" (p. 4). Gender socialization is the tendency for boys and girls to be socialized differently. Traditionally, boys are socialized to conform to a male gender role, while girls are socialized to adhere to a female gender role. A *gender role* is a set of attitudes and behaviors expected of a person based on her or his sex (Blackmore, 2003; Greendorfer, 2001). Within North America, boys are expected to be assertive, strong, tough, brave, and independent, while girls are to be submissive, dependent, polite, dainty, and fearful. Gender inappropriate behavior is deemed deviant and those not in compliance are subject to being ostracized and ridiculed for not abiding by societal expectations. Gender role–appropriate behaviors are so ingrained in our culture that they are rarely questioned (Krane, 2001).

Feminism

Feminism carries with it varied meanings and interpretations, and, for many in society, it is a term people fear, reject, or reluctantly adopt. Due to the mediated and mainstream portrayals of feminism that focus on the extreme and threatening, many absorb a stereotypical and inaccurate representation of feminism.

Feminism is a broad social movement that encompasses a variety of perspectives, all of which are under the umbrella of working for women's rights and against female oppression. The beliefs of those who identify as feminists can differ considerably. *Liberal feminism*, which emerged during the women's movement of the 1960s, emphasizes equality. From a liberal perspective, to achieve equality, one must work within the existing system. Liberal feminists "believe in the importance of public law in changing private attitudes; hence they seek to repeal laws that provide differential rights, responsibilities, and opportunities to females and males" (Costa & Guthrie, 1994, p. 236). In the United States, liberal feminism is the most mainstream form of feminism. *Socialist feminism*, also

referred to as *Marxist feminism*, emphasizes that equality cannot be achieved without a complete overhaul of the existing system, particularly from an economic perspective. Socialist feminists argue that fundamental inequalities are built into a capitalist society because power and capital are distributed unevenly. As such, it's not enough for women to individually work to rise to powerful positions in society; rather, power needs to be redistributed throughout society. Whereas liberal feminists focus on individual empowerment, socialist feminists focus on collective change and empowerment. Like socialist feminism, *radical feminism* emphasizes the need for dramatic social change in order to achieve real equality for women. Radical feminists believe that we exist in a patriarchal society, and until patriarchy is transformed at all levels, the system will remain unjust.

bell hooks, a feminist theorist and cultural studies scholar, defined feminism as "a movement to end sexist inequality, sexist exploitation, and oppression" (hooks, 2000, p. viii). Although many think of feminism as a movement that works toward women's equality (to men), hooks (1984) reminds us that gender is not the only identity that shapes one's place and status in society. As she explained,

> Implicit in this definition of women's liberation is a dismissal of race and class as factors that, in conjunction with sexism, determine the extent to which an individual will be discriminated against, exploited, or oppressed.
> (p. 18)

A central aspect of hooks' (1984, 2000) definition of feminism is acknowledging the complexity of oppression and analyzing the intersection of one's varied identities (e.g., race, ethnicity, class, ability, nationality, sexuality), thus allowing for a more accurate picture of women's experiences and realities. Certainly, feminism works toward equality, but equality becomes an arbitrary term when you consider the following: "Which men do women want to be equal to? Do women share a common vision of what equality means?" (hooks, 1984, p. 18).

In addition to studying women's experiences, a feminist approach can also be used to examine the ways in which men's roles in society are constructed and the ways these roles have changed and continue to transform. Although women are in a unique place to critically assess the patriarchal culture due to their marginalized status, men can adopt a feminist (or pro-feminist) approach by acknowledging the injustices faced by women, advocating for the rights of women (and other minorities), and engaging in a radical questioning of men's privileged position (while also acknowledging the complexity of their own identity) (Messner & Sabo, 1990).

A critical component of feminism is *praxis*, a "commitment to work toward ending the oppression" (Kappeler, 1992, p. 382). More than simply understanding the problem, feminism is interested in determining strategies to change or improve the situation. Praxis blends theory and practice together and involves an attempt to bring about progressive change. As Mies (1983) points out, "social change is the starting point of science, and in order to understand the content, form, and consequences of patriarchy, the researcher must be actively involved in the fight against it; one has to change something before it can be understood" (p. 125).

Women's "Herstory" in Sport

For professionals and students in sport and performance psychology it is imperative that we have an understanding of women's "herstory"[1] in sport and physical activity. The more one knows about the social climate of sport for girls and women, the more one will be able to work toward improving their athletic opportunities and experiences. As Gill (2001) stated, "we cannot fully understand the individual without considering the larger world" (p. 366). Understanding the social context is particularly important for feminist work.

Prior to passage of Title IX in 1972, it was not deemed acceptable for a female to participate in athletics due to the societal assumptions surrounding women's perceived frailty and in particular the notion that physical activity might harm the female reproductive system. Although organized sport forms did not exist in the ways we are familiar with today, many women were physically active and involved in athletics prior to Title IX (Priest, 2003).

Title IX of the Educational Amendments of 1972, states "No person in the U.S. shall, on the basis of sex be excluded from participation in, or denied the benefits of, or be subjected to discrimination under any educational program or activity receiving federal aid." To be in compliance with Title IX, an institution must work toward the following: (1) providing opportunities that are proportionate to the student enrollment, (2) expanding opportunities for the underrepresented sex, and (3) working to fully accommodate the athletic interests and abilities of the underrepresented sex (Coakley, 2009). Title IX has significantly helped increase participation opportunities for girls and women in sports. Since passage of Title IX, female high school sport participation has increased by 1000%, and female college participation has increased 574% (Acosta & Carpenter, 2008; The Tucker Center for Research on Girls & Women in Sport, 2007). Despite such increases, however, researchers have found that women and girls continue to confront barriers and stereotypes surrounding their involvement in sport.

A 2007 report by the Tucker Center for Research on Girls and Women in Sport highlighted three important trends in girls' (under age 18) physical activity patterns. First, although girls and women are participating at record high levels in sport at all levels of competition (youth, high school, college and professional), girls' participation has declined in team sports, pick-up play, and multisport activities (National Federation of State High School Associations [NFHS], 2007). Second, girls' participation in moderate to vigorous physical activities has also declined. This decline is especially significant due to the myriad of health benefits (e.g., enhanced cardiovascular endurance, flexibility, and muscular strength; disease prevention; enhanced mental health and self-confidence; and decreased morbidity and premature mortality) associated with such activity. Third, girls have been found to "consistently lag behind boys" in sport participation (The Tucker Center for Research on Girls & Women in Sport, 2007, p. 3). The National Federation of State High School Associations (NFHS) High School Participation Survey reported that 2.95 million girls and 4.21 million boys participated in high school sports (The Tucker Center for Research on Girls & Women in Sport, 2007; NFHS, 2007). Moreover, according to the Women's Sports Foundation, although girls comprise 49.7% of the high school population, they receive only 41.2% of all athletic participation opportunities.

At the college level, females constitute 54% of the college population, whereas female student athletes represent only 45% of the athletic population (Cheslock, 2007). Furthermore, 45% of athletic scholarship dollars and 32% of sport team recruitment dollars are allocated to women's athletics, translating to $166 million and $50 million less than men's athletics, respectively. In their longitudinal study examining the status of women in intercollegiate sport, Acosta and Carpenter (2008) found promising data pertaining to participation rates of female collegiate student athletes. The 2008 data reported the highest ever number of women teams (per school). In 1970, there were only 2.5 women's teams per school; today's (2008) data reveal 8.65 women's teams per school. The status of women coaches, however, remains low, with only 42.8% of women's teams and 2–3% of men's teams coached by a female head coach. Female athletic directors were found to represent only 21.3% of all athletic directors. Furthermore, only 27.3% of head athletic trainers and 11.3% of sports information directors are female (see Acosta & Carpenter, 2008, for complete data). As evident in the data, sport is a gendered institution in which men typically occupy the more powerful positions and women the less powerful ones. It is a context that has long been dominated by men, and there is ample documentation to support the continuing domination of men in positions of power in sport (Acosta & Carpenter, 2008; Cheslock, 2007; NFHS, 2007).

Barriers to Gender Equity

Although the landscape of women's sport has significantly changed, societal barriers, stereotypes, and expectations continue to restrict women's participation and experiences in sport. There are numerous reasons to be cautious when predicting the future trends in sport participation for females (Coakley, 2009).

The threat of being labeled a lesbian has been found to influence female athletes' sport involvement (Coakley, 2009; Griffin, 1998; Krane, 1997). The sport in which a female participates remains a significant determinant as to how she will be portrayed and perceived (by fans, media, peers, etc.) (Kauer & Krane, 2006). Our society maintains a level of discomfort with women's involvement in traditionally "masculine" sports (e.g., rugby, ice hockey, body building, boxing, basketball, football). Involvement in such sports carries with it assumptions and stereotypes regarding a female athlete's sexuality (Kauer & Krane, 2006). These stereotypes serve as a way to control all women by discouraging females from pursuing traditionally "masculine" activities out of fear of being labeled a lesbian (Griffin, 1998).

In addition to characterizing sports as "masculine" and "feminine," many argue that limitations also are placed on female athletes' physicality. For instance, in debates about the inclusion of women's ski jumping in the Olympic Games, Gran Franco Kasper, President of the International Ski Federation and a member of the International Olympic Committee (IOC), suggested that women should not ski jump because it "seems not to be appropriate for ladies

from a medical point of view" (www.time.com/time/nation/article/0,8599,1963447,00.html). Anita DeFrantz, chair of the IOC's Women and Sports Commission described the situation as "a textbook case of discrimination" (www.time.com/time/nation/article/0,8599,1963447,00.html). This case is reminiscent of the 800 m finals in the 1928 Summer Olympics, when several female runners collapsed from fatigue after completing the race; the sight of exhausted women forced officials to restrict women's participation in the 800 m run for 32 years. Such limits and methods of "protection" are placed on female bodies from birth—these restrictions, which persist even today, serve to hinder women's opportunities, physical development, and the perceptions and use of their bodies.

Another roadblock to women's equity in sport is the backlash directed toward Title IX. Critics of Title IX often blame women's sport, female athletes, and in particular Title IX, for the decline (cutting) of men's "minor" sport programs (e.g., wrestling, tennis, track and field, and gymnastics). Cheslock (2007) found that whereas men's collegiate tennis and wrestling experienced declines (1,166 athletes) between 1995 and 2005, men's football, basketball, lacrosse, and soccer grew by more than 7,400 student athletes. Moreover, only Division I-A schools were found to experience declines in men's participation levels. The problem is not that Title IX takes resources away from men's sports, but that resources are misallocated among men's sports. Men's athletics often inequitably distributes resources among men's sports. For example, it was found that 74% of Division I operating budgets are devoted to men's basketball and football, which leaves all other men's sports to compete for the remaining funds. Although the realities and experiences of those male athletes and coaches who have had programs cut should not to be discounted or ignored, the blame should not be directed toward Title IX. Rather, it is due to the disproportionate amount of the budget being directed toward men's basketball and football. Athletic budget decisions—although dictated by a variety of factors—are made by athletic department administrators (Cheslock, 2007; Coakley, 2009).

Gender and Sport

Gender plays a pervasive part in how sport and exercise are experienced (Hasbrook, 1999). The attributes commonly associated with sport—strength, power, dominance, competitiveness, aggression—are socially defined as masculine traits/

qualities. As a result, female participation in sport creates numerous challenges.

Although attitudes toward women and girls participation in sport has improved since passage of Title IX, the ways in which girls and boys are taught to understand and physically use their bodies is quite different. Researchers have found that whereas boys are encouraged to experience and push their bodies and master complex patterns of skill development, girls are socialized to restrict and protect their bodies (Young, 1990). Girls learn early that they should take up less space and refrain from overly physical acts or run the risk of being perceived as less feminine. While boys gain status and popularity as a result of their involvement in sport, girls who are physically aggressive, tough, strong, and/or display an overly competitive persona are often ridiculed, labeled as lesbians, and/or sexually harassed (Griffin, 1998; Krane, 2001; Lenskyj, 1992). Athletic adolescent females are often referred to as "tomboys," a term used to describe a female who engages in socially defined "masculine" activities. Such labeling works to establish sport involvement as an "abnormal"— and anti-feminine—component of female identity (Hall, 1996). It is during adolescence that such gender norms and expectations intensify, which in part explains the decrease in girls' sport participation during adolescence (Fredricks & Eccles, 2002; Hasbrook, 1999; Shakib, 2003).

In addition to the physical health benefits, a myriad of psychological and social benefits also are associated with sport involvement for girls and women. Females involved in sport gain confidence, learn their physical capabilities, have higher states of psychological well-being, develop important relationships, build mental toughness, develop leadership skills, and acquire a sense of satisfaction that comes from setting and working toward goals. Females also enjoy the challenges associated with sport and describe it as an empowering experience. Girls and women who participate in sport also report a more positive body image (The Tucker Center for Research on Girls and Women in Sport, 2007).

The psychological study of gender has significantly evolved over the years. Whereas the initial research in psychology focused on sex differences, the work of Bem (1974, 1978) and Spence and Helmreichs (1978) in the 1970s shifted the focus to studying masculinity, femininity, and gender roles. In the 1980s, another shift pushed researchers to acknowledge the social context. Carolyn Sherif was a strong advocate for the integration of social context into the psychological study of gender (Gill, 1995). Within sport psychology, however, we have historically focused on sex differences, failing to consider the ways in which gender relations are socially constructed. In 1992, Gill argued for the importance of analyzing the social context, suggesting that such an analysis "could advance our overall understanding of gender and sport" (p. 156). Even more recently, in 2001, however, there remained a "slow move beyond isolated studies of sex differences to more complex issues of gender relations" (Gill, 2001, p. 366). As Gill (2001) further explains,

> Despite the pervasiveness and power of gender in sport, and the infinite number of psychological questions we could ask, sport psychology research on gender is limited in all ways…our research questions and methods focus on differences and neglect complex gender issues and relations, and we lack guiding conceptual frameworks to help us understand the complexities of gender in sport and exercise contexts.
>
> (p. 366)

With the emergence of feminist sport psychology, we have seen an increase in the number of studies examining the role of gender in sport and exercise contexts. However, little attention has been directed to the ways in which gender is influenced by race, class, sexuality, and ability (among other identities). As Hall (2001) argued, "one only needs to look at the sport psychology and the feminist sport psychology literature to confirm that feminism and race are only gingerly embraced as a necessary and important variable within sport psychology" (p. 395). To continue moving toward feminist sport psychology, we must "heed the call of the sport studies scholars and consider the many intersections of gender, race, class and other power dynamics" (Gill, 2001, p. 369).

In addition to the historical focus on biologically based sex differences and psychologically based gender differences, the study of gender in sport psychology is often relegated to "special" sections that provide only minor discussion of the topic. As Fisher, Butryn, and Roper (2005) suggested, examination of an introductory sport psychology text provides a clear representation of the constructs (e.g., personality, anxiety, motivation, psychological skills training) considered our primary areas of knowledge and those that are marginal (e.g., gender, race, sexuality, class, ability). As Hall (2001) suggested, "sport psychology books, texts, and journal articles must integrate the social aspects of sport, including race and gender, and allow for more than two pages" (p. 397). Analysis of gender (and race, sexuality, class, ability, nationality, etc.) must be present within research in all areas of sport psychology, including motivation, anxiety, personality, leadership, group dynamics, and so on.

Studying Women's Bodies

The ways in which females experience and view their bodies is an important component in understanding their physical activity and sport behaviors. From a very young age, girls learn—through a variety of socializing agents (e.g., media, peers, family members, toys—Barbie)—the importance of appearance. Today's culture places a tremendous emphasis on the body and physical attractiveness, with specific norms that males and females are expected to model. When girls reach adolescence, the pressure to conform to the ideal feminine body intensifies. A significant amount of research has suggested that women hold inaccurate and negative ideas about their physical appearance, generally viewing themselves as overweight, and hold a desire to become thinner (Cohn & Adler, 1992; Rozin & Fallon, 1985). *Body image* is defined as an individual's perception of and ideas about her or his body (e.g., weight, height, shape). *Social physique anxiety* is defined as the feeling that others are negatively evaluating one's body.

Social physique anxiety has been found to relate to unhealthy eating and exercise behaviors and body dissatisfaction in females (Davis, 1990). Researchers have found that low body image is linked with risky behavior (e.g., eating disorders, disordered eating) among girls (Wild, Flisher, Bhana, & Lombard, 2004). Females in sports that emphasize appearance and body weight show more concern about body weight (Davison, Earnest, & Birch, 2002). However, research has also indicated that before becoming involved in aesthetic sports, their body image did not differ from those not in aesthetic sports (Poudevigne et al., 2003).

Feminist researchers in sport sociology and sport and exercise psychology have advocated for the incorporation of a feminist cultural studies perspective to enhance our understanding of the physically active body (Cole, 1993; Hall, 1996; Krane et al., 2001a). Feminist cultural studies examines the ways in which culture influences our beliefs about gender. As Krane et al. (2001a) suggests, "culture encompasses everything from our eating habits and the clothes we wear, to our conversation styles and daily activities" (p. 117). Masculinity and femininity are connected with one's physical appearance;

"our bodies become the text of femininity or masculinity" (Krane et al., 2001a, p. 117). The ideal feminine body is described by Markula (1995) as a series of contradictions—"firm but shapely, fit but sexy, strong but thin" (p. 424). To achieve the ideal feminine body, which most women never do, women use diet and exercise. In addition, women must constantly survey their bodies for flaws or problems and often engage in unhealthy eating or exercise patterns in an attempt to attain the ideal body (Duncan, 1994). As Krane et al. (2001a) suggested, "Western culture socializes women to monitor their body shapes, strive for the cultural ideal body shape, and engage in self-blame when they do not attain the ideal body" (p. 118).

Female athletes are presented with a number of unique pressures related to their bodies. Research reports that female athletes live in two cultures: a sport culture that is defined as "masculine" and the larger social culture that emphasizes "hegemonic femininity," the "socially privileged form of femininity" (Kauer & Krane, 2006, p. 44; Krane et al., 2004; Krane et al., 2001a). Although the ideal white feminine body is thin and toned, it creates an interesting paradox for the athletic female body that is supposed to be muscular and strong. The conflict between the two has the potential to negatively affect an athlete's self-esteem, health, and self-presentation (Krane et al., 1998). Grounded in feminist cultural studies, Krane et al. (2001c) examined the relationships among body image, eating, and exercise in female exercisers and athletes. Eight female athletes and ten female exercisers were interviewed regarding the ways in which they socially constructed their bodies and how these constructions influenced them psychologically and behaviorally. Both groups of women were very aware of the culturally defined standards of beauty and how their own bodies were measured by such standards. The athletes, although proud of the strength and power of their athletic bodies, expressed less positive self-esteem when talking about their bodies in relation to the larger social context. For example, in settings outside the sport context, the athletes described feeling "too big" or "too muscular." In 2004, Krane, Choi, Baird, Aimar, and Kauer interviewed 21 female collegiate athletes (all Caucasian, all heterosexual) about body image and perceptions of femininity and muscularity. The purpose of the study was to examine how female athletes negotiate and reconcile the social expectations of femininity with their athletic muscularity. Consistent with earlier research (Krane et al., 2001a), the participants indicated that being feminine was in contrast to being athletic; having muscles was considered unfeminine. As such, the participants considered themselves different from "normal girls," with *normal* representing nonathletic females. Their muscularity and athleticism, although acceptable within the sport context, was considered inappropriate outside of sport. Those participants who wore "revealing" uniforms (e.g., swimming, volleyball, distance running) described feeling uncomfortable and concerned about how they looked in their uniforms. The uniforms became a unique source of distress for several of the participants. These series of studies illustrate the challenges female athletes confront as they attempt to negotiate the societal expectations related to their bodies. Such challenges have the potential to lead to such behaviors as negative body image, eating disorders, disordered eating patterns, and low self-esteem. Research suggests that female athletes who feel dissatisfied with their bodies have a higher likelihood that they will engage in negative eating and exercise behaviors (Petrie, 1996). In fact, the eating and exercise behaviors of some of the female athletes in Krane et al.'s study (2001) were found to correspond with the descriptions of subclinical eating behaviors (e.g., distorted body image, weight dissatisfaction, excessive exercise, purging, bingeing) (Petrie, 1993).

Homonegativism in Sport

Heterosexism is defined as "an ideological system that denies, denigrates, and stigmatizes any non-heterosexual form of behavior, identity, relationship or community" (Herek, 1992, p. 89). Heterosexism assumes that everyone is heterosexual (Herek, 1992). The term *homophobia* is used to refer to the irrational fear of individuals who identify as gay, lesbian, bisexual, and transgender (LGBT). In more recent years, however, scholars have shifted to a more comprehensive term—homonegativism—which also incorporates "negative stereotypes, prejudice, and discrimination" against LGBT individuals (Krane, 1997, p. 145).

A significant amount of research has documented the homonegative and heterosexist climate of sport (Griffin, 1998; Krane, 1997; Pronger, 1990; Young, 1995). Within the university context, the athletic department has been described as "the most homophobic place on campus" (Jacobson, 2002, A33). An athletic director quoted in *The NCAA News* stated, "athletics has been the last bastion of homophobia. It's one of the few places left where homophobia is tolerated...the reality is that for many of our gay, lesbian, and bisexual athletes, it's not safe in intercollegiate athletics" (Hawes, 2001, 14). The bias and marginalization LGBT athletes face has been found to occur through a variety of means, including "negative stereotypes, verbal comments and harassment, discrimination in team selection, social isolation, negative media attention, and loss of resources" (Barber & Krane, n.d.).

HOMONEGATIVISM IN WOMEN'S SPORT

Sport has historically been defined as a male domain and, as such, female and male involvement in sport is interpreted quite differently. As previously noted, female participation in sport contradicts stereotypical notions of what it means to be "feminine." Whereas the heterosexist assumption is that people are heterosexual, when a female participates in a stereotypically unfeminine context, her sexuality is questioned. As a result, female athletes often find their sexuality is called into question just because they participate in sport. Kauer and Krane (2006) interviewed college female athletes about the perceived stereotypes surrounding women's sport, how they reacted to such stereotypes, and what strategies they employed to cope with the stereotypes. The findings revealed that the female athletes were commonly stereotyped as lesbians and masculine, with the lesbian stereotype evoking the strongest emotional response. To cope with the stereotypes, the heterosexual athletes described disassociating from their athletic identity (e.g., not wearing team athletic gear outside of the sport context) and emphasizing their heterosexuality (e.g., talking about their boyfriends) and femininity (e.g., wearing make-up, nails done). The lesbian and bisexual athletes described trying to conceal their sexual identity by using vague language, lying about their sexuality, or providing limited personal information. As Griffin (1998) suggested, "a lesbian participating in a hostile climate must be prepared to deny her lesbian identity and act in ways that lead others to believe that she is heterosexual" (p. 94). The fear of being labeled or identified as a lesbian has the potential to intimidate and limit all women in sport (regardless of sexuality) and forces many female athletes to go to extreme lengths to hide their sexuality or prove their heterosexuality (Griffin, 1998; Kauer & Krane, 2006; Krane, 2001). Consistent with Kauer and Krane (2006), female athletes involved in masculine sports use a variety of methods to "feminize" their appearance (e.g., wearing ribbons, wearing pink, growing their hair long; Griffin, 1998). In addition, athletes have been found to engage in sexual activity (with men) as a way in which to prove their heterosexuality (Krane, Surface, & Alexander, 2005). These athletes, especially those who feel compelled to prove their heterosexuality, are particularly vulnerable to sexual harassment (Lenskyj, 1992). Researchers also report that some female athletes will drop out of sport altogether or choose to participate in "feminine" sports to avoid the lesbian label (Griffin, 1998; Shakib, 2003).

Team climate can also be affected by the lesbian label. Researchers have reported that athletes will model the attitudes and behaviors of coaches and their peers. Griffin (1998) outlines three climates for lesbians in sport: hostile, conditionally tolerant, and open and inclusive. Much of the literature has focused on the hostile environments, those that discriminate against lesbians (Griffin, 1998; Krane, 1997). Lesbians in a hostile environment must be especially careful about revealing their identity as severe ramifications often are associated with "coming out" (e.g., reduction of playing time, loss of scholarships, harassment, loss of job). In recent years, however, a growing amount of research has described open and inclusive sport climates (Kauer & Krane, 2006; Roper & Halloran, 2007. For example, in a 2006 CHAMPS Life Skills program evaluation, it was found that 71% of the college athletes surveyed were comfortable having a gay or lesbian teammate, and 57% of the athletes indicated they would speak out against anti-gay slurs within the team setting. Roper and Halloran (2007) surveyed heterosexual male and female student athletes regarding their attitudes toward gay men and lesbians and found that those with contact with openly GLBT individuals held significantly more positive attitudes toward gay men and lesbians. Similarly, Kauer and Krane (2006) reported that exposure to out lesbians within the team setting positively affected the heterosexual athletes' attitudes. These results reflect a changing climate for GLBT athletes.

A female athlete's body and frame also raises issues surrounding sexuality. Female athletes who are muscular are often perceived to be lesbians (Kauer & Krane, 2006). To combat this association, women athletes have been found to engage in unhealthy eating patterns in an attempt to alter their bodies. Krane et al. (2005) reported that female athletes will limit their strength training regimen as a way in which to avoid muscular development. As Krane et al. suggest, avoiding the necessary strength training of a sports program has the potential to increase the risk of injury and limit sport skill development

due to insufficient strength. It becomes clear that the homonegative and heterosexist climate of sport creates an environment in which "female athletes' physical and psychological health may be at greater jeopardy than their peers not faced with such discrimination" (Barber & Krane, n.d.; http://www.aahperd.org/nagws/publications/news/loader.cfm?csModule=security/getfile&pageid=28762). In fact, as Barber and Krane suggest, such sport environments have the potential to "inhibit intrinsic motivation [and] the desire to participate for the enjoyment of the activity" (Barber & Krane, n.d.).

In addition to the work focused specifically on female athletes, researchers have also examined the experiences of lesbian collegiate coaches (Griffin, 1998; Krane & Barber, 2005). Lesbian coaches are confronted with a unique set of issues. In extreme cases, although not uncommonly, lesbian coaches are fired if an athletic director finds out about their sexual identity (Griffin, 1998; Wellman & Blinde, 1997). Coaches' fears associated with public harassment in the media or trouble securing a new coaching position work to silence the coach who has been wrongfully fired. Griffin (1998) outlined a continuum of identity management strategies ranging from "completely closeted" to "publicly out." Most coaches are somewhere in the middle of the continuum (passing as heterosexual, covering their lesbian identity, implicitly out, explicitly out). As a result, "many lesbian coaches are constantly assessing and monitoring how to present themselves depending on who they are with and where they are" (Griffin, 1998, p. 137). Similar to female athletes, some lesbian coaches attempt to pass as heterosexual by emphasizing or constructing a stereotypically heterosexual image (e.g., changing pronouns of significant relationships, having a male escort to events, emphasizing their role as a mother). Although some lesbian coaches are completely out, most who are out still face discrimination, particularly in terms of public support. Krane and Barber (2005) examined the experiences of 13 lesbian intercollegiate coaches. The interview data reveals the various tensions faced by lesbian coaches. All of the coaches were encouraged to remain silent about their identity and expressed fear that, if discovered, they would lose their job. Assistant coaches in the study expressed specific concern regarding professional mobility if their sexuality were disclosed or discovered. As a result of being silenced, the coaches were forced to negotiate multiple identities—being a coach and identifying as a lesbian. To do so, the coaches compartmentalized their lives and rationalized their need to do so. As a result, the lesbian coaches studied were found to develop two separate social identities (Krane & Barber, 2005).

HOMONEGATIVISM IN MEN'S SPORT

For males, sport plays an important role in male social development and is considered to be one of the primary sites for men to demonstrate their dominance and masculinity (Messner, 2002). The hypermasculine sport culture often adheres to the most socially accepted form of masculinity—hegemonic masculinity (Anderson, 2008). Hegemonic masculinity is commonly associated with the attributes found in mainstream, team sport—strength, dominance, aggression, intimidation, and (hyper)heterosexuality (Anderson, 2008). By demonstrating physical and psychological attributes associated with success in athletic contests, boys gain status in most adolescent and preadolescent male groups. Boys who are more artistic, attracted to traditionally "feminine" sport forms, or uninterested in sport, however, are forced to find alternate ways to claim their masculinity or face being labeled gay or effeminate (Anderson, 2008; Messner, 2002). Men's involvement in dance, for example, carries with it various stereotypical assumptions regarding male sexuality. Polasek and Roper (2011) examined the ways in which male ballet and modern dancers negotiated the gay stereotype associated with men's involvement in dance. The dancers were found to employ a variety of methods to challenge the stereotypes associated with men in dance. To combat the pervasive stereotype, several of the dancers, both heterosexual and gay, described working to present an overly "masculine" image when outside of the dance space. The participants described wearing stereotypically masculine clothing (baggy, less fashion conscious), talking about their girlfriends when around strangers, and disconnecting from their career as a dancer (not wearing dance clothing outside the dance space and not talking about their dance career). Several of the gay dancers also described examples of homonegativism within the dance community. For example, there was an assumption within some companies that for a performance between a man and woman to be "believable," a stereotypically "masculine" and "feminine" presentation was necessary. The participants also described companies that actively discriminated against men who were openly gay, some even being known as having a "no gays" policy. These findings, although clearly homonegative, are particularly interesting considering the meaning and significance

of dance—especially ballet and modern—within the gay community (Risner, 2009).

Research addressing the homophobic nature of sport has also consistently noted the especially hostile atmosphere of men's mainstream team sports (i.e., basketball, baseball, football, and hockey; Curry, 1991, 1998; Kimmel & Messner, 2001). Researchers (both within and outside sport) have found that the most extreme homonegativism is often found among tightly knit groups of men, who need both to deny any sexual component to their bonding and who can increase their solidarity by turning violently on minority groups/individuals (i.e., LGBT individuals; Curry, 1991, 1998; Kimmel & Messner, 2001).

INCLUSIVE SPORT ENVIRONMENTS

As an escape from the hetereosexist and homonegative mainstream sport climate, gay-friendly sport spaces began developing in the 1970s and '80s (Young, 1995). Such spaces provide an opportunity for LGBT individuals to socialize with other GLBT individuals and participate in sport in a safe and inclusive environment. Research indicates the importance of having a sense of comfort and community among LGBT individuals (Krane et al., 2002; Roper & Polasek, 2006; van Ingen, 2004). For the individual who identifies as LGBT, finding space where one feels comfortable is rare as individuals learn that most space is heterosexual (and primarily male-dominated) (Griffin, 1998).

The most prominent organized gay sporting event are the Gay Games, an international, Olympic-style event that occurs every 4 years. In contrast to the tenets of mainstream sport, the emphasis of the Gay Games is on inclusion, participation, and personal achievement (Coakley, 2009; Krane, Barber, & McClung, 2002; Young, 1995). Participation in the Gay Games has been described as empowering (Krane & Romont, 1997) and personally transformative (Young, 1995). Lesbians surveyed described feeling valued and having freedom to personally express themselves (Krane et al., 2002). When asked about the primary reasons that they participated in the Gay Games, lesbian and bisexual athletes discussed the significance of being with other LGBT individuals and the strong sense of community (Krane & Romont, 1997).

Social identity theory has been used to study and understand the ways in which gay-friendly sport settings (e.g., the Gay Games, GLBT sport leagues, gay fitness facilities) can promote salient and positive social and personal identity development among gay and lesbian individuals (Krane et al., 2002). Krane, Barber, and McClung (2002) examined the social psychological benefits of participation in the Gay Games. Consistent with previous research examining lesbian and bisexual athletes' motives and experiences at the Gay Games, Krane et al. (2002) found that participation in the Gay Games strengthened their personal identity in a variety of ways, including increased self-esteem and pride in their sexuality and community. The participants also enhanced their collective esteem, evident in the use of "we" when describing their experience—"we are proud," "we're winners—all of us" (p. 36). The participants also noted the importance of learning about the LGB community and indicated an enhanced desire to work toward social change after participating in the Gay Games. Similarly, Roper and Polasek (2006) examined the experiences and perceptions of being a member of a predominately gay fitness facility and found that the LGB members specifically noted the desire to be a member of a predominately gay gym—"I wanted to be around other gay people" (p. 20). In contrast to the mainstream, "straight" facilities, the members described working out at the predominately gay facility as a positive and comforting experience as a LGB individual.

WORKING WITH LGBT POPULATIONS

Although researchers in sport psychology, specifically Vikki Krane and Heather Barber, have conducted research examining the homonegative climate of sport—and specifically lesbians' experiences in sport—little direct application of this knowledge has been connected to applied sport psychology. The one exception is Mark Andersen's (2005) text, *Sport Psychology in Practice*, which included two chapters devoted to working with gay (Martens & Mobley, 2005) and lesbian athletes (Barber & Krane, 2005). Martens and Mobley addressed issues practitioners may confront when working with gay male athletes. Specifically, the authors urged practitioners to have an understanding of the coming out process, an awareness of one's own assumptions and bias associated with LGBT individuals, and an understanding of the ways in which performance may be influenced by the homonegative context of sport (and society). As Martens and Mobley stated, "given the issues that gay athletes must deal with in the world of sport (e.g., contempt for gays, fear of being outed), it is difficult to believe these factors in some way do not affect athletic performance" (p. 252). Framing their chapter from a social identity perspective, Barber and Krane (2005) presented three

consultation scenarios dealing with sexual orientation and incorporated strategies for practitioners working with lesbian, bisexual, and transgender athletes and coaches. Consistent with Martens and Mobley, Barber and Krane assert that sexual orientation is a performance issue that has the potential to influence team climate, psychological readiness (e.g., focus, stress), coach credibility, and coach/athlete satisfaction. Consistent with the tenets of feminist praxis, Barber and Krane note the unique position sport psychology practitioners are in to "challenge the heterosexist norms in women's sport" (p. 266) and "create environments where athletic achievement and positive social growth can occur" (p. 265).

Creating an open and inclusive sport climate requires those in positions of authority (coaches, sport psychology practitioners, team captains, athletic directors/administrators) to make a stand against discrimination toward LGBT individuals. As Barber and Krane (2005) note, "when coaches regard homonegative comments as unacceptable, it sends a strong message, especially to the LGB athletes" (p. 272). Silence does not signify a positive climate. Those in positions of power must actively speak out against discrimination and harassment and use inclusive language (Barber & Krane, 2005; Griffin, 2010). It is important for individuals to work toward becoming an agent of social change rather than an agent of oppression, which involves acknowledging one's unearned privileges and status, and working to eliminate or change privileges into rights that all people enjoy (Adams, Bell, & Griffin, 1997).

Institutional policies also play an important role in establishing an inclusive climate. For example, the National Collegiate Athletics Association (NCAA) recently included sexual orientation in their nondiscrimination policy. A number of resources also are available for sport and performance professionals. *It Takes A Team! Education Campaign for Lesbian, Gay, Bisexual and Transgender Issues in Sport* is an education project sponsored by the Women's Sport Foundation that focuses on "eliminating homophobia as a barrier to all women and men participating in sport." The program provides practical resources for athletic administrators, coaches, parents, and athletes at the high school and college levels to make sport safe and welcoming for all. In early 2011, the Gay Lesbian and Straight Education Network launched *Changing the Game: The GLSEN Sport Project*, an education and advocacy initiative that provides information about best practices for sport professionals on how to make K–12 athletics and physical education safe, respectful, and inclusive for students of all sexual orientations and gender identities (http://sports.glsen.org). Such resources provide valuable and practical information for sport and performance professionals. As Fisher, Butryn, and Roper (2005) suggested, "sport psychology researchers, teachers and consultants have the potential to regulate and prevent discrimination and abuses of power from happening to athletes and even fight on their behalf" (http://www.athleticinsight.com/Vol7Iss3/DiversifyingPoliticizing.htm).

Feminist Sport Psychology

Carole Oglesby's 1978 book, *Women and Sport: From Myth to Reality*, is considered one of the first feminist approaches to women and sport. Her feminist voice in sport psychology has continued to the present day (Oglesby, 1993; Oglesby, 2001a,b; Oglesby & Hill, 1993). Although the field of sport psychology "lacks guiding frameworks and provides few opportunities to engage in [feminist] dialogue" (Gill, 2001, p. 363), those in sport psychology who have taken a feminist perspective have pulled concepts from other disciplines including women's studies, cultural studies, and sport studies. With the exception of Bredemeier's et al. (1991) work on the epistemological perspectives of women who participate in physical activity, there was a "long silence" (Krane, 1994, p. 405) in feminist work in sport psychology between 1978 and 1994. Within the last 20 years, however, feminist work in sport psychology has witnessed "sporadic advances" (Roper, Fisher, & Wrisberg, 2005, p. 34).

In 1994, Krane and Gill each published papers addressing feminist approaches to sport psychology research and practice, respectively. When Martens (1987) and Dewar and Horn (1992) both called for new epistemological perspectives and methodological approaches to sport psychology research, Krane (1994) proposed feminism as an alternative approach to researchers in sport psychology. Feminist research, as Krane suggested, "acknowledges the sexist bias in the knowledge base and reexamines knowledge through the experiences of women...plac[ing] women at the center of analysis, not on the periphery" (p. 397). The participants in feminist research, often referred to as co-participants to reflect the dialectic and reciprocal relationship between the researcher and women (Lather, 1988), are viewed as the experts of their own experiences. Beyond simply describing "the problem," feminist research aims to "challenge the hegemonic practices and asks, what

is it about gender relations in sport and exercise that leads to various inequities?" (Krane, 1994, p. 398). For example, research in sport psychology indicates (and is published in many major sport psychology textbooks) that female athletes report lower levels of confidence than do male athletes (Corbin, Landers, Feltz, & Senior, 1983; Feltz & Petlichkoff, 1983). Such findings have the potential to perpetuate the perception that males are "naturally" better athletes. A feminist analysis would attempt to articulate *why* females underestimate their sport abilities. An understanding of the social context for women is pertinent to the analysis of these research findings. Also, it is important that those in sport psychology examine the measurements used to assess such constructs as confidence. As Krane (1994) noted, "perhaps current measurement instruments do not adequately tap into females' conceptions of constructs such as competitiveness and confidence" (p. 403).

In the same issue of *The Sport Psychologist* and also in *Sport Psychology Interventions* (Murphy, 1995), Gill (1994, 1995) addressed the ways in which sport psychology practitioners may employ a feminist approach to their applied work with athletes, teams, and coaches. Gill urged practitioners to begin by questioning how gender influences their responses, stressing the notion that gender matters. As Gill suggested, "gender influences reactions, expectations, and options a consultant might consider...trying to 'treat everyone the same' does a disservice to the athletes" (1994, p. 413). Recognizing the significance of gender is, as Gill (1994) suggested, the first step in feminist practice. Moving beyond this step involves valuing women's experiences, understanding the social context rather than focusing entirely on the individual, and emphasizing egalitarian relationships (Gill, 1994, 1995; Worrell & Remer, 1992). Emphasizing equalitarian relationships is particularly challenging within the sport context, a hierarchical setting often dominated by rigid power structures (e.g., coach–athlete, athletic director–coach, coach–sport psychology practitioner). A feminist approach to practice would allow practitioners to work toward a more inclusive, safe, and empowering environment for all sport participants.

In 2001, a special issue of *The Sport Psychologist*, edited by Diane Gill, was devoted to feminist sport psychology (In search of feminist sport psychology: Then, now and always). As Ryba (2005) stated, "it is a testimony to the importance and growing influence of feminist work in the field that apart from individual essays, an entire issue of *The Sport Psychologist* was recently devoted to the topic of feminist sport psychology" (www.athleticinsight.com). In this special issue, professionals and students in the field shared their personal feminist journeys and the feminist frameworks that guided their work in sport and exercise psychology. As Gill (2001) noted in the introductory article of the issue, "each author contributes her own insights and interpretations...the variations and differing perspectives are the strength of feminist sport psychology" (p. 364).

Oglesby (2001b) begins the issue with discussion of women's absence in the documented, mainstream histories of sport psychology and highlights the many contributions of feminist women in sport sciences during the formative years of sport psychology (1950–1975) (see Chapter 1, this volume, for further discussion). Ruth Hall addresses the absence of feminist attention to women of color within the sport psychology literature, calling for critical attention to the following three "fundamental issues":(a) white women are not the norm and should not be used to represent all women, (b) race must move beyond mere description; an understanding of the cultures of women of color are what is important, and (c) increased sport opportunities must be made available for women of color. Vikki Krane outlines three feminist perspectives—feminist standpoint, queer theory, and feminist cultural studies—that have guided her extensive research on lesbians in sport and women's bodily experiences (Krane, 1994, 1997, 2001; Krane & Barber, 2002, 2003, 2005 Krane et al. 2001; Krane et al., 2004; see earlier in this chapter for a discussion of her work in these areas). Brenda Bredemeier (2001) outlines the importance of feminist praxis to sport psychology researchers, using her work on moral development as an example of feminist research to practice. Whaley (2001) reviews the complexities of feminist methods and methodologies, highlighting the issues of particular relevance for those in sport and exercise psychology. The feminist perspectives and influences of five students in sport psychology (now all professionals) are also incorporated into the special issue (Greenleaf & Collins, 2001; Roper, 2001; Semerjian & Waldron, 2001). Consistent with the professionals' papers, each student raises important and unique perspectives and questions.

Career Experiences of Women in Sport Psychology

Career opportunities are an important area of discussion within any profession. Such a discussion is of particular relevance to this chapter as the sport setting has a poor record of hiring, promoting, and working toward equal representation in many sport careers—coaching, administration, athletic training, and media relations. Women in each of the aforementioned professions have been found to confront various forms of discrimination, marginalization, and harassment (Acosta & Carpenter, 2008; Depatie, 1997; Gillette, 2000; Theberge, 1993).

Within sport psychology, growing amount of research has been devoted to the career experiences of prominent professionals (Gould, Tammen, Murphy, & May, 1989; Roper, 2008; Roper et al., 2005; Simons & Andersen, 1995; Straub & Hinman, 1992). The majority of the early research in this area focused on male professionals, with little to no attention devoted to the experiences and perceptions of female professionals. Although certainly not independent of one another, it is important to distinguish between *academic* (university setting—teaching, research, service) and *applied* (practitioner—clinical and educational) sport and performance psychology.

In 2002, I questioned whether there existed a gender bias in applied sport psychology. I suggested that whereas women do exist in great numbers within the field of sport psychology, they are often "marginalized, not recognized for their work, and/or tend to work in less visible arenas" (Roper, 2002; p. 55). I addressed the ways in which gender inequality in sport, homonegativism within sport, the lack of prestige women receive within academic circles, and the lack of female role models each impact women's opportunities, status, and experiences working within the applied realm. In 2003, Williams and Scherzer surveyed the training and careers of sport psychology graduates and found no support for a pro-male bias within applied sport psychology. However, Williams and Scherzer found that more females (than males) reported "gender bias" as a frustration to making progress within applied sport psychology.

In 2005, using a feminist standpoint approach, Roper, Fisher, and Wrisberg qualitatively examined the career experiences of female professionals in *academic* sport psychology. Eight professional women (co-participants) in sport psychology were interviewed regarding their experiences as women (one component of their multiple identities) in the field. Feminist standpoint explores the world from the perspective of those who are oppressed and marginalized (Harding, 2004; Hill Collins, 1997) and "begins with the assumption that knowledge is socially situated and that there are multiple 'truths' emanating from the different sociopolitical situations faced by different social groups" (Krane, 2001, p. 402). Feminist standpoint theorists suggest that, in order to understand women's experiences, we must hear from the women themselves (Harding, 2004). The co-participants in this study provided in-depth descriptions of their career development and experiences. Consistent with Gill (1995) and Oglesby (2001), all the co-participants noted the preponderance of male professionals and the subsequent absence of female professionals in the written history of sport psychology. Regardless of the lack of representation, all of the co-participants suggested that there were a sizeable number of female professionals in the field. The specific obstacles the co-participants described confronting were specific to working in academia and not in the field of sport psychology (e.g., unfair hiring practices/job searches, glass ceiling, salary discrepancies, challenges associated with having a family, homophobic academic culture). All of the co-participants identified as feminists and stressed the importance of equality for women (both in sport and academia). The co-participants shared examples of the ways in which their work was feminist, including mentoring women and promoting women' opportunities (as athletes, students, faculty members), establishing the classroom as a feminist space (e.g., diversity of content/readings, collaborative approach rather than hierarchical teaching style, respect for all), and being active in women's organizations on campus. The importance of social networks for women was another important theme. Very often, female academicians understand the isolating nature of academia for women and are therefore willing to provide support and guidance for other women.

As a follow-up to Roper et al. (2005), I (2008) examined the ways in which women's career experiences in *applied* sport psychology were influenced by their gender. Eight professional women in applied sport psychology were interviewed. The participants all held a doctorate in clinical/counseling psychology (6) or sport science (2). At the time the data were collected, the participants worked in a variety of applied settings including in college sport, the United States Olympic Committee, the Canadian Sport Centre, private practice, and in professional men's sports. Consistent with Roper et al. (2005), the participants' personal involvement and interest in sport played a significant role in their decision to pursue a career in sport psychology. As was the case in academic sport psychology, all of the participants acknowledged that the majority of "recognized," high-profile practitioners were male. Due to the overemphasis on male practitioners in the field, several participants suggested that students may be less aware of the work being done by female practitioners. As a result, several of the participants acknowledged the importance of highlighting the work of women consultants at annual conferences. Although several of the participants indicated that their access to many of their applied opportunities developed as a result of "being in the right place at the right time" (p. 416), it was found that male professionals played a significant role in assisting six of the participants gain access to their initial applied opportunities. Certainly, male professionals should work to promote women within the field; however, it is important to consider the privilege male professionals possess that grants them the ability to assist women in gaining access. Moreover, in maintaining such positions of power, "men remain the gatekeepers to entry into advanced sport psychology positions" (Roper, 2008, p. 421). Consistent with Roper et al. (2005), it was also important to several of the participants to nurture and support other women in the field—both students and professionals. Seven of the eight participants described experiencing gender discrimination working in the sport context, which included experiencing sexist language from some male coaches, instances of sexual harassment by male athletes, feeling a need to downplay their appearance, having greater expectations placed upon women, and feeling excluded and isolated as a result of not being "one of the boys" (p. 415).

The findings from each of these studies provide insight into some of the unique experiences and challenges women may encounter when pursuing a career within the field of sport psychology. Although the findings are not generalizable to all women within the field, it is possible that other women may share similar experiences. Future research is needed to examine the gender biases in the field of academic and applied sport psychology and the ways the field might broaden the meaning of "traditional" applied sport psychology (e.g., elite, competitive mainstream sport forms) to include "nontraditional" forms of applied work, such as work with athletes with disabilities, senior-aged participants, youth, and other forms of movements or performance (e.g., dance, music, business). The emergence of social support networks was another important theme that characterized the experiences of the participants in both studies. Further investigation is needed to explore the mentoring process and the needs of female students and professionals, as they may be somewhat different than those of males. Continued attention must be directed toward career opportunities and patterns in the field of sport psychology.

Conclusion

It is clear that gender matters in sport and performance psychology, influencing our attitudes, interpretations, responses, and strategies. However, the field of sport and performance psychology is only beginning to critically examine gender relations in our research and practice. Although there are examples of work being conducted in the field that have employed relational analyses of gender and questioned the power relations imbedded within the sport context, sport and performance professionals continue to ignore gender issues and relations in their work. Researchers are encouraged to use alternative frameworks and paradigms to extend our knowledge base. Employing a feminist approach, for example, "challenges assumptions of traditional scientific research and emphasizes alternative methodologies that incorporate a wider range of methods of inquiry and forms of knowledge" (Gill, 1994, p. 411). It is also important that professionals in the field understand the social context in which they are working in and/or studying. The more one understands the social climate of sport, the more one will be able to work toward improving the opportunities and experiences of all sport participants.

Note

1. "Herstory" is a feminist term used to represent women's experiences and roles, rather than the "his"torical emphasis on men's experiences. As Oglesby (2001) stated, "the published history of sport psychology is precisely 'his story'" (p. 375).

References

Acosta, V., & Carpenter, L. (2008). *Women in sport: A longitudinal, national study.* Retrieved June 2, 2008, from http://www.acostacarpenter.org/

Andersen, M. (2005). *Sport psychology in practice.* Champaign, IL: Human Kinetics.

Adams, M., Bell, L. A., & Griffin, P. (Eds.) (1997). *Teaching for diversity and social justice: A sourcebook.* New York: Routledge.

Anderson, E. (2008). "Being masculine is not about who you sleep with…:" Heterosexual athletes contesting masculinity and the one-time rule of homosexuality. *Sex Roles, 58,* 104–115.

Barber, H., & Krane, V. (n.d.). *Creating inclusive and positive climates in girls' and women's sport: Position statement on homophobia, homonegativism, and heterosexism.* Retrieved from http://www.aahperd.org/nagws/publications/news

Barber, H., & Krane, V. (2005). The elephant in the locker room: Opening the dialogue about sexual orientation on women's sport teams. In M. Andersen (Ed.), *Sport psychology in practice* (pp. 259–279). Champaign, IL: Human Kinetics.

Bem, S. L. (1974). The measurement of psychological androgyny. *Journal of Consulting and Clinical Psychology, 42,* 155–162.

Bem, S. L. (1978). Beyond androgyny: Some presumptuous prescriptions for a liberated sexual identity. In J. Sherman & F. Denmark (Eds.), *Psychology of women: Future directions for research* (pp. 1–23). New York: Psychological Dimensions.

Blackmore, J. E. O. (2003). Children's beliefs about violating gender norms: Boys shouldn't look like girls, and girls shouldn't act like boys. *Sex Roles, 48,* 411–419.

Bredemeier, B., Desertrain, G., Fisher, L., Getty, D., Slocum, N., Stephens, D., & Warren, J. (1991). Epistemological perspectives among women who participate in physical activity. *Journal of Applied Sport Psychology, 3,* 87–107.

Bredemeier, B. (2001). Feminist praxis in sport psychology research. *The Sport Psychologist, 15,* 412–418.

Cheslock, J. (2007). *Who's playing college sports? Trends in participation.* East Meadow, NY: Women's Sport Foundation.

Coakley, J. (2009). *Sports in society: Issues and controversies* (10th ed.). New York: McGraw-Hill.

Cohn, L.D., & Adler, N.E. (1992). Female and male perceptions of ideal body shapes: Distorted views among Caucasian college students. *Psychology of Women Quarterly, 16,* 69–79.

Cole, C. L. (1993). Resisting the canon: Feminist cultural studies, sport, and technologies of the body. *Journal of Sport and Social Issues, 17,* 77–97.

Corbin, C. B., Landers, D., Feltz, D., & Senior, K. (1983). Sex differences in performance estimates. Female lack of confidence versus male boastfulness. *Research Quarterly for Exercise and Sport, 54,* 407–410.

Costa, D. M., & Guthrie, S. R. (1994). Feminist perspectives: Intersections with women and sport. In D. M. Costa & S. R. Guthrie (Eds.), *Women and sport: Interdisplinary perspectives* (pp. 235–252). Champaign, IL: Human Kinetics.

Curry, T. (1991). Fraternal bonding in the locker room: A profeminist analysis of talk about competition and women. *Sociology of Sport Journal, 8,* 119–135.

Curry, T. (1998). Beyond the locker room: Campus bars and college athletes. *Sociology of Sport Journal, 15,* 205–215.

Davis, C. (1990). Body image and weight preoccupation: A comparison between exercising and non-exercising women. *Appetite, 15,* 13–21.

Davison, K., Earnest, D., & Birch, L. (2002). Participation in aesthetic sports and girls' weight concerns at ages 5 and 7 years. *International Journal of Eating Disorders, 31,* 312–317.

Depatie, C. (1997). *Employment equity in Canadian equity newspaper sports journalism: A comparative study of the work experiences of women and men sports reporters.* Unpublished thesis, University of British Columbia.

Dewar, A., & Horn, T. (1992). A critical analysis of knowledge construction in sport psychology. In T. Horn (Ed.), *Advances in sport psychology* (pp. 13–22). Champaign, IL: Human Kinetics.

Duncan, M.C. (1994). The politics of women is body images and practices: Foucault, the panopticon, and *Shape* magazine. *Journal of Sport and Social Issues, 18,* 48–65.

Feltz, D., & Petlichkoff, L. (1983). Perceived competence among intercollegiate sports participants and dropouts. *Canadian Journal of Applied Sport Science, 8,* 231–235.

Fisher, L. A., Butryn, T. M., & Roper, E. A. (2005). Diversifying (and politicizing) sport psychology through cultural studies: A promising perspective revisited. *Athletic Insight, 7*(3).

Fredricks, J. A., & Eccles, J. S. (2002). Children's competence and value beliefs from childhood through adolescence. Growth trajectories in two male sex-typed domains. *Developmental Psychology, 38*, 519–533.

Gill, D. (1992). Gender and sport behavior. In T. S. Horn (Ed.), *Advances in sport psychology* (pp. 143–160). Champaign, IL: Human Kinetics.

Gill, D. (1994). A feminist perspective on sport psychology practice. *The Sport Psychologist, 8*, 411–426.

Gill, D. (1995). Women's history in sport psychology. *The Sport Psychologist, 9*, 418–433.

Gill, D. (2001). Feminist sport psychology: A guide for our journey. *The Sport Psychologist, 15*, 363–372.

Gill, D., & Kamphoff, C. S. (2010). Gender and cultural considerations. In J. Williams (Ed.), *Applied sport psychology: Personal growth to peak performance* (pp. 417–439). Dubuque, IA: McGraw Hill.

Gillette, C. J. (2000). *Perceptions of discrimination in athletic training education programs*. Unpublished thesis, University of Wisconsin.

Gould, D., Tammen, V., Murphy, S., & May, J. (1989). An examination of U.S. Olympic sport psychology consultants and the services they provide. *The Sport Psychologist, 3*, 300–312.

Greendorfer, S. L. (2001). Gender role stereotypes and early childhood socialization. In G. Cohen (Ed.), *Women in sport: Issues and controversies* (pp. 3–23). Oxon Hill, MD: AAHPERD Publications.

Greenleaf, C., & Collins, K. (2001). In search of our place: An experiential look at the struggles of young sport and exercise psychology feminists. *The Sport Psychologist, 15*, 431–437.

Griffin, P. (1998). *Strong women, deep closets: Lesbians and homophobia in sport*. Champaign, IL: Human Kinetics.

Griffin, P. (2010). When gay coaches and athletes come out. Retrieved August 5, 2010, fromhttp://ittakesateam.blogspot.com/2010/05/when-gay-coaches-and-athletes-come-out.html.

Hall, A. (1996). *Feminism and sporting bodies: Essays on theory and practice*. Champaign, IL: Human Kinetics.

Hall, R. (2001). Shaking the foundation: Women of color in sport. *The Sport Psychologist, 15*, 431–437.Harding, S. (2004). *The feminist standpoint theory reader*. London: Routledge.

Hasbrook, C. A. (1999). Young children's social constructions of physicality and gender. In J. Coakley & P. Donnelly (Eds.), *Inside sports* (pp. 7–16). London: Routledge.

Hawes, K. (2001). H—The scarlet letter of sports: More people in athletics say it's time to start talking openly about homophobia. *NCAA news, 38*(21), 13–14.

Herek, G. (1992). The social context of hate crimes: Notes on cultural heterosexism. In G. M. Herek & K. T. Berrill (Eds.), *Hate crimes: Confronting violence against lesbians and gay men* (pp. 89–104). Newbury Park, CA: Sage.

Hill Collins, P. (1997). Comment on Heckman's 'Truth and method: Feminist standpoint theory revisited: Where's the power?' *Signs, 22*, 375–381.

hooks, b. (1984). *Feminist theory: From margin to center*. Boston: South End Press.

hooks, b. (2000). *Feminism is for everybody: Passionate politics*. Cambridge, MA: South End Press.

Jacobson, J. (2002). The loneliest athletes. *Chronicle of Higher Education, 11*(1), A33–A34.

Kappeler, S. (1992). Pornography unmodified. In C. Kramerae & D. Spender (Eds.), *The knowledge explosion: Generations of feminist scholarship* (pp. 379–385). New York: Teachers College Press.

Kauer, K., & Krane, V. (2006). "Scary dykes" and "feminine queens": Stereotypes and female collegiate athletes. *Women in Sport and Physical Activity Journal, 15*, 42–55.

Kimmel, M., & Messner, M. (2001). Boyhood, organized sports and the construction of masculinities. In M. Kimmel & M. Messner (Eds.), *Men's lives*. Boston: Allyn and Bacon.

Krane, V. (1994). A feminist perspective on sport psychology research. *The Sport Psychologist, 8*, 393–410.

Krane, V. (1997). Homonegativism experienced by lesbian collegiate athletes. *Women in Sport and Physical Activity Journal, 6*(1), 141–163.

Krane, V. (2001a). We can be athletic and feminine, but do we want to? Challenging hegemonic femininity in women's sport. *Quest, 53*, 115–133.

Krane, V. (2001b). One lesbian feminist epistemology: Integrating feminist standpoint, queer theory, and feminist cultural studies. *The Sport Psychologist, 15*, 401–411.

Krane, V., & Barber, H. (2003). Lesbian experiences in sport: A social identity perspective, *Quest, 53*, 115–133.

Krane, V., & Barber, H. (2005). Identity tensions in lesbian college coaches. *Research Quarterly for Exercise and Sport, 76*, 67–81.

Krane, V., Barber, H., & McClung, L. (2002). Social psychological benefits of gay games participation: A social identity theory explanation. *Journal of Applied Sport Psychology, 14*, 27–42.

Krane, V., Choi, P., Baird, S., Aimar, C., & Kauer, K. (2004). Living the paradox: Female athletes negotiate femininity and muscularity. *Sex Roles, 50*, 315–329.

Krane, V., & Romont, L. (1997). Female athletes' motives and experiences at the Gay Games. *Journal of Gay, Lesbian, and Bisexual Identities, 2*, 123–138.

Krane, V., Surface, H., & Alexander, L. (2005). Health implications of heterosexism and homonegativism for girls and women in sport. In L. Randall & L. Petlichkoff (Eds.), *Ensuring the health of active and athletic girls and women* (pp. 327–346). Reston, VA: National Association for Girls and Women in Sport.

Krane, V., Waldron, J., Michalenok, J., & Stiles-Shipley, J. (2001c). Body image concerns in female exercisers and athletes: A feminist cultural studies perspective. *Women in Sport and Physical Activity Journal, 17*.

Lather, P. (1988). Feminist perspectives on empowering research methodologies. *Women's Studies International Forum, 11*(6), 569–581.

Lensky, H. (1992). Unsafe at home base: Women's experiences of sexual harassment in university sport and physical education. *Women in Sport and Physical Activity Journal, 1*, 19–33.

Markula, P. (1995). Firm but shapely, fit but sexy, strong but thin: The postmodern aerobicizing female bodies. *Sociology of Sport Journal, 12*, 424–453.

Martens, M. P., & Mobley, M. (2005). Straight guys working with gay guys: Homophobia and sport psychology service delivery. In M. B. Andersen (Ed.), *Sport psychology in practice* (pp. 249–263). Champaign, IL: Human Kinetics.

Martens, R. (1987). Science, knowledge, and sport psychology. *The Sport Psychologist, 1*, 39–55.

Messner, M. A. (2002). *Taking the field: Men and women in sports*. Minneapolis, MN: University of Minnesota Press.

Messner, M., & Sabo, D. (1990). *Sport, men, and the gender order: Critical feminist perspectives*. Champaign, IL: Human Kinetics

Mies, M. (1983). Towards a methodology of feminist research. In G. Bowles & R. D. Klein (Eds.), *Theories of women's studies* (pp. 117–139). London: Routledge & Kegan Paul.

Murphy, S. (1995). *Sport psychology interventions*. Champaign, IL: Human Kinetics.

National Federation of State High School Associations (NFHS). (2007). *2005–2006 NFHS high school athletics participation survey*. Retrieved July 16, 2010, from http://www.nfhs.org/2006/09/participation_in_high_school_sports

Oglesby, C. (1978). *Women and sport: From myth to reality*. Philadelphia: Lea & Febiger.

Oglesby, C. (1993). Changed times or different times—what happened with "women's ways" of sport? *Journal of Physical Education and Recreation, 64*, 60–64.

Oglesby, C. (2001a). Leaving it all on the field: Journeys of growth and change for women and sport. In G. Cohen (Ed.), *Women in sport: Issues and controversies* (2nd ed., pp. 441–444). Oxen Hill, MD: AAHPERD.

Oglesby, C. (2001b). To unearth the legacy. *The Sport Psychologist, 15*, 373–385.

Oglesby, C. A., & Hill, K. L. (1993). Gender and sport. In R. N. Singer, M. Murphy, & L. K. Tennant (Eds.), *Handbook on research in sport psychology* (pp. 718–728). New York: Macmillan.

Petrie, T. (1993). Disordered eating in female collegiate gymnasts: prevalence and personality/attitudinal correlates. *Journal of Sport and Exercise Psychology, 15*, 424–436.

Petrie, T. (1996). Differences between male and female college lean sport athletes, non-lean sport athletes and non-athletes on behavioral and psychological indices of eating disorders. *Journal of Applied Sport Psychology, 8*, 218–230.

Polasek, K. M., & Roper, E. A. (2011). *Negotiating the gay stereotype in men's ballet and modern dance. Research in Dance Education, 12*(2), *173–193*.

Priest, L. (2003). The whole IX yards: The impact of Title IX: The good, the bad and the ugly. *Women in Sport and Physical Activity Journal, 12*, 27–44.

Pronger, B. (1990). *The arena of masculinity: Sports, masculinity, and the meaning of sex*. New York: St. Martins Press.

Poudevigne, M., O'Connor, P., Laing, E., Wilson, A., Modlesky, C., & Lewis, R. (2003). Body images of 4 to 8 year old girls at the outset of their first artistic gymnastic class. *International Journal of Eating Disorders, 34*, 244–250.

Risner, D. (2009). *Stigma and perseverance in the lives of boys who dance: An empirical study of male identities in Western theatrical dance training*. Lewiston, NY: Edwin Mellen Press.

Roper, E. A. (2001). The personal becomes political: Exploring the potential of feminist sport psychology. *The Sport Psychologist, 15*, 445–449.

Roper, E. A. (2002). Women working in applied sport psychology: Examining the gender bias in the applied domain. *Journal of Applied Sport Psychology, 14*, 53–66.

Roper, E. A. (2008). Career experiences of women working in applied sport psychology. *Journal of Applied Sport Psychology, 19*, 32–50.

Roper, E. A., Fisher, L. A., & Wrisberg, C. (2005). Women's career experiences in sport psychology: A feminist standpoint approach. *The Sport Psychologist, 19*, 32–50.

Roper, E. A., & Halloran, E. (2007). Attitudes toward gay men and lesbians among heterosexual male and female student-athletes. *Sex Roles, 57*, 919–928.

Roper, E. A., & Polasek, K. M. (2006). Negotiating the space of a predominately gay fitness facility. *Women in Sport and Physical Activity Journal, 15*(1), 14–27.

Rozin, P., & Fallon, A. E. (1985). Sex differences in perceptions of desirable body shape. *Journal of Abnormal Psychology, 94*,102–105.

Ryba, T. (2005). Sport psychology as cultural praxis: Future trajectories and current possibilities. *Athletic Insight, 7*(3). Retrieved from www.athleticinsight.com

Semerjian, T., & Waldron, J. (2001). The journey through feminism: Theory, research and dilemmas from the field. *The Sport Psychologist, 15*, 438–444.

Shakib, S. (2003). Female basketball participation. *American Behavioral Scientist, 46*, 1405–1422.

Simons, J., & Andersen, M. (1995). The development of consulting practice in applied sport psychology: Some personal perspectives. *The Sport Psychologist, 9*, 449–468.

Spence, J. T., & Helmreichs, R. L. (1978). *Masculinity and femininity*. Austin, TX: University of Texas Press.

Straub, W., & Hinman, D. (1992). Profiles and professional perspectives of 10 leading sport psychologists. *The Sport Psychologist, 6*, 297–312.

Theberge, N. (1993). The construction of gender in sport: Women, coaching, and the naturalization of difference. *Social Problems, 40*, 301–313.

The Tucker Center for Research on Girls & Women in Sport. (2007). *Executive Summary. The 2007 Tucker Center Research Report, Developing physically active girls: An evidence-based multidisciplinary approach*. University of Minnesota, Minneapolis.

van Ingen, C. (2004). Therapeutic landscapes and the regulated body in the Toronto Front runners. *Sociology of Sport Journal, 21*, 253–269.

Wellman, S., & Blinde, E. (1997). Homophobia in women's intercollegiate basketball: Views of women coaches regarding coaching careers and recruitment of athletes. *Women in Sport and Physical Activity Journal, 6*(2), 63–73.

Whaley, D. (2001). Feminist methods and methodologies in sport and exercise psychology: Issues of identity and difference. *The Sport Psychologist, 15*, 419–430

Wild, L., Flisher, A., Bhana, A., & Lombard, C. (2004). Associations among adolescent risk behaviors and self-esteem in six domains. *Journal of Child Psychology and Psychiatry, 45*, 1454–1467.

Williams, J. M., & Scherzer, C. B. (2003). Tracking the training and careers of graduates of advanced degree programs in sport psychology, 1994 to 1999. *Journal of Applied Sport Psychology, 15*, 335–353.

Worrell, J., & Remer, P. (1992). *Feminist perspectives in therapy: An empowerment model for women*. Chichester, UK: Wiley.

Young, I. M. (1990). *Throwing like a girl and other essays in feminist philosophy and social theory*. Bloomington, IN: Indiana University Press.

Young, P. (1995). *Lesbians and gays and sports*. New York: Chelsea House.

Relationships and Sport and Performance

Sam Carr

Abstract

Human relationships play a fundamental role in shaping our psychological experiences. In sport and performance, researchers are beginning to recognize the significance of relationships with regards to the development of an array of contextual psychological responses, and it is becoming clear that the study of relationships in the context of human performance is worthy of attention. In this chapter, I briefly review the sport and performance literature that has explored athlete and performer relationships with peers, coaches, parents, and sport psychologists; and offer some conceptual pathways that can serve to further develop this important research area as it unfolds in sport and performance psychology. Specifically, I forward sets of ideas from attachment theory, transference, and actor–partner models as particularly useful frameworks within which to examine the sport relationship literature and attempt to illustrate where I see these ideas directing the sport and performance domains.

Key Words: Relationships, sport, performance, attachment, coaches, peers, parents

The psychiatrist Harry Sullivan, whose work laid the foundation for the field of interpersonal psychoanalysis, recognized the importance and inevitability of interpersonal relationships in human life. Specifically, he outlined how the field of psychology "*is* the field of interpersonal relations…a personality can never be isolated from the complex of interpersonal relations in which the person lives and has his being" (Sullivan, 1940, p. 10). For Sullivan, human beings have a fundamental *need* for interpersonal relations, and nothing is a more significant determinant of psychological well-being and quality of experience than the nature of our connections to the people around us. Indeed, the centrality of human relationships has been a defining feature of the works of numerous significant thinkers in psychology, such as Sigmund Freud, John Bowlby, Harry Harlow, Alfred Kinsey, and Melanie Klein.

By virtue of the fact that sport is often a microcosm of broader human existence, interpersonal relationships in sport are of critical import with regards to psychological functioning within sport and wider experiences of life itself. As such, calls have been made to recognize the significance of interpersonal relationship research within the sporting literature (e.g., Carr, 2009a; Jowett & Wylleman, 2006; Poczwardowski, Barott, & Jowett, 2006; Smith, 2003; Wylleman, 2000). Jowett and Wylleman (2006) have identified that sport researchers "are fortunate enough to have at our disposal such a large array of psychological theories about interpersonal relationships, their application in understanding relationships in sport and exercise would be paramount and could in turn bring about insights to the broader social psychological phenomena" (p. 122). In this chapter, I seek to provide an insight into the array of social relationship research that has been conducted in the field of sport and performance. The predominant aims of the chapter are to review and critique existing research on relationships, sport, and performance; and to highlight avenues for future research that can serve to further develop existing lines of enquiry in sport and performance. I begin by briefly reviewing existing research in sport social relationships, organizing my review around some of the major relationships that have been investigated by sport and performance psychologists. It is beyond the scope of this chapter to provide a complete review of the literature relating to each of these social relationships in sport (e.g., peers, coaches, parents, sport psychologists). Here, I seek simply to provide readers with an insight into the array of underpinning conceptual ideas, research questions, and methodological approaches that serve to highlight the complexity inherent in the investigation of sport relationships.

Peer Relationship Research in Sport and Performance

Peer Relationship Research in Sport

Weiss and her colleagues (e.g., Weiss, Smith, & Theeboom, 1996; Weiss & Smith, 1999, 2002; Smith, 2003) have recognized that youngsters' relationships with peers in sport-related contexts merit research attention. They have suggested that "the sport context is riddled with examples of peer interactions that impinge upon children's enjoyment and attraction to physical activity.... These include the social context surrounding arguments among or negative treatment from peers...and feelings of self-worth that emanate from peer evaluation" (Weiss et al., 1996, p. 348). However, studies targeting peer relationships in children and adolescents have conceptualized the issue in a variety of ways, referring to peer acceptance; the perceived quality of mutual, dyadic friendships involving a degree of affection; and levels of general popularity within a broader circle of peers to whom affective ties are not as strong (Newcomb & Bagwell, 1995). The perceived quality of *dyadic friendships* has been a particularly useful way of looking at peer relationships in the context of sport, specifically focusing on features of dyadic bonds that might be seen as indicators of relationship quality (such as the level of support, companionship, or conflict). Research in developmental contexts has consistently identified such friendship quality as a critical determinant of a variety of important variables, such as overall satisfaction with peer relationships, contextual emotional responses, peer acceptance and rejection, enhanced

motivation, behavioral difficulties, and enhanced achievement (e.g., Coie & Cillessen, 1993; Hartup, 1989; Ladd, 1999; Newcomb & Bagwell, 1995; Parker & Asher, 1993; Parker & Gottman, 1989). Accordingly, Weiss and her colleagues saw a need to explore the specific aspects of friendship quality that are pertinent to youth sport participation.

Weiss and Smith (1999) conceptualized six major dimensions of friendship quality in youth sport: companionship, emotional support, loyalty and intimacy, similarity, conflict resolution, and experiences of conflict, reflecting the main aspects by which youth sport friendship quality tends to be experienced. They developed and validated the Sport Friendship Quality Scale (SFQS; Weiss & Smith, 1999) to assess youngsters' perceptions of these friendship dimensions in their peer relationships in sport. The SFQS is a self-report measure that reflects children's perceptions of relationship quality experienced with a nominated best friend in sport. The work of Weiss and colleagues has stimulated research that has sought to demonstrate that the perceived dimensions of friendship quality tapped by the SFQS have important implications for cognitive, affective, and behavioral outcomes in the context of youth sport. Weiss and Smith (2002) identified that youngsters' perceptions of *ability to resolve conflict* and *companionship* with a nominated best friend in tennis were positively associated with their commitment and enjoyment of the sport. Similarly, Ullrich-French and Smith (2006) also showed that perceptions of positive dimensions of friendship quality from the SFQS were positively associated with enjoyment and levels of self-determined motivation in youth soccer. Furthermore, Ullrich-French and Smith (2009) identified that the likelihood of children remaining involved in soccer was significantly predicted by the perceived positive soccer friendship quality they had reported a year earlier, with those reporting more positive friendship dimensions being more likely to have continued their involvement.

The SFQS is therefore proving a popular and useful assessment of children's self-reports of the quality of friendship relations. However, there are still important points for researchers to consider when employing such tools. For example, the inventory requires children to make judgments about a nominated "best friend" in a sporting context. There may be little opportunity to check the validity or reciprocation of friendship for a child's nominated "best friend," and researchers should be cautious that the inventory could, at times, be more reflective of children's projected fantasies and wishes with regards to a nominated individual than of genuine friend-ship (Carr, 2009a). For example, in a recent study, I (Carr, 2009b) identified that the "best sporting friend" children had nominated and rated accord-ing to the SFQS was reciprocated (i.e., the best friend children had nominated had also nominated them) in 57% of cases. Although it is not necessar-ily the case that SFQS best friend ratings are only meaningful when both friends have nominated each other (e.g., it is feasible that child A may nominate child B as their "best friend" and not be nominated as child B's "best friend," yet the pair might still enjoy a close friendship that renders child A's SFQS ratings "worth examining"), it is worth considering that a nonreciprocal friendship dyad may in certain cases hold less significance as an antecedent or out-come variable. In my (Carr, 2009b) investigation, children's perceived friendship quality in *reciprocal* friendship dyads was significantly related to the characteristics of the attachment bonds children shared with their parents. However, this was not the case for perceived friendship quality in *nonreciprocal* dyads. This is potential evidence that only recipro-cated relationships were close enough for children's deeper attachment relationships with their parents to infiltrate the friendship experience.

The research reported above also reflects a ten-dency (Smith, 2003) to focus on individuals' reports of the friendship quality they experience with a nominated "best friend," paying particular atten-tion to individual perceptions of a single dyadic relationship. However, in an insightful review on the nature of the research on peer relationships in sport and physical activity, Smith (2003) has rec-ognized that it is also important to note that youth sport friendship can be examined on different levels of social complexity. For example, researchers might examine individual, relationship, or group perspec-tives, focusing on how individuals interact within a single, significant dyad or on their role in the con-text of a larger group. Furthermore, beyond indi-vidual perceptions of friendship quality, significant avenues of research are related to issues such as the role of athletic competence and physical appear-ance as factors that enhance or inhibit the devel-opment and quality of peer relationships in sport (e.g., Chase & Dummer, 1992; Evans & Roberts, 1987; Weiss & Duncan, 1992). Initial findings in this area have suggested that lack of athletic ability and physical appearance may be significant barriers to social status and opportunity, with lower ability children being significantly less likely to be afforded the opportunity to occupy central roles in physical

activity, to develop their motor competence, and to be accepted socially (see Smith, 2003, for a more thorough review).

Peer Relationship Research in Performance Contexts

Some significant investigations also shed light on aspects of peer relations in other performance con-texts. In the context of professional dance, Bailey and Oberschneider (1997) focused upon the issue of sexuality and friendship formation among pro-fessional dancers. In an environment in which the proportion of homosexual men is generally reported to be significantly higher (Bailey & Oberschneider, 1997; Billy, Tanfer, Grady, & Klepinger, 1993; Gebhard, 1972) than societal norms, the research-ers were interested in the experiences of dancers in relation to friendship formation as a consequence of homosexual population characteristics. They sug-gested that "professional dance is a useful laboratory to study interactions between gay and heterosexual dancers, as well as how dancers cope with any result-ing conflict and tension" (Bailey & Oberschneider, 1997, p. 443). Results identified interesting issues related to social relationships, including the fact that a sizeable minority of heterosexual male dancers suggested that it was often difficult for them to form friendships with homosexual dancers due to ten-sions with relationship boundaries. They reported being "assumed to be gay" or "being propositioned" as factors that made it difficult for them to form friendships with homosexual dancers comparable with their heterosexual friendships. Additionally, the vast majority of female dancers indicated that they found it "significantly easier" to form friendships with homosexual male dancers than with hetero-sexual dancers. Such findings raise interesting ques-tions about issues such as the role of sexuality in the formation of adult friendships (e.g., to what extent are the boundaries between sexual relationships and platonic friendships "blurred" or "tensioned" as a simple function of sexual orientation compatibility within the dyad?) and highlight dance as a poten-tially useful context in which to learn more about these features of human relationships.

Patrick et al. (1999) examined the role of peer relationships with regards to adolescents' contin-ued involvement in domains in which they had been identified as particularly talented. The study addressed this purpose in a sample of adolescents who were involved in a variety of performance con-texts, including sport, music, dance, drama, and art. An additional purpose of the investigation was to examine contextual differences between the various performance contexts. First, results supported the notion that adolescents' peer relationships served a significant motivational function in helping them to maintain their commitment to and involvement in their area of talent. Furthermore, when adolescents did not believe that the context afforded them the opportunity to make friendships and meet their social goals, they were inclined to decrease interest and commitment. Second, although there were no clear differences identified between the various performance domains, there were interesting differences between talent activities that were cited as "school-based" (i.e., sport teams, band, choir) and "non-school-based" (i.e., dance and piano). Specifically, adolescents involved in talent contexts that were not developed and conducted within a school-based setting were more likely to see themselves as facing a choice between continued involvement in their talent activity and an attractive social life. For school-based activities, this was less of a concern as adolescents felt that the relationships that formed a critical part of their social life could be simultaneously maintained while developing their talents. Such findings raise interesting issues related to the role of certain non–school-based performance contexts with regards to inhibiting the maintenance of peer relationships in young people.

Coach–Athlete Relationship Research in Sport

Poczwardowski et al. (2006) have suggested that another fruitful area of research in sport social relationships is the coach–athlete dyad. Research in this area (e.g., Jowett & Cockerill, 2003; Poczwardowski, Barott, & Henschen, 2002; Wylleman, 2000) has forwarded coach–athlete dyadic relationships as a central influence on the quality of both coaches' and athletes' experiences and sporting performance. Jowett (Jowett, 2003; Jowett & Clark-Carter, 2006; Jowett & Cockerill, 2002, 2003; Jowett & Meek, 2000; Jowett & Ntoumanis, 2004) has recognized the importance of a number of critical interpersonal relationship characteristics in the coach–athlete dyad. Her "3 Cs" model (see, for example, Jowett & Cockerill, 2002; Jowett, 2003), integrating ideas from dyadic relationship models (e.g., Berscheid, Snyder, & Omoto, 1989; Kiesler, 1997; Newcomb, 1953), has identified the higher order factors of *closeness* (including polar dimensions of *closeness* such as feelings of trust/distrust in the other, a liking/disliking of the other, feelings of attachment/isolation, feelings of respect/disrespect, and

emotional closeness/emotional distance), *coorientation* (including communicational dimensions such as self-disclosure, information exchange, shared understanding, acceptance, and connection/disconnection), and *complementarity* (including behavioral interactions such as helping transactions, instructional or emotional support, and power balance) as a fundamental way of conceptualizing coach–athlete dyadic relations. There have been significant developments (e.g., the Coach-Athlete Relationship-Questionnaire; CART-Q; Jowett & Ntoumanis, 2003, 2004) in terms of the provision of a quantitative measure of the quality of the coach–athlete dyad. Specifically, the CART-Q was developed as a self-report instrument assessing coaches' and athletes' perceptions of the quality of closeness, commitment (commitment replaced coorientation in the development of the instrument and reflects both parties' intentions to maintain their athletic relationship), and complementarity that are experienced in the coach–athlete dyad.

The coach–athlete relationship research has been particularly mindful of the fact that "a relationship does not reside within the individual but is a product and process shared by two people" (Jowett & Wylleman, 2006, p. 121) and has tended to advocate a dyadic approach to studying coach–athlete relationships, recognizing the manner in which both parties reciprocally influence each other. Much of the earlier reviewed research on peer relationships has tended to focus heavily upon the individual unit of analysis by utilizing *individuals'* self-reports of the relationship (e.g., "My friend and I can talk about anything") as the sole measure of relationship quality. Jowett's work has extended this analysis beyond individual perceptions.[1] For example, Jowett and Chaundy (2004) employed the CART-Q to assess athletes' self-perceptions *and* meta-perceptions of their relationship with their coach. The concepts of self-perceptions and meta-perceptions were borrowed from the social psychological literature (e.g., Laing, Phillipson, & Lee, 1966). Self-perceptions referred to an individual's direct perceptions toward the other in the relationship (e.g., "I trust my coach"). Meta-perceptions reflected inferences about the other's perceptions toward the self (e.g., "I think my coach trusts me"). Jowett and Chaundy (2004) sought to examine how athletes' self- and meta-perceptions (in addition to reports of coaches' leadership behaviors) related to levels of task and social cohesion. Results revealed that only self-perceptions of coach–athlete relationships had a unique predictive influence on task cohesion.

Beyond the 3Cs model, Lorimer and Jowett (2009) recently examined the empathic accuracy of coach–athlete dyads from a selection of team and individual sports. The study was grounded on the assumption that getting empathically alongside athletes and understanding "what makes them tick" is often cited as one of the most critical elements of the coaching process (Jones & Cassidy, 2004; Jones, Armour, & Potrac, 2004). Lorimer and Jowett (2009) video recorded the unstructured dyadic interactions between coach–athlete dyads over the course of a typical training session and asked members of each dyad to independently report on what both they and their partner had been thinking and feeling during the array of interactions that had taken place. Interesting findings included the fact that coaches of athletes in individual sports were more empathically accurate in their perceptions of athletes' thoughts and feelings than were coaches of athletes in team sports. Furthermore, increased length of training sessions was also found to increase coaches' sense of empathic accuracy with regards to their athletes. Such findings raise interesting points for discussion in relation to factors that would appear to enhance and inhibit coaches being able to develop an empathic understanding of athletes, suggesting that issues such as the team/individual nature of the sport and the amount of time athletes and coaches are able to spend together can play an important role in developing key relationship features that may have a critical influence on performance and well-being.

Parental Relationship in Sport and Performance
Research on Parental Influences in Sport and Physical Activity

Due to the fact that relationships with parents are likely to form the bulk of many children's socialization experiences (i.e., most children will likely spend significant proportions of their time in the company of parents prior to the onset of adolescence) (Brustad, 1993; Greendorfer, 1992), it is unsurprising that researchers have devoted attention to parental relationships in the contexts of sport and physical activity. Parental influence has been explored in the sporting literature in a number of ways. First, there have been investigations exploring a *role modeling* hypothesis, suggesting that children *reproduce* their parents' sport and physical activity behaviors via mechanisms central to social learning (e.g., Bandura, 1986). Support for this hypothesis has been mixed, with some studies supporting a correlation between parent and child levels of physical activity (e.g., Bois, Sarrazin, Brustad, Cury, & Trouilloud, 2005; Freedson & Evenson, 1991; Moore et al., 1991) and others providing no support (Brustad, 1993; Dempsey, Kimiecik, & Horn, 1993; Jago, Fox, Page, Brockman, & Thompson, 2010; Kimiecik & Horn, 1998). Bois et al. (2005) have suggested that much of the inconsistency in the literature can be attributed to methodological differences between studies (e.g., studies have relied upon objective activity data, children's self-reports, and parents' self-reports as indicators of activity levels). Gustafson and Rhodes (2006) reviewed 24 studies investigating the parental role modeling hypothesis and found that in 18 studies the methods used were not objective measures of child and parent physical activity and that in 12 studies the methods employed did not even report the validity of physical activity assessment methods employed. They, therefore, concluded that definitive conclusions are difficult to draw from the research in this area. This is not only due to the methodological differences outlined above but also to a reliance on samples limited to North American Caucasians, who are not representative of the population in terms of socioeconomic status or ethnicity (Gustafson & Rhodes, 2006). Even some of the most recent studies have failed to provide support for the role modeling hypothesis. Jago et al. (2010) studied 986 10-year-old children and their parents in the United Kingdom and found no association between accelerometer data from children and parents. Again, this may be a reflection of the developmental status of the sample (it may be that at 10 years, the development of independence and quest for individuation make an association less likely than in a younger sample). It is clear that the complex issues that need to be considered to address a hypothesis such as parental role modeling in children's sport and physical activity have yet to be adequately addressed, and future research is needed to further advance knowledge in this area.

Additional explanations exist for the lack of a consistently identified association between the physical activity levels of young people and their parents. One explanation that has been forwarded is the suggestion that role modeling in relation to physical activity is perhaps dependent upon the specific quality of the parental relationship in question. From this perspective, it is unwise to assume that because a relationship is parental it will necessarily follow that youngsters will be inclined to model the physical activity or health-related behaviors of the significant other. For example, Vilhjalmsson and Thorlindsson's (1998) study of over 1,000 Icelandic adolescents suggested that role modeling in relation to physical activity behavior was dependent upon the degree of emotional closeness that adolescents reported with the relationship referent concerned. Specifically, adolescents' physical activity behavior was more likely to correlate with a significant other when they reported a higher degree of emotional closeness to that other. Foshee and Bauman (1992) identified that for adolescents' with a parent who smokes, smoking behavior increases as felt emotional attachment to that parent increases, whereas for adolescents with a parent who does not smoke, smoking decreases as felt emotional attachment increases. In short, role modeling of health behaviors in adolescents was more likely when the relationship between the parties was an emotionally close attachment. Such findings support Bandura's (Bandura & Walters, 1963) initial predictions that modeling is likely to be dependent upon the quality of the relationship within which it takes place.

Other avenues of research have focused upon the manner in which parental *belief systems* are linked to children's experiences of and involvement in sport and physical activity (e.g., Eccles, Wigfield, & Schiefele, 1998; Fredricks & Eccles, 2004). From this perspective, the beliefs that parents hold in relation to children's (and to their own) sport and physical activity involvement are likely to be linked to children's experiences and psychological responses. Research that has addressed questions allied to this school of thought has provided evidence that parents' perceptions of their child's competence in sport are related to the child's perceived physical competence (e.g., Babkes & Weiss, 1999; Bois et al., 2005, Bois, Sarrazin, Brustad, Trouilloud, & Curry, 2002; Felson & Reed, 1986); that children's perceptions of the motivational climate emphasized by parents in sport are related to their achievement goals, levels of intrinsic motivation, and experiences of sport anxiety (e.g., Carr & Weigand, 2001; Carr, Weigand, & Hussey, 1999; Carr, Weigand, & Jones, 2001; White, 1996, 1998); and that children's perceptions of their parents' beliefs about the causes of success in sport are related to their personal goal orientations and own beliefs about sport success (e.g., White, Kavussanu, Tank, & Wingate, 2004). Such findings suggest that parental beliefs in relation to children's sport involvement are "felt" by children and play a role in the development of children's own contextual cognition, affect, and behavior.

Parent–Child Attachment

Although the study of relationships often adopts a focus on the characteristics of dyadic relationships that individuals experience in the *present*, there is also much to be gained from considering the lingering influence of significant relationships from the *past*. Classic ideas from psychodynamic, clinical, and developmental psychology (e.g., Ainsworth, Blehar, Waters, & Wall, 1978; Bowlby, 1969/1982, 1988; Freud, 1895, 1900, 1905, 1925) have stimulated large bodies of literature in support of the notion that the quality of early significant relationships plays an important role in how later relationships are "played out." In my own research on parent–child relationships (e.g., Carr, 2009a,b, 2011; Carr & Fitzpatrick, 2011), I have tried to view parental influence on sport-related experiences through these alternative lenses. In attachment theory, John Bowlby (1973) hypothesized that the internal working models of attachment children construct as a consequence of initial attachment relationships (typically with parents) will serve to organize future patterns of cognition, affect, and behavior. Bodies of attachment literature (e.g., George, Kaplan, & Main, 1984–1996; Main, Kaplan, & Cassidy, 1985; Main & Goldwyn, 1998) therefore afford particular importance to childhood relationships with parents in regulating adolescent and adult states of mind in relation to attachment. This is a conceptual reflection of the evolutionary importance of the parent–child relationship (Bowlby, 1969/1982). In the psychodynamic literature, Pincus, Freeman, and Modell (2007) have argued that,

> The human infant's immaturity at birth and extensive dependency on caregivers cannot be underestimated. Humans create ("find") themselves through others, and this cannot be more clearly seen than in human infancy: For an infant to become a self, he or she is dynamically constituted, to a profound extent, through others. A psychological "self" is shaped out from an immersion with others. Infant studies have documented the degree of this immersion. (p. 635)

Initial attachment experiences with parental caregivers play a significant role in "carving out" an internal psychological template that serves as a cognitive map for relevant cognition, affect, and behavior in the future.

In my own research, I sought to explore the significance of the parent–child attachment bond in regulating psychological experiences of sport. I hypothesized that adolescents' attachment relationships with key parental caregivers reflect the nature of internal working models that may function as a psychological template during the construction of new, close relationships in sport (Carr, 2009b). For example, insecure children may develop a self-protective distancing strategy with caregivers in order to avoid dealing with the rejection and unavailability that they perceive as a likely occurrence. Subsequently, such children seek less intimacy, proximity, and social support from peer relationships, in line with the framework of emotional responses to close relationships that they have developed in the context of the parental bond (Weimer, Kerns, & Oldenburg, 2004). In support of these predictions, an initial investigation (Carr, 2009b) identified that adolescents' self-reported levels of attachment security in relation to a nominated key caregiver significantly predicted their reports of sporting friendship quality with a nominated best friend. Features of attachment security with a key caregiver were positively related to a number of the features of positive sport friendship quality outlined in the SFQS. This suggests that attachment theory may also provide a useful framework within which to explore the specifics of parental influence in relation to psychological experiences of sport.

Parental Research in Performance Contexts

There have also been interesting studies relating to parent–child relationships in performance contexts other than sport. For example, Rapport and Meleen (1998) examined the recollections of parent–child bonds in a sample of adults who had shown early talent in the field of screen acting and had been considered "child celebrities" between the ages of 6 months and 18 years. Of particular interest in this study was the nature of the self-reported parent–child relationship in child celebrities whose parents had also served as the child's manager. Data suggested that former child performers whose parents (it was almost exclusively mothers who had fulfilled this role in the investigated sample) had served as their professional manager viewed the parental figure as less caring and more controlling than did performers whose caregivers were not their managers. The researchers argued that their data hint that the inherent *role* of managing a child celebrity may conflict with many of the fundamental aspects of caregiving typically associated with the parent–child relationship. For example, "managing" a child performer may require parents to adopt a more emotionally distant and objective perception of the child (e.g., in the managerial role, perhaps

the child is viewed as a "source of income" or as "the means to an end") that is incompatible with features of a caring and secure parental bond. Some of these conflicts related to parental roles have also been identified in parent–coach/child–athlete dyads in the context of sport (e.g., Weiss & Fretwell, 2005). However, studies in sport have also identified that children and parents report many positive issues to such dyadic relationships too.

Sport Psychologist–Athlete Relationships

Numerous fields of psychology have highlighted the therapeutic relationship as a critical element of the work that practicing psychologists are engaged in. Freud argued that a positive attachment between client and analyst was essential in helping the client to develop a sense of self-belief and confidence to deal with the painful emergence of traumatic experiences that arise during psychoanalysis (Horvath, 2000). In Carl Roger's (1951) seminal book, *Client-Centred Therapy*, a theoretical argument was developed proposing that it was the relationship that therapists provide, rather than the techniques they apply, that was largely responsible for the very effectiveness of therapy itself. Given the centrality of the psychologist–client relationship in other domains of psychology, coupled with the increasing body of knowledge in support of the importance of athletes' relationships in the context of sport, it is perhaps surprising that the sport psychologist–athlete relationship has been given relatively little attention in the literature. Andersen's (e.g., Andersen, 2000; Stevens & Andersen, 2007a,b) work has provided some of the most illuminating insights into some of the important issues that arise in the sport psychologist–athlete relationship. He (Andersen, 2000) has outlined how some of the central ideas from psychodynamic approaches to psychology have formed the core of much of his applied work as a sport psychologist. From this perspective, he has outlined how,

> [T]he core of psychodynamic theory outlines how past patterns of relationships with significant others have a profound impact on current functioning...past conflicts are likely to play themselves out with current authority figures (e.g., coaches, teachers, sport psychologists). (*Andersen*, 2000, p. 8)

Hence, for Andersen, the sport psychologist–athlete relationship is likely to be an extremely informative site, where psychologists are able to enhance their understanding of athletes on a deeper level. Stevens and Andersen's (2007a,b) interesting case studies from sport psychologist–athlete dyads have identified how fundamental psychodynamic concepts such as transference (an unconscious projection of relationship patterns onto figures in the present that are repetitions of how they have responded to significant others in the past or of fantasies that they have constructed previously) may permeate the sport psychologist's relationship with his or her athlete clients. This may be highly informative both in the psychologist's development of understanding about the athlete and for development of the athlete's self-insight.

Development of a secure and beneficial working relationship between a sport psychologist and athlete is by no means a given and is likely to be influenced by an array of other variables, including ethnicity, sex, personality characteristics, and attachment styles of both members of the dyad. Yambor and Connelly's (1991) account of the experiences that female sport psychology consultants have faced when working with male athletes highlights some of these issues. For example, they outlined how one male athlete was reluctant to engage in a working relationship with his female sport psychologist, commenting "You know how women are...they tell everything they know" (Yambor & Connelly, 1991, p. 307). Such ingrained beliefs and prejudices in relation to factors such as a consultant's gender or ethnicity might also play a substantial role in detracting from the development of an optimal working relationship, and more research is needed to explore such issues further.

Finally, it may also be important for sport psychologists to recognize that, in developing a working relationship with athletes, it may be useful to understand that the athlete is also strongly situated within a familial environment. Hellstedt (1995) wrote about the significance for consultants of developing an understanding of the dynamics of the family systems in which athletes are intertwined. He suggested that "the family provides the primary social environment where the athlete can develop an identity, self-esteem, and the motivation for athletic success...athletes often credit their families for encouragement, discipline, valuing achievement and, above all, love and support" (Hellstedt, 1995, p. 117). Accordingly, Hellstedt (1995) offered a useful model by which consultants can involve athletes' family units as a significant part of their work with athletes. Such ideas are extremely interesting in the sense that they facilitate a view of the sport psychologist as not only engaged in an exclusive dyadic relationship with the athlete but as integrating into the network of relationships in which the athlete is entwined. The advantages such approaches afford consultants and the challenges they face in the context of such models of practice have yet to be thoroughly explored in the literature.

Research Summary and Brief Considerations for Future Research

Reviewing the literature on peer, coach, parent, and sport psychologist relationships in the context of sport and performance highlights a diverse array of research questions, conceptual assumptions, and methodological approaches, and a series of important theoretical and applied implications. This has undoubtedly served to enrich our understanding of relationships and to reinforce the significance of relational experiences in sport and performance contexts. It can be viewed as a major strength that researchers have begun to scrutinize each of these specific sporting relationships. In so doing, the field of sport and performance psychology is beginning to identify and dissect the important conceptual features of the various relationships that permeate sport and performance, to develop measurement tools that help to investigate key features of these relationships, and to design studies that help us to better understand the antecedents and consequences of such relationships within the contextual arena of sport and performance.

However, there is still much to be learned in what is a relatively fledgling area of research within the field of sport psychology itself. Notable by their absence (particularly in the sport psychology literature) have been the roles of important issues such as ethnicity, gender, and sexuality in the context of sport relationships. For example, Bailey and Oberschneider's (1997) investigation of homosexuality in the context of elite dance (discussed earlier) provides evidence in support of the significant role sexuality might play in the context of peer relationship formation. The sociological literature (e.g., Clarke, 1998; Messner, 1992) has suggested that organized sport remains "a highly homophobic institution" and "a place where hegemonic masculinity is reproduced and defined" (Anderson, 2002, p. 860). The formation of peer and coach relationships for sexual minorities within such institutional restraints may be an important area for future investigation. Furthermore, isolated studies such as Jowett and Frost's (2007) provided evidence that some black athletes felt that the quality of the relationship they were able to develop with their white coaches was significantly hindered by their ethnic differences. Given their link with wider society, there is a need to further explore how these important sociocultural issues are linked to the development of sport relationships.

In the context of sport and performance, it is also worth considering some of the applied implications that arise when one considers the notion of human relationships. On a number of levels, there are some important issues for consideration in relation to this issue. For example, linked to the material on parent–child attachment described above, perhaps issues such as the motivational climate in which children's sporting friendships are situated create a contextual barrier to the expression, manifestation, or activation of deeply rooted internal relationship templates that children have constructed through parental relations. This could render such deep-rooted models less likely to be active and thus "exert an influence on" friendships. Ommundsen et al. (2005) have identified that performance-oriented motivational climates seem to inhibit positive friendship quality, and future studies might explore whether such a climate also dampens the likelihood that sport friendships are infiltrated by deeper relationship models. It is possible that a competitive sporting environment, which encourages the perception that teammates are rivals, dampens the likelihood of intimacy and closeness in sporting relations and makes it less likely that internal models of attachment (typically related to experiences of more intimate parental bonds) will be called upon for guidance. From an applied perspective, if such models were less "active" in the context of sport and performance, they may also be less accessible from an intervention perspective, making it more difficult to develop interventions designed to "rework" deeper models of attachment (e.g., in children with maladaptive beliefs about relationships) through the medium of sporting relationships (as opposed to other contexts that are framed differently).

Additionally, it is interesting to consider the intervention issues that arise when we consider the social and emotional isolation that often accompanies high-level performance. Murphy (2009) has suggested that those considered to be high performers in various contexts (from business to sport) may be liable to be isolated from peers in a hierarchical sense (they are quickly promoted to management and senior positions, rising above their former peers), and to dedicate their emotional and personal resources to the further development of their talent (taking them away from social activities and other aspects of their development). The social and emotional isolation that results from such factors may be an important area of consideration for practitioners working with those considered to be high performers and is another important area for future research. Combating such isolation and its psychological implications may be a central role of the consultant when working with high-level performers.

There has been a tendency to think about interpersonal sporting relationships in isolation, as opposed to as an interconnected network. In sport psychology, the literature has investigated questions that recognize the influence of relationships with a variety of significant others as important in the construction of various outcome variables. In achievement goal research (e.g., Carr et al., 1999, 2000; Vazou, Ntoumanis, & Duda, 2006), the combined influence of multiple social agents in the construction of important motivational variables, such as self-perception and achievement goal orientations, has been highlighted. Such research questions are important because they recognize that individuals in sport are simultaneously engaged in a number of significant relationships, each of which having the potential to contribute to psychological experiences within and beyond the context. However, less attention has been devoted to broader questions related to the manner in which these individual relationships may be interwoven. When individuals are engaged in close interpersonal relationships with parents, peers, and coaches, one might consider the individual him- or herself as a "common denominator," a "psychological participant" in each dyadic relationship. Consequently, the psychological effects of one dyadic relationship on an individual can reverberate via the individual, surfacing in other close relationships in which he or she is simultaneously engaged. In my own research, I have been interested in exploring conceptual frameworks that can help sport researchers develop understanding of how athletes' and performers' experiences of interpersonal relationships in the context of sport might be better understood by considering the nature of other key relationships they have been party to in the course of their lives. Some fruitful conceptual frameworks and ideas that hold potential to enhance such understanding are located in the attachment theory and transference literature. In the section that follows, I intend to provide an outline of how these ideas provide a logical rationale for understanding how close interpersonal relationships in sport may be linked to experiences of close relationships in the course of child development.

Furthermore, given that the vast majority of sport relationship research has focused upon dyadic interactions, I also briefly discuss new frameworks, such as the *actor–partner interdependence model* (APIM, Cook & Kenny, 2005; Kashy & Kenny, 2000; Kenny & Cook, 1999), from the social relationships literature and demonstrate how such models will prove invaluable in developing our understanding of dyadic sport and performance relationships.

Moving Relationship Research in Sport and Performance Forward: Promising Conceptual Frameworks and Ideas
Attachment Theory

The sport psychology literature has begun to recognize attachment theory (e.g., Bowlby, 1969/1982, 1973, 1980) as a significant conceptual framework for advancing the understanding of social relationships in the context of sport and exercise (e.g., Carr, 2009a,b, 2011; Davis & Jowett, 2010; Forrest, 2008). In short, Bowlby's (1969/1982, 1973, 1980) theory hypothesized infants to be biologically predisposed to form selective bonds with special and proximate caring figures in their environment and suggested that formative discrimination of attachment figures begins in infancy, where proximity to significant others is of critical importance to the maintenance and restoration of safety. Attachment theorists (e.g., Ainsworth et al., 1978; Bowlby, 1973; Sroufe & Waters, 1977) have argued that different patterns of cognition, affect, and behavior develop in response to caregivers' sensitivity, availability, and responsiveness to infants' desire for proximity.

As young children develop, attachment theory predicts that the experiences of care and support provided by key caregivers (typically parents) help them to construct (or not) "a feeling of security and help-seeking behaviors that function to protect them in situations of distress and to facilitate their exploration of the social world in general" (Duchesne & Larose, 2007, p. 1502). These systems of cognition, affect, and behavior are reflections of what Bowlby termed *internal working models* that are constructed in response to the attachment experiences that children encounter. These internal working models can be thought of as a psychological organization that serves to guide children's beliefs with respect to important issues such as the availability of key attachment figures as a source of comfort and security, judgments about their own self-worth and deservedness in attachment relations, and how best to deal with distress within the constraints of the attachment environment in which they find themselves (Cook, 2000; Duchesne & Larose, 2007; Sroufe & Waters, 1977). When youngsters develop a secure working model, they adopt a positive internal representation of themselves in attachment contexts, viewing attachment figures as psychologically available and responsive and developing a positive sense of their self-worth in attachment contexts. However, when they develop an insecure working model, they adopt a negative internal representation, fearing rejection and inconsistent responses from attachment figures and adopting a negative sense of self in attachment contexts (Duchesne & Larose, 2007; Kobak & Hazan, 1991). Florian, Mikulincer, and Bucholtz (1995) have suggested that insecurely attached children, who grow up with a sense of uncertainty surrounding the availability of attachment figures (Ainsworth et al., 1978), are likely to develop a generalized belief in a "non-supportive world" (p. 666).

Ainsworth et al. (1978) forwarded a number of distinct categories of attachment that are differentially related to the attachment histories of infants and caregivers; the most illustrious perhaps being secure, ambivalent, and avoidant styles of attachment. *Secure attachment* is thought to result from caregivers' availability and responsiveness to infants' proximity needs. A secure attachment style is expected to result in a more trusting, social, and confident child because the child is neither concerned nor preoccupied with a lack of caregiver responsiveness, support, and security. Anxious or ambivalent attachment is suggested to stem from inconsistency of responsiveness to infants' needs and is expected to result in a child who is more uncertain, anxious, and "clingy," due to anxiety about the caregiver's availability. Finally, avoidant attachment is suggested to stem from caregiver neglect and rejection, resulting in a child who is emotionally distant and less likely to express affection and emotional need. Bowlby (1973) hypothesized that the internal working models of attachment children construct as a consequence of initial attachment relationships (typically with parental caregivers) will serve as a psychological template for future patterns of cognition, affect, and behavior in close relationships.

In my own work, I have sought to employ these conceptual assumptions as a means of helping to understand adolescents' peer relationships in sport as a reflection of the critical and affectively charged attachment relationships they have shared with parental caregivers. I have hypothesized that adolescents' parental attachment relationships are likely to reflect the nature of internal working models that may well function as a psychological template during the construction of close peer relationships in sport. This is because adolescents whose early experiences enable them to develop a secure attachment model are more likely to develop internal perceptions of themselves (e.g., "I am worthy of being loved") and others (e.g., "Others typically want to be close to me") that facilitate positive relationships with peers, that adolescents often develop a style of interaction with others that closely reflects the attachment relationship that they experience with caregivers (e.g., an individual whose mother is rejecting and withholds support and affection may come to respond in a similar manner toward his or her friends) (Youngblade & Belsky, 1992; Weimer et al., 2004), and that adolescents can internalize complex patterns of emotional regulation (e.g., self-protective distancing strategies that help them to avoid dealing with anticipated rejection or unavailability if they seek proximity) developed in early attachment relationships and subsequently reproduce these strategies in their relationships with their peers (e.g., Contreras & Kerns, 2000; Contreras, Kerns, Weimer, Gentzler, & Tomich, 2000). In support of these predictions, an early investigation (Carr, 2009b) identified that adolescents' self-reported levels of attachment security in relation to a key parental caregiver significantly predicted their reports of sporting friendship quality with a nominated best friend. Features of attachment security with a key caregiver were positively related to a number of the features of positive sport friendship quality forwarded by Weiss and Smith (1999).

Of particular interest was that the *goal-corrected partnership* dimension of adolescents' reported caregiver attachment was the most significant predictor of all positive dimensions of friendship quality in sport. Bowlby (1969/1982) outlined that goal-corrected partnership is a central feature of secure working models of attachment, and it reflects the fact that adolescents have developed the ability to think of their caregiver as a separate human being with needs, feelings, and goals to which the adolescent is able to respond with empathy and understanding (this is in some ways a reciprocation of the type of care that adolescents have themselves been exposed to from caregivers in a typical secure attachment bond). In insecure attachment bonds, the development of this feature is less likely because the children have themselves been less frequently exposed to this type of caregiver model in response to their own needs and desires, and residual anger and frustration at a lack of caregiver availability and

responsiveness to the children's needs make it less likely that these children will be sympathetic to the needs of their caregivers (Bowlby, 1969/1982). This dimension of adolescent–parent attachment may be a critical indicator of important features of internal working models that could significantly enhance or impede adolescents' close friendship quality in sport.

Other studies from the sport psychology literature have also provided evidence in support of the promise of attachment theory as a framework to enhance the understanding of sport relationships. For example, Davis and Jowett (2010) used attachment theory as a way of conceptualizing the coach–athlete relationship. Athletes reported that coaches served some of the key relational functions hypothesized (Bowlby, 1969/1982, 1988) to underpin attachment relationships in early childhood (e.g., provision of a secure base, safe haven, and proximity maintenance on the part of the attachment figure) and further identified that when athletes experienced such attachment bonds with coaches, as characterized by higher levels of attachment-related avoidance and anxiety, then they were less likely to be satisfied with the coach–athlete relationship and with sport in general. This suggests that it is possible to view the fundamental relationship characteristics that attachment theory posits as essential to healthy development in childhood as important ingredients in adult sport relationships.

It is worth recognizing the distinctions between Davis and Jowett's (2010) study and my own (Carr, 2009b) work reported above. The predominant distinctions are reflected in the underpinning conceptual assumptions surrounding attachment theory in each study. In my study, I sought to support the assumption that parental attachment bonds reflect key features of adolescents' internal working models that have been constructed as a function of what has been considered the most fundamental (i.e., the parent–child) human relationship (Bowlby, 1969/1982, 1988; Freud, 1940; Pincus et al., 2007). Consequently, I hypothesized that such internal working models consist of mental structures, cognitive scripts, and core beliefs developed from fundamental parental relationships and that feature as a template when individuals try to build close peer relationships (I do not make the assumption that such peer relationships are *themselves* attachment bonds) in sporting contexts. Davis and Jowett (2010) conceptualize the coach–athlete relationship itself as a potential attachment bond, arguing that the relational features central to attachment bonds (e.g., provision of a secure base, safe haven, and proximity maintenance on the part of the attachment figure) may also be features of coach–athlete relationships. Their data suggest that athletes are able to view such relationships in accordance with these attachment features, and this has significance for how the relationship is experienced for athletes.

Transference

According to Sandler, Dare, and Holder (1973), *transference* can be defined as

> [A] specific illusion which develops in regard to another person...which represents in some of its features a repetition of a relationship towards an important figure in the person's past.... This is felt...not as repetition of the past, but as strictly appropriate to the present and to the particular person involved.
> (p. 671)

In a classic Freudian sense, such transference illusions (Freud, 1912/1958) have been understood as the superimposition of a patient's childhood fantasies, wishes, and conflicts onto a psychoanalyst by integrating "the figure of the physician into one of the 'series' already constructed in his [the patient's] mind" (Freud, 1912/1963, see also Andersen & Glassman, 1996; Andersen & Berk, 1998). By the patient "drawing the analyst into" (Andersen & Berk, 1998, p. 83) his or her own subconscious conflicts and wishes, the analyst is able to investigate by bringing displaced conflicts and their childhood origins to the patient's awareness (Andersen & Glassman, 1996; Luborsky & Crits-Christoph, 1998).

However, beyond psychoanalysis, Freud (1925/1961) also recognized the implications of the transference phenomenon for social functioning in general, concluding,

> It must not be supposed, however, that transference is created by analysis and does not occur apart from it. Transference is merely uncovered and isolated by analysis. It is a universal phenomenon of the human mind...and in fact dominates the whole of each person's relations to his human environment.
> (p. 42)

It is this ubiquitous notion that active, unconscious mental representations of the past "reach into" the present and shape how we experience ourselves and others that holds particular appeal for sport relationship research (Pincus et al., 2007). This idea is one of Freud's (1895, 1900, 1905, 1925) most

significant contributions to the field of psychology and has implications that extend far beyond its traditional psychoanalytical birthplace.

Sport psychology has devoted relatively little attention to the transference phenomenon. Ogilvie (e.g., Ogilvie, 1993; Ogilvie, Tofler, Conroy, & Drell, 1998) first outlined the potential importance of transference in sport-related relationships, calling for an increased awareness of the idea of transference and countertransference[2] in coaches and sport psychology consultants on the grounds that the sporting domain is a potential arena for the unconsciously motivated activation of unresolved relationship issues from individuals' past to be projected onto significant relationship figures such as coaches, athletes, and sport psychologists in the present. Strean and Strean (1998) have also supported this assertion and provided a number of clinical examples that demonstrate how transference is likely to feature in the relationships that athletes share with their coaches and sport psychologists. They provide examples such as idealization transference, in which athletes can subconsciously believe they have found in their coach or consultant an authority who responds to them in an empathic manner, does not judge them, and expects nothing in return. The feelings and emotions that this "discovery" can evoke in some athletes may be powerful and can certainly influence their behavior within the dynamics of the relationship (and also the behavior of the "other," who may respond to such idealization in various ways). The potential significance that such transference reactions could have with regards to maladaptive functioning and therapeutic intervention are important to recognize. Stevens and Andersen (2007a,b) provided case study evidence of how the transference phenomenon is significantly involved in how sporting dyadic relationships are "played out." They supported the idea that individuals' relationship pasts may well be "triggered," "projected," "repeated," or "played out again" in present relationships, such as coach–athlete or sport psychologist–athlete dyads, thus influencing the manner in which these relationships (and sport itself) are "experienced" for those involved. Furthermore, their research also helped to outline the potentially damaging effects that can ensue when sport relationships are excessively driven by such transference reactions and rightly called for greater awareness of the issue.

Additionally, it has been suggested that sport psychology has paid minimal attention to the "human deliverer" (Andersen, 2000, p. xiv) of its interventions (i.e., the consultant). From this perspective, it may be equally important for consultants to be "self-aware" in relation to their own countertransference (i.e., transference directed from practitioner to client). Winstone and Gervis (2006) have highlighted that consultants should be particularly aware of their own feelings and emotions being projected onto athletes and have highlighted that a lack of self-awareness in relation to such issues could well place consultants in situations in which they are ethically compromised.

Other Theoretical Frameworks Significant to Relationships in Sport and Performance: The Actor–Partner Interdependence Model

Much of the sport relationship literature has been limited to exploring dyadic relationships from an *intrapersonal* perspective. That is, the influence of a particular characteristic an individual possesses has been linked to a particular outcome in the same individual (e.g., an individual's attachment style has been linked to his or her perceptions of friendship quality in a sporting dyad, or an individual's relationship satisfaction has been linked to his or perceptions of key relationship characteristics). Recent research in the broader sphere of relationships has recognized that perceptions of dyadic relationships are constructed as a consequence of both intrapersonal and *interpersonal* processes and should be considered as a multilevel phenomenon (e.g., Cillessen, Lu Jiang, West, and Laszkowski, 2005). In the broader literature on relationships, researchers have provided evidence that characteristics of both the self and one's partner are likely to predict the self's perception of the relationship and behavior within it (Campbell, Simpson, Kashy, & Rholes, 2001). In the context of sport peer relationships, for example, this would suggest that adolescents' perceptions of friendship quality may depend not only on their own characteristics but also on various characteristics of their friends.

However, there is also a methodological impetus to such a multilevel investigation (Liu, 2009). Previous studies of dyadic relations have often attempted to analyze individual responses from each dyad member, assuming independent observations (e.g., 50 dyads might be analyzed as 100 individual cases, predicting each individual's outcome variable from both her own predictor variable and that of her partner). However, Kashy and Kenny (2000) have outlined that ignoring the nonindependent nature of dyadic data in this way poses significant threats to the accuracy of analyses (see Kenny, Kashy, & Cook, 2006). Kenny and his colleagues have developed the

actor–partner interdependence model (APIM, Cook & Kenny, 2005; Kashy & Kenny, 2000; Kenny & Cook, 1999) as a promising method for tackling the issue of interdependence in dyadic research. The APIM enables researchers to distinguish between *partner effects* (i.e., the extent to which specified characteristics of the self are a function of specified characteristics of one's partner in a given dyad) and *actor effects* (i.e., the extent to which specified characteristics of the self are a function of specified characteristics of the self). In the sport and performance literature, it will be important to explore the extent to which individuals' perceptions of relationship quality or satisfaction (which have been shown to be important predictors of a variety of critical outcomes) are constructed not only from variables that reside from within the self but also from those that reside within one's partner.

In a recent investigation, my colleague and I (Carr & Fitzpatrick, 2011) attempted to recognize the argument (e.g., Collins, 2002) that the dyad is an essential unit of analysis in social relationship research by employing the APIM (e.g., Kashy & Kenny, 2000) approach to examining both actor and partner attachment effects on perceived friendship quality. Our analyses enabled us to examine how adolescents' own attachment characteristics contributed not only to their own perceptions of the quality of their sport friendship but also to their friend's perception. Results suggested that both actor and partner effects played a role in the prediction of perceived sport friendship quality. Of most interest was that partner effects were identified for total positive friendship quality and "things in common" dimensions of the SFQS, suggesting that, on certain levels, individuals' perceptions of the quality of their relationships are significantly affected by the attachment characteristics of their friends.

The fact that the "things in common" dimension of perceived friendship quality was significantly predicted by partner attachment style but not by actor attachment style is interesting and suggests that certain aspects of perceived sport friendship quality may be particularly susceptible to partner influence. The "things in common" subscale of the SFQS taps into perceptions that one shares "common interests," has "similar values," and "thinks the same way" as one's friend. Our findings suggest that the construction of such perceptions in a dyadic sporting friendship may be more heavily dependent upon the partner's attachment characteristics than the actor's. It may be that for adolescents to develop the perception that a friend shares their interests, values, and ways of thinking it may be necessary for their friends to possess certain cognitive and emotional characteristics. The attachment literature has suggested that key features of constructs such as empathy involve factors such as perspective-taking (i.e., a cognitive ability related to taking other people's point of view) and empathic concern (i.e., the tendency to feel sympathy or concern for other people), and there is evidence in support of the claim that insecure attachment bonds and poor care experiences with parents are linked to hindered perspective-taking and empathic concern (e.g., Britton & Fuendeling, 2005; Reti et al., 2002). The partner effect in relation to "things in common" in our study can be explained by the fact that decreased attachment security in relation to parental relationships reflects less-developed cognitive and emotional capacities in relation to such empathic features, and this seems to be felt by relationship partners in sport friendships, hindering their construction of a perception that common values, interests, and ways of being are shared. These findings are an exciting insight into the manner in which sport relationships are co-constructed, and future research in sport and performance relationships may find it productive to further utilize the APIM.

Conclusion

In summary, a burgeoning and diverse literature is devoted to the study of human relationships in the context of sport and performance. Such literature has served to underline the significance of relationships as critical to the psychological experience of sport and performance, to help us recognize the unique conceptual features of these critical relationships and the manner in which such features can regulate the contextual experience, to develop useful measurement tools that will serve to guide future research efforts, and to begin to unravel the complex nature of the various antecedents that underpin the construction of sport and performance relationships. Accordingly, the sport and performance relationship research has served to substantiate Sullivan's (1940, p. 10) claim that "a person can never be isolated from the complex of interpersonal relations in which the person lives and has his being." In this sense, the centrality of relationships in human existence dictates that their influence, development, and significance will be inevitably woven into the fabric of sport and performance experiences. As such, the field of sport not only can benefit from the ideas and concepts central to relationship research but can also contribute in a reciprocal fashion to

the expansion of a broader understanding of human relationships. In this chapter, I sought to outline how fundamental concepts and ideas that have significantly advanced understanding of humans in a relational context might be integrated into the sport and performance literature. My recommendations for future research therefore focus on this integrative aim.

Future Directions

• In seeking to understand the construction, development, and nature of key relationships in sport and performance contexts, researchers might look to frameworks and ideas such as attachment theory and transference from the psychodynamic and developmental literature. These ideas may help to shed light on how the nature of present relationships in specific contexts is often a reflection of the influence of critical relationships from the past. In this sense, researchers can develop a more critical awareness of the developmental significance of early relationships through the lifespan and appreciate how individuals' relationships are often inextricably interlinked (as opposed to isolated social relationships).

• Beyond an understanding of how developmental issues relate to sport and performance relationship experiences, there is a need to develop our understanding of how issues such as ethnicity, sexuality, and gender contribute to the construction and experience of relationships in sport and performance contexts.

• Given the focus on dyadic relationships in the context of sport and performance, employment of frameworks such as the APIM from relationship research may be extremely useful in helping to unravel the complexities involved in dyadic relationship research. Such models will help to reveal how individual perceptions of relationship quality are co-constructed as a function of self and partner characteristics. In this way, sport relationships can be appreciated as truly co-constructed phenomena.

Notes

1. This is not to say that individual perceptions of relationship quality are not important. Rather, assessment of relationship quality may be more fully captured with the use of additional outcome measures.

2. Countertransference can be thought of as a similar transferal of previous relationship patterns, fantasies, and behavior projected by the therapist or consultant onto the client (Andersen, 2000).

References

Ainsworth, M. D. S., Blehar, M. C., Waters, E., & Wall, S. (1978). *Patterns of attachment: A psychological study of the strange situation*. Hillsdale, NJ: Erlbaum.

Andersen, M. B. (2000). Beginnings: Intakes and the initiation of relationships. In M. B. Andersen (Ed.), *Doing sport psychology* (pp. 3–16). Champaign, IL: Human Kinetics.

Andersen, S. M., & Berk, M. S. (1998). Transference in everyday experience: Implications of experimental research for relevant clinical phenomena. *Review of General Psychiatry, 2*, 81–120.

Andersen, S. M., & Glassman, N. S. (1996). Responding to significant others when they are not there: Effects on interpersonal inference, motivation and affect. In R. M. Sorrentino & E. T. Higgins (Eds.), *Handbook of motivation and cognition* (Vol. 3, pp. 262–321). New York: Guilford.

Anderson, E. (2002). Openly gay athletes: Contesting hegemonic masculinity in a homophobic environment. *Gender and Society, 6*, 860–877.

Babkes, M. L., & Weiss, M. R. (1999). Parental influence on children's cognitive and affective responses to competitive soccer participation. *Pediatric Exercise Science, 11*, 44–62.

Bailey, M. J., & Oberschneider, M. (1997). Sexual orientation and professional dance. *Archives of Sexual Behavior, 26*, 433–444.

Bandura, A. (1986). *Social foundations of thought and action: A social cognitive theory*. Englewood Cliffs, NJ: Prentice Hall.

Bandura, A. & Walters, R. (1963). *Social Learning and Personality Development*. New York: Holt, Rinehart & Winston.

Berscheid, E., Snyder, M., & Omoto, A. M. (1989). Issues in studying close relationships: Conceptualising and measuring closeness. In C. Hendric (Ed.), *Close relationships* (pp. 63–91). Newbury Park, CA: Sage.

Billy, J. O. G., Tanfer, K., Grady, W. R., & Klepinger, D. H. (1993). The sexual behaviour of men in the United States. *Family Planning Perspectives, 25*, 52–60.

Bois, J. E., Sarrazin, P. G., Brustad, R. J., Cury, F., & Trouilloud, D. O. (2005). Elementary schoolchildren's perceived competence and physical activity involvement: The influence of parents' role modeling behaviors and perceptions of their child's competence. *Psychology of Sport and Exercise, 6*, 381–397.

Bois, J. E., Sarrazin, P. G., Brustad, R. J., Trouilloud, D. O., & Cury, F. (2002). Mothers' expectancies and young adolescents perceived physical competence: A year long study. *Journal of Early Adolescence, 22*, 384–406.

Bowlby, J. (1969/1982). *Attachment and loss, Vol. 1. Attachment*. New York: Basic.

Bowlby, J. (1973). *Attachment and loss, Vol. 2. Separation: Anxiety and anger*. New York: Basic.

Bowlby, J. (1980). *Attachment and loss. Loss: Sadness and depression* (Vol. 3). London: Pimlico.

Bowlby, J. (1988). *A secure base: Parent–child attachment and healthy human development*. New York: Basic Books.

Britton, P. C., & Fuendeling, J. M. (2005). The relations among the varieties of adult attachment and the components of empathy. *Journal of Social Psychology, 145*, 519–530.

Brustad, R. J. (1993). Who will go out to play? Parental and psychological influences on children's attraction to physical activity. *Journal of Sport and Exercise Psychology, 14*, 59–77.

Campbell, L., Simpson, J. A., Kashy, D. A., & Rholes, W. S. (2001). Attachment orientations, dependence, and behaviour in a stressful situation: An application of the Actor-Partner Independence Model. *Journal of Social and Personal Relationships, 18*, 821–843.

Carr, S. (2009a). Implications of attachment theory for sport and physical activity research: Conceptual links with achievement goal and peer relationship models. *International Review of Sport and Exercise Psychology, 2*, 95–115.

Carr, S. (2009b). Adolescent-parent attachment characteristics and quality of youth sport friendship. *Psychology of Sport and Exercise, 10*, 653–661.

Carr, S. (2011). *Attachment in sport, exercise, and wellness*. London: Routledge.

Carr, S., & Fitzpatrick, N. (2011). Experiences of dyadic sport friendships as a function of self and partner attachment characteristics. *Psychology of Sport and Exercise, 12*, 383–391.

Carr, S., & Weigand, D. A. (2001). Parental, peer, teacher, and sporting hero influence on the goal orientations of children in physical education. *European Physical Education Review, 7*, 305–328.

Carr, S., Weigand, D. A., & Hussey, W. (1999). The relative influence of parents, teachers, and peers on children and adolescents' achievement and intrinsic motivation and perceived competence in physical education. *Journal of Sport Pedagogy, 5*, 28–50.

Carr, S., Weigand, D. A., & Jones, J. (2000). The relative influence of parents, peers and sporting heroes on goal orientations of children and adolescents in sport. *Journal of Sport Pedagogy, 6*, 34–55.

Chase, M. A., & Dummer, G. M. (1992). The role of sports as a social status determinant for children. *Research Quarterly for Exercise and Sport, 63*, 418–424.

Cillessen, A. H. N., Lu Jiang, X., West, T. V., & Laszkowski, D. K. (2005). Predictors of dyadic friendship quality in adolescence. *International Journal of Behavioural Development, 29*, 165–172.

Clarke, G. (1998). Queering the pitch and coming out to play: Lesbians and physical education in sport. *Sport, Education, and Society, 3*, 145–160.

Coie, I. D., & Cillessen, A. H. N. (1993). Peer rejection: Origins and effects on children's development. *Current Directions in Psychological Science, 2*, 89–92.

Collins, W. A. (2002). Historical perspectives on contemporary research in social development. In P. K. Smith & C. H. Hart (Eds.), *Blackwell handbook of childhood social development* (pp. 3–23). Malden, MA: Blackwell.

Contreras, J. M., & Kerns, K. A. (2000). Emotion regulation processes: Explaining links between parent–child attachment and peer relationships. In K. A. Kerns, J. M. Contreras, & A. M. Neal-Barnett (Eds.), *Family and peers: Linking two social worlds* (pp. 1–25). Westport, CT: Praeger.

Contreras, J. M., Kerns, K. A., Weimer, B. L., Gentzler, A. L., & Tomich, P. L. (2000). Emotion regulation as a mediator of associations between mother–child attachment and peer relationships in middle childhood. *Journal of Family Psychology, 14*, 111–124.

Cook, W. L. (2000). Understanding attachment security in family context. *Journal of Personality and Social Psychology, 78*, 285–294.

Cook, W. L., & Kenny, D. A. (2005). The Actor-Partner Interdependence Model: A model of bidirectional effects in developmental studies. *International Journal of Behavioural Development, 29*, 101–109.

Davis, L., & Jowett, S. (2010). Investigating the interpersonal dynamics between coaches and athletes based on fundamental principles of attachment. *Journal of Clinical Sport Psychology, 4*(1), 112–132.

Dempsey, J. M., Kimiecik, J. C., & Horn, T. S. (1993). Parental influence on children's moderate to vigorous physical activity participation: An expectancy-value approach. *Pediatric Exercise Science, 5*, 151–167.

Duchesne, S., & Larose, S. (2007). Adolescent parental attachment and academic motivation and performance in early adolescence. *Journal of Applied Social Psychology, 37*, 1501–1521.

Eccles, J. S., Wigfield, A., & Schiefele, U. (1998). Motivation to succeed. In W. Damon (Series Ed.), N. Eisenberg (Vol. Ed.), *Handbook of child psychology: Vol. 3 Social, emotional and personality development* (5th ed., pp. 1017–1094). New York: Wiley.

Evans, J., & Roberts, G. C. (1987). Physical competence and the development of children's peer relations. *Quest, 39*, 23–35.

Felson, M. B., & Reed, M. (1986). The effect of parents on the self-appraisals of children. *Social Psychology Quarterly, 49*, 302–308.

Florian, V., Mikulincer, M., & Bucholtz, I. (1995). Effects of adult attachment style on the perception and search for social support. *The Journal of Psychology, 129*, 665–676.

Forrest, K. (2008). Attachment and attention in sport. *Journal of Clinical Sport Psychology, 2*, 242–258.

Foshee, V., & Bauman, K. (1992). Parental and peer characteristics as modifiers of the bond-behaviour relationship: An elaboration of control theory. *Journal of Health and Social Behaviour, 33*, 6–76.

Fredricks, J. A., & Eccles, J. S. (2004). Parental influences on youth involvement in sports. In M. R. Weiss (Ed.), *Developmental sport and exercise psychology: A lifespan perspective* (pp. 144–164). Morgantown, WV: Fitness Information Technology.

Freedson, P. S., & Evenson, S. (1991). Familial aggregation in physical activity. *Research Quarterly for Exercise and Sport, 62*, 384–389.

Freud, S. (1895). The psychotherapy of hysteria. *S.E., 2*, 253–305.

Freud, S. (1900). The interpretation of dreams. *S.E., 5*, 550–572.

Freud, S. (1905). Fragment of an analysis of a case of hysteria. *S.E., 1*, 7–122.

Freud, S. (1925). An autobiographical study. *S.E., 20*, 7–74.

Freud, S. (1940). *An outline of psychoanalysis.* New York: Norton.

Freud, S. (1912/1958). The dynamics of transference. In J. Strachey (Ed. and Trans.), *The standard edition of the complete psychological works of Sigmund Freud* (Vol. 12, pp. 97–108). London: Hogarth Press. (Original work published 1912.)

Freud, S. (1925/1961). An autobiographical study; inhibitions, symptoms, and anxiety; lay analysis; and other works. In J. S. Strachey (Ed. & Trans.), *The standard edition of the complete psychological works of Sigmund Freud* (Vol. 20, pp. 7–71). London: Hogarth Press. (Original work published 1925–1926.)

Freud, S. (1912/1963). The dynamics of transference. *Therapy and technique* (pp. 105–115). New York: Macmillan. (Original work published 1912.)

Gebhard, P. (1972). Incidence of overt homosexuality in the United States and western Europe. In J. M. Livingood (Ed.), *National Institute of Mental Health task force on homosexuality: Final report and background papers* (pp. 22–29). Washington, DC: U.S. Government Printing Office.

George, C., Kaplan, N., & Main, M. (1984–1996). *Attachment interview for adults.* Unpublished manuscript, University of California, Berkeley.

Greendorfer, S. L. (1992). Sport socialisation. In T. S. Horn (Ed.), *Advances in sport psychology* (pp. 201–218). Champaign, IL: Human Kinetics.

Gustafson, S. L., & Rhodes, R. E. (2006). Parental correlates of physical activity in children and early adolescents. *Sports Medicine, 36*, 79–97.

Hartup, W. W. (1989). Behavioral manifestations of children's friendships. In T. J. Bemdt & G. W. Ladd (Eds.), *Peer relationships in child development* (pp. 46–70). New York: Wiley.

Hellstedt, J. (1995). Invisible players: A family systems model. In S. M. Murphy (Ed.), *Sport psychology interventions* (pp. 117–146). Champaign, IL: Human Kinetics.

Horvath, A. O. (2000). The therapeutic relationship: From transference to alliance. *Journal of Clinical Psychology, 56*, 163–173.

Jago, R. P., Fox, K. R., Page, A. S., Brockman, R., & Thompson, J. L. (2010). Parent and child physical activity and sedentary time: Do active parents foster active children? *BMC Public Health, 10*, 194–203.

Jones, R., Armour, K., & Potrac, P. (2004). *Sports coaching cultures.* London: Routledge.

Jones, R., & Cassidy, T. (2004). *Understanding sports coaching: The social, cultural and pedagogical foundations of coaching practice.* London: Routledge.

Jowett, S. (2003). When the honeymoon is over: A case study of a coach—athlete relationship in crisis. *The Sport Psychologist, 17*, 444–460.

Jowett, S., & Chaundy, V. (2004). An investigation into the impact of coach leadership and coach-athlete relationship on group cohesion. *Group Dynamics: Theory, Research, and Practice, 8*, 302–311.

Jowett, S., & Clark-Carter, D. (2006). Perceptions of empathic accuracy and assumed similarity in the coach–athlete relationship. *British Journal of Social Psychology, 45*, 617–637.

Jowett, S., & Cockerill, I. M. (2002). Incompatibility in the coach–athlete relationship. In I. M. Cockerill (Ed.), *Solutions in sport psychology* (pp. 16–31). London: Thomson Learning.

Jowett, S., & Cockerill, I. M. (2003). Olympic medallists' perspective of the athlete–coach relationship. *Psychology of Sport and Exercise, 4*, 313–331.

Jowett, S., & Frost, T. (2007). Race/ethnicity in the all male coach-athlete relationship: Black footballers' narratives. *International Journal of Sport and Exercise Psychology, 3*, 255–269.

Jowett, S., & Meek, G. A. (2000). The coach-athlete relationship in married couples: An exploratory content analysis. *The Sport Psychologist, 14*, 157–175.

Jowett, S., & Ntoumanis, N. (2003). The Greek coach–athlete relationship questionnaire (GrCART-Q): Scale development and validation. *International Journal of Sport Psychology, 34*, 101–124.

Jowett, S., & Ntoumanis, N. (2004). The coach–athlete relationship questionnaire (CART-Q): Development and initial validation. *Scandinavian Journal of Medicine and Science in Sports, 14*, 245–257.

Jowett, S., & Wylleman, P. (2006). Interpersonal relationships in sport and exercise settings: Crossing the chasm. *Psychology of Sport and Exercise, 7*, 119–123.

Kashy, D. A., & Kenny, D. A. (2000). The analysis of data from dyads and groups. In H. T. Reis & C. M. Judd (Eds.), *Handbook of research methods in social and personality psychology* (pp. 451–477). Cambridge, UK: Cambridge University Press.

Kenny, D. A., & Cook, W. (1999). Partner effects in relationship research: Conceptual issues, analytic difficulties, and illustrations. *Personal Relationships, 6*, 433–488.

Kenny, D. A., Kashy, D. A., & Cook, W. (2006). *Dyadic data analysis*. New York: Guilford.

Kiesler, D. J. (1997). *Contemporary interpersonal theory research and personality, psychopathology, and psychotherapy*. New York: Wiley.

Kimiecik, J. C., & Horn, T. S. (1998). Parental beliefs and children's moderate-to-vigorous physical activity. *Research Quarterly for Exercise and Sport, 69*, 163–175.

Kobak, R. R., & Hazan, C. (1991). Attachment in marriage: Effects of security and accuracy of working models. *Journal of Personality and Social Psychology, 60*, 861–869.

Ladd, G. W. (1999). Peer relationships and social competence during early and middle childhood. *Annual Review of Psychology, 50*, 333–359.

Laing, R. D., Phillipson, H., & Lee, A. R. (1966). *Interpersonal perception: A theory and a method of research*. New York: Harper & Row.

Liu, M. (2009). The intrapersonal and interpersonal effects of anger on negotiation strategies: A cross-cultural investigation. *Human Communication Research, 35*, 148–169.

Lorimer, R., & Jowett, S. (2009). Empathic accuracy in coach-athlete dyads who participate in team and individual sports. *Psychology of Sport and Exercise, 10*, 152–158.

Luborsky, L., & Crits-Christoph, P. (Eds.). (1998). *Understanding transference: The Core Conflictual Relationship Theme method* (2nd ed.). Washington, DC: American Psychological Association

Main, M., Kaplan, N., & Cassidy, J. (1985). Security in infancy, childhood, and adulthood: A move to the level of representation. *Monographs of the Society for Research in Child Development, 50* (1–2, Serial No. 219).

Main, M., & Goldwyn, R. (1998). *Adult attachment interview scoring and classification system*. Unpublished manuscript, University of California, Berkeley.

Messner, M. (1992). *Power at play: Sports and the problem of masculinity*. Boston: Beacon.

Moore, L. L., Lombardi, D. A., White, M. J., Campbell, J. L., Oliveira, S. A., & Ellison, R. C. (1991). Influence of parents physical activity levels on activity levels of young children. *Journal of Pediatrics, 118*, 215–219.

Murphy, S. M. (2009). Isolation. In K. Hays (Ed.), *Performance psychology in Action: Casebook for working with athletes, performing artists, business leaders, and professionals in high-risk occupations*. Washington DC: American Psychological Association.

Newcomb, A. F., & Bagwell, C. L. (1995). Children's friendship relations: A meta-analytic review. *Psychological Bulletin, 117*, 306–347.

Newcomb, T. M. (1953). An approach to the study of communicative acts. *Psychological Review, 60*, 393–404.

Ogilvie, B. C. (1993). *Transference phenomena in coaching and teaching*. In S. Sarpa, J. Alves, V. Ferreira, & A. Paula-Brito (Eds.), *Proceedings: VIII World Congress of Sport Psychology* (pp. 262–266). Lisbon, SP.

Ogilvie, B. C., Tofler, I. R., Conroy, D. E., & Drell, M. J. (1998). Comprehending role conflicts in the coaching of children, adolescents, and young adults. *Sport Psychiatry, 7*, 879–890.

Ommundsen, Y., Roberts, G., Lemyre, P., & Miller, B. W. (2005). Peer relationships in adolescent competitive soccer: Associations to perceived motivational climate, achievement goals, and perfectionism. *Journal of Sports Sciences, 23*, 977–989.

Parker, J. G., & Asher, S. R. (1993). Friendship and friendship quality in middle childhood: Links with peer group acceptance and feelings of loneliness and social dissatisfaction. *Developmental Psychology, 29*, 611–621.

Parker, J. G., & Gottman, J. M. (1989). Social and emotional development in a relational context: Friendship interaction from early childhood to adolescence. In T. J. Berndt & G. W. Ladd (Eds.), *Peer relationships in child development* (pp. 95–131). New York: Wiley.

Patrick, H., Ryan, A. M., Alfeld-Liro, C., Fredricks, J. A., Hruda, L. Z., & Eccles, J. S. (1999). Adolescents' commitment to developing talent: The role of peers in Continuing motivation for sports and the arts. *Journal of Youth and Adolescence, 28*, 741–763.

Pincus, D., Freeman, W., & Modell, A. (2007). A neurobiological model of perception: Considerations for transference. *Psychoanalytic Psychology, 24*, 623–640.

Poczwardowski, A., Barott, J. E., & Henschen, K. P. (2002). The athlete and coach: Their relationship and its meaning. Results of an interpretive study. *International Journal of Sport Psychology, 33*, 116–140.

Poczwardowski, A., Barott, J. E., & Jowett, S. (2006). Diversifying approaches to research on athlete-coach relationships. *Psychology of Sport and Exercise, 7*, 125–142.

Rapport, L. J., & Meleen, M. (1998). Childhood celebrity, parental attachment, and adult adjustment: The young performers study. *Journal of Personality Assessment, 70*, 484–505.

Reti, I. M., Samuels, J. F., Eaton, W. W., Bienvu, O. J., Costa, P. T., & Nestadt, G. (2002). Adult antisocial personality traits are associated with experience of low parental care and maternal overprotection. *Acta Psychoactica Scandinavica, 106*, 126–133.

Rogers, C. (1951). *Client-centred therapy: Its current practice, implications, and theory*. London: Constable.

Sandler, J., Dare, C., & Holder, A. (1973). *The patient and the analyst: The basis of the psychoanalytic process*. New York: International Universities Press.

Smith, S. (2003). Peer relationships in physical activity contexts: A road less travelled in youth sport and exercise psychology research. *Psychology of Sport and Exercise, 4*, 25–39.

Sroufe, L. A., & Waters, E. (1977). Attachment as an organizing construct. *Child Development, 48*, 1184–1199.

Stevens, L. M., & Andersen, M. B. (2007a). Transference and countertransference in sport psychology service delivery: Part I. A review of erotic attraction. *Journal of Applied Sport Psychology, 19*, 253–269.

Stevens, L. M., & Andersen, M. B. (2007b). Transference and countertransference in sport psychology service delivery: Part II. Two case studies on the erotic. *Journal of Applied Sport Psychology, 19*, 270–287.

Strean, W. B., & Strean, H. S. (1998). Applying psychodynamic concepts to sport psychology practice. *The Sport Psychologist, 12*, 208–222.

Sullivan, H. (1940), *Conceptions of modern psychiatry*. New York: Norton.

Ullrich-French, S., & Smith, A. L. (2006). Perceptions of relationships with parents and peers in youth sport: Independent and combined prediction of motivational outcomes. *Psychology of Sport and Exercise, 7*, 193–214.

Ullrich-French, S., & Smith, A. L. (2009). Social and motivational predictors of continued youth sport participation. *Psychology of Sport and Exercise, 10*, 87–95.

Vazou, S., Ntoumanis, N., & Duda, J. L. (2006). Predicting young athletes' motivational indices as a function of their perceptions of the coach- and peer-created climate. *Psychology of Sport and Exercise, 7*, 215–233.

Vilhjalmsson, R., & Thorlindsson, T. (1998). Factors related to physical activity: A study of adolescents. *Social Science and Medicine, 47*, 665–675.

Weimer, B. L., Kerns, K. A., & Oldenburg, C. M. (2004). Adolescents' interactions with a best friend: Associations with attachment style. *Journal of Experimental Child Psychology, 88*, 102–120.

Weiss, M. R., & Duncan, S. C. (1992). The relationship between physical competence and peer acceptance in the context of children's sport participation. *Journal of Sport and Exercise Psychology, 14*, 177–191.

Weiss, M. R., & Fretwell, S. D. (2005). The parent-coach/child-athlete relationship in youth sport: Cordial, contentious, or conundrum? *Research Quarterly for Exercise and Sport, 76*, 286–305.

Weiss, M. R., & Smith, A. L. (1999). Quality of youth sport friendships: Measurement development and validation. *Journal of Sport and Exercise Psychology, 21*, 145–166.

Weiss, M. R., & Smith, A. L. (2002). Friendship quality in youth sport: Relationship to age, gender, and motivation variables. *Journal of Sport and Exercise Psychology, 24*, 420–437.

Weiss, M. R., Smith, A. L., & Theeboom, M. (1996). "That's what friends are for": Children's and teenagers' perceptions of peer relationships in the sport domain. *Journal of Sport and Exercise Psychology, 18*, 347–379.

White, S. A. (1996). Goal orientation and perceptions of the motivational climate initiated by parents. *Pediatric Exercise Science, 8*, 122–129.

White, S. A. (1998). Adolescent goal profiles, perceptions of the parent-initiated motivational climate and competitive trait anxiety. *The Sport Psychologist, 12*, 16–32.

White, S. A., Kavussanu, M., Tank, K. M., & Wingate, J. M. (2004). Perceived parental beliefs about the causes of success in sport: Relationship to athletes' achievement goals and personal beliefs. *Scandinavian Journal of Medicine and Sports Sciences, 14*, 57–66.

Winstone, W., & Gervis, M. (2006). Countertransference and the self-aware sport psychologist: Attitudes and patterns of professional practice. *The Sport Psychologist, 20*, 495–511.

Wylleman, P. (2000). Interpersonal relationships in sport: Uncharted territory in sport psychology research. *International Journal of Sport Psychology, 31*, 555–572.

Yambor, J., & Connelly, D. (1991). Issues confronting female sport psychology consultants working with male student-athletes. *The Sport Psychologist, 5*, 304–312.

Youngblade, L. M., & Belsky, J. (1992). Parent–child antecedents of 5-year-olds' close friendships: A longitudinal analysis. *Developmental Psychology, 28*, 700–713.

Culture/Ethnicity and Performance

Anthony P. Kontos

Abstract

The purpose of the current chapter is to examine the role of culture/ethnicity on performance. After beginning with an overview of culture/ethnicity issues in the United States, the remainder of the chapter is organized into three sections: cultural/ethnic factors related to performance, factors that influence culture/ethnicity, and strategies for integrating culture/ethnicity into performance-based practice. The first section examines cultural/ethnic awareness and understanding related to historical issues, acculturation, and worldview. Challenges that affect the performance of cultural/ethnic groups, including "crossing-over" and racism, are explored. In the second section, factors including age, gender, and socioeconomic status that interact with culture/ethnicity to influence performance are reviewed. The third section discusses strategies to integrate culture/ethnicity with performance enhancement, including communication, cultural exchange, and cultivating opportunities for under-represented groups. A model for understanding the role of culture/ethnicity in regard to performance is proposed.

Key Words: Culture, ethnicity, sport, performance, gender, socioeconomic status (SES)

Darius is a 19-year-old African American student athlete from a larger urban area in the Midwestern United States. He is now a first-year scholarship American football player at a major university. He was an all-state performer in high school and was highly sought after among college recruiters, but he has struggled to adjust to the competition level since arriving at school. When he arrived on campus, Darius quickly realized that he was one of only a handful of African American male students on the predominately white, rural, and geographically isolated campus. He also has a lot of pressure from his stepfather and friends to succeed in his football career, and he misses his friends and family. Although Darius is the first individual from his family to attend university, he is doing well in his classes. However, his family and friends are interested primarily in his athletic performance. Lately,

he has been struggling to maintain focus on the field and has decided to seek performance enhancement services from the university's sport psychology professional.

Michelle is a 17-year-old Southeast Asian youth soccer player in California. She is an excellent player and has just been invited to spend the summer at a highly competitive residential soccer training center in Florida. Michelle is at a critical point in her soccer career, as the sport is demanding more of her and her family's time and support. She really wants to go to Florida and is excited about the opportunity. However, in spite of her considerable talent, her family is reticent to allow her to go to Florida to train, as they view her studies and family roles as being more important than her soccer career. Michelle's current soccer coach has asked the club's sport psychology professional to meet with

Michelle and her family to discuss the opportunity in Florida.

My point in starting this chapter with these two disparate examples from sport is to provoke the reader into pondering the role that culture/ethnicity may play in performance and opportunity. For some athletes, like Darius, culture/ethnicity may have encouraged and reinforced his sport participation, perhaps to the exclusion of other avenues of performance, resulting in concomitant pressure to succeed. However, his cultural/ethnic isolation on campus is not providing an ideal environment in which to excel. For Michelle, her culture/ethnicity has created barriers to her soccer opportunities. As a result, she is struggling with a decision between conforming to cultural roles and maintaining her cultural identity by not leaving to continue her soccer career, or continuing to pursue her performance opportunities in soccer, while going against her cultural values and social expectations.

Factors such as the sport, the performer's gender, and socioeconomic status (SES) may all play a role in how culture/ethnicity affects performance and opportunities to perform. Membership in a cultural/ethnic group sometimes reinforces sports participation, as it seems to for the Canadian hockey player, the Latino baseball player, and the African American basketball or American football player, as in Darius' case. Juxtaposed with these examples are individuals like Michelle, who might be playing a sport that is neither expected nor supported for someone from her culture/ethnic background. Culture and ethnicity can strongly influence both a player's perceptions and expectations and those of important others in their sports career, such as a coach, manager, fan, and trainer. How might culture/ethnicity shape these athletes' choices and opportunities, and enhance or detract from their performance?

The goal of the current chapter is to explore the cultural/ethnic factors that may influence performance. *Ethnicity* is defined as the shared cultural heritage (e.g., traditions, background) of a group of people (Coakley, 2004). Ethnic groups in the United States might include African Americans, Greek Americans, or Japanese Americans. Individuals within these socially distinct groups may share many cultural characteristics, but are not homogeneous in their cultural expression. As such, it is important to avoid the "sensitive stereotyping" of individuals from particular cultural/ethnic groups that can lead to overgeneralizations (Andersen, 1993; Kontos, 2009; Kontos & Breland-Noble,

2002). Culture refers to information and practices that describe how a group of people live in relation to their environment (Reber, 1995). When the term *minority* or *under-represented* is added to the mix, it refers to groups of people who experience discrimination, which in the United States includes African Americans, American Indians, Asians, Latinos, Native Hawaiians, and Pacific Islanders. Other cultural/ethnic groups who may have been discriminated against historically, such as Jews, Italians, or Irish, are no longer referred to as minority groups in the United States. However, there still exist biases, stereotypes, and subtle discrimination against these groups that must be considered by anyone working with individuals from these and other cultural/ethnic groups.

For the purposes of this chapter, I have combined the terms as *culture/ethnicity*, and use the term minority or under-represented where appropriate to refer to specific groups (e.g., African Americans, Latinos) with a history of discrimination in the United States. Rather than become mired in the ongoing debates about culture/ethnicity (and race for that matter) regarding issues such as semantics (e.g., use of the terms black vs. African American), I adopt a positive approach that focuses on developing awareness/understanding and strategies to enhance performance among individuals across cultural/ethnic groups. Throughout the chapter, I illustrate key issues using cases, and I provide practical insight with examples of effective strategies for integrating culture/ethnicity to enhance performance. In combining the terms culture and ethnicity, I hoped to promote a comprehensive look at their relationship to performance rather than focusing on the infinite permutations of specific cultural/ethnic groups. However, throughout the chapter, I provide specific examples that involve culturally/ethnically unique individuals whose characteristics and situations may differ significantly from individuals from other cultures/ethnicities. Moreover, the within-group variability of cultural/ethnic groups is substantial (Lloyd, 1987). As such, the reader should note that each individual is culturally/ethnically unique, and as with any performance enhancement intervention or treatment, an individualized approach is warranted. The chapter begins with a brief overview of ethnicity and culture in the United States, wherein I emphasize current trends in culture/ethnicity and cultural/ethnic representation within specific sports, rather than cultural/ethnicity-specific characteristics, which are reviewed elsewhere (see Kontos, 2009; Kontos & Breland-Noble, 2002).

Snapshot of Ethnicity and Culture in the United States

In the United States, over 107 million Americans represent at least one of several ethnic minority groups (e.g., African American, American Indian, Alaskan Native, Asian, Hispanic, Native Hawaiian, and/or Pacific Islander), and nearly 267 million Americans claim ancestry to one or more cultural (e.g., Arabic, Greek, Russian) groups (U.S. Census Bureau, 2001). Traditionally, the United States has been referred to as a "melting pot" or mosaic of cultures and peoples. This moniker is not surprising, given the preceding numbers and the fact that 31 million Americans are foreign-born (U.S. Census Bureau, 2001). However, in a less idealized but realistic analogy, culture in the United States is more reflective of a patterned, patch-work quilt, wherein various cultural groups have aggregated into strong but relatively separate, often geographically isolated communities that share similar values, beliefs, and customs. Each cultural/ethnic group can be broadly characterized as sharing certain cultural aspects such as language, religion, food, and values. However, the permutations in each individual's cultural practices, beliefs, and values result in significant variability within any one cultural/ethnic group (Kontos & Breland-Noble, 2002). Moreover, these communities may have limited cultural exchanges with other culturally/ethnically different groups. In addition, the geographic size (9.6 million square km) of the United States and its suburban sprawl beyond urban areas allows substantial distance and space for cultural separation.

It is important to note that ethnicity in the United States varies significantly with geography. For example, the Southwestern and Southeastern United States are characterized by large Latino communities. In contrast, the Northwestern United States consists of large Asian populations. Substantial African American populations are clustered around urban areas of the United States such as Detroit, Chicago, and Los Angeles, and are also scattered throughout rural and urban areas of the Southeast. Culturally/ethnically diverse populations in the United States tend to be clustered in or near large urban areas such as Seattle, Houston, and New York City. As such, the interactions among regional geography, community, and culture will infuse cultural practices and values (e.g., language, attire, food, music) with colloquial influences (e.g., sport opportunities, customs) that drive regional differences in attitudes, values, and behaviors among cultural/ethnic groups in the broad geographical area of the United States.

Cultural/ethnic representation in the general United States population is not mirrored in sports, particularly at higher levels of competition. In fact, certain sports such as professional American football and basketball have majority African American populations (both with nearly 70% representation) (Lapchick, 2004). Other sports, such as professional baseball and soccer, have burgeoning Latino immigrant populations. Other cultural/ethnic groups are generally represented at lower levels in sport than they are in the general population. Given these trends, sports with higher representation from under-represented cultural/ethnic groups may reflect values, beliefs, and practices that are reflective of the minority group and distinct from those of the majority cultural/ethnic group, which in the United States is predominately white.

Cultural/Ethnicity Factors Related to Performance

Many factors, such as language, religion, and geography, shape the influence of culture on behavior and performance through their effects on the development of cultural perspective and identity. As such, it is important to develop an understanding of the key cultural/ethnic factors related to performance. The following sections address the key issues that shape an individual's development, including historical context, acculturation/enculturation, and worldview. Next, the challenging issues of "crossing-over/tokenism" and racism/xenophobia are presented to explore the pertinent issues of discrimination and social identity than can influence performance among cultural/ethnic groups.

Awareness and Understanding of Culture

As advocated elsewhere (see Kontos, 2009), cultural self-awareness should be at the core of any multiculturally competent psychology professional's practice. Without knowing one's own cultural/ethnic identity, values, beliefs, and particularly biases, one cannot work effectively with, let alone relate to, culturally/ethnically different individuals. For the purposes of this chapter, I will focus on developing an understanding of culture/ethnicity that is predicated on the reader already being aware of his or her cultural self. To develop an understanding of culture, one should first consider the historical context and events that have shaped a cultural/ethnic group and its constituents.

HISTORICAL ISSUES

Historical forces play a significant role in shaping the cultural milieu of cultural/ethnic groups and the concomitant societal perceptions of their respective cultures. Most of these historical issues, such as slavery for African Americans, the concentration camps for Japanese living in the United States during World War II, or the forced relocation and assimilation of American Indians can be linked to specific cultural/ethnic groups and are attributed to the dominant cultural group (i.e., whites). The influence of these historical time periods and events continue to shape cultural/ethnic groups and must be considered when examining the relationship of culture to performance or any other behavior (see Kontos, 2009; Kontos & Breland-Noble, 2002, for a review of some of these issues). Moreover, the fact that many historical issues affecting cultural/ethnic groups in the United States are directly attributable to the dominant cultural/ethnic group has led to longstanding cultural/ethnic tensions, stereotypes, and prejudices, which are discussed in the racism/xenophobia section of this chapter.

History involves both group and individual processing. Groups of culturally/ethnically similar individuals may share a respective history, but the way in which each individual in the group experiences that history will vary as a product of many factors including exposure, SES, and age. In addition, individuals have their own histories apart from their group's history. For example, a poignant negative (or positive) encounter with someone from the dominant cultural group for an individual from a cultural/ethnic minority group will become part of that individual's personal history and drive perceptions of group history. Finally, history can be experienced through direct exposure to an event or time period, or it can be experienced indirectly through storytelling or other cultural reinforcement. Here, I will focus on one recent historical issue affecting an expanding ethnic/cultural group in the United States. Again, the reader should note that the relevance and importance ascribed to this historical issue to any one individual from the cultural/ethnic group discussed below is determined by an individual's exposure and personal history.

9/11 and Arab Americans

The tragic events of September 11, 2001 (9/11) have altered the perceptual landscape for Muslims, Arab Americans, and immigrants from Middle Eastern countries or those with similar cultural backgrounds, practices, and appearances. Prior to the events of 9/11, these individuals lived in relative anonymity in the United States. However, following the events of 9/11 and subsequent global episodes, such as the wars in Iraq and Afghanistan, their visibility and status changed dramatically. The predominantly negative response and perceptions in the United States toward Muslims and Arabs since 9/11 extend to individuals with similar skin color, appearance, and cultural beliefs and practices. For example, a Hindi from India might be perceived as being Muslim or Arabic by some, and, as such, will be subjected to the same negative affect and stereotypes. This misperception is based on the tendency of people to form first impressions based largely on skin color and appearance rather than on cultural awareness (Rule et al., 2010). The effects of the heightened exposure to Muslim and Arabic culture since 9/11 are particularly relevant to sport, in which participants are on public display. As a result, competition between non-Arabic/Christian and Arabic or Muslim nations/teams may take on exaggerated cultural importance. For example, in the 2010 World Cup in South Africa, the soccer match between Algeria and the United States was portrayed as a clash of cultures and values in the media. Such cultural pressures have the potential to affect the performance of athletes and are likely to persist until post-9/11 perceptions change both in the United States and abroad. As such, researchers should examine these issues to determine the effects that such cultural pressures might have on performance.

ACCULTURATION/ENCULTURATION

The manifestation of an individual's culture/ethnicity within a different dominant culture (e.g., white culture in the United States) exists on a continuum from highly acculturated to highly enculturated. *Acculturation* refers to the extent to which an individual has adopted or changed to reflect the dominant culture/ethnicity's values, beliefs, and practices (Marín, 1992). At the other end of the continuum is *enculturation*, which refers to the extent to which, in the presence of a dominant culture/ethnicity, an individual maintains affiliation with and acts in accordance with his or her own cultural/ethnic values, beliefs, and practices (Berry, 1993). An individual's level of acculturation toward or away from the dominant culture plays a significant role in determining what, if any effects, culture/ethnicity will have on performance. However, acculturation/enculturation is neither linear nor static, and within a multicultural society in a disparate country such as the United States, factors such as geographic location might influence significantly one's acculturation level. For example, a Latino baseball player may embrace the language, appearance, and customs of the dominant cultural group while playing for a team in the Northeastern United States. However, a year later, when he is traded to a team in Los Angeles, California, he may re-embrace his own culture. Other factors, such as time since immigration and generational status (first or second generation) may also influence acculturation levels. Finally, although acculturation encompasses numerous factors, language provides the most overt of example of acculturation. As such, in the United States, acculturation is typically easier among groups who already speak English. However, as illustrated in the case that follows, degrees of acculturation and enculturation are not always as they appear.

Case 1: Acculturated on the Surface; Enculturated at Heart

Maria, a 19-year-old first year Division I women's tennis player in the Southeastern United States, was referred to me for issues related to her "consistent decline in performance" (as described by her coaches) since arriving at school in the fall. Maria was a top recruit and was expected to be the No. 1 singles player. However, she has struggled to maintain the form that earned her numerous tennis scholarship offers from Division I schools and has performed progressively worse in each of her first three matches. Most of Maria's life has been spent in Colombia, where she lived with her father (her mother and father divorced, and she no longer has contact with her mother) and two older brothers, both of whom played competitive tennis. Maria spent the previous two summers in Miami, Florida, training, competing, and learning English to prepare her for tennis and school in the United States. After arriving at school in the fall, her performance has steadily decreased to the point at which she was struggling to maintain her playing position as the No. 3 singles player. Her style of playing has also not been effective, and Maria has been reticent to alter her approach.

Surprisingly, Maria's performance in the classroom has been excellent and according to coaches and teammates she has adjusted (i.e., acculturated) well to life at school in the Southeast. She lives with a "southern girl" and has developed an affinity for all things American—clothing, food, and music. At first, her performance issues seemed to be related to her

self-imposed expectations to win ("Winning is very important to me. I don't lose"), and performance anxiety ("Yes, I have been feeling more nervous before the last couple of matches than usual, but I will get through this") rather than culture per se. However, in the middle of our first session together, we began to discuss her family relationships and communication. Maria indicated that her father called her every night using an internet video connection to pass along updates and tips regarding her practice and match performances. She also received constant text messages and e-mails from her brothers, many of which inquired about her tennis performance. In spite of her outward acculturation in language, fashion, and lifestyle, Maria's strong connection to family and paternal cultural milieu reflected a more enculturated worldview. Much of Maria's performance anxiety and decrements stemmed from her obligation to follow her father's and brothers' advice and to please them. She expressed that she felt uncomfortable challenging their suggestions, even though she believed that they were counterproductive and in opposition to her coaches' advice. She was also concerned that her father would not want to talk with her unless it was about tennis, and she enjoyed speaking with him and missed her family. This statement was reflective of her general feeling that she "missed her family and friends in Colombia," something that had surfaced during the first summer she spent in Miami 2 years ago. Maria was especially uncomfortable speaking directly to her father (reflective of gender roles in Colombian culture) about changing her style of play, practice, or anything else tennis-related. She was also afraid that if she challenged her father, she might lose her connection to family and home.

I arranged to first speak with her father separately to discuss the situation and suggest that it would be in the best interest of Maria's tennis career that we talk together with Maria. We arranged a 2-hour internet video conference call, during which Maria's father and brothers agreed to let Maria's coaches—who were introduced toward the end of the call—work with Maria on her game. During the call, Maria expressed her concern about losing touch with her family and Colombia in general if they were not talking about tennis. They agreed to have two internet video calls per week that were devoted to personal, family, school, and other topics, and to have one call on Sundays devoted to tennis updates and discussion, but without the previous coaching/advice focus. Similar arrangements were made with her brothers regarding the text messages and e-mails. Her brothers also started to join their father on one of the personal calls each week and sent Maria positive encouraging text messages before each match. After a few weeks of the new communication and tennis coaching patterns, Maria began to return to her previous form and by the end of the season she had returned to No. 1 singles and placed second in an open invitational tournament. More importantly, Maria was having fun playing tennis again and had managed to strengthen her familial connection to her father and brothers in the process.

Case 1 illustrates how overt aspects of acculturation (e.g., language, food, fashion) may not accurately reflect underlying manifestations of enculturation (e.g., importance of family, cultural roles) that are affecting performance. Moreover, Maria's case highlights the role of awareness and communication in understanding culture/ethnicity's role in regard to performance and opportunities.

WORLDVIEW

We all look at individuals or groups of people through our own unique individual worldview (Kehe & Smith, 2004). This lens through which we view the world frames our perceptions of individuals who are culturally/ethnically different from us. Our worldview is built upon experience (direct and indirect) and our own cultural/ethnic identity (Sue et al., 1998). In particular, a worldview is shaped by poignant encounters, and, much as our nightmares are more memorable than our dreams, so too do negative encounters affect our worldview more so than positive ones. For example, a young soccer player who is African American may experience a racial slur from a white opponent in front of a large crowd with no direct resolution early in his life. As a result of this poignant negative encounter, he may develop a worldview with negative perceptions of whites that will be difficult to change even through subsequent positive encounters with whites. Later, this athlete may experience subtle biases playing with white teammates or for a white coach that might adversely influence his performance. Such encounters may also be indirect, such as those experienced by the millions of individuals who watched the media's coverage of African Americans stranded in New Orleans following Hurricane Katrina. Of course, as mentioned earlier, our worldview is built upon our cultural/ethnic identity. Hence, an individual's culture/ethnicity would have influenced the perception of the images from Hurricane Katrina.

However, our worldview is also influenced by the social (sport, school) and cultural (religion, values) institutions to which we ascribe allegiance. Consequently, our cultural/ethnic belief systems will add additional focus to our worldview lens.

Performance Challenges for Cultural/Ethnic Groups
THE ISSUES OF "CROSSING-OVER," "TOKENISM," AND "SELLING OUT"

Consider the following examples of athletes from specific cultures/ethnicities and their respective sports: an African American woman who plays professional tennis, a Chinese man who plays professional basketball, and a Latino man who plays professional hockey. Depending on your familiarity with current American sports performers, you may have already thought of athletes who represent each of the above examples, such as Venus or Serena Williams, Yao Ming, or Scott Gomez. Each of these athletes represents an example of "crossing-over," which refers to an athlete who plays a sport that is not traditionally played by his or her cultural/ethnic group (Coakley, 2004). Many sports that are non-traditional for certain cultural/ethnic groups are that way because of historical discrimination and lack of access and opportunity for cultural/ethnic minority groups in the United States. Examples of sports with such discriminatory histories include golf, tennis, swimming, and alpine skiing. On the other hand, cultural/ethnic groups may emphasize certain sports, resulting in a narrowed perception of destiny and encouraged participation in only select sports (Coakley, 2004). For example, African American males may be encouraged to focus on American football and basketball, whereas Latino males may be encouraged to focus instead on soccer and baseball. As alluded to later in the chapter, factors such as gender—and particularly SES—may play a significant role in determining sport expectations. For example, as a result of different gender role expectations, both Latina and African American females would not have a cultural/ethnic impetus to focus on the same sports as their male counterparts.

Once an athlete has "crossed over" to a nontraditional sport, that athlete must contend with the issues of being a "token" representative of his or her cultural/ethnic group (Coakley, 2004). Athletes in this position are often resented by teammates, as their inclusion on the team is perceived by the majority cultural/ethnic group's athletes as acquiescence to some unwritten cultural/ethnic quota system. However, at the same time, these athletes might be viewed as "sell-outs" by members of their own cultural/ethnic group and feel alienation from their own cultural/ethnic group (Kontos, 2009). As such, these athletes are in a challenging situation, and their resilience in dealing with such stress is probably critical to sustaining their performance and maximizing their opportunity. A recent example of such resiliency was evident in the challenges and ultimate success of Shani Davis, the first African American Olympic gold medalist in long-track speed skating, a sport long dominated by white athletes (although the recent success of South Korean, Chinese, and Japanese skaters suggests that this trend is changing). Shani grew up on the south side of Chicago, where speed skating is largely unknown and no facilities for the sport exist, and where most of his classmates were playing basketball, baseball, or American football. To cross-over into a sport like long-track speed skating required significant resilience. In referring to his selection of speed skating and his success in crossing over in the sport, Shani Davis stated, "To me, personally, it doesn't matter what color I am. Black or white, Asian or Hispanic, it doesn't matter to me as long as the message I'm portraying to people that watch me on TV is positive and it shows that they can do things that are different besides catching a football, hitting a baseball, or shooting a basketball. I'm just showing them that stepping outside the bubble is OK and they can be successful at it" (Wise, 2006, para. 14). It is important to note that much of what we know about the effects of crossing-over in sports is based on anecdotes such as this. As such, researchers should begin to examine empirically the nature of crossing-over and its potential effects—both positive and negative—on performance and performers.

RACISM/XENOPHOBIA

Sport provides an environment wherein, ideally, cultural/ethnic biases are wiped away and the focus instead is on performance. In practice, however, cultural/ethnic biases pervade sport through *race logic*, which is the stereotype that only certain racial/ethnic groups should play certain sports. Such cultural/ethnic bias is often referred to as *racism* in the United States or *xenophobia* (meaning literally fear of foreigners) in Europe. Racism can be subtle, as indicated in statements about performance and attributions for performance by media commentators (Coakley, 2004). Such comments are not restricted to the media. In fact, just the other day, I overheard a parent at a youth soccer game point out how "quick" one young player, who happened to be

African American, was. A few moments later, when a white player ran past the African American player, the same parent quipped about the white player, "he sure does hustle and read the game well." The first comment attributes performance to an innate physical attribute of speed, whereas, the second comment attributes performance to mental acuity and hard work. In the United States, we are often more tolerant of such subtle or "closed-door" racism than of overt forms of racism, as these subtle forms are viewed by those who are biased in such ways as something that does not harm anyone directly. However, such an attitude feeds the undercurrent of racial stereotypes, caricatures, and prejudice in the United States and can adversely affect performers' perceptions and confidence. Individuals are often unaware that they engage in subtle racism. A good litmus test for subtle racism is the "Would you say it aloud in mixed company?" question. Examples of somewhat less subtle racism can also be seen in the images and perceptions that advertisers and the media use. A recent example is the image of LeBron James, an African American player from the National Basketball Association hugging Giselle Bündchen, a white, Brazilian fashion model, on the cover of a 2008 *Vogue* magazine. This image, which represented the first African American male on the cover of *Vogue*, was perceived by some scholars and sports columnists as a racist portrayal of an African American male athlete as "animalistic" and a threat to white women in the United States (National Public Radio, 2008).

Unfortunately, some forms of racism in the United States are even less subtle. A now infamous recent example of overt racism in the United States was evidenced by radio personality Don Imus. He used racially prejudiced descriptions when referring to African American members of the Rutgers University women's basketball team, who at the time had just finished competing for the national championship. His comments were so overtly racist that even his colleagues were demonstrably uncomfortable, as evidenced by their on-air silence following Imus' comments. Although, these comments came after their performance, imagine the effects—both positive and negative—they might have had had they been made prior to their competition.

Both subtle and overt examples of racism reinforce performance stereotypes and can result in socially imposed performance and opportunity restrictions. Performers are often placed into sport positions based on racial stereotypes (Coakley, 2004). This practice is referred to as *stacking*.

For example, a coach may place an African American baseball player at center field due to racial stereotypes about his speed and athleticism, which are essential for that position. A related construct, *propinquity*, which refers to being close to the action, pertains to the tendency for positions of power/control in sport to be occupied by the dominant cultural group (i.e., whites). Examples of this practice include assigning white performers to be point guards in basketball, catchers in baseball, goalies or central defenders in soccer, and quarterbacks in American football. The restrictions in performance opportunity and exposure that result from stacking, together with the lack of performance awareness and influence from propinquity and other forms of racism in sport, can lead to a reduction in mentoring and exposure, and a subsequent reduction in opportunities in performance-related pursuits (e.g., coaching, administration, sport psychology). Hence, performers should be given the opportunity and encouraged to develop the skills required of different positions in sport regardless of ethnic/cultural background.

Factors That Influence Culture/Ethnicity

In this section, I discuss two factors that are known to influence the effects of culture/ethnicity on performance: gender and SES. Although both factors are addressed independently here, they often intersect to influence the effect of culture/ethnicity on performance. For example, girls from certain cultural/ethnic groups have different expectations placed upon them based on their parents' SES, which influences their cultural/ethnic roles and ability to participate in sport and other areas of performance. Such a process is evident to some degree in Alima's case, described in Case 2. Another example of the interaction between these factors pertains to the sport of boxing, in which culture/ethnicity (i.e., African Americans, Latinos), class (i.e., education), and gender (i.e., male) drive current and future participation patterns and rates in the United States (Wacquant, 1995). Therefore, the reader is cautioned to consider the following factors in combination rather than looking at any single factor in isolation to explain the relationship of culture/ethnicity to performance.

Gender

The area in which gender and culture/ethnicity interact to have the greatest impact is in the opportunity to perform. Researchers have suggested that opportunity in sport is influenced significantly by males, who control sport access and opportunities, particularly at the youth/sandlot level (Elling & Knoppers, 2005). Interestingly, male cultural/ethnic minorities follow the same prejudicial patterns as their male cultural/ethnic majority counterparts. As such, female cultural/ethnic minorities must overcome the prejudices of being both female and from a cultural/ethnic minority to have opportunity and succeed in sport. However, as Elling and Knoppers caution, it is important not to generalize or use sensitive stereotypes (Kontos & Breland-Noble, 2002) in assuming that all members of one group share the same biases or predispositions. For example, Muslim cultures are assumed to provide and encourage few opportunities for women in sport due to cultural gender role expectations. However, such a generalization overly simplifies the role of gender across Muslim cultures. For example, Moroccans and Surinamese Muslim females were more likely (~40%) to play sports compared to those of Turkish (~18%) background (Elling & Knoppers, 2005). Moreover, as noted by Walseth (2006), playing sports (i.e., being healthy) is consistent with Islamic ideals and is therefore more common among women who identify with their religion more so than with their culture per se. Therefore, in addition to treating each individual uniquely, one must consider the nature of the subgroups (e.g., Moroccans) within a larger group (e.g., Muslims).

Some researchers (e.g., Myers & Spencer, 2006) have argued for examining gender's role in regard to culture/ethnicity on a continuum, with masculine and feminine at either end. Certain cultures, such as Latin American and Middle Eastern, are more patriarchal and may, therefore, have more rigid sex roles, which may affect performance and opportunity to perform. The film *Bend It Like Beckham* highlighted the interaction between culture/ethnicity and gender in regard to performance opportunity. In the film, which is set in England, the lead female character, who is Pakistani (a culture that is more masculine on the continuum), plays soccer in spite of her family's cultural objections. Similarly, the following case demonstrates how the effects of culture/ethnicity on performance interact with gender roles to influence performance opportunity and access in the United States.

Case 2: Playing in the Shadows: Culture and Gender Roles

Alima, a talented 16-year-old high school soccer player at an ethnically mixed high school in a suburban area of the Midwestern United States, suddenly stopped coming to practice during the preseason of her junior year, and her teammates are not sure what it is going on. Alima was one of the best players on the team during the past two seasons—earning all–conference and area honors—and was expected to be an all-state candidate this season. As Alima's coach, I was concerned that she was in some sort of trouble—academic or personal. I checked with the school counselor, Mary, who indicated that Alima was doing well in class and that she was not aware of any personal issues involving Alima. Earlier that year, Alima's younger cousin Jamil began attending the same high school, where he played on my boy's high school soccer team. Jamil would occasionally come to watch the girls practice, and it was then that he learned that Alima was playing soccer. He informed his parents about this and they, in turn, informed Alima's parents. It was at this point that the gender roles and expectations from Alima's culture interacted to effectively end her soccer career. As a young, Middle Eastern, Muslim woman coming of age in America, Alima was expected to start assuming the traditional gender and family roles of women from her culture. In so doing, she was expected to avoid masculine physical activities and to start working as a hostess in her family's restaurant. Alima was certainly not expected to be running around and playing soccer, a sport reserved for males in her culture. Apparently, unbeknown to her teammates and myself, Alima had been playing soccer without the approval or knowledge of her family for nearly 2 years. In retrospect, I had never seen Alima's parents at the team meetings, as they were not mandatory, and Alima did not attend team social events or the end-of-season banquet. It is important to note that the school she attended did have a signed consent and physical exam on file for her to participate in physical activities, including physical education courses, and club and varsity sports. After learning about Alima's situation, I contacted her family to inquire about her status and possible return to the team. Her father explained to me that he was sorry, but that Alima would no longer be playing soccer as she was not permitted to do so. He also indicated that Alima had played soccer with her male siblings and cousins when she was younger—which helped to explain why she was so talented—but that it was no longer appropriate for her to be playing. I did not attempt to change her father's mind, as it was not my place to challenge his cultural beliefs. However, I did express to him that she was an excellent player—my best in fact—and that her talents would be missed, and I wished Alima and her family well.

Alima's situation provides an example of how gender can interact with culture to influence performance opportunity or, in this case, access to sport. Had Alima been a male in the same situation, her actions would have been supported and encouraged by her family's cultural values. However, in spite of her talent, her cultural gender roles would not afford her the opportunity to perform in a sport such as soccer. As an anecdotal aside, several of Alima's teammates who were from Middle Eastern cultures with more Westernized views of gender roles were allowed to play on the team. These divergent perspectives on gender roles are evidence of the substantial within-group cultural/ethnic variation alluded to earlier.

Socioeconomic Status

Socioeconomic status or *class* as it is often referred to in Europe, can influence opportunity and perceptions of destiny, and cause stress associated with performance and outcomes in sport (Kontos, 2009). Another issue with regard to SES and performance pertains to the erroneous assumption in the United States that being a member of certain under-represented groups (e.g., African Americans, Latinos) is linked to a low SES (Ford, 1997). For example, at one institution I worked at, a faculty colleague was admiring how one of her African American students had managed to develop good writing and analytical skills despite his disadvantaged background. Unknown to my colleague, this particular athlete was born and raised in a middle-income suburban community and had attended high-performing educational institutions since primary school. Of course, the converse can also be true in that certain under-represented groups might be assumed to be from higher SES families, when in fact, they represent a lower SES. The notion that all individuals from a certain cultural/ethnic minority group must be of low SES furthers the social stratification of individuals from these groups and reinforces negative stereotypes of cultural/ethnic minority groups.

Socioeconomic status can exacerbate or underlie issues typically attributed to culture/ethnicity. A good example of the interaction of SES and culture/ethnicity was provided in the case of Darius, presented at the beginning of the chapter. As in Darius' case, there may be significant stress and expectations from family and friends to perform in certain sports such as American football and basketball as a means of increasing SES and class standing (Coakley, 2004).

These perceptions can reinforce prevailing sport participation patterns, thus limiting other performance opportunities among current and future generations of cultural/ethnic minorities. At a recent session on career transitions out of sport that I presided over at a sport psychology conference, an audience member asked the presenter, a graduate student in sport psychology who had interviewed former National Football League (NFL) players, if the players were driven by money when they retired, to which the presenter replied, "Not when they retire. But they definitely were when they came into the League."

Typically, when we discuss the role of SES in sport performance and opportunity, we focus on low SES levels. In an interesting look at the effect of moderate SES and soccer performance, Kuper and Szymanski (2009) concluded that, at least in England (where they conducted their research), the majority of high-level (i.e., national team members) soccer players were from the working classes. As such, the middle class was all but left out (only 15% of the players came from this SES level) of high-level soccer. This finding would suggest that individuals of moderate to high SES are not encouraged to pursue sport beyond amateur levels. In contrast, in the United States, soccer is primarily played by individuals from moderate SES levels and has struggled to gain hold with individuals at lower SES levels, as it has in Europe, South America, and elsewhere in the world. In this regard, the sport and regional geography must also be considered when examining the role of SES on culture/ethnicity and performance and opportunity.

Strategies for Integrating Culture/Ethnicity into Performance-Based Practice

In the following sections, I present three strategies and an integrated approach for enhancing performance when working with individuals from diverse cultural/ethnic backgrounds. For each of the three strategies, I discuss a specific example of an effective strategy for enhancing performance. The first and perhaps most critical issue that I examine is communication. Second, I review strategies for enhancing cultural exchange and respect. In the cultural exchange section, I discuss briefly the power of exchange in enhancing communication and performance and provide examples from youth sports, as well as from my own collegiate athletic experience. Third, I examine the issues pertaining to leadership, mentoring, and action opportunities for underrepresented cultural/ethnic groups in sport and psychology. In the final section, I present an integrated approach to understanding culture/ethnicity's role in performance.

Communication: Bridging the Gaps

Anecdotally, I would estimate that over 75% of all of my sport/exercise psychology consulting cases have involved ineffective communication between athlete and coach, athlete and family, or athlete and athlete. Cultural/ethnic differences can exacerbate communication issues (McNamara, 2004). Language in particular can present a barrier to effective communication. Many professional sports leagues now employ interpreters and offer language lessons to non-English speaking athletes. However, interpreters and standard language lessons rarely address the sport-specific language needs critical for successful communication for performance. A coach of many Latin American baseball players with whom I worked developed a system of "baseball language lessons" that involved contextual language specific to the sport of baseball. He developed a slide show of baseball language using photos of his players (also reinforcing names and faces) that he would show to players who were also taking English lessons. He would constantly reinforce their learning by asking his newly arrived players from Venezuela and the Dominican Republic questions like, "Hey, what is that?" to which his players replied variously, "squeeze play," "pitch out," or "fielder's choice." Unfortunately, many efforts to enhance communication among culturally/ethnic minority groups focus only on learning English and rarely address the cultural communication issues that go beyond language.

Cultural communication involves the transfer of traditional cultural values and beliefs through verbal and nonverbal means. Cultural communication between different cultural/ethnic groups can foster cultural awareness and exchange, and create an environment of inclusion and belonging. One example of cultural communication is the Haka dance performed by the All-Blacks national rugby team from New Zealand. The dance was later adopted by the University of Hawaii and several high school American football teams as far removed as Texas. This dance, which is a traditional Maori war dance that has been adopted by other Polynesian cultural groups, serves to reinforce traditional cultural values and connections among the Maori athletes, while also providing a unique opportunity for cultural awareness among non-Maori teammates. Unfortunately, the Haka has been adopted by many teams without regard to its cultural meaning. In fact, the University of Hawaii no longer uses the dance before games because it was not representative of Hawaiian culture. Nonetheless, dance, music, and sport (see ethnic sport information in the following section) provide excellent vehicles for cultural communication. It is important for individuals working with diverse teams of individuals representing multiple cultures to promote such cultural communication opportunities by creating an open and supportive performance environment in which individuals are comfortable sharing aspects of their culture without criticism.

A Culture of Exchange and Respect: Using Sport as a Vehicle of Cultural Sharing and Understanding

Occasionally, cultural exchange will occur as a result of circumstance. For example, during an overnight stay for a tournament when I was a first-year collegiate soccer player, my coach (literally) drew straws to see who would room together that night (I still believe this was some sort of social experiment!). I drew straws with a 20-year-old Nigerian player named John. I had not spoken with John off the field in the 2 weeks since training camp started, and I knew nothing of him personally, or of his culture. Both he and I were quite tentative and uncertain going into the hotel room, as we had no idea what to expect. The first few minutes of silence seemed to go on forever, until I said, "So, where in Nigeria are you from?" Much to our collective surprise, the conversation that followed provided a vehicle for cultural exchange and understanding both on and off the field. He shared his experiences as part of the majority cultural group living just outside of Lagos, Nigeria, contrasted with the unfamiliar experience in the United States of being a cultural/ethnic minority. I discussed a poignant example of attending a concert in Detroit where my friend and I were the only two white males in the theater, and we contrasted these and other experiences. We also discussed the nuances of soccer playing styles in Nigeria compared to those in the United States. As a result of this "chance" cultural encounter, John and I not only became friends, but began to communicate and anticipate each other's movements and styles more effectively on the field as well. It is important to note that such serendipitous cultural exchanges can be structured into performer's lives through overnight hotel stays, practice partnering, team building, and other activities.

An often overlooked strategy for cultural sharing is *ethnic sport*. Ethnic games are games or competitions played by specific cultural/ethnic groups that reflect traditional culture and help reinforce cultural identity (Sogawa, 2006). Such games might include traditional cultural sports such as lacrosse for Iroquois American Indians, martial arts in certain Asian cultures, or wrestling in Kazakhstan, or they may involve sports that have been "culturally adopted" by groups or countries, such as cricket in Pakistan and India, and rugby for the Maori culture. A fourth-grade teacher I know has used ethnic games as a way to instill cultural awareness and appreciation through cultural exchange. In her class, she has asked each child and parent to research and implement an ethnic sport. Children may select a game representing their own cultural/ethnic group or one from another group. At the conclusion of this experience, the teacher conducts a week-long cultural/ethnic sport Olympics, wherein the children exchange the information about each culture/ethnicity and then participate in the game (or some similar derivative thereof; after all, the caber toss—a Scottish sport involving heaving a 5 m, 70 kg wooden pole—can be a bit daunting with fourth graders!). The resulting cultural exchange involving more common cultural/ethnic sports like lacrosse, cricket, and rugby, to less common sports such as ulama (an Olmecan-Mexican ball game), kite fighting, and kendo (Japanese sword fighting) exposes children to new sport opportunities and serves to create awareness of culture/ethnicity. As a side note, ethnic sports can also be used to foster culturally reinforced physical activity among individuals from a particular cultural/ethnic group.

It is important to note that forced cultural exchanges, such as those I witnessed during a cultural team building session for a collegiate women's basketball team, can backfire. In this instance, the athletes, who represented several nationalities, cultures, and ethnicities, were subjected to a contrived cultural exchange, introduction, and subsequent problem-solving activity that was met with nervous laughter and snide comments, and only served to reinforce the cultural distance among the team members. The individual who designed this intervention was not invited back the following year. The following year, we employed a partner cultural potluck and sport exchange for the first few weeks of the season. It was such a hit that the players decided to continue doing it each week, and it continues to be used to this day. It is also important to mention that the use of the strategies outlined here can be effective at any level or age. However, the earlier we introduce performers to cultural exchange, the more likely they are to develop respect for other cultures and be proud of their own unique cultural/ethnic identities.

Cultivating Leadership, Mentoring, and Action Opportunities for Underrepresented Groups

For the past two decades, professionals in the field of sport/exercise psychology have advocated for the expansion of opportunities for leadership in sport/exercise psychology involving under-represented groups (e.g., Duda & Allison, 1990; Kontos & Arguello, 2005; Martens, Mobley, & Zizzi, 2000). I believe that *targeted mentoring* is the most effective strategy for increasing opportunities for leadership among culturally/ethnically under-represented groups. Targeted mentoring can be informal (e.g., pairing up an under-represented student athlete with a graduate student mentor) or formal (e.g., recruitment via scholarships for specific under-represented groups to enter an educational program). Formal strategies can be effective, but often feel contrived and recreate many of the issues of "selling-out" and "tokenism" described earlier. An excellent strategy for increasing informal mentoring is for sport/exercise psychology professionals, coaches, and instructors to immerse themselves in the world of culturally/ethnically under-represented groups in sport. As Terry (2009) suggested, such a strategy, whether working with a performer or mentoring him or her toward a career after sport, can help dispel stereotypes, create understanding of subcultural norms, and enhance trust. From a mentoring perspective, it is equally important for a sport/exercise psychology professional, instructor, or coach to provide the same immersion experience for the mentee. For example, I frequently invite students and student athletes from my sport/exercise psychology undergraduate classes to sit in on individual sessions I have with athletes or participate in graduate student research club discussions. Following these experiences, I discuss with the mentee the issues of culture/ethnicity (e.g., worldview, racism, acculturation) related to working with a particular athlete or research topic. As such, both the mentor and mentee can experience both sides of the fence, so to speak. However, as Terry later pointed out, such informal contact is not appropriate with all cultures, such as within the coach–athlete hierarchy of Japanese culture, the teacher–student relationship in Korean culture, or for a male sport/exercise psychology professional or coach working with female Muslim athletes. Nonetheless, immersing one's self

in a culturally/ethnically different world demonstrates a true commitment to the performer or mentee and provides insights that could not otherwise be obtained from reading information contained in publications (such as this chapter).

Another area in which we can cultivate opportunity is through our work in under-represented cultural/ethnic communities. In so doing, we create opportunities for community members to become involved in sport/exercise psychology, coaching, or sport, and we can leverage resources from cultural/ethnic communities for later partnerships. Schinke et al. (2009) described an ideal community model for working with aboriginal athletes in Canada. In their approach, Schinke and colleagues addressed many of the issues presented in this chapter, including acculturation and communication. They also addressed the importance of relevant cultural practices, such as those used by performers in daily training, and cultural resources, such as those provided by aboriginal elders and other community leaders.

Currently, here at the University of Pittsburgh, my colleagues and I are working on a program designed to address health disparities in under-represented groups, specific to mild traumatic brain injury or concussion care. Specifically, we have designed a program that involves partnering with key "gatekeepers" in the African American community here in Pittsburgh to provide educational, assessment, treatment, and other concussion-related outreach services. We undertook this process after we noticed that African American athletes, particularly youth American football players, were under-represented as patients in our sports-related concussion program. We found this to be peculiar given that African Americans are represented in concussion-risk sports such as American football at higher levels than in the overall population of the United States (Kontos, Elbin, Covassin, & Larson, 2010) and that certain neighborhood American football programs in Pittsburgh are comprised of 90–100% African American participants. Using an approach similar to that described by Schinke et al. (2009), my colleagues and I have begun to develop a cultural network of outreach in these underserved neighborhoods. The key to success in this and any similar endeavor is partnering with key cultural representatives or gatekeepers (e.g., religious leader, coaches, former athletes, youth community center activists) and fostering a two-way street of cultural communication and exchange, as described earlier. Additionally, we have used the strong cultural ties to American football in these neighborhoods, together with our program's access to professional- and collegiate-level players, to create initial community interest in the program. As part of our program, we have begun to recruit and support financially African American undergraduate students to work with us in providing concussion outreach services. In addition, the program itself has spurned several inquiries from administrators, coaches, and parents to learn more about concussion and be able impart that information to other members of their communities. Fortunately, we have been able to secure funding for this program. However, initially our efforts were pro bono and were designed to demonstrate a strong commitment regardless of financial support. Although this is challenging to do, it is an important part of demonstrating an altruistic commitment to and partnership with a cultural/ ethnic group, one that also is perceived as mutually beneficial. We also plan to sustain our partnership beyond the scope of our project regardless of future funding. The primary goals of our program are to foster awareness of concussion among athletes, parents, coaches, and community members; cultivate and sustain community partnerships and resources to enhance access to and use of concussion services; and provide empirical data regarding the health disparity in concussion awareness and care within the African American communities in the greater Pittsburgh area. Our program incorporates much of what was discussed in the chapter (e.g., acculturation, SES, communication, cultural exchange) and offers one example of how community partnerships can lead to positive action within underrepresented cultural/ethnic groups.

An Integrated Approach

Previously, I have advocated for an integrated model for multicultural competency within sport psychology (Kontos, 2009). For the purposes of this chapter, I have adapted the model to provide an integrated approach to understanding the role of culture/ethnicity on performance (see Figure 22.1). This approach begins with a base of understanding of one's cultural self, including awareness (e.g., insight into own and others' cultures), identity (e.g., developmental stage of ethnic identity), and practices and beliefs (e.g., religion, language, stereotypes). For example, Abdu, a male distance runner who recently emigrated from Kenya to the United States to run for a collegiate track-and-field team has limited insight into culture in the United States, as he has never been outside of Africa during his competitions. On the surface, one might assume that

Abdu is keenly aware of ethnic identity in relation to others since Kenya is a very multicultural society, with over 40 tribal groups; however, Abdu has limited awareness of other ethnic identities as he is used to living in a monocultural Sunni Islamic/ Swahili area in Kenya's coastal region. Therefore, his cultural practices include daily prayers and a largely vegetarian diet, and although he speaks English very well, he is subjected to racial stereotypes that are exacerbated in the United States because he also practices Islam. Our understanding of our cultural self is then in constant contact with and influenced by our ever-changing worldview (i.e., how we view cultural different individuals and groups) and levels of enculturation and acculturation.

In the preceding example, the stereotypes and racism Abdu experienced in the United States are familiar to him, as he was a religious minority in Kenya, which is predominately (50%) Christian. However, he did not expect such perceptions to persist in the United States, and it has adversely affected his worldview of Americans in general. Moreover, Abdu is very enculturated toward Swahili and Islamic values and practices. Consequently, it is challenging for him to adjust to American culture. The nature of our worldview and cultural self is in turn influenced by demographics (i.e., gender, age, SES), history (personal and group), and experience (tokenism, racism) within a performance context. In Abdu's case, as a male from a high-SES family in Kenya, he has lived a generally privileged life and will be the third member of his four siblings to attend

Figure 22.1 Integrated approach to understanding ethnicity/ culture and performance.

college abroad. His personal experiences with other cultural groups have been generally positive, but he has experienced some racism both at home and in the United States as a result mostly of his religion and skin color. Ultimately, an integrated approach is needed to understand how the complexities of culture/ethnicity might influence performance for an athlete or other performer such as Abdu.

Conclusion

The goal of this chapter was to provide the reader with an overview of some of the key issues related to culture/ethnicity and performance and opportunity. Such a goal was challenging, as the literature in this area is limited and at best disparately connected. Regardless, the reader should take away from this chapter three key principles: (1) awareness of the effects of acculturation, crossing-over, and racism on a performer is critical to understanding a performer's worldview; (2) each performer represents a unique combination of culture/ethnicity, gender, and SES that demands an individualized approach from consultants and counselors; and (3) strategies that foster communication, cultural exchange, and increased opportunities for performers should be implemented whenever possible. In addition, I challenge practitioners to adopt an integrated approach to their work in the area of culture/ethnicity and performance. In conclusion, I hope that this chapter has started you on a path toward understanding and employing cultural/ethnic strategies for performance and opportunity in sport, and I encourage you to explore new strategies for cultivating sensitivity to culture/ethnicity as an integral part of performance enhancement.

Future Directions

From an applied perspective, practitioners should challenge themselves to go beyond the information and training about culture/ethnicity in performance provided in publications such as this chapter or presentations and workshops, and engage in true cultural immersion and exchange. Such opportunities might be provided for future practitioners as part of internship or practicum training, wherein a cross-cultural training model is implemented. However, among current practitioners, such opportunities may be challenging to locate or create. Hence, we, as a field, need to cultivate avenues for immersion through sustained outreach efforts, such as the one described earlier in this chapter. Members of the American Psychological Association's Division 47 (Exercise and Sport Psychology) and Association of

Applied Sport Psychology (AASP) should be encouraged to devise programs aimed at under-represented groups during their annual conferences and at other accessible times. However, we need to go beyond "one-time" initiatives and attempt to develop a sustainable framework for cultural immersion and exchange. Finally, we must create opportunities for individuals from under-represented cultural/ethnic groups in our field. My colleagues and I (Kontos & Breland-Noble, 2002; Kontos, 2009) have made repeated calls for enhanced scholarships, academic and professional opportunities, and representation among under-represented cultural/ethnic groups in academic and training programs. A key component of these efforts is the mentoring of undergraduate students from under-represented groups into our field. Hence, I challenge each of us as professionals or academicians to mentor (e.g., professional "shadowing," involvement in research, participation in journal clubs, etc.) one or more undergraduate students from an under-represented culture/ethnicity each year.

With regard to research, the area of culture/ethnicity and performance is rife with opportunities and challenges for researchers. Within the sport context, we know little about many of the issues discussed in this chapter, including acculturative stress in sports and the effects of crossing-over. Moreover, we know little about how specific cultural/ethnic groups perceive the issues presented in this chapter, or how such perceptions might differ within and across groups. Hence, qualitative research, involving focus groups and interviews with members within and across cultural/ethnic groups, is warranted. Finally, researchers should examine the role of culture/ethnicity in performance outside of the sport context, in areas such as the performing arts, entertainment, and business. Hopefully, the focus of new journals such as the APA Division 47's *Sport, Exercise, and Performance Psychology* will provide a vehicle for research beyond the realm of sport.

References

Andersen, M. B. (1993). Questionable sensitivity: A comment on Lee and Rotella. *Sport Psychologist, 7*, 1–3.

Berry, J. W. (1993). Ethnic identity in plural societies. In M. E. Bernal & G. P. Knight (Eds.), *Ethnic identity: Formation and transmission among Hispanics and other minorities* (pp. 271–296). Albany, NY: State University of New York Press.

Coakley, J. (2004). *Sport in society: Issues and controversies* (8th ed.). New York: McGraw-Hill.

Duda, J. L., & Allison, M. T. (1990). Cross-cultural analysis in exercise and sport psychology: A void in the field. *Journal of Sport and Exercise Psychology, 12*, 114–131.

Elling, A., & Knoppers, A. (2005). Sport, gender, and ethnicity: Practises of symbolic inclusion/exclusion. *Journal for Youth and Adolescence, 24*(3), 257–268.

Ford, D. Y. (1997). Counseling middle class African Americans. In C. Lee (Ed.), *Multicultural issues in counseling: New approaches to diversity* (2nd ed., pp. 81–108). Alexandria, VA: American Counseling Association.

Kehe, J. V., & Smith, T. B. (2004). Glossary. In T. Smith (Ed.), *Practicing multiculturalism: Affirming diversity in counseling and psychology* (pp. 325–337). Boston: Pearson.

Kontos, A. P. (2009). Moving toward multicultural competency in sport psychology in the USA. In R. Schinke & S. Hanrahan (Eds.), *Cultural sport psychology: From theory to practice* (pp.103–116). Champaign, IL: Human Kinetics.

Kontos, A. P. & Arguello, E. (2005, September). Sport psychology consulting with Latin American athletes. *Athletic Insight: The Online Journal of Sport Psychology, 7*(3). Retrieved from http://www.athleticinsight.com/Vol7Iss3/LatinAmerican.htm

Kontos, A. P., & Breland-Noble, A. M. (2002). Racial/ethnic diversity in applied sport psychology: A multicultural introduction to working with athletes of color. *Sport Psychologist, 16*, 296–315.

Kontos, A. P., Elbin III, R. J., Covassin, T., & Larson, E. (2010, October). *Exploring differences in computerized neurocognitive concussion testing between African American and White athletes.* Paper session presented at the meeting of Association of Applied Sport Psychology, Providence, RI.

Kuper, S., & Szymanski, S. (2009). *Soccernomics.* New York: Nation Books.

Lapchick, D. (2004). *2004 race and gender report card.* Orlando, FL: University of Central Florida.

Lloyd, A. P. (1987). Multicultural counseling: Does it belong in a counselor education program? *Counselor Education and Supervision, 26*, 164–167.

Marín, G. (1992). Issues in the measurement of acculturation among Hispanics. In K. F. Geisinger (Ed.), *Psychological testing of Hispanics* (pp. 235–251). Washington, DC: American Psychological Association.

Martens, M. P., Mobley, M., & Zizzi, S. J. (2000). Multicultural training in applied sport psychology. *Sport Psychologist, 14*, 81–97.

McNamara, J. B. (2004). The crucial role of research in multicultural and cross-cultural communication. *Journal of Communication Management, 8*, 322–334.

Myers, D. G., & Spencer, S. J. (2006). *Social psychology* (3rd ed.). New York: McGraw Hill.

National Public Radio. (2008, March 27). Some call LeBron James' 'Vogue' cover offensive. *National Public Radio.* Retrieved from http://www.npr.org/templates/story/story.php?storyId=89151096

Reber, A. S. (1995). *Dictionary of psychology* (2nd ed.) Victoria, AU: Penguin.

Rule, N. O., Nalini, A., Adams, R. B., Ozono, H., Nakashima, S., Yoshikawa, S., & Watabe, M. (2010). Polling the face: Prediction and consensus across cultures. *Journal of Personality and Social Psychology, 98*, 1–15.

Schinke, R., Blodgett, A., Ritchie, S., Pickard, P., Michel, G., Peltier, D., et al. (2009). Entering the community of Canadian indigenous athletes. In R. Schinke & S. Hanrahan (Eds.), *Cultural sport psychology: From theory to practice* (pp. 91–102). Champaign, IL: Human Kinetics.

Sogawa, T. (2006). Ethnic sport, its concept and research perspective. *International Journal of Sport and Health Science, 4*, 96–102.

Sue, D. W., Carter, R. T., Casas, J. M., Fouad, N. A., Ivey, A. E., Jensen, M., et al. (1998). *Multicultural counseling competencies: Individual and organizational development.* Thousand Oaks, CA: Sage.

Terry, P. C. (2009). Strategies for reflective cultural sport psychology practice. In R. Schinke & S. Hanrahan (Eds.), *Cultural sport psychology: From theory to practice* (pp. 79–90). Champaign, IL: Human Kinetics.

U. S. Census Bureau. (2001). *Census briefs.* Census 2000 Redistricting (Public Law 94–171) Summary. Washington, DC: U. S. Census Bureau.

Wacquant, L. J. D. (1995). The pugilistic point of view: How boxers think and feel about their trade. *Theory and Society, 24*, 489–535.

Walseth, K. (2006). Young Muslim women and sport: The impact of identity work. *Leisure Studies, 25*(1), 75–94.

Wise, M. (2006, February 24). Way off the mark on diversity. *The Washington Post.* Retrieved from http://www.washingtonpost.com

PART 4

Human Development and Performance

A Developmental Approach to Sport Expertise

Jean Côté and Bruce Abernethy

Abstract

This chapter examines the personal and contextual factors of youth sport that affect sport expertise and developmental outcomes. The *developmental model of sport participation* (DMSP) is used as a comprehensive framework that outlines different pathways of involvement in sport. Activities and contexts that promote continued sport participation and expert performance are discussed as the building blocks of all effective youth sport programs. This chapter provides evidence that performance in sport, participation, and psychosocial development should be considered as a whole instead of as separate entities by youth sport programmers. Adults in youth sport (i.e., coaches, parents, sport psychologists, administrators) must consider the differing implications of concepts such as deliberate play, deliberate practice, sampling, specialization, and program structure at different stages of an athlete's talent development. Seven postulates are presented regarding important transitions in youth sport and the role that sampling and deliberate play, as opposed to specialization and deliberate practice, can have during childhood in promoting continued participation and elite performance in sport.

Key Words: Performance, expertise, talent development, sport programs, youth sport

Talent development in sport is achieved through many years of preparation and requires a great deal of interaction between personal and contextual resources. Individuals vary in performance and participation because of different learning opportunities, the instructional methods experienced, and the environment in which learning takes place throughout development. Issues of participation, learning, and performance become important when trying to understand the types of experience children have and what should be taught at various stages of involvement in sport. In fact, several qualitative studies underscore the major influence of myriads of personal (play, practice, etc.), social (coaches, peers, parents, etc.), and contextual variables (e.g., facilities, equipment, etc.) affecting the achievement of elite performance in sport and other domains (Bloom, 1985; Carlson, 1988; Côté, 1999).

Although similarities exist between cognitive domains of expertise such as music, chess, and sport, the physical/motor component of sport provides unique challenges that need to be considered developmentally when explaining expert performance in sport (Abernethy, Farrow, & Berry, 2003). The objective of this chapter is to review and summarize those factors that promote the development of talent in sport by considering the interaction of personal, social, and contextual variables. The chapter is organized into six major sections. The first section provides statistics about sport participation in youth and the probability of becoming an elite athlete. The second section briefly reviews different sport-specific models of expertise and focuses mainly on the *developmental model of sport participation* (DMSP) as a framework to account for long-term athlete development in sport. The DMSP focuses on the specific activities and contexts of sport at different ages of an athlete's development. The next three sections highlight the relevance of particular sporting activities (e.g., play and practice) and contexts (e.g., birthplace, early specialization, sampling) that are known to lead to elite performance in sport. Finally, the last section of the chapter provides a review and a summary of different pathways of involvement in sport and their probable outcomes.

Sport Expertise in the Life of Children and Adolescents

Reviews of the literature on talent detection and identification in sport (e.g., Vaeyens, Gullich, Warr, & Philippaerts, 2009) show that the long-term prediction of talent in athletes is unreliable, especially when talent detection is attempted during the prepubertal or pubertal periods. Brown and Potrac (2009) illustrated some of the negative effects of early talent identification by interviewing four dedicated young soccer players in England soon after they were deselected from their teams. These four players began specializing in soccer during childhood, and their professional careers started between the ages of 10 and 13, when they signed contracts with professional clubs. In their late teens, each of them was asked to spend 3 years in a scholarship program with their club, in which they received full-time training. Although only 15% of the players who receive this scholarship eventually play professional soccer, the players were treated as if they would make it, with little consideration and preparation for an alternative scenario. Each of the four players failed to receive a senior professional contract, and the professional club treated the players' situation as "collateral damage" along the road to winning.

In the United States, statistics show that for every 10,000 high school student athletes in basketball and American football, only 12 will become professional. With respect to predicting talent from childhood achievement in sport, the odds of a professional contract are even smaller, considering that more than 38 million school-aged children participate in recreational youth sports throughout the United States. In Canada, Parcels (2002) calculated the odds of becoming a professional ice hockey player and showed that the translation rate from youth sport participation to elite-level performance in ice hockey is extremely low. As an example, 33,000 males born in 1975 began their hockey careers by registering with the Ontario Minor Hockey Association, likely with a glimmer of hope that they would play in the National Hockey League (NHL). Of the 33,000 original players, only 48 (0.15%) were drafted by an NHL team; 32 (0.09%) played one NHL game; 15 (0.04%) played more than one full NHL season; and just six of the 33,000 (0.01%) played enough NHL games (400) to qualify for the NHL Player's Pension. As a result, when measuring the quality of youth sport programs, it is important to account not only for those who are making it to the top of the performance pyramid, but also for the majority of the youth who are denied the opportunity to participate—often because of an unreliable selection process during childhood.

A pyramid approach to sport development is a reality of adult competitive sports that is characterized by a limited number of available spots in the highest level of competition, be this professional leagues or Olympic teams. Implicit within this approach is the assumption that earlier and increased training during childhood will provide a performance advantage to children by allowing them to be chosen for "select" teams and will eventually increase their chances to climb to the top in adult sports. Although organized youth sport has the potential to promote performance in young people's development, it is also an important activity to enhance youth health and personal development (Côté & Fraser-Thomas, 2007). The application of a pyramid approach to talent development mainly focuses on the short-term performance outcome of a selected number of youth. Considering the unreliable nature of predicting talent from performance measures in youth sport, it is important that youth sport programs focus also on the health and personal development of all youth in sport.

The application of a pyramid approach to youth sport programs may be effective for the development of talent in sports with a large base of participants (such as soccer in England, baseball and basketball in the United States, or ice hockey in Canada); however, it excludes a large number of children from opportunities for developing into elite-level athletes and reduces the pool of potential elite athletes from an early age (Fraser-Thomas & Côté, 2009). A pyramid approach to children's sport provides an early advantage to a selected number of children who are often chosen because of their accelerated maturity (Cobley, Baker, Wattie, & McKenna, 2009). Many "elite" youth sport programs largely down-play the psychosocial (i.e., dropout, burnout, lack of enjoyment) and physical (i.e., injuries) costs associated with an increased amount of training and with the selection of "talented" children because of the large number of children who are ready to try out for these programs. Despite the evidence against early talent identification and the fact that adult expert performance in sports is difficult to predict from sport performance in childhood, the quality of effective youth sport programs continues to be measured by the performance of those few athletes who reach the top of the pyramid, with little attention being provided to those other youth who could also eventually develop into elite-level athletes given the appropriate training and environment. For instance, Pearson, Naughton, and Torode (2006) reported that professional sports clubs in England continue to selectively invest substantial resources into attempts to identify talented athletes at a young age instead of providing opportunities to a larger number of young athletes.

Considering that performance in a given sport in childhood is a poor predictor of adult performance (Vaeyens et al., 2009), it is important that sport programs in childhood focus on retaining athletes by focusing on their level of efficiency. Sport programs with a strict emphasis on early selection, skill acquisition, and training during childhood might eliminate someone who, through growth, maturation, and training, could later develop into an elite-level athlete. The underpinning principle of highly efficient sport programs for childhood is to provide equipment, space, and playing and training opportunities for a large number of children across various sports as a mechanism to select the best athletes from among a large pool of motivated adolescents (Côté, 2009). The most important aspects of childhood sport is to attract children and motivate them to stay involved, so that they can intentionally choose a recreational or elite pathway at approximately age 13 (Côté, Lidor, & Hackfort, 2009). This approach to talent development in sport is consistent with a developmental perspective that considers talent as an entity that is inherently multidimensional, difficult to assess during childhood, and requires for its realization input from various levels of personal and social variables over a long period of time.

Models of Expertise Development in Sport

Over the last three decades, a number of athlete development models that consider talent as a multidimensional concept have been proposed. A review by Alfermann and Stambulova (2007) highlighted the emergence of five research-based models (Bloom, 1985; Côté, 1999; Salmela, 1994; Stambulova, 1994; Wylleman & Lavallee, 2004). More recently, Bruner, Erickson, Wilson, and Côté

(2010) conducted a citation network analysis and revealed two additional models published in peer-reviewed journals (Abbott & Collins, 2004; Bailey & Morley, 2006). The citation analysis exposed two distinct bodies of research related to athlete development: *talent development,* including five models of athlete development (Abbott & Collins, 2004; Bailey & Morley, 2006; Côté, 1999; Durand-Bush & Salmela, 2001; Morgan & Giacobbi Jr., 2006); and *career transitions,* including two models of athlete development (Stambulova, 1994; Wylleman & Lavallee, 2004). The career transitions models were designed to depict key transitions in an athlete's career and encourage researchers to not only consider athlete development within the sport context, but to also take into account athletes' demands and transitions outside of the sport environment. Chapter 25 of this book provides an in-depth discussion of Wylleman and Lavallee's model.

Athlete development models based upon the *talent development* literature have been influenced by the fields of cognitive psychology, skill acquisition, and expertise in domains such as music, art, and chess. The work of Bloom (1985), Chase and Simon (1973), and Ericsson (e.g., Ericsson, Chase, & Faloon, 1980; Ericsson, Krampe, & Tesch-Römer, 1993) have profoundly affected talent development research in sport over the last 40 years and, subsequently, the conceptualization of talent development models for sport. In their pioneering research, Bloom (1985) inferred a general pattern of development that appeared necessary to reach elite performance in sport, science, mathematics, music, and art. Building on Bloom's qualitative work, Ericsson and his colleagues (Ericsson, 1996; Ericsson et al., 1993; Ericsson & Lehmann, 1996) used an expert performance approach (Chase & Simon, 1973) to suggest that expert performance in music, chess, sport, and other domains should be viewed as a consequence of attaining a sequence of increasingly challenging goals through extended deliberate practice rather than through any innate talents.

A sizable body of evidence from sport researchers supports Ericsson and colleagues' contention about the role of deliberate practice in the attainment of expertise in sport (e.g., Deakin & Cobley, 2003; Helsen, Starkes, & Hodges, 1998; Hodges & Starkes, 1996; Starkes, Deakin, Allard, Hodges, & Hayes, 1996). Consequently, athlete development models based on talent development research tend to include deliberate practice as one of the most important elements of becoming an elite-level athlete. However, specific studies (e.g., Baker, Côté, & Abernethy, 2003b; Carlson, 1988; Orlick & Partington, 1988; Soberlak & Côté, 2003) examining athletes' pathways toward performance or continued participation in sport have identified additional key elements of talent development, such as deliberate play, early diversification, and roles of parents and peers, that have been integrated into more contemporary, conceptual models of athlete development (Abbott & Collins, 2004; Bailey & Morley, 2006; Côté, 1999; Durand-Bush & Salmela, 2001; Morgan & Giacobbi, 2006).

Citation analysis studies (Bruner, Erickson, McFadden, & Côté, 2009; Bruner et al., 2010) show that the DMSP (Côté, 1999; Côté, Baker, & Abernethy, 2007) is the most prominent conceptualization of athletes' development in the sport literature. The DMSP is a conceptual framework that integrates the developing person in his or her environment and therefore is consistent with a developmental perspective. The DMSP has been developed and refined over the last 12 years and presents a set of concepts about athletes' development that are quantifiable and testable.

The DMSP was developed in a series of four steps. The first step involved an initial conceptualization of athletes' development resulting from interviews with parents, coaches, and athletes (Côté, 1999). This original model was in line with results from other qualitative studies of athletes' development (e.g., Bloom, 1985; Carlson, 1988), while providing explicit and original propositions that could be quantified and tested empirically. In a second step, a quantitative methodology was developed over several years (Côté, Ericsson, & Law, 2005) to test the main assumptions of the DMSP. Using this methodology, a series of studies were conducted with groups of expert and nonexpert athletes (e.g., Baker, Côté, & Abernethy, 2003a,b; Baker, Côté, & Deakin, 2006; Berry, Abernethy, & Côté, 2008; Law, Côté, & Ericsson, 2007; Soberlak & Côté, 2003) to test, retrospectively, the main assumptions of the DMSP. Third, the retrospective method was adapted and used to test the DMSP in terms of other outcomes associated with long-term sport participation (e.g., personal development, dropout, continue participation; Fraser-Thomas, Côté, & Deakin, 2008a; Robertson-Wilson, Baker, Derbyshire, & Côté, 2003; Strachan, Côté, & Deakin, 2009b; Wall & Côté, 2007; Wright & Côté, 2003). This holistic approach to athletes' development has been further substantiated with new qualitative studies with athletes who have achieved various outcomes in sport (Fraser-Thomas & Côté, 2009; Fraser-Thomas et al., 2008). Finally, a fourth step involved the refinement of the DMSP through the writing of theoretical papers (Côté, Baker, & Abernethy, 2007; Côté, Strachan, & Fraser-Thomas, 2008; Fraser-Thomas, Côté, & Deakin, 2005) and the creation of seven postulates related to the DMSP and its various outcomes (Côté, 2007; Côté et al., 2009) (see Table 23.1).

The postulates of the DMSP feature characteristics of sport programs that not only promote expertise development, but also physical health and

Table 23.1 Postulates associated with the developmental model of sport participation (DMSP)

Postulate 1: Early diversification (sampling) does not hinder elite sport participation in sports in which peak performance is reached after maturation.

Postulate 2: Early diversification (sampling) is linked to a longer sport career and has positive implications for long-term sport involvement.

Postulate 3: Early diversification (sampling) allows participation in a range of contexts that most favorably affect positive youth development.

Postulate 4: High amounts of deliberate play during the sampling years build a solid foundation of intrinsic motivation through involvement in activities that are enjoyable and promote intrinsic regulation.

Postulate 5: A high amount of deliberate play during the sampling years establishes a range of motor and cognitive experiences that children can ultimately bring to their principal sport of interest.

Postulate 6: Around the end of primary school (about age 13), children should have the opportunity to either choose to specialize in their favorite sport or to continue in sport at a recreational level.

Postulate 7: Late adolescents (around age 16) have developed the physical, cognitive, social, emotional, and motor skills needed to invest their efforts into highly specialized training in one sport.

psychosocial development for all involved in sport. In contrast to most talent development programs that use a pyramid approach to develop elite performance in adulthood, the postulates do not support elitist programs or the early selection of talent during childhood. The DMSP is based on a developmental approach to talent development that features the interaction of variables at the contextual and activity (program) levels. These two levels (activities and context) and how they specifically relate to the seven postulates will be reviewed next.

Developmental Activities: Play and Practice

Developmental activities in youth sport can be conceptualized along a continuum that shows how much instruction and input is vested by the adult (i.e., coach) versus the youth. At one end of the continuum are activities in which adults play little role in providing instructions, as happens in play. The absence of instruction and explicit knowledge in play activities suggests an implicit learning process that has been shown to be an important feature for developing expertise in sport (Farrow & Abernethy, 2002; Maxwell, Masters, & Eves, 2000). At the other end of the continuum are sport activities in which adults set the direction and provide the instruction in a structured environment, such as the planned practices and competitions of organized sport. A mix of both children-led and adult-led activities appears to be important for the development of expertise in sport.

Reviews of the play literature in psychology (Pellegrini & Smith, 1998) suggest a developmental sequence in physical activity play. This sequence involves "rhythmic stereotypes" during the first year of life, "exercise play" between the ages of 2 and 5, "rough and tumble play" from ages 5 to 9, and a simultaneous stage labeled as "games with rules" after age 5. Smith (2010) suggests that games with rules represent the most advanced type of play and is characteristic of organized sports and activities that are initiated and controlled by adults. "Games with rules" is adult-led and consequently shares more characteristics with organized sports than with play activities.

Recognizing that athletes tend to first experience sport through fun and playful games, Côté (1999) coined the term *deliberate play* to characterize a form of sporting activity that involves early developmental physical activities that are intrinsically motivating, provide immediate gratification, and are specifically designed to maximize enjoyment. Deliberate play activities, such as street hockey or backyard soccer, are regulated by rules adapted from standardized sport rules and are set up and monitored by the children or by an adult involved in the activity as a participant instead of a leader. Deliberate play has unique properties, outcomes, and context that are different from rhythmic stereotypes, exercise play, rough-and-tumble play, and organized sport. Deliberate play is a form of activity that is self-chosen and self-directed, and it provides immediate reward and enjoyment (Côté, 1999; Côté et al., 2007). Deliberate play requires an adaptable frame of mind and involves a focused but unstressed approach to sport. Deliberate play encourages children to be creative, giving them the opportunity to experiment with new skills that they might be afraid to attempt under the critical eyes of coaches or parents. Further, deliberate play often involves an age-mixed context, in which younger children can model skills toward which to strive and older children provide scaffolding and expand their knowledge through teaching.

In contrast, organized sport occurs within a structured environment, most often led by a coach. Adults and coaches, in organized sport, segregate groups by age or skill level to facilitate discipline and instruction and keep the learning focused on the specific demands of the particular sport. Consistent with this explicit approach to learning, Ericsson, Krampe, and Tesch-Römer (1993) concluded that the most effective learning occurs through involvement in the highly structured activity that they defined as *deliberate practice*. According to Ericsson et al. (1993), engagement in deliberate practice requires effort, generates no immediate rewards, and is motivated by the goal of improving performance rather than inherent enjoyment. Deliberate practice focuses on promoting performance and sport expertise during childhood by having adults set up the learning environment with the ultimate goal of improving children's sport skills. In their writing, Ericsson and colleagues (1993) suggest that it would be next to impossible for a late starter to overcome the early advantage gained by those who begin deliberate practice at a young age and maintain high amounts of deliberate practice over time.

Although there are obvious advantages to having a coach who provides athletes with feedback about their performance, monitors success, and provides immediate instruction, it is unclear whether, during early stages of development, the benefits of this structured environment are superior to the benefits one gains from engagement in deliberate play activities. Furthermore, the overly structured, competitive, and adult-driven aspect of organized sport and deliberate practice during childhood can lead to negative outcomes such as early exclusion of late-maturing athletes and the increased prevalence of overuse injuries and dropout, all of which can potentially limit the talent development pool for certain sports. Highly structured, adult-driven approaches to skill learning may also result in an overdependency on explicit forms of skill learning and, with this, limits on the extent to which skill performance can remain robust under various psychological and physiological stressors (Masters & Maxwell, 2004). Postulates 4, 5, 6, and 7 of the DMSP (Table 23.1) specifically address the importance of deliberate play during childhood and the transition periods during an athletic career to more intense training and higher amounts of deliberate practice. Postulates 6 and 7 also speak to the dilemma of early specialization versus early sampling—a topic that we will review next.

The Sampling Approach to Sport Expertise

Support for both early specialization in one sport and the engagement, during childhood, in high amounts of deliberate practice is based on two assumptions that have yet to be confirmed by empirical evidence. The first assumption is that future experts distinguish themselves from future nonexperts with regard to training quantity and quality during childhood. Although experts typically accumulate more hours of sport-specific practice than do nonexperts by the time they reach national-level competition as an adult, retrospective studies that assess sport-specific practice patterns throughout development generally indicate that these differences between elite and less elite athletes do not occur until adolescence (Baker et al., 2003b; Helsen et al., 1998; Hodges & Starkes, 1996). Exceptions exist in sports in which peak performance occurs before biological maturation or adulthood, such as women's gymnastics (Law et al., 2007) and women's figure skating (Deakin & Cobley, 2003). However, as will be indicated later on, this level of involvement during early periods of development can have significant negative consequences for continued sport participation.

A second assumption for promoting early specialization in one sport is that this type of involvement is superior to involvement in diverse sporting activities. However, there is evidence from several studies that elite athletes who experience a diversified sport background can still reach an elite level of performance in sport (Baker et al., 2003b; Baker,

Côté, & Deakin, 2005; Bloom, 1985; Carlson, 1988) and, indeed, for some team ball sports, diversity of experience seems to be more prevalent among the more successful athletes (Baker et al., 2003b; Berry & Abernethy, 2009). Postulates 1, 2, and 3 of the DMSP state the benefits of early sampling as it relates to performance, participation, and personal development in sport.

Empirical evidence has also revealed a troubling link between early specialization and increased sport attrition—a link that has been reasonably well established across ability levels (Fraser-Thomas, Côté, & Deakin, 2008a; Gould, Udry, Tuffey, & Loehr, 1996; Wall & Côté, 2007). In contrast, Robertson-Wilson, Baker, Derbyshire, and Côté's (2003) study of physically active and inactive adult females indicated that sampling numerous sports and physical activities in childhood was associated with being more physically active during adulthood. Sampling promotes prolonged engagement in sport by limiting overuse injuries (Fraser-Thomas et al., 2005; Law et al., 2007) and providing the skills foundation for a range of recreational sports options in later life. A sampling approach to youth sport may help prevent excessive and repeated stress to a specific area of the body that often results from performing the same movement patterns repeatedly. In fact, a sampling approach in child-led activities (e.g., deliberate play) rather than adult-led activities (e.g., deliberate practice) has been proposed as a strategy to limit overuse and other sport-related injuries (Micheli, Glassman, & Klein, 2000).

Recent studies with youth have also found that those who are involved in a variety of extracurricular activities (e.g., sports, volunteering, arts) score more favorably on personal development measures such as academic performance (as measured by grade point average) and positive peer relationships than do youth who participate in fewer activities (Fredricks & Eccles, 2006). These patterns are thought to exist due to each extracurricular activity bringing its own distinct pattern of socialization experiences that reinforce certain behaviors and/or teach a variety of important skills (Rose-Krasnor, Busseri, Willoughby, & Chalmers, 2006). This contention is corroborated by studies of children's and youths' experiences in extracurricular activities, indicating that these activities each provide unique experiences that facilitate development (Hansen, Larson, & Dworkin, 2003; Larson, Hansen, & Moneta, 2006; Strachan, Côté, & Deakin, 2009a,b).

The evidence is clear that all future expert athletes must adopt a program of training that is sport-specific after adolescence in order to be internationally competitive and successful (postulates 6 and 7). However, coaches and parents should consider the consequences of high levels of sport-specific training during childhood as these experiences may have a profound influence on subsequent involvement in sport and physical activity later in life. The next section will review environmental variables that have been linked to elite performance in sport and will shed some light on the types of environment that appear to be best for promoting play and sampling in the early years of an athlete's involvement in sport.

Context of Youth Sport

To provide a broader perspective of athletic talent development, researchers have increasingly focused on attempting to understand the context of the athlete's environment at a macro level (Henriksen, Stambulova, & Roessler, 2009). Notably, macro-level research has demonstrated that birth date (Cobley et al., 2009) and the population size of an athletes' birthplace influences the likelihood of playing professional sports (Baker & Logan, 2007; Côté, MacDonald, Baker, & Abernethy, 2006; MacDonald, Cheung, Côté, & Abernethy, 2009; MacDonald, King, Côté, & Abernethy, 2009).

The birth date or *relative age effect* is a phenomenon that favors athletes born early in their sport-year, and it has been observed in sports that typically encourage the selection of athletes for "competitive" teams at a young age (i.e., the pyramid approach discussed earlier). The most compelling hypothesis about the relative age effect suggests that older children within a group will be provided with environments that facilitate the improvement of their skills early in their development because they are more mature or physically larger (Musch & Grondin, 2001). Cobley and colleagues (2009) recently published an in-depth review and discussion of those studies that have examined the relative age effect in sport.

Another contextual variable that has recently received attention in sport expertise research is the city size where elite athletes gain their formative experiences. A series of studies of over 4,000 professional athletes showed a *birthplace bias* toward smaller cities in North American sports: professional athletes were over-represented in cities of less than 500,000 and under-represented in cities of more than 500,000 (Côté et al., 2006; MacDonald, Cheung, et al., 2009; MacDonald, King, et al., 2009). Although this so-called birthplace effect is strong in some countries and sports systems,

evidence of a birthplace effect is not always found in different countries, sports and levels of performance, indicating that the effect may be buffered by broader sociocultural mechanisms (Baker, Schorer, Cobley, Schimmer, & Wattie, 2009; Schorer, Baker, Lotz, & Büsch, 2010). The relationship between relative age and birthplace was examined by Côté et al. (2006), and no evidence of moderation/mediation was found. Furthermore, Côté et al. showed that birthplace has a considerably stronger influence on talent development than does relative age in major U.S. and Canadian sports.

Evidence of the existence of the birthplace effect, in some countries at least, provides support for the notion that environments vary in their capacity to promote the development of talent and that "talent hotspots" are a reality. Furthermore, the birthplace effect underlines the importance of the early years of the child's involvement in sport in providing the foundation for the development of motivation and talent in sport. Researchers have proposed several hypotheses that may partially explain the birthplace effect and the existence of talent hotspots. Interestingly, most of the hypotheses proposed are consistent with the view that childhood talent development environments should be structured to support developmental activities that focus on deliberate play and sampling. For example, the quantity of deliberate play activities may be greater in smaller communities in North America due to fewer safety concerns, more access to open spaces, and less competition for children's leisure time activities (Côté et al., 2006; MacDonald, King, et al., 2009). Also, smaller communities may be more conducive to deliberate play activities that incorporate a variety of different aged children, adolescents, and adults (Côté et al., 2006). In contrast, the organized sport programs in bigger cities often reflect what adults think youth sport should be; they are often highly structured by parents, coaches, and other adults; they are more likely to focus on organized practice activities; and in turn, may limit the time children spend actually playing sports (Côté et al., 2006).

In addition, the intimate setting of small communities, in which the number of children competing for a spot on a team is less, may be more conducive to fostering a less competitive psychosocial environment and a greater variety of sport experiences. This argument is in line with Barker's (1968) behavior setting theory and concept of "underpopulated" settings. Studies comparing big schools and small schools (Barker & Gump, 1964) show that students in small schools show better attendance and participation in the school activities, get involved in different roles, support each other, increase their effort, and show higher levels of competence, satisfaction, and enjoyment. Sport policy research has supported the benefits of underpopulated settings in youth sport (Hill & Green, 2008; Green, 2005). In sum, Barker's attempt to define behavior settings at a level of analysis that includes the person in its environment offers a compelling framework to shed light on the mechanisms that are taking place in talent development hotspots, such as the small cities in North America.

Although past birthplace studies have focused primarily on performance outcomes of athletes from smaller and larger communities, a recent study (Fraser-Thomas, Côté, & MacDonald, 2010) examined the processes of youth sport that may explain the link between community size and long-term sport involvement. The Developmental Assets Profiles (Search Institute, 2004) of current and recently withdrawn competitive swimmers competing in small and big cities were compared. Results showed that athletes from smaller cities had significantly higher developmental asset scores for support, commitment to learning, and boundaries/expectations. Furthermore, athletes from bigger cities were significantly more inclined to withdraw from swimming. This study highlights the more subtle psychosocial differences between programs in smaller and larger communities (i.e., intimacy, relationship building, motivational climate, learning opportunities) and suggests a youth sport environment for the development of performance and long-term participation in sport that focuses on the needs of the child athlete rather than the performance of the child athlete.

The consideration of personal, social, and physical factors is necessary to fully understand the processes through which the birthplace effect occurs and to eventually foster a supportive developmental environment for athletes living in cities, towns, and rural settings of all different sizes. It appears that the physical and psychosocial sport context of talent development hotspots are consistent with the principles of positive youth development and the eight setting features identified by the National Research Council and Institute of Medicine (NRCIM, 2002; Table 23.2). The NRCIM's (2002) eight setting features should be at the foundation of any youth sport program and context designed to promote performance, participation, and personal development in sport. The inclusion of the factors inherent in the eight setting features of the NRCIM helps to clarify

Table 23.2 Features of positive development settings

1. Physical and psychological safety
2. Appropriate structure
3. Supportive relationships
4. Opportunities to belong
5. Positive social norms
6. Support for efficacy and mattering
7. Opportunities for skill building
8. Integration of family, school, and community efforts

Adapted from *Community Programs to Promote Youth Development*, by the National Research Council and Institute of Medicine, 2002, Washington, DC: National Academy Press.

the context in which the birthplace effect occurs. It also allows us to suggest concrete applications to consider when implementing youth sport programs that foster the same essential characteristics of sport participation in all communities, regardless of population size.

Linking Developmental Activities and Context: Trajectories and Outcomes of Sport Involvement

The different stages within a trajectory of the DMSP and its seven postulates are based on changes in the type and amount of involvement in sport, deliberate play, and deliberate practice, as well as changes in the context in which sport is practiced (Côté et al., 2007). Two of these trajectories—recreational participation and elite performance through early sampling—have the same foundation from ages 6 to 12. After the sampling years, sport participants can either choose to stay involved in sport at a recreational level (recreational years, age 13+) or embark on a path that focuses primarily on performance (specializing years, age 13–15; investment years, age 16+). These two trajectories have different outcomes in terms of performance, but are likely to lead to similar psychosocial and physical health benefits. A third possible trajectory consists of elite performance through early specialization. Although this trajectory leads to elite performance, it has also been shown to result in a reduction in both physical health (i.e., overuse injuries) and enjoyment (e.g., Law et al., 2007). In the next section, we review some of the longitudinal data for sport participants who have achieved different outcomes, highlighting changes in sporting activities throughout development. The outcomes that will be reviewed include elite performance, dropout, recreational participation, and personal development.

Elite Performance

Retrospective studies of expert performers in sport underscore two distinct pathways towards elite performance: elite performance through early sampling, and elite performance through early specialization.

ELITE PERFORMANCE THROUGH EARLY SAMPLING

During the sampling years (typically ages 6–12), athletes participate in a variety of sports and get involved in a high amount of deliberate play activities. The DMSP suggests that specialization begins around age 13, after the sampling years. The specializing years (age 13–15) are seen as a transitional stage to the investment years (age 16+). During the specializing years, youth engage in fewer activities (which include both deliberate play and deliberate practice), while during the investment years, youth commit to only one activity, and engage primarily in deliberate practice. This trajectory toward elite performance in sport has been documented in a variety of qualitative and quantitative studies (e.g., Baker et al., 2003b; Baker, Côté, & Deakin, 2005; Bloom, 1985; Carlson, 1988; Côté, 1999; Soberlak & Côté, 2003). Athletes who follow this trajectory tend to experience positive physical and psychosocial outcomes (e.g., physical health, sport enjoyment; see Côté et al., 2007, for a review).

ELITE PERFORMANCE THROUGH EARLY SPECIALIZATION

In sports in which peak performance is achieved before puberty (e.g., women's gymnastics, figure skating), early specialization is often necessary to reach elite performance. Some studies support early specialization as a suitable path toward elite performance (e.g., Law et al., 2007; Ward, Hodges, Williams, & Starkes, 2004). Elite performers who specialize at an early age usually skip the sampling years and, consequently, do not always experience the enjoyment associated with sampling and playing (Law et al., 2007). In fact, there is reasonable empirical support for the notion that early specialization can also be associated with higher levels of attrition (Fraser-Thomas et al., 2008a; Gould et al., 1996; Wall & Côté, 2007).

Dropout

Although the positive relationship between training and elite performance is consistent in sport research (Helsen et al., 1998; Hodge & Deakin, 1998; Hodges & Starkes, 1996; Starkes et al., 1996), recent studies show that sport programs that focus on large amounts of deliberate practice during childhood are more likely to lead to dropout (Fraser-Thomas et al., 2008a; Wall & Côté, 2007). These results, along with qualitative data of dropout and burnout athletes (e.g., Carlson, 1988; Fraser-Thomas et al., 2008b; Gould et al., 1996), indicate that sport programs that focus solely on the accumulation of vast amounts of deliberate practice during childhood may have more psychological and physical costs than do childhood sport programs that focus more on deliberate play and sampling.

Recreational Participation

The recreational outcome of the DMSP was examined in a retrospective study of active and inactive adult females (Robertson-Wilson et al., 2003). Results indicated that active females participated in significantly more physical activities than did inactive females from age 6 to 18, whereas no significant differences were found between the two groups in terms of their involvement in other structured nonphysical leisure activities, such as music or art. From ages 6 to 12 (i.e., sampling years), the active females participated in a variety of sports. These years were considered essential building blocks for their continued recreational sport participation. The recreational years (age 13+) are usually seen as an extension of the sampling years, with the primary goals being enjoyment and health. Activities during the recreational years can involve deliberate play and deliberate practice, with sport programs being flexible enough to adapt to individual interests and ages.

Personal Development

Sport has the potential to contribute to personal development if delivered within an appropriate developmental framework and monitored by responsible and informed adults (Fraser-Thomas & Côté, 2009; Holt, 2008). In fact, the focus on personal assets, such as empowerment, a positive identity, and a supportive environment, has been explicitly linked to increased competency and enjoyment and decreased burnout in elite youth sport programs (Strachan et al., 2009a). The role of coaches and parents in the development of elite athletes is more than simply promoting motor skill development and performance outcomes. Parents and coaches have a significant impact on the personal and social development of children involved in sport and therefore must promote an environment that considers healthy youth development over time. Coaches and parents in elite sport settings must look beyond the next game or the season finale, to also focus on the long-term positive developmental outcomes of the young athlete. Personal development and performance outcomes are not mutually exclusive; however, the structure of competitive sport can sometimes lead to behaviors such as insensitive coaches, aggression, and pressuring parents that are inconsistent with climates of personal growth in sport (Fraser-Thomas & Côté, 2009). Youth sport programs should include interactions between children, and between children and adults, that are based on principles of inclusion, play, and opportunities to try out different roles within a sport and in various forms of sporting activities (Côté, et al. 2008). Furthermore, the eight setting features of the NRCIM (Table 23.2), discussed earlier in this chapter, should be implemented in sport programs to provide youth with a context that promotes developmental assets and the growth of life skills, competency, and responsibility.

Conclusion

The achievement of expertise in sport is not the result of a particular physical, psychological, or sociological factor—rather, it arises from the integration of factors specific to both the individual and his or her developmental context. Understanding talent development and the emergence of expertise in different sports therefore requires a developmental approach that focuses on personal, social, and contextual variables. The DMSP (Côté et al., 2007; Côté & Fraser-Thomas, 2007) provides a comprehensive framework that outlines different pathways of involvement in sport.

Early sampling can lead to either recreational participation or elite performance in sport and is based on two main elements of childhood sport participation: involvement in various sports and participation in deliberate play. On the other hand, early specialization implies a focused involvement on only one sport, with high amounts of deliberate practice activities—the unambiguous goal being that of improving skills and performance in this sport during childhood. This pathway is likely to lead to elite performance for a select number of athletes, but also to more overuse injuries and dropout for a large number of young athletes. The seven postulates associated with the DMSP highlight the benefits of early sampling for continued sport participation, elite performance, and personal development through sport. Through early sampling and deliberate play, children have the opportunity to learn emotional, cognitive, and

motor skills in several contexts that will be important in their later participation or investment in sport. By the time athletes reach adolescence, they will have learned a variety of fundamental movement skills during the sampling years and will have the experiential base to develop more mature cognitive and emotional skills. The sampling pathway, although less direct, provides a platform for a potentially wider range of positive outcomes (from expert performance through to prolonged engagement in physical activity with its attendant health and social benefits) than are likely achieved through an early specialization route. The decision to choose an early sampling or early specialization pathway involves several tradeoffs. Accordingly, before embarking on a specific type of activity and training, athletes, parents, and coaches should weigh the potential health, psychological, sociological, and motor benefits and risks associated with early sampling or early specialization in children aged 6–12 years.

When coaches develop activities for youth practices, and when sport organizations design youth sport programs, they should consider the seven postulates of the DMSP and the outcomes associated with certain sport development pathways. In particular, coaches and programmers must consider the differing implications of deliberate play, deliberate practice, sampling, dropout, and early specialization. This chapter has shown that youth's health, psychosocial development, and motor skill development should and must be considered as a whole, instead of as separate entities, by youth sport programmers. Youth should be encouraged to participate in diverse sports and extracurricular activities that focus on fun, play, excitement, recreation, personal involvement, games, friendships, variety, and choice. Activities and contexts that promote regular participation, enjoyment, and skill acquisition are the building blocks of effective youth sport programs.

References

Abbott, A., & Collins, D. (2004). Eliminating the dichotomy between theory and practice in talent identification and development: Considering the role of psychology. *Journal of Sports Sciences, 22*, 395–408.

Abernethy, B., Farrow, D., & Berry, J. (2003). Constraints and issues in the development of a general theory of expert perceptual-motor performance. In J. L. Starkes & K. A. Ericsson (Eds.), *Expert performance in sports: Advances in research on sport expertise* (pp. 349–369). Champaign, IL: Human Kinetics.

Alfermann, D., & Stambulova, N. (2007). Career transitions and career termination. In G. Tenenbaum & R. Eklund (Eds.),

Handbook of sport psychology (pp. 712–733). New York: Wiley.

Bailey, R., & Morley, D. (2006). Towards a model of talent development in physical education. *Sport, Education, and Society, 11*(3), 211–230.

Baker, J., Côté, J., & Abernethy, B. (2003a). Learning from the experts: Practice activities of expert decision makers in sport. *Research Quarterly for Exercise and Sport, 74*(3), 342–347.

Baker, J., Côté, J., & Abernethy, B. (2003b). Sport-specific practice and the development of expert decision-making in team ball sports. *Journal of Applied Sport Psychology, 15*, 12–25.

Baker, J., Côté, J., & Deakin, J. (2005). Expertise in ultra-endurance triathletes early sport involvement, training structures, and the theory of deliberate practice. *Journal of Applied Sport Psychology, 17*, 64–78.

Baker, J., Côté, J., & Deakin, J. (2006). Patterns of involvement in expert and nonexpert master triathletes. *Research Quarterly for Exercise and Sport, 77*(3), 401–407.

Baker, J., & Logan, A. J. (2007). Developmental contexts and sporting success: Birth date and birthplace effects in national hockey league draftees 2000–2005. *British Journal of Sports Medicine, 41*, 515–517.

Baker, J., Schorer, J., Cobley, S., Schimmer, G., & Wattie, N. (2009). Circumstantial development and athletic excellence: The role of date of birth and birthplace. *European Journal of Sport Science, 9*(6), 329–339.

Barker, R. G. (1968). *Ecological psychology: Concepts and methods for studying the environment of human behaviour.* Stanford, CA: Stanford University Press.

Barker, R. G., & Gump, P. V. (1964). *Big school, small school.* Stanford, CA: Stanford University Press.

Berry, J., & Abernethy, B. (2009). Developmental influences on the acquisition of tactical decision-making expertise. *International Journal of Sports Psychology, 40*, 525–545.

Berry, J., Abernethy, B., & Côté, J. (2008). The contribution of structured activity and deliberate play to the development of expert perceptual and decision-making skill. *Journal of Sport and Exercise Psychology, 30*, 685–708.

Bloom, B. S. (1985). *Developing talent in young people.* New York: Ballantine.

Brown, G., & Potrac, P. (2009). 'You've not made the grade, son': De-selection and identity disruption in elite level youth football. *Soccer & Society, 10*(2), 143–159.

Bruner, M. W., Erickson, K., McFadden, K., & Côté, J. (2009). Tracing the origins of athlete development models in sport: A citation path analysis. *International Review of Sport and Exercise Psychology, 2*(1), 23–37.

Bruner, M. W., Erickson, K., Wilson, B., & Côté, J. (2010). An appraisal of athlete development models through citation network analysis. *Psychology of Sport and Exercise, 11*, 133–139.

Carlson, R. (1988). The socialization of elite tennis players in Sweden: An analysis of the players' backgrounds and development. *Sociology of Sport Journal, 5*, 241–256.

Chase, W. G., & Simon, H. A. (1973). Perception in chess. *Cognitive Psychology, 4*, 55–81.

Cobley, S., Baker, J., Wattie, N., & McKenna, J. (2009). Annual age-grouping and athlete development: A meta-analytical review of relative age effects in sport. *Sports Medicine, 39*, 235–256.

Côté, J. (1999). The influence of the family in the development of talent in sport. *The Sport Psychologist, 13*, 395–417.

Côté, J. (2007). Opportunities and pathways for beginners to elite to ensure optimum and lifelong involvement in sport. In S. Hooper, D. J. MacDonald, & M. Phillips (Eds.), *Junior sport matters: Briefing papers for Australian junior sport* (pp. 29–40). Belconnen, AU: Australian Sports Commission.

Côté, J. (2009). The road to continued sport participation and excellence. In E. Tsung-Min Hung, R. Lidor, & D. Hackfort (Eds.), *Psychology of Sport Excellence* (pp. 97–104). Morgantown, WV: Fitness Information Technology.

Côté, J., Baker, J., & Abernethy, B. (2007). Practice and play in the development of sport expertise. In R. Eklund & T. G. (Eds.), *Handbook of sport psychology* (3rd ed., pp. 184–202). Hoboken, NJ: Wiley.

Côté, J., Ericsson, K. A., & Law, M. P. (2005). Tracing the development of athletes using retrospective interview methods: A proposed interview and validation procedure for reported information. *Journal of Applied Sport Psychology, 17*, 1–19.

Côté, J., & Fraser-Thomas, J. (2007). Youth involvement in sport. In P. Crocker (Ed.), *Sport psychology: A Canadian perspective* (pp. 270–298). Toronto: Pearson.

Côté, J., Lidor, R., & Hackfort, D. (2009). ISSP position stand: To sample or to specialize? Seven postulates about youth sport activities that lead to continued participation and elite performance. *International Journal of Sport and Exercise Psychology, 9*, 07–17.

Côté, J., MacDonald, D. J., Baker, J., & Abernethy, B. (2006). When "where" is more important than "when": Birthplace and birthdate effects on the achievement of sporting expertise. *Journal of Sports Sciences, 24*(10), 1065–1073.

Côté, J., Strachan, L., & Fraser-Thomas, J. L. (2008). Participation, personal development, and performance through youth sport. In N. L. Holt (Ed.), *Positive youth development through sport* (pp. 34–45). London: Routledge.

Deakin, J., & Cobley, S. (2003). A search for deliberate practice: An examination of the practice environments in figure skating and volleyball. In J. L. Starkes & K. A. Ericsson (Eds.), *Expert performance in sport: Recent advances in research on sport expertise* (pp. 115–135). Champaign, IL: Human Kinetics.

Durand-Bush, N., & Salmela, J. H. (2001). The development of talent in sport. In H. A. Hausenblas & C. Janelle (Eds.), *Handbook of sport psychology* (pp. 154–171). New York: Wiley.

Ericsson, K. A. (1996). *The road to excellence: The acquisition of expert performance in the arts and sciences, sports and games.* Hillsdale, NJ: Lawrence Erlbaum Associates, Inc.

Ericsson, K. A., Chase, W. G., & Faloon, S. (1980). Acquisition of a memory skill. *Science, 208*, 1181–1182.

Ericsson, K. A., Krampe, R. T., & Tesch-Römer, C. (1993). The role of deliberate practice in the acquisition of expert performance. *Psychological Review, 100*(3), 363–406.

Ericsson, K. A., & Lehmann, A. C. (1996). Expert and exceptional performance: Evidence of maximal adaptation to task constraints. *Annual Review of Psychology, 47*, 273–305.

Farrow, D., & Abernethy, B. (2002). Can anticipatory skills be learned through implicit video-based perceptual training? *Journal of Sports Sciences, 20*, 471–485.

Fraser-Thomas, J., & Côté, J. (2009). Understanding adolescents' positive and negative developmental experiences in sport. *The Sport Psychologist, 23*, 3–23.

Fraser-Thomas, J., Côté, J., & Deakin, J. (2005). Youth sport programs: An avenue to foster positive youth development. *Physical Education and Sport Pedagogy, 10*(1), 19–40.

Fraser-Thomas, J., Côté, J., & Deakin, J. (2008a). Examining adolescent sport dropout and prolonged engagement from a developmental perspective. *Journal of Applied Sport Psychology, 20*, 318–333.

Fraser-Thomas, J., Côté, J., & Deakin, J. (2008b). Understanding dropout and prolonged engagement in adolescent competitive sport. *Psychology of Sport and Exercise, 9*, 645–662.

Fraser-Thomas, J., Côté, J., & MacDonald, D. J. (2010). Community size in youth sport settings: Examining developmental assets and sport withdrawal. *PHENex Journal, 2*(2), 1–9.

Fredricks, J. A., & Eccles, J. S. (2006). Extracurricular involvement and adolescent adjustment: Impact of duration, number of activities, and breadth of participation. *Applied Developmental Science, 10*(3), 132–146.

Gould, D., Udry, E., Tuffey, S., & Loehr, J. (1996). Burnout in competitive junior tennis players: I. A quantitative psychological assessment. *The Sport Psychologist, 10*, 322–340.

Green, B. C. (2005). Building sport programs to optimize athlete recruitment, retention, and transition: Toward a normative theory of sport development. *Journal of Sport Management, 19*, 233–253.

Hansen, D. M., Larson, R. W., & Dworkin, J. B. (2003). What adolescents learn in organized youth activities: A survey of self-reported developmental experiences. *Journal of Research on Adolescence, 13*(1), 25–55.

Helsen, W. F., Starkes, J. L., & Hodges, N. J. (1998). Team sports and the theory of deliberate practice. *Journal of Sport and Exercise Psychology, 20*, 12–34.

Henriksen, K., Stambulova, N., & Roessler, K. (2009). Holistic approach to athletic talent development environments: A successful sailing milieu. *Psychology of Sport and Exercise, 11*, 211–222.

Hill, B., & Green, B. C. (2008). Give the bench the boot! Using manning theory to design youth-sport programs. *Journal of Sport Management, 22*, 184–204.

Hodge, T., & Deakin, J. (1998). Deliberate practice and expertise in the martial arts: The role of context in motor recall. *Journal of Sport and Exercise Psychology, 20*, 260–279.

Hodges, N. J., & Starkes, J. L. (1996). Wrestling with the nature of expertise: A sport specific test of Ericsson, Krampe, and Tesch-Romer's (1993) theory of "deliberate practice." *International Journal of Sport Psychology, 27*, 400–424.

Holt, N. L. (Ed.). (2008). *Positive youth development through sport*. London: Routledge.

Larson, R. W., Hansen, D. M., & Moneta, G. (2006). Differing profiles of developmental experiences across types of organized youth activities. *Developmental Psychology, 42*(5), 849–863.

Law, M. P., Côté, J., & Ericsson, K. A. (2007). Characteristics of expert development in rhythmic gymnastics: A retrospective study. *International Journal of Sport and Exercise Psychology, 5*, 82–103.

MacDonald, D. J., Cheung, M., Côté, J., & Abernethy, B. (2009). Place but not date of birth influences the development and emergence of athletic talent in American football. *Journal of Applied Sport Psychology, 21*, 80–90.

MacDonald, D. J., King, J., Côté, J., & Abernethy, B. (2009). Birthplace effects on the development of female athletic talent. *Journal of Science and Medicine in Sport, 12*, 234–237.

Masters, R. S. W., & Maxwell, J. P. (2004). Implicit motor learning, reinvestment and movement disruption: What you don't know won't hurt you. In A. M. Williams & N. J. Hodges (Eds.), *Skill acquisition in sport: Research, theory and practice* (pp. 207–228). London: Routledge.

Maxwell, J. P., Masters, R. S. W., & Eves, F. F. (2000). From novice to know-how: A longitudinal study of implicit learning. *Journal of Sports Sciences, 18*(2), 111–120.

Micheli, L. J., Glassman, R., & Klein, M. (2000). The prevention of sports injuries in children. *Clinics in Sports Medicine, 19*(4), 821–834.

Morgan, T. K., & Giacobbi, P. R., Jr. (2006). Toward two grounded theories of the talent development and social support process of highly successful collegiate athletes. *The Sport Psychologist, 20*(3), 295–313.

Musch, J., & Grondin, S. (2001). Unequal competition as an impediment to personal development: A review of the relative age effect in sport. *Developmental Review, 21*, 147–167.

NRCIM. (2002). Features of positive developmental settings. In NRCIM (Ed.), *Community programs to promote community development* (pp. 86–118). Washington, DC: National Academy Press.

Orlick, T., & Partington, J. (1988). Mental links to excellence. *The Sport Psychologist, 2*(2), 105–130.

Parcels, J. (2002). Chances of making it in pro hockey. *Ontario Minor Hockey Association*. Retrieved from http://www.omha.net/flash.asp?page_name=flash.asp?page_id=242

Pearson, D., Naughton, G., & Torode, M. (2006). Predictability of physiological testing and the role of maturation in talent identification for adolescent team sports. *Journal of Science and Medicine in Sport, 9*, 277–287.

Pellegrini, A. D., & Smith, P. K. (1998). Physical activity play: Consensus and debate. *Child Development, 69*(3), 609–610.

Robertson-Wilson, J., Baker, J., Derbyshire, E., & Côté, J. (2003). Childhood physical activity involvement in active and inactive female adults. *Avante, 9*(1), 1–8.

Rose-Krasnor, L., Busseri, M. A., Willoughby, T., & Chalmers, H. (2006). Breadth and intensity of youth activity involvement as contexts for positive development. *Journal of Youth and Adolescence, 35*(3), 385–399.

Salmela, J. H. (1994). Stages and transitions across sport careers. In D. Hackfort (Ed.), *Psycho-social issues and interventions in elite sports* (pp. 11–28). Frankfurt am Main: Peter Lang.

Schorer, J., Baker, J., Lotz, S., & Büsch, D. (2010). Influence of early environmental constraints on achievement motivation in talented young handball players. *International Journal of Sport Psychology, 41*, 42–58.

Search Institute. (2004). *Developmental assets profile. Preliminary user manual*. Minneapolis, MN: Author.

Smith, P. K. (2010). *Children and play*. West Sussex, UK: Wiley-Blackwell.

Soberlak, P., & Côté, J. (2003). The developmental activities of elite ice hockey players. *Journal of Applied Sport Psychology, 15*, 41–49.

Stambulova, N. (1994). Developmental sports career investigations in Russia: A post-perestroika analysis. *The Sport Psychologist, 8*, 221–237.

Starkes, J. L., Deakin, J., Allard, F., Hodges, N. J., & Hayes, A. (1996). Deliberate practice in sports: What is it anyway? In K. A. Ericsson (Ed.), *The road to excellence: The acquisition of expert performance in the arts and sciences, sports and games*. Hillsdale, NJ: Lawrence Erlbaum Associates, Inc.

Strachan, L., Côté, J., & Deakin, J. (2009a). An evaluation of personal and contextual factors in competitive youth sport. *Journal of Applied Sport Psychology, 21*, 340–355.

Strachan, L., Côté, J., & Deakin, J. (2009b). "Specializers" versus "Samplers" in youth sport: Comparing experiences and outcomes. *The Sport Psychologist, 23*, 77–92.

Vaeyens, R., Gullich, A., Warr, C. R., & Philippaerts, R. (2009). Talent identification and promotion programmes of Olympic athletes. *Journal of Sports Sciences, 27*(13), 1367–1380.

Wall, M., & Côté, J. (2007). Developmental activities that lead to dropout and investment in sport. *Physical Education and Sport Pedagogy, 12*(1), 77–87.

Ward, P., Hodges, N. J., Williams, A. M., & Starkes, J. L. (2004). Deliberate practice and expert performance: Defining the path to excellence. In A. M. Williams & N. J. Hodges (Eds.), *Skill acquisition in sport: Research, theory, and practice* (pp. 231–258). London: Routledge.

Wright, A., & Côté, J. (2003). A retrospective analysis of leadership development through sport. *The Sport Psychologist, 17*, 268–291.

Wylleman, P., & Lavallee, D. (2004). A developmental perspective on the transitions faced by athletes. In M. R. Weiss (Ed.), *Developmental sport psychology: A lifespan perspective* (pp. 507–527). Morgantown, WV: FIT.

Training for Life: Optimizing Positive Youth Development Through Sport and Physical Activity

Maureen R. Weiss, Lindsay E. Kipp, *and* Nicole D. Bolter

Abstract

Using a positive youth development approach, we comprehensively review the literature on social, psychological, and physical outcomes of children's participation in sport and physical activity. Organizing topical areas around the *Five Cs* (Lerner & Lerner, 2006), we first discuss robust findings on social assets, including social relationships and competencies (parents, peers, coaches) and moral development. Second, we review the knowledge base on psychological assets, including self-perceptions (global self-worth, perceived competence), emotional outcomes (primarily enjoyment and anxiety), and motivational orientations and behaviors. Third, we discuss the unique set of physical assets that are possible from engaging in physical activity–based youth development programs, such as motor skill development, physical fitness, and physical health. Finally, we offer several avenues for future research studies that will provide even more definitive evidence of physical activity as a context for promoting positive youth development.

Key Words: Peer relationships, parental influence, coach behaviors, moral development, self-perceptions, emotions, motivation, motor skill development, physical health

I (Weiss) recently had an opportunity to visit Eton College, an exclusive boys' school just outside the skirts of Windsor Castle in England. I admired the famous playing fields where the phrase, "The battle of Waterloo was won on the playing fields of Eton," was conceived. It was not a stretch of imagination to make the connection of sport to life, as indeed sport is frequently referred to as a metaphor for life. Sport is a context in which knowledge, skills, and attributes *can* be learned and successfully transferred to other life domains, such as school, home, work, and peer groups. Yet such clichés ignore the complex reality that life skills and values are neither acquired automatically nor developed in a social vacuum. They need to be deliberately taught, nurtured, and reinforced within a climate featuring caring and competent adults and peers. As such, we couch our chapter on positive youth development

through sport in the form of "training for life"—by envisioning physical activity as a context for teaching important skills and values that transcend the proverbial "playing fields." Skills and values that are potentially learned through physical activity experiences can help youth navigate school, home, and peer domains with success, enjoyment, and feelings of competence.

Millions of children and adolescents participate in organized sports and physical activities worldwide, making these contexts ubiquitous for promoting developmental and health outcomes (De Knop, Engstrom, Skirstad, & Weiss, 1996; Hebestreit & Bar-Or, 2007; Smoll & Smith, 2002a; Weiss, 2004). Historical references communicate the long-held belief that sport participation provides opportunities for youth to develop physically, socially, emotionally, and spiritually (Wiggins, 1987, 2002).

Aside from historical accounts, substantial data-based evidence exists that sports and physical activities can promote skill development, health, and well-being when a mastery-oriented climate and supportive adult and peer relationships are emphasized (see Amorose, 2007; Smith & Biddle, 2008; Weiss, 2004).

Sports and physical activities can also act as a double-edged sword. Just as positive outcomes are available under optimal conditions, sport participation can lend itself to negative outcomes, such as poor sportsmanship, risky behaviors, and low self-esteem (e.g., Fraser-Thomas & Côté, 2009; Murphy, 1999; Weiss, Smith, & Stuntz, 2008). Negative experiences may lead youth to discontinue activity and fail to achieve physical and psychosocial health benefits. Thus, it is important to identify the social and environmental factors that optimize children's emotional, cognitive, social, and physical development, as well as those conditions that foster a positive attitude toward and behavioral commitment to physical activity. Only then can the potential of physical activities to promote "training for life" be realized.

Children and youth participate in a wide variety of developmentally appropriate *structured* (e.g., organized youth sport, school physical education) and *unstructured* physical activities (e.g., free play, recess, leisure time activity). We refer to "sports and physical activities" as an inclusive set of contexts salient to youth, including organized youth sport, out-of-school-time programs, school physical education, recreational activities, and motor development programs, among others. The bulk of empirical research on youth development has been conducted in structured physical activity contexts, notably organized sport and physical education, so most of the studies we review will reflect this trend.

Our chapter summarizes and integrates the knowledge base on youth development through sport and physical activity. Specifically, we focus on physical activity as a context for promoting social, psychological, and physical assets, values, attributes, and healthy outcomes. Our roadmap starts with the conceptual framework—positive youth development—that we use as an organizing tool for presenting developmentally appropriate theories and research on youth physical activity. Second, we review physical activity as a context for developing social assets among youth, including social attributes and relationships and moral growth and development. Third, we review psychological assets afforded youth through physical activity, notably self-perceptions, emotions, and motivation. Fourth, we review the unique set of physical assets accessible through participating in physical activity—motor skills, physical activity, physical fitness, and physical health. Throughout, we translate research to offer evidence-based best practices for promoting positive youth development through physical activity. Finally, we identify areas for future research that emphasize intervention, evaluation, and longitudinal studies.

A Framework for Promoting Psychosocial and Behavioral Development Through Sport

Positive youth development is a relatively recent framework that transformed the traditional view of child development as problem-centered to one focused on equipping youth with sustainable competencies that lead to healthy outcomes (e.g., Benson, 2006; Catalano et al., 2004; Damon, 2004; Larson, 2000; Lerner, Almerigi, Theokas, & Lerner, 2005; Roth, Brooks-Gunn, Murray, & Foster, 1998). The focus is on *promoting* development of psychosocial and behavioral assets, competencies, and characteristics that optimize opportunities for youth to become socially conscious, engaged, and healthy individuals in many domains (family, school, work, peer groups) over the lifespan. Acquiring life skills, core values, and healthy habits is also seen as a means of *preventing* unhealthy and risky behaviors. Learning and mastering competencies, such as self-regulation, social responsibility, and interpersonal relationships, provides youth with the tools for making informed life decisions and evolving into contributing citizens.

Scholars identify common features or components of youth development programs that are likely to make a positive impact on acquisition of life skills and core values (Benson, 2006; Eccles & Gootman, 2002; Larson, 2000; Lerner & Lerner, 2006; Mahoney, Larson, Eccles, & Lord, 2005; Roth & Brooks-Gunn, 2003). These components include a focus on developing personal assets or goals; intentional, structured activities aimed at building and nurturing skills; supportive adult and peer relationships; and a climate or atmosphere that empowers youth to develop initiative and leadership. Given these components, the positive youth development approach is consistent with the body of knowledge in youth sport psychology that has evolved over the past 75 years (see Murphy, 1999; Smoll & Smith, 2002a; Weiss, 2004, 2008; Weiss & Gill, 2005). The literature on youth development through sport participation has embraced theories that focus on promoting psychosocial and behavioral outcomes, identifying how significant others enable healthy development, and defining the types of environments that optimize development. Thus, the positive youth development framework offers an appropriate way of organizing our review.

When developmental psychologists conceived of a positive youth development approach, social, psychological, and cognitive assets were highlighted as processes for providing youth with the resources to achieve healthy functioning. Benson (2006) calls these *developmental assets* and specifies 20 internal (e.g., school engagement, interpersonal competence, self-esteem) and 20 external assets (e.g., family support, adult role models, positive peer influence) that promote positive behaviors and protect youth from high-risk behaviors. Larson labels assets *developmental or growth experiences* that teach youth new skills, attitudes, or ways of interacting with others (e.g., Dworkin, Larson, & Hansen, 2003; Larson, Hansen, & Moneta, 2006). Developmental experiences are classified as *personal development* (e.g., initiative, emotion management, goal setting) and *interpersonal development* (e.g., peer relationships, prosocial norms, leadership skills). Lerner coined the *Five Cs* to represent positive youth development goals: namely, *competence, confidence, connection, caring,* and *character* (Lerner et al., 2005; Lerner & Lerner, 2006). A sixth C, *contribution* (to community and society), is achievable after demonstrating all *Five Cs*. The *Five Cs* are compatible with mainstream topics on youth development through physical activity, so throughout our review we situate areas of study within the *Five Cs*. *Physical assets and competencies* are also paramount in *physical activity contexts,* such as motor skills that enable a physically active lifestyle, physical activity and fitness levels, and optimal physical health (Weiss, 2011; Weiss & Wiese-Bjornstal, 2009).

Skill-building activities, positive social relationships, and *caring, supportive climates* represent essential environmental ingredients for achieving developmental assets and goals (Catalano et al., 2004; Lerner et al., 2005; Roth & Brooks-Gunn, 2003). Eccles and Gootman (2002) identified, defined, and provided examples of essential contextual features of effective youth development programs that optimize attainment of competencies, values, and attributes. These features are consistent with research in youth physical activity contexts that emphasize an *intentional curriculum* to teach skills, *coach and teacher behaviors* characterized by positive and informational feedback and an autonomy-supportive style, *peer relationships* that contribute to a sense of belonging, and *supportive climates* that reflect caring and compassion by adults and peers and emphasize mastery, improvement, effort, and cooperative learning (i.e., mastery motivational climate) (e.g., Ames, 1992; Ebbeck & Gibbons, 1998; Gano-Overway et al., 2009; Gibbons, Ebbeck, & Weiss, 1995; Smoll, Smith, Barnett, & Everett, 1993).

Petitpas and colleagues (2005) adapted positive youth development features for the physical activity domain, accentuating *context* (e.g., a mastery motivational climate), *external assets* (e.g., caring coaches and teammates), and *internal assets* (e.g., perceived physical competence). Their adaptation incorporates the features of assets/goals, skill building activities, positive social relationships, and supportive climates emphasized by positive youth development scholars. Weiss and Wiese-Bjornstal (2009) applied this framework to review research evidence for physical activity as a context for youth development and made recommendations for how stakeholders (e.g., physical activity leaders, family members, health care providers, community leaders) can optimize positive youth development through physical activity. They concluded, "A caring and mastery-oriented climate, supportive relationships with adults and peers, and opportunities to learn social, emotional, and behavioral life skills—these are the nutrients for promoting positive youth development through physical activity" (p. 6).

Given the compatibility of the positive youth development framework with empirical research in youth sport psychology, it's not surprising that this framework has recently been embraced for organizing, interpreting, conducting, and translating research in youth physical activity settings (e.g., Fraser-Thomas & Côté, 2009; Gould & Carson, 2008; Hellison, 2003; Weiss, 2008, 2011). Up2Us (http://www.up2us.org/), a national coalition and advocacy group for sports-based youth development, was created to educate the general public, identify exemplary programs, and promote evaluation research. Some physical activity–based youth development programs have produced data-based evidence of effectiveness, such as the *Teaching Personal and Social Responsibility Model* (e.g., Hellison, 2003), *The First Tee* (e.g., Weiss, 2008), *PowerPlay* (Markowitz, 2010), and *Girls on the Run* (e.g., DeBate, Gabriel, Zwald, Huberty, & Zhang, 2009). Application of the positive youth development framework to physical activity contexts is in its infancy but has shown promising results so far.

In sum, the positive youth development framework exemplifies a compatible, intuitive, and developmentally appropriate means of reviewing the literature on youth physical activity as a context for promoting psychosocial and behavioral competencies. Given the robust features of personal assets, skill-building activities, positive social relationships, and supportive climates, we review mainstream topics in youth sport psychology organized along social, psychological, and physical assets attainable through physical activity. When possible, we adopt a developmental perspective that seeks to describe change in cognitive, psychosocial, and behavioral processes over time, and identify processes and mechanisms that explain such change (Horn 2004a; Weiss, 2008).

Social Assets

Youth have opportunities to attain numerous social assets through participating in physical activity. These include external assets, such as social support and other forms of positive influence from significant adults and peers, and internal assets, such as feeling connected to or accepted by peers; developing close, meaningful friendships; and having opportunities to demonstrate leadership skills. These areas resemble Lerner's *Five Cs* of connection (positive exchanges with peers and adults), competence (in interpersonal situations), and confidence (perceived social acceptance). Attainment of social assets also includes learning appropriate moral attitudes and behaviors, such as cooperation, respect, responsibility, honesty, courtesy, integrity, and civic engagement—indices of character (respect for societal and cultural norms), caring (demonstrating empathy and sympathy), and contribution (sense of civic engagement and social justice). In this section, we synthesize and discuss relevant research on social assets in two categories—social relationships and attributes (peers, parents, and coaches/teachers) and moral development and character (attitudes, attributes, and behaviors).

Social Relationships and Competencies

PEER INFLUENCE ON POSITIVE YOUTH DEVELOPMENT

Teammates and sport friends contribute significantly as external assets to youth participants' psychosocial and behavioral outcomes (A. L. Smith, 2003, 2007; Weiss & Stuntz, 2004). Peers are important sources of self-perceptions, emotional responses, and motivational orientations and behaviors. Because sports and physical activities are unique contexts in which one's behaviors are clearly visible, social comparison to and evaluation by peers are frequently used by youth to judge how physically competent they are (Horn, 2004b; Horn & Amorose, 1998). In turn, youths' perceived physical competence, social acceptance, and self-esteem are related to the importance they place on peer comparison and evaluation as sources of information (see Horn, 2004b; Weiss, Bhalla, & Price, 2007).

The degree to which youth feel accepted by their peer group or share a close friendship in physical activity is related to cognitive, affective, and behavioral outcomes (e.g., Cox, Duncheon, & McDavid, 2009; Cox & Ullrich-French, 2010; A. L. Smith, 1999; A. L. Smith, Ullrich-French, Walker, & Hurley, 2006; Weiss & Duncan, 1992). For example, in a series of studies in physical education classrooms, Cox and colleagues found that adolescent students who reported higher peer acceptance were higher in perceived autonomy, relatedness, enjoyment, self-determined motivation, and physical activity than were those lower in peer acceptance. A. L. Smith tested a model of relationships between peer and motivational variables for adolescent male and female participants. For both boys and girls, higher perceived peer acceptance and having a close friendship in physical activity contexts were related to higher physical self-worth, positive affect, and intrinsic motivation. For girls only, having a close physical activity friend was associated with greater physical activity levels through mediation of the psychological variables.

Social support is another mechanism by which peers positively influence developmental outcomes through physical activity (e.g., Coakley & White, 1992; Garcia Bengoechea & Strean, 2007; Stuntz & Spearance, 2010; Ullrich-French & Smith, 2006, 2009; Weiss & Smith, 1999, 2002; Weiss, Smith, & Theeboom, 1996; W.M. Weiss & Weiss, 2003, 2006, 2007). Youth who report greater companionship, esteem, loyalty, and emotional support from sport friends express greater enjoyment, perceived competence, self-determined motivation, and commitment, and are more likely to continue participation, than do those reporting lower support. For example, Weiss and Smith (2002) found that 10- to 18-year-old tennis players scoring higher on positive friendship qualities (e.g., companionship, loyalty, similarity of interests) reported greater enjoyment of and commitment to playing tennis than did those scoring lower in friendship quality.

Peer modeling is a powerful mechanism for influencing skill development, psychosocial responses, and physical activity behaviors (e.g., McCullagh & Weiss, 2002; Weiss, Ebbeck, & Rose, 1992; Weiss, McCullagh, Smith, & Berlant, 1998). According to Schunk (1998), peer models inform and motivate others through a process of model–observer similarity (e.g., age, gender, skill level). Youth who view others with similar characteristics perform a skill, enact a behavior, or display an attitude may emulate them because they identify with the peer model. Researchers have assessed relationships between an individual's physical activity level and possession of a friend who is physically active (e.g., Davison, 2004; Denault & Poulin, 2009; Garcia Bengoechea & Strean, 2007; King, Tergerson, & Wilson, 2008; Sabiston & Crocker, 2008; Schofield, Mummery, Schofield, & Hopkins, 2007). Highly active youth have active friends, are physically active with their friends, and value physical activity. Collectively, these studies suggest that peer modeling is a significant predictor of youths' physical activity competence beliefs, values, and behaviors.

In sum, the youth sport psychology literature consistently shows that peers occupy an important status as external social assets through processes of social comparison, social evaluation, social approval, social support, and modeling. We now move from discussing peers as external social assets to promotion of internal social assets through physical activity, such as feelings of social acceptance or belonging, close friendship, and leadership skills.

PROMOTING PEER ACCEPTANCE, CLOSE FRIENDSHIP, AND LEADERSHIP SKILLS

Extensive research on participation motivation shows that children and adolescents view sports and physical activities as an avenue for being with and making friends, attaining peer acceptance and approval, and feeling connected to a group (see Weiss & Petlichkoff, 1989; Weiss & Williams, 2004). That is, youth are motivated to continue participating in physical activity to attain, demonstrate, and improve social assets. Other research shows a strong linkage between sport ability and peer acceptance— youth who display better athletic skills are more popular among their peers than are those who are less skilled (e.g., Adler, Kless, & Adler, 1992; Chase & Dummer, 1992; Weiss & Duncan, 1992). Social aspects of sport involvement keep youth engaged and provide opportunities to strengthen peer relationships (A. L. Smith, 2003, 2007).

To better understand youths' conceptions of friendships in sport, Weiss and Smith conducted several interrelated studies (A. L. Smith, 1999;

A. L. Smith et al., 2006; Weiss & Smith, 1999, 2002; Weiss et al., 1996). Interviews with 8- to 16-year-old boys and girls about their expectations and positive and negative aspects of their sport friendships revealed 12 positive dimensions (Weiss et al., 1996). These included companionship, self-esteem enhancement, loyalty, intimacy, emotional support, prosocial behaviors, things in common, help and guidance, and conflict resolution. These dimensions characterize the social assets, benefits, and qualities of friendships that youth come to appreciate and desire from their sport experiences. Conflict and betrayal among friends also emerged, although less frequently, and characterized negative qualities of sport friendships. Higher order themes derived from this study assisted Weiss and Smith (1999) in developing a quantitative measure of sport friendship quality that has been used in many studies investigating external and internal social assets (e.g., Cox & Ullrich-French, 2010; Moran & Weiss, 2006; A. L. Smith et al., 2006; Weiss & Smith, 2002).

Developing leadership skills within sport teams is a topic of keen interest from a positive youth development perspective. Studies with adolescent athletes show that peer leaders use both instrumental (task-oriented) and expressive (social-oriented) behaviors to inspire and motivate their teammates toward achieving goals and creating team harmony (e.g., Glenn & Horn, 1993; Moran & Weiss, 2006; Price & Weiss, 2011). Athletes who score higher on leadership behaviors also score higher on peer group acceptance, friendship quality, interpersonal attraction, perceived competence, and behavioral conduct. Thus, peer leaders are associated with being sociable, concerned with social and task goals, and liked by and friendly with teammates. Moran and Weiss suggested that social competence might be the common attribute that connects these peer variables together. That is, youth who possess social skills are likely to be popular, develop quality friendships, respect others, be confident in their social abilities, and be identified as team leaders. However, until recently, few studies have investigated *development* of social competence and leadership skills in sport.

Evaluation studies of physical activity-based youth development programs show improved interpersonal skills when trained coaches deliver an intentional, structured curriculum within a mastery motivational climate. Using mixed methods, Weiss and colleagues found support for *The First Tee* program in effectively teaching social competencies to adolescent participants, such as meeting and greeting, appreciating diversity, resolving peer conflicts, and cooperating with group members (Weiss, 2008; Weiss, Bhalla, Bolter, & Price, 2008; Weiss, Bolter, Bhalla, & Price, 2007; Weiss, Bolter, et al., 2008; Weiss, Bolter, Price, & Bhalla, 2007). Program participants compared favorably to youth in other out-of-school-time activities (e.g., sports, band/music, clubs), and participants' use and transfer of social skills to other domains were stable over a 3-year period. Also using mixed methods, Markowitz (2010) found support for *PowerPlay*, a girls' sports-based youth development program, as an effective context for developing participants' feelings of connection to others, or connectedness. The program successfully fostered positive relationships between participants, as well as between the girls and program staff, resulting in feelings of connectedness, social support, and self-esteem.

Social assets are also targeted in Hellison's (2003; Hellison & Walsh, 2002) *Teaching Personal and Social Responsibility* model, a physical activity–based youth development program designed to promote social skills and prosocial norms. The program consists of trained teachers who deliver a structured curriculum within a caring and mastery-oriented climate. Respecting others lays the foundation for developing social responsibility, controlling negative emotions, resolving conflicts, and recognizing the rights of all participants. Evaluation studies show that programs based on the responsibility model are effective in developing and improving social assets (e.g., Hellison & Walsh, 2002; Hellison & Wright, 2003; Wright & Burton, 2008).

In sum, peer relationships, such as group acceptance and friendship, and interpersonal skills, such as leadership and social responsibility, connote important social assets. Considering youths' entire social network is important and can be embraced within an ecological or systems approach (Garcia Bengoechea, 2002; Garcia Bengoechea & Strean, 2007; Horn, 2004a). As such, we need to consider peer relationships independently and jointly with parent and coach relationships to fully understand their impact on positive youth development.

PARENTAL INFLUENCE ON POSITIVE YOUTH DEVELOPMENT

Parents are especially important social assets during early and middle childhood, but remain salient sources of information and support throughout childhood and adolescence (Fredricks & Eccles, 2004; Harter, 1999; Horn & Horn, 2007). Children's connection with parents bears important consequences for their social, psychological,

and physical competencies, health, and well-being. Research on processes and mechanisms of parental influence on youth development through physical activity is largely inspired by developmental theories that situate parents as key socializers of children's experiences in achievement domains (e.g., Eccles et al., 1983; Eccles, Wigfield, & Schiefele, 1998; Harter, 1978, 1981). In particular, parents influence youths' competence beliefs, emotional responses, motivational orientations, and moral development (i.e., competence, confidence, character, caring) through a wide range of expressed beliefs and behaviors. These include providing support and encouragement, giving feedback and reinforcement, modeling attitudes and behaviors, and expressing beliefs about their child's ability and the value of physical activity (see Fredricks & Eccles, 2004; Horn & Horn, 2007).

Most studies investigating relationships between parent and child beliefs and behaviors include multiple mechanisms of parental influence and multiple child outcomes. Children whose parents provide greater social support, encouragement, and positive feedback about performance, and who exemplify physical activity role models (e.g., are active, show enjoyment of activity, practice with child, are parent-coaches), report higher perceived competence, enjoyment, value toward physical activity, intrinsic motivation, and physical activity levels than do children reporting lower parental influence (e.g., Babkes & Weiss, 1999; Bhalla & Weiss, 2010; Bois, Sarrazin, Brustad, Trouilloud, & Cury, 2005b; Brown, Frankel, & Fennell, 1989; Brustad, 1993, 1996; Davison, 2004; Davison, Cutting, & Birch, 2003; Davison & Jago, 2009; Davison, Symons Downs, & Birch, 2006). For example, Babkes and Weiss (1999) found that young female and male soccer players who rated parents higher in responding positively to performance and exemplifying activity role models reported greater perceived competence, enjoyment, and intrinsic motivation toward participation. In a series of studies by Davison and colleagues, adolescent girls were more physically active and maintained activity levels over time when they reported parents higher in modeling physical activity (e.g., being active with children, frequently engaging in activity) and social support (e.g., taking children to sporting events, watching children perform at events).

Another robust finding is the relation of parents' competence beliefs for their child and value toward physical activity with children's beliefs and behaviors (e.g., confidence, enjoyment, motivation, physical activity). Parents who believe their child is physically capable and express that physical activity is a valuable achievement domain are associated with youth who report greater perceived competence, subjective values (importance, utility, interest), and motivated behaviors (e.g., Babkes & Weiss, 1999; Bhalla & Weiss, 2010; Bois, Sarrazin, Brustad, Chanal, & Trouilloud, 2005a; Bois, Sarrazin, Brustad, Trouilloud, & Cury, 2002; Dempsey, Kimiecik, & Horn, 1993; Eccles & Harold, 1991; Fredricks & Eccles, 2002, 2005; Kimiecik & Horn, 1998; Kimiecik, Horn, & Shurin, 1996). In a series of studies by Kimiecik and colleagues, adolescents who perceived that their parents held high competency beliefs for them (or parents reported high perceptions of child's physical competence) and valued physical activity and fitness recorded higher moderate to vigorous physical activity than did peers who rated parents lower in these beliefs. Bois et al. (2002, 2005a,b) found that reflected appraisals (child's perceptions of parents' beliefs about competence) and actual appraisals (parents' rating of child's physical competence) were significantly related to children's own perceived physical competence (self-appraisals) and activity levels. In another series of studies, Fredricks and Eccles (2002, 2005; Eccles & Harold, 1991; Jacobs & Eccles, 1992) found strong associations between parent and child competence beliefs and subjective values related to physical activity, concurrently and over the childhood and adolescent years.

Some studies explored how parents, as external assets, teach life skills and values through sport, including interpersonal assets (Bhalla, 2009; Kremer-Sadlik & Kim, 2007). Bhalla assessed adolescent girls' perceptions of how parents taught them life skills through basketball (e.g., goal setting, interpersonal skills, emotion management). Themes included providing general advice (respect everyone, be a team player), social support (focus on the positive, persevere through hard times), and specific strategies (set team goals, make a plan to overcome challenges). Kremer-Sadlik and Kim videotaped family interactions during formal participation (organized youth sport), informal participation (pick-up games), and passive participation (watching sports on TV). Analysis revealed that parents took an active role in socializing children about moral values and desirable interpersonal qualities by modeling prosocial behaviors and explicitly teaching about socially acceptable actions. The authors concluded, "The goal of parents' extensive investments of time and effort is not only to cultivate children's moral values for application to the realm of sports activities. Leadership, teamwork, loyalty, competitiveness, confidence, ingenuity and other values gained through sports activities also apply to life; they are seen as requisites for raising children into successful, healthy adults" (p. 50).

Recognizing that parents represent only one piece of the social jigsaw puzzle, some studies have examined the interactive effects of parents and peers or parents and coaches/teachers on positive youth development (e.g., Bhalla, 2009; Cox et al., 2009; Cox & Ullrich-French, 2010; Davison, 2004; Davison & Jago, 2009; Garcia Bengoechea & Strean, 2007; Keegan, Harwood, Spray, & Lavallee, 2009; Sabiston & Crocker, 2008; Stuntz & Spearance, 2010; Ullrich-French & Smith, 2006, 2009; W.M. Weiss & Weiss, 2003, 2006, 2007). For example, Sabiston and Crocker found strong relationships among parent and best friend influence (emotional support, competence beliefs, role modeling), expectancy-value constructs (perceived competence and subjective values), and physical activity level among adolescent girls and boys. W.M. Weiss and Weiss (2007) examined social and psychological determinants of sport commitment (psychological desire and resolve to continue involvement) among female gymnasts. For the 8- to 11-year-old group, perceptions of lower costs, lower constraints from parents (i.e., feelings of obligation to continue), and greater constraints from best friend were predictors of commitment, whereas lower costs, higher personal investments, and lower parent constraints predicted commitment for middle adolescents (11- to 14.5-year-olds).

In sum, parents represent important sources of sport-related information and motivation for youth. Parents directly or indirectly influence children's social, psychological, and physical competencies and attributes (e.g., social skills, competence beliefs, physical activity level) through provision of social support, role modeling, feedback, social reinforcement, and beliefs about the child's competence and value of physical activity. Soon after parents enroll their children in organized sports and physical activities, coaches and teachers become credible and valuable sources of competence information and motivation.

COACH INFLUENCE ON POSITIVE YOUTH DEVELOPMENT

Youth sport coaches and activity instructors represent external social assets who can promote physical skill, social, and psychological development (see Amorose, 2007; Horn, 2008; Weiss, 2011).

Coaches are key sources of competence information, based on their performance feedback, leadership decisions, structure of practices, and relationships formed with athletes (e.g., Amorose & Smith, 2003; Amorose & Weiss, 1998; Horn, Glenn, & Wentzell, 1993). In positive youth development terms, coaches and teachers are instrumental in developing competence, confidence, connection, character, and caring among participants. In this section, we summarize the mechanisms by which instructors influence behavioral competencies and psychosocial outcomes among youth.

Informational feedback and social reinforcement are predominant coaching behaviors required for teaching and improving physical and psychosocial competencies and attributes (see Amorose, 2007; Conroy & Coatsworth, 2006; Horn, 2008). In a line of research that spans four decades, Smoll and Smith (1989, 2002b) have set the gold standard for designing and implementing intervention studies that demonstrate the impact of coaching behaviors on positive youth development. Following an intervention in which youth baseball coaches were trained to respond more frequently with praise following success and encouragement plus instruction following errors, and to respond less frequently with punitive instruction, players from intervention and control groups were compared from pre- to postseason on psychosocial and behavioral variables. More frequent positive and informational feedback following performance, and infrequent punishing tactics, successfully enhanced self-esteem, perceived competence, interpersonal attraction among teammates, enjoyment, and continued participation, and decreased performance anxiety and attrition rates among youth participants (Barnett, Smoll, & Smith, 1992; R. E. Smith, Smoll, & Barnett, 1995; R. E. Smith, Smoll, & Cumming, 2007; R. E. Smith, Smoll, & Curtis, 1979; Smoll et al., 1993).

Smith and Smoll's groundbreaking research sparked many studies that expanded upon sample demographics, coaching behavior types, study designs, and outcome variables (e.g., Amorose & Smith, 2003; Amorose & Weiss, 1998; Black & Weiss, 1992; Coatsworth & Conroy, 2006; Conroy & Coatsworth, 2004; Horn, 1984, 1985; Weiss, Amorose, & Wilko, 2009). For example, Horn studied coaches' behaviors in relation to 13- to 15-year-old female softball players' perceptions of competence over the course of a season. Players who received more frequent praise following successful performance scored *lower* in perceived competence, whereas players who received greater criticism for

errors reported *higher* perceived competence. These paradoxical results were explained by the nature of the feedback given. Praise was not given *contingently or appropriately* for demonstrating specific, challenging skills but rather for mastering easy skills or exhibiting mediocre performance. In contrast, criticism was *contingent* upon specific performance levels and *appropriately* combined with information on how to improve on subsequent mastery attempts. To support this inference, Horn (1984) reported data that showed lower skilled players were given more praise and talented athletes more criticism for their efforts, thus explaining associated changes in perceived competence over the season. These results highlight that quality, rather than type, of informational and evaluative feedback is essential to promoting positive youth outcomes (see Horn, 1987; Horn, Lox, & Labrador, 2010). Coach praise that is contingent and appropriate to successful performance, and encouragement combined with informational feedback following skill errors, are associated with positive self-perceptions, affective responses, and motivated behaviors among youth.

Interpersonal leadership style has been a productive means of assessing coaches' impact on positive youth development through physical activity (e.g., Bartholomew, Ntoumanis, & Thøgersen-Ntoumani, 2009; Deci & Ryan, 1987; Mageau & Vallerand, 2003). *Autonomy-supportive behaviors* include those that provide athletes choice within limits, provide a rationale for activities and rules, acknowledge athletes' feelings, provide opportunities to develop initiative, and avoid guilt-induced criticism. *Controlling behaviors* include using rewards to control participants, giving overly critical feedback, emphasizing social comparison as a measure of success, and paying less attention to athletes who perform poorly. Studies consistently show that an autonomy-supportive style is associated with greater perceived competence, enjoyment, self-determined motivation, and well-being (e.g., Amorose & Anderson-Butcher, 2007; Coatsworth & Conroy, 2009; Gagné, Ryan, & Bargmann, 2003; Lim & Wang, 2009; Price & Weiss, 2000; Reinboth, Duda, & Ntoumanis, 2004; Standage, Duda, Ntoumanis, 2006). For example, Reinboth and colleagues found that greater perceived autonomy support by coaches was related to feelings of self-determination, subjective vitality, and intrinsic satisfaction among male adolescent athletes. Coatsworth and Conroy found that adolescent swimmers who reported greater coach autonomy support were higher in perceived competence and relatedness, which in turn predicted self-esteem, initiative, and identity reflection. By contrast, a controlling style is associated with lower self-determined motivation and well-being and higher dropout (e.g., Blanchard, Amiot, Perreault, Vallerand, & Provencher, 2009; Pelletier, Fortier, Vallerand, & Briere, 2001).

Coaches and teachers can also promote positive youth development through the motivational climate they create in the gym or on the field (see Ames, 1992; Weiss, Amorose, & Kipp, 2012). A mastery motivational climate is created when a coach or teacher defines success in self-referenced terms and emphasizes and reinforces effort, improvement, and cooperative learning. A performance motivational climate is created when a coach or teacher defines success in norm-referenced terms and emphasizes and reinforces favorable social comparison, such as winning and outperforming others. Research in youth physical activity contexts shows strong support for the psychosocial and behavioral benefits of participating within a mastery climate (e.g., Ferrer-Caja & Weiss, 2000, 2002; Keegan et al., 2009; Newton, Duda, & Yin, 2000; Sarrazin, Vallerand, Guillet, Pelletier, & Cury, 2002; Theeboom, De Knop, & Weiss, 1995; Weiss, Amorose, & Wilko, 2009). These studies show that youths' perceptions of a higher mastery climate are associated with greater perceived competence and autonomy, enjoyment, self-determined motivation, and physical activity behaviors (effort, persistence, skill development, lower dropout).

A *caring climate* is another attribute of the social environment that contributes to positive youth development, defined as "the extent to which individuals perceive a particular setting to be interpersonally inviting, safe, supportive, and able to provide the experience of being valued and respected" (Fry & Gano-Overway, 2010, p. 296). In two studies, sport participants rated the degree to which they perceived coaches and teammates valued, cared, and respected one another. Athletes' perceptions of a caring climate were related to frequency of athletes' caring behaviors (respecting and being kind to teammates), positive attitudes toward coaches and teammates, confidence in managing emotions, empathy toward others, and prosocial behaviors (Fry & Gano-Overway, 2010; Gano-Overway et al., 2009). A caring climate is complementary to a mastery climate, in that both highlight the atmosphere surrounding participants' ability to learn social and psychological competencies and values.

Researchers have interviewed coaches about how they teach life skills, and surveyed or interviewed athletes about how coaches teach them life skills, such as interpersonal competence, emotion management, and goal setting (e.g., Bhalla, 2009; Camiré, Trudel, & Forneris, 2009; Fraser-Thomas & Coté, 2009; Gould, Collins, Lauer, & Chung, 2007; Holt, Tink, Mandigo, & Fox, 2008; Weiss, 2008; Weiss, Bolter, Price, & Bhalla, 2007). Some studies (Gould et al., 2007; Holt et al., 2008) indicate that coaches assert a philosophy that entails teaching athletes life skills, but the coaches were not observed to verify if and how they teach these skills. Coaches also described how they taught life skills in general or vague terms (e.g., emphasize importance of academic progress, talk to players about being disciplined). Other studies (Bhalla, 2009; Camiré et al., 2009; Weiss, Bolter, et al., 2007) reveal that coaches taught specific strategies (e.g., how to manage emotions, set goals), modeled desirable behaviors (e.g., stay calm under pressure), provided social support (e.g., built rapport and trust with youth), used positive feedback (e.g., encouragement plus future-oriented instruction), and provided opportunities for self-regulated behavior (e.g., use of instructional aids) for promoting youth development. Some studies reported incidents of negative coaching behaviors that detracted from positive youth development (Bhalla, 2009; Camiré et al., 2009; Fraser-Thomas & Coté, 2009). Clearly, more research is needed to document how coaches teach life skills and how to train coaches to successfully teach life skills (Gould & Carson, 2008; Petitpas, Cornelius, Van Raalte, & Jones, 2005).

In sum, coaches and teachers are important external assets who can promote positive youth development through use of feedback, instruction, and opportunities for decision-making and cooperative learning. The structure and climate of practices and quality of coaching behaviors are key mechanisms for promoting youths' social, psychological, and physical competencies and healthy developmental outcomes. Research is consistent in showing that coaches should focus on positive and informational feedback, an autonomy-supportive style, and mastery, caring climates to achieve youth development goals. We now turn to a social asset that has long been held as a consequence of sport participation—moral development or *character*.

Moral Development

Moral or character development is another social asset that children and adolescents must acquire to become caring and contributing members of society. Moral development refers to the changes that occur over time in individuals' moral thoughts and actions (see Weiss, Smith, & Stuntz, 2008). Youth demonstrate moral development by understanding the difference between right and wrong, showing integrity, displaying empathy, and helping others (Lerner et al., 2005; Shields & Bredemeier, 2007). Moral development is an inherently social process because moral dilemmas occur when the rights and interests of one person conflict with the rights and interests of another. In turn, moral dilemmas are resolved by behaving in ways that show consideration for others' interests and well-being.

Sport and physical activity contexts are rich social environments that provide numerous opportunities for youth to develop and display moral character. Moral development in physical activity contexts can include a variety of concepts, such as sportsmanship, character, prosocial behavior, and fair play, among others (Weiss, Smith, & Stuntz, 2008). According to Martinek and Hellison (1997), physical activity contexts are "active, interactive, and highly emotional" (p. 44) and thus provide an excellent setting for teamwork and conflict resolution. Youth sport participants must often decide whether to help an opponent after they've fallen, tease a less skilled teammate or opponent, or act respectfully toward the referee after a bad call. Thus, physical activity contexts present an incredible opportunity to enhance youths' development of character.

Several conceptual approaches explain how moral development occurs in physical activity contexts. According to social learning theory (Bandura, 1986), children learn morally appropriate or inappropriate behaviors through observation of and reinforcement from significant others, such as parents, coaches, and peers. Structural developmental theorists (e.g., Haan, 1977; Kohlberg, 1969; Rest, 1986) propose that moral development occurs when youth demonstrate more mature levels of moral reasoning, which occurs as a result of experiencing moral dilemmas and dialoging with others to find balance among their own and others' interests. According to the positive youth development approach, youth develop character by participating in intrinsically motivating activities that provide opportunities to learn transferable life skills and interact with positive and supportive mentors (e.g., Gould & Carson, 2008; Petitpas et al., 2005; Weiss & Wiese-Bjornstal, 2009). Adult leaders facilitate moral growth by creating high expectations for behavior, providing opportunities for leadership, and holding youth accountable for their actions (e.g., Hansen & Larson, 2007; Roth &

Brooks-Gunn, 2003). In turn, youth demonstrate moral or character development by accepting personal and social responsibility, showing integrity, and contributing to society (Damon, 2004; Lerner et al., 2005). These conceptual approaches demonstrate that children's moral development is significantly influenced by the surrounding social context and personal competencies.

SOCIAL CONTEXTUAL FACTORS INFLUENCING MORAL GROWTH AND BEHAVIOR

A number of key social contextual factors influence youths' moral and character development through physical activity participation. First, observational learning or modeling is a powerful means by which significant adults and peers influence youths' moral reasoning and behaviors in sport (e.g., Bolter & Weiss, 2011, 2012; Mugno & Feltz, 1985; M.D. Smith, 1974, 1978). M.D. Smith (1978) found that 12- to 18-year-old ice hockey players reported that they learned to hit illegally from watching professional hockey, and over 60% said they had used these observed tactics during games. Mugno and Feltz found similar results with youth league and high school football players. These studies suggest that youth sport participants can learn immoral behaviors from watching others.

Perceived social approval from significant others for attitudes and behaviors represents another powerful mechanism of influence on youths' decisions about good and poor sporting behavior (e.g., Bolter & Weiss, 2011, 2012; Guivernau & Duda, 2002; Mugno & Feltz, 1985; Stuart & Ebbeck, 1995). For example, Stuart and Ebbeck created five hypothetical moral dilemmas in basketball (e.g., injuring another player, arguing with official) and assessed 9- to-15-year-old male and female players on moral judgment, reasoning, intention, and behavior. Perceived social approval was assessed by asking participants to rate the extent to which their coach, mother, father, and teammates would approve of them engaging in the behaviors depicted in the dilemmas. Perceived approval from *all* significant others was related to indices of youths' moral functioning. These findings indicate that social approval from coaches, parents, and teammates is an important predictor of youths' sportsmanlike attitudes and behaviors.

The moral atmosphere can also make an impact on youth sport participants' moral intentions and behaviors. According to Power, Higgins, and Kohlberg (1989), moral atmosphere reflects the norms for acceptable behavior that develop among individuals within the same community or group. Research suggests that norms for acceptable behavior may be specific to sport type and competitive level. Youth who participate in contact sports (e.g., ice hockey, football) were more likely to approve of and engage in physically aggressive behaviors than were those who participate in noncontact sports (e.g., track and field, tennis) (Bredemeier, Weiss, Shields, & Cooper, 1986, 1987; Conroy, Silva, Newcomer, Walker, & Johnson, 2001; Loughead & Leith, 2001). In addition, youth who compete at higher competitive levels reported greater endorsement of physically aggressive actions compared to those at lower competitive levels (Conroy et al., 2001; Loughead & Leith, 2001).

Norms that develop specific to one's team also influence youths' choices about moral sport behavior (Chow, Murray, & Feltz, 2009; Shields, LaVoi, Bredemeier, & Power, 2007; Stephens, 2000; Stephens & Bredemeier, 1996; Stephens & Kavanagh, 2003). Stephens and Bredemeier found that 12- to 14-year-old female athletes who reported a greater number of teammates would aggress against an opponent and perceived their coach higher in ego goal orientation were more likely to engage in aggressive behaviors. Shields et al. found that youths' poor sport behaviors were predicted by players' perceptions of team, coach, and parent norms, as well as by coach and spectator behaviors. Collectively, studies suggest that youths' perceptions of norms for acceptable behavior establish the moral atmosphere that influences youths' moral reasoning and behaviors.

Perceptions of the motivational climate are also related to moral attitudes and behaviors in physical activity contexts. Some studies have shown a negative relationship between a coach-created performance climate and moral reasoning and sportsmanlike behaviors (e.g., Boixados, Cruz, Torregrosa, & Valiente, 2004; Miller, Roberts, & Ommundsen, 2005; Ommundsen, Roberts, Lemyre, & Treasure, 2003). These findings suggest that coaches' emphasis on norm-referenced success, such as winning, that is evident in performance climates may encourage players to believe that unsportsmanlike attitudes and behaviors are legitimate to achieving the end goal of winning. In comparison, a coach-created mastery climate has been consistently related to displays of sportsmanlike behavior and mature moral reasoning (e.g., Boixados et al., 2004; Miller et al., 2005; Ommundsen et al., 2003).

INDIVIDUAL DIFFERENCES INFLUENCING MORAL GROWTH AND BEHAVIOR

Several individual difference factors affect the ways in which youth develop character through sport. First, cognitive development/age influences youths' capabilities to make moral judgments. Younger children cannot reason abstractly or see others' perspectives and thus use more egocentric moral reasoning. In contrast, older children and adolescents acquire the ability to reason abstractly and feel empathy, and therefore reason at higher levels (Solomon, 2004). For example, Jantz (1975) found that 7- to 8-year-old children reasoned at less mature levels, whereas 9- to 12-year-old children reasoned at higher, more cooperative levels when asked about the rules of basketball.

Second, gender is a contributing factor to sportsmanlike attitudes and play. Male sport participants are more likely to legitimize aggression or take part in unsportsmanlike aggressive behaviors (e.g., Bredemeier et al., 1986, 1987; Conroy et al., 2001). These gender differences may be attributed to different socialization processes through sport for male and female participants. Bredemeier et al. (1987) suggested that the normative structure of high-contact sports can often encourage aggressive play for male athletes and reward boys who play more aggressively.

Third, level of moral reasoning within sport contexts influences moral intentions and behaviors. Lower levels of moral reasoning are associated with a greater display and endorsement of aggressive behaviors in sport (e.g., Bredemeier, 1985, 1994; Bredemeier et al., 1986, 1987). These results indicate that individuals who reason at an egocentric level of moral reasoning are more likely to engage in and approve of unsportsmanlike aggression. Studies have also shown differences in how individuals reason about sport and life moral dilemmas (e.g., Bredemeier, 1995; Bredemeier & Shields, 1984). Bredemeier and Shields assessed moral reasoning about sport and life dilemmas among youth who varied in age (high school, college), gender (male, female), and athlete status (athlete, nonathlete). Sport moral reasoning was lower than life reasoning across the entire sample, suggesting that self-interest is more acceptable in sport than in nonsport contexts. Shields and Bredemeier (2007) used the term "game reasoning" to explain that individuals reason at a lower level in sport contexts because they see sport as separate from daily life and free from the constraints of everyday morality. In this way, sport participants may feel that aggressive or rule-breaking behaviors are justified in the name of winning.

Fourth, achievement goal orientation is another individual difference factor related to youths' moral thoughts and behaviors in sport. Higher ego goal orientation and lower task goal orientation are associated with greater endorsement of and engagement in unsportsmanlike play (e.g., Duda, Olson, & Templin, 1991; Dunn & Causgrove Dunn, 1999; Kavussanu & Ntoumanis, 2003). Individuals who primarily define success as comparing favorably to others may do whatever it takes to win, even cheating or injuring a competitor. Comparatively, individuals who adopt a stronger task orientation are focused on personal improvement and do not need to win to feel accomplished. Recent studies show that social goal orientations help explain moral judgments as well (e.g., Sage & Kavussanu, 2007; Stuntz & Weiss, 2003). For example, Stuntz and Weiss found that 11- to 15-year-old boys who defined success in terms of having a close friendship or being accepted by peers were more likely to approve of unsportsmanlike behaviors when peers similarly condoned unfair play. Together, these studies suggest that how individuals define success in sport contributes to their moral thoughts and intentions.

Finally, researchers have examined moral disengagement as an important predictor of moral thoughts and actions. Moral disengagement in sport occurs when individuals switch off their moral standards and disconnect themselves psychologically and emotionally from immoral acts (Boardley & Kavussanu, 2007). For example, an athlete might justify breaking the rules if he or she perceives that everyone else is doing so, or believe that fighting is okay if it is being done to protect a teammate. A few studies show that moral disengagement is related to fewer prosocial and more antisocial behaviors toward teammates and opponents (Boardley & Kavussanu, 2009, 2010).

PHYSICAL ACTIVITY–BASED INTERVENTIONS AND PROGRAMS

Developmental sport psychology researchers have implemented theory-driven studies with the goal of enhancing moral development in physical activity contexts (see Weiss, Smith, & Stuntz, 2008). For example, Romance, Weiss, and Bockoven (1986) designed a curriculum for a fifth-grade physical education class including situations that created moral dilemmas (e.g., uneven playing time, unfair rules) and provided opportunities for dialogue

and balance. After 8 weeks, post-test scores on life, sport, and overall moral reasoning for the experimental group were significantly higher than for the control group. Gibbons, Ebbeck, and Weiss (1995; Gibbons & Ebbeck, 1997) found similar results for an intervention with fourth-, fifth-, and sixth-graders based on Canada's *Fair Play for Kids* guidelines. Applied to both physical education and academic classes, the curriculum focused on respecting others, controlling one's emotions, and emphasizing equal participation for all while experiencing moral dilemmas, dialogue, and balance. Gibbons et al. found that moral judgment, reasoning, intention, and prosocial behavior increased for the experimental groups after the 7-month intervention, whereas no change was observed in the control group.

The First Tee (www.thefirsttee.org) uses golf as a vehicle for enhancing youths' life skill learning and developmental outcomes, including sportsmanship, respect, responsibility, honesty, integrity, and courtesy. Coaches teach golf and life skills seamlessly by emphasizing principles of doing versus telling (e.g., getting kids involved in activity immediately), creating optimal challenges for mastering skills, empowering youth (e.g., matching feedback to individual needs), and optimizing learning through a positive approach to feedback. Evaluation research shows *The First Tee* to be effective in teaching for and developing character. Interview responses with youth, coaches, and parents indicated that youth had learned positive character attributes (Weiss, 2008), and survey data (Weiss, Bolter, Bhalla, & Price, 2007) showed that youth participants in *The First Tee* demonstrated greater responsibility, honesty, and integrity compared to youth participating in other out-of-school-time activities. In addition, scores for respect, responsibility, and integrity remained high and stable over time (Weiss, Bolter, et al., 2008). Success in promoting character can be attributed to supportive adult leaders and a deliberate life skills curriculum that are designed to promote positive youth development. Physical activity–based youth development programs show promise for enhancing moral development and citizenship.

Psychological Assets

Participating in sports and physical activities affords youth many opportunities to attain psychological assets and positive attributes, such as perceived competence and self-esteem, feelings of autonomy and choice, positive affect and stress relief, and self-determined motivation (Horn, 2004b; Weiss & Wiese-Bjornstal, 2009). These areas resemble Lerner's *Five Cs* of competence (motivated behaviors) and confidence (global self-worth, perceived competence, self-efficacy). Significant adults and peers are instrumental in helping youth attain psychological assets and outcomes, thus connection is also one of the *Five Cs* that comes into play. In this section, we synthesize research on psychological assets and outcomes—self-perceptions, emotional responses, and motivational orientations and behaviors.

Self-Perceptions

We focus our review on two self-perceptions that hold significance for children and adolescents—global self-esteem and perceived physical competence. *Global self-esteem* is an individual's overall evaluation of him- or herself as worthy and significant, whereas *perceived competence* refers to beliefs about abilities in particular achievement domains (e.g., sports, music, arts; Horn, 2004b; Weiss, Bhalla, & Price, 2007). Physical self-perceptions are significant because they strongly predict cognitive, affective, and behavioral outcomes, such as positive and negative emotions, motivational orientations, performance, and health-related behaviors (e.g., Amorose, 2001; Crocker, Sabiston, Kowalski, McDonough, & Kowalski, 2006; Ebbeck & Weiss, 1998; Marsh, Gerlach, Trautwein, Ludtke, & Brettschneider, 2007; A. L. Smith, 1999). Thus, understanding how positive self-perceptions can be fostered in physical activity contexts is important for informing practitioners of effective strategies to ensure healthy developmental outcomes among youth.

In the physical domain, youth form judgments about their abilities based on several sources of available information. These include feedback from parents and coaches; peer evaluation; social comparison to teammates and friends; self-referenced criteria such as effort, enjoyment, and skill improvement; and norm-referenced sources such as performance statistics and event outcome (Horn, 2004b; Horn & Amorose, 1998; Weiss, Bhalla, & Price, 2007). Importance placed on these particular sources varies by age, cognitive development, competitive level, sport experience, and psychological characteristics (e.g., Amorose & Smith, 2003; Amorose & Weiss, 1998; Halliburton & Weiss, 2002; Horn et al., 1993; Horn & Weiss, 1991; McKiddie & Maynard, 1997; Weiss & Amorose, 2005; Weiss, Ebbeck, & Horn, 1997). Young children show preference for parental feedback, early and middle adolescents rate peer evaluation and comparison as more important,

and older adolescents use a variety of social, self-, and norm-referenced sources of information.

Significant adults and peers represent salient sources of physical competence judgments and global self-esteem (Horn, 2004b; Weiss, Bhalla, & Price, 2007). Reflected appraisals by parents, coaches, and peers are associated with youths' self-appraisals of physical ability and self-worth (e.g., Amorose, 2002; Babkes & Weiss, 1999; Bois et al., 2005a; Harter, Waters, & Whitesell, 1998). That is, youths' perceptions of important others' beliefs about their abilities and personal worthiness are strongly associated with their own perceived competence and global self-esteem. As reported earlier on external social assets, parents and coaches also influence youths' self-perceptions through beliefs and behaviors that reflect positive and informational feedback, social approval and support, role modeling, autonomy-oriented styles, and climates focused on mastery and improvement (see Amorose, 2007; Fredricks & Eccles, 2004; Horn, 2008; Smoll & Smith, 1989, 2002b). Mechanisms of peer influence affecting self-perceptions include perceived group acceptance, close friendship, social support, and observational learning (see A. L. Smith, 2003, 2007; Weiss & Stuntz, 2004).

Intervention studies have employed deliberate curricula and coach/teacher training for enhancing youths' sense of self (e.g., Bruening, Dover, & Clark, 2009; Coatsworth & Conroy, 2006; Ebbeck & Gibbons, 1998; Marsh & Peart, 1988; R. E. Smith et al., 1979; Smoll et al., 1993). Smoll and colleagues trained 10- to 12-year-old boys' baseball coaches to emphasize reinforcement for good performance and effort, mistake-contingent encouragement, and corrective and technical instruction, and to minimize using punishment strategies. At season's end, boys who played for the trained coaches and started the season with low self-esteem showed significant increases in self-esteem over the season, whereas those in the control group did not. These results suggest that children who had the most to gain from a positive sport experience (i.e., those low in self-esteem) benefited greatly from having a coach who used positive forms of instruction and evaluative feedback.

In an intervention study targeting promotion of physical self-perceptions and global self-esteem, Ebbeck and Gibbons (1998) employed an intentional curriculum focused on team-building challenges and trained physical education teachers to effectively implement the curriculum with middle school students over the course of a school year. Group differences and pre-/post-intervention differences in the intervention group emerged for global self-worth and perceptions of athletic competence, physical appearance, and social acceptance for girls and boys. A physical activity–based intervention that required effective teaching, cooperative goals, and optimal challenges was successful in modifying global and domain-specific self-evaluations.

Some studies incorporated physical activity and health promotion interventions to increase psychological, social, and behavioral assets in youth and adolescents (Bruening et al., 2009; Crews, Lochbaum, & Landers, 2004; Schneider, Fridlund Dunton, & Cooper, 2008; Taymoori & Lubans, 2008). For example, Bruening and colleagues conducted a 12-week physical activity program for preadolescent girls, incorporating a deliberate curriculum of physical activities, life skills, and healthy choices, and utilized social assets in the form of female college athlete role models. At post-intervention, interviews revealed that girls improved in self-esteem, self-responsibility, connection to community, sense of belonging, and knowledge and application of life skills to healthy living.

In sum, self-perceptions are psychological assets that can be fostered in structured physical activity settings that include deliberate strategies and competent and supportive adults and peers. Positive change in competence and confidence through connection in physical activity settings provides youth with assets that are beneficial throughout their lifetimes. The developmental significance of global self-esteem and perceived physical competence resides in a consistent relationship with emotional responses, motivational orientations, and physical activity behaviors.

Emotions

One of the most robust findings is that youth participate in sports and physical activities for enjoyment reasons (i.e., have fun, be with friends, learn new skills) and discontinue participation when it no longer remains enjoyable (see Weiss & Petlichkoff, 1989; Weiss & Williams, 2004). Youth can experience many positive emotions such as joy and pride, and negative emotions such as anxiety and stress, from physical activity participation (Crocker, Hoar, McDonough, Kowalski, & Niefer, 2004; Gould, 1993; Scanlan, Babkes, & Scanlan, 2005; R. E. Smith, Smoll, & Passer, 2002). Understanding sources of enjoyment and anxiety is developmentally significant because positive and negative emotions are related to motivational, performance, and health-related outcomes.

Of the many positive emotions youth can experience through sport, enjoyment has been the central construct of empirical research (see Crocker et al., 2004; Scanlan et al., 2005; Scanlan & Simons, 1992). Sources of enjoyment in youth sport can be classified along interpersonal, intrapersonal, and situational lines. Interpersonal sources include experiencing positive interactions with teammates, having a close friendship, feeling accepted by one's peer group, and engaging in positive parent and coach relationships. Intrapersonal sources include perceived competence, task goal orientation, effort, and mastering and improving skills. Situational sources include optimally challenging tasks and skills, competitive achievement, and social recognition and opportunities. These sources of sport enjoyment are robust across youth populations (e.g., age, gender, sport type, competitive level; Brustad, 1988; Scanlan, Carpenter, Lobel, & Simons, 1993; Scanlan, Stein, & Ravizza, 1989; Stephens, 1998; Wankel & Kreisel, 1985).

Sources of competitive anxiety and stress can also be aligned with interpersonal, intrapersonal, and situational factors (Crocker et al., 2004; Gould, 1993; Scanlan et al., 2005). Interpersonal sources include negative evaluative feedback from parents, coaches, and teammates; perceived parental or coach pressure to perform; and low social support by significant adults and peers. Intrapersonal sources include low self-perceptions, high trait anxiety, fear of failure, and perfectionism. Situational sources include the evaluative nature of the sport or situation, importance of the competition, situational criticality, and competition outcome (e.g., Brustad, 1988; Gould, Horn, & Spreeman, 1983; Scanlan & Passer, 1978, 1979; Scanlan, Stein, & Ravizza, 1991; Simon & Martens, 1979). Raedeke and Smith (2004) found that adolescent swimmers with higher levels of competitive stress reported higher levels of burnout, and that stress mediated the relationship of coping behaviors and social support satisfaction with burnout. Coping behaviors and social support are strategies to reduce stress that, in turn, can reduce propensities to burn out (i.e., emotional and physical exhaustion, reduced sense of accomplishment, sport devaluation).

Enjoyment and anxiety have also been studied as predictors of psychological and behavioral outcomes, such as self-determined motivation, sport commitment, and physical activity participation (e.g., Barr-Anderson et al., 2007; Schneider, Dunn, & Cooper,

2009; A. L. Smith, 1999; W.M. Weiss & Weiss, 2003, 2006, 2007; W.M. Weiss, Weiss, & Amorose, 2010). For example, Weiss and Weiss (2003, 2006) used cluster analysis to group 10- to 18-year-old gymnasts into commitment profiles. Gymnasts with an adaptive profile (committed to sport for attraction reasons) reported higher enjoyment and benefits and lower costs of participation compared to gymnasts with a maladaptive profile (committed to sport because they feel entrapped). Attracted gymnasts reported higher intrinsic motivation and behavioral commitment than did entrapped gymnasts. In another study, Schneider et al. studied associations between affective states and physical activity levels. Greater moderate to vigorous physical activity was associated with positive change in affect during activity, leading the authors to recommend that youth programs include enjoyable activities to promote greater physical activity participation.

Several intervention studies provide evidence that sport and physical activity participation fosters emotional well-being (e.g., MacPhail, Gorely, Kirk, & Kinchin, 2008; R.E. Smith et al., 1995, 2007; Theeboom et al., 1995). Smith and colleagues, in two studies, successfully trained youth coaches to provide frequent social support, reinforce effort and mastery, and de-emphasize the importance of winning, which in turn reduced athletes' performance anxiety. MacPhail et al. incorporated a 16-week sport education unit in elementary physical education classes. The program consisted of activities that encouraged students' autonomy, such as choosing a role on the team and determining winners in the tournament. Students were interviewed about their experiences throughout the program, and several themes emerged: fun and enjoyment, team affiliation, autonomy, perceived sport competence, and formal competition. Survey responses reinforced past research on sources of enjoyment: affiliation, autonomy, competition, and learning skills. These intervention studies show that participation in physical activity programs that include intentional curricula and trained coaches/teachers can enhance positive and decrease negative emotional outcomes.

In sum, physical activity is a context that can offer youth opportunities for positive emotional assets (e.g., enjoyment), but it can also provoke anxiety and stress in participants. Understanding the interpersonal, intrapersonal, and situational sources of enjoyment and anxiety allows for interventions, strategies, and behaviors that can maximize positive and minimize negative affect in youth sport. Successfully fostering emotional well-being can ultimately influence positive social, psychological, and physical development among youth and adolescents.

Motivation

Adaptive motivational attitudes and behaviors are desirable psychological assets attainable through participation in physical activities (see Weiss & Amorose, 2008; Weiss & Williams, 2004). Youth engage in physical activities for many different reasons, but self-determined forms of motivation (e.g., to derive pleasure, to identify as a physically active person, to attain benefits from participation) are related to greater effort, persistence, and health and well-being (see Weiss, Amorose, & Kipp, 2012). Sport and physical activity contexts can contribute to positive youth development by encouraging and reinforcing self-determined motivational orientations to ensure attainment of skill and health benefits.

Early research on youth participation motives uncovered main reasons for engaging in sports and physical activities (see Weiss & Amorose, 2008; Weiss & Williams, 2004). These reasons included being with and making friends, doing something well, having fun, attaining approval and acceptance from adults and peers, learning and improving skills, and becoming physically fit. The various reasons have been categorized into three consistent themes: to develop or demonstrate competence, to gain social acceptance or approval, and to enjoy one's experiences. These reasons highlight perceptions of competence, social influence, and positive affect as important predictors of participation motivation. The early descriptive research shifted to theory-driven studies using frameworks that include these key constructs.

Since the early participation motivation studies of the 1970s, most studies on motivational orientations and behaviors in sport have been based on developmentally appropriate theoretical frameworks. Studies based on Harter's (1978) competence motivation theory have shown that parents' and coaches' informational and evaluative feedback are associated with youths' perceived competence, enjoyment, and intrinsic motivation (e.g., Babkes & Weiss, 1999; Black & Weiss, 1992; Bois et al., 2005a; Weiss, Amorose, & Wilko, 2009). Studies based on Nicholls' (1984, 1989) achievement goal theory have shown that individuals with higher task-oriented goals (defining success as learning, mastery, effort, and improvement) are associated with more adaptive outcomes (e.g., intrinsic motivation, enjoyment, continued participation, performance) than are those with higher ego-oriented goals (defining success as favorable comparisons to others) (e.g., Duda, Chi, Newton, Walling, & Catley, 1995; Duda & Nicholls, 1992; Harwood & Swain, 2001; Swain, 1996).

Ryan and Deci's (2000, 2002) self-determination theory has triggered much research on motivational orientations and physical activity behaviors in youth physical activity contexts (see Amorose, 2007; Weiss & Amorose, 2008). According to self-determination theory, motives for participating in physical activity (e.g., to gain skills, make friends, have fun) can be situated along a continuum of more controlling (e.g., "Because I feel I *have to*") to more self-determined regulations (e.g., "Because I *want to*"). Several studies have examined predictors of self-determined motivation among youth physical activity participants, such as coaches' behaviors, peer acceptance, friendship quality, motivational climate, and teaching style (e.g., Amorose & Anderson-Butcher, 2007; Cox et al., 2009; Cox & Ullrich-French, 2010; Kipp & Amorose, 2008; Standage et al., 2006). In general, an autonomy-supportive coaching style, mastery motivational climate, greater peer acceptance, and positive friendship quality are related to greater perceived competence, autonomy, and relatedness, which in turn predict self-determined motivation.

Researchers have also studied psychosocial and behavioral outcomes associated with self-determined motivation, indicating its significance for physical activity participation. These outcomes include effort and persistence (Ferrer-Caja & Weiss, 2000, 2002; Pelletier et al., 2001; Sarrazin et al., 2002; Standage et al., 2006), physical activity level (Hagger, Chatzisarantis, Culverhouse, & Biddle, 2003; Parish & Treasure, 2003; Taylor, Ntoumanis, Standage, & Spray, 2010), enjoyment (Cox et al., 2009; Vierling, Standage, & Treasure, 2007), well-being (Blanchard et al., 2009; Gagné et al., 2003) and quality of life (Standage & Gillison, 2007). For example, Standage and Gillison found significant relationships between teachers' autonomy-supportive behaviors and adolescent physical education students' self-determined motivation, self-esteem, and quality of life. Collectively, studies provide support for individual and social predictors of self-determined motivation and cognitive, affective, and behavioral outcomes of self-determined motivation.

From early research on participation motives to theory-driven studies, it is clear that youth participate in physical activities for many reasons and that participating for more self-determined reasons is most beneficial. Youth who are involved in physical activities because it's fun or because they value the benefits gained are more likely to exert greater effort and persistence, be more physically active, and experience greater well-being compared to those who participate for more controlling reasons (e.g., to please parents, to reduce feelings of guilt). Coaches, teachers, and parents can promote a climate that facilitates improvement, choice, and social interactions (i.e., needs for competence, autonomy, and relatedness) to foster self-determined motivation. Because of the benefits of participating for autonomous reasons, self-determined motivation for being physically active is a psychological asset that can be attained through deliberate activity programs led by competent adults.

Physical Assets

Physical activity contexts, such as organized sport, physical education, and sports-based out-of-school-time programs, are distinct from other youth development contexts (e.g., academic clubs, performing arts programs, non-sport after-school programs) in contributing to *physical assets and outcomes*, such as motor skill development, movement literacy, sport-specific competencies, physically active lifestyles, physical fitness, and physical health (Clark, 2007; Payne & Isaacs, 2012; Strong et al., 2005; Weiss & Wiese-Bjornstal, 2009). We briefly review the knowledge base on physical assets attainable through sport and physical activity, and refer readers to detailed sources for more information on physical assets, outcomes, and interventions (Haywood & Getchell, 2009; Payne & Isaacs, 2012; Rink, Hall, & Williams, 2010; U.S. Department of Health and Human Services [USDHHS], 2008; Ward, Saunders, & Pate, 2007). In the following paragraphs we explain how physical assets reflect competence in Lerner's *Five Cs*.

Fundamental motor skills (e.g., throwing, catching, kicking, striking), postural control and balance, and locomotor skills (e.g., running, jumping, skipping) must be mastered by early or middle childhood to provide the requisite abilities for developing sport-specific skills necessary to adopt a physically active lifestyle (Clark, 2007; Haywood & Getchell, 2009; Payne & Isaacs, 2012). School physical education, parks and recreation, and after-school physical activity programs (e.g., *The Little Gym*) are prime contexts in which children can learn motor abilities and skills. Physical education is the most likely place to encounter an intentional curriculum and trained teachers to carry out developmental goals

(Bailey, 2006; Clark, 2007). As Clark points out, "If a child does not have good balance and has had limited experience and few locomotor skills, then he or she is not likely to accompany other children to a roller-skating or ice-skating party. A strong motor skill foundation at the start provides for new movement opportunities later in life such as skiing, rock climbing, tennis, golf and many others that arise as we continue on our motor development journey" (p. 43). In positive youth development terms, motor skill competence leads to other physical competencies, confidence in mastering challenges, and connecting with peers in shared activity experiences.

Physical health benefits of regular physical activity have been established with children and adolescents, including cardiovascular and metabolic health, cardiorespiratory and muscular fitness, improved bone health, and favorable body composition (USDHHS, 2008). Physically active youth are less likely to become overweight or obese, or develop heart disease, hypertension, type 2 diabetes, or osteoporosis as they grow older. As such, considerable interest and concern revolves around getting youth to engage in sufficient amounts and types of physical activity to accrue physical (and social and emotional) health benefits (Ennis, 2011; Pate, O'Neill, & McIver, 2011; Payne & Morrow, 2009). This concern stems from the consistent finding that physical activity levels decline over the adolescent years, especially among girls and youth of color, thus limiting health benefits afforded from regular activity (Strong et al., 2005; USDHHS, 1996, 2008).

The *Physical Activity Guidelines for Americans*, published by USDHHS in 2008, reflects the efforts of kinesiology and public health scholars and educators to produce a comprehensive and accessible set of recommendations for physical activity type, frequency, intensity, and duration that align with healthy living. The guidelines for children and adolescents (ages 6–17 years) include 60 minutes or more of physical activity daily, including moderate- or vigorous-intensity aerobic activities, as well as muscle- and bone-strengthening physical activities. The guidelines also state, "Adults play an important role in providing age-appropriate opportunities for physical activity. In doing so, they help lay an important foundation for life-long, health-promoting physical activity. Adults need to encourage active play in children and encourage sustained and structured activity as children grow older" (p. 15). This point accentuates our focus on significant others as essential sources of positive youth development

through physical activity—in this case, applied to physical assets and health outcomes.

Evidence for promoting physical activity levels among youth stems from programs that feature positive youth development characteristics, notably an intentional curriculum for developing personal assets, skill-building activities, positive social relationships, and caring, supportive climates (e.g., DeBate et al., 2009; DeBate, Zhang, & Thompson, 2007; Pate et al., 2005; Pate, Ward, O'Neill, & Dowda, 2007; Ward et al., 2006; see Ward et al., 2007, for other physical activity interventions). DeBate and colleagues found significant pre- to post-intervention change (12 weeks) in physical activity commitment and frequency in third- through eighth-grade girls participating in the *Girls on the Run* (www.girlsontherun.org) programs. This out-of-school-time organization, conducted within the school setting, is a physical activity–based youth development program with a structured curriculum focused on issues relevant for 8- to 13-year-old girls (e.g., physical activity, self-esteem, body image, social relationships, eating attitudes and behaviors). Physical activity leaders are trained in strategies and behaviors that empower, support, and teach girls physical, social, and psychological assets that will result in healthy developmental outcomes. Participants in *Girls on the Run* also show improvements in global self-esteem, physical ability self-concept, eating attitudes, and body size satisfaction (DeBate et al., 2009; DeBate & Thompson, 2005; Martin, Waldron, McCabe, & Choi, 2009).

Pate and colleagues conducted a comprehensive, school-based intervention with adolescent girls (*Lifestyle Education for Activity Project* [LEAP]), designed to increase physical activity and health outcomes (e.g., Dishman et al., 2005; Dishman, Saunders, Motl, Dowda, & Pate, 2009; Kelly et al., 2010; Pate et al., 2005, 2007; Ward et al., 2006). LEAP consisted of customizing traditional physical education curricula to meet the developmental needs and interests of adolescent girls, such as girls-only classes, opportunities for choice and variety of physical activities, value placed on social interactions and relationship building, access to nontraditional and lifetime activities, and providing behavioral skills and community resources to maximize continued physical activity once the intervention ended. Physical education teachers were explicitly trained through formal workshops, one-on-one mentoring, and instructional aids to implement the LEAP intervention. In positive youth development language, LEAP targeted personal assets within a structured curriculum, provided skill-building activities, and trained teachers to achieve curricular goals within a supportive and mastery climate. The intervention spanned the 2-year period when girls were in eighth and ninth grades. Results showed that LEAP was effective in promoting vigorous physical activity levels, and that girls' enjoyment of activity, perceived physical competence, and social support were factors mediating the effect of the intervention on physical activity levels.

Despite limited data-based evidence of increased physical activity levels through youth participation, it is clear that physical assets are achieved in programs that include structured, deliberate goals; developmentally appropriate skill-building activities; and trained instructors who implement curricular goals within a supportive and mastery climate. More rigorous intervention and longitudinal studies are needed to provide evidence-based benefits of youth sport and physical activity programs regarding motor skill development, physical activity levels, and physical health outcomes. Not only would these studies contribute to knowledge about best practices for positive youth development, but they would also provide a platform for policy change and advocacy for greater political, educational, and community support for physical activity–based youth development programs.

Future Directions

Weiss' (1998) presidential address for the Association for the Advancement of Applied Sport Psychology projected major issues facing sport and exercise psychology researchers in the 21st century. These issues revolved around measurement development, intervention studies, and lifespan development. How have we fared over the past 15 years in these areas as they apply to youth development through physical activity? First, a number of valid, age-appropriate measures of social, psychological, and behavioral assets were developed (e.g., friendship quality, coaching behaviors, motivational orientations, physical activity). Still, a measure in hand does not a rigorous study make. We need to move beyond cross-sectional studies and pre-test/post-test designs with no control group to longitudinal designs with appropriate comparison groups. Such designs will allow us to identify predictors of personal assets, explain variations in outcomes, and assess retention effects based on program involvement (i.e., were improvements short-lived or enduring?).

Second, intervention studies have increased over time but have done so at a slower pace compared to studies of relationships among variables or those deriving interview themes using qualitative methods. To demonstrate the effectiveness of physical activity contexts on positive youth development, more intervention and evaluation studies using mixed methodologies are necessary. Weiss (1998) stated that, "our theoretical and empirical knowledge base is strong enough to inspire informed intervention programs such as the coach education research conducted by Smith and Smoll" (p. S19). The knowledge base today is much stronger, given the review in this chapter. Thus, clinicians and researchers have access to many exemplary intervention study designs. In addition to intervention studies, evaluation research can be conducted, which entails assessing the efficacy of an existing sport-based youth development program. Because physical activity is currently a hot commodity (no doubt mostly due to the obesity epidemic), greater opportunities for external funding exist such as recent calls by the National Institutes of Health, the Robert Wood Johnson Foundation, and the William T. Grant Foundation for innovative evaluation and intervention research assessing the effectiveness of existing or new youth programs on developmental and health outcomes. The financial, time, and energy demands of intervention and evaluation research might be tempered with opportunities for multiyear funding.

Third, Weiss (1998) singled out lifespan development issues as needing more research. She indicated that the empirical knowledge base has informed us about 8- to 14-year-old youth and college-aged student athletes, but relatively much less about youth under age 8, adolescents 14–18 years of age, and middle-aged and older adults. Since that time, considerably more research has been conducted with middle and older adolescents (high school age), as noted in our chapter review. This knowledge is important because we know that physical activity declines steeply over the teenage years and, along with the decline, greater risk-taking and unhealthy behaviors occur. Future research should continue to assess, monitor, and track adolescents concurrently and over time; indeed, the positive youth development framework is especially suited for this age group. We are still in dire need of research on the role of physical activity on developmental outcomes during early and middle childhood. Perhaps the dearth of research in this area is linked with difficulty in assessing young children using survey or interview methods. Alternative assessment techniques, such as observational data, parent-reported data, and qualitative methods, can supplement traditional means of gathering data from youth in this age range.

Several controversial topics merit attention in future research efforts. First, the meaning of the phrase "the social network" means something different to today's youth than as used in this chapter, and "friending" has become a new verb courtesy of Facebook. What effect do social media (texting, tweeting, other web-based technologies) have on physical activity levels and positive youth development? Do youth spend more time engaged in virtual social interactions rather than being engaged in face-to-face interactions, and what are the implications for developing personal assets and health-related outcomes? How does participation in "social network" activities complement or detract from real-time physical activities? Related to the social media topic is the effect of video and computer games on youths' physical, social, and psychological assets and outcomes. Popularity of the Nintendo Wii and subsequent development of other movement-based video game systems, such as Microsoft Xbox 360 Kinect and Sony PlayStation Move, has led to questions about how the amount and type of physical activity invoked with such games compares to traditional forms of physical activities. Does this depend on an adolescent's current physical activity level and health status? Can "social online" games contribute to teamwork, leadership, and communication (Murphy, 2007)?

Another controversial topic is the trend toward early sport specialization (see Landers, Carson, & Blankenship, 2010; Wiersma, 2000). Youth traditionally changed sports and physical activities with the changing of the seasons, but it has become commonplace to play one sport year-round (especially in climates that allow for such practice) or to choose a sport early in which to develop exclusive expertise. Early sport specialization would appear to have associated benefits (e.g., sport skill and high-level performance) and costs (e.g., feelings of pressure, potential to burn out, less time for other social activities). However, we have little empirical data to determine the benefit–cost tradeoff of early specialization and its effects on positive youth development. We can design studies that identify youth who play one sport versus youth who play multiple sports (and other activities), and track individuals over time to gauge the pros and cons of early sport specialization.

Several other youth development topics merit attention by researchers. One issue entails the escalating importance placed on winning and consequent unethical behaviors such as cheating, using performance-enhancing drugs (notably steroids), and other forms of unsportsmanlike behavior. Given the extensive research showing that self-referenced definitions of success lead to the most adaptive developmental outcomes, can we really modify a win-oriented society to a philosophy of athletes first, winning second? Perhaps our most challenging issue is how to stem the tide of declining physical activity levels across childhood and adolescence to maximize positive social, psychological, and physical health benefits. Physical activity interventions such as LEAP and others (see Ward et al., 2007) have been successful in promoting increases in physical activity frequency and intensity by using theoretical frameworks to guide curricular content and teaching strategies that effect change in behavioral and psychosocial outcomes. Considerably more intervention research is needed with various demographics (age, gender, race, ethnicity, culture) to apply the *Physical Activity Guidelines for Americans* (USDHHS, 2008) and observe effects on positive youth development.

Conclusion

Can sport and physical activity contexts provide "training for life," as our title suggests? Based on our review of research on developing physical, social, and psychological competencies through physical activity, it's indeed possible but not automatic. As the positive youth development framework contends, programs must be structured to meet age-appropriate needs and interests, possess an intentional curriculum with designated personal goals, include caring and supportive adults and peers, and be delivered in a climate that is psychologically and physically safe (Eccles & Gootman, 2002; Mahoney et al., 2005). The current knowledge base is promising, especially findings from evaluation and intervention studies, but much more work lies ahead to definitively show that sport and physical activity contexts are effective for promoting youth development.

Our comprehensive review uncovered many robust findings. Social assets include external resources, such as peer, parent, and coach influence, and personal competencies, such as peer group acceptance, close friendship, and peer leadership. Psychological assets include self-perceptions, emotions, and motivational orientations and behaviors. Physical assets include motor skill development, physical activity and fitness, and physical health. Studies consistently show that coaches/teachers promote positive youth development through positive and informational feedback, an autonomy-supportive interpersonal style, and creation of a mastery and caring climate. Parents influence youth through beliefs and behaviors that impart confidence in their child's abilities, positive value toward physical activity, social support, and positive role modeling. Peers influence one another through evaluative feedback, social comparison, observational learning, and social support. Interventions that included features of a positive youth development approach were effective in improving social, physical, and psychological assets.

Still, much more research is needed to provide data-based evidence that guides best practices with youth in physical activity contexts. The roadmap is there—we need to expand and extend current research and "turn up the volume" with more frequent use of intervention and evaluation designs, mixed methodologies, and multiple assessments to establish which personal competencies and outcomes are affected, to what degree, and for how long. We need data that track youth into emerging, young, and middle adulthood to determine the enduring effect of physical activity experiences on social, psychological, and physical health outcomes.

Is sport a metaphor for life? It can be, by promoting competencies and attributes that lead to healthy developmental outcomes in multiple domains and across the lifespan. We are optimistic about the future of positive youth development research in physical activity contexts, with new generations of scholars trained in interdisciplinary and collaborative ways, including innovative research designs, methods, and measures. These researchers, along with the practitioners who apply evidence-based best practices, will have the knowledge, skills, and motivation to continue existing efforts to make a difference in the lives of children and adolescents through sport and physical activity.

References

Adler, P. A., Kless, S. J., & Adler, P. (1992). Socialization to gender roles: Popularity among elementary school boys and girls. *Sociology of Education, 65*, 169–187.

Ames, C. (1992). Achievement goals, motivational climate, and motivational processes. In G. C. Roberts (Ed.), *Motivation in sport and exercise* (pp. 161–176). Champaign, IL: Human Kinetics.

Amorose, A. J. (2001). Intraindividual variability of self-evaluations in the physical domain: Prevalence, consequences, and antecedents. *Journal of Sport and Exercise Psychology, 23*, 222–244.

Amorose, A. J. (2002). The influence of reflected appraisals on middle school and high school athletes' self-perceptions of sport competence. *Pediatric Exercise Science, 14*, 377–390.

Amorose, A. J. (2007). Coaching effectiveness: Exploring the relationship between coaching behavior and motivation from a self-determination theory perspective. In M. S. Hagger & N. L. D. Chatzisarantis (Eds.), *Intrinsic motivation and self-determination in exercise and sport* (pp. 209–227). Champaign, IL: Human Kinetics.

Amorose, A. J., & Anderson-Butcher, D. (2007). Autonomy-supportive coaching and self-determined motivation in high school and college athletes: A test of self-determination theory. *Psychology of Sport and Exercise, 8*, 654–670.

Amorose, A. J., & Smith, P. J. K. (2003). Feedback as a source of physical competence information: Effects of age, experience and type of feedback. *Journal of Sport and Exercise Psychology, 25*, 341–359.

Amorose, A. J., & Weiss, M. R. (1998). Coaching feedback as a source of information about perceptions of ability: A developmental examination. *Journal of Sport and Exercise Psychology, 20*, 395–420.

Babkes, M. L., & Weiss, M. R. (1999). Parental influence on cognitive and affective responses in children's competitive soccer participation. *Pediatric Exercise Science, 11*, 44–62.

Bailey, R. (2006). Physical education and sport in schools: A review of benefits and outcomes. *Journal of School Health, 76*, 397–401.

Bandura, A. (1986). *Social foundations of thought and action: A social cognitive theory.* Englewood Cliffs, NJ: Prentice-Hall, Inc.

Barnett, N. P., Smoll, F. L., & Smith, R. E. (1992). Effects of enhancing coach-athlete relationships on youth sport attrition. *The Sport Psychologist, 6*, 111–127.

Barr-Anderson, D. J., Young, D. R., Sallis, J. F., Neumark-Sztainer, D. R. Gittelsohn, J., Webber, L., et al. (2007). Structured physical activity and psychosocial correlates in middle-school girls. *Preventive Medicine, 44*, 404–409.

Bartholomew, K. J., Ntoumanis, N., & Thøgersen-Ntoumani, C. (2009). A review of controlling motivation strategies from a self-determination theory perspective: Implications for coaches. *International Review of Sport and Exercise Psychology, 2*, 215–233.

Benson, P. L. (2006). *All kids are our kids: What communities must do to raise caring and responsible children and adolescents* (2nd ed.). San Francisco: Jossey-Bass.

Bhalla, J. A. (2009). *Coaches and parents as sources of positive youth development: Caucasian and African American girls' life skills learning through sport.* Unpublished doctoral dissertation, University of Virginia, Charlottesville.

Bhalla, J. A., & Weiss, M. R. (2010). A cross-cultural perspective of parental influence on achievement beliefs and behaviors in sport and school domains. *Research Quarterly for Exercise and Sport, 81*, 494–505.

Black, S. J., & Weiss, M. R. (1992). The relationship among perceived coaching behaviors, perceptions of ability, and motivation in competitive age-group swimmers. *Journal of Sport and Exercise Psychology, 14*, 309–325.

Blanchard, C. M., Amiot, C. E., Perreault, S., Vallerand, R. J., & Provencher, P. (2009). Cohesiveness, coach's interpersonal style and psychological needs: Their effects on self-determination and athletes' subjective well-being. *Psychology of Sport and Exercise, 10*, 545–551.

Boardley, I. D., & Kavussanu, M. (2007). Development and validation of the moral disengagement in sport scale. *Journal of Sport and Exercise Psychology, 29*, 608–628.

Boardley, I. D., & Kavussanu, M. (2009). The influence of social variables and moral disengagement on prosocial and antisocial behaviors in field hockey and netball. *Journal of Sports Sciences, 27*, 843–854.

Boardley, I. D., & Kavussanu, M. (2010). The effects of goal orientation and perceived value of toughness on antisocial behavior in soccer: The mediating role of moral disengagement. *Journal of Sport and Exercise Psychology, 32*, 176–192.

Bois, J. E., Sarrazin, P. G., Brustad, R. J., Chanal, J. P., & Trouilloud, D. O. (2005a). Parents' appraisals, reflected appraisals, and children's self-appraisals of sport competence: A yearlong study. *Journal of Applied Sport Psychology, 17*, 273–289.

Bois, J. E., Sarrazin, P. G., Brustad, R. J., Trouilloud, D. O., & Cury, F. (2002). Mothers' expectancies and young adolescents' perceived physical competence: A yearlong study. *Journal of Early Adolescence, 22*, 384–406.

Bois, J. E., Sarrazin, P. G., Brustad, R. J., Trouilloud, D. O., & Cury, F. (2005b). Elementary schoolchildren's perceived competence and physical activity involvement: The influence of parents' role modeling behaviours and perceptions of their child's competence. *Psychology of Sport and Exercise, 6*, 381–397.

Boixados, M., Cruz, J., Torregrosa, M., & Valiente, L. (2004). Relationship among motivational climate, satisfaction, perceived ability, and fair play attitudes in young soccer players. *Journal of Applied Sport Psychology, 16*, 301–317.

Bolter, N. D., & Weiss, M. R. (2011, December 12). Coaching for character: Development of the Sportsmanship Coaching Behaviors Scale (SCBS). *Sport, Exercise and Performance Psychology*. Advance online publication. doi: 10.1037/a0026300.

Bolter, N. D., & Weiss, M. R. (2012). Coaching behaviors and adolescent athletes' sportsmanship outcomes: Further validation of the Sportsmanship Coaching Behaviors Scale (SCBS). Manuscript submitted for publication.

Bredemeier, B. J. (1985). Moral reasoning and the perceived legitimacy of intentionally injurious sport acts. *Journal of Sport Psychology, 7*, 110–124.

Bredemeier, B. J. (1994). Children's moral reasoning and their assertive, aggressive, and submissive tendencies in sport and daily life. *Journal of Sport and Exercise Psychology, 16*, 1–14.

Bredemeier, B. J. (1995). Divergence in children's moral reasoning about issues in daily life and sport specific contexts. *International Journal of Sport Psychology, 26*, 453–464.

Bredemeier, B. J., & Shields, D. L. (1984). Divergence in children's moral reasoning about sport and everyday life. *Sociology of Sport Journal, 1*, 348–357.

Bredemeier, B. J., Weiss, M. R., Shields, D. L., & Cooper, B. A. (1986). The relationship of sport involvement with children's moral reasoning and aggression tendencies. *Journal of Sport Psychology, 8*, 304–318.

Bredemeier, B. J., Weiss, M. R., Shields, D. L., & Cooper, B. A. (1987). The relationship between children's legitimacy judgments and their moral reasoning, aggression tendencies, and sport involvement. *Sociology of Sport Journal, 4*, 48–60.

Brown, B. A., Frankel, F., & Fennell, M. (1989). Hugs or shrugs: Parental and peer influence on continuity of involvement in sport by female adolescents. *Sex Roles, 20*, 397–412.

Bruening, J. E., Dover, K. M., & Clark, B. S. (2009). Preadolescent female development through sport and physical activity: A case study of an urban after-school program. *Research Quarterly for Exercise and Sport, 80*, 87–101.

Brustad, R. J. (1988). Affective outcomes in competitive youth sport: The influence of intrapersonal and socialization factors. *Journal of Sport and Exercise Psychology, 10*, 307–321.

Brustad, R. J. (1993). Who will go out and play? Parental and psychological influences on children's attraction to physical activity. *Pediatric Exercise Science, 5*, 210–223.

Brustad, R. J. (1996). Attraction to physical activity in urban schoolchildren: Parental socialization and gender influences. *Research Quarterly for Exercise and Sport, 67*, 316–323.

Camiré, M., Trudel, P., & Forneris, T. (2009). High school athletes' perspectives on support, communication, negotiation and life skill development. *Qualitative Research in Sport and Exercise, 1*, 72–88.

Catalano, R. F., Berglund, M. L., Ryan, J. A. M., Lonczak, H. S., & Hawkins, J. D. (2004). Positive youth development in the United States: Research findings on evaluations of positive youth development programs. *Annals of the American Academy of Political and Social Science, 591*, 98–124.

Chase, M. A., & Dummer, G. M. (1992). The role of sports as a social status determinant for children. *Research Quarterly for Exercise and Sport, 63*, 418–424.

Chow, G. M., Murray, K. E., & Feltz, D. L. (2009). Individual, team, and coach predictors of players' likelihood to aggress in youth soccer. *Journal of Sport and Exercise Psychology, 31*, 425–443.

Clark, J. E. (2007). On the problem of motor skill development. *Journal of Physical Education, Recreation, and Dance, 78*(5), 39–44.

Coakley, J. J., & White, A. (1992). Making decisions: Gender and sport participation among British adolescents. *Sociology of Sport Journal, 9*, 20–35.

Coatsworth, J. D., & Conroy, D. E. (2006). Enhancing self-esteem of youth swimmers through coach training: Gender and age effects. *Psychology of Sport and Exercise, 7*, 173–192.

Coatsworth, J. D., & Conroy, D. E. (2009). The effect of autonomy-supportive coaching, need satisfaction, and self-perceptions on initiative and identity in youth swimmers. *Developmental Psychology, 45*, 320–328.

Conroy, D. E., & Coatsworth, J. D. (2004). The effects of coach training on fear and failure in youth swimmers: A latent growth curve analysis from a randomized, controlled trial. *Journal of Applied Developmental Psychology, 25*, 193–214.

Conroy, D. E., & Coatsworth, J. D. (2006). Coach training as a strategy for promoting youth social development. *The Sport Psychologist, 20*, 128–144.

Conroy, D. E., Silva, J. M., Newcomer, R. R., Walker, B. W., & Johnson, M. S. (2001). Personal and participatory socializers of perceived legitimacy of aggressive behavior in sport. *Aggressive Behavior, 27*, 405–418.

Cox, A. E., Duncheon, N., & McDavid, L. (2009). Teachers as sources of relatedness perceptions, motivation, and affective responses in physical education. *Research Quarterly for Exercise and Sport, 80*, 765–773.

Cox, A. E., & Ullrich-French, S. (2010). The motivational relevance of peer and teacher relationship profiles in physical education. *Psychology of Sport and Exercise, 11*, 337–344.

Crews, D. J., Lochbaum, M. R., & Landers, D. M. (2004). Aerobic physical activity effects on psychological well-being in low-income Hispanic children. *Perceptual and Motor Skills, 98*, 319–324.

Crocker, P. R. E., Hoar, S. D., McDonough, M. H., Kowalski, K. C., & Niefer, C. B. (2004). Emotional experience in youth sport. In M. R. Weiss (Ed.), *Developmental sport and exercise psychology: A lifespan perspective* (pp. 197–221). Morgantown, WV: Fitness Information Technology.

Crocker, P. R. E., Sabiston, C. M., Kowalski, K. C., McDonough, M. H., & Kowalski, N. (2006). Longitudinal assessment of the relationship between physical self-concept and health-related behavior and emotion in adolescent girls. *Journal of Applied Sport Psychology, 18*, 185–200.

Damon, W. (2004). What is positive youth development? *Annals of the American Academy of Political and Social Science, 591*, 13–24.

Davison, K. K. (2004). Activity-related support from parents, peers, and siblings and adolescents' physical activity: Are there gender differences? *Journal of Physical Activity and Health, 1*, 363–376.

Davison, K. K., Cutting, T. M., & Birch, L. L. (2003). Parents' activity-related parenting practices predict girls' physical activity. *Medicine and Science in Sports and Exercise, 35*, 1589–1595.

Davison, K. K., & Jago, R. (2009). Change in parent and peer support across ages 9 to 15 yr and adolescent girls' physical activity. *Medicine and Science in Sports and Exercise, 41*, 1816–1825.

Davison, K. K., Symons Downs, D., & Birch, L. L. (2006). Pathways linking perceived athletic competence and parental support at age 9 years to girls' physical activity at age 11 years. *Research Quarterly for Exercise and Sport, 77*, 23–31.

DeBate, R. D., Gabriel, K. P., Zwald, M., Huberty, J., & Zhang, Y. (2009). Changes in psychosocial factors and physical activity frequency among 3rd to 8th grade girls who participated in a developmentally focused youth sport program: A preliminary study. *Journal of School Health, 79*, 478–484.

DeBate, R. D., & Thompson, S. H. (2005). *Girls on the Run*: Improvements in self-esteem, body size satisfaction, and eating attitudes/behaviors. *Eating and Weight Disorders, 10*, 25–32.

DeBate, R. D., Zhang, Y., Thompson, S. H. (2007). Changes in commitment to physical activity among 8-to11-year-old girls participating in a curriculum-based running program. *American Journal of Health Education, 38*, 277–284.

Deci, E. L., & Ryan, R. M. (1987). The support of autonomy and the control of behavior. *Journal of Personality and Social Psychology, 53*, 1024–1037.

De Knop, P., Engstrom, L. M., Skirstad, B., & Weiss, M. R. (Eds.). (1996). *Worldwide trends in youth sport*. Champaign, IL: Human Kinetics.

Dempsey, J. M., Kimiecik, J. C., & Horn, T. S. (1993). Parental influence on children's moderate to vigorous physical activity participation: An expectancy-value approach. *Pediatric Exercise Science, 5*, 151–167.

Denault, A-S., & Poulin, F. (2009). Predictors of adolescent participation in organized activities: A five-year longitudinal study. *Journal of Research on Adolescence, 19*, 287–311.

Dishman, R. K., Motl, R. W., Saunders, R., Felton, G., Ward, D. S., Dowda, M., & Pate, R. R. (2005). Enjoyment mediates effects of a school-based physical-activity intervention. *Medicine and Science in Sports and Exercise, 37*, 478–487.

Dishman, R. K., Saunders, R. P., Motl, R. W., Dowda, M., & Pate, R. R. (2009). Self-efficacy moderates the relation between declines in physical activity and perceived social support in high school girls. *Journal of Pediatric Psychology, 34*, 441–451.

Duda, J. L., Chi, L., Newton, M. L., Walling, M. D., & Catley, D. (1995). Task and ego orientation and intrinsic motivation in sport. *International Journal of Sport Psychology, 26*, 40–63.

Duda, J. L., & Nicholls, J. G. (1992). Dimensions of achievement motivation in schoolwork and sport. *Journal of Educational Psychology, 84*, 290–299.

Duda, J. L., Olson, L. K., & Templin, T. J. (1991). The relationship of task and ego orientation to sportsmanship attitudes and the perceived legitimacy of injurious acts. *Research Quarterly for Exercise and Sport, 62*, 79–87.

Dunn, J. G. H., & Causgrove Dunn, J. C. (1999). Goal orientations, perceptions of aggression, and sportspersonship in elite male youth ice hockey players. *The Sport Psychologist, 13*, 183–200.

Dworkin, J. B., Larson, R., & Hansen, D. (2003). Adolescents' accounts of growth experiences in youth activities. *Journal of Youth and Adolescence, 32*, 17–26.

Ebbeck, V., & Gibbons, S. L. (1998). The effect of a team building program on the self-conceptions of grade 6 and 7 physical education students. *Journal of Sport and Exercise Psychology, 20*, 300–310.

Ebbeck, V., & Weiss, M. R. (1998). Determinants of children's self-esteem: An examination of perceived competence and affect in sport. *Pediatric Exercise Science, 10*, 285–298.

Eccles, J. S., Adler, T. E., Futterman, R., Goff, S. B., Kaczala, C. M., Meece, J. L., & Midgley, C. (1983). Expectancies, values, and academic behaviors. In J. T. Spence (Ed.), *Achievement and achievement motivation* (pp. 75–146). San Francisco: W. H. Freeman.

Eccles, J. S., & Gootman, J. A. (2002). Features of positive developmental settings. In J. S. Eccles & J. A. Gootman (Eds.), *Community programs to promote youth development* (pp. 86–118). Washington, DC: National Academy Press.

Eccles, J. S., & Harold, R. D. (1991). Gender differences in sport involvement: Applying the Eccles' expectancy-value model. *Journal of Applied Sport Psychology, 3*, 7–35.

Eccles, J. S., Wigfield, A. W., & Schiefele, U. (1998). Motivation to succeed. In W. Damon (Series Ed.), & N. Eisenberg (Vol. Ed.), *Handbook of child psychology: Vol. 3. Social, emotional, and personality development* (5th ed., pp. 1017–1095). New York: Wiley.

Ennis, C. D. (2011). Physical education curriculum priorities: Evidence for education and skillfulness. *Quest, 63*, 5–18.

Ferrer-Caja, E., & Weiss, M. R. (2000). Predictors of intrinsic motivation among adolescent students in physical education. *Research Quarterly for Exercise and Sport, 71*, 267–279.

Ferrer-Caja, E., & Weiss, M. R. (2002). Cross-validation of a model of intrinsic motivation with students enrolled in high school elective courses. *The Journal of Experimental Education, 71*, 41–65.

Fraser-Thomas, J., & Côté, J. (2009). Understanding adolescents' positive and negative developmental experiences in sport. *The Sport Psychologist, 23*, 3–23.

Fredricks, J. A., & Eccles, J. S. (2002). Children's competence and value beliefs from childhood through adolescence: Growth trajectories in two male-sex-typed domains. *Developmental Psychology, 38*, 519–533.

Fredricks, J. A., & Eccles, J. S. (2004). Parental influences on youth involvement in sports. In M. R. Weiss (Ed.), *Developmental sport and exercise psychology: A lifespan perspective* (pp. 145–164). Morgantown, WV: Fitness Information Technology.

Fredricks, J. A., & Eccles, J. S. (2005). Family socialization, gender, and sport motivation and involvement. *Journal of Sport and Exercise Psychology, 27,* 3–31.

Fry, M. D., & Gano-Overway, L. A. (2010). Exploring the contribution of the caring climate to the youth sport experience. *Journal of Applied Sport Psychology, 22,* 294–304.

Gagné, M., Ryan, R. M., & Bargmann, K. (2003). Autonomy support and need satisfaction in the motivation and well-being of gymnasts. *Journal of Applied Sport Psychology, 15,* 372–389.

Gano-Overway, L. A., Newton, M., Magyar, T. M., Fry, M. D., Kim, M., & Guivernau, M. R. (2009). Influence of caring youth sport contexts on efficacy-related beliefs and social behaviors. *Developmental Psychology, 45,* 329–340.

Garcia Bengoechea, E. (2002). Integrating knowledge and expanding horizons in developmental sport psychology: A bioecological perspective. *Quest, 54,* 1–20.

Garcia Bengoechea, E., & Strean, W. B. (2007). On the interpersonal context of adolescents' sport motivation. *Psychology of Sport and Exercise, 8,* 195–217.

Gibbons, S. L., & Ebbeck, V. (1997). The effect of different teaching strategies on the moral development of physical education students. *Journal of Teaching in Physical Education, 17,* 85–98.

Gibbons, S. L., Ebbeck, V., & Weiss, M. R. (1995). Fair play for kids: Effects on the moral development of children in physical education. *Research Quarterly for Exercise and Sport, 66,* 247–255.

Glenn, S. D., & Horn, T. S. (1993). Psychological and personal predictors of leadership behavior in female soccer athletes. *Journal of Applied Sport Psychology, 5,* 17–34.

Gould, D. (1993). Intensive sport participation and the prepubescent athlete: Competitive stress and burnout. In B. R. Cahill & A. J. Pearl (Eds.), *Intensive participation in children's sports* (pp. 19–38). Champaign, IL: Human Kinetics.

Gould, D., & Carson, S. (2008). Life skills development through sport: Current status and future directions. *International Review of Sport and Exercise Psychology, 1,* 58–78.

Gould, D., Collins, K., Lauer, L., & Chung, Y. (2007). Coaching life skills through football: A study of award winning high school coaches. *Journal of Applied Sport Psychology, 19,* 12–37.

Gould, D., Horn, T., & Spreeman, J. (1983). Sources of stress in junior elite wrestlers. *Journal of Sport Psychology, 5,* 159–171.

Guivernau, M., & Duda, J. L. (2002). Moral atmosphere and athletic aggressive tendencies in young soccer players. *Journal of Moral Education, 31,* 67–85.

Haan, N. (1977). *Coping and defending: Processes of self-environment organization.* New York: Academic Press.

Hagger, M. S., Chatzisarantis, N. L. D., Culverhouse, T., & Biddle, S. J. H. (2003). The process by which perceived autonomy support in physical education promotes leisure-time physical activity intentions and behavior: A trans-contextual model. *Journal of Educational Psychology, 95,* 784–795.

Halliburton, A. L., & Weiss, M. R. (2002). Sources of competence information and perceived motivational climate among adolescent female gymnasts varying in skill level. *Journal of Sport and Exercise Psychology, 24,* 396–419.

Hansen, D. M., & Larson, R. W. (2007). Amplifiers of developmental and negative experiences in organized activities: Dosage, motivation, lead roles, and adult-youth ratios. *Journal of Applied Developmental Psychology, 28,* 360–374.

Harter, S. (1978). Effectance motivation reconsidered. *Human Development, 21,* 34–64.

Harter, S. (1981). A model of intrinsic mastery motivation in children: Individual differences and developmental change. In W. A. Collins (Ed.), *Minnesota symposium on child psychology* (Vol. 14, pp. 215–255). Hillsdale, JN: Erlbaum.

Harter, S. (1999). *The construction of the self: A developmental perspective.* New York: Guilford.

Harter, S., Waters, P., & Whitesell, N. R. (1998). Relational self-worth: Differences in perceived worth as a person across interpersonal contexts among adolescents. *Child Development, 69,* 756–766.

Harwood, C., & Swain, A. (2001). The development and activation of achievement goals in tennis: I. Understanding the underlying factors. *The Sport Psychologist, 15,* 319–341.

Haywood, K. M., & Getchell, N. (2009). *Lifespan motor development* (5th ed.). Champaign, IL: Human Kinetics.

Hebestreit, H., & Bar-Or, O. (Eds.). (2007). *The encyclopaedia of sports medicine, Vol. X: The young athlete.* Oxford, UK: Blackwell Science, Ltd.

Hellison, D. (2003). Teaching personal and social responsibility in physical education. In S. J. Silverman & C. D. Ennis (Eds.), *Students learning in physical education: Applying research to enhance instruction* (pp. 241–254). Champaign, IL: Human Kinetics.

Hellison, D., & Walsh, D. (2002). Responsibility-based youth programs evaluation: Investigating the investigations. *Quest, 54,* 292–307.

Hellison, D., & Wright, P. (2003). Retention in an urban extended day program: A process-based assessment. *Journal of Teaching in Physical Education, 22,* 369–381.

Holt, N. L., Tink, L. N., Mandigo, J. L., & Fox, K. R. (2008). Do youth learn life skills through their involvement in high school sport? A case study. *Canadian Journal of Education, 31,* 281–304.

Horn, T. S. (1984). Expectancy effects in the interscholastic athletic setting: Methodological considerations. *Journal of Sport Psychology, 6,* 60–76.

Horn, T. S. (1985). Coaches' feedback and changes in children's perceptions of their physical competence. *Journal of Educational Psychology, 77,* 174–186.

Horn, T. S. (1987). The influence of teacher-coach behavior on the psychological development of children. In D. Gould & M. R. Weiss (Eds.), *Advances in pediatric sport sciences, Vol. 2: Behavioral issues* (pp. 121–142). Champaign, IL: Human Kinetics.

Horn, T. S. (2004a). Lifespan development in sport and exercise psychology: Theoretical perspectives. In M. R. Weiss (Ed.), *Developmental sport and exercise psychology: A lifespan perspective* (pp. 27–71). Morgantown, WV: Fitness Information Technology.

Horn, T. S. (2004b). Developmental perspectives on self-perceptions in children and adolescents. In M. R. Weiss (Ed.), *Developmental sport and exercise psychology: A lifespan perspective* (pp. 101–143). Morgantown, WV: Fitness Information Technology.

Horn, T. S. (2008). Coaching effectiveness in the sport domain. In T. S. Horn (Ed.), *Advances in sport psychology* (3rd ed., pp. 240–267). Champaign, IL: Human Kinetics.

Horn, T. S., & Amorose, A. J. (1998). Sources of competence information. In J. L. Duda (Ed.), *Advances in sport and exercise psychology measurement* (pp. 49–64). Morgantown, WV: Fitness Information Technology.

Horn, T. S., Glenn, S. D., & Wentzell, A. B. (1993). Sources of information underlying personal ability judgments in high school athletes. *Pediatric Exercise Science, 5,* 263–274.

Horn, T. S., & Horn, J. L. (2007). Family influences on children's sport and physical activity participation, behavior, and psychosocial responses. In G. Tenenbaum & R. C. Eklund (Eds.), *Handbook of sport psychology* (3rd ed., pp. 685–711). Hoboken, NJ: John Wiley & Sons.

Horn, T. S., Lox, C. L., & Labrador, F. (2010). The self-fulfilling prophecy theory: When coaches' expectations become reality. In J.M. Williams (Ed.), *Applied sport psychology: Personal growth to peak performance* (6th ed., pp. 81–105). Palo Alto, CA: Mayfield.

Horn, T. S., & Weiss, M. R. (1991). A developmental analysis of children's self-ability judgments. *Pediatric Exercise Science, 3,* 312–328.

Jacobs, J. E., & Eccles, J. S. (1992). The impact of mothers' gender-role stereotypic beliefs on mothers' and children's ability perceptions. *Journal of Personality and Social Psychology, 63,* 932–944.

Jantz, R. K. (1975). Moral thinking in male elementary pupils as reflected by perception of basketball rules. *Research Quarterly, 46,* 414–421.

Kavussanu, M., & Ntoumanis, N. (2003). Participation in sport and moral functioning: Does ego orientation mediate their relationship? *Journal of Sport and Exercise Psychology, 25,* 501–518.

Keegan, R. J., Harwood, C. G., Spray, C. M., & Lavallee, D. E. (2009). A qualitative investigation exploring the motivational climate in early career sports participants: Coach, parent and peer influences on sport motivation. *Psychology of Sport and Exercise, 10,* 361–372.

Kelly, E. B., Parra-Medina, D., Pfeiffer, K. A., Dowda, M., Conway, T. L., Webber, L. S., et al. (2010). Correlates of physical activity in Black, Hispanic, and White middle school girls. *Journal of Physical Activity and Health, 7,* 184–193.

Kimiecik, J. C., & Horn, T. S. (1998). Parental beliefs and children's moderate-to-vigorous physical activity. *Research Quarterly for Exercise and Sport, 69,* 163–175.

Kimiecik, J. C., Horn, T. S., & Shurin, C. S. (1996). Relationships among children's beliefs, perceptions of their parents' beliefs, and their moderate-to-vigorous physical activity. *Research Quarterly for Exercise and Sport, 67,* 324–336.

King, K. A., Tergerson, J. L., & Wilson, B. R. (2008). Effect of social support on adolescents' perceptions of and engagement in physical activity. *Journal of Physical Activity and Health, 5,* 374–384.

Kipp, L. E., & Amorose, A. J. (2008). Perceived motivational climate and self-determined motivation in female high-school athletes. *Journal of Sport Behavior, 31,* 108–129.

Kohlberg, L. (1969). Stage and sequence: The cognitive-developmental approach to socialization. In D. Gosling (Ed.), *Handbook of socialization theory and research* (pp. 347–480). Chicago, IL: Rand McNally.

Kremer-Sadlik, T., & Kim, J. L. (2007). Lessons from sports: Children's socialization to values through family interaction during sports activities. *Discourse and Society, 18,* 35–52.

Landers, R. Q., Carson, R. L., & Blankenship, B. T. (Eds.). (2010). The promises and pitfalls of sport specialization in youth sport. *Journal of Physical Education, Recreation, and Dance, 81*(8), 14–39.

Larson, R. W. (2000). Toward a psychology of positive youth development. *American Psychologist, 55,* 170–183.

Larson, R. W., Hansen D. M., & Moneta, G. (2006). Differing profiles of developmental experiences across types of organized youth activities. *Developmental Psychology, 42,* 849–863.

Lerner, R. M., Almerigi, J. B., Theokas, C., & Lerner, J. V. (2005). Positive youth development: A view of the issues. *Journal of Early Adolescence, 25,* 10–16.

Lerner, R. M., & Lerner, J. V. (2006). Toward a new vision and vocabulary about adolescence: Theoretical, empirical, and applied bases of a "Positive Youth Development" perspective. In L. Balter & C. S. Tamis-LeMonda (Eds.), *Child psychology: A handbook of contemporary issues* (pp. 445–469). New York: Psychology Press.

Lim, B. S. C., & Wang, C. K. J. (2009). Perceived autonomy support, behavioural regulations in physical education and physical activity intention. *Psychology of Sport and Exercise, 10,* 52–60.

Loughead, T. M., & Leith, L. M. (2001). Hockey coaches' and players' perceptions of aggression and the aggressive behavior of players. *Journal of Sport Behavior, 24,* 394–407.

MacPhail, A., Gorely, T., Kirk, D., & Kinchin, G. (2008). Children's experiences of fun and enjoyment during a season of sport education. *Research Quarterly for Exercise and Sport, 79,* 344–355.

Mageau, G. A., & Vallerand, R. J. (2003). The coach-athlete relationship: A motivational model. *Journal of Sports Sciences, 21,* 883–904.

Mahoney, J. L., Larson, R. W., Eccles, J. S., & Lord, H. (2005). Organized activities as development contexts for children and adolescents. In J. L. Mahoney, R. W. Larson, & J. S. Eccles (Eds.), *Organized activities as contexts of development* (pp. 3–22). Mahwah, NJ: Erlbaum.

Markowitz, E. S. (2010). *Exploring connectedness and self-esteem in a girls' sports-based youth development program: How the ingredients fit together.* Unpublished doctoral dissertation, University of Virginia, Charlottesville.

Marsh, H. W., Gerlach, E., Trautwein, U., Ludtke, O., & Brettschneider, W. -D. (2007). Longitudinal study of preadolescent sport self-concept and performance: Reciprocal effects and causal ordering. *Child Development, 78,* 1640–1656.

Marsh, H. W., & Peart, N. D. (1988). Competitive and cooperative physical fitness training programs for girls: Effects on physical fitness and multidimensional self-concepts. *Journal of Sport and Exercise Psychology, 10,* 390–407.

Martin, J. J., Waldron, J. J., McCabe, A., & Choi, Y. S. (2009). The impact of "Girls on the Run" on self-concept and fat attitudes. *Journal of Clinical Sport Psychology, 3,* 127–138.

Martinek, T. J., & Hellison, D. R. (1997). Fostering resiliency in underserved youth through physical activity. *Quest, 49,* 34–49.

McCullagh, P., & Weiss, M. R. (2002). Observational learning: The forgotten psychological method in sport psychology. In J. Van Raalte & B. W. Brewer (Eds.), *Exploring sport and exercise psychology* (2nd ed., pp. 131–149). Washington, DC: American Psychological Association.

McKiddie, B., & Maynard, I. W. (1997). Perceived competence of schoolchildren in physical education. *Journal of Teaching in Physical Education, 16,* 324–339.

Miller, B. W., Roberts, G. C., & Ommundsen, Y. (2005). Effect of perceived motivational climate on moral functioning, team moral atmosphere perceptions, and the legitimacy of intentionally injurious acts among competitive youth football players. *Psychology of Sport and Exercise, 6,* 461–477.

Moran, M. M., & Weiss, M. R. (2006). Peer leadership in sport: Links with friendship, peer acceptance, psychological characteristics, and athletic ability. *Journal of Applied Sport Psychology, 2,* 97–113.

Mugno, D. A., & Feltz, D. L. (1985). The social learning of aggression in youth football in the United States. *Canadian Journal of Applied Sport Sciences, 10,* 26–35.

Murphy, S. M. (1999). *The cheers and the tears: A healthy alternative to the dark side of sports.* San Francisco: Jossey-Bass.

Murphy, S. M. (2007). A social meaning framework for research on participation in social online games. *Journal of Media Psychology, 12.* Retrieved from http://www.calstatela.edu/faculty/sfischo/A_Social_Meaning_Framework_for_Online_Games.html

Newton, M., Duda, J. L., & Yin, Z. N. (2000). Examination of the psychometric properties of the Perceived Motivational Climate in Sport Questionnaire-2 in a sample of female athletes. *Journal of Sports Sciences, 18,* 275–290.

Nicholls, J. G. (1984). Achievement motivation: Conceptions of ability, subjective experience, task choice, and performance. *Psychological Review, 91,* 328–346.

Nicholls, J. G. (1989). *The competitive ethos and democratic education.* Cambridge, MA: Harvard University Press.

Ommundsen, Y., Roberts, G. C., Lemyre, P. N., & Treasure, D. (2003). Perceived motivational climate in male youth soccer: Relations to social-moral functioning, sportspersonship and team norm perceptions. *Psychology of Sport and Exercise, 4,* 397–413.

Parish. L. E., & Treasure, D. C. (2003). Physical activity and situational motivation in physical education: Influence of the motivational climate and perceived ability. *Research Quarterly for Exercise and Sport, 2,* 173–182.

Pate, R. R., O'Neill, J. R., & McIver, K. L. (2011). Physical activity and health: Does physical education matter? *Quest, 63,* 19–35.

Pate, R. R., Ward, D. S., O'Neill, J. R., & Dowda, M. (2007). Enrollment in physical education is associated with overall physical activity in adolescent girls. *Research Quarterly for Exercise and Sport, 78,* 265–270.

Pate, R. R., Ward, D. S., Saunders, R. P., Felton, G., Dishman, R. K., & Dowda, M. (2005). Promotion of physical activity among high-school girls: A randomized controlled trial. *American Journal of Public Health, 95,* 1582–1587.

Payne, V. G., & Isaacs, L. D. (2012). *Human motor development: A lifespan approach* (8th ed.). Boston: McGraw-Hill.

Payne, V. G., & Morrow, J. R., Jr. (2009). School physical education as a viable change agent to increase youth physical activity. *President's Council on Physical Fitness and Sports Research Digest, 10*(2), 1–8.

Pelletier, L. G., Fortier, M. S., Vallerand, R. J., & Briére, N. M. (2001). Associations among perceived autonomy support, forms of self-regulation, and persistence: A prospective study. *Motivation and Emotion, 25,* 279–306.

Petitpas, A. J., Cornelius, A. E., Van Raalte, J. L., & Jones, T. (2005). A framework for planning youth sport programs that foster psychosocial development. *The Sport Psychologist, 19,* 63–80.

Power, F. C., Higgins, A., & Kohlberg, L. (1989). *Lawrence Kohlberg's approach to moral education.* New York: Columbia.

Price, M. S., & Weiss, M. R. (2000). Relationships among coach burnout, coach behaviors, and athletes' psychological responses. *The Sport Psychologist, 14,* 391–409.

Price, M. S., & Weiss, M. R. (2011). Peer leadership in sport: Relationships among personal characteristics, leader behaviors, and team outcomes. *Journal of Applied Sport Psychology, 23,* 49–64.

Raedeke, T. D., & Smith, A. L. (2004). Coping resources and athlete burnout: An examination of stress mediated and moderation hypothesis. *Journal of Sport and Exercise Psychology, 26,* 525–541.

Reinboth, M., Duda, J. L., & Ntoumanis, N. (2004). Dimensions of coaching behavior, need satisfaction, and the psychological and physical welfare of young athletes. *Motivation and Emotion, 28,* 297–313.

Rest, J. R. (1986). *Moral development: Advances in research and theory.* New York: Praeger.

Rink J. E., Hall, T. J., & Williams, L. H. (2010). *Schoolwide physical activity: A comprehensive guide to designing and conducting programs.* Champaign, IL: Human Kinetics.

Romance, T. J., Weiss, M. R., & Bockoven, J. (1986). A program to promote moral development through elementary school physical education. *Journal of Teaching in Physical Education, 5,* 126–136.

Roth, J. L., & Brooks-Gunn, J. (2003). What exactly is a youth development program? Answers from research and practice. *Applied Developmental Science, 7,* 94–111.

Roth, J., Brooks-Gunn, J., Murray, L., & Foster, W. (1998). Promoting healthy adolescents: Synthesis of youth development program evaluations. *Journal of Research on Adolescence, 8,* 423–459.

Ryan, R. M., & Deci, E. L. (2000). Self determination theory and the facilitation of intrinsic motivation, social development, and well being. *American Psychologist, 55,* 68–78.

Ryan, R. M., & Deci, E. L. (2002). An overview of self-determination theory: An organismic-dialectical perspective. In E. L. Deci & R. M. Ryan (Eds.), *Handbook of self-determination research* (pp. 3–33). Rochester, NY: The University of Rochester Press.

Sabiston, C. M., & Crocker, P. R. E. (2008). Exploring self-perceptions and social influences as correlates of adolescent leisure-time physical activity. *Journal of Sport and Exercise Psychology, 30,* 3–22.

Sage, L., & Kavussanu, M. (2007). Multiple goal orientations as predictors of moral behavior in youth soccer. *The Sport Psychologist, 21,* 417–437.

Sarrazin, P., Vallerand, R., Guillet, E., Pelletier, L., & Cury, F. (2002). Motivation and dropout in female handballers: A 21-month prospective study. *European Journal of Social Psychology, 32,* 395–418.

Scanlan, T. K., Babkes, M. L., & Scanlan, L. A. (2005). Participation in sport: A developmental glimpse at emotion. In J. L. Mahoney, R. W. Larson, & J. S. Eccles (Eds.), *Organized activities as contexts of development* (pp. 275–309). Mahwah, NJ: Erlbaum.

Scanlan, T. K., Carpenter, P. J., Lobel, M., & Simons, J. P. (1993). Sources of enjoyment for youth sport athletes. *Pediatric Exercise Science, 5,* 275–285.

Scanlan, T. K., & Passer, M. W. (1978). Factors related to competitive stress in young male youth sports participants. *Medicine and Science in Sports, 10,* 103–108.

Scanlan, T. K., & Passer, M. W. (1979). Sources of competitive stress in young female athletes. *Journal of Sport Psychology, 1,* 151–159.

Scanlan, T. K., & Simons, J. P. (1992). The construct of sport enjoyment. In G. C. Roberts (Ed.), *Motivation in sport and exercise* (pp. 199–216). Champaign, IL: Human Kinetics.

Scanlan, T. K., Stein, G. L., & Ravizza, K. (1989). An in-depth study of former elite figure skaters: Sources of enjoyment. *Journal of Sport and Exercise Psychology, 11,* 65–83.

Scanlan, T. K., Stein, G. L., & Ravizza, K. (1991). An in-depth study of former elite figure skaters: II. Sources of stress. *Journal of Sport and Exercise Psychology, 13,* 102–120.

Schneider, M., Dunn, A., & Cooper, D. (2009). Affect, exercise, and physical activity among healthy adolescents. *Journal of Sport and Exercise Psychology, 31,* 706–723.

Schneider, M., Fridlund Dunton, G., & Cooper, D. M. (2008). Physical activity and physical self-concept among sedentary adolescent females: An intervention study. *Psychology of Sport and Exercise, 9,* 1–14.

Schofield, L., Mummery, W. K., Schofield, G., & Hopkins, W. (2007). The association of objectively determined physical activity behavior among adolescent female friends. *Research Quarterly for Exercise and Sport, 78,* 9–15.

Schunk, D. H. (1998). Peer modeling. In K. Topping & S. Ehly (Eds.), *Peer-assisted learning* (pp. 185–202). Mahwah, NJ: Erlbaum.

Shields, D. L., & Bredemeier, B. L. (2007). Advances in sport morality research. In G. Tenenbaum & R. C. Eklund (Eds.). *Handbook of sport psychology* (3rd ed., pp. 662–684). Hoboken, NJ: Wiley.

Shields, D. L., LaVoi, N. M., Bredemeier, B. L. & Power, F. C. (2007). Predictors of poor sportspersonship in youth sports: Personal attitudes and social influences. *Journal of Sport and Exercise Psychology, 29,* 747–762.

Simon, J. A., & Martens, R. (1979). Children's anxiety in sport and nonsport evaluative activities. *Journal of Sport Psychology, 1,* 160–169.

Smith, A. L. (1999). Perceptions of peer relationships and physical activity participation in early adolescence. *Journal of Sport and Exercise Psychology, 21,* 329–350.

Smith, A. L. (2003). Peer relationships in physical activity contexts: A road less traveled in youth sport and exercise psychology research. *Psychology of Sport and Exercise, 4,* 25–39.

Smith, A. L. (2007). Youth peer relationships in sport. In S. Jowett & D. Lavallee (Eds.), *Social psychology in sport* (pp. 41–54). Champaign, IL: Human Kinetics.

Smith, A. L., & Biddle, S. J. (2008). *Youth physical activity and sedentary behavior.* Champaign, IL: Human Kinetics.

Smith, A. L., Ullrich-French, S., Walker, E., II, & Hurley, K. S. (2006). Peer relationship profiles and motivation in youth sport. *Journal of Sport and Exercise Psychology, 28,* 362–382.

Smith, M. D. (1974). Significant others' influence on the assaultive behavior of young hockey players. *International Review of Sport Sociology, 3–4,* 45–56.

Smith, M. D. (1978). Social learning of violence in minor hockey. In F. L. Smoll & R. E. Smith (Eds.), *Psychological perspectives in youth sports* (pp. 91–106). Washington, DC: Hemisphere.

Smith, R. E., Smoll, F. L., & Barnett, N. P. (1995). Reduction of children's sport performance anxiety through social support and stress-reduction training for coaches. *Journal of Applied Developmental Psychology, 16,* 125–142.

Smith, R. E., Smoll, F. L., & Cumming, S. P. (2007). Effects of a motivational climate intervention for coaches on young athletes' sport performance anxiety. *Journal of Sport and Exercise Psychology, 29,* 39–59.

Smith, R. E., Smoll, F. L., & Curtis, B. (1979). Coach effectiveness training: A cognitive-behavioral approach to enhancing relationship skills in youth sport coaches. *Journal of Sport Psychology, 1,* 59–75.

Smith, R. E., Smoll, F. L., & Passer, M. W. (2002). Sport performance anxiety in young athletes. In F. L. Smoll & R. E. Smith (Eds.), *Children and youth in sport: A biopsychosocial perspective* (2nd ed., pp. 501–536). Dubuque, IA: Kendall/Hunt.

Smoll, F. L., & Smith, R. E. (1989). Leadership behaviors in sport: A theoretical model and research paradigm. *Journal of Applied Social Psychology, 19,* 1522–1551.

Smoll, F. L., & Smith, R. E. (Eds.). (2002a). *Children and youth in sport: A biopsychosocial perspective.* Dubuque, IA: Kendall/Hunt.

Smoll, F. L., & Smith, R. E. (2002b). Coaching behavior research and intervention in youth sport. In F. L. Smoll & R. E. Smith (Eds.), *Children and youth in sport: A biopsychosocial perspective* (2nd ed., pp. 211–231). Dubuque, IA: Kendall/Hunt.

Smoll, F. L., Smith, R. E., Barnett, N. P., & Everett, J. J. (1993). Enhancement of children's self-esteem through social support training for youth sport coaches. *Journal of Applied Psychology, 78,* 602–610.

Solomon, G. B. (2004). A lifespan view of moral development in physical activity. In M. R. Weiss (Ed.), *Developmental sport and exercise psychology: A lifespan perspective* (pp. 453–474). Morgantown, WV: Fitness Information Technology.

Standage, M., Duda, J. L., & Ntoumanis, N. (2006). Students' motivational processes and their relationship to teacher ratings in school physical education: A self-determination theory approach. *Research Quarterly for Exercise and Sport, 77,* 100–110.

Standage, M., & Gillison, F. (2007). Students' motivational responses toward school physical education and their relationship to general self-esteem and health-related quality of life. *Psychology of Sport and Exercise, 8,* 704–721.

Stephens, D. E. (1998). The relationship of goal orientation and perceived ability to enjoyment and value in youth sport. *Pediatric Exercise Science, 10,* 236–247.

Stephens, D. E. (2000). Predictors of likelihood to aggress in youth soccer: An examination of coed and all-girls teams. *Journal of Sport Behavior, 23,* 311–325.

Stephens, D. E., & Bredemeier, B. J. (1996). Moral atmosphere and judgments about aggression in girls' soccer: Relationships among moral and motivational variables. *Journal of Sport and Exercise Psychology, 18,* 158–173.

Stephens, D. E., & Kavanagh, B. (2003). Aggression in Canadian youth hockey: The role of moral atmosphere. *International Sports Journal, 7,* 109–119.

Strong, W. B., Malina, R. M., Blimkie, C. J. R., Daniels, S. R., Dishman, R. K., Gutin, B., et al. (2005). Evidence based physical activity for school-age youth. *Journal of Pediatrics, 146,* 732–737.

Stuart, M. E., & Ebbeck, V. (1995). The influence of perceived social approval on moral development in youth sport. *Pediatric Exercise Science, 7,* 270–280.

Stuntz, C. P., & Spearance, A. L. (2010). Cross-domain relationships in two sport populations: Measurement validation including prediction of motivation-related variables. *Psychology of Sport and Exercise, 11,* 267–274.

Stuntz, C. P., & Weiss, M. R. (2003). The influence of social goal orientations and peers on unsportsmanlike play. *Research Quarterly for Exercise and Sport, 74,* 421–435.

Swain, A. (1996). Social loafing and identifiability: The mediating role of achievement goal orientations. *Research Quarterly for Exercise and Sport, 67*, 337–344.

Taylor, I. M., Ntoumanis, N., Standage, M., & Spray, C. M. (2010). Motivational predictors of physical education students' effort, exercise intentions, and leisure-time physical activity: A multilevel linear growth analysis. *Journal of Sport and Exercise Psychology, 32*, 99–120.

Taymoori, P., & Lubans, D. R. (2008). Mediators of behavior change in two tailored physical activity interventions for adolescent girls. *Psychology of Sport and Exercise, 9*, 605–619.

Theeboom, M., De Knop, P., & Weiss, M. R. (1995). Motivational climate, psychosocial responses, and motor skill development in children's sport: A field-based intervention study. *Journal of Sport and Exercise Psychology, 17*, 294–311.

Ullrich-French, S., & Smith, A. L. (2006). Perceptions of relationships with parents and peers in youth sport: Independent and combined prediction of motivational outcomes. *Psychology of Sport and Exercise, 7*, 193–214.

Ullrich-French, S., & Smith, A. L. (2009). Social and motivational predictors of continued youth sport participation. *Psychology of Sport and Exercise, 10*, 87–95.

U.S. Department of Health and Human Services (USDHHS). (1996). *Physical activity and health: A report of the Surgeon General*. Atlanta, GA: Centers for Disease Control and Prevention.

U.S. Department of Health and Human Services (USDHHS). (2008). *2008 Physical activity guidelines for Americans*. Washington, DC: Author.

Vierling, K. K., Standage, M., & Treasure, D. C. (2007). Predicting attitudes and physical activity in an "at-risk" minority youth sample: A test of self-determination theory. *Psychology of Sport and Exercise, 8*, 795–817.

Wankel, L. M., & Kreisel, P. S. J. (1985). Factors underlying enjoyment of youth sports: Sport and age group comparisons. *Journal of Sport Psychology, 7*, 51–64.

Ward, D. S., Saunders, R., Felton, G. M., Williams, E., Epping, J. N., & Pate, R. R. (2006). Implementation of a school environment intervention to increase physical activity in high school girls. *Health Education Research, 21*, 896–910.

Ward, D. S., Saunders, R. P., & Pate, R. R. (2007). *Physical activity interventions in children and adolescents*. Champaign, IL: Human Kinetics.

Weiss, M. R. (1998). "Passionate collaboration": Reflections on the status and future directions of applied sport psychology in the coming millennium. *Journal of Applied Sport Psychology, 10*, S11–S24.

Weiss, M. R. (2004). *Developmental sport and exercise psychology: A lifespan perspective*. Morgantown, WV: Fitness Information Technology.

Weiss, M. R. (2008). "Field of dreams": Sport as a context for youth development. *Research Quarterly for Exercise and Sport, 79*, 434–449.

Weiss, M. R. (2011). Teach the children well: A holistic approach to developing psychosocial and behavioral competencies through physical education. *Quest, 63*, 55–65.

Weiss, M. R., & Amorose, A. J. (2005). Children's self-perceptions in the physical domain: Between- and within-age variability in level, accuracy, and sources of perceived competence. *Journal of Sport and Exercise Psychology, 27*, 226–244.

Weiss, M. R., & Amorose, A. J. (2008). Motivational orientations and sport behavior. In T. S. Horn (Ed.), *Advances in sport psychology* (3rd. ed., pp. 115–155). Champaign, IL: Human Kinetics.

Weiss, M. R., Amorose, A. J., & Kipp, L. E. (2012). Youth motivation and participation in sport and physical activity. In R. M. Ryan (Ed.), *The Oxford handbook of human motivation* (pp. 520–553). New York: Oxford University Press.

Weiss, M. R., Amorose, A. J., & Wilko, A. M. (2009). Coaching behaviors, motivational climate, and psychosocial outcomes among female adolescent athletes. *Pediatric Exercise Science, 21*, 475–492.

Weiss, M. R., Bhalla, J. A., Bolter, N. D., & Price, M. S. (2008). Lessons learned and core values adopted in a sport-based youth development program: A longitudinal qualitative analysis [Abstract]. *Journal of Sport and Exercise Psychology, 30*, S208.

Weiss, M. R., Bhalla, J. A., & Price, M. S. (2007). Developing positive self-perceptions through youth sport participation. In H. Hebestreit & O. Bar-Or (Eds.), *The encyclopaedia of sports medicine, Vol. X: The young athlete* (pp. 302–318). Oxford, UK: Blackwell Science, Ltd.

Weiss, M. R., Bolter, N. D., Bhalla, J. A., & Price, M. S. (2007). Positive youth development through sport: Comparison of participants in The First Tee life skills programs with participants in other organized activities. *Journal of Sport and Exercise Psychology, 29*(Suppl.), S212.

Weiss, M. R., Bolter, N. D., Bhalla, J. A., Price, M. P., & Markowitz, E. S. (2008). Life skills, youth development, and sport participation: Retention effects over a one-year period. *Journal of Sport and Exercise Psychology, 30*(Suppl.), S209–S210.

Weiss, M. R., Bolter, N. D., Price, M. S., & Bhalla, J. A. (2007). More than a game: Impact of The First Tee life skills programs on positive youth development. *Research Quarterly for Exercise and Sport, 78*(Suppl.), A9.

Weiss, M. R., & Duncan, S. C. (1992). The relation between physical competence and peer acceptance in the context of children's sport participation. *Journal of Sport and Exercise Psychology, 14*, 177–191.

Weiss, M. R., Ebbeck, V., & Horn, T. S. (1997). Children's self-perceptions and sources of competence information: A cluster analysis. *Journal of Sport and Exercise Psychology, 19*, 52–70.

Weiss, M. R., Ebbeck, V., & Rose, D. J. (1992). "Show and tell" in the gymnasium revisited: Developmental differences in modeling and verbal rehearsal effects on motor skill learning and performance. *Research Quarterly for Exercise and Sport, 63*, 292–301.

Weiss, M. R., & Gill, D. L. (2005). What goes around comes around: Re-emerging themes in sport and exercise psychology. *Research Quarterly for Exercise and Sport, 76*(Suppl.), S71–S87.

Weiss, M. R., McCullagh, P., Smith, A. L., & Berlant, A. R. (1998). Observational learning and the fearful child: Influence of peer models on swimming skill performance and psychological responses. *Research Quarterly for Exercise and Sport, 69*, 380–394.

Weiss, M. R., & Petlichkoff, L. M. (1989). Children's motivation for participation in and withdrawal from sport: Identifying the missing links. *Pediatric Exercise Science, 1*, 195–211.

Weiss, M. R., & Smith, A. L. (1999). Quality of youth sport friendships: Measurement development and validation. *Journal of Sport and Exercise Psychology, 21*, 145–166.

Weiss, M. R., & Smith, A. L. (2002). Friendship quality in youth sport: Relationship to age, gender, and motivation variables. *Journal of Sport and Exercise Psychology, 24*, 420–437.

Weiss, M. R., Smith, A. L., & Stuntz, C. P. (2008). Moral development in sport and physical activity: Theory, research, and intervention. In T. S. Horn (Ed.), *Advances in sport psychology* (3rd ed., pp. 187–210). Champaign, IL: Human Kinetics.

Weiss, M. R., Smith, A. L., & Theeboom, M. (1996). "That's what friends are for": Children's and teenagers' perceptions of peer relationships in the sport domain. *Journal of Sport and Exercise Psychology, 18*, 347–379.

Weiss, M. R., & Stuntz, C. P. (2004). A little friendly competition: Peer relationships and psychosocial development in youth sport and physical activity contexts. In M. R. Weiss (Ed.), *Developmental sport and exercise psychology: A lifespan perspective* (pp. 165–196). Morgantown, WV: Fitness Information Technology.

Weiss, M. R., & Wiese-Bjornstal, D. M. (2009). Promoting positive youth development through physical activity. *President's Council on Physical Fitness and Sports Research Digest, 10*(3), 1–8.

Weiss, M. R., & Williams, L. (2004). The *why* of youth sport involvement: A developmental perspective on motivational processes. In M. R. Weiss (Ed.), *Developmental sport and exercise psychology: A lifespan perspective* (pp. 223–268). Morgantown, WV: Fitness Information Technology.

Weiss, W. M., & Weiss, M. R. (2003). Attraction- and entrapment- based commitment among competitive female gymnasts. *Journal of Sport and Exercise Psychology, 25*, 229–247.

Weiss, W. M., & Weiss, M. R. (2006). A longitudinal analysis of sport commitment among competitive female gymnasts. *Psychology of Sport and Exercise, 7*, 309–323.

Weiss, W. M., & Weiss, M. R. (2007). Sport commitment among competitive female gymnasts: A developmental perspective. *Research Quarterly for Exercise and Sport, 78*, 90–102.

Weiss, W. M., Weiss, M. R., & Amorose, A. J. (2010). Sport commitment among competitive female athletes: Test of an expanded model. *Journal of Sports Sciences, 28*, 423–434.

Wiersma, L. D. (2000). Risks and benefits of youth sport specialization: Perspectives and recommendations. *Pediatric Exercise Science, 12*, 13–22.

Wiggins, D. K. (1987). A history of organized play and highly competitive sport for American children. In D. Gould & M. R. Weiss (Eds.), *Advances in pediatric sport sciences, Vol. 2: Behavioral issues* (pp. 1–24). Champaign, IL: Human Kinetics.

Wiggins, D. K. (2002). A history of highly competitive sport for American children. In F. L. Smoll & R. E. Smith (Eds.), *Children and youth in sport: A biopsychosocial perspective* (2nd ed., pp. 19–37). Dubuque, IA: Kendall/Hunt.

Wright, P. M., & Burton, S. (2008). Implementation and outcomes of a responsibility-based physical activity program integrated into an intact high school physical education class. *Journal of Teaching in Physical Education, 27*, 138–154.

Talent Development: The Role of the Family

Chris G. Harwood, Julie P. Douglas, *and* Antoinette M. Minniti

Abstract

The process of talent development has been a theme within sport psychology that has consistently stimulated research for over 30 years. Commercial, professional, and economic developments that characterize competitive sport have significantly raised the profile and fiscal impact of this process. There is an increasing emphasis within national sport organizations to develop bigger talent pools and achieve success. On an international level, that means economic and pride rewards for athletes and their countries. Results matter in the high-performance sport industry and, thus, our understanding of the mechanisms behind talent development is crucial. This chapter considers the diverse roles of the family in talent development by drawing together research that underpins our current understanding of the family's significant influence on this complex process. Recent developments in the literature and proposed new directions for the research are also discussed, alongside applied implications.

Key Words: Talent development, family, parents, siblings, social support, parenting styles

Talent development has been a prominent theme within the field of sport and performance psychology that has consistently stimulated research for over 30 years (Bailey & Morley, 2006; Bloom, 1985; Côté, 1999; Ericsson, Krampe, & Tesch-Römer, 1993; Martindale, Collins, & Abraham, 2007; Vaeyens, Güllich, Warr, & Philippaerts, 2009; Wylleman, & Lavallee, 2004). The area of research is very closely allied with the theme of "expertise" in sport (see Chapter 23, this volume; Starkes & Ericsson, 2003; Starkes, Helsen, & Jack, 2001 for reviews), where the core focus has been on systematically investigating the array of factors (e.g., perceptual, cognitive, physical, and strategic skills) that differentiate expert performers (and performance) from their less skilled counterparts. Both fields of research appear to share the common goal of understanding the development of expertise or talent, and the economic popularity of this goal at the present time cannot be overestimated.

In recent years, the commercial, professional, and economic developments that continue to characterize elite competitive sport have significantly raised the profile and potential fiscal impact of the talent development process. Within national sport organizations, an increasing emphasis is placed on developing larger talent pools and improved results on a global stage. Success at an international level means huge economic rewards and pride for both the individual athlete and the country he or she is representing (Martindale et al., 2007). Further, positions on medal tables within major games are increasingly linked to continued government funding and job security for coaching and support staff. Results matter in the high-performance sport industry (Abbott & Collins, 2004; Vaeyens et al., 2009) and therefore understanding the mechanisms behind successful talent development and talent transition has become popular, challenging, and critical.

Simonton (1999) defines talent as "any innate capacity that enables an individual to display exceptionally high performance in a domain that requires special skills and training" (p. 436). More recently, Bailey and Morley (2006) identify the development of particular abilities; namely, psychomotor, interpersonal, intrapersonal, cognitive, and creative, defining these abilities as the "building blocks of talent" (p. 215) that are nurtured when the child "experiences a period of structured learning" (p. 215). The combination of these definitions, although not always explicitly stated, appears to describe what authors are referring to when they discuss talent and its development.

Interestingly, as noted by Lauer, Gould, Roman, and Pierce (2010), those seemingly most responsible for talent development (i.e., teachers and coaches) do not have direct control over the process. Côté, Baker, and Abernethy (2003) posited that children who become experts have already been involved in hundreds of hours of deliberate play and practice prior to age 8. In these early stages, a child's parents are believed to have a significant socializing influence on the young athlete's developmental experiences in sport (Greendorfer, Lewko, & Rosengren, 1996), and contextual factors may moderate both the rate and outcome of the overall process. This latter statement forms the essence of a social-psychological approach to talent development, whereby the developmental roles, beliefs, values, skills, and behavior of the family (e.g., parents, siblings, grandparents) may heavily influence athletic transitions toward an expert level.

The influence of family members, particularly parents, on youth sport participation and performance has been well established in the sport psychology literature (Fredricks & Eccles, 2004; Horn & Horn, 2007; see Côté & Hay, 2002; Wylleman, De Knop, Verdet, & Cecič-Erpič, 2006; see also Chapter 24, this volume, for reviews). A large proportion of our overall body of knowledge has tended to accumulate through a process of distinct studies or investigations (often cross-sectional) about parental influence on specific psychosocial constructs (e.g., children's perceptions of competence, self-esteem, enjoyment, achievement motivation, precompetitive anxiety; see Babkes & Weiss, 1999). These studies are important in facilitating our understanding of the theoretical mechanisms via which family members may impact on psychological constructs that are potentially central to the talent development process. Nevertheless, this body of literature does not target talent development per se, nor does

it illustrate the dynamic family processes that might occur with regard to a talented athlete's transitions to an elite level. Other researchers, therefore, have adopted more retrospective, qualitative perspectives as a means to gain a descriptive and holistic understanding of parental and sibling involvement at different stages of elite athlete development (e.g., Bloom, 1985; Côté, 1999; Durand-Bush, Salmela, & Thompson, 2004).

With these points in mind, we will pursue several distinct aims in this chapter. First, we will offer a brief overview of the prominent talent development models (e.g., Bloom, 1985; Côté, 1999; Ericsson et al., 1993; Wylleman & Lavallee, 2004), including the descriptions of the family role that are ascribed through this research. Second, drawing from Eccles's work (Eccles et al., 1983; Fredricks & Eccles, 2004), we will drill down further into the developmental research that supports the roles of parents as providers, interpreters, and role models through the progressive stages of talent development. Third, we will evaluate the more limited body of research that relates to the role of siblings in sport, before turning to the emergence of conceptual perspectives in developmental science and positive youth development that informs the role of the family. Finally, we will consider further applied research advances that may assist practitioners, coaches, and organizations in their program management of the family within talent development initiatives.

Talent Development Models: A Historical Overview

Over the past 25 years, a number of models have been developed that relate either directly or indirectly to talent development (Côté, 1999; Salmela, 1994; Stambulova, 1994; Wylleman & Lavallee, 2004). The earliest, however, are those of Bloom (1985) and Ericsson et al. (1993) in their proposition of two distinctly unique frameworks that revolutionized and advanced understanding of the potential mechanisms of talent development. Importantly to this text's focus on sport and performance psychology, both studies examined the development of expertise across a variety of performance domains including the arts, sport, and science.

Ericsson et al. (1993) proposed that the development of talent and the consequent attainment of expert status would take 10 years or 10,000 hours of what Ericsson et al. called *deliberate practice*, a figure that was established after extensive retrospective interviews with expert performers across a variety of domains, including music, sports, ballet, and chess. Their concept of deliberate practice sought to disprove the theory of innate abilities leading to expert success by instead emphasizing the integral role of extended, effortful, and purposeful practice. Ericsson (1996) noted that not only is deliberate practice influenced by what he referred to as motivational, effort, and resource constraints (e.g., access to teachers, coaches, and facilities), but that family environment also served as a critical variable in this developmental process.

Prior to this, Bloom (1985) had also challenged the innate talent theory through his pioneering research across the domains of music, art, sport, mathematics, and science. Bloom's interviews with 120 world-class performers in a variety of these activities (e.g., artists, musicians, mathematicians, tennis players, swimmers) revealed three distinct phases of talent development; namely, the early years, the middle years, and the late years. His detailed interpretations of the home environment during these developmental stages sought to highlight the influential roles played by parents. Within his investigation of the sport domain, we see that, in the early years, parents introduced their child to a variety of sports with an emphasis on play and fun. Although there was family involvement in supporting the activity, including provision of early instruction, parents attempted to ensure higher quality coaching for their child. Early parent–coach–child relationships were characterized by supporting the coach in creating a learning climate with process-oriented training and an absence of competitive pressure on the child. Parents invested time in taking their child to introductory competitions, with the emphasis on fun as opposed to results. In the middle years, the emphasis shifted from fun in a variety of activities to greater sport specialization and higher levels of training and competition. Parents supported their children in more intense, demanding, and result-oriented environments, accepting of and adjusting to the inevitable sacrifices required of them (e.g., increased financial demands, transport needs, social sacrifices). This also included adjustments to the whole family routine, whereby family activities would center on the child's sport activity to ensure their presence at training and competitions. In the later years, with athletes progressing toward an elite level, parents played the role of an emotional support system for their increasingly independent child. Although less involved in practice settings and logistical support, the family home functioned as a refuge from the ups and downs of athletic life,

and parents were the unconditional providers of social support.

In summarizing the findings from his extensive investigation of talent development across the six unique domains of expertise, Bloom (1985) highlights the lack of contextual importance that exists in talent development. He asserts that the key objective of expert skill development is congruent across performance domains, with a large degree of similarity in the process of seeking this expert skill level, no matter what the actual skill entails. Bloom went on to explain that parents must first value both the notion of achievement and the chosen talent area. They must then work to develop those same values in their children, with the aim of creating and maintaining a long-term commitment to learning in their chosen talent area.

MacNamara, Holmes, and Collins (2006, 2008) recently investigated talent development pathways in music. Their findings supported those of Bloom, and the authors additionally noted the large degree of similarity between sport and music domains. MacNamara et al. investigated the use of what they refer to as *psychological characteristics for developing excellence* (PCDEs), examples of which include commitment, time management, and goal setting. These are effectively a number of different psychological strategies that individuals can use to assist with the attainment of excellence in a chosen domain. In a similar vein to Bloom, they assert that the attainment and development of these PCDEs as the "promoters of talent" (2008, p. 338) is important for creating and maintaining this long-term commitment to the development process. Their suggestions are further supported by Csikszentmihalyi, Rathunde, and Whalen (1993).

Csikszentmihalyi et al. conducted research with 208 outstanding students in art, music, athletics, science, and mathematics. Their findings illustrated how the development of learned habits and characteristics, such as the aforementioned PCDEs, can be conducive to fostering talent, thus leading to a smoother developmental pathway for young adolescents. Overall, similarities of talent development pathways suggest that the most salient features of the process can be discussed through any chosen domain, although some of the subtle nuances in the talent development process within different achievement domains necessitate attention to the particular combination and application of these psychological characteristics. Sport is used as the primary point of reference for the remainder of this chapter, and a wealth of literature examines talent development in this domain.

Returning to Bloom's model, although the stages appear to occur in line with certain chronological ages, he never explicitly matched ages with his stages. Bloom noted the importance of the length of time spent doing the activity, rather than making reference to the age of the performer. Nevertheless, by specifically focusing on the influence of the family in athletic talent development, Côté (1999) later advanced a sport-specific framework that comprised three distinct chronological categories.

Côté's (1999) *developmental model of sport participation* (DMSP) was based on gathering qualitative data from retrospective interviews with four 18-year-old national-level athletes, four siblings, and seven parents. His findings revealed that athletic talent development occurred through stages of participation, which he referred to as the *sampling, specializing,* and *investment* years. The specific behaviors associated with the family were congruent with Bloom's observations across other activity domains. Specifically, during the sampling years (ages 6–13), parents encouraged their children to get involved in a wide range of enjoyable sporting activities and took a leadership role in valuing and providing these opportunities. They also recognized a gift in their child athlete and ensured that they supported this gift. Within the specializing years (ages 13–15), athletes made a commitment to one or two sports, with parents making increased financial and time commitments to the child athlete. Although parents also developed a growing interest in their child athlete's sport as committed followers and facilitators, they continued to emphasize the value of school, as well as sport achievement. Interestingly, older siblings also served as a role model for work ethic in this stage. Finally, during the investment years (ages 15–18), athletes became committed to achieving an elite level in one sport. Parents' roles in terms of tangible and emotional support intensified as parents made greater sacrifices to ensure optimal training conditions and to help their son or daughter deal with setbacks. These sacrifices also included strained relationships with younger siblings provoked not only by differential behavior to the athletic sibling, but also due to bitterness and jealousy at the older sibling's achievements.

A final model, which takes a more holistic, lifespan approach to the sports and the post-sports career of elite athletes, was recently proposed by Wylleman and Lavallee (2004). Entitled the *developmental lifespan model*, Wylleman and Lavallee's framework focuses on four stages of athletic development: initiation, development, mastery, and discontinuation. Their model views the athletic career as a progression of normative stages or transitions in which athletes not only progress in terms of level and commitment to the sport, but concurrently face developments in psychological/cognitive, psychosocial, and academic and/or vocational domains (see Wylleman et al., 2006). Athletes must not only cope successfully with the tasks and challenges of each career stage, but these challenges exist in multiple domains of development that need to be recognized by coaches, parents, practitioners, and organizations (e.g., a 17-year-old athlete who is transitioning from a development to mastery stage may also be coping with the academic/vocational demands of schoolwork and examinations). Derived from research with elite and formerly elite athletes, this model explicitly integrates significant others (coaches, parents, peers, siblings, partners) and attempts to specify those who are the most salient influences at each stage of an individual's psychosocial development. Congruent with Bloom (1985) and Côté (1999), and in support of Greendorfer and Lewko's (1978) views on the early sport socialization of children by their parents, Wylleman and Lavallee assert that parents and siblings (as proximal family members) have the most influential roles during the initiation stage, from 6 to 13 years. During this phase, the young athlete is heavily reliant on parents for informational and emotional support as the primary caregivers. In the development stage, the influence of parents, particularly with respect to competence-related information (Horn & Weiss, 1991), is believed to lessen compared with the value that children ascribe to this information in the initiation stage. During the development stage, adolescents are cognitively able to compare themselves to peers more accurately and are more responsive to expert information that will enhance their competence. Therefore, coaches and peers are believed to have a more prominent influence on the athlete during this stage. In the mastery stage, the coach and potential partners (spouse, girlfriend/boyfriend) are believed to carry the greatest valence or influence over the elite athlete with respect to his or her athletic career.

In summary, these aforementioned talent development models are currently the most popular in the psychology literature, and they provide the basic descriptions of family-related involvement at each stage. However, to better understand the subsequent research that supports these models, it is important to conceptualize the exact roles of the parent in a manner that illustrates how their roles change over time.

Parental Roles: Provider, Interpreter, and Role Model

Fredricks and Eccles (2004) focus on how an understanding of parental influence in youth sport can be achieved by ascribing three key roles to parents. These three roles have become popularized in the sport parenting literature over the past decade. First, parents serve as *providers* of a young athlete's sport experience, not only with respect to introducing their child to sport and supporting their child financially and logistically, but also with respect to offering much needed emotional, esteem, and informational support in training and competition environments (Côté & Hay, 2002; Rees & Hardy, 2000; Wolfenden & Holt, 2005). Second, they function as *interpreters* of their child's sport experience by transmitting their beliefs and values not only about the goals of sport (and its attribution-related outcomes), but also about the competencies of their child athlete. Drawing from Eccles et al.'s (1983) expectancy-value model of achievement, we know that parents influence their children's motivation and perceptions of competence via their own expectations, attributions, and beliefs about their child's competence (Babkes & Weiss, 1999; Brustad, 1993; Woolger & Power, 2000). A positive belief and value system in parents, with respect to the benefits of competitive sport and the necessary psychological characteristics for progression, will help young athletes interpret information from parents that will fast-track their development and coping responses. Finally, parents operate as *role models* for their son or daughter by providing adaptive models of proactive and reactive behavior in both sport and nonathletic situations (e.g., competing in sport themselves with a dedicated work ethic; showing a calm temperament when observing sports and interacting with others; letting their children problem-solve when overseeing them in challenging situations to build their competence, independence, and autonomy). As we will discuss later in this chapter, numerous psychosocial characteristics can underpin successful talent development, and parental role modeling of these characteristics can serve as an internalization mechanism for such qualities to develop within the athlete (Bandura, 1977; see also Chapter 13, this volume). By using the conceptual lens of these three key roles, we can refine our understanding of parental roles at each key stage of talent development, deciphering the

prominence and content of each during an athlete's development.

The Early Years: Sampling and Initiation Roles

Research into elite athletes that has addressed their introduction into sport supports the view that all three parental roles are of central importance at this stage (e.g., Australian Sports Commission, 2003; Baxter-Jones & Maffulli, 2003; Durand-Bush et al., 2004; Gibbons, 2002; Gould, Dieffenbach, & Moffett, 2002). An Australian National Athlete Development Survey (Australian Sports Commission, 2003) reported that 15% of 673 high-level athletes' parents had competed at a pre-elite level, and 5% at an elite level. Athletes reported their parents to be highly sport-minded, with a positive empathy for sport that fostered encouragement, a finding echoed both in Durand-Bush et al.'s (2004) study of the factors underpinning the development and maintenance of expertise in ten Olympic or World Champions, and Gould et al.'s (2002) study of the psychological characteristics of a similarly elite population. In these studies, athletes (and parents) retrospectively reflected on parents' participation-inducing roles in a variety of sporting activities at an early age, and there was typically a presence of positive "parental push" achieved by motivating and encouraging the athlete while abstaining from excessive pressure or control.

The provision of tangible support (e.g., finance, equipment, transport) also blends in with the role modeling activities of parents who additionally offered early instruction and coaching to their child, as reported by Durand-Bush and colleagues (2004). This finding was supported by Keegan, Harwood, Spray, and Lavallee (2009) in a qualitative investigation of the motivational climate perceived by young athletes from 7 to 12 years of age. Specifically, these children appeared to value the "play-and-teach" behaviors of parents (e.g., within the garden), their presence at competitions as a supporter and spectator, and the reinforcement that parents provided when children showed them a new skill. In addition, although these young athletes were able to pick up on both positive feedback and evaluative behavior of parents, they also referred to negative, demotivating behaviors and styles. Children referred to a parent's propensity for anger, their use of rewards as a mechanism for control, and result-contingent reinforcement (see also Gould et al., 2002). These maladaptive role behaviors are congruent with Weiss and Fretwell's (2003) study of the dual role parent–son/coach–player relationship, and speak to the importance of establishing clear role separation and an unconditional parent–child relationship.

Most recently, Lauer et al. (2010) conducted a retrospective study of parental behaviors across the three stages of development within professional tennis. Nine tennis triads (player, parent, and coach) were interviewed separately on the parental behaviors and attitudes that helped and hindered development in the three stages. In the early years, congruent with other studies, parents' tangible and emotional support provisions were highly evident, alongside a focus on instilling positive values, emphasizing fun, actively playing with their child, and making sport and play a family experience. Successful parents helped their children develop effective stress management strategies, for example by having emotionally intelligent discussions of new situations and challenges. Few negative, controlling behaviors were reported in this period, although there was some evidence reported of overly pushy behavior and degrees of struggle with the coach–parent dual role in some participants. In summary, within the early years, research suggests that parents have somewhat of a triangular foundation to build in terms of establishing a talent-nourishing family environment. This is an environment in which sport is a family value that is facilitated by action in terms of parental participation (role modeling) and parental initiative and resourcing (provider). In turn, internal parental values of hard work, encouragement, praise, and discipline (Gould et al., 2002) function to guide the talented athlete's early experiences of skill development and competition as parents behave as interpreters of such experiences for them. Perhaps the role of the parent during these early years is most appropriately articulated by an athlete in Connaughton, Wadey, Hanton, and Jones' (2008) retrospective study of the development and maintenance of mental toughness in Olympic and international level athletes. The athlete reflects on these early years by stating:

> I had a lot of friends in my sport that had parents who were really over-involved and pushy in their training, but I was lucky. My parents provided me with the tools that I needed, in terms of getting to practice, being supportive, and providing an optimal level of interest in what I was doing in those early days. They also believed in me and encouraged every progression that I made, which turned me into a confident kid.
> (p. 86)

The Middle Years: Specializing and Development Roles

When talented athletes ostensibly begin to specialize in one sport, from 12 to 15 years of age, research suggests that their amount of training increases to between 12 and 19 hours per week over 75% of the year (Australian Sports Commission, 2003; Gibbons, 2002). During this time, parents experience an intensive pressure and responsibility to provide all forms of social support, in addition to acting as suitable role models (Côté & Hay, 2002; Rees & Hardy, 2000; Wolfenden & Holt, 2005). First, research suggests that parents of talented athletes appear to "step up" and be more proactively involved with their child's sport specialization (Connaughton et al., 2008; Durand-Bush et al., 2004; Ewing, Hedstrom, & Weisner, 2004; Gould et al., 2002; Hellstedt, 1990; Wuerth, Lee, & Alfermann, 2004). This support appears to reflect a developmental milestone, whereby the child athlete becomes the more autonomous driver of his or her sport progression, and parents model the role of close, proactive guardians within the support team. For example, Durand-Bush and colleagues note how parents respected and supported their child's decision to progress in terms of commitment to his or her sport. Further, Kay's (2000) research into the family dynamics of 20 sport families illustrated how, beyond material and emotional support, the ability to adapt family life to the athlete's sporting commitments was central to continued success.

The intensity of demands required of parents in their support role during the specializing stage was recently illustrated via two in-depth qualitative studies of the stressors experienced by parents within tennis and soccer environments (Harwood & Knight, 2009a; Harwood, Drew, & Knight, 2010). Within tennis, parents cited numerous organizational, competitive, and developmental stressors, substantiating a view that the specializing stage was extremely demanding compared to the sampling and investment stages of development. Work–tennis role conflict, lack of family/partner time, organizational and tennis administration roles, and financial impact on the family and siblings represented but a few of the organizational stressors experienced. In addition to competitive stressors when watching matches, dealing with the emotions of the result, and interacting with other tennis parents, these parents also referred to the difficulties of ensuring their child's best interests for the future. These developmental stressors included actively managing conflicts with the school (due to their sport involvement) while maintaining the value of education, and ensuring that they had the best and most up-to-date information for assisting their child in tennis-related decisions (Harwood & Knight, 2009a).

Sport–family role conflict due to the heavy travel routine, disrupted and missed holidays, differential treatment of siblings, and one-dimensional personal life (usually of fathers) also served as evidence of the consequences of the parental support role within elite youth soccer (Harwood et al., 2010). In a similar vein to tennis, these parents cited the need for consistent emotional support to their son in matches, and they took a proactive interest in the quality of communication and feedback that they received from the club and coaches. In addition, they also actively tried to manage school–soccer conflicts and education issues on behalf of their son (see Donnelly, 1993). This level of positive, highly functional involvement was also noted by Wuerth and colleagues (2004), who concluded that athletes who had made a more effective transition through sport were supported by parents who showed more directive behavior with greater sport-related advice and emotional support than did parents of less successful athletes.

The salient emotional and esteem support of parents to their adolescent son or daughter during this phase appears to be very much interlinked with their "teachings" as an interpreter of the more challenging situations and demands that their child will face. Based on their interviews with ten Olympic champions and their respective parents, Gould et al. (2002) summarized how parents kept success in perspective, helped to evaluate performance as opposed to outcome, taught psychological skills to their child, and "lived" family values, in which hard work pays off and people follow through on their commitments. In their follow-up investigation with specializing stage athletes, Keegan, Spray, Harwood, and Lavallee's (2010) findings also suggested that parents' leadership, feedback/evaluation, pre-performance motivational, and support/facilitation roles were more prominent than in their sampling stage research (Keegan et al., 2009). Last, Lauer et al.'s (2010) exploration of developmental parental behavior in tennis speaks to similar resource demands. Parents' logistical, emotional, and esteem support during the specializing years were more significant than in the early years. Although life skills, education, and positive value-development were maintained, parents were required to make critical developmental decisions for their child. Negative behaviors were also most evident during this stage,

with overpressurizing and involvement, poor emotional match reactions, and embarrassing behavior, with too much tennis talk, a restricted social life, and parental approval tied to results.

All of these studies point to an often frenetic experience for the family in the presence of a talented adolescent sibling, an experience that demands multiple coping skills and resources within parents. Some parents appear ill-equipped to deal with these experiences. Therefore, although there is a natural tendency to assume that coaches and peers play the more prominent roles in terms of influencing athlete development (Wylleman & Lavallee, 2004), the reality of what is going on behind the scenes may be exceptionally different. Not only do the parents of many talented athletes appear to commit to their child in a healthy, resourceful manner, and sacrifice unselfishly in the process, but they do so while striking the balance between fostering their autonomy and safeguarding their best interests. Relating back to Connaughton et al.'s (2008) study of mental toughness development, another athlete offers an excellent example of the influence of the interpreter role that was played by his father in the middle years:

> I remember one of my first competitions where I dropped the ball. I started crying my eyes out.... I thought my world was going to cave in, but my dad and I talked afterwards and he said, "You've got to concentrate and carry on with your performance no matter what happens. You've got to be able to pick yourself up after making mistakes." He drove into me that it was part of development and part of growing up and because I respected him so much, I took everything on board. As a result, I learned to rationalize my thoughts and feelings as I started to realize that how I thought and felt would influence my performance.
> (p. 90)

The Later Years: Investment and Mastery Roles

During the mastery and investment stages of talent development, the athlete is most probably training between 19 and 22 hours per week on average (Australian Sports Commission, 2003; Gibbons, 2002). The start of this stage marks the demanding transition from elite junior to elite senior performance as the athlete progresses toward attaining professional status. In many cases, the athlete may spend long periods away from home while focusing on training and competition, and, although the family may still be called upon for financial support, it is the emotional and esteem support provision that markedly characterizes this phase. Holt and Dunn (2004) put forward a grounded theory of the psychosocial competencies necessary for successful transition into senior professional soccer. Guided by multiple interviews with U.K. professional youth academy players and U-20 Canadian national soccer team members, four core competencies emerged. Alongside requirements for the talented player to demonstrate intrapersonal attributes associated with discipline, commitment, and resilience, such a transition was also dependent on the social support received and utilized by players. Holt and Dunn noted that three specific types of social support were apparent, and these were typically associated with facilitating resilience in the players. Both parents provided emotional support, evidenced when players were able to turn to their parents for comfort, moral support, and security during times of stress. Informational support was accessed by players seeking guidance, often from fathers, about possible solutions to soccer-related problems. Finally, tangible support, again provided by both parents, related to concrete assistance, such as travel and financial backing. These findings were equally reminiscent of Rees and Hardy's (2000) investigation into the social support experiences of international senior performers and the reflections of Olympic champions (Durand-Bush & Salmela, 2002; Durand-Bush et al., 2004) on key developmental factors. Parents provided a haven of emotional support and a consistent presence during setbacks, a refuge from the stress of competition, confidence building during slumps, and financial assistance in real times of need. Lauer et al. (2010) reported that, during the elite tennis years, positive parents provided emotional support to players in a context of "independence fostering" and helped on financial management and balanced lifestyle advice. They pulled back from any coaching role, a behavior that was not followed by overinvolved parents, who continued to demonstrate excessively controlling, critical, and independence-thwarting behaviors.

In sum, the investment years are potentially highly stressful and career-defining for athletes as they make the transition to elite level performance. It appears from this body of research that parents continue to play many significant roles that we should not underestimate as researchers and practitioners. However, perhaps the most central role is one of unconditional love and support during the athlete's goal of independence-striving as a young adult. This role forms a critical resource for an athlete's coping arsenal as he or she attempts to make the transition into adulthood and elite sport (Schlossberg, 1984).

A Family Affair: The Role of Siblings

Although scientific investigations of sport parents and parental influence on talent development are burgeoning, the role of the intact family remains limited by a lack of focus on sibling influences. Both Côté and Hay (2002) and Horn and Horn (2007) lament the paucity of sport-related research into sibling–sibling relationships and the family dynamics associated with differential sibling socialization patterns. The sibling relationship is often the longest relationship that one will experience in a lifetime, and they are unique in terms of their ascribed (i.e., one doesn't choose to be a sibling) and often intimate nature in childhood and adolescence, resulting in mutual socialization effects (Côté, 2002). Further, sibling relationships represent a subsystem of the family that can affect the entire climate of the family (Côté & Hay, 2002). The addition of a sibling to a family unit can be a distressing and challenging time for both the older child and parents. According to Shaffer (2002), sibling rivalry exhibited through competition, jealousy, and/or resentment often begins immediately, although parents can minimize the effects by continuing with established routines and encouraging the involvement of older siblings in the care and attention of the new arrival. Rivalry is thought to occur due to competition for resources such as parental time, attention, and finances. Sulloway's (1996) popular "ecological theory" of the family posits that first-born and later-born children develop different talents and characteristics from each other because they are required to compete with each other to find their own ecological niche in the family. For younger siblings, this might include a niche not already occupied by an older sibling, pursuing interests where they have a strong chance of competitive superiority as a means of maximizing attention and approval from a parent.

Nevertheless, although there is a tendency to view sibling relationships as inherently conflicting, several studies within sport offer insights into the positive roles played by siblings and how parents might maximize cooperation among siblings for mutually beneficial outcomes. In the same way as parents serve as providers, interpreters, and role models, siblings have also been reported to act in similar roles. Stevenson (1990) discusses how older siblings can introduce their younger siblings to their chosen sport. This may occur not only through the emotional or social support offered to a younger sibling, but also through the younger sibling's desire to emulate their older sibling whom they observe to be having positive and enjoyable experiences through sport. Côté's (1999) research reported earlier in this chapter also affirmed that older siblings served as role models for work ethic and commitment for younger, adolescent siblings during the specializing stage of sport development. Interestingly, however, reverse modeling effects can also exist. Namely, Wold and Andersen (1992) found that adolescents whose same-sex older siblings were physically inactive and nonparticipants in sport were themselves less likely to participate in sport compared to those adolescents who did not have an older sibling at all. Likewise, Stuart's (2003) qualitative study of adolescents' sources of value in sport found that an older sibling's negative experiences of sport can negatively influence the value that the younger sibling places on sport.

Research suggests that a talented and physically active older sibling in a family can put great strain upon the family unit, particularly during the later specializing/early investment years. Côté's (1999) investigation found that younger siblings possessed a sense of bitterness and jealousy toward their adolescent older sibling, created by the uneven distribution of parental resources during the investment years. Congruent responses were recently articulated by parents within the in-depth parental stress studies conducted by Harwood and colleagues (Harwood et al., 2010; Harwood & Knight, 2009a,b). Specifically, parents reported significant sport–family role conflict within both soccer and tennis, associated with the travel and organizational demands of supporting a talented child athlete. Sibling stressors emerged as a core theme within an investigation of 123 British tennis parents, 28% of whom cited unequal time, money, and attention to their tennis-playing sibling as stressful (Harwood & Knight, 2009b). Further, perceptions of sibling resentment and jealousy, a one-dimensional personal life, split-family lifestyles, a lack of partner/spousal time, and personal guilt characterized some of the risks to the highly committed family. As one soccer parent in Harwood and colleagues' (2010) study stated:

> It's hard to give the other children the attention when you're away Tuesday, Thursday nights and Saturday mornings. We've got two girls aged 7 and they do feel their noses are being pushed past. Then they play up

when you do see them and they wind you up even more, so it's a vicious circle. (p. 49)

When referring to the behavior of younger versus older siblings, the impact of birth order itself is another interesting phenomenon that has relevance to the talent development process in the context of parental style. Parents typically have high expectations for their first-borns (Furman, 1995), and their inexperience in the role of parenting means that they may be overly affectionate, supportive, cautious, overprotective, or punitive. However, it is considered that later-born children experience differences in parenting styles due to a "learning from mistakes" mentality that guides parents toward offering their child greater freedom. These differences in parenting are thought to account for some of the differences observed in the nature and temperament of first-born in comparison to later-born children (Kail & Cavanaugh, 2007). First-born children are more likely to score higher on intelligence tests, go to university, and be more conforming to parents' requests than their younger siblings, who are less concerned with pleasing adults, are generally more popular with peers, and more innovative, according to Kail and Cavanaugh. There is limited research within sport to scientifically substantiate the effects of birth order on talent development as influenced by the family. However, Flowers and Brown (2002) demonstrated that first-born athletes reported significantly higher cognitive and somatic state anxiety as opposed to later-born athletes. They speculated that this may have been due to the differential patterns of parenting styles and behaviors that give rise to first-borns perceiving increased pressure to lead by example and attain a high level of performance.

Perhaps the most interesting sport-related research, vividly illustrating the paradoxical nature of the sibling relationship, was recently conducted by Davis and Meyer (2008) in their qualitative investigation of sibling competition in elite sport. The authors interviewed ten same-sex siblings about the nature of their sibling relationship in the context of competing against each other in the same sport. Athletes referred to the positive source of motivation and often self-imposed pressure related to outperforming their sibling, alongside some of the negative feelings that accompanied such pressure. However, they also spoke deeply of having a positive regard for their siblings' feelings, possessing a clear awareness of their presence, and engaging in both emotional and instructional support as highly cooperative behaviors that characterized their relationship.

Connaughton et al. (2008) also highlighted the positive role that sibling rivalry can assume in the development of mental toughness during the middle years. Therefore, it does appear that, within a supportive family environment, sport can encourage a sense of emotional connection, cooperation, positive rivalry, and role modeling between siblings (Davis & Meyer). In this respect, although the presence of siblings can offer additional stressors for parents and create a challenging family dynamic for the parent provider in youth sport, siblings may also serve highly functional and supportive roles in the overall talent development process.

The Family As an Asset to Positive Youth Development

Thus far in this chapter, we have drawn substantially from the literature in sport psychology to offer in-depth descriptions of potential parental and sibling roles within athletic talent development. However, it is important to acknowledge how contemporary perspectives from applied developmental scientists have begun to inform and stimulate avenues of research that directly implicate the influence of the family on youth development in sport and life. This section will, therefore, introduce how key work from the field of developmental science and positive youth development has the potential to merge with the application of sport and performance psychology in the context of familial facilitation of optimal talent development.

Bronfenbrenner's Bioecological Perspective

The family tends to be the greatest source of socialization through our most formative years, and developmental psychologists have adopted a systems approach to explain the forces of influence that occur to shape development within this complex social system. Bronfenbrenner's (1977, 2005) bioecological systems approach is one interpretation of systems theory that has been widely accepted; it considers how both individual difference and contextual variables operate in conjunction with one another to influence the direction and power of development over time. With this approach in mind, relationships between individuals are considered to be reciprocal. As such, parents are thought to have an effect on children, but children are also considered to influence the ways in which parents may interact with that child. For example, a temperamental and outgoing child may cause a parent

to be more controlling and less supportive of autonomy in his or her behaviors and interactions with that child (Kail & Cavanaugh, 2007). These reciprocal effects also extend to sibling relationships and can be both *direct* (i.e., behavior from one family member, such as the parent, distinctly affects and is affected by another family member, such as the child) and *indirect* (i.e., behavior between two individuals, such as mother and child, is modified by that of a third individual, such as the father). In this respect, a mother who is happily married and enjoys a supportive relationship with her husband will tend to interact more patiently and sensitively with her child compared to a mother who does not receive the support of her husband and feels she is bringing up the child on her own (Cox, Owen, Henderson, & Lewis, 1989; Cox, Owen, Henderson, & Margand, 1992). A systems theory approach also assumes that such systems are dynamic in nature, so that change is inevitable, necessary, and required in order for development to occur.

Bronfenbrenner (2005) classified the contexts of development into ecological niches that either directly or indirectly influence the development of the child. Contexts that directly affect the child are those in which the child participates, such as school, youth sport, and family. These contexts are labeled *microsystems*. In contrast, those contexts that indirectly affect the child, including the parent's place of work and their network of friends, are labelled *exosystems*. Within microsystems, the influence of significant others is considered to be particularly important, as their dispositional characteristics may influence the reciprocal interaction between the developing child and the significant other. Familial interactions then significantly influence the expression of dominant personality traits over others and nurture the development of more socially productive and culturally accepted assets in young people.

Although Bronfenbrenner's theory is widely accepted within developmental science, it has been largely neglected within family and talent development research in sport. A notable exception is a recent study by Holt, Tamminen, Black, Sehn, and Wall (2008), who adopted an ecological systems approach to investigate the nature of parental involvement within competition and training settings in youth soccer. Through extensive fieldwork and interviewing, the authors employed a grounded theory methodology to understand parental involvement in soccer, illustrating the wide range of verbal reactions to their child's performance and how these were influenced by contextual and personal factors, such as overall policy issues, empathy with their child, the emotional intensity of the event, and their perceived knowledge and experience of soccer. The study did not consider the impact of such parental involvement on talent development per se, or indeed any other psychological construct. However, the nature of parental interactions with their child athlete, and parents' use of more supportive versus more controlling feedback reactions according to personal and situational factors, reinforced how talent development environments can be highly complex systems.

Clarifying Key Developmental Assets

Bronfenbrenner's model has resonated most in recent years within positive youth development. Within this field of study, Benson and colleagues (Benson, Leffert, Scales, & Blyth, 1998) identified 40 assets that were integral to positive youth development outcomes in society. These developmental assets were divided into 20 internal and 20 external assets. Internal assets represent attributes of the individual, such as commitment to learning (e.g., achievement motivation), interpersonal competence (e.g., communication skills), restraint, self-esteem, and positive identity formation. Conversely, external assets are characterized by the quality of the external environment that supports the shaping of these internal assets in the child. These assets include access to positive role models, social support, clear setting of boundaries, opportunities for learning, and positive peer influence. In combination, the presence of these internal and external assets within a specific youth setting (i.e., microsystem) are thought to play protective, enhancement, and resiliency roles (Benson et al., 1998). In youth sport, for example, children high in developmental assets protect themselves against engaging in high-risk, illegal, and/or antisocial behaviors; they are more successful and likely to show enhanced leadership skills, optimism, and enjoyment; and finally, they are believed to develop greater resilience in difficult and adverse situations (e.g., positive responses to setbacks and failure). In a closely allied approach within developmental psychology, Lerner, Fisher, and Weinberg (2000) refer to the *6 Cs* of positive youth development: competence, character, connection, confidence, caring and, ultimately, contributions. These reflect the desired outcomes within their model of national youth policy toward the development of a civilized society.

Translating these approaches into youth sport, Fraser-Thomas, Côté, and Deakin (2005) provide a compelling argument for the importance of programs built on fostering key developmental assets. By drawing from Bronfenbrenner (2005), they affirm that it is the regularity and quality of *reciprocal social relationships* experienced by talented athletes with parents, coaches, and peers that underpin successful development and that are integral to effective youth sport program design. Nevertheless, few (if any) studies in sport have specifically defined or agreed upon the key internal assets associated with athletic talent development, nor have sport programs specifically identified, targeted, and resourced the key external assets in order to facilitate optimal psycho-socio-emotional development. What we do know is that a wide variety of psychological, social, and emotional qualities and characteristics are considered important for the child athlete from both a performance enhancement/talent development perspective and from a personal/positive youth development perspective. However, the development of both these objectives within a coaching program can be potentially conflicting due to time and other resource constraints that often force coaches to make the decision to focus on one over the other. Coaches may often choose to focus on sport performance and results at the expense of attention to an athlete's personal development. Time, perceived swimmer interest levels, coach knowledge, and coach confidence may serve as barriers to enhancing the psychosocial development of their athletes.

In recent years, a number of authors have referred to psychosocial characteristics that are important for one or both of these potentially conflicting developmental objectives. Holt and Dunn (2004) refer to the importance of discipline, resilience, and commitment in elite youth soccer transitions; Côté (2002) refers to qualities such as cooperation, assertion, responsibility, empathy, and social control; Holt, Tink, Mandigo, and Fox (2008) speak to the value of initiative, respect, leadership, and teamwork. Harwood (2008) focuses on the fostering of commitment, communication, concentration, control, and confidence within specializing stage players in a youth soccer academy. Meanwhile, the introduction of the PDCEs (referred to earlier in this chapter) by MacNamara and colleagues—encompassing constructs such as goal setting, realistic performance evaluations, imagery, planning and organizational skills, commitment, competitiveness, focus and distraction control, coping with pressure, and self-awareness—extend the breadth of desirable attributes and strategies within current research in elite athlete development (Bailey et al., 2009; MacNamara et al., 2006, 2008; MacNamara, Button, & Collins, 2010a,b). Nevertheless, few studies in talent development and psychology have taken an asset-based perspective and investigated the processes and mechanisms by which family members may help to shape a specific internal asset in their child or sibling.

Conclusion

The primary aim of this chapter was to consider the variety of ways in which the family plays a vital role in shaping the talent of athletes. In light of this aim, we first reviewed some of our foremost talent development models in psychology (Bloom, 1985; Ericsson et al., 1993) and more recently in sport (Côté, 1999), which clearly highlights the range of approaches available to us for understanding talent development. In the context of youth sport, the consideration of Eccles and colleagues' developmental research (Eccles et al., 1983; Fredricks & Eccles, 2004) further suggests that parents can influence their child athletes via acting as providers, interpreters, and role models, and this influential process will vary in quantity and quality across key stages of talent development. Although researchers provide slightly different categorical names and/or age ranges for identifiable key stages of talent development, there is general agreement that these stages exist and also that parents and siblings (although less is known about the latter) can contribute to an athlete's development in sporting families. It must be noted that specific research into the role of grandparents in talent development and youth sport is nonexistent, to the authors' knowledge.

The final sections of this chapter addressed emergent research within developmental science and positive youth development that reflect current thinking about relevant concepts that can be used to inform the role of the family. In the last sections of the chapter, we will provide future directions for applied research and urge the consideration of unique approaches to understanding this complex area. For example, we refer to the importance of mixed-methodological designs, extending our knowledge base via examination of parenting styles and practices, ensuring collaborative practice within the family, and targeted efforts on the "right" assets or competencies for talent development.

One of the greatest challenges or, at the very least, important considerations that talent development researchers (and practitioners) must be mindful of is the ever-evolving configuration of the modern family. However, no matter what the distinct makeup of each particular family, Csikszentmihalyi et al.'s (1993) suggestion of a complex family in which a child experiences a consistent and supportive environment from which he or she feels able to "develop their individuality by seeking out new challenges and opportunities" (p. 155) is considered the most adaptive to talent development. This environment appears similar to that advocated within the attachment literature as one that enhances the development of the favorable secure attachment dimension (Bowlby, 1969). In other words, when children are sufficiently challenged and supported, in equal measure, then it seems they are far more likely to develop into good people and—in consideration of athletic talent development—ideally, they will become individuals who have skills that make them better people and/or talented athletes.

Although our knowledge in this area is developing, we have only scratched the surface in terms of fully understanding the mechanisms of talent development as driven by the family. The most pertinent measures and processes associated with developing talented athletes are of significance not only on an individual level, but are also increasingly recognized by national governing bodies and through international competitive sport, whereby economic and pride rewards are highly public and reflect a sort of status or esteem. The fact that we have identified so many new areas for consideration in this chapter as we have reviewed the previously conducted research reveals just how much work remains to be done in this area.

Future Directions

Although research into the role of siblings within talent development environments has remained limited and descriptive, investigations of parental processes in elite youth sport have burgeoned in recent years (Gould, Lauer, Rolo, Jannes, & Pennisi, 2008; Harwood et al., 2010; Harwood & Knight, 2009a,b; Holt, Tamminen, Black, Mandigo, & Fox, 2009; Holt et al., 2008; Knight, Boden & Holt, 2010; Lauer et al., 2010). Each of these investigations has adopted a qualitative methodology suggesting that researchers recognize that the complexity of parenting and of being parented as a talented athlete cannot be fully understood by traditional, cross-sectional quantitative designs. Moreover, the contextual richness of data that have been generated by studying positive and negative parenting practices (Gould et al., 2008; Lauer et al., 2010), parenting styles and verbal reactions (Holt et al., 2008, 2009), parental stressors (Harwood & Knight, 2009a,b), and child's parental behavior preferences (Knight et al., 2010) offer a treasure trove of applied recommendations and case examples for practitioners within family-based intervention work.

Nevertheless, it must be acknowledged that longitudinal, prospective research of family influence upon the talented athlete is limited. Such research would most probably require a very sophisticated mixed-methods approach. However, several avenues of applied research could aim to extend upon the rather descriptive insights of past studies and, subsequently, aim to inform applied practice. This final section focuses attention on these specific areas.

PARENTING STYLES AND FAMILIAL SOCIAL SUPPORT

Past research has championed the role of the parent as a key provider of social support, both in terms of emotional and esteem support, as well as tangible and informational support (Rees & Hardy, 2000; Wolfenden & Holt, 2005). However, social support researchers consider this multidimensional construct in one of two ways; either the social support that an athlete actually receives in a given period of time from a parent or the social support that the athlete perceives to be available to him or her should he or she require it. These two types of social support are called "received" and "perceived," respectively. In terms of the latter, perceived social support availability can be further divided into general perceptions of perceived support availability—an individual's perception of how approachable and helpful people are in general—and interpersonal perceptions of support availability, which are specific to individual relationships with specific people such as mother, father, brother, sister, and grandparents (Pierce, Sarason, & Sarason, 1991).

In terms of optimizing a talent development environment, parents are particularly influential in the development of a child's perception of perceived support availability. This is due to the belief that it is a more stable personality trait related to one's sense of acceptance that is, in turn, determined by an individual's attachment style (Sarason, Pierce, & Sarason, 1990). Drawing from Bowlby's (1969) attachment theory, attachment styles are developed within individuals during childhood as a direct consequence of the behaviors of the primary caregiver. Dependent upon the amount of attention that is given to the child in a time of stress or need, the child will develop an anxious, secure, or avoidant style (Bowlby, 1969; for a more detailed explanation, see Chapter 21, this volume). The parenting behaviors that shape the development of this attachment style are governed by the parenting style that that parent adopts, based on his or her values, expectations, and sense of appropriate ways to interact with his or her child. Baumrind (1971) identified two dimensions of parenting behaviors: acceptance/responsiveness, and demandingness/control. Responsiveness refers to the sensitivity, supportiveness, and involvement exhibited by parents, whereas demandingness refers to the amount of control exerted by the parent on the child, often influenced by their high expectations of the child. These two dimensions result in four parenting styles: authoritative (high in both responsiveness and control), authoritarian (high in control but low in responsiveness), indulgent-permissive (high in responsiveness but low in control), and neglectful-uninvolved (low in responsiveness and low in control). Of these, authoritative is accepted as being the most beneficial to psychosocial development, in which parents exercise the firm-but-fair concept. However, criticisms of the Baumrind typology have led to alternative perspectives, such as Grolnick's (2003) view of three dimensions of parenting behavior; namely, autonomy support versus control, structure, and involvement.

Recent support for the existence of Grolnick's parenting styles and the practices associated with them in sport was provided by Holt and colleagues (2009), in an in-depth investigation with 56 parents and 34 of their female child athletes. However, the role, relevance, and development of parenting styles; their potential associations with perceived support availability; received social support; psychosocial assets; and attachment styles in athletes have not been scientifically investigated at any level. For family-based talent development research to move beyond the descriptive, there is a greater need to investigate the early-stage processes and mechanisms related to how and why parents, grandparents, and siblings interact with a child athlete in a certain manner. Drawing from quality of relationship theories (Pierce, Sarason, Sarason, Solky-Buzel, & Nagle, 1997), assessments of the support, depth, and conflict in the parent–child relationship (see Jowett & Cramer, 2010) and sibling–sibling relationship as perceived by the athlete may also assist in our understanding of optimal talent development environments. These fields of research will help us to more scientifically substantiate the social-psychological mechanisms by which some athletes thrive in certain stages of talent development whereas others potentially struggle.

FAMILY COLLABORATION IN ASSET DEVELOPMENT

Anecdotal reports from coaches, personal experience, and recent research suggest that families are sometimes viewed as hindrances to coaches as opposed to being embraced as key facilitators and stakeholders of talent development outcomes (see Gould et al., 2008; Knight & Harwood, 2009). Few intervention studies in sport have taken the intentional angle of coaches, parents, and, indeed, grandparents, working together on relevant psychosocial outcomes or developmental assets from a positive youth development perspective. Yet, one starting point for researchers is to develop greater clarity related to those specific internal assets that are deemed relevant and critical to athletic development/performance, as well as important to wider personal development. The clearer the asset framework for athletic development in sport, the greater the likelihood is that a family may be educated to play an intentional role in facilitating and supporting such prescribed assets.

Recently, Douglas, Harwood, and Minniti (under review) undertook a two-stage approach to proposing an internal asset framework in youth swimming. Stage 1 involved a content analysis of terminology within the youth sport and youth development literature, leading to 17 constructs that represented similar psychosocial terms. Stage 2 incorporated an in-depth consensus validation and external audit of these constructs and their definitions through multiple interviews with ten elite swim coaches and academic experts. Their final framework coalesced into five developmental categories representing 17 psychosocial assets. These categories were self-perceptions, behavioral skills, approach characteristics, social skills, and emotional competence. These psychosocial assets were considered by the experts to be of significant importance for both personal development and for successful talent development in youth swimming.

A subsequent step for applied researchers may be to determine the beliefs, competencies, and barriers to development that are perceived by parents about these key psychosocial assets. For example, the recent research on parental stressors (see Harwood & Knight, 2009a) suggests individual differences in parental knowledge and efficacy in supporting their child through certain competitive experiences. It is therefore important for talent development researchers to not only understand which psychosocial competencies parents value, but also to ascertain if parents have the knowledge, skills, or confidence to help develop such competencies in their child athlete. A further layer of complexity may then be added to establish the relevant developmental periods in which parents, siblings, and grandparents may most effectively contribute to the growth of each asset. In sum, the holistic question of "which assets, when, and primarily shaped by whom?" remains pivotal but largely unexplored in sport (to the authors' knowledge) from an empirical standpoint. Once this is better understood, it will be possible to establish the most effective ways to help parents and families foster key assets and, thus, athletes' psychosocial development.

RESEARCHING THE BROADNESS OF THE MODERN FAMILY

In the developing world, our understanding of what constitutes a family is ever-changing and evolving. In Western societies, such as in the United States and the United Kingdom, where social change was extensive in the second half of the 20th century, families are much more dynamic and varied than ever before. Whereas the traditional nuclear family of spouses and their biological or adoptive children remain extant, cohabitation and the birth of children within a committed hetero- or homosexual relationship are now much more commonplace and socially acceptable. In addition, an increasing female population in the workforce, a higher divorce rate, more single-parent families, and an increase in the *blended family* (in which a child or children, their parent, and another stepparent blend children from two families into a new family system) can have consequences on the dynamic and interactive nature of families on development (Shaffer, 2002). For talent development researchers, a number of more idiosyncratic questions now exist if one seeks to research the influence of the modern family on athletic talent. For example, what specific psychological roles do grandparents play within the wider family unit, given their potential for intensive and differential involvement (when compared to parents) in childhood and adolescence? What are the effects of being an only child in the absence of siblings, and do those athletes with siblings benefit and achieve a higher level of success than only children? Do differential parenting styles experienced between first-born and later-borns and between those athletes with siblings and only-borns transfer into the need for differential coaching styles? Additionally, the growing variety of family configurations has received no attention within the context of talent development. For example, we know that although adoption is a highly successful and mutually beneficial arrangement, children who have been adopted have been found to display more learning difficulties and emotional problems than those who are raised with biological parents (Shaffer, 2002). We also know that family conflict and divorce can have significant and long-term negative implications for the children caught up in the crisis, resulting in increased aggression toward others, academic difficulties, and psychological distress. In addition, there can be significant gender differences in regards to how both sexes deal with the break-up of the family. Females may display a lack of confidence toward their own future relationships with males and become depressed or withdrawn, as opposed to males, who are more likely to act out their frustrations and fears (for more detailed reviews of the effect of gender, culture, and race on talent development please refer to Freeman, 2000; Horowitz, Subotnik, & Matthews, 2009; and Reis & Hébert, 2008). Again, although all of this knowledge is useful in determining our understanding of these seemingly negative life experiences on child development, no attempt has been made to understand the effects of adoption and/or divorce on the promotion of talent within children and adolescents (Shaffer, 2002).

We end our chapter with a series of questions that may be useful in guiding readers through this complex area.

- What is talent?
- How has our understanding of talent evolved (historically and methodologically)?
- What does the current research tell us about how it can best be nurtured?
- What is the relevance of understanding key stages of talent development?
- How can future research help us to better understand the complex process of talent development?

References

Abbott, A., & Collins, D. (2004). Eliminating the dichotomy between theory and practice in talent identification and development: Considering the role of psychology. *Journal of Sports Sciences, 22*, 395–408.

Australian Sports Commission. (2003). *How do elite athletes develop? Look through the 'rear-view mirror': A preliminary report from the National Athlete Development Survey.* Canberra, AU: Australian Sports Commission.

Babkes, M. L., & Weiss, M. R. (1999). Parental influence on children's cognitive and affective responses to competitive soccer participation. *Pediatric Exercise Science, 11*, 44–62.

Bailey, R., Collins, D., Ford, P., MacNamara, A., Toms, M., & Pearce, G. (2009). *Participant development in sport: An academic review.* London: SportscoachUK.

Bailey, R., & Morley, D. (2006). Towards a model of talent development in physical education. *Sport, Education and Society, 11*, 211–230.

Bandura, A. (1977). Self-efficacy: Toward a unifying theory of behavioural change. *Psychological Review, 84*, 191–215.

Baumrind, D. (1971). Current patterns of parental authority. *Developmental Psychology, 4*, 1–103.

Baxter-Jones, A. D., & Maffulli. N. (2003). Parental influence on sport participation in elite young athletes. *Journal of Sports Medicine and Physical Fitness, 43*, 250–255.

Benson, P. L., Leffert, N., Scales, P. C., & Blyth, D. A. (1998). Beyond the "village" rhetoric: Creating healthy communities for children and adolescents. *Applied Developmental Science, 2*, 138–159.

Bloom, B. S. (1985). *Developing talent in young people.* New York: Ballantine.

Bowlby, J. (1969). *Attachment and loss: Vol.1. Attachment.* New York: Basic Books.

Bronfenbrenner, U. (1977). Toward an experimental ecology of human development. *American Psychologist, 32*, 513–531.

Bronfenbrenner, U. (2005). The bioecological theory of human development. In U. Bronfenbrenner (Ed.), *Making human beings human: Bioecological perspectives on human development* (pp. 3–15). Thousand Oaks, CA: Sage.

Brustad, R. J. (1993). Who will go out and play? Parental and psychological influences on children's attraction to physical activity. *Pediatric Exercise Science, 5*, 210–223.

Connaughton, D., Wadey, R., Hanton, S., & Jones, G. (2008). The development and maintenance of mental toughness: Perceptions of elite performers. *Journal of Sports Sciences, 26*, 83–95.

Côté, J. (1999). The influence of family in the development of talent in sport. *The Sport Psychologist, 13*, 395–417.

Côté, J. (2002). Coach and peer influence on children's development through sport. In J. M. Silva & D. E. Stevens (Eds.), *Psychological foundations of sport* (pp. 520–540). Boston, MA: Allyn and Bacon.

Côté, J., Baker, J., & Abernethy, B. (2003). From play to practice: A developmental framework for the acquisition of expertise in team sport. In J. Starkes & K. A. Ericsson (Eds.), *Expert performance in sports: Advances in research on sport expertise* (pp. 89–114). Champaign, IL: Human Kinetics.

Côté, J., & Hay, J. (2002). Children's involvement in sport: A developmental perspective. In J. M. Silva & D. E. Stevens (Eds.), *Psychological foundations of sport* (pp. 484–502). Boston, MA: Allyn and Bacon.

Cox, M. J., Owen, M. T., Henderson, V. K., & Lewis, J. M. (1989). Marriage, adult adjustment, and early parenting. *Child Development, 60*, 1015–1024.

Cox, M. J., Owen, M. T., Henderson, V. K., & Margand, N. A. (1992). Prediction of infant-father and infant-mother attachment. *Developmental Psychology, 28*, 474–483.

Csikszentmihalyi, M., Rathunde, K., & Whalen, S. (1993). *Talented teenagers: The roots of success and failure.* New York: Cambridge.

Davis, N. W., & Meyer, B. B.(2008). When sibling becomes competitor: A qualitative investigation of same-sex sibling competition in elite sport. *Journal of Applied Sport Psychology, 20,* 220–235.

Donnelly, P. (1993). Problems associated with youth involvement in high performance sport. In B. R. Cahill & A. J. Pearl (Eds.), *Intensive participation in children's sport* (pp. 95–126). Champaign, IL: Human Kinetics.

Douglas, J. P., Harwood, C. G., & Minniti, A. M. (under review). Positive youth development in swimming: Clarification and consensus of key psychosocial assets. *Manuscript submitted for publication.*

Durand-Bush, N., & Salmela, J. H. (2002). The development and maintenance of expert athletic performance: Perceptions of world and Olympic champions. *Journal of Applied Sport Psychology, 14,* 154–171.

Durand-Bush, N., Salmela, J. H., & Thompson, K. A. (2004). Le role joue´ par les parents dans le developpement et le maintien de la performance athletique experte. *Sciences et Techniques des Activités Physiques et Sportives, 64,* 15–38.

Eccles (Parsons), J., Alder, T. E., Futterman, R., Goff, S. B., Kaczala, C. M., Meece, J. L., & Midgley, C. (1983). Expectancies, values and academic behaviours. In J. T. Spence (Ed.), *Achievement and achievement motivations* (pp. 76–146). San Francisco, CA: W. H. Freeman & Co.

Ericsson, K. A. (1996). *The road to excellence: The acquisition of expert performance in the arts and sciences, sports, and games.* Mahweh, NJ: Erlbaum.

Ericsson, K. A., Krampe, R., & Tesch-Römer, C. (1993). The role of deliberate practice in the acquisition of expert performance. *Psychological Review, 100,* 363–406.

Ewing, M., Hedstrom, R. A., & Wiesner, A. R. (2004). Perception de l'engagement des parents dans la pratique du tennis de leur enfant. *Sciences et Techniques des Activités Physiques et Sportives, 64,* 53–70.

Fraser-Thomas, J., Côté, J., & Deakin, J. (2005). Youth sport programs: An avenue to foster positive youth development. *Physical Education and Sport Pedagogy, 10,* 19–40.

Fredricks, J. A., & Eccles, J. S. (2004). Parental influences on youth involvement in sports. In M. R. Weiss (Ed.), *Developmental sport and exercise psychology: A lifespan perspective* (pp. 145–164). Morgantown, WV: Fitness Information Technology, Inc.

Freeman, J. (2000). Teaching for talent: Lessons from the research. In C. F. M. van Lieshout & P. G. Heymans (Eds.), *Developing talent across the lifespan* (pp. 231–248). Philadelphia: Taylor & Francis.

Flowers, R. A., & Brown, C. (2002). Effects of sport context and birth order on state anxiety. *Journal of Sport Behaviour, 25,* 41–56.

Furman, W. (1995). Parenting siblings. In M. H. Bornstein (Ed.), *Handbook of parenting. Vol.1. Child and parenting* (pp. 143–162). Mahwah, NJ: Erlbaum.

Gibbons, T. (2002). The path to excellence: A comprehensive view of development of U.S. Olympians who competed from 1984–1998. *Initial report: Results of the Talent Identification and Development Questionnaire to U.S. Olympians.* Colorado Springs, CO: United States Olympic Committee.

Greendorfer, S., & Lewko, J. (1978). Role of family members in sport socialization of children. *Research Quarterly, 49,* 146–152.

Greendorfer, S. L., Lewko, J. H., & Rosengren, K. S. (1996). Family and gender-based influences in sport socialization of children and adolescents. In F. L. Smoll & R. E. Smith (Eds.), *Children and youth in sport: A biopsychosocial perspective* (pp. 89–111). Madison, WI: Brown & Benchmark.

Grolnick, W. S. (2003). *The psychology of parental control: How well-meant parenting backfires.* Hillsdale, NJ: Erlbaum.

Gould, D., Dieffenbach, K., & Moffett, A. (2002). Psychological talent and their development in Olympic champions. *Journal of Applied Sport Psychology, 14,* 172–204.

Gould, D., Lauer, L., Rolo, C., Jannes, C., & Pennisi, N. (2008). The role of parents in tennis success: Focus group interviews with junior coaches. *The Sport Psychologist, 22,* 18–37.

Harwood, C. (2008). Developmental consulting in a professional football academy: The 5Cs coaching efficacy program. *The Sport Psychologist, 22,* 109–133.

Harwood, C., Drew, A., & Knight, C. J. (2010). Parental stressors in professional youth football academies: A qualitative investigation of specialising stage parents. *Qualitative Research in Sport and Exercise, 2,* 39–55.

Harwood, C. G., & Knight, C. J. (2009a). Stress in youth sport: A developmental examination of tennis parents. *Psychology of Sport and Exercise, 10,* 447–456.

Harwood, C. G., & Knight, C. J. (2009b). Understanding parental stressors: An investigation of British tennis players. *Journal of Sports Sciences, 27,* 339–351.

Hellstedt, J. C. (1990). Early adolescent perceptions of parental pressure in the sport environment. *Journal of Sport Behavior, 13,* 135–144.

Holt, N. L., & Dunn, J. G. H. (2004). Toward a grounded theory of the psychosocial competencies and environmental conditions associated with soccer success. *Journal of Applied Sport Psychology, 16,* 199–219.

Holt, N. L., Tamminen, K. A., Black, D. E., Mandigo, J. L., & Fox, K. R. (2009). Youth sport parenting styles and practices. *Journal of Sport and Exercise Psychology, 31,* 37–59.

Holt, N. L., Tamminen, K. A., Black, D. E., Sehn, Z. L., & Wall, M. P. (2008). Parental involvement in competitive youth sport settings. *Psychology of Sport and Exercise, 9,* 663–685.

Holt, N. L., Tink, L. N., Mandigo, J. L., & Fox, K. R. (2008). Do youth learn life skills through their involvement in high school sport? A case study. *Canadian Journal of Education, 31,* 281–304.

Horn, T. S., & Horn, J. L. (2007). Family influences on children's sport and physical activity participation, behaviour, and psychosocial responses. In G. Tenenbaum & R. Eklund (Eds.), *Handbook of sport psychology* (3rd ed., pp. 685–711). Hoboken, NJ: Wiley & Sons Inc.

Horn, T. S., & Weiss, M. R. (1991). A developmental analysis of children's self-ability judgements in the physical domain. *Pediatric Exercise Science, 3,* 310–326.

Horowitz, F. D., Subotnik, R. F., & Matthews, D. J. (2009). *The development of giftedness and talent across the lifespan.* Washington, DC: American Psychological Association.

Jowett, S., & Cramer, D. (2010). The prediction of young athletes' physical self from perceptions of relationships with parents and coaches. *Psychology of Sport and Exercise, 11,* 140–147.

Kail, R. V., & Cavanaugh, J. C. (2007). *Human development: A life-span view*. Belmont, CA: Thomas Wadsworth.

Kay, T. (2000). Sporting excellence: A family affair? *European Physical Education Review, 6*, 151–169.

Keegan, R., Harwood, C. G., Spray, C. M., & Lavallee, D. (2009). A qualitative investigation exploring the motivational climate in early-career sports participants: Coach, parent and peer influences on sport motivation. *Psychology of Sport and Exercise, 10*, 361–372.

Keegan, R., Spray, C. M., Harwood, C. G., & Lavallee, D. (2010). The 'motivational atmosphere' in youth sport: Coach, parent and peer influences on sport motivation in specializing sports participants. *Journal of Applied Sport Psychology, 22*, 87–105.

Knight, C., & Harwood, C. (2009). Exploring parent-related coaching stressors in British tennis: A developmental investigation. *International Journal of Sports Science and Coaching, 4*, 545–585.

Knight, C. J., Boden, C. M., & Holt, N. L. (2010). Junior tennis players' preferences for parental behaviors. *Journal of Applied Sport Psychology, 22*, 377–391.

Lauer, L., Gould, D., Roman, N., & Pierce, M. (2010). Parental behaviours that affect junior tennis player development. *Psychology of Sport and Exercise, 11*, 487–496.

Lerner, R. M., Fisher, C. B., & Weinberg, R. A. (2000). Toward a science for and of the people: Promoting civil society through the application of developmental science. *Child Development, 71*, 11–20.

MacNamara, Á., Button, A., & Collins, D. (2010a). The role of psychological characteristics in facilitating the pathway to elite performance. Part 1: Identifying mental skills and behaviours. *The Sport Psychologist, 24*, 52–73.

MacNamara, Á., Button, A., & Collins, D. (2010b). The role of psychological characteristics in facilitating the pathway to elite performance. Part 2: Examining environmental and stage related differences in skills and behaviours. *The Sport Psychologist, 24*, 74–96.

MacNamara, A., Holmes, P., & Collins, D. (2006). The pathway to excellence: The role of psychological characteristics in negotiating the challenges of musical development. *British Journal of Music Education, 23*, 285–302.

MacNamara, A., Holmes, P., & Collins, D. (2008). Negotiating transitions in musical development: The role of psychological characteristics of developing excellence. *Psychology of Music, 36*, 335–352.

Martindale, R. J. J., Collins, D., & Abraham, A. (2007). Effective talent development: The elite coach perspective in UK sport. *Journal of Applied Sport Psychology, 19*, 187–206.

Pierce, G. R., Sarason, I. G., & Sarason, B. R. (1991). General and relationship-based perceptions of social support: Are two constructs better than one? *Journal of Personality and Social Psychology, 61*, 1028–1039.

Pierce, G. R., Sarason, I. G., Sarason, B. R., Solky-Butzel, J. A., & Nagle, L. C. (1997). Assessing the quality of personal relationships. *Journal of Social and Personal Relationships, 14*, 339–356.

Rees, T., & Hardy, L. (2000). An investigation of the social support experiences of high-level sports performers. *The Sport Psychologist, 14*, 327–347.

Reis, S. M., & Hébert, T. P. (2008). Gender and giftedness. In S. I. Pfeiffer (Ed.), *Handbook of giftedness in children: Psycho-educational theory, research and best practices* (pp. 271–292). New York: Springer.

Salmela, J. H. (1994). Phases and transitions among sport careers. In D. Hackfort (Ed.), *Psycho-social issues and interventions in elite sport* (pp. 11–28). Frankfurt, DE: Lang.

Sarason, B. R., Pierce, G. R., & Sarason, I. G. (1990). Social support: The sense of acceptance and the role of relationships. In B. R. Sarason, I. G. Sarason & G. R. Pierce (Eds.), *Social support: An interactional view* (pp. 97–128). New York: Wiley.

Schlossberg, N. (1984). *Counseling adults in transition*. New York: Springer.

Shaffer, D. R. (2002). *Developmental psychology: Childhood and adolescence* (6th ed.). Belmont, CA: Wadsworth/Thomson Learning.

Simonton, D. K. (1999). Talent and its development: An emergent and epigenetic model. *Psychological Review, 106*, 435–457.

Stambulova, N. (1994). Developmental sports career investigations in Russia: A post- perestroika analysis. *The Sport Psychologist, 8*, 221–237.

Starkes, J. L., & Ericsson, K. A. (2003). *Expert performance in sports: Advances in research on sport expertise*. Champaign, IL: Human Kinetics.

Starkes, J. L., Helsen, W., & Jack, R. (2001). Expert performance in sport and dance. In R. N. Singer, H. A. Hausenblas, & C. M. Janelle (Eds.), *Handbook of sport psychology* (pp. 174–201). New York: Wiley.

Stevenson, C. L. (1990). The early careers of international athletes. *Sociology of Sport Journal, 1990*, 238–253.

Stuart, M. E. (2003). Sources of subjective task value in sport: An examination of adolescents with high or low value for sport. *Journal of Applied Sport Psychology, 15*, 239–255.

Sulloway, F. (1996). *Born to rebel*. New York: Pantheon Books.

Vaeyens, R., Güllich, A., Warr, C. R., & Philippaerts, R. (2009). Talent identification and promotion programmes of Olympic athletes. *Journal of Sports Sciences, 27*, 1367–1380.

Weiss, M. R., & Fretwell, S. (2003). The parent-coach phenomenon in youth sport: Perspectives from the child, teammates, and parent-coach. *Journal of Sport and Exercise Psychology, 25*, S138.

Wold, B., & Andersen, N. (1992). Health promotion aspects of family and peer influences on sport participation. *International Journal of Sport Psychology, 23*, 343–359.

Wolfenden, L. E., & Holt, N. L. (2005). Talent development in elite junior tennis: Perceptions of players, parents and coaches. *Journal of Applied Sport Psychology, 17*, 108–126.

Woolger, C., & Power, T. G. (2000). Parenting and children's intrinsic motivation in age group swimming. *Journal of Applied Developmental Psychology, 21*, 595–607.

Wuerth, S., Lee, M. J., & Alfermann, D. (2004). Parental involvement and athletes' career in youth sport. *Psychology of Sport and Exercise, 5*, 21–33.

Wylleman, P., De Knop, P., Verdet, M. C., & Cecić-Erpič, S. (2006). Parenting and career transitions of elite athletes. In S. Jowett & D. Lavallee (Eds.), *Social psychology in sport* (pp. 233–247). Leeds: Human Kinetics.

Wylleman, P., & Lavallee, D. (2004). A developmental perspective on transitions faced by athletes. In M. Weiss (Ed.), *Developmental sport and exercise psychology: A lifespan perspective* (pp. 507–527). Morgantown, WV: Fitness Information Technology.

Expert Masters Sport Performers: Perspectives on Age-Related Processes, Skill Retention Mechanisms, and Motives

Bradley W. Young *and* Nikola Medic

Abstract

An exceptional cohort of *masters athletes* extensively train for and compete in sport during middle- and older-ages of the lifespan. This chapter, which examines the empirical research and emerging inquiry pertaining to this cohort, is specifically informed by modeling approaches to lifelong performance, psychomotor expertise perspectives, and a social-cognitive perspective on motivation. First, studies documenting optimistic trends of age-related performance decline among aging athletes are reviewed and evaluated to understand which processes might underscore retention. Second, theoretical mechanisms pertaining to the preservation of aged skilled performance are presented, for which various aspects of masters athletes' training are integral. The third section outlines perspectives on the exceptional commitment and competitive motives that serve to perpetuate masters athletes' extensive sport involvement. Avenues for future research and applied implications are integrated throughout the chapter.

Key Words: Aging, sport, masters athletes, skill retention, expertise, motivation, commitment

A wealth of lifespan research has demonstrated the deteriorative effects of aging. Patterns of age-related decline for middle-aged and older adults have been well documented for speeded perceptual- or cognitive-motor (Salthouse, 1992), memory (Henry, MacLeod, Phillips, & Crawford, 2004), neural processing (Cerella, 1990), and physiological/motor performance measures (Reaburn & Dascombe, 2008), thus implying an inevitable downward spiral of functional ability with age. Such patterns would appear to collectively support the notion that the performance potential of middle-aged and older adults is substantially compromised. Moreover, we could be easily convinced that this notion should extend to how we conceive the potential for sport performance as athletes advance beyond the traditionally-held age of peak function.

However, emerging evidence from the sport domain provides a more optimistic picture. Anecdotally, one may be impressed by stories of older athletes such as golfer Tom Watson, swimmer Dana Torres, and football quarterback Brett Favre, who continue to compete on the biggest competitive stages against far younger peers, winning medals or vying for prestigious championships. Evidence shows that contemporary sporting achievements by certain middle- and older-aged athletes far surpass similarly-aged peers from past decades, and in some cases, better Olympic performances of yesteryear (Ericsson, 1990). Moreover, stories abound in the popular press of today's aging athletes performing remarkably well over youthful standards; the number of older athletes accomplishing such feats appears to be growing, and stories commonly relate to athletes ranging in age from their 30s into their 90s. These stories challenge long-held notions of what can be expected from aging athletes. They also precipitate certain questions: How can we account for such skilled performance and expertise in older athletic domains? How might an examination of skilled older sport performers inform us about the nature of age-related processes that underscore instances of performance retention?

Without denying that aging effects occur even among exceptional aged performers, we submit that a study of these athletes—whom we refer to as *masters athletes*, can inform a better understanding of how aging effects are negotiated, and the psychosocial conditions related to aging persons' adaptive potential. They represent the physical and functional elite of an ever-aging society. Masters athletes continue to train systematically for, and compete in, various sport disciplines well beyond the typical age of peak performance. Masters sport usually begins at age 35 (although it varies depending on sport), and participants older than 55 are referred to as seniors athletes. Masters athletes typically acknowledge that they engage in practice to prepare themselves for a competitive sport event. Events occur at regional to international levels of competition, and usually require formal registration of some type to local jamborees or tournaments, adult leagues, inclusive and recreationally competitive events called *games*, or more exclusive competitive *championships*. Notably, masters have a unique motivation to do sport at life stages when most others either have dropped out, are under-committed to sport, or are unable to commit because social circumstances and life demands constrain such opportunities.

The purpose of this chapter is to review empirical research and emerging lines of inquiry pertaining to this sporting cohort. We discuss the mechanisms by which aging sport performers manage to retain performance, including the characteristics of sport involvement and the remarkably extensive investment in training required for preserving high levels of skill. We present perspectives on how motives and commitment serve to perpetuate sport involvement. While reviewing relevant research, we attempt to integrate avenues for future research and applied implications of results throughout the chapter. As a point of departure, we begin by reviewing research that documents patterns of age-related performance decline among aging athletes; these studies afford evidence of performance retention with advancing age and offer insight into how sustained sport training over the years tempers the expected rates of decline. We restrict our review to works that have appraised patterns for sport performance generally (and not simply physiological indices), thereby acknowledging that sport performance is a product of multifaceted components (including cognitive elements) and is greater than the sum of physiological capacities.

Trends for Age-Related Decline in Sport Performance

A collection of studies has explored age trends in an attempt to determine expected (or normal) rates of decline among aging sport populations, and how individual, task, or societal factors might influence rates (see Stones, 2009, for a review). Across studies, Stones noted that performance decline becomes accelerated with age, is greater for females, is greater for longer (endurance) than shorter distance events within any sport, and is greater for events with higher peak power costs. Overall, there is greater variability in rates of decline with increasing age. Ericsson (1990) identified several important performance trends associated with aging, which have since been replicated. First, there are consistent decrements in peak performance with age, which appear linear for younger elite masters athletes and become increasingly larger (or exponentially accelerated) for athletes over 60–65 years of age (e.g., Reaburn & Dascombe, 2008). Similar trends occur with seniors athletes, although accelerated decline in this latter group of less competitively serious and less-skilled athletes may emerge later, around age 75 (e.g., Wright & Perricelli, 2008). Second, performance data for record holders in any cohort appear to show less pronounced decline compared to rates obtained for a collection of participants from the same cohort, and this is especially the case among the oldest age groups. Third, the mean age of peak performance occurs between 20–30 years but differs systematically depending on the event or task factors. Performance peaks at later ages and is more likely retained with age for sport tasks demanding motor accuracy rather than peak power (e.g., driving for accuracy, or putting skill in golf vs. driving for distance; Baker, Deakin, Horton, & Pearce, 2007), and sport tasks demanding endurance compared to power costs (e.g., distance vs. sprint swimming; Schulz & Curnow, 1988). Tasks reflecting cognitive-motor or decision-making aspects, which rely on experience, knowledge, and strategy (e.g., baseball batters' skill in drawing walks) are more likely to be retained than are tasks representing physiological/power aspects (e.g., hitting and base running performance; Bradbury, 2009).

To this point, we have primarily discussed trends derived from cross-sectional data. Cross-sectional data are typically taken from archived records such that the performance of athletes of different ages is compared at a particular point in time and no two points in a dataset reflect the same individual. Due to an absence of within-person training effects, cross-sectional masters' data therefore are believed to represent normative rates of age-decline in a performance for a particular cohort. Ericsson (1990) noted that cross-sectional studies yield a different pattern of age-related decline than that from longitudinal studies, an observation also noted by Stones (2009), who found that decline is consistently greater with cross-sectional data than with longitudinal data. This is important, because longitudinal data are hypothesized to reflect within-participant experiences and training effects over time, and comparisons of cross-sectional and longitudinal data using similarly matched athletic cohorts have been advocated as a means to isolate how within-subject experiences and training influence age-decline (Starkes, Weir, & Young, 2003; Stones & Kozma, 1982).

Comparing Cross-Sectional and Longitudinal Trends

In a seminal study of elite Canadian track-and-field athletes aged 40–74 years, the mean yearly performance decline for cross-sectional data was 1.58%, compared to a longitudinal decline of 0.76% (Stones & Kozma, 1982). More recent studies employed age-on-performance regressions, guided by the proposition that quadratic β coefficients arising from separate second-order polynomial models

for cross-sectional and longitudinal data can be used to interpret whether training moderates age-decline. Hypothetically, moderation is supported when longitudinal data demonstrate non-significant or attenuated quadratic components (which indicate accelerated decline with age) compared to cross-sectional data (Starkes, Weir, Singh, Hodges, & Kerr, 1999; Starkes et al., 2003; see Figure 26.1). Collectively, inspection of the regression results for longitudinal samples in 11 of the 16 comparative analyses in track and field (Starkes et al., 1999; Young & Starkes, 2005; Analysis 2 in Young, Weir, Starkes, & Medic, 2008) and swimming (Weir, Kerr, Hodges, McKay, & Starkes, 2002) supports this hypothesis. Cross-sectional data consistently demonstrate significant quadratic β coefficients, with weights ranging from $\beta = .01$ to .50. Longitudinal analyses less frequently demonstrate significant quadratic coefficients, but when they have, values ranged from $\beta = .01$ to .08. On the whole, cross-sectional samples representing normal trends show stronger evidence for accelerated age-related decline, providing evidence that continuously trained cohorts enjoy moderated age-decline trends (i.e., better performance retention). Authors have prominently discussed features of career-span training to explain comparatively tempered decline

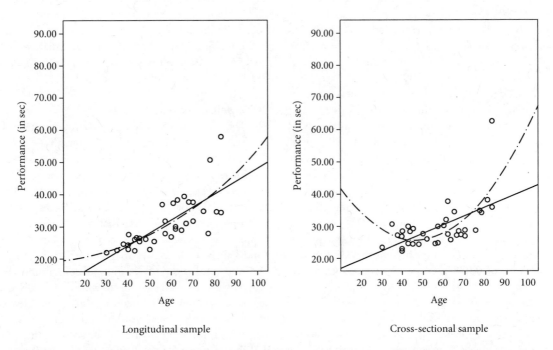

Longitudinal sample   Cross-sectional sample

Figure 26.1 A comparison of age-decline patterns for 200 m running performance from Young, Weir, Starkes, and Medic (2008) shows more accelerated quadratic decline (*broken line*) for the cross-sectional sample compared to the longitudinal sample. The quadratic decline curve is nonsignificant for the longitudinal sample, which is instead best represented by a linear rate of decline (*solid line*).

for longitudinal data, however, other factors associated with immersion in the sport, such as recent historical trends giving older adults increasing access to coaching and available competitive programs over the long term, especially among older age groups (e.g., over age 50), have been attributed as well.

Although methodological rigor has improved in recent studies (see Fairbrother, 2007; Young, Weir, et al., 2008), Stones (2009) encouraged greater analytic rigor by recommending the future use of mixed linear modeling to address across-athlete (i.e., cross-sectional) effects and within-athlete (i.e., longitudinal) effects within the same dataset. Future research would also offer a more reliable examination of practice effects if analyses considered individual differences in age *and* lifespan training data to explain performance. This would remedy a major limitation to date since, up to now, researchers have generally *inferred* a moderating role of training on age-decline based on the assumption that highly active longitudinal samples had indeed engaged in high practice volumes over time.

Finally, another approach to inferring the role of continued sport involvement for the retention of aging performance has involved the comparison of masters performance trends against standard biomarkers of aging. According to estimates from wide-ranging biological indices, Bortz (1997) estimated that a general rate for the aging process in normative (non-athletic) populations is 2% per year. In contrast, sport performance declines at only 0.5% per year from age 35 to 70 based on cross-sectional data taken from archived national masters records (Bortz & Bortz, 1996), and this rate might be considered the standard rate of decline among fit aging athletes. Insomuch as strenuous sporting events are subtended by most of the major body systems and are therefore rate-limited by them all, investigators contended that no supporting system could decline faster than this rate. Furthermore, when performance decline rates are derived longitudinally for continuously involved aging athletes, decrements are far less than this 0.5% standard annual decline rate. For example, long-time professional golfers yielded a mean annual decline in performance of 0.07% between 35 and 49 years, and 0.25% for ages 51 to 60 (Baker, Horton, Pearce, & Deakin, 2005). Based on longitudinal career statistics for 96 professional golfers from peak age until 50 years, mean annual decline rates for scoring average, driving distance, driving accuracy, greens in regulation, and putts per round all ranged from no significant decline to 0.36%, indicating moderated age effects (Baker, Deakin, Horton, & Pearce, 2007). Investigators concluded that golfers' modest performance retention reflected the inherently elite capabilities of these golfers, but importantly, their continued immersion in the sport and practice that they maintained over decades.

In sum, the distinction between what can be inferred from masters' cross-sectional and longitudinal data is important because it allows the influence of continued sport training on age-related decline to be isolated and examined. Evidence largely points to a moderating effect of continuous training by masters athletes on age-related performance decline. Moderation suggests that performance is being retained into the middle and older ages among exceptional sport performers.

Mechanisms for Retention of Skilled Performance in Older Athletes

Whereas the prior section discussed trends for age and sport performance, this section addresses potential mechanisms that may explain how middle- and older-aged athletes retain high levels of skilled performance that seem to fly in the face of expected age-related decline. Literature in this regard is framed within the sport expertise approach, the scientific study of inter-individual differences associated with expert performance, and a field that is influenced by psychomotor researchers who subscribe to an information processing approach to explain experts' decisions and behavior (see Starkes & Ericsson, 2003). We present three specific explanations for retention: the *compensatory*, *selective maintenance*, and *preserved differentiation* accounts.

Compensation Explanation

The compensatory explanation contends that it is possible for overall performance to remain relatively stable with age, despite declines in some aspects of functioning, due to increased reliance on other aspects of functioning that have increased or become more refined (Baltes, 1987; Baltes & Baltes, 1990). This perspective recognizes that development, even among aging populations, can entail both losses and gains; furthermore, that performance is multifaceted and is the net product of several underlying/constituent skills, some of which may decline while others remain refined or evolve in nature. As an analogy, researchers examining the aging of intelligence captured the essence of the account this way. With age, two systems of intelligence are differentiated: knowledge-free fluid mechanics, and knowledge-rich crystallized pragmatics (see Horn, 1982).

As the capacity for high-level performance in the mechanics of intelligence (e.g., reaction time, recall from short-term memory) is reduced with age, the pragmatics of intelligence (e.g., forms of procedural and declarative knowledge, or strategies like mnemonics) can continue to evolve, thus allowing individuals to maintain efficacy, but only in the select domain in which they have been immersed and for which they have amassed knowledge. In this manner, evolved "pragmatics" compensate for slowing "mechanics" in a very context-specific fashion.

Evidence of such compensation is reported in two classic studies with typists and chess players. Salthouse (1984) found that expert typists' speeded performance remained virtually unchanged across the adult lifespan, in spite of the fact that tests for general processing (e.g., finger tapping rate, choice reaction time) demonstrated slowing with age. Older experts maintained strong typing performance by increasing their eye–hand span, and this unique mechanism of "advance preview" of the to-be-transcribed text afforded greater anticipation of impending characters. Charness (1981) found that experts' chess moves did not diminish in quality with advancing age. Despite the fact that older experts engaged in a less extensive cognitive search to find a candidate move, they selected equally optimal moves in the same amount of time because they dispensed with the redundancies of a verification phase used by younger experts. This finding is consistent with the notion that older adults maintain performance by effectively reducing the complexity of a decision task—in the case of older chess experts, they perform as well as younger players by making decisions in a different manner, perhaps by using a heuristic that allows them to use a smaller set of information variables better than their younger peers. In each of the aforementioned studies, the continued domain-specific experiences of aging typists and chess players were advocated as the means by which individuals acquired compensatory mechanisms.

Given that sport performance is comprised of physiological and strength components, but also several psychomotor constituent skills that are specific to the sport domain in question (e.g., perceptual detection, speeded diagnosis of game play characteristics, anticipatory decision-making, and strategy use based on probabilities), it is possible that functioning on these latter sport-specific perceptual-motor processing skills may compensate for the expected slowing on physiological/strength components. Whereas "advance preview" and arresting the decision verification phase were important, respectively, for older skilled typists and chess players to keep pace with the young, researchers have only begun to examine the proposition that masters athletes require equally, if not more, attuned perceptual anticipation processes to perform at levels similar to their younger peers. An example of this is an exploratory study of five age groups of elite handball goaltenders, in which researchers used eye-tracking and temporal occlusion methods to examine defensive responses to an oncoming shooter (Schörer & Baker, 2009). Senior (M age = 47 years) goaltenders demonstrated equal reaction quality to younger adult (M = 27 years) goalies, and, although they were perceptually similar with respect to eye fixations, seniors appeared to initiate movements earlier than young adult elites. Trends suggested possibly more efficient response selection by seniors, although reliable conclusions were limited by small sample sizes. Pesce, Cereatti, Casella, Baldari, and Capranica (2007) contrasted experienced orienteers and non-athletes, age-matched in their mid-60s, on laboratory tasks that simulated orienteering demands. Investigators contended that experienced orienteers had adapted compensatory mechanisms related to attentional flexibility, and these effects were domain-specific and related to their extensive practice in the sport. Specifically, orienteers who were under time pressure were able to "zoom in" on local features of a target and react quickly when making a decision, despite incongruent pre-trial cues (i.e., when they were cued for global features and needed to make a decision on local features of a stimulus display), whereas non-athletes suffered significant costs in responding due to incongruent cuing and were therefore much slower to react. Investigators suggested that experienced orienteers may have developed a new skill to strategically modulate automatic attentional processes, which helps them during orientation competition when they must rapidly shift attention between global (e.g., features of the broader landscape, features on the map) and local features (e.g., specific items on the map).

The age-related processes of national-level golf putters have been investigated in a series of studies (see Molander & Bäckman, 1996). Findings show that putters in their 50s generally perform as well as their counterparts in their 20s and that older performers likely accomplish this with putting-specific compensatory skills related to diagnostics (i.e., reading the green) and decisions (e.g., stance and shot direction) that counteract age-related functional decline. Results suggest, interestingly, that compensatory mechanisms negate age differences only under relatively relaxed performance conditions, and that compensatory mechanisms may not function as well for older skilled putters when they perform when inundated with cognitive "distractions" (e.g., background noise competing for attentional resources) and conditions of high arousal, which interrupt their selective attention mechanisms and memory for diagnostic elements related to the putting task (also see Chapter 6, this volume, for attention degradation under conditions of high anxiety). Their findings do not deny the notion of compensation, but rather suggest that compensation may contribute less to aged sport performance under more stressful competitive conditions.

The use of the psychomotor expertise paradigm to investigate the skilled information processing mechanisms that allow older experts to retain exceptional performance is still in its infancy. The field is ripe for future research, and the prospects are stimulating. Consider, for example, the notion that an aging National Hockey League hockey defenseman may react equally well as younger players to oncoming attackers because he can read the play earlier and/or make more accurate decisions regarding trajectories to intercept an attacker, despite having slower foot speed and less accelerative power in general. In this case, compensation would involve unconscious processing mechanisms. There is also the notion, however, that older experts consciously compensate by invoking strategies to maximize their performance—this is referred to as the *selective optimization with compensation* principle (Baltes, 1987). Baltes proposed that, as individuals age, to remain expert, they must *select* fewer domains/tasks in which they wish to be highly efficacious because of a restriction in the range of tasks for which an individual can demonstrate adaptation to aging constraints. The example of an aging expert pianist choosing to focus his performance repertoire on a smaller number of pieces, or the aging actor who elects for shorter filmed performances involving subtler dramatic interpretations rather than full-length plays, are suitable illustrations, as is the marathon runner who forfeits other activities to almost exclusively focus her investment of time on running.

Optimization refers to the view that people engage in behaviors to strategically enrich their adaptive capacities and to maximize their performance on chosen tasks. The pianist who chooses to practice more often on a smaller number of pieces and the athlete who strategically chooses to invest in only the most relevant practice activities (e.g., deliberate practice), help to illustrate this principle. The marathoner who increases her knowledge about optimizing conditions, such as the influence of daily rhythms or dieting, is also pursuing optimization. With respect to specific *conscious compensation* strategies, examples include an older expert pianist slowing down his speed of playing prior to fast movements in order to produce a contrast that enhances the impression of speed in the fast movements. For the older marathoner, it may be using cold tank immersion to regenerate following workouts, or buying certain shoes to avoid injury. Experts who maintain superior aged performance likely enact elements of selection, optimization, and compensation in combination and in a highly personalized fashion. Langley and Knight (1999) documented how one older elite tennis player chose to maximize personal sporting success as he aged. Specifically, he focused efforts on tennis rather than other peripheral sports (selection), he searched out strong doubles partners and began using an oversized racquet (optimization), and, finally, he joined a new tennis club with a softer playing surface to reduce wear on his body, used lobs instead of backhand drives when under pressure during game play, and set a more intermittent competitive schedule to keep himself prepared to play at his best (compensation). Future research employing similar narrative approaches to understand aspects of selective optimization and compensation is essential; these efforts might uncover the richness of strategies that are utilized by exceptional aging performers and which may be sport-specific and highly personal in nature. Studies that catalogue how sports people or performers in music, dance, or the arts conquer the weaknesses of aging are important, so that accounts are not derived anecdotally from remarks in the press or from biographical accounts, but rather have empirical and conceptual grounding.

Selective Maintenance Explanation

Like compensation, this account contends that pronounced age-decline in performance results from insufficient practice and that individuals need to sustain appropriate amounts of domain-specific (or "deliberate") practice for superior performance to be maintained (Ericsson, 2000; Krampe & Ericsson, 1996). Provided that deliberate practice persists, this account claims that older experts will use the *same* domain-specific skill mechanisms to process information *in the same way* as younger experts (e.g., Morrow, Leirer, Altieri, & Fitzsimmons, 1994), unlike compensation, which advocates older experts acquiring *new* skills to offset decline in other areas. According to this explanation, skilled performance is retained into older ages when individuals accumulate great amounts of deliberate practice early in a career (prior to expected age-slowing), then sustain the specificity, intensity, and volume of practice as they age (beyond onset of "normal" age-decline).

To examine the role of deliberate practice for maintaining cognitive-motor skills, Krampe and Ericsson (1996) tested four groups of pianists (young/old amateurs, young/old experts) on general processing speed tasks and piano playing tasks. Amateurs and experts both showed large age-related decline on general tasks. Although older experts showed slower general processing speed, they were reliably better than young amateurs and still comparable to the younger experts for most piano tasks. Individual differences in piano performance were strongly accounted for by deliberate practice accumulated during career-long training, with these practice data significantly reducing the unique effects attributed to age in hierarchical regression models. Deliberate practice data during the past 10 years explained virtually all age-related differences in piano performance among experts (between 31% and 40%), compared to less than 2% for age. In contrast, age uniquely accounted for 32–39% of piano performance among young and old amateurs, with 2–3% explained by practice. Thus, for experts compared to amateurs, evidence of age-related decline was negligible after controlling for practice. Investigators attributed this to the fact that older experts (*M* = 60 years) had engaged in more deliberate training compared to novices at each period of their careers, but particularly in the most recent 10 years.

Young, Medic, Weir, and Starkes (2008) examined the contributions of training and age to the explanation of elite middle-aged running performance. Results showed that ongoing training data accounted for performance better than age, and when practice and age data were combined in the same model, ongoing running practice (28%) explained more performance variance than did age (15%). Findings were similarly replicated using training amounts from past periods in a career, in that the predictive power of a model based on past cumulative running training was stronger than one based solely on age. Although running performance slows with age overall, the reduction of age-related variance in performance by practice variables supports the selective maintenance account.

Although selective maintenance and compensatory perspectives take different positions on whether young and old experts share the same skilled processing mechanisms, both perspectives on performance retention are experiential in nature, leading Baker and Schörer (2009) to suggest that they might be better integrated in future research. To this end, future work comparing young/old and expert/novice groups should use criterion tasks that validly capture underlying skills necessary for expert performance in a sport (Ericsson, 2000), including tests of near-maximal levels of cognitive skill (Baltes & Baltes, 1990). These skill tasks should mimic domain-specific decision-making demands, with information presented in the ecologically valid context for which participants continue to have a lot of experience; age-related differences are typically minimized when skill tasks are presented in this manner (Walker, Fain, Fisk, & McGuire, 1997). Furthermore, the same repertoire of skill tests should be presented to different cross-sectional age cohorts—this might uncover whether expert/novice differences involve the same (supporting selective maintenance) or different processing mechanisms (supporting compensation) as a function of age. Second, researchers might employ methods to collect reliable and valid retrospectively recalled life-long practice data, which can then be submitted to analyses to explain performance on skill tasks; most compensation studies have not done this, instead subscribing to group (class) comparisons in the absence of individual deliberate practice data. Analyses that inspect practice by life-stage interactions will help determine whether training during particular career periods is more important for retention than during others (Hodges, Kerr, Starkes, Weir, & Nananidou, 2004). Full affirmation of the selective maintenance account relies on demonstrable contributions of practice from various life stages, yet evidence attesting to the contribution of cumulative practice from earlier life stages is lacking compared to contributions from the most recent stages of lifespan training (Krampe & Ericsson, 1996; Young, Medic, Weir, et al., 2008).

Preserved Differentiation Account

Some have speculated that blind adherence to experiential explanations is oversimplified. For example, Baker and Schörer (2009, p. 74) commented that "simple maintenance of training does not seem enough to stave off age-related declines in some areas" and Horton, Baker, and Schörer (2008) questioned whether individual factors influence the capacity to sustain voluminous training, to accommodate wear-related degradations, and to recuperate. Many studies demonstrate a selection effect by including masters athletes who have been uninjured and who have been able to sustain training (Young, Medic, Weir, et al., 2008). If such individual factors were proven to be stable and inherent capacities, they would be aligned with the primary tenet of the *preserved differentiation* account. Also called the "general factor" account, it asserts that fixed capacities predispose certain individuals toward exceptional performance (Salthouse, Babcock, Skovronek, Mitchell, & Palmon, 1990). Unlike the prior two accounts that tied expertise to the acquisition of "software" skills, it hypothesizes that aged experts have always had superior hardware components or abilities, that these abilities are fixed, that they existed prior to the development of expertise in the domain, and that they account for the superior performance at every stage in the expert's career. If one subscribes to a general slowing phenomenon in which all persons suffer age-decline at a similar rate, then those individuals who possessed higher indices for pertinent requisite abilities before age-related slowing would always remain superior to less-endowed peers across the lifespan; in this manner, the ability/capacity differentials underscoring expertise are preserved. Age effects are independent of experience, and older experts excel because of a selection bias for general processing abilities.

Contrary to this account, research from diverse fields shows that expertise is manifested with a high degree of domain-specificity; that is, an expert's advantage appears for criterion tests that reflect the structure or context of a particular domain, and this advantage disappears on tests that are out of context (see Ericsson, Charness, Feltovich, & Hoffmann, 2006). As a corollary, studies have found that abilities initially thought to be fixed explain significantly less performance variance on criterion tasks over time, with this variance increasingly assumed by within-task factors relating to domain-specific experience (e.g., Fleishman & Rich, 1963). Similarly, correlations between general psychometric abilities (e.g., IQ) and occupational performance weakens the longer one has been involved in the domain (Krampe & Charness, 2006). Preserved differentiation is further challenged by the fact that age differences are minimized when criterion tests reflect content with which aging persons are highly familiar, and when information is presented in an enriched manner that is faithful to the domain for which they have continued experience (Fisk & Kirlik,

1996). Where evidence for preserved differentiation is found, protocol has not necessarily reflected these characteristics (Salthouse et al., 1990). On the whole, evidence supports the contribution of experiential factors toward skilled older performance more so than preserved abilities. Consequently, it is important to better understand the domain-specific activities in which experts need to engage in order to maintain a high level of achievement.

What Is It About Training That Is Important for Retention of Skilled Performance?

In this section, we discuss a small body of work pertaining to masters athletes' training to elucidate aspects that might be particularly salient for retention, including extent, continuity, types of practice, specificity and variety of involvement, and potentially evolving microstructures of practice with age. To illustrate, most studies on masters athletes report extensive weekly training amounts ranging from 5 to 11 hours per week, with regional-level (e.g., Weir et al., 2002) and international-level competitors (e.g., Young & Medic, 2011a) averaging on the lower and upper ends of this range, respectively. Data are commonly skewed, and it is not uncommon to find as much as 20% of international-level masters swimming and track-and-field samples in their 50s with weekly training values surpassing 16 hours (e.g., Young & Medic, 2011b). From a lifespan perspective, average training amounts do typically decline for each subsequent stage of life, perhaps reflecting compromised trainability, health considerations, or the need for greater recuperation time between bouts of practice, or inadequate time for training due to other competing roles and duties in life. Still, exceptional older competitors report extensive involvement; for example, national-level Senior Olympians (*M* age = 67 years) reported 54 minutes of aerobic training daily, four times per week, complemented by 14 minutes of anaerobic training, 2 days per week (Smith & Storandt, 1997). In terms of continuity, national-level masters runners train 50 weeks per year (Young, Medic, Weir, et al., 2008) and often train for more than 15 years consecutively during the middle decades of life (Young & Starkes, 2005). National-level Masters Games competitors have participated in sport on average for 33 out of 48 years of their life (Hodge, Allen, & Smellie, 2008). Continuous involvement is critical for gradually building up the amount of training that can be accommodated without burnout or injury, building fitness, acquiring and refining mechanisms, and optimizing performance. This practice advantage characterizing elite masters performers can appear in the 30s (Baker, Côté, & Deakin, 2006) but is likely pronounced as masters athletes age. For example, a sample of national-level 10 km runners in their 50s had, on average, accumulated more than 93,000 km of lifelong running training (Young, Medic, Weir, et al., 2008).

Research identifies deliberate practice (Ericsson, Krampe, & Tesch-Römer, 1993) as the form of training required to maintain adaptive fitness and retain performance during middle and older adulthood (Ericsson, 2000). By definition, deliberate practice is highly specific to the domain. A complementary notion exists, however, that less specific activity—akin to cross-training—either in the form of different sports, fitness, or vigorous active leisure pursuits, may also help to preserve performance with advancing age. Many older athletes do at least one other sport event besides their primary activity (Smith & Storandt, 1997), suggesting a strategically diversified "sampling" approach to sport participation. Shuttling between different but related competitive activities may be important to circumvent wear-and-tear, to circumvent seasonal barriers to participation in certain climates, and to buoy motivation over time, while at the same time capitalizing on transfer of skill mechanisms or common fitness attributes between related activities. Future research is necessary to determine the instrumentality of such an approach among middle- and older-aged athletes.

As an additional consideration beyond sheer training amounts, Starkes et al. (2003) contended that one must consider athletes' relative investment in the constituent activities of their training repertoire and how this *microstructure* changes as a function of age and expertise. They detailed one longitudinal case study to show how a present-day 69-year-old world record holder in distance running changed his training over the past 25 years in order to increasingly "narrow" the scope of training activities to focus on the most pertinent activities for performance improvement as he aged. This narrowing of practice is not apparent to the same extent in cross-sectional studies of older sport experts nor is it evident in younger experts. Such strategic evolutions may be necessary to foster a more efficient use of overall dwindling training time, to minimize lost training time due to injury (Horton et al., 2008), to maintain continuity, and to avoid doldrums associated with the most common timeframe for motivational lapses among masters athletes—that is, after

an injury (Medic, Starkes, Young, Weir, & Giajnorio, 2005a). Future research that focuses on the microstructure of practice and the training regimens of exceptional older performers, particularly how they change at different life stages, may provide insight into what is possible for athletes as they age. Do elite aging athletes achieve superior status because they consciously evolve their microstructure to focus on the most pertinent activities for improving performance? That is, do they compensate by maximizing their adaptive fitness based on one or a few select activities? If so, do elite aging performers feel compelled to make such changes due to immutable age-related processes that compromise trainability? Finally, might masters athletes alter their training patterns because they are motivated to make practice less effortful and more enjoyable, by opting for the comfort zone afforded by practice on already well-learned skills, rather than expending more effort to refine unstable skills? If evidence attests to this latter notion, then the trainability and possible preservative influence of practice for older elite athletes may still remain underestimated, especially considering that deliberate practice should be effortful and relatively less enjoyable even as it evolves.

The extensive training that characterizes exceptional masters performers is not accomplished easily, especially considering the taxing nature of such activities and the negotiations of competing life demands and responsibilities that must be accomplished in order to find the time and energy to invest in voluminous practice (Hastings, Kurth, & Meyer, 1989). With this in mind, another valuable area of inquiry is to better understand the psychosocial conditions that facilitate the motivation for performing as a masters athlete, but more importantly, for fostering the commitment that appears critical for sustaining the many years of uninterrupted practice, the shorter off-season periods, and the higher weekly practice amounts required for preserving expertise with advancing age. Lessons learned about the quantities and quality of practice needed to retain expertise, and how one maintains the resolve to undergo such training, are important for understanding superior aged performance in any domain, be it sport, music, chess, or dance.

Older Sport Performers and Motivation Across the Lifespan

In light of the fact that masters and seniors athletes participate in sport at life stages when the majority of the population has either dropped-out, failed to re-engage, or remains under-committed, aging sport performers offer a unique opportunity for researchers to better understand competitive motivations across the lifespan. In this section, we consider how the exceptional continuity of training and involvement that characterizes elite aging sport performers might be related to motives. We concern ourselves with questions such as why some middle- to older-aged athletes remain particularly motivated to train and perform competitively, and what motivates these athletes to train harder or longer. We examine the multidimensional nature of motivation by focusing our discussion on four theoretical frameworks, including *achievement goal theory* (Nicholls, 1992), *self-determination theory* (Ryan & Deci, 2000), the *passion model* (Vallerand et al., 2003), and the *sport commitment model* (Scanlan, Russell, Beals, & Scanlan, 2003). Throughout, we highlight opportunities for future research and recommend applied strategies that can be used to favorably start and maintain sport involvement throughout life, as well as ways to optimize the sport performance of middle- to older-aged athletes.

Achievement Goals of Masters Athletes

Research suggests that masters athletes structure their training around one or two major annual competitions that they consider to be of highest importance. From a motivational perspective, this finding is valuable for at least two reasons. First, Hanranah and Gross (2005) have shown that masters athletes rate their performances (e.g., times) as more successful, and due to more internal and intentional causes, than their outcomes (e.g., rankings in competition). They also believe that their performances are a more direct result of their own internal resources and intentions than their ability to place. Research indicates that masters athletes report high levels of task goal orientation and moderate to low levels of ego goal orientation, findings that have been replicated among national-level track-and-field athletes (Medic, Starkes, Weir, Young, & Giajnorio, 2005b), national-level Seniors Olympians (Newton & Fry, 1998; Steinberg, Grieve, & Glass, 2000), and World Masters Games participants (Hodge et al., 2008). By definition, those with a high task goal orientation are more likely to see themselves as competent because they tend to judge their performance in self-referenced terms, and they are prone to feel autonomous, since they get more satisfaction from mastering a sport skill or improving their own personal standards of performance than from attaining a certain outcome relative to others. Seriously-minded adult marathoners who held mastery motives endorse personal challenge and improvement motives, and recognize mastery as a means to enhance personal self-esteem through sport (Ogles & Masters, 2003). On the other hand, masters athletes who are high in ego goal orientation are more focused on anticipated outcomes, such as rewards and acknowledgment, rather than on the inherent aspects of sport or task mastery. Together, these results suggest that focusing on performance to attain a certain time, for example, rather than focusing on outcomes like winning medals or defeating others, may give masters athletes more gratification and help them sustain their involvement in sport.

Self-Determination of Masters Athletes

A number of studies conducted to date have shown that masters athletes, regardless of the sport, have a variety of motives for continued participation, including enjoyment of the sport, opportunities to test skills, health and fitness concerns, social reasons, and extrinsic rewards (e.g., Medic et al., 2005a,b; Tantrum & Hodge, 1993). In addition, a number of studies have shown that masters athletes tend to be self-determined, reflecting the process of autonomy or choice in human functioning. For example, most masters athletes report engaging in sport primarily because of an inherent enjoyment and satisfaction derived from the activity and because the activity is valued and coherent with other aspects of the self. In addition, most participants have no intentions to stop participating in sport.

Studies have suggested that masters athletes' motives for sport differ across *age, relative age within a competitive age grouping,* and *gender.* For example, Dodd and Spinks (1995) found that older masters athletes (65+ years) place greater importance on extrinsic rewards, implying that they have a tendency to be attracted by external reinforcers such as athletic awards, medals, and social recognition for their achievements. Some research shows that older athletes (50+ years) may take on a broader health orientation and become more concerned about social affiliation, either while becoming no less competitive and still equally valuing motives related to social recognition of their achievements (Ogles & Masters, 2000), or while diminishing their competitive orientation and motives associated with extrinsic reinforcers (Steinberg et al., 2000). This said, there is evidence among masters athletes that more extrinsically-oriented motives are important. Medic, Starkes, Young, Weir, and Giajnorio (2004) compared motivational regulations of 64 masters runners (35–86 years old) to 35 university runners and found that masters runners were more externally regulated (e.g., extrinsic rewards were more important to them) and less amotivated. In a later study, a survey of 319 masters athletes from track and field and swimming determined that high levels of external regulation were the most important factor distinguishing those 65 years and older from other age groups (Medic, Starkes, Young, & Weir, 2005). Given that masters athletes can have a large age range, and the fact that the only existing cross-sectional studies suggest that their motives differ across age, it remains unclear whether motives for sport change over time. Future longitudinal research is needed to shed light on this issue.

Relative age in the context of masters sport is determined by an athlete's birth-year, and it refers to whether an athlete is relatively younger or relatively older than his or her opponents in the competitive registration groupings that characterize masters sports. A motivational strategy aimed at establishing a fair playing field in many masters sports is the use of competitive categories that generally progress in 5-year age intervals (e.g., 35–39, 40–44, 45–49, etc.). Nevertheless, Medic et al. (2005b) found that relatively older athletes in any 5-year registration category (e.g., 49-year-olds in the 45–49-year grouping) demonstrate higher amotivation scores than do relatively younger athletes (e.g., 45-year-olds) against whom they compete. Athletes who are amotivated typically feel incapable of succeeding, do not know the reasons why they are involved, and do not really think that their place is in the sport—a profile that leads to withdrawal from the activity. Thus, motivational reasons may explain why cross-sectional studies of registrations at masters competitive events consistently show strong bias in participation numbers favoring relatively younger athletes (see Medic, Starkes, Weir, Young, & Grove, 2009; Medic, Starkes, & Young, 2007), findings that have been replicated longitudinally in a 6-year sliding sample of American national-level masters swimmers (Medic, Young, & Medic, 2011). In this latter study, the odds of a masters swimmer competitively participating during the first constituent year of any 5-year age category was more than two times greater than the odds of that athlete returning to participate during the fifth constituent year. In other words, preliminary evidence suggests that masters swimmers tend to disengage from competition toward the end of an age cycle (e.g., at age 59 in a 55–59 year category). This study also found that about eight out of 10 swimmers who participated in the national championship event failed to return to the same competitive event at any point in the next 6 years. Thus, disruptions in competitive participation appear to be linked to relative age and may be underscored by motivational factors—these disruptions in competitive participation may threaten the continuously active lifestyle of masters sport participants. An area in which research is needed relates to an examination of the psychological, social, and physiological mechanisms that may explain such relative age effects in masters sports and the effects of such a phenomenon on the critical mass of participants longitudinally.

Results from studies that have examined masters athletes' motives as a function of gender suggest that females assign greater importance to intrinsic rewards, enjoyment, and health/fitness and less importance to extrinsic rewards, competition, and achievement goals (Gill, Williams, Dowd, Beaudoin, & Martin, 1996; Medic, 2009). Similarly, Tantrum and Hodge (1993) found that male masters swimmers rated winning, and females rated losing weight, respectively, as more important. Hastings, Kurth, Schloder, & Cyr (1995) found that female masters swimmers rated enjoyment, sociability, and fitness as more important than did male swimmers. Gender differences clearly exist, however, Young (2011) identified a future challenge to determine whether the genders differ broadly (e.g., Toepell, Guilmette, & Brooks, 2004, in which masters rowers showed gender differences on seven motives) or on select motives (e.g., Etnier, Sidman, & Hancock, 2004, in which adult soccer players showed gender differences on one motive). Generally, further research is needed to more definitively understand the factors that contribute to motivational differences between male and female, as well as between younger and older masters athletes. From an applied perspective, research that has examined competitive masters athletes' motives suggests that to gain the most benefits (e.g., performance, well-being, flow, creativity, self-esteem) from their participation in masters sports, motivational strategies for masters athletes need to be individualized, and personal reasons for participation require consideration.

Passion for Masters Sport

The passion model helps to explain psychological forces that lead individuals to sustain intense engagement in a passionate activity like sport (Vallerand et al., 2008). Passion is a strong inclination toward an activity that individuals love, find important, invest time and energy in, and consider an important part of their identity. People can have two types of passion toward an activity. *Obsessive passion* refers to the motivational force that pushes people toward activities and produces compulsions due to internal forces that seem to control them. For example, an athlete with an obsessive passion for running would report having no choice but to attend a scheduled running workout despite acknowledging other duties or priorities that remain neglected. *Harmonious passion*, on the other hand, refers to the motivational force that leads a person to engage in an activity willingly and produces a sense of volition and personal endorsement about pursuing the activity. For example, an athlete with harmonious passion would be able to put aside a running workout if the need arose and devote him- or herself to other necessary activities and interests.

One of the only studies on passion among masters athletes surveyed 138 (95 male; 43 female) national-level masters track-and-field athletes (Medic, Starkes, Weir et al., 2007). Results showed that masters athletes scores were very high for harmonious passion and moderate to low for obsessive passion. Masters athletes whose sport motives were autonomous (intrinsically motivated) and highly internalized (integrated within the individual's self) were those who also had high levels of harmonious passion, corresponding to a high sense of personal endorsement and volition for engaging in sport. For these athletes, sport involvement is likely to be in harmony with other aspects of their lives, but at the same time it does not overpower their identities and take over their personal lives. Findings further suggested that masters athletes whose sport motives were internalized into their identities by external agents (e.g., pressures from significant others) were those who had high levels of obsessive passion. These internal compulsions (e.g., feelings that one absolutely has to do sport) are likely to lead to guilt and/or anxiety if one is prevented from engaging in the activity, or to lead masters athletes to engage in sport activity even when they should not (e.g., when injured). With this internal pressure controlling their sport engagement, masters athletes who have high levels of obsessive passion may find it difficult to disengage from thinking about, and participating in, their sport. Masters athletes who have high levels of obsessive passion, when faced with demands to curtail or cease training and competition, will likely do one of two things: continue engaging in their sports despite unfavorable circumstances (e.g., overtraining syndrome, sport-related injuries), or consequently experience negative feelings similar to psychological withdrawal when they are prevented from participating in their sports. Future research is needed to determine the salience and conflicted nature of emotions arising when masters athletes with high levels of obsessive passion are prevented from doing their sport activity and whether consequences exclusively relate to the athlete or also impact significant others. Another possible area for research is whether obsessive passion interacts with age; for example, does obsessive passion cause more or less complications for the older athlete and their family, or is obsessive passion more likely to be accepted in younger athletes than in older ones? One applied implication of the findings to date is that, when working with obsessively passionate masters athletes, it may be important to reassess short- and long-term goals, to consider doing some cross-training and/or resting, to consider spending more time working on mental skills, and/or to consider reflecting on salient feelings surrounding one's sport experience in a training log.

Commitment to Masters Sport

The sport commitment model (Scanlan et al., 2003) is a framework that can be used to understand psychosocial factors underlying persistence in sport. Sport commitment is defined as a psychological state representing the desire and resolve to continue sport participation over time. According to the original model, sport commitment can be enhanced by higher enjoyment, personal investment, involvement opportunities, social support, and social constraints, whereas the attractiveness of alternative opportunities decreases an athlete's commitment. *Functional commitment* is a construct defined as the desire to continue sport involvement because of volitional feelings of choice, whereas a second construct, *obligatory commitment,* represents the resolve to continue involvement because one feels that one "has to" invest further. Different psychosocial factors are proposed to explain each of functional and obligatory commitment, respectively (Wilson et al., 2004).

Although most extant research on the model has been conducted in youth sport, recent efforts have been directed at understanding sport commitment of masters athletes. To date, studies on masters athletes that have examined influences on the two sport commitment types have been almost exclusively cross-sectional in nature, examining various samples of bowlers (Weir, Medic, Baker, & Starkes, 2008), marathon runners (Starkes, Medic, & Routledge, 2007), summer sport athletes at the regional level (Wigglesworth, Young, & Medic,

2010), golfers (Starkes et al., 2007) track-and-field athletes (Medic, Starkes, Young, & Weir, 2006) at the national level, and international-level swimmers (Young, Medic, Piamonte, Wigglesworth, & Grove, 2008) (see Table 26.1). One of the repeated findings is that masters athletes have high levels of functional commitment and moderate to low levels of obligatory commitment. Thus, they are committed to their sport mainly because they feel that they want to continue their participation, and, to a lesser extent, because they feel that they have to continue. This suggests that both types of commitment are relevant to masters athletes, but that functional commitment predominates. This is important because research has shown that functional commitment is likely healthier, more adaptive, and more likely to be positively related to persistent training and participation behavior (Carpenter & Coleman, 1998) and negatively related to burnout and dropout (Weiss & Weiss, 2006).

Using the proposed determinants, researchers have been able to predict between 48% and 85% of variance in masters' athletes functional commitment to sport. In each of the investigations, sport enjoyment/satisfaction was found to be the strongest predictor of functional commitment (see Table 26.1). Furthermore, perceptions of high investment of personal resources in sport have commonly predicted higher functional commitment of masters athletes. Anticipation of having enjoyable experiences as a result of future sport involvement and anticipation of special occasions arising from continued sport activity (i.e., involvement opportunities), as well as lower perceptions of other attractive alternatives besides sport (i.e., involvement alternatives), have also frequently predicted higher levels of functional sport commitment among more elite-level masters competitors. Finally, social support only proved to be related to increased feelings of wanting to continue sport among national-level masters golfers.

With respect to athletes' obligatory commitment, the various factors have predicted between 22% and 62% of variance. In each of the sports, levels of social constraints (i.e., high expectations

Table 26.1 Summary of variables from cross-sectional studies found to be predictive of masters athletes' functional and obligatory commitment to sport

	Regional Bowlers	Regional Summer Sports Athletes	National Golfers	National Marathon Runners	National Track-and-Field Athletes	International Swimmers
Functional commitment						
Enjoyment	+	+	+	+	+	+
Personal investment	+	+			+	+
Involvement opportunities				+	+	+
Involvement alternatives				−	−	−
Social support			+			
Obligatory commitment						
Social constraints	+	+	+	+	+	+
Social support			−		−	−
Enjoyment	+		+		+	
Personal investment	+	+				+
Involvement alternatives	+					+
Involvement opportunities						+

+, the determinant significantly and positively predicts the sport commitment dimension; −, the determinant significantly and negatively predicts the sport commitment dimension and pressure from significant others) were consistently the strongest predictors of high obligatory commitment. For masters athletes in golf, track and field, or swimming, significant others play an even more important role—when athletes from these sports perceive that their sport participation is not supported, their feelings that they have to continue participating in sport increase. In addition to being predictors of functional commitment, enjoyment and personal investment also have predicted obligatory commitment at times, depending on the sample in question. Finally, the obligatory commitment levels of masters swimmers and bowlers increased when these athletes reported greater perceptions of attractive activities besides their sport.

In the lone longitudinal study with masters athletes to date, Young, Piamonte, Grove, and Medic (2011) surveyed 190 international-level swimmers on two occasions, 1 year apart. Results demonstrated that 18% of variance in increases in obligatory commitment levels was explained by increases in personal investments and involvement alternatives, and decreases in social support. Thirty-nine percent of variance in increases in functional commitment levels was explained by increases in sport enjoyment and personal investments, however, age also significantly interacted with personal investments, involvement opportunities, and social constraints to predict changes in functional commitment. Specifically, increases in the amount of time, energy, and effort put into one's sport were positively related to functional commitment, but more pronouncedly as masters swimmers got older. Increases in involvement opportunities positively predicted changes in functional commitment for younger masters, but inversely predicted functional commitment among older cohorts. Finally, constraints from significant others were associated with increased resolve to continue sport among older masters and decreased resolve among younger masters. Although these longitudinal findings mostly complement findings obtained by cross-sectional studies and provide support for the efficacy of the model for capturing the dynamics of change in commitment types over time, the age-moderated findings are unique. With respect to the few prior studies on SCM and age, results showed that adult tennis players older than 45 years had higher commitment levels and lower levels of attractive alternate activities than did players aged 19–44 years (Casper & Stellino, 2008). In a study of regional-level Senior Games participants (55–74 years) (Young, Carey, & Medic, 2010), enjoyment and personal investment positively predicted

functional commitment, whereas increases in social constraints, personal investments, and involvement alternatives led to increases in obligatory commitment. Further evidence from this sample showed that functional commitment may be solely predicted by enjoyment in participants older than 65 years. Finally, emerging research indicates that mean levels for determinant constructs and commitment types vary by gender, but differently depending on the sample (Casper & Stellino, 2008; Wigglesworth et al., 2010; Wigglesworth, Young, Medic, & Grove, in press). Findings consistently suggest that males have higher obligatory commitment, and there is also evidence that males have lower functional commitment and enjoyment. Distinct regression analyses by gender have demonstrated that personal investment uniquely predicts both commitment types for international-level masters female swimmers (Wigglesworth et al., in press) and uniquely predicts functional commitment for female regional-level Seniors Games participants (Young et al., 2010).

Overall, the results of sport commitment studies with masters athletes suggest that differential patterns of determinants underlie each commitment dimension. These differential patterns of associations likely develop from heterogeneous experiences within different sports. One recurring finding, however, is that sport enjoyment seems to be an important determinant for both dimensions of commitment, especially functional commitment, and this is not surprising considering the voluntary nature of sporting activity. However, in terms of sport enjoyment's importance in predicting obligatory commitment, it could be that masters athletes feel that they have to continue participating in their sport in order to have the opportunity to experience something that they enjoy doing, which is participation in their sport. This finding is also in line with previous research from the youth setting that has consistently found that sport enjoyment is a major reason why athletes participate in sport, as well as with several previous studies that have demonstrated that sport enjoyment is positively related to personal effort, persistence, and future intentions to participate in sport. The concept of enjoyment has, however, been conceptualized as a *unidimensional* construct within the sport commitment literature. Such an approach is not entirely in line with the broader literature on sport motivation that advocates for a differentiated view of enjoyment or intrinsic motivation. Also, considering that multiple sources of enjoyment (Scanlan, Stein, & Ravizza,

1989) have been identified within youth sport settings, future studies may wish to examine greater differentiation between sources of enjoyment that may be applicable to understanding commitment issues in masters sport.

Social Influences on Masters Sport Involvement

In addition to individual motives that propel masters athletes to compete and engage in voluminous training amounts, social influences also play a large role in fostering extensive and persistent involvement. Socialization processes likely explain why athletes first become involved in masters sport, including why certain athletes re-engage in masters sport after a time away (Harada, 1994). A survey of over 450 masters athletes from track and field and swimming found that there were three common ways by which athletes entered masters sports (Medic et al., 2005a). First, many masters athletes had been socialized into competitive sport at a young age and maintained this activity throughout their lives; specifically, 49% of them were continuously involved in their sports since they were young, and 22% switched to their current sports from a different one. Another common means for entrance into masters sports was through social networks, which included recommendations from doctors (18%), friends (15%), family (10%), and coaches (8%). The final means of entering masters sport was through community recreational involvement as fans/coaches/officials (9%), after becoming members of community sport programs or local masters clubs (21%), and by learning of opportunities from the local media (9%).

Social influences serve to consolidate the identity of an athlete, especially as he or she becomes socially recognized and identifiable by others for his or her achievements and investments in sport (Stevenson, 2002). If an athlete's identity becomes inextricably defined by his or her sport involvement, that athlete will likely seek out further sport activity to maintain the coherency of this identity (Yair, 1992). Many masters athletes believe that sport offers them an opportunity for social recognition of achievement that cannot be found elsewhere, and, thus, they are committed to realizing such a benefit from their participation in sport (Dionigi & O'Flynn, 2007). In exercise contexts, social support in adults has been associated with sustained coping, behavioral persistence and greater adherence to physical activity. In light of relatively greater demands imposed by masters athletes' extensive sporting activity, the

role of social support might be further accentuated among this cohort compared to more recreational or leisure-oriented active adults. For example, Golding and Ungerleider (1991) discovered a positive association between perceived social support from friends and frequency of training among 50-year-old runners. National-level masters runners (M age = 57 years) who train with a coach reported a more adaptive motivational (i.e., high levels of intrinsic motivation, low levels of amotivation) and goal orientation (low ego orientation) profile (Medic, Young, Starkes, & Weir, 2012) than those without a coach, and these profiles typically benefit one's overall motivation and psychological well-being and predict sport persistence. Furthermore, 23% of national-level masters runners claim that "training in groups" is a strategy they use to overcome motivational lapses (Medic et al., 2005a).

The results from sport commitment research also point to the importance that significant others play with regards to aging athletes' involvement in sport. Specifically, results consistently suggest that social pressure and lack of support from significant others is associated with higher levels of obligatory commitment for masters athletes. To date, research has not frequently shown a predictive role for social support in explaining feelings of wanting to continue sport (see Table 26.1). Such findings might only relate specifically to masters athletes from individual sports (e.g., bowling, golf, marathon, and track and field), and future research is required to determine whether they generalize to team sports. Still, these findings intimate that individual factors, rather than social influences, are more important for wanting to continue sport, a notion consonant with findings from prior studies wherein masters runners demonstrated a preference for being alone, shaping family time around sport, and allowing training to consume "family time" (Barrell, Chamberlain, Evans, Holt, & Mackean, 1989; Yates, Shisslak, Allender, Crago, & Leehey, 1992).

Research has begun to identify critical social agents that influence masters' sport commitment. A survey of 424 international-level swimmers (M age = 54 years) found 11% and 39% of variance in functional and obligatory commitment, respectively, could be explained by a combination of social support and social constraint factors (Young & Medic, 2011a). Furthermore, for subsets of masters swimmers who reported a broad social network around them, the four most important agents for influencing sport commitment were one's spouse (or significant other), one's own children, training partners, and one's health professional. This suggests that sport programming interventions to retain a critical mass of elite participants over time might focus on ways to increase adaptive forms of social influence from these agents. Although swimmers' obligatory commitment levels were lower than functional commitment levels, they were predicted by perceived pressure from one's spouse and from training partners, such as the anticipated disapproval from these agents should they quit their sport. Endorsement of sport participation from one's physician, on the other hand, was associated with lower obligatory commitment. Pressure from one's children to continue in sport was a salient perception explaining both obligatory and functional commitment. Although literature suggests that obligatory commitment is not necessarily suited for promoting long-term involvement, investigators did propose that highly committed masters athletes might possibly reframe aspects of obligation in such a way that they are viewed through a functional lens. For example, they might reframe pressuring influences from their own children in a manner consistent with their own values and needs (e.g., the importance of pleasing and earning the approval of one's children, the importance of a sporting lifestyle) and is therefore consistent with a self-determined motivational profile (e.g., high levels of identified and integrated regulation). Finally, it is possible that future research might demonstrate that a different set of social agents or a certain social agent is heavily influential in promoting sport commitment for those masters swimmers who have a narrower social network, such as the 26% of the sample without children and the nearly 20% without a spouse.

Overall, the four theoretical models used to explain sport participation and commitment in masters-level sport suggest that masters athletes tend to be more task goal than ego goal oriented, highly autonomous in their decisions to pursue sport, and are driven by volitional constructs such as functional commitment and harmonious passion to continue in their sport. Such a motivational profile may explain their longstanding persistence and their motivational capacity to engage in a large amount of training and, specifically, the appropriate types of demanding training. The research also shows a dichotomous (or perhaps, a complementary) profile—masters athletes report lower yet relevant scores reflecting obligatory commitment and obsessive passion for their sport. Additionally, elite samples of masters athletes can be highly competitive, and certain subsets of masters athletes are either

externally regulated or motivated by the pursuit of extrinsic awards and social recognition. These findings inform about the strategies that can be used to keep masters athletes optimally motivated and committed. For example, sporting environments in which masters athletes train and compete need to: be individualized, so that they complement personal reasons and the specific needs for continuing to train and compete; emphasize training sessions and competitive events that are intrinsically motivating and enjoyable; emphasize the development of new skills and techniques; and provide high support and low pressure from significant others.

Conclusion and Future Directions

Whilst acknowledging the biological nature of human aging and increasing limits on the overall range of possibilities for exceptional performance in old age, Baltes and Baltes (1990, p. 27) stated that "the adaptive task of the aging individual is to select and concentrate on those domains that are high priority and that involve a convergence of environmental demands and individual motivations, skills, and biological capacity." By studying masters athletes, researchers have been able to discover an exceptional cohort that has selected and focused their energies and personal investments on sport activity in middle- and older ages of the lifespan. Sport—as a competitive pursuit and a venue for enjoying oneself, testing personal skills, gaining extrinsic rewards, social affiliation, and health—is a priority for masters athletes. This priority is understood when one considers that exceptional masters athletes typically choose to pursue excellence in one sport domain. This considerable priority can be further gleaned from the athletes' self-reported levels of passion and commitment, and from the voluminous amounts of time that they have devoted to sport activity for extended periods across their lifespan.

The research reviewed herein portrays a critical role for environmental demands in producing exceptional masters sport performers and for preserving high levels of performance over time. Despite potential differences in individual biological capacities that interact to influence masters athletes' adaptations to training and resilience to injury across time, most evidence from existing literature on masters athletes suggests an experiential explanation for their exceptional performance. Central to these explanations are the selective maintenance and compensatory accounts, which specify how deliberate, context-specific practice sustained over long periods of time refines information processing mechanisms responsible for elite performance. Although masters athletes show decreases in performance when measured on generic physical/physiological attributes with advancing age, these accounts contend that specialized perceptual-motor and cognitive mechanisms may evolve to substantially moderate or offset this slowing. These mechanisms—such as being able to read the field of play to anticipate moves earlier, or being able to know the probabilities of opponents' shot selections to pre-plan an early response—are "software skills" that masters athletes have developed and employ effectively. From a psychosocial perspective, it is possible that these athletes have benefited from "the formation and nurturance of social convoys" (Baltes & Baltes, 1990, p. 20) responsible for the socialization process that initially propelled them into masters sport and that continue to recognize them for their achievements and reinforce their sport identity.

Studies on the individual motivations of masters athletes for continued sport participation show heterogeneous reasons for sport involvement that are mostly characterized by high task goal orientation, self-determined motivation, functional commitment, and harmonious passion. Although future research is needed to further clarify motivational profiles and to explain longitudinal persistence in sport as a function of such profiles, it is clear that individual motivations are associated with exceptional instances of aged sport performance. Masters athletes are motivated to compete, and the expectation that one will compete at a future event engenders motivation to engage in systematic training over time; reciprocally, short-term motives to do one's sport may translate into longer-term competitive aspirations.

The study of masters athletes' trends for performance decline with advancing age in various sports is appealing and affords optimism, especially when one considers longitudinal data reflecting inherent training effects. Particular studies that have derived data from continuously active, more-elite masters athletes, who have reported involvement for long stretches of the lifespan while avoiding serious injury, provide strong evidence of moderated age-decline trends. In essence, these findings underscore the exceptional aging processes of masters athletes and their remarkable adaptive fitness in the face of expected decline. In sum, studies on masters athletes reflect a growing field that is ripe for future investigation. Questions relating to age-related processes, skill retention mechanisms, and motives for competition/training pertain to researchers from different perspectives (e.g., modeling, psychomotor expertise, social-cognitive) who, together, may continue to help us better understand masters sport performers and the conditions underlying their exceptional nature.

Acknowledgments

The writing of this chapter was supported by a Strategic Initiative Grant from the Social Sciences and Humanities Research Council of Canada and Sport Canada. The authors would like to thank Cassandra Sparks for her work on a secondary literature search and synthesis in support of this chapter.

References

Baker, J., Côté, J., & Deakin, J. (2006). Expertise in ultra-endurance triathletes early sport involvement, training structure, and the theory of deliberate practice. *Journal of Applied Sport Psychology, 17,* 64–78.

Baker, J., Deakin, J., Horton, S., & Pearce, G. W. (2007). Maintenance of skilled performance with age: A descriptive examination of professional golfers. *Journal of Aging and Physical Activity, 15,* 300–317.

Baker, J., Horton, S., Pearce, W., & Deakin, J. (2005). A longitudinal examination of performance decline in champion golfers. *High Ability Studies, 16,* 179–185.

Baker, J., & Schörer, J. (2009). Maintenance of skilled performance with age: Lessons from the Masters. In J. Baker, S. Horton, & P. Weir (Eds.), *The masters athlete: Understanding the role of sport and exercise in optimizing aging* (pp. 66–78). London: Routledge.

Baltes, P. B. (1987). Theoretical propositions of life-span developmental psychology: On the dynamics between growth and decline. *Developmental Psychology, 23,* 611–626.

Baltes, P. B., & Baltes, M. M. (1990). Psychological perspectives on successful aging: The model of selective optimization with compensation. In P. B. Baltes & M. M. Baltes (Eds.), *Successful aging: Perspectives from the behavioural sciences* (pp. 1–34). Cambridge, UK: Cambridge University Press.

Barrell, G., Chamberlain, A., Evans, J., Holt, T., & Mackean, J. (1989). Ideology and commitment in family life: A case study of runners. *Leisure Studies, 8,* 249–262.

Bortz, W. M. (1997). Geriatrics: The effect of time in medicine. *Western Journal of Medicine, 166,* 313–318.

Bortz, W., & Bortz, W. M. (1996). How fast do we age? Exercise performance over time as a biomarker. *Journal of Gerontology: Medical Sciences, 51,* 223–225.

Bradbury, J. C. (2009). Peak athletic performance and aging: Evidence from baseball. *Journal of Sports Sciences, 27,* 599–610.

Carpenter, P. J., & Coleman, R. (1998). A longitudinal study of elite youth cricketers' commitment. *International Journal of Sport Psychology, 29,* 195–210.

Casper, J. M., & Stellino, M. B. (2008). Demographic predictors of recreational tennis participants' sport commitment. *Journal of Park and Recreation Administration, 26,* 93–115.

Cerella, J. (1990). Aging and information processing rates in the elderly. In J. E. Birren & K. W. Schaie (Eds.), *Handbook of the psychology of aging* (3rd ed., pp. 201–221). San Diego, CA: Academic Press.

Charness, N. (1981). Aging and skilled problem solving. *Journal of Experimental Psychology: General, 110*, 21–38.

Dionigi, R. A., & O'Flynn, G. (2007). Performance discourses and old age: What does it mean to be an older athlete? *Sociology of Sport Journal, 24*, 359–377.

Dodd, J. R., & Spinks, W. L. (1995). Motivations to engage in masters sport. *ANZALS Leisure Research Series, 2*, 61–75.

Ericsson, K. A. (1990). Peak performance and age: An examination of peak performance in sports: In P. B. Baltes & M. M. Baltes (Eds.), *Successful aging: Perspectives from the behavioural sciences* (pp. 164–195). New York: Cambridge University Press.

Ericsson, K. A. (2000). How experts attain and maintain superior performance: Implications for the enhancement of skilled performance in older individuals. *Journal of Aging and Physical Activity, 8*, 366–372.

Ericsson, K. A., Charness, N., Feltovich, P. J., & Hoffmann, R. (2006). *Cambridge handbook of expertise and expert performance*. New York: Cambridge University Press.

Ericsson, K. A., Krampe, R. Th., & Tesch-Römer, C. (1993). The role of deliberate practice in the acquisition of expert performance. *Psychological Review, 100*, 363–406.

Etnier, J. L., Sidman, C. L., & Hancock, L. C., II. (2004). An examination of goal orientation profiles and motivation in adult team sport. *International Journal of Sport Psychology, 35*, 173–188.

Fairbrother, J. T. (2007). Prediction of 1500-m freestyle swimming times for older masters All-American swimmers. *Experimental Aging Research, 33*, 461–471.

Fisk, A. D., & Kirlik, A. (1996). Practical relevance and age-related research: Can theory advance without practice? In W. A. Rodgers, A. D. Fisk, & N. Walker (Eds.), *Aging and skilled performance: Advances in theory and application* (pp. 1–15). Mahwah, NJ: LEA.

Fleishman, E. A., & Rich, S. (1963). Role of kinesthetic and spatial-visual abilities in perceptual- motor learning. *Journal of Experimental Psychology, 66*, 6–11.

Gill, D., Williams, L., Dowd, D. A., Beaudoin, C. M., & Martin, J. J. (1996). Competitive orientations and motives of adult sport and exercise participants. *Journal of Sport Behavior, 19*, 307–318.

Golding, J. M., & Ungerleider, S. (1991). Social resources and mood among masters track and field athletes. *Journal of Applied Sport Psychology, 3*, 142–159.

Hanrahan, S. J., & Gross, J. B. (2005). Attributions and goal orientations in masters athletes: Performance versus outcome. *Revista de Psicologia del Deporte, 14*, 43–56.

Harada, M. (1994). Early and later life sport participation patterns among the active elderly in Japan. *Journal of Aging and Physical Activity, 2*, 105–114.

Hastings, D. W., Kurth, S. B., & Meyer, J. (1989). Competitive swimming careers through the life course. *Sociology of Sport Journal, 6*, 278–284.

Hastings, D. W., Kurth, S. B., Schloder, M., & Cyr, D. (1995). Reasons for participating in a serious leisure career: Comparison of Canadian and U.S. masters swimmers. *International Review for the Sociology of Sport, 30*, 101–119.

Henry, J. D., MacLeod, M. S., Phillips, L. H., & Crawford, J. R. (2004). A meta-analytic review of prospective memory and aging. *Psychology and Aging, 19*, 27–39.

Hodge, K., Allen, J. B., & Smellie, L. (2008). Motivation in Masters sport: Achievement and social goals. *Psychology of Sport and Exercise, 9*, 157–176.

Hodges, N. J., Kerr, T., Starkes, J. L, Weir, P. L., & Nananidou, A. (2004). Predicting performance times from deliberate practice hours for triathletes and swimmers: What, when and where is practice important? *Journal of Experimental Psychology: Applied, 10*, 219–237.

Horn, J. L. (1982). The theory of fluid and crystallized intelligence in relation to concepts of cognitive psychology and aging in adulthood. In F. I. M. Craik & S. E. Trehub (Eds.), *Aging and cognitive processes* (pp. 847–870). New York: Plenum Press.

Horton, S., Baker, J., & Schörer, J. (2008). Expertise and aging: Maintaining skills through the lifespan. *European Review of Aging and Physical Activity, 5*, 89–96.

Krampe, R. T., & Charness, N. (2006). Aging and expertise. In K. A. Ericsson, N. Charness, P. J. Feltovich, & R. Hoffmann (Eds.), *Cambridge handbook of expertise and expert performance* (pp. 723–742). New York: Cambridge University Press.

Krampe, R. T., & Ericsson, K. A. (1996). Maintaining excellence: Deliberate practice and elite performance in young and older pianists. *Journal of Experimental Psychology: General, 125*, 331–359.

Langley, D. J., & Knight, S. M. (1999). Continuity in sport participation as an adaptive strategy in the aging process: A lifespan narrative. *Journal of Aging and Physical Activity, 7*, 32–54.

Medic, N. (2009). Understanding masters athletes' motivation for sport. In J. Baker, S. Horton, & P. Weir (Eds.), *The masters athlete: Understanding the role of sport and exercise in optimizing aging* (pp. 105–121). London: Routledge.

Medic, N., Starkes, J. L., Weir, P. L., Young, B. W., & Grove, J. R. (2009). Relative age effect in masters sports: Replication and extension. *Research Quarterly for Exercise and Sport, 80*, 669–675.

Medic, N., Starkes, J. L., Weir, P. L., Young, B. W., Wilson, P., Mack, D. E., & Elferink-Gemser, M. (2007). *Do motives for sport predict sport commitment and passion for sport in a sample of highly skilled masters athletes?* Proceedings of the 3rd International Conference on Self-Determination Theory, Toronto, ON, Canada.

Medic, N., Starkes, J. L., & Young, B. W. (2007). Examining relative age effects on performance achievement and participation rates of masters athletes. *Journal of Sports Sciences, 25*, 1377–1384.

Medic, N., Starkes, J. L., Young, B. W., & Weir, P. L. (2005). Motivational differences of masters athletes participating in various track events. *Canadian Society for Psychomotor Learning and Sport Psychology Abstracts*, Niagara Falls, ON, Canada.

Medic, N., Starkes, J. L., Young, B. W., & Weir, P. L. (2006). Testing the sport commitment model with masters runners. *Journal of Sport and Exercise Psychology, 28*, s132–s133.

Medic, N., Starkes, J. L., Young, B. W., Weir, P. L., & Giajnorio, A. (2004). Motivational orientation of masters athletes: Comparison to young adult athletes. *Canadian Society for Psychomotor Learning and Sport Psychology Abstracts*, Saskatoon, SK, Canada.

Medic, N., Starkes, J. L., Young, B. W., Weir, P. L., & Giajnorio, A. (2005a). *Master athletes' motivation to train and compete: First order themes.* Proceedings of the International Society of Sport Psychology (ISSP) 11th World Congress of Sport Psychology, Sydney, Australia.

Medic, N., Starkes, J. L., Young, B. W., Weir, P. L., & Giajnorio, A. (2005b). *Multifaceted analyses of masters athletes' motives to continue training and competing*. Proceedings of the ISSP 11th World Congress of Sport Psychology, Sydney, Australia.

Medic, N., Young, B. W., & Medic, D. (2011). Participation-related relative age effects in Masters swimming: A 6-year retrospective longitudinal analysis. *Journal of Sports Sciences, 29*, 29–36.

Medic, N., Young, B. W., Starkes, J. L., & Weir, P. L. (2012). Relationship between having a coach and masters athletes' motivational regulations for sport and achievement goal orientations. *International Journal of Coaching Science, 6*, 65–79.

Molander, B., & Bäckman, L. (1996). Cognitive aging in a precision sport context. *European Psychologist, 1*, 166–179.

Morrow, D., Leirer, V., Altieri, P. & Fitzsimmons, C. (1994). When expertise reduces age differences in performance. *Psychology and Aging, 9*, 134–148.

Newton, M., & Fry, M. D. (1998). Senior Olympians' achievement goals and motivational responses. *Journal of Aging and Physical Activity, 6*, 256–270.

Nicholls, J. G. (1992). The general and the specific in the development and expression of achievement motivation. In G. C. Roberts (Ed.), *Motivation in sport and exercise* (pp. 31–56). Champaign, IL: Human Kinetics.

Ogles, B. M., & Masters, K. S. (2000). Older vs. younger male marathon runners: Participative motives and training habits. *Journal of Sport Behavior, 23*, 130–143.

Ogles, B. M., & Masters, K. S. (2003). A typology of marathon runners based on cluster analysis of motivations. *Journal of Sport Behavior, 26*, 69–85.

Pesce, C., Cereatti, L., Casella, R., Baldari, C., & Capranica, L. (2007). Preservation of visual attention in older expert orienteers at rest and under physical effort. *Journal of Sport and Exercise Psychology, 29*, 78–99.

Reaburn, P., & Dascombe, B. (2008). Endurance performance in masters athletes. *European Review of Aging and Physical Activity, 5*, 31–42.

Ryan, R. M., & Deci, E. L. (2000). Self-determination theory and the facilitation of intrinsic motivation, social development, and well-being. *American Psychologist, 55*, 68–78.

Salthouse, T. (1984). Effects of age and skill in typing. *Journal of Experimental Psychology: General, 113*, 345–371.

Salthouse, T. A. (1992). *Mechanisms of age-cognition relations in adulthood*. Hillsdale, NJ: LEA.

Salthouse, T. A., Babcock, R. L., Skovronek, E., Mitchell, D. R. D., & Palmon, R. (1990). Age and experience effects in spatial visualization. *Developmental Psychology, 26*, 128–136.

Scanlan, T. K., Russell, D. G., Beals, K. P., & Scanlan, L. A. (2003). Project on elite athlete commitment (PEAK): II. A direct test and expansion of the sport commitment model with elite amateur sportsmen. *Journal of Sport and Exercise Psychology, 25*, 377–401.

Scanlan, T. K., Stein, G. L., & Ravizza, K. (1989). An in-depth study of former elite figure skaters: II. Sources of enjoyment. *Journal of Sport and Exercise Psychology, 11*, 65–83.

Schörer, J., & Baker, J. (2009). An exploratory study of aging and perceptual-motor expertise in handball goalkeepers. *Experimental Aging Research, 35*, 1–19.

Schulz, R., & Curnow, C. (1988). Peak performance and age among superathletes: Track and field, swimming, baseball, tennis and golf. *Journal of Gerontology: Psychological Sciences, 43*, 113–120.

Smith, C. L., & Storandt, M. (1997). Physical activity participation in older adults: A comparison of competitors, noncompetitors, and nonexercisers. *Journal of Aging and Physical Activity, 5*, 98–110.

Starkes, J. L., & Ericsson, K. A. (2003). *Expert performance in sports: Advances in research on sport expertise*. Champaign, IL: Human Kinetics.

Starkes, J. L., Medic, N., & Routledge, R. (2007, July). *Retaining expertise: What does it take for older expert athletes to continue to excel?* Keynote presentation at the Congress of European College of Sport Science, Jyväskylä, Finland.

Starkes, J. L., Weir, P. L., Singh, P., Hodges, N. J., & Kerr, T. (1999). Aging and the retention of sport expertise. *International Journal of Sport Psychology, 30*, 283–301.

Starkes, J. L., Weir, P. L., & Young, B. W. (2003). What does it take for older athletes to continue to excel? In J. L. Starkes & K. A. Ericsson (Eds.), *Expert performance in sports: Advances in research on sport expertise* (pp. 251–272). Champaign, IL: Human Kinetics.

Steinberg, G., Grieve, F. G., & Glass, B. (2000). Achievement goals across the lifespan. *Journal of Sport Behavior, 23*, 298–306.

Stevenson, C. L. (2002). Seeking identities: Toward an understanding of the athletic careers of masters swimmers. *International Review for the Sociology of Sport, 37*, 131–146.

Stones, M. (2009). Statistical modeling of age trends in masters athletes. In J. Baker, S. Horton, & P. Weir (Eds.), *The masters athlete: Understanding the role of sport and exercise in optimizing aging* (pp. 15–38). London: Routledge.

Stones, M. J., & Kozma, A. (1982). Cross-sectional, longitudinal, and secular age trends in athletic performance. *Experimental Aging Research, 8*, 185–188.

Tantrum, M., & Hodge, K. (1993). Motives for participating in masters swimming. *New Zealand Journal of Health Physical Education and Recreation, 26*, 3–7.

Toepell, A. R., Guilmette, A. M., & Brooks, S. (2004). Women in masters rowing: Exploring healthy aging. *Women's Health and Urban Life Journal, 5*, 74–95.

Vallerand, R. J., Blanchard, C., Mageau, G. A., Koestner, R., Ratelle, C., Leonard, M., et al. (2003). Les passions de l'âme: On obsessive and harmonious passion. *Journal of Personality and Social Psychology, 85*, 756–767.

Vallerand, R., Mageau, G., Elliot, A., Dumais, A., Demers, M., & Rousseau, F. (2008). Passion and performance attainment in sport. *Psychology of Sport and Exercise, 9*, 373–392.

Walker, N., Fain, B., Fisk, A. D., & McGuire, C. L. (1997). Aging and decision making: Driving-related problem solving. *Human Factors, 39*, 438–444.

Weir, P. L., Kerr, T., Hodges, N. J., McKay, S. M., & Starkes, J. L. (2002). Master swimmers: How are they different from younger elite swimmers? An examination of practice and performance patterns. *Journal of Aging and Physical Activity, 10*, 41–63.

Weir, P., Medic, N., Baker, J., & Starkes, J. (2008). Understanding sport commitment in Senior bowlers. *Journal of Sport and Exercise Psychology, 30*(June), s208.

Weiss, W. M., & Weiss, M. R. (2006). A longitudinal analysis of commitment among competitive female gymnasts. *Psychology of Sport and Exercise, 7*, 309–323.

Wigglesworth, J. C., Young, B. W., & Medic, N. (2010). Exploring the sport commitment of regional-level masters athletes as a function of gender and age. *Canadian Society for Psychomotor Learning and Sport Psychology Abstracts,* Ottawa, ON, Canada.

Wigglesworth, J. C., Young, B. W., Medic, N., & Grove, J. R. (in press). Examining gender differences in the determinants of masters swimmers' sport commitment. *International Journal of Sport and Exercise Psychology.*

Wilson, P. M., Rodgers, W. M., Carpenter, P. J., Hall, C., Hardy, J., & Fraser, S. N. (2004). The relationship between commitment and exercise behavior. *Psychology of Sport and Exercise, 5,* 405–421.

Wright, V. J., & Perricelli, B. C. (2008). Age-related rates of decline in performance among elite senior athletes. *The American Journal of Sports Medicine, 36,* 443–450.

Yair, G. (1992). What keeps them running? The 'circle of commitment' of long distance runners. *Leisure Studies, 11,* 257–270.

Yates, A., Shisslak, C. M., Allender, J., Crago, M., & Leehey, K. (1992). Comparing obligatory runners to nonobligatory runners. *Psychosomatics, 33,* 180–189.

Young, B. W. (2011). Psycho-social perspectives on the motivation and commitment of Masters athletes. In N. Holt & M. Talbot (Eds.), *Lifelong engagement in sport and physical activity* (pp. 125–138). London: Routledge & International Council of Sport Science and Physical Education.

Young, B. W., Carey, S., & Medic, N. (2010). Predictors of recreational sport commitment among Ontario Seniors Games participants. *Canadian Society for Psychomotor Learning and Sport Psychology Abstracts,* Ottawa, ON, Canada.

Young, B. W., & Medic, N. (2011a). Examining social influences on the sport commitment of masters swimmers. *Psychology of Sport and* Exercise, *12,* 168–175.

Young, B. W., & Medic, N. (2011b). Veteraaniurheilijat: Tutkimuksia merkittävästä panostuksesta, motivaatiosta ja mahdollisuuksista [Masters athletes: Studies on remarkable investments, motives, and opportunities]. In Finnish Veterans´ Athletic Association (Eds.), *Erilainen tapa vanheta [Different ways of aging in sport]* (pp. 45–58). Lappeenranta, Finland: KS-Paino.

Young, B. W., Medic, N., Piamonte, M., Wigglesworth, J., & Grove, J. R. (2008). Examining the determinants of sport commitment in competitive masters swimmers. *Canadian Society for Psychomotor Learning and Sport Psychology Abstracts,* Canmore, AB, Canada.

Young, B. W., Medic, N., Weir, P. L., & Starkes, J. L. (2008). Explaining performance in elite middle-aged runners: Contributions from age, ongoing and past training factors. *Journal of Sport and Exercise Psychology, 30,* 1–20.

Young, B. W., Piamonte, M. E., Grove, J. R., & Medic, N. (2011). A longitudinal study of masters swimmers' commitment. *International Journal of Sport Psychology, 42,* 436–460.

Young, B. W., & Starkes, J. L. (2005). Career-span analyses of track performance: Longitudinal data present a more optimistic view of age-related performance decline. *Experimental Aging Research, 31,* 1–22.

Young, B. W., Weir, P. L., Starkes, J. L., & Medic, N. (2008). Does lifelong training temper age-related decline in sport performance? Interpreting differences between cross-sectional and longitudinal data. *Experimental Aging Research, 34,* 1–22.

Transitions: Ending Active Involvement in Sports and other Competitive Endeavors

Albert J. Petitpas, Taunya Marie Tinsley, *and* Amy S. Walker

Abstract

All elite performers eventually face the end of their careers. Whether individuals are athletes, performance artists, politicians, or businesspersons, their performance demands are often intense and require a high level of awareness, knowledge, and skills to effectively manage the challenges that they face. Ironically, most elite performers have not prepared or planned for their transition from the competitive arena. This chapter focuses on the transitions that performers face as they end their careers. In particular, the authors discuss conceptual and theoretical frameworks for sport career transitions; developmental factors related to effective and healthy transitions during, and out of, performance; psychological reactions to performance transitions; suggestions for assisting individuals with preparing for and coping with transitions; and ethical considerations involved when providing services to individuals ending active involvement in competition.

Key Words: Athletes, performing artists, businesspeople, transition, retirement

Individuals whose careers demand performance at optimal levels under high pressure will eventually transition and end active involvement in their competitive endeavors. Whether these individuals are athletes, performing artists, politicians, or business executives, they have demonstrated the skills and personal know-how to manage the challenges and other systemic factors associated with performance excellence (Aoyagi & Portenga, 2010; Hays 2009). Ironically, most of these elite performers are underprepared to manage their eventual career transition (Lavallee, Park, & Tod, 2010).

The purpose of this chapter is to examine the transition that occurs during the process of ending active involvement in sport or other competitive endeavors. In particular, the authors discuss conceptual and theoretical frameworks for sport career transitions; developmental factors related to effective and healthy transitions during, and out of, performance; psychological reactions to performance transitions; suggestions for assisting individuals with preparing for and coping with transitions; and ethical considerations involved when providing services to individuals ending active involvement in competition. The theoretical frameworks that inform this chapter come from the fields of sport psychology, organizational psychology, and sports counseling.

In this chapter, we use the term *helping professional* interchangeably with counselor, psychologist, and sports counseling or sport psychology consultants to describe the variety of service providers and practitioners who work with athletes and performers. Helping professionals may also include sports medicine professionals and graduate students from the above-mentioned domains.

Types of Performers Addressed in this Chapter

The focal group of this chapter is elite athletes. It should be pointed out, however, that much of the information addressed would also be applicable to other professions that demand high standards of performance in high-pressure contexts. Performing arts, business management, and high-risk (i.e., life-or-death) occupations are three additional domains that place incredible pressure on those who participate. Although clear differences exist in the performance issues and the consequences of actions in sport and each of these other domains, participants also share some common features. As described by Hays (2009, p. 4), individuals in these occupations perform in front of an actual or implied audience, bring their talents and skills into proficient action, display a public face that may be different from their ordinary self, meet certain performance standards, respond to high external demands, demonstrate appropriate coping skills under pressure, handle judgments regarding their proficiency or excellence, and face performance consequences. In addition, these individuals also face transitions while they are performing and must eventually end their active involvement in an activity that has likely fulfilled many needs and become a significant part of their personal identities (Peterson, 2009). Although the bulk of this chapter discusses athletic career transitions, resources are available for those who work with high performers in other fields (Hays, 2009; Hays & Brown, 2003).

Conceptual and Theoretical Frameworks of Career Transitions

Interest in and publications on the topic of career transitions and career termination in sport in the psychological and sociological literature have increased dramatically over the last several decades (Alfermann & Stambulova, 2007). Although there were a handful of articles on career termination prior to 1985, most simply adapted theoretical models from social gerontology and depicted sport retirement as a type of social death experience (e.g., Lerch, 1982; McPherson, 1980; Rosenberg, 1982). Several authors suggested that retirement from sport was similar to a grieving process, and athletes in this situation would go through stages of adjustment similar to those experienced by a dying person. As such, they adapted Kubler-Ross's (1969) stage model of grief and loss and suggested that, when faced with career termination, athletes would pass through stages of shock, denial, anger, bargaining, depression, and acceptance (e.g., Astle, 1986; Lynch, 1988; Ogilvie, 1987; Rotella & Heyman, 1986). Although there is some anecdotal evidence in support of a stage model explanation of athletic

transition (Gordon, Milios, & Grove, 1991; Ogilvie, 1987), this theory has not stood up to empirical scrutiny (Baillie, 1993; Brewer, 1993; Kleiber & Brock, 1992) and has been criticized for failure to take into account individual, environmental, and social differences (Crook & Robertson, 1991; Danish, Petitpas, & Hale, 1993; Pearson & Petitpas, 1990; Taylor & Ogilvie, 1994). Nonetheless, knowledge of the stages of the Kubler-Ross model can assist helping professionals in understanding the range of reactions that can occur during the disengagement process.

During the early 1990s, several new models appeared in the literature that examined transitions from a variety of domains, taking into account the diversity of individual and environmental factors present. These new models evolved out of the *adaptation to transitions model* proposed by Schlossberg (1981). This model provided a framework for understanding adult life transitions. Schlossberg defined a transition as "an event or nonevent that results in a change in assumptions about oneself and the world and thus requires a corresponding change in one's behavior and relationships" (Schlossberg, 1981, p. 5). Transitions were said to be hastened by events such as a change in physical context, taking on a new social role, or physiological changes.

According to Schlossberg (1981), adaptation to transition is a factor of individuals' cognitive appraisals of the situation, their personal characteristics, and their environment. Gardner and Moore (2006) suggested that, based on the Schlossberg model, transitions can be understood by examining a common set of variables. Was the transition expected to occur ("on-time," e.g., planned retirement) or was it unexpected ("off-time," e.g., career-ending injury in rookie year)? Was the onset of the transition gradual or sudden? Was the transition permanent, temporary, or uncertain? How much stress was experienced? Did the transition involve the need for a role change? What emotions were experienced? Although these factors are important, other individual and environmental considerations are likely to come into play and can have either a facilitating or debilitating affect on the transition (Schlossberg, 1984).

Among these individual characteristics are age, sex, life stage, health, race/ethnicity, socioeconomic status, value orientation, psychosexual competence, sex role identification, and prior experience with similar transitions. Environmental factors include the interpersonal support system, institutional supports, and the pre- and post-transitional physical settings. In addition to the individual and environmental characteristics listed above, several sport-specific factors, such as status loss (Gorbett, 1984); strength and exclusivity of the athletic identity, confidence, locus of control, anticipatory socialization, and coaches (Crook & Robertson, 1991); entitlement (Pearson & Petitpas, 1990); and education, skills, interests, and unanticipated support (Swain, 1991) have also been proposed as having significant impact upon the course of career transitions in sport.

Pearson and Petitpas (1990, p. 9) extrapolated from the Schlossberg model and predicted that the transition process would be most difficult for student athletes who have most strongly and exclusively based their identity on athletic performance, have the greatest gap between level of aspiration and level of ability, have had the least prior experience with the same or similar transitions, are limited in their general ability to adapt to change because of emotional and/or behavioral deficits, are limited in their ability to form and maintain supportive relationships, and who must deal with the transition in a context (social and/or physical) lacking material and emotional resources that could be helpful. In any event, the Schlossberg model addressed many of the criticisms of the adapted Kubler-Ross loss and grief stage model and spawned several sport-specific athletic career termination frameworks (Stambulova, 1997, 2003; Taylor & Ogilvie, 1994, 2001).

Another framework that has much in common with the Schlossberg model is the *life development intervention* (LDI) model (Danish et al., 1993). Transitions, or "critical life events," are viewed as multidimensional events with many biopsychosocial components. These events are not discrete. They first occur when individuals begin to anticipate them, continue during their occurrence, and conclude only when the post-transition aftermath has been determined. Critical life events, like transitions, have their own characteristics (e.g., timing, duration, contextual purity), and individuals' reactions to them are often a factor of their individual and support resources, their level of preparation (pre-event priming), and their past experience dealing with similar events. Although the LDI framework has much in common with Schlossberg's model, it also links transitional theory to an intervention framework that will be examined later.

Stambulova (1994) formulated a model in which sports career transitions are also considered critical life events, but they are described on three levels (i.e., general, specific, and individual). These levels distinguish between typical phases and principles by taking into account different sport events, gender, cross-cultural differences, and athletes' personality and experiences. The goal is to provide assistance in times of crisis or difficult moments (Stambulova, 1994; Wylleman, Lavallee, & Alfermann, 1999). Stambulova's (1994) model provides support for creating a continuous system of psychological assistance to athletes within each level and in different periods.

Ogilvie and Taylor's (1993) framework focused on the sport to post-career transition. They hypothesized that the difference between a "healthy" and a "distressful" career transition could be determined by examining the reasons for the sport career termination (i.e., forced or voluntary), factors related to adaptation (i.e., life experiences, self-identity, social-identity, and perceptions of control), and resources available (i.e., coping skills, social support, level of career planning). The framework includes suggestions for how to cope with the transition in the event of a career termination marked by distress.

More recently, Wylleman, Alfermann, and Lavallee (2004) introduced a developmental career model that examined the normative and non-normative transitions that athletes will face during and after retirement from sport participation. They proposed that it is important to explore athletes' development across a number of different life cycle domains; namely, physical, psychological, psychosocial, educational, and vocational. Each of these domains has its own unique developmental tasks, but each domain is also influenced by the other domains. For example, as athletes progress through the stages of the physical domain (i.e., initiation, development, mastery, discontinuation), their sources of primary support in the psychosocial domain may shift from parents and siblings to coaches and partners. This "whole person" approach enables helping professionals to see athletes' developmental progression in the sport context, and also to understand the demands and transitions they face outside of sport.

Factors Related to Healthy Transitions from Sport Careers

Unlike the career longevity of business executives and many other professions, most athletes face the inevitable decline of their abilities to compete both physically and mentally at a relatively young age (Baillie, 1993). Elite athletes typically end their sport career at about the same time most of their age-mates are reaching the establishment stage in their work careers (Ward, Sandstedt, Cox, & Beck, 2005). Although the obvious reason for retirement from sport is the decline of physical skills, there is general consensus among sport researchers that retirement is typically a result of multiple factors (e.g., Alfermann, Stambulova, & Zemaityte, 2004; Baillie, 1993; Baillie & Danish, 1992; Pearson & Petitpas, 1990; Sinclair & Orlick, 1993; Stambulova, 1994; Stambulova, Alfermann, Statler, & Côté, 2009).

Most conceptual models of athlete career transition identify deselection, injury, and free choice as the three most direct causes of sport career termination (e.g., Danish et al., 1993; Ogilvie & Taylor, 1993). Failure to be selected for a team and career-ending injuries are not under the direct control of athletes and are typically classified as unplanned or involuntary terminations. Athletes who experience an involuntary termination of their sport career usually face more challenges and are more vulnerable to distress than are athletes who retire by their own choice (Gardner & Moore, 2006). Freely chosen retirement is often a more thoughtful and lengthy process in which athletes are better prepared to adapt to the transition out of elite sport (Alfermann & Stambulova, 2007). Differentiating between athletes whose sport career termination was involuntary as opposed to freely chosen has proven to be quite useful in identifying those individuals who may have difficulty adjusting to the end of their sport career and for planning and implementing programs to prepare individuals for this transition (Lavallee et al., 2010).

Athletes who freely choose to retire from competition usually have the easiest transition in adjusting to their nonactive athlete status (Alfermann & Stambulova, 2007). Often, athletes who voluntarily leave their sport have planned for the transition and have lined up a new career or thought through how they will invest their time and energy post-sport. Their disengagement from sport is on their own timetable and would meet Schlossberg's (1981) description of an "on-time" transition. Typically, for athletes, on-time transitions occur when they are at an appropriate age, have achieved their major sport goals, and have prepared for and planned what they will do after they retire from sport (Danish et al., 1993). Those athletes who freely choose to retire are likely to have a degree of control and predictability during their transition experiences that would be expected to reduce the level of anxiety and uncertainty that could otherwise be expected in any major career transition (Alfermann et al., 2004; Meichenbaum, 1985).

Being deselected from a team is the most frequent cause of involuntary disengagement from sport. Whether it is preseason tryouts or competitive trials, many athletes are "cut" from or fail to make teams each year. Deselection can cause emotional reactions ranging from mild upset to anger, depression, or despair (Alfermann & Stambulova, 2007; Alfermann et al., 2004; Pearson & Petitpas, 1990; Petitpas, 2009; Wippert & Wippert, 2010). Ironically, athletes who are most vulnerable to the selection process because of borderline or declining physical abilities are likely to increase their training in hopes of making the team, thus pushing educational or career planning further into the background (Petitpas, 2009). As a result, athletes who are likely to be most vulnerable to deselection are often those who are least prepared to cope with the end of their sport career.

The second major cause of forced or involuntary termination from competitive sport is a career-ending injury. Peterson (2009) reported that between 14% and 24% of athletes identify injury as the primary reason for retirement from sport. Career-ending injuries have been shown to be the most difficult to manage and can lead to the most severe reactions (Webb, Nasco, Riley, & Headrick, 1998). An acute career-ending injury is unpredictable, sudden, and out of a person's control, all factors associated with increased levels of anxiety and stress (Meichenbaum, 1985). As a result, it is not surprising that those former athletes who report the most life dissatisfaction after their sport career has ended are those who experienced career-ending injuries (Kleiber & Brock, 1992).

In addition, a number of situational factors can lead to sport career termination. Drug use, gambling, or other significant league policy infractions; boycotts; lockouts; financial problems; and family crises can cause a voluntary or involuntary retirement from active sport participation. In general, the process of sport career termination from elite competitive sport, whether freely chosen or forced, requires individuals to deal with many changes. How athletes react to these changes can vary in many ways.

As with any transition, athletes who retire from active competition will be forced to adjust to change and to reconsider how they view themselves and the world. Most athletes cope with these changes relatively easily, but a review of 14 studies that examined athletes' reactions to career termination revealed that 20.1% showed psychological difficulties (Lavallee, Nesti, Borkoles, Cockerill, & Edge,

2000). Although identifying those athletes who are likely to have the most difficulty adjusting to sport retirement is difficult at best, several developmental and multicultural factors have been shown to lead to higher levels of vulnerability to distress during sport career termination.

Developmental Factors

ATHLETIC IDENTITY AND ENGAGEMENT IN EXPLORATORY BEHAVIOR

Most athletes go through a period of specialization in which they narrow their focus on sport participation (see also Chapter 24, this volume).

This devotion and commitment is necessary for athletes to perfect their techniques and enhance their performance, but can become detrimental to other aspects of personal and career development (Petitpas & France, 2010). If the strength and exclusivity of this specialization becomes too great, athletes can fail to engage in other activities that have been shown to be critical in developing a cogent sense of personal identity during their adolescent years (Gardner & Moore, 2006).

The primary developmental task of late adolescence and early adulthood is to explore different occupational, ideological, and life roles to gain the experiences necessary to develop one's personal identity. Exploratory behavior not only provides individuals with the self-knowledge necessary to make commitments to a personal identity, but also exposes them to situations that increase their abilities to cope effectively with life transitions and other stressors. Unfortunately, sport specialization, with its inherent time commitments and psychological and physical demands, can prevent many elite athletes from engaging in exploratory behavior, an activity that is critical for subsequent personal and career development (Jordaan, 1963; Super, 1957).

Role experimentation (Miller & Kerr, 2003), *selective optimization* (Danish, 1983), and *athletic identity* (Brewer, 1993) are examples of terms that have been used to describe the process through which athletes give exclusive attention to their sport at the expense of all other interests. This concept is closely linked to a developmental status called *identity foreclosure* (Marcia, 1966). Several studies have shown that the strength and exclusivity of an athletic identity is related to negative consequences when athletes disengage from sport roles because of retirement, injury, or the selection process (Brewer, 1993; Hinitz, 1988; Kleiber & Brock, 1992).

Pearson and Petitpas (1990) contend that individuals who have a strong athletic identity and the greatest gap between their level of aspiration and level of ability may be particularly vulnerable when faced with the threat of the loss of sport. These athletes fear that any time or attention devoted away from sport might jeopardize their playing career. They essentially put all of their hopes and dreams in their athletic pursuits, and ignore objective feedback about their chances of achieving their goals, withdraw from their athletic social support network, and devote even more time and effort into practicing their sport skills (Gardner & Moore, 2006). As a result, the occurrence of a career-ending injury or deselection can be particularly traumatic.

PLANNING

Another factor related to adjustment to sport career termination is the amount and quality of life/work planning athletes engage in prior to leaving sport (Alfermann & Stambulova, 2007). Athletes often believe that they are years behind their agemates in establishing themselves in the workplace and often have a limited sense of their values, needs, nonsport interests, or skills. Yet, the majority of athletes do not plan for their retirement or life after sports (Alfermann et al., 2004). Without planning or a sense of direction, athletes often report feeling a sense of emptiness and have difficulty taking the initial steps necessary to engage in career exploration. On the other hand, athletes who do plan for retirement have been shown to adapt to the transition more quickly and report greater life satisfaction (Torregrosa, Boixados, Valiente, & Cruz, 2004).

SOCIAL SUPPORT AND RESOURCES

Although athletes' personal dynamics play a significant role in adjusting to sport career termination, the importance of the quality and availability of a person's social support network and the resources available within the individual's environment should not be underestimated. As individuals progress through the athletic life cycle, their social support network becomes heavily weighted with coaches, teammates, and other people who are involved in elite sport (Wylleman & Lavallee, 2004). Although these sources of support are quite beneficial during the sport career, they may be less helpful during the retirement process (Petitpas, 2009).

Density is a term commonly used to describe the level of similarity among support group members. Individuals within a high-density support group tend to know each other and hold similar values and beliefs about what is needed in specific situations (Pearson, 1990). Elite athletes are often surrounded by a high-density support group comprised primarily or exclusively of athletes, coaches, and sport administrators. It is not surprising that a sport-centric support group would be more invested in keeping athletes involved with sport, rather than in facilitating their transition into retirement. In addition, coaches and teammates are typically more comfortable offering informational support and challenge than they are in providing emotional support (Rosenfeld, Richman, & Hardy, 1989). As a result, many athletes find themselves without the emotional support necessary to assist in making the difficult decisions that are frequently involved in the process of ending a career as an elite athlete (Gardner & Moore, 2006; Petitpas, 2009).

ORGANIZATIONAL SUPPORT

Another factor that can influence the impact and consequences of ending a sport career is the resources available within the athlete's environment. Sport settings with appropriate medical, counseling, or other athlete assistance programs can provide the support and resources necessary to assist athletes with the transition out of competitive sport. These services are particularly vital in situations in which the individual athlete lacks the internal resources or social support required to cope effectively with sport career termination (Wylleman & Lavallee, 2004).

Psychological Reactions to Sports Career Transitions
Individual Reactions

Most individuals make a relatively smooth transition out of sport competition. Nonetheless, many former elite athletes report that they miss the competition, the camaraderie with teammates and coaches, the adulation of fans, and the total experience of participating in high-intensity sports (Werthner & Orlick, 1986). Often, a sense of loss and feelings of sadness are associated with disengagement from sport that may stem from the realization that nothing will be able to duplicate the experiences inherent in being an elite athlete (Lavallee et al., 2000). Although about 20% of athletes are likely to experience psychological difficulties during their transition out of competitive sport (Lavallee et al., 2000), many others will second-guess their decision to retire or express some bitterness over being forced to leave sports before they had achieved all their athletic goals (Werthner & Orlick, 1986).

Confusion or questioning of one's self-identity is a common reaction to the end of a sport career (Peterson, 2009), and many athletes find it necessary to make significant social adjustments when they leave competition (Wylleman & Lavallee, 2004). As athletes move further away from their sports, the need to develop a new identity or to learn to define one's self other than strictly in athletic terms becomes greater (Brewer, Van Raalte, & Petitpas, 2000). Often, individuals' attempts at redefinition will meet resistance from their sport-centric social support network as it struggles to understand why they are retiring from competition (Petitpas, 2009). Add geographic changes and separation from teammates, and it is not hard to understand that athletes may also experience some loneliness or boredom as they readjust to life without elite sport.

Another potential issue is what has been referred to as the *Olympic self-image* (Petitpas, Danish, McKelvain, & Murphy, 1992). Whether Olympian, professional, or other type of elite athletes, individuals who are accustomed to the spotlight can have a difficult time imagining themselves in anything but exciting and high-visibility careers. These athletes often fail to acknowledge all of the time and hard work they put into their sport and simply accept their lofty positions as the status quo. This feeling of status can be exacerbated when athletes also develop a sense of entitlement. Athletes who have been overprotected and overindulged because of their physical skills may not be willing to engage in career and life planning because they assume that the sport system will simply take care of them. When individuals have high visibility and/or a sense of entitlement, they are reluctant to start at the bottom level of a new career progression and can experience anger and disappointment at what they believe is a sport system that has abandoned them (Petitpas, 2009).

Athletes often make many sacrifices in order to reach high levels of achievement. They put in countless hours and become accustomed to heavily regimented schedules built around a set routine of practices, competitions, and other related commitments. As a result, a significant number of athletes who are forced to retire from competition are not prepared to cope with the ambiguity of an uncertain future and lose confidence in their abilities to meet the demands of establishing themselves in a nonsport career (Petitpas et al., 1992).

Most athletes have a clear sense of direction and purpose that brings a focus and meaning to their lives. However, for athletes who have not reached their sport goals, the end of the sport career can bring about a feeling of emptiness or lack of purpose (Werthner & Orlick, 1986). With unfulfilled dreams, athletes in the process of disengagement from sport can feel empty inside and question if all the time, effort, and struggles were really worth it. Some athletes, particularly those who feel they were forced to retire before they engaged in any type of self-examination, can drift from activity to activity in hopes of finding a new sense of direction. Some may become bitter at the sport system and disown their entire sport experience (Petitpas et al., 1992). Still others will hold onto their sport identity through coaching, broadcasting, or sport administration. Whatever the case, those athletes who have planned for retirement—or at least been able to put their sport participation in perspective—are in the best position to harness the positive energy from their sport experiences to ease the transition into their next career (Alfermann et al., 2004).

Assisting Individuals with Sport Career Termination

When planning support programs for athletes to assist them during the career transition process, sport organizations should consider several types of services. The LDI model (Danish et al., 1993) provides a helpful format for planning multipurpose support programs for athletes. As discussed previously, the LDI perspective views transitions as a process rather than as a discreet event. For example, sport career terminations start when athletes begin thinking about ending their sport career and continue through retirement and the aftermath of adjusting to life without competitive sport. As such, a comprehensive support program should have different components that are available before, during, and after a transitional event. Programs that assist athletes in preparing for a future event are called *enhancement strategies*. Those programs that take place during the event in efforts to buffer the impact of the transition are called *support strategies,* and those that take place after the event to help athletes cope with the aftermath of the transition are called *counseling strategies.*

The cornerstone of the LDI approach is enhancement. The general objectives of enhancement type services are to prepare athletes for their sport career termination by helping them to identify skills they have acquired through sport, showing them how these skills could be used in different life areas, and teaching new skills that would enhance their abilities to cope with all the changes that can occur as a result of their disengagement from sport (Danish

et al., 1993). Enhancement services exemplify the type of planning activity that has been linked to a smoother transition out of competitive sport (Alfermann & Stambulova, 2007). Athletes who plan for their retirement from sport are better able to anticipate some of the changes that they might experience and gain confidence in their ability to cope with these changes.

The importance of enhancement strategies that focus on the acquisition of life skills can be seen in the increasing number of Olympic Committees that have created programs to assist athletes. Although each of these programs is structured differently, they all share some common goals. In general, these programs aim to assist elite athletes by providing a supportive environment in which they can share their concerns; helping them to identify their values, needs, interests, and skills; assisting them with life/ career planning; building their confidence in their abilities to make a successful transition into a new career; and establishing an accessible support group of other athletes, coaches, or sport administrators (Anderson & Morris, 2000). In particular, athletes who participated in a U.S. Olympic Committee–sponsored career development program report that they found activities in which they identified their transferable skills and learned how to transfer these skills into nonsport careers to be very beneficial (Petitpas et al., 1992). It appears that when athletes believe that they have skills that are valued in nonsport domains, they gain confidence in their abilities and experience less anxiety when confronting their retirement from elite sport.

Unfortunately, enhancement programs can be a hard sell to professional sport organizations. There appears to be a pervasive fear among many sport organizations, coaches, and athletes that any activity not directly related to improving sport performance may distract athletes' focus from their sport goals. However, there is research that challenges the validity of this fear. Anderson and Morris (2000) found that Australian Olympic athletes who participated in a comprehensive life skills education program performed better during Olympic Games than did their athletic peers who did not participate. In fact, Anderson's study suggests that life skills development programs might actually provide performance benefits to elite athletes.

Self-awareness is another benefit of enhancement programs. As athletes engage in the self-assessment activities that are typically part of the life/work planning process, they learn about their values, needs, interests, and skills. This information can often lead to a more well-rounded self-assessment through which athletes begin to see themselves as more than simply an athlete (Lavallee, 2005). Athletes who engage in exploratory behavior are typically more self-aware and, therefore, in a better position to make informed decisions about their transition out of elite sport (Petitpas & France, 2010). Individuals with a strong and exclusive athletic identity are more apt to avoid enhancement programs and put off their sport career termination as long as possible. When this is the case, support or counseling interventions may be required to help these athletes cope during or after their sport career termination (Danish et al., 1993).

Approximately 20% of athletes, particularly those who have not participated in any enhancement-type programs, are likely to experience some strong emotions while they are disengaging from elite competition (Lavallee et al., 2000). Unfortunately, many athletes report that they are hesitant to disclose their feelings because very few people understand what they are going through (Petitpas et al., 1992). Athletes who have not attended to their feelings and beliefs about the end of their sport career are unlikely to be in a position to begin planning for their future (Petitpas, Champagne, Chartrand, Danish, & Murphy, 1997). Therefore, it is important for sports organizations to make available support services for those athletes who are in the midst of the sport career termination process.

Lavallee (2005) found that the support and counseling components of the LDI model were effective in helping athletes manage their transitions out of elite competition. He assessed participants' readiness to cope with their transition using a personality and an interest inventory. He then used the findings of the assessment to assist participants in identifying their skills and helping them see how these skills could be transferred to other careers. These interactions were enhanced by an empathetic counseling relationship that empowered participants to use goal setting and other strategies to move beyond their sport career.

Athletes in transition typically need to address how they are feeling in a forum where they believe that others understand what they are going through. This need can be fulfilled by organizing support groups of athletes who are also in or have gone through the process of retiring from sport. The purpose of the group would be to create a safe place where athletes can own their emotions and garner the support of people who understand what they are experiencing. Although simply sharing emotions may not resolve any of the issues involved in the transition, it is often a necessary first step for those athletes who might otherwise become emotionally paralyzed by the strong feelings that leaving sport can evoke.

In situations in which support groups are not feasible or available, helping professionals can provide individual counseling. Lavallee and colleagues (2010) suggested that helping professionals who build relationships based on empathetic understanding can create a psychologically safe environment in which athletes become comfortable sharing their emotions and beliefs about their career termination. During the counseling relationship, a helping professional can also evaluate the level and exclusivity of athletes' identification with the sport role. In cases in which the athlete has not engaged in exploratory behavior and identity foreclosure is indicated, it is important to differentiate between situational versus psychological types (Lavallee, Park, & Tod, 2010; Gardner & Moore, 2006). In *situational foreclosure*, individuals lack the information and self-knowledge necessary to make informed choices about what career decisions are in their best interests. They have moved through the stages of their athletic development without giving sufficient thought to their educational or career plans. In contrast, athletes in *psychological foreclosure* make an unwavering commitment to sport to avoid identity crises, and their sport identity becomes the central component of their intrapsychic defensive systems. Athletes in psychological foreclosure view their sport successes as the only means of maintaining their coaches' approval and defend against any threats to their ego identities by avoiding people or situations that might challenge the salience of athletic participation (Petitpas & France, 2010). Whereas individuals with situational foreclosure are likely to benefit from the information and support provided in enhancement and support interventions, those who are psychologically foreclosed are likely to need professional counseling interventions (Gardner & Moore, 2006).

Sports organizations that provide enhancement and support services can help buffer some of the emotional distress or self-image problems that can arise during sport career termination. All athletes will experience a number of normative transitional periods as they progress through the stages of athletic development. However, sport participation is just one of several lifespan developmental considerations. Wylleman and Lavallee's (2004) "whole person" approach examines athletic transitions in light of other developmental demands; namely, psychological, psychosocial, academic, and career. Evaluating athletes' development across each of these domains provides helping professionals with a better understanding of the support and information necessary to facilitate a smooth transition from one stage to the next. It is also important to monitor participants' progress across domains because a major roadblock or event in one area can affect all the other areas.

As described earlier, a small number of athletes will experience so much distress over their sport career termination that they will develop problems such as substance abuse, eating disorders, depression, or other clinical issues. Therefore, sports organizations should develop a referral network of professionals who can provide the counseling interventions required. Ideally, these professionals would not only specialize in dealing with individuals with the specific issue, but also have the sport counseling competencies necessary to understand how factors like athletic identity can impact functioning.

In summary, the LDI model provides a useful framework for planning comprehensive support service to assist athletes who are experience sport career termination. Programs should include components that help athletes anticipate and prepare for their retirement, provide an appropriate support network for athletes during the transition, and establish a referral network of professionals who can assist athletes with specific problems that can arise in the aftermath of the transition. Clearly, enhancement strategies that help athletes identify transferable skills, acquire life skills, increase self-awareness, and plan for transitions are the best means of facilitating a smooth sport career termination. Sport organizations that build these services into the normative experiences of their athletes are likely to have the most far-reaching impact.

Ethical Considerations

Ethical practice in counseling, psychology, and consultation is the foundation of principled, high-quality service delivery (Watson, Etzel, & Shapiro, 2009). At any point in their career, helping professionals who work with athletes can encounter ethically challenging dilemmas that will test their values and behaviors (Aoyagi & Portenga, 2010; Watson et al., 2009). Helping professionals who work with the athlete population may face a number of ethical dilemmas, including multiple relationships, confidentiality, competence, marketing, unique service settings, self-regulation, and use of technology for service provision (Aoyagi & Portenga, 2010; Ward, Sandstedt, Cox, & Beck, 2005; Watson et al., 2009). Awareness of the common ethical challenges inherent in working with athletes is essential to responsible, effective, and competent service provision (Aoyagi & Portenga, 2010; Kocet, 2006; Watson et al., 2009; see also Chapter 3, this volume). It is critical and important that helping professionals who assist athletes and other high performers through career transitions be familiar with ethical decision-making models that can guide their decisions (Watson et al., 2009).

Conclusion

The purpose of this chapter was to examine the process of transitions and career termination of athletes and other individuals who perform at optimal levels under high pressure. In general, adjustment to ending a sport or high-pressured career is influenced by a large number of factors. Chief among these factors is the amount of planning and preparation individuals engage in prior to the transition, the degree to which they explore other roles and broaden their self-identity, the availability and quality of support services, and whether the decision to transition and terminate one's career was voluntary or forced. Organizations that offer comprehensive enhancement, support, and counseling services are in the best position to ensure that their people will have relatively smooth transitions during and through the end of their competitive careers.

References

Alfermann, D., & Stambulova, N. (2007). Career transition and career termination. In G. Tenenbaum & R. C. Eklund (Eds.), *Handbook of sport psychology* (3rd ed., pp. 712–733). New York: Wiley.

Alfermann, D., Stambulova, N., & Zemaityte, A. (2004). Reactions to sport career termination: A cross-national comparison of German, Lithuanian, and Russian athletes. *Psychology of Sport and Exercise, 5,* 61–75. doi:10.1016/S1469-0292(02)00050-X

Anderson, D., & Morris, T. (2000). Athlete lifestyle programs. In D. Lavallee & P. Wylleman (Eds.), *Career transitions in sport: International perspectives* (pp. 59–80). Morgantown, WV: Fitness Information Technology.

Aoyagi, M. W., & Portenga, S. T. (2010). The role of positive ethics and virtues in the context of sport and performance psychology service delivery. *Professional Psychology: Research and Practice, 41*(3), 253–259. doi: 10.1037/a0019483

Astle, S. J. (1986). The experience of loss in athletics. *Journal of Sports Medicine and Physical Fitness, 26,* 279–284.

Baillie, P. H. F. (1993). Understanding retirement from sports: Therapeutic ideas for helping athletes in transition. *The Counseling Psychologist, 21*(3), 399–410.

Baillie, P. H. F., & Danish, S. J. (1992). Understanding the career transition of athletes. *The Sport Psychologist, 6,* 77–98.

Brewer, B. W. (1993). Self-identity and specific vulnerability to depressed mood. *Journal of Personality, 61*, 343–364.

Brewer, B., Van Raalte, J., & Petitpas, A. (2000). Self-identity issues in sport career transitions. In D. Lavallee & P. Wyllemann (Eds.), *Career transitions in sport: International perspectives* (pp. 29–43). Morgantown, WV: Fitness Information Technology.

Crook, J. M., & Robertson, S. E. (1991). Transitions out of elite sport. *International Journal of Sport Psychology, 22*, 115–127.

Danish, S. J. (1983). Musings about personal competence: The contributions of sport, health, and fitness. *American Journal of Community Psychology, 11*, 221–240.

Danish, S. D., Petitpas, A. J., & Hale, B. D. (1993). Life development intervention for athletes: Life skills through sports. *The Counseling Psychologist, 21*, 352–385.

Gardner, F., & Moore, Z. (2006). *Clinical sport psychology.* Champaign, IL: Human Kinetics

Gorbett, F. J. (1984). Psycho-social adjustment of athletes to retirement. In L. Bunker, R. J. Rotella, & A. S. Reilly (Eds.), *Sport psychology: Psychological considerations in maximizing sport performance* (pp. 288–294). Ithaca, NY: Mouvement.

Gordon, S., Milios, D., & Grove, J. R. (1991). Psychological aspects of the recovery process from sport injury: The perspective of sport physiotherapists. *Australian Journal of Science and Medicine in Sport, 23*, 53–60.

Hays, K. F. (Ed.). (2009). *Performance psychology in action: A casebook for working with athletes, performing artists, business leaders, and professionals in high-risk occupations.* Washington, DC: American Psychological Association.

Hays, K. F., & Brown, C. H. (2003). *You're on! Consulting for peak performance.* Washington, DC: American Psychological Association.

Hinitz, D. R. (1988). *Role theory and the retirement of collegiate gymnasts.* Unpublished doctoral dissertation, University of Nevada, Reno.

Jordaan, J. P. (1963). Exploratory behavior: The foundation of self and occupational concepts. In D. E. Super, R. Starishevsky, N. Matlin, & J. P. Jordaan (Eds.), *Career development: Self- concept theory* (pp. 46–57). New York: CEEB Research Monographs.

Kleiber, D. A., & Brock, S. C. (1992). The effect of career-ending injuries on the subsequent well-being of elite college athletes. *Sociology of Sport Journal, 9*, 70–75.

Kocet, M. M. (2006). Ethical challenges in a complex world: Highlights of the 2005 ACA codes of ethics. *Journal of Counseling and Development, 84*, 228–234.

Kubler-Ross, E. (1969). *On death and dying.* New York: Macmillan.

Lavallee, D. (2005). The effect of a life development intervention on sports career transition adjustment. *The Sport Psychologist, 19*, 193–202.

Lavallee, D., Nesti, M., Borkoles, E., Cockerill, I., & Edge, A. (2000). Intervention strategies for athletes in transition. In D. Lavallee, & P. Wylleman (Ed.), *Career transitions in sport: International perspectives* (pp. 111–130). Morgantown, WV: Fitness Information Technology.

Lavallee, D., Park, S., & Tod, D. (2010), Career termination. In S. J. Hanrahan, & M. B. Andersen (Eds.), *Routledge handbook of applied sport psychology* (pp. 242–249). New York: Routledge.

Lerch, S. H. (1982). Athletic retirement as social death: An overview. In N. Theberge & P. Donnelly (Eds.), *Sport and the sociological imagination* (pp. 259–272). Fort Worth, TX: Texas Christian University Press.

Lynch, G. P. (1988). Athletic injuries and the practicing sport psychologist: Practical guidelines for assisting athletes. *The Sport Psychologist, 2*, 161–167.

Marcia, J. (1966). Development and validation of ego-identity status. *Journal of Personality and Social Psychology, 3*, 551–558.

McPherson, B. P. (1980). Retirement from professional sport: The process and problems of occupational and psychological adjustment. *Sociological Symposium, 30*, 126–143.

Meichenbaum, D. (1985). *Stress inoculation training.* New York: Pergamon Press.

Miller, P. S., & Kerr, G. A. (2003). The role experimentation of intercollegiate student athletes. *The Sport Psychologist, 17*, 196–219.

Ogilvie, B. C. (1987). Counseling for sports career termination. In J. R. May & M. J. Asken (Eds.), *Sport psychology: The psychological health of the athlete* (pp. 213–230). New York: PMA Publishing.

Ogilvie, B. C., & Taylor, J. (1993). Career termination in sports: When the dream dies. In J. Williams (Ed.), *Applied sport psychology: Personal growth to peak performance* (2nd ed., pp. 356–365). Palo Alto, CA: Mayfield.

Pearson, R. (1990). *Counseling and social support: Perspectives and practice.* Thousand Oaks, CA: Sage Publications.

Pearson, R. E., & Petitpas, A. J. (1990). Transitions of athletes: Developmental and preventative perspectives. *Journal of Counseling and Development, 69*, 7–10.

Peterson, K. M. (2009). Overtraining, burnout, injury, and retirement. In K. F. Hays (Ed.), *Performance psychology in action: A casebook for working with athletes, performing artists, business leaders, and professionals in high-risk occupations* (pp. 225–243). Washington, DC: American Psychological Association.

Petitpas, A. (2009). Sport career termination. In B. W. Brewer (Ed.), *Handbook of sports medicine and science: Sport psychology* (pp. 113–120). West Sussex, UK: Wiley-Blackwell.

Petitpas, A., Champagne, D., Chartrand, J., Danish, S., & Murphy, S. (1997*). Athlete's guide to career planning.* Champaign, IL: Human Kinetics.

Petitpas, A., Danish, S., McKelvain, R., & Murphy, S. (1992). A career assistance program for elite athletes. *Journal of Counseling and Development, 70*, 383–386.

Petitpas, A., & France, T. (2010). Identity foreclosure in sport. In S. J. Hanrahan, & M. B. Andersen (Eds.), *Routledge handbook of applied sport psychology* (pp. 282–291). New York: Routledge.

Rosenberg, E. (1982). Athletic retirement as social death: Concepts and perspectives. In N. Theberge & P. Donnelly (Eds.), *Sport and the sociological imagination* (pp. 245–258). Fort Worth, TX: Texas Christian University Press.

Rosenfeld, L., Richman, J., & Hardy, C. (1989). Examining social support networks among athletes: Descriptions and relationship to stress. *The SportPsychologist, 3*(1), 23–33.

Rotella, R. J., & Heyman, S. R. (1986). Stress, injury, and the psychological rehabilitation of athletes. In J. M. Williams (Ed.), *Applied sport psychology: Personal growth to peak performance* (pp. 343–364). Palo Alto, CA: Mayfield.

Schlossberg, N. K. (1981). A model for analyzing human adaptation to transition. *The Counseling Psychologist, 9*(2), 2–18. doi: 10.1177/001100008100900202

Schlossberg, N. K. (1984). *Counseling adults in transition.* New York: Springer.

Sinclair, D. A., & Orlick, T. (1993). Positive transitions from high-performance sport. *The Sport Psychologist, 7,* 138–150.

Stambulova, N. (1997). Sociological sports career transitions. In J. Bangsbo, B. Saltin, H. Bonde, Y. Hellsten, B. Ibsen, M. Kjaer, et al. (Eds.), *Proceedings of the 2nd Annual Congress of the European College of Sport Science* (Vol. I, pp. 88–89). Copenhagen, DK: University of Copenhagen.

Stambulova, N. (2003). Symptoms of a crisis-transition. In N. Hassmen (Ed.), *SIPF yearbook, 2003* (pp. 97–109). Örebro, SE: Örebro University Press.

Stambulova, N., Alfermann, D., Statler, T., & Côté, J. (2009). ISSP position stand: Career development and transitions of athletes. *International Journal of Sport and Exercise Psychology, 7*(4), 292–308. Retrieved from http://www.fitinfotech.com/IJSEP/IJSEPbackissueWVU.tpl

Stambulova, N. B. (1994). Developmental sports career investigations in Russia: A post- perestroika analysis. *The Sport Psychologist, 8,* 221–237.

Super, D. E. (1957). *The psychology of careers.* New York: Harper & Row.

Swain, D. A. (1991). Withdrawal from sport and Schlossberg's model of transitions. *Sociology of Sport Journal, 8,* 152–160.

Taylor, J., & Ogilvie, B. C. (1994). A conceptual model of adaptation to retirement among athletes. *Journal of Applied Sport Psychology, 6,* 1–20.

Taylor, J., & Ogilvie, B. C. (2001). Career termination among athletes. In R. N. Singer, H. A. Hausenblas, & C. M. Janelle (Eds.), *Handbook of sport psychology* (2nd ed., pp. 672–291). New York: Wiley.

Torregrosa, M., Boixados, M., Valiente, L., & Cruz, L. (2004). Elite athletes' image of retirement: The way to relocation in sport. *Psychology of Sport and Exercise, 5,* 35–44.

Ward, D. G., Sandstedt, S. D., Cox, R. H., & Beck, N. C. (2005). Athlete-counseling competencies for U.S. psychologists working with athletes. *The Sport Psychologist, 19,* 318–334.

Watson, J., Etzel, E. F., & Shapiro, J. (2009). Ethics and counseling practice with college student-athletes. In E. F. Etzel (Ed.), *Counseling and psychological services for college student-athletes* (pp. 85–111). Morgantown, WV: Fitness Information Technology.

Webb, W., Nasco, S., Riley, S., & Headrick, R. (1998). Athletic identity and reactions to retirement from sports. *Journal of Sports Behavior, 21,* 338–362.

Werthner, P., & Orlick, T. (1986). Retirement experiences of successful Olympic athletes. *International Journal of Sport Psychology, 17,* 337–363.

Wippert, P., & Wippert, J. (2010). The effects of involuntary athletic career termination on psychological distress. *Journal of Clinical Sport Psychology, 4,* 133–149.

Wylleman, P., Alfermann, D., & Lavallee, D. (2004). Career transitions in sport: European perspectives. *Psychology of Sport and Exercise, 5,* 7–20.

Wylleman, P., & Lavallee, D. (2004). A developmental perspective on transitions faced by athletes. In M. Weiss (Ed.), *Developmental sport and exercise psychology: A lifespan perspective* (pp. 507–527). Morgantown, WV: Fitness Information Technology.

Wylleman, P., Lavallee, D., & Alfermann, D. (Eds.). (1999). *Career transitions in competitive sports* [Monograph]. Retrieved from http://www.fepsac.com/index.php/download_file/-/view/31

PART 5

Interventions in Sport and Performance Psychology

Counseling Performers in Distress

Zella E. Moore

Abstract

Counseling performers in distress is a highly gratifying yet complex professional endeavor that requires the practitioner to be flexible, self-aware, and committed to engaging in evidence-based practice regularly guided by the ever-evolving scientific literature. Performers come to the attention of sport/performance psychologists with an array of personal needs and levels of psychological distress. To effectively meet their needs, practitioners must have a conceptual understanding of the construct of distress, be able to assess distress along the continuum of severity, determine appropriate targets of intervention, and choose an efficacious intervention that remediates subclinical or clinical concerns while promoting psychological health and well-being. This chapter therefore provides a conceptual and practical understanding of the nonclinical, subclinical, and clinical needs of performers; describes an evidence-based approach to assessment and treatment; and highlights how setting, counselor, client, and cultural variables can affect the counseling process.

Key Words: Counseling, performer, distress, clinical, subclinical, MCS-SP, psychological treatment, performance enhancement

The pursuit of performance excellence is at the heart of the aspirations and day-to-day activities of countless thousands in diverse performance fields such as sport, the performing arts, the military, and business. Indeed, achievement and high performance are some of the defining motivations in modern society. Since performance is impacted by a myriad of variables, including issues or distress that warrant psychological interventions broadly related to overall functioning across numerous life domains, a variety of subdisciplines within professional psychology have sought to understand the psychology of human performance in order to better assess and intervene in the performance process. These efforts have led to much research on a wide array of constructs and related strategies and techniques, hoping to enhance the development of elite human performance.

Understanding the Psychology of Human Performance

Research in diverse topics such as goal setting, mental imagery, task versus ego orientation, attention, operant learning of complex skills, cognitive stages of motor learning, and many more has been conducted to develop a clear and consistent means of helping those desiring optimal performance to consistently attain their goals (Hanrahan & Andersen, 2010). What these approaches generally have in common is the supposition that the reduction of "negative" thoughts, emotions, feeling states, and/or physiological activity would ultimately culminate in enhanced human performance. A fundamental assumption of this approach within sport psychology is that teaching the various self-control skills noted above would, over time, allow the performer to respond better to the inevitable stressors and pressures associated with high-level human performance (see Chapter 38, this volume). Such intervention efforts utilize the skills-building approach developed in the 1970s by such notable cognitive-behavioral theorists as Donald Meichenbaum (1977) and have been widely accepted as the foundation of sport psychology interventions (Andersen, 2009).

Although these self-control based strategies have often been viewed as the intervention gold standard in sport/performance psychology, recently, the efficacy of these interventions has been challenged (Gardner & Moore, 2006, 2007; Moore, 2003). Also, there has been an absence of empirical study examining the proposed mechanism of change of these intervention strategies. This exclusion impairs our ability to fully understand which intervention components actually have utility and which do not.

As a result, a colleague and I have previously suggested that the psychology of human performance should be reconsidered based on a more contemporary model in which a wide variety of previously overlooked factors are seen as relevant to both the understanding and enhancement of human performance processes and outcomes (Gardner & Moore, 2004b, 2007). Although a complete description of this model is beyond the scope of this chapter (see Gardner & Moore, 2007, for a complete discussion), we assert that factors such as emotion regulation, self/other attentional processes, rumination, and experiential avoidance (all core processes in both adaptive and maladaptive behavior) all have direct relevance to human performance.

It is clear, after years of research, that human performance is a complex human activity that involves multiple internal and external factors. The wide array of factors that should be considered to understand the psychology of human performance include (Gardner & Moore, 2006, 2007) *instrumental competencies*, which include individual physical, sensorimotor, and/or cognitive skills and abilities; *environmental stimuli and performance demands*, which include the situational and interpersonal/social circumstances and contexts that performers experience and to which they must respond; *dispositional characteristics*, which include the intrapersonal characteristics from which performers respond to their world; and *behavioral self-regulation*, which is the outcome of a variety of cognitive, affective, physiological, and behavioral processes that are central to goal-directed behavior within any performance domain.

Understanding both human performance in general and the individual performer in particular requires a consideration of all of these important factors, which intersect to determine how one functions and performs in a given context (Gardner & Moore, 2006). Careful perusal of these factors also underscores the numerous ways in which optimal performance can be disrupted by psychological distress at all levels of intensity.

Defining Distress

Why do we need to define distress? Why can't we just talk about counseling techniques? Well, a physician would not prescribe a medication without fully understanding the patient's medical pathology first. Although symptoms can be very similar, the medication would obviously be different for pneumonia than for HIV/AIDS. Likewise, a contractor would not install bolts into a wall without knowing whether the wall is concrete or plaster. If the wrong bolts are utilized, they will not support the installation. So, effectively understanding distress allows practitioners to choose the best interventions available to remediate clients' specific concerns and promote intrapersonal and interpersonal health and well-being. Within sport psychology, it has long been suggested, though, that athletes are generally psychologically healthy (Vealey, 1994). Traditional models of sport psychology consultation have subsequently argued that performance enhancement should be an educational endeavor due to the assumed psychological health of athletes (or other performers, especially those functioning at high levels), and that only when clear and diagnosable psychological conditions develop would the performer need psychological counseling/treatment of any type (Silva, 1989). This supposition is based upon a binary categorical way of thinking about psychological distress, proposing that individuals either have a full diagnosable condition (and thus consideration of distress is warranted) or they do not (and therefore focusing on that distress is essentially irrelevant at best and contraindicated at worst). Based upon this premise, a brief review of classification is warranted, which may help highlight the need for a reconsideration of the construct of distress.

Categorical Versus Dimensional Models of Classification

The ultimate function of classification systems in the health professions is to guide systematic research, comprehensive assessment, and ethical decision-making in evidence-based practice. These functions are achieved by a classification system that is able to accurately delineate categories of problem areas (i.e., disorders) and the interrelationship of such categories. Classification systems such as the *Diagnostic and Statistical Manual of Mental Disorders, Fourth Edition, Text Revision* (*DSM-IV-TR*; American Psychiatric Association [APA], 2000) are highly embedded in the day-to-day practice of professional psychologists. In this regard, clinical syndromes (i.e., categories) are described and defined, thus allowing both researchers and clinicians to communicate with each other with regard to typical clinical presentations. Yet, within sport/performance psychology, this categorical system has unfortunately been functionally reduced even further, such that the presence or absence of a *DSM-IV-TR* diagnosis has often been used as the primary factor in determining whether an "educational" or "clinical" approach to service provision is utilized. As such, the presence or absence of a diagnosable condition has become a two-factor, de facto categorical system, and it has been suggested that widespread acceptance of this simplistic categorical dichotomy (healthy/nondistressed/no diagnosis vs. unhealthy/distressed/diagnosis) as a means of understanding performers is a weakness for sport psychology (Gardner & Moore, 2006, 2007). Recent data have in fact suggested that subclinical levels of psychological distress (which refers to psychological issues not quite meeting criteria for diagnosis according to the *DSM* but nevertheless manifesting in one form or another) have a negative impact on both athletic performance and performance enhancement efforts (Wolanin & Schwanhausser, 2010). These data support the position that psychological distress should be viewed beyond simple categorical models of diagnosis, and that researchers and practitioners should consider a more dimensional view of distress. A dimensional approach "acknowledges that there may be important individual differences among those who fall above, and among those who fall below, a categorical diagnostic threshold" (Helzer, Kraemer, & Krueger, 2006, p. 1672). Although both categorical and dimensional models have useful and valid components (Brown, 2007; Helzer et al., 2006), a more dimensional model maintains an appreciation for the degrees and nuances of the client's overall psychological well-being, distress levels, and general levels of human functioning, and it takes into account subclinical psychological barriers as well.

The limitations of categorical models of classification have been recognized for quite some time within clinical and counseling psychology (First,

2010; Waldman & Lilienfeld, 1995). Although categorical models do have strengths when utilized correctly, they are still generally ineffective at capturing individual differences in disorder severity and clinically significant features falling below conventional *DSM* thresholds. Of importance, the value of including dimensional elements in the *DSM* has recently been a focus of professional attention (Brown, 2007). Yet, unfortunately, even with burgeoning interest in adopting a dimensional view of distress, the recent draft iteration of the upcoming *DSM-5* (American Psychiatric Association, 2011, http://www.dsm5.org; First, 2010) has thus far made little progress in this regard, although some attempt has been made to introduce dimensional severity ratings to the extant diagnostic categories and criteria sets. As noted previously, sport/performance psychology has similarly been inclined to view performers in the same categorical manner, by viewing performers as either healthy or clinically diagnosable. This bifurcated view of performers is both theoretically and empirically problematic, as it makes little sense to believe that only upon reaching a particular cutoff point (i.e., officially meeting diagnostic criteria) do psychological characteristics/factors such as worry, rumination, and avoidance become problematic with regard to personal well-being and/or performance.

Multilevel Classification System for Sport Psychology

In response to the absence of a structured and standardized system to understand the full range of internal and external psychological factors facing performers, the Multilevel Classification System for Sport Psychology (MCS-SP; Gardner & Moore, 2004b, 2006) was developed as a dimensional system to comprehensively evaluate and consider the relevant factors that may need to be increased or reduced in order to enhance human performance. As further described below, the use of the MCS-SP allows the practitioner to move beyond the traditional view that a performer's "distress" is out of the purview of sport/performance psychology and recognize that psychological interventions (such as counseling) for the purpose of distress reduction can enhance both performance and overall well-being.

The MCS-SP is a classification system that provides a step-by-step working framework for assessing/evaluating, conceptualizing, and planning interventions for performers. The benefit of the MCS-SP is that it is a comprehensive model that maintains a dimensional perspective and appreciates the numerous personal variables and subclinical issues that impact the performance and overall well-being of clientele. Of significant importance, it then sets the stage for the practitioner to choose the most effective intervention to meet the performer's needs (a discussion of counseling performers in distress follows the discussion of classification). Researchers and practitioners (Bennett, 2007; Hack, 2007; Wolanin, 2007; Wolanin & Schwanhausser, 2010) have utilized the MCS-SP as a central component of their practice of sport/performance psychology over the last several years.

To help clarify any confusion as to how the MCS-SP can be a dimensional model if it uses categorical descriptors, consider that a categorical system can be thought of as being on a horizontal plane in which different categories can exist independently or can co-occur with each other. Our system is essentially a more vertical system whereby individuals fall on different levels of severity. For ease of understanding and use, we have named the different levels of severity. However, although it has the typography of a categorical system, it actually functions as a dimensional system.

According to the MCS-SP, the performer needs to be understood (and in turn interventions should be chosen) not simply by a consideration of outcome-based performance goals, but rather by a careful and systematic consideration of instrumental competencies, environmental stimuli and performance demands, dispositional characteristics, and behavioral self-regulation abilities that were noted previously. The practitioner then utilizes the MCS-SP to understand the performer's issues from the perspective of one of four broad classifications, each of which contains two subtypes. These four classifications are performance development (PD), performance dysfunction (Pdy), performance impairment (PI), and performance termination (PT). What follows is a brief description of the dimensional MCS-SP classifications, followed by a discussion of targeted counseling interventions and variables that affect the counseling process. Readers interested in a more complete description of the MCS-SP, including the MCS-SP semi-structured interview, are referred to Gardner and Moore (2006).

Performance Development

Including dimensional aspects of classification, the MCS-SP consists of categories that span the spectrum of distress type and severity. The title of the first classification, PD, suggests minimal psychological barriers and a greater focus on the development and maintenance of performance. The PD classification is reserved for performers whose needs are those in which:

• The client's primary goal is the enhancement and/or full development of realistic skills and performance.

• The client at this time experiences no *significant* developmental, transitional, behavioral, interpersonal, or intrapersonal psychological barriers that could impede performance or overall well-being. Of course, clients can *state* that they have no such barriers, but the practitioner must actually assess for these factors instead of assuming that the client's self-report is accurate.

• Developing or refining a variety of relevant psychological skills can be reasonably expected to enhance skill sets and performance.

• Based on the above variables, distress alleviation is not a necessary goal. Instead, the primary intervention goals are the enhancement of performance and continued development of psychological strengths.

Within the PD category, there are two distinct subtypes, as there are with all subsequent categories as well. PD-I refers to those performers for whom skill development is still *ongoing*, and the development or enhancement of specific psychological skills may aid in that development and in turn enhance performance. PD-II refers to performers for whom performance abilities are *already developed* to a large/nearly complete degree. For these individuals, employing specific psychological skills may assist or even be necessary for the performer to attain and maintain optimal performance states.

The PD category includes the types of client issues that psychological skills training techniques such as imagery, goal setting, arousal control, precompetitive routines (stimulus control), cognitive control, refocusing, and mindfulness- and acceptance-based strategies were developed to assist. It is important to understand, though, that the reason for assuming that both traditional and newer approaches to performance enhancement may in fact be effective in these cases is the critical absence of either clinical or subclinical (subthreshold for a *DSM* disorder) issues negatively impacting the client. It is much more difficult for psychological skills to improve performance if significant psychological barriers are in the way. So, in cases of PD, the absence of clinical or subclinical issues makes the application of self-regulatory processes to assist in performance a rational choice. There is no need for more intensive intervention, as there are no psychological barriers to be ameliorated at this time.

A perusal of the sport/performance psychology literature would suggest that since the PD classification requires no discernible psychological barriers, this category would represent the large majority of performers. Yet, despite the common misconception that all or almost all performers are psychologically healthy, they are actually no less likely than the average person to experience psychological distress and dysfunction. PD clients are in fact merely a subset of the clients with whom we work. Thus, with an ongoing appreciation for the continuum upon which all people, including performers fall, I turn to the second MCS-SP classification.

Performance Dysfunction

Further along the severity of distress dimension, Pdy is the next classification. Performance *dysfunction* does not mean *disorder*, nor does it imply that no psychological barriers exist. So, the Pdy category describes client issues in which:

- The desire to improve performance is stated as either a primary or secondary goal of intervention.
- The client's performance development/ progress may have been slowed or delayed, or performance may have previously been consistently greater than the performer's current level of performance.
- The performer is generally psychologically healthy, but psychological barriers are negatively impacting her or him. These barriers can include, for example, developmental, interpersonal, intrapersonal, transitional, and dispositional issues.
- Overall psychological, general behavioral, or performance functioning may be somewhat reduced.
- Although the performer may benefit from developing self-regulatory strategies for enhancing performance as a *secondary* intervention, counseling and/or psychological treatment would be the primary intervention option to best meet the performer's overall needs.

Although the PD classification is used for clients without current psychological issues, the Pdy category represents subclinical psychological barriers. Although Pdy clients do not meet criteria for a psychological disorder (*DSM*), they are still struggling with endogenous or exogenous factors that impede performance and/or valued functioning in other important life domains. In essence, this category is more in the middle of the healthy/ unhealthy continuum and appreciates the specific nuances and degrees of distress. The Pdy category also includes two distinct subtypes. Pdy-I refers to performers for whom *exogenous* (external) factors, such as interpersonal/social, developmental, and transitional issues, lead to psychological reactions and result in dysfunctional performance. Pdy-II refers to athletes who possess underlying *endogenous* (internal) psychological vulnerabilities that are triggered by a multitude of life circumstances, which in turn disrupt functioning in a variety of domains. Such endogenous psychological vulnerabilities can include, for example, subclinical levels of distress; cognitive schemas about performance, failure, and disappointing others/need for approval; unrelenting standards; worry/rumination; and distress intolerance. Although these are not "clinical" issues in the technical sense of the term (as a diagnosable condition is absent), such vulnerabilities often result in varying degrees of performance disruption and may cause disruption in other life domains. In this regard, the practitioner may note that both endogenous and exogenous factors are present for a client. That is not uncommon, because internal (endogenous) factors understandably lead to external (exogenous) behavioral manifestations for many clients. In such cases, the client is classified as Pdy-II because the primary and most critical elements to resolve are the endogenous concerns. Thus, the intervention focus will be on remediating the client's subclinical psychological barriers/vulnerabilities, which should also residually reduce the outward behavioral consequences (such as interpersonal disputes, difficulty adjusting to a new environment, etc.). I should also note that just as clients can have endogenous-only concerns, and simultaneous endogenous and exogenous concerns, clients can also have exogenous-only concerns. An example of a client with more externally focused Pdy concerns could be a psychologically healthy college freshman who becomes sad and withdrawn after moving away from home, not based on significant psychological vulnerabilities, but on more normative developmental/transitional demands.

For Pdy cases, there is no clear theoretical basis for nor empirical evidence of efficacy for traditional self-regulatory–based psychological skills training procedures as the most appropriate, or even as a necessary, intervention. The psychological issues and the underlying processes represented by Pdy have typically been ignored in sport/performance psychology research and practice. This may be because they lie outside of the binary delineation of the clinical–nonclinical view of performers, which I previously discussed. Yet, it has been frequently noted that *most* performers come to the sport/performance psychologist with exactly these types of problems, and, although at first glance, they may appear to be exclusively performance-based issues (suggestive of a PD classification), deeper investigation unveils that these often subtle, but very real issues (Pdy) are actually at the heart of the problem (Bauman, 2000; Bond, 2001; Gardner, 2001; Gardner & Moore, 2004b, 2006; Giges, 2000). An illustration of this type of client could be a gymnast who comes to the sport/performance psychologist complaining that she has lost her focus and is unhappy with her performance levels. At first, she may be mistakenly classified as PD due to a respectable performance history, demonstration of dedication, and her own report that there is "nothing wrong" with her. However, further investigation reveals that she has unrealistic performance demands based on a history of unrelenting and dysfunctional levels of perfectionism. This has led her to ruminate heavily about her performance (self-focused attention) and subsequently lose her ability to maintain task-focused attention, thereby resulting in performance decrements. Since significant endogenous psychological vulnerabilities/schemas are the triggering causative factors, a classification of Pdy is warranted.

Performance Impairment

Moving from one end of the distress continuum (PD), through the middle (Pdy), and now toward the other side the continuum, the next classification is PI. The PI category describes client issues in which:

• Clinical issues exist that, in most circumstances, would warrant a *DSM* diagnosis. These issues cause the performer significant emotional distress and/or behavioral dysregulation, likely resulting in reduced performance or an inability to compete due to institutional and/or outside agency involvement (e.g., organizational action, judicial involvement).
• The clinical issues significantly impair at least one (but typically more) major life domain, such as family, interpersonal, educational, and occupational domains (performance would be considered "occupational" for elite performers).
• Performance enhancement, although possibly and understandably desired by the client, is secondary in importance to overall life adjustment as a priority for the sport/performance psychologist.

• The significance of the clinical issue(s) makes it unlikely that psychological skills training procedures would have a substantial effect on performance at this time, without resolution of the critical impairment issues.
• Intensive psychological treatment (which may possibly include psychotropic medication) is indicated as the intervention of choice.

The PI category can be viewed as the "clinical" end of the continuum. The psychological dysfunction is clear, diagnosable, and significant, and it takes precedence over performance-related issues. The PI category is made up of two distinct subtypes. PI-I refers to those cases in which clinical disorders (such as mood, anxiety, and/or eating disorders) significantly disrupt a performer's life functioning, and, in turn, are very likely to significantly impair his or her performance life as well. PI-II refers to cases of clinical personality disorders, anger/impulse control disorders, and/or substance abuse in which substantial behavioral dysregulation (often outward) results in significant impairment in overall life and performance functioning. For performers who fall in the PI category, appropriate psychological interventions would be the same as for the nonperformer experiencing a *DSM* condition, although the implications of the consequences for the high-performer's lifestyle (e.g., for an elite athlete or business executive) may be substantial. Thus, treatment plans must take into account the role of performance consequences for the client. The treatment options available to those individuals (including performers) requiring such services can be found in a number of comprehensive texts on clinical sport psychology (Gardner & Moore, 2006) and clinical psychology (Nathan & Gorman, 2007; Roth & Fonagy, 2005).

Although the distinctions among PD, Pdy, and PI are clear, I stress that these classifications are best conceptualized by the practitioner as occurring along a continuum and not as three rigid categorical boxes that have no relationship to each other. As performer's lives evolve, endogenous and exogenous changes regularly occur. As such, clients may from time to time possess different levels of distress, and may move from one classification to another. It is certainly not uncommon for any given person to develop situational, transitional, interpersonal, intrapersonal, or developmental issues when he or she has previously been functioning at higher levels.

At this point, readers may be thinking of a particular client who seems to be represented by more than one classification, such as PD and Pdy, and wondering if it is possible to distinguish the appropriate classification. For example, consider a National Collegiate Athletic Association (NCAA) Division 1 football quarterback who is an excellent performer but has been referred because of concerns over his peer group, who coaches fear may be sabotaging his development. Is this PD or Pdy? This is just a hypothetical example and much more information would be needed to determine classification, but for the sake of illustration, I suggest that this is Pdy. It is not a performance issue; it is an interpersonal adjustment issue (whether it is his "fault" or not). He is functioning very well from a performance standpoint, but the important variable to address is an interpersonal concern that has the potential to significantly disrupt the maintenance of performance success. Pdy is the more appropriate classification, as psychological barriers (of an interpersonal nature in this particular case) are risking performance success or overall well-being. The client would not warrant a PD classification because PD is reserved for clients who simply need to reach and maintain consistent quality performance (and, as such, interventions for PD are generally more educational in nature). To assist in classification decision-making, I often ask myself, "If X is changed in the client's life, is it likely to also resolve [or how will it impact] Y?," or "What is the pivotal variable that is likely to alter the client's system? And is that variable more of a PD, Pdy, or PI variable?" With a firm understanding of the client's macro and micro functioning, symptom sets, underlying processes, and outcomes, classification can in fact be determined even when a client *seems* at first glance to fit more than one classification.

Finally, there is one additional MCS-SP classification, which is rarely confused with the first three.

Performance Termination

This final MCS-SP classification is reserved for issues in which:

• The primary concern centers around stressors and issues related to the termination of a performance career. The career termination is usually the result of the natural career process, or injury or deselection that leads to a premature career termination.

• Psychological distress reactions reflecting either a normative or exceptional grieving process (often including anger, anxiety, and depression)

may be present. Such reactions may necessitate individual and/or family attention.

• Career realities suggest that performance enhancement efforts are contraindicated.

• Counseling/psychological treatment is the clear intervention of choice to address emerging stressors and issues. Referrals for career counseling and financial planning may be helpful as well.

As sport/performance psychologists know, the termination process actually involves its own interesting continuum, as some performers comfortably withdraw from the performance milieu, others moderately struggle, and others experience extreme distress reactions (see Chapter 27, this volume). As it is such a unique issue, the MCS-SP allocates a specific category for it instead of subsuming it into the other three classifications.

There are two subtypes within the PT category. PT-I refers to cases in which a career ends relatively expectedly (possibly voluntarily) due to increasing age, personal choice, and/or a gradual decline of physical skills. It is not uncommon for newly retired performers to struggle with identity issues during this time, or to face a variety of interchangeable emotional experiences such as shock, denial, anger, bargaining, depression, and acceptance, as one may following the death of a loved one or loss of a significant relationship. I should point out, though, that although some of these emotional experiences have been described by Kubler-Ross (Hopson & Adams, 1977; Kubler-Ross, 1969) as occurring linearly, more recent evidence suggests that these and any other common emotional reactions are interchangeable and can flexibly shift on a moment-to-moment basis. As such, it appears that they should not be conceptualized as *stages*, but as elastic and vacillating emotional consequences (Copp, 1998).

PT-II includes cases in which the performer faces an unexpected and involuntary end to his or her performance career due to serious injury- or non–injury-based termination. Because this form of termination is unexpected, these performers often have no clear career options in mind and may immediately lose the performance "family" they have been a part of, often for many years. Understandably, interventions for PT are likely to vary depending on the specific nature of the case. Typically, PT-I clients will benefit from career and supportive counseling, whereas PT-II individuals may likely require more intensive psychological interventions. However, it is important to consider that both clients who voluntarily retire and those whose careers involuntarily end can have emotional reactions that span the spectrum of severity, from a smooth integration into the nonperformance world to suicidality.

Understanding the construct of distress from a more dimensional perspective such that is provided by the MCS-SP allows for an appreciation of the nuances of the human condition that a dichotomous framework inadvertently underappreciates. When practitioners have such a framework to help them recognize factors such as instrumental competencies, environmental stimuli and performance demands, the performer's dispositional characteristics and behavioral self-regulation patterns, and nuanced levels of distress along the continuum, there is a great opportunity to subsequently choose and utilize the evidence-based intervention strategies that are most likely to directly target and meet the client's performance and overall psychological needs. What follows is a discussion of approaches to counseling performers in distress, followed by a discussion of setting, counselor, client, and cultural variables that can impact the counseling process.

Approaches to Counseling Performers in Distress
Traditional Approaches to Counseling Performers in Distress

A myriad of specific therapeutic modalities are utilized by psychological health care providers. Although a complete review of therapeutic modalities in beyond the scope of this chapter, numerous theoretical models have been presented with various levels of professional acceptance and demonstrable treatment efficacy (see Nathan & Gorman, 2007). The list of therapeutic modalities is vast, from psychoanalytic models and their various iterations that seek to alter intrapsychic conflicts; to a wide array of humanistic/existential models and their efforts to unblock the human's natural desire for growth and personal development; to behavioral, cognitive-behavioral, and neo-behavioral models and their efforts to modify cognition and behavior in its various forms.

The field of psychotherapy was dominated for nearly the entire 20th century by the development of "schools of psychotherapy." During that time, treatment developers and their adherents presented their various models as being the ultimate treatment for most, if not all, psychological distress. The near blind allegiance to schools of psychotherapy led to an inevitable "horse-race" mentality, in which proponents would attempt to justify their adherence to a particular model—some by appeals to authority, in which the prominence of the developers were used as evidence of efficacy; some by case examples used as evidence of efficacy; and some by conducting randomized controlled trials demonstrating the supposed superiority of one method over another as evidence of efficacy. The result has been a fragmented field that, to date, cannot agree on either the relative efficacy of the various schools of psychotherapy, the most appropriate definition of "evidence," or even the proper role of scientific inquiry in the future development of psychotherapy (American Psychological Association Presidential Task Force on Evidence-based Practice, 2006).

In addition, although many have argued that different psychotherapies have different levels of efficacy based upon condition/problem area (Siev, Huppert, & Chambless, 2009) due to the targeting of problem-specific psychological variables (i.e., fears in phobias vs. worry in generalized anxiety), others have suggested that all treatments work about the same for all conditions/problem areas by virtue of nonspecific therapist–client relationship factors present in all treatments and conditions (Wampold, 2001). It is fair to say that the differences in thinking about this seemingly easy-to-answer question loop back to the difference in definition of the term "evidence" and the role of science. Some scholarly camps (i.e., Wampold, 2001) rely exclusively on meta-analyses, with all of the inherent strengths and weaknesses of these procedures, as the basis of their evidence with respect to specificity of treatment effects versus nonspecific effects of treatment. Other scholarly camps (i.e., Barlow, 2010) offer a serious critique of meta-analyses as a means of determining efficacy, especially when not used by independent and impartial groups/organizations, due to the ease by which slight modifications in procedure can result in vastly different results. This large camp instead suggests that, ultimately, only carefully constructed randomized controlled trials can determine the efficacy and specificity of psychological treatments.

One unifying reality, however, has been the fact that consistently lacking through most of the 20th century was a consideration of the mechanisms by which psychotherapy procedures worked. Rarely were important questions asked, such as, "Exactly *through what means* do treatments work?," and "What changes, in what time frame, and why?" For an example of mechanisms of change, let's consider the field of medicine once again. It is fairly well understood in medicine that antibiotics work for conditions like nonviral pneumonia by way of reducing levels of infectious organisms in the body. Similarly, the reason antibiotics do not work in cases of viral pneumonia is that they do not reduce the presence and volume of viral organisms in the body. As such, the mechanism of change of antibiotics is reduction of infectious organisms in the body.

Accompanied by strong support in the clinical psychology domain, it has been suggested that only by fully understanding the *mechanisms of change* (also referred to as *mechanisms of action*) can any psychological treatment be fully understood and, in turn, appropriately utilized (Gardner, 2009; Kazdin, 2007; Moore, 2007; Moore & Gardner, 2011). Also, for optimal efficacy, the mechanisms of change for any given treatment should be inextricably tied to the specific nature of the psychopathology in question. For example, because studies in experimental psychopathology suggest that generalized anxiety disorder is characterized by an excessive use of worry (as a ruminative process) to avoid the full experience of moment-to-moment anxiety (Borkovec, Alcaine, & Behar, 2004), then effective treatments for this condition should be able to demonstrate that reductions in the worry process precede and are directly associated with positive outcomes in treating such conditions. The early 21st century has seen the beginnings of a connection between experimental psychopathology and the search for mechanisms of change within psychological treatments and, with it, a more systematic and targeted approach to client treatment. With the rapid development of this line of research, some are already suggesting both that "schools of psychotherapy" are a prescientific notion whose time has passed and that the field of psychology is moving toward a more unified or integrative approach to understanding psychopathology and its treatment (Barlow & Carl, 2011; Boswell et al., 2011). This targeted approach to psychological intervention also has enormous relevance to the psychological care of performers in distress.

An Evidence-Based Approach to Counseling Performers in Distress

As a scientific discipline, psychology is currently in an age of accountability in which (a) clients, with increasing knowledge fueled at least in part by the internet; (b) health care organizations, with their pressure to provide services within the context of shrinking availability of health care dollars; and (c) institutions/organization, with their need to demonstrate positive outcomes from the services that they provide, all expect health service providers to utilize interventions with demonstrable efficacy and efficiency. Within this context of accountability, the concept of evidence-based psychological care has permeated the fields of clinical and counseling psychology worldwide.

Evidence-based psychological practice may be best understood as the delivery of psychological services in which assessment and intervention modalities and strategies are selected based upon the following guidelines (Moore, 2007):

- *Best available scientific evidence.* The individual practitioner is expected to be aware of ongoing and ever-changing empirical findings, their meaning, implications, and limitations.
- *Clinical skill and judgment.* The practitioner is expected to be capable of effectively utilizing those interventions that the best available scientific evidence suggests are appropriate, while also being able to make judgments about the contraindications and/or limitations of these procedures for individual cases.
- *Client values.* The practitioner should be able to provide appropriate informed consent, including a clear presentation of benefits and risks involved with differing procedures and help clients connect their individual needs and desires with the most recent and available scientific evidence.

When adopting an evidence-based approach to providing care to performers in distress, the practitioner has a series of tasks to address prior to beginning the intervention process. First, the practitioner needs to carefully assess the presenting request for service. This is more complex than it may appear, as much has been written regarding the frequency with which performers presenting requests for service focus on the desire to enhance performance when, over time, it becomes apparent that subclinical or even clear clinical issues (not easily discussed and presented) are at the core of their performance issues (Bauman, 2000; Bond, 2001; Gardner, 2001; Gardner & Moore, 2004b, 2006). Second, the practitioner must ensure that he or she knows the most up-to-date empirical data surrounding interventions for that class of problem/issue and not simply assume that what he or she knows or has done in the past is still part of the prevailing body of knowledge. This is challenging, in that it is quite easy to become comfortable with a particular approach or strategy and fail to remain current with the ever-evolving body of professional knowledge. Third, the practitioner must ask him- or herself if he or she is knowledgeable and professionally comfortable with delivering specific services and interventions (even if it means having to refer a client elsewhere).

With an evidence-based practice philosophy as the guide, what follows are guidelines for an evidence-based approach to providing psychological services to performers in distress.

IDENTIFYING THE TARGET OF INTERVENTION AND SELECTING THE INTERVENTION

Utilizing the MCS-SP as the starting point is suggested as a way of determining the precise target of psychological intervention, and subsequently selecting the most appropriate intervention to impact the identified target. As an easy vehicle for adopting the MCS-SP into practice, a semi-structured interview for the MCS-SP is available (see Gardner & Moore, 2006), which allows for simple and quick determination of MCS-SP classification. If time and/or practice style does not permit the use of a formal interview, a 10-item self-report measure called the Performance Classification Questionnaire (PCQ; Gardner & Moore, 2006; Wolanin, 2005) is also available and can be quickly administered in a variety of settings. The PCQ is used to readily distinguish (by an established cutoff score) between the PD and Pdy classifications, which appear to be the two most frequently seen classifications in sport/performance psychology practice settings. As the PCQ is not designed to be a clinical diagnostic tool, PI is not assessed with this measure. Highly reliable and valid measures for the assessment of clinical disorders are widely available.

Although the MCS-SP offers a broad understanding of the general needs of the performer, the specific information gleaned from the MCS-SP interview or PCQ must then be followed-up to gain a complete understanding of the intervention targets. In developing this understanding, the practitioner develops a case formulation in which the information related to instrumental competencies, relevant environmental stimuli and performance demands, dispositional characteristics, and behavioral self-regulation skills/deficits noted earlier in this chapter are systematically considered, thus resulting in a clear target for intervention efforts (Gardner & Moore, 2005).

Recent empirical findings in clinical psychology have identified a number of psychological variables that appear to be transdiagnostic and, in fact, central to the development and maintenance of a large variety of clinical and subclinical difficulties (Kring & Sloan, 2010). Identified as core psychological processes are rumination (in all of its forms,

such as worry, perfectionism, and brooding), emotional avoidance, self-focused attention, and deficits in emotion regulation. In turn, interventions that directly target these processes appear to offer greater efficacy and efficiency than many traditional intervention strategies (Barlow, Allen, & Choate, 2004; Boulanger, Hayes, & Pistorello, 2010; Kashdan, Barrios, Forsyth, & Steger, 2006). In fact, emotional avoidance, which is a particularly pernicious core pathological process, has been shown to better explain psychological distress and lower levels of functioning than coping strategies and cognitive reappraisal, the mechanisms by which traditional cognitive-behavioral interventions are thought to work (Kashdan et al., 2006).

Using a previous example, findings in experimental psychopathology over the last decade have demonstrated that generalized anxiety disorder, which is a chronic and pervasive anxiety disorder, appears to have at its core significant deficits in emotion regulation. These emotion regulation deficits in turn result in substantial efforts to control, reduce, or inhibit the full experience of emotion (particularly anxiety), and, as such, individuals suffering from this condition engage in substantial amounts of concentrated attention on future possibilities (i.e., worry). By doing so, these individuals attenuate the full in-the-moment experience of anxiety (particularly the physiological component of anxiety), which results in negative reinforcement of this action (i.e., immediate reduction of anxiety) and, over time, the further maintenance of this process with all its negative life outcomes (Borkovec et al., 2004). Importantly, studies have likewise demonstrated that subclinical forms of generalized anxiety disorder (which consists of moderate levels of worry and often perfectionism) have a significant and negative impact on quality of life, not unlike that seen in clinical levels of this disorder (Heimberg, Turk, & Mennin, 2004). In essence, psychological interventions for this disorder or its subclinical variations necessitate a targeting of these specific processes. Failure to do so would likely result is less positive outcomes.

Of course, the implication of this approach is the need to focus on the presence, absence, and significance of these (and other) core psychological processes and not simply to determine the presence or absence of signs and symptoms of diagnoses. For the sport/performance psychologist, the implication is clear as well. Processes such as worry, dysfunctional perfectionism, and the like, even if not reaching levels consistent with a diagnosable disorder, should be assessed and, when necessary targeted for intervention (see also Chapter 9, and 15, this volume).

With this discussion in mind, let's consider the psychological interventions most relevant for performers manifesting the various MCS-SP classifications. As this chapter is concerned with counseling performers in distress, there is no need for a discussion of intervention efforts for those warranting a PD classification (but see, for example, Chapter 38, this volume).

COUNSELING PERFORMANCE DYSFUNCTION

Recall that for Pdy, although overall functioning is typically adequate to strong, difficulties in specific life or performance-related areas are reported. Pdy denotes subclinical difficulties that include intrapersonal, interpersonal/social, transitional, and/or dispositional issues/demands. The intervention choices thus should be directly related to those particular aspects and should be informed by the psychological processes related to the presenting problem area(s). For example, in the case of adjustment difficulties in response to new environments, such as an athlete's freshman year at college, brief situational counseling targeting obstacles to expected social adjustment would be the likely intervention of choice. Likewise, in the case of a performer whose worry or dysfunctional perfectionism is interfering with the ability to meet personal or team performance expectations, an intervention geared toward acceptance of emotional experiences, reduction of the use of cognitive processes such as worry and perfectionism (Santanello & Gardner, 2007) as a form of emotional avoidance, and reconnection to those actions that are directly related to performance success would be indicated. This approach to psychological intervention would look much like that provided to clients experiencing levels of distress meeting criteria for formal diagnoses. Yet, that fact should not at all turn the practitioner away from its use, as subclinical issues for high performers can be effectively remediated by the same evidence-based strategies used for clinical variants.

It is important to emphasize that psychological interventions for performers in distress meeting criteria for the Pdy (subclinical) classification would not differ markedly from interventions often seen as "clinical" in nature. Actually, these interventions are as likely to result in performance enhancement as they are in the enhancement of general psychological well-being. The binary distinction of clinical versus nonclinical when viewing performers has blurred the reality that clients' performances can be impacted by a myriad of variables, including issues/distress that require psychological interventions broadly related to overall functioning across many life areas. Recent empirical data have in fact supported this position. In a study of Division I collegiate athletes, Wolanin and Schwanhausser (2010) found that efforts at performance enhancement using Gardner and Moore's (2004a, 2007) mindfulness-acceptance-commitment (MAC) approach were differentially effective with athletes predetermined to meet criteria for PD or Pdy. These findings indicated that a more clinically oriented version of the intervention protocol was more appropriate for those with subclinical psychological issues (Pdy), whereas a more educational version of the intervention protocol was appropriate for those not experiencing any (including subclinical) psychological issues (PD).

Particularly interesting cases of Pdy are those situations in which performers experience psychological reactions to serious injury (see also Chapter 32, this volume). Intense reactions may have much in common with post-traumatic stress disorder (PTSD), but may not meet the *DSM-IV-TR* Criterion A (confronted a potential loss of life or a severely disabling injury) necessary for a full diagnosis of PTSD. Findings in experimental psychopathology indicate that trauma-related disorders have as a core feature the incomplete experience and processing of intense emotions related to the traumatic event. Emotion is inhibited or avoided via a variety of cognitive and behavioral methods (i.e., avoiding thinking about the event, avoiding situations related to the event, and emotional numbing). Practitioners are therefore encouraged to approach the performer's distress in much the same way they would if dealing with an identified (i.e., diagnosed) PTSD case. The treatment should include systematic exposure to the feared/traumatic event, so that the emotion can be fully experienced and processed effectively, a treatment component with substantial empirical support (Foa, Keene, & Friedman, 2004). Other empirically supported treatments incorporating such procedures can be found in the cognitive-behavioral literature (see Barlow, 2008).

The take-home message is to not forget the practice of *psychology* and its utility with all individuals as we focus on the performance issues and needs of our clients. Personal distress and reductions in overall psychological well-being are inextricably connected to performance concerns (Gardner & Moore, 2004b, 2006; Giges, 2000). This message is important when working with performers who do not meet criteria for *DSM* diagnoses. Assess carefully the needs of those clients meeting criteria for Pdy. The core personal issues and intervention needs of subclinical (Pdy) clients are likely to be more similar to the core personal issues and intervention needs of more distressed clients (PI) than they are to those clients whose performance needs are without the presence of clinical or subclinical issues (PD). Although clients (and often psychologists as well) emphasize desired performance outcomes, psychological interventions that deal with interpersonal processes, intrapersonal and dispositional characteristics, and transitional life circumstances are very often targeting the mechanisms of change for both enhanced performance and enhanced personal well-being.

COUNSELING PERFORMANCE IMPAIRMENT

Performance impairment includes difficulties that meet criteria for *DSM* diagnoses and lead to a significant negative impact on overall psychological functioning. PI clients are also almost certain to experience significant performance difficulties, either via decrements in overt performance or by way of external limitations on their performance (i.e., suspensions, loss of job or position). The major focus of intervention should be on the psychological difficulties directly related to the distress and functional impairment. The treatment strategy for performers should be no different than for the nonperformer because what matters most is choosing the treatment that is likely to improve overall psychological well-being and promote enhanced life functioning, and in the shortest possible time.

Examples of PI are many, from major depressive disorder and bulimia nervosa—both of which result in significant personal distress as well as reductions in the ability to handle day-to-day life demands and performance-related responsibilities—to the full range of personality disorders, which typically include extreme and often inappropriate interpersonal behaviors often resulting in serious external consequences (suspension, firing, incarceration, etc.). In choosing appropriate psychological interventions, a wide variety of officially empirically supported interventions are available. For example, efficacious treatments for major depression include behavioral (activation) therapy (Dimidjian, Martell, Addis, & Herman-Dunn, 2008), cognitive therapy (Young, Rygh, Weinberger, & Beck, 2008), interpersonal psychotherapy (IPT; Bleiberg & Markowitz, 2008), and mindfulness-based cognitive therapy (specifically for clients who have experienced three or more episodes of depression; Teasdale et al.,

2002). Efficacious treatments for bulimia include cognitive-behavioral therapy (CBT) and IPT (please note that IPT is a very specific treatment modality and is not the old interpersonal psychodynamic approach), whereas evidence-based treatments for specific personality disorders include dialectical behavior therapy (Linehan, 1993), schema therapy (Young, Klosko, & Weishaar, 2003), and a few very specific forms of psychodynamic psychotherapy (Bateman, & Fonagy, 2004; Clarkin et al., 2001). As seen in these few examples, the choices are wide. However, this does not mean that any treatment can be used with any client, or in any manner. Very specific treatment protocols are recommended for each condition, and it is not enough to simply assume that generic forms of each of these treatments would be appropriate (Nathan & Gorman, 2007). It is the responsibility of the practitioner to carefully consider the scientific data and choose the specific variants of these treatments that have demonstrated efficacy.

Likewise, the breadth of treatment choices does not mean that it does not matter which of the empirically supported treatments are used. For example, although CBT and IPT are both efficacious treatments for major depression, data suggest that individuals with serious interpersonal difficulties respond better to CBT, whereas those with substantial cognitive distortions respond better to IPT (Craighead, Hart, Craighead, & Ilardi, 2002). Yes, you read that correctly, even though it does not make intuitive sense! Clearly, these counterintuitive findings, and many others like them, strongly suggest that practitioners must depend on the accumulated scientific data and not simply rely on their personal assumptions, opinions, and comfort levels to make intervention decisions.

The issues of knowing the existing scientific data and best-practice guidelines and practicing within one's area of competence are not just important for the practitioner working with *DSM*-diagnosable (PI) performers (see Chapter 3, this volume). Rather, these are important considerations for practitioners working with performers who experience distress along the continuum due to the impending, expected, or unexpected end of their performance careers. This brings us to a discussion of the psychological intervention options relevant to the final MCS-SP classification of PT.

COUNSELING PERFORMANCE TERMINATION

Recall that PT refers to those circumstances in which performers are confronted with either expected (e.g., age-related) or unexpected (e.g., injury) termination of their performance careers. Most often, counseling such individuals should allow for the expression of concerns and emotions related to the termination of the career (usually much earlier in life than nonperformers would expect to retire), with some time provided for consideration of alternative career choices, predicted impact on relationships and personal identity, and financial considerations. It is not uncommon, however, for practitioners to confront more difficult situations in which the performer experiences what has been termed "identity foreclosure" (Danish, Petitpas, & Hale, 1995). Identity foreclosure is a situation in which the client's identity has been so strongly connected to being a performer that career termination, and the subsequent loss of that identity, leads to significant questions about personal identity and the meaning of life. Although no single intervention has been empirically demonstrated to be efficacious for such intense difficulties related to PT, interventions should provide a safe environment for the full discussion and processing of the meaning (internal and external) of the career termination, the emotions that it may generate (spanning the spectrum of severity), and the interpersonal consequences that may be expected to ensue. Although no specific treatment approach can claim efficacy with this very specific issue, a variety of brief psychological interventions would seem to be particularly appropriate for use, such as IPT (Bleiberg & Markowitz, 2008), with its specific focus on the impact of role changes in life; mindfulness- and acceptance-based behavioral therapies (Gardner & Moore, 2004a, 2007, 2012; Roemer & Orsillo, 2009), with their emphasis on mindful awareness of present-moment experiences and focus on commitment to the pursuit of valued-directed behavior; and emotion-focused therapy (Elliott, Watson, Goldman, & Greenberg, 2004), with its emphasis on emotional experiencing and personal growth. All seem appropriate for counseling performers whose distress is related to issues of PT.

At this point, I have considered the various MCS-SP classifications and types of difficulties that find their way into the work of the sport/performance psychologist, and have considered an evidence-based approach to treatment decision-making along the way. But, one thing is certain: Interventions with high performers do not happen in a bubble. A number of variables, both endogenous and exogenous, can, at times, have a significant impact on the effectiveness or even the efficient delivery of psychological interventions with athletes and other performers.

Variables Affecting Treatment

Psychological interventions, including those utilized in sport/performance settings and contexts, are rarely simple and easy to deliver. A wide array of variables may impact the efficiency and effectiveness of these interventions. Where we work, how we work, who we are, who our clients are, what they think about counseling/psychotherapy, and how they think about their needs all influence the intervention process. Earlier in this chapter, I noted the intraprofessional debate between those who believe that psychological treatment is specific to disorders and, as such, requires the targeting of disorder-specific psychological processes, and those who believe that essentially all bona fide treatments work for all problems due to the primacy of nonspecific factors in psychotherapy. Interestingly, both nonspecific factors, such as the therapist–client relationship and a client's belief that treatment has a reasonable chance of success, as well as an appropriate matching of disorder and treatment type, ultimately impact treatment outcome. Few within professional psychology would challenge the fact that, at the very least, nonspecific factors such as those just noted are necessary, albeit probably not sufficient, for optimal treatment efficacy. What follows is an overview of some of the variables that may impact intervention efforts, with an emphasis on these variables in the context of sport/performance psychology.

SETTING VARIABLES

Sport/performance psychologists often work across numerous settings including private offices, hospitals/clinics, and a variety of performance-related settings (i.e., training facilities, performance venues, buses). These settings offer different advantages and disadvantages (Gardner, 2001; Moore, 2003), and practitioners must remain mindful of the fact that differing settings inevitably result in differing impacts on the relationship with the client. The relationship dimension, and the power differential (if you will), is vastly different when working with performers in their world (i.e., in a small room adjacent to the physical therapy offices within a large stadium) or within the confines of the practitioner's private office. Although there is no simple or single way to deal with these different circumstances and their impact on the practitioner–client relationship, the mistake would be to ignore these differences and act as though all settings are created equal. Astute practitioners will consider the setting, the type of clients with whom they work, and the issues involved, and will both draw reasonable hypotheses about the possible impact and maintain vigilant mindful attention for signs that the setting may be negatively impacting the intervention process (Murphy & Murphy, 2010). This theme of mindful-awareness and willingness to respond when necessary is the hallmark of a competent practitioner who is considering and effectively handling nonspecific factors in the treatment context.

We must consider whether the setting in which we work impacts our ability to do so adequately (i.e., Do the settings provide privacy and relative comfort for clients to adequately share their thoughts and feelings?). We must also consider whether the setting impacts what clients expect of us, or how much they value our services. Namely, do clients believe that our efforts at reducing their distress are in fact "treatment," or is it seen as "a once-in-a-while (when I am free for 15 minutes) occasion to tell you how I'm feeling," with an expectation that this will somehow make an impact on their distress? A direct and important implication of this is that, if we cannot structure our environment so that we have adequate time/opportunity to deliver interventions, we have to make sure that we do not oversell what the impact will be from these brief and sometimes informal meetings. It is our responsibility to ensure that clients understand that if they come to us periodically for 15 minutes, they may not be getting the correct "dose" of the intervention and should, therefore, not have faulty expectations of effective and sustainable change.

COUNSELOR VARIABLES

Practitioners, like clients, span the entire spectrum of human personality, beliefs, values, and interpersonal styles. This is important to recognize, as psychological care providers should be catalytic in the change process for our clients. That is, the process should not engage our own issues, nor should we change in any fundamental way (as it is not our own therapy) due to work with a given client (Moore, 2003). After all, it is their treatment, not ours. We cannot alter who we are as human beings, but as professionals we can do a variety of things to ensure that who and what we are does not interfere with our intervention efforts. First, there is the simple recognition that no matter what treatment model or strategy we employ, psychological counseling is, by its very nature, an interpersonal enterprise. Our clients' actions within a session are likely to be consistent in one form or another with their actions outside of a session. As such, part of our task is to be aware of these behaviors, make observations when appropriate, and promote clinically relevant behavior change when necessary (Kohlenberg & Tsai, 1991). It is also expected that we maintain awareness of our own personal stimulus functions for our clients, and theirs to us; specifically: what we represent to our clients, how our behaviors impact them, what our clients represent to us, and how their behaviors impact us. Most importantly, we must place a premium on maintaining appropriate boundaries and behaving in a professional, ethical manner. Successful practitioners working in this milieu will ultimately be those who are mindful of their choices, actions, and motivations, therefore allowing them to ultimately provide effective counseling services to performers in distress.

CLIENT VARIABLES

A variety of client variables similarly impact the treatment process (Gardner & Moore, 2006). Personality and previous history with and beliefs about therapy and its likely effectiveness can all have some impact on treatment outcome. It is worthwhile to state that these variables are most likely to affect the practitioner–client relationship and can, subsequently, have an effect on treatment outcome.

However, within sport/performance psychology, there is a very different and unique variable that the practitioner dealing with performers in distress must be mindful of and attend to as needed. Specifically, it is the critical issue of acceptability of being distressed. Put another way, I am referring to the acceptability of having a psychological issue/problem/disorder of any kind that needs professional attention, and the personal meaning and acceptability of receiving psychological intervention. This issue is not insignificant; because I strongly believe that subclinical distress is the reason that a large percentage of performers seek services from sport/performance psychologists, we need to remain open to discussing the acceptability of distress with performers. Clients with subclinical or clinical issues must be open to the fact that they have a psychological barrier in need of attention, so that they can actually deal with the issue.

Many performers who do not meet criteria for a clear psychological disorder, and who subsequently do not have the type of life impairment that typifies such disorders, will come to the sport/performance psychologist requesting help for performance-related issues. Upon careful assessment, or even over time as the client becomes more comfortable, subclinical issues will often become evident and require attention. The practitioner must then carefully navigate between the client's performance-related request for services and the reality that the most effective performance enhancement intervention would likely be focused counseling/psychological treatment targeting the subclinical barriers. In my experience in working with performers and supervising trainees, the difficulties with navigating the client's stated desire and his or her actual intervention needs are typically more in the mind of the practitioner. The performer is typically much more accepting of this direction than the practitioner expects. Of course, how professional services are *presented* to the client significantly contributes to breaking down any concerns or misconceptions held by the client, such as those related to the identified problem/issue in question, the way that the issue impacts performance (and possibly other spheres of life), and the specific facets of the proposed intervention. This client variable is often based upon misconceptions and stereotypes that must be confronted in an empathic, knowledgeable, and professional manner by the practitioner.

Finally, the sport/performance psychology practitioner is encouraged to carefully consider the developmental level of his or her client and answer several questions: Do I have the proper education and training to counsel performers of different developmental levels, and, as is sometimes the case, entire families? How can I best understand the performer's needs, based upon knowledge of both normal development and developmental psychopathology? And, do I possess a solid understanding of the empirical literature with regard to treatment efficacy in general, and across developmental levels in particular?

CULTURAL VARIABLES

Countless factors comprise the cultural makeup of the client, including, though certainly not limited to, race, ethnicity, socialization, socioeconomic background and current status, religion, sexual orientation, geographic location, and gender (Comas-Dias, 2011; Schinke & Moore, 2011). These intersecting, overlapping, and sometimes deeply held personal factors can impact the therapeutic relationship between the client and practitioner, can influence the intervention strategies we choose, and, of great importance, can impact intervention outcomes. Although effective interventions for many psychological difficulties are available, less research

has been conducted to determine whether these interventions are effective in treating those from diverse backgrounds. Recent reviews in clinical psychology show that in about half of the studies considering this important issue, ethnic minorities do as well as Caucasians, and half of the studies signal worse treatment outcomes (Lam & Sue, 2001). It has been suggested that, to improve care for those from diverse backgrounds, Western-developed psychotherapies may need to be culturally modified or adapted to become more effective in treating cultural minorities (Griner & Smith, 2006; Lam & Sue, 2001). Specifically, although the mechanisms of change of these evidence-based treatments appear to remain the same across cultural groups, the manner and style of delivering these empirically supported treatment processes may need to be modified to better meet cultural norms, expectations, and sensitivities (Comas-Dias, 2011; Muñoz & Mendelson, 2005; Schinke & Moore, 2011).

How, then, do we, as sport/performance psychologists, make the determination as to how to apply evidence-based interventions to cultural minority populations? The answer is to look at the extant scientific knowledge base in both sport/performance psychology (Kontos, 2009; Marks, 2011; Schinke & Hanrahan, 2009; Schinke & Moore, 2011) and allied disciplines, such as clinical psychology, which has considered these issues for 50 years (American Psychological Association, 2003; Wrenn, 1962). In the case of treatment efficacy and ethnic and cultural diversity, the practitioner can expect regular changes in the scientific knowledge base. Any reviews done to date will inevitably need to be reconsidered in the years that follow. When working with clients from minority ethnic or cultural backgrounds, the empirical data may offer only guidance, rather than definitive directions (see Chapter 22, this volume; Parham, 2011). For example, a clinical study by Hwang (2006) highlighted a program that adapted the delivery of evidence-based mental health services for an Asian American population with great success. Although at present no absolute strategies or guidelines exist, we can state the following:

• Delivering treatments without relevant consideration for cultural diversity may decrease the likelihood that those treatments will provide the assumed and desired benefits.
• No evidence suggests that mechanisms of change are different among ethnic/cultural groups, but rather, the delivery of these approaches should

be considered and possibly modified to be more acceptable to ethnic/cultural groups with different attitudes, beliefs, and histories. Sport/performance psychologists have a wonderful opportunity in this regard, as many practitioners work with performers in their own unique cultural context (e.g., the sport culture or the performing arts culture) and can therefore pay special attention to cultural issues, when appropriate. Clinical studies have even found that clients who perceive that their psychologist is culturally aware and competent are actually more likely to complete a treatment protocol and also state greater levels of perceived satisfaction with the treatment (Comas-Diaz, 2011). Data such as these certainly highlight the importance of cultural considerations.

• A growing body of empirical data exists to which the practitioner can refer with respect to efficacy of treatment strategies and cultural diversity. For example, the current evidence suggests that women have as good or better outcomes from psychological interventions as do men, and furthermore, no evidence suggests that men or women systematically respond better or worse to same- or opposite-gender counselors (Lam & Sue, 2001). As the literature is changing rapidly, the burden is on the practitioner to remain current and understand the nuances of implementation of psychological interventions, consistent with the spirit of evidence-based practice.

• The practitioner should remember that within-cultural differences can be as important as between-cultural differences (Marks, 2011; Schinke & Moore, 2011). For example, the meaning and experience of psychological interventions to performers from rural poor cultures (e.g., the Appalachian area of the United States) can be much different than it is for athletes from major urban areas, even if basic ethnic background (e.g., Anglo-American) is the same.

Conclusion

Providing counseling services to performers in distress can be a highly gratifying yet complex professional endeavor. The practitioner must be flexible, self-aware, and committed to engaging in evidence-based practice, regularly guided by the ever-evolving scientific literature. To best understand and intervene with performers in distress, practitioners are encouraged to avoid the tendency to view performers as either presenting with or without clinical problems and to instead adopt a more dimensional view of psychological

distress that appreciates how subclinical issues can negatively impact both performance and overall psychological well-being. In this chapter, the practitioner has been provided with an overview of how to appreciate the distress continuum; to assess the client's performance, subclinical, and clinical needs; to select the most appropriate and efficacious interventions to meet those needs; and to consider a host of variables that can impact intervention selection, delivery, and client assimilation. I close with some important questions that await investigation in this field.

Future Directions

1. What is the relationship between performance enhancement and enhanced psychological well-being?

2. How do adapted forms of psychological treatment compare to traditional performance enhancement techniques in terms of performance and well-being outcomes?

3. How common is it for sport/performance psychology cases to fall somewhere between the traditional binary "clinical" versus "nonclinical" categories?

4. How will the publication of the upcoming DSM-5 impact psychology's conceptualization of distress?

5. How best should a multidisciplinary field deal with subclinical cases?

References

American Psychiatric Association (APA). (2000). *Diagnostic and statistical manual of mental disorders* (4th ed., text revision). Washington, DC: Author.

American Psychiatric Association. (2011). *SM-5: The future of psychiatric diagnosis*. Retrieved from http://www.dsm5.org

American Psychological Association. (2003). Guidelines on multicultural education, training, research, practice, and organizational change for psychologists. *American Psychologist, 58*, 377–402.

American Psychological Association Presidential Task Force on Evidence-based Practice. (2006). Evidence-based practice in psychology. *American Psychologist, 61*, 271–285. doi: 10.1037/0003-066X.61.4.271

Andersen, M. B. (2009). The "Canon" of psychological skills training for enhancing performance. In K. Hays (Ed.), *Performance psychology in action* (pp. 35–56). Washington, DC: APA.

Barlow, D. H. (2010). The Dodo bird–again–and again. *The Behavior Therapist, 33*, 15.

Barlow, D. H. (Ed.). (2008). *Clinical handbook of psychological disorders: A step-by-step treatment manual* (4th ed.). New York: Guilford Press.

Barlow, D. H., Allen, L. B., & Choate, M. L. (2004). Toward a unified treatment for emotional disorders. *Behavior Therapy, 35*, 205–230.

Barlow, D. H., & Carl, J. R. (2011). The future of clinical psychology: Promises, perspectives, and predictions. In D. H. Barlow (Ed.), *Oxford handbook of clinical psychology* (pp. 891–911). New York: Oxford University Press.

Bateman, A. W., & Fonagy, P. (2004). Mentalization-based treatment of BPD. *Journal of Personality Disorders, 18,* 36–51.

Bauman, J. (2000, October). Toward consensus on professional training issues in sport psychology. In E. Dunlap (Chair), *Toward consensus on professional training issues in sport psychology.* Panel discussion presented at the conference for the Association for the Advancement of Applied Sport Psychology, Nashville, TN.

Bennett, G. (2007). The role of a clinical psychologist in a Division I athletic program. *Journal of Clinical Sport Psychology, 1,* 261–269.

Bleiberg, K. L., & Markowitz, J. C. (2008). Interpersonal psychotherapy for depression. In D. H. Barlow (Ed.), *Clinical handbook of psychological disorders: A step-by-step treatment manual* (4th ed., pp. 306–327). New York: Guilford Press.

Bond, J. W. (2001). The provision of sport psychology services during competition tours. In G. Tenenbaum (Ed.), *The practice of sport psychology* (pp. 217–239). Morgantown, WV: Fitness Information Technology.

Borkovec, T. D., Alcaine, O., & Behar, E. (2004). Avoidance theory of worry and generalized anxiety disorder. In R. G. Heimberg, C. L. Turk, & D. S. Mennin (Eds.), *Generalized anxiety disorder: Advances in research and practice* (pp. 77–108). New York: Guilford Press.

Boswell, J. F., Sharpless, B. A., Greenberg, L. S., Heatherington, L., Huppert, J. D., Barber, J. P., et al. (2011). Schools of psychotherapy and the beginnings of a scientific approach. In D. H. Barlow (Ed.), *Oxford handbook of clinical psychology* (pp. 98–127). New York: Oxford University Press.

Boulanger, J. L., Hayes, S. C., & Pistorello, J. (2010). Experiential avoidance as a functional contextual concept. In A. M. Kring & D. M. Sloan (Eds.), *Emotional regulation and psychopathology: A transdiagnostic approach to etiology and treatment* (pp. 107–136). New York: Guilford Press.

Brown, T. A. (2007). Temporal course and structural relationships among dimensions of temperament and DSM-IV anxiety and mood disorders. *Journal of Abnormal Psychology, 116,* 313–328.

Clarkin, J. F., Foelsch, P. A., Levy, K. N., Hull, J. W., Delaney, J. C., & Kernberg, O. F. (2001). The development of a psychodynamic treatment for patients with borderline personality disorder: A preliminary study of behavioral change. *Journal of Personality Disorders, 15,* 487–495.

Comas-Diaz, L. (2011). Interventions with culturally diverse populations. In D. H. Barlow (Ed.), *The Oxford handbook of clinical psychology* (pp. 868–887). New York: Oxford University Press.

Copp, G. (1998). A review of current theories of death and dying. *Journal of Advanced Nursing, 28,* 382–390.

Craighead, W. E., Hart, A. B., Craighead, L. W., & Ilardi, S. S. (2002). Psychosocial treatments for major depressive disorder. In P. E. Nathan & J. M. Gorman (Eds.), *A guide to treatments that work* (2nd ed., pp. 245–261). New York: Oxford University Press.

Danish, S. J., Petitpas, A., & Hale, B. D. (1995). Psychological interventions: A life development model. In S. M. Murphy (Ed.), *Sport psychology interventions* (pp. 19–38). Champaign, IL: Human Kinetics.

Dimidjian, S., Martell, C. R., Addis, M. E., & Herman-Dunn, R. (2008). Behavioral activation for depression. In D. H. Barlow (Ed.), *Clinical handbook of psychological disorders: A step-by-step treatment manual* (4th ed., pp. 328–364). New York: Guilford Press.

Elliott, R., Watson, J., Goldman, R. N., & Greenberg, L. S. (2004). *Learning emotion-focused therapy: The process-experiential approach to change.* Washington, DC: American Psychological Association.

First, M. B. (2010). Clinical utility in the revision of the *Diagnostic and Statistical Manual of Mental Disorders (DSM). Professional Psychology: Research and Practice, 41*(6), 465–473.

Foa, E. B., Keene, T. M., & Friedman, M. J. (Eds.). (2004). *Effective treatments for PTSD: Practice guidelines from the international society for traumatic stress studies.* New York: Guilford Press.

Gardner, F. (2001). Applied sport psychology in professional sports: The team psychologist. *Professional Psychology: Research and Practice, 32,* 34–39.

Gardner, F. L. (2009). Efficacy, mechanisms of change, and the scientific development of sport psychology. *Journal of Clinical Sport Psychology, 3*(2), 139–155.

Gardner, F. L., & Moore, Z. E. (2012) A scientific revolution in sport psychology: Challenges and opportunities in the assimilation and delivery of acceptance-based behavioral interventions. *Athletic Insight, 4*(1).

Gardner, F. L, & Moore, Z. E. (2001, October). *The Multilevel Classification System for Sport Psychology (MCS-SP): Toward a structured assessment and conceptualization of athlete-clients.* Symposium presented at the annual conference of the Association for the Advancement of Applied Sport Psychology, Orlando, Florida.

Gardner, F. L., & Moore, Z. E. (2004a). A Mindfulness-Acceptance-Commitment based approach to athletic performance enhancement: Theoretical considerations. *Behavior Therapy, 35,* 707–723.

Gardner, F. L., & Moore, Z. E. (2004b). The Multi-level Classification System for Sport Psychology (MCS-SP). *The Sport Psychologist, 18*(1), 89–109.

Gardner, F. L., & Moore, Z. E. (2005). Using a case formulation approach in sport psychology Consulting. *The Sport Psychologist, 19,* 430–445.

Gardner, F. L. & Moore, Z. E. (2006). *Clinical sport psychology.* Champaign, IL: Human Kinetics.

Gardner, F. L., & Moore, Z. E. (2007). *The psychology of enhancing human performance: The Mindfulness-Acceptance-Commitment (MAC) approach.* New York: Springer Publishing.

Giges, B. (2000). Removing psychological barriers: Clearing the way. In M. B. Andersen (Ed.), *Doing sport psychology* (pp. 17–32). Champaign, IL: Human Kinetics.

Griner, D., & Smith, T. B. (2006). Culturally adapted mental health interventions: A meta-analytic review. *Psychotherapy: Theory, Research, Practice, Training, 43,* 531–548.

Hack, B. (2007). The development and delivery of sport psychology services within a university sports medicine department. *Journal of Clinical Sport Psychology, 1,* 247–260.

Hanrahan, S. J., & Andersen, M. B. (Eds.). (2010). *Routledge handbook of applied sport psychology: A comprehensive guide for students and practitioners.* New York: Routledge.

Heimberg, R. G., Turk, C. L., & Mennin, D. S. (Eds.). (2004). *Generalized anxiety disorder: Advances in research and practice.* New York: Guilford Press.

Helzer, J. E., Kraemer, H. C., & Krueger, R. F. (2006). The feasibility and need for dimensional psychiatric diagnoses. *Psychological Medicine, 36,* 1671–1680.

Hopson, B., & Adams, J. (1977). Toward an understanding of termination: Defining some boundaries of termination. In J. Adams, J. Hayes, & B. Hopson (Eds.), *Transition: Understanding and managing personal change* (pp. 3–25). Montclair, NJ: Allanheld & Osmun.

Hwang, W. (2006). The psychotherapy adaptation and modification framework: Application to Asian Americans. *American Psychologist, 61*, 702–716.

Kashdan, T. B., Barrios, V., Forsyth, J. P., & Steger, M. F. (2006). Experiential avoidance as a generalized psychological vulnerability: Comparisons with coping and emotion regulation strategies. *Behavior Research and Therapy, 44*, 1301–1320.

Kazdin, A. E. (2007). Mediators and mechanisms of change in psychotherapy research. *Annual Review of Clinical Psychology, 3*, 1–27.

Kohlenberg, R. J., & Tsai, M. (1991). *Functional analytic psychotherapy: Creative intense and curative therapeutic relationships.* New York: Plenum Press.

Kontos, A. P. (2009). Multicultural sport psychology in the United States. In R. J. Schinke & S. J. Hanrahan (Eds.), *Cultural sport psychology* (pp. 103–116). Champaign, IL: Human Kinetics.

Kring, A. M., & Sloan, D. M. (Eds.). (2010). *Emotion regulation and psychopathology: A transdiagnostic approach to etiology and treatment.* New York: Guilford Press.

Kubler-Ross, E. (1969). *On death and dying.* New York: Macmillan.

Lam, A. G., & Sue, S. (2001). Client diversity. *Psychotherapy: Theory, Research, Practice, Training, 38*, 479–486.

Linehan, M. M. (1993). *Skills training manual for treating borderline personality disorder.* New York: Guilford Press.

Marks, D. R. (2011). The polyphonic self: Interactivism and the examination of culture in clinical sport psychology. *Journal of Clinical Sport Psychology, 5*(4), 294–308.

Meichenbaum, D. (1977). *Cognitive behaviour modification: An integrative approach.* New York: Plenum Press.

Moore, Z. E. (2003). Ethical dilemmas in sport psychology: Discussion and recommendations for practice. *Professional Psychology: Research and Practice, 34*(6), 601–610.

Moore, Z. E. (2007). Critical thinking and the evidence-based practice of sport psychology. *Journal of Clinical Sport Psychology, 1*(1), 9–22.

Moore, Z. E., & Gardner, F. L. (2011). Understanding models of performance enhancement from the perspective of emotion regulation. *Athletic Insight, 3*(3), 247–260.

Muñoz, R. F., & Mendelson, T. (2005). Toward evidence-based interventions for diverse populations: The San Francisco General Hospital prevention and treatment manuals. *Journal of Clinical and Consulting Psychology, 73*, 790–799.

Murphy, S. M., & Murphy, A. I. (2010). Attending and listening. In S. J. Hanrahan & M. B. Andersen (Eds.), *Comprehensive applied sport psychology: A handbook for professionals and students* (pp. 12–20). London: Routledge.

Nathan, P. E., & Gorman, J. M. (2007). *A guide to treatments that work* (3rd ed.). New York: Oxford University Press.

Parham, W. D. (2011). Research vs. me-search: Thinking more of thee and less of me when working within the context of culture. *Journal of Clinical Sport Psychology, 5*(4), 309–323.

Roemer, L., & Orsillo, S. M. (2009). *Mindfulness- and acceptance-based behavioral therapies in practice.* New York: Guilford Press.

Roth, A., & Fonagy, P. (2005). *What works for whom?: A critical review of psychotherapy research* (2nd ed.). New York: Guilford Press.

Santanello, A. W., & Gardner, F. L. (2007). The role of experiential avoidance in the relationship between maladaptive perfectionism and worry. *Cognitive Therapy and Research, 31*(3), 319–332.

Schinke, R. J., & Hanrahan, S. J. (Eds.). (2009). *Cultural sport psychology.* Champaign, IL: Human Kinetics.

Schinke, R. J., & Moore, Z. E. (2011). Culturally informed sport psychology: Introduction to the special issue. *Journal of Clinical Sport Psychology, 5*(4), 283–293.

Siev, J., Huppert, J. D., & Chambless, D. L. (2009). The Dodo bird, treatment technique, and disseminating empirically supported treatments. *The Behavior Therapist, 32*(4), 69–76.

Silva, J. (1989). Toward the professionalization of sport psychology. *The Sport Psychologist, 3*(3), 265–273.

Teasdale, J. D., Moore, R. G., Hayhurst, H., Pope, M., Williams, S., & Segal, Z. V. (2002). Meta-cognitive awareness and prevention of relapse in depression: Empirical evidence. *Journal of Consulting and Clinical Psychology, 70*, 275–287.

Vealey, R. S. (1994). Current status and prominent issues in sport psychology interventions. *Medicine and Science in Sport and Exercise, 26*, 495–502.

Waldman, I. D., & Lilienfeld, S. O. (1995). Diagnosis and classification. In M. Hersen & R. T. Ammerman (Eds.), *Advanced abnormal child psychology* (pp. 21–36). Hillsdale, NJ: Erlbaum.

Wampold, B. E. (2001). *The great psychotherapy debate: Models, methods, and findings.* Mahwah, NJ: Lawrence Erlbaum Publishers.

Wolanin, A. T. (2005). Mindfulness-acceptance-commitment (MAC) based performance enhancement for Division I collegiate athletes: A preliminary investigation. *Dissertation Abstracts International-B, 65*, 3735–3794.

Wolanin, A. T. (2007). Clinical sport psychology services based in a doctoral training clinic. *Journal of Clinical Sport Psychology, 1*, 270–280.

Wolanin, A. T., & Schwanhausser, L. A. (2010). The moderating effects of level of psychological functioning on the effectiveness of the mindfulness-acceptance-commitment (MAC) approach to performance enhancement. *Journal of Clinical Sport Psychology, 4*, 312–322.

Wrenn, C. G. (1962). The culturally encapsulated counselor. *Harvard Educational Review, 32*, 441–449.

Young, J. E., Klosko, J. S., & Weishaar, M. E. (2003). *Schema therapy.* New York: Guilford Press.

Young, J. E., Rygh, J. L., Weinberger, A. D., & Beck, A. T. (2008). Cognitive therapy for depression. In D. H. Barlow (Ed.), *Clinical handbook of psychological disorders: A step-by-step treatment manual* (4th ed., pp. 250–305). New York: Guilford Press.

Appearance and Performance Enhancing Drug Use

Thomas B. Hildebrandt, Eleanna Varangis, *and* Justine K. Lai

Abstract

Appearance and performance enhancing drugs (APEDs) include a wide range of substances borrowed from a wide range of medical disciplines and associated fields and have a long history in sport and competition. The defining features of APED use are discussed and include polypharmacy, body image disturbance, and disturbances in diet and exercise. Appearance and performance enhancing drugs are unique among substances of abuse in their biological action, as well as in the basic motivations for their use. Although there are a wide range of potentially serious physical and psychiatric side effects, APEDs continue to be used by millions of men and women and to a greater degree by those engaged in sport and fitness activities. It is still unclear how individuals become illicit APED users, but it is possible that legal APEDs act as a gateway substance for illicit APED use. There are few empirically supported prevention programs for APED use and a complete absence of empirically supported interventions for those using APEDs. The engagement of APED users in treatment is complicated by the ethical-legal obstacles and mistrust between the APED-using and health services communities. Future research will need to overcome these barriers to provide effective and useful interventions for those APED users in the sport or performance fields.

Key Words: Anabolic-androgenic steroid, testosterone, appearance and performance enhancing drug, drug dependence, exercise, body image disturbance

Appearance and performance enhancing drugs (APEDs) are substances used to enhance outward appearance by promoting muscle growth and fat loss or improving one's performance in athletic or social domains. The current scientific literature, along with media coverage, has focused on anabolic-androgenic steroids (AASs), a family of synthetic hormones derived from sex hormones, such as testosterone and dihydrotesterone (DHT), even though AASs are rarely used by themselves to achieve the desired effects (Hildebrandt, Langenbucher, Carr, & Sanjuan, 2007). Rather, polypharmacy, or the use of substances from multiple drug classes, is a characteristic feature of APED use, an umbrella under which AAS use falls. Most associate the phenomena of APED use with AAS because of the public interest generated from scandals involving professional and Olympic athletes (Catlin, Fitch, & Ljungqvist, 2008; Tsitsimpikou et al., 2009), as well as tragedies involving APED users that include, but are not limited to, suicide/homicide, cardiac events, or other severe psychiatric or medical complications (Cowan, 1994; Dickerman, Schaller, Prather, & McConathy, 1995; Hausmann, Hammer, & Betz, 1998; Huie, 1994; Patil, O'Donohoe, Loyden, & Shanahan, 2007; Peet & Peters, 1995; Santamarina, Besocke, Romano, Ioli, & Gonorazky, 2008; van Breda, Keizer, Kuipers, & Wolffenbuttel, 2003). However, the use of AASs in sport- or performance-related fields is just the tip of the iceberg. Illicit AAS use developed out of a long history of legitimate use in medicine and related disciplines, such as behavioral endocrinology, and their transition from medicine to cosmetic or performance enhancer is not unique. Thousands of other substances share the same history as AASs—they are abused by those looking to feel better about their appearance or gain an edge in sport or performance.

History of Appearance and Performance Enhancing Drugs Use

Since the introduction of formal competition, humans have sought ways to achieve an "edge" over their competitors. The potential ability of APEDs to provide a competitive advantage of strength, speed, and enhanced recovery time has always been an attractive option to those who wish to attain an unnatural edge. Performance enhancing substances date back to ancient times, when they were primarily derived from sources such as plants, animals, and at times, humans. In fact, the use of testosterone as a potential anabolic agent was discovered based on ancient humans' observation of animal behavior following castration; it has been reported that animal or human testes were often eaten in order to improve or heal the owner's own organs (Holt, Erotokritou-Mulligan, & Sönksen, 2009). As is true now, APED use was not restricted to anabolic-androgenic agents. In ancient Greece, a diet of dried figs purportedly promised similar performance enhancing effects, and stimulants in the form of brandy or wine potions were often used by athletes as part of their training routine. Roman gladiators also used stimulants in the form of plants during training to help facilitate their recovery from battle (Bahrke & Yesalis, 2002). However, unlike present attitudes toward performance enhancing drug use, none of these methods was considered unethical or cheating.

Until the 19th century, little had changed in terms of APED technology or use. In the 1800s, caffeine and other stimulants were the most widely used performance enhancing substances, and were often combined with brandy, wine, or morphine by athletic trainers to make "doping cocktails" for their athletes (Yesalis & Bahrke, 2002). Since doping was still not technically illegal, athletes didn't conceal their substance use, and, as a result, doping accounts from that time are quite detailed and accurate. In the late 19th century, scientists discovered amphetamines, and doctors began using testosterone extract for medicinal purposes, but it wasn't until the 20th century that these substances reached the athletic world and became a significant impediment to fair competition (Kuhn, 2002).

In the 20th century, the use of steroids became more widespread, with athletes using any number of different types of AAS, stimulants, opioids, and various other hormones and pro-hormones to try to compete with their increasingly larger and more muscular opponents. In 1928, the International Amateur Athletic Federation (IAAF) became the first sporting body to ban doping in an attempt to prevent certain athletes with access to these performance enhancing drugs from having an unfair advantage over nondoping competitors. Many other similar agencies followed suit, but without available tests to detect whether an athlete had been doping, the move was largely ineffective (Yesalis & Bahrke, 2002). In the meantime, the use of AAS and amphetamines increased dramatically as the drugs spread outside of the medical community and began to be used recreationally and in competition by athletes. In response to this very apparent proliferation of APEDs in the sporting world, both the International Federation of Association Football (FIFA) in 1966 and the International Cycling Union (ICU) in 1967 introduced antidoping tests for its athletes. The next year, the International Olympic Committee (IOC) convened to create a medical commission charged with administering and processing drug tests for all Olympic athletes. In 1974, the first truly reliable doping test was introduced, which was followed by a significant increase in the number of drug disqualifications in competitions using the test (Holt et al., 2009). Athletes were now finding it harder and harder to find APEDs not yet detectable by these newer drug tests, and, as a result, discovered the anabolic effects of human growth hormone (hGH), a drug so similar to endogenous human growth hormone that it was able to go undetected by drug tests. The athletic community soon caught on to hGH use and banned it entirely for athletic use by 1991. Although *blood doping* (in which an athlete uses certain drugs to increase his or her red blood cell count in order to increase oxygen availability throughout the body) had been used by distance runners, cyclists, cross-country skiers, and biathletes for decades, by the 1990s, this form of abuse also became an increasingly popular form of APED use. As a result, in 1994, the IOC mandated a blood drug test, as opposed to the traditional urine test, and in November 1999, the IOC decided to further their crusade against the use of APEDs in sport by creating the World Anti-Doping Agency (WADA), the first international body created solely for the purpose of combating and detecting the use of doping agents in competition (Bahrke & Yesalis, 2002). Despite these increasing efforts to control APED use, athletes were still able to hide their use of hGH. In response to growing concerns about this trend, the IOC introduced an isoform test at the 2004 Athens summer Olympic Games to test for the use of hGH. However, this test is only able to detect hGH that has been administered in the prior 24 hours, and consequently has never detected the presence of hGH in any Olympic athlete from its introduction until present (Holt et al., 2009).

Although APED use seems to be pervasive within the athletic community, its use patterns vary greatly from sport to sport. As a result, testing administration schedules adopted by the different sporting bodies may either make doping nearly impossible or passively support it. Traditionally, drug testing protocols have lagged behind athletes' pursuit of a pharmacological edge, thus giving rise to scandals and public disappointment. Of even more concern are those performance professions that have no standardized regulation of APED use. For example, modeling, dance, "pro" (entertainment) wrestling, or acting contracts don't traditionally include APED testing, but they often include requirements for characteristics such as weight and appearance. Given the financial incentives associated with these fields and their high appearance or performance standards, APED use has undoubtedly become an issue for this population.

Scope of Appearance and Performance Enhancing Drugs Use

Due to the international nature of most formal sporting competitions, APED use is a global phenomenon. Based on research and surveys conducted on adolescents, Australia, Sweden, France, Norway, Germany, and Brazil tend to report incidences of AAS use ranging from about .1% to 3.6%, whereas the United States and Poland tend to report higher steroid use prevalence, ranging from about 1.4% to 14.3% (Handelsman & Gupta, 1997; Harmer, 2010). A recent large-scale U.S. study (Monitoring the Future) indicated that a general decrease in steroid use occurred among middle and high school students since the late 1990s (by about .4%), but still ranged between 1% and 6% (NIDA, 2006). In a more recent report, the nationwide Youth Risk Behavior Surveillance (YBRS) study estimated that nonprescription steroid use was present in 3.3% of students (CDC, 2010).

Field studies generally suggest greater use among gym attendees and athletes; incidence reports vary from 11% to 70% for males and 1% to 9% for females (e.g. Bolding, Sherr, & Elford, 2002; Frankle, Cicero, & Payne, 1984; Green, Uryasz, Petr, & Bray, 2001; Kersey, 1993; Lindstrom, Nilsson, Katzman, Janzon, & Dymling, 1990). In a recent study conducted in South Wales, researchers documented a 70% prevalence rate of illicit APED use (Baker, Graham, & Davies, 2006), suggesting that some gyms may have a culture particularly amenable to APEDs. Specific sports may also be at higher risk; in a study conducted on the U.S. Powerlifting Federation, Wagman, Curry, and Cook (1995) found that roughly two-thirds of the U.S. powerlifting team respondents admitted to having used AASs. Thus, those engaged in weightlifting for recreation, sport, or training may be more likely to use AASs, especially when engaged in activities in which there is a high demand on power or strength. The prevalence of other illicit APEDs is poorly documented and remains largely unknown. It is reasonable to hypothesize that some individuals in certain performing professions, such as dance, modeling, or acting, would be drawn to illicit APED use to increase outward appearance or to alter the body quickly for the demands of a specific role or job. However, there are no published prevalence estimates of illicit APED use among these groups, and it is possible that their pattern of illicit APED use differs from those of athletes or weightlifters. Specifically, it is possible that these users may be more likely to abuse weight loss or fat burning substances to increase the visual appearance of their muscle.

Most of the prevalence studies rely on self-report and are subject to a number of methodological concerns, which may explain why usage estimates vary from 10% to 90% (National Center on Addiction and Substance Abuse, 2000). Illegal APEDs carry both the stigma of cheating and legal repercussions associated with breaking the law. This context is likely to lead to an under-reporting by many illicit APED users. Other issues include the types of questions asked: The majority of prevalence estimates are based on an understanding by the respondent as to what is and is not an AAS. The sophistication of the nutritional supplement market may lead to some over-reporting of AAS use, and others who are taking AASs at someone else's direction, without knowledge of the substance, may under-report. A related issue is the focus on simply AASs. Doping includes a much wider range of substances, which can lead to an underestimation of illicit APED use. More sophisticated screening methods, such as liquid chromatography/tandem mass spectrometry and gas chromatography/combustion/isotope-ratio mass spectrometry have been developed but are limited by costs, test sensitivity, and the short half-lives of certain substances (Bowers, 2009). A significant portion of the APED market has evolved in response to the need to evade these testing procedures, and this will continue to be the case as long as doping and drug testing exist. These factors continue to complicate interpretation of basic epidemiological data gathered on APEDs.

Conceptual Foundations of Appearance and Performance Enhancing Drugs Use

The cornerstone substances of most illicit APED use are the AAS; thus, much of what we know about APED use originates from observational studies conducted with small groups of self-reported AAS users. However, the foundation of most APED use is a targeted form of polypharmacy (Hildebrandt, Langenbucher, Carr, & Sanjuan, 2007) including other anabolics, fat burning agents, stimulants, anti-impotence drugs, hair loss remedies, prescription pain killers, fertility agents, synthetic metabolic hormones, or sleep aids. Appearance and performance enhancing drugs are often taken in prescribed patterns termed *cycles*, which can vary greatly in length, severity, and complexity. The APED cycle is often followed by an intentional period of drug discontinuation that is designed to help restore homeostatic balance for the major endocrine systems. For AAS users, this means attempts to re-regulate their hypothalamic-pituitary-gonadal (HPG) axis. Often, cycles are timed to coincide with periods when the benefits will peak when performance peaks are needed or to evade scheduled drug tests (e.g., offseason vs. in-season). Appearance and performance enhancing drugs cycles can last anywhere from weeks to months, with averages reported in field trials suggesting the typical user is "on-cycle" for about 3 months and uses approximately 1,300 mg/week of AAS (Hildebrandt et al., 2011). Typical cycles often include multiple AASs and up to 60% of substance use can involve taking nonsteroidal anabolics (e.g., hGH, insulin, etc.). This polypharmacy is often referred to as *stacking*, and sophisticated users may also gradually increase and taper these substances, a practice known as *pyramiding*. The exact pattern of APED use is likely dictated by the physical starting point of the user and the demands of the given sport or performance. Such

diversity has been documented in community samples of weightlifting men (Hildebrandt, Alfano, & Langenbucher, 2010; Hildebrandt, Langenbucher, Carr, & Sanjuan, 2007; Hildebrandt, Schlundt, Langenbucher, & Chung, 2006).

These subtyping studies suggest that there are at least four subtypes of APED user. The first group is characterized by an expansive use of APEDs, including higher risk substances and combinations administered over longer durations. The majority of these users identify as bodybuilders, but are likely to include any individual whose goal is hypermuscularity and simultaneously low body fat. A second group self-identifies primarily as powerlifters, and these men report taking primarily AASs; their goals are more exclusively related to power and strength. A third group has a greater likelihood of identifying as fitness or endurance athletes. Although members of this group often take AASs, they report the highest rate of use of fat burning or weight loss drugs. This pattern of drug use includes the incorporation of prescription stimulants, thyroid medications, or other appetite suppressing drugs. This group may be more likely to include performers not typically captured in APED using samples. A fourth group identifies as recreational weightlifters, and these individuals are generally taking only AAS, but for shorter durations and in smaller amounts than the other groups. This last group also tends to experience the least body image disturbance.

Three core features of all APED use provide the best markers of risk and impairment: polypharmacy, body image disturbance, and disturbances in diet and exercise. Problematic APED use has generally been conceptualized in terms of a classic substance abuse model, despite the fact that the use patterns, motivations for use, and associated lifestyle vastly differ from that of traditional drugs of abuse. We would argue, rather, that based upon the research to date, problematic APED use is characterized by a unique cluster of symptoms that indicates a problem with a distinct pathogenesis. Appearance and performance enhancing drugs use is not currently defined in any psychiatric diagnostic system, although a recent proposal suggests maintenance of the classic drug dependence model (Kanayama, Brower, Wood, Hudson, & Pope, 2010). Our approach suggests that psychopathology be defined around these core symptoms of polypharmacy, body image disturbance, and disturbances in diet and exercise (Hildebrandt et al.,2011).

Polypharmacy has a specific meaning for APED nosology, and it is considered present when multiple drug classes with unique pharmacological properties are purposefully combined such that the combination of substances is preferred over the use of a single substance or a set of substances with the same pharmacological properties. In this context, when multiple substances are used simultaneously, it is difficult to determine a primary drug. This inability to determine a primary drug of abuse may be particularly true for the different AASs. Although all share some affinity for androgen receptors (ARs), and thus share a common mechanism of action, they can differ significantly in their metabolization and interact with each other to affect reward neurocircuitry. For instance, testosterone can aromatize into estradiol and convert to DHT or other androgens naturally in the brain or other tissue (Shahidi, 2001). These metabolites may have very different effects on reward processes and have differential dose-dependent relationships on self-administration (DiMeo & Wood, 2006). A number of metabolites of testosterone or different AAS have demonstrated reinforcing properties, working through distinctly different targets within addiction neurocircuitry (Fryc, 2007; Frye, Rhodes, Rosellini, & Svare, 2002). When compared, AASs that do not aromatize and have low AR affinity, such as stanozolol, yield reduced AR binding, whereas aromatizable androgens, such as testosterone and nandrolone decanoate, yield increased AR binding, and stanozolol can inhibit the nandrolone increase in AR binding when administered together (Wesson & McGinnis, 2006). Stanozolol, a commonly used AAS, also shows no evidence for self-administration, whereas nandrolone shows the greatest evidence for self-administration among AAS (Ballard & Wood, 2005). Given the breadth of available AASs, their differential reinforcement properties, different mechanisms for reward, and potential for synergistic and antagonistic effects, using multiple drugs from this class could be considered a unique form of polysubstance use.

Descriptive studies on AAS users have typically consisted of both small field studies, as recruited from targeted populations such as gym users or adolescent athletic teams (Perry, Andersen, & Yates, 1990; Pope & Katz, 1994) and, more recently, larger internet samples via fitness, bodybuilding, and AAS discussion boards (Hildebrandt, Langenbucher, Carr, Sanjuan, & Park, 2006; Perry, Lund, Deninger, Kutscher, & Schneider, 2005). These samples have noticeable selection biases and are often assessed using nonstandardized anonymous questionnaires or brief interviews. Although AAS is the primary substance of choice, the majority of users often

endorse use of central nervous stimulants, thyroid hormones, nonsteroidal anabolics (e.g., human chorionic gonadotropin [hCG]), and ancillary agents (e.g., antiestrogens; Evans, 1997; Hildebrandt et al., 2007; Kanayama, Hudson, & Pope, 2010; Parkinson & Evans, 2006; Perry et al., 2005). Even when measured as part of a "typical" use pattern, 60% reported non-AAS use (Hildebrandt et al., 2007b), suggesting that polypharmacy is a central feature of APED use. Since very little data exist on these non-AAS agents, the degree to which these APEDs are misused, their interactive effects, or their role in the prevention and/or creation of psychiatric or medical problems remains unknown and underappreciated.

Body image disturbance among APED users appears to be a robust psychiatric feature (Cafri et al., 2005) and is mainly defined as including obsessive-compulsive symptoms similar to those found in body dysmorphic disorder (BDD; Olivardia, 2001). The culmination of this research has been the suggestion of a unique subtype of body dysmorphic disorder termed *muscle dysmorphia* (Pope, Gruber, Choi, Olivardia, & Phillips, 1997). This differs from traditional BDD in that the obsessions and compulsions are specific to increasing muscle or lean muscularity. Men meeting criteria for this disorder report higher rates of APED use (Cafri, Olivardia, & Thompson, 2008; Pope et al., 2005). Defining body image disturbance more broadly, there is evidence of significant variability in the severity of disturbances among APED users. For instance, Hildebrandt et al. (2010) found that nearly half of their sample of APED users had low levels of body image disturbance, but those with high levels also reported the heaviest and most dangerous APED use.

A heavy investment in controlling ones diet and the use of strict or intense exercise to bring about the effects of APEDs makes this form of drug use distinct. Classic drugs of abuse provide a clear and immediate form of reinforcement or drug "high" that is absent among most APEDs, including AAS (Kanayama, Hudson, & Pope, Jr., 2010). However, the desired effects of APEDs typically involve changes to external appearance or tissues outside the brain. For athletes, the intense exercise regimens and potential for overtraining may place them at increased risk for developing problems with AASs and other APEDs. This risk has a biological basis related to the ability of AASs to stimulate recovery and balance the hormonal response to exercise (Hildebrandt, Alfano, & Yehuda, 2011). Thus, compulsive or excessive exercise patterns may be a reliable marker and risk factor of dangerous APED use.

Medical and Psychiatric Consequences of Appearance and Performance Enhancing Drugs

Anabolic-Androgenic Steroids

Anabolic-androgenic steroid use directly affects the endocrine system by introducing large doses of exogenous androgens, thus forcing adaptation by the HPG axis. Potential effects include physical feminization (e.g., gynecomastia), testicular shrinkage, hair growth, acne, loss/increase in libido, and water retention (Evans, 2004; Hartgens & Kuipers, 2004). Some of these effects result from aromatization, or the conversion of androgens into estrogens; once AAS use ceases, these effects tend to reverse, although some continue to experience these effects even after cessation (Kanayama et al., 2009a). Within the APED user community, a wide array of ancillary agents are often utilized to combat these effects, such as tamoxifen or clomiphene citrate, which suppress aromatization effects or stimulate endogenous testosterone production (Hildebrandt, Langenbucher et al., 2006). In females, the side effects are primarily masculinizing (e.g., deepening voice, clitoral enlargement, hair growth, etc.) and often deter most women from chronic or persistent use.

Anabolic-androgenic steroid use has been linked to impaired liver function and disease through animal studies (e.g., Ishak, 1981) and various case studies of AAS use (e.g., Cabasso, 1994); however, systematic research has not shown a consistent relationship between long-term liver damage and AAS use for healthy adults. Anabolic-androgenic steroids have also been associated with hypertension (American College of Sports Medicine [ACSM], 1987), but several studies have not been able to find any effects (Friedl, Hannan, Jones, & Plymate, 1990; Pope, & Katz, 1994). Anabolic-androgenic steroids that affect water retention or increase blood volume may potentially raise blood pressure, but the lack of empirical research makes it difficult to make a conclusive determination. Some forms of AASs have been shown to definitively affect serum cholesterol levels (Alen, Rahkila, Reinila, & Vihko, 1987; Hurley et al., 1984), but there is no evidence to suggest that this effect is more than transitory or persists after cessation of AAS use (Lenders et al., 1988). Anabolic-androgenic steroid -using athletes have documented higher rates of hypertrophic cardiomyopathy (HCM), but it is unclear whether this is due to the actual substances or to the intensity and particular type of exercise training associated with its use. However, research findings on HCM and AAS have been mixed (Salke, Rowland, & Burke, 1985; Urhausen, Albers, & Kindermann, 2004; Zuliani et al., 1989), and there is some evidence to suggest that some types of AAS might even reduce independent risk factors for heart disease (Albers et al., 1984; Cohen, Hartford, & Rogers, 1996; Crook, Sidhu, Seed, O'Donnell, & Stevenson, 1992). Other potential effects on the circulatory system include clotting abnormalities (Ferenchick, Hirokawa, Mammen, & Schwartz, 1995), leading to higher frequencies of thrombotic stroke (Laroche, 1990; Shiozawa et al., 1982).

Although AASs are abused for their effects on muscle tissue, AASs directly affect the central nervous system (CNS) through AR binding and indirectly through increases in estrogen and their metabolites. They may also increase the reinforcing effects of other drugs of abuse (Clark & Henderson, 2003). There are observed links between testosterone levels and hypomania/mania (Freinhar & Alvarez, 1985; Pope & Katz, 1988, 1994; Pope, Kouri, & Hudson, 2000), increased aggression (Daly, 2001; Daly et al., 2003; Perry et al., 2003), violence (Beaver, Vaughn, Delisi, & Wright, 2008; Klotz, Petersson, Isacson, & Thiblin, 2007)), substance use disorders (Brower, 2002; Kanayama, Hudson, & Pope, 2009b), and depression (Gray et al., 2005; Yates, Perry, MacIndoe, Holman, & Ellingrod, 1999), although the exact causal relationships are unclear.

Although the most commonly associated stereotype of the AAS user is one of "roid rage," the evidence for a significant relationship between aggression and AAS is mixed. Some cross-sectional and case studies indicate that a significant relationship exists (Galligani, Renck, & Hansen, 1996; Lefavi, Reeve, & Newland, 1990; Moss, Panazak, & Tarter, 1992; Perry et al., 2003; Pope, & Katz, 1994), whereas other research has been unable to find differences in aggression between AAS users and nonusers (Bahrke, Wright, Strauss, & Catlin, 1992; Bond, Choi, & Pope, 1995; Perry et al., 1990). Most of these studies are limited by methodological issues, such as selection bias and lack of control for confounding factors; however, randomized controlled studies with normal male volunteers prescribed supraphysiological doses of AAS have found evidence to support the link between aggression and AASs. Table 29.1 summarizes these studies; seven out of nine studies report evidence for increased aggression among those in the active drug

Table 29.1 Summary of controlled studies of supraphysiological doses of anabolic-androgenic steroids (AAS) on mood and aggression.

Study	Sample Size	Drug	Dose	Mood Outcomes	Baseline Measures of Mood[a] M (SD)	Post-Dose Measures of Mood[a] M (SD)
Matsumoto (1990)	51 M	TE	Placebo, 25, 50, 100, or 300 mg/wk	"Minor behavior disturbance" (n = 3)	n/a	n/a
Su et al. (1993)	20 M	MT vs. PLC	3 days each of placebo, 40, 240 mg/day	Increase in positive & negative moods (HD)	General mood, behavioral and cognitive symptoms: VAS = 180.1 (51.47)	General mood, behavioral, and cognitive symptoms: VAS = 207.4 (92.66)
				Mania (HD, n = 1)	Aggression: VAS = 44 (27.04)	Aggression: VAS = 48.4(27.04)
Kouri, Lukas, Pope, & Oliva (1995)	8 M	TC vs. PLC	2 weeks each of 150, 300, 600 mg/wk, or placebo	Increased aggression	Aggression: VAS = 52.83 (12.08) PSAP = 89 (41)	Aggression: VAS = 59.17 (11.62) PSAP = 203.2 (48)
Bhasin et al. (1996)	43 M	TE vs. PLC	600 mg/wk	No change	n/a	n/a
Tricker et al. (1996)	43 M	TE vs. PLC	600 mg/wk	No change	NS	NS
Yates, Perry, MacIndoe, Holman, & Ellingrod (1999)	42 M (11 DO)	TC vs. PLC cross-over design	Placebo followed by 100, 250, or 500 mg/wk	Some mania & depression	Psychiatric Rating: BPRS = 18.7 (1.1)	Psychiatric Rating: BPRS = 19.7 (2.6)
					Depression: HDRT = 0.8 (1.5)	Depression: HDRT = 2.4 (3.0)
					Mania: MMRS = 1.4 (2.0)	Mania: MMRS = 3.5 (3.9)
Pope et al. (2000)	53 M	TC	6 weeks: 2 weeks each of 150, 300, 600 mg/wk), or placebo; 6 weeks "washout"	Increased mania and aggression (n = 8)	Mania: YMRS = 0.5 (1)	Mania: YMRS = 3.9 (4.9)
					Aggression: PSAP = 208 (235)	Aggression: PSAP = 362 (301)
Daly et al. (2003)	20 M	MT	3 days each of placebo, 40, 240 mg/day	Increased aggression	Aggression: VAS = 14.6 (9.9)	Aggression: VAS = 18.5 (12.3)
Perry et al. (2003)	28 M	Any APEDs	Variable	Increased aggression	[Nonusers] Cluster B: PDQ-R = 9.3 (5.6)	[Users] Cluster B: PDQ-R = 16.1 (8.3)

BPRS, Brief Psychiatric Rating Scale; DO, drop out; N/A, not available; NS, nonsignificant difference; LD, low dose; HD, high dose; HDRT, Hamilton Depression Rating Scale; MMRS, Modified Mania Rating Scale; MT, methyltestosterone; PDQ, Personality Disorder Questionnaire; PLC, placebo; PSAP, Point Subtraction Aggression Paradigm; TE, testosterone enanthate; TC, testosterone cypionate; VAS, Visual Analogue Scale; YMRS, Young Mania Rating Scale. [a] Unless noted otherwise condition. Other mood effects were less robust, with few identifying depression or mania/hypomania even with prolonged use. The lack of a consistent relationship suggests that mood disturbances in APED users may be due to an interaction effect with environment, existing psychiatric history, or personality characteristics (Perry et al., 2003) or expectation effects due to culturally generated beliefs on AAS use (Björkqvist, Nygren, Björklund, & Björkqvist, 1994).

Fat Burning and Weight Loss Appearance and Performance Enhancing Drugs

Perhaps the most overlooked non-AAS APEDs are CNS stimulants used to boost energy for workouts or to burn body fat. Large-scale studies indicate that up to 80% of users are using some form of these drugs (Hildebrandt et al., 2007; Parkinson & Evans, 2006; Perry et al., 2005). The side effects (Caplan, Epstein, Quinn, Stevens, & Stern, 2007; Samenuk et al., 2002), abuse potential (Tinsley & Watkins, 1998), and reinforcing properties of these drugs are well documented (Li, Wessinger, & McMillan, 2005; Stoops, 2008). It has been noted (Lukas, 1996), but subsequently absent in clinical discussions of AAS use, that the effects of AASs may increase the reinforcing nature of stimulants. Animal work on the interactive effects of stimulants and AASs indicates that exposure to various AASs increased the rewarding properties of amphetamines (Clark, Lindenfeld, & Gibbons, 1996) and potentiated aggressive responding in response to stimulants (Steensland, Hallberg, Kindlundh, Fahlke, & Nyberg, 2005). Given the widespread use of legal and illegal stimulants, the interaction between these two drug classes is of particular relevance to defining problematic APED use. Stimulants activate the sympathetic nervous system, potentially resulting in anxiety, sleep disorders, or withdrawal syndrome, along with affected cardiac function and metabolism, with psychosis occurring in extreme circumstances (Silverman, Evans, Strain, & Griffiths, 1992; Spriet, 2002; Maglione et al., 2005; Philibert & Mac, 2004; Walton & Manos, 2003).

Thyroid hormones (e.g., T3) and similar substances are less frequently used, but they are also used to reduce body fat or maintain leanness. These hormones are known to have particularly robust physiological and psychological effects. Hyperthyroidism has been implicated in long-term continuous use of thyroid hormones (Cooper, 2005), but the lack of empirical evidence on prolonged T3 use makes it difficult to determine if normal thyroid function resumes over time. Altered thyroid function has strong correlations with psychopathology, particularly mood disorders (Bauer, Goetz, Glenn, & Whybrow, 2008; Bunevicius, 2009), and thus these substances are likely to play a role in the mood dysregulation found in problematic APED use. Increased thyroid levels also have been observed in conjunction with aggressive and violent behavior (Stalenheim, von Knorring, & Wide, 1998), although the causal direction is unknown. There is some evidence that high AAS dosages raise levels of endogenous thyroid hormones (Daly et al., 2003) and that men with hyperthyroidism have elevated levels of sex hormones (Zahringer et al., 2000), but the direct implications of this interaction between thyroid and sex hormones for mood and behavior has yet to be determined.

A particularly dangerous substance, dinitrophenol (DNP), could also be included under the fat-burning or weight loss category, although it is pharmacologically distinct. This drug is known for its acute toxicity (McFee, Caraccio, McGuigan, Reynolds, & Bellanger, 2004), although the mechanism of action for this substance (mitochondrial protein uncoupling) has become a target for innovative obesity interventions (Crowley & Vidal-Puig, 2001; Harper, Dickinson, & Brand, 2001).

There is evidence to suggest that women may be more susceptible to using fat burning and weight loss APEDs; Gruber and Pope (2000) found that in a sample of 25 female APED users, at least 80% had used some sort of erogenic substance, the most common being ephedrine and diuretics. Like certain subgroups of male APED users who are focused on achieving leanness as opposed to muscularity (Hildebrandt et al., 2007), it is reasonable to suppose that women would also be more likely to use APEDs for this purpose, in order to achieve the societal thin ideal. These female users also had a high rate of disordered eating (84%) and past eating disorder history (44%), suggesting that, for women, the use of these substances may be more closely related to traditional eating disorder pathology than for men; however, further research is necessary to understand the distinction between genders. These women were specifically recruited from gym and bodybuilding communities, but it may be that equivalent rates may be found in women engaged in appearance-based careers, such as modeling and dance or performance sports in which where a certain ideal is valued (i.e., figure skating, diving, gymnastics, track).

Ancillary Appearance and Performance Enhancing Drugs

Also of interest are ancillary drugs used to eliminate training-related pain. A series of case studies have noted a link between AAS use and opiates, in particular the ancillary pain killer nalbuphine hydrochloride (Arvary & Pope, 2000; McBride, Williamson, & Petersen, 1996; Wines, Gruber, Pope, & Lukas, 1999). However, concurrent opioid use by AAS users appears to be rare in field studies, but may be more frequent among professional athletes. Other ancillaries more commonly used by APED users include substances that block estrogen receptor activation or the aromatization of an AAS into estrogen (e.g., anastrozole citrate, letrozole citrate, etc.), as well as substances to stimulate endogenous testosterone production post-cycle (e.g., hCG). Given the prevalence of this type of drug use, particularly among those men classified as AAS-dependent (Kanayama et al., 2009b) or engaged in heavy polypharmacy (Hildebrandt et al., 2007), linking its presence to definitions of problematic use may be important. This behavior would be particularly important for identifying high-risk APED use, in which the drug effects are only tolerated with use of an increasingly complex system of pharmacological intervention. There is some evidence that, among regular users, the use of ancillary drugs increases satisfaction with APED use and predicts intentions for long-term use (Hildebrandt, Langenbucher, Carr, Sanjuan, & Park, 2006). Such a pattern raises the possibility that prolonged APED use evolves out of a growing sophistication for managing side effects and negative consequences to use. It remains unclear whether this relationship is due to unique reinforcing properties or secondary effects that contribute to a sense of drug mastery. Alternatively, it may be that many who use ancillaries are at reduced risk for problematic APED use because ancillaries are not used to push the limits of APED use, but are part of a more normative pattern in which side effects are effectively managed.

Nonsteroidal Appearance and Performance Enhancing Drugs

A number of classes of nonsteroidal anabolic drugs are used primarily to increase muscle mass. These include hormones such as insulin and hGH, but also other related substances such as insulin-like growth factors. Evidence from our examination of APED use severity (Hildebrandt et al., 2007) suggests that both insulin and hGH are good indicators of heavy polypharmacy and drug use severity. This is evidenced by correlations with significant side effects, including mood dysregulation and cardiac effects (Hildebrandt et al., 2007). The relationship between use of these drugs and problematic use is not surprising, given the potentially negative cardiac effects (Klein & Ojamaa, 1992) or intestinal growth (De Palo, Gatti, Lancerin, Cappellin, & Spinella, 2001) associated with hGH and the mood dysregulation related to insulin (Reagan, 2007). In fact, hyperglycemia (which is possible during acute insulin use) may exacerbate the likelihood of acute cardiac events (Gilmore & Stead, 2006) while leaving an individual vulnerable to coma or death. To our knowledge, no acute risks are associated with AASs that equate to the risks of insulin use. Given the concurrent use of these substances with AASs, overlap in desired effects (i.e., improve appearance or performance), and evidence linking them to drug use severity, they are likely to have important diagnostic properties.

How Do People Become Appearance and Performance Enhancing Drugs Users?

The typical transition from nonuser to illicit APED user is still a mystery, but is likely to be a complex process. Several theoretical risk factors for APED use have emerged from the literature, although it is important to note that none has been empirically derived. Several large-scale epidemiological studies have established significant correlates of adolescent AAS use. However, there are few longitudinal datasets with adequate information to test for specific illicit APED use risk factors or causal factors that promote or protect individuals from becoming illicit APED users. The sum of epidemiological studies suggests that young illicit users are either impulsive, risk-taking illicit substance users or athletes/gym attendees who are highly invested in their shape, weight, or body. Both groups likely reflect unique sources of risk that promote their respective transition from nonuser to illicit APED user. However, broad prevention programs or other interventions aimed at these two large groups of at-risk youth are expensive, difficult to administer, and too broad for the specific goal of preventing illicit APED use. Thus, targeting those at highest risk within these general risk factors would be a priority for prevention efforts.

Data collected through the Youth Behavior Risk Survey (YBRS) suggest that adolescent AAS use is associated with a range of high-risk behaviors including fighting, unprotected sex, number of sexual partners, driving while intoxicated, and not wearing a seatbelt (Middleman, Faulkner, Woods, Emans, & DuRant, 1995). The YBRS data also indicate increased illicit substance use broadly among adolescent AAS users, including alcohol, injection drug use, cocaine, and marijuana (DuRant, Escobedo, & Heath, 1995; DuRant, Rickert, Ashworth, Newman, & Slavens, 1993) and that this broader pattern of illicit drug use is stable over short periods of time (DuRant, Ashworth, Newman, & Rickert, 1994). Nationally representative data on college males from 1993 to 2001 suggest a similar stability in this relationship between illicit APED use and other forms of illicit substance use over time (McCabe, Brower, West, Nelson, & Wechsler, 2007) and also suggest a relationship between weightlifting, power sports, and AAS use (Tahtamouni et al., 2008; Tanner, Miller, & Alongi, 1995). Findings from Project EAT (Eating Among Teens) and Project EAT-II, a series of longitudinal studies of adolescents in Minnesota, suggest a relationship between strategies to increase weight and muscle mass, sports that emphasize weight, and AAS use (vandenBerg, Neumark-Sztainer, Cafri, & Wall, 2007; Vertalino, Eisenberg, Story, & Neumark-Sztainer, 2007). Among those endorsing AAS use, these adolescents reported poorer self-esteem, more depression, suicide attempts, and eating or weight-related concerns (Irving, Wall, Neumark-Sztainer, & Story, 2002). Thus, the traits of impulsivity, aggression, low self-esteem, and body image disturbance could be conceptualized as general risk factors for illicit APED use among youth. However, specific risk factors have not been clearly identified, but may include the types of sport, exercise habits, and the overlooked potential for legal APED use to increase illicit APED risk. These missing links have served to limit a clear conceptual model for the emergence of illicit APED use among youth.

Legal APED use, which primarily consists of nutritional supplements, pro-hormones, and over-the-counter fat burning drugs, could be an essential part of the missing model of illicit APED use. Conceptualizing these substances as gateway substances provides for a specific and tenable hypothesis about how illicit APED use develops among youth. This "gateway hypothesis," which originated in theories of adolescent drug abuse development (Kandel, 1975, 1980) posits that the use of one drug can bring about the use of other drugs. For a substance to be considered a gateway drug, it must meet three criteria: the gateway drug precedes use of another drug, a strong correlation demonstrates that use of the gateway drug increases the

risk of use of another drug, and a causal link exists whereby use of the gateway drug brings about the use of another drug. Applied to illicit APEDs, nutritional supplements are potential gateway substances in that they precede use of illegal APEDs including AASs; APED users rarely begin using AASs or other pharmaceutical-grade APEDs without having established some pattern of nutritional supplement use. The use of illegal APEDs also is likely to occur in conjunction with the use of nutritional supplements, indicating a strong correlation. Finally, there are a number of ways in which nutritional supplements may bring about illegal APED use. As much as 10–15% of legal substances are contaminated with illegal APEDs (Martello, Felli, & Chiarotti, 2007), thus facilitating inadvertent exposure to illegal APEDs. Also, APED users are generally members of specific APED or exercise communities, in which they can easily exchange information about various APEDs (legal and illegal; Monaghan, 2002) and achieve access to illegal APEDs. Therefore, through this medium, norms about illicit use, the associated risks, and the transition from legal to illegal APED use are transferred to the individual via socialization.

Interventions for Appearance and Performance Enhancing Drugs

Existing interventions for APED use currently focus on male and female adolescents participating in organized sports teams. The Adolescents Training and Learning to Avoid Steroids (ATLAS) Prevention Program is focused on reducing intentions to use APEDS, alcohol, and other illicit drugs through educating participants on the effects of these substances, alternatives to APED use, strength training and sports nutrition techniques, and media awareness (Goldberg et al., 1996). The program was run in three cohorts from 1994 to 1996; Cohort 1 received seven classroom and seven weight-room sessions, whereas participants in cohorts 2 and 3 received the same content in a compressed version of five classroom and three weight-room sessions (Goldberg et al., 2000). The classroom peer-led sessions addressed risk factors of AASs and other drugs, nutritional education, and media awareness, along with weight-room sessions for strength training techniques. In the two cohorts available for long-term follow-up (1 and 2), ATLAS was shown to have significant effects on attitudes toward AASs, showing that, at both school and subject level, intervention participants were more likely to perceive AAS adverse effects as severe and perceive themselves as more vulnerable to these effects versus controls (Goldberg et al., 2000). They also had greater knowledge of the effects of AASs, alcohol, supplement use, and exercise. Individual-level analyses showed reduced intentions to use AAS, although these effects were not found to be significant at a school-wide level. At long-term follow-up, 19 control participants had initiated AAS use since entering the program, as opposed to nine intervention participants; however, this difference was not found to be significant between the two conditions despite significant differences in illicit drug use between groups at 1-year follow-up.

Athletes Targeting Healthy Exercise and Nutrition Alternatives (ATHENA) was developed as a similar intervention specifically targeting female adolescent athletes. Surveys administered to a sample of female adolescent athletes were used to identify factors that contribute to or identify individuals at risk for unhealthy behaviors (Elliot et al., 2006). These 11 factors, which correctly identified risk for 73.1% of the total sample, were used as the curriculum elements for the ATHENA program. The program therefore incorporated these results with features from the ATLAS program, with a targeted gender-specific focus on positive body image, prevention of disordered eating, and nutritional information (Elliot et al., 2004). A depression prevention program was also incorporated to address the negative affect associated with disordered eating (Ranby et al., 2009). Unlike ATLAS, ATHENA did not incorporate an exercise component; the eight 45-minute sessions over the course of 8 weeks were incorporated into each team's usual practice activities, in which approximately 70% of activities were led by an appointed peer leader. In a mediation analysis of the ATHENA intervention, no effects were found in the intervention group on actual steroid or creatine use, or unhealthy weight loss behaviors at 9-month follow-up; however, ATHENA participants endorsed fewer intentions to use steroids and creatine, with a similar trend for intentions to engage in unhealthy weight loss (Ranby et al., 2009). Fifteen constructs were included in the analyses, based on pre-test, post-test, and long-term follow-up questionnaires. ATHENA had the intended effect on 7 of 11 putative mediators. Social norms were the strongest mediator for intentions to use APEDS and engage in unhealthy weight loss practices, followed by self-efficacy or ability to control eating to enhance athletic performance. Outcome expectancies were also found to mediate intentions for weight loss behaviors, whereas knowledge of steroid effects played a role on intentions for APED use. Interestingly, peer norms for steroids, peer norms for eating disorders, and belief in ability to resist unhealthy weight loss were not included in the multiple mediator model; these mediators were not affected by ATHENA.

The ATLAS and ATHENA programs have been shown to be effective as primary prevention programs for reducing intentions to engage in unhealthy body shaping behaviors, although they do not seem to have efficacy for affecting actual behaviors. A unique feature of both interventions is that they are implemented within an athletic team setting among peers who share a common identity and common goals, as compared to other adolescent drug prevention programs, which generally take place in a health class setting where these factors are less controllable. Because of the already time-intensive nature of athletic team participation, coaches are also a formative influence in the lives of these adolescents and thereby play an important part in the implementation of the interventions. However, the time-intensive nature of the training and program setting may make it difficult to generalize to communities that lack resources or are not invested in the prevention of anabolic steroid use. These programs also do not address the problem of older APED users.

Kanayama et al. have suggested different potential psychological and pharmacological treatments for the adverse effects of APEDS based on a proposed model of APED dependence (Kanayama, Brower, Wood, Hudson, & Pope, 2010). Potential pharmacological treatments include hCG and clomiphene for treating suppression of the HPG axis, or traditional treatments for substance use, such as methadone, buprenorphine, or naltrexone. Potential nonpharmaceutical treatments include cognitive-behavioral therapy for body image concerns, along with psychological treatments that have been traditionally used for treating substance use disorders. There is little evidence that these treatments work, and it is unclear if the APED-using population can be engaged in these traditional forms of intervention.

Ethics of Steroid Use

Appearance and performance enhancing drug use is a complicated ethical issue, in which the dilemma of how to ensure fair competition by banning their use from sporting competitions and testing athletes for potential use is of central debate and importance. Any discussion of steroids inevitably revolves around whether steroids should be banned from sporting competitions and whether doping testing should be enforced because of the unfair advantage provided to the athletes who use these substances. As a result, the ethical dilemma in the world of sport pertains to how to ensure fair competition in a society in which steroid use is rampant and its benefits are highly attractive to the average athlete. To outside observers, it may seem obvious that APEDs should be banned and that athletes should be tested regularly to ensure that doping bans are enforced and violations are acted upon. However, for athletes, the struggle lies in balancing a need for fair competition with the desire to win at all costs.

Modern media plays a large role in the ethics of steroid use—both in enticing athletes to use steroids to be the best, in order to achieve fame and prestige, but also by very publicly decrying those who test positive for APEDs. Media images of highly visible and wealthy athletes who have achieved unnatural levels of muscularity may play an undue role in encouraging up-and-coming athletes to take steroids in order to achieve a similar level of success (Ehrnborg & Rosén, 2009). Increasingly, media reports focus on famous athletes who have been accused of doping, such as Ben Johnson in 1988 and again in 1993 (Thomsen, 2003), Mark McGwire in 2005 (O'Keefe, Red, & Quinn, 2005), Barry Bonds in 2007 (Quinn, 2007), and countless others. Specific federal investigations ("BALCO investigation: key players," 2006) have raised the public's awareness of this issue. However, considering that these players only retroactively admitted to AAS use after having already attained a successful career, the punishment or chastisement they might receive may seem slightly less serious. In addition, the punishments administered to athletes caught doping are often insignificant, further trivializing the drug offense. However, although these incidents are front page news, the likelihood of a false-positive test result is another serious issue to consider. For many athletes, regular drug testing is a routine procedure, and the fear of a false-positive result and the related stigma and bad press poses a major threat to the ethical administration of drug tests (Browne, Lachance, & Pipe, 1999). No blood or urine drug test is 100% accurate, and the potential for contamination of the sample or even detection of normally elevated levels of naturally occurring endogenous hormones are not unrealistic concerns. In these cases, a false-positive result stemming from inaccurate test results could present a huge obstacle in the developing career of an athlete.

Another facet to the ethics of steroid use is that of protecting the health and privacy of the athlete. In addition to the fact that APEDs give athletes an unfair advantage in competition, they also pose health risks (Miah, 2005). The IOC's original motivation in banning APEDs was because of their potential for morbidity and mortality (Ferstle, 2000). From this standpoint, trainers and physicians place an individual's health in danger by suggesting APED use as an option and are not upholding medical ethical principles. Although physicians may reason that APED use protects an athlete from training injuries by helping promote recovery, the potential long-term side effects that may occur when APEDs are abused or used incorrectly is a more serious concern (Hoberman, 2002). However, there remains an interesting counterargument that, under the correct supervision and with realistic goals, APEDs can be used to enhance life in much the same way that Botox or plastic surgery is used to treat the physical breakdown of the body.

A final issue to consider is the invasive nature of drug testing. For some, blood testing may be uncomfortable or put the athlete at risk for bruising, infection, or other common side effects associated with blood draws. In addition, taking and testing someone's blood can provide the tester with private information about the athlete (such as HIV status) that may be considered an invasion of his or her privacy (Browne et al., 1999). These rights are important to consider throughout the testing process, along with refraining from final conclusions until a thorough investigation has been completed. Athletes are often immediately penalized for violations without the chance for self-defense (Ferstle, 2000). Such an environment of paranoia and penalization is likely to cause significant barriers for those health professionals tasked with caring for those who do use APEDs and leads to a fundamental question: Have the moral standards linked to cheating and fair play interfered with the ability of health professionals to aid and intervene with those at risk for significant harm from APED use?

Conclusion

Appearance and performance enhancing drug use is a complex phenomenon heavily influenced by an evolving athletic environment that has the potential for lucrative salaries and endorsement possibilities. It differs from other drugs of abuse in many important ways, but APED misuse continues to be conceptualized as an addiction rather than a hybrid of substance, body image, and diet or exercise-based problems. Viewing APED use through the lens of drug addiction is likely to be inconsistent with the experience of most users. Sport and performance-based professionals will undoubtedly encounter individuals who are involved with APEDs and will need to have some understanding of this culture to effectively intervene. Among the many difficulties they will encounter are a constantly evolving APED market, problems with quantifying or measuring the severity of APED use, users' secrecy and their mistrust of health professionals, lack of effective intervention strategies, and a mixture of ethical and legal obstacles that inhibit users from seeking help. Despite these obstacles, sport and performance professionals are well positioned to be helpful in engaging those who are in need of services.

Future Directions

The research agenda for this area is diverse and complex. A multidisciplinary approach that aims to address a few fundamental issues will be necessary to move the field forward. These priorities include standardized assessment of APED use, risk, and impairment; delineating the long-term effects of APEDs and separating these effects from those caused by sport, training, or diet; identifying clear causal factors (biological, social, and psychological) that help bring about illicit APED use; delineating and describing individual differences in APED use (e.g., gender differences) and associated risk or impairment; and measuring the impact of drug testing on the evolution of the APED market and the relevance of this interplay between attempts to "catch" cheaters and the stimulation of a larger APED industry to the ethics of APED use in sport.

References

Albers, J. J., Taggart, H. M., Applebaum-Bowden, D., Haffner, S., Chesnut, C. H., 3rd, & Hazzard, W. R. (1984). Reduction of lecithin-cholesterol acyltransferase, apolipoprotein D and the Lp(a) lipoprotein with the anabolic steroid stanozolol. *Biochimica et Biophysica Acta, 795*(2), 293–296.

Alen, M., Rahkila, P., Reinila, M., & Vihko, R. (1987). Androgenic-anabolic steroid effects on serum thyroid, pituitary and steroid hormones in athletes. *American Journal of Sports Medicine, 15*(4), 357–361.

American College of Sports Medicine (ACSM). (1987). American College of Sports Medicine position stand on the use of anabolic-androgenic steroids in sports. *Medicine and Science in Sports and Exercise, 19*(5), 534–539.

Arvary, D., & Pope, H. G. (2000). Anabolic-androgenic steroids as a gateway to opioid dependence. *New England Journal of Medicine, 342*(20), 1532.

Bahrke, M. S., Wright, J. E., Strauss, R. H., & Catlin, D. H. (1992). Psychological moods and subjectively perceived behavioral and somatic changes accompanying anabolic-androgenic steroid use. *American Journal of Sports Medicine, 20*(6), 717–724.

Bahrke, M. S., & Yesalis, C. E. (Eds.). (2002). *Performance-enhancing substances in sport and exercise.* Champaign, IL: Human Kinetics.

Baker, J. S., Graham, M. R., & Davies, B. (2006). Steroid and prescription medicine abuse in the health and fitness community: A regional study. *European Journal of Internal Medicine, 17*(7), 479–484.

BALCO investigation: key players. (2006, April 27). *USA Today.* Retrieved from: http://www.usatoday.com/sports/balco-players.htm

Ballard, C. L., & Wood, R. I. (2005). Intracerebroventricular self-administration of commonly abused anabolic-androgenic steroids in male hamsters (Mesocricetus auratus): Nandrolone, drostanolone, oxymetholone, and stanozolol. *Behavioral Neuroscience, 119*(3), 752–758.

Bauer, M., Goetz, T., Glenn, T., & Whybrow, P. C. (2008). The thyroid-brain interaction in thyroid disorders and mood disorders. *Journal of Neuroendocrinology, 20*(10), 1101–1114.

Beaver, K. M., Vaughn, M. G., Delisi, M., & Wright, J. P. (2008). Anabolic-androgenic steroid use and involvement in violent behavior in a nationally representative sample of young adult males in the United States. *American Journal of Public Health, 98*(12), 2185–2187.

Bhasin, S., Storer, T. W., Berman, N., Callegari, C., Clevenger, B., Phillips, J., Bunnell, T. J., Tricker, R., Shirazi, A., & Casaburi, R. (1996). The effects of supraphysiologic doses of testosterone on muscle size and strength in normal men. *The New England Journal of Medicine, 335*, 1–7.

Björkqvist, K., Nygren, T., Björklund, A., & Björkqvist, S. (1994). Testosterone intake and aggressiveness: Real effect or anticipation? *Aggressive Behavior, 20*(1), 17–26.

Bolding, G., Sherr, L., & Elford, J. (2002). Use of anabolic steroids and associated health risks among gay men attending London gyms. *Addiction, 97*(2),195–203.

Bond, A. J., Choi, P. Y., & Pope, H. G., Jr. (1995). Assessment of attentional bias and mood in users and non-users of anabolic-androgenic steroids. *Drug and Alcohol Dependence, 37*(3), 241–245.

Bowers, L. D. (2009). The analytical chemistry of drug monitoring in athletes. *Annual Review of Analytical Chemistry (Palo Alto, Ca.), 2*, 485–507.

Brower, K. J. (2002). Anabolic steroid abuse and dependence. *Current Psychiatry Reports, 4*(5), 377–387.

Browne, A., Lachance, V., & Pipe, A. (1999). The ethics of blood testing as an element of doping control in sport. *Medicine and Science in Sports and Exercise, 31*(4), 497–501.

Bunevicius, R. (2009). Thyroid disorders in mental patients. *Current Opinion in Psychiatry, 22*(4), 391–395.

Cabasso, A. (1994). Peliosis hepatis in a young adult bodybuilder. *Medicine and Science in Sports and Exercise, 26*(1), 2–4.

Cafri, G., Olivardia, R., & Thompson, J. K. (2008). Symptom characteristics and psychiatric comorbidity among males with muscle dysmorphia. *Comprehensive Psychiatry, 49*(4), 374–379.

Cafri, G., Thompson, J. K., Ricciardelli, L., McCabe, M., Smolak, L., & Yesalis, C. (2005). Pursuit of the muscular ideal: Physical and psychological consequences and putative risk factors. *Clinical Psychology Review, 25*(2), 215–239.

Caplan, J. P., Epstein, L. A., Quinn, D. K., Stevens, J. R., & Stern, T. A. (2007). Neuropsychiatric effects of prescription drug abuse. *Neuropsychology Review, 17*(3), 363–380.

Catlin, D. H., Fitch, K. D., & Ljungqvist, A. (2008). Medicine and science in the fight against doping in sport. *Journal of Internal Medicine, 264*(2), 99–114.

Center for Disease Control. (2010). Youth Risk Behavior Surveillance – United States, 2009. *Morbidity and Mortality Weekly Report, 59*, 1–146.

Clark, A. S., & Henderson, L. P. (2003). Behavioral and physiological responses to anabolic-androgenic steroids. *Neuroscience and Biobehavioral Reviews, 27*(5), 413–436.

Clark, A. S., Lindenfeld, R. C., & Gibbons, C. H. (1996). Anabolic-androgenic steroids and brain reward. *Pharmacology Biochemistry and Behavior, 53*(3), 741–745.

Cohen, L. I., Hartford, C. G., & Rogers, G. G. (1996). Lipoprotein (a) and cholesterol in body builders using anabolic androgenic steroids. *Medicine and Science in Sports and Exercise, 28*(2), 176–179.

Cooper, D. S. (2005). Antithyroid drugs. *New England Journal of Medicine, 352*(9), 905–917.

Cowan, C. B. (1994). Depression in anabolic steroid withdrawal. *Irish Journal of Psychological Medicine, 11*(1), 27–28.

Crook, D., Sidhu, M., Seed, M., O'Donnell, M., & Stevenson, J. C. (1992). Lipoprotein Lp(a) levels are reduced by danazol, an anabolic steroid. *Atherosclerosis, 92*(1), 41–47.

Crowley, V., & Vidal-Puig, A. J. (2001). Mitochondrial uncoupling proteins (UCPs) and obesity. *Nutrition, Metabolism and Cardiovascular Diseases, 11*(1), 70–75.

Daly, R. C. (2001). Anabolic steroids, brain and behaviour. *Irish Medical Journal, 94*(4), 102.

Daly, R. C., Su, T. P., Schmidt, P. J., Pagliaro, M., Pickar, D., & Rubinow, D. R. (2003). Neuroendocrine and behavioral effects of high-dose anabolic steroid administration in male normal volunteers. *Psychoneuroendocrinology, 28*(3), 317–331.

De Palo, E. F., Gatti, R., Lancerin, F., Cappellin, E., & Spinella, P. (2001). Correlations of growth hormone (GH) and insulin-like growth factor I (IGF-I): Effects of exercise and abuse by athletes. *Clinica Chimica Acta, 305*(1–2), 1–17.

Dickerman, R. D., Schaller, F., Prather, I., McConathy, W. J. (1995). Sudden cardiac death in a 20-year-old bodybuilder using anabolic steroids. *Cardiology, 86*(2), 172–3.

DiMeo, A. N., & Wood, R. I. (2006). Self-administration of estrogen and dihydrotestosterone in male hamsters. *Hormones and Behavior, 49*(4), 519–526.

DuRant, R. H., Ashworth, C. S., Newman, C., & Rickert, V. I. (1994). Stability of the relationships between anabolic steroid use and multiple substance use among adolescents. *Journal of Adolescent Health, 15*(2), 111–116.

DuRant, R. H., Escobedo, L. G., & Heath, G. W. (1995). Anabolic-steroid use, strength training, and multiple drug use among adolescents in the United States. *Pediatrics, 96*(1 Pt 1), 23–28.

DuRant, R. H., Rickert, V. I., Ashworth, C. S., Newman, C., & Slavens, G. (1993). Use of multiple drugs among adolescents who use anabolic steroids. *New England Journal of Medicine, 328*(13), 922–926.

Ehrnborg, C., & Rosén, T. (2009). The psychology behind doping in sport. *Growth Hormone and IGF Research, 19*(4), 285–287.

Elliot, D. L., Goldberg, L., Moe, E. L., Defrancesco, C. A., Durham, M. B., & Hix-Small, H. (2004). Preventing substance use and disordered eating: Initial outcomes of the ATHENA (athletes targeting healthy exercise and nutrition alternatives) program. *Archives of Pediatrics and Adolescent Medicine, 158*(11), 1043–1049.

Elliot, D. L., Moe, E. L., Goldberg, L., DeFrancesco, C. A., Durham, M. B., & Hix-Small, H. (2006). Definition and outcome of a curriculum to prevent disordered eating and body-shaping drug use. *Journal of School Health, 76*(2), 67–73.

Evans, N. A. (2004). Current concepts in anabolic-androgenic steroids. *American Journal of Sports Medicine, 32*(2), 534–542.

Evans, N. A. (1997). Gym and tonic: A profile of 100 male steroid users. *British Journal of Sports Medicine, 31*, 54–58.

Ferenchick, G. S., Hirokawa, S., Mammen, E. F., & Schwartz, K. A. (1995). Anabolic-androgenic steroid abuse in weight lifters: Evidence for activation of the hemostatic system. *American Journal of Hematology, 49*(4), 282–288.

Ferstle, J. (2000). Evolution and politics of drug testing. In C. E. Yesalis (Ed.), *Anabolic steroids in sport and exercise* (2nd ed., pp. 363–413). Champaign, IL: Human Kinetics.

Frankle, M., Cicero, G., & Payne, J. (1984). Use of androgenic anabolic steroids by athletes. *Journal of the American Medical Association, 252*, 482.

Freinhar, J. P., & Alvarez, W. (1985). Androgen-induced hypomania. *Journal of Clinical Psychiatry, 46*(8), 354–355.

Friedl, K. E., Hannan, C. J., Jr., Jones, R. E., & Plymate, S. R. (1990). High-density lipoprotein cholesterol is not decreased if an aromatizable androgen is administered. *Metabolism, 39*(1), 69–74.

Frye, C. A. (2007). Some rewarding effects of androgens may be mediated by actions of its 5alpha-reduced metabolite 3alpha-androstanediol. *Pharmacology Biochemistry and Behavior, 86*(2), 354–367.

Frye, C. A., Rhodes, M. E., Rosellini, R., & Svare, B. (2002). The nucleus accumbens as a site of action for rewarding properties of testosterone and its 5 alpha-reduced metabolites. *Pharmacology Biochemistry and Behavior, 74*(1), 119–127.

Galligani, N., Renck, A., & Hansen, S. (1996). Personality profile of men using anabolic androgenic steroids. *Hormones and Behavior, 30*(2), 170–175.

Gilmore, R. M., & Stead, L. G. (2006). The role of hyperglycemia in acute ischemic stroke. *Neurocritical Care, 5*(2), 153–158.

Goldberg, L., Elliot, D., Clarke, G. N., MacKinnon, D. P., Moe, E., Zoref, L., et al. (1996). Effects of a multi-dimensional anabolic steroid prevention intervention: The Adolescents Training and Learning to Avoid Steroids (ATLAS) program. *Journal of the American Medical Association, 276*, 1555–1562.

Goldberg, L., MacKinnon, D. P., Elliot, D. L., Moe, E. L., Clarke, G., & Cheong, J. (2000). The adolescents training and learning to avoid steroids program: Preventing drug use and promoting health behaviors. *Archives of Pediatrics and Adolescent Medicine, 154*(4), 332–338.

Gray, P. B., Singh, A. B., Woodhouse, L. J., Storer, T. W., Casaburi, R., Dzekov, J., et al. (2005). Dose-dependent effects of testosterone on sexual function, mood, and visuospatial cognition in older men. *Journal of Clinical Endocrinology and Metabolism, 90*(7), 3838–3846.

Green, G. A., Uryasz, F. D., Petr, T. A., & Bray, C. D. (2001). NCAA study of substance use and abuse habits of college student-athletes. *Clinical Journal of Sport Medicine, 11*(1), 51–56.

Gruber, A. J., & Pope, H. G., Jr. (2000). Psychiatric and medical effects of anabolic-androgenic steroid use in women. *Psychotherapy and Psychosomatics, 69*(1), 19–26.

Handelsman, D. J., & Gupta, L. (1997). Prevalence and risk factors for anabolic-androgenic steroid abuse in Australian high school students. *International Journal of Andrology, 20*(3), 159–164.

Harmer, P. A. (2010). Anabolic-androgenic steroid use among young male and female athletes: Is the game to blame? *British Journal of Sports Medicine, 44,* 26–31.

Harper, J. A., Dickinson, K., & Brand, M. D. (2001). Mitochondrial uncoupling as a target for drug development for the treatment of obesity. *Obesity Reviews, 2*(4), 255–265.

Hartgens, F., & Kuipers, H. (2004). Effects of androgenic-anabolic steroids in athletes. *Sports Medicine, 34*(8), 513–554.

Hausmann, R., Hammer, S., & Betz, P. (1998). Performance enhancing drugs (doping agents) and sudden death – a case report and review of the literature. *International Journal of Legal Medicine, 111*(5), 261–164.

Hildebrandt, T., Alfano, L., & Langenbucher, J. (2010). Body image disturbance among 1000 appearance and performance enhancing drug users. *Journal of Psychiatric Research, 44*(13), 841–846.

Hildebrandt, T., Alfano, L., & Yehuda, R. (2011). What can allostasis tell us about anabolic-androgenic steroid addiction. *Development and Psychopathology, 23*(3), 907–919.

Hildebrandt, T., Lai, J. K., Langenbucher, J. W., Schneider, M., Yehuda, R., & Pfaff, D. W. (2011). The diagnostic dilemma of appearance and performance enhancing drug misuse. *Drug and Alcohol Dependence, 114*(1), 1–11.

Hildebrandt, T., Langenbucher, J. W., Carr, S. J., & Sanjuan, P. (2007). Modeling population heterogeneity in appearance- and performance-enhancing drug (APED) use: Applications of mixture modeling in 400 regular APED users. *Journal of Abnormal Psychology, 116*(4), 717–733.

Hildebrandt, T., Langenbucher, J., Carr, S., Sanjuan, P., & Park, S. (2006). Predicting intentions for long-term anabolic-androgenic steroid use among men: A covariance structure model. *Psychology of Addictive Behaviors, 20*(3), 234–240.

Hildebrandt, T., Schlundt, D., Langenbucher, J., & Chung, T. (2006). Presence of muscle dysmorphia symptomology among male weightlifters. *Comprehensive Psychiatry, 47*(2), 127–135.

Hoberman, J. (2002). Sports physicians and the doping crisis in elite sport. *Clinical Journal of Sports Medicine, 12*(4), 203–208.

Holt, R. I. G., Erotokritou-Mulligan, I., & Sönksen, P. H. (2009). The history of doping and growth hormone abuse in sport. *Growth Hormone and IGF Research, 19,* 320–326.

Huie, M. J. (1994). An acute myocardial infarction occurring in an anabolic steroid user. *Medicine and Science in Sports and Exercise, 26*(4), 408–13.

Hurley, B. F., Seals, D. R., Hagberg, J. M., Goldberg, A. C., Ostrove, S. M., Holloszy, J. O., et al. (1984). High-density-lipoprotein cholesterol in bodybuilders v powerlifters. Negative effects of androgen use. *Journal of the American Medical Association, 252*(4), 507–513.

Irving, L. M., Wall, M., Neumark-Sztainer, D., & Story, M. (2002). Steroid use among adolescents: Findings from Project EAT. *Journal of Adolescent Health, 30*(4), 243–252.

Ishak, K. G. (1981). Hepatic lesions caused by anabolic and contraceptive steroids. *Seminars in Liver Disease, 1*(2), 116–128.

Kanayama, G., Brower, K. J., Wood, R. I., Hudson, J. I., & Pope, H. G. (2009a). Anabolic-androgenic steroid dependence: An emerging disorder. *Addiction, 104*(12), 1966–1978.

Kanayama, G., Brower, K. J., Wood, R. I., Hudson, J. I., & Pope, H. G., Jr. (2010). Treatment of anabolic-androgenic steroid dependence: Emerging evidence and its implications. *Drug and Alcohol Dependence, 109*(1–3), 6–13.

Kanayama, G., Hudson, J. I., & Pope, H. G. (2009b). Features of men with anabolic-androgenic steroid dependence: A comparison with nondependent AAS users and with AAS nonusers. *Drug and Alcohol Dependence, 102*(1–3), 130–137.

Kanayama, G., Hudson, J. I., & Pope, H. G., Jr. (2010). Illicit anabolic-androgenic steroid use. *Hormones and Behavior, 58*(1), 111–121.

Kandel, D. B. (1975). Stages in adolescent involvement with drugs. *Science, 190,* 912–914.

Kandel, D. B. (1980). Developmental stages in adolescent drug involvement. *NIDA Research Monographs, 30,* 120–127.

Kersey R. (1993). Anabolic-androgenic steroid use by private health club/gym athletes. *Journal of Strength and Conditioning Research, 7,* 118–126.

Klein, I., & Ojamaa, K. (1992). Cardiovascular manifestations of endocrine disease. *Journal of Clinical Endocrinology and Metabolism, 75*(2), 339–342.

Klotz, F., Petersson, A., Isacson, D., & Thiblin, I. (2007). Violent crime and substance abuse: A medico-legal comparison between deceased users of anabolic androgenic steroids and abusers of illicit drugs. *Forensic Science International, 173*(1), 57–63.

Kouri, E. M., Lukas, S. E., Pope, H. G., & Oliva, P. S. (1995). Increased aggressive responding in male volunteers following the administration of gradually increasing doses of testosterone cypionate. *Drug and Alcohol Dependence, 40*(1), 73–79.

Kuhn, C. (2002). Anabolic steroids. *Recent Progress in Hormone Research, 57,* 411–434.

Laroche, G. P. (1990). Steroid anabolic drugs and arterial complications in an athlete—a case history. *Angiology, 41*(11), 964–969.

Lefavi, R. G., Reeve, T. G., & Newland, M. C. (1990). Relationship between anabolic steroid use and selected psychological parameters in male bodybuilders. *Journal of Sport Behavior, 13*(3), 157–166.

Lenders, J. W., Demacker, P. N., Vos, J. A., Jansen, P. L., Hoitsma, A. J., van 't Laar, A., et al. (1988). Deleterious effects of anabolic steroids on serum lipoproteins, blood pressure, and liver function in amateur body builders. *International Journal of Sports Medicine, 9*(1), 19–23.

Li, M., Wessinger, W. D., & McMillan, D. E. (2005). Effects of amphetamine CNS depressant combinations and of other CNS stimulants in four-choice drug discriminations. *Journal of the Experimental Analysis of Behavior, 84*(1), 77–97.

Lindstrom, M., Nilsson, A. L., Katzman, P. L., Janzon, L., & Dymling, J. F. (1990). Use of anabolic-androgenic steroids among body builders-frequency and attitudes. *Journal of Internal Medicine, 227*(6), 407–411.

Lukas, S. E. (1996). CNS effects and abuse liability of anabolic-androgenic steroids. *Annual Review of Pharmacology and Toxicology, 36,* 333–357.

Maglione, M., Miotto, K., Iguchi, M., Jungvig, L., Morton, S. C., & Shekelle, P. G. (2005). Psychiatric effects of ephedra use: An analysis of Food and Drug Administration reports of adverse events. *American Journal of Psychiatry, 162*(1), 189–191.

Martello, S., Felli, M., & Chiarotti, M. (2007). Survey of nutritional supplements for selected illegal anabolic steroids and ephedrine using LC-MS/MS and GC-MS methods, respectively. *Food Additives and Contaminants, 24*(3), 258–265.

Matsumoto, A. M. (1990). Effects of chronic testosterone administration in normal men: safety and efficacy of high dosage testosterone and parallel dose-dependent suppression of luteinizing hormone, follicle-stimulating hormone, and sperm production. *Journal of Clinical Endocrinology and Metabolism, 70*(1), 282–287.

McBride, A. J., Williamson, K., & Petersen, T. (1996). Three cases of nalbuphine hydrochloride dependence associated with anabolic steroid use. *British Journal of Sports Medicine, 30*(1), 69–70.

McCabe, S. E., Brower, K. J., West, B. T., Nelson, T. F., & Wechsler, H. (2007). Trends in non-medical use of anabolic steroids by U.S. college students: Results from four national surveys. *Drug and Alcohol Dependence, 90*(2–3), 243–251.

McFee, R. B., Caraccio, T. R., McGuigan, M. A., Reynolds, S. A., & Bellanger, P. (2004). Dying to be thin: A dinitrophenol related fatality. *Veterinary and Human Toxicology, 46*(5), 251–254.

Miah, A. (2005). From anti-doping to a 'performance policy' sport technology, being human, and doing ethics. *European Journal of Sport Science, 5*(1), 51–57.

Middleman, A. B., Faulkner, A. H., Woods, E. R., Emans, S. J., & DuRant, R. H. (1995). High-risk behaviors among high school students in Massachusetts who use anabolic steroids. *Pediatrics, 96*(2 Pt 1), 268–272.

Monaghan, L. F. (2002). Vocabularies of motive for illicit steroid use among bodybuilders. *Social Science and Medicine, 55*(5), 695–708.

Moss, H. B., Panazak, G. L., & Tarter, R. E. (1992). Personality, mood, psychiatric symptoms among anabolic steroid users. *The American Journal on Addictions, 1*(4), 315–324.

National Center on Addiction and Substance Abuse. (2000). *Winning at any cost: Doping in Olympic sports* (1st ed.). New York, NY: The CASA National Commission on Sports and Substance Abuse.

National Institute on Drug Abuse. (2006). *Research reports: Anabolic steroid abuse* (NIH Publication Number 06-3721). Bethesda, MD: NIDA.

O'Keefe, M., Red, C., & Quinn, T. (2005, March 13). Hitting the Mark: FBI informants say McGwire was juiced. *Daily News*. Retrieved from: http://www.nydailynews.com/archives/sports/hitting-mark-fbi-informants-mcgwire-juiced-article-1.559684

Olivardia, R. (2001). Mirror, mirror on the wall, who's the largest of them all? The features and phenomenology of muscle dysmorphia. *Harvard Review of Psychiatry, 9*(5), 254–259.

Parkinson, A. B., & Evans, N. A. (2006). Anabolic androgenic steroids: A survey of 500 users. *Medicine and Science in Sports and Exercise, 38*(4), 644–651.

Patil, J. J., O'Donohoe, B. O., Loyden, C. F., & Shanahan, D. (2007). Near-fatal spontaneous hepatic rupture associated with anabolic steroid use: A case report. *British Journal of Sports Medicine, 41*, 462–463.

Peet, M., & Peters, S. (1995). Drug-induced mania. *Drug Safety, 12*(2), 146–53.

Perry, P. J., Andersen, K. H., & Yates, W. R. (1990). Illicit anabolic steroid use in athletes. A case series analysis. *American Journal of Sports Medicine, 18*(4), 422–428.

Perry, P. J., Kutscher, E. C., Lund, B. C., Yates, W. R., Holman, T. L., & Demers, L. (2003). Measures of aggression and mood changes in male weightlifters with and without androgenic anabolic steroid use. *Journal of Forensic Sciences, 48*(3), 646–651.

Perry, P. J., Lund, B. C., Deninger, M. J., Kutscher, E. C., & Schneider, J. (2005). Anabolic steroid use in weightlifters and bodybuilders—An internet survey of drug utilization. *Clinical Journal of Sport Medicine, 15*(5), 326–330.

Philibert, R., & Mac, J. (2004). An association of Ephedra use with psychosis and autonomic hyperactivity. *Annals of Clinical Psychiatry, 16*(3), 167–169.

Pope, C. G., Pope, H. G., Menard, W., Fay, C., Olivardia, R., & Phillips, K. A. (2005). Clinical features of muscle dysmorphia among males with body dysmorphic disorder. *Body Image, 2*(4), 395–400.

Pope, H. G., Jr., Gruber, A. J., Choi, P., Olivardia, R., & Phillips, K. A. (1997). Muscle dysmorphia. An underrecognized form of body dysmorphic disorder. *Psychosomatics, 38*(6), 548–557.

Pope, H. G., Jr., & Katz, D. L. (1988). Affective and psychotic symptoms associated with anabolic steroid use. *American Journal of Psychiatry, 145*(4), 487–490.

Pope, H. G., Jr., & Katz, D. L. (1994). Psychiatric and medical effects of anabolic-androgenic steroid use. A controlled study of 160 athletes. *Archives of General Psychiatry, 51*(5), 375–382.

Pope, H. G., Jr., Kouri, E. M., & Hudson, J. I. (2000). Effects of supraphysiologic doses of testosterone on mood and aggression in normal men: A randomized controlled trial. *Archives of General Psychiatry, 57*(2), 133–140; discussion 155–136.

Quinn, T. (2007, January 11). Caught in the act: Bonds failed amphetamine test, blamed teammate. *Sports Illustrated*. Retrieved from: http://sportsillustrated.cnn.com/2007/baseball/mlb/01/11/bonds.amphetamines/

Ranby, K. W., Aiken, L. S., Mackinnon, D. P., Elliot, D. L., Moe, E. L., McGinnis, W., et al. (2009). A mediation analysis of the ATHENA intervention for female athletes: Prevention of athletic-enhancing substance use and unhealthy weight loss behaviors. *Journal of Pediatric Psychology, 34*(10), 1069–1083.

Reagan, L. P. (2007). Insulin signaling effects on memory and mood. *Current Opinion in Pharmacology, 7*(6), 633–637.

Salke, R. C., Rowland, T. W., & Burke, E. J. (1985). Left ventricular size and function in body builders using anabolic steroids. *Medicine and Science in Sports and Exercise, 17*(6), 701–704.

Samenuk, D., Link, M. S., Homoud, M. K., Contreras, R., Theohardes, T. C., Wang, P. J., et al. (2002). Adverse cardiovascular events temporally associated with ma huang, an herbal source of ephedrine. *Mayo Clinic Proceedings, 77*(1), 12–16.

Santamarina, R. D., Besocke, A. G., Romano, L. M., Ioli, P. L., Gonorazky, S. E. (2008). *Clinical Neuropharmacology, 31*(2), 80–85.

Shahidi, N. T. (2001). A review of the chemistry, biological action, and clinical applications of anabolic-androgenic steroids. *Clinical Therapeutics, 23*(9), 1355–1390.

Shiozawa, Z., Yamada, H., Mabuchi, C., Hotta, T., Saito, M., Sobue, I., et al. (1982). Superior sagittal sinus thrombosis associated with androgen therapy for hypoplastic anemia. *Annals of Neurology, 12*(6), 578–580.

Silverman, K., Evans, S. M., Strain, E. C., & Griffiths, R. R. (1992). Withdrawal syndrome after the double-blind cessation of caffeine consumption. *New England Journal of Medicine, 327*(16), 1109–1114.

Spriet, L. L. (2002). Regulation of skeletal muscle fat oxidation during exercise in humans. *Medicine and Science in Sports and Exercise, 34*(9), 1477–1484.

Stalenheim, E. G., von Knorring, L., & Wide, L. (1998). Serum levels of thyroid hormones as biological markers in a Swedish forensic psychiatric population. *Biological Psychiatry, 43*(10), 755–761.

Steensland, P., Hallberg, M., Kindlundh, A., Fahlke, C., & Nyberg, F. (2005). Amphetamine-induced aggression is enhanced in rats pre-treated with the anabolic androgenic steroid nandrolone decanoate. *Steroids, 70*(3), 199–204.

Stoops, W. W. (2008). Reinforcing effects of stimulants in humans: Sensitivity of progressive-ratio schedules. *Experimental and Clinical Psychopharmacology, 16*(6), 503–512.

Su, S., Pagliaro, M., Schmidt, P. J., Pickar, D., Wolkowitz, O., & Rubinow, D. R. (1993). Neuropsychiatric effects of anabolic steroids in male normal volunteers. *JAMA, 269*(21), 2760–2764.

Tahtamouni, L. H., Mustafa, N. H., Alfaouri, A. A., Hassan, I. M., Abdalla, M. Y., & Yasin, S. R. (2008). Prevalence and risk factors for anabolic-androgenic steroid abuse among Jordanian collegiate students and athletes. *European Journal of Public Health, 18*(6), 661–665.

Tanner, S. M., Miller, D. W., & Alongi, C. (1995). Anabolic steroid use by adolescents: Prevalence, motives, and knowledge of risks. *Clinical Journal of Sport Medicine, 5*(2), 108–115.

Thomsen, I. (1993, March 6). IAAF Bans Johnson for life after his 2d doping offense. *The New York Times*. Retrieved from: http://www.nytimes.com/1993/03/06/sports/06iht-ben_.html

Tinsley, J. A., & Watkins, D. D. (1998). Over-the-counter stimulants: Abuse and addiction. *Mayo Clinic Proceedings, 73*(10), 977–982.

Tricker, R., Casaburi, R., Storer, T. W., Clevenger, B., Berman, N., Shirazi, A., Bhasin, S. (1996). The effects of supraphysiologic doses of testosterone on angry behavior in healthy eugonadal men – A clinical research center study. *The Journal of Clinical Endocrinology and Metabolism, 81*(10), 3754–3758.

Tsitsimpikou, C., Tsiokanos, A., Tsarouhas, K., Schamasch, P., Fitch, K. D., Valasiadis, D., & Jamurtas, A. (2009). Medication use by athletes at the Athens 2004 summer Olympic games. *Clinical Journal of Sport Medicine, 19*(1), 33–38.

Urhausen, A., Albers, T., & Kindermann, W. (2004). Are the cardiac effects of anabolic steroid abuse in strength athletes reversible? *Heart, 90*(5), 496–501.

van Breda, E., Keizer, H. A., Kuipers, H., & Wolffenbuttel, B. H. R. (2003). Androgenic anabolic steroid use and severe hypothalamic-pituitary dysfunction: A case study. *International Journal of Sports Medicine, 24*(3), 195–196.

vandenBerg, P., Neumark-Sztainer, D., Cafri, G., & Wall, M. (2007). Steroid use among adolescents: Longitudinal findings from Project EAT. *Pediatrics, 119*(3), 476–486.

Vertalino, M., Eisenberg, M. E., Story, M., & Neumark-Sztainer, D. (2007). Participation in weight-related sports is associated with higher use of unhealthful weight-control behaviors and steroid use. *Journal of the American Dietetic Association, 107*(3), 434–440.

Wagman, D. F., Curry, L. A., Cook, D. L. (1995). An investigation into anabolic androgenic steroid use by elite US powerlifters. *Journal of Strength and Conditioning Research, 9*(3), 149–154.

Walton, R., & Manos, G. H. (2003). Psychosis related to ephedra-containing herbal supplement use. *Southern Medical Journal, 96*(7), 718–720.

Wesson, D. W., & McGinnis, M. Y. (2006). Stacking anabolic androgenic steroids (AAS) during puberty in rats: A neuroendocrine and behavioral assessment. *Pharmacology Biochemistry and Behavior, 83*(3), 410–419.

Wines, J. D., Gruber, A. J., Pope, H. G., & Lukas, S. E. (1999). Nalbuphine hydrochloride dependence in anabolic steroid users. *American Journal on Addictions, 8*(2), 161–164.

Yates, W. R., Perry, P. J., MacIndoe, J., Holman, T., & Ellingrod, V. (1999). Psychosexual effects of three doses of testosterone cycling in normal men. *Biological Psychiatry, 45*(3), 254–260.

Yesalis, C. E., & Bahrke, M. S. (2002). History of doping in sport. In M. S. Bahrke & C. E. Yesalis (Eds.), *Performance-enhancing substances in sport and exercise* (pp. 1–20). Champaign, IL: Human Kinetics.

Zahringer, S., Tomova, A., von Werder, K., Brabant, G., Kumanov, P., & Schopohl, J. (2000). The influence of hyperthyroidism on the hypothalamic-pituitary-gonadal axis. *Experimental and Clinical Endocrinology and Diabetes, 108*(4), 282–289.

Zuliani, U., Bernardini, B., Catapano, A., Campana, M., Cerioli, G., & Spattini, M. (1989). Effects of anabolic steroids, testosterone, and HGH on blood lipids and echocardiographic parameters in body builders. *International Journal of Sports Medicine, 10*(1), 62–66.

Burnout: A Darker Side to Performance

Kate I. Goodger *and* Martin I. Jones

Abstract

The struggle of the human spirit to fulfil potential and accomplish excellence in the competitive and challenging environments of high performance is at the heart of sport and performance psychology. However, a lurking negative consequence of an individual's effortful striving is the possibility of burnout. The concept originated in the health care domain as a syndrome that scholars and practitioners believe results from chronic exposure to stress. It is characterized by three key dimensions: exhaustion, inefficacy, and cynicism. Since its inception, the concept of burnout has been transposed across a range of social contexts, with a growing literature that has examined burnout specifically among athletes and coaches. This chapter seeks to compare the sport psychology and professional burnout literatures to provide an overview of how to recognize, avoid, and reduce and remove burnout. Burnout intervention approaches have shifted from mitigating burnout to enhancing "engagement," which is its conceptual opposite (i.e., energy, efficacy, and involvement). Consequently, the concept of engagement is explored and proposed as an important intervention strategy to consider for those working with performers across domains. The chapter concludes with a summary and look at future directions in this field.

Key Words: Burnout, overtraining, stress, job stress, depression, fatigue, exhaustion, health, performance, motivation, commitment, engagement, disengagement, positive psychology, identity

The strivings of an individual to fulfil potential and accomplish excellence in the competitive and challenging environments of high performance is at the heart of sport and performance psychology. The concept of burnout seems antithetical in the context of commitment and striving, but research suggests that burnout may in fact be the dark side of striving, the result of perhaps too much caring, commitment, and stress. Within burnout research on professional occupations, in which the concept originated, there has been a recent move to position burnout on a continuum from engagement to burnout (Maslach & Leiter, 2008). Historically, attention has focused on the negative end of the continuum and on burnout as a psychological syndrome that results from exposure to chronic stressors associated with work

(Maslach & Leiter). Pragmatically, the goal of this research was not only to understand what burnout is but also what to do about it (Maslach & Goldberg, 1998). The growth of interest in the positive end of the continuum—engagement—has arisen from the proposition that as the conceptual opposite of burnout, the promotion of engagement in one's work is the best strategy for burnout prevention (Maslach, Schaufeli, & Leiter, 2001; Schaufeli, Martínez, Marques Pinto, Salanova, & Bakker, 2002).

Engagement has been variously defined within the burnout literature as an energetic state of involvement with a personally fulfilling activity (Leiter & Maslach, 1998); a persistent, pervasive, positive, fulfilling, work-related state of mind (Schaufeli, Salanova, Gonzalez-Romá, & Bakker, 2002); and a persistent, positive, cognitive-affective experience, characterized by confidence, dedication, and vigor (Lonsdale, Hodge, & Raedeke, 2007). The purpose of this chapter is to provide an overview of burnout and to describe current concepts regarding intervention in cases of burnout. Rather than framing burnout as simply what happens to individual performers "when things go wrong," the principles of positive psychology (Seligman & Csikszentmihalyi, 2000) suggest that, ultimately, burnout can be prevented by applying the notion of engagement to support positive human functioning and thriving.

Research exploring burnout was initially restricted to "helping professions," in which the term was coined to describe a type of exhaustion observed by Herbert Freudenberger (1974) among young volunteers working at a New York drug addiction clinic. The concept has since been extended to apply to virtually all occupations (Maslach et al., 2001) and some nonvocational settings, such as sport and marital relationships (Shirom, 2002). Within the parent domain of professional burnout, the breadth of occupations explored is vast and although subgroups that could be considered "performers" (such as doctors, business leaders, and military personnel) have been examined, no discernible subdivision sits neatly under the banner of performance psychology. In sport psychology, a growing body of research has studied burnout in athletes and coaches. In early work in this domain, Smith (1986) asked a question that remains pertinent today concerning the extent to which the nature, causes, and consequences of athlete burnout were unique and to what extent they are shared by those who suffer burnout in various other domains. To support those working with performers in a variety of domains, this chapter will contrast research from athlete and coach burnout with that of professional burnout to establish commonalities and differences.

The chapter is structured into three broad sections addressing recognizing burnout, avoiding burnout, and reducing and removing burnout. In the first section, burnout is defined, associated symptoms are described, it is differentiated from related concepts (e.g., fatigue and overtraining), and its measurement is discussed. The second section discusses the consequences of burnout and its relationship with performance, examines explanations of burnout, and presents findings about the antecedents and correlates of burnout. In the final section, management and intervention approaches for working with performers encountering burnout is examined, and the role of organizations in prevention is discussed.

The chapter concludes with a look at future intervention and research directions.

Recognizing Burnout
Defining and Measuring Burnout

Progress in burnout research has been hindered by conceptual ambiguity and confusion, leading to measurement problems (Cresswell & Eklund, 2006a; Dale & Weinberg, 1990; Maslach et al., 2001). The most widely accepted conceptualization of professional burnout is a multidimensional perspective originally proffered by Maslach and Jackson (1981). According to this definition, burnout is described as a psychological syndrome comprising three key dimensions: exhaustion–energy, cynicism–involvement, and inefficacy–efficacy (Leiter & Stright, 2009; Maslach, 2003). The exhaustion dimension captures the component of strain and feeling overextended and depleted in one's emotional and physical resources. Cynicism (or depersonalization) describes a negative, callous, or excessively detached response toward different aspects of work and comprises the interpersonal component of burnout. Finally, the third dimension of inefficacy (or reduced accomplishment) represents the self-evaluation component of burnout and encapsulates feelings of incompetence, lack of achievement, and decreased productivity at work (Maslach & Leiter, 2008).

Emotional exhaustion has repeatedly been identified as the central component of burnout (Taris, Le Blanc, Schaufeli, & Schreurs, 2005), to such an extent that debate has been raised as to whether the other dimensions are needed in recognizing burnout (Schaufeli & Taris, 2005). Maslach and Leiter (2008) explain that exhaustion does not capture the whole story of burnout. Exhaustion is not simply experienced but rather it prompts action by the individual to distance him- or herself emotionally and cognitively from work as a coping strategy. This leads to the onset of the second dimension of cynicism and an attempt to gain distance from work. In an earlier review, Maslach and Leiter (2005) reported that cynicism was such an immediate response to exhaustion that a strong and consistent relationship with burnout has been found across work and organizational settings. The relationship between inefficacy and the other dimensions appears less clear, which has led to it being marginalized in comparison (Cox, Tisserand, & Taris, 2005). Engagement, the conceptual opposite of burnout, has also been proposed as encompassing three dimensions, and there is consensus that *vigor* or *energy* (high levels of physical and mental resources and willingness to invest effort) is the conceptual opposite of the exhaustion dimension, and that dedication (sense of significance, enthusiasm, inspiration and challenge) is the opposite of cynicism (Lonsdale et al., 2007). There is no consensus on the equivalent engagement dimension for inefficacy, with competing conceptualizations of absorption (being immersed and happily absorbed in one's work; Schaufeli & Bakker, 2003) and efficacy (sense of confidence in one's ability to be effective at work; Maslach & Leiter, 1997) battling for acceptance by researchers. As this efficacy–inefficacy dimension of burnout and engagement relates directly to performance, we will return to a more detailed discussion of this concept shortly.

Because Maslach and Jackson's (1981) conceptualization was originally developed for helping professions, Maslach and Schaufeli (1993) have warned of overextending the definition outside the human services and suggest that modification based upon salient contextual influences may be required. Likewise, Schutte and colleagues (Schutte, Toppinen, Kalimo, & Schaufeli, 2000) observed that although underlying characteristics (i.e., exhaustion) remain constant, the syndrome may manifest differently across settings. The first research examining burnout in the sport context focused on coaches (Caccese & Mayerberg, 1984). This research stemmed from the observation that coaching represented a "people-oriented" profession with human relationships as a central component. Due to the perceived parallels between coaching and other helping professions, contextual interference is considered to be low and the burnout dimensions have transposed readily from professional burnout to coach burnout. Even contemporary research has continued to employ this conceptualization with limited modification (e.g., Hjalm, Kentta, Hassmen, & Gustafsson, 2007; Raedeke, 2004).

Greater sensitivity to contextual differences has been necessary for athlete populations. Maslach and Schaufeli (1993) advise that, when applying the three dimensions of burnout to other domains, researchers must first assess the core elements of a particular domain and customize the dimensions to align with these elements. The provider–recipient relationship is at the core of how Maslach and Jackson (1981) have conceptualized burnout. Athletes are considered to be on the receiving end of this relationship, and therefore it is not the most central element of the sport context for athletes (Raedeke, 1997). Raedeke argues that the core element of the sport

context for athletes is their performance, and hence the dimensions should be defined in relation to athletic performance. Through Raedeke's endeavors (i.e., Raedeke, 1997; Raedeke, Lunney, & Venables, 2002; Raedeke & Smith, 2001) a specific definition of athlete burnout has emerged and is becoming the most widely utilized within sport psychology research. The exhaustion dimension has been modified to *physical and emotional exhaustion* (PEE) and is associated with intense training and competition. Reduced sense of athletic accomplishment (*reduced accomplishment,* RA) replaces the inefficacy dimension and relates to an athlete's skills and abilities. Failures to achieve personal goals or performances that are below expectations are thought to contribute to RA. Finally cynicism (depersonalization) was not identified as salient within athlete experiences, and *sport devaluation* (DV) became the third dimension in athlete burnout. Devaluation refers to a loss of interest, a "don't care" attitude, or resentment toward performance and the sport.

In burnout research with athletes, exhaustion has emerged again as a central feature of the syndrome but, given the physical demands of intense sports participation, some degree of exhaustion would be expected (Cresswell & Eklund, 2006b). Cresswell and Eklund explain that expected levels of exhaustion are transient in that they are relieved following routine recovery periods, whereas exhaustion associated with burnout is enduring and remains following routine recovery. The relationship between exhaustion and the other dimensions of athlete burnout is not yet fully understood (Gustafsson, Kentta, Hassmen, Lundqvist, & Durand-Bush, 2007). However, some research has indicated that the interrelationships among these dimensions, and specifically the sequential order in which the dimensions occur, may differ from occupational settings (Gustafsson et al., 2007). Studies have consistently identified that exhaustion emerges as the earliest of the dimensions, but this is closely followed by reduced accomplishment. Devaluation is experienced later (Cresswell & Eklund, 2007a; Goodger, Wolfenden, & Lavallee, 2007a; Gustafsson et al., 2007). This ordering is attributed to the balance of resources and demands leading to exhaustion. As athletes experience feelings of insecurity about their performance and inefficacy, they respond by working harder, which exacerbates levels of exhaustion. The combined experience of an enduring state of exhaustion and low or declining performance leads to accomplishment frustrations and changes in motivation, and, eventually, to devaluation.

Cresswell and Eklund speculated that devaluation may serve to protect an athlete's self esteem. Self-esteem has also been linked to the reduced accomplishment dimension in that, for some athletes, this becomes contingent on effective performance and is intimately linked to issues of athletic identity (Goodger et al., 2007a; and Gustafsson et al., 2007). The emphasis on achievement and results, and the public nature of evaluation in sport, suggests that the inefficacy dimension of athlete burnout is much more significant than it is considered to be in the professional domain. Cresswell and Eklund also propose that it may be appropriate to further subdivide this dimension into professional efficacy (relating to feelings of confidence) as well as reduced accomplishment. In their study of professional rugby players, they reported that reduced accomplishment was associated with past and present performance, whereas low professional efficacy referred to doubts in a player's abilities to continue to perform at a high level. This distinction has important implications for applied practice and intervention work. Although more research is needed, these early observations infer potential key differences in the interrelationship between the dimensions of burnout in cases of professional versus athlete burnout and also suggest that the role of the inefficacy dimension may require further development.

Alongside the challenges in developing a universally agreed upon definition of burnout, the attainment of a valid and reliable measurement tool has been equally difficult. Self-report measures have been the tool of choice in burnout research (Goodger, Lavallee, Gorely, & Harwood, 2007b). In part, the popularity of Maslach and Jackson's (1981) three dimensions of burnout are attributed to successful operationalization through the development of the Maslach Burnout Inventory (MBI; Maslach & Jackson, 1981). Although not devoid of critics, this instrument has "almost been universally accepted as the gold standard" in assessing burnout (Schutte et al., 2000, p. 53). In addition, further versions of the MBI have been advanced for utilization outside the helping profession context, including the MBI-General Survey (MBI-GS: Schaufeli, Leiter, Maslach, & Jackson, 1996) and MBI- Educators Survey (MBI-ES: Maslach, Jackson, & Leiter, 1996). These measures have also been employed in coach burnout research with limited modification (e.g., Kelley, 1994; Kelley & Gill, 1993).

Raedeke's (1997) three dimensions of athlete burnout have been operationalized in the sport context with the publication of the Athlete Burnout Questionnaire (ABQ; Raedeke & Smith, 2001). The ABQ comprises three five-item subscales that assess levels of perceived burnout across physical and emotional exhaustion, sport devaluation, and reduced sense of athletic accomplishment. Responses to each item are scored on a 5-point Likert scale ranging 1 (almost never) to 5 (almost always). Research using the ABQ has reported acceptable internal consistency (α between .85 and .91), test–retest reliability, and construct validity (Cresswell & Eklund, 2005a,b; Raedeke & Smith, 2001, 2004). Furthermore, in a direct assessment of convergent, discriminant, and construct validity of the ABQ with the MBI-GS (Schaufeli et al., 1996), Cresswell and Eklund (2006c) reported acceptable convergent validity and satisfactory internal discriminant validity and concluded that the ABQ should be the recommended self-report measure for athlete burnout. Despite the apparent popularity of the ABQ, a current limitation is associated with the measure that should be acknowledged. The utility of the MBI has been aided by the establishment of norms and cutoff points indicating levels of burnout, as well as clinical cutoffs to support a diagnosis of clinical burnout (Schaufeli, Bakker, Hoogdum, Schaap, & Kladler, 2001). At present there is no guidance as to how to interpret scores of the ABQ, and cutoff points been not been established. Consequently, practitioners and researchers are advised to proceed with caution when classifying burnout levels with athletes (Hodge, Lonsdale, & Ng, 2008).

Burnout and Related Constructs

Burnout exhibits a shared symptomatology with a number of related constructs across professional and sport domains, including fatigue, depression, job stress, and overtraining. These constructs have been used interchangeably and sometimes inappropriately in the research literature.

FATIGUE

To distinguish between cases of fatigue and burnout, Schaufeli and Taris (2005) cite the basic tenet of Thorndike's (1914) *psychological fatigue*. According to Thorndike, psychological fatigue is the "intolerance of any effort." Specifically, this concerns both the inability and unwillingness to expend effort. Inability (energy/exhaustion) relates to the depletion of energy resources, whereas unwillingness (motivation/depersonalization) is associated with withdrawal and manifests through increased resistance to the activity, reduced commitment, and lack of interest and disengagement. Withdrawal prevents further depletion and hence is a protective strategy. Schaufeli and Taris stated that in episodes of "normal" occupational fatigue, withdrawal is highly functional in allowing the individual to recuperate and reduce fatigue. In the burnout case, it is part of the problem, not a solution, because it becomes habituated into relatively permanent impaired motivation. Exhaustion (inability) and withdrawal (unwillingness) comprise two inseparable features of burnout extending beyond simple fatigue.

Burnout has also been discussed in relation to chronic fatigue syndrome (CFS). Chronic fatigue syndrome is highly pervasive, with the potential to affect any of the body's major systems (i.e., neurological, immunological, endocrine, and musculoskeletal). Schaufeli and Buunk (2003) argue that accompanying psychological symptoms can occur, but CFS is generally considered to be primarily a physical complaint, and, although physical symptoms are not uncommon in burnout cases, symptoms are largely psychological. A further point of distinction is that, in CFS, the origin of fatigue is unclear, whereas in burnout cases fatigue is work related. Also, the development of negative attitudes and behaviors toward work characteristic of burnout are not always observed in individuals with CFS (Schaufeli & Buunk, 2003).

DEPRESSION

To differentiate burnout from depression, Freudenberger (1983) explains that burnout tends (initially at least) to be associated with the social environment at work (or, in the case of athlete burnout, sport). In contrast, depression is seen to be more pervasive and generalizes across all aspects of an individual's life. Sadness, guilt, hopelessness, and feelings of worthlessness are also considered basic features of depression but are not necessarily observed in burnout (Shirom, 2005). Research has further identified the two constructs as distinguishable (e.g., Glass & McKnight, 1996; Leiter & Durup, 1994; Schaufeli & Enzmann, 1998). In the sport setting, Cresswell and Eklund (2006c) examined whether the ABQ could demonstrate appropriate convergence with and discrimination from depression and anxiety measures. Findings confirmed acceptable convergent and discriminant validity and supported research from nonsporting populations that burnout and depression should be regarded as separate constructs. Shirom (2005) advocates assessing the possible impact of depression in studies of burnout by routinely including a measure of depressive symptomatology.

JOB STRESS

Job stress is recognized as a significant occupational hazard that can impair physical health, psychological well-being, and work performance (Maslach & Leiter, 2008). Schaufeli and Enzmann (1998) describe job stress as a term applied to "any affect-laden negative experience that is caused by an imbalance between job demands and the response capability of the worker" (p. 8). Burnout is considered to be a particular type of job stress characterized by negative, dysfunctional, job-related attitudes and behaviors, and stemming from prolonged interpersonal demands at work (Schaufeli & Buunk, 2003).

Within the sport context, the term *job stress* resonates readily with coaching as a profession and is recognizable in coach burnout research in psychological and situational correlates that include coaching issues (e.g., timetabling and budgets), role conflict, perceived stress, perceived success (including win–loss record), social support, and commitment (Goodger et al., 2007b). In studies of professional athletes (e.g., Cresswell & Eklund, 2007a, 2007b, 2006b) concerns over "low job-security" and the "threat of nonselection" are associated with the incidence of burnout. Furthermore, Schaufeli and Taris (2005), in debating whether burnout is a general or work-related phenomenon, suggested that it can occur outside the work context but should fundamentally "refer to a phenomenon that occurs in response to activities that are psychologically similar to work" (p. 260). They characterize these types of activities as work-like because they are structured, coercive in nature, and directed toward specific goals, and they suggest that the activities of athletes, artists, students, and volunteers may, from a psychological perspective, be similar to work. These observations suggest that athletes can experience burnout as a form of job stress, but further research is needed to confirm this.

OVERTRAINING

Overtraining is a sport-specific construct that has historically been confused with burnout. Cresswell and Eklund (2006a) argue that experiential characteristics that are identical across burnout and overtraining—such as exhaustion, lethargy, and negative mood—make distinguishing between them difficult. Moreover, they are perceived to be so intimately related to one another that one (burnout) may be simply a more severe manifestation of the other (overtraining). Cresswell and Eklund maintain, however, that it is critical to preventative and intervention strategies to attempt to differentiate them. They argue that, at the conceptual level, overtraining is considered to be an endpoint, whereas burnout is an experiential state (and hence an athlete could be overtrained but may not burn out). Overtraining is also associated with physical training and issues of under-recovery, whereas burnout can occur in the absence of excessive physical loads (e.g., Gould, Tuffey, Udry, & Loehr, 1996). From a more pragmatic standpoint, Peterson (2005) makes a distinction between the two constructs on the basis of motivation. She states that the overtrained athlete is one who is attempting to balance a continued drive to train with a reduced ability to do so, whereas the burned-out athlete is one who has lost that motivation to train (and, ultimately, to participate in their sport).

Characteristics of Burnout

Burnout is described as a psychological/psychosocial syndrome, and a syndrome refers to a group of signs and symptoms that occur together and characterize a particular abnormality (Shirom, 2005). Identifying clearly discernible signs and symptoms of burnout has, however, been an ongoing challenge with respect to professional, coach, and athlete burnout. This is attributed to its shared symptomatology with related constructs, conceptual confusion surrounding what burnout is and what it is not, a lack of methodological rigor in early research that led to an all-encompassing approach (i.e., an A to Z of burnout symptoms; Schaufeli & Enzmann, 1998), and difficulty in distinguishing between symptoms and consequences, in which a symptom such as decreased motivation may also be considered a consequence of the syndrome. This section of the chapter focuses on reviewing the efforts of researchers to provide clarity regarding the characteristics and symptomatology of burnout. Consequences of the syndrome will be examined in more detail in the Avoiding Burnout section that follows.

Instead of being stuck wading through treacle, trying to clearly delineate between signs, symptoms, characteristics, and consequences, professional burnout researchers have begun to employ more collective descriptors such as "concomitants" (i.e., effects of burnout; Schaufeli & Enzmann, 1998) and "manifestations" (Schaufeli & Buunk, 2003). Schaufeli and Buunk outline five main groups of manifestations; these include affective, cognitive, physical, behavioral, and motivational manifestations. *Affective manifestations* in burnout cases typically include a suppressed mood state (e.g., gloomy, tearful, and

depressed) but can also involve significant shifts in mood, such as aggressive- and anxiety-based states resulting from frustration, diminished tolerance, and oversensitivity. *Cognitive manifestations* can incorporate impaired functioning in information processing, memory, attention, and concentration, as well as rigid and detached thinking stemming from compromised voluntary or executive control (Van Der Linden, Keijsers, Eling & Van Schaijk, 2005). Research examining *physical manifestations* has provided contradictory evidence regarding the relationship between burnout and health. Schaufeli and Buunk (2003) stated that empirical support for such a relationship is weak when objective measures such as cholesterol and cortisol levels are employed, but when self-report measures are used, a significant correlation emerges. Physical symptoms generally associated with burnout include headaches, nausea, restlessness, sleep disturbance, ulcers, high blood pressure, disrupted menstrual cycle, and frequent and prolonged colds (Schaufeli & Enzmann, 1998). There is also inconsistency in the professional literature with regard to *behavioral manifestations* associated with burnout. Behaviors that have been identified are increased substance use (e.g., alcohol, drugs, and smoking), over- and undereating, high risk-taking behavior, avoidance, impulsivity, and procrastination. In turn, consequences linked to these behaviors have raised concern for interpersonal relationships away from work (i.e., families), as well as for organizations through staff turnover, absenteeism, and impaired performance and productivity (Schaufeli & Enzmann). Finally, under *motivational manifestations*, the burned out individual is considered to be experiencing a motivational crisis in which drive has vanished, to be replaced by disillusionment and despondence. Behavioral responses to this crisis include, ultimately, withdrawal, which leads to feelings of isolation and alienation and the possible breakdown of relationships, resentment, and conflict (Schaufeli & Enzmann, 1998).

In the sport context, researchers examining athlete burnout have attempted to differentiate between symptoms and consequences. Goodger et al. (2007a) defined symptoms as physical or mental characteristics of burnout (i.e., experienced when an athlete has burnout) and consequences as the result or outcome of burnout. Research exploring the characteristics of athlete burnout has, in recent years, tended to focus attention on characterizing each of the three dimensions of PEE, RA, and DV (e.g., Cresswell & Eklund, 2006b; Goodger et al., 2007a; Raedeke et al., 2002). Characteristics associated with PEE include negative affect, feeling trapped or unable to escape sport, constant tiredness, and longer recovery periods being required. For RA, typical characteristics reported are inconsistent or up and down performance, low feeling of achievement/accomplishment, training hard but seeing no improvement, and internalization of external feedback (e.g., coach). Finally, DV is characterized as a loss of motivation and enthusiasm, perceptions of few benefits to sport, looking forward to time away from the sport, resentment, and being sick of playing/competing.

To support the work of practitioners consulting with athletes, and to aid the early identification of cases of burnout, there has been an emergence of research outlining early signs of burnout (e.g., Cresswell, 2009; Cresswell & Eklund, 2003). These early signs are believed to precede burnout and can help to identify potential at-risk athletes. Readers are referred to Cresswell and Eklund's (2003) *Practitioner Guide* to athlete burnout for a more in-depth account. In a longitudinal study, Maslach and Leiter (2008) conducted research on early signs of professional burnout and early signs of engagement. They propose that, due to the strength of the relationship between exhaustion and cynicism, the presence of higher or lower reported scores for both dimensions would be predictive of early signs of burnout and engagement, respectively. Their findings indicate that higher levels in only one of the dimensions could be considered an early warning sign, but this indicator was less stable and subject to change. The direction of the change toward burnout or engagement was influenced by the level of congruence/incongruence in different work life areas, the most significant being perceptions of fairness. Research on early warning signs of burnout is limited but has significant potential value in preventing the development of burnout, as well as in shaping the type of intervention employed in sport and performance settings.

Avoiding Burnout

The introduction to this chapter highlighted the concept that burnout is the potential dark side of personal striving. This section aims to explore this proposition further through understanding why burnout should be avoided (i.e., consequences), as well as examining what the literature tells us about how it can be avoided (i.e., antecedents).

Consequences of Burnout

It may appear superfluous to consider why burnout should be avoided when the potential negative consequences seem obvious. However, within both professional and sport burnout literature few studies have actually looked at the consequences of burnout, and, subsequently, a number of claims relating to consequences have not yet been substantiated (Schaufeli & Enzmann, 1998). For the purpose of this chapter, two key areas in which consequences are assumed to have particular gravitas with performers will be discussed in detail: namely, health and performance. Consequences are defined here as outcomes of the burnout experience (Goodger et al., 2007a).

As alluded to earlier in the discussion on physical manifestations, professional burnout research has been inconsistent and inconclusive in determining the relationship between burnout and health problems (Schaufeli & Buunk, 2003; Schaufeli & Enzmann, 1998), and in the sport literature, a notable gap in research is the limited focus that has been placed on health-related consequences of burnout. In a recent special issue of *Stress and Health* (2009), a series of studies were published that focused on employee burnout and its relationship to different facets of physical health. These studies have advanced the knowledge base regarding this relationship via higher levels of research rigor relative to past studies (i.e., longitudinal designs, advanced statistical analysis, and control of confounders; Shirom, 2009).

In one of these special issue articles, Vinokur and colleagues (Vinokur, Pierce, & Lewandowski-Romps, 2009) conducted a longitudinal study investigating self-rated health (i.e., an assessment of one's overall health status) and burnout, and observed that, over time, burnout predicted a decrease in perceived health. In isolation, this finding is not surprising, but the authors also reported that perceived health predicted decreases in burnout and that this causative relationship was stronger. The implications of this are that an individual's assessment of his or her own health status will impact his or her feelings of burnout, and hence could be an important consideration for both research and intervention. A second noteworthy observation reported in the special issue was in the study by Leone and colleagues (Leone, Huibers, Knottnerus, & Kant, 2009), which looked at burnout and fatigue. Findings indicated that burnout and prolonged fatigue predicted each other and that there appears to be a dose–response relationship between them. The implication is that they impact each other in a downward spiral, and early intervention is critical to prevent the co-occurrence of these conditions and a resulting worsening outcome. Leone et al.'s (2009) work reinforces the notion that a hallmark of burnout is its chronicity. That is, the state of exhaustion and its associated symptoms are not relieved by routine recovery (i.e., daily or weekly rest), and it does not simply get better but takes time and appropriate management to do so. Health-related problems associated with the incidence of burnout are therefore a major concern, and the maintenance of a positive perceived health status should be a priority.

Alongside health, another key consequence of burnout for the performer is its impact on performance. Similarly to health and burnout, the relationship between performance and burnout is poorly understood. Taris (2006) stated that research has been scant and has relied heavily on "subjective" assessments of performance, with participants judging their own performance. He argued that although self-report data have value, these are also susceptible to a number of biases. As a result, he questions if such assessment can be used to reliably and validly measure performance. Biases include negative affectivity, personal conceptualizations of performance, personal meanings of performance to self-worth, and self-protection (i.e., making performance appear more favorable to protect job security). Taris conducted a meta-analysis of 16 studies employing objective performance measures, and his findings confirmed a negative correlation between exhaustion and job performance, but results were inconclusive for cynicism and professional inefficacy. In his conclusions, Taris proposes that intervention strategies should first target a reduction in exhaustion. But he also suggests that performance and burnout appear to reflect a bidirectional process in which burnout dimensions and performance mutually influence each other. Consequently, he states that there is value in the old adage that a happy worker equals a productive worker. To both aid performance and offset burnout, satisfaction and reduced exhaustion should be targeted.

Pertinent to any discussion of performance and burnout is the question of the *meaning* of performance to both the individual and the organization. On one level, the impact of burnout on performance has significant practical implications and relates in large part to issues of productivity. On another level, however, it can be much more personal in nature. In the sport context, Feigley (1984) argued that burnout impacts the quality of the performance of national teams through the retirement or attrition of young performers before fulfilling their athletic potential. Equivalent concerns are raised by Raedeke (2004) about coaches; he references the annual discontinuation of 35% of U.S. swimming coaches' membership and posits possible links to burnout. A similar story is also evident in the professional literature. Sharma and colleagues (Sharma, Sharp, Walker, & Monson, 2008) report on the early retirement of senior colorectal and vascular surgical consultants working in the U.K. National Health Service due to burnout and the ramifications of this for performance in terms of the quality of patient service delivery and the training of junior consultants. Therefore, both present and future performance can be influenced by withdrawal associated with burnout. Moreover, there may be wider-reaching consequences beyond those for the burned-out individual and his or her organization, such as those for persons who are impacted by the performance itself (e.g., patients, clients, coworkers, or teammates). Williams and colleagues (Williams, Manwell, Konrad, & Linzer, 2007) give an example of this through the MEMO study (Minimizing Error and Maximizing Output), in which stressed, dissatisfied, and burned-out physicians reported a greater likelihood of making errors and providing suboptimal patient care.

A popular metaphor for burnout is the sputtering flame (Raedeke, 1997), flickering and then extinguishing its light as it is overcome. The importance of this metaphor is that the dying flame emphasizes not only the gradual depletion of personal resources (which is at the core of burnout) but also the concept that that the flame must be lit in order to provide light. Pines (1993) explained that an individual's basic need for meaning and significance in life is critical because "in order to burnout, one has first to be 'on fire'" (p. 41). Those who expect to derive a sense of significance from their work are therefore probably more susceptible to burnout. Although meaning may be derived from participation in an activity, an individual may also attach huge meaning to the outcome of participation and to performance.

In the professional context, Pines and Keinan (2005) argued that workers may experience stress but not necessarily burnout. A key differential is the importance and significance they place on their work. In a sample of police officers, the authors reported burnout correlated more strongly than stress with outcome variables including job dissatisfaction, desire to quit the job, physical and emotional symptoms, and perceived performance level. Among athlete populations, Lemyre, Hall, and Roberts (2008) proposed the existence of a maladaptive motivational profile comprising how athletes define success in achievement settings, their dispositional perfectionism, and the salient motivational climate, which can leave them vulnerable to burnout. Such a maladaptive profile is high in achievement striving and ego-oriented in nature, in which competence *must* be demonstrated alongside self-validation. Burnout is consequently engendered through feelings of entrapment and threats to self-worth. This avenue of research suggests that there may be much gain in proactively supporting performers to develop a healthy (adaptive) perspective (i.e., task oriented) to the personal meaning they derive from being a performer and from performing.

Antecedents of Burnout

Examining the burnout literature across professional and sport settings for what is known about antecedents of the syndrome, one is confronted by a significant methodological problem—the overwhelming bias toward cross-sectional research designs (Cresswell & Eklund, 2006a; Goodger et al., 2007b). By virtue of being a snapshot in time, cross-sectional research is not well suited to answer questions about antecedents, in which determining causality is fundamental. In an attempt to make sense of the literature, some researchers have moved away from antecedents as a descriptor and use "possible causes" (e.g., Schaufeli & Buunk, 2003) and "attributions" (e.g., Cresswell & Eklund, 2006b) instead. In this section, we will look at some of the most salient possible causes and correlates of burnout and examine the pertinent theoretical perspectives that have been proffered to explain burnout.

In their overview of 25 years of professional burnout research, Schaufeli and Buunk (2003) identify five major areas as possible causes of burnout: quantitative job demands, role problems, lack of social support, lack of self-regulatory activity, and client-related demands. Quantitative job demands essentially refer to workload and time pressures. Burnout is reported to occur more in employees when they work more hours per week, interact frequently with clients, have high case loads, and deal with severe client problems. Role problems associated with the incidence of professional burnout include role conflict (i.e., when conflicting demands of the job have to be met) and role ambiguity (i.e., when there is inadequate information available to do the job well), and a lack of social support has consistently shown a positive relationship with burnout. It is suggested that social support may act as a buffer that protects against stressors linked to job demands, enabling those who experience social support to cope better with demands. Self-regulatory activities related to work include participation in decision-making, autonomy, and feedback. Together, these comprise job "resources" that are considered fundamental to ensuring productivity at work. Finally, the concept of client-related demands stems from the original conceptualization of burnout as specific to helping professions. Burnout was thought to be triggered by chronic exposure to client-related stressors, such interaction with difficult clients, problems in interacting with clients, and frequency of contact with chronically or terminally ill clients. Although these factors are believed to contribute to the development of burnout, Schaufeli and Enzmann (1998), in a comparison of 16 studies, reported that correlations were higher for *job-related* stressors including workload, time pressure, and role conflict.

Goodger and colleagues (2007b) conducted a systematic review of the literature covering burnout in sport. It was the first major review in the field in more than 15 years, and, in addition to examining characteristics of sample populations and research designs, the authors summarized correlates of both athlete and coach burnout research. The term *correlate* was adopted as there were insufficient numbers of longitudinal studies to identify antecedents. Three groups of correlates emerged from the review: psychological, demographic, and situational. The authors summarized the direction of the association with a summary code as follows:

+ Positive correlation (potential causal factor)
– Negative correlation (potential preventive factor)
0 No association with burnout
?? Inconclusive (contradictory or insufficient research)

Only the main themes under each of the correlate groups will be summarized here. For more detail, the reader is referred to the original review. Psychological correlates of athlete burnout included motivation (- and ?? for extrinsic motivation); coping with adversity (–); response to training and recovery (+ for mood disturbance and - for recovery); role of significant others (?? and - for social support); and identity (+ for athletic identity). For coach burnout, psychological correlates identified were perceived stress (+), commitment (–), and social support (–). Few studies of situational and demographic variables were conducted with athlete populations, and, as a result, the review identified only training load/volume (+) as a situational correlate. No demographic correlates emerged. Three situational correlates of coach burnout emerged in the review: coaching issues (+, e.g., timetabling and budgets), role conflict (+), and perceived success (??). Finally, the demographic correlates of coach burnout established included gender (??), age (??), marital status (??), experience (??), and type of sport (??). The authors attributed the lack of conclusive results for many variables to a lack of sufficient data and inconsistency in the quality of reporting in some studies.

It is challenging to find commonalities across professional, athlete, and coach burnout studies; however, there does appear to be overlap in that work demands, role problems, lack of social support, and lack of self-regulation (autonomy) play a significant role in the incidence of burnout across domains.

A variety of theoretical approaches to professional burnout exist, but they can be grouped into individual, interpersonal, and organizational approaches (Schaufeli & Buunk, 2003). These three main approaches will be summarized next. There has been some testing of models to explain coach burnout (e.g., Kelley, 1994; Kelley & Gill, 1993), but there are currently no specific theories pertaining to coaches.

Individual approaches to professional burnout emphasize the role of intrapersonal processes, a strong conscious or unconscious motivation (including expectations and aspirations) toward work activity, and a discrepancy between expectations and reality. The mismatch between intention and reality results in job stress, which can eventually lead to burnout when inadequate or inappropriate coping strategies/resources are adopted. Interpersonal approaches highlight the importance of emotional demands in relationships with recipients (i.e., client, patient) and the dynamic of social relationships in the workplace. Schaufeli and Buunk (2003) explained that, within interpersonal approaches, it is the lack of reciprocity between provider and recipient or worker and organization that is at the root of burnout. Other social psychological processes playing a role include social comparison and emotional contagion. The third group, organizational approaches, interprets burnout in terms of "undesired" organizational behavior that impacts both individuals and the organization itself. Examples of undesirable behaviors include job demands, lack of autonomy, lack of rewards, lack of social support or community, and incongruent institutional goals or values.

Within sport psychology, explanations of athlete burnout have traditionally been divided into stress-induced and non–stress induced perspectives. Simply, stress-induced perspectives consider burnout to manifest through exposure to chronic stress, and non–stress induced perspectives acknowledge that stress plays a role (i.e., it is a symptom) but cannot be seen as the causal agent. The major models of burnout in sport psychology are presented next.

Models of Burnout in Sport Psychology
The Cognitive-Affective Model

One of the most comprehensive explanations of athlete burnout is Smith's (1986) *cognitive–affective model* (Gould et al., 1996). Smith's model can be squarely placed as a stress-induced perspective in that stress is perceived as the key causal factor, and burnout manifests as a product of chronic exposure. The model is conceptually grounded in Thibaut and Kelley's (1959) *social exchange theory* (SET). According to this theory, human behavior is governed by the desire to maximize positive and minimize negative experiences. Participation in activities continues as long as they are favorable, and favor is determined by the balance of costs and rewards and how these compare to the outcomes of alternative activities (Weinberg & Gould, 2003). Withdrawal is likely if activities fall below the comparison level for alternatives. In burnout cases, Smith argues that previously enjoyed activities become an aversive source of stress, and individuals withdraw as a result perceptions of increased stress-induced costs associated with the present activity.

Smith proposed a four-stage model of stress and burnout. The model considers the impact of individual difference factors, including personality and motivation, which are seen to influence the different stages. The first stage comprises situational demands that the performer faces. Demands are cognitively appraised in the second stage against the athlete's personal resources (i.e., perceived ability to meet demands), and appraisal in turn governs the nature and intensity of emotional responses. If appraisal is negative (i.e., perceived imbalance between demands and resources), physiological responses in the third stage are initiated in readiness. Behavioral responses (e.g., coping behaviors) occur in the final stage. In addition to the sequential process associated with progression through the four stages, a recursive relationship is proposed to exist between stages, and behavioral responses are also thought to feed back into the situational demands stage (Gould et al., 1996). The process is initiated through a perceived imbalance between demands and resources over time (i.e., a sense of chronic overload or conflict between demands and resources), and physiological responses such as lethargy, tension, fatigue, or illness result. Ultimately, behavioral responses are observed as performance decrements and eventual withdrawal.

Smith's (1986) model has been one of the most well supported in the literature (e.g., Cresswell & Eklund, 2006b; Gould et al., 1996). Gould and colleagues (1996) argue that the model can be applied effectively to most cases of athlete burnout and, as such, is the most useful explanation of the syndrome available. They cited the strengths of the model as its comprehensiveness, together with the emphasis placed on athletes' own interpretations as a root cause of the process.

The Negative Training Stress Response Model

Another early explanation of athlete burnout was advanced by Silva (1990); namely, the *negative training stress response model*. The model, as the title suggests, also represents a stress-induced perspective. According to Silva, physical training places an athlete under stress that may be both positive and negative. Adaptations and training gains are the product of positive stress, whereas negative stress (e.g., too much training) can cause negative training responses. These include staleness, overtraining, and burnout, which occur across a psychophysiological continuum. Staleness develops as an initial negative response to training demands and, if unmanaged, progresses to overtraining as the body's adaptive mechanisms fail to respond effectively. Through the experience of overtraining, the body's response system can eventually become depleted and exhausted, and it is at this stage that burnout develops.

Support for Silva's (1990) model in the literature has been limited (e.g., Gould et al., 1996), and critics argue that the model describes possible antecedents or consequences of burnout rather than the key characteristics of the experience itself (Cresswell & Eklund, 2006a). The model's proposition that withdrawal from sport is inevitable is thought to be inaccurate as there have been several reported cases of burnout in active athletes (e.g., Cresswell & Eklund, 2007a, 2007b; Gould et al, 1996; Raedeke, 1997). Despite the criticism levied at Silva's model, the focus on the relationship between training and physical demands and the development of athlete burnout has experienced resurgence in recent years through the stress-recovery approach.

The Stress-Recovery Perspective

The stress-recovery perspective posits that burnout is the product of an accumulating imbalance between stress (training and non–training based) and adequate recovery (Kallus & Kellmann, 2000). The authors of this approach state that overtraining initially develops as athletes are unable to recover from the stress they are exposed to, and, as a widening gap between stress and sufficient recovery continues, staleness is experienced, potentially followed by burnout if the balance is not redressed. Kellmann and Kallus have developed a multidimensional self-report measure—the Recovery Stress Questionnaire (RESTQ)— to assess stress-recovery in athletes (RESTQ-Sport; Kellmann & Kallus, 2001) and coaches (RESTQ-Coach; Kallus & Kellmann, 1995). The instrument contains stress and recovery subscales and assesses the recovery state of individuals. The recovery state indicates the extent to which the individual is physically and/or mentally stressed, his or her capacity to use individual strategies for recovery, and the strategies used. Following assessment, a multidimensional intervention approach is encouraged to combat the stress-recovery imbalance and the conditions that may result (i.e., overtraining, staleness, and burnout). Physiological, emotional, cognitive, behavioral/performance, and social aspects are encompassed in this multidimensional approach. The reader is referred to Kellmann (2002) for a comprehensive overview of this work.

Kentta and Hassmen (1998) advanced a second stress-recovery model, *total quality recovery*, which places greater emphasis on the role of sufficient (and quality) recovery in preventing overtraining, staleness, and burnout. According to their model, under-recovery and conditions such as overtraining are grounded in a psycho-socio-physiological framework. This framework comprises three subsystems affecting the individual: physiological, psychological, and sociological. An individual's adaptation or maladaptation (i.e., under-recovery, overtraining, etc.) to training demands is affected by stress (training and non-training), quality of recovery, and stress tolerance. To monitor appropriate quality recovery, the authors have also developed the Total Quality Recovery instrument (TQR; Kentta & Hassmen).

The stress-recovery approach is not exclusive to burnout in that it can be applied equally to cases of staleness and overtraining. However, its value to this syndrome, in which exhaustion is a core element, is the emphasis placed on recovery as a process performers can actively engage in and work to self-manage. Furthermore, proponents of this approach advocate that intervention is multifaceted. It is not simply about physical recovery but rather looks at the whole performer and the social context in which he or she is located.

We now examine three approaches that utilize a non–stress induced perspective of athlete burnout.

The Sport Commitment Model

The first non–stress induced model, proposed by Schmidt and Stein (1991), interprets burnout as a consequence of entrapment. The *sport commitment model* is based upon earlier work on commitment by Kelley (1983) and Rusbult (1983), which sought to explain why individuals maintain or persist in a given course of action. In this model, commitment is determined by three factors: satisfaction (rewards and costs), attractiveness of alternative options, and resources invested. These factors combine to indicate a profile of a commitment "type." In the sport context, there are two types of commitment (Raedeke, 1997): *sport attraction* (individual "wants to" be involved) and *sport entrapment* (individuals feel they "have to" be involved). Schmidt and Stein assert that the difference between athletes who experience burnout and those who do not is the nature of their commitment profile. Burnout is more likely to manifest among athletes displaying an entrapment profile (i.e., high cost and low reward, low alternative activities, and high investment). This leads them to doubt the value of sport, and they feel fenced in and stifled, unable to leave. The model has generated significant interest and has been empirically supported across both athlete and coach populations (e.g., Raedeke, 2004; Raedeke, 1997; Raedeke, Granzyk, & Warren, 2000; Raedeke & Smith 2001).

The Unidimensional Identity Development and External Control Model

A second popular non–stress induced perspective of burnout is Coakley's (1992) *unidimensional identity development and external control model*. In contrast to all other models, Coakley applies a sociological view to athlete burnout, arguing that it is a social problem stemming from the way sports are organized. During qualitative interviews with athletes, Coakley observed that organizational constraints prevented the development of a multifaceted identity, and, due to exclusive involvement in sport, athletes experienced identity foreclosure. Sport becomes their identity and identity in turn hinges upon sporting success. Alongside these identity concerns, Coakley also recorded athlete accounts of a sense of autonomy constrained by the organization of sport, in which decision-making was in the hands of others, not the athletes. Combined, these observations led Coakley to advance his model of athlete burnout in which the syndrome is believed to be the product of the strains associated with a unidimensional identity and a lack of control over one's own life. The eventual consequence is withdrawal from sport. There has been debate in reference to the latter point, about whether withdrawal is inevitable (Cresswell & Eklund, 2006a), but, on the whole, research has supported the tenets of Coakley's model (e.g., Black & Smith, 2007; Cresswell & Eklund, 2007a; Gould et al, 1996; Gustafsson et al., 2007).

Self-Determination Theory

Finally, a third and relatively new addition to the non–stress induced perspectives of athlete burnout has been the application of self-determination theory (SDT; Ryan & Deci, 2000). The earlier contention in this chapter that individuals must be lit up in order to burn out (Pines, 1993) highlights the importance of motivation in understanding the burnout syndrome. Gould et al. (1996) recognized the importance of exploring the role of motivation in burnout, but it has not been until the last decade that this has become a stand-alone avenue of research (e.g., Cresswell and Eklund, 2005a,b; Lemyre, Roberts, & Treasure, 2006).

Self-determination theory proposes that the basis of human well-being and personal growth is the satisfaction of three basic needs (autonomy, competence, and relatedness). The level of perceived need satisfaction also influences individuals in an achievement setting to adopt a more or less self-determined motivational style. Self-determination theory proposes that motivational styles occur on a continuum from individuals who are more self-determined (internally regulated) to those who are less self-determined (externally regulated by outside influences). Individuals who are self-determined experience more control over their own behaviors and have a greater likelihood of a positive outcome in the achievement setting. In contrast, maladaptive outcomes, such as burnout, are associated with circumstances in which need satisfaction is thwarted, and these occur among individuals who are more externally regulated than self-determined (Lemyre, Roberts, & Stray-Gundersen, 2007; Lemyre et al., 2006). The application of SDT to cases of athlete burnout is quickly becoming a popular approach; it has not yet, however, been applied to coaching populations. Self-determination theory not only contributes to the conceptual understanding of the relationship between burnout and motivation but also supports those working with burnout cases. Hodge, Lonsdale, and Ng (2008) argue that practitioners can support athletes and coaches by encouraging the establishment of a need-satisfying climate and the utilization of a need-supporting coaching style.

Reducing and Removing Burnout

Cox and colleagues (2005) affirmed that the ultimate goal of burnout research is "its [burnout] prevention, its treatment and the rehabilitation into the workplace of people who have been severely burned out" (p. 191). The reality of the literature is that efforts to develop effective intervention strategies have ranged from "extensive, albeit kaleidoscopic, and rather scattered" (Schaufeli & Buunk, 2003, p. 414) to research that is accused of remaining more conceptual and theoretical in nature, leading to the potential "paralysis of practical action" (Cox et al., 2005, p. 190). In the work setting, considerable effort has been made to undertake and evaluate the effectiveness of intervention programs and strategies but conceptual and methodological inadequacies have limited the conclusiveness and generalizability of findings. In the sport context, no researchers have undertaken intervention studies. Rather, researchers have made recommendations that provide guidance about early warning signs, and suggested strategies for prevention and management, based largely upon information extrapolated from retrospective discussion with athletes who have experienced burnout (e.g., Cresswell & Eklund, 2003; Gould et al., 1996).

Across performance domains, interventions for burnout essentially comprise two general approaches: prevention and management. These approaches may be directed at changing the individual or changing the job environment/organization. The majority of authors acknowledge that a combined approach of both individual and organizational intervention should be most effective, but the bulk of interventions have been conducted at the individual level (Schaufeli & Buunk, 2003). Schaufeli and Buunk argued that negatives are associated with this bias in that a "blame the victim" mindset can develop, and Maslach and colleagues (Maslach et al., 2001) observed that this situation is somewhat paradoxical because research has identified that organizational factors play a bigger part in burnout than do individual ones. They describe pragmatic and

philosophical reasons underpinning the focus on the individual, including individual causality and responsibility, and an assumption that it is easier and cheaper to change the individual than to make changes to an organization.

Individual-centered interventions aim primarily to enhance a person's capacity to cope with work by strengthening internal resources and coping skills. Interventions utilize techniques such as relaxation, stress management, time management, and work–life balance changes. Counselors often focus on changing work-related cognitions (i.e., expectations) and behaviors (i.e., interactions with others). Due to the progressively debilitative nature of the burnout syndrome, early intervention and prevention strategies are important to prevent the situation from worsening. However, burnout's erosive character does in itself raise several challenges that impact intervention. Cresswell and Eklund (2003) asserted that prevention and management approaches rely on a number of possibly questionable assumptions, including that individuals are self-aware enough to identify that they are actually experiencing burnout; that they are interested in developing strategies to combat this; that they have the ability to learn and implement change strategies; and that they are motivated to do so. Maslach and colleagues (Maslach et al., 2001) added that the effectiveness of individual strategies in the workplace is limited by the amount of control individuals have over organizational change or exposure to stressors, a situation echoed in professional sport (e.g., Cresswell & Eklund, 2007b).

For those working with performers, there is good news in that reviews conducted in the professional intervention literature suggest that there is benefit in this approach and there is evidence for the efficacy of individual stress management interventions (Schaufeli & Buunk, 2003). Van der Klink and colleagues (2001) carried out a meta-analysis of 48 studies that incorporated three individual focused interventions (e.g., cognitive-behavioral, relaxation, and multimodal or combination) and one work-focused type of intervention. Findings revealed a significant effect for all individual-focused interventions, with greatest effect sizes (medium) being reported for cognitive-behavioral and multimodal. No significant effects were observed for workplace interventions. More recently Awa, Plaumann, and Walter (2010) reviewed 25 intervention studies (68% person-directed interventions, 8% organization-directed, and 24% a combination of both) and concluded that person-directed interventions were effective in reducing burnout in the short term (6 months or less). Combination interventions (person and organization) have longer lasting positive effects (12 months and over). Positive intervention effects decreased over time, which seems to indicate a need for some form of refresher. Finally, one of the major conclusions of the literature is that the core element of burnout—namely, exhaustion—can be reduced by training individuals to apply skills such as relaxation, stress management, and cognitive restructuring. The dimensions of inefficacy and cynicism seem more resistant to change and present an important focus for future research (Maslach et al., 2001; Schaufeli & Buunk, 2003).

From a sociological perspective, Coakley (2009) proposed that although burnout happens to the individual and is experienced through both psychological and physiological manifestations, it is always situated in particular situations and social contexts. The role of the organization and social context are considered to be more significant to burnout than are individual difference factors alone (Maslach et al., 2001), but the reality of the literature is that greater attention has focused on the latter. Just as with individual oriented approaches to intervention, sport burnout research that has focused on "changing the organization" has been essentially "advisory" in nature (e.g., Cresswell & Eklund, 2007b, 2003; Gould et al., 1996).

Leiter and Maslach (2004) offered a useful structured intervention approach to working with organizations that could be applied equally to the sport context through what they describe as "six areas of work life" that comprise the major predictors of job burnout. Leiter and Maslach propose that burnout occurs when there is a disconnect between the individual and the organization in any of these six identified areas: workload, control, reward, community, fairness, and values. Work overload can occur when job demands exceed an individual's capacity, and intervention should focus on assuring adequate resources are available to meet demands, as well as addressing work–life balance to encourage recovery and revitalization of energy resources. Personal control (autonomy) is important in the workplace, and issues of role conflict and ambiguity have in particular been linked to a perceived lack of control. Participation in organizational decision-making is associated with more positive perceptions of control. The potential for burnout occurs when there is insufficient reward or a lack of recognition in the workplace, leading to feelings of inefficacy. Congruence between effort and reward creates greater opportunity for personal satisfaction and pride and a lower incidence of burnout. The overall quality of social interactions in the workplace defines the community factor, and burnout has been shown to be less likely in positive and supportive work environments. Fairness is the extent to which decision-making is seen to be just and equitable (Maslach & Leiter, 2008), and perceptions of reciprocity, support, fairness, and balanced social exchanges are associated with lower burnout rates. Finally, the values of the organization represent the motivating connection that drew the worker to the organization in the first place. These affect the worker's job goals and expectations, and a disconnect occurs when value conflict exists between the individual and the organization. Conversely, consistency across personal and organizational values is conducive to job engagement.

A further important component of this approach is the premise of *job–person congruity* (Maslach & Leiter, 2008). A consistent theme across the literature examining organizational risk factors and burnout has been the problematic relationship between the person and environment. Originally, this was conceptualized around the notion of the *job–person fit,* in which an imbalance or misfit was thought to generate a greater likelihood of strain and potential for burnout. Maslach and Leiter (1997) advanced a model proposing that the degree of congruence between the person and key aspects of the organizational environment (i.e., the six areas of work life) predict burnout or engagement, and assert that it is the individual's appraisal of congruence that is critical. In reality then, this approach is based upon a combination of individual- and organization-oriented interventions and thus offers a comprehensive model for those working with performers across domains. Within the performance context of professional rugby, Cresswell and Eklund (2007b) found that players who were exposed to equivalent rugby-related events but who subsequently differed in their self-reported burnout experiences differed on the interpretation of these events and their appraisal of demands and perceived challenges. Moreover, Cresswell and Eklund state that although players have little power to effect organizational changes in sport, they do have power to control how they appraise events.

This chapter began with an emphasis on sport and performance psychology as a vehicle to support individual growth and striving. A stated intention was to provide knowledge of burnout research that could be utilized by those working with performers within the positive psychology paradigm (Seligman & Csikszentmihalyi, 2000). It is at this juncture that we return full circle to this expressed intention. In their landmark article in *American Psychologist*, Seligman and Csikszentmihalyi observed that, prior to the millennium, psychology had largely focused on pathology and had come to understand much about how people survived and endured conditions of adversity but little about what made life worth living. They explained that at the forefront of the advancement of positive psychology was a growing momentum within psychology directed at prevention. Yet the focus of applied psychology on personal weakness, malfunction, and the damaged brain rendered the field poorly equipped to do effective prevention. Research on prevention has identified that human strengths act as buffers against mental illness (e.g., future-mindedness, hope, interpersonal skill, work ethic, perseverance, etc.), and Seligman and Csikszentmihalyi proposed that, in the future, the task of prevention is to develop a science of human strength, virtue, and optimal functioning in order to learn how to foster these attributes in young people. Researchers within the professional burnout field (and to a lesser extent in sport) have adopted the tenets of positive psychology through the advancement of engagement as the best prevention of burnout (Maslach et al., 2001; Schaufeli & Bakker, 2004; Schaufeli et al., 2002).

Employee engagement has become a popular and expanding field of study in its own right and is believed to predict employee outcomes, organization success, and financial performance. Scholars and practitioners do not consider employee engagement to be simply an attitude but rather the individual's total approach to the performance of his or her job role physically, emotionally, and cognitively (Saks, 2006). It is about being *psychologically present* when occupying or performing a job role, which is characterized by the degree to which an individual is *attentive* (i.e., cognitive availability and the amount of time spent thinking about the work role) and *absorbed* (i.e., being engrossed in a role and the intensity of focus on a role; Kahn, 1990; Rothbard, 2001; Saks, 2006). The concept of disengagement is also relevant to our discussion. Kahn (1990) described this as "the uncoupling of selves from work roles: in disengagement, people withdraw and defend themselves physically, cognitively or emotionally, during work roles" (p. 694). Three psychological conditions are associated with engagement versus disengagement at work. Employees are more engaged when experiencing psychological meaningfulness, psychological safety, and psychological availability (Kahn, 1990). Expanding on Kahn's work, May and colleagues (May, Gilson, & Harter, 2004) reported meaningfulness was predicted by job enrichment and role fit, safety by rewarding coworkers and supportive supervisor relations, and availability by resources.

Maslach and colleagues (Maslach & Leiter, 1997; Maslach et al., 2001) have championed the drive to incorporate engagement into the professional burnout field. They contend that burnout is the erosion of engagement and, as such, the two can be considered conceptual opposites positioned on opposing poles of a continuum. There is, however, an alternate perspective on burnout and engagement that scholars and practitioners should consider. Schaufeli and Bakker (2004) contend that, rather than being polar opposites, burnout and engagement are actually independent states of mind that, although negatively correlated, should be treated separately. They also offer a model that attempts to simultaneously explain the two concepts and associated predictors and consequences. For those supporting performers, this model may provide useful guidance on how to enhance engagement and offset burnout.

Maslach, Jackson, and Leiter's (1996) original model is descriptive, hypothesizing that the presence of specific demands (i.e., workload and personal conflict) and absence of specific resources (i.e., social support, autonomy, and involvement in decision) predict burnout. Demerouti and colleagues (Demerouti, Bakker, Nachreiner, & Schaufeli, 2001) attempted to further describe the processes underpinning burnout and disengagement by employing the *job demand-resources model* (J D-R). This model posits that exhaustion is associated with job demands and that disengagement is associated with an absence or lack of job resources. Schaufeli and Bakker (2004) have in turn built upon Demerouti et al.'s work to proffer their model of burnout and engagement. This model is considered to be a "positive" approach as it encompasses both health-enhancing (engagement) aspects of positive job characteristics, as well as the negative aspects that lead to health impairment (Van den Broeck, Vansteenkiste, De Witte, & Lens, 2008). According to J D-R, psychosocial job characteristics can be divided into two broad categories of job demands and job resources. Job demands are aspects of the work context that tax individual's personal capacities (i.e., physical demands, shift work) and hence are associated with certain psychological and/or physiological costs. They are not necessarily negative as long as they do not exceed the individual's capacities. If capacities are strained and exceeded, they then can become stressors and associated with health impairment and burnout (Van den Broeck et al., 2008).

Job resources are physical, psychological, social, or organizational aspects of the work context that can reduce the health-impairing impact of job demands. These resources empower individuals to achieve work goals and stimulate personal growth, development, and learning (Schaufeli & Bakker, 2004). Job demands and job resources are theorized to be associated with burnout and engagement through two processes: an energetic process and a motivational process. The *energetic process* refers to an overtaxing or wearing out, in which job demands can exceed and exhaust an individual's capacity. This is associated with health problems and possible burnout. The *motivational process* refers to job resources that, through an intrinsic motivational role, aid employee growth, development, and learning. Through an extrinsic motivational role they aid in the attainment of work goals and promote well-being and engagement. Schaufeli and Bakker concluded by proposing that preventive measures to combat burnout should include a reduction in job demands and a strengthening of job resources (and through this, engagement), although they suggested the former is likely to have a greater impact. More recently, Van den Broeck et al. (2008) employed SDT (Deci & Ryan, 2000) as a framework to explain the mechanisms underpinning the processes enveloped within the J D-R model and their associations with burnout and engagement. Findings confirmed that need satisfaction/thwarting (i.e., autonomy, relatedness, and competence) was able to explain the relationship among job demands, job resources, burnout, and engagement via the energetic and motivational processes. The authors emphasized the utility of SDT to intervention strategies that promote need-enhancing and need-satisfying climates (e.g., Cresswell & Eklund, 2006a; Lonsdale, et al., 2007).

In conclusion, researchers appear to agree upon the fact that the best intervention is likely to be preventive and involve a combined approach of working with the affected individual and the organization (e.g., Cresswell & Eklund, 2006a; Maslach et al., 2001; Raedeke & Smith, 2004; Schaufeli & Buunk, 2003). Engagement is a concept that accommodates both these features and, indeed, is likely to be more attractive to organizations as it aligns more closely with their objectives of growth, performance, and productivity.

Conclusion

Burnout research, especially in sport, is still in its relative infancy. An observable shift has occurred in the last decade, such that researchers in athlete burnout have turned increasingly to the professional literature for guidance on the conceptual development of the field (e.g., Cresswell & Eklund, 2006a; 2006b; Raedeke, 1997; Raedeke et al., 2002). Two historical challenges have impaired the advancement of burnout research, both in the professional and sport domains: conceptual agreement on how to define burnout and development of a valid measurement tool (Dale & Weinberg, 1990; Schaufeli & Enzmann, 1998). Thanks to the pioneering work of Raedeke (Raedeke, 1997; Raedeke & Smith, 2001), a definite opportunity for greater conceptual clarity and consensus is available through the development of the three dimensions of athlete burnout and the ABQ.

Over thirty years ago, Jackson, Schwab, and Schuler (1986) commented on the professional burnout literature by stating that more data did not automatically yield more knowledge or understanding. To further our understanding of burnout in performers such as athletes, and to ultimately develop effective intervention approaches, sport and performance psychology researchers must be mindful that their thinking is conceptually grounded, that research is guided by sound theoretical rationales, and that methodological designs are rigorous. Fundamental for those working with performers affected by burnout is to understand the *meaning* of performance to the individual and to mesh this with an appreciation of the performance *context*. As Coakley (2009) explained, burnout is situated and embedded within the interplay between the person and the environment. The opportunity for either burnout or engagement to germinate is always present.

Future Directions

Many future avenues are open for performer-related burnout research, but we wish to highlight some salient gaps in the literature that deserve attention. First, although Raedeke's (1997) conceptualization of athlete burnout and the ABQ have made a significant contribution to the field, further work is needed to validate these concepts across athlete (and perhaps other performance) populations. Critical to the continued utility of the ABQ is the development of valid cutoffs for identifying clinical burnout and establishing population norms (Hodge et al., 2008). Second, the field needs more systematic testing of the models and theories of athlete burnout. There seems to be an encouraging future in employing the SDT framework to understand athlete burnout, but, at present, only a handful of studies have explored this avenue. Third, as Cox et al. (2005) proposed, the principal objective of burnout research must be the development of successful interventions. A glaring dearth of studies have conducted and evaluated intervention programs among any sport populations; this must become a critical focus of future research. Without offering research-based intervention programs, why carry out research on burnout at all? With the shift toward engagement (e.g., Lonsdale et al., 2007), a range of new "positive" avenues for intervention efforts have opened up.

Fourth, the field of sport and performance psychology offers a tremendous opportunity to study different dimensions of burnout and engagement across different performance groups. Researchers have begun to explore the interaction between athlete burnout dimensions, and a possible sequential ordering has been proposed in an attempt to capture burnout as a developmental process (e.g., Cresswell & Eklund, 2006b; Goodger et al., 2007a; Gustafsson et al., 2007). Developmental approaches will require a greater investment in longitudinal research designs that are able to capture these events over time. Earlier work within the professional domain has already highlighted differences in burnout profiles across occupations and cultures. Schaufeli and Enzmann (1998) reported that higher exhaustion and inefficacy are associated more frequently with professions such as social workers and nurses, whereas cynicism is higher among law enforcement. Conducting similar analyses across various performance domains—such as athletics, coaching, executive leadership, music, theater, and dance—will give us a deeper understanding of burnout and help us enhance the quality of our interventions.

References

Awa, W. L., Plaumann, M., & Walter, U. (2010). Burnout prevention: A review of intervention programs. *Parent Education and Counselling, 78*, 184–190.

Black, J. M., & Smith, A. L. (2007). An examination of Coakley's perspective on identity, control, and burnout among adolescent athletes. *International Journal of Sport Psychology, 38*, 417–436.

Caccese, T. M., & Mayerberg, C. K. (1984). Gender differences in perceived burnout of college coaches. *Journal of Sport and Exercise Psychology, 6*, 279–288.

Coakley, J. A. (1992). Burnout amongst adolescent athletes: A personal failure or social problem. *Sociology of Sport Journal, 9*, 271–285.

Coakley, J. A. (2009). From the outside in: Burnout as an organizational issue. *Journal of Intercollegiate Sports, 2*, 35–41.

Cox, T., Tisserand, M., & Taris, T. (2005). The conceptualization and measurement of burnout: Questions and directions. *Work and Stress, 19*, 187–191.

Cresswell, S. L. (2009). Possible early signs of athlete burnout: A prospective study. *Journal of Science and Medicine in Sport, 12*, 393–398.

Cresswell, S. L., & Eklund, R. C. (2003). The athlete burnout syndrome: A practitioner's guide. *New Zealand Journal of Sports Medicine, 31*, 4–9.

Cresswell, S. L., & Eklund, R. C. (2005a). Motivation and burnout among top amateur rugby players. *Medicine and Science in Sports and Exercise, 37*, 469–477.

Cresswell, S. L., & Eklund, R. C. (2005b). Changes in athlete burnout and motivation over a 12-week league tournament. *Medicine and Science in Sports and Exercise, 37*, 1957–1966.

Cresswell, S. L., & Eklund, R. C. (2006a). Athlete burnout: Conceptual confusion, current research, and future directions. In S. Hanton & S. D. Mellalieu (Eds.), *Literature reviews in sport psychology* (pp. 91–126). New York: Nova Science.

Cresswell, S. L., & Eklund, R. C. (2006b). The nature of athlete burnout: Key characteristics and attributions. *Journal of Applied Sport Psychology, 18*, 219–239.

Cresswell, S. L., & Eklund, R. C. (2006c). The convergent and discriminant validity of burnout measures in sport: A multi-method multi-trait analysis. *Journal of Sports Sciences, 24*, 209–212.

Cresswell, S. L., & Eklund, R. C. (2007a). Athlete burnout: A longitudinal qualitative study. *The Sport Psychologist, 21*, 1–20.

Cresswell, S. L., & Eklund, R. C. (2007b). Athlete burnout and organizational culture: An English rugby replication. *International Journal of Sport Psychology, 38*, 365–387.

Dale, J., & Weinberg, R. S. (1990). Burnout in sport: A review and critique. *Journal of Applied Sport Psychology, 2*, 67–83.

Deci, E. L., & Ryan, R. M. (2000). The "what" and "why" of goal pursuits: Human needs and the self-determination of behavior. *Psychological Inquiry, 11*, 319–338.

Demerouti, E., Bakker, A. B., Nachreiner, F., & Schaufeli, W. B. (2001). The job demands-resources model of burnout. *Journal of Applied Psychology, 86*, 499–512.

Feigley, D. A. (1984). Psychological burnout in high-level athletes. *The Physician and Sports Medicine, 12*, 109–119.

Freudenberger, H. J. (1974). Staff burnout. *Journal of Social Issues, 30*, 159–165.

Freudenberger, H. J. (1983). Hazards of psychotherapeutic practice. *Psychotherapy in Private Practice, 1*, 83–89.

Glass, D. C., & McKnight, J. D. (1996). Perceived control, depressive symptomatology, and professional burnout: A review of the evidence. *Psychology and Health, 11*, 23–48.

Goodger, K. I., Lavallee, D. E., Gorely, P. J., & Harwood, C. G. (2007b). Burnout in sport: A systematic review. *The Sport Psychologist, 21*, 127–151.

Goodger, K. I., Wolfenden, L., & Lavallee, D. (2007a). Symptoms and consequences associated with three dimensions of burnout in junior tennis players. *International Journal of Sport Psychology, 38*, 342–364.

Gould, D., Tuffey, S., Udry, E., & Loehr, J. (1996). Burnout in competitive junior tennis players: II. Qualitative analysis. *The Sport Psychologist, 10*, 341–366.

Gustafsson, H., Kentta, G., Hassmen, P., Lundqvist, C., & Durand-Bush, N. (2007). The process of burnout: A multiple case study of three elite endurance athletes. *International Journal of Sport Psychology, 38*, 388–416.

Hjalm. S., Kentta, G., Hassmen, P., & Gustafsson, H. (2007). Burnout among elite soccer coaches. *Journal of Sport Behavior, 30*, 415–427.

Hodge, K., Lonsdale, C., & Ng, J. (2008). Burnout in elite rugby: Relationships with basic psychological needs fulfillment. *Journal of Sports Sciences, 26*, 835–844.

Jackson, S. E., Schwab, R. L., & Schuler, R. S. (1986). Toward an understanding of the burnout phenomenon. *Journal of Applied Psychology, 71*, 630–640.

Kahn, W. A. (1990). Psychological conditions of engagement and disengagement at work. *Academy of Management Journal, 33*, 692–794.

Kallus, K. W., & Kellmann, M. (1995). The recovery-stress questionnaire for coaches. In R. Vanfraecham-Raway & Y. Vanden Auweele (Eds.), *Proceedings of the IXth European Congress on Sport Psychology in Brussels* (Vol. 1, pp. 26–33). Brussels: FEPSAC/Belgian Federation of Sports Psychology.

Kallus, K. W., & Kellmann, M. (2000). Burnout in athletes and coaches. In Y. L. Hanin (Ed.), *Emotions in sport* (pp. 209–230). Champaign, IL: Human Kinetics.

Kelley, B. C. (1994). A model of stress and burnout in collegiate coaches: Effects of gender and time of season. *Research Quarterly for Exercise and Sport, 65*, 48–58.

Kelley, H. H. (1983). Love and Commitment. In H. H. Kelley, E. Berscheid, A Christensen, J. H., Harvey, T. L. Huston, G. Levinger, E. McClintock, L. A, Peplau, & D. R. Peterson (eds) *Close Relationships* (pp. 265–314). New York: W. H. Freeman.

Kelley, B. C., & Gill, D. L. (1993). An examination of personal and situational variables, stress appraisal, and burnout in collegiate tennis coaches. *Research Quarterly for Exercise and Sport, 64*, 94–102.

Kellmann, M. (Ed.). (2002). *Enhancing recovery: Preventing underperformance in athletes.* Champaign, IL: Human Kinetics.

Kellmann, M., & Kallus, K. W. (2001). *Recovery-Stress questionnaire for athletes: User manual.* Champaign IL: Human Kinetics.

Kentta, G., & Hassmen, P. (1998). Overtraining and recovery: A conceptual model. *Sports Medicine, 26*, 1–16.

Leiter, M. P., & Durup, J. (1994). The discriminant validity of burnout and depression: A confirmatory factor analytic study. *Anxiety, Stress, and Coping, 7*, 357–373.

Leiter, M. P., & Maslach, C. (1998). Burnout. In H. Freidman (Ed.), *Encyclopedia of mental health* (Vol. 1, pp. 202–215). San Diego, CA: Academic Press.

Leiter, M. P., & Maslach, C. (2004). Areas of work life: A structured approach to organizational predictors of job burnout. In P. L. Perrewe & D. C. Ganster (Eds.), *Research in occupational stress and well-being* (Vol. 3, pp. 91–134). Oxford, UK: Elsevier.

Leiter, M. P., & Stright, N. (2009). The social context of work-life: Implications for burnout and engagement. In C. L. Cooper, J. C. Quick, & M. J. Schabracq (Eds.), *International handbook of work and health psychology* (3rd ed., pp. 25–47). Chichester, UK: Wiley-Blackwell.

Lemyre, P. N., Hall, H. K., & Roberts, G. C. (2008). A social cognitive approach to burnout in elite athletes. *Scandinavian Journal of Medicine and Sciences in Sport, 18*, 221–234.

Lemyre, P. N., Roberts, G. C., & Stray-Gundersen, J. (2007). Motivational, overtraining and burnout: Can self-determined motivation predict overtraining and burnout in elite athletes. *European Journal of Sport Sciences, 7*, 115–126.

Lemyre, N., Treasure, D., & Roberts, G.C. (2006). Influence of athlete variability in motivation and affect on burn-out. *Journal of Sport and Exercise Psychology, 28*, 32–48.

Leone, S. S., Huibers, M. J. H., Knottnerus, A. J., & Kant, L. (2009). The temporal relationship between burnout and prolonged fatigue: A 4 year prospective cohort study. *Stress and Work, 25*, 365–374.

Lonsdale, C., Hodge, K., & Raedeke, T. (2007). Athlete engagement: I. A qualitative investigation of relevance and dimensions. *International Journal of Sport Psychology, 38*, 451–470.

Maslach, C. (2003). Job burnout: New directions in research and intervention. *Current Directions in Psychological Science, 12*, 189–192.

Maslach, C., & Goldberg, J. (1998). Prevention of burnout: New perspectives. *Applied and Preventive Psychology, 7*, 63–74.

Maslach, C., & Jackson, S. E. (1981). The measurement of experienced burnout. *Journal of Occupational Behavior, 2*, 99–113.

Maslach, C., Jackson, S. E., & Leiter, M. P. (1996). *Maslach burnout inventory manual* (3rd ed.). Palo Alto, CA: Consulting Psychologists Press.

Maslach, C., & Leiter, M. P. (1986). *Maslach burnout inventory manual* (2nd ed.). Palo Alto, CA: Consulting Psychologists Press Inc.

Maslach, C., & Leiter, M. P. (1997). *The truth about burnout.* San Francisco: Jossey-Bass.

Maslach, C., & Leiter, M. P. (2005). Stress and burnout: The critical research. In C. L. Cooper (Ed.), *Handbook of stress medicine and health* (2nd ed., pp.153–170). Boca Raton, FL: CRC Press LLC.

Maslach, C., & Leiter, M. P. (2008). Early predictors of job burnout and engagement. *Journal of Applied Psychology, 93*, 498–512.

Maslach, C., & Schaufeli, W. B. (1993). Historical and conceptual development of burnout. In W. B. Schaufeli, C. Maslach, & T. Marek (Eds.), *Professional burnout: Recent developments in theory and research* (pp. 1–16). Washington, DC: Taylor & Francis.

Maslach. C., Schaufeli, W. B., & Leiter, M. P. (2001). Job burnout. *Annual Review of Psychology, 52*, 397–422.

May, D. R., Gilson, R. L., & Harter, L. M. (2004). The psychological conditions of meaningfulness, safety, and availability, and the engagement of the human spirit at work. *Journal of Occupational and Organizational Psychology, 77*, 11–37.

Peterson, K. (2005). Overtraining: Balancing practice and performance. In S. Murphy (Ed.), *The sport psych handbook* (pp. 49–70). Champaign, IL: Human Kinetics.

Pines, A. (1993). Burnout: An existential perspective. In W. B. Schaufeli, C. Maslach, & T. Marek (Eds.), *Professional burnout: Recent developments in theory and research* (pp. 33–51). Washington, DC: Taylor & Francis.

Pines, A. M., & Keinan, G. (2005). Stress and burnout: The significant difference. *Personality and Individual Differences, 39*, 625–635.

Raedeke, T. D. (1997). Is athlete burnout more than just stress? A sport commitment perspective. *Journal of Sport and Exercise Psychology, 19*, 396–417.

Raedeke, T. D. (2004). Coach commitment and burnout: A one year follow-up. *Journal of Applied Sport Psychology, 16*, 333–349.

Raedeke, T. D., Granzyk, T. L., & Warren, A. (2000). Why coaches experience burnout: A commitment perspective. *Journal of Sport and Exercise Psychology, 22*, 85–105.

Raedeke, T. D., Lunney, K., & Venables, K. (2002). Understanding athlete burnout: Coach perspectives. *Journal of Sport Behavior, 25*, 181–206.

Raedeke, T. D., & Smith, A. L. (2001). Development and preliminary validation of an athlete burnout measure. *Journal of Sport and Exercise Psychology, 23*, 281–306.

Raedeke, T. D., & Smith, A. L. (2004). Coping resources and athlete burnout: An examination of stress mediated and moderation hypothesis. *Journal of Sport and Exercise Psychology, 26*, 525–541.

Rothbard, N. P. (2001). Enriching or depleting? The dynamic of engagement in work and family roles. *Administrative Science Quarterly, 46*, 655–684.

Rusbult, C. E. (1983). A longitudinal of the Investment Model: The development (and deterioration) of satisfaction and commitment in heterosexual involvements. *Journal of Personality and Social Psychology, 45*, 101–17.

Ryan, R. M., & Deci, E. L. (2000). The darker and brighter sides of human existence: Basic psychological needs as a unifying concept. *Psychological Inquiry, 11*, 319–338.

Saks, A. M. (2006). Antecedents and consequences of employee engagement. *Journal of Management Psychology, 21*, 600–619.

Schaufeli, W. B., & Bakker, A. B. (2003). *The Utrecht work engagement scale (UWES). test manual.* Utrecht, NL: The Netherlands: Department of Social & Organizational Psychology.

Schaufeli, W. B., & Bakker, A. B. (2004). Job demands, job resources, and their relationship with burnout and engagement: A multi-sample study. *Journal of Organizational Behavior, 25*, 293–315.

Schaufeli, W. B., Bakker, A. B., Hoogdum, K., Schaap, C., & Kladler, A. (2001). On the clinical validity of the Maslach burnout inventory and the burnout measure. *Psychology and Health, 16*, 565–582.

Schaufeli, W. B., & Buunk, B. P. (2003). Burnout: An overview of 25 years of research and theorizing. In M. J. Schabracq, J. A. M., Winnubst, & C. L. Cooper (Eds.), *The handbook of work and health psychology* (2nd ed., pp. 383–425). Chichester, UK: Wiley.

Schaufeli, W. B., & Enzmann, D. (1998). *The burnout companion to study and practice: A critical analysis.* London: Taylor & Francis.

Schaufeli, W. B., Leiter, M. P., Maslach, C., & Jackson, S. E. (1996). Maslach burnout inventory—general survey. In C. Maslach, S. E. Jackson, & M. P. Leiter (Eds.), *The Maslach burnout inventory—test manual* (3rd ed., pp. 204–220). Palo Alto, CA: Consulting Psychologists Press.

Schaufeli, W. B., Martínez, I., Marques Pinto, A. Salanova, M., & Bakker, A. B. (2002). Burnout and engagement in university students: A cross national study. *Journal of Cross- Cultural Psychology, 33*, 464–481.

Schaufeli, W. B., Salanova, M., González-Romá, V., & Bakker, A. B. (2002). The measurement of engagement and burnout: A confirmative analytic approach. *Journal of Happiness Studies, 3*, 71–92.

Schaufeli, W. B., & Taris, T. W. (2005). Commentary: The conceptualization and measurement of burnout: Common ground and worlds apart. *Work and Stress, 19*, 256–262.

Schmidt, G. W., & Stein, G. L. (1991). A commitment model of burnout. *Journal of Applied Sport Psychology, 8*, 323–345.

Schutte, N., Toppinen, S., Kalimo, R., & Schaufeli, W. (2000). The factorial validity of the Maslach burnout inventory—general survey (MBI-GS) across occupational groups and nations. *Journal of Occupational and Organizational Psychology, 73*, 53–66.

Seligman, M., & Csikszentmihalyi, M. (2000). Positive psychology: An introduction. *American Psychologist, 55*, 5–14.

Sharma, A., Sharp, D. M., Walker, L. G., & Monson, J. R. T. (2008). Stress and burnout in colorectal and vascular surgical consultants working in the UK national health service. *Psycho-Oncology, 17*, 570–576.

Shirom, A. (2002). Employee burnout and health: Current knowledge and future research paths. In J. Houdmont & S. Leka (Eds.), *Contemporary occupational health psychology: Global perspectives on research and practice* (pp. 59–76). Chichester, UK: Wiley.

Shirom, A. (2005). Reflections on the study of burnout. *Work and Stress, 19*, 263–270.

Shirom, A. (2009). Burnout and health: Expanding our knowledge. *Stress and Work, 25*, 281–285.

Silva, J. M. (1990). An analysis of the training stress syndrome in competitive athletics. *Journal of Applied Sport Psychology, 2*, 5–20.

Smith, R. E. (1986). Toward a cognitive-affective model of athlete burnout. *Journal of Sport Psychology, 8*, 36–50.

Taris, T. W. (2006). Is there a relationship between burnout and objective performance? A critical review of 16 studies. *Work and Stress, 20*, 316–334.

Taris, T. W., Le Blanc, P. M., Schaufeli, W. B., & Schreurs, P. J. (2005). Are there causal relationships between the dimensions of the Maslach burnout inventory? A review and two longitudinal tests. *Work and Stress, 19*, 238–255.

Thibaut, J. W. & Kelley, H. H. (1959). *The social psychology of groups.* New York: John Wiley

Thorndike, E. L. (1914). *Educational Psychology: Mental work and fatigue and individual differences and their causes*(Vol 3). New York, NY: Teachers College.

Van den Broeck, A., Vansteenkiste, M., De Witte, H., & Lens, W. (2008). Explaining the relationships between job characteristics, burnout, and engagement: The role of basic psychological need satisfaction. *Work and Stress, 22*, 277–294.

Van der Klink, J. J., Blonk, R. W., Schene, A. H., & Van Dijk, F. L. (2001). The benefits of interventions for work-related stress. *American Journal of Public Health, 91*, 270–276.

Van der Linden, D., Keijsers., G. P. J., Eling, P., & Van Schaijk, R. (2005). Work stress and attentional difficulties: An initial study on burnout and cognitive failures. *Work and Stress, 19*, 23–36.

Vinokur, A. D., Pierce, P. F., & Lewandowski-Romps, L. (2009). Disentangling the relationships between job burnout and perceived health in a military sample. *Work and Stress, 25*, 355–363.

Weinberg, R. S., & Gould, D. (2003). *Foundations of sport and exercise psychology* (4th ed.). Champaign, IL: Human Kinetics.

Williams, E. S., Manwell, L. B., Konrad, T. R., & Linzer, M. (2007). The relationship of organizational culture, stress, satisfaction, and burnout with physician-reported error and suboptimal patient care: Results from the MEMO study. *Health Care Management Review, 32*, 203–212.

The Body and Performance

William B. Strean *and* Joseph P. Mills

Abstract

In this chapter, we explore various understandings of the body, including philosophical perspectives and information from cognitive science. Following a theoretical overview, we give examples of how an integrated, somatic approach to perceiving the body can be applied in sport and performance psychology. Much of sport and performance psychology seems to rely on both dualistic and cognitive approaches to understanding human behavior. We suggest that the perspective gained from the integration of thinking, feeling, and acting can enhance both research and application in the field. We offer specific examples of somatic practices that can be used in sport and performance interventions.

Key Words: Body, somatics, sport, performance, psychology

> Philosophy lives in words, but truth and fact well up into our lives in ways that exceed verbal formulation. There is in the living act of perception always something that glimmers and twinkles and will not be caught, and for which reflection comes too late.
> —*James*, 1902, pp. 446–447

As you begin to read this chapter, what's your mood? What are you thinking about? We might call that your current narrative or the story you are in. What sensations are you having (e.g., hot/cold, pulsing, streaming, tension/relaxation)? Consider that your overall experience could be represented by the color brown. Consider that each construct of your mood, thoughts, and sensations could be represented by a primary color. Although the constituent parts are useful analytic categories, imagine what it would be like to extract just the red from the brown.[1] You couldn't do it. Although it may be useful to talk about the parts, phenomenologically

they cannot be separated from the whole. Some years ago, we invented cognition, affect, and behavior, and we have come to operate as if they can be distinguished. Yet, when we are dealing with the complex experiences of sport and performance, our thinking, feeling, and acting are all embodied and integrated. Although so many examples from research and practice seem to suggest that there is such a thing as cognition that exists distinct from emotion and embodiment, experience shows that this is not the case.

Recognizing that we are whole is the basis of somatics (from *soma*, the body in its wholeness).

Consider that this recognition may be like shifting your view from what seemed like a flat earth to a perspective in which you see your world as round. Whole, new possibilities emerge, and your former way of observing, perceiving, and acting is no longer satisfying.

As you step into your role in sport and performance psychology, imagine adopting a somatic orientation and how it might influence your interactions with clients. Where you previously may have had conversations with an underlying assumption that mental activity could be extracted from emotion and the rest of the body/self, you now see that there is a mood to every conversation. You recognize that mind and body are not *connected* parts, but your analytic categories appeared to reify the separation that you had created. You begin to see how the person in front of you is a shape generated by history, which shifts subtly with each piece of your dialogue. You start to pay attention to how each of you is breathing. You notice how breathing, thinking, feeling, and shape are unified.

You might start your performance enhancement session by asking the same three questions that began this chapter. Then you might lead your client through a centering exercise with these instructions (feel free to follow along):

This is a simple centering exercise. Stand comfortably. Allow your breath to drop toward your belly. Let your jaw go. Let your shoulders drop. Feel the length of your body. Pay attention without feeling like you have to stretch yourself. Feel your feet on the ground. Notice the length of the long bones of your legs, your spine, all the way to the top of your head. Simply become aware of the dimension of length.

Now, pay attention to the width of the body: across the collarbone, the pelvis, from side to side. Simply feel the distance and space.

Next, attend to depth. You can't see the back of your head, down the back, or the back of the legs, but you can feel them. You can feel the front of your face and torso and legs, and you can feel or notice the distance from the front to the back. We exist in the dimension of depth. You can also think of having your past behind you, your future in front of you, and from the back to the front of the body is the present.

We also have a center. There is a physical center. It's like an organizing principle. If you go to your bellybutton and go 2 inches down and 2 inches back, that's your center. It may help to put two fingers on the spot 2 inches below your belly button, feel 2 inches

behind your fingers; that's your center. Now, feel your breath going in to your center. As you breathe out, soften your ribcage and feel your ribs drop toward the center, feel this process helping you to maintain this position with ease. As you're breathing in, think "I'm breathing in," and, as you're breathing out, think "I'm breathing out." If your attention is on breathing in when you're breathing in and if your attention is on breathing out when you're breathing out, then you're present. You're present, open, and connected. Present in this moment, open to possibility, and connected to yourself and what you care about. This is a very simple exercise yet very powerful.

At the end of the centering exercise, you might explore how intentionally moving one's attention and slowing and deepening the breath develops awareness and changes one's experience, and that this can be observed through the lenses of thoughts, moods, and sensations. A centering practice could be adopted as a commitment to self-awareness and as part of a foundation for enhanced performance. By expanding attention to the whole person (including the aspects of thinking, feeling, and acting), we expand our awareness and create greater possibilities for effective interventions.

We tend to forget that a long-held assumption does not thereby become a fact, and we often even resent being reminded.
(*Goswami*, 1993, p. 10)

To paraphrase Maslow's oft-quoted remark, if all sport and performance psychologists have is a hammer, all our clients are going to look like nails. You might smile politely at that thought, yet consider the ramifications of your perspective. What if the fundamental way in which you have viewed your clients has limited your effectiveness? It's a provocative and unpleasant consideration. Being told that the world was round was unlikely much of a picnic at first either. But when a new way of observing and perceiving became available, it became empowering.

It's not personal. We have all grown up in a materialist culture in which mind–body dualism is built into our language. Even if we embrace monistic idealism intellectually, we continue to be pulled back into habituated ways of sensing and distinguishing. Consider that it's a challenge worth taking on. What if what we've been taught is separate, is not? What if we overcome the supposed problem of the connection of mind and body by realizing they were never separate in the first place?

What Is "The Body"?: A Somatic Perspective

Theoretical Overview

Before we go further into the possibly esoteric question of the body, it may be useful to explore the even more esoteric question of the nature of reality. Throughout the ages, people had been admonished to know themselves. Once modern science embraced materialism, with its inherent dualisms, we lost much of our unity with nature and we began to see consciousness as separate from nature. Psychology was separated from physics. We created our own alien world. Our materialist view contributes to our soiling of the planet. If we see the environment as separate from ourselves, we are more likely to exploit or damage it. If we are separate from the environment or other people, we can have enemies. Getting back together—reassembling the components of our self, which have been disjointed by our default language—emerges with a shift from a materialist view to monistic idealism, or a quantum worldview. We reintegrate our world and ourselves (Goswami, 1993).

The context in which we consider something different for sport and performance psychology is an ingrained backdrop of material realism with its five core principles of strong objectivity, causal determinism, locality, physical or material monism, and epiphenomenalism, which posits all mental phenomena can be explained as secondary phenomena of matter by a suitable reduction to antecedent physical conditions. The basic idea is that what we call consciousness is simply a property (or group of properties) of the brain when the brain is viewed at a certain level.

Now to untangle those philosophical musings, so that we can get into the body and sport psychology. Most simply stated, "cognitive science shows that our minds are not, and cannot be disembodied" (Lakoff & Johnson, 1999, p. 563). The concept of mind separate from the body is a metaphorical concept.

The term *somatics*, as noted above, comes from the word *soma*—the body in its wholeness. From a somatic perspective, we cannot distinguish the self from the body. The characteristics that constitute the self (emotions, actions, beliefs, interactions, perception, ethics, morals, and drive for dignity) all emerge from the physical form (Strozzi-Heckler, 2003, 2007a). Somatics rejects the notion that there is a disembodied, self-contained self that is separate from the life of one's body. Clearly, these ideas depart drastically from pervasive Cartesian discourses that have dominated and also posited a determinable, objective reality disconnected from subjective experience (Strean & Strozzi-Heckler, 2009). The loss of somatic knowing and the worldview derived from Descartes' dualism carries its own logical conclusion: Since I do not have immediate contact with any of the realities of my ordinary life, I can be deluded about any of them (Johnson, 1983).

Most of our understanding of the mind and rationality is based on metaphors that are not supported by cognitive science. Take, for example, the enduring notion that rational thought is dispassionate. We know this to be false from studies in neuroscience (Damasio, 1994). Those who have lost the capacity to be emotionally engaged in their lives cannot reason appropriately about moral issues. The traditional Western conception of the person with disembodied reason and an objective world must be replaced with the concept of an embodied person. After 550 pages of reviewing the history of philosophy and showing the problems based on cognitive science, Lakoff and Johnson (1999) provided some key points about the new view of the person that emerges from a plenitude of research results. To summarize, we have embodied reason with *embodied concepts*—our conceptual system is grounded in, makes neural use of, and is shaped by our perceptual and motor systems; *conceptualization only through the body*—all of our understandings can only be framed in terms of concepts shaped by our bodies; *basic concepts* that use our perceptual, imaging, and motor systems to characterize optional functioning in everyday life; *embodied reason*—major forms of rational inference are sensorimotor inference; *embodied truth and knowledge*—because our ideas are framed from unconscious embodied conceptual systems, truth and knowledge depend on embodied understanding; and *embodied mind*—concepts and reason derive from and use the sensorimotor system, so that the mind is not separate from or independent of the body.

Reconsidering "Body"

Our perceptions of "body" and ourselves are tied to our cultural heritage and our individual experiences. We live in societies in which people tend to experience themselves as disembodied (e.g., McKenna & Bargh, 2000; Rawls, 1999). We frequently experience the body as an object that carries us from our computer to the next meeting. Although dualistic conceptions have prevailed and dominated to the present day, thinkers such as Dewey (1916, 1925) and Merleau-Ponty (1945) asserted embodied perspectives many years ago. Just as our educational systems might be more effective if we followed Dewey's ideas about learning, we might be further ahead in other applied fields if his commentary on the body–mind guided our thinking. We are still falling short of embracing the lovely notion put forth by Merleau-Ponty, "Our own body is in the world as the heart is in the organism... it forms with it a system" (translated by Hilditch, 1995). Polanyi (1958) also espoused these views, and he asserted that all knowledge and thought has bodily roots. One of the key figures to take up the tradition of embodiment and become essential in catalyzing the discourse of somatics, Thomas Hanna (1988, p. xii) commented, "Everything we experience in our lives is a bodily experience." Lorenz (1996) described how the ancient Chinese philosopher K'ung Fu-tzu used a wonderful metaphor for the mind and the living body: The two form a connection that's like that existing between a cutting edge and a knife; a cutting edge without a knife is inconceivable, whereas a knife without a cutting edge lacks the most essential feature inherent in the concept of a knife.

Although we intellectualize and theorize in various ways, sport psychology tends to treat the body as an object. We see the body as something about which we have an image (often a negative one, leading to phrases like "social physique anxiety") or like a machine we use to achieve performance, one that sometimes breaks down. Bodies have alternatively been considered in sundry ways as bearers of value (Sparkes, Partington, & Brown, 2007) and as sites of knowledge (e.g., Ryba, 2008). More sociological analyses of the body in sport have viewed the body as "a site for aesthetic freedom" (Markula, 2009) and, in case of a specific sport like swimming, for example, offered thoughts on topics such as "how to look good (nearly) naked" and the performative regulation of the swimmer's body, in which "the swimmer's body presents a potential threat to the interaction order, insofar as social encounters may be misconstrued as sexual, and so rituals are enacted to create a 'civilized' definition of the situation" (Scott, 2010, p. 143).

POLITICAL SOMATICS: THE BODY IN SOCIAL CONTEXT

Elaborate explorations have been undertaken about the meanings, social constructions, and sociology of the body that are beyond the scope of this chapter. It may be useful, however, to note that a full reconsideration of the body would include the social body. C. Wright Mills (1959) declared that we are "trapped" by our limited understanding of the relationship between private experience and social context. Studies indicate that the body is not only a biological phenomenon, but also a social construction (Turner, 1984); a site of state control (Foucault, 1990); the origin of transgressive capacities (Bakhtin, 1986); carries symbolic value (Bourdieu, 1991); is a text (Derrida, 1978); and, in education, serves as a terrain of struggle, conflict, and contradiction (McLaren, 1987). When embodiment has been considered in sport psychology, there frequently remains a clinging to a cognitive perspective (e.g., van Quaquebeke & Giessner, 2010) and dualisms in how the body is conceptualized (e.g., Baum & Trubo, 1999; Lussier-Ley, 2010). By recognizing that "the body" is both socially constructed and cannot be parceled out into constituent components, a more useful phenomenological picture of what it is like to be a person performing in sport (or other contexts) could be proffered. Rather than a detached mental analysis predicated on a mind viewing a body as object, the lived experience of the socially situated self could be provided.

THE PROMISE OF RECONSIDERING THE BODY

Although the application of the perspective shift here is ultimately relevant to sport and performance contexts, for many reading this text, the academic world is closer to our everyday experience.

> It is anybody's guess as to how many of us... walk around in schools and universities with feelings of bodily and emotional stress because of the disembodiment involved in how we are taught to teach, to learn, and to do research. Probably there are hordes of us. As we become adults, we learn how to repress somatic awareness, and many of us can no longer tell when our stomachs know better than our minds, when our bodies feel completely wrong, or why we develop headaches. We cover up the stress caused by the disembodiment of our work by still more work, or by still another cup of coffee. Lack of meaning, which points, by definition, to the loss of a participatory way of knowing, to lack of somatic and emotional involvement (see Berman, 1989; Johnson, 1983; Tarnas, 1991), is no longer accurately felt, understood, and acted on.
> (*Heshusius & Ballard*, 1996, p. 3)

The Foundations

According to Thomas Hanna (1988), it is easy to see how modern life produces so many individuals with a negative self-image. The progress of technology and medicine that keeps us alive longer is based on progressively deteriorating structures that cause unrelenting discomfort. All too quickly, we reach a stage in life filled with numerous problems. We can no longer do what we once did. We are often in discomfort and sometimes pain. We are often tired, especially by mid-afternoon, and without energy. Our oxygen supply is unknowingly limited. Finally, we are continually told that this process is an inevitable effect of aging.

It would be hard to dispute the relatively simple statement that the physical challenges of modern life are unrepresentative of the sorts of movements in which our ancestors were forced to engage. We evolved hunting and gathering, movements that involved a complete use of our bodies. Crucially, we no longer have that need, and, as a result, the responses of the human body are liable to be entirely different. We spend time in "pre-human postures unsuitable to our physiological evolution" (Colgan, 2002, p. 6). Hanna (1988) described how if one motto was to be pinned on your wall, it should be: "function maintains structure" or more simply, "use it or lose it." Our brain, which is a highly responsive organ of adaptation, adjusts to this lack of activity. If certain actions are no longer part of our behavioral inventory, our brain crosses them off; it forgets.

Some of the 20th century's greatest minds have commented on the challenges that face us in our rapidly changing social world. The ethologist Konrad Lorenz (1996) described how humans had become domesticated, a process that makes fewer demands on our instinctual equipment. One of America's leading psychologists, James Gibson (1979), stated that behaviors that were once adaptive might become maladaptive if the environment changes. Contemporary societies are dominated by increasingly specialized activities that require prolonged periods of sitting: in schools as a child or at desktop workplaces as an adult (Kendall, McCreary, Provance, Rodgers & Romani, 2005). The misuse of the body destroys bone, muscle, and connective tissue (Colgan, 2002).

Professionals trained in bodywork, such as Body Control Pilates teachers, are taught that the lack of movement in contemporary society causes atrophy of the deep-lying foundational muscles. This requires more work (contraction/tension) for the peripheral muscles, as they take on the stabilizing role in addition to their mobilizing one (we can't escape gravity) and causes them to weaken as they shorten or lengthen to accommodate the gradual postural collapse. Movement becomes inefficient as the brain selects the strongest team of muscles or the path of least resistance to move the body, bypassing the foundation muscles. If we consider the analogy of buildings, the importance of structure may become easier to grasp. New buildings appear almost overnight after months spent undercover. Why? Because the foundations are so crucial to the structure, they take longer to construct than the building itself. If we were told that a building had improper foundations, it wouldn't take most of us long to leave. More vitally, builders *never* strengthen buildings from the outside by putting more bricks on the outer walls with little account of the overall structure. This is why traditional gym-based resistance training can hasten, not reverse, decline. Constant contraction of big muscles on the outside of the body is more likely to pull joints onto each other, increasing, not decreasing, wear and tear (Colgan, 2002). How would we rather perform, as the Empire State Building, or the Leaning Tower of Pisa? It may be that we are performing in spite of our posture and elements of our training.

Holding unnecessary tension in this way is essentially tiring, and when combined with anxiety in a performance setting, is likely to prevent appropriately coordinating movements (Williams & Harris, 2001). Everyone—elite athletes included—is subjected to these processes of our environment. Similarly, we become accustomed to shallow breathing and remain unaware that our fatigue and ennui is largely a result of no longer taking sufficiently deep breaths. When the same bodily response occurs over and over, its pattern is gradually learned at an unconscious level. This is a slow, relentless act ingrained into the functional patterns of the central nervous system, an act that Hanna (1988) calls "habituation" (p. 53). It could also be called normalization. The brain accepts the wrong muscle length as correct, and consequently poor postural movement patterns feel normal to the individual. The body is simply unaware of any other way of being; we have become disembodied. If we add a load to this structure—such as sporting performance—it is easy to see how the sporting body, with shortened and over-recruited muscles (remember, in the event of postural collapse, these muscles are forced to take on both stabilizing and mobilizing roles), breaks down so frequently. This is why bodywork professionals report that even world-class sprinters cannot perform simple pelvic stability exercises. Over-recruitment means that these athletes' brains cannot isolate deeper lying stabilizing muscles, such as the pelvic floor and transversus abdominus, and keep the pelvis stable when the legs move.

Good posture is the state at which the body's joints are free and balanced, all its muscles are working in harmony, and it becomes an integrated unit, naturally and mechanically designed to self-adjust with the minimum of strain under all conditions (Stirk, 1988). A *tensegral structure*, a concept from the field of engineering, in which the integrity of structures are based *synergistically* between balanced tension and compression, is the most efficient method for dealing with gravity (Myers, 2004). It is designed with efficiency in mind, and therefore is the state that affords maximal chances of survival. If the body were designed to break down with the frequency that it does in top-level sport, it is worth questioning whether we would have survived as long as we have.

When seen in the context of modern-day sport, good posture is, by extension, a centered state that affords maximum performance. This is a state in which a performer's collapsed emotional state is not mirrored by her posture, because her posture can't collapse. It is a state in which coaches will not have to demand, usually toward the end of competitions, that their athletes "run tall," "suck in their stomachs," or "relax" because it's what they already are, it's their state of effortless being. It will also afford maximum protection against illness and injury, and, as a result, slowly the athlete will gain confidence. One of science's most robust findings is that performance improves as a function of practice (Ericsson, Krampe, & Tesch-Römer, 1993); more time spent doing sport, and less time resting and recovering from injury, can only lead to improved performance and increased confidence. More crucially, if we can accept that we may *feel* like the Empire State Building even though we see and feel the world as the Leaning Tower of Pisa, what would our sporting world look like if we really were the Empire State Building?

Dismantling Dualism: An Integrative Approach

Figuratively, at least, the knowledge practices that characterize modernity began on the day that Rene Descartes severed his body from his head. The attempt he records in the *Meditations* to create reliable procedures for creating knowledge was founded on the assumption that "I [that is, my mind, by which I am what I am] is entirely and truly distinct from my body" and that "body, figure, extension, motion, and place are merely fictions of

my mind" (Descartes, 1960 [1637], pp. 165, 118). In performing that act of willed self-dismemberment, Descartes bequeathed to modernity a knowing subject for whom epistemological agency requires the rejection of the physicality of the self. Saved from emotion by the clear light of reason, able to separate moral judgments from personal desires and loyalties, and undisturbed by the implacable demands of the body, the knowing subject is what Descartes called "precisely speaking, only a thinking thing" (1960 [1637], p.121).

(as cited in *Michelson*, 1998, pp. 217–218)

From Descartes on, the guiding question in Western philosophy has been whether body and mind are one or two distinct substances and what the ontological relation between them is. Varela, Thompson, and Rosch (1991) suggested that Descartes' conclusion "was the product of his question and that question was a product of specific practices—those of disembodied, unmindful reflection" (p. 28).

In contrast, Japanese philosophers conceive the body not as two disparate parts but as a unit capable of increasing levels of integration. Rather than asking how the mind and body are related, the Japanese have more often asked how the mind and body become increasingly interrelated. The Japanese philosopher Yasuo Yuasa remarked, "One starts from the experiential assumption that the mind–body modality changes through the training of the mind and body by means of cultivation (*shugyo*) or training (*keiko*). Only after assuming this experiential ground does one ask what the mind–body relation is. That is, the mind–body issue is not simply a theoretical speculation but it is originally a practical, lived experience (*taiken*), involving the mustering of one's whole mind and body. The theoretical is only a reflection on this lived experience" (cited in Varela et al., 1991, p. 30).

We can benefit from the recognition that our human being and experience is visceral, embodied, and emotional. It is the mistake of people overidentified with their intellect to suppose that intelligence and emotion are at odds, and that the latter is a subversive nuisance. We should not allow ourselves to be fooled by those who are out of touch with their own feelings into believing that separating thinking from feeling is a good, a "higher," thing to do (Claxton, 2006).

One of the challenges of an integrative approach is finding language that deviates from the existing dualistic expressions. Varela et al. (1991) proposed the term *enactive* to emphasize the growing conviction that cognition is not the representation of a pregiven world by a pregiven mind, but is rather the enactment of a world and a mind on the basis of a history of the variety of actions that a being in the world performs.

Each individual then might be conceptualized in relation to others. The self (some call "embodied mind") is passionate, desiring, social, and has a major empathic function. The ability to imitate and imagine the world of another is crucial. Empathic projection leads to an ecological and embodied spirituality that "requires an aesthetic attitude to the world that is central to self-nurturance, to the nurturance of others, and to the nurturance of the world itself" (Lakoff & Johnson, 1999, p. 566).

Lessons from Cognitive Science

In a continued exploration of cognitive science, we find further support to repudiate the notion that the mind is a disembodied logical reasoning device. Influenced by Varela et al. (1991), Clark (1997) followed three stages of cognitive science to extend the case. The first stage of classical cognitivism depicted the mind as a central logical engine and the body as an input device. In the connectionist (artificial neural network) or second stage, there was tacit acceptance of the "classical marginalization of body and world" (p. 83). Only in the third stage was the body and world taken seriously, and an *emergentist* perspective saw adaptive success as inhering as much in the complex interactions among body, world, and brain as in the inner processes constrained by skin and skull.

A separation of cognitive knowledge from embodied knowledge and the distrust and denigration of bodily knowing have dominated Western culture (Strozzi-Heckler, 2007b). Through recognition of the advances in cognitive science and by recognizing the progression in philosophical thought, we can begin to apply an integrated perspective in sport and performance psychology.

Somatics as Harmonizing Body, Mind, Emotions, and Spirit

As psychology has traditionally considered the mind and cognitive processes, we have favored explicit knowledge—the quantifiable and definable information that we use in our academic lives. Part of what broadening our perspective accomplishes is including "what we know in our bodies." We also value hunches, intuition, and nonintellectual qualities that inform performance.

A great deal of perception, communication, and intention for action takes place outside of (symbolic) language. Arnheim (1969) showed how language was unnecessary and perhaps irrelevant for artistic thought. Visual thinking is now generally seen as autonomous from language. Many aspects of other nonliterate activities, such as musical invention, dance, and sports, are learned to a large extent without language. Mimetic skill or mimesis rests on the capacity to produce conscious, self-initiated, representational acts that are intentional but not linguistic and is fundamentally different from imitation and mimicry in that it involves the invention of intentional representations. Mimesis can recruit a wide variety of actions and modalities to its purpose. Tones of voice, facial expressions, eye movements, manual signs and gestures, postural attitudes, patterned whole-body movements of various sorts, and long sequences of these elements can express many aspects of how we perceive the world. Most modern art forms, even those that rely heavily on oral and written language, are cognitive hybrids. Cinema, which started out in imitation of the theater, has become overwhelmingly mimetic in style; very little of what a good film communicates can be captured in words. Although it is logically prior to language, mimetic representation has characteristics that are essential to language and would thus have set the stage for the later emergence of speech. The important properties of individual mimetic acts include intentionality, generativity, communicativity, reference, autocueing, and the ability to model an unlimited number of objects (Donald, 1991). "We make sense of the world in a distinctly human way that is not linguistic" (Egan, 1997, p. 166). To enhance sport performance, it may be useful to consider where coaching and sport psychology err toward being overly analytic; the X's and O's may distract from developing the kinds of instinctive reactions and skills that coaches really desire.

A developing theme is the "embodied form of personal experience that is an inevitable but seldom-examined part of the process of doing educational and social research" (Eisner, 1996, p. ix). Berman (1989) pointed out that we have only analytic methodologies, not methodologies of feeling and sensing.

The process of arriving at this approach exemplifies it. Before we can account for it intellectually, there arises discomfort or a feeling that there is something off. This follows Polanyi's (1966) famous notion about tacit knowledge; we know we know something, but we cannot tell because it is initially visceral and internal. Although we can make rational sense of dominant assumptions, they no longer make sense somatically and affectively. "Something *felt* wrong. Our bodies told us so…it became overwhelmingly clear to us that somatic and affective modes of awareness came prior to and informed changes at the intellectual level" (Heshusius & Ballard, 1996, p. 2). "[K]nowledge depends on being in a world that is inseparable from our bodies, our language, and our social history—in short, form our *embodiment*" (Varela et al., 1991, p. 149).

This somatic knowing (Hanna, 1970; Berman, 1989) is different from, but not exclusive of, what cognitive psychologists refer to as "kinesthetic knowing." It is an experiential knowing that involves sense, precept, and mind–body action and reaction—a knowing, feeling, and acting that includes more of the broad range of human experience than that delimited within the traditionally privileged, distanced, disembodied range of discursive conceptualization (Matthews, 1998).

In the context of dance education, Erskine (2009, p. 1) noted, "Somatic methods are orientated towards general optimum functioning and perceived as developing awareness of bodymind connections (Green, 1999; Jackson, 2005)…. Integrating somatic methods results in a change of consciousness in attitude to persons, moving, performance, and the creation of works" (Bannon & Sanderson, 2000; Hämäläinen, 2002).

Within sport psychology, the specific discourse of somatics is new (Strean & Strozzi-Heckler, 2009). Yet, we have known that when our interventions assist people to have greater awareness of feeling and sensation, their aliveness begins to grow (Ravizza, 2001). The fact that so many people—even athletes—live in their heads makes it relatively easy to make a big impact with some simple somatic practices. It is profound to see how a basic centering practice can allow individuals "feel into themselves" in a way they haven't in years (Hardy & Fazey, 1990).

Key Distinctions from a Somatic Discourse

There are many ways in which the core ideas of somatics could be brought to light and used to improve practice. Let us consider, from the perspective of the practitioner, meeting with a client or group of clients as a way to witness the application of some fundamental somatic concepts. These particular distinctions (Strozzi-Heckler, 2007b) have roots in aikido, and, like aikido, an athlete's participation in a psychology consultation is a departure

from competition. These distinctions provide ways of observing and altering interactions, and they offer ways of establishing partnerships rather than determining winners and losers.

Centering

The "how" of centering was seen in the opening exercise of this chapter. A practice of centering might be considered as a commitment to self-awareness. Centering is the foundation for effective action—whether that action is a physical movement made by an athlete or performer, or whether it is a conversational move made by a sport psychology professional. We always want to begin our interactions from a place of center. Being centered includes aligning oneself physically by attending to length, width, depth, and breath. It also involves returning to an emotional center of acceptance and a cognitive/language center of calm and quiet. Our engagement begins from an intentional move to center. Consider how action is compromised, physically or conversationally, when it begins from a place of imbalance. Practicing centering and teaching our clients this practice is a way in which somatic exercises can assist applied consulting.

Facing

If we were to consider ourselves as biological creatures, we might note quickly that we are distinct from other animals in that we stand with our organs exposed, and we are able to face another member of our species in a way that others cannot. Our first move of creating connection is to face. In a biological sense, this is no small step as we have both a very fundamental desire to connect with other creatures and a concomitant fear of being hurt by others. If we are aware of this dynamic in our clients and ourselves, we can attend to the biological and emotional melee that rushes beneath the surface of our conversational greetings. We can think of facing those we encounter as a commitment to integrity.

Entering

Our first action toward creating a conversation is entering. By being centered and creating an intention to connect by facing, we can read the client to feel for an openness to step in. We begin to connect with the client. In this moment, our focus shifts and we move toward engagement. Entering includes the whole self; we are present, we bring our energy, attention, and intention. We are aware of our mood and sensations as parts of our whole, somatic self.

Extending

From a centered presence, we move our energy into the world. Although there is the more apparent notion of extending a hand as a way of greeting, extension includes listening, moving one's energy toward the client, and fostering a deeper connection. Like all other moves, we are assessing how much is too much and how much is not enough. We notice our impact on the client, and we stay present with ourselves.

Blending

When our energy mixes with that of the client, it is like forming a knot. We continue to ask ourselves what amount of extension and reception facilitates a working dynamic. We are monitoring to create harmony with another's energy. Various somatic practices, such as two-step (see the section Standing Practices for a description), that involve physically moving and coordinating with another body can cultivate our ability to blend with a client. The ongoing relationship can be seen as a continuous process of giving and receiving, cycles of reciprocity.

Applying Somatic Practices for Performance Enhancement

Practices

From a somatic perspective, a great deal of value of sport and performance psychology interventions is derived by assisting individuals to develop, refine, and consistently engage in practices.[2] Practices enable one to reshape the body, which has great plasticity. Learning is embodied through practice and repetition. If we want to learn to be adept at a sport skill, for example, we seem to understand that it will be insufficient to read a book about the sport. We will not become competent by memorizing the sequence of movements. To be able to move effectively without having to plan our actions consciously takes practicing the moves over time. When we think of how we learn to drive, this concept becomes clear. We first learned the various components of gas pedal, brake, steering wheel, and turn signals. Then, as we began to drive under the instruction of a teacher (often a certified driving instructor, sometimes an older friend, sibling, or parent), we drove deliberately and self-consciously. Now, we drive and converse with other passengers, plan our days, listen to music, daydream, and even talk on the phone (and hopefully not send text messages). The ability to drive a car has become embodied. It's invisible to us. It is so transparent to us that

it may even be difficult to teach. It's something we just do. Through a practice of recurrent actions, we've embodied the capacity to drive without having to consciously reflect on how we're doing it. We can now say we have embodied the skill of driving a car.

One of the greatest lessons available from the study of somatics is understanding the foundational importance of practices. In a sense, this concept should be apparent to those of us from sport and performance backgrounds. We acknowledge that a physical change, such as skilful performance, requires many repetitions. Yet, we sometimes relate to the mental aspects of performance with an implied belief that an insight or realization is enough for an enduring change. Although we are aware of examples in which a paradigm shifts and resulting changes persist, the vast majority of cases seem to suggest that continuing actions must occur to shift the self. Although each individual person or case requires specific practices to support what he or she is up to, some somatic practices are frequently beneficial. Many athletes and other performers have reported that the centering practice described above has been valuable to them. Other common somatic practices include sitting/attention training and standing practices. Consistent with other forms of mental and physical learning, including psychological skills, practice is necessary for effective development (e. g., Schmidt & Wrisberg, 2008).

Sitting/Attention Training

One can look at many cultures and traditions over human history and find support for practices that involve becoming still and focusing inward. Most athletes (and sport psychology practitioners) will find that they are more effective in their active lives when they take on a practice such as sitting or meditating. Although there are many places to learn these practices in much greater depth, it can be as simple as following the instruction to sit comfortably with the eyes closed, the back straight, and pay attention to breath (in and out at the nostrils or abdomen). Having struggled with a meditation practice for most of the past 25 years and with the experience of inviting many and varied clients to explore such a practice, I have arrived at several conclusions: (a) it is likely that nothing else is as simple, yet as challenging; (b) there is probably little else that can be more useful for more people—no single practice tends to provide such large payoffs across individuals; and (c) it is astounding how many people will report both how beneficial the practice is and resist doing it at the same time. Meditation teacher Steven Sashen (personal communication, June 17, 2007) reported that, in speaking with thousands of people, he discovered almost nobody wants to meditate, but all want the results of meditation such as a deep abiding peace, a feeling of connection to others and the world, and for some, the ability to simply relax. Perhaps disrupting the high-paced flow of our lives is, paradoxically, one of the best ways to spend more time having flow experiences.

Standing Practices

A variety of movement practices can be personalized to the client to help with increasing awareness and with making vital shifts. One of my favorites that can both detect and develop coordination of action is called a "two-step." This practice involves having two people face each other, each with the same leg forward and the other leg back. The front foot slides slightly forward, the back leg steps forward, each person pivots, and then steps back with the other foot. The pair finishes facing with the other leg forward. It is captivating to see relationship dynamics appear with this exercise. Whether it is two infielders trying to turn a double play, a setter and a hitter, or skating pairs, the way that the two "body/selves" move together in a two-step tells a story about how they move together in other contexts (this practice also applies when working with couples or co-workers). The two-step can both disclose what happens in a relationship and also offer a tool to play with and develop new coordinated actions. For example, one partner may always take the lead and direct the other partner, or the two partners may collide as they both try to assert themselves. After observing the pattern, alternatives can be suggested and attempted. Many other standing practices—some as simple as paying attention and changing postures when walking—develop greater awareness and self-control. Other practices can involve working through the body on balance, sensation, breath, and mood to develop a self that can take new, effective action.

Examples of Somatic Sport and Performance Psychology Interventions

In the context of dance education, Fortin (1998) found that by focusing on the lived experience of the body, teachers were able to nurture their students' own empowerment. Similarly, in a sport context, athletes frequently report greater awareness and improved performance following an introduction to somatic practices (for thorough accounts of an elite softball player using somatics, see Strean & Strozzi-Heckler, 2009). Key features of using somatics in sport and performance intervention include (a) *global attention to clients*—during an initial session, the practitioner may observe "the story" the body tells, how clients carry themselves, and strengths they embody, and we might note areas of learning and development that our assessments suggest; we may notice where they are "armored" (Reich, 1960); (b) *enhancing clients' awareness* of feeling, emotion, sensation, how the body is shaped, how historical influences are embodied, and how to use breathing and moving to create more optimal states; and (c) *working with the client to develop and select somatic practices,* such as centering, two-step, or standing practices with partners or teammates.

Conclusion

How we understand the body has intimate and profound ramifications for both theoretical advancement and effective application in sport and performance psychology. The dualistic conceptions that have dominated our thinking and action fall short when considered in comparison to understanding the integrated nature of human beings. By recognizing that thinking, feeling, and acting are all embodied, we will expand our attention, increase our awareness, and become more successful in our research and practice.

Future Directions

What if we were to reorient part of our work to shift our perspective from the business deal mentality depicted in the Tragedy of the Commons to shaping and supporting greater compassion? There is probably no one right way to go about it, and spontaneous compassion follows no rules. There are no axiomatic ethical systems or practical moral injunctions. What if we were to be completely responsive to the needs of the particular situation or client? Nagarjuna (cited in Varela et al., 1991, p. 250) conveys this attitude of responsiveness:

Just as the grammarian makes one study grammar,
A Buddha teaches according to the tolerance of his students;
Some he urges to refrain from sins, others to do good,
Some to rely on dualism, others on non-dualism;
And to some he teaches the profound,
The terrifying, the practice of enlightenment,
Whose essence is emptiness that is compassion.

For more than 99% of human history, the world was enchanted, and human beings saw themselves as an integral part of it. The complete reversal of this perception in a mere 400 years or so has destroyed the continuity of human experience and the integrity of the human psyche. It has very nearly wrecked the planet as well. The only hope, or so it seems, is the re-enchantment of the world (Berman, 1984). Steps along that path may include understanding the primacy of consciousness and embodiment. Perhaps the continued survival of the species in a habitable environment is the greatest "performance" challenge facing us today.

Notes

1. From a printing perspective, brown is made up of black, yellow, cyan, and magenta.

2. Much of the content of this section appeared in Strean & Strozzi-Heckler (2009).

References

Arnheim, R. (1969). *Visual thinking*. Berkeley: University of California Press.

Bakhtin, M. M. (1986). *Speech genres and other late essays* (C. Emerson & M. Holquist, Eds.). Austin: University of Texas Press.

Baum, K., & Trubo, R. (1999). *The mental edge: Maximize your sports potential with the mind-body connection*. New York: Berkeley Pub. Group.

Bannon, F., & Sanderson, P. (2000). Experience every movement: Aesthetically significant dance education. *Research in Dance Education, 1*(1), 9–26.

Berman, M. (1984). *The reenchantment of the world*. New York: Bantam.

Berman, M. (1989). *Coming to our senses: Body and spirit in the hidden history of the West*. New York: Simon and Schuster.

Bourdieu, P. (1991). *The logic of practice*. Cambridge, UK: Polity Press.

Clark, A. (1997). *Being there: Putting brain, body, and world together again*. Cambridge, MA: MIT Press.

Claxton, G. (2006). Nirvana and neuroscience: The self-liberating brain. In D. K. Nauriyal (Ed.), *The Buddha's way: The confluence of Buddhist thought, contemporary psychology and consciousness studies in the post-modern age* (pp. 93–111). London: Routledge Curzon.

Colgan, M. (2002). *Perfect posture: The basis of power*. Vancouver: Apple Publishing Company.

Damasio A. R. (1994). *Descartes' error: Emotion, reason and the human brain*. New York: Grosset/Putnam.

Derrida, J. (1978). *Writing and difference*. Chicago: University of Chicago Press.

Dewey, J. (1916). *Democracy and Education: An introduction to the philosophy of education*. New York: Macmillan.

Dewey, J. (1925). *Experience and nature*. Chicago: Open Court Publishing.

Donald, M. (1991). *Origins of the modern mind: Three stages in the evolution of culture and cognition*. Cambridge, MA: Harvard University Press.

Egan, K. (1997). *The educated mind: How cognitive tools shape our understanding*. Chicago: University of Chicago Press.

Eisner, E. (1996). Foreward. In L. Heshusius & K. Ballard (Eds.), *From positivism to interpretivism and beyond: Tales of transformation in educational and social research (the mind-body connection)* (pp. ix-xi). New York: Teachers College Press.

Ericsson, K. A., Krampe, R. T., & Tesch-Römer, C. (1993). The role of deliberate practice in the acquisition of expert performance. *Psychological Review, 100*, 363–406.

Erskine, S. (2009). The integration of somatics as an essential component of aesthetic dance education (pp. 1–11). In C. Stock (Ed.), *Dance dialogues: Conversations across cultures, artforms and practices*. Proceedings of the 2008 World Dance Alliance Global Summit, Brisbane, July 13–18. On-line publication, QUT Creative Industries and Ausdance, http://www.ausdance.org.au

Fortin, S. (1998). Somatics: A tool for empowering modern dance teachers. In S. B. Shapiro (Ed.), *Dance, power, and difference: Critical and feminist perspectives on dance education* (pp. 49–74). Champaign, IL: Human Kinetics.

Foucault, M. (1990). *The history of sexuality. Vol. 1*. New York: Vintage Books.

Gibson, J. J. (1979). *The ecological approach to visual perception*. Boston: Houghton Mifflin.

Goswami, A. (1993). *The self-aware universe: How consciousness creates the material world*. New York: Penguin.

Green, J. (1999). Somatic authority and the myth of the ideal body in dance education. *Dance Research Journal, 31*(2), 80–100.

Hämäläinen, S. (2002). Evaluation in choreographic pedagogy. *Research in Dance Education, 3*(1), 35–45.

Hanna, T. (1970). *Bodies in revolt: A primer in somatic thinking*. New York: Holt, Rinehart and Winston.

Hanna, T. (1988). *Somatics: Reawakening the mind's control of movement, flexibility, and health*. Reading, MA: Addison-Wesley.

Hardy, L., & Fazey, J. A. (1990). *Mental training*. Leeds, England: National Coaching Foundation.

Heshusius, L., & Ballard, K. (Eds.). (1996). *From positivism to interpretivism and beyond: Tales of transformation in educational and social research (the mind-body connection)*. New York: Teachers College Press.

Hilditch, D. (1995). *At the heart of the world*. Doctoral dissertation, Washington University, St. Louis, MO.

Jackson, J. (2005). My dance and the idea body: Looking at ballet practice from the inside out. *Research in Dance Education, 6*(1/2), 25–40.

James, W. (1902). *The varieties of religious experience*. New York: The Modern Library.

Johnson, D. (1983). *Body*. Boston: Beacon Press.

Kendall, F. P., McCreary, E. K., Provance, P. G., Rodgers, M., & Romani, W. (2005). *Muscles: Testing and function with posture and pain* (5th ed.). Baltimore: Lippincott Williams & Wilkins.

Lakoff, G., & Johnson, M. (1999). *Philosophy in the flesh*. New York: Basic Books.

Lorenz, K. (1996). The natural science of the human species: An introduction to comparative behavioural research. In A. V. Cranach (Ed.), *The "Russian" manuscript (1944–1948)*. Cambridge, MA: MIT Press.

Lussier-Ley, C. (2010). Dialoguing with body: A self study in relational pedagogy through embodiment and the therapeutic relationship. *The Qualitative Report, 15* (1), 197–214.

Markula, P. (2009, May 1). 'Sculpt Your Body with a Killer Workout': Exercise as a technique of body management. In *Symposium: The body as object: The human as material culture*. Presented at the Material Culture Institute's 3rd Annual Symposium, Edmonton, AB.

Matthews, J. C. (1998). Somatic knowing and education. *Educational Forum, 62*, 236–242.

McKenna, K. Y. A., & Bargh, J. A. (2000). Plan 9 from cyberspace: The implications of the internet for personality and social psychology. *Personality and Social Psychology Review, 4*, 57–75.

McLaren, P. (1987). Schooling the postmodern body. Critical pedagogy and the politics of enfleshment. In H. Giroux (Ed.), *Postmodernism, feminism and cultural politics* (pp. 144–173). Albany, NY: State University of New York Press.

Merleau-Ponty, M. (1945). *Phenomenogie de la perception*. Paris: Gallimard.

Michelson, E. (1998). Re-membering: The return of the body to experiential learning. *Studies in Continuing Education, 20*(2), 217–233.

Mills, C. W. (1959). *The sociological imagination*. New York: Oxford University Press.

Myers, T. W. (2004). *Anatomy trains myofascial meridians for movement therapists*. London: Churchill Livingstone.

Polanyi, M. (1958). *Personal knowledge: Towards a post-critical philosophy*. London: Routledge & K. Paul.

Polanyi, M. (1966). *The tacit dimension*. London: Routledge & Kegan.

Ravizza, K. (2001). Increasing awareness for sport performance. In J. M. Williams (Ed.), *Applied sport psychology: Personal growth to peak performance* (4th ed., pp. 179–189). Mountain View, CA: Mayfield.

Rawls, J. (1999). *A theory of justice* (rev. ed.). Cambridge, MA: Harvard University Press.

Reich, W. (1960). *Selected writings: An introduction to orgonomy*. New York: Farrar, Straus & Cudahy.

Ryba, T. V. (2008). Researching children in sport: Methodological reflections. *Journal of Applied Sport Psychology, 20*, 334–348.

Schmidt, R. A., & Wrisberg, C. A. (2008). *Motor learning and performance: A situation-based approach* (4th ed.). Champaign, IL: Human Kinetics.

Scott, S. (2010). How to look good (nearly) naked: The performative regulation of the swimmer's body. *Body and Society, 16*, 143–168.

Sparkes, A. C., Partington, E., & Brown, D. H. K. (2007). Bodies as bearers of value: The transmission of jock culture via the 'Twelve Commandments'. *Sport, Education and Society, 12*(3), 295–316.

Stirk, J. (1988). *Functional fitness*. London: Elm Tree Books.

Strean W. B., & Strozzi-Heckler, R. (2009). (The) Body (of) Knowledge: Somatic contributions to sport psychology. *Journal of Applied Sport Psychology, 21*(1), 91–98.

Strozzi-Heckler, R. (2003). *Being human at work: Bringing somatic intelligence into your professional life*. Berkeley, CA: North Atlantic Books.

Strozzi-Heckler, R. (2007a). Leadership dojo. In P. Holman, T. Devane, & S. Cady (Eds.), *The change handbook* (2nd ed., pp. 239–243). San Francisco: Berrett-Koehler.

Strozzi-Heckler, R. (2007b). *The leadership dojo: Build your foundation as an exemplary leader*. Berkeley, CA: Frog Books.

Tarnas, R. (1991). *The passion of the western mind: Understanding the ideas that have shaped our world view*. New York: Ballantine.

Turner, B. (1984). *The body and society. Explorations in social theory*. Oxford, England: Basil Blackwell.

van Quaquebeke, N. & Giessner, S. R. (2010). How embodied cognitions affect judgments: Height-related attribution bias in football foul calls. *Journal of Sport and Exercise Psychology, 32*, 3–22.

Varela, F. J., Thompson, E., & Rosch, E. (1991). *The embodied mind: Cognitive science and human experience*. Cambridge, MA: MIT Press.

Williams, J. M., & Harris, D. V. (2001). Relaxation and energizing techniques for regulation of arousal. In J. M. Williams (Ed.), *Applied sport psychology: Personal growth to peak performance* (4th ed., pp. 229–246). Mountain View, CA: Mayfield.

Injury and Performance

John Heil *and* Leslie Podlog

Abstract

Injury is a disruptive event in the life of the dedicated recreational athlete and the elite performer alike. Crucial to the success of injury management is an understanding of the role of psychosocial factors in injury. This chapter reviews the psychology of sport injury literature with the aim of informing intervention efforts among key service providers. The literature review presents models that have provided the framework for research and intervention, reviews scholarship pertaining to a broad range of injury (musculoskeletal injuries, head injury and concussion, catastrophic and fatal injury), illuminates the sporting subcultures in which injuries occur and are managed, and offers suggestions for future scholarship with attention to implications for applied practitioners. Although written explicitly for the psychologist, the roles of others who influence the psychology of injury, including the physician and sports medicine therapist, the coach, and athlete, are highlighted.

Key Words: Injury models, musculoskeletal, concussion, catastrophic and fatal injury, culture of risk, intervention, psychologist, service delivery

The goal of a psychology of sport injury is to identify best practices and the strategies that guide their implementation. This begins with identifying best knowledge and concludes with a presentation of appropriate roles for service providers. The challenge lies in the diverse literature that is of relevance to this discipline, the varied settings in which providers work, and the range of skills they potentially offer. In this chapter, injury is defined as any physical functional or medical condition that inhibits optimal performance. A service provider is anyone who is positioned to provide a significant psychological impact on injury management. The psychology of injury is broadly conceived to include any psychological state associated with actual or potential injury. With these definitions in mind, the aim of the chapter is to review the psychology of sport injury literature in order to inform intervention efforts among key service delivery providers. The chapter has three sections, including a review of the psychosocial injury literature, a discussion of the role of various service providers in injury intervention, and, finally, a discussion of future directions in service delivery provision for injured athletes and performers.

Literature Review: Injury

Research in psychology of sport injury proper (defined as a literature catalogued by the three keywords *psychology, sport, injury*) is a fledgling enterprise, limited in scope. In contrast, the literature relevant to a psychology of sport injury (defined as literature catalogued by at least two of the three keywords *psychology, sport, injury*) is widely dispersed across subspecialties within psychology, medicine, and sociology. Given the breadth of scholarship on the psychosocial aspects of injury, the literature is challenging to monitor and access. Consequently, this review will draw from various bodies of scholarly literature (e.g., sport psychology, sociology of sport, sport and general medicine, clinical and health psychology, performance psychology) in highlighting the "best knowledge" required by service delivery personnel for effective injury management.

The review is divided into four sections: injury models that have provided the framework for research and intervention, scholarship pertaining to three broad injury categories (musculoskeletal injuries, head injury and concussion, catastrophic and fatal injury), the particular context and sporting subcultures in which injuries occur and are managed, and suggestions for future scholarship, with attention to applied practitioners.

Models of Injury Research and Intervention

Various psychological models have been proposed as guides to research and intervention, and these focus on injury risk, rehabilitation, and return to sport. These are summarized below.

Stress-Injury Model

Andersen and Williams (Anderson & Williams, 1988; Williams & Andersen, 1998) proposed the *stress-injury model* to examine injury vulnerability and resilience. This a broadly based view of the interplay of stress, psychological coping skills, and injury. It is a sport-specific variant of the stress-injury model of Holmes and Rahe (1967), which looked at life change stress as a predictor of injury and illness. It suggests that a combination of a stress-prone personality, a recent history of stressors, and relatively weak coping resources predict a more significant stress response and hence greater injury risk. The stress response is mediated by interrelated cognitive appraisal and physiological response and is moderated by psychological skills (which are trainable via typical sport psychology mental training methods). The efficacy of this model in sport injury was first demonstrated in the research of Smith, Smoll, and Ptacek (1990). It has been widely tested and offers substantial support for the notion of an at-risk injury profile. Although theoretically relevant, congruent with stress-injury research and supportive of the efficacy of psychological skills, it is of little utility as an intervention guide.

Psychophysiological Model of Injury Risk

The *psychophysiological model of injury risk* (Heil, 1993) focuses specifically on performance in high-threat environments, in which fear of injury (or reinjury) is a factor. Heil (1993) proposed

that perceptions of stress—in particular, fear of injury—elicit diminished performance and heightened injury risk via change in behavior (disrupted biomechanics, poor physiological resource utilization, decreased attention to performance cues) mediated by physiological and psychological mechanisms. Psychological changes may be skill-related (e.g., decreased concentration, increased distractibility) or interpretive alterations (e.g., decreased self-confidence and increasing pain awareness). Physiological alterations may include interrelated changes at the muscular (i.e., muscle guarding/bracing, generalized muscle tension), autonomic (i.e., increased heart rate), and neurochemical levels. The model complements the work by Anderson and Williams, in that it offers a circumscribed set of cause–effect links and makes direct hypotheses about the interplay of psychological, behavioral, and physiological factors. As such, it is of utility as an applied behavioral assessment tool, offering both a strategy for observing sport behavior and a guide to structure clinical inquiry with an at-risk athlete. Because of its pragmatic nature and practical language, it can be used by a wide range of providers, including the psychologist, medical specialist, and coach. This type of model—that is, one that offers more direct hypotheses of the real-time interplay of psychological, physiological, and behavioral factors—will likely guide the next generation of sport injury research.

Grief-Loss and Stage Models of Injury Rehabilitation

The underlining assumption of the grief-loss premise is that injury represents a loss of some aspect of the self, whereas the stage element suggests that psychological responses follow a predictable pattern (Brewer, 2007; Evans & Hardy, 1995). Several stage models have been applied to sport injury, all of which have evolved from the seminal work *On Death and Dying* by Elizabeth Kubler-Ross (1969). She hypothesized that individuals moved through a series of stages during the progression of terminal illness: disbelief, denial, and isolation; anger; bargaining; depression; and finally acceptance and resignation. Rotella (1982), Astle (1986), and Gordon, Milios, and Grove (1991) were among the first sport psychologists to embrace this model, suggesting that athletes may experience a similar emotional response to injury. The appeal of this model rests in its forward thinking "positive psychology" assumption that emotional discord is not necessarily a reflection of pathology but rather an appropriate response to a disruptive event. Although the Kubler-Ross model initially resonated with sport psychologists, other models followed that sought to address the criticisms of the Kubler-Ross model (absence of empirical support for a rigid stage progression) and to more directly reflect the experience of the injured athlete (Evans & Hardy, 1995). McDonald and Hardy (1990), for example, suggested a two-stage grief process. The initial "reactive phase," which includes shock (feeling of detachment) and encounter (panic and helplessness), is followed by a second adaptive stage of "retreatment and acknowledgment" as the athlete either returns to play or adjusts to the protracted consequences of illness.

This second generation of stage theories typically debunked the concept of denial. This debunking is a consequence of the use of a relatively crude research measurement methodology and reflects a disconnect between researchers and clinicians, a problem endemic to applied science. Although a well-established and time-honored concept in clinical practice, the subtle nature of denial leads it to be resistant to quantification. Although professional consensus is no guarantee, the case study and anecdotal literature on denial is so deep and so compelling that it is literally undeniable. As elusive as denial is, simply reframing it conceptually can bring it into focus. For example, in a qualitative research study on severe injury in elite skiers, Gould, Udry, Bridges, & Beck(1997a&b) identify an information processing theme that can be easily read as denial. Heil (2000) looks in detail at the concept, making the point that the absence of (empirical) proof is not the proof of absence.

Affective Cycle of Injury Rehabilitation

The *affective cycle of injury model* (Heil, 1993) reflects a clinical perspective that maintains the core idea of dynamic emotional response found in stage theory. The hypothesized "engine of emotion" that drives psychological response to the challenges of rehabilitation has three components: distress (e.g., anxiety, depression), denial (unacknowledged distress), and determined coping (vigorous, proactive, goal-driven behavior). The distress and denial processes described by Heil are akin to the reactive phase proposed by McDonald and Hardy (1990), whereas determined coping appears analogous to their adaptive phase.

Unlike earlier stage theories that describe a sequential set of psychological states, this model is rooted in the empirically grounded, medically based stages of injury and rehabilitation. For example,

Steadman (1993) offers a psychologically sensitive medical model that encompasses six stages of rehabilitation: immediate postinjury, treatment decision and implementation, early postoperative/rehabilitation, late postoperative/rehabilitation, specificity, and return to play. It also includes a preinjury stage that is congruent with the concepts of injury risk and prevention. Unlike the sequential steps prescribed in stage models, Heil asserts that shifts in emotional response from denial to distress to determined coping can occur at any point in the rehabilitation process depending upon specific rehabilitation experiences (e.g., a rehabilitation setback, pain flare-ups), as well as on the athlete's subjective sense of rehabilitation progress.

A Biopsychosocial Model of Injury Rehabilitation

Brewer et al.'s (2002) *biopsychosocial model* identifies seven key components, including injury characteristics (e.g., severity, location, history), sociodemographics factors (e.g., age, gender, socioeconomic status), biological factors (e.g., circulation, tissue repair, neurochemistry), psychological factors (personality, cognition, affect, and behavior), social/contextual factors (e.g., social support, life stress, rehabilitation environment), intermediate biopsychological outcomes (e.g., range of motion, pain, strength, rate of recovery), and sport injury rehabilitation outcomes (e.g., functional performance, quality of life, readiness to return to sport).

It suggests that the characteristics of the injury and sociodemographics influence biological, psychological, and social/contextual factors. Psychological factors are posited to have a reciprocal relationship with biological and social/contextual factors, all of which influence intermediate biopsychological rehabilitation outcomes. Psychological factors and intermediate rehabilitation outcomes influence sport injury rehabilitation outcomes. The strength of the model is its scope. However, it does not provide a coherent explanation of how variables within and across categories interact to produce different return to sport outcomes. Given this limitation, examining other injury rehabilitation models is worthwhile.

Integrated Model of Psychological Response to Sport Injury and Rehabilitation

Wiese-Bjornstal, Smith, Shaffer, and Morrey (1998) incorporate Andersen and Williams' (1988) stress injury model into their post-injury cognitive appraisal model. As initially proposed in the stress-injury model, personality characteristics, a history of stressors, coping resources, and interventions interact with or work in isolation to influence athletes' stress response and the subsequent likelihood of injury occurrence. They propose that the same factors that determine injury risk also influence athletes' psychological response to injury, drawing on Lazarus and Folkman's (1984) cognitive appraisal theory of stress and coping. The key premises of this model are that individual differences in response to injury are the consequence of differing appraisals or perceptions of the injury; and that cognitive appraisals influence not only athletes' psychological responses to injury but also physical recovery and psychosocial status. Although the integrated model of response to injury has received a great deal of empirical support, the model intentionally focuses on responses to sport injury and the rehabilitation process. However, it does not detail athletes' ultimate post-injury performance goals or the processes involved in their attainment. For a more detailed examination of athletes' recovery and return to sport outcomes, Taylor and Taylor's (1997) model is instructive.

Return to Sport Model

Taylor and Taylor's (1997) *return to sport model* identifies a series of five successive physical and psychological stages, including the initial return, recovery confirmation, return of physical and technical abilities, high-intensity training, and return to competition. These stages unfold as the athlete moves through a progressive series of mind–body challenges.

The first stage, the initial return, tests whether the injury is healed. It is essential for enhancing athlete efficacy about the ability to achieve future athletic goals. Like the initial stage, the second stage—recovery confirmation—is more psychological than physical in nature as it involves athletes obtaining feedback that the healed injury is capable of withstanding the demands of training and competition. The third stage, the return of physical and technical abilities, focuses on restoring athletes' levels of physical conditioning and technical proficiency, signifying the end of rehabilitation and healing. The penultimate stage, high-intensity training, marks the psychological transformation from injured to healed. The final phase, the return to competition, may provide a mixture of excitement regarding the ability to publicly demonstrate one's skills and trepidation about putting oneself back in the same situation where injury occurred. Taylor and Taylor's (1997) model provides a useful heuristic for sport

medicine professionals and coaches. The criticisms lodged against other stage models are, however, relevant to the return to sport model.

Interestingly, few of the preceding models incorporate components from those developed in the health psychology literature that look at prediction of healthy behaviors. For example, the *theory of planned behavior*, examining the impact of personal beliefs and attitudes on intentions (i.e., motivation) to engage in health-related behaviors, appears relevant in an injury context. Given the importance of motivation to the recovery process, examining the factors influencing motivations to engage in injury recovery warrants consideration. In the next section, we review research findings, organized into three categories or injury types: musculoskeletal injuries, head injuries, and catastrophic or fatal injuries.

Scholarship on Three Injury Types: Musculoskeletal, Head, and Catastrophic Injury

The vast majority of the research focuses on musculoskeletal injuries, likely because they are most frequent, are more limited in duration, and show greater professional consensus on treatment protocols. Head injury has garnered increasing attention is recent years and seen progress toward standardization in assessment and treatment. In contrast, catastrophic and fatal injury, unfortunately, continue to receive relatively little systematic attention from the sports medicine professions.

Musculoskeletal Injury

Research examining the psychosocial aspects of musculoskeletal injury has focused on three phases including: the period preceding injury occurrence (i.e., injury antecedents), the rehabilitation phase, and the return to sport transition. The review of injury antecedents is structured in accord with Williams and Andersen's stress-injury model (1998).

INJURY ANTECEDENTS
History of Stressors

Researchers testing injury vulnerability have found fairly consistent support for a relationship between injury and stressors (defined as major life events, daily hassles, and previous injury history). Many studies show a relationship between major life change events and injury (e.g., Holmes, 1970; Bramwell, Masuda, Wagner, & Holmes, 1975; Cryan & Alles, 1983; Ford, Eklund, & Gordon, 2000; Williams & Roepke, 1993). There are far fewer research studies and much less consistent support for the role of daily stressors in injury (e.g., Byrd, 1993; Fawkner, McMurray, & Summers, 1999). This may reflect methodological weaknesses in the studies, specifically the failure to obtain measures of daily hassles of sufficient frequency or duration (Williams & Andersen, 2007). Several studies have found a positive relationship between prior injury and subsequent injury (e.g., Lysens et al., 1984; Van Mechelen et al., 1996; Williams, Hogan, & Andersen, 1993). However, it is unclear the extent to which this is a function of psychological factors relative to increased biomechanical vulnerability from prior injury.

Personality

The research on the relationship between personality factors (including mood states) and injury shows inconsistent results. Of the investigations showing a positive association, competitive trait anxiety (e.g., Lavallee & Flint, 1996; Petrie, 1993) and an external locus of control (Pargman & Lunt, 1989) have been linked with injury vulnerability. Similarly, Fields, Delaney, and Hinkle (1990) and Nigorikawa et al. (2003) found that runners scoring high on type A behaviors experienced significantly more injuries compared to runners scoring lower on this measure. In contrast, those using nonsport measures showed no relationship between personality traits and injury occurrence (e.g., Hanson, McCullagh, & Tonymon, 1992; Kerr & Minden, 1988; McLeod & Kirkby, 1995; Passer & Seese, 1983).

Support exists for including mood states as potential correlates of injury occurrence. Fawkner (1995) noted increases in negative mood disturbance immediately prior to injury, whereas Lavallee and Flint (1996) reported that higher tension/anxiety, anger/hostility, and total negative mood state correlated with higher severity of injury. One reason for the contradictory findings may be that many of the personality variables tested were not selected on the basis of particular models and were not always related to sport or stress specific concerns.

Coping Resources

Testing of coping resources has revealed that athletes (and dancers) with poor coping resources and weak social support networks are at increased risk for injury (Byrd, 1993; Hanson et al., 1992; Noh, Morris, & Andersen, 2005; Rogers & Landers, 2005; Petrie, 1992; Smith, Smoll, & Ptacek, 1990; Williams, Tonymon, & Wadsworth, 1986). In summary, sufficient evidence supports the Williams and Andersen (1998) hypothesis that there is an identifiable "injury risk" profile. Specifically, the research suggests that an athlete's history of stressors, certain personality traits (e.g., competitive trait anxiety, type A), and poor coping resources increase injury susceptibility.

Stress Response

Research on the stress response is limited in both amount and scope, focusing primarily on change in visual information processing. In several studies, athletes experiencing a high volume of life change events during the preceding year reported relatively higher state anxiety and greater peripheral vision narrowing during high-stress conditions (Andersen, 1988; Williams, Tonymon, & Andersen, 1990, 1991). Similarly, Williams and Andersen (1997) found that athletes with high negative life event scores experienced slower central vision reaction time, in addition to peripheral narrowing. Andersen and Williams (1999) found that for athletes with low social support, negative life events along with changes in peripheral narrowing accounted for 26% of the variance in injury frequency. Similarly, Rogers and Landers (2005) found that peripheral narrowing during stress mediated 8.1% of the negative life events–athletic injury relationship.

Preventive Intervention

Researchers have found consistent support for the benefit of psychological intervention in reducing injury susceptibility (Johnson, Ekgenren, & Andersen, 2005; Kerr & Goss, 1996; Maddison & Prapavessis, 2005; May & Brown, 1989; Perna, Antoni, Baum, Gordon, & Schneiderman, 2003). May and Brown (1989) found that attention control, imagery, and various psychological skills led to reduced injuries, increased self-confidence, and enhanced self-control among skiers in the 1998 Winter Olympics. Johnson et al. (2005) found that athletes receiving a psychological skills training intervention (e.g., somatic and cognitive relaxation, stress management skills, goal setting skills, attribution and self-confidence training) experienced significantly fewer injuries (i.e., three injuries across three players) compared to a control group (i.e., 21 injuries across 13 players) during the subsequent competitive soccer season. Maddison and Prapavessis (2005) used a cognitive-behavioral stress management program for athletes identified as at risk (either low in social support or high in avoidance coping or both). Athletes in the treatment group reported less injury time loss than an at-risk athlete control group, as well as decreases in worry and improved coping. Although not all studies have shown psychological interventions to be effective in reducing injury risk (e.g., Amason, Engerbretsen, & Bahr, 2005), targeting at-risk athletes may be worthwhile from a cost and time perspective.

THE REHABILITATION PHASE

Although stage theories played a seminal role in thinking about athletic injury, they have been deemed largely inadequate for capturing the complexity and range of athletes' psychological response to injury. Empirically, it appears that the scholarship clusters into two areas: intrapersonal psychological responses and interpersonal interactions in injury rehabilitation.

Intrapersonal Psychological Responses

Research on psychological factors has focused on cognitive appraisals, emotional reactions, and behavioral responses. Substantial support has accumulated for cognitive appraisal models in general and the integrated model in particular (Brewer, 2007).

Cognitions. A range of post-injury cognitions has been identified, including attributions for injury occurrence, self-perceptions following injury, cognitively based coping strategies, and perceived injury benefits. Athletes have attributed their injuries to behavioral (San Jose, 2003; Tedder & Biddle, 1998) and mechanical/technical factors (Brewer, 1999b). Self-perceptions of esteem and worth have been shown to diminish following injury in some studies (e.g., Leddy, Lambert, & Ogles, 1994) but not in others (e.g., Smith et al., 1993). Cognitive appraisals of the potential benefits of injury have been described (e.g., opportunity to develop nonsport interests, viewing injury as a test of character, and enhanced appreciation for sport; Podlog & Eklund, 2006; Rose & Jevne, 1993; Tracey, 2003; Gould et al.1997a&b).

Quinn and Fallon (1999) found time differences in sport self-confidence over the course of rehabilitation, with confidence levels high at the commencement of injury, declining during rehabilitation, and increasing on attaining recovery. Unfortunately, there is little other study of change in appraisal over time and how this is related to recovery.

Emotions. Athletes' emotional reactions to injury (loss, denial, frustration, anger, and depression)

are consistent with those described in the original Kubler-Ross stage models (Gordon & Lindgren, 1990; Mainwaring, 1999; Sparkes, 1998; Tracey, 2003, Gould et al., 1997a&b). Positive emotions, such as happiness, relief, and excitement, have been reported as well (Podlog & Eklund, 2010). The attainment of rehabilitation goals and the prospect of recovery may engender a host of positive emotional responses throughout the course of rehabilitation. It appears these responses are influenced by a wide array of personal and situational factors (e.g., athletic identity, previous injury experience, injury severity, injury type, current injury status, life stress, social support satisfaction, timing of the injury; Albinson & Petrie, 2003; Alzate Saez de Heredia, Ramirez, & Lazaro, 2004; Bianco, Malo, & Orlick, 1999; Brewer, 1993; Green & Weinberg, 2001; Johnston & Carroll, 1998a; Manuel et al., 2002; Smith, Scott, O'Fallon, & Young, 1990; Smith et al., 1993; Sparkes, 1998).

In support of the integrated model and the affective cycle of injury, it has been shown that emotions typically fluctuate in response to rehabilitation progress and/or setbacks (Crossman, Gluck, & Jamieson, 1995; Leddy et al., 1994; Macchi & Crossman, 1996). As would be expected from both models, emotional states move from negative to positive as athletes progress through their rehabilitation and return to competition draws nearer (see Brewer, 2007, for a review). Interestingly, studies have shown an increase in negative affect as the return to sport approaches, owing possibly to anxieties over reinjury and the uncertainty of what lies ahead, as well as concerns that post-injury goals may be unrealized (Crossman et al., 1995; Ford & Gordon, 1998; Johnston & Carroll, 1998b; Johnston & Carroll, 2000; Morrey, Stuart, Smith, & Wiese-Bjornstal, 1999). Alternately, return to sport may be viewed as a functional reality check, challenging denial that may have falsely bolstered athlete expectation. In summary, individual differences in emotional response over the course of rehabilitation are varied, complex and non-sequential.

Behaviors. The use of psychological coping skills and adherence to rehabilitation have received the greatest amount of research attention. Personal factors linked to adherence including pain tolerance (Byerly, Worrell, Gahimer, & Domholdet, 1994; Fisher, Domm, & Wuest, 1988), self-motivation (Brewer, Daly, Van Raalte, Petitpas, & Sklar, 1999; Duda, Smart, & Tappe, 1989; Fields, Murphey, Horodyski, & Stopka, 1995), tough-mindedness

(Wittig & Schurr, 1994), perceived injury severity (Taylor & May, 1996), internal health locus of control (Murphy, Foreman, Simpson, Molloy, & Molloy, 1999), self-efficacy (Milne, Hall, & Forwell, 2005; Daly, Brewer, Van Raalte, Petitpas, & Sklar, 1995), and self-esteem (Lampton, Lambert, & Yost, 1993) have all been positively associated with rehabilitation adherence. In contrast mood disturbance (Alzate Saez de Heredia et al., 2004; Daly et al., 1995) and fear of reinjury (Pizzari, McBurney, Taylor, & Feller, 2002; Walker, Thatcher, & Lavallee, 2010) are negatively associated.

Adherence has been positively associated with clinical outcome (e.g. proprioception, range of motion, muscular endurance) in a number of investigations (e.g., Alzate Saez de Heredia et al., 2004; Brewer et al., 2004; Pizzari, Taylor, McBurney, & Feller, 2005). However, nonsignificant (Brewer et al., 2000; Feller, Webster, Taylor, Payne, & Pizzari, 2004) and negative relationships (Feller et al., 2004; Pizzari et al., 2005; Shelbourne & Wickens, 1990) have also been found. The negative relationship in particular is likely a function of methodological problems. Although it is a simple matter to get measures of compliance (e.g., attendance), assessing the more subtle elements (e.g., motivation and psychological coping behaviors) is much more difficult. In fact, active coping responses, such as use of positive self-talk (Scherzer et al., 2001), imagery (Milne et al., 2005; Scherzer et al., 2001), goal-setting (Penpraze & Mutrie, 1999; Evans & Hardy, 2002), and seeking out additional information about injury (Udry, 1997), are also associated with adherence.

In addition, situational factors, mostly related to perception of treatment, also predict adherence. These include belief in the efficacy of the treatment (Brewer et al., 2003a; Duda et al., 1989; Taylor & May, 1996), information about rehabilitation (Pizzari et al., 2002), the clinical environment (Fields et al., 1995; Fisher et al., 1988; Pizzari et al., 2002), value of rehabilitation to the athlete (Taylor & May, 1996), and hours per week of sport involvement (Johnston & Carroll, 2000).

Psychological interventions that have demonstrated efficacy in enhancing the rate or quality of sport injury rehabilitation include goal setting (Theodorakis, Beneca, Malliou, & Goudas, 1997; Theodorakis, Malliou, Papaioannou, Beneca, & Filactakidou, 1996) imagery and relaxation (Cupal & Brewer, 2001), and stress inoculation (Ross & Berger, 1996). Similarly, the use of self-directed cognitive coping strategies predicts favorable outcomes (accepting injury, focusing on getting better,

thinking positive and using imagery; Bianco et al., 1999; Gould et al., 1997b1997; Rose & Jevne, 1993; Quinn & Fallon, 1999). There is also speculation that psychological factors may expedite the recovery process through neurochemical or physiological changes (e.g., increased blood flow, enhanced proprioception, muscular endurance and strength, coordination), but empirical support is lacking (Cupal, 1998; Heil, 1993; Bianco & Eklund, 2001).

Interpersonal Interactions

Patient–practitioner interactions, mainly those between the athlete and athletic trainer/sport physiotherapist, have been found to be crucial factors influencing athletes' psychological state, the quality of their rehabilitation experiences, and eventual treatment outcomes (Brewer, Van Raalte, & Petitpas, 2007; Francis, Andersen, & Maley, 2000; Larson, Starkey, & Zaichkowsky, 1996; Wiese, Weiss, & Yukelson, 1991). Given the close proximity and regularity of contact, sport medicine professionals are uniquely positioned to play an influential role in the psychological well-being of injured athletes, through behavioral intervention, as well as through effective psychological triage and referral (Gordon, Potter, & Ford, 1998; Larson et al., 1996). Positive behaviors exhibited by rehabilitation specialists include the provision of social support (Bianco & Eklund, 2001; Hardy, Burke, & Crace, 1999; Robbins & Rosenfeld, 2001); building patient alliances based on acceptance, genuineness, and empathy (Petitpas & Cornelius, 2004); effective communication (Wiese-Bjornstal, Gardetto, & Shaffer, 1999); and counseling (Ray, Terrell, & Hough, 1999). Conversely, poor athletic trainer–athlete relations and a lack of effective communication were perceived barriers to rehabilitation adherence (Granquist, Podlog, & Engel, 2010). The influence of the medical professional can (and should) go beyond treatment of the physical ramifications of injury to address the psychosocial consequences.

Additionally, it is important for sport medicine practitioners to facilitate psychological referral when confronted with issues (e.g., clinical depression) beyond their expertise (Brewer, Petitpas, & Van Raalte, 1999; Heil, 1993). Although they are well positioned to complement physical rehabilitation and believed capable of doing so, rehabilitation specialists have indicated they do not always feel adequately prepared or skilled to address such concerns (Ford & Gordon, 1998; Gordon et al., 1991, 1998). In recognition of this, organizations such as the National Athletic Trainers Association (NATA) now require demonstrated competence in dealing with the psychosocial aspects of injury. Clearly, sport medicine professionals require a range of skills in promoting effective patient–practitioner interactions and in ensuring the holistic (physical and psychological) recovery of injured athletes.

THE RETURN TO SPORT TRANSITION

Increasing recognition that physical healing does not necessarily coincide with psychological readiness for return to play has spawned research on the return to play transition (Glazer, 2009; Podlog & Eklund, 2005, 2006; 2007a,b, 2009; Walker et al., 2010). Return to sport challenges include heightened performance anxiety (Gould et al., 1997b), anxieties over reinjury (Kvist, Ek, Sporrstedt, & Good, 2005), diminished physical self-efficacy (Andersen, 2001), concerns about performing at pre-injury levels (Evans, Hardy, & Fleming, 2000), and uncertainties about meeting the expectations of others (Taylor, Stone, Mullin, Ellenbecker, & Walgenbach, 2003). Further complicating the return to sport transition are loss of identity, feelings of disconnectedness from teammates (Petitpas & Danish, 1995), and, coercive and/or subtle pressures to return from coaches, teammates, and family members (Andersen, 2001). For example, Canadian national team skiers indicated that they returned to competition prematurely to avoid negative judgments from coaches and to meet specific return deadlines (Bianco, 2001).

Podlog and Eklund (2005, 2006, 2007a,b, 2009, 2010) conducted a series of investigations examining the role of motivation in return to play following injury using self-determination theory (SDT; Ryan & Deci, 2000). High-level athletes from Canada, Australia, and England ($n = 180$) reported greater intrinsic motivation to return to sport (e.g., the joy of the game, desire to achieve, and personal satisfaction) than extrinsic motivations (e.g., the need to please others or to avoid feelings of guilt; Podlog & Eklund, 2005). These quantitative findings were bolstered in a longitudinal qualitative investigation in which 12 elite Australian and Canadian athletes reported a predominance of intrinsic motives to return to sport (Podlog & Eklund, 2006). In a subsequent investigation with 225 professional Australian football league players, Podlog and Eklund (2010) found that greater intrinsic (vs. extrinsic) motivations resulted in more positive appraisals and emotions and diminished perceptions of threat, unfairness, and potential ego damage. Podlog and

Eklund (2005) found that intrinsic motivation was positively associated with a "renewed perspective on sport" (e.g., greater sport appreciation, heightened motivation for success, enhanced mental toughness), whereas extrinsic motivation was positively associated with "return concerns" (e.g., diminished confidence, unsatisfying performances, heightened competitive anxiety).

Podlog, Lochbaum, and Stevens (2010) examined the need satisfaction components of SDT, predicting that higher satisfaction of the needs for competence, autonomy, and relatedness (i.e., interconnectedness) during rehabilitation would predict greater well-being and enhanced return to sport outcomes (e.g., greater sport appreciation, enhanced mental toughness, heightened motivation for sport success). They found that positive affect partially mediated the relationship between competence and autonomy need satisfaction and a renewed perspective on sport, and that negative affect, self-esteem, and vitality fully mediated the relationship between relatedness need satisfaction and return concerns.

The Psychological Readiness to Return to Sport Scale (I-PPRS; Glazer, 2009) and the Re-Injury Anxiety Inventory (RIA; Walker et al., 2010) have been developed to assess athletes' psychological mind set during the re-entry period. The I-PPRS consists of six items in which athletes are asked to rate dimensions of confidence on a scale from 0 to 100. Initial validation of the instrument suggests that it is a reliable and valid measure. Given its concise nature, the I-PPRS can be easily administered by health practitioners in the rehabilitation setting. The RIA is a 28-item measure of two factors: anxieties regarding rehabilitation (RIA-R: 15 items) and anxieties regarding reinjury at return to play (RIA-RE: 13 items). Walker et al. (2010) take care to differentiate fear (a flight or fight response to danger) from anxiety (uncertainty, worry or concern), believing that anxiety more precisely captures the athletes state of mind. Reliability measures, as well as face, content, and factorial validity, provide strong preliminary evidence for the psychometric utility of this inventory, rendering it a useful tool in the identification of at-risk athletes.

Head Injury and Concussion

Head injury and concussion have become a topic of widespread public interest, with increasing media attention devoted to the short- and long-term effects of concussive incidents. For example, in a *Time* magazine article entitled "Our Favorite Sport Is Too Dangerous; How to Make the game Safer",

Sean Gregory highlighted the concussive dangers present in professional football and suggested a number of changes for making the game safer, including rule changes, changes in equipment and training, and concussion management for youth coaches (Gregory, 2010). However, Gregory suggests that these measures would be insufficient without a significant change in the culture of professional football whereby "bravery," "bravado" and "machismo" (p. 42) lead to denial of pain and injury, ultimately jeopardizing health needlessly. It appears that the admirable ethics of fraternal bonds and commitment to the team are unfortunately enmeshed with poorly calculated risk taking and the idea of injury as a badge of courage. As troublesome as the consequences of head injury are in the professional game, the greater concern lies with youth and developmental athletes for whom pro players are role models. A more balanced and better informed risk–benefit approach to pain and injury management is likely to benefit both health and performance from the top to the bottom of the game. A more detailed discussion of the culture of injury risk is provided in a subsequent section.

The widespread media attention devoted to head injury and concussion is not mere journalistic sensationalism. On the contrary, epidemiological studies indicate that sport-related concussion occurs at a troublesome rate across a wide variety of sports, particularly in contact sports such as rugby (Kahanov, Dusa, Wilksinson, & Roberts, 2005; Koh, Cassidy, & Watkinson, 2003), ice-hockey (Tegner & Lorentzon, 1996; Williamson & Goodman, 2006), and football (Guskiewicz et al., 2003). Although the clinical course is typically of short duration (i.e., 10–14 days) and may resolve spontaneously, long-term problems can occur including cognitive deficit, depression, and cumulative deterioration in brain function (Straume-Naesheim, Andersen, Dvorak, & Bahr, 2005). Unfortunately, uncertainties regarding the extent of damage and the limitations of measures of recovery make the diagnosis, treatment, and return to play decision surrounding head injury particularly challenging (Makdissi, 2010). Further complicating the matter is the need for service providers to rely on athletes to truthfully and accurately report their symptoms. Athletes may fail to report their symptoms given a strong desire to compete and the belief that one must play with pain and injury. Alternatively, athletes may be unaware that they have suffered a concussion, given a lack of understanding of its signs and symptoms (Valovich McLeod, Heil, McVeigh, & Bay, 2006). However,

the increasing array and sophistication of assessment methods, along with innovative research linking force of impact to symptom production (Rowson, Goforth, Dietter, Brolinson, & Duma, 2009) show great promise in identifying severity of injury and in decision-making regarding safe return to play.

Taking into account the individual nature of the concussion experience and the range of assessment methods, it is not surprising that no single assessment and management plan has been adopted by injury practitioners. For example, Notebaert and Guskiewicz (2005) found that certified athletic trainers employed a range of concussion assessment methods, including clinical examination (95%), symptom checklists (85%), Standardized Assessment of Concussion (48%), neurological testing (18%), and the Balance Error Scoring System, a measure of postural stability (16%). When deciding whether to return an athlete to play, most trainers used the clinical examination (95%), return to play guidelines (88%), symptom checklists (80%), and player self-report (62%). Interestingly, only 3% of all athletic trainers surveyed complied with the NATA position statement, which advocated using symptom checklists, neuropsychological testing, *and* balance testing for managing sport-related concussions (Guskiewicz, Bruce, Cantu, Ferrara, Kelly, McCrea, et al., 2004). These results highlight the need to ensure that concussion diagnosis and treatment plans include a combination of methods and tools to ensure athlete's readiness to return to play and to diminish the likelihood of sustaining a repeated concussion (Eckner & Kutcher, 2010).

Although a comprehensive concussion management plan is beyond the scope of this chapter, researchers currently suggest the combined use of symptom checklists, neuropsychological testing, and postural stability assessment (Broglio & Guskiewicz, 2009; Guskiewicz & Cantu, 2004; Oliaro, Anderson, & Hooker, 2001). Baseline testing on all measures should be conducted whenever feasible to establish the individual athlete's "normal" preinjury performance and to provide reliable benchmarks against which to measure postinjury recovery (Guskiewicz et al., 2004). Symptom checklists determine concussion severity and persistence based on assessment of retrograde and anterograde amnesia, loss of consciousness, headache, concentration problems, dizziness, and blurred vision. To assist in this process, commonly employed checklists such as the Graded Symptom Checklist (GSC) are recommended for use at initial evaluation and at subsequent follow-up assessment (Guskiewicz et al., 2004).

Neuropsychological testing should also be conducted using some combination of paper-and-pencil (e.g., controlled oral Word Association Test, Hopkins Verbal Learning Test, Trail Making: Parts A & B) and computerized neuropsychological tests (e.g., CogSport, Concussion Resolution Index, Immediate Postconcussion Assessment and Cognitive Testing—ImPACT). Assessment protocols should include measures of cognitive abilities that are commonly disrupted after concussion, including attention and concentration, cognitive processing speed and efficiency, learning and memory, working memory, executive function, and verbal fluency (Guskiewicz et al., 2004). Neuropsychological assessments have been demonstrated to be more sensitive than most standard medical diagnostic imaging (i.e., magnetic resonance imagery [MRIs]) in detecting cognitive deficits following concussion (see Guskiewicz et al., 2004, for a description of commonly used neuropsychological tests). Postural stability/balance testing, such as the Sensory Organization Test (SOT) and the Balance Error Scoring System (BESS), should accompany the use of symptom checklists and neuropsychological testing. Research with these measures shows that the greatest postural deficits were seen 24 hours post-concussion, with athletes demonstrating a gradual recovery during a 5-day period to within 6% of baseline scores (Guskiewicz, Ross, & Marshall, 2001; Peterson, Ferra, Mrazik, & Piland, 2003).

Comprehensive concussion management plans are detailed by Camiolo Reddy and Collins (2009), Guskiewicz et al. (2004), and Oliaro, Anderson, and Hooker (2001). The 2004 NATA position statement (Guskiewicz et al., 2004) includes recommendations for defining and recognizing concussion, making return to play decisions, and a discussion of concussion assessment tools. It also provides guidance on when to refer an athlete to a physician after concussion, when to disqualify an athlete from further sport involvement, special considerations for the young athlete, home care, and, finally, equipment issues.

Because head injury is a relatively common event, often occurring in the absence of medical personnel, it requires grass roots attention. Given the significance of cognitive symptoms in head injury, the skill set and knowledge of the sport psychologist is well suited to identification and management. Consequently, it would be prudent, at a minimum, to include training in head injury assessment sufficient for the sport psychologist to be an effective "first responder" in head injury situations.

Catastrophic and Fatal Injury

Catastrophic sport injury includes fatality, as well as nonfatal brain or spinal cord injury, and skull or spinal fracture (Zemper, 2009). Unlike head injury and concussion, which occur with unfortunate and sometimes predictable regularity, the incidence of catastrophic and fatal injuries in sport is quite low, even in collision sports (Fuller, 2008; Zemper, 2009). For example Fuller (2008) reports the following injury rates: ice hockey (4/100,000 per year), rugby league (2/100,000 per year), and American Football (2/100,000 per year). The National Center for Catastrophic Injury Research at the University of North Carolina indicates that catastrophic injuries among young athletes are rare (Zemper, 2009).

The impact of catastrophic injury is often psychologically devastating for both the athlete and those in his or her inner circle (Zemper, 2009). In a series of recent investigations, Brett Smith and Andrew Sparkes documented the complex challenges associated with disablement by sport-induced spinal cord injury (Rees, Smith, & Sparkes, 2003; Smith & Sparkes, 2002; Sparkes & Smith, 2005, 2002). In interviews with 14 male rugby union players, the core challenge was identified as "restorying" a life and constructing new body–self relationships and identities (Sparkes & Smith, 2005). Three narrative types emerged: restitution (centered on the return to a "former self" and the "fight to make a comeback"), chaos (a "shattered" sense of self), and quest (accept impairment and disability and *use* the disability to gain from the experience). In embracing a quest narrative, one former rugby player invoked the metaphors of being reborn, stating "My life has changed since the accident and I'm now on a journey. This isn't a tragic journey though. No, I've been reborn, and have become a better person since becoming disabled" (p. 85).

Noncatastrophic career-ending medical injuries may have a catastrophic psychological impact, initiating existential uncertainties about one's life purpose, identity crises, and questions about one's value as a human being (Kleiber & Brock, 1992; Thomas & Rintala, 1989; Sparkes & Smith, 2002). Injury is potentially the most distressful path to career cessation (Lavallee, 2000) and is most disruptive in those with strong athletic identity (Brewer, 1993).

Although fortunately infrequent, fatal injuries are more common in high-risk sports, such as extreme mountaineering, and among those who are high-risk takers. Whatever the setting, the impact of fatal injury is potentially devastating for survivors (e.g., teammates, coaches, family members; Krakauer, 1998;

Henschen & Heil, 1992; Vernacchia, Reardon, & Templin, 1997). Henschen and Heil (1992) conducted follow-up interviews with ten collegiate football players 4 years after they witnessed the death of a teammate during weight training. They reported having continued memories of their deceased teammate and described specific triggering events (e.g., the interview itself, the word "Hawaii"—the deceased teammates birthplace) that continued to elicit "deep emotions" and memories of the event. The athletes commented: "I now appreciate what I have," and "I wonder about how frail our existence really is" (p. 222). The research study was triggered by observation of an usually high level of injury reported the week following the event.

Vernacchia et al. (1997) examined the emotional reactions of teammates and coaches following the heart-attack death of a collegiate basketball player. Confounding the grief process was the need to make a decision about competing even as they moved through a grieving process. A series of stages of grief and recovery were identified including shock, confusion, and denial; performance resolve; realization of loss; glorification and memorialization; closure and relief; avoidance and debriefing; and, finally, reentry and acceptance.

Mass-casualty and high-profile sport-centered catastrophic events may also exert a potent influence on athletes, even though they or their teammates may not be directly victimized. The horror of the hostage taking and killing of Israeli athletes at the Munich Olympics in 1972 had a profound impact, with the Games suspended for 34 hours and with many athletes experiencing ambivalence regarding competing (Wallechinsky, 1984). Similarly, the 2007 Virginia Tech Shootings had a profound impact on the athletic programs, even though no athletes were directly threatened by the shooter. Subsequently, the sports medicine team engaged in a "lessons learned" exercise to gain perspective on the event, identify best practices, and offer advice to other athletic programs that might encounter similar events (Heil, Bennett, Brolinson, & Goforth, 2009). Key themes identified include sports medicine team members immediate personal response and protracted period of emotional adjustment; the need to redefine professional roles, given the scope and severity of the crisis; and the importance of balancing respect for the dead and care for the living as athletic teams returned to training and competition. The report highlights the critical function played by sports events as turning points in the process of healing and recovery for the university community,

along with the unique burden thus placed on student athletes. The experience led the sport medicine practitioners to rethink their assumptions about what constitutes a sport-related trauma—from an event that occurs on the playing field to one that has a significant impact on athlete well-being.

Methods for critical incident stress management, initially developed by trauma specialists for response to public safety critical incidents and high-profile catastrophes, have been adopted for response to sports-related incidents (Malone, Fox, & Mulvey, 2008; Stapleton, Heil, Bennett, & Hankes, 2007). The nature of the intervention varies greatly based on the specific nature of the event, the timeline of service delivery, intervention setting, and the relationship between the providers and the traumatized group. The methods range from the pragmatic, like Psychological First Aid (Brymer et al., 2006) to the philosophic. Fisher and Wrisberg (2005) suggest that sports medicine professionals can help athletes cope with catastrophic injury by cultivating a Buddhist perspective; that is by embracing the "middle path"—teaching athletes how to grieve and let go, accepting what happens and learning from it, having a philosophic attitude toward loss, and allowing the natural pain to occur and working through it.

Athletes and sports organizations face difficult choices in times of catastrophe, as demonstrated by the impact on sport of the September 11, 2001 (9/11) terrorist attacks in the days after. U.S. Fencing was the first American national team to travel outside the United States. After a lively open e-mail debate that focused on the possible risk of travel versus the certain loss of succumbing to terrorism, the team went forward, albeit with extra security precautions (e.g., Soter, personal communication). Remarkably, athletes also have the potential to be agents for positive influence in times of great crisis. Consider the role played by soccer star Didier Drogba and the Ivory Coast Soccer Team in defusing the tensions of civil war in their nation, and then, in 2010, stepping up to help salvage the African Cup of Nations after a terrorist attack (Martin, 2010). Given the gravity, complexity, and emotional tone of such events, there is clearly a role for psychology.

Performance Psychology

To a significant extent, the measure of the worth of a discipline is its ability to reach beyond its apparent scope to make a broader contribution. For all the opportunities for change and improvement that have been thus far identified within sport psychology, the psychology of sport injury has much to offer other performing disciplines, such as dance and the performing arts, the military, and public safety. In addition, there is much to offer general medical populations, especially when vigorous physical rehabilitation is critical to recovery and when there is pressure for timely return to performance, for instance with injured workers (Heil, Wakefield, & Reed, 1998).

The link between psychological factors and injury has been examined among performing artists, military, and public safety personnel, with results quite similar to athletes (Gregg, Banderet, Reynolds, Creedon, & Rice, 2002). Sport and performance psychologists have devoted much of their research focus to ballet dancers, likely because of the similarities in physical and performance demands between dancers and athletes (e.g., Adam, Brassington, Steiner, & Matheson, 2004; Liderbach & Compagno, 2001; Novaco, 2005). Findings suggest that negative life events, competitive anxiety, sleep disturbance, negative mood, fatigue, eating disorders, and obsessive passion (vs. harmonious passion; Rip, Fortin, & Vallerand, 2006) are associated with increased injury risk among dancers. Dancers with an internal locus of control are more likely to train through and perform with injury (Allen, 2000). Psychological intervention, including use of autogenic training, imagery, and self-talk, led to reduced time spent injured among ballet dancers (Morris & Noh, 2007). Finally, social support has been shown to moderate the stress–injury relationship among dancers (Patterson, Smith, & Everett, 1998).

Injury Context: A Culture of Risk

Although injury is an individual experience, its impact is shared, experienced, and modulated via social relationships on the field of play, in the treatment setting, and within the athlete's personal circle of confidants and family members. Although injury may have a profound impact on the athlete's psychological well-being, it also affects coaches, teammates, and others whose goals and ambitions may suffer along with the injured athlete. Moreover, coaches, teammates, training partners, and health practitioners form a social network upon which athletes rely as they cope with injury (Andersen, 2007).

It is also important to appreciate the influence of sport institutions on athletes' values, attitudes, and injury-related behaviors. Sport is a collective enterprise with a dizzying array of stakeholders, including sports organizations (from local clubs to professional teams) and national governing bodies, as well as fans, the media, and marketers of sports equipment. Each of these entities is a potential agent of change, with a unique and distinct investment in the prevailing culture. Their stake in the game varies dramatically from the well-being of the players, to personal entertainment, to the financial viability of a commercial product, with the inevitable clashes that such diverse goals engender.

Over the past 20 years, a growing body of sociological research has contributed to a greater understanding of the sport norms, values, and environments that are linked to injury occurrence (e.g., Hughes & Coakley, 1991; Messner, 1992; Nixon, 1992, 1993, 1994, 1996; Roderick, 1998; Young, 2004). Much of this research examines the personal experiences of injured athletes (Smith & Sparkes, 2002), the ways in which athletes internalize "macho" and gendered beliefs about playing with pain and injury (e.g., Messner, 1992; Young, McTeer, & White, 1994), and the "normalization" of pain and injury (Albert, 1999; Nixon, 1993). From a sociological perspective, injury risk increases to the extent that a culture narrowly defines success according to win–loss records, values external forms of success (e.g., prize money, scholarships, media attention, etc.) over intrinsic achievement, and promotes an unquestioning adoption or overconformity to the norms of a "sport ethic" that cultivates a culture of risk.

The "sport ethic" promotes laudable values, such as sacrifice for the game, demonstrating character by playing with pain and injury, seeking distinction through achievement, and challenging limits (Hughes & Coakley, 1991). However, when these values are paired with a shortsighted and overly simplistic approach (e.g., "Winners never quit and quitters never win") to assessing the cost–benefit of risky behaviors, the athlete may suffer needlessly, with both compromised health and diminished performance (Frey, 1991; Nixon, 1994a,b; Young & White, 1999). This simplistic thinking can result in a rigid conformity to the sport ethic, overidentification with one's role as an athlete, poor decision-making regarding risk, and, ultimately, the occurrence of avoidable health-damaging behaviors (Curry, 1993; Curry & Strauss, 1994; Malcom, 2006; Messner, 1990, 1992; Nixon, 1992, 1993). This may include failure to adopt injury prevention measures (such as use of safety equipment and appropriate warm-up), pushing through pain when a signal of impending injury is present, or exacerbating existing injury by disregarding medical limits

(Brewer, Van Raalte, & Linder, 1993; Curry, 1993; Frey, 1991; Hughes & Coakley, 1991; Kleiber & Brock, 1992; Malcolm, 2006; Nixon, 1992; Pike, 2004; Roderick, 2006).

Research offers insight into the role coaching practices may play in inadvertently undermining athlete well-being. In a study of British women rowers, Pike (2004) notes that women's risk-taking behaviors were exacerbated by negligent coaching practices as a performance-efficiency ethos took precedence over health and well-being. Similar coaching practices have been highlighted in professional English soccer, among cyclists (Albert, 2004), football and rodeo athletes (Frey, Preston, & Bernhard, 2004), and English female university athletes (Charlesworth & Young, 2004). In one of the few quantitative investigations, Shipherd and Eklund (2010) found that adolescent athletes typically exhibited a high degree of internalization of sport ethic norms and values. The high (vs. low) overconformers experienced a greater total number of injuries, greater injury severity, and more missed days of practice and competition.

The phenomenon of sacrificing one's body reaches to the roots of the Western sport experience, as evidenced in the legend of Pheidippides, whose death at the end of a run from Marathon to Athens to announce a military victory is memorialized in the modern marathon run. This all-out focus on victory over personal well-being has been documented in a series of qualitative investigations (Loland, 2006; Spitzer, 2006; Young, 2004). In a case study of Cold War era East German athletes, Spitzer (2006) describes how athletes were systematically doped and coerced to train through debilitating pain and injury in pursuit of Olympic glory, revealing a worst-case scenario of the coercive powers of a preemptive sport culture.

Although deeply entrenched, sports' culture of risk is not without its checks and balances, and is not impervious to change. In the 2009–2010 season, the National Football League implemented a shift in policy in head injury assessment and management, tantamount to a fundamental change in culture. The tipping point seems to have been the head injury suffered by prominent quarterback, Ben Roethlisberger. Following his reluctance to play until fully recovered, a controversy unfurled in the court of public opinion with input from the broad array of stakeholders (Sanserino, 2009). Previously, head injury (like any injury) was assessed and treated by team medical staff. Going forward, medical status and readiness for return to play will be addressed by independent examiners (Davis, 2011). This change is all the more noteworthy for the longstanding and recurrently resurgent concern with athlete safety (Guskiewicz et al., 2007) that has thus far met with only limited success—even with input from iconic figures like Hall of Fame player Johnny Unitas (Stewart & Kennedy, 2010) and legendary "ironman" Jim Otto (Couturie, Else, & Witte, 1986).

Negotiating the best path through the risk of athletic demise to the joys of high performance is a daunting task. Ideally, coaches should function as arbiters of the sport ethic on behalf of the athlete and in service of the goals for excellence that they share jointly. Health care providers, including psychologists, can assist coaches in this endeavor, by providing consultation to coaches on injury risk situations. Safai (2003) provides a model for managing overconformity to a "culture of risk" in her study of Canadian university athletes. She describes the ways in which athletes and medical team members (e.g., sport medicine doctors, physiotherapists) negotiated treatment through a three-way interplay among "a culture of risk," "a culture of precaution," and the promotion of the concept of "sensible risks." Safai's research suggests that this "culture of precaution" effectively balances risk taking when the notion of commitment to the desire to heal is central to the treatment plan.

To serve athletes effectively, sport injury specialists need an in-depth knowledge of the sporting subcultures and specific contexts in which injury occurs and recovery unfolds. Ultimately, all health practitioners must be willing to ask critical questions about the "culture of risk" that fosters sport injury. The psychologist is uniquely positioned to contribute to the debate on the implicit influence of culture and expectations on behavior, the means by which subtle incentives drive the system, and the spin-down impact of high-profile professional sport role models on youth, high school, and college athletes.

Future Directions for Research and Scholarship

Researchers from a variety of scholarly traditions have contributed to an ever-expanding body of knowledge of injury in sport and performance domains. However, there remains a need to develop more ecologically relevant investigative methodologies, to focus attention on injury populations that have been relatively neglected, and to complement the traditional pathology-focused thinking that permeates injury research with a positive psychology focus. Below, we outline ten salient, but by no means exhaustive, areas in need of further development.

First, the epistemological assumption that injury is a pathological condition neglects the positive elements of recovery and survivorship. Although, injury may undoubtedly elicit negative psychological states, it can be a learning experience that yields unanticipated benefits of personal growth and development. For instance, heightened motivation, a greater appreciation of one's sport, an elevated awareness of the need for injury prevention measures, and extra time to develop non–sport related capacities have been reported by athletes (Loberg, Houston, & Heil, 2008; Podlog & Eklund, 2005; Udry, 1999). Simply reframing injury rehabilitation as a competitive challenge may illuminate the ways in which injury can be a constructive or transformative event. The phenomenon of remarkable recovery (Heil, 2009; O'Connor, Heil, Harmer, & Zimmermann, 2005) is a compelling area of study with broad applicability in rehabilitation and high-performance training.

Second, while embracing a biopsychosocial model, researchers have typically examined physical, psychological, and social components of injury in isolation. There is a need for interdisciplinary collaborative research that illuminates the mind–body linkage, such as the studies on the role of peripheral vision change in injury risk (Williams & Andersen, 1997) and the impact of meditation on pain management (Astin, 2004). The increasing availability of functional brain scanning technologies (such as functional MRI [fMRI]) offers significant promise (Davis et al., 2008).

Third, future injury research would also profit from an expanded set of research methodologies that are more ecologically relevant and that provide a window into the lived experience of injury. This would mean continuing the trend toward qualitative approaches (e.g., Bianco, 2001; Johnston & Carroll, 1998; Tracey, 2003), as well as use of novel methodologies such as participant observation, action research (Gilbourne & Taylor, 1998), ethnodrama, emotional disclosure and journaling (Mankad, Gordon, & Wallman, 2009a,b), autoethnography (Sparkes, 1998), lessons-learned methodology (Heil et al., 2009), and narrative analysis (Smith & Sparkes, 2002). Mankad et al. (2009a), for example, conducted a 3-day writing intervention, consisting of three 20-minute writing sessions, during which athletes disclosed negative emotions associated with injury and rehabilitation. A psycholinguistic analysis of writing samples revealed that increasing self-awareness correlated with improved psychological status, thus reinforcing the value of emotional disclosure and cognitive integration in injury.

Fourth, there are obvious ethical and pragmatic limitations on true experimental designs based on manipulation of independent variables (e.g., creating more or less favorable circumstances under which athletes return to sport, applying pressure to return on some athletes but not others). However, use of cross-sectional and longitudinal analyses offer a unique insight into the impact of events over a longer time horizon (Young, 2004). Although challenges are associated with multiple time point data collections, the increasing deployment of injury surveillance systems offers an excellent opportunity for gathering applied clinical data using quasi-experimental and repeated measures designs (Campbell & Stanley, 1966). Work by Van Heerden on a clinical assessment system that collects contemporaneous, psychological self-report data and is designed for use in medical settings shows promise (e.g., Van Heerden & Potgieter, 2003)

Fifth, there is a need for research with concrete dependent variables. Sport psychology research needs to move beyond associations of "pen-and-paper" tests with other "pen-and-paper" tests (e.g., McDonald & Hardy, 1990). It is essential to determine if interventions result in behavioral outcomes, such as reduced reinjury occurrence, enhanced functional rehabilitation (e.g., greater proprioception), or improved post-injury performance. Researchers need to capitalize on the penchant of competitive sport for putting behavior to numbers and find a way to integrate the ready-made datasets into research.

Sixth, there is a need for critical sociologically based investigations on the role of competitive sport environments in the adoption of sport norms and values that may increase injury risk. Young (2004) highlights some specific concerns, including the role of the media in reporting and influencing expectations about pain tolerance and risk taking, the role of sport in behaviors such as eating disorders and the use of performance enhancing drugs, and variations in cultural norms based on gender and level of competitive play. Investigation into "best practice" communication and intervention strategies for health practitioners who may encounter health-compromising situations in athletes driven by sport values has obvious pragmatic value.

Seventh, most work has focused on acute injury, leaving the unique challenges faced by athletes with chronic injuries relatively neglected. It appears that chronically injured athletes are more likely to experience pressures to return to sport as a consequence of poor understanding of the mechanisms underlying such injury and uncertain rehabilitation timelines (Pike, 2004; Podlog & Eklund, 2007). Coaches, teammates, and others may express greater skepticism toward the "legitimacy" of chronic injury, thus setting up a destructive interpersonal dynamic that can further complicate recovery. Malingering also remains a controversial issue in sport and medical populations, one plagued by poor understanding and generating highly charged and potentially destructive encounters between athlete and providers (Heil, 1993; Rotella, Ogilvie & Perrin, 1999).

Eighth, research has focused on highly competitive athletes at the peak of physical prowess. There is a need to identify age-specific differences regarding the subjective experience and consequences of injury, particularly in younger, developing athletes (Wiese-Bjornstal, 2004). Children, adolescents, and adults of various ages differ in their psychological response to injury (Weiss, 2004), with important age-related differences in psychological readiness for surgery (Udry, Shelbourne, & Gray, 2003), postoperative pain (Tripp, Stanish, Reardon, Coady, & Sullivan, 2003), and adherence to rehabilitation following knee surgery (Brewer, Cornelius, Van Raalte, & Petitpas, 2003a; see special edition of *Athletic Training*, 2003). There is also a need to identify age-appropriate interventions, especially for children (Donnelly, 2003; Loberg, Houston, & Heil, 2008). With increasing involvement in formal sports competition across the lifespan and the growth of the Senior Games, there is also cause to give attention to the unique needs of the graying athlete (Dionigi, 2006). The Paralympic movement is also on the rise. The combination of functional limits and complex medical needs renders this group unique among athletes, even as the competitive zeal and commitment to training of some give them much in common with their elite able-bodied counterparts (Wu & Williams, 1999).

Ninth, head injury and concussion, as well as catastrophic injury, have seen vigorous and extensive research and innovation in treatment within the medical professions. However, sport psychology has lagged in addressing the concerns associated with head injury and catastrophic injury, as well as with career-ending injury. These athlete groups have both significant medical and psychological issues. Given the frequency of head injury and its significant but often subtle psychological sequelae, sport

psychologists need to define a role for themselves in the evolving head injury management systems.

Finally, there is a need to move forward with theory-driven research (e.g., self-regulation theory, personal investment theory, SDT). For example, Podlog and Eklund (2007) outlined the value of SDT (see also Chapter 12, this volume) as a framework for interpreting and bringing coherence to the diverse array of findings regarding the return to sport from injury. The many and varied injury models (e.g., Williams & Andersen's [1998] stress-injury model; Wiese-Bjornstal et al.'s [1998] integrated model of response to sport injury) provide a useful framework for conceptualizing research and intervention. However, a model is not a theory, and as a consequence does not (and cannot) provide an internally consistent, coherent explanation that affords specific predictions and assists in outlining intervention strategies.

Significant gains in the psychology of sport injury have been made regarding knowledge of injury antecedents, cognitive and emotional responses to injury, and the factors influencing injury rehabilitation and the return to sport. Knowledge of effective methods for reducing and effectively treating the various types of injuries (i.e., acute musculoskeletal, chronic, head, fatal and catastrophic) remains an essential task for injury researchers and applied practitioners. Collaborative and cross-disciplinary scholarship employing a range of research methodologies that focus on age-appropriate interventions and that adopt a positive psychology perspective would assist toward this end.

Intervention

Because injury implicitly elicits a sense of threat and loss, it is a psychologically laden experience. Within the last 20 years, psychologists have defined a role as injury management providers, making significant advances in knowledge base, treatment methods, and service delivery. Sport-specific injury intervention has developed from a synthesis of cognitive-behavioral therapy and high-performance psychology. This is reflected in a series of texts focused specifically on the psychology of injury (Heil, 1993; Pargman, 1993, 1999; Taylor & Taylor, 1997). Psychologists were also quick to recognize the critical psychological role played by sports medicine providers, with each of the works referenced including specific content for medical providers. Furthermore, training in sport psychology skills has empowered athletes not only in performance but also in injury rehabilitation. An overview of the current state of practice and identification of specific roles in the psychology of injury for this broad array of potential service providers follows.

Psychologists

Practically speaking, few clinical or sport psychologists are true sport injury specialists. Psychologists who work with injured athletes are not a homogenous group, do not typically share a common set of knowledge and skills, and bring varying resources to injury intervention. In addition, sport injury providers' relationships within the medical and sport systems uniquely influence their accessibility to athletes, their opportunity to intervene with other potential service providers, and the nature of the service they can deliver. Hence, they will have knowledge and skills that are diverse, relative to the norm in traditional medical practice.

Physician and Sports Medicine Therapists

The sports medicine therapist and physician often function as primary care providers for psychological distress in the injured athlete. Bringing psychological mindedness to injury management will help improve outcomes and enhance quality of care. Triage and timely referral for formal psychological intervention will enhance the ability of the sports medicine system to provide an effective service. The NATA has recognized the importance of psychology in the skill set of the athletic trainer and has instituted specific psychological certification and training criteria (Stiller-Ostrowski, Gould, & Covassin, 2009). Thus, it is useful to think of the sports medicine specialist as a "first responder" to psychological issues in injury.

Coaches

More injuries are witnessed by coaches than any of the sports medicine providers, as the vast majority of sports events lack the medical support typical of high-level sport. The coach is first responder to injury and often must decide whether to remove the athlete from competition or to allow the athlete to continue to play. Coaches' responses to injury also have a potentially significant impact from the first moment injury is noted until complete recovery and return to play. Training for coaches in all aspects of injury management, including psychological care, would improve the health and well-being of athletes.

Athletes

The many injuries that are mild in nature do not need and will not receive intervention from any

health professional. However, some injuries may still carry a psychological burden and benefit from psychological self-management. The athlete is not simply the recipient of the injury but also an important agent in providing care. The effectiveness of injury rehabilitation depends on many small day-to-day decisions and actions. These range from compliance with rehabilitation to attention to sport-specific training practices to psychological adjustment to the impact of injury. Consequently, it is important to provide the athlete with pragmatic knowledge and skills in self-management of psychological (and medical) symptoms and behaviors. Ideally, this can and probably should come from all other providers, each of whom brings a unique perspective and skill set to the understanding and management of injury in a sport environment. To the extent that injury care is comprehensive, the athlete is best served.

Performance Intervention

It is useful to think of athletes as the "test pilots" of rehabilitation whose physical skill set, goal orientation, and motivation to recover quickly allow them to pioneer new and better methods of rehabilitation. The psychology of sport injury is transferable to other populations (Heil et al., 1998). This is most apparent in the training room or rehabilitation center, which is a common ground of sorts, shared by athlete and artist, soldier and citizen. The designation of athlete is a comfortable one for those in military and public safety settings. Although driven by an aesthetic sensibility, there is a fundamental athleticism to dance and the performing arts, captured by legendary ballet master Joffrey, in his description of the dancer as artistic athlete. Although general medical patients are least likely to think of themselves as athletes, the concept is a pragmatic one and has been applied to the injured worker who must return to a physically demanding occupation (Heil et al., 1998).

For those (e.g., the military) who perform outside the arena and the playing field, in settings that carry the threat of mortal danger, there are unique needs, challenges, and opportunities. For example, the writing techniques employed effectively by Mankad et al. (2009a&b) with athletes were found to be counterproductive in soldiers with a high level of combat experience. Lt. Col. Paul Bliese of the Walter Reed Army Institute of Research, citing internal research indicates that, "soldiers in the emotional writing group who had high levels of combat experience scored higher on an anger scale compared to soldiers not asked to write" (Cited in

Munsey, C. 2009, October. Writing about wounds. APA Monitor, p. 59). The dynamics of performance under the threat of death and continued action when injured are of apparent and compelling relevance (Grossman, 2004; Heil & Fine, 1999). Because the definitive answers to these issues lie outside the bounds of empirical research, it is essential to identify and apply appropriate methods of study to outdoor sports athletes, the military, and police—such as the structured interview methodology employed by Klinger (2004) with police in deadly force encounters. In similar fashion, it is also of value to apply the knowledge thus gained to training programs for pain and injury management in these groups (Heil & Lee, 1999).

Future Directions in Service Delivery

The goals for an applied sport psychology of injury include expanding the skills of the psychologist, the role for psychology, and the means of service delivery. The ideal is to develop interventions and service delivery models that are grounded in scientifically proven, theory-based research. Where this knowledge base in not forthcoming, there is a need to look to conceptual models and to assimilate varied resources to enable the applied practitioner to meet the needs of the moment. In summary, this implies designing practices based on best knowledge available.

Expanding Psychologists' Skill Sets

Any psychologist who works in the sport setting will encounter injury. Yet few psychologists are true injury specialists, possessing the expansive knowledge and skill set that such a designation would imply. Thus, expanding professional skills is important to the efficacy and credibility of the psychologist—especially since injury management is a traditionally medical enterprise. For example, Stirling and Kerr (2010) suggest that sport psychologists view themselves as agents of child protection, as it relates to injury and other issues relevant to the overall health and well-being of children. The role of the psychologist needs to reach beyond that of direct service provider. The ability to provide indirect services through consultation and training with other psychological providers is critical. For this to be effective, appropriate training materials need to be developed to guide practitioners in triage and intervention. The applied sport psychology texts by Heil (1993), Pargman (1993, 1999, 2007), and Taylor and Taylor (1997) have begun to address this, but much work remains to be done.

Moving from Injury Management to Health Psychology

Psychologists are finding a role in injury management, most typically with musculoskeletal injuries. However, the profession has yet to embrace the many other injuries and medical conditions that may arise in the sport environment. This is especially important when the role of the psychologist implies oversight of the psychological well-being of an identified group, such as the university-based applied sport psychologist. Ideally, the sport psychologist should be prepared to conduct head injury assessment and triage, given the relatively common occurrence of head injury (often in the absence of a sports medicine provider) and in light of its potential negative health impact. A ready-made literature is available to assimilate from sports medicine, which draws heavily on neuropsychology and which is comprehensible to the psychologist. Although relatively infrequent, catastrophic and fatal injuries clearly call for psychological intervention and deserve professional attention. Like the general population, many athletes bring medical problems with them to the field of play, such as asthma, diabetes, and functional gastrointestinal disorders. There is an existing substantial body of literature in behavioral medicine for the psychologist to assimilate and apply.

Enhancing Multidisciplinary Service Delivery

Bringing a deliberate psychologically minded approach to injury management is the overarching goal of the psychology of sport injury as an applied discipline. The diverse range of service delivery providers recasts the psychological management of sport injury into a systems framework, with the psychologist playing a dual role as both direct and indirect service provider. From this, it follows that psychologists expand their role beyond that of direct provider to encompass training of other medical professionals. Consider also that many injured athletes will not receive services from any health care provider, although some will certainly benefit from psychological intervention. Therefore, it is necessary to put relevant information and skills into the hands of the coach and athlete. This expanded array of potential providers increases accessibility and enables comprehensive and timely intervention.

Training in the psychology of injury is complicated by the differences in the knowledge base of potential psychological providers and their established roles in the sport environment. For the professional psychologist, this should rest heavily on state-of-the-art theory, research, and practice. In contrast, for the coach and athlete, it is relatively more important that material be engaging, practical, and immediately relevant. What is needed is a set of distinctly designed learning curricula for each of the identified service provider groups that includes a framework for understanding the psychological dynamics underlying injury, a means for assessing the psychological status of a given athlete, and a set of principles to guide decision-making and action in response to injury.

In like fashion, it appears prudent for psychologists to similarly cross-train, gaining knowledge of fundamentals in medical care and rehabilitation. This will not only increase the potential effectiveness of psychologists but also facilitate interdisciplinary collaboration. Where there is a common language and shared understanding, the potential for true teamwork is enhanced.

Conclusion

This chapter reviews the psychology of sport injury research literature and highlights key issues in intervention. A diverse set of injury models that have guided both research and intervention are presented and critiqued. The scholarship pertaining to musculoskeletal injuries, head injury and concussion, as well as catastrophic and fatal injury are reviewed in detail, and discussed in the context of the performance subcultures in which injuries occur and are managed. Directions for future scholarship are identified with attention to implications for applied practitioners.

References

Adam, M. U., Brassington, G. S., Steiner, H., & Matheson, G. O. (2004). Psychological factors associated with performance-limiting injuries in professional ballet dancers. *Journal of Dance Medicine and Science, 8,* 43–46.

Albert, E. (1999). Dealing with danger: The normalization of risk in cycling. *International Review for the Sociology of Sport, 34,* 157–171.

Albert, E. (2004). Normalising risk in the sport of cycling. In K. Young (Ed.), *Sporting bodies, damaged selves: Research in the sociology of sports-related injury* (pp. 181–194). Oxford, England: Elsevier.

Albinson, C. B., & Petrie, T. (2003). Cognitive appraisals, stress, and coping: Preinjury and postinjury factors influencing psychological adjustment to athletic injury. *Journal of Sport Rehabilitation, 12,* 306–322.

Allen, K. S. (2000). *The relationship between locus of control and dance injury in university dance students.* Unpublished master's thesis, Eugene, OR.

Alzate Saez de Heredia, R., Ramirez, A., & Lazaro, I. (2004). The effect of psychological response on recovery of sport injury. *Research in Sports Medicine, 12,* 15–31.

Amason, A., Engerbretsen, L., & Bahr, R. (2005). No effect of a video-based awareness program on the rate of soccer injuries. *American Journal of Sports Medicine, 33,* 77–84.

Andersen. M. B. (2001). Returning to action and the prevention of future injury. In J. Crossman (Ed.), *Coping with sports injuries: Psychological strategies for rehabilitation.* Melbourne: Oxford University Press.

Andersen, M. B. (2007). Collaborative relationship in injury rehabilitation: Two case examples. In D. Pargman (Ed.), *Psychological bases of sport injuries* (3rd ed., pp. 219–236). Morgantown, WV: Fitness Information Technology.

Andersen, M. B., & Williams, J. M. (1988). A model of stress and athletic injury: Prediction and prevention. *Journal of Sport and Exercise Psychology, 10,* 294–306.

Andersen, M. B., & Williams, J. M. (1999). Athletic injury, psychosocial factors, and perceptual changes during stress. *Journal of Sports Sciences, 17,* 735–741.

Astin, J. A. (2004). Mind-body therapies for the management of pain. *The Clinical Journal of Pain, 20,* 27–32.

Astle, S. J. (1986). The experience of loss in athletes. *Journal of Sports Medicine and Physical Fitness, 26,* 279–284.

Bianco, T. (2001). Social support and recovery from sport injury: Elite skiers share their experiences. *Research Quarterly for Exercise and Sport, 72,* 376–388.

Bianco, T., & Eklund, R. C. (2001). Conceptual considerations for social support research in sport and exercise settings: The instance of sport injury. *Journal of Sport and Exercise Psychology, 2,* 85–107.

Bianco, T., Malo, S., & Orlick, T. (1999). Sport injury and illness: Elite skiers describe their experiences. *Research Quarterly for Exercise and Sport, 70,* 157–169.

Bramwell, S. T., Masuda, M., Wagner, N. H., & Holmes, T. H. (1975). Psychological factors in athletic injuries: Development and application of the Social Athletic Readjustment Rating Scale (SARRS). *Journal of Human Stress, 1,* 6–20.

Brewer, B. W. (2007). Psychology of sport injury rehabilitation. In G. Tenenbaum & R. C. Eklund (Eds.), *Handbook of sport psychology* (3rd ed., pp. 404–424). Hoboken, NJ: John Wiley & Sons, Inc.

Brewer, B. W. (1993). Self-identity and specific vulnerability to depressed mood. *Journal of Personality, 61,* 343–364.

Brewer, B. W. (1999b). Casual attribution dimensions and adjustment to sport injury. *Journal of Personal and Interpersonal Loss, 4,* 215–224.

Brewer, B. W., Andersen, M. B., & Van Raalte, J. L. (2002). Psychological aspects of sport injury rehabilitation: Toward a biopsychosocial approach. In D. L. Mostofsky & L. D. Zaichkowsky (Eds.), *Medical and psychological aspects of sport and exercise* (pp. 41–54). Morgantown, WV: Fitness Information Technology.

Brewer, B. W., Cornelius, A. E., Van Raalte, J. L., Petitpas, A.J., Sklar, J.H., Pohlman, M.H., et al. (2003a). Age-related differences in predictors of adherence to rehabilitation after anterior cruciate ligament reconstruction. *Journal of Athletic Training, 38,* 158–162.

Brewer, B. W., Cornelius, A. E., Van Raalte, J. L., Brickner, J. C., Tennen, H., Sklar, J. H., et al. (2004). Comparison of concurrent and retrospective pain ratings during rehabilitation following anterior cruciate ligament reconstruction. *Journal of Sport and Exercise Psychology, 26,* 610–615.

Brewer, B. W., Cornelius, A. E., Van Raalte, J. L., Petitpas, A. J., Sklar, J. H., Pohlman, M. H., et al. (2000). Attributions for recovery and adherence to rehabilitation following anterior cruciate ligament reconstruction: A prospective analysis. *Psychology and Health, 15,* 283–291.

Brewer, B. W., Daly, J. M., Van Raalte, J. L., Petitpas, A. J., & Sklar, J. H. (1999). A psychometric evaluation of the Rehabilitation Adherence Questionnaire. *Journal of Sport and Exercise Psychology, 21,* 167–173.

Brewer, B. W., Petitpas, A. J., & Van Raalte, J. L. (1999). Referral of injured athletes for counseling and psychotherapy. In R. R. Ray & D. M. Wiese-Bjornstal (Eds.), *Counseling in sports medicine* (pp. 127–141). Champaign, IL: Human Kinetics.

Brewer, B. W., Van Raalte, J. L., & Linder, D. E. (1993). Athletic identity: Hercules' muscles or Achilles heel? *International Journal of Sport Psychology, 24,* 237–254.

Brewer, B. W., Van Raalte, J. L., & Petitpas, A. J. (2007). Patient-practitioner interactions in sport injury rehabilitation. In D. Pargman (Ed.), *Psychological bases of sport injuries* (3rd ed., pp. 79–94). Morgantown, WV: Fitness Information Technology.

Broglio, S. P., & Guskiewicz, K. M. (2009). Concussion in sports: The sideline assessment. *Sport Health, A Multidisciplinary Approach, 1,* 361–369.

Brymer, M., Jacobs, A., Layne, C., Pynoos, R., Ruzek, J., Steinberg, A., Vernberg, E., & Watson, P. (2012, February 21). *Psychological first aid: Field operations guide* (2nd ed.). National Child Traumatic Stress Network and National Center for PTSD. Retrieved from http://www.ptsd.va.gov/professional/manuals/manual-pdf/pfa/PFA_2ndEditionwithappendices.pdf.

Byerly, P. N., Worrell, T., Gahimer, J., & Domholdt, E. (1994). Rehabilitation compliance in an athletic training environment. *Journal of Athletic Training, 29,* 352–355.

Byrd, C. W. (1993). *The relationship of history of stressors, personality, and coping resources, with the incidence of athletic injuries.* Unpublished master's thesis, University of Colorado, Boulder.

Camiolo Reddy, C., & Collins, M. W. (2009). Sports concussion: Management and predictors of outcome. *Current Sports Medicine Reports, 8,* 10–15.

Campbell, D. T., & Stanley, J. C. (1966). *Experimental and quasi-experimental designs for research.* Chicago: Rand McNally.

Charlesworth, H., & Young, K. (2004). Why English female university athletes play with pain: Motivations and rationalizations. In K. Young (Ed.), *Sporting bodies, damaged selves: Research in the sociology of sports-related injury* (pp. 163–180). Oxford, England: Elsevier.

Couturie, B., Else, J. (Directors) & Witte, K. (Producers). (1986). *Disposable heroes* [Videotape]. Los Angeles: Active Home Video.

Crossman, J., Gluck, L., & Jamieson, J. (1995). The emotional responses of injured athletes. *New Zealand Journal of Sports Medicine, 12,* 1–2.

Cryan, P. O., & Alles, E. F. (1983). The relationship between stress and football injuries. *Journal of Sports Medicine and Physical Fitness, 10,* 103–123.

Cupal, D. D. (1998). Psychological interventions in sport injury prevention and rehabilitation. *Journal of Applied Sport Psychology, 10,* 103–123.

Cupal, D. D., & Brewer, B. W. (2001). Effects of relaxation and guided imagery on knee strength, reinjury anxiety, and pain following anterior cruciate ligament reconstruction. *Rehabilitation Psychology, 46,* 28–43.

Curry, T. J. (1993). The effects of receiving a college letter on the sport identity. *Sociology of Sport Journal, 10,* 73–87.

Curry, T. J., & Strauss, R. H. (1994). A little pain never hurt anybody: A photo-essay on the normalization of sport injuries. *Sociology of Sport Journal, 11,* 195–208.

Daly, J. M., Brewer, B. W., Van Raalte, J. L., Petitpas, A. J., & Sklar, J. H. (1995). Cognitive appraisal, emotional adjustment, and adherence to rehabilitation following knee surgery. *Journal of Sport Rehabilitation, 4,* 23–30.

Davis, H., Liotti, M., Ngan, E. T. C., Woodward, T. S., Van Snellenberg, J. X., van Anders, S., et al. (2008). fMRI bold signal changes in elite swimmers while viewing videos of personal failure. *Brain Imaging and Behavior.* DOI 10.1007/s11682-007-9016-x

Davis, J. (2011, July 27). Head injuries in football. *The New York Times.* Retrieved from http://topics.nytimes.com/top/reference/timestopics/subjects/f/football/head_injuries/index.html

Dionigi, R. (2006). Competitive sport and aging: The need for qualitative sociological research. *Journal of Aging and Physical Activity, 14,* 365–379.

Donnelly, P. (2003). *Marching out of step: Sport, social order and the case of child labour.* Keynote address, Second World Congress of Sociology of Sport, Cologne, Germany, June 18–21.

Duda, J. L., Smart, A. E., & Tappe, M. K. (1989). Predictors of adherence in rehabilitation of athletic injuries: An application of personal investment theory. *Journal of Sport and Exercise Psychology, 11,* 367–381.

Eckner, J. T, & Kutcher, J. S. (2010). Concussion symptom scales and sideline assessment tools: A critical literature update. *Current Sports Medicine Reports, 9,* 8–15.

Evans, L., & Hardy, L. (1995). Sport injury and grief responses: A review. *Journal of Sport and Exercise Psychology, 17,* 227–245.

Evans, L., & Hardy, L. (2002a). Injury rehabilitation: A goal-setting intervention study. *Research Quarterly for Exercise and Sport, 73,* 310–319.

Evans, L., Hardy, L., & Fleming, S. (2000). Intervention strategies with injured athletes: An action research study. *The Sport Psychologist, 14,* 188–206.

Fawkner, H. J. (1995). *Predisposition to injury in athletes: The role of psychosocial factors.* Unpublished master's thesis, University of Melbourne, Australia.

Fawkner, H. J., McMurray, N. E., & Summers, J. J. (1999). Athletic injury and minor life events: A prospective study. *Journal of Science and Medicine in Sport, 2,* 117–124.

Feller, J. A., Webster, K. E., Taylor, N. F., Payne, R., & Pizzari, T. (2004). Effect of physiotherapy attendance on outcome after anterior cruciate ligament reconstruction: A pilot study. *British Journal of Sports Medicine, 38,* 74–77.

Fields, J., Murphey, M., Horodyski, M., & Stopka, C. (1995). Factors associated with adherence to sport injury rehabilitation in college-age recreational athletes. *Journal of Sport Rehabilitation, 4,* 172–180.

Fields, K. B., Delaney, M., & Hinkle S. (1990). A prospective study of Type A behavior and running injuries. *Journal of Family Practice, 30,* 425–429.

Fisher, A. C., Domm, M. A., & Wuest, D. A. (1988). Adherence to sports-injury rehabilitation programs. *Physician and Sportsmedicine, 16,* 47–52.

Fisher, L. A., & Wrisberg, C. A. (2005). The "Zen" of career-ending-injury rehabilitation. *Athletic Therapy Today, 10,* 44–45.

Ford, I. A., Eklund, R. C., & Gordon, S. (2000). An exami-nation of psychosocial variables moderating the relationship between life stress and injury time-loss among athletes of a high standard. *Journal of Sports Sciences, 18*, 310–312.

Ford, I., & Gordon, S. (1998). Perspective of sport trainers and athletic therapists on the psychological content of their prac-tice and training. *Journal of Sport Rehabilitation, 7*, 79–94.

Francis, S. R., Andersen, M. B., & Maley, P. (2000). Physiotherapists' and male professional athletes' views on psychological skills for rehabilitation. *Journal of Sport Sciences and Medicine in Sport, 3*, 17–29.

Frey, J. (1991). Social risk and the meaning of sport. *Sociology of Sport Journal, 8*, 136–145.

Frey, J. H., Preston, F. W., & Bernhard, B. J. (2004). Risk and injury: A comparison of football and rodeo subcultures. In K. Young (Ed.), *Sporting bodies, damaged selves: Research in the sociology of sports-related injury* (pp. 211–222). Oxford, England: Elsevier.

Fuller, C. W. (2008). Catastrophic injury in rugby union is the level of risk acceptable? *Sports Medicine, 38*, 975–986.

Gilbourne, D., & Taylor, A. H. (1998). From theory to practice: The integration of goal perspective theory and life develop-ment approaches within an injury-specific goal-setting pro-gram. *Journal of Applied Sport Psychology, 10*, 124–139.

Glazer, D. D. (2009). Development and preliminary validation of the Injury-Psychological Readiness to Return to Sport (I-PRRS) Scale. *Journal of Athletic Training, 44*, 185–189.

Gordon, S., & Lindgren, S. (1990). Psycho-physical rehabilita-tion from a serious sport injury: Case study of an elite fast bowler. *Australian Journal of Science and Medicine in Sport, 22*, 71–76.

Gordon, S., Milios, D., & Grove, R. J. (1991). Psychological aspects of the recovery process from sport injury: The per-spective of sport physiotherapists. *The Australian Journal of Science and Medicine in Sport, 23*, 53–60.

Gordon, S., Potter, M., & Ford, I. W. (1998). Toward a psy-choeducational curriculum for training sport-injury reha-bilitation personnel. *Journal of Applied Sport Psychology, 10*, 140–156.

Gould, D., Udry, E., Bridges, D., & Beck, L. (1997a) Coping with season-ending injuries. *Sport Psychologist, 11*, 379–399.

Gould, D., Udry, E., Bridges, D., & Beck, L. (1997b). Stress sources encountered when rehabilitating from season-ending ski injuries. *The Sport Psychologist, 11*, 361–378.

Granquist, M., Podlog, L., & Engel, J. (2010). *Is poor rehabili-tation adherence a common occurrence within collegiate athletic training settings? Certified athletic trainers' perspectives.* Paper presented at the Association for Applied Sport Psychology (AASP), Providence, Rhode Island.

Green, S. L., & Weinberg, R. S. (2001). Relationships among athletic identity, coping skills, social support, and the psy-chological impact of injury in recreational participants. *Journal of Applied Sport Psychology, 13*, 40–59.

Gregg, R. L., Banderet, L. E., Reynolds, K. L., Creedon, J. F., & Rice, V. J. (2002). Psychological factors that influence traumatic injury occurrence and physical performance. *Work: A Journal of Prevention Assessment and Rehabilitation, 18*, 133–139.

Gregory, S. (2010). The problem with football. Our favorite sport is too dangerous. How to make the game safer. *Time, 175*, 36–43.

Grossman, D. (2004). *On combat: The psychology and physiology of deadly conflict in war and in peace.* USA: PPCT Research Publications.

Guskiewicz, K. M., & Cantu, R.C. (2004). The concussion puz-zle: Evaluation of sport-related concussion. *American Journal of Medicine and Sports, 6*, 13–21.

Guskiewicz, K. M., Marshall, S. W., Bailes, J., McCrea, M., Harding, H. P., Jr., Matthews, A., et al. (2007). Recurrent concussion and risk of depression in retired professional foot-ball players. *Medicine and Science in Sports and Exercise, 39*, 903–909.

Guskiewicz, K. M., McCrea, M., Marshall, S. W., Cantu, R. C., Randolph, C., Barr, W., et al. (2003). Cumulative effects associated with recurrent concussion in collegiate football players: The NCAA concussion study. *The Journal of the American Medical Association, 290*, 2549–2555.

Guskiewicz, K. M., Bruce, S.L., Cantu, R.C., Ferrara, M.S., Kelly, J.P., McCrea, M., et al. (2004). National Athletic Trainers' Association position statement: Management of sport related concussion. *Journal of Athletic Training, 39*, 280–297.

Guskiewicz, K. M., Ross, S. E., & Marshall, S. W. (2001). Postural stability and neuropsychological deficits after con-cussion in collegiate athletes. *Journal of Athletic Training, 36*, 263–273.

Hanson, S. J., McCullagh, P., & Tonymon, P. (1992). The rela-tionship of personality characteristics, life stress, and cop-ing resources to athletic injury. *Journal of Sport and Exercise Psychology, 14*, 262–272.

Hardy, C., Burke, K., & Crace, K. (1999). Social support and injury: A framework for support-based interventions with injured athletes. In D. Pargman (Ed.), *Psychological bases of sport injuries* (2nd ed., pp. 175–198). Morgantown, WV: Fitness Information Technology.

Heil, J. (1993). *Psychology of sport injury.* Champaign, IL: Human Kinetics Publishers.

Heil, J. (2000). The injured athlete. In Y. L. Hanin (Ed.), *Emotion in sport* (pp. 245–265). Champaign, IL: Human Kinetics.

Heil, J. (2009). Turning injury to advantage: Rapid recovery on game day. *Athletic Therapy Today, 14*, 13–15.

Heil, J., Bennett, G., Brolinson, P. G., & Goforth, M. (2009). *Sports medicine response to the Virginia Tech shootings: Lessons learned* [PDF Document]. Retrieved from http://www.cpsvp.vt.edu/pdf/VTSportLessonsLearnedJun09.pdf

Heil, J., & Fine, P. (1999). Pain in sport: A biopsychological perspective. In D. Pargman (Ed.), *Psychological bases of sport injuries* (2nd ed., pp. 13–28). Morgantown, WV: Fitness Information Technology.

Heil, J., & Lee, J. (2009, September). *Sport psychology applied to law enforcement training.* Workshop at Association for Applied Sport Psychology Conference, Salt Lake City, UT.

Heil, J., Wakefield, C., & Reed, C. (1998). Patient as athlete: A metaphor for injury rehabilitation. *Psychotherapy Patient, 10*, 21–39.

Henschen, K. R., & Heil, J. (1992). A retrospective study of the effect of an athlete's sudden death on teammates. *Omega: Journal of Death and Dying, 25*, 217–223.

Holmes, T. H. (1970). Psychological screening. In *Football inju-ries: Paper presented at a workshop* (pp. 211–214). Washington, DC: National Academy of Sciences. (Sponsored by Sub-committee on Athletic Injuries, Committee on the Skeletal System, Division of Medical Sciences, National Research Council, February 1969).

Holmes, T. H., & Rahe, R. H. (1967). The social readjustment scale. *Journal of Psychosomatic Research, 11*, 213–218.

Hughes, R., & Coakley, J. (1991). Positive deviance among athletes: The implications of overconformity to the sport ethic. *Sociology of Sport Journal, 4,* 307–325.

Johnson, U., Ekengren, J., & Andersen, M. B. (2005). Injury prevention in Sweden: Helping soccer players at risk. *Journal of Sport and Exercise Psychology, 27,* 32–38.

Johnston, L. H., & Carroll, D. (1998a). The context of emotional responses to athletic injury: A qualitative analysis. *Journal of Sport Rehabilitation, 7,* 206–220.

Johnston, L. H., & Carroll, D. (1998b). The provision of social support to injured athletes: A qualitative analysis. *Journal of Sport Rehabilitation, 7,* 267–284.

Johnston, L. H., & Carroll, D. (2000). Coping, social support, and injury: Changes over time and the effects of level of sports involvement. *Journal of Sport Rehabilitation, 9,* 290–303.

Kahanov, L., Dusa, M. J., Wilkinson, S., & Roberts, J. (2005). Self-reported headgear use and concussions among collegiate men's rugby union players. *Research in Sports Medicine, 13,* 77–89.

Kerr, G., & Goss, J. (1996). The effects of a stress management program on injuries and stress levels. *Journal of Applied Sport Psychology, 8,* 109–117.

Kerr, G., & Minden, H. (1988). Psychological factors related to the occurrence of athletic injuries. *Journal of Sport and Exercise Psychology, 10,* 167–173.

Kleiber, D. A., & Brock, S. C. (1992). The effect of career-ending injuries on the subsequent well-being of elite college athletes. *Sociology of Sport Journal, 9,* 70.

Klinger, D. (2004). *Into the kill zone: A cop's eye view of deadly force.* San Francisco: Josey Bass.

Koh, J. O., Cassidy, J. D., & Watkinson, E. J. (2003). Incidence of concussion in contact sports: A systematic review of the evidence. *Brain Injury, 17,* 901–917.

Krakauer, J. (1998). *Into thin air: A personal account of the Mount Everest disaster.* New York: Villard.

Kvist, J., Ek, A., Sporrstedt, K., & Good, L. (2005). Fear of re-injury: A hindrance for returning to sports after anterior cruciate ligament reconstruction. *Knee Surgery, Sports Traumatology, Arthroscopy, 13,* 393–397.

Kubler-Ross, E. (1969). *On death and dying: What the dying have to teach doctors, nurses, clergy, and their own families.* New York: Macmillan.

Lampton, C. C., Lambert, M. E., & Yost, R. (1993). The effects of psychological factors in sports medicine and rehabilitation adherence. *Journal of Sports Medicine and Physical Fitness, 33,* 292–299.

Larson, G. A., Starkey, C. A., & Zaichkowsky, L. D. (1996). Psychological aspects of athletic injuries as perceived by athletic trainers. *The Sport Psychologist, 10,* 37–47.

Lavallee, D. (2000). Theoretical perspectives on career transition in sport. In D. Lavallee & P. Wylleman (Eds.), *Career transitions in sport: International perspectives* (pp. 1–28). Morgantown, WV: Fitness Information Technology.

Lavallee, L., & Flint, F. (1996). The relationship of stress, competitive anxiety, mood state, and social support to athletic injury. *Journal of Athletic Training, 31,* 296–299.

Lazarus, R. S., & Folkman, S. (1984). *Stress, appraisal, and coping.* New York: Springer.

Leddy, M. H., Lambert, M. J., & Ogles, B. M. (1994). Psychological consequences of athletic injury among high-level competitors. *Research Quarterly for Exercise and Sport, 65,* 347–354.

Liderbach, M., & Compagno, J. M. (2001). Psychological aspects of fatigue-related injuries in dancers. *Journal of Dance Medicine and Science, 5,* 116–120.

Loberg, L., Houston, M., & Heil, J. (2008, September). Children's experiences with a sport-related injury [Abstract]. In *Association for Applied Sport Psychology 2008 Conference Proceedings* (p. 33). Madison, WI: AASP.

Loland, S. (2006). Olympic sport and the ideal of sustainable development. *Journal of the Philosophy of Sport, 33,* 144–156.

Lysens, R., Steverlynck, A., Vanden Auweele, Y., Lefevre, J., Renson, L., Claessens, A., et al. (1984). The predictability of sports injuries. *Sports Medicine, 1,* 6–10.

Macchi, R., & Crossman, J. (1996). After the fall: Reflections of injured classical ballet dancers. *Journal of Sport Behavior, 19,* 221–234.

Maddison, R., & Prapavessis, H. (2005). A psychological approach to the prediction and prevention of athletic injury. *Journal of Sport and Exercise Psychology, 27,* 289–310.

Mainwaring, L. (1999). Restoration of self: A model for the psychological response of athletes to severe knee injuries. *Canadian Journal of Rehabilitation, 12,* 145–156.

Makdissi, M. (2010). Sports related concussion management in general practice. *Australian Family Physician, 39,* 12–17.

Malcolm, D. (2006). Unprofessional practice? The status and power of sport physicians. *Sociology of Sport Journal, 23,* 376–395.

Malcom, N. L. (2006). 'Shaking it off' and 'toughing it out': Socialization to pain and injury in girls' softball. *Journal of Contemporary Ethnography, 35,* 495–525.

Malone, T. D., Fox, B. D., & Mulvey, A. (2008). Catastrophic injuries and the role of the athletic trainer. In J. M. Mensch & G. M. Miller (Eds.), *The athletic trainer's guide to psychosocial intervention and referral* (pp. 219–238). Thorofare, NJ: Slack Incorporated.

Mankad, A., Gordon, S., & Wallman, K. (2009a). Psycholinguistic analysis of emotional disclosure: A case study in sport injury. *Journal of Clinical Sport Psychology, 3,* 182–196.

Mankad, A., Gordon, S., & Wallman, K. (2009b). Psycho-immunological effects of written emotional disclosure during long-term injury rehabilitation. *Journal of Clinical Sport Psychology, 3,* 205–217.

Manuel, J. C., Shilt, J. S., Curl, W. W., Smith, J. A., DuRant, R. H., Lester, L., & Sinal, S. H. (2002). Coping with sports injuries: An examination of the adolescent athlete. *Journal of Adolescent Health, 31,* 391–393.

Martin, B. (2010, May 24). Ivory Coast soccer savior. *Sports Illustrated, 112,* pp. 52–55.

May, J. R., & Brown, L. (1989). Delivery of psychological services to the U.S. Alpine ski team prior to and during the Olympics in Calgary. *The Sport Psychologist, 3,* 320–329.

McDonald, S. A., & Hardy, C. J. (1990). Affective response patterns of the injured athlete: An exploratory analysis. *The Sport Psychologist, 4,* 261–274.

McLeod, S., & Kirkby, R. J. (1995). Locus of control as a predictor of injury in elite basketball players. *Sports Medicine, Training and Rehabilitation, 6,* 201–206.

Messner, M. (1990). When bodies are weapons: Masculinity and violence in sport. *International Review for the Sociology of Sport, 25,* 203–219.

Messner, M. A. (1992). *Power at play: Sports and the problem of masculinity.* Boston, MA: Beacon Press.

Messner, M. A., & Sabo, D. F. (1990). *Sport, men, and the gender order: Critical feminist perspectives.* Champaign, IL: Human Kinetics Publishers

Milne, M., Hall, C., & Forwell, L. (2005). Self-efficacy, imagery use, and adherence to rehabilitation by injured athletes. *Journal of Sport Rehabilitation, 14,* 150–167.

Morrey, M. A., Stuart, M. J., Smith, A. M., & Wiese-Bjornstal, D. M. (1999). A longitudinal examination of athletes' emotional and cognitive responses to anterior cruciate ligament injury. *Clinical Journal of Sport Medicine, 9,* 63–69.

Morris, T., & Noh, Y. E. (2007). Research-based injury prevention intervention in sport and dance. In D. Pargman (Ed.), *Psychological bases of sport injuries* (3rd ed., pp. 3–24). Morgantown, WV: Fitness Information Technology.

Munsey, C. (2009, October). Writing about wounds. *APA Monitor, 40,* pp.58–59.

Murphy, G. C., Foreman, P. E., Simpson, C. A., Molloy, G. N., & Molloy, E. K. (1999). The development of a locus of control measure predictive of injured athletes' adherence to treatment. *Journal of Science and Medicine in Sport, 2,* 145–152.

Nigorikawa, T., Oishi, E., Tasukawa, M., Kamimura, M., Muramaya, J., & Tanaka, N. (2003). Type A behavior pattern and sports injuries. *Japanese Journal of Physical Fitness and Sports Medicine, 52,* 359–367.

Nixon, H. L. (1992). A social network analysis of influences on athletes to play with pain and injuries. *Journal of Sport and Social Issues, 16,* 127–135.

Nixon, H. L. (1993). Accepting the risks of pain and injury in sport: Mediated cultural influences on playing hurt. *Sociology of Sport Journal, 10,* 183–196.

Nixon, H. L. (1994a). Coaches' views of risk, pain, and injury in sport with special reference to gender differences. *Sociology of Sport Journal, 11,* 79–87.

Nixon, H. L. (1994b). Social pressure, social support, and help seeking for pain and injuries in college sports networks. *Journal of Sport and Social Issues, 13,* 340–355.

Nixon, H. L. (1996). *Principles and models for sports policy and programs for disabled people.* New York: Sociological Association.

Noh, Y. E., Morris, T., & Andersen, M. B. (2005). Psychosocial factors and ballet injuries. *International Journal of Sport and Exercise Psychology, 3,* 79–90.

Notebaert, A. J., & Guskiewicz, K. M. (2005). Current trends in athletic training practice for concussion assessment and management. *Journal of Athletic Training, 40,* 320–325.

Novaco, R. W. (2005). Clinical problems of anger and its assessment and regulation through a stress coping skills approach. In W. O'Donohue & L. Krasner (Eds.), *Handbook of psychological skills training: Clinical techniques and applications* (pp. 320–338). Boston: Allyn & Bacon.

O'Connor, E. A., Heil, J., Harmer, P., & Zimmermann, I. (2005). Injury. In J. Taylor & G. Wilson (Eds.), *Applying sport psychology: Four perspectives* (pp. 187–206, 281–283). Champaign, IL: Human Kinetics.

Oliaro, S., Anderson, S., & Hooker, D. (2001). Management of cerebral concussion in sports: The athletic trainer's perspective. *Journal of Athletic Training, 36,* 257–262.

Pargman, D. (1993). (Ed.). *Psychological bases of sport injuries.* Morgantown, WV: Fitness Information Technology.

Pargman, D. (Ed.). (1999). *Psychological bases of sport injuries* (2nd ed.). Morgantown, WV: Fitness Information Technology.

Pargman, D. (2007). (Ed.). *Psychological bases of sport injuries* (3rd ed.). Morgantown, WV: Fitness Information Technology.

Pargman, D., & Lunt, S. D. (1989). The relationship of self-concept and locus of control to the severity of injury in freshman collegiate football players. *Sports Medicine, Training and Rehabilitation, 1,* 201–208.

Passer, M. W., & Seese, M. D. (1983). Life stress and athletic injury: Examination of positive versus negative events and three moderator variables. *Journal of Human Stress, 9,* 11–16.

Patterson, E. L., Smith, R. E., & Everett, J. J. (1998). Psychosocial factors as predictors of ballet injuries: Interactive effects of life stress and social support. *Journal of Sport Behavior, 21,* 101–112.

Penpraze, P., & Mutrie, N. (1999). Effectiveness of goal setting in an injury rehabilitation programme for increasing patient understanding and compliance [Abstract]. *British Journal of Sports Medicine, 33,* 60.

Perna, F. M., Antoni, M. H., Baum, A., Gordon, P., & Schneiderman, N. (2003). Cognitive behavioral stress management effects on injury and illness among competitive athletes: A randomized clinical trial. *Annals of Behavioral Medicine, 25,* 66–73.

Peterson, C. L., Ferrara, M. A., Mrazik, M., & Piland, S. G. (2003). An analysis of domain score and posturography following cerebral concussion. *Clinical Journal of Sport Medicine, 13,* 230–237.

Petitpas, A., & Cornelius, A. (2004). Practitioner-client relationships: Building working alliances. In G. S. Kolt & M. B. Andersen (Eds.), *Psychology in the physical and manual therapies* (pp. 57–70). Edinburgh, SCT: Churchill Livingstone.

Petitpas, A., & Danish, S. J. (1995). Caring for injured athletes. In S. Murphy (Ed.), *Sport psychology interventions* (pp.255–281). Champaign, IL: Human Kinetics.

Petrie, T. A. (1992). Psychosocial antecedents of athletic injury: The effects of life stress and social support on female collegiate gymnasts. *Behavioral Medicine, 18,* 127–138.

Petrie, T. A. (1993a). Coping skills, competitive trait anxiety, and playing status: Moderating effects of the life stress-injury relationship. *Journal of Sport and Exercise Psychology, 15,* 261–274.

Pike, E. (2004). Risk, pain and injury: A natural thing in rowing? In K. Young (Ed.), *Sporting bodies, damaged selves: Sociological studies of sports-related injury* (pp. 151–162). Oxford, England: Elsevier.

Pizzari, T., McBurney, H., Taylor, N. F., & Feller, J. A. (2002). Adherence to anterior cruciate ligament reconstruction: A qualitative analysis. *Journal of Sport Rehabilitation, 11,* 90–102.

Pizzari, T., Taylor, N. F., McBurney, H., & Feller, J. A. (2005). Adherence to rehabilitation after anterior cruciate ligament reconstructive surgery: Implications for outcome. *Journal of Sport Rehabilitation, 14,* 201–214.

Podlog, L., & Eklund, R. C. (2005). Return to sport following serious injury: A retrospective examination of motivation and outcomes. *Journal of Sport Rehabilitation, 14,* 20–34.

Podlog, L., & Eklund, R. C. (2006). A longitudinal investigation of competitive athletes' return to sport following serious injury. *Journal of Applied Sport Psychology, 18,* 44–68.

Podlog, L., & Eklund. R. C. (2007a). The psychosocial aspects of a return to sport following serious injury: A review of the literature. *Psychology of Sport and Exercise, 8,* 535–566.

Podlog, L., & Eklund, R. C. (2007b). Professional coaches perspectives on the return to sport following serious injury. *Journal of Applied Sport Psychology, 1*, 44–68.

Podlog, L., & Eklund, R. C. (2009). High-level athletes' perceptions of success in returning to sport following injury. *Psychology of Sport and Exercise, 10*, 535–544.

Podlog, L., & Eklund, R. C. (2010). Returning to competition following a serious injury: The role of self-determination. *Journal of Sports Sciences, 28*, 819–831.

Podlog, L., Lochbaum, M., & Stevens, T. (2010). Need satisfaction, well-being and perceived return-to-sport outcomes among injured athletes. *Journal of Applied Sport Psychology, 22*, 167–182.

Quinn, A. M., & Fallon, B. J. (1999). The changes in psychological characteristics and reactions of elite athletes from injury onset until full recovery. *Journal of Applied Sport Psychology, 11*, 210–229.

Ray, R., Terrell, T., & Hough, D. (1999). The role of the sports medicine professional in counseling athletes. In R. Ray & D. Wiese-Bjornstal (Eds.), *Counseling in sports medicine* (pp. 3–20). Champaign, IL: Human Kinetics.

Rees, T., Smith, B., & Sparkes, A. (2003). The influence of social support on the lived experiences of spinal cord injured sportsmen. *The Sport Psychologist, 17*, 135–156.

Rip, B., Fortin, S., & Vallerand, R. J. (2006). The relationship between passion and injury in dance students. *Journal of Dance Medicine and Science, 10*, 14–20.

Robbins, J. E., & Rosenfeld, L. B. (2001). Athletes' perceptions of social support provided by their head coach, assistant coach, and athletic trainer, pre-injury and during rehabilitation. *Journal of Sport Behavior, 24*, 277–297.

Roderick, M. (1998). The sociology of risk, pain, and injury: A comment on the work of Howard L. Nixon II. *Sociology of sport journal, 15*, 64–79.

Roderick, M. (2006). The sociology of pain and injury in sport: Main perspectives and problems. In S. Loland, I. Waddington, & B. Skirstad (Eds.). *Pain and injury in sport: Social and ethical analysis* (pp. 17–33). Leicester, England: Routledge.

Rogers, T. J., & Landers, D. M. (2005). Mediating effects of peripheral vision in the life events stress/athletic injury relationship. *Journal of Sport and Exercise Psychology, 27*, 271–288.

Rose, J., & Jevne, R. F. J. (1993). Psychosocial processes associated with sport injuries. *The Sport Psychologist, 7*, 309–328.

Ross, M. J., & Berger, R. S. (1996). Effects of stress inoculations on athletes' postsurgical pain and rehabilitation after orthopedic injury. *Journal of Consulting and Clinical Psychology, 64*, 406–410.

Rotella, R. J. (1982). Psychological care of the injured athlete. In D. N. Kulund (Ed.), *The injured athlete* (pp. 213–224). Philadelphia: Lippincott.

Rotella, R. J., Ogilvie, B. C., & Perrin, D. H. (1999). The malingering athlete: Psychological considerations. In D. Pargman (Ed.), *Psychological bases of sport injuries* (2nd ed., pp.111–112) Morgantown, WV: Fitness Information Technology.

Rowson, S., Goforth, M.W., Dietter, D., Brolinson, P.G., & Duma, S. M. (2009). Correlating cumulative sub-concussive head impacts in football with player performance -biomed 2009. *Biomedical Science Instrumentation, 45*, 113–118.

Ryan. R., & Deci, E. L. (2000). Self-determination Theory and the facilitation of intrinsic motivation, social development and well-being. *American Psychologist, 55*, 68–78.

Safai, P. (2003). Healing the body in the "Culture of Risk": Examining the negotiation of treatment between sport medicine clinicians and injured athletes in Canadian intercollegiate sport. *Sociology of Sport Journal, 20*, 127–146.

San Jose, A. (2003). Injury of elite athletes: Sport- and gender-related representations. *International Journal of Sport and Exercise Psychology, 1*, 434–459.

Sanserino, M. (2009, December 1). Tough-guy culture in NFL on playing hurt is changing: Ex-players, even fans, hope erring on the side of caution takes priority. *Pittsburgh Post-Gazette*, pp.1–4. Retrieved from http://www.post-gazette.com/pg/09335/1017514-66.stm

Scherzer, C. B., Brewer, B. W., Cornelius, A. E., Van Raalte, J. L., Petitpas, A. J., Sklar, J. H., et al. (2001). Psychological skills and adherence to rehabilitation after reconstruction of the anterior cruciate ligament. *Journal of Sport Rehabilitation, 10*, 165–172.

Shelbourne, K. D., & Wickens, J. H. (1990). Current concepts in anterior cruciate ligament rehabilitation. *Orthopaedic Review, 19*, 957–964.

Shipherd, A. M., & Eklund, R. C. (2010). *Over conformity to the sport ethic among adolescent athletes and injury.* Manuscript submitted for publication.

Smith, A. M., Scott, S. G., O'Fallon, W. M., & Young, M. L. (1990). Emotional responses of athletes to injury. *Mayo Clinic Proceedings, 65*, 38–50.

Smith, A. M., Stuart, M. J., Wiese-Bjornstal, D. M., Milliner, E. K., O'Fallon, W. M., & Crowson, C. S. (1993). Competitive athletes: Preinjury and postinjury mood states and self-esteem. *Mayo Clinic Proceedings, 68*, 939–947.

Smith, B., & Sparkes, A. C. (2002). Men, sport, spinal cord injury and the construction of coherence: Narrative practice in action. *Qualitative Research, 2*, 143–171.

Smith, R. E., Smoll, F. L., & Ptacek, J. T. (1990). Conjunctive moderator variables in vulnerability and resiliency research: Life stress, social support and coping skills, and adolescent sport injuries. *Journal of Personality and Social Psychology, 58*, 360–369.

Sparkes, A. C. (1998). An Achilles heel to the survival of self. *Qualitative Health Research, 8*, 644–664.

Sparkes, A. C., & Smith, B. (2002). Sport, spinal cord injury, embodied masculinities, and the dilemmas of narrative identity. *Men and Masculinities, 4*, 258

Sparkes, A. C., & Smith, B. (2005). When narratives matter: Men, sport, and spinal cord injury. *Men and Masculinities, 6*, 1095.

Spitzer, G. (2006). Sport and the systematic infliction of pain: A case study of state-sponsored mandatory doping in East Germany. In S. Loland, I. Waddington, & B. Skirstad (Eds.), *Pain and injury in sport: Social and ethical analysis* (pp. 109–126). Leicester, England: Routledge.

Stapleton, A., Heil, J., Bennett, G., & Hankes, D. (2007, October). Fatal injury in sport: Lessons learned. Presented at *Colloquium on crisis intervention in sport.* Association for Applied Sport Psychology Conference, Louisville, KY.

Steadman, J. R. (1993). A physician's approach to the psychology of injury. In J. Heil (Ed.), *Psychology of sport injury* (pp. 25–31). Champaign, IL: Human Kinetics Publishers.

Stewart, M., & Kennedy, M. (2010). *Touchdown: The power and precision of football's perfect play.* Minneapolis, MN: Millbrook Press.

Stiller-Ostrowski, J. L., Gould, D. R., & Covassin, T. (2009). An evaluation of an educational intervention in psychology of injury for athletic training students. *Journal of Athletic Training, 44,* 482–489.

Stirling, A., & Kerr, G. (2010). Sport psychology consultants as agents of child protection. *Journal of Applied Sport Psychology, 22,* 305–319.

Straume-Naesheim, T. M., Andersen, T. E., Dvorak, J., & Bahr, R. (2005). Effects of heading exposure and previous concussions & on neuropsychological performance among Norwegian elite footballers. *British Journal of Sports Medicine, 39,* 70–77.

Taylor, A. H., & May, S. (1996). Threat and coping appraisal as determinants of compliance to sports injury rehabilitation: An application of protection motivation theory. *Journal of Sports Sciences, 14,* 471–482.

Taylor, J., Stone, K. R., Mullin, M. J., Ellenbecker, T., & Walgenbach, A. (2003). *Comprehensive sports injury management: From examination of injury to return to sport.* Austin, TX: Pro-ed.

Taylor, J., & Taylor, S. (1997). *Psychological approaches to sports injury rehabilitation.* Gaithersburg, MD: Aspen.

Tedder, S., & Biddle, S. J. H. (1998). Psychological processes involved during sports injury rehabilitation: An attribution-emotion investigation. [Abstract]. *Journal of Sports Sciences, 16,* 106–107.

Tegner, Y., & Lorentzon, R. (1996). Concussions among Swedish elite ice hockey players. *British Journal of Sports Medicine, 30,* 251–255.

Theodorakis, Y., Beneca, A., Malliou, P., & Goudas, M. (1997). Examining psychological factors during injury rehabilitation. *Journal of Sport Rehabilitation, 6,* 355–363.

Theodorakis, Y., Malliou, P., Papaioannou, A., Beneca, A., & Filactakidou, A. (1996). The effect of personal goals, self-efficacy, and self-satisfaction on injury rehabilitation. *Journal of Sport Rehabilitation, 5,* 214–223.

Thomas, C., & Rintala, J. (1989). Injury as alienation in sport. *Journal of the Philosophy of Sport, 16,* 44–58.

Tracey, J. (2003). The emotional response to the injury and rehabilitation process. *Journal of Applied Sport Psychology, 15,* 279–293.

Tripp, D. A., Stanish, W. D., Reardon, G., Coady, C., & Sullivan, M. J. L. (2003). Comparing postoperative pain experiences of the adolescent and adult athlete after anterior cruciate ligament surgery. *Journal of Athletic Training, 38,* 154–157.

Udry, E. (1997). Coping and social support among injured athletes following surgery. *Journal of Sport and Exercise Psychology, 19,* 71–90.

Udry, E. (1999). The paradox of injuries: Unexpected positive consequences. In D. Pargman (Ed.). *Psychological bases of sport injuries* (2nd ed., pp. 379–388). Morgantown, WV: Fitness Information Technology.

Udry, E., Gould, D., Bridges, D., & Beck, L. (1997). Down but not out: Athlete responses to season-ending injuries. *Journal of Sport and Exercise Psychology, 19,* 224–248.

Udry, E., Shelbourne, K. D., & Gray T. (2003). Psychological readiness for anterior cruciate ligament surgery: Describing and comparing the adolescent and adult experience. *Journal of Athletic Training, 38,* 167–171.

Valovich McLeod, T. C., Heil J., McVeigh S. D., & Bay R. C. (2006). Identification of sport and recreational activity concussion history through the pre-participation screening and a symptom survey in young athletes. *Journal of Athletic Training, 41*(4), 470–472.

Van Heerden, J. C., & Potgieter, J. R. (2003). A computerized programme for monitoring athletes' emotional stress and pain perception. *South African Journal for Research in Sport, Physical Education and Research, 25,* 93–103.

Van Mechelen, W., Twisk, J., Molendijk, A., Blom, B., Snel, J., & Kemper, H. C. G. (1996). Subject-related risk factors for sports injuries: A 1-yr prospective study in young adults. *Medicine and Science in Sports and Exercise, 28,* 1171–1179.

Vernacchia, R. A., Reardon, J. P., & Templin, D. P. (1997). Sudden death in sport: Managing the aftermath. *The Sport Psychologist, 11,* 223–235.

Walker, N., Thatcher, J., & Lavallee, D. (2010). A preliminary development of the Re-Injury Anxiety Inventory (RIAI). *Physical Therapy in Sport, 11,* 23–29.

Wallechinsky, D. (1984). *The complete book of the Olympics.* New York: Viking Penguin.

Weiss, M. R. (2004). *Developmental sport and exercise psychology: A lifespan perspective.* Morgantown, WV: Fitness Information Technology.

Wiese, D. M., Weiss, M. R., & Yukelson, D. P. (1991). Sport psychology in the training room: A survey of athletic trainers. *The Sport Psychologist, 5,* 15–24.

Wiese-Bjornstal, D. M. (2004). Psychological responses to injury and illness. In G. S. Kolt & M. B. Andersen (Eds.), *Psychology in the physical and manual therapies* (pp. 21–38). Edinburgh, SCT: Churchill Livingstone.

Wiese-Bjornstal, D. M., Gardetto, D. M., & Shaffer, S. M. (1999). Effective interaction skills for sports medicine professionals. In R. Ray & D. M. Wiese-Bjornstal (Eds.), *Counseling in sports medicine* (pp. 55–74). Champaign, IL: Human Kinetics.

Wiese-Bjornstal, D. M., Smith, A. M., Shaffer, S. M., & Morrey, M. A. (1998). An integrated model of response to sport injury: Psychological and sociological dynamics. *Journal of Applied Sport Psychology, 10,* 46–69.

Williams, J. M., & Andersen, M. B. (1997). Psychosocial influences on central and peripheral vision and reaction time during demanding tasks. *Behavioral Medicine, 26,* 160–167.

Williams, J. M., & Andersen, M. B. (1998). Psychosocial antecedents of sport injury: Review and critique of the stress injury model. *Journal of Applied Sport Psychology, 10,* 5–25.

Williams, J. M., & Andersen, M. B. (2007). Psychosocial antecedents of sport injury and interventions for risk reduction. In R. C. Eklund & G. Tenenbaum (Eds.), *Handbook of sport psychology* (3rd ed., pp. 379–403). Hoboken, NJ: John Wiley & Sons, Inc.

Williams, J. M., Hogan, T. D., & Andersen, M. B. (1993). Positive states of mind and athletic injury risk. *Psychosomatic Medicine, 55,* 468–472.

Williams, J. M., & Roepke, N. (1993). Psychology of injury and injury rehabilitation. In R. N. Singer, M. Murphey, & L. K. Tennant (Eds.), *Handbook of research on sport psychology* (pp. 815–839). New York: Macmillan.

Williams, J. M., Tonymon, P., & Andersen, M. B. (1990). Effects of life-event stress on anxiety and peripheral narrowing. *Behavioral Medicine, 16,* 174–181.

Williams, J. M., Tonymon, P., & Andersen, M. B. (1991). Effects of stressors and coping resources on anxiety and peripheral narrowing in recreational athletes. *Journal of Applied Sport Psychology, 3,* 126–141.

Williams, J. M., Tonymon, P., & Wadsworth, W. A. (1986). Relationship of stress to injury in intercollegiate volleyball. *Journal of Human Stress, 12*, 38–43.

Williamson, I. J. S., & Goodman, D. (2006). Converging evidence for the under-reporting of concussions in youth ice hockey. *British Journal of Sports Medicine, 40*, 128–132.

Wittig, A. F., & Schurr, K. T. (1994). Psychological characteristics of women volleyball players: Relationships with injuries, rehabilitation, and team success. *Personality and Social Psychology Bulletin, 20*, 322–330.

Wu, S. K., & Williams, T. (1999). Paralympic swimming performance, impairment, and the functional classification system. *Adapted Physical Activity Quarterly, 16*, 251–270.

Young, K. (2004). Sports-related pain and injury: Sociological notes. In K. Young (Ed.), *Sporting bodies, damaged selves: Research in the sociology of sports-related injury* (pp. 1–25). Oxford, England: Elsevier.

Young, K., & Charlesworth, H. (2004). Injured female athletes: Experiential accounts from England and Canada. In S. Loland, I. Waddington, B. Skirstad (Eds.), *Pain and injury in sport: Social and ethical analysis* (89–106). Leicester, England: Routledge.

Young, K., McTeer, W., & White, P. (1994). Body talk—Male athletes reflect on sport, injury, and pain. *Sociology of Sport Journal, 11*, 175–194.

Young, K., & White, P. (1999). Threats to sport careers: Elite athletes talk about injury and pain. In J. Coakley (Ed.), *Inside sport* (pp. 203–213). London: Routledge.

Zemper, E. D. (2009). Catastrophic injuries among young athletes. *British Journal of Sports Medicine, 44*, 13–20.

Pain and Performance

John Heil *and* Leslie Podlog

Abstract

Pain is a prevalent factor in competitive sport and physical performance domains such as dance, military operations, and outdoor adventure activities. This chapter synthesizes pain scholarship from various performance domains, drawing from medical research, sport science, and case study reports to identify best pain assessment and intervention practices. The chapter also examines the function of pain at the extremes of performance. Seven topic areas are covered: the psychosocial/performance literature on pain appraisal and coping, principles of pain science and practice, psychological intervention, psychological perspectives on pain medication, chronic pain and injury, remarkable feats of pain tolerance, and concluding comments and suggestions for future research.

Key Words: Pain, injury, psychology, sport, performance, military, remarkable feats, intervention, assessment, research

The experience of pain is ubiquitous in sport, influencing training and competition, as well as injury rehabilitation and prevention. The athlete's experience of pain is an encounter with core issues in the ethos of sport, including personal sacrifice, meeting adversity, and heroic behavior. As such, pain behavior not only influences performance but also is seen as defining character. Expectations regarding pain tolerance are imbedded in the culture of sport and bear heavily on injury risk and rehabilitation. Although long on lore and legend, the meaning of pain and the means to pain management are short on science in the sport research literature. Fortunately, medical science has embraced the study of pain, albeit from a pathology-oriented perspective.

This chapter reviews the relatively sparse sport science literature and presents foundation concepts from medical research and practice. Although the sport literature sheds light on the interplay of pain, injury, and performance, it offers little insight into its underlying science. Medical scholarship has made great strides in recent years in illuminating the biological, psychological, and social dynamics of the pain experience, but with little study of high-performance environments. The phenomenology of pain and performance is exceptionally well articulated in personal anecdote and case study in sport and high-performance domains, but does not reference the underlying science of behavior. Given the critical impact of pain in high-performance settings, the relative absence of directly relevant scientific research, and the inherent difficulties in scientifically studying uniquely occurring pain performance experiences, the case study literature merits attention—if only to help generate hypotheses for future research. The synthesis of medical scholarship, sport science, and case study reports will serve as the basis for identifying intervention practices and understanding the function of pain at the extremes of performance.

This chapter both complements and extends Chapter 32 of this volume by identifying best knowledge and practices for pain assessment and intervention. Because all treatment providers play a role in pain management, a cross-disciplinary perspective is embraced. Pain is defined by the International Association for the Study of Pain as a sensory and emotional experience associated with actual or potential tissue damage, or described in terms of such damage (Merskey & Bogduk, 1994). The chapter is divided into seven sections: the psychosocial/performance literature on pain appraisal and coping, principles of pain science and practice, psychological intervention, psychological perspectives on pain medication, chronic pain and injury, remarkable feats of pain tolerance, and concluding comments and future research directions.

Literature Review: Pain Appraisal and Coping

Pain is integral to the sport experience, on and off the field of play. The central mechanism guiding athlete behavior is the meaning assigned to pain (Fordyce, 1976; Loeser, 1991). Addison, Kremer, and Bell (1998) offer a continuum of pain experienced by athletes: *fatigue and discomfort*—normal or routine sensations associated with competition, training, and rehabilitation; *positive training pain*—nonthreatening, typically occurring during endurance activity, and believed to be under the athlete's control; *negative training pain*—perceived as threatening and an indication that continued training is no longer beneficial; *negative warning pain*—similar to negative training pain, but more threatening, signaling potential injury and prompting the athlete to evaluate its cause and take appropriate action; *negative acute pain*—indicates injury and is perceived as intense and specific; *numbness*—the absence of sensation, interpreted as highly negative and typically a cause for concern.

Fatigue, discomfort, and positive training pain should be expected during rehabilitation and ideally perceived as evidence that athletes are at beneficial levels of intensity. When pain is not readily classifiable by athletes, or is mistakenly believed to be negative acute pain, it may lead to distress and decreased compliance with rehabilitation, even if benign (Sullivan, Stanish, Waite, Sullivan, & Tripp, 1998). Alternately, when incorrectly interpreting negative pain, athletes are at risk for treatment setbacks and reinjury. When pain elicits strong negative emotional reactions, a vicious pain cycle can develop in which pain causes increased distress that in turn causes increased pain, and so on (Fordyce, 1976; Heil, 1993). Depression and anxiety enhance pain perception through increased physiological arousal and interference with positive coping behaviors (Adler & Gattaz, 1993; Heil, 1993).

Athletes can manage their reaction to pain by managing cognitions and behaviors. Muscular relaxation, goal setting, education regarding injury, following prescribed physical functional limits, and adherence to prescribed exercise are positive choices that facilitate rehabilitation and healing (Heil, 1993, Taylor & Taylor, 1997). Conversely, *catastrophizing* is a maladaptive cognitive coping strategy (Jones, Rollman, White, Hill, & Brooke, 2003) that increases pain perception and undermines function. Unfortunately, catastrophic thinking (such as, "The pain is killing me") is a common reaction to athletic injury (e.g., Udry, Gould, Bridges, & Beck, 1997). Catastrophizing is characterized by an excessive focus on pain (rumination), with an exaggeration of threat (magnification) and the perception of not being able to cope with the pain (helplessness) (Sullivan, Bishop, & Pivik, 1995). This thinking style is associated with a more intense pain experience and increased psychological distress in general medical patients (Sullivan et al., 2001), and athletes (Sullivan, Tripp, Rodgers, & Stanish, 2000). Catastrophizing increases muscle tension and anxiety, and stimulates neural systems that produce increased sensitivity to pain or *hyperalgesia* (Grau & Meagher, 1999). Catastrophizing can impair the ability of performers to make good decisions and to take appropriate action in response to their pain.

Pain perceptions and coping styles have also been examined among performing artists, in particular, ballet dancers (Anderson & Hanrahan, 2008; Encarnacion, Meyers, Ryan & Pease, 2000; Paparizos, Tripp, Sullivan, & Rubenstein, 2005; Thomas & Tarr, 2009). In a study of professional ballet and contemporary dancers, Anderson and Hanrahan (2008) investigated the relationships between the type of pain experienced (performance pain vs. injury pain), the cognitive appraisal of pain, and pain coping styles. They found that neither the cognitive appraisal of pain nor pain coping style differ according to the type of pain experienced or the severity of pain. However, dancers with performance pain of either high or low severity were more likely to dance in pain than were dancers experiencing injury pain. Moreover, the appraisal of pain as threatening was predictive of avoidance and catastrophizing pain coping styles (Anderson & Hanrahan, 2008). The researchers concluded that dancers may not differentiate between performance pain and injury pain, or alter their appraisal and coping strategies according to the characteristics of the pain experienced. Their findings highlight an opportunity for educating dancers about the difference between routine pain that is considered a normal part of training, and pain that is a signal of serious injury.

Encarnacion et al. (2000) examined the role of gender and skill level (i.e., academy level, preprofessional and professional) in pain coping styles among ballet dancers. Although no significant differences were found across skill levels, a more positive pain coping style was identified among females. Encarnacion and colleagues (2000) suggest that the nonsignificant differences in response styles between skill levels may be a consequence of the high level of psychological uniformity of individuals who are drawn to a competitive dance environment. In contrast with these findings, Paparizos et al. (2005) found that high-skill dancers (M years training = 15.24) had higher pain tolerance than did low-skill dancers (M years training = 4.36) who, in turn, had greater tolerance than nondancers. This suggests that dancers may develop tolerance to pain as they progress through the dance hierarchy and are socialized into the dance subculture.

Although athletes and performing artists interpret and cope with pain on an intrapsychic level, pain is experienced and managed in a social context that is unique to their sport or performance domain. In sport and high-performance subcultures, behavior is guided by a unique set of principles that are implicitly observed and are perceived as fundamental to success. Such principles are reflected in subtleties of language and in expectations regarding behavior—what Coakley and Hughes (1991) term the "sport ethic." The sport ethic is a set of norms accepted as the dominant criteria for defining what is accepted, expected, or required of an athlete or high performer. Adoption of the sport ethic is promoted by coaches, sports fans, and the media, all of whom glorify the heroism of athletes who "accept risks and play through pain" and who praise athletes who compete with injury for their "dedication to the game" (Hughes & Coakley, 1991). This can drive athletes to internalize the belief that pain tolerance and injury risk are essential measures of personal worth, to overcommit to the notion that one must sacrifice the body for success and, tragically, trade short-term gains (in the form of avoidable injury) for long-term success (Curry, 1993; Curry & Strauss, 1994; Malcom, 2006; Nixon, 1992, 1993).

Within sport and high-performance domains, special privileges and recognition are afforded to the elite competitor, with the path to elite status guided by a "survival of the fittest" mentality. From youth sport through high school and college, to elite and professional status, the climb up the ladder of competitive excellence becomes steeper and more challenging, leaving room for fewer and fewer athletes. Skills in pain management figure significantly in who will survive. Athletes are reminded of the dictum "no pain, no gain, no fame." They are encouraged to play with pain, to give 110%, and to be mentally tough. The expectation for high performance and maximal effort permeates the world of sport. In high-visibility sports, the fans and media join the athlete and coach in evaluating performance by these standards. As a consequence, the athlete is implicitly encouraged to take risks that potentially influence both physical and mental well-being.

Risk-taking behaviors were clearly documented in interviews with female British rowers, some of whom believed pain and injury to be a desirable part of rowing (Pike, 2004, p. 155). Many rowers felt that they must push their physical limits and tended to rely on the principle "no pain, no gain," even stating that "rowing training can never hurt enough" (Pike, 2004, p.155). According to Pike (2004), some athletes displayed their injury as a symbolic indicator of their commitment to training and to the sport ethic. Coaches reinforced this mentality by relaying to their athletes personal injury- or pain-related stories emphasizing how "down" or depressed they were as a result of "enforced rest" periods. According to Pike (2004), women's risk-taking behaviors were exacerbated by negligent coaching practices and a performance-efficiency ethos that took precedence over health and well-being.

Within the performance-efficiency ethos, athletes are often discouraged from expressing pain, and those who communicate pain freely may be perceived as "weak." Such constraints on communication can isolate injured athletes from coaches or teammates and encourage athletes to hide pain. In contrast, pain may elicit excessive social support and attention from friends and family, or allow athletes to avoid challenging workouts. These secondary gains can maintain pain. The assessment of pain by the provider is as challenging as it is critical to successful rehabilitation (Heil, 1993).

Principles of Pain Science and Practice

Widely held implicit assumptions regarding pain abound in medicine and sport, reflecting the training and culture of these distinct perspectives. Unfortunately, many of the fundamental assumptions are incorrect, resulting in the misinterpretation of pain behavior and misguided pain intervention. At the core of much thinking is a strong tendency in both the medical and sport communities to define pain either as physical or mental—that is, as real or in one's head. There are three commonly held misconceptions: that there is a pain center in the brain, that pain is solely an objective physical sensation, and that there is a one-to-one relationship between tissue damage and the personal experience of pain (e.g., Bonica,1991; Chapman, Tuckett, & Song, 2008; Melzack & Wall, 1965).

Anesthesiologist John Bonica (Chapman, 2011) was one of the first to begin to challenge these assumptions and, in so doing, pioneered the discipline of pain medicine. The first of his many significant innovations in pain management was the development of waking anesthesia–based pain control techniques (nerve blocks) for soldiers wounded in combat in World War II. Coincidentally, Bonica was motivated by the need to better care for injuries suffered as a professional wrestler while working his way through medical school. Bonica (1991) has suggested that these common misconceptions are rooted in a widely held but simplistic assumption he calls "telephone line" theory, which has driven implicit thinking about pain in medical practice. The telephone line theory conceptualizes pain as transmitted from periphery to the brain, much like a telephone signal, and assumes a linear relationship between pain stimulus and pain intensity, and between tissue damage and pain intensity. The best evidence now describes pain as a highly plastic phenomenon, with pain stimuli subject to an array of influences from the moment a sensory input is triggered until it is perceived in the brain (Chapman et al., 2008; Melzack & Wall, 1965).

Furthermore, it appears that the operation of the pain system changes as pain persists over time, as if it were a computer rewriting its own software (Chapman et al., 2008). There is no specific pain center in the brain. Rather, it appears that several brain centers in the cortical and limbic systems function in a complementary fashion to regulate distinct aspects of the phenomenology of pain (Jensen, 2010) These areas include the prefrontal cortex (PFC), the anterior cingulate cortex (ACC), the sensory cortex (SC), and the insula (IN) (Jensen,

2010). The prefrontal cortex seeks to give "meaning" to pain. It is the source of executive decision-making regarding pain coping and exerts a top-down effect via descending neural pathways, inhibiting pain and thus reducing its severity. The ACC, within the limbic system, mediates the affective/emotional component of pain, modulating the fear response and priming motor behavior. The SC provides information regarding pain location and quality (burning, aching etc.). The IN has been described as the sensory input to the limbic system. It conveys a sense of physical threat and triggers survival response.

The Biopsychology of Pain

Without a clear understanding of the function of the pain system, the ability to understand pain behavior, to direct intervention, or to conduct research is seriously curtailed. The following is a brief synopsis of the biological processes thought to underlie the pain experience. For a more extensive explanation written for a sport psychology audience, the reader is referred to Fine (1993) and Heil and Fine (1999).

THE BIOLOGY OF PAIN

The pain processing system is currently conceived of as a supersystem integrating inputs from the neurological, endocrine, and immune systems, mediated by overlapping sets of neural circuitry and biochemical messengers (Chapman et al., 2008). The neurological core of the pain system is the nociceptive system, which includes peripheral nerves, the spinal cord, and the brain.

Pain and other sensory stimuli from the periphery converge at the spinal cord, along with information received (via descending tracts) from the brain. Consequently, the spinal cord functions like a neurosensory switching station. Melzack and Wall (1965) proposed the *gate control theory of pain*, which suggests that processing centers in the spinal cord may either decrease or increase the intensity of pain as a neuroelectric phenomenon, with the result that individuals may perceive relatively less or more pain than that initially signaled in the periphery. Melzack and Wall (1965) use the metaphor of the spinal cord as a "gate," opening and closing in response to an array of potential inputs. This theory, which revolutionized thinking about pain, is used to explain the efficacy of pain control modalities (ranging from cryotherapy to ultrasound to acupuncture), as well as an array of pain behaviors, including remarkable feats of pain tolerance (Heil & Fine, 1999).

Even as the neuroelectric signaling reaches the brain, the final perception of pain is deferred momentarily as input from multiple ascending pathways are received at brain centers in the cortical and limbic systems and integrated into a psychologically meaningful message. Even at its initial awareness, pain gains some of its meaning from prior experience, present state of mind, and future expectations (Heil & Fine, 1999).

PSYCHOLOGICAL FACTORS

Pain has long been characterized as a biopsychosocial phenomenon (Fordyce, 1976) in recognition of its potent psychological and social components. What begins as a nociceptive input gives rise to a sequence of psychological events that begin with perception, culminate in the determination of meaning, and in turn give rise to action (Heil & Fine, 1999). The single most important element of meaning is the assumed status of pain as benign or, alternately, as a sign of injury (O'Connor, Heil, Harmer, & Zimmerman, 2005).

As pain gains meaning, it also gains complexity as social and psychological factors build upon pain's nociceptive imprint. Pain is essentially a private subjective experience, unknown to others until it is expressed via words or behaviors (Fordyce, 1988). Once the nature of pain is communicated, it takes on an added social dimension as significant others (teammates, coaches, friends, health providers) react to the athlete's expression of pain (Craig, Versloot, Goubert, & Verhoort, 2010).

Often, pain is experienced as a transient phenomenon and an essentially inconsequential event. Alternately, it may take a pathological form leading to a highly disruptive life-altering disease process of indeterminable proportions—or, it may be the herald of behavior that reveals the depths of the human spirit.

Pain Assessment

Because of the fundamentally subjective nature of pain, large individual differences in pain sensitivity and pain tolerance, and varying influences of genetic and environmental factors, pain assessment is challenging in both clinical and research settings (Arendt-Nielsen & Yarnitsky, 2009; Nielsen, Staud, & Price, 2009; Turk & Melzack, 2010). For example, the *Handbook of Pain Assessment* (Turk & Melzack, 2010) includes 25 chapters and over 500 pages of text. Assessment itself is a multimodal process blending art and science. It typically incorporates various forms of self-report, blended with observation—and, in complex situations, should include psychological testing and the report of significant others (Turk & Melzack, 2010).

Experimental pain research incorporates measures of threshold (smallest stimulus intensity perceived as painful) and tolerance (maximum pain subject is willing to endure) with more complex sensory scaling methods, which are less subject to unique psychological factors (Arendt-Nielsen & Yarnitsky, 2009; Nielsen et al., 2009). Distinct approaches to clinical assessment have been developed for pediatric versus adult pain sufferers (e.g., McGrath, 1990, 2008) in both applied and research settings.

SELF-REPORT MEASURES

The diagnostic interview should provide information regarding quantitative and qualitative aspects of pain, the meaning that is attached to it by the athlete, and its impact on behavior. The simplest approach to the quantitative assessment is the use of a verbal and/or written numerical self-report scale (e.g., the 0 to 10 scale rating "no pain" to "worst possible pain"). Separate ratings are commonly made for "intensity" and "bothersomeness," which are hypothesized to assess the relative roles played by distinct brain centers (specifically, the SC and the ACC) in the subjective experience of pain (Jensen, 2010).

Qualitative pain assessment includes open-ended questions that provide a description of pain quality (e.g., burning, stabbing, electric, aching, etc.). This approach offers the benefit of a projective style of self-report that offers insight into the personal distress associated with pain. For example, report of muscles "tearing apart" versus "feeling tight" suggests catastrophizing.

Assessment of pain across varying settings functions as a form of behavioral analysis, revealing the impact of pain, its meaning to the athlete, and the scope of the athlete's coping methods. By identifying factors that increase or decrease pain, it identifies the specific moments of distress and the particular challenges posed by sport, rehabilitation, and day-to-day life activities. Contrasting behavior in the company of coaches, teammates, and rehabilitation providers offers insight into how the athlete is perceiving and responding to the expectations of others.

OBSERVATION

Attention to the expression of pain behaviors should be a routine aspect of pain assessment (Turk

& Melzack, 2010). Pain behaviors are observable across a variety of dimensions including vocal (e.g., sighing), facial (e.g., grimacing), gestural (e.g., rubbing), and postural (e.g., guarding; Keefe, Williams, & Smith, 2010). Muscular guarding (also called *bracing* or *splinting*) can be particularly problematic. It is a natural protective response to injury that isolates or decreases the mobility of the injured area through postural adjustment, functioning like a brace or sling. Although potentially adaptive during the initial phase of injury, guarding can become habituated, leading to both increased injury risk and poor performance by inhibiting proper body mechanics (Heil, 1993).

PSYCHOLOGICAL TESTING

A variety of assessment tools are available, some focused on pain specifically (including fear of pain, pain anxiety, pain catastrophizing) and others that have broad application but have been found to be of particular utility in pain assessment (e.g., measuring generalized anxiety, depression, and negative affect). Mounce, Keogh, and Eccleston (2010) examined a wide range of measures commonly used in pain assessment, including the Pain and Negative Affect Schedule, the Spielberger State-Trait Anxiety Inventory, the Depression Anxiety and Stress Scale (Short form), the Pain Catastrophizing Scale, the Pain Anxiety Symptom Scale, the Fear of Pain Questionnaire III, the Brief Fear of Negative Evaluation Scale, and the Anxiety Sensitivity Index. In a factor analytic study with 508 pain-free participants, three dimensions of pain assessment were identified: general distress, fear of pain from injury, and cognitive intrusion of pain.

Commonly used measures include the Multidimensional Pain Inventory (MPI; Junghaenel, Keefe, & Broderick, 2010) and the McGill Pain Questionnaire (MPQ; Melzack,1975; Melzack & Katz, 2010). The MDI is a 61-item self-report instrument that classifies each patient into one of three adaptational styles: adaptive, dysfunctional, or interpersonally distressed. Although designed specifically for chronic pain sufferers, the comprehensive and face valid nature of the questions renders it a useful tool for any longstanding pain problem.

The MPQ and its variants include an extensive pain-related history, as well as a pain drawing and a listing of pain words. The pain words are a series of 78 terms that are categorized as either sensory (e.g., sharp, burning, aching) or affective-evaluative (e.g., exhausting, fearful, agonizing). The ease of administration and face validity of the instrument has long made it a standard in psychological assessment in pain treatment settings (Melzack & Katz, 2010; Ransford, Cairns, & Mooney, 1976).

In complex injury situations, a multidimensional measure of personality, such as the Minnesota Multiphasic Personality Inventory (MMPI; Hathaway & McKinley, 1989), may prove useful. Research utilizing the MMPI with athletes has generally found a positive correlation between psychological health and performance (LeUnes & Nation, 1989). The MMPI is especially useful in the evaluation of severe injury or when there appears to be an overlay between psychological and medical factors (Fordyce, 1979). It has been used in presurgical evaluations to predict difficulties in rehabilitation following surgery (Spengler & Freeman, 1979; Wise, Jackson, & Rocchio, 1979).

Pain assessment does not require a complex methodology or use of formal assessment. In the everyday performance environment, pragmatism and ease of administration trump complexity and psychometric rigor. Simply asking for pain ratings (verbal or written) across varied time and circumstances offers insight into the links among pain, behavior, and environment. In addition, observations of pain behavior and emotional distress across performance and rehabilitation environments offer a wealth of data. The information gathered in this way is unobtrusive, thus averting the feeling of being evaluated. Sharing of impressions by providers (and coaches), whether congruent or discordant, offers useful information, triggers constructive dialogue, and facilitates a team-oriented approach to rehabilitation.

Frequent repeat measures are particularly useful for tracking subtle changes in injury, revealing how effectively the athlete is meeting the successive challenges of rehabilitation and return to play. Van Heerden and Potgieter (2003) have designed a computer-based self-report instrument that records and summarizes contemporaneous reports of pain and mood and is easily incorporated in a rehabilitation setting.

Psychological Intervention

Pain and pain management are important performance issues and an integral aspect of rehabilitation. To be effective, pain interventions must integrate principles of high performance and rehabilitation. This section provides an overview of mental training relevant to pain management, identifies situations in which pain may function as a barrier to treatment, and proposes an intervention strategy that integrates management of performance- and injury-related pain.

Mental Training

The mental training methods that are well established within sport and other high-performance environments share much in common with pain management techniques used in clinical settings. For example, cognitive-behavioral methods, such as stress inoculation (e.g., Turk, Meichenbaum, & Genest, 1983), are readily transferrable from sport performance to injury management. Similarly, methods used for relaxation and intensity control are of comparable utility in either setting. A variety of pain management interventions have been devised for use in general medical settings (Fordyce, 1976; Kabat-Zinn, 1982; Turk & Gatchel, 2002). However, these methods can be reconfigured for an action-oriented high-performance setting. For example, Petras (2009) reports on a novel mental training intervention done in collaboration with an orthopedic surgeon. By effectively managing pain and distress, a fracture was set immediately after injury at the sport venue, rather than delaying the procedure until the athlete was transported to a hospital.

Research on the mental strategies used by distance runners during training and competition (e.g., Morgan, 1978; Schomer, 1986, 1987) offers insight into approaches to pain management that are suitable for athletic performance. These methods entail either focusing on selected somatic perceptions or, alternately, dissociating from these inputs. This will be discussed in detail subsequently, when presenting the pain matrix concept.

Jensen (2010) proposes an innovative neuropsychological model of pain management that offers hypotheses on the neurological mechanisms underlying the efficacy of specific methods of self-regulation. This model, although reflective of a clinical perspective, is pragmatically congruent with the methods underlying mental training in that its intent is to empower with skills and knowledge. Jensen (2010) identifies a three-component typology of pain management methods distinguished by the specific focus of intervention: changing thoughts about pain (e.g., cognitive restructuring and acceptance based treatments), modifying behavior in response to pain (e.g., operant conditioning and motivational interviewing), and altering the sensory experience of pain (e.g., relaxation training and self-hypnosis).

Meeting the simultaneous demands of pain control in injury and in high performance poses a formidable challenge. As complex as this task can be with healthy athletes, it is even more demanding for those who are injured because of the simultaneous and sometimes conflicting needs of performance and safety. Mastering this doubly complex focus challenge lies at the heart of understanding the difference between pain and injury, which is itself an enigma. In the subsequent sections, the potential role of pain as a barrier to rehabilitation is discussed and a model for integrating pain management across performance and rehabilitation settings is presented.

Pain As a Barrier to Rehabilitation

Pain may emerge as a barrier to rehabilitation: as a potent distractor, as a trigger of anxiety or fear about recovery, or as a cue to question the efficacy of treatment. Conversely, failure to recognize and accept the limits that pain is signaling can also complicate recovery.

Problems with adherence to rehabilitative regimens are well documented in the medical and health psychology literature and may reflect a broad range of underlying psychological and interpersonal dynamics (Brewer, 2007). Catastrophizing has emerged as a widespread and difficult problem in the medical literature (Mounce et al., 2010). Given the complexities of reporting and assessing pain, the potential exists for compliance issues to become intertwined with problems in the provider–patient relationship. Consider the situation in which an athlete fears that pain experienced during rehabilitation is a sign of reinjury, when in fact it is benign pain associated with recovery. This may result in athlete's reluctance or refusal to comply with rehabilitation protocols (O'Connor et al., 2005). This may be perceived by providers as a lack of motivation, leading treatment providers to question the athlete's sincerity, or even to challenge complaints of pain (Ford & Gordon, 1993). Such questioning may further undermine trust in the ability of treatment providers to safely direct rehabilitation. As a consequence, the athlete–provider relationship may be compromised, thus further interfering with recovery.

An excessive focus on pain and the exaggerated sense of threat associated with negative self-talk can increase the severity of pain (Sullivan et al., 2000) and thus limit athletes' activity levels (Sullivan et al., 1998). The emotional distress associated with catastrophizing (e.g., "I'll never recover,") can inhibit athletes' motivations to remain committed to their rehabilitation programs. Negative self-talk and catastrophizing can become habitual when doubt, uncertainty, and fear guide athletes' thinking (Taylor & Taylor, 1997). Fortunately, negative thinking can be unlearned with conscious attention, frequent challenge, and replacement with realistically positive self-talk.

Individuals who are better able to minimize pain persist longer in painful activities, including rehabilitation (Lysholm & Wiklander, 1987). Although positive self-talk can minimize pain and increase rehabilitation performance (Theodorakis et al., 1997), statements that are simply optimistic are not effective. Self-talk must be realistic and meaningful. An accurate injury assessment and medical facts about the injury and pain provide the evidence to counter negative self-talk and encourage "realistically positive" self-talk. In situations in which the athlete can be assured that pain is benign, any of a variety of methods that refocus attention can be useful, including deliberate use of mental training techniques, as well as informal methods as simple as occupying oneself with another task.

Failure to respond to pain as a signal of danger or otherwise set reasonable limits on physical activity may be a consequence of underlying maladaptive psychological dynamics. Among injured athletes, failure to accept the limitations signaled by pain may be a manifestation of denial or lack of understanding regarding the severity of injury (O'Connor et al., 2005). Rehabilitating athletes may also push needlessly into pain as a signal of effort or proof of courage, reflecting either a counterphobic response to fear or a strong self-punitive orientation motivated by a poor sense of self-worth (Ogilvie & Tutko, 1966). Overexercise may be seen in conjunction with anorexia nervosa and bulimia, in which compulsive adherence to activity regimens are practiced as weight loss measures without proper regard to the impact on overall health and well-being. The so-called "addicted athlete," typically a recreational runner, also demonstrates a mix of compulsive adherence to activity and failure to set effective limits when injured (Chapman & De Castro, 1990; Pierce, McGowan, & Lynn, 1993).

Misunderstanding or miscommunication about pain between athlete and provider can undermine rehabilitation. When the athlete perceives that pain complaints are minimized, or when the provider sees pain as exaggerated, the treatment relationship may become strained and the quality of care compromised. In either case, it is the primary responsibility of the treatment provider to lead the conversation about pain, keeping in mind that by definition pain is a sensory and emotional experience. Furthermore,

the provider is specifically cautioned about moving too quickly to make an assumption about malingering (Heil, 1993).

Pain Sport Matrix

Pain management in both sport and rehabilitation shares a common skill set: to effectively assess the meaning of pain perceptions, to maintain an appropriate focus in the face of distractions (such as pain perception or catastrophizing cognition), to engage in informed decision-making regarding a best course of action, and to regulate the autonomic and other physiologic mechanisms of the pain system.

Research on long-distance runners has identified association–dissociation as a method for managing the collective discomfort of pain, fatigue, and exertion during performance (Brewer, Van Raalte, & Linder, 1996; Crust, 2003; Heil, 1990; Masters & Lambert, 1989; Masters & Ogles, 1998; Morgan, 1978; Schomer, 1986, 1987). In this literature, *association* refers to a focus on relevant performance cues (Masters & Ogles, 1998). For example, runners would use association to be aware of their pace and rate of perceived exertion, as well as of fatigue, and pain. *Dissociation* is described as the intentional use of distraction as a way of coping with the mental and physical demands of the sport (Masters & Ogles, 1998). For instance, runners would talk to another runner or look at their surroundings to keep their mind off of the discomfort.

The association–dissociation strategy assumes an implicit role for assessment, decision-making, and self-regulation. The research suggests that elite distance runners rely more heavily on association, are more facile at shifting attention according to the demands of the sport (e.g., from a dissociative, distractive mode to an associative, focusing mode), and better able to tune into performance cues as needed despite pain.

Research by Heil (1990) uses a survey method to examine perspectives of sport psychologists and medical pain management specialists on association and dissociation. It challenges the assumption that dissociation from pain demands simultaneous dissociation from sport performance and suggests that the athlete may choose to associate (or dissociate) to pain or to sport independently. Furthermore, the results indicate that the interpretation of whether a given cognition is associative or dissociative is subjective, varying by individual. From this, it follows that a given cognitive strategy may have a divergent impact on pain tolerance and sport performance for different individuals and that cognitive strategies need to be devised based on their unique meaning to the individual athlete.

The *pain-sport attentional matrix* (Heil, 1993) assumes that pain and performance are independent dimensions (rather than a unitary dimension, as assumed by Morgan and others), both of which are subject to the application of associative and dissociative strategies. The matrix identifies a four-dimensional strategy that addresses pain assessment, decision-making, focusing, and self-regulation. Each strategy is defined by whether the athlete "focuses on" or "focuses away from" pain and sport and represents a starting point for a mental training intervention.

1. *Associating to both pain and sport* can be beneficial when pain signals proper technique. If, instead, the athlete changes movement patterns to avoid pain, then compensatory injury could result.

2. *Dissociating from both pain and sport* during performance is problematic because focus is sacrificed for the sake of pain management. Alternately, this approach could be beneficially applied during natural breaks from activity as a way of getting psychological rest from pain or the cognitive demands of sport.

3. *Dissociating from pain while associating to sports performance* is appropriate when pain is understood as routine (or, in medical terms, *benign*); otherwise pain becomes a distraction and undermines performance.

4. *Associating to pain and dissociating from sport* is of value in the management of overuse and chronic injury. Because sport performance can fully absorb attention, pain signals may be suppressed to the detriment of athletes' physical well-being. This strategy can be used in breaks between activities to assess pain or, for example, be used as a check on muscular guarding.

Psychological Perspectives on Pain Medication

The use of medications by injured athletes presents a challenge to the sports medicine physician given the culture of risk in sport, the potential for ergolytic (or performance-diminishing) side effects, the hazards of inadvertent anti-doping violations, and the controversial medical milieu that both guides and constrains prescription of pain medications. Inadequate prescription of medication to manage acute pain can undermine the injury recovery process, even as overuse of opioid analgesics is at the heart of a society-wide drug problem (American Pain Society, 2008; Chou et al., 2009a,b).

Further complicating proper care of athletes is their tendency to be risk takers and to attempt continued play even when injured (Bergandi, 1985; Malcolm, 2006; Pike, 2004). When athletes receive opioids for pain due to acute injuries, there is the risk that they may not allow the injuries to heal fully before resuming vigorous physical activity, essentially using medication to block the pain-driven danger signal. This can result in exacerbation of injury and ongoing pain, creating a mutually exacerbating cycle of medication and injury (Lipman, 1993).

The so-called weaker opioids, such as hydrocodone and oxycodone, are the most commonly prescribed drugs for moderate to severe pain due to injury, but they are also potentially dangerous in overdose. Football player John Matuszak was a headliner as an athlete, but news of his death from an accidental overdose of pain medication was only briefly noted on the back pages of the sports section ("Overdose caused death," 1989).

For anti-doping test-eligible athletes, the central question is whether opioid use is ergogenic (performance enhancing) or ergolytic (performance reducing). However, this question is rendered more complex by the potential performance-diminishing impact of nonuse. For example, athletes deprived of access to appropriate opioids may suffer a performance inhibiting effect. Opioids may be perceived as ergogenic in that they relieve pain and anxiety about pain and enhance sleep and neuromuscular tone—but whether they confer an unfair advantage is open to question. In contrast, when opioids mask pain, the athlete may be at undue risk for injury. Further, the opioids' side-effect profile of physiological depression and diminished concentration may undermine performance (i.e., be ergolytic). Although in the final analysis the choice remains with the athlete, the decision can be a complex one as the athlete must consider the relative influence of therapeutic benefit, side effects, and injury risk.

Decision-making regarding use of pain medication is complicated by issues related to quality of care, regulatory guidelines for prescribers, the constraints of anti-doping testing, and a culture that embraces "no pain, no gain." The ethical dilemmas that thus arise regarding athlete safety and fair play are likely to continue to be a part of the day-to-day delivery of athlete health care and part of the larger debate of the role of sport in society. The psychologist has a key role to play in assisting physicians by monitoring compliance, side effects, and efficacy; assessing psychological status as influenced by injury and medication use; and providing nonmedication-based alternatives to pain management.

Pain at the Extremes of Performance

Remarkable feats of acute pain tolerance, in which the pain system functions at its optimum, are the stuff of legend. Chronic pain, in contrast, is an aberration of a system designed to enhance survival in the face of threat to the physical integrity of the organism. Acute pain evolves into chronic pain as the nociceptive system is derailed from the survival imperative that has driven its operation. It is well noted that both phenomena are very much a function of the context within which the experience unfolds and of the mind-set of the individual.

Chronic Pain and Injury

Chronic pain is pain that persists beyond the routine healing process or is present in the absence of apparent structural pathology. The hallmark of chronic pain syndromes is an increasing role of psychological factors over time and progressively complex engagement of the pain supersystem (Chapman et al., 2008). The assumption held in some quarters of the medical community that chronic pain is a psychological rather than medical condition has been debunked by neuroimaging research that reveals differential brain processing of pain signals in healthy versus chronic pain patients (Apkarian, Baliki, & Geha, 2009; Tracey & Bushnell, 2009; Williams & Clauw, 2009). There is also evidence linking fibromyalgia, a common chronic pain condition, to mitochondrial dysfunction (Teitlebaum, Johnson, & St Cyr, 2006).

Societally, *chronic pain syndrome* is a problem of enormous proportion. Gregorian, Gasik, Winghan, Voeller, and Kavanagh (2010) estimate an annual health care cost in the United States of $86 billion for back and neck pain alone. Annual lost productivity from common pain-related conditions has been estimated at about $61 billion (Stewart, Ricci, Chee, Morgenstein, & Lipton, 2003). Lost productivity defines pain as a performance problem in the United States and throughout industrialized nations (Fordyce, 1988; Kiesler & Finholt, 1998). Fordyce (1998) traces the increasing incidence of pain and disability to the rise of disability entitlement programs and the way in which such programs are managed, essentially characterizing pain as a "biopsychosocial" and "economic" problem. Kiesler and

Finholt (1998) offer an incisive multidimensional case study analysis on the relatively abrupt increase of repetitive strain injury (an overuse injury) in transcriptionists. They identify a multitude of contributing factors that span change in work tasks and ergonomics, as well as social and cultural elements of the work environment.

The role of physical activity is critical in the return to productive functioning. In a simple but pivotal study on the role of rest versus activity Deyo, Diehl, and Rosenthal (1986) found that 2 days of rest for a nonsurgical back injury led to a better outcome than did 7 days of rest. In an often-cited study, Bortz (1984) identified the compelling effects of disuse syndrome that span multiple body systems and that is understood to be a critical factor in the evolution of acute pain into chronic pain syndromes. The term "industrial athlete" has been applied to the rehabilitating worker, in recognition of the inherent physical functional demands of the industrial workplace. Thus, the application of a sport performance approach to this clinical population appears prudent. A multidisciplinary model has been proposed that blends a traditional rehabilitation-oriented approach with sport performance principles (Heil, Wakefield, & Reed, 1998). The transferability of sport and rehabilitation concepts in serious illness and injury are well articulated, for example, by Lance Armstrong (2000) in *Its Not About the Bike.*

Although chronic pain syndromes have been recognized in military personnel (Gatchel et al., 2009), the role of chronic pain and injury in sport is not well recognized and is poorly understood. This may reflect a natural selection process for those who fall prey to chronic pain or injury, preventing them from reaching the highest levels of competitive sport. Clearly, poor performance will take an athlete off the field of play and out of the spotlight. Furthermore, there is a tendency to forget yesterday's heroes. The full impact of injury may not be seen until long after sport careers are over. Consider the *Sports Illustrated* (Nack, 2001) cover story featuring football great Johnny Unitas, who spent the latter years of his life in chronic pain. Increasing attention to the long-term impact of head injury in sport may reveal an unseen epidemic of chronic pain and disability after competitive careers are completed. The now dated football documentary, *Disposable Heroes,* which details the chronic injuries of legendary "iron man" Jim Otto may prove to be of enduring relevance (Couturie, Else, & Witte, 1989).

Remarkable Feats of Pain Tolerance

Remarkable feats of pain tolerance have long been described in diverse literatures, including competitive sport (e.g., Heil, 1998), outdoor adventure (e.g., Hansel, 1985; Ralston, 2004), military action (Beecher, 1946; Grossman, 2004), and, police and fire fighting (Klinger, 2004; Maclean, 1992). Although athletes' remarkable feats are recognized within the pain literature (e.g., Beecher, 1946, 1956; Loeser, 1991), attempts to explain such phenomena are limited. During World War II, military surgeon Beecher (1946, 1956) observed that soldiers wounded in combat needed less opioid analgesics for relief of pain compared to civilians who suffered similar injuries. He concluded that medication use is a function not only of the severity of a wound but also of the emotional response associated with it. The role of situational factors in pain perception and evidence of large interindividual differences in response to analgesic medication is well supported in subsequent research (American Pain Society, 2008).

A psychological model of acute pain tolerance in high-performance environments is proposed that integrates sport psychology and the medical literature, as well as anecdotal reports in the outdoor sport, public safety, and survival literatures. The model suggests that remarkable feats are typically associated with the following elements (Heil, 1993):

• Expectations that pain can and will be tolerated
• Reframing of pain as a positive factor
• Strong goal focus
• Absorption in the "work in progress"; that is, a focus on sport or performance over pain
• Altered consciousness as ego-syntonic; that is, acceptance of cognitive and perceptual change under stress
• Assumption of limited pain duration
• Survival context (literal or metaphorical)

The manner in which these seven factors may be manifested in sport and high-performance are detailed below.

PAIN TOLERANCE

Training typically entails some degree of pain and privation in tandem with skill building behavior and, as such, provides training in pain management. Paparizos et al. (2005) found differences in pain perceptions among ballet dancers of different levels, suggesting that pain tolerance is either trained or is a selection factor in success. In some settings, for example military special forces, pain tolerance challenges are systematically integrated into training. For example, Navy SEAL training specifically incorporates fatigue and hypothermia tolerance (Orr, 1992). Expectations that athletes will tolerate pain permeate sport. Consider the legend of the Greek soldier, Pheidippides, who is said to have run from the battlefield on the Plains of Marathon to the city of Athens to announce a critical victory over an invasion force—only to collapse and die upon delivering the news. His efforts today are honored in the Marathon, which covers the 26 miles and 385 yards he allegedly covered in his run. Endurance events, such as the Tour de France and the Iditarod, which require high degrees of pain tolerance, are widely celebrated.

The *placebo analgesia response* in medical research (Geers, Wellman, Fowler, Helfer, & France, 2010; Sauro & Greenberg, 2005) offers insight into the complex interacting physiological and psychological mechanisms that appear to underlie pain tolerance in high-performance environments. Research supports a role for a positive mind-set, defined by a combination of expectation and optimism, in the placebo response (Geers et al., 2010). The placebo effect has been shown to be mediated by endogenous opioids, thus revealing the intricate interplay between mind and body in pain management (Sauro & Greenberg, 2005). Furthermore, specific neuropsychological correlates have been identified in the placebo response (i.e., increased activity in the PFC, decreased activity in the ACC; Jensen, 2010). Similarly, the *nocebo response* (opposite of the placebo response, in which atypically severe pain is experienced in response to a medical intervention) is also evoked by expectation. As in the placebo response, specific neurophysiological mediators (cholecystokinin as a facilitator; proglumide as an inhibitor) have been identified (Benedetti, Amanzio, Casadio, Oliaro, & Maggi, 1997).

PAIN REFRAMED

In training and competitive situations, pain is often reframed and interpreted as a positive element. This is not to suggest that pain is a goal in itself (as in "no pain, no gain"), but rather that the tolerance of pain in the pursuit of sport goals is expected. In endurance sports (e.g., running, swimming, rowing, cycling), pain can be equated with effort and thus interpreted positively. Research by Peterson, Durtschi, and Murphy (1990) demonstrates that, at a comparable level of exertion, elite-level athletes are more likely to describe aerobic discomfort as exertion, in contrast to the less elite runners who are more likely to report pain. Coincidentally, the process of relabeling of pain—that is, of interpreting pain as an alternate and less aversive sensation—is a common hypnotic intervention and has been deliberately applied in sport performance settings (Henschen & Gordin, 2010; Petras, 2009; Syrjala & Abrams, 2002). It appears that normalizing pain, either by reframing or by embracing the expectation that pain will be tolerated, triggers a top-down neurological effect of closing the pain gate to neuroelectric signaling (Jensen, 2010; Melzack & Wall, 1965)

GOAL FOCUS

The importance of goal focus is deeply rooted in coaching theory and practice, and is ingrained in the elite athlete through repeated training over many years. Goal focus is typically strongest during competition, when there is close proximity to compelling sport goals. Overlearning associated with almost countless repetitions automates sport skills, making them reflexive and facilitating their execution under stress. In *Young Men and Fire,* Maclean (1992), a fire fighter and wild fire survivor, investigates the Mann Gulch Wild Fire in which 12 of the U.S. Forest Services' elite airborne fire fighters, the Smoke Jumpers, died. At the conclusion of the book, he describes the fatal fire ground and offers this compelling observation of the power of a strong goal focus:

> After the bodies had fallen, most of them had risen again, taken a few steps, and fallen again; this time like pilgrims in prayer facing the top of the hill…The evidence then is that at the very end beyond thought and beyond fear and beyond even self compassion and divine bewilderment, there remains some firm intention to continue doing forever and ever what we last hoped to do on earth.

ABSORPTION IN THE "WORK"

In *Beyond Boredom and Anxiety*, Csikszentmihalyi (1975) described "flow" as a psychological state with a focus so intense that it approaches absolute absorption in the activity at hand. In a field study with police officers, Heil and Lee (2009) administered a cold pressor challenge in conjunction with high-fidelity simulation training. They found that typically the perception of cold rapidly fell out of awareness with onset of the training scenario in the absence of any specific effort to mediate pain, usually returning promptly at the conclusion of the

scenario when the officers were no longer absorbed with the challenging task. Can mental training help performers achieve flow states that might also help them manage pain? In a study using functional magnetic resonance imaging (fMRI), Davis (2008) demonstrated the efficacy of mental skills training in elite swimmers as a behavioral vector driving underlying neurophysiological processes. Jensen (2010) offers insight into the mind–body machinery that the high performer can access to modulate the pain response. In his neuropsychology theory of pain, he articulates a role for executive decision-making in pain management, with the PFC exerting top-down control of the periaqueductal gray (PAG), effectively reducing pain severity. The ACC also appears implicated, in that it is involved in the initiation and facilitation of behavioral coping efforts. In support of the potential trainability of this mind–body function is a laboratory pain study by Grant and Rainville (2009) comparing skilled Zen mediators. They observed that mediators had higher pain tolerance than nonmeditators, and that pain tolerance was further enhanced when meditating. In a related study (using conventional MRI), Grant, Courtemanche, Duerden, Duncan, and Rainville (2010) identified structural differences in specific brain regions between meditators and nonmeditators.

ALTERED CONSCIOUSNESS

Alterations in pain perception are part of a broader phenomenon of perceptual and cognitive alteration in high-performance environments, including competitive sport (Gordin & Reardon, 1995; Heil, 2003), police deadly force encounters (Klinger, 2004), and combat (Grossman, 2004). A listing of perceptual changes by Grossman (2004) includes visual tunneling and enhanced visual clarity, auditory exclusion and intensified sounds, slow motion and fast motion time effects, intrusive thinking and dissociation, memory loss and distortion, and temporary paralysis and automated behavior. These apparently contrasting effects may be performance enhancing or performance diminishing, depending upon personal and situational factors. It appears that alterations in consciousness are performance enhancing to the extent they are perceived as ego-syntonic—that is, consistent with one's ideal self-image. Consequently, training in military and police settings that focuses on accepting and normalizing such effects is beneficial (Grossman, 2004; Heil & Lee, 2009; Klinger, 2004).

These findings are consistent with research in sport examining the ideal performance state (see Chapter 38, this volume), including the experience of flow (Jackson & Csikszentmihalyi, 1999), the zone of optimal functioning (Hanin, 2000), and the concept of peak performance (Ravizza, 1977).

LIMITED DURATION

Most notable feats of pain tolerance are of limited duration, standing in poignant contrast to chronic pain, the hallmark of which is the prospect of no relief. In the competitive context, the athlete is able to look ahead to a time when the event will be over and pain will cease. The realization that performance pain will eventually pass but that the emotional cost of failure can endure indefinitely is a potent motivator to tolerate the pain of the moment in the pursuit of a more enduring sense of satisfaction with achievement. Concentration is more easily sustained and pain control more easily attained when an end is in sight. A laboratory-based pain study by Wiech, Kalisch, Weiskopf, Pleger, Stephan, and Dolan (2006) reveals the influence of duration on pain tolerance. They found that subjects with direct control over the duration of a noxious stimulus reported less pain (with identification of neurological correlates) when compared to subjects whose pain duration was manipulated by the experimenter.

SURVIVAL CONTEXT

Many of the anecdotal reports of remarkable pain tolerance are in a true survival context—in life-threatening conditions (Grossman; 2004; Klinger, 2004). Given the obvious limitations on human research on performance under the threat of death, it is instructive to examine studies using animal models. Kelly's (1986) review of the stress analgesia literature reveals underlying physiological changes in pain processing in response to stress, including potentially life-threatening stressors. These findings are consistent with Jensen's (2010) neuropsychological model of pain, in which the emergence of a perceived threat to the organism increases activity of the IN potentially mediating a survival response of the sort described by Kelly (1986).

Although sport seldom devolves into a true life-or-death situation, the athlete's survival at sport may depend upon a successful outcome. Given the sense of investment in success and the personal cost of failure when an athletic contest is "win or go home," sport can be viewed as a metaphorical survival situation. Research in sport has revealed changes in pain processing under the stress of training. Early research by Janal, Colt, Clark, and Glusman (1984) identified underlying neurophysiological change (endorphin increase) mediating postexercise reduction in pain perception. This is consistent with a large body of research (Berger & Owen, 1988; Head, Kendall, Ferner, & Eagles, 1996), which has documented perception of enhanced mood following exercise.

In *Between a Rock and a Hard Place*, climber Aron Ralston (2004) recounts his experience of being trapped for 127 hours by a rock slide in a remote wilderness setting. His description of a sense of impending doom and eventual self-rescue offers unique insights into the survival function of the pain system. The adaptive value of pain changes in a true survival situation. For example, pain routinely functions as a warning sign, as a signal of impending danger. In so doing, it typically mobilizes the organism to reduce pain by avoidance or escape, ideally before tissue damage ensues. However, in a true survival situation, the threat of loss of life appears to supersede the threat of pain, per se, and the prospect of non–life threatening tissue damage. In survival situations, the organism may be better served by the suppression of pain—enabling the person to literally sacrifice the part to save the whole.

As days passed and Ralston's condition deteriorated, he vacillated between a goal-directed task focus (working at freeing his arm from the rock, even though the prospects were increasingly unlikely) and a sense of impending doom. Then came a moment of transformation, a change in mindset that opened the door to survival. He states:

> I leave behind my prior declaration that severing my arm is nothing but a slow act of suicide and move forward on a cresting wave of emotion. Knowing the alternative is to wait for a progressively more certain but assuredly slow demise, I choose to meet the risk of death in action.
> (pp. 280–281)

Recognizing that his survival is on the line, and accepting that pain will come, he absorbs himself in the task of methodically detaching his arm from his body. As he does so, his consciousness alters and the experience of pain is transformed, facilitating his work at survival. Ralston began to systematically and methodically sever his arm, structure by structure. About 40 minutes into the task he notes:

I clear out the last muscle surrounding the tendon and cut a third artery. I still haven't even uttered an "Ow!" I don't think to verbalize the pain; it's a part of this experience, no more important to the procedure than the color of my tourniquet.

(p. 283)

Once freeing his arm, he is buoyed by a cascade of emotions, understanding that survival is at hand and the end of his ordeal is in sight.

Conclusion

The scholarly discipline and applied practice of pain and injury management are intimately intertwined. Thus, the future directions for practice and research detailed in Chapter 32, Injury and Performance, are much the same as those for pain management, with the following cautions noted. Although the science and art of injury management are complex, issues related to pain assessment and management are perhaps more so. Threat of injury is always present as a risk factor for athletes, but pain is a true constant in the sport environment. There is a great deal of controversy and even misunderstanding about the fundamentals of nociception, the efficacy of medication, the etiology of various pain syndromes, and the way in which personal suffering factors into the diagnosis and treatment of injury (Argoff, Barland, Arnold, Kroenke, & Russel, 2010; Bonica, 1991; Fordyce, 1988). Because pain is fundamentally a subjective experience, it is difficult to assess and manage from the perspective of objective medical science. Furthermore, pain spans performance and injury, where the same word can convey a multitude of meanings, and where its expression is influenced by an array of cultural factors. Determining the meaning of pain is a communication challenge (Fordyce, 1976) and, as such, speaks to a role for psychology. However, to effectively embrace this role, the psychologist needs an understanding of the full scope of the biopsychosocial process of pain and the opportunity to join in the pain conversation with athlete, coach, and medical providers (Fordyce, 1976; Turk et al., 1983, Turk & Gatchel, 2002). As has been suggested with injury, there is a need for cross-training and interdisciplinary collaboration by all treatment providers who wish to provide optimal care for the athlete. The sport and performance psychologist who is prepared to direct mental training with the athlete when healthy and guide rehabilitation when injured is uniquely positioned to enhance health and performance in sport.

References

Addison, T., Kremer, J., & Bell, R. (1998). Understanding the psychology of pain. *Irish Journal of Psychology, 19*, 486–503.

Adler, G., & Gattaz, W. F. (1993). Pain perception threshold in major depression. *Biological Psychiatry, 34*, 687–689.

American Pain Society. (2008). *Principles of analgesic use in the treatment of acute pain and cancer pain* (6th ed.). Glenview, IL: American Pain Society.

Anderson, R., & Hanrahan, S. J. (2008). Dancing in pain: Pain appraisal and coping in dancing. *Journal of Dance Medicine and Science, 12*, 9–16.

Apkarian, A. V., Baliki, M. N., & Geha, P. Y. (2009). Towards a theory of chronic pain. *Progress in Neurobiology, 87*, 81–97.

Arendt-Nielsen, L., & Yarnitsky, D. (2009). Experimental and clinical applications of quantitative sensory testing applied to skin, muscles and viscera. *Journal of Pain, 10*, 556–572.

Argoff, C. E., Barland, P., Arnold, L. M., Kroenke, K., & Russel, I. J. (2012, February 21). Best practices in fibromyalgia diagnosis and multimodal management: Insights from the Fibromyalgia Working Group. *Pain Clinician*. New York: Albert Einstein College of Medicine, Montefiore Medical Center & Asante Communications. Retrieved from http://painclinician.com/education/activity/id/46/

Armstrong. L. (2000). *It's not about the bike: My journey back to life*. New York: Putnam.

Beecher, H. K. (1946). Pain in men wounded in battle. *Annals of Surgery, 123*, 96–105.

Beecher, H. K. (1956). Relationship of significance of wound to pain experienced. *Journal of the American Medical Association, 161*, 1609–1613.

Benedetti, F., Amanzio, M., Casadio, C., Oliaro, A., & Maggi, G. (1997). Blockade of nocebo hyperalgesia by the cholecystokinin antagonist proglumide. *Pain, 71*, 125–140.

Bergandi, T. A. (1985). Psychological variables relating to the incidence of athletic injury: A review of the literature. *International Journal of Sport Psychology, 16*(2), 141–149.

Berger, B. G., & Owen, D. R. (1988). Stress reduction and mood enhancement in four exercise modes: Swimming, body conditioning, hatha yoga, and fencing. *Research Quarterly for Exercise and Sport, 59*, 148–159.

Bonica, J. (1991). Pain management: Past and current status including role of the anesthesiologist. In T. H. Stanley, M. A. Ashburn, & P. G. Fine (Eds.), *Anesthesiology and pain management* (pp. 1–30). Boston: Kluwer.

Bortz, W. M. (1984). The disuse syndrome [Commentary]. *The Western Journal of Medicine, 141*, 691–694.

Brewer, B. W. (2007). Psychology of sport injury rehabilitation. In G. Tenenbaum & R. C. Eklund (Eds.), *Handbook of sport psychology* (3rd ed., pp. 404–424). Hoboken, NJ: John Wiley & Sons, Inc.

Brewer, B. W., Van Raalte, J. L., & Linder, D. E. (1996). Attentional focus and endurance performance. *Applied Research in Coaching and Athletics*, 1–14.

Chapman, C. L., & De Castro, J. M. (1990). Running addiction: Measurement and associated psychological characteristics. *Journal of Sports Medicine and Physical Fitness, 30*, 283–290.

Chapman, C. R. (2011, September 11). Reflections on the life of John Bonica. Retrieved from http://painresearch.utah.edu/crc/CRCpage/Bonica.html

Chapman, C. R., Tuckett, R. P., & Song, C. W. (2008). Pain and stress in a systems perspective: Reciprocal neural, endocrine, and immune interactions. *Journal of Pain, 9*, 122–145.

Chou, R., Franciullo, G. J., Fine, P. G., Adler, J. A., Ballantyne, J. C., Davies, P., et al. (2009a). Clinical guidelines for the use of chronic opioid therapy in chronic noncancer pain. *Journal of Pain, 10*, 113–130.

Chou, R., Franciullo, G. J., Fine, P. G., Miaskowski, C., Passik, S. D., & Portenoy, R. K. (2009b). Opioids for chronic non-cancer pain: Prediction and identification of aberrant drug-related behaviors: A review of the evidence for the American Pain Society and American Academy of Pain Medicine Clinical Practice Guideline. *Journal of Pain, 10*, 131–146.

Couturie, B., Else, J. (Directors), & Witte, K. (Producers). (1986). *Disposable heroes* (Videotape). Los Angeles: Active Home Video.

Csikszentmihalyi, M. (1975). *Beyond boredom and anxiety: Experiencing flow in work and play.* San Francisco: Jossey–Bass.

Craig, D. C., Versloot, J., Goubert, L., & Verhoort, T. (2010). Perceiving pain in others: Automatic and controlled mechanisms. *Journal of Pain, 11*, 101–108.

Crust, L. (2003). Should distance runners concentrate on their bodily sensations, or try to think of something else? *Sports Injury Bulletin, 30*, 10–12.

Curry, T. J. (1993). The effects of receiving a college letter on the sport identity. *Sociology of Sport Journal, 10*, 73–87.

Curry, T. J., & Strauss, R. H. (1994). A little pain never hurt anybody: A photo-essay on the normalization of sport injuries. *Sociology of Sport Journal, 11*, 195–208.

Davis, H., Liotti, M., Ngan, E. T. C., Woodward, T. S., Van Snellenberg, J. X., van Anders, S., et al. (2008). fMRI BOLD signal changes in elite swimmers while viewing videos of personal failure. *Brain Imaging and Behavior.* DOI 10.1007/s11682-007-9016-x

Deyo, R. A., Diehl A. K., & Rosenthal M. (1986). How many days of bed rest for acute low back pain? A randomized clinical trial. *New England Journal of Medicine, 315*, 1064–1070.

Encarnacion, M. L. G., Meyers, M. C., Ryan, N. D., & Pease, D. G. (2000). Pain coping styles of ballet performers. *Journal of Sport Behavior, 23*, 20–32.

Fine, P. G. (1993). The biology of pain. In J. Heil (Ed.), *The psychology of sport injury* (pp. 269–280). Champaign, IL: Human Kinetics.

Ford, I. W., & Gordon., S. (1993). Social support and athletic injury: The perspective of sport physiotherapists. *Journal of Science and Medicine in Sport, 25*, 17–25.

Fordyce, W. E. (1976). *Behavioral methods for chronic pain and illness.* St. Louis, MO: C. D. Mosby.

Fordyce, W. E. (1979). Use of the MMPI in the assessment of chronic pain. In J. Butcher, G. Dahlstrom, M. Gynther, & W. Schofield (Eds.), *Clinical notes on the MMPI* (pp. 2–13). Nutley, NJ: Hoffmann-LaRoche.

Fordyce, W. E. (1988). Pain and suffering: A reappraisal. *American Psychologist, 43*, 276–283.

Gatchel, R. J., McGeary, D. D., Peterson, A., Moore, M., LeRoy, K., Isler, W. C., et al. (2009). Chronic pain in active-duty military personnel: Preliminary findings of a randomized controlled trial of an interdisciplinary functional restoration program. *Military Medicine, 174*, 1–8.

Geers, A. L., Wellman, J. A., Fowler, S. L., Helfer, S. G., & France, C. R. (2010). Dispositional optimism predicts placebo analgesia. *Journal of Pain, 11*, 1165–1171.

Gordin, R. D., & Reardon, J. (1995). Achieving the zone: The study of flow in sport. In K. P. Henschen & W. Straub (Eds.), *Sport psychology: An analysis of athlete behavior* (3rd ed., pp. 223–230). Ithaca, NY: Mouvement Publications.

Grant, J. A., Courtemanche J., Duerden, E. G., Duncan G. H., & Rainville, P. (2010). Cortical thickness and pain sensitivity in zen meditators. *Emotion, 10*, 43–53.

Grant, J. A., & Rainville, P. (2009). Pain sensitivity and analgesic effects of mindful states in zen meditators: A cross-sectional study. *Psychosomatic Medicine, 71*, 106–114.

Grau, J. W., & Meagher, M. W. (1999). Pain modulation: It's a two-way street. *Psychological Science Agenda, 12*, 10–12.

Gregorian, R. S., Gasik, A., Winghan, J. K., Voeller, S., & Kavanagh, S. (2010). Importance of side effects in opioid treatment: A trade-off analysis with patients and physicians. *Journal of Pain, 11*, 1095–1119.

Grossman, D. (2004). *On combat: The psychology and physiology of deadly conflict in war and in peace.* IL: PPCT Research Publications.

Hanin, Y. L. (Ed.). (2000). *Emotion in sport.* Champaign, IL: Human Kinetics.

Hansel, T. (1985). *You gotta keep dancing.* Elgin, IL: David C. Cook Publishing.

Hathaway, S. R., & McKinley, J. C. (1989). *Minnesota multiphasic personality inventory-2* [Manual]. Minneapolis: University of Minnesota Press.

Head, A., Kendall, M. J., Ferner, R., & Eagles, C. (1996). Acute effects of beta blockade and exercise on mood and anxiety. *British Journal of Sports Medicine, 30*, 238–242. [doi:10.1136/bjsm.30.3.238]

Heil, J. (1990). *Association-dissociation: Clarifying the concept.* Paper presented at the Association for the Advancement of Applied Sport Psychology Annual Conference, San Antonio, TX.

Heil, J. (1993). *Psychology of sport injury.* Champaign, IL: Human Kinetics.

Heil, J. (1998). *Remarkable feats: Of pain tolerance, injury rehabilitation, and coping with adversity in sport.* Keynote presentation at the Second International Meeting of Psychology Applied to Sport and Exercise, Braga, Portugal.

Heil, J. (2003, Winter). Mind on winning, Part III: Hughes & Marsh. *American Fencing Magazine,* p. 13.

Heil, J., & Fine, P. (1999). Pain in sport: A biopsychological perspective. In D. Pargman (Ed.), *Psychological bases of sport injuries* (2nd ed., pp. 13–28). Morgantown, WV: Fitness Information Technology.

Heil, J., & Lee, J. (2009, September). *Sport psychology applied to law enforcement training.* Workshop at Association for Applied Sport Psychology Conference, Salt Lake City, UT.

Heil, J., Wakefield, C., & Reed, C. (1998). Patient as athlete: A metaphor for injury rehabilitation. *The Psychotherapy Patient, 10*, 21–39.

Henschen, K., & Gordin, R. (2010). Hypnosis and sport performance. In *Encyclopedia of sports medicine.* Thousand Oaks, CA: Sage Publications (http://www.sage-ereference.com/sportsmedicine/article_n258.html; retrieved 3/15/2011).

Hughes, R., & Coakley, J. (1991). Positive deviance among athletes: The implications of overconformity to the sport ethic. *Sociology of Sport Journal, 4*, 307–325.

Jackson, S., & Csikszentmihalyi, M. (1999). *Flow in sports: The keys to optimal experiences and performances.* Champaign, IL: Human Kinetics.

Janal, M. N., Colt, E. W. D., Clark, W.C., & Glusman, M. (1984). Pain sensitivity, mood, and plasma endocrine levels in man following long-distance running: Effects of Naloxone. *Pain, 19*, 13–25.

Jensen, M. P. (2010). A neuropsychological model of pain: Research and clinical implications. *Journal of Pain, 11*, 2–12.

Jones, D. A., Rollman, G. B., White, K. P., Hill, M. L., & Brooke, R. I. (2003). The relationship between cognitive appraisal, affect, and catastrophizing in patients with chronic pain. *The Journal of Pain, 4,* 267–277.

Junghaenel, D. U., Keefe, F. J., & Broderick, J. E. (2010). Multi-modal examination of psychological and interpersonal distinctions among MPI coping clusters: A preliminary study. *Journal of Pain, 11,* 87–96.

Kabat-Zinn, J. (l982). An outpatient program in behavioral medicine for chronic pain patients based on the practice of mindfulness meditation: Theoretical considerations and preliminary results. *General Hospital Psychiatry, 4,* 313–347.

Keefe, F. G., Williams, D. A., & Smith, S. J. (2010). Assessment of pain behaviors. In D. C. Turk & R. Melzack (Eds.), *Handbook of pain assessment* (3rd ed., pp. 170–190). New York: Guilford Press.

Kelly, D. D. (1986). Stress-induced analgesia [Special issue]. *Annals of the New York Academy of Sciences, 467.*

Kiesler, S., & Finholt, T. (1998). The mystery of RSI. *American Psychologist, 43,* 1004–1015.

Klinger, D. (2004). *Into the kill Zone: A cop's eye view of deadly force.* San Francisco: Josey Bass.

LeUnes, A. D., & Nation, J. R. (1989). *Sport psychology: An introduction.* Chicago: Nelson Hall.

Lipman, A. G. (1993). Medications in the treatment of pain and injury. In J. Heil (Ed.), *The psychology of sport injury* (pp. 269–280). Champaign, IL: Human Kinetics.

Loeser, J. (1991, February). *Pain management: Past and current status including the role of the anesthesiologist.* Presentation at the 36th Annual Postgraduate Course in Anesthesiology, Snowbird, UT.

Lysholm, J., & Wiklander, J. (1987). Injuries in runners. *American Journal of Sports Medicine, 15,* 168–171.

Maclean, N. (1992). *Young men and fire.* Chicago: University of Chicago Press.

Malcom, N. L. (2006). 'Shaking it off' and 'toughing it out': Socialization to pain and injury in girls' softball. *Journal of Contemporary Ethnography, 35,* 495–525.

Masters, K. S., & Lambert, N. J. (1989). The relationship between cognitive coping strategies, reasons for running, injury, and performance of marathon runners. *Journal of Sport and Exercise Psychology, 11,* 161–170.

Masters, K. S., & Ogles, B. M. (1998). Associative and dissociative cognitive strategies in exercise and running: 20 years later, what do we know? *The Sport Psychologist, 12,* 253–270.

McGrath, P. J. (1990). *Pain in children: Nature, assessment, and treatment.* New York: Guilford.

McGrath, P. J., Walco, G. A., Turk, D. C., Dworkin, R. H., Brown, M. T., Davidson, K., et al. (2008). Core outcome domains and measures for pediatric acute and chronic/recurrent pain clinical trials: PedIMMACT recommendations. *Journal of Pain, 9,* 771–783.

Melzack, R. (l975). The McGill pain questionnaire: Major properties and scoring methods. *Pain, 1,* 277–299.

Melzack, R., & Katz, J. (2010). The McGill pain questionnaire: Appraisal and current status. In D. C. Turk & R. Melzack (Eds.), *Handbook of pain assessment* (3rd ed., pp. 35–52). New York: Guilford Press.

Melzack, R., & Wall, P.D. (1965). Pain mechanisms. A new theory. *Science, 150,* 971–979.

Merskey H., & Bogduk, N. (1994). Part III: Pain terms, a current list with definitions and notes on usage. In *Classification of chronic pain* (2nd ed., pp. 209–214). IASP Task Force on Taxonomy. Seattle: IASP Press.

Morgan, W. P. (1978, April). The mind of the marathoner. *Psychology Today,* pp. 38–40, 43, 45–46, 49.

Mounce, C., Keogh, E., & Eccleston, C. (2010). A principal components analysis of negative affect-related constructs relevant to pain: Evidence for a three component structure. *The Journal of Pain, 11,* 710–717.

Nack, W. (2001, May 7). The wrecking yard. *Sports Illustrated.* Retrieved 12/20/10 from http://sportsillustrated.cnn.com/vault/article/magazine/MAG1022464/2/index.htm

Nielsen, C. S., Staud, R., & Price, D. D. (2009). Individual differences in pain sensitivity: Measurement, causation, and consequences. *Journal of Pain, 10,* 231–237.

Nixon, H. L. (1992). A social network analysis of influences on athletes to play with pain and injuries. *Journal of Sport and Social Issues, 16,* 127–135.

Nixon, H. L. (1993). Accepting the risks of pain and injury in sport: Mediated cultural influences on playing hurt. *Sociology of Sport Journal, 10,* 183–196.

O'Connor, E. A., Heil, J., Harmer, P., & Zimmermann, I. (2005). Injury. In J. Taylor & G. Wilson (Eds.), *Applying sport psychology: Four perspectives* (pp. 187–206, 281–283). Champaign, IL: Human Kinetics.

Ogilvie, B. C., & Tutko, T. A. (1966). *Problem athletes and how to handle them.* London: Pelham Books.

Orr, K. (1992). *Brave men—dark waters.* New York: Simon and Schuster.

Overdose caused death of Matuszak. (1989, June 28). *The Washington Post,* p. F4.

Paparizos, A. L., Tripp, D. A., Sullivan, M. J. L., & Rubenstein, M. L. (2005). Catastrophizing and pain perception in recreational ballet dancers. *Journal of Sport Behavior, 28,* 35.

Peterson, K., Durtschi, S., & Murphy, S. (1990, September). *Cognitive patterns and conceptual schemes of elite distance runners during submaximum and maximum running effort.* Paper presented at the annual meeting of the Association for the Advancement of Applied Sports Psychology, San Antonio, Texas.

Petras, R. J. (2009). Reducing pain and anxiety during reduction of a fracture. *Practical Pain Management, 9,* 16–18.

Pierce, E. F., McGowan, R. W., & Lynn, T. D. (1993). Exercise dependence in relation to competitive orientation of runners. *Journal of Sports Medicine and Physical Fitness, 33,* 189–193.

Pike, E. (2004). Risk, Pain and Injury: "A Natural Thing in Rowing"? In K. Young (Ed.), *Sporting bodies, damaged selves: Sociological studies of sports-related injury* (pp. 151–162). Oxford, England: Elsevier.

Ralston, A. (2004). *Between a rock and a hard place.* New York: Atria Books.

Ransford, A. O., Cairns, D., & Mooney, V. (1976). The pain drawing as an aid to the psychologic evaluation of patients with low-back pain. *Spine, 1,* 127–134.

Ravizza, K. (1977). Peak experiences in sport. *Journal of Humanistic Psychology, 17,* 35–40.

Sauro, M. D., & Greenberg, R. P. (2005). Endogenous opiates and the placebo effect: A meta-analytic review. *Journal of Psychosomatic Research, 58,* 115–120.

Schomer, H. H. (1986). Mental strategies and perception of effort in marathon runners. *International Journal of Sport Psychology, 17,* 41–49.

Schomer, H. H. (1987). Mental strategy training programme for marathon runners. *International Journal of Sports Psychology, 18*, 133–151.

Spengler, D. M., & Freeman, C. W. (1979). Patient selection for lumbar discectomy: An objective approach. *Spine, 4*, 129–134.

Stewart, W. R., Ricci, J. A., Chee, E., Morgenstein, D., & Lipton, R. (2003). Lost productivity time and cost due to common pain conditions in the US workforce. *Journal of the American Medical Association, 290*, 2443–2454.

Sullivan, M. J. L., Bishop, S. R., & Pivik, J. (1995). The Pain Catastrophizing Scale: Development and validation. *Psychological Assessment, 7*, 524–532. ·

Sullivan, M. J. L., Stanish, W., Waite, H., Sullivan, M., & Tripp, D. A. (1998). Catastrophizing, pain, and disability in patients with soft-tissue injuries. *Pain, 77*, 253–260.

Sullivan, M. J. L., Thorn, B., Haythornthwaite, J. A., Keefe, F., Martin, M., Bradley, L. A., & Lefebvre, J. C. (2001). Theoretical perspectives on the relation between catastrophizing and pain. *The Clinical Journal of Pain, 17*, 52–64.

Sullivan, M. J. L., Tripp, D. A., Rodgers, W., & Stanish, W. (2000). Catastrophizing and pain perception in sport participants. *Journal of Applied Sport Psychology, 12*, 151–167.

Syrjala, K. L., & Abrams, J. R. (2002). Hypnosis and imagery in the treatment of pain. In D. C. Turk & R. J. Gatchel (Eds.), *Psychological approaches to pain management: A practitioner's handbook* (2nd ed., pp. 187–209). New York: Guilford Publications.

Taylor, J., & Taylor, S. (1997). *Psychological approaches to sports injury rehabilitation.* Gaithersburg, MD: Aspen.

Teitlebaum, J. E., Johnson, C., & St Cyr, J. (2006). The use of D-ribose in chronic fatigue syndrome and fibromyalgia: A pilot study. *Journal of Alternative and Complementary Medicine, 12*, 857–862.

Theodorakis, Y., Beneca, A., Malliou, P., Antoniou, P., Goudas, M., & Laparidis, K. (1997). The effect of a self-talk technique on injury and rehabilitation. *Journal of Applied Sport Psychology, 9*, 164.

Thomas, H., & Tarr, J. (2009). Dancers' perceptions of pain and injury: Positive and negative effects. *Journal of Dance Medicine and Science, 13*, 51–59.

Tracey, I., & Bushnell, M. C. (2009). How neuroimaging studies have challenged us to rethink: Is chronic pain a disease? *Journal of Pain, 10*, 1113–1120.

Turk, D. C., & Gatchel, R. J. (Eds.). (2002). *Psychological approaches to pain management: A practitioner's handbook* (2nd ed.). New York: Guilford Publications.

Turk, D. C., Meichenbaum, D., & Genest, M. (1983). *Pain and behavior medicine: A cognitive behavioral perspective.* New York: Guilford Press.

Turk, D. C., & Melzack, R. (Eds.). (2010). *Handbook of pain assessment* (3rd ed.). New York: Guilford Press.

Udry, E., Gould, D., Bridges, D., & Beck, L. (1997). Down but not out: Athlete responses to season-ending injuries. *Journal of Sport and Exercise Psychology, 19*, 224–248.

Van Heerden, J. C., & Potgieter, J. R. (2003). A computerized programme for monitoring athletes' emotional stress and pain perception. *South African Journal for Research in Sport, Physical Education and Research, 25*, 93–103.

Wiech, K., Kalisch, R., Weiskopf, N., Pleger, B., Stephan K. E., & Dolan, R. J. (2006). Anteriolateral prefrontal cortex mediates the analgesic effect of expected and perceived control over pain. *Journal of Neuroscience, 26*, 11501–11509.

Williams, D. A., & Clauw, D. J. (2009). Understanding fibromyalgia: Lessons from the broader pain research community. *Journal of Pain, 10*, 777–791.

Wise, A., Jackson, D. W., & Rocchio, P. (1979). Preoperative psychologic testing as a predictor of success in injury: A preliminary report. *The American Journal of Sports Medicine, 7*, 287–292.

Eating Disorders in Sport

Trent A. Petrie *and* Christy Greenleaf

Abstract

This chapter describes eating disorders (EDs) among male and female athletes. Prevalence rates of clinical (i.e., anorexia nervosa, bulimia nervosa, and ED not otherwise specified) and subclinical EDs and related conditions (i.e., female athlete triad, muscle dysmorphia, exercise dependence) are presented, and factors within the sport environment associated with pathogenic eating and weight control behaviors, including performance demands, sport type, competitive level, and coach/parent/ peer influences, are explained. As a framework for synthesizing previous research and theoretical conceptualizations, a sociocultural conceptual model of disordered eating for athletes is included. General sociocultural and sport-specific pressures are thought to be associated with internalization of body ideals, body dissatisfaction and drive for muscularity, negative affect and dietary restraint, and bulimic symptomatology. Research supporting the model is presented and suggestions for future research are offered. The chapter concludes with recommendations for prevention of problematic eating and weight control behaviors and issues regarding identification and treatment of EDs.

Key Words: Male and female athletes, body image, drive for muscularity, eating disorders, sociocultural pressures, interventions, prevention

Risk factors associated with eating disorders (EDs) are many and include familial, sociocultural, personality/psychological, biological, developmental, and genetic factors (Jacobi, Hayward, de Zwaan, Kraemer, & Agras, 2004; Polivy & Herman, 2002; Striegel-Moore & Bulik, 2007). Among these, sociocultural factors have been highlighted, which underscores the pervasive influence of Western cultures' feminine beauty ideal (i.e., extreme thinness) and sexual objectification of women (Striegel-Moore & Bulik, 2007). Although initially developed to explain the occurrence of disordered eating and body image concerns among women, this approach has been extended to men as the sociocultural environment has shifted over the last 20–30 years and has begun to focus on men's appearance, defining masculinity through body size and shape (Cafri et al., 2005; Ricciardelli & McCabe, 2004; Soban, 2006). Now,

researchers understand that both women *and* men have specific societally based expectations about how they should look, what they should eat, how they should behave, and what they should think and feel. These ideals are embedded in the socialization process (i.e., learning what it means to be a woman or a man) and are transmitted through the media, families, and peers. The communication of body ideals starts early in life, with children as young as 8–9 years worrying about not being thin enough (girls) and wondering if they are sufficiently muscular (boys) (McCabe & Ricciardelli, 2003).

Several key ideas define the sociocultural approach to understanding ED risk. First, in Western societies, physical appearance (in particular the size and shape of one's body) is central in determining individual's attractiveness, social and personal worth, and gender status (femininity vs. masculinity). For women, there are two body ideals: tall, thin, and tubular, like a runway model, and thin, but slightly curvaceous with ample breasts, like a *Sports Illustrated* swimsuit model. If a woman's body approximates either of these ideals, then she is viewed as attractive, feminine, and a person of worth, and is imbued with many positive personal characteristics (e.g., intelligent, socially active). For men, the body ideal is lean, but also highly muscular—a mesomorphic body type. The closer a man's body is to the ideal, the more he is viewed as masculine, independent, rugged, powerful . . . a "winner." Second, diet, particularly in the form of extreme restraint, is the primary mechanism for achieving the female beauty ideal. Women who are able to sufficiently restrict their food intake to attain the thin ideal are viewed as virtuous and feminine. Physical activity, particularly in the form of high-level strength training and conditioning, is the avenue for attaining the male body ideal. Men who do not work out or whose bodies are not exemplars of the muscular somatotype may be derided as unmanly and lacking in important masculine characteristics. Third, as boys and girls develop, these messages about body, self, and eating are communicated through all forms of the media (e.g., magazines, television), and by friends and family (Stice, 1994). In time, boys and girls (and ultimately men and women) internalize these messages about what it means to be masculine and feminine (and what their bodies should look like). These schema become the lens through which they compare themselves with the rest of the world and evaluate their bodies and personal worth. Fourth, because societal body ideals are unattainable for the majority of men and women (e.g., Brownell & Napolitano, 1995; Pope, Olivardia, Gruber, & Borowiecki, 1999), comparisons between one's actual body and the internalized ideal results in dissatisfaction and psychological distress in relation to one's body and, for some, attempts to modify the body through pathogenic behaviors, such as extreme dietary restraint, excessive exercising (including, for men, weightlifting), and use of muscle building supplements (see also Chapter 29, this volume, for a discussion of polypharmacy, body image disturbance, and disturbances in diet and exercise as risk factors for appearance and performancing enhancing drug [APED] abuse).

In addition to highlighting these societal pressures and processes, the sociocultural approach identifies certain environments that may exacerbate risk in already vulnerable groups or establish risk in groups that might otherwise be considered relatively immune. Sports and related performance domains, such as ballet, represent such environments. Researchers (e.g., Thompson & Sherman, 2010) have suggested that specific pressures/factors within sport environments may encourage an unhealthy focus on weight and body shape. These factors include sport-sanctioned or coach-encouraged weight limits; judging criteria that emphasize and reward certain body types, such as thin and stereotypically attractive body builds among female athletes in aesthetic sports; team "weigh-ins" that are conducted in public and use shame/embarrassment as a motivating factor for weight loss and emphasize obtaining specific weight as opposed to being physically healthy; stereotypes regarding what bodies of athletes in different sports "should" look like; performance demands that encourage a very low percentage body fat; peer pressure to lose weight or gain muscle and to adopt specific behaviors (e.g., diet) to do so; revealing uniforms/costumes that may increase body consciousness and dissatisfaction; direct and subtle comments by coaches and other sport personnel concerning weight, body size/shape, and appearance; and personality characteristics, such as mental toughness, pursuit of excellence, playing with pain, and "coachability," that also define a person with an ED. Because of these pressures and other factors, theoretically, female *and* male athletes and performers, such as ballet dancers, would be at increased risk for the development of body image concerns and disordered eating behaviors due to their immersion in environments in which weight and body size/shape are considered to be central to success and where being competitive and pursuing excellence (perfection) is valued.

In this chapter, we examine the extant literature on EDs among athletes and other performers (where available) to define the influence of the sport environment. Although research has focused primarily on female athletes and performers, in the last decade, more studies have examined male athletes, so we will include information on them as well. We begin our review by defining EDs and related conditions/syndromes, and by providing a brief overview of the prevalence of these disorders in the general population. Next, we focus on prevalence rates in sport and discuss related conditions that often are seen among athletes and those who are physically active. Third, we offer a more detailed examination of the factors within the sport environment that may be related to levels of disordered eating. Fourth, we refine Petrie and Greenleaf's (2007) sociocultural model, incorporating findings from recent studies and expanding it to address features unique to male athletes. Fifth, we address the issue of prevention, focusing on how sport environments can be changed to become more "body healthy" and on intervention programs that have been shown to reduce putative ED risk factors and can be implemented with appearance-conscious athletes. Sixth, we focus on the issue of identification and treatment, particularly with regard to the unique situation of working with athletes who still may be training and competing. Finally, although we consider research issues throughout the chapter, in the final section, we offer directions that we hope will guide and advance future eating disorder studies.

What Are Eating Disorders and What Is Their Prevalence?
Clinical Disorders

Clinical EDs are psychiatric disorders that involve pathogenic eating and weight control behaviors and disturbed weight-related cognitions and perceptions (American Psychiatric Association [APA], 2000). Individuals with clinical EDs have distorted body images (e.g., seeing themselves as fat when they are actually underweight) and problematic attitudes toward and beliefs about food (e.g., believing that some foods are "good" and others are "bad"). Secretive and ritualized eating behaviors and rigid beliefs often characterize clinical EDs. The three primary clinical EDs are anorexia nervosa (AN), bulimia nervosa (BN), and ED not otherwise specified (EDNOS).

ANOREXIA NERVOSA

Currently, AN involves maintaining low body weight for age and height, having a distorted body image and inaccurate perceptions of body weight, being extremely fearful of gaining weight, and overvaluing body weight for self-evaluation (APA, 2000); proposed criteria in the *Diagnostic and Statistical Manual—V* (DSM-V) are similar, but do not include loss of menstruation for girls and women. Individuals with AN may engage in caloric restriction and limit the types of food they eat to control their body weight and shape. Although the prevalence of AN is low, adult women (0.5% to 0.9%) have slightly higher rates than do men (0.05% to 0.3%; APA, 1994; Hudson, Hiripi, Pope, & Kessler, 2007). In a community sample of men and women from the United Kingdom, Currin, Schmidt, Treasure, and Jick (2005) reported an incidence of 0.7 and 8.6 (per 100,000), respectively,

and found that rates of AN remained stable during the 1990s. Research in the United States and Europe has shown that rates are higher among adolescents than among young to middle-aged adults (Currin et al., 2005), and for girls more so than boys (Ackard, Fulkerson, & Neumark-Sztainer, 2007; Isomaa, Isomaa, Marttunen, Kaltiala-Heino, & Bjorkqvist, 2009). For example, Ackard et al. found that, in a sample of middle and high school students, 0.4% of girls and 0% of boys met diagnostic criteria.

BULIMIA NERVOSA

Bulimia nervosa involves episodic binge eating and subsequent compensatory behavior, as well as an extreme influence of body weight and shape on self-evaluation (APA, 2000). Individuals with BN often feel a lack of control over their binge eating and engage in behaviors such as self-induced vomiting, dieting or fasting, and excessive exercise to regain feelings of control over their bodies and their weight. Proposed criteria in the *DSM-V* are similar, although the frequency of binge eating will be lower than is required in the *DSM-IV*. Among adults, the lifetime prevalence of BN is 1% to 3% for women and 0.1% to 0.5% for men (APA, 1994; Hudson et al., 2007). Incidence rates (per 100,000) in the United Kingdom have ranged from 0.7 (males) to 12.4 (females); rates were considerably higher among boys and girls aged 10–19 years than in those older than 20 (Currin et al., 2005). Among female college students in the United States, prevalence decreased during the 1980s, but remained stable from the 1990s to the early 2000s, when rates ranged from 1.3% to 2.2% (Crowther, Armey, Luce, Dalton, & Leahey, 2008; Keel, Heatherton, Dorer, Joiner, & Zalta, 2006).

EATING DISORDER NOT OTHERWISE SPECIFIED

Individuals with EDNOS have some of the symptoms of AN or BN, but either not all, or all but not at the needed level of severity for classification as AN or BN. A woman, for example, may have regular menstrual cycles yet experience many of the symptoms of AN, such as severe caloric restriction, feeling fat despite low body weight, and having poor self-esteem. A lifetime prevalence rate of 9.0% for 18-year-old female Finns (Isomaa et al., 2009) and point prevalence rates from 2.5% to 3.3% for female undergraduates in the United States (Crowther et al., 2008) have been reported.

Binge eating disorder (BED), currently classified as an EDNOS, involves episodic binge eating without engaging in compensatory behaviors and often follows weight loss and restrictive eating (APA, 2000). In the *DSM-V*, BED is proposed as a separate disorder. Few large scale studies have examined BED prevalence, although lifetime prevalence rates of BED are estimated between 0.7% and 4% (APA, 2000); higher rates have been found for women (3.5%) than men (2%) (Hudson et al., 2007).

Subclinical Disorders

Subclinical EDs include disturbed eating behaviors and attitudes that are problematic and unhealthy but less severe in nature than clinical EDs. Similar to clinical EDs, subclinical EDs involve psychological and physical symptoms, such as distorted body image, negative self-beliefs, and the use of pathogenic eating and weight control behaviors, such as restricting caloric intake, binge eating, excessive exercising, and/or self-induced vomiting. Subclinical EDs may develop into clinical EDs, thus putting individuals at greater psychological and physical risk (Kotler, Cohen, Davies, Pine, & Walsh, 2001; Stice, Marti, Shaw, & Jaconis, 2009). In fact, some symptoms of psychological disturbance associated with clinical and subclinical EDs, such as pathogenic eating attitudes and weight control behaviors, as well as negative affect and self-concept, seem to be similar. For example, in a study with female college students, women classified as either eating disordered or subclinical reported similar levels of disturbance in mood, confidence, and self-esteem, as well as internalization of social ideals of appearance and body satisfaction (Cohen & Petrie, 2005).

Subclinical prevalence rates generally are higher than clinical, for both men and women (Crowther et al., 2008; Isomaa et al., 2009; Keel et al., 2006; Tylka & Subich, 2002). For example, among male and female U.S. undergraduates, subclinical rates have ranged from 37% to 39%, respectively (Cohen & Petrie, 2005; Tylka & Subich). Keel et al. reported lifetime binge eating rates of 8.1% and 28.7% for male and female undergraduates, respectively.

Clinical and Subclinical Eating Disorders (and Related Conditions) Among Athletes and Other Performers

Prevalence rates of clinical EDs among athletes are slightly higher than in the general population (Hausenblas & Carron, 1999; Smolak, Murnen, & Ruble, 2000). Among U.S. female collegiate and international elite athletes, AN rates are estimated between 0% and 6.7%, BN between 0% and 12.1%, and EDNOS between 2% and 13.4% (Greenleaf, Petrie, Carter, & Reel, 2009; Johnson, Powers, &

Dick, 1999; Sundgot-Borgen & Torsveit, 2004). Among U.S. male collegiate and international elite athletes, AN rates are low (0%), whereas BN (0–7.5%) and EDNOS (0–9.7%) are somewhat higher (Petrie, Greenleaf, Reel, & Carter, 2008; Johnson et al., 1999; Sundgot-Borgen & Torsveit, 2004). Comparing across studies with different samples, elite athletes appear to have higher prevalence rates of clinical EDs than do collegiate athletes (Greenleaf et al., 2009; Johnson et al., 1999; Petrie et al., 2008; Sundgot-Borgen & Torsveit, 2004). Although some researchers have focused on adolescent athletes in relation to disordered eating attitudes and behaviors (e.g., Fulkerson, Keel, Leon, & Dorr, 1999) or have included them as part of larger sample (e.g., Torstveit, Rosenvinge, & Sundgot-Borgen, 2008), there is no separate and credible prevalence data for adolescents with respect to clinical disorders.

Similar to nonathletes, subclinical EDs, as well as individual pathogenic weight control behaviors, are more prevalent than clinical EDs (e.g., Greenleaf et al., 2009; Johnson et al., 1999; Petrie et al., 2008; Torstveit et al., 2008). Among U.S. collegiate athletes, Greenleaf et al. and Petrie et al. found that 25.5% of the women and 19.2% of the men were subclinical. Furthermore, they reported that these athletes engaged in a wide range of eating and weight control behaviors, including binge eating (two or more times/week: 7.8% females and 9.3% males), exercising to burn calories (two or more hours/day: 25.2% females and 37% males), and dieting or fasting (two or more times/year: 15.6% females and 14.2% males). More extreme behaviors, such as self-induced vomiting (one or more times/week: 2.5% females and 5% males), diuretics (two or more times/month: 1.5% females and 7% males), and laxatives (two or more times/ week: 1% females and 7.9% males) were less prevalent. Sundgot-Borgen and Torsveit (2004) reported prevalence rates of *anorexia athletica* (AA), a subclinical disorder that is characterized by low body weight for age and height, pathogenic eating behaviors, and excessive concern about body weight and shape, to range from 1% (males) to 4% (females) among elite Norwegian athletes.

Although studies with adolescent athletes have been limited in quality and number, recent research suggests that athletes may be at less risk than their nonathlete peers (Martinsen, Bratland-Sanda, Eriksson, & Sundgot-Borgen, 2010; Rosendahl, Bormann, Aschenbrenner, Aschenbrenner, & Strauss, 2009). For example, in a study of high school students in

Germany, the prevalence rate of disordered eating symptoms among athletes was 16.3% compared to 26.1% of nonathletes (Rosendahl et al., 2009). Similar results were reported by Martinsen et al. (2010) for Norwegian adolescents. In subsequent sections, we address the mechanisms through which participation in sport during adolescence may offer protective effects against problematic eating attitudes and behaviors and discuss how athletes who compete at the collegiate or elite level are more at risk.

Similar to athletes, dancers may also be at increased risk of problematic eating. In a small study of national ballet companies in the United States and China, Hamilton, Brooks-Gunn, Warren, and Hamilton (1988) reported lifetime prevalence of eating problems (defined as self-reported AN, BN, and/or purging behavior) of 11% for U.S. and 24% for Chinese female dancers. In another small but more recent sample of female U.S. ballet dancers, there was a 3.4% lifetime prevalence of AN, 6.9% of BN, and 55.2% of EDNOS (Ringham et al., 2006). Among Israeli dancers (type not specified), Bachner-Melman, Zohar, Ebstein, Elizur, and Constantini (2006) found lifetime prevalence rates of 4.5% (AN), 1.8% (BN), and 11.7% (EDNOS). In a recent review, Hincapié and Cassidy (2010) suggested that more scientifically sound research examining problematic eating and related conditions among dancers was needed, and they identified methodological concerns, small samples, and vague operational definitions as common limitations of previous research. As dancers experience appearance and weight pressures similar to those of athletes, it makes sense to extend ED research in this population.

In addition to clinical and subclinical EDs, a number of related conditions occur among athletes, exercisers, and other performers, in part because of the centrality of the body within the athletic and exercise environment. Like the previously described disorders, these related conditions can be quite serious and negatively affect physical and psychological functioning.

FEMALE ATHLETE TRIAD

The *female athlete triad* ("triad") occurs in women and involves three interrelated conditions: disordered eating, amenorrhea, and osteoporosis. Female athletes, often in attempts to enhance performance and control their bodies, restrict caloric intake and engage in other behaviors such as exercising to maintain a low body weight. These weight control efforts result in reduced energy availability

that can disrupt menstrual functioning and reduce bone mineral density (American College of Sports Medicine [ACSM], 2007; Rauh, Nichols, & Barrack, 2010; Warren & Chua, 2008). The triad is associated with increased risk of injury (e.g., stress fractures), medical complications (e.g., infertility), and psychological problems (e.g., anxiety, depression) (ACSM, 2007). In a study of female high school athletes, Rauh et al. (2010) found that all three components of the triad increased the risk of injury.

The relatively few triad prevalence studies that exist have shown a fairly low co-occurrence of all three conditions, ranging from 1.2% in high school athletes (Hoch et al., 2009; Nichols, Rauh, Lawson, Ji, & Barkai, 2006) to 2.7% at the college level (Beals & Hill, 2006; Reel, SooHoo, Doetsch, Carter, & Petrie, 2007) to 4.3% among elite Norwegian athletes (Torstveit & Sundgot-Borgen, 2005). Across all competitive levels, rates appear to be highest among athletes from lean-build, endurance, and/or aesthetics sports. Even though prevalence is relatively low, rates are similar to AN and to BN and clinically important, meaning that a considerable number of girls and women will suffer from this syndrome. When considering the presence of only two of the three conditions, which does increase female athletes' risk of developing the triad and experiencing negative physical and psychological symptoms, prevalence rates have been higher. For example, rates have ranged from 5.9% (high school; Nichols et al., 2006) to 8.9% (college; Beals & Hill, 2006) to 5.4–26.9% (elite; Torstveit & Sundgot-Borgen, 2005) to 27% (adult triathletes; Hoch, Stavrakos, & Schimke, 2007).

MUSCLE DYSMORPHIA

Muscle dysmorphia (MD), which is not a psychiatric diagnosis within the *DSM* system and was originally identified by Pope and his colleagues (e.g., Pope, Gruber, Choi, Olivardia, & Phillips, 1997), involves an extreme preoccupation with a perceived lack of muscularity and distorted body image (Olivardia, 2001). Individuals with MD perceive and fear that their bodies are small and weak even though in reality they are of average or above average musculature (Grieve, Truba, & Bowersox, 2009; Leone, Sedory, & Gray, 2005). Additionally, individuals with MD often engage in excessive exercise and weight training, have highly restrictive eating routines, often hide or cover up their physiques, and may take nutritional supplements, as well as illegal substances such as steroids, in order to increase their musculature (Murray, Rieger, Touyz, & de la Garza Garcia, 2010; Pope, Pope, Menard, Fay, Olivardia, & Phillips, 2005). Muscle dysmorphia can have serious mental health risks, including depression and suicidal ideology (Pope et al., 2005). McFarland and Kaminski (2009), for example, found that among college men MD was associated with depression, anxiety, interpersonal sensitivity, and poor self-concept.

Muscle dysmorphia is more prevalent among men, although some women do experience it. It is thought to develop primarily during late adolescence (Murray et al., 2010) when boys may experience a great deal of social pressure to attain a muscular and powerful body. Reported prevalence rates for MD vary. Pope, Katz, and Hudson (1993), in a study of male body builders, found that 8% reported symptoms of MD, whereas Maida and Armstrong (2005) found that 25% of male weightlifters sampled reported symptoms. Cafri, van den Berg, and Thompson (2006) reported 9.8% of boys aged 13–18, used substances, including steroids, to enhance their muscularity, and that use of these types of substances was associated with MD symptoms. In terms of risk associated with sport type, higher rates generally are found among body builders (Baghurst & Kissinger, 2005; Maida & Armstrong, 2005). In a study examining the dimensions of MD, Baghurst and Lirgg (2009) found that college football players were less likely to monitor their diets (i.e., restrict intake), use muscle supplements for energy and recovery from workouts, and be concerned with the size and shape of their muscles than either natural or non-natural body builders (MD may be an aspect of the body image disturbance discussed in Chapter 29 as a risk factors for APED abuse).

EXERCISE DEPENDENCE

Exercise dependence, which is not considered a psychiatric disorder within the DSM system and which emerged from earlier research on obligatory exercise (e.g., Pasman & Thompson, 1989), involves a strong preoccupation with being physically active and has been characterized by three or more of the following symptoms: exercise tolerance, whereby there is a need for increasing amounts of physical activity; withdrawal symptoms, such as anxiety and depression, when unable to exercise; intentions to limit amount of exercise; a perceived loss of control when not able to exercise; spending a great deal of time exercising; experiencing conflict with other social, work, and family obligations or activities because of time spent exercising; and continuing to exercise

even when ill or injured (Cook & Hausenblas, 2008; Hamer & Karageorghis, 2007; Hausenblas & Symons Downs, 2002).

When exercise dependence occurs without disordered eating, it is considered "primary"; when it co-occurs with pathological eating attitudes and behaviors, it is considered "secondary" (Adams, 2009; Cook & Hausenblas, 2008). Prevalence rates among college students indicate that 21–62% report some symptoms of exercise dependence, but that few are at risk (5%) and even fewer are actually dependent (Garman, Hayduk, Crider, & Hodel, 2004; Symons Downs, Hausenblas, & Nigg, 2004). Symptoms of exercise dependence may be more common among men than women (Symons Downs et al., 2004). Among individuals with clinical EDs, compulsive exercise is associated with AN, although male and female athletes report using exercise as their primary means for weight loss and/or maintenance (Greenleaf et al., 2009; Petrie et al., 2008).

The Influence of the Sport and Performance Environment

Societal ideals of appearance, body size/shape, and attractiveness are pervasive in Western society and clearly communicated via friends, family, and the media (e.g., Derenne & Beresin, 2006; Strahan, Wilson, Cressman, & Buote, 2006). Women are expected to be thin, yet curvaceous, whereas men are expected to be muscular and lean. Adopting these unrealistic body ideals is associated with poor body image and disturbed eating (Grossbard, Lee, Neighbors, & Larimer, 2009; Moradi, Dirks, & Matteson, 2005). Athletes and other performers are not immune to these general sociocultural weight and physique pressures. In fact, female collegiate athletes who were classified as having a clinical or subclinical ED reported feeling more pressures to achieve a certain body size and weight from parents, friends, romantic partners, TV/movies, and magazines than did athletes who were asymptomatic (Petrie, Greenleaf, Reel, & Carter, 2009a). Furthermore, Petrie, Greenleaf, Reel, and Carter (2009b) found that female collegiate athletes' investment in how they look and motivation to exercise to improve their physical appearance were the best predictors of whether they had a subclinical ED. Male athletes, like their nonathletic counterparts, want to gain weight and muscularity, whereas female athletes are concerned about reducing weight and body fat (Muller, Gorrow, & Schneider, 2009; Raudenbush & Meyer, 2003).

Because athletes' (and other similar performers, such as dancers) bodies are the central focus within the competitive environment, and their bodies are the means through which performance outcomes and results are achieved, they also experience a set of pressures and factors unique to their environment. These pressures may lead to some athletes engaging in unhealthy eating and weight control behaviors and others to experience subclinical and clinical EDs. Such pressure/factors include sport environment and performance demands; type of sport; level of competition; and coach, parent, and peer influences.

Sport Environment and Performance Demands

Within competitive environments, such as sport and dance, athletes' and performers' bodies are constantly on display and evaluated, not only based on what they can do, but on how attractive they appear to others (e.g., judges, fans). The uniforms and costumes that athletes and dancers wear may increase the pressures they feel to lose weight and/or reshape their bodies. Athletic uniforms in sports like swimming, synchronized swimming, cross-country running, cheerleading, and volleyball are often quite revealing and skimpy, which may lead to increased body consciousness and social comparisons (Greenleaf, 2002; Krane, Choi, Baird, Aimar, & Kauer, 2004). Among female high school and male and female college athletes, including cheerleaders, uniforms were rated as one of the primary pressures they experienced in relation to their weight and body image (Galli & Reel, 2009; Reel & Gill, 1996; Reel, SooHoo, Petrie, Greenleaf, & Carter, 2010). It is likely that some athletes, in an effort to look and feel good in their uniforms and in comparison to their teammates and/or competitors, engage in weight control behaviors that may be pathogenic.

In almost all sports, a body type is thought to be "ideal" both in terms of performance and aesthetics (Thompson & Sherman, 2010). For example, cross-country runners are expected to have very lean, thin bodies whereas defensive football players are expected to have large, muscular bodies. Gymnasts are thought to be tiny and thin, whereas basketball players tall and big. Coaches, athletes, sport personnel (e.g., judges), and even fans come to expect athletes to have a specific body type if they play a certain sport; exceptions are viewed as odd and, in some cases, problematic. These sport-specific ideals are a source of body and weight

pressure for athletes, particularly for those athletes who do not fit the stereotype for their sport, and can negatively influence how they eat, train, and think about themselves and their bodies (e.g., Monsma, Malina, & Feltz, 2006; Russell, 2004; Stewart, Benson, Michanikou, Tsiota, & Narli, 2003). It may also be the case that some athletes have physiques ideal for their sport but that may not be socially ideal. A female ice hockey player with strong and muscular legs, which are advantageous for her sport performance, may be quite self-conscious and dissatisfied with her body in social situations (Russell, 2004). Similarly, a male diver who maintains a slim physique for his sport may feel unhappy with his smaller body size in social settings. The potential conflict between an athletic versus socially ideal body may contribute to pathogenic behaviors.

The sport environment, with its demands, may reward (or at least tolerate) behaviors that otherwise might be considered abnormal. For example, some behaviors among athletes, such as dieting, playing through pain, being focused on perfection, and excessive exercise, may be perceived in the sport environment as "desirable" qualities (Thompson & Sherman, 1999). However, outside of sport, these same behaviors may be indicative of disordered eating. As Filair, Rouveix, Pannafieux, and Ferrand (2007) suggested, "athletes may tread a fine line between optimal competitive attitudes and detrimental health behaviors" (p. 50). Thus, the sport environment, through the comments and behaviors of coaches, teammates, and judges, and the expectations of fans, may directly and subtly nurture characteristics and behaviors that are associated with (or may lead to) disordered eating attitudes and behaviors.

Athletes' goal orientations, as well as the motivational climate within the sport environment, may have a strong influence on athletes' behaviors and how they view their bodies. Athletes with a strong ego goal orientation define success in reference to others' performances, whereas those with a strong task goal orientation define success based upon personal improvement and effort (Roberts, Treasure, & Conroy, 2007; see also Chapter 12, this volume); similarly, the motivational climate may be performance (i.e., emphasis is on performance outcome) or mastery (i.e., emphasis is on athlete improvement and effort) oriented (see Chapter 25, this volume). Although there is not a great deal of research specifically examining goal orientations and motivational climate in relationship to disordered eating among athletes, one recent study provides some initial support. For female athletes in gymnastics and dance, an ego goal orientation, as well as a performance-focused sport environment, was related to more frequent dieting, stronger focus on weight control, higher levels of perfectionism, and more weight-related pressures from coaches and peers (de Bruin, Bakker, & Oudejans, 2009). Similarly, Peden, Stiles, Vandehey, and Diekhoff (2008) found a strong relationship between pressures to succeed in sport and to be the most attractive and characteristics of EDs among female collegiate athletes. Wanting to outperform others may lead athletes to compare themselves constantly to teammates and competitors to determine their status as the thinnest, most in shape, and/or most attractive. If they believe they fall short, they then may adopt extreme weight control measures to modify their body size and shape to be the "best."

Sport Type

Athletes in sports that are judged (i.e., aesthetic), in sport and artistic performances that emphasize a lean physique (i.e., endurance), and in sports with weight restrictions may experience additional pressures that increase their risk for problematic eating attitudes and behaviors. Athletes in aesthetic sports, such as cheerleading, figure skating, synchronized swimming, and gymnastics, experience considerable weight-related pressures (Reel & Gill, 1996; Ziegler et al., 2005; Zucker, Womble, Williamson, & Perrin, 1999). For example, Ginsberg and Gray (2006) found that cover models of "judged" sports (e.g., *Dance Spirit*, *USA Gymnastics*) were thinner than the models used in magazines of "nonjudged" sports, conveying a consistent message about the body size and shape of athletes from these sports. It may be that the evaluative nature of these types of sports, coming from the media and within the sport itself, contributes to an environment in which weight and body consciousness is heightened. In a study of retired gymnasts, Kerr and Dacyshyn (2000) found that some gymnasts reported that weigh-ins and punishment by their coaches for being "overweight" was a constant source of stress. Kerr, Berman, and De Souza (2006) found evidence of problematic eating behaviors among gymnasts who received disparaging comments about their weight and body from coaches. In the same study, gymnastics judges reported being aware of dangerous weight control behaviors and that the "ideal" body for gymnasts was not necessarily healthy. Moreover, researchers have found elevated prevalence rates for athletes

from these sports: 8% of female figure skaters met disturbed eating criteria for body dissatisfaction and drive for thinness (Monsma & Malina, 2004); 6.1% and 28.9% of female collegiate gymnasts in the United States, respectively, were classified as clinical or subclinical in terms of EDs (Anderson & Petrie, 2012); and 38% of rhythmic gymnasts scored as "at-risk" on a measure of disordered eating (Ferrand, Champely, & Filaire, 2009).

Lean, or endurance, sport environments also may contribute to athletes' risk for disordered eating behaviors and attitudes (Beals & Manore, 2000; Petrie, 1996; Picard, 1999; Zucker et al., 1999). Endurance sports are typically those in which a thin, small physique is thought to be advantageous; for example, distance running and swimming are considered lean sports. Because of the purported performance advantages associated with leaner bodies, coaches, teammates, and even parents may directly and/or subtly encourage athletes to drop weight in order to gain an edge over their competition. Unfortunately, this belief that a lower weight directly leads to improved performances is not supported empirically (Thompson & Sherman, 2010), although many coaches hold the idea as sacrosanct. This pressure to lose weight and attain a leaner physique may lead athletes to engage in pathogenic weight loss behaviors as they fight against their body's natural size and weight. For example, in a large, nationally based sample of U.S. female collegiate swimmers, 6.7% were classified with a clinical ED; 20.9% were classified as subclinical (Anderson & Petrie, 2012). Furthermore, over half the swimmers reported exercising for one or more hours each day specifically to burn calories and lose weight.

Athletes in sports with weight restrictions or weight classifications, such as wrestling, powerlifting, and taekwondo, report unhealthy and pathogenic weight control behaviors including fluid restriction, purposeful dehydration, self-induced vomiting, and diuretic and laxative use (Filair at al., 2007; Fleming & Costarelli, 2009; Kiningham & Gorenflo, 2001). Athletes in these types of sports must achieve a specific weight in order to compete in their desired division or weight classification, often aiming to be in a weight class one or two levels below their natural body weight and size (to achieve a competitive advantages). In the United Kingdom, Caulfield and Karageorghis (2008) found that jockeys reported the highest levels of disturbed eating when they were trying to quickly reduce their weight. In the United States, wrestling has been a prime example of a sport in which athletes have used pathogenic and life-threatening behaviors, such as exercising in rubber suits, intentionally dehydrating, and self-induced vomiting, to quickly lose weight in order to qualify for a specific weight division (Gibbs, Pickerman, & Sekiya, 2009; Kiningham & Gorenflo, 2001). In 1997, three college wrestlers died after engaging in these types of behaviors (Gibbs et al., 2009), and the National Collegiate Athletic Association (NCAA) subsequently made changes to weigh-in policies and implemented new rules promoting healthier approaches to weight loss (Gibbs et al., 2009; Oppliger, Utter, Scott, Dick, & Klossner, 2006).

Not all research, though, supports the notion that aesthetic, endurance, and weight class sport athletes are at increased risk (Petrie et al., 2008, 2009a; Greenleaf et al., 2009). For example, Petrie and his colleagues found no relationship among sport type and ED classification in male and female college athletes. Their samples, though, did not include large numbers of typical "at-risk" sports, such as gymnastics or swimming. In addition, because different systems have been used to categorize sport type, it is difficult to make comparisons across studies and come to any final conclusions. To better determine the extent to which sport type plays a role in the development and/or maintenance of disordered eating, large, single-sport studies need to be conducted in which researchers use validated measures.

Competitive Level

At elite levels of sport and performance, significant time, effort, and training are required. Internal and external pressures to be the best (perhaps perfect) are quite real. Athletes and performers often internalize an identity and sense of value/worth/self that is closely linked to their successes and accomplishments (e.g., Jones, Glintmeyer, & McKenzie, 2005). The competitive nature and physical (and psychological) demands of high-level performance may contribute to athletes doing whatever they believe is necessary, such as changing their bodies to be leaner and/or more muscular, to be the best. As noted previously, athletes and performers who determine their success in relation to being better than others report high levels of disordered eating attitudes and behaviors (de Bruin et al., 2009). To date, though, few studies have compared athletes and performers at different competitive levels. Sundgot-Borgen and Torstveit (2004) found a much higher level of EDs among male and female Norwegian national team athletes in comparison to age-matched nonathlete controls. Among adolescents, athletes and nonathletes either do not differ from one another, or athletes report healthier profiles (e.g., feel more personally effective) on measures of disordered eating (Fulkerson et al., 1999; Smolak et al., 2000). Less intensely involved athletes and performers may accrue many of the positive benefits (e.g., increased self-worth) of being physically active and involved in a sport (Greenleaf, Boyer, & Petrie, 2009). However, athletes who compete and train at higher levels may be at increased risk as they (and the sport environment) focus more on their bodies and the "need" to excel. More research is needed to determine the extent to which competitive level is associated with ED risk.

Coach, Parent, and Peer Influences

As general ED research has indicated, significant others' attitudes about eating, body size/shape, and appearance can reinforce societal ideals (i.e., lean, muscular) and be a source of weight pressures (e.g., Peterson, Paulson, & Williams, 2007; Stice, 1998). Within sport, the social environment created by coaches, parents, and peers also can play a strong and influential role in determining athletes' and performers' levels of disordered eating attitudes and behaviors (Kerr et al., 2006; Martinsen et al., 2010; Muscat & Long, 2008). Coaches are powerful social agents in athletes' lives, having control over their physical training, playing time, food intake, interpersonal relationships, psychological well-being, and body image. As such, athletes and performers generally want to please their coaches so as to reap the rewards that they control (e.g., playing time, attention) and are in a vulnerable position when it comes to comments coaches may make about them, their bodies, and their performances. Kerr et al. (2006) found that female gymnasts who were told to lose weight by a coach or had a coach make negative weight-related comments reported more disturbed eating attitudes than did gymnasts who had not been told anything about their weight; half of the gymnastics coaches indicated that they made judgments about the need for gymnasts to lose weight based only on appearance. Similarly, in a sample of young adult female athletes, over half had received negative comments about their appearance, body shape, and/or weight (such as being too fat) and indicated that such comments made them quite upset and more focused on and self-conscious of their bodies (Muscat & Long, 2008); most critical comments were made in front of others, including at family dinners or team practices.

Within the sport environment, teammates and competitors also may influence athletes' attitudes about themselves, their bodies, their appearance, and their eating. Social comparison of weight, body shape/physique, and eating behaviors may lead to unhealthy weight control efforts. In fact, female collegiate athletes identified "teammates noticing if I have put on weight" as the primary weight-related pressure they experience in the sport environment (Reel et al., 2010). Additionally, modeling of attitudes and pathogenic weight-control behaviors within sport and performance environments may show athletes and performers what is expected of them (e.g., lose weight) and how such changes can be accomplished (e.g., diet, exercise in addition to normal training). Among U.S. female collegiate athletes, teammate weight control behaviors have been found to partially predict restrictive eating behaviors (Engel et al., 2003), whereas high school female athletes commonly engage in "fat talk" even though they reported generally positive body image (Smith & Ogle, 2006).

Peers and parents also can be sources of pressure concerning body size/shape and eating behaviors. Muscat and Long (2008) found that among female collegiate athletes, 42% of the critical comments they received about body, weight, and eating were from family members; 33% were from friends. Further, pressures from parents and friends regarding body size and weight are higher among female collegiate athletes who are clinical or subclinical, in comparison to those who are asymptomatic (Petrie et al., 2009a). Peers and parents can be positive influences too. Scoffier, Maïano, and d'Arripe-Longueville (2010) found that peer acceptance and strong parent–athlete relationships offered a protective effect against disordered eating attitudes in a sample of elite adolescent female athletes. How parents and peers structure the relationship with athletes and performers (e.g., supportive) and what they communicate (e.g., care vs. pressure) appears to be related to how athletes respond and potentially whether they develop negative body attitudes and engage in unhealthy weight control behaviors.

The majority of research examining the influence of weight, appearance, and body pressures within the sport environment has focused on female athletes. Male athletes, however, are not immune to such pressures from coaches, parents, teammates, and peers. Galli and Reel (2009) found that the adult male athletes in their sample identified coaches, teammates, women (in general), and significant others as individuals who were sources of pressures about weight and who influenced how they felt about their bodies. Similarly, among U.S. male collegiate athletes, coaches were listed as being the strongest source of pressure concerning body size and weight (Petrie, Greenleaf, Carter, & Reel, 2007). In considering male athletes and performers and the pressures they may experience, it is necessary to acknowledge that different body ideals exist. Overall, male athletes want to be lean, but depending on the sport, they also may want to gain muscle and strength to improve their performances and achieve the mesomorphic societal ideal (Hinton, Sanford, Davidson, Yakushko, & Beck, 2004; Raudenbush & Meyer, 2003; Stewart et al., 2003). More research is needed concerning the potential influence of sport pressures on male athletes.

A Sociocultural Model of Disordered Eating for Male and Female Athletes

In 2007, Petrie and Greenleaf presented a psychosocial model to explain the development of EDs among athletes. Because of the dearth of studies on potential risk factors for athletes, they (a) drew from the general ED literature (e.g., Jacobi et al., 2004; Stice, 2002; Striegel-Moore & Bulik, 2007) to support and illustrate the pathways and factors included in their model, and (b) acknowledged that their model was based on research conducted primarily with women and thus would apply best to the experiences of female athletes. Since the introduction of their model, considerably more research on athletes (male and female) has been conducted; some studies have addressed the specific variables in the model, others have tested directly the proposed pathways, and still others have examined potential moderators. In this section, we revise and expand the Petrie and Greenleaf model, integrating findings from recent studies that suggest changes be made to the originally proposed pathways. We also more directly address the unique experiences of male athletes, drawing upon existing models of EDs and body image for men (e.g., Cafri et al., 2005; Ricciardelli & McCabe, 2004) and including the factor "drive for muscularity" in the model. We recognize that this model focuses primarily on psychosocial influences and does not incorporate all potential risk factors (e.g., biological, genetic, personality) and that it will likely continue to evolve as more research, particularly longitudinal and experimental, is conducted. Thus, we view it as an organizational starting point for examining the development of EDs among male and female athletes, and we encourage researchers to consider other empirically supported factors in their studies as well.

Sociocultural Model

With one exception (i.e., Doughty & Hausenblas, 2005), studies with athletes have been cross-sectional in design. Thus, for athletes, it is premature to view the variables in the model as "risk" factors, and more correct to refer to them as "correlates" (see Striegel-Moore & Bulik, 2007; Jacobi et al., 2004; or Stice, 2002, for a detailed discussion of risk factors in ED research). Because relationships among potential risk factors found within nonathlete samples do not always translate to athletes, examining correlations is a useful first step and should be the current focus of research on athletes, EDs, and the sport environment. Once these relationships are empirically established (across multiple studies and populations), Stice (2002) has suggested that researchers include longitudinal designs (to determine if the potential risk factor predicts onset of the outcome, disordered eating) and multiple potential risk factors (to examine mediating and moderating effects; see Frazier, Tix, & Barron, 2004, for a detailed discussion). As researchers establish temporal relationships among the risk factors, experimental designs then can be implemented to determine causality.

The general (nonsport) factors in the Petrie and Greenleaf (2007) model (see Figure 34.1) included six constructs determined to be risk, or causal risk, factors (in studies with nonathletes) in the development of binge eating and bulimic symptomatology (Jacobi et al., 2004; Stice, 2002): general societal pressures to be thin or achieve a societally determined body shape (e.g., lean and muscular for men);

internalization of societal body or appearance ideals; body dissatisfaction; negative affect (e.g., anger, guilt, sadness); dietary restraint; and modeling of disordered eating and other weight control behaviors by peers and family. To address the uniqueness of the sport environment, Petrie and Greenleaf added "sport-specific pressures regarding weight, body-shape, and performance" to their model. They suggested that general societal and sport-specific pressures operated through internalization to affect athletes' levels of body dissatisfaction. Body dissatisfaction's effects on bulimic symptomatology were hypothesized to occur through either increases in negative affect (referred to as the "affect-regulation" pathway; Stice, 2001a) or increases in intention to restrict food consumption (referred to as the "dietary restraint" pathway). Singly, or in combination, changes in affect or diet were hypothesized to increase the individual's likelihood of binge eating and, potentially, subsequent purging. A recurrent cycle of bingeing and purging is the immediate precursor of BN. They also hypothesized that seeing significant others, such as family members, friends, and/or teammates, engage in binge eating or pathogenic weight control behaviors would lead directly to the adoption of similar behaviors and ultimately the development of bulimic symptoms.

In this revision of the Petrie and Greenleaf (2007) model, we will not review the general ED research they cited to support the inclusion of the original constructs. Instead, we evaluate it through the lens of recent research on athletes, body image, and disordered eating to determine what constructs and pathways are supported and which should be changed (pathways) and added (constructs). This revision and expansion represents the current state

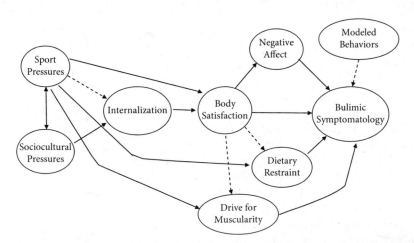

Figure 34.1 A sociocultural model for the development of bulimic symptomatology for male and female athletes.

of disordered eating among athletes, which unfortunately still is limited by a paucity of research. We hope, though, that this model (see Figure 34.1), with its focus on multivariate influences (and potential moderators), will stimulate a more sophisticated approach to studying EDs among athletes and advance research programs in this area.

GENERAL SOCIETAL PRESSURES REGARDING WEIGHT, BODY SIZE, AND APPEARANCE

As individuals who live and function within the broader society, male and female athletes (and artistic performers, such as ballet dancers) are not immune to societal pressures—weight and eating, body size/shape, attractiveness, and what it means to be masculine or feminine—that are communicated through the media (e.g., TV, magazines) and by family and friends. Although historically such societal ideals have been ubiquitous for girls and women, promoting an unrealistically thin (yet buxom) body, over the last 20 years, boys and men have been exposed to similar pressures and are experiencing similar increases in body dissatisfaction as a result (e.g., Cafri et al., 2005; Leit, Gray, & Pope, 2002). Now, men also are exposed to a body ideal (i.e., lean, yet highly muscular) that is unrealistic and achievable only through extreme measures, such as excessive exercising (e.g., weight lifting) and use of supplements (e.g., steroids). Through the socialization process and repeated exposure to these societal body, appearance, and behavioral pressures, male and female athletes are likely to internalize the ideals and then use them as the framework through which they evaluate their own bodies and behaviors. Theoretically, athletes who have strongly internalized specific physical ideals and overemphasize weight, body size/shape, and appearance in their self-evaluation will be most at risk for the development of increased body dissatisfaction.

The effects of general societal pressures on disordered eating attitudes and behaviors have been documented for girls and women (e.g., Stice, 2002) and boys and men (e.g., Ricciardelli & McCabe, 2004), but only a few studies have examined this construct with athletes. In a series of studies with male and female collegiate athletes, Petrie and his colleagues (Anderson, Petrie, & Neumann, 2011; Petrie et al., 2007; 2009a) have demonstrated relationships between general societal pressures and different ED outcomes. For example, in a mixed-sport sample, women who were classified as having either a subclinical or clinical ED reported more pressures from parents, friends, romantic partners, TV/movies, and magazines to be a certain weight or achieve body size/shape than did those who were asymptomatic (Petrie et al., 2009a). For male athletes, pressures about weight from these same groups were related to a stronger psychological drive to achieve a more muscular body and higher levels of bulimic symptomatology (Petrie et al., 2007). Galli and Reel (2009) found that male athletes received comments from friends and family and through the media about appearance, and that these messages influenced their self-expectations about how they should look. Even more compelling, however, are the findings from Anderson et al., who examined the Petrie and Greenleaf (2007) model in a nationally based sample of female collegiate gymnasts and swimmers/divers. As hypothesized, they found that the more strongly athletes experienced sociocultural pressures, the more likely they were to internalize those societal ideals about weight, body size, and appearance; in fact, pressures accounted for 26–41% of the variance in internalization scores. These studies provide initial support that male and female collegiate athletes do experience general sociocultural pressures about weight and body, and these pressures may lead to internalization and, ultimately, to increases in disordered eating.

SPORT-SPECIFIC PRESSURES REGARDING WEIGHT AND BODY

As discussed previously in this chapter, within the sport environment, specific pressures exist, such as judging criteria, body weight categories, coach expectations, and wearing revealing uniforms, that may contribute to athletes feeling conscious about their weight and body size/shape. In the last 5–10 years, considerable research has been conducted on sport-specific pressures and their potential influences on disordered eating attitudes and behaviors (Anderson et al., 2011; de Bruin, Oudejans, & Bakker, 2007; Ferrand et al., 2009; Galli, Reel, Petrie, Greenleaf, & Carter, 2011; Monsma et al., 2006; Muller et al., 2009; Peden et al., 2008; Petrie et al., 2007, 2009a; Reel et al., 2010). Although cross-sectional, these studies suggest that athletes experience pressures concerning weight, self-reported dieting, body size, and appearance that are communicated by coaches, teammates, and judges (e.g., Reel et al.; Galli et al., 2011); these pressures are associated with increases in body image concerns, self-reported dieting behavior, drive for muscularity, and disordered eating behaviors (de Bruin et al., 2007; Ferrand et al., 2009; Petrie et al., 2007, 2009a); female *and* male athletes are subject to such pressures, although the focus for boys and men may be more related to achieving a muscular physique (e.g., Galli & Reel, 2009); and the pressures, and the strength of their effects, may be greatest among higher level, elite performers (e.g., de Bruin et al., 2007; Ferrand et al., 2009).

In the Petrie and Greenleaf (2007) model, a pathway between sport-specific pressures and internalization was proposed. That is, the effects of sport pressures were thought to be mediated through the extent to which they increased athletes' internalization of body and appearance ideals. Subsequent research by Anderson et al. (2011), however, did not support this initial conceptualization and suggested that other pathways may better represent the potential influence of these pressures. Across two independent samples of female gymnasts and swimmers, Anderson et al. found that sport-specific pressures were related directly to body dissatisfaction and dietary restraint. For these female athletes, the more negative pressure they felt from their coaches and teammates about how they looked and how much they weighed, the more likely they were to feel badly about their current body size and shape and to try to lose weight by severely reducing their food intake. Although this study is the first to directly examine these linkages, the results are sufficiently compelling to warrant modifying pathways within the Petrie and Greenleaf model. Our modifications include adding pathways from sport pressures to body dissatisfaction and to dietary restraint, and making the path from sport pressures to internalization a dotted line to indicate the tentativeness of this relationship.

INTERNALIZATION OF THE MALE OR FEMALE BODY IDEAL

Theoretically, athletes who have internalized unrealistic and generally unattainable societal body ideals and have made physical appearance a central part of their self-evaluation will perceive a discrepancy between how they actually appear and how they would really like to look. That is, they will compare their bodies to this ideal referent and, for many, find themselves lacking. When this discrepancy is sufficiently large, athletes may feel dissatisfied (even disgusted) with their current physical appearance. Even though athletes generally have a more positive body image than do nonathletes (Hausenblas & Symons-Downs, 2001), they still may be affected negatively, in terms of being self-conscious about and dissatisfied with their bodies, through this self-evaluation process.

Few empirical studies have been conducted with athletes in relation to the influence of internalization, although the results of these studies are supportive of the proposed model. In 1993, Petrie found that female collegiate gymnasts who were classified as bulimic reported higher scores on a measure of internalization than did those who were described as normal eaters. Similarly, in two independent mixed-sport samples of female collegiate athletes, those classified as having a subclinical or clinical ED more strongly endorsed the societal value of being physically fit and in shape and of being attractive and thin than did the women who were asymptomatic (Petrie et al., 2009a), and greater internalization of societal ideals was related to increased levels of body dissatisfaction, negative affect, dietary restraint, and bulimic symptomatology (Greenleaf, Petrie, Carter, & Reel, 2010). As expected, female collegiate swimmers/divers and gymnasts who took on as their own society's ideals concerning appearance reported being dissatisfied with their current body size and shape (Anderson et al., 2011). Although male athletes have not been studied with respect to internalization, we would expect that those who evaluate their bodies in relation to the mesomorphic ideal also would experience more body image concerns. Thus, inclusion of this variable in the model appears warranted for female *and* male athletes, although additional research is needed to confirm this hypothesis.

BODY DISSATISFACTION (AND DRIVE FOR MUSCULARITY)

Body dissatisfaction has been linked directly to EDs, as well as through its influence on negative affect and dieting (Stice, 2001b). Athletes who perceive a substantial real–ideal body discrepancy, and subsequent body dissatisfaction, are hypothesized to react behaviorally and affectively. In terms of behaviors, female athletes may restrict their food intake as a means to lose weight and shrink their body size. Although some male athletes also may intend to engage in dietary restraint, given that the masculine ideal incorporates muscularity, we would expect them primarily to be focused on behaviors that can increase their strength and muscle mass, such as increasing food intake, ingesting muscle enhancing products (legal and illegal), and raising the intensity and duration of physical workouts (particularly weight training). Affectively, because physical appearance is a central component in their overall self-evaluation, male and female athletes may experience negative emotions, such as anger, guilt, shame, and sadness (Stice, 2002).

Body image concerns have been related directly to severity of eating pathology in both male and female athletes (Anderson et al., 2011; Brannan, Petrie, Greenleaf, Reel, & Carter, 2009; Ferrand et al., 2009; Greenleaf et al., 2010; Petrie, 1993; Petrie et al., 2007, 2009a; Williamson et al., 1995). For example, Brannan et al. found that, even after controlling for social desirability and body mass index, body dissatisfaction accounted for 24% of the variance in bulimic symptomatology in a mixed-sport sample of female collegiate athletes. Anderson et al. reported a strong, direct relationship between body dissatisfaction and scores on the Bulimia Test–Revised, a measure of bulimic symptomatology. They also found an association with negative affect (as expected), but not so with dietary restraint, which they attributed to the fact that weight and appearance pressures from the sport environment also were related directly to dietary restraint and accounted for a significant portion of its variance. For male collegiate athletes, a fear of becoming fat was significantly higher among those who were subclinical in comparison to athletes classified as asymptomatic (Petrie et al., 2007).

For male athletes, body dissatisfaction also appears to be related to drive for muscularity, which is related to muscle dysmorphia, and defined as "attitudes and behaviors that reflect the degree of people's preoccupation with increasing their muscularity" (McCreary & Sasse, 2000, p. 300). The extent to which young men were invested in and committed to their appearance was related to a more intense pursuit of a muscular physique (Davis, Karvinen, & McCreary, 2005). Similarly, male collegiate athletes who were body dissatisfied reported an increased drive for muscularity, which, in turn, was associated with higher levels of bulimic symptomatology (Petrie et al., 2007). Athletes, particularly males, who are focused on making their bodies larger and more muscular may engage in pathological eating behaviors that result in bingeing and purging and other bulimic-related attitudes and behaviors. Thus, drive for muscularity is a correlate of, and may be considered a potential risk factor for, the development of disordered eating, particularly BN.

Given these recent body image findings with male and female athletes, modifications to the Petrie and Greenleaf (2007) model are warranted. First, we added a path between body dissatisfaction and bulimic symptomatology. Although body dissatisfaction's influence appears to be indirect, such as through negative affect, there also is strong evidence of a direct relationship between it and disordered eating. Second, we included the factor "drive for muscularity" to account for the different experiences of male athletes, and we delineated paths from sport-specific pressures and body dissatisfaction to it. Third, we added a direct path from drive for muscularity to disordered eating. Fourth, we designated the paths from body dissatisfaction to dietary restraint and to drive for muscularity with a dotted line to highlight the tentativeness of these potential relationships. Body dissatisfaction may be associated with an increased focus on dieting and engaging in muscle enhancing behaviors, but when considered in conjunction with pressures regarding body size and shape emanating from the sport environment, these effects may be diminished. Additional research is needed to determine the relative influences of these factors.

NEGATIVE AFFECT AND DIETARY RESTRAINT

Several studies with athletes have demonstrated connections between negative affect and self-reported dietary restraint and indices of disordered eating (Anderson et al., 2011; Hinton & Kubas, 2005; Greenleaf et al., 2010; Krane, Stiles-Shipley, Waldron, & Michalenok, 2001; Petrie, 1993; Petrie et al., 2007, 2009a). Specifically, higher levels of eating pathology have been associated with lower self-esteem, higher levels of guilt, greater intention to restrict food intake, and more stress. Across two different studies of female collegiate athletes, self-reported dietary intent was the strongest predictor of level of disordered eating (Greenleaf et al., 2010; Hinton & Kubas, 2005). In their test of the Petrie and Greenleaf (2007) model, Anderson et al. (2011) found the expected relationships between negative affect and self-reported dietary restraint and higher levels of bulimic symptomatology; combined with body dissatisfaction, these three variables explained 55–58% of the bulimia variance. These studies provide support for these two variables as correlates (and possible risk factors) of disordered eating, particularly bulimic symptomatology.

MODELED BEHAVIORS

Modeling and social conformity are processes that explain the acquisition of some behaviors, particularly for individuals who are part of cohesive units, such as sport teams or dance companies (see Chapter 13, this volume). In such situations, athletes (and other performers) may see teammates engage in behaviors such as binge eating or purging, then be reinforced directly or indirectly by a coach or by hearing teammates make negative evaluative comments about their bodies, appearance, and/or eating behaviors. Through this exposure, athletes may begin to act or think in similarly pathological ways.

In support of modeled behaviors, Engel et al. (2003) surveyed male and female collegiate athletes and found that having teammates who either excessively dieted or used various purging behaviors (e.g., vomiting) was related to the athletes' own binge eating, body dissatisfaction, purging, and/or dietary restraint. Anderson et al. (2011), however, found no relationship between female collegiate gymnasts and swimmers/divers seeing teammates engage in extreme dieting and excessive exercising or hearing them express concerns about their bodies and their own level of bulimic symptomatology. Because the potential influence of others' is equivocal, we leave modeled behaviors in the model, but designate the pathway to disordered eating with a dotted line to indicate the tentativeness of the relationship.

POTENTIAL MODERATORS

Moderators change the direction and/or strength of a relationship between two variables (Frazier et al., 2004), which suggests that each pathway within the revised model may vary depending on the presence or absence of specific factors (see Petrie & Greenleaf, 2007, for a detailed explanation of the mechanisms underlying potential moderators). Although some studies have shown sport type, competitive level, age, gender, and race/ethnicity to be moderators of relationships among disordered eating variables (e.g., de Bruin et al., 2007), we could locate only one study that has directly examined the effects of psychological variables as potential moderators of a specific pathway in this model. Brannan et al. (2009) examined the potential moderating effects of perfectionism, optimism, self-esteem, and reasons for engaging in exercise. In a mixed-sport sample of female collegiate gymnasts, they found that concerns about mistakes and exercising to improve appearance worsened the effects of body dissatisfaction on bulimic symptoms; self-esteem, however, buffered its deleterious effects. This study suggests that the strength of the different relationships within the model may vary in conjunction with specific personality and psychological variables, such as perfectionism, self-esteem, social support, intrinsic motivation, neuroticism, goal orientation, reasons for exercising, appearance orientation, instrumentality, appearance comparisons, inadequate coping skills, life stress, and impulse control, to name a few. Although we do not include them directly in the model, we encourage researchers to examine moderators in relation to the pathways we have described in this chapter (see Figure 34.1).

Summary and Directions for Future Research

Our revised model extends the work of Petrie and Greenleaf (2007), incorporating recent athlete research. Although not all potential risk factors, such as age of menarche or competitive level, are included directly in the model, it can serve as an organizational catalyst for investigating EDs in athletes from a sociocultural perspective. To further advance research, we offer the following suggestions:

• Researchers should move beyond between-group comparisons (e.g., athlete group vs. nonathlete group) to within-group analyses of the relationships among putative risk factors. This model provides direction for such studies: (a) validate the relationships, initially using correlational designs, among the factors in the model, (b) examine the interrelationships among the potential risk factors (i.e., mediational pathways) in multivariate designs, and (c) test personality and psychological variables that potentially moderate the relationships among the factors. Including both general sociocultural and sport-specific pressures focuses researchers' attention on the potential influence that these environments, messages, and ideals have on the development of body image concerns and disordered eating. By directly testing the pathways in this model, researchers can determine what variables increase the risk for which athletes. Examining potential moderators will uncover the circumstances when risk is highest. Information from such studies is crucial for the development of effective prevention programs.

• When the relationships in the model are empirically supported across different studies and within different populations (e.g., male and female athletes; elite and nonelite), researchers should use longitudinal designs to establish temporal precedence among the variables. Although we have presented a theoretical model that suggests a directionality that is supported by studies with female nonathlete, the reality is that current research with athletes does not allow for a definitive determination of which variable leads to another.

• Initially, research on the model might focus on certain groups of athletes and performers in whom prevalence is high, such as elite female athletes from aesthetic and endurance sports. But studies also need to focus on different groups of athletes, such as men, women from other sport types, and girls who are participating at a less elite level. For example, studies are needed to validate the inclusion of drive for muscularity in the model. It only will be through testing the model with samples representing different populations that its validity and generalizability can be determined. At present, we suggest that the model be used as a starting point for studies with all athlete groups, but encourage researchers to make modifications (based on evolving research findings) to fit the specific needs of the population being studied.

• Although our previous suggestions are specific to quantitative investigations, which are needed to test etiological models and establish temporal precedence, we advocate the use of the model to guide qualitative research. Such studies can help us understand of how male and female athletes' experience of the sport environment influences their lives. In particular, in-depth interviews with athletes can shed light on other potential risk factors and moderators that could then be tested via more traditional quantitative methodologies.

Intervention

In this section, we cover the three different, yet related components of intervention: prevention, identification, and treatment. In discussing prevention, we start with what can be done at the socio-environmental level to minimize the sport-specific pressures that exist. We recognize, though, that such environmental changes may be difficult to achieve, so we also present information on prevention programming that can be implemented with athletes and performers directly. We discuss identification and treatment together because they represent two sides of the same coin, with the former being the pathway to the latter.

Creating a Body-Healthy Training Environment

Initial research with athlete samples (e.g., Anderson et al., 2011; Galli et al., 2011) suggests that sport-specific pressures, those that originate from the behaviors, attitudes, values, and messages of important social agents in the sport environment (e.g., coaches and teammates), are related negatively to body image and eating behaviors. Although the connections between pressures and subsequent disordered eating attitudes and behaviors have not

been examined (and borne out) yet in longitudinal and experimental research, results from nonathlete studies of pressures suggest targeting them will ultimately reduce ED risk. That is, by making the sport environment less weight- and body-focused, "downstream" variables in the model (see Stice, 2002), such as internalization and body dissatisfaction, would be improved. So, changing the sport environment as a means of reducing athletes' and performers' risk is suggested by our model as well as by initial research on the effects of sport-specific pressures.

By a "body-healthy" environment we mean that athletes' and performers' physical and psychological well-being is central to all decisions, recommendations, and requirements regarding training. Such an approach requires changing the perception that maximizing performance is sine qua non, no matter the ultimate physical or psychological cost to the athlete. Healthy athletes—in terms of weight, physical status, physiological functioning, nutrition, and psychological well-being—will perform better than those who are compromised in any of these areas. Unfortunately, many coaches and many athletes/performers themselves, believe that a direct, and even magical, connection exists between weight change and improved performance (Thompson & Sherman, 2010). Thus, the pursuit of this goal may lead athletes to engage in unhealthy eating and weight control (or gain) behaviors that, in the end, compromise their performance.

To bring about such environmental change (and how coaches, dance instructors, parents, and administrators, to name a few, think about weight and performance), we offer several suggestions based on the work of Petrie and Greenleaf (2010). We also refer the reader to Bonci et al. (2008), who provided detailed information regarding the identification, prevention, and management of EDs in U.S. collegiate athletic departments.

DISCONNECTING WEIGHT AND PERFORMANCE

No ideal body weight or body fat percentage translates into superior performances (Bonci et al., 2008); in fact, within any given sport, there is considerable variability in the body sizes, shapes, and weights of high-level performers (Thompson & Sherman, 2010). Despite this reality, many coaches still monitor eating patterns, track weight, and assess the body fat of their athletes in hopes of helping the athlete reach this magical target (Heffner, Ogles, Gold, Marsden, & Johnson, 2003). These behaviors put an unhealthy focus on weight and body size/shape and pressure athletes to exercise excessively, take muscle-gain supplements, restrict caloric intake, and/or vomit, which can lead to physical problems, such as menstrual irregularities and/or the loss of lean body mass. When these problems occur, performances may be compromised because of inadequate energy supplies, insufficient strength and coordination, fatigue, and/or lack of confidence in their body. By disconnecting weight and performance, de-emphasizing weight change, and encouraging healthier avenues for improving performance (e.g., skill development, proper nutrition, mental toughness), coaches can take a step in creating a body-healthy environment.

ELIMINATING WEIGH-INS AND WEIGHT REQUIREMENTS

Weight requirements and weigh-ins stem from the misguided belief that weight change leads directly to performance improvements. From our perspective, these behaviors are unnecessary and in almost all instances should be eliminated. Instead, we suggest that athletes only be weighed for medical reasons (e.g., training in humid environment and monitoring hydration); weigh-ins, if done, be conducted by medical personnel (e.g., athletic trainers) and *never* by coaches; athletes be informed of the weigh-ins' purpose and given the opportunity to *not* be told their weight; weigh-ins be done privately with the medical personnel; and weight be kept private/confidential and *never* posted publicly (e.g., in the locker room). In addition, coaches and other personnel should refrain from making direct, or even subtle, comments about an athlete's weight or body shape.

If weight change (gain or loss) could be beneficial for the athlete's health, well-being, and potentially, performance, decisions to proceed should be made by a sport management team (SMT) that comprises various professionals, such as strength and conditioning staff, medical personnel, nutritionist, exercise physiologist, mental health practitioner, etc. Before recommending weight change strategies, the SMT would evaluate all aspects of the athlete's current physical condition and training to determine if other behavioral changes are warranted instead. If a weight change plan is recommended because of expected health benefits, the athlete should be involved in its implementation and monitoring of progress (Bonci et al., 2008). Throughout, the focus should be on the athlete's health, not on the weight change per se.

CHANGING WEIGHT/BODY-FOCUSED NORMS

Expectations about weight, eating, body size/shape, and appearance may exist within an entire sport (e.g., jockeys cutting weight) or be specific to one team (e.g., a field hockey coach expecting his players to look "feminine"). Such expectations may be communicated by coaches and through teammates, both directly and indirectly, leading to the development of norms that can reinforce existing unhealthy beliefs and influence the adoption of new pathogenic behaviors. For example, athletes may exercise in addition to normal workouts, not eat dinner after training, vomit after a large meal, not be satisfied with their body size and shape, and/or ingest muscle-enhancing supplements, such as steroids. The underlying message is conformity.

Although organizational change, such as the adoption of policies regarding not weighing athletes or the use of a nutritionist for meal planning, can address unhealthy norms, change also can occur by helping coaches and athletes/performers modify their attitudes and beliefs about weight, body, and appearance, as well as the behaviors (unhealthy) that they believe are acceptable because they may bring about weight change. By understanding a team's cultural norms, practitioners will know what to address, who to target, and how to proceed. For example, practitioners could help coaches see the connection between their seemingly innocuous comments about an athlete's body size (or weight) and his loss of confidence. Because norms can be entrenched, change may take time and considerable effort and attention by the practitioner.

EDUCATING COACHES

Although most collegiate-level coaches have received some training regarding EDs (e.g., attended a workshop), they still recognize the need for additional assistance when it comes to identifying, referring, and/or assisting athletes (Sherman, Thompson, Dehass, & Wilfert, 2005). To help, practitioners can provide coaches with information about the effects of body image concerns and EDs on performance. Practitioners also might utilize athletic trainers (and other medical staff) to help educate coaches about normal physiological functioning (e.g., menstruation) and how proper training and nutrition (and not excessive weight change) may contribute to improvements in athletes' performances. Such educational efforts can be ongoing and informal, such as by talking at practices, or more formal and time-limited, such as through scheduled presentations.

CREATING AN INTEGRATED TRAINING ENVIRONMENT

If they cannot focus on weight change, then coaches will want to know what they can do to improve performances. Practitioners can address this issue and help coaches create an integrated training environment. Although the services available will vary by team, program, etc., when practitioners have established working relationships with strength and conditioning coaches, nutritionists, and sport psychologists, they can ensure that consideration is given to strength training, speed and conditioning work, nutrition, and mental skills by coaches and athletes. When evaluating athletes' poor performances, practitioners can help coaches consider various potential causes (and solutions), instead of focusing entirely (and unduly) on body weight, size, or shape.

Prevention Programming

Changing the sport culture takes time and effort, and coaches and other sport personnel may be resistant. Thus, practitioners also can offer programming directly to athletes and performers, such as those who have body image concerns. Because pressures, general societal and sport-specific, have been identified as potential risk factors for athletes, targeting those is important. In addition, programs that address athletes' tendencies to internalize body, weight, and appearance-related messages would be useful. Reducing these potential risk factors, in theory, would lead to improvements in body image, reductions in negative affect, dietary restraint, and the need to attain a muscular physique, and, ultimately, decreases in binge eating and/or bulimic symptomatology.

Primary prevention programs are designed to prevent new cases of a disorder or condition from emerging in a targeted population. Over the last 20 years, considerable research has been conducted on such programs with nonathletes, and recent meta-analyses have shown that they have small to moderate effects in reducing risk factors, such as internalization, body dissatisfaction, and negative affect (Fingeret, Warren, Cepeda-Benito, & Gleaves, 2006; Stice, Shaw, & Marti, 2007). More specifically, these meta-analyses found that the most effective programs targeted high-risk groups, such as women who are body dissatisfied, included participants who are 15 years or older, used interactive and experiential formats, and incorporated content that focused on body-acceptance or reduction of the thin-ideal through the creation of cognitive-

dissonance, such as when women argue against (or behave in a manner contrary to) societal ideals regarding weight, body, and appearance.

Controlled prevention research in the sport environment, however, has been limited. For example, Abood and Black (2000) examined an 8-week, interactive prevention program that focused on increasing knowledge and skills in self-esteem, handling performance pressures, improving nutrition, and managing stress, but did not address disordered eating. In comparison to a control group, female collegiate athletes who completed the program reported lower drive for thinness and body dissatisfaction and higher self-esteem and nutrition knowledge; no follow-up data were collected. Similarly, Elliot et al. (2004) found that at the end of their sport seasons, high school female athletes who had completed the 8-week, peer-led Athletes Targeting Healthy Exercise and Nutrition Alternative (ATHENA) program reported healthier behaviors (e.g., decrease in diet pill use), increased knowledge (e.g., consequences of EDs), improved mood, and fewer future behavioral intentions (e.g., vomiting) than athletes in the control condition.

More recently, Smith and Petrie (2008) extended a traditional dissonance-based prevention program (e.g., Stice et al., 2007) to female collegiate athletes. They compared the cognitive dissonance (CD) program to two alternatives—psychoeducationally based healthy weight management (HWM) and wait-list control. Athletes were matched on body dissatisfaction and then randomly assigned to the HWM, CD, or control group; the athletes in the HWM or CD programs attended three 1-hour sessions. Although there was no overall intervention by time effect, which may have been due to the small sample (and thus low power), post hoc analyses revealed the CD group reported decreases in sadness, internalization, and body dissatisfaction over the 3 weeks. Combined, these studies provide initial support for the effectiveness of primary prevention programs with high school and collegiate female student athletes, particularly when the format is interactive and the content addresses the unique needs of this population.

Determining the effectiveness of primary prevention programs among athletes is a necessary next step. Because numerous programs exist for nonathletes (e.g., Fingeret et al., 2006; Stice et al., 2007), researchers will not have to develop interventions from scratch, but rather can utilize the most effective components of existing programs and modify them to address the unique pressures and features of the sport environment. To guide research on such programs, we make the following recommendations (Fingeret et al., 2006; Stice et al., 2007). First, programs should address variables that have been demonstrated to be risk factors in the development of disordered eating attitudes and behaviors. Etiological models, such as the one presented in this chapter, provide for testable hypotheses and allow researchers to determine what causes (and mediates) change in the outcomes. Second, researchers should modify existing programs to fit the needs and experiences of athletes and performances, and address the unique pressures in the performance environment. Researchers also should incorporate other approaches that may increase the persuasiveness (and likelihood it is internalized) of the message, such as adding booster sessions (e.g., 6 months after completion of intervention) or integrating principles of motivational interviewing in the program itself (Stice et al., 2007). Third, researchers should include wait-list and placebo control groups and follow athletes for 6 months to a year post intervention. Fourth, researchers should target subgroups of athletes who are perceived to be most at risk, such as those from aesthetic sports or more generally those who are body dissatisfied. Fifth, as more is learned about the experiences (and risk factors) of male athletes, programming may be developed and tested for them as well.

Identification and Treatment

There are two distinct time frames during which screening and identification of athletes and performers for EDs might occur, and this process can be facilitated through a strong partnership with the sport or performance organization's medical staff. First, during their pre-participation physical examinations, all athletes (or performers) can provide information regarding their eating and nutritional status, body- and weight-related attitudes, and psychological well-being and, for girls and women, their menstrual functioning (Bonci et al., 2008). This information can be obtained through interviews, paper-and-pencil questionnaires, or a combination of the two (see Bonci et al., 2008 for a review). Regardless of how information is collected, care must be taken to maintain confidentiality (e.g., not sharing responses with coaches). Second, throughout the year, athletes' behaviors, attitudes, mood states, and physical and psychological functioning can be monitored by coaches and medical staff for signs and symptoms of EDs. Multiple signs and symptoms are associated with EDs (see Bonci

et al. 2008; Petrie & Greenleaf, 2007, for more information) that can be used to identify athletes who may need assistance.

Whether as a result of initial screening or ongoing monitoring during the season, when athletes are identified as experiencing disordered eating attitudes and/or behaviors, a meeting should be scheduled with a member of the SMT to gather more information. Although it is beyond the scope of this chapter to provide detailed information about the initial meeting (see Thompson & Sherman, 2010), setting it up should be done confidentially and directly with the athlete, done with someone who has a good relationship with the athlete (e.g., athletic trainer), and focused on the athlete's health and well-being (as opposed to weight and/or performance). If the SMT member who holds this initial meeting is not a mental health professional with experience in diagnosing an ED, a focus of the meeting should be on helping the athlete feel comfortable talking with someone who does (see Bonci et al., 2008). The desired outcome of this initial meeting is a determination of the extent to which the observed symptoms indicate an ED or related psychological problem and a referral for treatment if needed.

Early identification is helpful for two reasons. First, it can limit the negative effects of the suspected disorder and facilitate the athlete receiving treatment. If the athlete is subclinical or just engaging in pathogenic weight control behaviors, the development of more severe problems, such as the triad or a clinical ED, may be avoided. Second, sport institutes, sport organizations, ballet companies, and coaches/trainers are ethically and legally responsible for the athletes/performers under their guidance, and should make health and well-being the primary concern. Creating a body-healthy training environment, having a screening program in place, and developing explicit policies regarding identification and treatment are three ways to demonstrate that responsibility, which may help to reduce legal liability.

Because it is beyond the scope of this chapter to discuss in depth effective ED treatments, we recommend several other sources for review (see Moore, Ciampa, Wilsnack, & Wright, 2007; Wilson, Grilo, & Vitousek, 2007). We do, though, want to highlight a few issues that may arise in the treatment of an athlete or performer with an ED. First, in most instances, the mental health providers (e.g., psychologist, psychiatrist, nutritionist) who provide the ED treatment are likely not to be part of the

SMT nor part of the immediate sport environment. Thus, confidentiality and how information will be shared (or not) with the SMT must be considered and addressed at the outset. Sharing information with the SMT may be needed so that decisions can be made about continued physical training and/or participation in competitions. The athlete who is in treatment, if an adult, must provide explicit consent for such communication to occur, unless the consent has been made previously as part of a medical care agreement with the sport/performance organization. If consent has been granted, the athlete always should be informed about what is communicated, to whom it is communicated, and the purpose of the communication. Whenever possible, the athlete should be aware of such communications before they occur.

Second, subclinical or clinical EDs can compromise physical health, so decisions about continuing training and competition (performance) while in treatment must be made. Athletes may continue *if* their overall health and nutritional status and the treatment itself are not compromised by the training/competing (Thompson & Sherman, 2010). Such decisions should not be made lightly and should involve input from all the professionals who are involved in the athletes' treatment, including physician, psychologist, and nutritionist. Mechanisms to effectively monitor health status and treatment goals need to be established and implemented when they enter treatment. If, at any time, their health and/or treatment progress is compromised, then training should be limited immediately.

Finally, athletes and other performers are part of broader systems (e.g., teams, organizations, companies), so absences from training are likely to be noticed and commented upon by teammates, other personnel, and potentially even the press. Thus, athletes who are undergoing treatment will need to think through how (and what) they will communicate with others about their treatment or potential absence. The SMT or the mental health practitioner who is working with the athlete can assist in this decision-making, developing a plan of action that is comfortable for the athlete. It can be useful to view an ED as an injury and the treatment as rehabilitation. Such an approach normalizes the process and can destigmatize the disorder.

Conclusion

Eating disorders are psychological disorders that have serious medical and physical complications and involve body image concerns, disruptions in normal eating, and decrease in self-worth. Even with their high levels of physical activity and fitness, and lean and toned bodies, athletes are not immune to these problems. In fact, male and female athletes (and some artistic performers, such as ballet dancers), particularly those at more elite levels and from domains that emphasize physique and leanness, may experience clinical and subclinical EDs and engage in pathogenic weight control behaviors at rates higher than nonathletes.

Although risk factor research with athletes lags far behind what has been conducted with nonathlete samples, similar variables appear to play a role in the development of disordered eating, such as internalization, general societal pressures about physique and appearance, body dissatisfaction, negative affect, and dietary intent. Because athletes are subject to unique pressures within the sport environment that appear to increase risk, this factor is considered as well in our sociocultural model. For male athletes, drive for muscularity (i.e., a psychological desire and engagement in behaviors to attain a more muscular physique) also is included to address the fact that men's physical ideal is both lean *and* muscular. The manner in which these factors interact to promote risk has evolved as a result of recent research (e.g., Anderson et al., 2011) and is likely to continue to do so as researchers move to longitudinal and experimental designs to test the factors.

Over the last two decades, prevention programming with nonathletes has expanded and research has demonstrated its basic effectiveness in reducing putative risk factors (e.g., Stice et al., 2007). Because only a handful of similar studies have been conducted with athletes, this area should be explored in future research. Etiological models, such as the one presented in this chapter, offer direction not only for basic risk factor research, but for the development and evaluation of prevention programs. Such programs, to be effective, will need to address the unique pressures, messages, attitudes, and values that exist within the sport or performance environment and give athletes knowledge and skills for handling them.

References

Abood, D., & Black, D. (2000). Health education prevention for eating disorders among college female athletes. *American Journal of Health Behavior, 24,* 209–220.

Ackard, D. M., Fulkerson, J. A., & Neumark-Sztainer, D. (2007). Prevalence and utility of DSM-IV eating disorder diagnostic criteria among youth. *International Journal of Eating Disorders, 40,* 409–417.

Adams, J. (2009). Understanding exercise dependence. *Journal of Contemporary Psychotherapy, 39*, 231–240.

American College of Sports Medicine. (2007). The female athlete triad. *Medicine and Science in Sports and Exercise, 39*, 1867–1882.

American Psychiatric Association. (1994). *Diagnostic and statistical manual of mental disorders* (4th ed.). Washington, DC: Author.

American Psychiatric Association. (2000). *Diagnostic and statistical manual of mental disorders, text revision*. Washington, DC: Author.

Anderson, C., & Petrie, T. A. (2012). Prevalence of disordered eating and pathogenic weight control behaviors among NCAA Division I female collegiate gymnasts and swimmers. *Research Quarterly for Exercise and Sport, 83*, 120–124.

Anderson, C., Petrie, T. A., & Neumann, C. (2011). Psychosocial correlates of bulimic symptomatology among NCAA Division I female collegiate gymnasts and swimmers/divers. *Journal of Sport and Exercise Psychology, 33*, 483–505.

Bachner-Melman, R., Zohar, A. H., Ebstein, R., Elizur, Y., & Constantini, N. (2006). How anorexic-like are the symptoms and personality profiles of aesthetic athletes? *Medicine and Science in Sports and Exercise, 38*, 628–636.

Baghurst, T., & Kissinger, D. B. (2009). Perspectives on muscle dysmorphia. *International Journal of Men's Health, 8*, 82–89.

Baghurst, T., & Lirgg, C. (2005). Characteristics of muscle dysmorphia in male football, weight training, and competitive natural and non-natural bodybuilding samples. *Body Image, 6*, 221–227.

Beals, K. A., & Hill, A. K. (2006). The prevalence of disordered eating, menstrual dysfunction, and low bone mineral density among US collegiate athletes. *International Journal of Sport Nutrition and Exercise Metabolism, 16*, 1–23.

Beals, K. A., & Manore, M. M. (2000). Behavioral, psychological, and physical characteristics of female athletes with subclinical eating disorders. *International Journal of Sport Nutrition and Exercise Metabolism, 10*, 128–143.

Bonci, C., Bonci, L., Granger, L., Johnson, C., Malina, R., Milne, L. W., et al. (2008). National Athletic Trainers' Association position statement: Preventing, detecting, and managing disordered eating in athletes. *Journal of Athletic Training, 43*, 80–108.

Brannan, M., Petrie, T., Greenleaf, C., Reel, J., & Carter, J. (2009). The relationship between body dissatisfaction and bulimic symptoms in female collegiate athletes. *Journal of Sport and Exercise Psychology, 3*, 103–126.

Brownell, K., & Napolitano, M. (1995). Distorting reality for children: Body size proportions of Barbie and Ken dolls. *International Journal of Eating Disorders, 18*, 295–298.

Cafri, G., Thompson, J. K., Ricciardelli, L., McCabe, M., Smolak, L., & Yesalis, C. (2005). Pursuit of the muscular ideal: Physical and psychological consequences and putative risk factors. *Clinical Psychology Review, 25*, 215–239.

Cafri, G., van den Berg, P., & Thompson, J. K. (2006). Pursuit of muscularity in adolescent boys: Relations among biopsychosocial variables and clinical outcomes. *Journal of Clinical Child and Adolescent Psychology, 35*, 283–291.

Caulfield, M. J., & Karageorgehis, C. I. (2008). Psychological effects of rapid weight loss and attitudes towards eating among professional jockeys. *Journal of Sports Sciences, 26*, 877–883.

Cohen, D. L., & Petrie, T. A. (2005). An examination of psychosocial correlates of disordered eating among undergraduate women. *Sex Roles, 52*, 29–42.

Cook, B. J., & Hausenblas, H. A. (2008). The role of exercise dependence for the relationship between exercise behavior and eating pathology. Mediator or moderator? *Journal of Health Psychology, 13*, 495–502.

Crowther, J., Armey, M., Luce, K., Dalton, G., & Leahey, T. (2008). The point prevalence of bulimic disorders from 1990 to 2004. *International Journal of Eating Disorders, 41*, 491–497.

Currin, L., Schmidt, U., Treasure, J., & Jick, H. (2005). Time trends in eating disorder incidence. *British Journal of Psychiatry, 186*, 132–135.

Davis, C., Karvinen, K., & McCreary, D. (2005). Personality correlates of a drive for muscularity in young men. *Personality and Individual Differences, 39*, 349–359.

de Bruin, A. P., Bakker, F. C., & Oudejans, R. R. D. (2009). Achievement goal theory and disordered eating: Relationships of disordered eating with goal orientations and motivational climate in female gymnasts and dancers. *Psychology of Sport and Exercise, 10*, 72–79.

de Bruin, A. P., Oudejans, R. R. D., & Bakker, F. C. (2007). Dieting and body image in aesthetic sports: A comparison of Dutch female gymnasts and non-aesthetic sport participants. *Psychology of Sport and Exercise, 8*, 507–520.

Derenne, J. L., & Beresin, E. V. (2006). Body image, media, and eating disorders. *Academic Psychiatry, 30*, 257–261.

Doughty, J., & Hausenblas, H. (2005). A longitudinal examination of disordered eating correlates in collegiate gymnasts. *Women in Sport and Physical Activity Journal, 14*, 52–61.

Elliot, D., Goldberg, L., Moe, E., DeFrancesco, C., Durham, M., & Hix-Small, H. (2004). Preventing substance use and disordered eating: Initial outcomes of ATHENA (Athletes Targeting Healthy Exercise and Nutrition Alternatives) program. *Archives of Pediatric Medicine, 138*, 1043–1049.

Engel, S. G., Johnson, C., Powers, P. S., Crosby, R. D., Wonderlich, S. A., Wittrock, D. A., & Mitchell, J. E. (2003). Predictors of disordered eating in a sample of elite Division I college athletes. *Eating Behaviors, 4*, 333–343.

Ferrand, C., Champely, S., & Filaire, E. (2009). The role of body-esteem in predicting disordered eating symptoms: A comparison of French aesthetic athletes and non-athlete females. *Psychology of Sport and Exercise, 10*, 373–380.

Filair, E., Rouveix, M., Pannafieux, C., & Ferrand, C. (2007). Eating attitudes, perfectionism and body-esteem of elite male judoists and cyclists. *Journal of Sports Science and Medicine, 6*, 50–57.

Fingeret, M., Warren, C., Cepeda-Benito, A., & Gleaves, D. (2006). Eating disorder prevention research: A meta-analysis. *Eating Disorders, 14*, 191–213.

Fleming, S., & Costarelli, V. (2009). Eating behaviours and general practices used by Taekwondo players in order to make weight before competition. *Nutrition and Food Science, 39*, 16–23.

Frazier, P., Tix, A., & Barron, K. (2004). Testing moderator and mediator effects in counseling psychology research. *Journal of Counseling Psychology, 51*, 115–134.

Fulkerson, J. A., Keel, P. K., Leon, G. R., & Dorr, T. (1999). Eating-disordered behaviors and personality characteristics of high school athletes and nonathletes. *International Journal of Eating Disorders, 26*, 73–79.

Galli, N., & Reel, J. J. (2009). Adonis or Hephaestus? Exploring body image in male athletes. *Psychology of Men and Masculinity, 10*, 95–108.

Galli, N., Reel, J., Petrie, T., Greenleaf, C., & Carter, J. (2011). Preliminary development of the weight pressures in sport scale for male athletes. *Journal of Sport Behavior, 34*, 47–68.

Garman, J. F., Hayduk, D. M., Crider, D. A., & Hodel, M. M. (2004). Occurrence of exercise dependence in a college-aged population. *Journal of American College Health, 52*, 221–228.

Gibbs, A., Pickerman, J., & Sekiya, J. K. (2009). Weight management in amateur wrestling. *Sports Health: Multidisciplinary Approach, 1*, 227–230.

Ginsberg, R., & Gray, J. (2006). The differential depiction of female athletes in judged and non-judged sport magazines. *Body Image, 3*, 365–373.

Greenleaf, C. (2002). Athletic body image: Exploratory interviews with former competitive female athletes. *Women in Sport and Physical Activity Journal, 11*, 63–88.

Greenleaf, C., Boyer, E. M., & Petrie, T. A. (2009). Psychological well-being and physical activity: The role of high school physical activity and sport participation. *Sex Roles, 61*, 714–726.

Greenleaf, C., Petrie, T. A., Carter, R., & Reel, J. J. (2009). Female collegiate athletes: Prevalence of eating disorders and disordered eating behaviors. *Journal of American College Health, 57*, 489–495.

Greenleaf, C., Petrie, T. A., Carter, R., & Reel, J. J. (2010). Psychosocial risk factors of bulimic symptomatology among female athletes. *Journal of Clinical Sport Psychology, 4*, 177–190.

Grieve, F. G., Truba, N., & Bowersox, S. (2009). Etiology, assessment, and treatment of muscle dysmorphia. *Journal of Cognitive Psychotherapy: An International Quarterly, 23*, 306–314.

Grossbard, J. R., Lee, C. M., Neighbors, C., & Larimer, M. E. (2009). Body image concerns and contingent self-esteem in male and female college students. *Sex Roles, 3–4*, 198–207.

Hamer, M., & Karageorghis, C. I. (2007). Psychobiological mechanisms of exercise dependence. *Sports Medicine, 37*, 477–484.

Hamilton, L., Brooks-Gunn, J., Warren, M., & Hamilton, W. (1988). The role of selectivity in the pathogenesis of eating problems in ballet dancers. *Medicine and Science in Sports and Exercise, 20*, 560–565.

Hausenblas, H. A., & Carron, A. V. (1999). Eating disorder indices and athletes: An integration. *Journal of Sport and Exercise Psychology, 21*, 230–258.

Hausenblas, H. A., & Symons Downs, D. (2002). Exercise dependence: A systematic review. *Psychology of Sport and Exercise, 3*, 89–123.

Hausenblas, H. A., & Symons Downs, D. (2001). Comparison of body image between athletes and nonathletes: A meta-analytic review. *Journal of Applied Sport Psychology, 13*, 323–339.

Heatherton, T., & Baumeister, R. (1991). Binge eating as an escape from self-awareness. *Psychological Bulletin, 110*, 86–108.

Heffner, J., Ogles, B., Gold, E., Marsden, K., & Johnson, M. (2003). Nutrition and eating in female college athletes: A survey of coaches. *Eating Disorders, 11*, 209–220.

Hincapié, C. A., & Cassidy, J. D. (2010). Disordered eating, menstrual disturbances, and low bone mineral density in dancers: A systematic review. *Archives of Physical Medicine and Rehabilitation, 91*, 1777–1789.

Hinton, P., & Kubas, K. (2005). Psychosocial correlates of disordered eating in female collegiate athletes: Validation of the ATHLETE questionnaire. *Journal of American College Health, 54*, 149–156.

Hinton, P., Sanford, T., Davidson, M., Yakushko, O., & Beck, N. (2004). Nutrient intakes and dietary behaviors of male and female collegiate athletes. *International Journal of Sport Nutrition and Exercise Metabolism, 14*, 389–405.

Hoch, A. Z., Stavrokos, D. E., & Schimke, J. E. (2007). Prevalence of female athlete triad characteristics in a club triathlon team. *Archives of Physical Medicine Rehabilitation, 88*, 681–682.

Hoch, A. Z, Pajewski, N. M., Moraski, L., Carrera, G. F., Wilson, C., Hoffman, R. G., et al. (2009). Prevalence of the female athlete triad in high school athletes and sedentary students. *Clinical Journal of Sports Medicine, 19*, 421–428.

Hudson, J. I., Hiripi, E., Pope, H. G., & Kessler, R. C. (2007). The prevalence and correlates of eating disorders in the National Comorbidity Survey replication. *Biological Psychiatry, 61*, 348–358.

Isomaa, R., Tsomaa, A., Marttunen, M., Kaltiala-Heino, R., & Bjorkqvist, K. (2009). The prevalence, incidence and development of eating disorders in Finnish adolescents—A two-step 3-year follow-up study. *European Eating Disorders in Review, 17*, 199–207.

Jacobi, C., Hayward, C., de Zwaan, M., Kraemer, H., & Agras, W. S. (2004). Coming to terms with risk factors for eating disorders: Application of risk terminology and suggestions for a general taxonomy. *Psychological Bulletin, 130*, 19–65.

Johnson, C., Powers, P. S., & Dick, R. (1999). Athletes and eating disorders: The National Collegiate Athletic Association study. *International Journal of Eating Disorders, 26*, 179–188.

Jones, R. L., Glintmeyer, N., & McKenzie, A. (2005). Slim bodies, eating disorders and the coach-athlete relationship: A tale of identity creation and disruption. *International Review for the Sociology of Sport, 40*, 377–391.

Keel, P., Heatherton, T., Dorer, D., Joiner, T., & Zalta, A. (2006). Point prevalence of bulimia nervosa in 1982, 1992, and 2002. *Psychological Medicine, 36*, 119–127.

Kerr, G., Berman, E., & De Souza, M. J. (2006). Disordered eating in women's gymnastics: Perspectives of athletes, coaches, parents, and judges. *Journal of Applied Sport Psychology, 18*, 28–43.

Kerr, G., & Dacyshyn, A. (2000). The retirement experience of elite female gymnasts. *Journal of Applied Sport Psychology, 12*, 115–133.

Kiningham, R. B., & Gorenflo, D. W. (2001). Weight loss methods of high school wrestlers. *Medicine and Science in Sports and Exercise, 33*, 810–813.

Kotler, L. A., Cohen, P., Davies, M., Pine, D. S., & Walsh, B. T. (2001). Longitudinal relationships between childhood, adolescent, and adult eating disorders. *Journal of the American Academy of Child and Adolescent Psychiatry, 40*, 1434–1440.

Krane, V., Choi, P. Y. L., Baird, S. M., Aimar, C. M., & Kauer, K. L. (2004). Living the paradox: Female athletes negotiate femininity and muscularity. *Sex Roles, 5–6*, 315–329.

Krane, V., Stiles-Shipley, J., Waldron, J., & Michalenok, J. (2001). Relationships among body satisfaction, social physique anxiety, and eating behaviors in female athletes and exercisers. *Journal of Sport Behavior, 24*, 247–264.

Leit, R., Gray, J., & Pope, H. (2002). The media's representation of the ideal male body: A cause of muscle dysmorphia? *International Journal of Eating Disorders, 31*, 334–338.

Leone, J. E., Sedory, E. J., & Gray, K. A. (2005). Recognition and treatment of muscle dysmorphia and related body image disorders. *Journal of Athletic Training, 40*, 352–359.

Maida, D. M., & Armstrong, S. L. (2005). The classification of muscle dysmorphia. *International Journal of Men's Health, 4*, 73–91.

Martinsen, M., Bratland-Sanda, S., Eriksson, A. K., & Sundgot-Borgen, J. (2010). Dieting to win or to be thin? A study of dieting and disordered eating among adolescent elite athletes and non-athlete controls. *British Journal of Sports Medicine, 44*, 70–76.

McCabe, M., & Ricciardelli, L. (2003). Body image and strategies to lose weight and increase muscle among boys and girls. *Health Psychology, 22*, 39–46.

McCreary, D., & Sasse, D. (2000). An exploration of the drive for muscularity in adolescent boys and girls. *Journal of American College Health, 48*, 297–304.

McFarland, M. B., & Kaminski, P. L. (2009). Men, muscles, and mood: The relationship between self-concept, dysphoria, and body image disturbances. *Eating Behaviors, 10*, 68–70.

Monsma, E. V., & Malina, R. M. (2004). Correlates of eating disorders risk among female figure skaters: A profile of adolescent competitors. *Psychology of Sport and Exercise, 5*, 447–460.

Monsma, E. V., Malina, R. M., & Feltz, D. (2006). Puberty and physical self-perceptions of competitive female figure skaters: An interdisciplinary approach. *Research Quarterly for Exercise and Sport, 77*, 158–166.

Moore, Z., Ciampa, R., Wilsnack, J., & Wright, E. (2007). Evidence-based interventions for the treatment of eating disorders. *Journal of Clinical Sport Psychology, 1*, 371–378.

Moradi, B., Dirks, D., & Matteson, A. V. (2005). Roles of sexual objectification experiences and internalization of standards of beauty in eating disorder symptomatology: A test and extension of Objectification Theory. *Journal of Counseling Psychology, 52*, 420–428.

Muller, S., Gorrow, T., & Schneider, S. (2009). Enhancing appearance and sports performance: Are female collegiate athletes behaving more like males? *Journal of American College Health, 57*, 513–520.

Murray, S. B., Rieger, E., Touyz, S. W., & de la Garza García, Y. (2010). Muscle dysmorphia and the DSM-V conundrum: Where does it belong? A review paper. *International Journal of Eating Disorders, 43*, 483–491.

Muscat, A. C., & Long, B. C. (2008). Critical comments about body shape and weight: Disordered eating of female athletes and sport participants. *Journal of Applied Sport Psychology, 20*, 1–24.

Nichols, J. F., Rauh, M. J., Lawson, M. J., Ji, M., & Barkai, H. S. (2006). Prevalence of the female athlete triad syndrome among high school athletes. *Archives of Pediatric and Adolescent Medicine, 160*, 137–142.

Olivardia, R. (2001). Mirror, mirror on the wall, who's the largest of them all? The features and phenomenology of muscle dysmorphia. *Harvard Review of Psychiatry, 9*, 254–259.

Oppliger, R. A., Utter, A. C., Scott, J. R., Dick, R. W., & Klossner, D. (2006). NCAA rule change improves weight loss among national championship wrestlers. *Medicine and Science in Sports and Exercise, 38*, 963–970.

Pasman, L., & Thompson, J. K. (1989). Body image and eating disturbance in obligatory runners, obligatory weightlifters, and sedentary individuals. *International Journal of Eating Disorders, 7*, 759–769.

Peden, J., Stiles, B., Vandehey, M., & Diekhoff, G. (2008). The effects of external pressures and competitiveness on characteristics of eating disorders and body dissatisfaction. *Journal of Sport and Social Issues, 32*, 415–429.

Peterson, K. A., Paulson, S. E., & Williams, K. K. (2007). Relations of eating disorder symptomology with perceptions of pressures from mother, peers, and media in adolescent girls and boys. *Sex Roles, 57*, 629–639.

Petrie, T. A. (1993). Disordered eating in female collegiate gymnasts: Prevalence and personality/attitudinal correlates. *Journal of Sport and Exercise Psychology, 15*, 424–436.

Petrie, T. A. (1996). Differences between male and female college lean sport athletes, nonlean sport athletes, and nonathletes on behavioral and psychological indices of eating disorders. *Journal of Applied Sport Psychology, 8*, 218–230.

Petrie, T. A., & Greenleaf, C. (2007). Eating disorders in sport: From theory to research to intervention. In G. Tenenbaum & R. Eklund (Eds.), *Handbook of sport psychology* (pp. 352–378). Hoboken, NJ: Wiley.

Petrie, T. A., & Greenleaf, C. (2010). Male and female athletes with eating disorders. In S. Hanrahan & M. Andersen (Eds.), *Routledge handbook of applied sport psychology* (pp. 224–232). New York: Routledge.

Petrie, T. A., Greenleaf, C., Carter, J., & Reel, J. (2007). Psychosocial correlates of disordered eating among male collegiate athletes. *Journal of Clinical Sport Psychology, 1*, 340–357.

Petrie, T. A., Greenleaf, C., Reel, J., & Carter, J. (2008). Prevalence of eating disorders and disordered eating behaviors among male collegiate athletes. *Psychology of Men and Masculinity, 9*, 267–277.

Petrie, T. A., Greenleaf, C., Reel, J., & Carter, J. (2009a). An examination of psychosocial correlates of eating disorders among female collegiate athletes. *Research Quarterly for Exercise and Sport, 80*, 621–632.

Petrie, T. A., Greenleaf, C., Reel, J., & Carter, J. (2009b). Personality and psychological factors as predictors of disordered eating among female collegiate athletes. *Eating Disorders, 17*, 302–321.

Picard, C. L. (1999). The level of competition as a factor for the development of eating disorders in female collegiate athletes. *Journal of Youth and Adolescence, 28*, 583–594.

Polivy, J., & Herman, C. P. (2002). Causes of eating disorders. *Annual Review of Psychology, 53*, 187–213.

Pope, C. G., Pope, H. G., Menard, W., Fay, C., Olivardia, R., & Phillips, K. A. (2005). Clinical features of muscle dysmorphia among males with body dysmorphic disorder. *Body Image, 2*, 395–400.

Pope, H. G., Gruber, A., Choi, P., Olivardia, R., & Phillips, K. (1997). Muscle dysmorphia: An underrecognized form of body dysmorphic disorder. *Psychosomatics, 38*, 548–557.

Pope, H. G., Katz, D. L., & Hudson, J. I. (1993). Anorexia nervosa and "reverse anorexia" among 108 male bodybuilders. *Comprehensive Psychiatry, 34*, 406–409.

Pope, H., Olivardia, R., Gruber, A., & Borowiecki, J. (1999). Evolving ideals of male body image as seen through action toys. *International Journal of Eating Disorders, 26*, 65–72.

Raudenbush, B., & Meyer, B. (2003). Muscular dissatisfaction and supplement use among male intercollegiate athletes. *Journal of Sport and Exercise Psychology, 25*, 161–170.

Rauh, M. J., Nichols, J. F., & Barrack, M. T. (2010). Relationships among injury and disordered eating, menstrual dysfunction, and low bone mineral density in high school athletes: A prospective study. *Journal of Athletic Training, 45*, 243–252.

Reel, J., & Gill, D. (1996). Psychosocial factors related to eating disorders among high school and college female cheerleaders. *The Sport Psychologist, 10*, 195–206.

Reel, J., SooHoo, S., Doetsch, H., Carter, J. E., & Petrie, T. A. (2007). The female athlete triad: Is the triad a problem among Division I female athletes? *Journal of Clinical Sport Psychology, 1*, 358–370.

Reel, J. J., SooHoo, S., Petrie, T. A., Greenleaf, C., & Carter, J. E. (2010). Slimming down for sport: Developing a weight pressures in sport measures for female athletes. *Journal of Clinical Sport Psychology, 4*, 99–111.

Ricciardelli, L. A., & McCabe, M. P. (2004). A biopsychosocial model of disordered eating and the pursuit of muscularity in adolescent boys. *Psychological Bulletin, 130*, 179–205.

Ringham, R., Klump, K., Kaye, W., Stone, D., Libman, S., Stowe, S. & Marcus, M. (2006). Eating disorder symptomatology among ballet dancers. *International Journal of Eating Disorders, 39*, 503–508.

Roberts, G. C., Treasure, D. C., & Conroy, D. E. (2007). Understanding the dynamics of motivation in sport and physical activity: An achievement goal interpretation. In G. Tenenbaum & R. C. Eklund (Eds.), *Handbook of sport psychology* (3rd ed., pp. 3–30). Hoboken, NJ: Wiley & Sons.

Rosendahl, J., Bormann, B., Aschenbrenner, K., Aschenbrenner, F., & Strauss, B. (2009). Dieting and disordered eating in German high school athletes and non-athletes. *Scandinavian Journal of Medicine and Science in Sports, 19*, 731–739.

Russell, K. (2004). On versus off the pitch: The transiency of body satisfaction among female rugby players, cricketers, and netballers. *Sex Roles, 51*, 561–574.

Scoffier, S., Maïano, C., & d'Arripe-Longueville, F. (2010). The effects of social relationships and acceptance on disturbed eating attitudes in elite adolescent female athletes: The mediating role of physical self-perceptions. *International Journal of Eating Disorders, 43*, 65–71.

Sherman, R., Thompson, R., Dehass, D., & Wilfert, M. (2005). NCAA coaches survey: The role of coach in identifying and managing athletes with eating disorders. *Eating Disorders, 13*, 447–466.

Smith, A., & Petrie, T. (2008). Reducing the risk of disordered eating among female athletes: A test of alternative interventions. *Journal of Applied Sport Psychology, 20*, 392–407.

Smith, P. M., & Ogle, J. P. (2006). Interactions among high school cross-country runners and coaches: Creating a cultural context for athletes' embodied experiences. *Family and Consumer Sciences Research Journal, 34*, 276–307.

Smolak, L., Murnen, S. K., & Ruble, A. E. (2000). Female athletes and eating problems: A meta-analysis. *International Journal of Eating Disorders, 27*, 371–380.

Soban, C. (2006). What about the boys? Addressing issues of masculinity within male anorexia nervosa in a feminist therapeutic environment. *International Journal of Men's Health, 5*, 251–267.

Stewart, A., Benson, P., Michanikou, E., Tsiota, D., & Narli, M. (2003). Body image perception, satisfaction and somatotype in male and female athletes and non-athletes: Results using a novel morphing technique. *Journal of Sports Sciences, 21*, 815–823.

Stice, E. (1994). Review of the evidence for a sociocultural model of bulimia nervosa and an exploration of the mechanisms of action. *Clinical Psychology Review, 14*, 633–661.

Stice, E. (1998). Modeling of eating pathology and social reinforcement of the thin ideal predict the onset of bulimic symptoms. *Behavior Research Journal, 36*, 931–944.

Stice, E. (2001a). A prospective test of the dual-pathway model of bulimic pathology: Mediating effects of dieting and negative affect. *Journal of Abnormal Psychology, 110*, 124–135.

Stice, E. (2001b). Risk factors for eating pathology: Recent advances and future directions. In R. Striegel-Moore & L. Smolak (Eds.), *Eating disorders: Innovative directions in research and practice* (pp. 51–73). Washington, DC: American Psychological Association.

Stice, E. (2002). Risk and maintenance factors for eating pathology: A meta-analytic review. *Psychological Bulletin, 128*, 825–848.

Stice, E., Marti, C. N., Shaw, H., & Jaconis, M. (2009). An 8-year longitudinal study of the natural history of threshold, subthreshold, and partial eating disorders from a community sample of adolescents. *Journal of Abnormal Psychology, 118*, 587–597.

Stice, E., Shaw, H., & Marti, C. (2007). A meta-analytic review of eating disorder prevention programs: Encouraging findings. *Annual Review of Clinical Psychology, 3*, 207–231.

Strahan, E. J., Wilson, A. E., Cressman, K. E., & Buote, V. M. (2006). Comparing to perfection: How cultural norms for appearance affect social comparisons and self-image. *Body Image, 3*, 211–227.

Striegel-Moore, R., & Bulik, C. (2007). Risk factors for eating disorders. *American Psychologist, 62*, 181–198.

Sundgot-Borgen, J., & Torstveit, M. K. (2004). Prevalence of eating disorders in elite athletes is higher than in the general population. *Clinical Journal of Sports Medicine, 14*, 25–32.

Symons Downs, D., Hausenblas, H. A., & Nigg, C. R. (2004). Factorial validity and psychometric examination of the Exercise Dependence Scale-Revised. *Measurement in Physical Education and Exercise Science, 8*, 183–201.

Thompson, R., & Sherman, R. (1999). Athletes, athletic performance, and eating disorders: Healthier alternatives. *Journal of Social Issues, 55*, 317–337.

Thompson, R., & Sherman, R. (2010). *Eating disorders in sport.* New York: Routledge.

Torstveit, M., Rosenvinge, J., & Sundgot-Borgen, J. (2008). Prevalence of eating disorders and the predictive power of risk models in female elite athletes: A controlled study. *Scandinavian Journal of Medicine and Science in Sports, 18*, 108–118.

Torstveit, M., & Sundgot-Borgen, J. (2005). The Female Athlete Triad exists in both elite athletes and controls. *Medicine and Science in Sports and Exercise, 37*, 1449–1459.

Tylka, T., & Subich, L. (2002). A preliminary investigation of the eating disorder continuum with men. *Journal of Counseling Psychology, 49*, 273–279.

Warren, M. P., & Chua, A. T. (2008). Exercise-induced amenorrhea and bone health in the adolescent athlete. *Annals of the New York Academy of Sciences, 1135*, 244–252.

Williamson, D., Netemeyer, R., Jackman, L., Anderson, D., Funsch, C., & Rabalais, J. (1995). Structural equation modeling of risk factors for the development of eating disorder symptoms in female athletes. *International Journal of Eating Disorders, 17*, 387–393.

Wilson, T., Grilo, C., & Vitousek, K. (2007). Psychological treatment of eating disorders. *American Psychologist, 62*, 199–216.

Ziegler, P. J., Kannan, S., Jonnalagadda, S. S., Krishnakumar, A., Taksali, S. E., & Nelson, J. A. (2005). Dietary intake, body image perceptions, and weight concerns of female US international synchronized figure skating teams. *International Journal of Sport Nutrition and Exercise Metabolism, 15*, 550–566.

Zucker, N. L., Womble, L. G., Williamson, D. A., & Perrin, L. A. (1999). Protective factors for eating disorders in female college athletes. *Eating Disorders, 7*, 207–218.

Physical Activity Interventions

Stuart J.H. Biddle *and* Trish Gorely

Abstract

Physical activity is a key behavior in modern public health and is a topic of great concern to governments and health agencies. Psychologists can contribute to a better understanding of physical activity behavior by studying and explaining factors associated with participation in physical activity and interventions to change such behaviors. This chapter outlines the evidence on correlates for physical activity across the age span, what mediators might be important for behavior change, and what current evidence on interventions is available to guide thinking on behavior change.

Key Words: Exercise, intervention, mediator, correlates, behavioral epidemiology

"Sport psychology" has evolved over the past 30 years into the broader of field of "sport and exercise psychology." This reflects psychologists' interests in investigating not only psychology in sport training and competition contexts but wider aspects of physical activity for health. Such "exercise" behaviors may include walking, fitness training, and physical activity for disease management. Although the psychology for sport and for exercise may appear similar, and indeed there are obvious overlaps, there is also a distinct literature that focuses on health behavior change that runs parallel to that of sport psychology. Indeed, much of the key literature for "exercise psychologists" is found in medical and behavioral medicine journals rather than "sport and exercise psychology" and we detect a widening of the gap between the two subfields as exercise psychologists adopt the broader behavioral medicine approach to their research.

In Western societies, changes in the way we live have created health problems that are different from those of previous generations. Modern society is plagued with noncommunicable disease, including cardiovascular disease, obesity, diabetes, and cancers, and these are considered lifestyle diseases. As such, behavioral scientists believe that we should be able to reverse such trends and improve physical and mental health by changing behaviors. One framework that places behavior change in the context of measurement and correlates of behavior is the *behavioral epidemiology framework* proposed by Sallis and Owen (1999).

Behavioral Epidemiology Framework

Behavioral epidemiology is concerned with the distribution and etiology of behaviors that may be associated with disease outcomes and how these relate to the occurrence of disease in the population. In relation to physical activity, this framework has five main phases:

• *Phase 1: to establish the link between physical activity and health outcomes.* This is now well documented for many diverse physical and mental health conditions across various population groups, including older adults (Chodzko-Zajko et al.,

2009), adults (Hardman & Stensel, 2009), and young people (Stensel, Gorely, & Biddle, 2008). If there were no health implications for physical activity, the field of exercise psychology would not exist.

• The report of the Chief Medical Officers of England, Scotland, Wales and Northern Ireland (2011) concluded that physical activity has preventive health effects on cardiovascular disease, overweight and obesity, type 2 diabetes, musculoskeletal health, psychological health, and some cancers. It is clear that physical activity is a significant behavior in public health (Hardman & Stensel, 2009). Within the context of this book, it is important to note that being physically active can boost performance in areas such as work or in cognitive function, thus having a wider value than just physical health (Colcombe & Kramer, 2003).

• *Phase 2: to develop methods for the accurate assessment of physical activity*. Often, large-scale surveillance of population trends rely on self-report, a method that has significant problems with validity and reliability. Recent objective methods, such as accelerometers, heart rate monitors, or pedometers, are useful but do not necessarily give all of the information required, such as type of activity or the setting in which the activity takes place. Nevertheless, it is recommended that objective assessment is undertaken, supplemented by other tools, including self-report or geographic information systems (GIS) and global positioning systems (GPS), if possible.

• *Phase 3: to identify factors that are associated with different levels of physical activity (correlates)*. It is important to identify factors that might be associated with the adoption and maintenance of behavior, so that such factors can be targeted in interventions. This area is referred to as the study of *correlates* of physical activity.

• *Phase 4: to evaluate interventions for changing physical activity behaviors*. Once a variable is identified as a correlate of physical activity (e.g., self-efficacy), then interventions can manipulate this variable to test if it is, in fact, a causal determinant (Baranowski, Anderson, & Carmack, 1998).

• *Phase 5: to translate findings from research into practice*. If interventions work, it is appropriate to translate and "roll out" such findings into ecologically valid settings.

Correlates of Physical Activity

One of the primary aims of research in exercise psychology is to find ways of increasing physical activity in those with low levels of such activity. Before successful interventions can be initiated, it is important to establish what factors might be associated with activity participation ("correlates" in phase 3 of the behavioral epidemiology framework). A great deal of literature exists in this area, and a number of reviews are available on young people (Sallis, Prochaska, & Taylor, 2000; van der Horst, Chin, Paw, Twisk, & Van Mechelen, 2007), adults (Trost, Owen, Bauman, Sallis, & Brown, 2002), and older adults (van Stralen, De Vries, Mudde, Bolman, & Lechner, 2009). Correlates are typically grouped into demographic, biological, psychological, sociocultural, and environmental factors.

Young People

For demographic correlates, age and gender have been consistent correlates of physical activity in youth, with males and children often reporting more activity than females and adolescents. Particularly in girls, participation falls steadily in the teenage years. Data on ethnicity are less, but trends suggest greater activity for white ethnic groups, but, clearly, this distinction is likely to mask many other possible differences and similarities.

The most frequently studied biological correlate for young people is weight status (e.g., body fat or body mass index [BMI]). This has not been shown to be related to physical activity when reviewed by Sallis et al (2000) and van der Horst et al (2007). Although an association between physical activity and overweight/obesity has been demonstrated (Steinbeck, 2001), and indeed would be expected, associations in childhood can be difficult to detect due to measurement issues such as maturity and measurement error, particularly for self-reported physical activity.

For children, there is little consistency in the data concerning psychological correlates of physical activity reported by Sallis et al. (2000) and van der Horst et al. (2007). Part of this may be explained by a simple lack of studies reported on some correlates. Across the two reviews, physical activity is positively associated with intentions and preference for physical activity. Recent studies have also shown self-efficacy (confidence) to be associated with greater levels of physical activity in children.

For adolescents, reviews show that higher levels of perceived competence and self-efficacy are associated with greater physical activity. Biddle et al. (2005) reported that the strength of the association between physical activity and perceived competence for adolescent girls was small, but small to moderate for self-efficacy. The construct of "Goal orientation/ motivation" or "achievement orientation" was identified by van der Horst et al. and Sallis et al. as being positively associated with physical activity in adolescents. This construct is likely to be some form of "task orientation," a concept familiar to sport and exercise psychologists.

The psychological literature is clear that the motivation to take part in behaviors of free choice, such as physical activity in leisure time, is predicted by strong intentions (Ajzen, 2001), and this was supported in the review by Sallis et al. (2000). Intentions to act are the immediate antecedent of behavior, and research supports an association between intentions and physical activity. This has mainly been tested through the use of the *theory of planned behavior* (Ajzen, 2001; Hagger, Chatzisarantis, & Biddle, 2002). Planning how best to implement intentions may strengthen this relationship further (Gollwitzer & Sheeran, 2006) and help close the gap between intentions and behaviors.

Issues of body image and appearance seem to be important for adolescent girls in the context of physical activity decision-making. Specifically, the correlates of perceived body attractiveness, importance of appearance, and physical self-worth were positive and small to moderate in their strength of association with physical activity in adolescent girls (Biddle et al., 2005).

Previous physical activity and healthy diet have been associated with physical activity in youth. These are considered to be *behavioral correlates*. The variable of "previous physical activity" suggests that some measure of tracking takes place; that is, the more active children remain so as they age. Evidence for tracking, however, is not as strong as we sometimes might think. Statistical associations for activity patterns between different ages are, at best, moderate and sometimes small. Of course, this will depend on the periods of the life course being studied, the type of physical activity or sedentary behavior being assessed, and the length of time between assessments. Associations are weaker between adolescence and adulthood than during childhood to adolescence (Malina, 1996), and associations decline as the length of assessment period increases (Telama et al., 2005); this also is true for sedentary behaviors (Biddle, Pearson, Ross, & Braithwaite, 2010).

Sedentary behavior during the after-school and weekend periods is associated with less physical activity in youth (Atkin, Gorely, Biddle, Marshall, & Cameron, 2008). For adolescents, including girls, sports participation is related to overall physical activity levels (Biddle, et al., 2005; Vilhjalmsson & Kristjansdottir, 2003).

Sallis et al. (2000) did not find any sociocultural variables associated with physical activity in children, whereas an association with parental support was identified in the review by van der Horst (2007). Peer and parental support were found to be correlates of physical activity for adolescents. One variable often thought to be associated with activity in young people is that of parental physical activity. However, the evidence for this is weak. A review by Gustafson and Rhodes (2006) showed that parental activity was most likely mediated in its influence on activity by parental support.

The study of environmental factors associated with physical activity is a more recent trend (Davison & Lawson, 2006). Reviews show that access to facilities (children) and opportunities to exercise (adolescents) are associated with higher levels of physical activity. In addition, time outdoors is associated with more activity in children, and this is likely related to spending less time on sedentary entertainment (Ferreira et al., 2006; Sallis et al., 2000).

In summary, a number of factors appear to be associated with young people's involvement in physical activity (Biddle, Atkin, Foster, & Cavill, 2011). Key factors that may be amenable to change are motivation through good intentions, feelings of competence and confidence, and a motivational style centered on effort and self-improvement. Moreover, parents are important in offering different forms of support for their children's activity. Finally, supportive environments are associated with greater activity.

Adults

Trost et al. (2002) updated a review of the correlates of physical activity in adults done by Sallis and Owen (1999). For adults, clear inverse associations were reported for age, and these also showed males to be more active than females. Education and related socioeconomic status markers showed that lower levels of these indicators were associated with less physical activity. For adults, however, an inverse association is evident between overweight/obesity and physical activity (Trost et al., 2002).

For psychological correlates of physical activity, Trost et al. reported that there was evidence for a consistent positive association with physical activity for enjoyment, expected benefits, intention, perceived health, self-motivation, self-efficacy, stage of behavior change (i.e., higher stages in the transtheoretical model), and self-schemata for exercise, and negative associations for barriers and mood disturbance. The strongest evidence is for self-efficacy and is likely to be more important for behaviors that require effort, such as structured fitness programs. The correlate of enjoyment is associated with intrinsic motivational states (Deci & Ryan, 2002).

Trost et al. (2002) reported that physical activity history in childhood/youth was not associated with adult activity, whereas an association was found for activity history in adulthood (i.e., adult activity has some degree of tracking). Other behavioral factors associated with physical activity for adults include smoking (negative) and healthy diet (positive). Moreover, social support is associated with physical activity in adults. For environmental factors, access to facilities and a positive environment, such as enjoyable scenery and neighborhood safety have been shown to be associated with greater physical activity.

Older Adults

Despite the benefits of regular physical activity in the health and daily functioning of adults as they age, knowledge and understanding of potential correlates of physical activity in older adults is relatively understudied (King, 2001; van Stralen et al., 2009). Van Stralen et al. (2009) reviewed the evidence for correlates of physical activity initiation and maintenance in older adults (50+ years). Their review only included longitudinal and experimental studies. The authors rated the evidence for potential correlates as convincing (i.e., >66% of the studies for that correlate reported a significant result in the same direction), probable (i.e., between 50% and 66% of the studies were in the same direction), and weak (<50% of the studies were in the same direction). Although many potential correlates emerged during the review, few of these had been studied frequently enough to enable meaningful conclusions to be drawn. Using the data provided by van Stralen et al. and applying a further criterion of a correlate having been examined within at least three separate studies (Sallis et al., 2000), Table 35.1 summarizes the correlates for which there is convincing (*bold*) and probable evidence during physical activity initiation and maintenance in older adults. Some similarities in correlates in initiation and maintenance can be seen, but there are also some differences. For example, outcome expectations are probably

Table 35.1 Convincing (*bold*) and probable correlates of physical activity initiation and maintenance in older adults

	Initiation	Maintenance
Personal and behavioral	**Physical activity level at baseline (+)** Physical health status (+) Smoking (−)	**Physical health status (+)** **Exercise habits (+)** **Physical activity level at baseline (+)** Physical fitness (+) Smoking (−)
Psychological	**Self-efficacy (+)** **Intention (+)** **Motivational readiness to change (+)** **Action planning (+)** Outcome expectations (+)	**Intention (+)** **Enjoyment (+)** **Motivational readiness to change (+)** **Realization of outcome expectations (+)** **Perceived benefits (+)** Self-efficacy (+) Perceived barriers (−) Mood status (+) Stress (−)
Social	Social support from significant others (+) Social norms (+)	
Physical environment	**Perceived access (+)** **Crime (safety) (+)** **Program format (Home) (+)**	**Program format (Home) (+)**

Adapted from van Stralen, M. M., De Vries, H., Mudde, A. N., Bolman, C., & Lechner, L. (2009). Determinants of initiation and maintenance of physical activity among older adults: A literature review. *Health Psychology Review, 3*(2), 147–207.

important during the initiation phase, but realization of these outcomes is probably important for maintenance. Sources of social support from family and friends are probably important during initiation of physical activity. It is clear from Table 35.1 that significant gaps exist in our understanding of influences on physical activity behavior in older adults. An acknowledged limitation of this review was that the studies included mostly involved healthy volunteers, and it is possible that those living with chronic illness, disability, or infirmity may have different correlates.

The Mediating Variable Framework

The previous section identified a number of potential influences—correlates—of physical activity participation for young people, adults, and older adults. Correlates research represents an important step in the design of effective interventions for at least two reasons: correlates of physical activity that cannot be changed (e.g., sex, age) can be used to identify target groups who may be at particular risk of low levels of physical activity, and correlates that can be changed become the focus of intervention strategies, as it is hypothesized that changes in these correlates will lead to changes in the desired behavior (Baranowski et al., 1998; Baranowski & Jago, 2005). For example, barriers to physical activity, such as lack of time, are often reported as negative correlates of participation (i.e., someone with high perceived barriers for physical activity will be less likely to undertake regular physical activity). Interventions should seek to help such individuals identify these barriers and seek ways to overcome them, which should then lead to increases in physical activity. In this case, the correlate (barriers to physical activity participation) acts as a mediator of physical activity behavior change. This mediating variable model has been put forward as a way of trying to understand behavior change as a result of interventions or programs (Baranowski et al., 1998; Rhodes & Pfaeffli, 2010).

The *meditating variable model* is represented in its simplest form in Figure 35.1. For physical activity interventions, the framework suggests that changes in physical activity are the result of changes in mediating variables (such as barriers), and these changes in mediating variables are the result of interventions that were designed to induce change in these variables (Baranowski & Jago, 2005). During evaluation of interventions, it is important that these hypothesized mediator pathways are assessed because this allows critical components of interventions to be

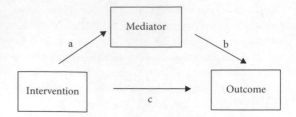

Figure 35.1 Simple form of the mediating variable model.

identified (MacKinnon, Krull, & Lockwood, 2000) and provides evidence of what works for changing behavior (Lubans, Foster, & Biddle, 2008). Such analyses have both practical and theoretical implications. At a practical level, correlates identified as mediators can then be employed in subsequent interventions, and those demonstrated to not mediate behavior change can be discarded. In this way, intervention content can be refined and the most efficient use of resources be made (Bauman, Sallis, Dzewaltowski, & Owen, 2002; MacKinnon & Fairchild, 2009). At a theoretical level, mediation analysis helps to improve theories of behavior change. For example, if an intervention results in physical activity behavior change, but this change is not explained by the hypothesized mediating variables within the underlying theoretical models, then this indicates that the theory is incomplete and needs further development (Baranowski et al., 1998).

According to Baron and Kenny (1986), to demonstrate that a variable functions as a mediator, certain conditions must be met. First, the intervention must result in changes in the hypothesized mediator (for example, the intervention results in decreases in perceived barriers to physical activity—*path a* in Figure 35.1). Second, variations in the proposed mediator are significantly related to variations in the dependent variable (for example, changes in barriers to physical activity are significantly related to changes in actual physical activity behavior—*path b*). Finally, when paths a and b are statistically controlled, a previously significant relation between the independent and dependent variables (e.g., between the intervention and physical activity behavior) is attenuated, with the strongest demonstration of mediation occurring when *path c* is zero.

Despite the theoretical and practical utility of conducting mediation analysis, it is frequently overlooked and omitted from the analysis of physical activity interventions (Baranowski et al., 1998; Lubans et al., 2008; Rhodes & Pfaeffli, 2010). This represents a significant limitation in the literature, and researchers are strongly encouraged to make consideration of mediators a fundamental component of intervention evaluation. This would enable the key mechanisms of behavior change to be identified and increase our understanding of how to facilitate physical activity behavior change (Lubans et al., 2008; Rhodes & Pfaeffli, 2010).

Psychological and Behavioral Theories of Physical Activity

Theory should underpin the planning and implementation of physical activity interventions (Bartholomew, Parcel, Kok, & Gottlieb, 2001). Typically, these are social psychological in nature and have been used to advance understanding of why people might choose to be active or not. Health psychology is a primary source of such frameworks. The most often referred to theories are *social cognitive theory* (SCT; Bandura, 1986), the *theory of planned behavior* (TPB; Ajzen, 2001; Hagger et al., 2002), and the *transtheoretical model* (TTM; Marshall & Biddle, 2001; Prochaska & Marcus, 1994). In addition, the *health action process model* (Schwarzer, 2008), *common sense model of illness perceptions* (Hagger & Orbell, 2003; Leventhal, Leventhal, & Contrada, 1998), *health belief model* (Harrison, Mullen, & Green, 1992; Rosenstock, 1974), and *behavioral choice theory* (Epstein & Roemmich, 2001) have also been used and have a place in intervention planning. Moreover, models, frameworks, and theories making reference to organizational change and communities are also needed, yet tend to be neglected in exercise psychology. A brief overview of selected psychological theories will be provided.

Social Cognitive Theory

Social cognitive theory can be attributed to the work of Albert Bandura (1977). Social cognitive theory suggests that we learn and modify our behaviors through an interaction among personal, behavioral, and environmental influences, or the so-called model of *reciprocal determinism*. That is, we are not merely a function of the environment, nor are we merely passive in following our psychological characteristics. Moreover, our own and others' behavior can influence us.

We regulate our behavior based on our own goals, behaviors, and feelings—a self-regulation component of SCT. For example, people may adopt a certain goal to be physically active that helps motivate action. In addition, we reflect on our behaviors, particularly in respect of thinking about the consequences of our behaviors. These are called *outcome expectancies*. We also reflect on our own capabilities to undertake certain behaviors, and these are our *efficacy expectancies*.

The element of SCT concerning self-reflection of our capability has led to the development of the construct of *self-efficacy*, a situation-specific confidence to undertake a certain behavior exemplified by the "Can I?" question. Research on self-efficacy in physical activity not only shows this to be an important antecedent of behavior (i.e., a correlate), but also an outcome of participation by showing that positive experiences in physical activity can enhance feelings of efficacy (McAuley & Blissmer, 2000; McAuley & Morris, 2007; also see Chapter 14, this volume).

There are four main sources of information that we might use to develop our levels of self-efficacy. These are prior behavior (success and performance attainment), watching others (modelling), encouragement (verbal and social persuasion), and creating feelings of relaxation and upbeat mood (judgements of physiological states), and these can form strategies for interventions.

Theory of Planned Behavior

The TPB assumes that intention is the immediate antecedent of behavior and that intention is predicted from three main constructs: attitude, subjective norm (normative beliefs), and perceptions of behavioral control (see Figure 35.2). Ajzen and Fishbein (1980) suggested that the attitude component of the model is constructed from the beliefs held about the specific behavior, as well as by the value perceived from the likely outcomes. Such beliefs can be instrumental (i.e., "Exercise helps me lose weight") and affective ("Exercise is enjoyable"). The latter may be more effective for sustainable behavior change (Rhodes, Fiala, & Conner, 2009).

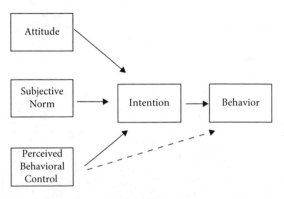

Figure 35.2 The theory of planned behavior.

The normative beliefs (subjective norm) component is comprised of the beliefs of significant others and the extent that one wishes to comply with such beliefs. Perceived behavioral control is defined by Ajzen (1988) as "the perceived ease or difficulty of performing the behavior" (p. 132) and is assumed "to reflect past experience as well as anticipated impediments and obstacles" (p. 132). The construct of perceived behavioral control is underpinned by a set of control beliefs and the perceived power of these beliefs. *Control beliefs* refer to the perceived presence of factors that may help or impede the behavior, and *perceived power* refers to the perceived impact that helping or inhibiting factors may have on the behavior. Perceived behavioral control is thought to accurately predict behavior under circumstances only when perceived control closely approximates actual control (hence the use of broken line in Figure 35.2). In a meta-analysis, Hagger and colleagues (2002) reported correlations of 0.35 between attitude and behavior, 0.60 between attitude and intention, and 0.51 between intention and behavior.

There is a less than perfect correlation between intentions and behavior. To help bridge the gap between intentions and behavior, "implementation intentions" have been proposed by Gollwitzer (1999). These are goals and plans that involve specifying when, how, and where performance of behavior will take place. This may be an important aspect of behavioral planning that places greater emphasis on behavior than preceding cognitions alone.

The Transtheoretical Model

The TTM proposes that behavior change involves moving through stages of change and is a framework that encompasses both the "when" (stages) and the "how" of behavior change. Most other models refer only to the "how" of change. Integral to the TTM are the *processes* (strategies) of change and *moderators* of change, such as decisional balance (pros and cons of change) and self-efficacy. Research concerning the TTM in physical activity is now quite extensive (Marshall & Biddle, 2001; Riemsma et al., 2002), although not without its critics (Adams & White, 2003, 2005).

Studies on physical activity assess the stages of precontemplation, contemplation, preparation, action, and maintenance, as described in Table 35.2. The stages of change are concerned with the temporal patterning of behavior change. By also identifying processes of change, we are able to better understand why and how this temporal shift might take place. Processes of change, therefore, are important for interventions because they help move people between stages. Processes of change are the various strategies and techniques that people use to help them progress through the stages. Ten processes of change have been identified, with five of these described as cognitive or "thinking" strategies and the other five as behavioral or "doing" strategies. Cognitive processes (e.g., increasing knowledge, being aware of health risks) are thought to peak during the action stage whereas behavioral processes (e.g., enlisting social support, reminding yourself) peak later, in the maintenance stage. The meta-analysis by Marshall and Biddle (2001) of physical activity TTM studies showed that movement from precontemplation to contemplation and from preparation to action are characterized by sharper increases in behavioral process use compared to

Table 35.2 Understanding the stages of the transtheoretical model in the context of physical activity

What is the name of the stage?	Does the person have an intention to meet the criterion level of physical activity?	Does the person meet the criterion level of physical activity?	What is his or her current behavior?
Precontemplation	No	No	Little or no physical activity
Contemplation	Yes	No	Little or no physical activity
Preparation	Yes	No	Small amounts, possibly infrequent, of physical activity, but not at criterion level
Action	Yes	Yes	Physically active at criterion for <6 months
Maintenance	Yes	Yes	Physically active at criterion for >6 months

other stage transitions and that nine of the ten processes followed similar patterns of change across the stages. This argues against the presence of a stage-by-process interaction, in which some processes are thought to be more important or likely at certain stages. This area requires further work.

One strategy that can assist people to make successful behavior change is to weigh up the advantages of change (pros) against the disadvantages or costs (cons). This "decisional balance" exercise (Prochaska, Norcross, & Di Clemente, 1994) is one that has been at the core of the TTM. Research suggests that in the early stages of behavior change, the cons outweigh the pros of change. Those in preparation see more equality between the pros and cons, whereas those who are in maintenance will perceive more pros than cons. Changing perceptions of pros and cons, therefore, may assist in behavior change.

Marshall and Biddle (2001) also showed that self-efficacy increases with each stage progression, as proposed by the model. The pattern of increase was not linear, however, with effects being moderate between precontemplation and contemplation, small to moderate from contemplation to preparation, moderate from preparation to action, and moderate to large from action to maintenance.

Riemsma et al. (2002) conducted a systematic review to assess the effectiveness of stage-based approaches in behavior change interventions. This included seven intervention trials concerning physical activity, and only one showed a positive effect for behavior change, with two showing mixed effects. Similarly, Adams and White (2005) have questioned the long-term effectiveness of such interventions. However, several commentators suggest that short-term effectiveness has been demonstrated, and that further work is required before dismissing the model or replacing it with something else (Brug et al., 2005).

Behavioral Choice Theory

One framework that has been used in the study of sedentary behavior in children is *behavioral choice theory* (Epstein & Roemmich, 2001). Based on behavioral economics (Zimmerman, 2009), behavioral choice theory proposes that choosing a specific behavior (e.g., playing a sport or being physically active in other ways) will be a function of (a) the accessibility and (b) the reinforcement value of the behavior. In using this approach to explain and modify young people's propensity for sedentary technological pursuits, Epstein and colleagues have shown that by making alternative active behaviors more accessible, and sedentary pursuits less reinforcing, reductions in sedentary behavior and increases in physical activity are possible (Epstein & Roemmich, 2001; Epstein, Saelens, & O'Brien, 1995). The challenge is to find ways of making physical activity more appealing (reinforcement value) and easy to do (accessible) relative to competing behaviors, such as sedentary behaviors. Perceived risk may also inhibit active travel, for example, thus making the behavior less attractive and "available" (Carver, Timperio, Hesketh, & Crawford, 2010).

Guidelines for Conducting Interventions

A framework for the development and evaluation of complex interventions has been proposed by the Medical Research Council (MRC) in the United Kingdom (Campbell et al., 2000; Craig et al., 2008). In the original version of the framework (Campbell et al., 2000), it was suggested that several stages of design and development are required for complex interventions (e.g., an intervention with many parts to it, such as one aimed at increasing physical activity in a community by a variety of means). In the framework, it is suggested that the first step in intervention development is to gain a thorough understanding of the existing evidence base so that the best theoretical base and intervention is chosen. Next steps involve identifying intervention strategies and demonstrating how they might influence the target behavior. Engaging with potential participants, conducting feasibility studies, and pilot work are all important elements during this development. The next major step is the conducting of a definitive trial to determine the effect of the intervention. This trial will usually involve randomization and a control group. The final stage of this framework involves the implementation of the findings in more real-world settings to determine if the intervention has the same effects in less controlled conditions. More recently, it has been recognized that this original framework was perhaps too rigid, and a revised version was developed (Craig et al., 2008). The revised framework still emphasizes that developing and evaluating interventions should proceed along a series of stages but highlights that the progress might not be as linear as suggested in the original guidance. The revised guidelines, although still favoring experimental designs, go beyond an emphasis and reliance on randomized controlled trials (RCTs) to offer a wider range of potentially suitable designs. Greater emphasis is also placed on process evaluation, although the authors note that outcomes are still the most critical element of intervention evaluation. Finally, the authors stress the importance of researchers reporting their interventions with enough detail to make replication possible.

In the first steps of the framework, interventionists face a significant challenge as they choose between competing theories of behavior. Basing an intervention on one theoretical perspective may make the design of an intervention easier, but, as no one theory includes all possible influences (correlates) of behavior, this single focus runs the risk of limiting intervention effectiveness as key constructs from other theories are ignored. Bartholomew et al. (2006) have proposed a process of intervention mapping to help guide these choices and assist in the planning, design, and evaluation of theoretically based interventions. Intervention mapping is a very detailed process, and space does not allow much expansion here; however, the broad steps involved include identifying program objectives, selecting theory-based methods that are relevant to the target behaviors, developing practical strategies based on the theory(s) chosen to achieve the objectives, developing adoption and implementation plans, and generating an evaluation plan.

One advantage of the MRC guidelines and intervention mapping is that they emphasize the explicit links between the theoretical constructs (e.g., self-efficacy, outcome expectations) and the techniques employed to change them (Michie & Abraham, 2004). If such links are subsequently demonstrated (or not), through, for example, mediation analysis, then greater understanding is gained of how behavior change actually occurs. Unfortunately, many existing physical activity interventions do not report these explicit links (Brug, Oenema, & Ferreira, 2005) nor conduct mediation analysis (Lubans et al., 2008), and these issues must be addressed if the field is to develop a range of theoretically sound and evidence-based behavior change techniques (Michie & Abraham, 2004).

Interventions
Young People

A substantial amount of work has examined physical activity interventions in children and adolescents, and this work has been synthesized in several reviews (see, e.g., (Dobbins, DeCorby, Robeson, Husson, & Tirilis, 2009; Salmon, Booth, Phongsavan, Murphy, & Timperio, 2007; Timperio, Salmon, & Ball, 2004; van Sluijs, McMinn, & Griffin, 2007). Although much of this work has been school based because of the large number of young people who can be reached through schools and the associated health and physical education curricula, there is increasing recognition of the importance of family- and community-based interventions. Evidence for interventions in each of these settings will be discussed.

SCHOOL-BASED INTERVENTIONS

Dobbins et al. (2009) reviewed the evidence for school-based physical activity programs. The studies included in the review employed different combinations of physical activity promotion strategies within the school setting (e.g., changes to school curriculum, teacher training, accessibility to equipment, educational materials), and some interventions also included promotion in the community or family. In general, the interventions provided participants with information about the benefits of physical activity, the risks associated with inactivity, and increased the amount of time and the intensity with which participants were engaged in activity during the school day. Three of six studies evaluating interventions in primary school children reported significant positive intervention effects for self-reported leisure time physical activity rates. There appeared to be little difference in the structure and content of effective and ineffective interventions. A further seven studies were identified that examined the effect of school-based interventions on time (duration) spent in physical activity. Of these, five reported a significant intervention effect in primary school-aged children ($n = 4$) and young adolescents ($n = 1$). The increase in physical activity duration varied from 6 to 50 minutes per week. Most of the studies used self-report measures of physical activity, but the two studies using objective measures also showed positive effects. The studies not reporting significant effects generally employed similar intervention strategies but were conducted over a shorter period of time. The authors concluded that some good evidence suggests that school-based physical activity interventions can impact duration of physical activity (particularly in primary school children), but the evidence does not suggest that school-based interventions are effective in increasing the percentage of children who are active in their leisure time. It was also noted that the long-term effects of school-based interventions are unknown as all but one study in the review evaluated outcomes in the very short term (e.g., 6 months or immediately post-intervention). In addition, there is limited evidence for the impact of school-based interventions in adolescent girls and no evidence for adolescent boys.

In an earlier systematic review of RCTs, van Sluijs et al. (2007) concluded that, for studies based in primary schools, there was inconclusive evidence for the effect of either school-only interventions and school interventions that also included family or community components. However, in secondary schools, there was strong evidence of an effect of school-based interventions that also included family or community involvement. Although these two reviews appear to reach different conclusions, the different inclusion criteria used may have led to the different findings. Regardless, both authors call for more adequately powered high-quality research to strengthen the evidence base.

FAMILY INTERVENTIONS

Reviews that have included an examination of the effectiveness of family-based physical activity interventions in children and adolescents have generally reported little consistent evidence for the effectiveness of such interventions (NICE Public Health Collaborating Centre—Physical Activity, 2007; O'Connor, Jago, & Baranowski, 2009; Salmon et al., 2007; van Sluijs et al., 2007). For example, in a narrative review, Salmon et al. (2007) reported three studies showing positive effects, three showing positive trends that approached significance, and three showing no effects. Likewise, van Sluijs et al. (2007) reported that only one out of four high-quality controlled trials reported a positive effect, and this favored the control group. The review by O'Connor et al. (2009) also sought to identify the best methods of involving parents in physical activity interventions. Lack of reporting of intervention fidelity, dose, and exposure made it difficult to draw conclusions, but sending material home from school or engaging family members in a physical activity/exercise program did not appear effective, whereas contacting families via organized activities or including parent training/family counseling or preventive messages during family visits may be more effective. Although the findings from these reviews are not necessarily encouraging, limitations in the included studies (e.g., low study quality, weak outcome measures) suggest we should not reach definitive conclusions about the effectiveness of family-based interventions. Given that parents are likely to be the main gatekeepers to their child's physical activity outside of school time (Salmon

et al., 2007) and correlates research has identified many family-based influences on young peoples' participation (Edwardson & Gorely, 2010), further attention should be given to identifying effective strategies for families in physical activity behavior change (O'Connor et al., 2009).

COMMUNITY INTERVENTIONS

There is increasing recognition that involvement of the community at all levels is important for physical activity interventions to be effective (Pate et al., 2000). Agencies such as general practitioners and community youth organizations have the potential to influence the attitudes and behavior of young people, and it seems logical that young people are more likely to adopt healthy physical activity habits if they receive consistent messages across a variety of settings and from a variety of sources. Reviews of interventions in community groups have typically identified only a small number of studies, and these have generally not been shown to be effective (NICE Public Health Collaborating Centre—Physical Activity, 2007; Salmon et al., 2007; van Sluijs et al., 2007). However, as with much of the work with physical activity interventions in other settings, methodological weaknesses make it difficult to draw anything but tentative conclusions. Having said that, interventions based within primary-care settings, involving tailored self-change plans based on an assessment of activity and food habits, show most promise, although further work with better designed studies is required (Salmon et al., 2007).

Adults

Physical activity promotion for adults has been a focus of researchers and public health practitioners for many years, and many reviews have examined the effectiveness of these physical activity interventions. Hillsdon et al. (2003) conducted a review of these reviews (published between 1996 and 2001) and subsequently updated this to include reviews published up until 2004 (Hillsdon, Foster, Cavill, Crombie, & Naidoo, 2005). The Hillsdon reviews were structured around three settings: the workplace, community settings, and health care settings, and the findings from these reviews will provide the main backbone for this section.

Workplace interventions may include exercise testing and prescription in workplace exercise facilities, health screening and counseling, active travel to work, and pedometer-based walking interventions. Hillsdon et al. (2003, 2005) concluded that findings for physical activity promotion in the workplace are inconsistent and that considerable methodological limitations (e.g., issues with sampling and selection of participants, attrition bias, and poor measurement of outcome variables) are present in the existing work. A more recent review (Dugdill, Brettle, Hulme, McCluskey, & Long, 2008) focusing just on workplace physical activity interventions was more positive and suggested that there is evidence that workplace walking interventions using pedometers in conjunction with goal setting, diaries, or self-monitoring can increase daily step counts. Likewise, they found some evidence that workplace counseling positively influenced physical activity behavior. Further work is required to fully understand the impact of workplace physical activity interventions, and emphasis needs to be placed on a broader range of worksites (for example, small- to medium-sized enterprises and the voluntary sectors; Dugdill et al., 2008).

Community interventions were defined as those that recruited from the general population rather than from a specific setting (e.g., workplace or primary health care). The interventions were typically based in the home or in fitness/leisure facilities and included one or more of the following strategies: weekly group-based counseling, mailed self-help materials, stage of change–based written materials, telephone education, advice and support, exercise testing and prescription, supervised and facility-based exercise, or behavior modification through self-monitoring, reinforcement, or relapse prevention. Based on the evidence, Hillsdon et al. (2003, 2005) concluded that targeting individuals in community settings is effective in producing short-term changes in physical activity and is likely to be effective in producing mid- to long-term change. Community-based interventions that have a strong theoretical base, teach behavioral skills tailored to individual needs, promote moderate intensity activity that is not facility dependent, and incorporate regular contact with an exercise specialist are associated with longer term changes in behavior.

Hillsdon et al. (2005) identified eight reviews that examined the effectiveness of physical activity interventions in health care settings. Interventions in this setting might include information and advice from a nurse or general practitioner, written prescriptions for physical activity, self-help materials, telephone follow-up, or referral to an exercise specialist. Based on the evidence in the reviews, Hillsdon et al. (2005) concluded that brief advice from a health care professional supported by written materials is likely to be effective in producing

short term (6–12 weeks) changes in physical activity behavior. Effectiveness is associated with a focus only on physical activity behavior change (i.e., not also including information on other health behaviors, such as diet or smoking) and the promotion of moderate intensity physical activity. Referring participants to an exercise specialist based in the community may lead to longer term (>8 months) changes.

In a recent review looking specifically at the long-term effectiveness of interventions to promote physical activity in adults, it was concluded that evidence exists for the long-term (>12 months) effectiveness of interventions to promote physical activity in healthy adults (Müller-Riemenschneider, Reinhold, Nocon, & Willich, 2008). However, high-quality comprehensive interventions using booster strategies, such as phone, mail, or Internet contact, were necessary to facilitate the most substantial long-term increases. It was also noted that, although there were significant gains in physical activity, only a few participants were actually meeting recommended physical activity targets at the end of the intervention, and this, combined with the fact that most participants were motivated volunteers, means that further strategies to reach the whole population and to reach recommended physical activity levels are necessary if public health goals are to be met.

The Internet has increasingly been viewed as a possible mode of delivery for physical activity interventions. Potential advantages of Internet delivery over traditional face-to-face interventions include reaching large numbers of people for lower cost, the potential for participants to access large amounts of information, and participants being able to choose when they would like to engage with the program and receive information (van den Berg, Schoones, & Vliet Vlieland, 2007). Van den Berg et al. (2007) reviewed RCTs that examined the effectiveness of interventions designed to promote physical activity by means of the Internet (defined to include both website and e-mail based strategies). The authors identified ten studies meeting their inclusion criteria, of which the majority tailored the intervention to the characteristics of the participants and used interactive self-monitoring and feedback tools. Three studies compared an Internet-based intervention to a wait-list control, and two of these reported significant differences between intervention and control groups. Seven studies compared two intervention groups in which either the intensity of contact or the type of treatment varied. In one of these studies, there was a significant effect in favor of the intervention group. The authors concluded that indicative evidence exists that Internet-based physical activity interventions are more effective than a wait-list control, but more work is needed to identify which components are key to the effectiveness of such interventions (e.g., amount of contact, type of treatment procedure).

Older Adults

Many interventions have been established to facilitate physical activity among older adults. Van der Bij et al. (2002) reviewed 38 RCTs reporting on 57 physical activity interventions to determine which interventions are most effective in initiating and maintaining physical activity behavior change in the older adult. Identified interventions were grouped as home-based ($n = 9$), group-based ($n = 38$), or education/counseling ($n = 10$). In the home-based interventions, participants were given an exercise prescription and asked to exercise at home according to this prescription. Most prescriptions required participation in at least three moderate intensity exercise sessions per week. Included within the home-based interventions were behavioral strategies for reinforcement, such as telephone calls, rewards, or feedback. Group-based interventions required participants to attend supervised group-based moderate to high intensity exercise programs, usually three times per week. A minority of these interventions also included behavioral strategies such as telephone call or mail reminders or rewards. The education/counseling interventions generally took place in a primary health care setting and involved some sort of health risk appraisal and then counseling on exercise and health, with participants being encouraged to engage in regular physical activity. All the education interventions included behavioral strategies (e.g., follow-up visits, telephone support, goal setting, feedback, behavioral contracting, or vouchers) to support the participants. Participation rates in the short term (<1 year) were high for both the home- (90%) and group-based (84%) interventions. However, these participation levels were not maintained in the long term (≥1 year) in either setting, although the decline in participation appeared lower in group-based interventions. This finding for declining participation with length of intervention was similar to that reported in an earlier review by King et al. (1998), which used similar inclusion and analysis criteria. The results for the education/counseling interventions were more variable, and few participants attended all sessions. Despite the low attendance rates, short-term results showed a significant increase in physical activity within the intervention group, but these effects were not maintained in the long term. The failure to show long-term effects regardless of intervention strategy suggests that new strategies need to be explored with older adults (Taylor et al., 2004). A limitation of the papers included in the review was that the majority only reported participation rates and did not report changes in actual physical activity levels. Van der Bij et al. (2002) also conclude that there is no clear evidence for the effectiveness of behavioral reinforcement strategies in facilitating the initiation or maintenance of physical activity in older adults.

Evaluation of Interventions

Reviews of intervention effectiveness highlighted in the previous section have shown that although physical activity behavior may be successfully changed in some situations or populations, in many cases, these changes are not sustained in the long term, and it is unclear exactly what intervention strategies led to any observed changes. Potential reasons for the gaps in the evidence base include limited or no description of the link between selected intervention activities and the behavioral outcomes, lack of consideration of the mediators/correlates of behavior change, lack of detail about the exposure of participants to the intervention content, and issues related to implementation fidelity, so that it is not clear to what extent the intervention was implemented as planned or in a consistent manner across sites (Figure 35.1). These reasons suggest that greater attention needs to be paid to intervention evaluation, so that it is possible to determine what works, with whom, and in what situation. This will require an explicit link between program planning and outcome and process evaluation, so that changes in behavior might be more convincingly explained and understood.

PROGRAM PLANNING

Program planning begins with a clear definition of the problem to be addressed. Having identified the problem, tools such as logic modelling (W.K. Kellogg Foundation, 2004), intervention mapping (Bartholomew, Parcel, Kok, & Gottlieb, 2006), or the RE-AIM framework (Estabrooks & Gyurcsik, 2003) can be used to enhance implementation plans. Such tools encourage "from right to left" planning, meaning that the plans first detail specific long-term outcomes, then the necessary interim and short-term outcomes that will be needed to achieve these. These outcomes then drive the selection of the activities. The activities/interventions are, in turn, influenced by evidence from theory or other work of their likely impact on the agreed outcomes and for specific target groups. Essentially, program planning is looking to develop a roadmap for the program by describing the core components, illustrating the connections between the program components and expected outcomes, and highlighting what activities need to occur when.

OUTCOME EVALUATION

Effective intervention planning will highlight the underlying theoretical assumptions about the psychological concepts and mediators that the planned intervention activities are trying to change. These theoretical perspectives then drive the design of the subsequent evaluation and the methods that it will use. Outcome evaluation (sometimes called *impact* or *summative evaluation*) measures the effects of the program on the short-term, intermediate, or long-term outcomes identified in the program planning phase. In physical activity interventions, this may be changes in physical activity behavior, attendance at sessions, or changes in fitness. However, outcome evaluation should also include measurement of the hypothesized mediators of behavior change identified in the planning phase, so that mechanisms behind behavior change can be elucidated and more effective intervention strategies developed in the future.

PROCESS EVALUATION

Process evaluation helps interventionists understand why a program was or was not successful. It is used to monitor the implementation of the intervention and helps in understanding the relationship between program elements and program outcomes (Baranowski & Jago, 2005; Saunders, Evans, & Joshi, 2005). The actual questions asked during this phase of evaluation are determined in part by the logic model developed during the planning phase, but address issues of fidelity or quality of implementation (e.g., Was the program delivered as planned?), dose (e.g., How much of the program was delivered? To what extent did participants receive and use materials or other resources), and reach (e.g., To what extent was the target audience reached?) (Saunders et al., 2005). Additionally, questions about the program context (e.g., other initiatives, staff turnover) that could affect intervention implementation or activities may be important. By better

understanding how an intervention works, programs can evolve and become increasingly effective.

A Brief Commentary on Sedentary Behavior Change

A recent trend in physical activity epidemiology is to study the measurement and health consequences of sedentary behavior, operationally defined as sitting time. Although not new, with Morris' seminal work from the 1950s investigating workplace physical activity and sedentary occupational time (Morris, Heady, Raffle, Roberts, & Parks, 1953), it is only in the past 10 years that a rapid rise in publications on the topic is evident. This has included data on young people (Marshall, Biddle, Gorely, Cameron, & Murdey, 2004; Tremblay, 2010) and adults (Dunstan et al., 2010; Katzmarzyk, Church, Craig, & Bouchard, 2009), and the field is summarized nicely by Owen and colleagues (2010).

The important point to note in the context of this chapter is that interventions to change sedentary behavior may be different from those targeted at increasing physical activity. Evidence exists for successful sedentary behavior change in children (Biddle, O'Connell, & Braithwaite, 2011; Epstein et al., 2008), but little is available on adults. Although some strategies might be a direct replacement of sitting time with physical activity, such as active computer games (Daley, 2009; Murphy, 2009), other strategies might involve less sitting and more standing, such as at work.

Conclusion

Sport and exercise psychologists have shown a great deal of interest in the psychology of sports competition and, more recently, in wider aspects of physical activity for health. A distinct literature focuses on health behavior change in health psychology and behavioral medicine, and sometimes this runs parallel to that of sport and exercise psychology. We encourage exercise psychologists to look at the behavior change literature and, to this end, have summarized what we see as key issues in this field. Physical activity is a major public health issue, and behavior change is a central feature of this.

Future Directions

• How can psychologists contribute to the pressing issue of behavioral maintenance?

• What are the best ways of prompting individuals for behavior change through self-monitoring?

- How can we enhance the fidelity of behavioral interventions?
- Can psychologists embrace new technologies for use in behavior change?

References

Adams, J., & White, M. (2003). Are activity promotion interventions based on the transtheoretical model effective? A critical review. *British Journal of Sports Medicine, 37*, 106–114.

Adams, J., & White, M. (2005). Why don't stage-based activity promotion interventions work? *Health Education Research, 20*(2), 237–243.

Ajzen, I. (1988). *Attitudes, personality and behaviour.* Milton Keynes, England: Open University Press.

Ajzen, I. (2001). Nature and operation of attitudes. *Annual Review of Psychology, 52*, 27–58.

Ajzen, I., & Fishbein, M. (1980). *Understanding attitudes and predicting social behaviour.* Englewood Cliffs, NJ: Prentice-Hall.

Atkin, A. J., Gorely, T., Biddle, S. J. H., Marshall, S. J., & Cameron, N. (2008). Critical hours: Physical activity and sedentary behavior of adolescents after school. *Pediatric Exercise Science, 20*, 446–456.

Bandura, A. (1977). *Social learning theory.* Englewood Cliffs, NJ: Prentice Hall.

Bandura, A. (1986). *Social foundations of thought and action: A social cognitive theory.* Englewood Cliffs, NJ: Prentice Hall.

Baranowski, T., Anderson, C., & Carmack, C. (1998). Mediating variable framework in physical activity interventions: How are we doing? How might we do better? *American Journal of Preventive Medicine, 15*(4), 266–297.

Baranowski, T., & Jago, R. (2005). Understanding mechanisms of change in children's physical activity programs. *Exercise and Sport Sciences Reviews, 33*(4), 163–168.

Baron, R. M., & Kenny, D. A. (1986). The moderator-mediator variable distinction in social psychological research: Conceptual, strategic, and statistical considerations. *Journal of Personality and Social Psychology, 51*, 1173–1182.

Bartholomew, L. K., Parcel, G. S., Kok, G., & Gottlieb, N. H. (2001). *Intervention mapping: Designing theory- and evidence-based health promotion programs.* Mountain View, CA: Mayfield.

Bartholomew, L. K., Parcel, G. S., Kok, G., & Gottlieb, N. H. (2006). *Planning health promotion programs: An intervention mapping approach* (2nd ed.). San Francisco: John Wiley.

Bauman, A., Sallis, J. F., Dzewaltowski, D., & Owen, N. (2002). Toward a better understanding of the influences on physical activity: The role of determinants, correlates, causal variables, mediators, moderators, and confounders. *American Journal of Preventive Medicine, 23*(2S), 5–14.

Biddle, S. J. H., Atkin, A., Cavill, N., & Foster, C. (2011). Correlates of physical activity in youth: A review of quantitative systematic reviews. *International Review of Sport and Exercise Psychology, 4*(1), 25–49.

Biddle, S. J. H., O'Connell, S., & Braithwaite, R. E. (2011). Sedentary behaviour interventions in young people: A meta-analysis. *British Journal of Sports Medicine, 45*, 937–942.

Biddle, S. J. H., Pearson, N., Ross, G. M., & Braithwaite, R. (2010). Tracking of sedentary behaviours of young people: A systematic review. *Preventive Medicine, 51*, 345–351.

Biddle, S. J. H., Whitehead, S. H., O'Donovan, T. M., & Nevill, M. E. (2005). Correlates of participation in physical activity for adolescent girls: A systematic review of recent literature. *Journal of Physical Activity and Health, 2*, 423–434.

Brug, J., Conner, M., Harre, N., Kremers, S., McKeller, S., & Whitelaw, S. (2005). The transtheoretical model and stages of change: A critique. Observations by five commentators on the paper by Adams, J. and White, M. (2004). Why don't stage-based activity promotion interventions work? *Health Education Research, 20*(2), 244–258.

Brug, J., Oenema, A., & Ferreira, I. (2005). Theory, evidence and intervention mapping to improve behavior nutrition and physical activity interventions. *International Journal of Behavioral Nutrition and Physical Activity, 2*(2).

Campbell, M., Fitzpatrick, R., Haines, A., Kinmonth, A. L., Sandercock, P., Spiegelhalter, D., et al. (2000). Framework for design and evaluation of complex interventions to improve health. *British Medical Journal, 321*(7262), 694–696.

Carver, A., Timperio, A., Hesketh, K., & Crawford, D. (2010). Are children and adolescents less active if parents restrict their physical activity and active transport due to perceived risk? *Social Science and Medicine, 70*(11), 1799–1805.

Chief Medical Officers of England, Scotland, Wales, and Northern Ireland. (2011). *Start active, stay active: a report on physical activity from the four home countries' Chief Medical Officers.* London: Department of Health (http://www.dh.gov.uk/en/Publicationsandstatistics/Publications/PublicationsPolicyAndGuidance/DH

Chodzko-Zajko, W. J., Proctor, D. N., Fiatarone Singh, M. A., Minson, C. T., Nigg, C. R., Salem, G. J., et al. (2009). Exercise and physical activity for older adults: American College of Sports Medicine position stand. *Medicine and Science in Sports and Exercise, 41*(7), 1510–1530.

Colcombe, S., & Kramer, A. F. (2003). Fitness effects on the cognitive function of older adults: A meta-analytic study. *Psychological Science, 14*(2), 125–130.

Craig, P., Dieppe, P., Macintyre, S., Michie, S., Nazareth, I., & Petticrew, M. (2008). Developing and evaluating complex interventions: The new Medical Research Council guidance. *British Medical Journal, 337*, a1655.

Daley, A. J. (2009). Can exergaming contribute to improving physical activity levels and health outcomes in children? *Pediatrics.* DOI: 10.1542/peds.2008–2357

Davison, K., & Lawson, C. (2006). Do attributes in the physical environment influence children's physical activity? A review of the literature. *International Journal of Behavioral Nutrition and Physical Activity.* Retrieved from http://www.ijbnpa.org/content/3/1/19

Deci, E. L., & Ryan, R. M. (Eds.). (2002). *Handbook of self-determination research.* Rochester, NY: The University of Rochester Press.

Dobbins, M., DeCorby, K., Robeson, P., Husson, H., & Tirilis, D. (2009). School-based physical activity programs for promoting physical activity and fitness in children and adolescents aged 6–18. *Cochrane Database of Systematic Reviews.* Retrieved from http://mrw.interscience.wiley.com/cochrane/clsysrev/articles/CD007651/pdf_fs.html

Dugdill, L., Brettle, A., Hulme, C., McCluskey, S., & Long, A. (2008). Workplace physical activity interventions: A systematic review. *International Journal of Workplace Health Management, 1*, 20–40.

Dunstan, D. W., Barr, E. L. M., Healy, G. N., Salmon, J., Shaw, J. E., Balkau, B., et al. (2010). Television viewing time and mortality: The Australian Diabetes, Obesity and Lifestyle Study (AusDiab). *Circulation, 121*, 384–391.

Edwardson, C. L., & Gorely, T. (2010). Parental influences on different types and intensities of physical activity in youth: A systematic review. *Psychology of Sport and Exercise, 11*(6), 522–535.

Epstein, L. H., & Roemmich, J. N. (2001). Reducing sedentary behaviour: Role in modifying physical activity. *Exercise and Sport Sciences Reviews, 29*(3), 103–108.

Epstein, L. H., Roemmich, J. N., Robinson, J. L., Paluch, R. A., Winiewicz, D. D., Fuerch, J. H., et al. (2008). A randomised trial of the effects of reducing television viewing and computer use on body mass index in young children. *Archives of Pediatric and Adolescent Medicine, 162*(3), 239–245.

Epstein, L. H., Saelens, B. E., & O'Brien, J. G. (1995). Effects of reinforcing increases in active behavior versus decreases in sedentary behavior for obese children. *International Journal of Behavioral Medicine, 2*, 41–50.

Estabrooks, P., & Gyurcsik, N. C. (2003). Evaluating the impact of behavioral interventions that target physical activity: Issues of generalizability and public health. *Psychology of Sport and Exercise, 4*, 41–55.

Ferreira, I., van der Horst, K., Wendel-Vos, W., Kremers, S., van Lenthe, F. J., & Brug, J. (2006). Environmental correlates of physical activity in youth: A review and update. *Obesity Reviews, 8*(2), 129–154.

Gollwitzer, P. M. (1999). Implementation intentions: Strong effects of simple plans. *American Psychologist, 54*(7), 493–503.

Gollwitzer, P. M., & Sheeran, P. (2006). Implementation intentions and goal achievement: A meta-analysis of effects and processes. *Advances in Experimental Social Psychology, 38*, 69–119.

Gustafson, S. L., & Rhodes, R. E. (2006). Parental correlates of physical activity in children and adolescents. *Sports Medicine, 36*, 79–97.

Hagger, M. S., Chatzisarantis, N. L. D., & Biddle, S. J. H. (2002). A meta-analytic review of the Theories of Reasoned Action and Planned Behaviour in physical activity: Predictive validity and the contribution of additional variables. *Journal of Sport and Exercise Psychology, 24*, 3–32.

Hagger, M. S., & Orbell, S. (2003). A meta-analytic review of the common-sense model of illness representations. *Psychology and Health, 18*, 141–184.

Hardman, A. E., & Stensel, D. J. (2009). *Physical activity and health: The evidence explained* (2nd Edition). London: Routledge.

Harrison, J. A., Mullen, P. D., & Green, L. W. (1992). A meta-analysis of studies of the Health Belief Model with adults. *Health Education Research: Theory and Practice, 7*, 107–116.

Hillsdon, M., Foster, C., Cavill, N., Crombie, H., & Naidoo, B. (2005). *The effectiveness of public health interventions for increasing physical activity among adults: A review of reviews* (2nd ed.). London: Health Development Agency.

Hillsdon, M., Foster, C., Naidoo, B., & Crombie, H. (2003). *A review of the evidence on the effectiveness of public health interventions for increasing physical activity amongst adults: A review of reviews.* London: Health Development Agency.

Katzmarzyk, P. T., Church, T. S., Craig, C. L., & Bouchard, C. (2009). Sitting time and mortality from all causes, cardiovascular disease, and cancer. *Medicine and Science in Sports and Exercise, 41*(5), 998–1005.

King, A. C. (2001). Interventions to promote physical activity by older adults. *Journals of Gerontology Series A-Biological Sciences and Medical Sciences, 56 Spec No 2*(2), 36–46.

King, A. C., Rejeski, W. J., & Buchner, D. M. (1998). Physical activity interventions targeting older adults: A critical review and recommendations. *American Journal of Preventive Medicine, 15*(4), 316–333.

Leventhal, H., Leventhal, E., & Contrada, R. J. (1998). Self-regulation, health and behaviour: A perceptual cognitive approach. *Psychology and Health, 13*, 717–734.

Lubans, D. R., Foster, C., & Biddle, S. J. H. (2008). A review of mediators of behavior in interventions to promote physical activity among children and adolescents. *Preventive Medicine, 47*, 463–470.

MacKinnon, D., & Fairchild, A. (2009). Current directions in mediation analysis. *Current Directions in Psychological Science, 18*, 16–20.

MacKinnon, D., Krull, J., & Lockwood, C. (2000). Equivalence of the mediation, confounding and suppression effect. *Prevention Science, 1*, 173–181.

Malina, R. M. (1996). Tracking of physical activity and physical fitness across the lifespan. *Research Quarterly for Exercise and Sport, 67*(3, Suppl.), S48–S57.

Marshall, S. J., & Biddle, S. J. H. (2001). The Transtheoretical Model of behavior change: A meta-analysis of applications to physical activity and exercise. *Annals of Behavioral Medicine, 23*, 229–246.

Marshall, S. J., Biddle, S. J. H., Gorely, T., Cameron, N., & Murdey, I. (2004). Relationships between media use, body fatness and physical activity in children and youth: A meta-analysis. *International Journal of Obesity, 28*, 1238–1246.

McAuley, E., & Blissmer, B. (2000). Self-efficacy determinants and consequences of physical activity. *Exercise and Sport Sciences Reviews, 28*, 85–88.

McAuley, E., & Morris, K. S. (2007). Advances in physical activity and mental health: Quality of life. *American Journal of Lifestyle Medicine, 1*(5), 389–396.

Michie, S., & Abraham, C. (2004). Interventions to changes health behaviours: Evidence based or evidence-inspired?. *Psychology and Health, 19*, 29–49.

Morris, J. N., Heady, J. A., Raffle, P. A. B., Roberts, C. G., & Parks, J. W. (1953). Coronary heart disease and physical activity of work. *The Lancet, 2*, 1053–1057, 1111–1120.

Müller-Riemenschneider, F., Reinhold, T., Nocon, M., & Willich, S. N. (2008). Long-term effectiveness of interventions promoting physical activity: A systematic review. *Preventive Medicine, 47*(4), 354–368.

Murphy, S. (2009). Video games, competition and exercise: A new opportunity for sport psychologists? *The Sport Psychologist, 23*, 487–503.

NICE Public Health Collaborating Centre—Physical Activity. (2007). *Promoting physical activity for children: Review 7—Family and community interventions.* London: NICE. Retrieved from http://www.nice.org.uk/guidance/PH17

O'Connor, T. M., Jago, R., & Baranowski, T. (2009). Engaging parents to increase youth physical activity: A systematic review. *American Journal of Preventive Medicine, 37*(2), 141–149.

Owen, N., Healy, G. N., Matthews, C. E., & Dunstan, D. W. (2010). Too much sitting: The population health science of sedentary behavior. *Exercise and Sport Sciences Reviews, 38*(3), 105–113.

Pate, R. R., Trost, S., Mullis, R., Sallis, J., Wechsler, H., & Brown, D. (2000). Community interventions to promote proper nutrition and physical activity among youth. *Preventive Medicine, 31*(Supplement), S138–S149.

Prochaska, J. O., & Marcus, B. H. (1994). The transtheoretical model: Application to exercise. In R. K. Dishman (Ed.), *Advances in exercise adherence* (pp. 161–180). Champaign, IL: Human Kinetics.

Prochaska, J. O., Norcross, J. C., & DiClemente, C. C. (1994). *Changing for good*. New York: Avon.

Rhodes, R. E., Fiala, B., & Conner, M. (2009). A review and meta-analysis of affective judgments and physical activity in adult populations. *Annals of Behavioral Medicine, 38,* 180–204.

Rhodes, R. E., & Pfaeffli, L. (2010). Mediators of physical activity behaviour change among adult non-clinical populations: A review update. *International Journal of Behavioral Nutrition and Physical Activity, 7*(1), 37.

Riemsma, R., Pattenden, J., Bridle, C., Sowden, A., Mather, L., Watt, I., et al. (2002). A systematic review of the effectiveness of interventions based on a stages-of-change approach to promote individual behaviour change. *Health Technology Assessment, 6*(24).

Rosenstock, I. (1974). Historical origins of the health belief model. *Health Education Monographs, 2,* 328–335.

Sallis, J. F., & Owen, N. (1999). *Physical activity and behavioral medicine*. Thousand Oaks, CA: Sage.

Sallis, J. F., Prochaska, J. J., & Taylor, W. C. (2000). A review of correlates of physical activity of children and adolescents. *Medicine and Science in Sports and Exercise, 32,* 963–975.

Salmon, J., Booth, M. L., Phongsavan, P., Murphy, N., & Timperio, A. (2007). Promoting physical activity participation among children and adolescents. *Epidemiologic Reviews, June,* 1–15. DOI: 10.1093/epirev/mxm010

Saunders, R., Evans, M., & Joshi, P. (2005). Developing a process-evaluation plan for assessing health promotion program implementation: A how-to guide. *Health Promotion Practice, 6*(2), 134–147.

Schwarzer, R. (2008). Modeling health behavior change: How to predict and modify the adoption and maintenance of health behaviors. *Applied Psychology: An International Review, 57,* 1–29.

Steinbeck, K. S. (2001). The importance of physical activity in the prevention of overweight and obesity in childhood: A review and an opinion. *Obesity Reviews, 2*(2), 117–130.

Stensel, D. J., Gorely, T., & Biddle, S. J. H. (2008). Youth health outcomes. In A. L. Smith & S. J. H. Biddle (Eds.), *Youth physical activity and sedentary behavior: Challenges and solutions* (pp. 31–57). Champaign, IL: Human Kinetics.

Taylor, A., Cable, N., Faulkner, G., Hillsdon, M., Narici, M., & van der Bij, A. (2004). Physical activity and older adults: A review of health benefits and the effectiveness of interventions. *Journal of Sports Sciences, 22,* 703–725.

Telama, R., Yang, X., Viikari, J., Valimaki, I., Wanne, O., & Raitakari, O. (2005). Physical activity from childhood to adulthood: A 21-year tracking study. *American Journal of Preventive Medicine, 28*(3), 267–273.

Timperio, A., Salmon, J., & Ball, K. (2004). Evidence-based strategies to promote physical activity among children, adolescents and young adults: Review and update. *Journal of Science and Medicine in Sport, 7*(1 Supplement), 20–29.

Tremblay, M. S. (2010). Assessing the level of sedentarism. In C. Bouchard & P. T. Katzmarzyk (Eds.), *Physical activity and obesity* (2nd ed., pp. 13–17). Champaign, IL: Human Kinetics.

Trost, S. G., Owen, N., Bauman, A. E., Sallis, J. F., & Brown, W. (2002). Correlates of adults' participation in physical activity: Review and update. *Medicine and Science in Sports and Exercise, 34,* 1996–2001.

van den Berg, M. H., Schoones, J. W., & Vliet Vlieland, T. P. M. (2007). Internet-based physical activity interventions: A systematic review of the literature. *Journal of Medical Internet Research, 9*(3), e26. Retrieved from http://www.jmir.org/2007/2003/e2026/HTML

van der Bij, A. K., Laurant, M. G. H., & Wensing, M. (2002). Effectiveness of physical activity interventions for older adults: A review. *American Journal of Preventive Medicine, 22*(2), 120–133.

van der Horst, K., Chin, A., Paw, M. J., Twisk, J. W. R., & Van Mechelen, W. (2007). A brief review on correlates of physical activity and sedentariness in youth. *Medicine and Science in Sports and Exercise, 39*(8), 1241–1250.

van Sluijs, E. M. F., McMinn, A. M., & Griffin, S. J. (2007). Effectiveness of interventions to promote physical activity in children and adolescents: Systematic review of controlled trials. *British Medical Journal, 335,* 703–707.

van Stralen, M. M., De Vries, H., Mudde, A. N., Bolman, C., & Lechner, L. (2009). Determinants of initiation and maintenance of physical activity among older adults: A literature review. *Health Psychology Review, 3*(2), 147–207.

Vilhjalmsson, R., & Kristjansdottir, G. (2003). Gender differences in physical activity in older children and adolescents: The central role of organised sport. *Social Science and Medicine, 56,* 363–374.

W. K. Kellogg Foundation. (2004). *W.K. Kellogg Foundation evaluation handbook*. Michigan: Author.

Zimmerman, F. J. (2009). Using behavioral economics to promote physical activity. *Preventive Medicine, 49*(4), 289–291.

The Role of the Sport and Performance Psychologist with the Coach and Team: Implications for Performance Consulting

Christopher M. Carr

Abstract

The complex and dynamic relationships among the sport psychologist, the coach, and the team (athletes and staff) are discussed in this chapter. The consultative nature of the work of the sport and performance psychologist and how psychological interventions are applied in organizational settings are addressed and discussed. Specific relationship issues and consultation strategies related to coaches, support staff (e.g., sports medicine personnel), the team, and individual athletes are presented. Several common consultation issues, such as role definition, professional challenges (e.g., isolation), managing conflicts, and dealing with successful/unsuccessful performance, are discussed. I use a number of examples from my own experiences with professional consultations at the collegiate, Olympic, and professional sports levels to identify and describe key issues in organizational consulting. Based on lessons drawn from these experiences and on the fundamental principles of systems theory as applied to organizations, I offer a number of practical strategies to enhance consultant effectiveness when working with elite, high-performing teams.

Key Words: Consultation, sport psychologist, coaches, athletics administrators, teams, Olympic sports, professional sports, journaling, confidentiality, collegial support, self-awareness

Psychological interventions addressing performance concerns can occur at many levels, including the individual, group (team), and system (organizational) levels. The purpose of this chapter is to explore the interaction among the sport psychologist, the coach (team leader), and the team, using a systems theory perspective (Senge, 1990) to provide a framework for understanding the multiple roles a sport psychologist takes on when providing consultation for a sports organization. There are many variables to consider when beginning a team/systemic consultation to enhance the performance of the team or to address a team-based psychological issue (e.g., recovery from traumatic events). It is important that the consultant have great awareness of the variety of systemic dynamics that occur during the consultation process, from point of entry to termination. The potential success or failure of a sport and performance psychology consultation will depend greatly on the interactive dynamics among the coach, the team, and the sport psychologist.

This chapter addresses three key issues that influence this unique and challenging dynamic (interaction of coach, team, sport psychologist) at all levels of sport and performance consultation. Whether the consultation is with a professional sports team, a collegiate team, a dance troupe, or a management team in a *Fortune 500* company, these issues apply. First, I will discuss how the consultant should organize the consultation when working in a high-performance team environment. Next, I will discuss the key subsystems that comprise the high-performance organization, utilizing sports as my main example. Building successful relationships within each of these subsystems is a key to success and survival in performance consulting. Finally, I will discuss the challenges and pitfalls facing psychologists working in high-performance settings, in which the emphasis is on results and demonstrated improvements. This chapter is a deeply personal exploration of the process of high-performance consulting. It is informed by my own experiences in the field, based on over 20 years of work with organizations in such diverse areas as collegiate and professional sports, business, and medicine. A great deal of learning takes place for the individual professional working in such settings, and my goal is to distill some general principles that can apply to all who work in this field. I do not have all (or even most) of the answers, but I have certainly identified some of the major mistakes that can be made!

The Sport and Performance Psychologist Working in a High-Performance Team Setting

The sport and performance psychologist (hereafter referred to as the S&P psychologist) must be able to clearly define and communicate to clients his or her training and competencies in the fields of sport and performance psychology in order to be an effective and impactful consultant. Unfortunately, many "gurus" and self-described motivational speakers are often utilized by teams and organizations to address their psychological functioning (e.g., mental toughness, resilience), and this has tended to confuse the issue of what a S&P psychologist is and does. Rather than explore the pros and cons of this area of debate (e.g., who is or isn't qualified), this section focuses on clarifying the consultant's role as he or she begins the process of engaging within a team and coaching staff dynamic.

Preparation and Training of the S&P Psychologist

The development and preparation needed to be effective in a high-performance program has been explored in depth in the sport and performance psychology literature (Hack, 2005; Hays & Brown, 2004; McCann, 2005). Issues discussed have included the professional (licensure status, certification), educational (type of degree, internships), and training (skill sets, experience with varied populations, training in different interventions) experiences necessary for optimal preparation. Some of these issues are also further explored in this Handbook (see Chapters 2, 3, 37, and 39, all in this volume).

Choice of Title

If someone is calling themselves a psychologist of any type, they should have the appropriate licensure within their state of practice. If not licensed as a psychologist, then the title of "consultant" has been suggested by organizations such as the Association for Applied Sport Psychology (Become a certified consultant, n.d.). The decision of what title the consultant uses influences his or her relationship with the client (e.g., organization and/or team). If an individual is using the title of psychologist, it may imply that the consultation will include multiple areas of service, including the typical individual consultation/counseling that is commonly utilized by psychologists in practice. A consultant may be perceived as focusing on more group-oriented consultation, such as workshops and small-group discussions, and on strictly performance issues. A psychologist must work within his or her competency, as defined by his/her state licensure regulations (these issues are explored in depth in Chapter 3, and the reader is referred to this thoughtful discussion).

The Structure of the Consultation

In defining his or her consultation role with a team or organization, the S&P psychologist should be clear from the onset about the goals and objectives of the consultation, including what the S&P psychologist can (and cannot) do during the course of consultation. This structure must be established early in the relationship and should clarify expectations for both consultant and client. Numerous issues may require clarification and sometimes careful negotiation, but some of the important initial tasks of consultation include defining

• Who is the client (e.g., organization, coach, administrator, team, athletes—or all?)
• What services will be provided (e.g., one-on-one consultations, observations, assessment)
• Length of the consultation (e.g., one-time workshop or year-long)
• When the services will be provided (e.g., weekly, quarterly, biannually)
• The fees associated with the consultation service provided (e.g., hourly, retainer)

Other structural issues that may require clarification include defining what is offered to the team members (e.g., individual consultation services, team presentations); issues of accessibility, such as whether the S&P psychologist has access to areas that only staff/team members may enter (e.g., locker rooms, training room); and how interactions with other support staff (e.g., athletic trainers, media staff) will be structured (regular meetings, reports, joint consultations, etc.). It is important that these structural issues be clarified prior to beginning the consultation relationship, as it helps to minimize potential conflicts and confusion once the consultation process begins. To provide an example, I have included as an Appendix to this chapter a letter I send out at the beginning of a season to players and staff of one of the professional teams I consult with.

Confidentiality

A critical issue for all S&P psychologists is confidentiality. Confidentiality includes the discussion of who hears what regarding the consultant's role with the team. In other words, is there any confidentiality regarding coach–consultant, management–consultant, team–consultant, or individual athlete–consultant interactions? This needs to be defined prior to beginning the consultation relationship, then communicated clearly to all coaches, managers, and team members. A licensed psychologist must understand that if he or she is providing any type of psychological counseling/consultation, all state laws and ethics regarding confidentiality (e.g., signed informed consent) must be adhered to during the consultation arrangement. In the author's experience, once the confidentiality questions are discussed and determined, the consultation arrangement can move ahead with limited conflict. However, if the confidentiality issue is vague (do all consultant–team member interactions get shared with the coach, for example?), then it may severely impair the consultant's outcome with the team and/or organization. This issue is, once again, thoughtfully discussed in Chapter 3; however, it must be emphasized here that clarifying confidentiality and communicating the established boundaries clearly within the organization early in the consultation process are critical in order to maximize the consultant's impact and effectiveness.

Although confidentiality can pose some difficult challenges to any consultant, relying on one's training/education and related professional licensure guidelines should be a good guide to making wise decisions. I have had the privilege of providing sport psychology consultation with two different national governing bodies (NGBs) as they prepared athletes for the elite competitive level in their sports (e.g., World Cups, World Championships, Olympic Games). In each of these consultations (one over a 10-year period; the other over 4 years), I developed clear guidelines regarding confidentiality issues, especially in my work with individual athletes (e.g., athlete needed a signed release of information to disclose relevant information to coaches/support staff). In each instance, education was provided to the coaching and administrative staffs regarding the impact of maintaining confidentiality with individual athlete consultations and the efficacy of the sport psychology relationship. With both NGBs, no major conflicts occurred due to misunderstandings about confidentiality, and the coaches/administrators demonstrated respect for these confidentiality/boundary issues. I believe the key was establishing this dialogue early in the consultation process.

Consulting with Members of the High-Performance Team

A systems-based approach to sport psychology consulting (Fletcher, Benshoff, & Richburg, 2003; Whelan, Meyers, & Donovan, 1995) provides several advantages for the S&P psychologist, including understanding of the interactive and circular nature of systems and the realization that complex systems are comprised of important subsystems (Minuchin, 1974). Senge (1990) provides an informal overview of some of the key principles of systems theory for consultants working in complex organizations, and, although his approach is informal, I have found it very useful during my consulting career. Here are a few of his key "laws" of systems thinking, applied to organizational consulting:

- *Today's problems come from yesterday's solutions.* Very often, I am called into a team to work on problems that turn out to be at least partially due to past attempts to solve basic, underlying organizational issues. Often, these underlying issues (of communication, trust, etc.) must be dealt with before long-term change can occur.
- *The harder you push, the harder the system pushes back.* All consultants seem to learn this lesson early in their careers. When you suggest and implement change, the team resists. This is not usually a conscious decision, but much more a function of natural processes (such as system homeostasis and organizational momentum), so it is very useful for the S&P consultant to remind him- or herself of this law and not take the pushback personally.
- *Behavior grows better before it grows worse.* Short-term solutions often produce short-term positive changes. But if long-term issues of vision, goals, teamwork, and a commitment to excellence

are not addressed, long-term success will not usually follow. This is a very powerful principle, but difficult for the consultant to adhere to because often the coach, players, or management are looking for quick results.

• *Small changes can produce big results—but the areas of highest leverage are often the least obvious.* This law is also a major reason why S&P consultants can be very effective—the areas in which a system needs to change are usually not obvious to those already in the system. The outsider can identify high-leverage opportunities more easily because of his or her emotional distance from the issues. It is typically no easy task to identify the major targets of change, but thinking in terms of the team's processes rather than snapshots of discrete events is a useful strategy. A corollary of this law is that as the S&P consultant becomes part of a team, he or she, too, may become blinded to the weaknesses of the system.

• *There is no blame.* It is so easy in sport and other competitive endeavors to blame some outside factor for our problems. The referees, the media, the fans, rivals, accrediting agencies, the government—all can be blamed for our failures. This final law reminds me to help a team understand that there is no outside force at work. Our problems are part of the system, and attaining success depends on developing effective strategies and relationships with your "enemies"—you are both part of a single system.

It is important for the S&P psychologist to differentiate and define these critical subsystems, so that he or she is aware of the organizational components that will potentially impact his or her consultation work. Three critical subsystems that are generally encountered when working with sports organizations are discussed in this section: the organization, management, and support staff; the coaching staff; and the sports team. The subsystems encountered in other performance domains (e.g., the performing arts, medicine) will vary according to context.

Organization, Management, and Support Staff

A typical sport psychology consultation involves an organization (e.g., NGB, Professional Team, National Collegiate Athletics Association [NCAA] Athletics Department), a specific team, and the staff associated with that specific team. The S&P psychology consultant may interact directly with only

a few, or perhaps all, of these staff members during the course of the consultation. It is important to recognize that, regardless of direct contact, the consultant will indirectly impact all staff members, so knowledge of these members' roles within the organization is of utmost importance to the consulting relationship. To highlight this role delineation, I can share an example of my current consulting role with an NCAA Division I collegiate football program. This relationship has developed over a 4-year period and includes the following staff members that I have had direct (face-to-face, individual consultation regarding team/athlete/coaching issues) contact with during the course of consultation:

• University athletics director (consultation regarding athlete behaviors)
• Associate athletics director for sport (consultation regarding team issues)
• Head football coach (weekly consultation regarding staff, team, athlete issues)
• Eight full-time assistant coaches, two graduate assistant coaches (player/team issues)
• Sports medicine staff of head team physician, two orthopedic consultants, one head football certified athletic trainer (ATC), two assistant football ATCs, multiple student athletic trainers, and other medical consultants (e.g., neurologist) (consultation regarding athlete medical issues and mental health issues)
• Strength and conditioning staff, including a head strength and conditioning coach and three assistant strength coaches (consultation regarding coaching, team dynamic, and individual athlete issues)
• Academic advising staff (four) specifically assigned to football (consultation regarding athlete mental health issues)
• Director of football operations (consultation regarding team travel and performance consultation room arrangements)
• Administrative staff of three professionals (consultation regarding travel, team meetings, preparation of team materials)

This list may not be exhaustive (although you may become exhausted reading it!), but it does nicely illustrate the significant number of different staff members who play important roles in the team's performance and thus come into direct contact with the S&P psychologist. There are other related professionals, involved individuals and groups, and service providers that the S&P psychologist may come into contact with during the consultation experience (e.g., media staff, travel staff, boosters, alumni, equipment staff, pastoral staff), but those listed above have had a direct and regular relationship with me.

It is therefore important for the consultant to have a clear understanding of the possibilities inherent in his or her interactions with the variety of staff members who may be involved in the consultation process, even if all such consults cannot be defined at the beginning of the relationship. I have found that, at times, the need to provide services or my own need to seek additional resources emerges only during consultation, but it is helpful to have a guide as to who may reasonably ask for services and what you are expected to provide to an organization over time. It is also important to set limits on what you are able to provide for the client within the context of the consultation. These limits must be communicated clearly to the client (and relevant contacts) in order to establish boundaries and an efficient process of consultation. For example, if the S&P consultant is contracted by a small business to provide team building, leadership training, and potential employee assessment, then it would be important to define the limits of the relationship early in the process. Of course, these specific behaviors/boundaries would best be guided by one's competencies (e.g., training, licensure). Thus, if your role is to provide quarterly team-building exercises that are based upon quarterly employee evaluations (e.g., performance-based feedback regarding work environment, communication, supervision, and challenges), then it would be important to define the expectations of who collects the evaluations, who reviews/summarizes the data, and who receives the specific feedback upon which the consultant creates the team-building session. The risk of not setting clear limits could greatly (and negatively) impact the consultant. For example, an employee believes that he or she was sharing confidential feedback, but the manager discloses the concern within the team-building session based upon his review of the data (which may not have been recommended by the consultant). If the consultant had set the limit that only he or she would review the evaluations and prepare a summary report (maintaining confidentiality of the responses), then this accidental exposure would have been avoided and the consultant would be perceived by the staff (team) as more trustworthy and valued. It is thus critically important for the S&P consultant to have an understanding of the unique culture of his or her client(s), whether it be an athletic team/organization, a performing arts group, or a business team. This is often achieved best by simply spending time with the organization and asking questions when knowledge is lacking (some excellent examples and descriptions of just this approach are provided in McCann, 2000; Price & Andersen, 2000; Tammen, 2000).

If the consultation involves a business, there may be management staff, a sales staff, a marketing staff, an accounting/finance staff, and perhaps other staff levels (e.g., secretarial, administrative) that will have direct contact with the consultant. In Olympic sports, there will be NGB administrators, high-performance directors, coaches, and support staff (e.g., ATCs, MDs, exercise physiologists, biomechanists) who will be involved with the team/athlete performance issues. At the professional level, the consultant may deal with owners, managing partners, general managers, head coaches, assistant coaches, medical staff, strength and conditioning staff, scouting departments, player development staffs (e.g., administering professional league programs, such as the National Football League [NFL] Player Programs), media relations staff, and administrative staffs (who often have the most important role in communications). It is best to learn about the systemic structure of the organizational client before beginning the hard work of performance enhancement. This is of great help to the S&P psychologist who must understand these staff roles and discover how they may impact the consultation. In some instances in which the consultant is hired by the management staff, there exists the potential conflict that athletes may view the consultant as a "spy" or "pipeline" to the management, and therefore the consultant finds little receptivity from the athletes in his or her work. This consultation arrangement may be sufficient for the consultant, but it must be noted that efficacy of the consultation (regarding team performance/success) may be greatly impacted by a skewed view of the consultant's role on the part of service recipients. It is also important to note that coaches/support staff often have preconceived opinions on the discipline of psychology, and these may involve a negative bias—so, be prepared to deal with those attitudes.

In some cases, it is the coach who "took a class in psychology" who may either enhance or disrupt the consultative process. An effective consultant will gather this information early in the process and utilize this information to assist in the ongoing consultation process. Do not be afraid to ask a staff member "What is your role with the team (organization)?" in your initial consultation process. If you maintain a journal, and take regular notes regarding the consultation, it will be relevant information that may impact your consultation process (e.g., determining who to include in workshops/meetings) in a very efficacious manner. I have found that if I am included in staff meetings early in the consultation process, I am very engaged in note-taking/journaling as members of the team/staff share content, ideas, and information regarding the organization and/or team. The journaling allows me to follow-up in later informal sessions (e.g., watching a practice) with other staff members to further identify their roles within the team. Often, staff members will share their beliefs about how you (the S&P consultant) may best enhance the performance of the team/organization.

Coaches

The coaching staff, in my experience, is the most influential resource for the ultimate success (or failure) of a performance-based consultation. Complicating consultation is the fact that there are multiple levels of coaches and responsibilities in many sports and high-performance organizations, and a single coach may play a variety of roles within the team system. The *head coach* is typically the most influential coach on staff, especially regarding the approval/support of the S&P consultant. Building a positive and collaborative relationship with the head coach is essential to an effective consultation outcome. But where should the S&P psychologist focus his or her consultation when working with the head coach? Perhaps an instructive example is the surprising team performance that occurred in 1980 at the Winter Olympic Games in Lake Placid, New York. As dramatized in the movie "Miracle," the U.S. men's hockey team won the gold medal in those Olympic Games, but more impressively, beat the almost-unbeatable Soviet Union team in the semifinals. The moment of victory against the Soviet team was captured forever on video when broadcaster Al Michaels exclaimed "Do you believe in miracles?" as the clock wound down to zero and the U.S. team won the game 4–3. But consider the unique and complex dynamics of team composition and the leadership of head coach Herb Brooks in that memorable achievement. In a letter that Coach Brooks sent to all team members 4 months after the games were over, he wrote: "This year was a challenge for all of us. A challenge to: Live and work as a unit; Play a positive game in a creative way; and, Make the most out of our dreams. You

met these challenges and conquered them. If there was ever any team I ever wanted to identify with on a personal basis, this was the team" (Coffey, 2005, p. 263). This comment reflects the very complex dynamics facing a head coach working with a high-performance team. Consider the challenges facing the coach as he selected his coaching staff, selected his team, defined the players' roles, and created a team dynamic in which each player's contribution was optimized. Which entry points would you, as a S&P psychologist, choose to work on with a coach in such a situation? There is no right answer, but there are a variety of performance-related areas that can benefit from a careful psychological analysis and intervention in such situations. As an S&P psychologist, it is important to understand and attend to the variety of roles that coaches must fulfill and optimize in order to facilitate team success.

As I mentioned, layers of coaching staffs often exist within athletic teams. For example, in the previously mentioned Division I collegiate football program, there is one head coach, one offensive coordinator (responsible for the team's offense), one defensive coordinator (responsible for the team's defense), two or three assistant coaches on offense, two or three assistant coaches on defense, one or two "operations" staff (a coach or administrator who typically organizes travel/team meals/lodging/recruit visits—an important individual for the consultant to know), two graduate assistant coaches (students in graduate school preparing for a career in coaching), and a number of student assistant coaches, for a total of nine to ten full-time coaches for one team! In addition, there is typically a strength/conditioning coaching staff of three or four coaches who will provide physical training for the team. Thus, the S&P consultant will invariably develop relationships, with varying degrees of sophistication and involvement, with at least 12–15 individual coaches, for just one Division 1 college football team! An effective consultant will take into consideration the relationship he or she has with all coaching staff members and understand that as long as a coach/staff member has contact with the athlete, then they can impact that athlete. Thus, relationship development gained through informal interactions, organized one-on-one meetings, staff meetings/presentations, and topic-specific consultations (e.g., coach asks consultant on how to "best" enhance cohesion within his position group) will benefit the S&P consultant's impact on the overall team performance issues. Such multiple relationships with coaches/managers/leaders are typical in most mid-size or large organizations such as companies, hospitals, or dance troupes.

A key learning skill for any S&P consultant is to familiarize him- or herself with the nuances and dynamics of coaching and coaching roles. (See also Chapter 18, this volume, in which the authors describe and discuss the rich history of sport psychology research on the psychology of coaching.) Senge (1990) talks about the necessity of creating a "learning organization" for a team or company to be successful, and it is the coach who has the responsibility for making this happen. It is important to find appropriate avenues to engage with coaches and understand their duties, roles, challenges, and the benefits they derive from their profession. Trust and rapport are established slowly, and respect may take even longer to earn, so patience and persistence are essential for the S&P psychologist to establish an effective consultation process. For example, when I began working with the U.S. alpine ski team in 1992, I spent most of my time during the first few camps I attended engaged in informal discussion (at breakfast, in the van rides, on the mountainside, at workouts) with all of the coaching staff to better understand the following: what is their title (e.g., head coach, speed team or head coach, technical team); what is their role (e.g., selection of U.S. team, setting up training, individual technical skill teaching); how long have they been coaching; did they have an athletic history (e.g., former U.S. ski team members/collegiate skiers); their current assessment (e.g., observed strengths/limitations/challenges) of the team; and their past history and, if they were willing, their perceptions of the role of S&P psychology with the team. Most coaches I have encountered in my 20-plus years of S&P consultation are more than glad to share their opinions of sport psychology.

As mentioned earlier, consultants must find an approach that is effective for them for integrating and understanding this informally collected information. Personally, I would find myself journaling in the evening, describing the variety of informative discussions and observations, so that I could better comprehend and assess the current dynamics within the team. For example, how did the coaches interact in team meetings? Did a coach protect an athlete during a player evaluation meeting? Were there any observed coaching cliques? All of these dynamics may be diagnostic of potential problems (or strengths) that an S&P consultant will want to consider during the consultation process. Once a consultant begins to better understand the role of the coach, regardless of his or her title, the consultant can more effectively facilitate performance-based interventions and assessment within the team/organizational consultation.

It is difficult to overemphasize how context-dependent coaching situations can be. This fact reinforces the notion that becoming familiar with—and perhaps a part of—a coaching subsystem offers the best path to effective consulting. During the first year of my 6-year consultation with a major league baseball team, I discovered that major league hitting coaches and pitching coaches often have unique styles of coaching and player assessment. Both of these performance-specific (pitching and hitting) coaching positions are an oasis for attributional (how people describe outcomes) theory and explanation. If a pitcher was throwing well, it may be attributed to a recent bullpen session or new mechanical adjustment in his throwing motion; yet, if the pitcher was not throwing well, it may be attributed to a tight strike zone by the umpire or the other team having "one of those days where they hit everything!" Although I was aware of the self-defensive, and often effective, nature of attributional explanations for poor performance (Gordon, 2008), it also allowed me to observe how fragile and unstable the coaches felt in their roles. I chose to listen and attend to the coaches (Murphy & Murphy, 2010), and then offer other explorative statements (e.g., "How has this pitcher handled adversity in the past…in the minors?") in order to encourage possible effective problem-solving and so that the coach would hopefully recognize that my role was to support, not criticize, his role in the development of a player. I believe this quiet attentiveness and collaborative exploration with these elite coaches allowed for the development of trust and rapport, which allowed me to be more effective in my consultation with players (during my last 3 years with the major league team, I averaged 14 player consultations on each 3- to 4-day consultation trip. With a roster of 25 active players, I was being utilized by over 50% of the roster).

In creating an effective consultation that enhances the overall performance of a team, business, or organization, the S&P consultant must make great efforts to approach the coaches and leaders with respect, attentiveness (via listening first rather than speaking first), clear boundaries, and appropriate availability (being available for consultation via in-person, e-mail, web-based, or phone platforms). Each S&P consultant needs to follow his or her own "moral compass" regarding how he or she approaches a consultative relationship with a coach.

The Team

As Carron, Martin, and Loughead discuss in Chapter 16 of this volume, understanding each individual team member's role is an essential part of building a high-performing team. How much this will be an integral aspect of an S&P psychologist's intervention with a team depends on the context of consultation and the consultant's goals. If the goal of the consultation is to provide two or three mental skills workshops, then a detailed examination of team member roles may not be an effective use of the consultant's time. However, if the sport psychologist is being contracted to consult with the team for a long period of time and/or if the team is aiming toward a major event (e.g., a 4-year plan in preparation for an Olympic Games), the ongoing process will require a thorough understanding of individual team member roles in order to best facilitate effective consulting in forums such as team meetings and individual consultations.

Clarity about team roles within a team is important for the S&P consultant because different roles may become the foci of differing intervention strategies and goals. There are few short-cuts for conducting a thorough role assessment. The consultant must come to understand the variety of performer roles within the team via interviewing, informal dialogue with team members, and perhaps formal assessment. Initial assumptions based on prior knowledge of a team from the perspective of an outside observer are often wrong or miss the mark. My own experience with a major league baseball team provides a good example. The initial team consultation meeting (after the interview with the general manager, assistant general manager, and player development director) was during spring training. Spring training is a major league baseball ritual, in which teams train and play games in the Grapefruit (Florida) and Cactus (Arizona) Leagues. This 4- to 5-week training period consists of a major and minor league camp. Every major league baseball team has five or six minor league affiliates, and teams have a variety of levels of experience and performance. Triple A teams are the next competitive level down from the major leagues, and there are Double A, Single A (High and Low), Rookie League, and developmental league teams. For major league spring training, 60–65 invited players are often invited to open camp; at the end of spring training a 25-man roster is assigned to the major league team for the season. In my first meeting, I addressed the major league camp participants and coaches. The room held over 75 players and staff. During the next 2 weeks, I focused on learning about each position on the field. I learned about the role of the pitcher (noting differences among starting pitchers, middle relief pitchers, and closers), the designated hitter (a specific position in the American League in which the player only bats and does not play the field, thus leading to increased emphasis on hitting performance), the various fielding positions, and so on. In my journal, I kept notes and observations about how players described their own position, how their teammates described their position, and how the coaching staff (multiple coaches ranging from hitting coaches to field/position instructors to pitching coaches) viewed each position. My purpose was to eventually understand how each team member's role fit within the performance paradigm of the team. I did not want to assume that my previous experience with the game of baseball, as a former player (youth leagues), as a fan, and as a sport psych consultant for collegiate and high school baseball, would bias my understanding of team roles and team organization. Indeed, this was an arduous task, took a great amount of time, consumed a large portion of my initial consultation, and required careful reflection, directed attention, keen observation, and a willingness to say "I don't know" when asked for advice about team roles I did not yet understand.

Perhaps I should emphasize that I believe that, if a consultant does not have experience within a specific sport or performance area, he or she must be honest about this lack of knowledge as he or she begins the consultation. "I don't know" is a perfectly fine answer to many questions, as long as you are open to follow-up exploration and assessment. A strong trend in sport and performance psychology is to see the athlete or performer as the expert; the role of the consultant is to come to understand the strengths and weaknesses of the individual and offer appropriate guidance. There is certainly a temptation to nod wisely and feign understanding as you are inundated with sport-specific information during the beginning stages of a consultation, but, in the long run, an attitude of humility and a keen appreciation of how much you don't know serves best in establishing a successful consulting relationship. A fond memory of my initial interview for the position as the consulting sport psychologist for the U.S. men's alpine ski team is that I was asked at the end of a very enjoyable interview, "So Chris, do you ski?" To which I replied, "Yes...but I'm terrible." In fact, I had only skied five or six times in my life. Upon attending my first "on-hill" training camp (at Beaver Creek, Colorado), it was obvious that I had "limited" alpine skiing skills. Fortunately, the staff and athletes knew what to expect thanks to my initial honesty and were cordial and also receptive to teaching me some skiing skills (mostly how to turn and stop!). Team members were all in agreement that I had been hired due to my sport psychology knowledge, and not my skiing abilities. Had I misrepresented my skiing ability or my knowledge of the sport, it would have been an obvious mistake. Instead, my lack of knowledge became a helpful assessment component of my consultation. It was amazing to discover how receptive an elite alpine athlete could be in discussing the basics of ski racing on a 20-minute chairlift ride. I believe that my early decision to admit my lack of knowledge, be humble in learning the sport, and be more of an "asker" than a "teller" during my first year led to my being able to maintain a 10-year relationship with the U.S. men's alpine team.

I have always believed that a "one size fits all" consultation model does not yield optimal results and, in fact, may invoke resistance and doubt among the clients if they believe that the consultants' interventions are not based on an appropriate understanding of their specific sport and culture. When the service provided does not match the specific needs of the client, the consultation is destined for conflict and challenge. There are several good discussions of the "what," "where," "when," "why," and "who" of an applied S&P consultation model (Andersen, 2000; Ravizza, 1988). Let me offer some suggestions based on my consulting experiences:

- Be a great listener. Ask questions about each member's role.
- Prior to the consultation, do research on the sport/culture/history of the team you are working with. Be wary of attending to the traditional media and to social websites such as blogs, listservs, or chat groups for your research, as these are often biased and inflammatory. I have found that team websites and organization websites (e.g., NBA.com) can give you some basic information regarding the prospective client, but the details you must get on your own.
- Ask direct and clear questions of the management (e.g., general manager) and coaching staff regarding the roles of the various team members.

- Speak directly with the team members (athletes/performers) and be engaged in informal dialogue and communication regarding their specific roles on the team. For example, "What do you see is the most important task you perform for your team?"
- Seek opportunities to interact without being intrusive. When an opportunity evolves (e.g., a player comes and sits next to you), engage with them informally regarding their position or role on the team. For example, "I noticed you played more minutes in the game last night. Does that change the confidence you have about your team role?"
- When in doubt concerning the nature of performance issues, seek an answer from players, coaches, or staff.
- Be aware of how much time you spend with any particular athlete or team member. There are often underlying team issues related to preferential treatment from coaches, etc. Make sure that you spend fair and equal time with team members you work with.
- Be aware of your interactions with coaches in the presence of team members. I have found it helpful to clarify with team members at initial meetings with them that I will be talking with coaches at practices and competitions, but that these conversations will concern overall team observations and coaching interactions. I emphasize that I will never discuss specific players with a coach without their permission. I have found it helpful to clarify this coach–consultant interaction dynamic early; otherwise, it may become an issue as team members worry, "Are they talking about me?"
- Trust your ethical training and your own moral compass. Occasionally re-read Doug Hankes' chapter on Ethics. Schedule regular supervision or peer consultation concerning your practice.

Challenges and Pitfalls

Many challenges and potential pitfalls are associated with the practice of applied S&P psychology consulting. One of the most challenging aspects of this profession is that performance consulting very often does not conform to the expectations of practice generated during graduate training and during postdoctoral experiences. Most performance consultants work with athletes, performing artists, or business organizations by going to their workplace. It is common to conduct evaluations, meetings, and team-building sessions on-site. The traditional

50-minute therapy hour in the practitioner's office simply does not apply to the world of performance consulting. Others have described the "outside-the-box" approach that must be utilized when working with high performers, often on the road, in very informal consultation settings, and sometimes under extreme time pressure (Ravizza, 2001; Andersen, Van Raalte, & Brewer, 2001). It is useful if the S&P consultant can anticipate some of these situations and be prepared to deal with them effectively. The following are some major challenges I have encountered and identified during my consultations across a variety of performance domains.

Am I a Performance Coach or a Psychologist?

A unique challenge was presented to me before my first interactions with the major league baseball team described earlier in this chapter. The assistant general manager wanted to present me to the organization as the new "performance coach." Because my role was to provide performance enhancement services, he believed that the title "psychologist" would engender possible avoidance by players. Interestingly, during my interactions with the coaching staff, I had noted in my journal that many of these major league baseball coaches had concerns about support staff (e.g., strength and conditioning coaches) who wore baseball uniforms as all the major league and minor league managers and coaches do. These coaches had expressed doubt about the practice to me, and they seemed resistant, and in some cases resentful, of the support staff in question. I suspected that if I used the word "coach" to describe myself in any form with this organization, I would be creating some resistance at the outset of the consultation. I had a respectful discussion with the assistant general manager regarding my concerns and suggested that "I'm a psychologist...how about calling my position a 'performance psychologist'?" He agreed, and that was the title I used.

The take-home message I drew from this experience is that, as professionals, we should clearly present and ethically market ourselves commensurate with our training and credentials. A licensed psychologist with specialized training in sport and performance psychology should be guided by licensure and professional standards at all times, even when performing in novel environments. Of course, practicing within one's area of competence is a fundamental principle that must be adhered to at all times.

"Castaway": Dealing with Isolation As an S&P Consultant

Doing S&P consulting is often isolating and lonely. Our work usually requires extensive travel, long periods spent away from home and family, and extended periods of informal interaction with clients, at all hours of the day. It is important that the S&P consultant utilize effective strategies and resources to cope with any associated emotional and social discomfort, which can be quite normal. Often, when traveling with a professional or elite team, I made a conscious decision to head alone to my hotel room upon our arrival in a new city, even though I had been invited by the coaches (and sometimes players) to meet in the hotel bar for drinks and food. By my own choice, I kindly declined and went to my room to order room service. Making this decision may have sometimes made me appear socially aloof to clients, but I always believed that this choice allowed me to avoid potential conflicts, such as dual relationship or perhaps confidentiality issues arising from socializing with athletes, coaches, or other performers. The cost was that I did have to manage feelings of isolation and loneliness. However, I feel that the benefits of the "better safe than sorry" approach outweighed the costs. In speaking with other consultants with similar working experiences, it is clear that these feelings of loneliness can potentially lead to behaviors that can be harmful to the consultative relationship. It is all too easy to justify behaviors that may be ethically questionable ("What could be wrong with a few drinks with the team to build rapport?"). To avoid the potential ethical pitfalls related to the consultant's feelings of isolation (being a "castaway"), a professional orientation and clarity concerning the consultation role will guide the S&P psychologist toward an optimal outcome. As I discuss below, regular peer consultation or supervision is also an excellent way to stay grounded.

Hack (2005) encourages consumer education regarding the selection of an S&P psychologist, including determining the "right fit" based on the personality, skill level, and experience of the consultant. Educated consumers, including sports organizations as well as individual coaches and athletes, also need to assess the background of potential S&P consultants, including their experience in providing consultation with teams, so that they can better assess the career maturity of the consultant.

Managing Conflict and Role Definition

It is important that the S&P consultant define his or her role clearly at the onset of the consultation.

A potential pitfall is presenting oneself as focusing on "performance" issues and mental training only, and then beginning to provide individual counseling on personal issues such as relationship counseling, substance abuse, or a mood disorder resulting from a season-ending injury. The more ambiguous the consultant presents him- or herself in the initial meetings and interactions, the more risk there is of role confusion. This confusion may create distance, suspicion, doubt, and distrust in the team members and coaching staff. One of the techniques I have used in past consultations is the development of a one-page information sheet regarding my role with the team. This has been very useful with teams/organizations that have either had no prior experience with a sport and performance psychologist, or a team that has had previous S&P consultation. In this brief one-page summary (see Appendix A), I provide all of my contact information (cell phone, office phone, e-mail address), my specific role with the team, some "do's and don'ts" of my role with the team, and how my consultation will occur (e.g., my availability and times I will be with the team). I believe that if you have provided the team members and coaches with this clearly defined role (which has been reviewed and approved by the management), then you may avoid the potential pitfall of role confusion and conflict.

Dealing with Success and Failure as a Consultant

In my early career, I spent 4 years as a substance abuse counselor for adolescent clients in both inpatient and outpatient settings. I learned in that field that "if you take credit for each patient who recovers, you have to take credit for each one who relapses." As the relapse rate in my area was over 80%, I learned how to focus my efforts on my therapeutic skills and interventions and not take therapy outcomes personally. The seductive side of sport and performance psychology is that it is all too easy to begin to take credit for client successes.

At sport psychology conferences, I find it perplexing that some speakers always highlight the successful consultations they have had with teams. Yet these same presenters never discuss situations when the team *was not successful*. The underlying message I believe is often conveyed in our field is that "my clients are successful because of my work with them." This is the seductive nature of sport and performance psychology consulting, that it is easy to associate with success and possible for consultants to take credit for an athlete's gold medal or a team's tournament victory.

I strongly suggest that consultants be wary of the attributions being made in the marketing of our services. Be careful of offering the message that: "If you use my services, your team will be successful, just like these other teams I've worked with (and then list the successful teams)." I believe our focus should be on our skill sets, our relationships, our professional behaviors, our intervention abilities, our assessment skills, and our ability to work in an ethical and competent manner. It is impossible for us to quantify or measure our role in the success of our clients, and I think it is potentially damaging to client relationships and to long-term success in this field to continually draw attention to successful relationships with athletes and other performers who have achieved high levels of success through dedication and sacrifice that most can only imagine.

Now, do I believe that sport and performance psychology applications and consultation are effective? Absolutely. But I caution against attributing too much of the success of our clients to the results of our consultation work. In fact, I have found that the best way to evaluate my consultation success is by measuring utilization (by coaches, athletes, teams) and successful implementation of consultation interventions. So many elements outside anyone's control influence the results of competitions and performance, that a more realistic evaluation of our programs and services can be obtained when a consultant measures his or her success based upon the controllable aspects of the consultation process. Tod and Andersen (2005) discuss the important components of successful consultation, including relationship-building skills, technical competence of the consultant, and satisfaction with the consultation based upon athlete and coach feedback. Success of the team is not mentioned as a characteristic of a successful consultant.

The other obvious risk of taking credit for a team's success is the inevitable blame placed on the consultant if the team loses. It may be helpful to accept and acknowledge that an S&P consultant may provide an excellent consultation experience (based upon collaborative relationships, working alliances, skilled interventions/assessment, team/coach satisfaction); however, his or her contract may still be terminated after a team's unsuccessful season as the new management attempts to rebuild the organizational structure of the team. Perhaps we should follow the advice we often give to our clients: "control the controllables." This approach allows the consultant to focus more appropriately on enhancing professional knowledge, relationship-building skills, and the ability to engage in an effective manner with a variety of clients.

Strategies to Enhance Consultant Effectiveness

The world of sport and performance psychology consultation is indeed multilayered, complex, and dynamic. Multiple relationships, competitive pressures, and achieving acceptance within the performance domain are all important issues to address. In reflecting on my own experiences in sport psychology, I am able to offer the following suggestions for strategies to maintain a high level of personal functioning and effectiveness in this challenging field. The rewards are certainly worth it. I once provided a 3-year consultation with the U.S. Navy Officer Candidate School (OCS), where I thought my biggest challenge would be convincing the U.S. Marine Corps Drill Instructors of the importance of mental skills training. In fact, they were my biggest supporters and served an invaluable role in helping me understand the performance tasks facing Naval officers, and the challenges and demands of an intense 13-week training period. When I shared my appreciation for their support after one of my staff briefings during an OCS visit, a gunnery sergeant smiled and replied, "Doc, if what you can teach them saves one Marine's life, then this is worth it." It was indeed a somber reminder that sometimes our work may impact an outcome other than on-the-field wins and losses. I hope the following suggestions and strategies will be useful for sport and performance consultants in a variety of domains.

Self-Awareness

In any consultation, effective implementation requires constant evaluation and self-assessment regarding the interplay of relationships among the S&P consultant and the coach, team, and support staff. What do I mean by "self" assessment? I am referring to one's ability to accurately monitor one's process dynamics in the multifaceted role of consultation. The consultant must be aware of his or her role with each of the elements within the team: the coach, the team members, and the staff. The fluid dynamics of these roles must be vigilantly monitored. How best to maintain this self-awareness? I have found that an effective process of maintaining self-awareness comes via journaling and peer/collegial consultation. These strategies allow me to establish a baseline of self-reflections and observations, and pair them with objective feedback and assessment from trusted colleagues.

JOURNALING

As part of my practice, I keep a number of reflective journals. Whenever I start a consultation with a new team/organization, I begin a new journal. It contains my initial reflections from the interview (phone, on-site), my impressions of the management, and my research on the team/organization history. As I prepare consultations, the journal becomes a reflective tool that I review to help determine appropriate interventions. It also contains my account of all interventions (e.g., team talks, individual consults). My reflections, observations, frustrations, and perceived successes are noted. I have found that journaling allows me to monitor my own motivation, enthusiasm, and conflicted emotions, and re-reading entries after a period of reflection often offers greater clarity on sometimes confusing situations.

I continue this self-monitoring as I receive feedback from coaches, team members, and other staff. For example, during one of my consultations with an Olympic sport team, I noted during a review of my journal (most likely on a long day of air travel) that I was addressing one coach's regular and consistent complaints about an athlete's lack of successful performance during each previous camp consultation. Yet, I discovered that I was quickly sharing solutions rather than listening. This journal review allowed me to set a goal of being an active and attentive listener during the upcoming camp, especially with this specific coach, which took our relationship to a more effective level. Describing the "spiritual fitness module" he helped develop with the U.S. Army, Martin Seligman states the importance of "self-awareness" (which I believe is the primary goal of journaling) as: "Self-awareness involves reflection and introspection to gain insights into life's pressing questions. These questions pertain to identity, purpose, meaning, truth in the world, being authentic, creating a life worth living, and fulfilling one's potential" (2011, p. 150). Isn't this our goal when working with our clients? If indeed it is, then wouldn't it make sense that the same intervention would enhance our own role as sport and performance psychologists?

Collegial Support and Consultation

An effective strategy to address the isolation, confusion of roles, and resolution of potential dual relationships or confusing ethical dilemmas facing S&P psychologists is asking for assistance from trusted peers and colleagues. Looking back on my career, my most important support has been the mentorship and guidance of colleagues. An effective consultant should develop a relationship with a trusted mentor, one who has engaged in S&P consultation, with whom they can arrange regular and consistent contacts (via phone, e-mail, in-person). When a consultant feels the isolation of being the sole provider of sport and performance psychology services with an organization, there can be a tendency to become myopic and tunnel-visioned concerning interventions. A mentor and colleague may be able to offer alternative perspectives to help break roadblocks, sharing intervention suggestions or further assessment strategies to help guide the consultation. This consultation is similar to but may not be the same as supervision, which has been discussed within the sport psychology literature (Van Raalte & Andersen, 2005). Peer-based collegial consultation is based on shared experiences, openness to feedback, an opportunity to self-disclose concerns about the consultation, and willingness seek guidance from a peer.

In my own career, I have sought peer feedback and consultation on at least a monthly basis. When dealing with difficult or confusing situations, or challenging moments during the consultation (e.g., a team's losing streak, or preparation for championships), I have found it extremely helpful to speak with a colleague and listen to his or her observations and reflections. The field of sport and performance psychology offers many opportunities to build collaborative relationships and supportive colleagues. Graduate faculty, graduate student peers, other peer professionals met via conferences, and even networking with active consultants may provide beneficial environments to create collegial networks. Although technology does support listservs, blogs, chat rooms, and the like, I think it is wise to arrange a face-to-face meeting with a potential collaborative colleague prior to engaging in any consultative relationship.

I can provide an example of an excellent collegial support group that developed accidentally in 2005, but which has led to an ongoing professional support process. In 2005, I was approached by members of the NCAA and asked to coordinate a seminar that focused on collegiate student athlete mental health issues. The NCAA had been dealing with member institution (Division I, II, III) concerns about sport psychology and the role of sport psychologists in addressing student athlete mental health concerns. I contacted approximately 25 colleagues who were licensed mental health providers (e.g., counseling/clinical psychologists) and who worked in full-time, part-time, or specifically defined (e.g., contracted as consultants) roles with collegiate athletics departments. The group met at the NCAA Headquarters in Indianapolis, Indiana, in February 2005, for one and a half days; the *NCAA News* published an overview of the meeting shortly after (Brutlag Hosick, 2005). During the meeting, many of us commented on how rewarding and rare it was to discuss the difficult issues we face at work with others who did the same type of work and had the same type of training. This collegial support and dialogue established during the meeting was to become the foundation of an ongoing support network.

Shortly after the conclusion of the NCAA seminar, a group of attendees discussed establishing an ongoing retreat for the group. Members felt a smaller, more informal gathering would engender more honest and direct dialogue and sharing. This commitment by the initial group has now led to an annual meeting, held for the past 6 years after the beginning of each year, in a Western ski resort. The initial meeting at this site gathered 23 professionals (using the same criteria initially utilized in the 2005 NCAA meeting); the most recent meeting in 2011 had 53 attendees, and the evidence suggests the meeting will continue to grow. Although the small and intimate nature of the initial meeting has changed somewhat (we still encourage smaller groups and discussions in lunch breaks, on ski chairlifts, and in après ski lounges), the rise in attendance demonstrates the increasing role of full-time/part-time licensed counseling/clinical sport psychologists and mental health providers in the collegiate athletics environment. More importantly, it provides a small (90–100 members) network of similarly trained and practicing professionals who can ask questions, collect data, share clinical forms/handouts, and seek confidential collegial consultation from each other. I coordinate the ongoing meeting (it is also supported by my employer), and attendees are invited based upon (1) meeting the criteria for the first meeting, (2) presenting on a topic that has been requested by the attendees/group dialogue (e.g., post-meeting evaluations), or (3) offering unique contributions to the specific issues related to psychological health issues of elite athletes. It is truly an enriching and professionally rewarding experience for all of us.

Continuing Education

The field of sport and performance psychology seems to change daily. Research from the positive psychology movement, the development of new positions within collegiate athletics, the evolution of sports medicine performance centers that incorporate sport and performance psychology as a core of their service provision—all represent both challenges and opportunities in our field. The American Psychological Association (APA), the Division of Exercise and Sport Psychology in APA (Division 47), the Association for Applied Sport Psychology (AASP), and the American College of Sports Medicine (ACSM) all have annual conferences, regional conferences, websites, and continuing education opportunities to further enhance a professionals' skills and consultation knowledge.

Technology

I admit that I'm an "old school" guy. When I was a graduate assistant football coach at Ball State University, I actually cut film to compile the special team's film review for each game. I would spend over 8 hours each Sunday just cutting film and then splicing it together, so that 20–25 film strips would be hanging in our office awaiting processing. Now, the video from a college football game is sitting on each coach's computer as soon as the game is finished. The rapid evolution of technology in our lifetimes is more than amazing.

An effective S&P consultant must have the ability to learn about new technology and potential applications within a consultation role. The ability to download video quickly onto an iPad device and review it with an athlete to reinforce an intervention is one example of incorporating technology into practice. I believe technological advances also create potential ethical concerns (e.g., client data storage, accessibility to data being visible to others) of which the consultant needs to be aware. Consultants must seek to learn or develop best practice procedures in this sphere to minimize potential harm to the client. Additionally, familiarity with technology allows consultants to stay abreast of events in the world of their clients. For example, each day, I review websites related to my consultation contracts: the team website, local news websites, national sports news websites, and other relevant media. This helps me to gather information and, often, find out about potential issues (e.g., an

athlete's injury) prior to my contact with the team. It is also a fact of life that most high performers are themselves "early adopters" of new technologies as they continually seek a performance edge, so it behooves us as consultants to be familiar with this rapidly changing area (Murphy, 2011). I highly recommend that consultants take due diligence in understanding the effectiveness of technology and how to incorporate it into their practice. To remain a "dinosaur" may in fact lead to your extinction as a consultant!

Conclusion

My goal in this chapter was to share insights gained from my consulting experiences and the relevant performance literature regarding some of the dynamics and challenges facing S&P psychology consultants, and potential strategies to address these issues and maximize consultant effectiveness. An important first step for consultants is to clarify their orientation and professional identity. I discussed how a consultant can best organize the consultation process when working in a high-performance team environment. I then discussed the key subsystems that comprise the high-performance organization, focusing on organization staff, the coaching staff, and the team itself, and discussed how to clarify one's role with each subsystem, utilizing a systems perspective. Finally, I discussed some of the challenges facing psychologists working in high-performance settings and offered strategies for dealing with issues such as isolation, confidentiality, dual relationships, and the seductive nature of performance consulting. Although challenging, I have found that a career in high-performance consulting is very satisfying and personally rewarding, and I hope that we can encourage many more new professionals to join us in further developing and enhancing this important field.

References

Andersen, M. (Ed.). (2000). *Doing sport psychology*. Champaign, IL: Human Kinetics Publishers.

Andersen, M. B., Van Raalte, J. L., & Brewer, B. W. (2001). Sport psychology service delivery: Staying ethical while keeping loose. *Professional Psychology: Research and Practice, 32*, 12–18.

Association for Applied Sport Psychology. (n.d.). *Become a certified consultant.* Retrieved from http://appliedsportpsych.org/consultants/become-certified

Brutlag Hosick, M. (2005). Forum places psychological focus on mental health issues. *NCAA News, February 28, 2005.*

Coffey, W. (2005). *The boys of winter.* New York: Crown Publishers.

Fletcher, T. B., Benshoff, J. M., & Richburg, M. J. (2003). A systems approach to understanding and counseling college student-athletes. *Journal of College Counseling, 6,* 35–45.

Gordon, R. A.(2008). Attributional style and athletic performance: Strategic optimism and defensive pessimism. *Psychology of Sport and Exercise, 9,* 336–350.

Hack, B. (2005). Qualifications: Education and experience. In S. Murphy (Ed.), *The sport psych handbook* (pp. 293–304). Champaign, IL: Human Kinetics Publishers.

Hays, K. F., & Brown, C. H. (2004). *You're on! Consulting for peak performance.* Washington, DC: American Psychological Association.

McCann, S. C. (2000). Doing sport psychology at the really big show. In M. Andersen (Ed.), *Doing sport psychology* (pp. 209–223). Champaign, IL: Human Kinetics Publishers.

McCann, S. (2005). Roles: The sport psychologist. In S. Murphy (Ed.), *The sport psych handbook* (pp. 279–291). Champaign, IL: Human Kinetics Publishers.

Minuchin, S. (1974). *Families and family therapy.* Cambridge, MA: Harvard University Press.

Murphy, S. M. (2011, August). Technology for performance and sport psychology consultants. In K. Hays (Chair), *Sport/performance psychology: How to expand in media, technology, and telecommunications.* Symposium conducted at the annual meeting of the American Psychological Association, Washington, DC.

Murphy, S. M., & Murphy, A. I. (2010). Attending and listening. In S. J. Hanrahan & M. B. Andersen (Eds.), *Routledge handbook of applied sport psychology: A comprehensive guide for students and practitioners* (pp. 12–10). London: Routledge.

Price, F. L., & Andersen, M. B. (2000). Into the maelstrom: A five-year relationship from college ball to the NFL. In M. Andersen (Ed.), *Doing sport psychology* (pp. 193–206). Champaign, IL: Human Kinetics Publishers.

Ravizza, K. (1988). Gaining entry with athletic personnel for season-long consulting. *The Sport Psychologist, 4,* 330–340.

Ravizza, K. (2001). Reflections and insights from the field on performance-enhancement consultation. In G. Tenenbaum (Ed.), *The practice of sport psychology* (pp. 197–215) Morgantown, WV: Fitness Information Technology.

Seligman, M. E. P. (2011). *Flourish: A visionary new understanding of happiness and well-being.* New York: Free Press.

Senge, P. M. (1990). *The fifth discipline: The art and practice of the learning organization.* New York: Doubleday.

Tammen, V. V. (2000). First internship experiences, or, what I did on holiday. In M. Andersen (Ed.), *Doing sport psychology* (pp. 181–192). Champaign, IL: Human Kinetics Publishers.

Tod, D., & Andersen, M. (2005). Success in sport psych: Effective sport psychologists. In S. Murphy (Ed.), *The sport psych handbook* (pp. 305–314), Champaign, IL: Human Kinetics Publishers.

Van Raalte, J. L., & Andersen, M. B. (2005). Supervision I: From models to doing. In M. B. Andersen (Ed.), *Doing sport psychology* (153–166). Champaign, IL: Human Kinetics Publishers.

Whelan, J. P., Meyers, A. W., & Donovan, C. (1995). Competitive recreational athletes: A multisystemic model. In S. M. Murphy (Ed.), *Sport psychology interventions* (pp. 71–116). Champaign, IL: Human Kinetics.

Appendix A

Sport Psychology Services

Indiana Fever Basketball Team
Chris Carr, Ph.D., HSPP
Sport and Performance Psychologist
St. Vincent Sports Performance
Indianapolis, IN 46260
(317) XXX-XXXX/office/private voicemail
(317) XXX-XXXX/cell
cmcarr@stvincent.org

Welcome to the 2010 Indiana Fever basketball season! In an effort to provide all players and coaches with the "tools" toward optimal performance, Dr. Carr will be available to provide sport and performance psychology consultation during the 2010 season. Dr. Carr is a sport psychologist and Coordinator of the Sport and Performance Psychology Program at St. Vincent Sports Performance in Indianapolis, Indiana. He was previously the sport psychologist at the Methodist Sports Medicine Center in Indianapolis (2000–2006) and was (1995–2000) at The Ohio State University, where he was the Director of Sport Psychology Services for the OSU Athletic Department. He was previously the sport psychologist at Arizona State University and Washington State University. He was the Sport Psychologist for the USA Diving National Team (2004–2008) and was the Sport Psychologist for the U.S. Men's Alpine Ski Team from 1992–2002; he has been involved in four Olympic Games. A former college football player and graduate assistant football coach, Dr. Carr was the Team Psychologist for the Arizona Cardinals of the NFL during the 1994 season. He is beginning his ninth season as the Sport Psychologist for the Indiana Fever, and will be available for any player who desires performance psychology consultation.

What is sport and performance psychology? It relates to the "mental" aspects of basketball, including concentration skills, confidence, pre-performance mental routines, and mental strategies for enhanced performance. Elite athletes are often very aware of their physical and technical skills and how to develop themselves into better athletes. However, the mental aspect of sport is often overlooked or assumed. Basketball players recognize the phrases such as "being in a slump," which often refers to confidence and focus. To develop mental skills that will enhance your performance is the goal of sport and performance psychology. This resource is offered by the organization to help players develop mental strategies that will enhance their basketball performance and personal well-being. Other issues related to performance, such as relationships, recovery from injury, self-confidence, and adjustment to a new team can be discussed as well.

Dr. Carr will be available for in-person consultations during the season. During the season, Dr. Carr will be at practices and some competitions. Any player can request an individual (confidential) meeting with Dr. Carr. Additionally, he will be available at all times via phone or e-mail with any interested player. There will be performance psychology materials made available to players during the season and upon request. When Dr. Carr is with the team, you can think of him as a "performance consultant," who is there to help you with mental skills preparation as a professional basketball player. His experience and knowledge will help you to create your own optimal mental routine for basketball and personal performance, as well as support you when personal issues cause stress and distraction in your life.

The Performance Coach

Dave Collins *and* Sara Kamin

Abstract

The performance coach (PC) is an increasingly ubiquitous feature of many performance environments. Often seen as having its genesis in the sport environment, this performance emphasis for PCs stands interestingly at odds with a groundswell of opinion against such a sole focus for sport practitioners. This chapter considers this tension, together with the objectives underpinning knowledge and modus operandi that can represent good practice in PCing. Through this means, we offer a position statement on the PC field, examining concerns and highlighting issues for its future progression.

Key Words: Expertise, professional practice, skill development, coaching, professional judgment and decision making

"A Rose by Any Other Name"

In addressing an apparently clear topic—performance coaching (PCing)—readers may ask why a debate about the job title is an appropriate or even necessary starting point. We would contend, however, especially in such a new and emerging area, that such exploration is a good way to clarify many salient points, including what we are trying to do, how, and on the basis of what training and bodies of knowledge. Thus, even though we employ the commonly used term *performance coach* (or PC) throughout, a number of issues emerge from this usage, all with implications for preparation, modus operandi, and outcome deliverables within this (potentially and presently?) amorphous new profession.

In simple terms, the issue may be conceptualized as the focus of the work. Should the practitioner (irrespective, for the moment, of training and theoretical orientation) focus on the client's issues, the performance outcome, or the variables affecting the performance outcome as the primary focus? Slightly more subtly, is the individual as a whole person, the individual in that particular domain, or the

performance in the domain the primary deliverable? We will explore the challenges of this "trichotomy" later. For the moment, note the complex permutations that result when this potentially orthogonal "triple thrust" interacts with the bewildering array of practitioners and clients. In this regard, we quote our distinguished editor (that's you Shane) in his original commissioning communication:

> The impetus for this chapter comes from the current situation where many sport psychologists, psychologists, and non-psychologists are working with clients in the performing arts, business, medicine and so on, using sport psychology concepts, theories and strategies.

Of course, Shane's statement is quite apart from all those therapists whose orientation could be said to focus *solely* on the individual and his or her personal welfare, irrespective of his other performance domain. For the majority of those who place themselves in the performance field (as apart from the clinical, psychotherapeutic, etc.), however, this issue has only recently emerged. For example, consider the sport-focused "debate" between Mellalieu and Lane (2009) or the interesting points made by Mark Andersen (2005, 2009). Despite this apparently recent emergence, we would have to say that it has been "bubbling under" for as long as we have been working in applied performance psychology. From our perspective, as we will hopefully demonstrate in this chapter, explicit consideration of the various components has commonly and historically been lacking. These authors are quite correct in highlighting the sensible and clear issues of professionalism (e.g., confidentiality) or conceptual clarity (e.g., anxiety, or the "purpose" of mental imagery as performance enhancer or therapeutic device—cf. Holmes & Collins, 2001). However, we feel that a more fundamental debate on what *performance* psychology is actually for seems necessary. After all, the questioning of the performance focus seems to generate some heat. Consider this quote, again from Andersen (2009).

> Foregrounding performance enhancement as our métier places a behaviour above the person, and that placement sits on a slippery slope that can lead to dehumanisation, exploitation, and other forms of abuse.
> (p. 13)

Accordingly, it would seem that consideration of the key elements of work as a PC would be useful. Since we are unlikely to arrive at definitive answers in one chapter, we take a broad and propositional stance, in that ideas are presented and discussed rather than definite positions arrived at—although we will indicate our own stance throughout.

Throughout the chapter, two clear sets of guidelines are developed. The first, emerging from a critical consideration of the content and mechanisms for PC interventions, will offer a digest of what we do and therefore what we need to know or to discover; one list caters more to practitioners, the other to researchers. The second set of guidelines will relate gaps in our knowledge, coupled with how we may best develop expertise in the field, and emerges from consideration of expert characteristics and abilities in psychologically based support. These lists will be populated throughout the chapter, so both scientists and practitioners should stay engaged. But first, as a basis for the whole debate, we want to briefly examine the history of our profession(s).

Where Have We Come From: Where Is the Knowledge Base Based?

Although listing the knowledge required is an important step to the effective delineation and future promotion of PCing, we would also suggest that some careful and critical consideration is paid to qualitative aspects of that knowledge; to what might be described as the epistemological origin of the knowledge and the techniques that consequently accrue. In this respect, our contention is that different aims for any science discipline (or more accurately subdiscipline) generate distinctly different "flavors" of knowledge. This is certainly the case in sport psychology, which could arguably be seen as the parent discipline to PCing. Consider what we have previously described as the "three ages of a support science" (Collins, 2008). These are:

- *Psychology through performance.* Psychology researchers test ideas in various laboratories, one of which is a performance domain (e.g., a psychologist tests if people have increased activation in the "happiness" areas in the brain after engagement in activities they like, such as exercise/musical performance/dance, etc.).
- *Psychology of performance.* Researchers investigate and develop sport (or dance or music or business, etc.) -specific theories or domain-named variants of mainstream theories through examination of performers (e.g., the development of a theory of "X construct for Y," such as a psychological skills inventory for dance).
- *Psychology for performance.* Researchers and support providers utilize psychological principles and methodologies to benefit the performance of specific individuals, teams or groups (e.g., intra-individual or team/group specific work focused on understanding and enhancing performance for this particular group rather than theory development).

This progression is certainly in part chronological, in that a mainstream "parent" discipline will usually host endeavors in different domains before such study begins to establish itself as a distinct subdiscipline. Only latterly do discipline-domain specialists start to emerge, developing their own distinct knowledge base, modus operandi, and ethical standards (cf. Carr, 1999). Readers are invited to consider the current evolutionary stage of knowledge in their own performance domain.

More pertinently for the purposes of this chapter, however, once a certain evolutionary stage is reached, all three stages will exist in parallel. Thus, peer-reviewed knowledge will be generated from all three perspectives; indeed, from an access perspective, more from the second than the other two. Accordingly, research-practitioner knowledge is more likely to be influenced by domain-specific "science" than on research focused on performance support, the third or "science for performance" stage. By contrast, more descriptive ideographic (but less publishable?) material from this third stage is most likely to drive forward support-practitioner behavior.

This key qualitative difference is pervasive across the literature of any PC domain and results in the generation of much that is publication-focused rather than on the applied implications per se. As an example, consider the wide diversity in the definition of "elite" applied to participant recruitment in the sport science literature. To our eyes, elite seems to cover a multitude of levels, from National Collegiate Athletics Association (NCAA) Division III to World/Olympic medalists, indeed multimedalists, with often little or no acknowledgment of the vast differentials that certainly apply between these extremes. Other performance domains demonstrate a similarly alarming span, particularly in the performing arts, where the appellation of "professional" dancer or musician (for example) can accurately be applied to a very broad ability span.

Our point here is not one of academic snobbery, but rather to highlight that significant qualitative and quantitative differences are likely to exist in many aspects of the knowledge upon which PCs may draw. Add to this the undoubted confounds that will be associated with the experimental design and interpretation of knowledge for these different approaches and the PC scientist-practitioner may well find the foundations of his knowledge to be less firm than first sight suggests.

So, as one specific issue, consider the initial objectives and consequent provenance of knowledge in sport psychology. Was it really grounded on a performance enhancement focus (our third "age") or rather grown out of psychologists' research through and of sport? As highlighted above, what about the nature of the subject pools on which our sport knowledge is based? It *may* be that many aspects of the older and more established discipline of sport psychology (at least from a performance enhancement perspective) also suffer from the concerns we raise for PCs. Be that as it may; on with developing the two sets of guidelines that we hinted at earlier.

What Is the PC Trying to Achieve, and What Does He or She Need to Know?
Performance Versus Individual Welfare: Which Is the Appropriate Focus?

We return to this emerging debate about the "correct" focus of the PC's efforts. In fact, until the idea of a focus other than performance for performance psychologists was highlighted by a reviewer on one of our submissions, it hadn't even occurred to us! Curse us as unfeeling philistines if you will; however, we submit that many of the arguments against a performance focus are based on other features of professional practice rather than just the curmudgeonly nature of practitioner that, some suggest, inevitably results (cf. the earlier quote from Mark Andersen). We offer a variety of exemplars and evidence for this contention throughout.

In our experience, the best answer to this particular conundrum is a focus on the quality of process. Long hours can be spent debating set standards for targets and outcomes but, in reality, these are likely to be as diverse as the clientele—and the clientele for PCing is already extremely diverse! As evidence, consider a recently completed survey into perceptions of business coaching, clearly for many practitioners a key component of their PC portfolio.

In a commissioned research report for the influential *Harvard Business Review*, Coutu and Kauffman (2009) provided a comprehensive picture of the extremely diverse expectations, views, purposes, and preferences of business coaches. An additional and positive feature of this report was the inclusion of short "commentaries" by leading members of the coaching community. The various detailed outcomes of the report can best be summarized in this quote: "Commentators and coaches alike felt that the bar needed to be raised in various areas for the industry to mature, but there was no consensus on how this could be done" (p. 92). We hope that this offers some endorsement to our proposed "process focus" as the best way forward. It is also relevant, however, to note the strong performance emphasis that, unsurprisingly to us at least, was stressed by this survey. A mere surface probe of the expectations of performance managers[1] in sport will reveal a similar and overriding concern with performance enhancement. This was certainly the case with a government-sponsored survey in England a few years back (Abbott et al., 1999). A similar focus was found more recently in dance (Botting & Collins, 2005). To get a completely current picture, one need only read the mission statements of sport science institutes, dance academies, and music conservatoires to see this performance focus made explicit.

The other factor to note from the Coutu and Kauffman (2009) report is the apparent lack of awareness in consumers of exactly what a PC is, how he or she is trained and accredited, and (therefore?)

perhaps how PC usage may best be employed (at least across the business setting, which is the focus for this report). There is a general lack of systematic research across other performance domains in this regard, although our personal experience would suggest that these confusions are far from unique to the business domain. Interestingly, when similar surveys have been completed, they yield equally confused pictures (e.g., Wilson, Gilbert, Gilbert, & Damanpour, 2006).

Of course, there is another possible explanation to our stance. It may well be that, as confirmed performance enhancers, we are the victims of social constructivism (cf. Shunk, 2000) and a Pygmalion or Rosenthal effect; in short, we see what we expect to see. Thus, to be completely certain, specific research is needed that pursues identification of the objectives and expectations of clients, while recognizing that they too are subject to these same pressures. For the moment, let us suggest that clients will normally move toward a specialist whose job title implies that their needs may be fulfilled. Reflecting this need-driven agenda, performance psychologists tend to be consulted by clients who wish to enhance their performance.

Although we await such specific investigation—despite feeling it rather pointless—another aspect of the Coutu and Kauffman (2009) survey may offer further insight. Figure 37.1 offers a schematic representation of the potential overlap between consulting (in this business context, a pure performance focus) and therapy (representative, perhaps, of the individual welfare focus espoused by Andersen). The central (representative of the PC) box offers some process markers that describe perceptions of a service that, while focused on improving future performance, acknowledges the need for individual critical reflection and development, both within and without the specific domain.

There are some issues that readers may raise (e.g., the "focuses on the past" label for therapy) but perhaps this is the best current answer: that working on performance will almost inevitably involve addressing other aspects of the individual: humanitarian, albeit with an additional (superordinate) purpose (cf. Whelan, Meyers & Donovan, 1995, although notably with recreational athletes). Certainly, this position reflects our own working style while still reflecting the performance emphasis that seems to drive clients to seek our support and/or why we may be employed by an interested or professionally engaged third party (e.g., parents, agents, coaches, managers, etc.). In short, the jury may still be out, but there seems to be strong evidence that a performance focus is the most logical for PCs, especially when contracted by a third party such as a team, company, or group.

So, What Should the Practitioner Know?

Just for the moment, accept the contention that a PC's role is to do with performance. As such, many of the mental skills developed and refined to

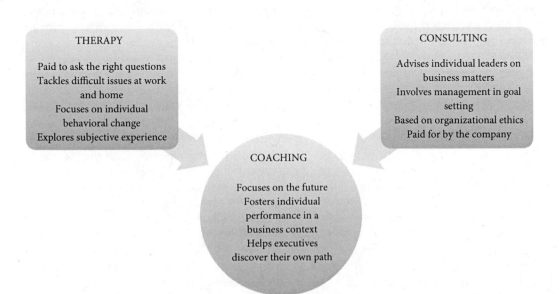

Figure 37.1 Performance coaching in a business context—links with consulting and therapy. Adapted from Coutu, D., & Kauffman, C. (2009), Research report: What can coaches do for you? *Harvard Business Review, January*, p. 97.

date across performance settings would seem relevant. An increasing range of publications attests to this relevance. For example, in a recent addition to this burgeoning literature (Collins, Button, & Richards, 2011), we used a "Performers Panel" of experts from the different domains, albeit all physical, to critique, test, and optimize the applied focus of the (mostly) sport-generated and/or applied techniques. Supporting our contention that such techniques are largely pan-domain, this approach worked with no issues, in that the Panel members were universal and comprehensive in their endorsement of both the philosophy and the methods espoused. In short, most of the techniques applied across the different domains. Notably, however, we did also include a few additional items that seemed to us to be crucial for a comprehensive picture of performance enhancement, representing knowledge streams additional to the usual emphasis on "mental skills."

First, and reflecting the multidimensionality of performance highlighted by so many authors, a broad swath of additional knowledge should come from both individual and social psychology. Fortunately, both these categories seem well established and accepted parts of the PC landscape, although the exact detail of the ideal makeup is a matter of much debate (cf. the second section of this chapter). Second, and less common, however, is an equally important component: knowledge on the acquisition, refinement, and execution of skills. For most performance domains, these will be largely physical and draw on the increasingly distinct (from sport psychology) disciplines of skill acquisition and motor control. In addition, reflecting the increasingly organizational component to performance domains, some understanding of the use (and possible abuse) of business setups would seem to represent another important consideration for PCs.

Just in passing, may we highlight how foolish and artificial the distinction between these extra subdisciplines and the rest of performance psychology can be, at least at the applied level. Execution of skills under pressure is absolutely fundamental to performance, and optimizing this process is surely the primary function of the performance-focused PC. Accordingly, the PC repertoire should surely include a large dose of motor control, skill acquisition, and even coaching science (to aid and facilitate change, or to help others in doing so), as well as the other two "frontal lobe" categories of mental skills and cognitive/social psychology (cf. MacPherson, Collins, & Obhi, 2009). Notably, this skill acquisition/execution/refinement tripos may also be central for PCs in nonphysical domains. Even (comparatively) low physicality performing arts such as singing are impacted by issues of execution, which such a knowledge base can usefully address. On the other hand, both physical (e.g., sport and dance) and comparatively less physical (e.g., business[2]) performance domains have a plethora of often neglected cognitive skills associated with them, most notably decision-making. Given the dearth of knowledge about how these skills are best developed and refined (cf. Yates & Tschirhart, 2006), we would suggest that the skill tripos should be required reading for PCs, especially those looking to work "off piste" (in novel environments) or pan-domain. In these all-too-common situations for the commercial PC, such knowledge is extremely useful in facilitating a grasp of the inherent challenges and, therefore, areas for attention in any particular performance domain.

Finally, we hope that the organizational strand is obvious. Support systems, management, satisfying sponsors, and generating an effective "high-performance environment" are all parts of the current *lingua franca* of performance—and that is without consideration of the explicitly business applications in, say, human resources, medicine, and finance. In summary, there is much more for the PC to know than just a few "mental strategies."

Transferring Knowledge: Possible Pitfalls

A final point relates to the uncritical export–import of ideas from one performance domain (and scientific "age") to another. This is all too common, especially when PCs move their work efforts seamlessly from one domain to another (and back again)[3]. Performance consultation companies built around retired performers, or retired business people deciding to work in performance are an example that *may* reflect poor practice. The social constructs, mores, expectations, and other key factors will almost inevitably be different; factors of which the PC may be completely unaware unless an expensive (time and money) period of acquaintance and prestudy is completed. The logical progression of ideas from one scenario to another will also represent a confound that has been shown to receive little consideration in a logical/chronological chain of empirical studies (e.g., imagery; Goginsky & Collins, 1996). Even though difficult, as such decision-making chains are much less available in applied work, it would be interesting to test the logic and coherence of concept progression intra (chronologically across career from domain to domain) and inter (through professional apprenticeship for example) PC practice.

We have certainly been very aware of these pitfalls in our own work. Accordingly, for example, in applying the idea of psychological characteristics of developing excellence as important building blocks for effective progression up the performance ladder, we have always initiated transfer to new environments with a check that both the generic idea *and* the specific constructs apply to the new environment. Thus, ideas developed in sport (e.g., MacNamara, Button, & Collins, 2010a,b) have been thoroughly explored in music, both classical/structured professional preparation (MacNamara, Holmes, & Collins, 2008), and popular/unstructured development (Kamin, Richards, & Collins, 2007) before transposition. Indeed, both transplanted and domain-specific applications can benefit from such "compare and contrast" studies that explore the commonalties and key differences of construct implications between environments (cf. MacNamara et al., 2010b). Perhaps the applied literature could also benefit from an explicit emphasis on confirming the principles, social construction, and mechanisms of PC "tools" in different performance domains.

These issues are extremely pertinent, and attention to the epistemological routes of knowledge may serve to counter concerns (both philosophical and pragmatic) expressed by one domain on the wholesale import of ideas from others. Certainly, we have always been careful to treat each as unique (as even surface exploration will usually demonstrate).

PCing from the Client Perspective: Who (and How) Exactly Are We Trying to Help?

This issue is the "vexed question" of most applied work across all domains. In fact, defining the client and the outcome deliverables makes up arguably the most crucial elements of establishing the working alliance between consultant and client, especially in a world where the professional title[4] of PC has yet to achieve any commonly accepted parameter.

Certainly, there is already good evidence that who is practically seen as the client (specifically who the PC "answers to") has significant implications for the modus operandi and efficacy of the work, a consideration that may also raise interesting and pertinent issues of conduct (Anderson, Van Raalte, & Brewer, 2001; Baltzell, Schinke, & Watson, 2010; Brown & Cogan, 2006). Figure 37.2 presents this idea in diagrammatic form.

Originally completed in a sports context, we have found that these principles apply equally well to PCs in other performance domains. They also seem to apply pretty well in less "formal" environments, as when considering potential "clashes" between employer–parent and client–child for example. The main point is on which side of the dotted line the PC (and other support team members) is perceived to sit. If seen as "management," performers will impression manage the information they share (cf. Leary, 1992; Leary & Tangney, 2003), effectively trying to use the PC as a (another) conduit to enhance perception and increase chances of selection/promotion. If, by contrast, the PC is seen as completely on the side of the performers, managers and other support staff can become worried about issues of confidentiality and professionalism, and also restrict their openness to the detriment of the PC's work.

As such, the PC treads a fine line between being seen as "one of us" or "one of them"; taking either stance will impact efficacy and, long term, will probably result in loss of the role. For example, work too much on the management side and the PC will be culled when a new system is employed; work too much for the performers and your loyalty to the bosses may be questioned. Our experience is that clear and open communication from the outset, with statements on client confidentiality publicly endorsed by management, represents the best way to quickly establish an effective and appropriate working alliance. Clearly, this is more directly applicable to organizational environments but the principles still apply to smaller scale, "family" situations. In this regard, we would suggest that *all* parts

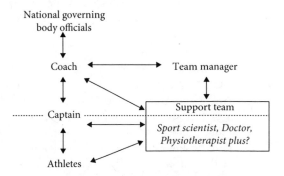

Figure 37.2 Basis of role conflicts among athletes, officials, and support teams. From Collins, D. J., Moore, P. M., Mitchell, D., & Alpress, F. (1999). Role conflict and confidentiality in multidisciplinary athlete support programmes. *British Journal of Sports Medicine, 33,* 208–211.

of the performance team are considered as clients.[5] The contractual client (the individual or organization who pays) is briefed to understand and accept the limitations on data flow as an essential precursor of the desired outcomes, whereas the "direct" client (although we suggest all should be) is aware that the PC is not a thoroughfare to management. Faking or bending this situation will only end in tears and lack of success, not to mention a few lawsuits.

Some other aspects to the client issue are worthy of more careful consideration pertaining to client expectations against a more "absolute" conception of what represents good conduct. As professionals in the caring profession(s), we need to consider the "client's perspective," in which client is, "code of conduct-wise," defined as the receiver of treatment/therapy. Crucially, however, there is a need to consider all the routes to support the client, while also conforming to our "all are clients" guideline outlined earlier. For example, consider the challenge of working with a young performance artist, "supported" by "demanding" parents. In such cases, do we as PCs act against the wishes (or even the confidentiality) of the direct client (the artist) by supporting the face-valid need to decrease the pressure on him or her, even if this may terminate the intervention contract? In short, do we need to place client welfare over self-stated client need? Having experienced several such cases, and in the search for ethical guidance, we have considered the advice framed for consultants becoming aware of the potential for illegal or self-harming behavior (cf. the British Psychological Society [BPS] Code of Conduct IV, 1.2, vi, b/c) Given the strength of personal identity and emotion tied into performance success, the future for PCing may require some careful extension to existing generic and more therapy-oriented codes of conduct, notwithstanding the focus-related issues of performance versus individual that permeate this chapter.

Our Professional Responsibility for Evidence of Impact: Do We Need to Test?

Once the "who and how" questions are answered and we are clear about the various levels of client responsibility, another professional component seems to hold some challenges for the wide variety of PCs in the marketplace. The need for accountability has grown substantially in recent years, and the need to "show that what I do is working" brings pressures to all support professionals. Undoubtedly, however, the pressures are greater for less objectifiable, multidimensional support sciences such as

PCing. As Mark Andersen (2009, p. 13) points out, data-driven accountability seems a lot simpler for, say, the strength and conditioning specialist ("As a result of my work, they now bench press X kg more") than for the mentally focused PC. Whether this drive has come from a more discerning/demanding clientele, or from increased numbers of administrators appointed to monitor all aspects of a performance environment (cf. features of practice in national institutes of sport), there is little doubt that all support staff are increasingly expected to demonstrate their unique contributions.

Is this really functional, or even positive, however? Consider the consequences of a broader drive for demonstrable quality assurance. As scientist-practitioners, we are all for applying rigor to our work, and, clearly, the scientific-ness should be apparent and explicitly presented to the client. This is an important proviso, which may do much to counter the charismatic con artists who represent a substantial threat to PCing becoming recognized as a respected and valid profession. "So long as it works, who cares" or "it's too complex to explain . . . you wouldn't understand" are all too commonly offered underpinnings by such charlatans. Nor should the cutting edge-ness of the method and the consequent lack of peer-reviewed proof of product (almost always essential when working with genuinely top-class performers who really need the latest edge) be used to cover up the need for addressing the "why" question. In *all* cases, we would suggest that clients are encouraged to inquire into—and PCs are required to demonstrate and explain—the scientific underpinnings of what they are suggesting. Not only is this a key feature of informed consent (would you swallow something just because some guy told you it would work ? You would? Is your name Alice??), it also represents a feature of good practice that we should strongly and unashamedly peddle to educate the market on what to expect from "proper" PCing.

Now slot this "informed science" perspective into the accountability drive highlighted earlier. From a quality viewpoint, ensuring that the scientific underpinnings of any work are always presented offers, we suggest, the best kind of accountability. Indeed, when working as part of a support team (an increasingly common, even desirable occurrence), such sharing of the declarative underpinnings as well as the procedural plans (in other words, the why as well as the what; see our ideas on this later) enables the team to maximize interactive impact. But what about the need to demonstrate each discipline's (or your own, if flying solo) unique contribution? Well, to be honest, we feel that this sort of accountability is at best illusionary and more usually detrimental. As one example, note the inherent limitation on evidence-based practice, even though *some* evidence is both highly desirable and ethically (to our view) essential.

Consider a multiagency support environment, such as that typically found in professional performance setups (sport, dance, etc.). In these circumstances, rivalries and interdisciplinary competition can inhibit the potential benefit of the support interventions, while each specialist, in an attempt to maintain his or her place in the sun (and on the payroll), works only to demonstrate his or her unique contribution. So, returning to our earlier example, the strength and conditioning specialist demonstrates greater strength on specific exercises, the nutritionist reports lower body fats, while the PC scrabbles about trying to show greater use of mental "strategies" or hangs on, leech-like, to often vulnerable (and also often second-tier) performers to keep up his or her contact hours.[6] Sounds familiar? It does to our experience. This is negative for the PC field because the snide in-fighting that often results inevitably limits the support team's impact and increases pressure on performers as each specialist ensures his or her quota of contact to show that he or she is contributing. Such discrete measures completely miss the point that performance, as a complex system, is rarely if ever going to be influenced by one or two such crude markers (Abbott, Button, Pepping, & Collins, 2005; Anderson, 1999). In fact, when increased strength is associated with decreased performance on domain-specific tasks (e.g., increased bench press against less effective hand-offs in rugby; Collins & MacPherson, 2007) or greater use of a highly structured pre-performance strategy is associated with increased error count (in dance; Collins & Collins, 2011), the potential dangers of an overemphasis on individual accountability become even clearer.

In summary, we suggest that, in the applied environment, it is often counterproductive to try and "partial out" the contributions made by each part of the support machine. It is probably not even a good idea to constantly monitor the performance impact of the PC. Of course, there is a need for performance psychology to become ever more "evidence based," but, reflecting the three ages idea expounded earlier, this is rarely if ever going to be done "distinctly" at the coal face of applied work. In fact, PCs who find themselves forced to "fight their corner" in this way

are not located in a high-performing environment, albeit they may be associated with a high-performance individual or organization. The bottom line is that such ill-considered and dysfunctional pressures characterize all that can be so potentially bad about the performance focus; simply, such expectations cannot be associated with getting the best from an individual specialist or the team. Rigor in the underpinning science, performance as the only meaningful measure, and working through and with others as much as possible are the watchwords for effective PCing.

Other Downsides of Professional Variance: Problems and Possible Solutions
Does Ambition Outstrip Professionalism? A Need for Greater Professionalism

Given the wide variety of professionals, paraprofessionals and nonprofessionals working in the PC field, there is a need to consider the impact this has on the consulting landscape. This also carries some potential responsibilities, both to clientele and accredited members, for the different professional bodies associated with the performance area. The bottom line here is perhaps best summarized as practitioner presentation against client expectation. Against this agenda, all pertinent bodies (e.g., in sport, BPS and the British Association of Sport and Exercise Sciences [BASES] or the American Psychological Association [APA] and the Association for Applied Sport Psychology [AASP]; in performance, the BPS/APA) must play a preferably integrated role in setting and publicizing standards.

A common example of such nonbehavior may help. It should surely be contrary to codes of conduct for PCs to name former illustrious clients; this should only be done by the clients themselves and not be solicited or "pushed for" by the PC. If consultants are good—that is, effective in raising performance and presenting a scientific rigor to what they do—then this will generate business in a healthier way than slick websites full of celebrity quotes.

In setting standards, however, professional organizations (such as the APA, AASP, etc.) must recognize the pressures and consequent behavior to which members may default. In this regard, we were drawn to work in organizational psychology, which considered the behavior of upwardly mobile business people. In a study of 139 Master of Business Administration (MBA) students, Kilduff and Day (1994) discerned two "types" of approach to promotion. Contrasting these types as "chameleons versus normals," Kilduff and Day observed that chameleons:

- Jumped from organization to organization, achieving 55% more cross-company promotions
- Were twice as likely to change employers
- Showed a preoccupation with analyzing their performance and focusing on their own interests
- Were extremely focused and adroit at avoiding blame
- Developed and more effectively utilized large networks, often playing one against another for personal advancement

Based on our experiences in practice, we would like to suggest (nonempirically) two additional subgenus of chameleons pertinent to PCing. First, those encountered in professional performance domains.

Performance organizations, even predominantly volunteer ones, are often very competitive and very faddish. The first feature is, perhaps, an inevitable hangover from retired performers, now administrators, continuing a now dysfunctional trait behavior. The second is the downside of the need for constant refinement, the search for that extra edge, which can lead the less-informed to seize on what we call "magic feather solutions" (cf. Dumbo). Wherever these two inclinations come from, however, they can often add to these individuals' paranoid need to justify/demonstrate their contribution, resulting in what might be best termed "beige chameleons." In our experience, this subgenus is quite common in performance organizations, changing "color" to fit with the latest trends but only just enough to keep in with the program (cf. Erwin & Garman, 2009). For PCs, such individuals can often prove a major block to innovation; they are driven by personal protection and are usually suspicious of new ideas and innovations. As a consequence, the fully educated PC will possess a good working knowledge of micro politics, a skill already identified as central to the toolkit of high-level sports coaches (Potrac & Jones, 2009). It is due to such individuals as the beige chameleon that many high-performance environments cannot really be said to be high performing. The knowledgeable PC will avoid the trap of thinking that outcome trappings (cups, medals, plaudits) equal top class process, although they may often encounter some trouble convincing their clients!

In fact, given that the PC's role may often (or should) involve change management, it is surprising that there isn't a more substantial literature base in this area across performance domains (Cruickshank & Collins, in press), nor even a greater perceived need to understand the theory and relative merits of different change mechanisms (e.g., Wischnevsky & Damanpour, 2006). There is increasingly good evidence from some performance domains for the performance process impact that can be made by improved management systems (e.g., dance; Bronner, Ojofeitimi, & Rose, 2003). Accordingly, performance-focused organizational behavior may be another useful area for a PC literature base. This would certainly act as another bridge for PCs working across domains as it would offer empirical guidelines for business-focused coaching in performance-focused environments. For the moment, recognizing that such change can be driven from above, but often more effectively from below (Butcher & Clarke, 2008), is an important factor in avoiding the mire of organizational politics that can represent the biggest block to (even) higher attainment.

The other (but clearly overlapping) subgenus of performance chameleon relates to the PC and his or her behavior with clients. We would suggest that some of the worst excesses manifested in the growing field of PCing, largely but not exclusively perpetrated by unqualified guru-style coaches, relate to chameleon-like behavior.[7] Indeed, these behaviors may underpin the concerns that scientist-practitioners such as Mark Andersen (e.g., 2009) appear to have with performance-focused interventions. Features of such behavior, which impact us all through loss of professional status/reputation and personal loss of business, can include:

- Websites and promotional material full of "big names," often mentioned tangentially without claim to have actually worked with them
- Offering the use of "special" techniques, often of their own concoction, with little or no mention of formal qualifications
- Extremely broad claims, offering solutions in (suspiciously) double-quick time
- A stronger experiential background in one domain but claims for efficacy in others, without critical consideration
- Use of a performer background to self-endorse efficacy as a support practitioner

Don't get us wrong. There is a clear need to advertise one's services, and there are several highly qualified, broadly experienced, and extremely effective PCs of our acquaintance who are in the "leaps tall buildings at a single bound" category. However, such claimed excesses from altogether more ordinary PCs seem to us a significant threat to the emerging PC profession. Accordingly, it may be time for professional associations to commence an aggressive marketing campaign against such. Tighter code of conduct guidelines on personal support statements or use of client names would seem a small price to pay for a genuinely higher ambient standard of professional and professional behavior. Against the general lack of common knowledge about what a PC is (e.g., Wilson et al., 2006), such brand marketing appears to be essential from all three parts of the relationship: client, practitioner, and profession.

A Potential Solution: Focusing on Professional Judgment and Decision-Making in Performance Consulting

What has emerged so far is the need for PCing to focus on raising the bar through an emphasis on process. Irrespective of the philosophical (but practical) questions that have occupied so much attention so far, the future of PCs is bound to better service. This, in turn, is firmly located in the PC's ability to enhance the accuracy and validity of his or her professional judgment and decision-making, the PJDM of professional practice.

We emphasize PJDM for a number of reasons, including the part that this construct plays in skill development across the caring professions—more specifically, however, because PJDM is *the* tool through which PCs can best develop and deploy a bespoke solution to optimally address the client's presenting condition and stated needs. Our brief overview of the PJDM approach, for which we should acknowledge the work of Amanda Martindale as a prime driver, is appropriate for PCing in a number of ways. First, consider the complexity and multidimensionality of practice in PCing, which is probably the clearest finding to emerge from a review of its current status. All acknowledge the need for accountability, while also recognizing the inherent difficulties of such when based on set guidelines (cf. Coutu & Kauffman, 2009). In this regard, PCs may learn from other, more established professions that are currently wrestling with similar dilemmas. For example, consider this quote from the medical field.

> Medical practice must be regulated, but the form this currently takes is increasingly based on a "technical" view, which wrongly assumes that practice is straightforward and that error is the result of individual failure. The metaphor of "delivery" is currently used to characterise medical practice but this usage is fundamentally flawed. An alternative is presented, supported by a growing literature, that shows that professional practice generally (and

medical practice in particular) is characterised by complexity, uncertainty and unpredictability. Practitioners use their judgement and wisdom, developed in their own practice and in their contacts with fellow practitioners. Often, practitioners choose between options that are not ideal, and may need to decide on what they believe is best for an individual rather than what is "right" in some absolute sense.
> (*Coles*, 2006, p. 397)

This quote, and the literature it represents, provides a strong drive toward careful and critical consideration of process decisions, exploiting the twin pillars of peer supervision and the rationale underpinning decisions taken. Not only can this approach cater well for the levels of diversity in philosophy, objective and methodology which seem to characterize current PCing (a clear picture of a lack of clarity!), it also advances and structures the profession's current preoccupation with "critical reflection" (cf. Accreditation guidelines for BASES and AASP. Questioning competence as merely technical ability, Schön (1983) sees professional practice more as artistry, whereas for Carr (1995) such practice:

> [I]s not "right" action in the sense that it has been proved to be correct. It is "right" action because it is reasoned action that can be defended discursively in argument and justified as morally appropriate to the particular circumstances in which it was taken.
> (p. 71)

In short, careful consideration of the "whys and why nots" of an action is crucial for the emerging but diverse PC profession (cf. Martindale & Collins, 2010). There would appear to be three essential steps to implementing such an approach. First, the introduction of peer supervision as a norm, or even an expectation, in PCing must be considered, a process that although increasingly common and implicit in some systems (e.g., clinical psychology and psychotherapy) has yet to receive an explicit push from "the authorities." Second, the need for one or more accreditation systems covering the span of PC activity that explicitly require critical consideration of PJDM steps, perhaps through the use of case studies, an already accepted feature. The final area is broader and more esoteric, although none the less important: an increasing consideration of PJDM in case study and other "how to do it" papers across the literature (cf. Martindale & Collins, 2010). In fact, we would see this approach as the best basis for an expanded applied emphasis reflecting the "psychology for performance" usage.

Procedural Implications and Advantages of the PJDM Emphasis

The second of several advantages (for a more comprehensive review, see Martindale & Collins, 2005) relates to the ways in which a PC may design and develop the plan for an intervention. As a general case in performance, and certainly across the broad spectrum of domains within which PCs are known to operate, the issues to be addressed are often both complex and not entirely within the consciousness of the client; this situation is obviously at odds with the usual situation in more traditional counseling (although we, of course, recognize that here, too, things can get very convoluted). The question is whether this level of complexity is inherent within the (as often presented) "straightforward performance agendas" that are said to characterize PCing.

Perhaps reflecting this complexity, some authors have noted that the issue conceptualization stage (in sport psychology, as an example) can be glossed over, with the practitioner moving directly from needs assessment to intervention, drawing more on well-known and preferred "recipes" than a bespoke plan for the exact parameters of that particular client's situation (Martindale & Collins, 2005; Poczwardowski, Sherman, & Henschen, 1998). Often referred to in counseling psychology as the configuration of the client's problem (Cormier & Cormier, 1991), this stage should represent an optimum meld of client need, practitioner philosophy (most crucially, the theoretical orientation), and the various components of the presenting condition. Reflecting the already identified complexity of performance domains, together with the vast array of stated orientation/background for practitioners, this meld becomes all the more important in determining the rigor and potential of the intervention cf. (Hill & O'Grady, 1995). As Martindale and Collins point out:

> It is the recognition of this phase as the "missing link" for determining the quality, and ultimately the success, of an intervention which has stimulated the current flow of research into PJDM in counseling psychology, and other fields such as medicine (e.g., Patel & Ramoni, 1997[8]), nursing (e.g., Husted & Husted, 1995), and teaching (e.g., Griffey & Housner, 1991).

Manifested as the "intentions for impact," careful consideration at this stage can generate a multilevel and multiobjective intervention plan that may, in fact, be much more reflective of the type of approach espoused by Andersen(2009) and other colleagues.

An example may make this advantage even clearer. Martindale (2010) reports a case study of a long-term intervention with a judo athlete, in which intentions for impact were carefully developed and used as the basis for design. Unfortunately, the athlete received a career-threatening injury after some progress had been made on the original plan. Reflecting these changed circumstances, however, while also maintaining the original intentions, work went on at a number of levels, addressing both the immediate need (rehab of and return from injury) and the longer term agenda. This process is reflected in Figure 37.3.

The point is that making such "intentions for impact" explicit, while also acknowledging the complexities that *should be* inherent in any real-life example, seems a good way to expose PJDM to professional debate and, consequently, raise standards through the more advantageous process emphasis.

The Nature and Development of Expertise in PCing

The final piece of the puzzle with regard to PCing and its promotion as a unique and well-run profession draws on a consideration of how expertise in the field should be developed, evaluated, and accredited. Once again, a great deal can be learned from other disciplines that, having acknowledged their importance a while back, are currently still striving with these issues. For example, to what extent are lessons learned in sport psychology smoothly transitioned into PCing? Or even, to what extent do we in sport "reinvent the wheel" rather than turn to our parent disciplines to check for their tried solutions?

Here, again, we feel that a focus on PJDM offers a great deal, whereas the explicit consideration of intentions for impact and the associated decision-making stream will also serve to highlight (and thence motivate the filling of) key gaps in the knowledge base pertaining to generic or specific performance domains. Stating and clarifying this decision-making process is an important developmental "tool" for any profession, a factor already been acknowledged (although not universally implemented) in sport. The recognition that evidence-based practice is important for "allowing sport psychologists to make informed decisions regarding the most effective interventions" (Gardner & Moore, 2006, p. 67) should surely have led to a greater acceptance of such evidence-based (with PJDM and other reasoning) papers in the literature. We await such a

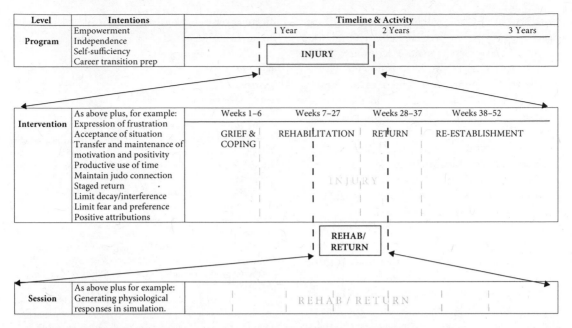

Figure 37.3 "Nested" agendas as intention for impact in a multidimensional performance intervention. From Martindale, A. (2010). *Developing professional judgement and decision making expertise in applied sport psychology.* Unpublished doctoral dissertation, University of Edinburgh, Scotland.

development, in tandem with a greater emphasis on the mechanisms and mediators of change that should surely underpin the PC's trade (cf. Gardner, 2009).

Supporting the focus on PJDM proposed by Martindale (2010) while also acknowledging the general dearth of knowledge in this area (Yates & Tschirhart, 2006), we contend that the advantages of such an approach are actually already embedded in the *lingua franca* of performance psychology. For example, and again stressing the almost ubiquitous endorsement of "reflection in action" a la Schön (1991), there have been several surprising but damaging omissions in the evolution of his original work into today's general practice. For example, his idea of on-the-spot experimentation (i.e., "nested within the larger problem-setting experiment, there are also local experiments of various sorts," p. 141) is supportive of the PC as scientist-practitioner; trying out new ideas (and transferring them from domain to domain) and evaluating against an a priori stated set of objectives (aka, "intentions for impact"; cf. Hill, 1992). Our point here is that active experimentation should be a much more accepted, even lauded feature of PC practice, but also that the basic tenets for such action are already broadly accepted.

Finally, in evaluating and accrediting expertise, we suggest that organizations may fall prey to some academic snobbery in terms of expectations for scientific rigor, or at least to a misplaced expectation on where this may fall. PCing has a great deal in common with other helping professions (such as clinical psychology, psychiatry, and psychotherapy); indeed, the last named is perhaps as much a constituent part of the current PC environment as the more traditional areas of sport or dance psychology. In much of the work in these disciplines, research has accepted that clear, black-and-white answers are often impossible to come by (cf. our earlier comments and Phillips, Klein, & Sieck, 2004). Where rigor should be expected, however—indeed, *required*—is in the reasons (and reasoning) underlying the design and execution of the intervention. In short, and yet again, we argue that this makes the case for accrediting the process of PJDM rather than the actions or even the outcomes of an intervention as the primary source.

Conclusion

Until now, performance enhancement has been thought to be the PC's primary task, and this seems a logical focus, with experts in agreement about the philosophy and methods that should be espoused by PCs across domains. However, although PCs are becoming a common fixture in sport and performance contexts, much remains unclear about exactly what this role entails and about the necessary underlying theoretical and practical foundation that may best prepare practitioners for this role. In this chapter, we have proposed what we believe to be comprehensive preparation for PCs: a background combining training in mental skills; counseling skills; individual, organizational, and social psychology; motor control; and skill acquisition, refinement, and execution. If clients seek to understand the scientific foundation underlying the techniques being suggested (and we hope they do!), a "proper" PC should demonstrate the ability to provide this information as required.

We also hope to have demonstrated the importance of PCs being keenly attuned to their clients' perspectives, as well as that of other invested parties whose demands, or even mere presence, may exert an influence on the client's own needs and expectations. By acknowledging the effect of significant others (e.g., coaches, family members, etc.) on the client, a clearer picture of the performance context can emerge, one in which each person's involvement in the client's overall performance is acknowledge and considered. Similarly, acknowledgment of the PC as a member of a performance team, rather than a lone entity working only with the performer in isolation, is equally important. If deliverables are not met, the team, and no one member in particular, should be held accountable. The ability to work through and with other members of the team, and an understanding of the social dynamics involved in this type of setting, is a key factor in effective PCing.

Future Directions

Moving forward, we suggest the following actions and activities in order to assist PCs in gaining credibility and continuing to set their role apart from other similar professions:

• Further training in organizational behavior (particularly change management) and PJDM, as both would be applicable for PCs across domains
• Advocating for professional organizations to come up with stricter guidelines about who can and cannot define and advertise themselves as PCs (this to be coupled with more "aggressive marketing" of the advantages such status should bring to the client)
• Peer supervision as an increasing norm to ensure PCs are conscientious when determining what techniques to employ with clients

Ultimately, PCs themselves may consider forming a new professional field, joining their colleagues from diverse backgrounds in working toward a more fully informed and more widely supported approach to client work.

Notes

1. Some may be unfamiliar with this term, although it is increasingly common across performance domains. The performance manager is the individual primarily concerned with the overall promotion of performance. This *may* include coaches (especially head coaches), managers (especially in the soccer sense), artistic directors (in dance companies for example) or performance directors.
2. We stress "comparatively." As several studies and many consultants will attest, PC in business often benefits from an emphasis on skill acquisition and physical issues, such as sleep and diet.
3. Note here the Code of Conduct requirement for sufficient professional development, experience and knowledge before extending work to another field (e.g., BPS Code of Conduct 2009, IV, 2.3, v).
4. At the time of writing, we are unaware of any professional accreditation schemes for PCing, although numerous courses (both formal and informal) are presented as addressing the skill set.
5. For example, the BPS Code of Conduct 2009, I, g "In this code the term 'client' refers to any person or persons with whom a psychologist interacts on a professional basis. For example, a client may be an individual (such as a patient, a student, or a research participant), a couple, a family group, an educational institution, or a private or public organisation, including a court. A psychologist may have several clients at a time including, for example, those receiving, commissioning and evaluating the professional activity."
6. Consider this all too common behavior against Code of Conduct guidance (e.g., BPS Code of Conduct 2009, IV, 3.2, iii).
7. And again, contrast such behavior with Code of Conduct guidelines (e.g., BPS Code of Conduct 2009, IV,4.1, vii).
8. See also Coles, 2005, cited elsewhere in this chapter.

References

Abbott, A., Button, C., Pepping, G. -J., & Collins, D. (2005). Unnatural selection: Talent identification and development in sport. *Nonlinear Dynamics, Psychology and Life Sciences, 9*(1), 61–88.

Abbott, A., Collins, D., Moore, P., Tebbenham, D., Burwitz, L., & Arnold, J. (1999). Consumer expectations of sport psychology. *Journal of Sports Sciences, 16,* 68–69.

Andersen, M. (2009). Performance enhancement as a bad start and a dead end: A parenthetical comment on Mellalieu and Lane. *The Sport and Exercise Scientist, 20 (June),* 12–14.

Andersen, M. B. (2005). "Yeah, I work with Beckham": Issues of confidentiality, privacy and privilege in sport psychology service delivery. *Sport and Exercise Psychology Review, 1*(2), 5–13.

Anderson, M., Van Raalte, J., & Brewer, B. (2001). Sport psychology service delivery: Staying ethical while keeping loose. *Professional psychology: Research and Practice, 32,* 12–18.

Anderson, P. (1999). Complexity theory and organization science. *Organization Science, 10*(3), 216–232.

Baltzell, A., Schinke, R. J., & Watson, J. (2010, Spring/Summer). Who is my client? *AASP Newsletter,*pp. 18–21.

Botting, M., & Collins, D. (2005). Optimising support in dance performance. *Dance UK News, 56,* 22–24.

Bronner, S., Ojofeitimi, S., & Rose, D. (2003). Injuries in a modern dance company: Effect of comprehensive management on injury incidence and time loss. *American Journal of Sports Medicine, 31*(3), 365–373.

Brown, J., & Cogan, K. (2006). Ethical clinical practice and sport psychology: When two worlds collide. *Ethics and Behavior, 16*, 15–23.

Butcher, D., & Clarke, M. (2008, August). Politics and worthy management agendas. *Management Online Review.* Retrieved from www.morexpertise.com ISSN 1996-3300.

Carr, D. (1999). Professional education and professional ethics. *Journal of Applied Philosophy, 16*(1), 33–46.

Carr, W. (1995) *For education: Towards critical educational inquiry.* Buckingham, England: Open University.

Coles, C. (2006). Uncertainty in a world of professional regulation. *Advances in Psychiatric Treatment, 12*, 397–403.

Collins, D. (2008, December). *Strange bedfellows: Why sport AND exercise psychology?* Invited keynote at the inaugural British Psychological Society DSEP Conference, London.

Collins, D., Button, A., & Richards, R. (2011). *Performance psychology: A practitioner's guide.* Oxford, England: Churchill Livingston.

Collins, D., & Collins, J. (2011). Putting them together: Skill packages to optimise team/group performance In D. Collins, A. Button, & H. Richards (Eds.), *Performance psychology: A practitioner's guide.* Oxford, England: Churchill Livingstone.

Collins, D., & MacPherson, A. (2007). Psychological factors of physical preparation. In B. Blumestein, R. Lidor, & G. Tenenbaum (Eds.), *Psychology of sport training.* Oxford, England: Myer & Myer Sport.

Collins, D. J., Moore, P. M., Mitchell, D., & Alpress, F. (1999). Role conflict and confidentiality in multidisciplinary athlete support programmes. *British Journal of Sports Medicine, 33*, 208–211.

Cormier, W. H., & Cormier, S. L. (1991). *Interviewing strategies for helpers. Fundamental skills and cognitive behavioural interventions* (3rd ed.). Pacific Grove, CA: Brooks/Cole.

Coutu, D., & Kauffman, C. (2009), Research report: What can coaches do for you? *Harvard Business Review, January*, 91–97.

Cruickshank, A. & Collins, D. (in press). Exploring Change Management in Elite Sport. *Journal of Change Management.*

Erwin, D. G., & Garman, A. N. (2009). Resistance to organisational change: Linking research and practice. *Leadership and Organization Development Journal, 31*(1), 39–56.

Gardner, F. L. (2009). Efficacy, mechanisms of change, and the scientific development of sport psychology. *Journal of Clinical Sports Psychology, 3*, 139–155.

Gardner, F. L., & Moore, Z. E. (2006). *Clinical sport psychology.* Champaign, IL: Human Kinetics.

Goginsky, A. M., & Collins, D. J. (1996). Research design and mental practice. *Journal of Sports Sciences, 14*(5), 381–392.

Griffey, D. C., & Housner, L. D. (1991). Differences between experienced and inexperienced teachers' planning decisions, interactions, student engagement and instructional climate. *Research Quarterly for Exercise and Sport, 62*(2), 196–204.

Hill, C. E. (1992). An overview of four measures developed to test the hill process model: Therapist intentions, therapist response modes, client reactions, and client behaviours. *Journal of Counseling and Development, 70*, 728–739.

Hill, C. E., & O'Grady, K. E. (1985). List of therapist intentions illustrated in a case study and with therapists of varying theoretical orientations. *Journal of Counseling Psychology, 32*, 3–22.

Husted, G. L., & Husted, J. H. (1995). *Ethical decision making in nursing.* New York: Mosby Inc.

Holmes, P. S., & Collins, D. (2001). The PETTLEP approach to motor imagery: A functional equivalence model for sport psychologists. *Journal of Applied Sport Psychology, 13*(1), 83–106.

Kamin, S., Richards, H., & Collins, D. (2007). Influences on the talent development process of non-classical musicians: Psychological, social and environmental influences. *Music Education Research, 9*(3), 449–468.

Kilduff, M., & Day, D. (1994). Do chameleons get ahead? The effects of self-monitoring on managerial careers. *Academy of Management Journal, 37*(4), 1047–1060.

Leary, M. R. (1992). Self-presentational processes in exercise and sport. *Journal of Sport and Exercise Psychology, 14*(4), 339–351.

Leary, M. R., & Tangney, J. P. (Eds.). (2003). *Handbook of self and identity.* New York: Guilford Press.

MacNamara, Á., Button, A., & Collins, D. (2010a). the role of psychological characteristics in facilitating the pathway to elite performance. Part 1: Identifying mental skills and behaviours. *The Sport Psychologist, 24*, 52–73.

MacNamara, Á., Button, A., & Collins, D. (2010b). The role of psychological characteristics in facilitating the pathway to elite performance. Part 2: Examining environmental and stage related differences in skills and behaviours. *The Sport Psychologist, 24*, 74–96.

MacNamara, Á., Holmes, P., & Collins, D. (2008). Negotiating transitions in musical development: The role of psychological characteristics of developing excellence. *Psychology of Music, 13*, 1–18.

MacPherson, A., Collins, D., & Obhi, S. (2009). The importance of temporal structure and rhythm for the optimum performance of motor skills: A new focus for practitioners of sport psychology. *Journal of Applied Sport Psychology, 21*(S1), S48–S61.

Martindale, A. (2010). *Developing professional judgement and decision making expertise in applied sport psychology.* Unpublished doctoral dissertation, University of Edinburgh, Scotland.

Martindale, A., & Collins, D. (2005). Professional judgment and decision making: The role of intention for impact. *The Sport Psychologist, 19*(3), 303–317.

Martindale, A., & Collins, D. (2010). But *why* does what works work? A response to Fifer, Henschen, Gould, and Ravizza. *The Sport Psychologist, 24*, 113–116.

Mellalieu, S., & Lane, A. (2009). Is studying anxiety interpretations useful for sport and exercise psychologists? *The Sport and Exercise Scientist, 20*(March), 28–30.

Patel, V. L., & Ramoni, M. F. (1997). Cognitive models of directional inference in expert medical reasoning. In P. J. Feltovich, K. M. Ford, & R. R. Hoffman (Eds.), *Expertise in context* (pp. 287–311). Cambridge, MA: MIT Press.

Phillips, J. K., Klein, G., & Sieck, W. R. (2004). Expertise in judgment and decision making: A case for training intuitive decision skills. In D. J. Koehler & N. Harvey (Eds.), *Blackwell handbook of judgment and decision making* (pp. 177–208). New York: Cambridge University Press.

Poczwardowski, A., Sherman, C. P., & Henschen, K. P. (1998). A sport psychology delivery heuristic: Building on theory and practice. *The Sport Psychologist, 12*, 191–207.

Potrac, P., & Jones, R. (2009). Power, conflict and cooperation: Toward a micropolitics of coaching. *Quest, 61*, 223–236.

Schön, D. A. (1983/1991). *The reflective practitioner: How professionals think in action*. London: Ashgate.

Shunk, D. H. (2000). *Learning theories: An educational perspective* (3rd ed.). Upper Saddle River, NJ.: Prentice-Hall.

Wilson, K. A., Gilbert, J. N, Gilbert, W. F. D., & Damanpour, F. (2006). College athletic directors' perceptions of sport psychology consulting. *The Sport Psychologist, 23*, 405–424.

Wischnevsky, J. D., & Damanpour, F. (2006). Organizational transformation and performance: An examination of three perspectives. *Journal of Managerial Issues, 18*(1), 104–128.

Whelan, J. P., Meyers, A. W., & Donovan, C. (1995). Competitive recreational athletes: A multisystemic model. In S. M. Murphy (Ed.), *Sport psychology interventions* (pp. 187–220). Champaign, IL: Human Kinetics.

Yates, J. F., & Tschirhart, M. D. (2006). Decision-making expertise. In K. A. Ericsson, N. Charness, P. J. Feltovich, & R. R. Hoffman (Eds.), *The Cambridge handbook of expertise and expert performance* (pp. 288–311). New York: Cambridge University Press.

Optimal Performance: Elite Level Performance in "The Zone"

Robert J. Harmison *and* Kathleen V. Casto

Abstract

Curiosity about and interest in optimal performance has grown markedly among researchers, practitioners, athletes, and performers over the past 30 years. Despite this interest, elite-level performance in "the zone" continues to be an elusive phenomenon for researchers and practitioners to understand. This chapter discusses the various psychological factors involved in optimal performance and summarizes the historical and current research and scholarly writings in the area. The subjective experience of optimal performance is defined and clarified, and the psychological profile of optimal performance is described and elaborated. Issues related to the assessment of psychological characteristics and skills associated with optimal performance are discussed, and a model for understanding the myriad of factors that impact optimal performance is provided. The application and effectiveness of psychological skills training to promote the occurrence of optimal performance is reviewed as well. Finally, directions and opportunities for future research are presented.

Key Words: Peak experience, peak performance, flow, psychological profile, mental toughness, ideal performance state, psychological assessment, psychological preparation, psychological skills training

Performing at one's best, fulfilling one's potential, or achieving one's dreams in a moment of personal glory serves as a major drive for many athletes and performers in their pursuit of excellence. Achieving such a reward is often so self-fulfilling in nature that it requires no audience or medal, yet is often accompanied by both. For some athletes and performers, an optimal performance occurs as a once-in-a-lifetime experience, whereas for the seasoned athlete or performer it can take the form of an effortless and fluid execution of a task that has been perfected through rigorous preparation. Jackson and Csikszentmihalyi (1999) state that to have this kind of performance is "to feel completely at one with what you are doing, to know you are strong and able to control your destiny at least for the moment, and to gain a sense of pleasure independent of results" (p. vi). Athletes describe

their optimal performances in unique and individualistic fashion. For example, U.S. Olympic miler Gabriel Jennings artfully described this experience as a synchronization of mind, body, and surroundings when he stated, "I feel the earth and the wind and the trees. I feel its spirit. It puts me in the moment. I feel the rhythm of the race." In contrast, Reggie Jackson, professional baseball Hall of Fame inductee and clutch hitter, more concretely described getting "in the zone" as an absence of distraction: "I step into the batter's box, I mumble 'All right, Reggie, just let it happen, just let it flow, now let it happen.' Then I am quiet." Similarly, National Basketball Association all-time leading scorer, Kareem Abdul-Jabbar, noting the importance of a lucid mind in peak performing, said, "You have to be able to center yourself, to let all of your emotions go."

Despite the widespread fascination with the achievement of optimal performance, much remains unknown regarding the how and why it occurs. What exactly is this moment, why is it experienced differently, and why doesn't it happen on command? Can it be captured, studied, viewed from the outside, taught, anticipated, or attained through sheer desire or will power? Does it result from a conscious awareness that the body is functioning in seamless harmony, or does it begin as a state of mind, setting the stage for a physical reaction of ideal execution? This chapter delves into these topics, as well as discusses the relevant research surrounding the all-powerful and mysterious state of perfection achieved in a crowning performance.

Although the dominant historical trend in applied psychology has been to focus on the amelioration of aversive states and conditions, more recently, the field has shifted to emphasizing the enhancement of experience (the "positive psychology" movement; Seligman & Csikszentmihalyi, 2000). In keeping with this trend, this chapter focuses on the psychological factors involved in optimizing performance. To understand the phenomenon of optimal performance, it is first necessary to define the experiences that are classified under the umbrella of optimal performance and how these related constructs are perceived together and separately among athletes and performers. Then, the psychological profile of athletes and performers who perform optimally and the assessment of psychological characteristics and skills will be discussed to provide a foundation for understanding the psychology of optimal performance. Next, a model of psychological preparation for optimal performance will be presented. Finally, typical psychological skills training methods to promote optimal performance and the effectiveness of these interventions will be described and reviewed. Potential future directions within the optimal performance area also will be shared.

Optimal Performance Defined

Research (e.g. Csikszentmihalyi, 1990; Jackson & Roberts, 1992; Privette, 1983; Ravizza, 1977) in the area of optimal performance has focused on three major and overlapping facets: peak experience, peak performance, and flow (see Figure 38.1). Since each of these facets describes optimal performance in slightly different ways, it is important that researchers and practitioners understand how these three experiences occur and the pertinent characteristics that differentiate the three facets from one another. Being armed with such knowledge will allow researchers to better design investigations of the phenomenon of optimal performance and practitioners to more effectively implement interventions to increase optimal performance within sport and other performance areas.

Peak Experience

On October 15, 1988, Kirk Gibson of Major League Baseball's Los Angeles Dodgers produced a performance that has been listed as being one of the most dramatic moments in U.S. sporting history in the past century. With his team trailing 4 runs to 3 and down to its last out in the bottom of the last inning in Game 1 of the World Series, an ailing Gibson hobbled to the batter's box for his only at-bat of the game, hoping to deliver an improbable game-tying pinch-hit against the Oakland A's dominant pitcher, Dennis Eckersley. At the end of the at-bat that lasted nearly 6 minutes and included several awkward and painful-looking swings by Gibson, who was nursing injuries to both of his legs, a determined and focused Gibson did the unthinkable and hit Eckersley's best pitch over the right field fence for a 2-run, walk-off home-run that won the game for his team. An elated Gibson lumbered toward first base with his right hand in a fist held high over his head, double-pumped his right arm at his waist after reaching second base, skipped gingerly as he passed third base, and limped his way to home plate, where his teammates and coaches were waiting to mob him in celebration. When asked to describe what he felt as he rounded the bases and crossed home, Gibson said, "No pain at all there. I mean that's all glory and that's all the reward for all the people that stuck behind me my whole career.... It's hard to describe. It's just one of coming through when it counts. Bottom of the ninth inning. What more can you ask for than to come through for your team in a situation like that?"

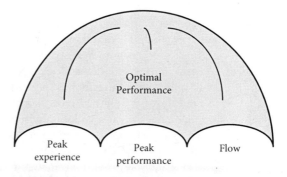

Figure 38.1 Optimal performance as an umbrella term for the subjective states of peak experience, peak performance, and flow.

In the context of understanding optimal performance, hitting that World Series game-winning home run can be categorized as a peak experience for Kirk Gibson. *Peak experience* is a broad term first described by Maslow (1968) as a fleeting and spontaneous event characterized by intense positive emotion and fulfillment. Thorne (1963) described it as "a subjective experiencing of what is subjectively recognized to be one of the high points of life, one of the most exciting, rich, and fulfilling experiences which the person has ever had" (p. 248). Similarly and more recently, Lanier, Privette, Vodanovich, and Bundrick (1996) defined peak experience as "a psychological experience that surpasses the usual level of intensity, meaning, and richness" (p. 781). After watching Gibson's performance unfold and listening to his descriptions of his thoughts and feelings of the event, it is rather easy to conclude that these definitions of peak experience match what Gibson experienced that October day.

Peak experience is important to understand in the present context due to its role in setting the stage for future research in optimal performance. Early studies (e.g., Maslow, 1968; Thorne, 1963) that focused on the psychological and philosophical interpretations of a climatic event preceded and are often cited in conjunction with more current literature related to optimal performance (e.g., Jackson & Kimiecik, 2008; Yeagle, Privette, & Dunham, 1989). In fact, some of the early research on peak experiences in sport (e.g., Ravizza, 1977) has been erroneously referenced to as evidence of the psychological characteristics of peak performance (see next section), adding some confusion and a lack of clarity to the construct of optional performance. It is important to note that optimal performance and peak experience are not synonymous terms. Although it is clearly plausible for a peak performance to result in feelings of highest happiness and ecstasy (i.e., peak experience), it also is quite possible for a relatively average performance to end in a spectacular outcome that produces feelings of elation such as those described by Gibson above.

Research suggests that certain personality characteristics or activity engagement are related to more frequent reports of peak experiences (e.g., Nelson, 1989), whereas others suggest that this is not the case (e.g., Panzarella, 1980; Gordon, 1985). For example, Yeagle, Privette, and Dunham (1989) demonstrated that both artists and an adult control group described their peak experiences similarly as characterized by words like "joy," "fulfillment," and "intensity." However, Kreutzer (1978) and others have shown a relationship between particular characteristics or personal abilities and the occurrence of peak experience, suggesting that those who are considered more in touch or entwined with the subject or skill that is being pursued may be more prone to reporting such climatic moments. As a result, people who regularly train and prepare for performances, such as performing artists and elite athletes, may be more likely to report these experiences as they are more often in a situation conducive to such an occurrence and are also evaluating these performances in order to judge value and meaning. This may explain evidence that has revealed that a peak experience can be a once-in-a-lifetime occurrence (Panzarella, 1980), whereas other researchers have found it to be regularly occurring (Ravizza, 1984). It is herein important to note that an emotionally resonant performance experience may not be necessarily accompanied by a technically excellent one, but it is possible that such an emotionally charged incident could serve as either a trigger for or an antecedent of the mechanical precision associated with positive performance outcomes. Furthermore, as people strive to satisfy innate needs for meaning and distinctiveness, the performance setting may serve as a canvas by which peak experiences come into fruition and thereby motivate the continued desire for excellence.

Peak experiences are thought to be initiated by particularly spiritual or inspiring events, unity with nature, or exceptionally aesthetic perceptions (Maslow, 1968). The resulting after-effects of these moments include therapeutic and intense feelings of satisfaction, positive personal growth, and self-actualization (Lanier et al., 1996). For example, Lipscombe (1999) showed that veteran sky divers reported undergoing peak experiences, and such experiences act as a motivational drive for continued participation. This study also highlights the relevance of peak experience as a motive for engaging in sport or other performance-based activities. Panzarella (1980) collected reports from individuals in music and visual arts settings that suggest that peak experience is a three-stage process including cognitive response and loss of self, climax with motor responses, and a final reflexive, self-transformation with an emotional response. This formulation of peak experience most clearly indicates an overlap with physical performance.

Collectively, research on peak experiences is conflicting, sparse, and based largely on self-reports. These problems may in part be due to the mysterious, obscure, and sometimes spiritual nature of this event. Despite these limitations, studies have demonstrated that a peak experience stands out and is an exemplary moment in time, with a lasting positive effect on the lives of those who encounter such a moment. Although this experience can be reported by all types of people, it can be theorized that elite athletes and performers may undergo similar events at one or more points in their performing careers that stand out far above normal performance experiences.

Peak Performance

In some performance situations, peak experiences can cross over into the domain of peak performance, defined as "superior functioning that exceeds an individual's probable performance quality, or full use of potential, in any activity" (Jackson & Kimiecik, 2008, p. 379). It is a "performance of a lifetime," one that stands out and defines the climax of a performer's career. Peak performance is differentiated from peak experience in that it is less emotion-centered and more dependent on action-oriented behaviors (Marotto, Roos, & Victor, 2007). Although a peak performance usually does coincide with positive emotions (Jackson & Kimiecik, 2008), these psychological responses are not the major outcome by which the term is operationally defined. Rather, performance-related outcomes, such as physical states and positive evaluative feedback regarding judgments of success, are thought to be causal factors for the occurrence of this experience. Due to the degree of personal investment people have in their performances, superior functioning results in positive emotions, such as fun and enjoyment and contentment and joy generated by achieving success. Furthermore, peak performance refers to human functioning as behavior that goes beyond the level at which a person normally functions (Privette & Landsman, 1983).

Concrete examples from sport include running a personal record in a race or scoring a record number of points in a game with relative ease. Likewise, in the performing arts, a peak performance could be hitting all the right notes or making all the right movements perfectly, as intended, or in a way that elicits a sense of greatness. Although these moments are usually more revered among the elite performers, individual differences in how a peak performance is classified allow for some performers to experience a peak performance not in comparison to standards set by others, but rather in surpassing personal expectations and prior achievements. Thus, more subtle performance outcomes resulting from a peak

performance could go unnoticed by an audience and may actually require no audience at all. It merely requires that performers function at their own personal best and be aware that this event is happening. For example, a track athlete could run the race of his or her life, but not win the race or even place. Likewise, experts, despite reliably performing more highly than others on their domain-specific task, can still have relative peak performances (Ericsson & Lehmann, 1996). This draws attention to the notion that peak performance is a highly subjective experience, determined by the performer alone, and based on a rich combination of incoming information such as physical sensations, perceived judgment of success, and cues from the surrounding environment (e.g., Carver, Blaney, & Scheier, 1979; Pennebaker & Lightner, 1980).

Some research suggests that skilled performers are more apt to experience these moments. For example, Harung, Heaton, Graff, and Alexander (1996) interviewed world-class performers in fields such as the performing arts, government, education, and business and found that they more frequently reported experiences of higher states of consciousness thought to be associated with peak performance than did a control sample of college students. Additionally, some researchers suggest that cognitive functioning in areas such as memory, attention, and the development of task achievement strategies differs as a function of skill on expert–novice continuum (Chase & Simon, 1973; Singer, 2000). This is thought to be a result of mental processing being more automatic due to development of well-formed neural pathways for experts while being more effortful, conscious, and slow in novice performers (Shiffrin & Schneider, 1977). Automaticity of both thought and body movements in experts may create this more ideal or conducive situation for the occurrence a peak performance.

In addition, how a peak performance is perceptually experienced may vary slightly based on the activity. Privette and Landsman (1983) surveyed a random sample of college students and found several major constructs associated with peak performance, including clear focus, intense involvement, intention, and spontaneous expression of power. Thornton, Privette, and Bundrick (1999) studied a group of business leaders who described peak performance as a moment of great significance and fulfillment associated with full focus and clear sense of self, but also reported that these individuals endorsed sociability and personal discipline as peak performance descriptors more than words used to describe peak performance by the control group. Although the state of experiencing a peak performance is important to understand, the focus of researchers and practitioners alike has appeared to shift to the process of getting there as opposed to solely describing the experience once it has been achieved. In the athletic setting, peak performance is illustrated by more action-oriented states such as high energy, confidence, control, relaxation, and enjoyment (Jackson & Kimiecik, 2008). These conditions, operating in concert, are capable of producing the equally elusive, yet more cognitive experienced state known as *flow*.

Flow

Flow is defined as an optimal psychological state achieved during an activity through a balance between the perceived challenge of the activity and the sense that one has the skills or ability to meet this challenge (Csikszentmihalyi, 1990). It is characterized by total immersion in an activity accompanied by feelings of enjoyment (Bakker, 2005). Furthermore, flow is often reported as an intrinsically motivated, intensely rewarding, and above average experience (Jackson, 1992). Our knowledge of the causes and characteristics of this experience are based on self-report and subjective personal accounts. Flow is not an uncommon state and can occur frequently in certain performance settings, especially at work. It seems to occur often in well-trained athletes (Csikszentmihalyi, 1990).

The originator of the concept, Csikszentmihalyi (1990) has resisted developing a straightforward definition of flow, but he has described eight major components that typically accompany the flow experience. These components, later termed "dimensions of flow" by Jackson and Kimiecik (2008), include the challenge–skill balance, merging action and awareness, clear goals and feedback, concentration on the task at hand, sense of control, loss of self-consciousness, transformation of time, and the autotelic experience. Each of these dimensions of flow is discussed in detail below.

The challenge–skill balance is the basis of all flow states. A challenging task that the performer nevertheless has the skills to achieve is essential for producing the intense focus characteristic of flow. If an activity is perceived as too challenging or overly difficult, then a feeling of anxiety or stress can curtail the positive mood states associated with flow (Jackson & Kimiecik, 2008). On the other hand, boredom and apathy can arise from a task perceived as too easy or requiring little skill. Having a sense that the

activity is challenging, yet having a complementary sense that the appropriate skill to meet these challenges is present, sets the foundation for initiation of a flow state. This explains why flow is more likely to result from a structured or competitive activity, such as work or sport, in which challenge and constant feedback are present (Csikszentmihalyi, 1990).

Merging action and awareness is the dimension of flow responsible for eliciting a sense of complete absorption, involvement, and focus on the task at hand (Csikszentmihalyi, 1990). Flow, in this sense, stems from the automaticity of action, something that is smooth, natural, uninterrupted, and associated with a sense of peacefulness. It is when behaviors become automatic and no longer require cognitive energy focused on the work aspect of the activity that fun and enjoyment can take place, allowing the performer to "get lost" in the task. This concept of flow is highly intertwined with the dimensions of "concentration on the task at hand," "loss of self-consciousness," and "transformation of time" because these experiences are possible consequences of one another, as well as of automaticity of action. When motor behaviors are so automatic that they are essentially unconscious, intense concentration and focus on the enjoyable and holistic aspects of the task at hand allow all other concerns or worries to fade from consciousness (Csikszentmihalyi, 1990). This ability to remove oneself from "reality" and become totally immersed in a task captures the idea of transcendence from self and changes in the perception of time. Csikszentmihalyi suggested that it is this total concentration and focus that serves as the most decisive indicator of flow. Additionally, these factors are thought to result in what is known as the "autotelic experience," in which a flow activity becomes an end in and of itself, being both enjoyable and intrinsically rewarding (Jackson & Kimiecik, 2008).

Clear goals and feedback have also been indicated as important dimensions of flow. Goals often serve as intrinsic motivational factors, whereas feedback relays information regarding the progress of goal achievement (Jackson & Kimiecik, 2008). These self-assessments of the likelihood of achieving goals may in turn influence flow—positive feedback may encourage flow while negative feedback may hinder flow. For example, a soccer player who misses a shot, gets the ball stolen away by a defender, or feels an injury creeping up may begin to negatively assess the likelihood of achieving the goal of playing well or winning the game and will thus be less likely to have a flow experience.

Control is a complex facet of flow that presents an interesting dichotomy in that it has been reported as both very present and completely absent during such an experience. Flow itself is not likely to be within the realm of control as this moment in performance is thought to be unpredictable. However, one study (Russell, 2001) conducted with athletes revealed that 64% of athletes reported that flow was controllable, and another study (Jackson, 1995) indicated that 79% of athletes reported having control over the occurrence of flow. Csikszentmihalyi (1990) brings some light to this conundrum by clarifying that what most performers classify as a "sense of control" is more likely the perceived *possibility* of control distinct from the *actuality* of control. Thus, what is experienced during flow is a sense of empowerment and the potential to determine one's own environment and performance outcomes. Furthermore, this sense is facilitated by the feeling that aversive states and potential risks are of no latent threat to ongoing functioning.

Evidence suggesting that most athletes report being able to control flow (e.g. Russell, 2001; Jackson, 1995) has led other researchers to investigate the possibility that certain qualities of a person (e.g. a certain skill or personality trait) could increase the likelihood or frequency of a flow experience. Jackson, Kimiecik, Ford, and Marsh (1998) found that, among athletes, perceived ability was positively related to flow. In addition Jackson, Thomas, Marsh, and Smethurst (2001) found a similar positive relationship between performance, self-concept, and the use of psychological training skills and perceived flow in athletes. Csikszentmihalyi (1990) suggested that flow may be more frequent in athletes because sports are designed in ways that are conducive to flow and distinct from boring or everyday experiences. However, Stein, Kimiecik, Daniels, and Jackson (1995) found that factors such as task-specific competence, confidence, and goal setting were unrelated to flow in the sport setting. In a study involving basketball shooting accuracy, Pates, Karageorghis, and Maynard (2003) demonstrated that shooting performance and perceptions of flow increased with increased lengths of exposure to self-selected music, hypothesizing that music may trigger emotions and other cognitive states associated with flow.

The experience of flow has been researched across a broad range of performance settings. For example, in the area of performing arts Hefferon and Ollis (2006) found among professional dancers that the flow dimensions of absorption, challenge–skill balance, and autotelic experience emerged as predominant themes in dance performance. The investigators also revealed other, more dance-specific factors that emerged as facilitators of flow, such as familiarity and comfort with the performance space, pre-performance routine, costumes, and confidence in the movements of the dance performance. Investigating the physiological perspective of flow in the arts, de Manzano, Harmat, Theorell, and Ullén (2010) suggested that pianists experienced flow during performance as a result of the interaction between emotional (i.e., the sympathetic branch of the autonomic nervous system) and attentional systems by demonstrating a relationship between perceived flow and factors such as blood pressure, heart rate variability, and respiratory depth. Similarly, in a military-based study, performance on sensory and cognitive vigilance tasks thought to be indicative of flow were predicted by cerebral blood flow velocity, as well as by the nonphysiological factors of task engagement and task focused coping (Matthews et al., 2010). One study of flow experiences on the job demonstrated that job resources, such as autonomy, feedback, social support, and supervisory coaching, were positively related to a perceived balance between challenges and skills indicative of flow in teachers. Interestingly, this study also found evidence that increased reports of flow among teachers was related to increased reports of flow among their students, suggesting a contagious aspect of flow (Bakker, 2005). Another job-related study on flow showed that elder care line managers and accountancy line managers reported experiencing more flow at work when engaged in tasks such as planning, problem-solving, and evaluation, indicating that the activity in which one is engaged predicts flow at work (Nielsen & Cleal, 2010).

Psychological Profile of Optimal Performance

Frequently, athletes, performers, coaches, and other performers refer to the importance of psychological factors in determining optimal performance. Despite these commonly held beliefs by those within the various performance domains, it is appropriate to ask if indeed there is a universal psychological profile related to optimal performance. Fortunately, a number of studies have investigated the psychological characteristics and skills related to optimal performance. For example, research has revealed that consciousness states considered ideal or often associated with peak experiences/performances are functional autonomy, spontaneity, loss of time and space, strong sense of self, union with the experience, and a feeling of effortlessness (Privette, 1983; Ravizza, 1977). More recently, Russell (2001) identified a set of factors in college athletes that facilitate flow (e.g., confidence and positive thinking, optimal physical preparation, focus, optimal precompetitive arousal level, motivation to perform), prevent flow (e.g., nonoptimal preparation/readiness, nonoptimal confidence, inappropriate focus, lacking motivation to perform, overarousal before competition), and disrupt flow (e.g., nonoptimal physical state, inappropriate shift in focus, self-administered pressure, self-doubt). A discussion of the universal psychological profile of optimal performance is presented below.

Psychological Characteristics of Optimal Performance

Attempting to summarize the research on the psychological characteristics of optimal performance in sport, Krane and Williams (2010) reviewed studies that assessed athletes' subjective experiences during peak performances (e.g., Privette & Bundrick, 1991; Ravizza, 1977; Robazza, Bortoli, & Hanin, 2004), compared psychological characteristics of successful and less successful athletes (e.g., Gould, Guinan, Greenleaf, Medbury, & Peterson, 1999; Mahoney & Avener, 1977; Robazza & Bortoli, 2003), and surveyed top sport people (e.g., coaches, scouts) about what it takes to achieve at a high level (e.g., Gould, Greenleaf, Guinan, & Chung, 2002; Orlick, 1980). Based on these studies, Krane and Williams concluded that certain psychological characteristics appear to be correlated with optimal performance for most athletes, consisting of feelings of high self-confidence and expectations of success, being energized yet relaxed, feeling in control, being totally concentrated, having a keen focus on the present task, having positive attitudes and thoughts about performance, and being strongly determined and committed. Conversely, the characteristics typically associated with poorer performances in sport seem to include feelings of self-doubt, lacking concentration, being distracted, being overly focused on the competition outcome or score, and feeling over- or underaroused. Although acknowledging that the set of psychological characteristics associated with optimal performance is highly idiosyncratic, Krane and Williams concluded that, for most athletes, the presence of these psychological characteristics is associated with performing to their potential.

Less is known about the psychological characteristics of optimal performance in performance domains other than sport. However, Hays and Brown (2004) interviewed performers and consultants representing the performance domains of business (e.g., lawyer, advertising executive), high-risk professions (e.g., surgeon, police officer), and performing arts (e.g., actor, dancer) regarding key psychological factors that influence successful performance in their respective performance domains. In addition to identifying unique aspects related to performance in each domain, Hays and Brown also uncovered some common psychological characteristics across the various performance domains related to high-level performance. Specifically, they found that expert performers in these nonsport domains have confidence in their abilities, express a sense of purpose and direction, and possess self-knowledge and a clear sense of identity. In addition, these performers reported experiencing performance stress related to the demands of performance, perceived the importance of the performance situation, and felt uncertainty in the performance situation similar to that which has been reported by athletes. Interestingly, a number of these expert performers indicated that their stress was positively experienced as exhilarating, motivating, and important for achieving optimal intensity for performance. Hays and Brown further noted that presenting oneself to others as confident, displaying emotions appropriate to the performance situation, being willing to take risks, and maintaining an optimal performance state were key psychological factors during high-level performance for these performers.

Mental Toughness

An alternative approach to studying the psychological characteristics of optimal performance is to consider the term *mental toughness* as a descriptor of high-level performance. Even a quick perusal of the popular literature will reveal that mental toughness is a widely used and valued label in sport and nonsport performance domains. Initial writings on mental toughness (e.g., Goldberg, 1998; Loehr, 1982) typically described the construct in relatively simplistic terms, often depicting mental toughness as a singular trait (e.g., resilience) and focusing primarily on the athletes' use of psychological skills (e.g., goal setting, visualization, positive thinking). In recent years mental toughness and its relationship to high-level performance has received an increased amount of scholarly interest and inquiry (for reviews, see Connaughton & Hanton, 2009; Gucciardi, Gordon, & Dimmock, 2009), although this research has been criticized for its atheoretical and less than scientifically rigorous nature (e.g., Crust, 2007, 2008). Despite these criticisms, a number of investigations collectively have provided greater conceptual clarity to the psychological construct of mental toughness, revealing a more conceptually refined and specific definition of mental toughness, along with a clearer picture of the characteristics of mentally tough athletes (see Gucciardi & Gordon, 2011).

As for a definition of mental toughness, Coulter, Mallett, and Gucciardi (2010) described mental toughness as:

> [T]he presence of some or the entire collection of experientially developed and inherent values, attitudes, emotions, cognitions, and behaviours that influence the way in which an individual approaches, responds to, and appraises both negatively and positively construed pressures, challenges, and adversities to consistently achieve his or her goals. (p. 715)

In addition, based on his review of the mental toughness literature, Harmison (2011) concluded that the research to date supports a view of mental toughness as a multidimensional personality construct that encompasses a number of common psychological attributes possessed by athletes that appear to not vary much from sport to sport. These common attributes include being confident; summoning motivation and desire; effectively dealing with adversity and failure; overcoming physical and/or emotional pain and hardship; successfully managing anxiety, pressure, and other emotions; staying focused; and finding balance and keeping perspective. Furthermore, Harmison theorized that the possession of these mentally tough attributes and the associated network of cognitions and emotions is what helps athletes to cope more effectively with the negative and positive aspects of competitive sport, allowing them to display the necessary mentally tough behaviors (e.g., consistently produce high-level performance when needed the most, exhibit positive body language when under duress) associated with optimal performance.

The Ideal Performance State

A central task for athletes and performers in their mental preparation for competition or performance is the achievement of an ideal performance state. The ideal performance state is an individualized and task-specific mental and emotional state that can best be thought of as the necessary mixture of cognitions (e.g., self-efficacy), emotions

(e.g., state anxiety), and physiological parameters (e.g., arousal) for athletes and performers to achieve at their best. The research reviewed above suggests that the psychological characteristics of the ideal performance state for most athletes and performers include thoughts and feelings related to being confident, motivated, determined, focused, and in control of their emotional responses related to anxiety, pressure, and the like.

The reality, however, is that ideal performance states for athletes and performers are highly subjective and likely vary from person to person. An alternative approach to such nomothetic attempts to define ideal performance states is the *individualized zone of optimal functioning* model (IZOF; Hanin, 1978, 1986, 1989, 1997, 2000a), developed to understand the relationship between subjective experiences and athletic performance. The IZOF model proposes that each individual athlete/ performer experiences a unique range of positive (i.e., pleasant) and negative (i.e., unpleasant) psychobiological states that either facilitate or diminish performance. Initially, the IZOF model was applied only to the study of precompetitive anxiety and its effect on performance (for reviews, see Hanin, 1995; Raglin & Hanin, 2000). Eventually, the IZOF model was extended beyond the single emotional state of anxiety to include an analysis of the optimal and dysfunctional patterns of positive and negative emotions affecting sport performance. According to the extended IZOF model (Hanin, 2000a), athletes will experience a unique, subjective set of emotions (e.g., confidence, frustration, fun) with varying levels of intensity that is associated with their more successful performances. Thus, an optimal intensity of these emotions will allow athletes to achieve peak performances. Hanin (2000a) also postulated that each emotion serves two primary functions: mobilizing and organizing energy. Therefore, emotions can either aid or prevent athletes and performers from sufficiently generating and efficiently using energy to accomplish their tasks within a given competition or performance.

Evidence from studies that have tested the in- or out-of-zone principle in predicting sport performance across different sports, age groups, sport experience, and competitive levels has indicated that idiosyncratic positive and negative emotions appear to be related to more and less successful performances (e.g., Hanin & Syrjä, 1995; Robazza, Bortoli, & Hanin, 2004a; Syrjä, Hanin, & Tarvonen, 1995). In addition, several intervention studies (e.g., Cohen, Tenenbaum, & English,

2006; Robazza, Pellizzari, & Hanin, 2004b) have provided some initial evidence for the efficacy of applying IZOF-based principles to guide emotion regulation in sport. For example, Cohen et al. found that a psychological skills training intervention was effective in helping two female college-aged golfers to achieve optimal emotional states and improved objective performance (e.g., lower scores, higher percentage of greens in regulation) over baseline measures. In addition, Robazza et al. (2004b) concluded that their individualized emotion self-regulation assessment and intervention program was effective in modifying the precompetition psychobiological states toward patterns more similar to best performance in the predicted directions for five out of six national-level, male Italian athletes.

Assessment of the Psychological Profile of Optimal Performance

Both researchers and practitioners alike have demonstrated a marked interest in being able to assess the psychological profile of optimal performance. A number of quantitative and qualitative methods have been utilized to gain a better understanding of the psychological characteristics and skills of athletes and performers when they are at their best. These methods have ranged from the use of formal, standardized psychological inventories to more informal checklists and interviews. Highlighted below are some of the more formal attempts to assess the psychological characteristics and skills associated with optimal performance, mental toughness in sport, and the ideal performance state.

Psychological Characteristics, Skills, and Methods

One of the challenges to understanding how to effectively assess the psychological profile related to optimal performance involves separating several terms that have been used interchangeably in the literature, namely psychological characteristics, psychological skills, and psychological methods. Typically, psychological characteristics refer to trait and state constructs such as motivation, confidence, arousal, and attention. Researchers and practitioners are most interested in the amount or intensity of these constructs possessed by athletes and performers. Psychological skills refer to the innate or learned abilities that athletes and performers possess to regulate their levels of motivation, confidence, arousal, etc. These skills include the ability to summon the necessary effort and persistence to overcome obstacles, think productively and manage one's thoughts, control one's feelings of anxiety and nervousness, and direct one's focus on the task-at-hand—to name just a few. Finally, psychological methods refer to the techniques and strategies practiced and employed by athletes and performers to master the necessary psychological skills and achieve the desired levels of the psychological characteristics of interest. Goal setting, relaxation strategies (e.g., deep breathing), self-talk techniques (e.g., thought stopping), imagery/visualization, and concentration training are considered to be the core methods taught by practitioners and coaches and used by athletes and performers.

A host of inventories have been developed over the years to measure the various psychological characteristics (e.g., motivation, confidence) associated with optimal performance, and a discussion of these measures is beyond the scope of this chapter (see Duda, 1998, for a review, and Ostrow, 2002, for a complete listing). In addition, a handful of useful inventories have been developed to measure the psychological skills possessed by athletes and performers and the psychological skills employed by them as well. Unfortunately, most of these measures assess the test-taker's psychological characteristics, skills, and use of methods within the same instrument, leading to some confusion with regard to what is actually being measured. The most commonly used inventories that have been reported in the literature include the Psychological Skills Inventory for Sports (Mahoney, Gabriel, & Perkins, 1987), the Athletic Coping Skills Inventory–28 (Smith, Schutz, Smoll, & Ptacek, 1995), the Test of Performance Strategies (Thomas, Murphy, & Hardy, 1999), and the Ottawa Mental Skills Assessment Tool–3 (Durand-Bush, Salmela, & Green-Demers, 2001). Since each of these inventories varies in terms of the theoretical foundation upon which it is based, the methods used to develop the measure, and the aspects of the psychological profile of optimal performance that it assesses, the interested reader is encouraged to review each instrument carefully prior to selecting a specific inventory for use in research or practice.

Mental Toughness

The assessment of mental toughness is an important issue for researchers and practitioners in their attempts to identify and develop mental toughness in athletes and performers. A number of attempts have been made over the past 25 years to create a reliable and valid measure of mental toughness in sport, but most of these attempts have been plagued by the lack of theory to guide the development of the questionnaires and faulty conceptualizations of the construct of mental toughness.

For example, the Psychological Performance Inventory (PPI; Loehr, 1986) has been the most often used questionnaire to assess mental toughness in sport as reported in the literature. The PPI is based on Loehr's definition of toughness as being able to perform at one's best regardless of the situation and his model of specific mental skills (e.g., self-confidence, attention control, visualization) required for toughness. In addition, the Mental Toughness 48 (MT48; Clough, Earle, & Sewell, 2002) was developed based on the application of the health psychology construct of hardiness to the conceptualization of mental toughness in sport. The MT48 has been utilized by researchers in a number of recent studies that have attempted to determine the relationship between mental toughness and a mix of other variables (e.g., physical endurance, sport injury rehabilitation, coping and optimism). More recently, Sheard, Golby, and van Wersch (2009) reported on their efforts to develop the Sport Mental Toughness Questionnaire (SMTQ), a multidimensional measure based on current conceptualizations of mental toughness in sport that taps into several important underlying dimensions of mental toughness in sport (e.g., confidence, motivation).

Despite the popularity of instruments such as the PPI and MT48 and rigorous attempts to develop measures such as the SMTQ, a need still exists to develop a reliable and valid measure of mental toughness to guide researchers and practitioners. Various criticisms (e.g., Connaughton & Hanton, 2009; Crust, 2007) have been levied against these previous attempts. These have ranged from calling the psychometric properties of the instruments into question, citing the unjust transfer of non–sport related psychological constructs into a more sport-specific setting, raising the issue of conceptualizations of mental toughness being based on hypothetical rather than research-related constructs, and acknowledging the general lack of sound theoretical frameworks to guide the development of the measures. Fortunately, recent advances in mental toughness theory and research are appearing in the literature (see Gucciardi & Gordon, 2011), and theoretical writings (e.g., Harmison, 2011) and instrument development efforts (e.g., Middleton, Martin, & Marsh, 2011) are being offered to guide the future assessment of mental toughness in sport.

Ideal Performance State

Given the highly individualized and task-specific nature of the ideal performance state, accurately assessing an athlete's or performer's mental and emotional state associated with optimal performance can be a challenging task. In addition to relying on state measures of sport confidence, performance anxiety, and the like, researchers and practitioners often utilize individual assessment methods to better understand the recipe of thoughts and emotions related to optimal performance. Orlick's (1986) competition reflections form and Butler and Hardy's (1992) performance profile are examples that have been widely used and written about in the literature. Although these qualitative methods are based on personal strengths and construct approaches to understanding human behavior, these methods sometimes are criticized for lacking standardization in the development of the assessment tools and their application in research and practice settings.

As referred to in the previous section, Hanin (1978, 1986, 1989, 1997, 2000a) has written extensively about idiographic approaches to understanding the relationship between subjective experiences and athletic performance. Hanin (2000b,c) developed a potentially useful assessment procedure for identifying patterns of optimal as well as dysfunctional emotions related to sport performance. A complete description of Hanin's assessment procedure is beyond the scope of this chapter, and the interested reader is encouraged to review Hanin's cited works, along with Harmison's (2006) application of the procedure with an elite-level athlete. In sum, the assessment process entails athletes selecting a set of individually relevant emotions from a list of both pleasant and unpleasant emotions that they associate with their best and worst performances. The athletes then indicate a level of intensity for each emotion selected to indicate the magnitude of the emotion they felt related to their best or worst performances. Optimal ranges for each emotion can be estimated via a simple calculation or systematically plotted over time, thereby establishing an optimal zone of emotions (i.e., ideal performance state) for athletes to target in their psychological preparation for performance.

Psychological Preparation for Optimal Performance

To this point in the chapter, the various aspects related to optimal performance have been described and discussed in relative isolation. Thus, what is needed is a unifying framework within which to understand the myriad of factors and variables that impact optimal performance. A pyramid model of athletic excellence (Gould & Damarjian, 1998; Hardy, Jones, & Gould, 1996) has been proposed to aid researchers and practitioners in this regard, and it would appear that this model easily can be applied to other performance domains as well. This unifying model of psychological preparation for optimal performance is grounded in two assumptions (Hardy et al., 1996). First, athletes (and performers) are multidimensional and complex beings, implying that a number of psychological, physical, technical, and tactical factors interact with one another to determine their performance. Second, athletes (and performers) do not compete or perform in a vacuum; that is, a host of environmental and contextual variables also will either facilitate or inhibit their attempts to achieve at their best.

Based on their comprehensive examination of the optimal performance literature, Hardy et al. (1996) identified a framework consisting of five components to help researchers and practitioners better understand the role that psychological factors play in achieving optimal performances (see Figure 38.2). These components are fundamental foundational attributes, psychological skills and strategies, adversity coping skills and strategies, the ideal performance state, and the environment. The components of the model are described briefly below (for a more detailed discussion, see Gould & Damarjian, 1998, and Hardy et al., 1996).

Starting at the base of the model, the fundamental foundational attributes component includes the personality traits, motivational orientations, and philosophical beliefs of the athlete or performer. For example, specific attributes that have been found to be related to performance in the sport psychology literature include trait sport confidence (Vealey, 1986), competitive trait anxiety (Martens, Vealey, & Burton, 1990), attentional style (Nideffer, 1976), task versus ego goal orientations (Duda, 2001), and mental toughness (Harmison, 2011). This component of the model serves to encourage researchers and practitioners to pay special attention to the various personality and dispositional attributes of athletes and performers, as they have both a direct and indirect influence on the extent to which they achieve their ideal performance state.

The components that appear on the right and left sides of the pyramid highlight the need for athletes and performers to possess psychological skills and adversity coping strategies to actively increase the probability of attaining and maintaining an ideal performance state. According to Hardy et al. (1996), the consistent use of various psychological skills and strategies, such as goal setting, imagery, and pre-performance routines, allows athletes (and performers) to prepare themselves mentally to perform, thus putting themselves in a psychological position to be successful. Although adversity coping skills and strategies (e.g., emotion-focused coping, realistic stress appraisal, social support) have not received the same amount of attention in the

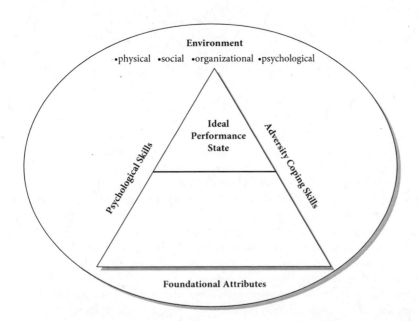

Figure 38.2 A unifying model of psychological preparation for peak athletic performance. Modified from Hardy, L., Jones, G., & Gould, D. (1996). A unifying model of psychological preparation for peak athletic performance. In *Understanding psychological preparation for sport: Theory and practice of elite performers* (pp. 239–248). Chichester, West Sussex: Wiley.

literature, athletes and performers would appear to need means by which to cope with all types of stressors (e.g., injury, performance demands, expectations of others) that may prevent or interrupt an ideal performance state.

At the top of the pyramid model is the ideal performance state. This component of the model implies that the right mixture of cognitions (e.g., self-efficacy), emotions (e.g., state anxiety), and physiological parameters (e.g., arousal) is needed for athletes (and performers) to achieve optimal performances (Hardy et al., 1996). The ability of athletes and performers to consistently attain and maintain an ideal performance state is the central feature of the pyramid model. Each component of the model—the foundational attributes, psychological and adversity coping skills, and environmental factors discussed below—contributes to and eventually determines whether or not the ideal performance state is achieved by the athlete or performer. Keeping in mind that the ideal performance state is highly subjective and idiosyncratic, researchers and practitioners should consider utilizing Hanin's (2000b,c) IZOF-based emotion profiling assessment procedure to identify individually relevant emotions and intensities that are associated with optimal performance.

Last, enveloping the pyramid is a set of physical, social, organizational, and psychological factors that can either increase or decrease the chances that athletes and performers will attain and maintain their ideal performance states (Hardy et al., 1996). For example, the physical environment of the competition site (e.g., basketball court placed on a stage with a 10-foot drop-off just beyond the sidelines) can influence the confidence and anxiety levels for some athletes. Also, the finding that some athletes draw their confidence from perceiving social support from significant others or believing in their coach's leadership and decision-making skills highlights the role that social factors can play in ideal performance states (Vealey, Hayashi, Garner-Holman, & Giacobbi, 1998). In addition, Woodman and Hardy (2001) identified a number of organizational factors (e.g., unfairness in team selection, lack of financial support) that are perceived by some athletes to be major sources of stress and likely interfere with their ability to achieve an ideal performance state in certain competitive situations. Finally, according to Hardy et al., athletes' performance accomplishments (e.g., winning vs. losing streak), the quality of their training (e.g., high vs. low), and the motivational climate (e.g., task vs. ego-oriented) in which they train and compete are among the contributors to the psychological environment that can lead to either an optimal or dysfunctional performance state.

Optimal Performance and Psychological Skills Training

The theoretical and empirical evidence presented above suggests that athletes and performers will perform best when they are able to achieve their ideal performance state. Thus, the question should be raised of whether athletes can learn how to create their ideal performance state in order to achieve consistent optimal performances. Many researchers and practitioners would agree that the ideal performance state is not a simple, one-dimensional state that is easily obtained (e.g., Hardy et al., 1996; Loehr, 1984). In fact, much of the sport psychology research over the past 40 years has examined the cognitive and affective processes related to performance, and the results indicate a complex network of relationships among a great variety of psychological variables that are related to successful performance in sport. In an effort to identify a common set of psychological skills related to optimal performance, Krane and Williams (2010) reviewed the research that focused on the mental preparation strategies used by successful athletes (e.g., Durand-Bush et al., 2001; Gould, Eklund, & Jackson, 1992; Greenleaf, Gould, & Dieffenbach, 2001). Krane and Williams concluded that an identifiable set of cognitive and behavioral skills and strategies is correlated with obtaining optimal performances, including goal setting, imagery, competition and refocusing plans, well-learned and automatic coping skills, thought control strategies, arousal management techniques, facilitative interpretations of anxiety, and attention control and refocusing skills. Similarly, Hays and Brown (2004) found expert performers in the business, high-risk profession, and performing arts domains to report the use of various psychological skills to contribute to their optimal performances, including goal setting, activation management, imagery, thought management, attention management, pre-performance mental preparation plans, well-developed performance focus plans, and refocusing or contingency plans. It has been argued that athletes and performers can learn these psychological skills and strategies through education and practice to enhance productive mind–body states and control unproductive mental states, resulting in a greater likelihood that they will perform at their best (Hays & Brown, 2004; Krane & Williams, 2010).

Effectiveness of Psychological Skills Training in Enhancing Performance

Although qualitative reviews (e.g., Meyers, Whelan, & Murphy, 1996; Vealey, 2007) have been generally optimistic regarding the role of psychological skills training in enhancing performance, attempts to uncover a link between psychological skills/strategies and optimal performance have been criticized on methodological and procedural grounds (e.g., Dishman, 1983; Landers, 1994; Morgan, 1997). Morgan has been particularly critical of the lack of research evidence to guide professional practice, pointing out that a very limited number of experimental studies exist to support the efficacy of applied sport psychology interventions and citing lack of external validity (e.g., nonsport research setting), inadequate experimental designs (e.g., lack of a control group), and behavioral artifacts (e.g., Halo effect). In addition, Morgan argued that when conventional scientific evidence exists in support of psychological interventions, the findings usually are equivocal. Collectively, three quantitative reviews (Greenspan & Feltz, 1989; Martin, Vause, & Schwartzman, 2005; Meyers et al.,1996) have painted a somewhat more positive view regarding the efficacy of applied sport psychology interventions.

In addition to presenting a qualitative review of the applied sport psychology literature that argued in favor of the effectiveness of various cognitive-behavioral interventions (i.e., goal setting, imagery, arousal management, and cognitive self-regulation) on athletic performance, Meyers et al. reported on a meta-analysis conducted by Whelan, Meyers, and Berman (1989) that consisted of 56 studies published between 1970 and 1989. The meta-analysis yielded an average effect size of.62 (standard deviation [SD] = .85) for cognitive-behavioral interventions compared to the control group. Meyers et al. also indicated that this positive result was observed across different treatment conditions (e.g., goal setting, anxiety management), control conditions (e.g., no control group, placebo control group), types of dependent measures (e.g., self-report, observer ratings), task characteristics (e.g., team sports, self-paced skills), context characteristics (e.g., competitive and noncompetitive situations), and participant characteristics (e.g., novice and skilled athletes). Meyers et al. concluded that the size of this effect supported the efficacy of cognitive-behavioral interventions to improve athletic performance.

For their review, Greenspan and Feltz (1989) searched the published and unpublished sport psychology literature for intervention research dating back to 1972. They selected studies to review that utilized athlete participants who competed on a regular and organized basis, and included designs in which the dependent variable was sport performance in a noncontrived competitive situation in which the participants regularly competed. Greenspan and Feltz analyzed and synthesized a total of 23 interventions across 19 published studies, addressing the efficacy of cognitive and behavioral interventions (e.g., relaxation, cognitive restructuring, self-monitoring) with athletes. In general, Greenspan and Feltz concluded that the psychological interventions utilized in the reviewed studies were effective in improving athletic performance in competitive situations. More specifically, 87% (20 of 23) of the interventions reported positive results, and 73% (8 of 11) of the interventions in which it was possible to infer causality were found to enhance performance. More cautiously, however, the reviewers noted that 35% (8 of 23) of the interventions failed to include some form of control (i.e., control group or appropriate single-subject design), causality could be inferred in less than half (11 of 23) of the interventions, and only 18% (4 out of 22) of the interventions utilized an adequate manipulation check of the intervention. In addition, Greenspan and Feltz acknowledged that most of the participants in the various studies were male, most of the studies utilized collegiate athletes as opposed to elite or youth athletes, and most of the interventions were conducted with individual sport athletes (e.g., tennis players) or on individual skills (e.g., basketball free-throw shooting) within team sports. The authors also expressed additional concerns related to the possibility of a bias toward the publication of studies with positive results, the lack of attention paid to ethnic/cultural variables, the neglect by researchers of the effects of interventions on nontargeted performance areas, and the failure to assess the maintenance of treatment effects.

Utilizing even more stringent selection criteria, Martin, Vause, and Schwartzman (2005) recently reviewed studies published in several behavioral and sport psychology journals that addressed the extent to which psychological interventions directly and reliably improved performance of athletes in competition. Martin et al. reanalyzed the studies reviewed by Greenspan and Feltz (1989) and extended their analysis to include the current state of published experimental studies through 2002. For their review, Martin et al. followed the selection criteria used by Greenspan and Feltz, but eliminated studies that assessed performance in mock competitions, relied on athlete self-reports of their performance as the dependent variable, or failed to incorporate appropriate single-subject or groups designs. Their conservative selection criteria yielded only 15 studies; however, 14 of these studies demonstrated a positive effect of the interventions on performance, with nine showing a substantial impact (mean improvement ranged from 3% to 80% over baseline or control). Martin et al. also noted that nearly all the participants in the single-subject designs showed improvement as the result of the intervention. In addition, they concluded that the studies that involved imagery (six of the seven studies) or goal setting (all three studies) as a component of the intervention were particularly successful in improving athletic performance. Similar to Greenspan and Feltz, Martin et al. shared a number of concerns related to their review, including finding no experimental studies that provided evidence of performance improvement with elite-level athletes, that demonstrated the positive effects of interventions on nontargeted behaviors, or that showed durable follow-up effects of interventions.

Conclusion

The phenomenon of optimal performance has received much theoretical and empirical interest over the years. Historically, athletes' and performers' peak experiences, peak performances, and flow states have been investigated in an attempt to better understand the psychology of optimal performance. In addition, researchers have focused on psychological constructs such as mental toughness and the ideal performance state to paint a clearer picture of the psychological characteristics of optimal performance and to increase the ability to describe, explain, and predict optimal performance. Several models exist depicting the various factors that impact optimal performance in athletes and performers, and a unifying model for psychological preparation for optimal performance (Gould & Damarjian, 1998; Hardy et al., 1996) was highlighted as a useful aid for researchers and practitioners interested in this area. The relationship between psychological skills training and optimal performance was explored, and evidence was presented to suggest that psychological skills training can be effective in enhancing the likelihood of optimal levels of performance. Next, future research directions for an enhanced understanding of the psychology of optimal performance are discussed.

Future Directions

Despite sustained and multiple efforts investigating the psychology of optimal performance, opportunities abound for researchers to continue to explore the role of psychological factors in the achievement of optimal performance by athletes and performers in other domains. One such opportunity that exists is related to the interaction between person and situational antecedents of optimal performance states. For the most part, the majority of the investigations to date have focused either on the person variables (e.g., use of psychological skills; Pates et al., 2003) or situational variables (e.g., social support; Matthews et al., 2010) associated with optimal performance, but rarely the interaction of the two. Although this type of research is complicated and challenging, it is reasonably possible to explore the relationships between optimal performances states, person variables, and situational factors (see Jackson et al., 2001). Furthermore, social-cognitive conceptualizations of various psychological constructs, such as mental toughness (Harmison, 2011) and sport confidence (Vealey & Chase, 2008), are emerging and provide a framework upon which various person–situational interactions can be explored. For example, Harmison recently proposed that mental toughness can best be understood as a social-cognitive personality construct that is conceptualized as a system of internal, mediating cognitive-affective processes that interact with each other and one's environment and manifest themselves in predictable patterns of situation–behavior relationships. Thus, determining the types of cognitions (e.g., belief in ability to respond to a mistake) and affects (e.g., feel in control of ability to be successful) experienced by mentally tough athletes, how they are organized within an athlete's personality system (e.g., self-belief interconnected to value placed on determination, which results in feelings of confidence), and the manner in which they interact with features of the competitive situations (e.g., history of responding successfully to mistakes) can allow for a better description, explanation, and prediction of the relationship between mental toughness and optimal performance.

Another research opportunity can be found in the feedback loops that exist between optimal performance states and psychophysiological functioning. Evidence exists to suggest that cognitive states and other psychological factors can have an effect on the physiology linked with performance and vice versa (e.g., Morgan & Pollock, 1977; Pennebaker & Skelton, 1981; Watson & Pennebaker, 1989). More specifically, previous research in the field of somatic interpretation has examined the effects of attention and distraction in a health or performance setting and the role that each plays in somatic awareness (Cioffi, 1991). For example, distraction in the form of a demanding or variable external environment (e.g., cross-country course vs. running track) has been found to lower the intensity of internal information, thereby decreasing symptom reporting and physical and psychological distress while also increasing performance (e.g., Pennebaker & Lightner, 1980). However, Morgan and Pollock's (1977) classic study of the use of association and dissociation strategies by elite-level runners suggests that awareness of internal stimuli may benefit more experienced runners by allowing them to utilize somatic amplification to make adjustments to their pace based on an accurate understanding of their physiological sensations. These studies highlight the role that awareness of certain physical sensations plays in self-regulation involving physical exertion. As with most volitional behavior, an initial task (i.e., physical performance) ignites a goal-directed response, such as conforming to a standard, which requires self-focus for one to constantly self-regulate behavior (Carver et al., 1979). For behaviors involving physical exertion, the self-regulation includes becoming more aware of certain physical sensations. Given the role of awareness in optimal performance constructs such as flow, a better understanding of how physical sensations impact psychological states would serve to enhance an understanding of optimal performance (see also Chapters 7,8, and 32, all in this volume).

When attempting to study the phenomenon of optimal performance, the majority of the research has focused on the psychological characteristics of athletes and performers when they are at their very best. Much less is known about optimal performance and the psychology of athletes who overcome difficult, challenging, and often negative performance situations. Incorporating further study of the construct of mental toughness into an understanding of the psychology of optimal performance would appear to hold some promise in this regard. As discussed earlier, theoretical models of mental toughness (e.g., Harmison, 2011) are beginning to emerge that can provide the foundation upon which researchers can investigate this popular and valued attribute. Uncovering the relationship between mental toughness attributes, mentally tough cognitions and affects,

and the mentally tough performance behaviors that result will add to our understanding of the psychological characteristics of optimal performance. Whereas almost a decade of research (see Connaughton & Hanton, 2009; Gucciardi et al., 2009) has produced a relatively clear conceptualization and definition of the mental toughness construct, opportunities remain for researchers to investigate how mental toughness impacts the achievement of optimal performance via the psychological and coping skills utilized by athletes in response to challenging and difficult performance situations. Possible research questions that can be explored include how mentally tough athletes/performers interpret difficult performance situations, how these interpretations influence athletes'/performers' expectations regarding their performance in that situation, what feelings and emotions are generated as a result of athletes'/performers' beliefs about difficult situations, and what specific mentally tough behaviors are produced from these cognitions and affects.

Finally, despite the general acceptance that optimal performance is characterized by a set of desirable psychological characteristics and is associated with the use of certain psychological skills, the reality remains that a limited amount of empirical, cause-and-effect evidence exists to support the effectiveness of interventions designed to create ideal performance states and enhance the objective performance of real athletes and performers in their actual performance settings. This presents a unique, albeit challenging opportunity for researchers to document the efficacy of psychological skills training in enhancing performance in sport and other performance domains. To overcome some of the inherent challenges in conducting methodologically sound intervention research with athletes and performers in their performance settings, Martin et al. (2005) offered a number of useful suggestions, including the use of videos to record performances to be objectively evaluated at a later time, selecting performance variables (e.g., performance statistics, well-defined performance behaviors) that can be reliably measured, and utilizing more single-subject designs. Researchers interested in uncovering the link between psychological skills training and optimal performance would be wise to heed Martin et al.'s recommendation to place a higher value on conducting empirical studies that utilize "real" athletes (or performers) in "real" competitions (or performances), include objective measures of performance, and incorporate empirical designs that allow for cause-and-effect to be determined (e.g., single-subject design, use of control group).

References

Bakker, A. B. (2005). Flow among music teachers and their students: The crossover of peak experiences. *Journal of Vocational Behavior, 66,* 26–44.

Butler, R. J., & Hardy, L. (1992). The performance profile: Theory and application. *The Sport Psychologist, 9,* 253–264.

Carver, C. S., Blaney, P. H., & Scheier, M. F. (1979). Reassertion and giving up: The interactive role of self-directed attention and outcome expectancy. *Journal of Personality and Social Psychology, 37,* 1859–1870.

Chase, W. G., & Simon, H. A. (1973). Perception in chess. *Cognitive Psychology, 4,* 55–81.

Cioffi, D. (1991). Beyond attentional strategies: A cognitive-perceptual model of somatic interpretation. *Psychological Bulletin, 109,* 25–41.

Clough, P., Earle, K., & Sewell, D. (2002). Mental toughness: The concept and its measurement. In I. Cockerill (Ed.), *Solutions in sport psychology* (pp. 32–45). London: Thomson.

Cohen, A. B., Tenenbaum, G., & English, R. W. (2006). Emotions and golf performance: An IZOF-based applied sport psychology case study. *Behavior Modification, 30,* 259–280.

Connaughton, D., & Hanton, S. (2009).Mental toughness in sport: Conceptual and practical issues. In S. D. Mellalieu & S. Hanton (Eds.), *Advances in applied sport psychology: A review* (pp. 317–346). London: Routledge.

Coulter, T. J., Mallett, C. J., & Gucciardi, D. F. (2010). Understanding mental toughness in Australian soccer: Perceptions of players, parents, and coaches. *Journal of Sports Sciences, 28,* 699–716.

Crust, L. (2007). Mental toughness in sport: A review. *International Journal of Sport and Exercise Psychology, 5,* 270–290.

Crust, L. (2008). A review and conceptual re-examination of mental toughness: Implications for future research. *Personality and Individual Differences, 45,* 576–583.

Csikszentmihalyi, M. (1990). *Flow: The psychology of optimal experience.* New York: Harper & Row.

de Manzano, Ö., Harmat, L., Theorell, T., & Ullén, F. (2010). The psychophysiology of flow during piano playing. *Emotion, 10,* 301–311.

Dishman, R. K. (1983). Identity crisis in North American sport psychology: Academics in professional issues. *Journal of Sport Psychology, 5,* 123–134.

Duda, J. L. (1998). *Advances in sport and exercise psychology measurement.* Morgantown, WV: Fitness Information Technology.

Duda, J. L. (2001). Achievement goal research in sport: Pushing the boundaries and clarifying some misunderstandings. In G. C. Roberts (Ed.), *Advances in motivation in sport and exercise* (pp. 129–182). Champaign, IL: Human Kinetics.

Durand-Bush, N., Salmela, J. H., & Green-Demers, I. (2001). The Ottawa Mental Skills Assessment Tool (OMSAT-3). *The Sport Psychologist, 15,* 1–19.

Ericsson, K. A., & Lehmann, A. C. (1996). Expert and exceptional performance: Evidence of maximal adaptation to task constraints. *Annual Reviews in Psychology, 47,* 273–305.

Goldberg, A. S. (1998). *Sports slump busting: 10 steps to mental toughness and peak performance.* Champaign, IL: Human Kinetics.

Gordon, R. D. (1985). Dimensions of peak communication experiences: An exploratory study. *Psychological Reports, 57,* 824–826.

Gould, D., & Damarjian, N. (1998). Mental skills training in sport. In B. Elliot (Ed.), *Training in sport: Applying sport science* (pp. 69–116). Chichester, West Sussex, England: Wiley.

Gould, D., Eklund, R. C., & Jackson, S. A. (1992b). 1988 U.S. Olympic wrestling excellence: II. Thoughts and affect occurring during competition. *The Sport Psychologist, 6,* 383–402.

Gould, D., Greenleaf, C., Guinan, D., & Chung, Y. (2002). A survey of U.S. Olympic coaches: Variables perceived to have influenced athlete performance and coach effectiveness. *The Sport Psychologist, 16,* 229–250.

Gould, D., Guinan, D., Greenleaf, C., Medbury, R., & Peterson, K. (1999). Factors affecting Olympic performance: Perceptions of athletes and coaches from more and less successful teams. *The Sport Psychologist, 13,* 371–394.

Greenleaf, C., Gould, D., & Dieffenbach, K. (2001). Factors influencing Olympic performance: Interviews with Atlanta and Nagano U.S. Olympian. *Journal of Applied Sport Psychology, 13,* 154–184.

Greenspan, M. J., & Feltz, D. L. (1989). Psychological interventions with athletes in competitive situations: A review. *The Sport Psychologist, 3,* 219–236.

Gucciardi, D. F., & Gordon, S. (2011). *Mental toughness in sport: Developments in research and theory.* London: Routledge.

Gucciardi, D. F., Gordon, S., & Dimmock, J. A. (2009). Advancing mental toughness research and theory using personal construct psychology. *International Review of Sport and Exercise Psychology, 2,* 54–72.

Hanin, Y. L. (1978). A study of anxiety in sport. In W. F. Straub (Ed.), *Sport psychology: An analysis of athletic behavior* (pp. 236–249). Ithaca, NY: Mouvement.

Hanin, Y. L. (1986). State-trait anxiety research in the USSR. In C. D. Spielberger & R. Diaz-Guerrero (Eds.), *Cross cultural anxiety* (pp. 45–64). Washington, DC: Hemisphere.

Hanin, Y. L. (1989). Interpersonal and intragroup anxiety in sports. In D. Hackfort & C. D. Spielberger (Eds.), *Anxiety in sports: An international perspective* (pp. 19–28). Washington, DC: Hemisphere.

Hanin, Y. L. (1995). Individual zones of optimal functioning (IZOF) model: An idiographic approach to performance anxiety. In K. Henschen & W. Straub (Eds.), *Sport psychology: An analysis of athlete behavior* (pp. 103–119). Longmeadow, MA: Mouvement.

Hanin, Y. L. (1997). Emotions and athletic performance: Individual zones of optimal functioning model. *European Yearbook of Sport Psychology, 1,* 29–72.

Hanin, Y. L. (2000a). Individual zones of optimal functioning (IZOF) model: Emotion–performance relationships in sport. In Y. L. Hanin (Ed.), *Emotions in sport* (pp. 65–89). Champaign, IL: Human Kinetics.

Hanin, Y. L. (2000b). Successful and poor performance and emotions. In Y. L. Hanin (Ed.), *Emotions in sport* (pp. 157–187). Champaign, IL: Human Kinetics.

Hanin, Y. L. (2000c). IZOF-based emotion-profiling: Step-wise procedures and forms. In Y. L. Hanin (Ed.), *Emotions in sport* (pp. 303–313). Champaign, IL: Human Kinetics.

Hanin, Y. L., & Syrjä, P. (1995). Performance affect in junior ice hockey players: An application of the individual zones of optimal functioning model. *The Sport Psychologist, 9,* 169–187.

Hardy, L., Jones, G., & Gould, D. (1996). A unifying model of psychological preparation for peak athletic performance.

In *Understanding psychological preparation for sport: Theory and practice of elite performers* (pp. 239–248). Chichester, West Sussex, England: Wiley.

Harmison, R. J. (2006). Peak performance in sport: Identifying ideal performance states and developing athletes' psychological skills. *Professional Psychology: Research and Practice, 37,* 233–243.

Harmison, R. J. (2011). A social-cognitive framework for understanding and developing mental toughness in sport. In D. F. Gucciardi & S. Gordon (Eds.), *Mental toughness in sport: Developments in theory and research* (pp. 47–68). London: Routledge.

Harung, H. S., Heaton, D. P., Graff, W. W., & Alexander, C. N. (1996). Peak performance and higher states of consciousness: A study of world-class performers. *Journal of Managerial Psychology, 11,* 3–21.

Hays, K. F., & Brown, C. H., Jr. (2004). *You're on! Consulting for peak performance.* Washington, DC: American Psychological Association.

Hefferon, K. M., & Ollis, S. (2006). 'Just clicks': An interpretive phenomenological analysis of professional dancers' experience of flow. *Research in Dance Education, 7,* 141–159.

Jackson, S. A. (1992). Athletes in flow: A qualitative investigation of flow states in elite figure skaters. *Journal of Applied Sport Psychology, 4,* 161–180.

Jackson, S. A. (1995). Factors influencing the occurrence of flow in elite athletes. *Journal of Applied Sport Psychology, 7,* 138–166.

Jackson, S. A., & Csikszentmihalyi, M. (1999). *Flow in sports: The keys to optimal experiences and performances.* Champaign, IL: Human Kinetics.

Jackson, S. A., & Kimiecik, J. C. (2008). The flow perspective of optimal experience in sport and physical activity. In T. S. Horn (Ed.), *Advances in sport psychology* (pp. 377–399). Champaign, IL: Human Kinetics.

Jackson, S. A., Kimiecik, J. C., Ford, S. K., & Marsh, H. W. (1998). Psychological correlates of flow in sport. *Journal of Sport and Exercise Psychology, 20,* 358–378.

Jackson, S. A., & Roberts, G. C. (1992). Positive performance states of athletes: Toward a conceptual understanding of peak performance. *The Sport Psychologist, 6,* 156–171.

Jackson, S. A., Thomas, P. R., Marsh, H. W., & Smethurst, C. J. (2001). Relationships between flow, self-concept, psychological skills, and performance. *Journal of Applied Sport Psychology, 13,* 129–153.

Krane, V., & Williams, J. M. (2010). Psychological characteristics of peak performance. In J. M. Williams (Ed.), *Applied sport psychology: Personal growth to peak performance* (pp. 169–188). New York: McGraw-Hill.

Kreutzer, C. S. (1978). Whatever turns you on: Triggers to transcendent experiences. *Journal of Humanistic Psychology, 18,* 11–80.

Landers, D. M. (1994). Performance, stress, and health: Overall reaction. *Quest, 46,* 123–135.

Lanier, L. S., Privette, G., Vodanovich, S., & Bundrick, C. M. (1996). Peak experiences: Lasting consequences and breadth of occurrences among realtors, artists, and a comparison group. *Journal of Social Behavior and Personality, 11,* 781–791.

Lipscombe, N. (1999). The relevance of the peak experience to continued skydiving participation: A qualitative approach to assessing motivations. *Leisure Studies, 18,* 267–288.

Loehr, J. E. (1982). *Athletic excellence: Mental toughness training for sports.* New York: Plume.

Loehr, J. E. (1984, March). How to overcome stress and play at your peak all the time. *Tennis, 21,* 66–76.

Loehr, J. E. (1986) *Mental toughness training for sports: Achieving athletic excellence.* Lexington, MA: Stephen Greene Press.

Mahoney, M. J., & Avener, M. (1977). Psychology of the elite athlete: An exploratory study. *Cognitive Therapy and Research, 1,* 135–142.

Mahoney, M. J., Gabriel, T. J., & Perkins, T. S. (1987). Psychological skills and exceptional athletic performance. *The Sport Psychologist, 1,* 181–199.

Marotto, M., Roos, J., & Victor, B. (2007). Collective virtuosity in organizations: A study of peak performance in an orchestra. *Journal of Management Studies, 44,* 388–413.

Martens, R., Vealey, R. S., & Burton, D. (1990). *Competitive anxiety in sport.* Champaign, IL: Human Kinetics.

Martin, G. L., Vause, T., & Schwartzman, L. (2005). Experimental studies of psychological interventions with athletes in competitions: Why so few? *Behavior Modification, 29,* 615–641.

Maslow, A. (1968). *Toward a psychology of being.* New York: Von Nostrand Reinhold Company.

Matthews, G., Warm, J., Reinerman-Jones, L., Langheim, L., Washburn, D., & Tripp, L. (2010). Task engagement, cerebral blood flow velocity, and diagnostic monitoring for sustained attention. *Journal of Experimental Psychology, 16,* 187–203.

Meyers, A. W., Whelan, J. P., & Murphy, S. M. (1996). Cognitive behavioral strategies in athletic performance enhancement. In M. Hersen, R. M. Eisler, & P. M. Miller (Eds.), *Progress in behavior modification* (pp. 137–164). Pacific Grove, CA: Brooks/Cole.

Middleton, S. C., Martin, A. J., & Marsh, H. W. (2011). Development and validation of the Mental Toughness Inventory (MTI): A construct validation approach. In D. F. Gucciardi & S. Gordon (Eds.), *Mental toughness in sport: Developments in theory and research* (pp. 91–107). London: Routledge.

Morgan, W. P. (1997). Mind games: The psychology of sport. In D. R. Lamb & R. Murray (Eds.), *Optimizing sport performance* (pp. 1–62). Carmel, IN: Cooper.

Morgan, W., & Pollock, M. (1977). Psychologic characterization of the elite distance runner. *Annals of the New York Academy of the Sciences, 301,* 382–403.

Nelson, P. L. (1989). Personality factors in the frequency of reported spontaneous paranatural experiences. *Journal of Transpersonal Psychology, 21,* 193–209.

Nideffer, R. M. (1976). *The inner athlete: Mind plus muscle for winning.* New York: Crowell.

Nielsen, K., & Cleal, B. (2010). Predicting flow at work: Investigating the activities and job characteristics that predict flow states at work. *Journal of Occupational Health Psychology, 15,* 180–190.

Orlick, T. (1980). *In pursuit of excellence.* Champaign, IL: Human Kinetics.

Orlick, T. (1986). *Psyching for sport: Mental training for athletes.* Champaign, IL: Human Kinetics.

Ostrow, A. (2002). *Directory of psychological tests in the sport and exercise sciences.* Morgantown, WV: Fitness Information Technology.

Panzarella, R. (1980). The phenomenology of aesthetic peak experiences. *Journal of Humanistic Psychology, 20,* 69–85.

Pates, J., Karageorghis, C. I., Fryer, R., & Maynard, I. (2003). Effects of asynchronous music on flow states and shooting performance among netball players. *Psychology of Sport and Exercise, 4,* 415–427.

Pennebaker, J. W., & Lightner, J. M. (1980). Competition of internal and external information in an exercise setting. *Journal of Personality and Social Psychology, 39,* 165–174.

Pennebaker, J. W., & Skelton, J. A. (1981). Selective monitoring of physical sensations. *Journal of Personality and Social Psychology, 41,* 213–223.

Privette, G. (1983). Peak experience, peak performance, and flow: A comparative analysis of positive human experiences. *Journal of Personality and Social Psychology, 45,* 1361–1368.

Privette, G., & Bundrick, C. M. (1991). Peak experience, peak performance, and flow. *Journal of Social Behavior and Personality, 6,* 169–188.

Privette, G., & Landsman, T. (1983). Factor analysis of peak performance: The full use of potential. *Journal of Personality and Social Psychology, 44,* 195–200.

Raglin, J. S., & Hanin, Y. L. (2000). Competitive anxiety. In Y. L. Hanin (Ed.), *Emotions in sport* (pp. 93–111). Champaign, IL: Human Kinetics.

Ravizza, K. (1977). Peal experiences in sport. *Journal of Humanistic Psychology, 17,* 35–40.

Ravizza, K. (1984). Qualities of the peak experience in sport. In J. M. Silva & R. S. Weinberg (Eds.), *Psychological foundations of sport* (pp. 452–462). Champaign, IL: Human Kinetics.

Robazza, C., & Bortoli, L. (2003). Intensity, idiosyncratic content and functional impact of performance-related emotions in athletes. *Journal of Sport Sciences, 21,* 171–189.

Robazza, C., Bortoli, L., & Hanin, Y. (2004a). Precompetition emotions, bodily symptoms, and task-specific qualities as predictors of performance in high-level karate athletes. *Journal of Applied Sport Psychology, 16,* 151–165.

Robazza, C., Pellizzari, M., & Hanin, Y. (2004b). Emotion self-regulation and athletic performance: An application of the IZOF model. *Psychology of Sport and Exercise, 5,* 379–404.

Russell, W. D. (2001). An examination of flow state occurrence in college athletes. *Journal of Sport Behavior, 24,* 83–107.

Seligman, M. E. P., & Csikszentmihalyi, M. (2000). Positive psychology: An introduction. *American Psychologist, 55,* 5–14.

Sheard, M., Golby, J., & van Wersch, A. (2009). Progress toward construct validation of the Sports Mental Toughness Questionnaire (SMTQ). *European Journal of Psychological Assessment, 25,* 186–193.

Shiffrin, R. M., & Schneider, W. (1977). Controlled and automatic human information processing: II. Perceptual learning, automatic attending and a general theory. *Psychological Review, 82,* 127–190.

Singer, R. N. (2000). Performance and human factors: Considerations about cognition and attention for self-paced and externally paced events. *Ergonomics, 43,* 1661–1680.

Smith, R. E., Schutz, R. W., Smoll, F. L., & Ptacek, J. T. (1995). Development and validation of a multidimensional measure of sport-specific psychological skills: The Athletic Coping Skills Inventory-28. *Journal of Sport and Exercise Psychology, 17,* 379–398.

Stein, G. L., Kimiecik, J. C., Daniels, J., & Jackson, S. A. (1995). Psychological antecedents of flow in recreational sport. *Personality and Social Psychology Bulletin, 21,* 125–135.

Syrjä, P., Hanin, Y., & Tarvonen, S. (1995). Emotion and performance relationship in squash and badminton players. In R. Vanfraechem-Raway & Y. Vanden Auweele (Eds.), *Proceedings of the 9th European Congress on Sport Psychology* (pp. 183–190). Brussels, Belgium: FEPSAC/Belgium Federation of Sport Psychology.

Thomas, P. R., Murphy, S. M., & Hardy, L. (1999). Test of performance strategies: Development and preliminary validation of a comprehensive measure of athletes' psychological skills. *Journal of Sport Sciences, 17,* 697–713.

Thorne, F. C. (1963). The clinical use of peak and nadir experience reports. *Journal of Clinical Psychology, 19,* 248–250.

Thornton, F., Privette, G., & Bundrick, C. M. (1999). Peak performance of business leaders: An experience parallel to self-actualization theory. *Journal of Business and Psychology, 14,* 253–264.

Vealey, R. S. (1986). Conceptualization of sport confidence and competitive orientation: Preliminary investigation and instrument development. *Journal of Sport Psychology, 8,* 221–246.

Vealey, R. S. (2007). Mental skills training in sports. In G. Tenenbaum & R.C. Eklund (Eds.), *Handbook of sport psychology* (pp. 287–309). New York: Wiley.

Vealey, R. S., & Chase, M. A. (2008). Self-confidence in sport. In T. S. Horn (Ed.), *Advances in sport psychology* (pp. 65–97). Champaign, IL: Human Kinetics.

Vealey, R. S., Hayashi, S. W., Garner-Holman, M., & Giacobbi, P. (1998). Sources of sport-confidence: Conceptualization and instrument development. *Journal of Sport and Exercise Psychology, 20,* 54–80.

Watson, D., & Pennebaker, J. W. (1989). Health complaints, stress, and distress: Exploring the central role of negative affectivity. *Psychological Review, 96,* 234–254.

Whelan, J. P., Meyers, A. W., & Berman, J. S. (1989, August). Cognitive-behavioral interventions for athletic performance enhancement. In M. Greenspan (Chair), *Sport psychology intervention research: Reviews and issues.* Symposium presented at the annual meeting of the American Psychological Association, New Orleans, LA.

Woodman, T., & Hardy, L. (2001). A case study of organizational stress in elite sport. *Journal of Applied Sport Psychology, 13,* 207–238.

Yeagle, E., Privette, G., & Dunham, F. (1989). Highest happiness: An analysis of artists' peak experience. *Psychological Reports, 65,* 523–530.

Supervision and Mindfulness in Sport and Performance Psychology

Mark B. Andersen

Abstract

The topic of supervision has been a late arrival in the applied sport psychology world of discussion and debate. The field of performance psychology is even newer than sport psychology, and there is little in this field that addresses useful models of supervision. This chapter focuses on supervision in applied sport psychology. Supervision in our field has borrowed extensively from mainstream counseling and clinical psychology models. There is no real, viable model of supervision based on the cognitive-behavioral therapy derived psychological skills training (PST) paradigm that seems to be dominant in our field. One of the current trends in counseling and clinical psychology has been the exploration of the usefulness of mindfulness in a variety of therapeutic settings. In this chapter, I review the applied sport psychology literature on supervision and how advancements in mindfulness and the field of interpersonal neurobiology (neural correlates of presence, attunement, and resonance between therapists and clients and supervisors and supervisees) can inform applied sport (and performance) psychology practice. As a psychodynamic/Buddhist philosophy-oriented psychotherapist and supervisor, I argue that a mindfulness approach to sport and performance psychology supervision (and treatment) service delivery is a transtheoretical model that could be applicable to almost any of the helping professions. I conclude this chapter with a case example of how a mindfulness-based psychodynamic approach to beginning supervision might sound and feel like for the practitioner and the supervisee.

Key Words: Supervision, mindfulness, presence, attunement, resonance, psychodynamic theory

In defining supervision, Bernard and Goodyear (1998) wrote that it is:

> An intervention provided by a senior member of a profession to a junior member, or members of that same profession. This relationship is evaluative, extends over time, and has the simultaneous purpose of enhancing the professional functioning of the junior member(s), monitoring the quality of professional services offered to those clients she, he, or they see(s) and acting as the gatekeeper for those who are to enter that particular profession.
> (p. 6)

This definition, however, is overly practitioner focused and seems curiously lacking in recognition of client welfare concerns. Authors in applied sport psychology supervision (e.g., Lubker & Andersen, in press; Van Raalte & Andersen, 2000; Watson, Zizzi, Etzel, & Lubker, 2004) have suggested that the primary purpose of supervision in applied sport (and performance) psychology service delivery is the health and welfare of clients in treatment. Only then comes the demi-primary goal of helping the supervisee become a competent and self-reflective practitioner. Although client welfare is primary, this other goal will be the focus of this chapter.

Regarding training in the field, numerous articles and book chapters have been written about what constitutes necessary and sufficient coursework and internship experiences for graduate students to be adequately prepared to enter the applied services arena (e.g., Andersen, 2002; Andersen & Tod, 2011 Andersen, Van Raalte, & Brewer, 2000; Andersen & Williams-Rice, 1996; Feltz, 1987; Morris, Alfermann, Lintunen, & Hall, 2003; Silva, Lerner, & Metzler, 2007; Tod, 2007; Tod, Andersen, & Marchant, 2009, 2011; Tod, Marchant, & Andersen, 2007), and I will not go into the arguments for and against the different pathways. Rather, I will limit the discussion of training to what happens, or should happen, within a central area of training (i.e., supervision of practica and internships). Also, there is no substantive literature on the supervision and training of performance psychologists. Therefore, I will draw from the extant literature in applied sport psychology and from the clinical and counseling psychology fields. In this chapter, I will cover the history of supervision in applied sport psychology, current models of supervision, how mindfulness relates to supervision, and why the features of interpersonal mindfulness of presence, attunement, and resonance are applicable in supervision and how they help ensure competent client care. I will end the chapter with an example of how my supervisees and I begin therapeutic psychodynamic/Buddhist philosophy supervision and mutually lay the ground rules for mindful supervision.

Brief History of Supervision

Supervision in applied sport psychology probably has a long history, but research on and academic discourse about supervision are relatively recent arrivals on the scene. Given that sport psychology as a field began within and grew up in the tradition of physical education (PE) programs in universities, it seems odd that supervision as a topic of discussion is a recent development. The PE discipline has a long history of supervision of student teachers that is part of probably every PE curriculum. Why exploring those teacher education processes did not flow on to applied sport psychology is, however, unknown. One of the earliest mentions of supervision came with the advent of the Association for Applied Sport Psychology (AASP, but at that time, AAASP) criteria for certified consultant status in 1989. The criteria were (are):

Supervised Experience Guidelines:

• A total of 400 hours of supervised experience, of which:

• 100 hours must be in direct contact hours with the clients

• 40 hours of supervision by an AASP approved supervisor, and all 400 hours must be verified by this supervisor

• Only those hours actually spent in the preparation and delivery of sport and exercise psychology services are eligible for inclusion (from http://appliedsportpsych.org/consultants/become-certified)

There was, however, no real discussion of what supervision would be or what models of supervision would be best for applied sport psychology work. The next mention of supervision I can find is a conference workshop in 1992 (i.e., Carr, Murphy, & McCann, 1992), but only an abstract is available. Two years later, Andersen, Van Raalte, and Brewer (1994) published the first quantitative research on assessing the skills of sport psychology supervisors. The picture that emerged from that research was not a good one. Many graduate students were not receiving enough practical work to meet AASP certified consultant criteria, and most supervisors had not gone through any formal training in supervision. More than a decade later, the picture had gotten better, but not by much.

In 21st-century research on practitioners, Watson et al. (2004) found that over 80% of sport psychology professionals were not receiving any supervision, and later, in a survey of U.K. sport psychology practitioners, Winstone and Gervis (2006) reported that 31% of their sample had received no supervision of their practice in the past 12 months, and 50% had received only one to five supervision sessions in the past year. Further, when asked about the need for supervision post accreditation (after obtaining licensure, registration), 71% thought it was important only "when needed—ad hoc," and 29% believed supervision was important and should occur monthly or fortnightly. Beliefs and behaviors in this study do not gel well because only 5% of the sample had had supervision sessions 11 or more times in the past year. Almost a third of the sample believed supervision was important enough to occur monthly or fortnightly, but only 5% behaved in ways that were congruent with those beliefs. It appears that supervision in applied sport psychology has not advanced much since its first mention as a best-practice guideline nearly two decades ago.

Except for the few studies mentioned above, there is little research into supervision in applied sport psychology contexts. The bulk of the literature is opinion and discussion articles and several works with case studies or case examples (e.g., Andersen, 1994, 2005; Andersen, Van Raalte, & Brewer, 2000; Andersen, Van Raalte, & Harris, 2000; Andersen & Williams-Rice, 1996; Barney, Andersen, & Riggs, 1996; Van Raalte & Andersen, 2000). In contrast, within counseling and clinical psychology, thousands of research articles, book chapters, opinion pieces, and whole books are dedicated to supervision models, processes, and training.

Models of Supervision

There are probably as many models of supervision as there are different psychotherapies and other helping professions. In general, and especially when working with beginning psychologists, the model of supervision used usually reflects, or parallels, the type of therapy model the supervisee is employing in service delivery. For example, if sport psychology trainees are using a psychological skills training (PST) model for performance enhancement, then the supervision of that service would probably involve training and refining the students' skills in teaching those interventions to their athletes. Also, the supervisor might help trainees with their own performance issues (anxiety, irrational thinking) regarding becoming a competent sport psychologist and encourage them to use the same interventions on themselves to address their professional development (e.g., relaxation for their anxieties [Kurpius & Morran, 1988], cognitive restructuring for irrational thinking [Bradley & Gould, 2001]). In psychodynamic supervision (Andersen, Van Raalte, & Harris 2000), in addition to examining the supervisee–client transference and countertransference configurations, the supervisor and supervisee would examine their own transference and countertransference dynamics and enactments to promote self-understanding and growth of the supervisee as a self-reflective and self-knowledgeable practitioner. One hopes that almost all supervision is therapeutic, but supervision is not therapy (see Van Raalte & Andersen, 2000, for a discussion of supervision vs. therapy in applied sport psychology).

For trainee and novice psychologists, this congruency between what happens in treatment and what occurs in supervision is probably the best path to take because the beginning psychologist is often anxious and even overwhelmed by the numerous tasks and challenges of working in a helping profession. Having supervision and practice stem from the same roots may provide a measure of stability and familiarity for student and novice practitioners.

This parallel fit between treatment and supervision, however, may not be the optimal approach for practitioners with several years experience under their belts. If practice and supervision stay firmly within one model for years, then the opportunities for professional growth become limited because the one model is reinforced over and over again. Choosing a supervisor with a different theoretical orientation than one's own may help practitioners see their clients in new ways, provide avenues for professional development, and expand their areas of competence. Models of supervision come in a variety of flavors. Some are primarily skills based and solution focused (e.g., behavioral supervision, PST-based supervision); others tend more toward the psychotherapeutic end of the spectrum (e.g., psychodynamic supervision, phenomenological supervision). One's choice of a supervision model is like one's choice of a therapeutic model of service. For most people, it is a matter of what models resonate with them. Psychodynamic theory and Buddhist philosophy have been part of my world view since my early undergraduate days, so my choice of this theory and this philosophy is part of how I interpret my environment and the people and interactions within it.

Central to Buddhist philosophy is the practice of mindfulness (Epstein, 1995; see the next section) in meditation and in daily living. Mindfulness, however, is not really a model of supervision. I see mindfulness as an overarching transtheoretical way *to be*, whether you are a supervisor, a nurse, a podiatrist, a psychoanalyst, or any other member of the helping professions. Being mindful in therapeutic encounters opens up an awareness of interpersonal issues that are at the crux of all supervision (and helping) relationships. For more in-depth discussions of some of the models of supervision that may apply to sport psychology practice, see Andersen and Williams-Rice (1996) and Van Raalte and Andersen (2000).

Mindfulness and Supervision

Mindfulness is the moment-to-moment nonjudgmental awareness of thoughts, perceptions, and feelings as they rise and fall away in an unceasing unfolding of conscious experience. Mindfulness is also one of the Eightfold Paths in the Fourth Noble Truth of Buddhism, practiced as one means of diminishing human suffering and letting go of clinging to impermanence and past hurts and injustices. In the 1990s, mindfulness was penetrating the general psychology discourse (see Langer, 1990), and it was also gaining ground in new models of treatment, such as dialectical behavior therapy (e.g., Linehan et al., 1999) and Epstein's (1995) marriage of Buddhism and psychoanalysis. There are hundreds of popular books on Zen Buddhism and mindfulness in sport (e.g., Parent, 2005), but mindfulness did not appear in the academic sport psychology discourse in any substantial way until the 2000s. It is surprising that mindfulness has made such a late entry into the academic applied sport psychology literature, given that most authors following PST approaches acknowledge that staying in present time is an important part of performance. This ancient practice of mindfulness seems to have been appropriated by some sport psychologists as a technique in service of performance enhancement. A whole book (Gardner & Moore, 2007) and several journal articles (e.g., Gardner, 2009; Gardner & Moore, 2004) in sport psychology have been dedicated to using mindfulness with athletes to enhance their performances. This rather narrow application of mindfulness has dominated the applied sport psychology literature until recently. Zizzi and Andersen (2010) took a different approach and discussed mindfulness in terms of the mindful sport psychology practitioner, and how being mindful during work with athlete clients may be one of the best ways to help establish a strong therapeutic relationship. Recently, Andersen and Mannion (2011) illustrated the importance of intra- and interpersonal mindfulness when working with clients and supervisees through their own therapy and supervision case examples. For this chapter, I want to look at mindfulness and what happens when two people sit down in supervision (or therapy) and at least one of them (supervisor, therapist) is present and mindful. In this interpersonal mindfulness setting, interesting things begin to happen that encompass some of the best features of caring and loving human relationships. The phenomena I would like to focus on are what Siegel (2010) has identified in his recent book, *The Mindful Therapist,* as presence, attunement, and resonance.

Presence

When supervisors and supervisees are being mindful in the therapy encounter or in the supervisor's office, they are situated nonjudgmentally in the present continually unfolding moment, observing the other's emotional, cognitive, and behavioral communications (both verbal and nonverbal) along with the changes in their own internal landscapes that rise, fall, and recede. One can't be mindful of everything all at once, and attention to the present

may shift from internal observations and responses (e.g., emotions the supervisee or client is evoking in the supervisor or therapist) to external supervisee (or client) moment-to-moment processes. Near the beginning of the 20th century, Freud (1912/1958) described the mindful stance of the therapist (or supervisor) in his analytic terms:

> As we shall see, it rejects the use of any special expedient (even that of taking notes). It consists simply in not directing one's notice to anything in particular and in maintaining the same "evenly suspended attention" (as I have called it) in the face of all that one hears.... The rule for the doctor may be expressed: "He should withhold all conscious influences from his capacity to attend, and give himself over completely to his 'unconscious memory.'" Or to put it purely in terms of technique: "He should simply listen, and not bother about whether he is keeping anything in mind."
> (pp. 111–112)

Freud's "doctor" is present with the client and nonjudgmental (i.e., "evenly suspended attention...in the face of all that one hears"). I can't think of a better stance for supervisors when they sit down with those therapists in their care. So, how does nonjudgmental presence benefit supervisees and clients?

Humans have evolved over time into highly social animals, and some of our potential abilities to connect closely with others of our species are probably hardwired. Iacobini (2008) has suggested that our abilities to connect with others (i.e., to attune with others; see following section on attunement) may have much to do with our *mirror neurons.* Much mirror neuron research has centered on their functions in imitating others' behaviors (e.g., Iacobini et al., 1999), but Iacobini has hypothesized that they also function to help us notice the outwards signs of another's internal state and then reproduce that state within ourselves. Mirror neurons may be one of the foundations of empathy. When a practitioner's head and heart are filled with negative thoughts and emotions, distracted by other concerns outside of supervision or therapy, and not nonjudgmentally present, then it becomes difficult to process the verbal and nonverbal information from the supervisee or the client. A traditional cognitive interpretation of this limited focus suggests that the practitioner will be less effective if cognitively distracted (see Chapter 6, this volume). The mirror neuron research suggests another consequence of limited presence: If we are not present, then we have, metaphorically, left the building. Clients and supervisees, because of their histories, are socially vigilant for a variety of signs. People who have histories of neglectful or absent significant others (e.g., parents) are usually more sensitive to signs of distance than are those with secure attachment histories. If we have left the building, some supervisees and clients will experience our nonpresence as a repetition of earlier hurtful (absent) encounters with others, to the detriment of the therapeutic relationship, and thus, supervision and therapy outcomes. Being present with a supervisee, and helping that supervisee be present with his clients, is one way that the overarching model of mindfulness and presence learned in supervision gets translated back to the health, happiness, and care of clients.

Attunement

A quotidian example of presence that almost all have experienced is becoming engrossed in something one is reading. For example, in reading a riveting novel, one is often present from sentence to sentence and page to page as one follows the developing characters and plot. One is right here, right now, maybe sitting in a comfortable chair, but engrossed "far-away" in the fantasy that is rolling off the pages. A similar example of attunement occurs when watching a movie in which one feels closely connected and emotionally invested in the life (or lives) of a character(s). When something wonderful happens to the character, one feels elation. When something terribly sad happens to the individual on the screen, and one sees all the emotional evidence displayed in the actor's face and verbal and nonverbal language, one may begin to feel one's eyes filling with tears. In these cases, one is not attuned to a "real" person but rather to a simulated, celluloid person. But it doesn't matter—real or imagined, we have the ability to tune into others' internal states.

To be able to make internal representations of another person's internal states would seem to be of great survival value for social animals such as humans, and there is substantial evidence from the field of interpersonal neurobiology on how our nervous systems, from our spinal cords, brainstems, limbic regions, posterior and anterior insula, and medial prefrontal cortex (among others) are involved in the process of attunement (Siegel, 2006, 2007, 2010). To be attuned to another, however, necessitates that one is also attuned to oneself. If, for some historical reason (e.g., being punished or shamed repeatedly for exhibiting emotions as a child), a person is cut off from his or her internal emotional states or suppresses emotions as soon as they start to arrive, then

that person is not well self-attuned and will have difficulties attuning with others.

One of my most common experiences as a supervisor is having a supervisee tell a story about working with a client who began to cry. I usually ask at that point, "And what was happening with you when your client started crying?" (I generally avoid the hackneyed question, "How did that make you feel?" because I do not want to prompt them that I am interested in their affective reactions. What I am interested in is whether they tell a cognitive [e.g., "I was thinking maybe I should just let him cry"], affective [e.g., "I started feeling embarrassed for him"], or behavioral [e.g., "I got him a tissue and said things would be all right"] story). I am also interested in what type of story the supervisee doesn't tell. To my question "What was happening?" I often hear cognitive linear stories relatively devoid of the supervisee's emotions. There seems to be a disconnect in how the supervisee is emotionally interacting with the client. This example may be one of poor self-attunement, and, without self-attunement, empathy will be elusive. As Rogers (1992) described,

> To sense the client's private world as if it were your own, but without ever losing the "as if" quality—this is empathy, and this seems essential to therapy. To sense the client's anger, fear, or confusion as if it were your own, yet without your own anger, fear, or confusion getting bound up in it.
> (p. 832)

One may be poorly attuned to oneself and clients, but one may also be overattuned. Rogers used the subjunctive mood (i.e., "as if it *were* your own") in his statement, but if the statement were in present tense (i.e., "as if it *is* your own"), then we would have an example of identity and personal boundary blurring—a kind of misalliance that is possibly damaging for both client and practitioner. My client's loss becomes "my loss," and then we are both truly lost. I have lost my "self," and my client has lost a caring, present, attuned other to hold her and her messiness and not disintegrate with her.

In supervision, I often hear tales of clients becoming rather upset at the emotional material that has surfaced, only to have the supervisee steer them away from the messy, discombobulating, affective experience and move back into a linear, cognitive (and safe) story. This shift may send a message back to the client that "You can't handle your emotions and neither can I, so let's talk about something else." Not a therapeutic message for a practitioner to send—a message of disattunement. Our job is to hold our clients in loving care, but if we cannot hold our own messiness, then we may have difficulties holding others'. Steering clients away from the emotional (or colluding with them to avoid the emotional) is common in beginning therapists.

To help supervisees in supervision, when I make a nonjudgmental observation that might be perceived as a personal criticism or my disappointment in the supervisee, and I see a trace of frustration, or embarrassment, or anger, I often ask, "What's happening for you right now?" And I listen for the stories that are told and not told. When I hear another linear cognitive story (e.g., "I was thinking that what you said hadn't even crossed my mind"), I then often say, "When I made that observation, I felt a sense of frustration, even embarrassment, and possible disappointment coming from you because maybe you missed something important. Maybe there was even a hint of being angry at me for pointing out what might have been missed. It's okay to be angry at me. Was there any unpleasant emotional content in your reactions?" What often ensues is a discussion of connecting with one's own and one's clients' emotional worlds and what it means to be attuned.

I am no expert in being present and attuned (see Siegel, 2010, for an in-depth discussion of attunement). My moment-to-moment stance and my attunement vectors collapse all the time. I sometimes find myself getting judgmentally angry and frustrated with my supervisees. Much of the time, but not always, I can recognize that I am off track and that my mindfulness has been defenestrated. Then I usually say, "Just then I got really mad at you and wanted to tell you to bugger off. Sorry about that. I wasn't being here. I got some buttons pushed, and your supervisor left the building. I am back now." I try to model that we are all fallible and can never be perfect therapists and supervisors, but by modeling presence and attunement and helping supervisees become more present and attuned with me (and I with them, and all the difficulties that that entails), then I hope that they can take those models of (fallible) presence and (inconsistent) attunement and be kinder to themselves as they work with clients. In time, just like practicing sport skills, they become better at it, and their clients come to know someone who is there for them, attuned to their hearts and heads; that is how therapeutic relationships grow and form foundations for healthy change. In a parallel-like process, we hope what happens with presence and attunement in supervision flows on to client–therapist relationships.

Resonance

Resonance is one product of interpersonal mindfulness, presence, and attunement. When two people are attuned to each other, some wonderful things can happen. As Siegel (2010) suggested:

> In many ways we feel "close" or "heard" or "seen" by another person when we can detect that he has attuned to us and has taken us inside of his own mind. When we ourselves register this attunement, either consciously or not, our own state can change. The observed takes in the observer having taken her in, and the two become joined. This is resonance.... This is how we feel "felt," and this is how two individuals become a "we."
> (pp. 54–55)

When we feel felt in a context of all those Rogerian qualities of effective therapists (e.g., positive regard, nonjudgment, empathy, genuineness, acceptance), then we are freed to be ourselves in all our messiness, knowing that, no matter what, we will be held in loving care. Another word for feeling felt and resonance is "love." As Freud wrote in a letter to Jung, "Psychoanalysis is in essence a cure through love." LOVE! I uppercase that word because I don't want to pussyfoot around it or be a shrinking violet when it enters the therapy room or the supervision session. Of course, I don't want it confused with romantic or sexual love; what occurs between therapists and clients and supervisors and supervisees is a kind of healing, caring love. To ameliorate some discomfort in using the word "love" to describe what can happen in therapy and supervision, maybe we can think of it in terms of St. Thomas Aquinas' definition, "To love is to will the good of another."

Most psychologists I know can relate several examples of resonance they have experienced in supervision or psychotherapy. One of the best examples occurs when a supervisee or client is telling a tale of some sort of sadness, frustration, or confusion, and the supervisor or therapist generates a metaphoric image that (he or she hopes) encapsulates what the person is feeling. When the metaphor hits the mark, a supervisee or client will often respond with an expressive sigh and say, "Exactly!!" It is in those "exactly" moments that the individual truly feels felt by the other. That is resonance.

Also, resonance often occurs when a practitioner makes an interpretation that lands home. For example, I worked with a Paralympian, Patrik, for a few years, and he was struggling with the end of his career (for the full case study of Patrik, see

Van Raalte & Andersen, 2007). He had probably overidentified with being an athlete, and his sporting success was a source of much longed-for attention and love. Being the upbeat, motivated "gimp" athlete, however, was also a source of resentment. He felt he had missed out on a lot of his adolescence and young adulthood (messing around with mates, cutting loose, going wild) because sport took up all his time and energy. He also resented that he did not feel loved for simply who he was. It was the "athlete" who got the love. It was apparent that he had an intense ambivalence about his sport. It was his vehicle to get the love he wanted, but it also meant he could not simply be himself and go out on the town with his mates and have a normal life. The internal and external pressures (and reinforcements) for being the upbeat, always-on role model for others was something he wanted to escape:

> One day I said to Patrik "It sounds like maybe what you would really like to be is a lazy, miserable slob."
> At first he looked rather shocked that I had said such a thing. Then a few seconds later he smiled, and with a sense of relief he said, "Yes, that would be wonderful."
> (p. 237)

With his shock, his smile, his relief, and his "that would be wonderful," I knew that Patrik knew that I knew how he felt. This feeling felt, this resonance, along with presence and attunement (the conditions for resonance) forms the loving glue that binds supervisees and supervisors together in their working alliances. This same glue is what we also want our supervisees to cultivate in their encounters with their clients. It seems, almost regardless of what model of supervision or psychotherapy one is using, that interpersonal mindfulness, feeling felt, being heard, and being held in loving, nonjudgmental care are the foundations for growth and healthy change in both supervisees and clients.

Resonance also works both ways. Supervisees and clients take in their mentors/practitioners (how they feel, how they think, how they behave), attune to them, resonate with them, and use them as models or "dress rehearsals" (Yalom, 1980) for their lives in the real world. Resonance may be one of the pathways for the internalization of the supervisor or therapist. The client or supervisee takes in the other and, in time, makes the other her own.

Meta-Supervision (Supervision of Supervision)

In this section, I examine the state of training in supervision in applied sport psychology. It will be a

short section. The literature on supervision training in performance psychology is nonexistent, but there is a huge literature on training supervisors in the clinical, counseling, and social work fields. Petitpas, Brewer, Rivera, and Van Raalte (1994) reported that 43% of professionals delivering supervision to practitioners and students had no formal training in supervision. Ten years later, Watson et al. (2004) found that, for sport psychology professionals who provide supervision, 47% reported having received no training in supervision, and 29% reported that their training was rather informal (e.g., workshops, independent study).

Only one model of supervision training exists in the applied sport psychology literature, and that is the one Barney et al. (1996) developed. In their model, advanced sport psychology doctoral students would undertake coursework in models, theories, and practice of supervision. After obtaining supervision knowledge, these students would then begin supervising master's level students in their early practica experiences. The doctoral students would then receive meta-supervision (supervision of their supervision of the master's students) from experienced staff. It sounds like a good model for training, but it is a fantasy. I know of no program in sport psychology training that incorporates this model.

Teaching Mindfulness, Presence, Attunement, and Resonance to Supervisees

How do we teach mindfulness? We start with the breath. Present moment-to-moment breath awareness is an excellent starting point (for a discussion of such a breathing intervention, see Chapter 31, this volume). In many applied sport psychology texts, diaphragmatic breathing is presented as a relaxation technique. It can be much more than that. Mindful awareness while "belly breathing" is a starting point for us to become present and attuned to ourselves. As we breathe, all sorts of images, thoughts, and emotions will rise and fall in between focusing on the breath. Sitting in nonjudgmental awareness of the chatter within our heads and returning to present awareness of the breath is also a practice that helps us stay present. We can then build on mindful breathing with a conscious shift of focus to various parts of the body. For example, one exercise would be to practice mindful breathing, then shift awareness to one's left foot, move the foot and notice the physical and kinesthetic sensations, then bring one's attention back to the breath. From this point, we can expand the practice to different parts of the body and other current internal states (e.g., present emotions). Practicing being present and aware of the breath, the body, and internal states of mind helps students begin the process of becoming attuned to themselves.

A beginning exercise I use with graduate students for interpersonal presence and attunement takes a bit of method acting. I usually demonstrate the exercise with me sitting in front of a student for maybe 5 minutes. No words are spoken. I am a bit of a ham (well, maybe more than "a bit"), and I use my role-playing/acting skills to show through my face, my breathing, and my body language a whole range of emotional and cognitive states. For example, I recall poignant or despairing memories that bring tears to my eyes. The student's main task is to stay focused on me as I go through joy, interest, surprise, deep sadness, curiosity, disgust, and several other states. The student's secondary task is to nonjudgmentally notice what is rising and falling within herself (e.g., her emotions, thoughts, images) as she sees me change before her. These tasks are quite difficult, especially when done in front of other students, so usually after I demonstrate the exercise I have students break into groups of three (i.e., roles of mindful practitioner, emoting client, and observer) and practice the exercise three times with each student taking on all three roles. After each of the three exercises, the students discuss with each other what happened for them. Then, when all three exercises have been completed, I pull the class back together and we discuss the exercises as a whole group.

In these exercises, as students attune to themselves and to another person, they begin to get a feel of what it is to take someone else's internal state into themselves and resonate with the other. These exercises are not easy, and students fall out of the present moment, retreat from attunement with themselves and the other, and often escape the practice with nervous laughter. But not to worry; the hows and whys of students struggling and stumbling through these exercises are also valuable data for self-exploration. This practice is one I introduce to students well before they even start role playing an intake interview with clients. Mindfulness, as I have stated, can be the transtheoretical foundation for many helping professions. It is where we start. I will now turn to some of the issues supervisors and supervisees face in beginning the dance of supervision.

Beginning Supervision

At the graduate student practicum and internship levels, supervision may hold real or perceived threats for the trainee. As Bernard and Goodyear (1998) stated in the opening quote for this chapter, the supervisor is in an evaluative position over the graduate student, and this large power differential can be an obstacle in the supervision dyad. Also, the supervisor-as-gatekeeper role may be anxiety provoking because the supervisor may have the power to terminate (fairly or unfairly) student career goals. Such real and perceived threats can twist supervisor–supervisee interactions. Supervisees may censor the stories they tell about their interactions with clients and report mainly positive encounters and results, glossing over real or potential difficulties. The threat of supervision often sits like an elephant in the counseling room that no one talks about. How does one obviate, as best one can, the problem of this impeding pachyderm? One path to reducing perceived threat and generally reduce anxiety in supervision is to lay out ground rules at the beginning and communicate that the supervision hour is one in which judgment is suspended, mistakes are expected and treated with loving care, and unconditional positive regard is always present. As in therapy, the main task of the first session (or sessions) is to see if a "we" can be established, a working alliance between supervisee and supervisor (or client and therapist). To illustrate the laying of ground rules and the "we establishing," I present a dialogue from a supervision intake.

A Performance Psychology Supervision Intake Session

A former student (I'll call her Pippa) in the master of applied psychology program that I coordinate called me a few years after she graduated. A friend of hers had referred a soprano (Chloë) to her, and the apparent issues centered on the singer having landed her first major role in a regional opera company. She was to sing the part of Micaëla in Bizet's *Carmen*, a substantial role in the opera. She was struggling to make the transition from an opera chorus singer and occasional small-role soloist to a large, supporting part. My former student recalled our discussions and role plays of working with performing artists and thought that I might be helpful in supervising her work with Chloë. We arranged a time to meet and discuss what she was looking for in supervision. Although she was a former student in our program, I had never supervised any of her practicum placements, but I had observed her in class role plays. The following dialogue (and commentary) from our supervision intake is what I recall.

Mark (M): Pip, good to see you. It has been a few years.

Pippa (P): Yes, it has. Thanks for taking time to see me. I am a bit anxious about this client. I have never worked with singers before.

M: Well, one of the great things about working with singers is that they already know how to breathe. I understand that moving into working with a new type of performer can be rather daunting, but maybe we can discuss your anxieties a little bit later. For now, let's discuss what you are looking for in supervision, what you want to get out of our sessions, and then after we have a good picture of what you want, I can let you know how I usually operate in supervision, and we can decide whether we would be a good fit. How does that sound?

Pippa has presented with the anxiety of being a stranger in a strange land ("never worked with singers before"). I also feel that she is anxious about coming to me for psychodynamic supervision. I do not want to address her anxieties directly at this point because that would be jumping into supervision mode before we have laid some groundwork. I do, however, address some of her anxiety indirectly by reminding her that she and the singer do have something in common: they are both knowledgeable about diaphragmatic breathing. My message is that the strange land she is about to traverse is not completely foreign. My general paternal countertransference to students (and former students) regularly leads me to offering assurance that "they are doing just fine, and things will be okay."

From stories that other psychologists and graduate students have told me, it seems fairly common that supervision relationships usually start with supervisees telling stories about clients with little or no ground rules or discussions of theoretical frameworks. If these early elements are not put into place, then the expectations of both parties remain at "default" status, and a supervisor's default expectations may not be the same as the supervisee's. This not laying groundwork, and running on defaults can lead to conflict, confusion, and unhappiness down the line. So, I ask Pippa to put the anxiety to the side for now and start to get down to the business of what she wants to happen in our potential supervision relationship.

P: That sounds good. I have been thinking about what I want from supervision, and I have a few things. First, I need your advice about opera, like what I should be reading. So, maybe you could give me some reading assignments, and then we could discuss them in session.

Pippa knew from her graduate classes with me that I have worked with performing artists, including opera singers. I get the impression that she may think I am some kind of expert on opera. I want to be helpful, but I need to disabuse her of the idea that I am more than a dilettante. Pip also knows from classroom discussions and role plays that I only do psychodynamic/mindfulness supervision, the thought of which can be anxiety provoking. She has started out talking about "safe" advice and educational needs. Maybe she is slowly building up to a request for a psychodynamic/mindful exploration of her professional relationships.

M: Yes, we could possibly do some of that in the beginning. Right off the top of my head, I think you would enjoy a biography of Maria Callas [see Huffington, 2002, in reference section] or Placido Domingo's new edition of his autobiography [see Domingo & Trewin, 2010]. I can get you those references. And it would probably be good to see the movie of the opera *Carmen* [see Von Normann & Rosi, 1984]. I am sure you can rent it at almost any large video store. I'll be as helpful as I can, but I am no expert, and you already have an expert. You might ask your client what she thinks is worth reading or seeing. Let her be your teacher. It's a great way to help build your relationship. Now, what else would you like from supervision?

P: Well, I could really use some help with mindfulness.

M: What kind of help would you like?

P: I think my client might really benefit from being mindful and staying in the moment, sitting with her anxieties. But, I need to know more about it all and how to teach her mindfulness.

M: It sounds like you are somewhat unsure about your knowledge and ability to teach mindfulness.

P: I have a lot to learn.

M: Yes, maybe, but I think you know a lot more about mindfulness than you think you know. What do you do when you teach someone diaphragmatic breathing?

P: I first have them put their hands on their bellies to get them to feel what it is like to belly breathe. Then, once they have that down, I have them count on the inhale and the exhale to get a rhythm going, and then I have them just focus on one part of the breath, maybe just the stomach rising and falling, or maybe just the sensation of air moving in and out of the nose.

M: And if their minds wander, what do you tell them?

P: I usually say something like, "Your thoughts may wander away from your focus on the breath. If they do, not to worry, just gently bring the focus back to the breath."

M: Can't get more mindful than that. It sounds like you have the first, and probably most important, mindful practice down pat.

P: Okay, but I don't feel confident beyond the breathing.

M: That's all right. It seems like you're a bit anxious about your skills in this area, and that's all right too, but it sure looks like you have a solid foundation for mindful practice. You know I do only psychodynamic/mindful supervision, so learning and using mindfulness with your client and on yourself as a therapist and as a supervisee would be a significant part of our work together in supervision.

P: That's a big part of why I thought of you for supervision.

M: If we enter into supervision, I'll want us to have an agreement that you will practice mindful sitting, mindful walking, mindful doing the dishes, mindful being with your client, and mindful being with me. You'll be listening to a lot of mindfulness exercises on your iPod and reading a lot of books on mindfulness. Are you up for all that?

P: Yes, that's what I really want to do.

M: That's fantastic! This could be a lot of fun.

A lot is going on in the above dialogue. At the start, I wanted to answer her question about advice and educational activities around opera, but also to redirect her to a better source—her client. Many early career psychologists want to appear knowledgeable to their clients, but admitting ignorance and asking clients for help can be much more therapeutic for both clients and practitioners than having psychologists furiously study up on the sport or performing art by themselves. The psychologist stands before the client as she is—human, relatively ignorant, but willing to learn and to enter into the client's world. The client gets to help out the psychologist, and that may bring some balance to the relationship. Everyone wins (usually).

My question of "what else" leads us closer to the heart of psychodynamic/mindful supervision, but we are still in the safe area of "learning about mindfulness." It seems she is not quite ready to discuss the possibly scary path (the psychodynamic bit). It also seems that Pippa has serious doubts about her abilities, and I, in a Socratic fashion, help her

tell a story of what she does know about breathing and mindfulness. My cheerleading is only marginally helpful, and she concedes that she knows something, but falls back to what amounts to a minor episode of despair with, "but I don't feel confident beyond the breathing." When she earlier stated, "I have a lot to learn," I also heard the questions, "Will you teach me? Will you please take me on as a supervisee?" With this "no-confidence" statement, I started to hear those questions again, "Will you help me become confident? Will you be my supervisor?" I feel that Pip really wants an answer to those questions. Before I fully answer the questions, I need to lay out some ground rules, at least for the mindfulness aspects of supervision and practice. She sounds committed, and I do a bit more cheerleading about supervision being fun to reinforce her commitment. In our conversation so far, however, the psychodynamic hydra has not yet raised its anxiety provoking heads.

P: Great, so when can we start?

M: We can probably start soon, but before we begin, I think we need to talk about the psychodynamic aspects of the supervision process. Just as we are committed to the mindfulness aspects of supervision, we also need to be committed to the psychodynamic ground rules and processes.

P: You mean like the rule of saying whatever is on my mind no matter how silly or embarrassing?

M: Exactly! That's actually a difficult task because we all censor. We all have thoughts and feelings that would make us uncomfortable if we voiced them. But I promise to let you know what is happening for me in supervision, if I think it will be helpful for you, and I would like you to promise to do your best at keeping the censorship to a minimum when we are talking about you and your relationships with your clients, because whatever pops into your head during supervision, even if it seems from left field, probably has something to tell us about what is either happening with you and your client or between you and me.

P: I'll give it my best shot.

M: Cool! And this saying whatever is on your mind or emotionally in your heart is another mindfulness exercise. It's moment-to-moment attention to whatever is unfolding in your thinking and feeling, just as Freud's free association is a type of mindfulness exercise. It's one part of being mindful in supervision.

Psychodynamic supervision can be daunting because the supervisors and supervisees examine sensitive material from the supervisees' pasts, their relationship patterns, their families of origin, their countertransferences to their clients, and their transferences to their supervisors. Psychodynamic supervision looks quite similar to psychodynamic psychotherapy, but there are significant differences. When supervisors and supervisees are discussing the supervisees' neuroses, relationship patterns, and countertransferences, it is done in the context of how these features of the supervisee might have an influence on the quality of care delivered to the client. The questions become: Can we recognize these neuroses or countertransferences? And can we walk around them, so that they do not negatively affect the therapeutic relationship? The questions in supervision are all ultimately related to client welfare. Digging deeper into the supervisee's neuroses and relationship patterns to get at their roots is reserved for the supervisee's own psychotherapy. I explained all of the above to Pippa, but I had a feeling that she was still anxious about revealing aspects of herself in supervision. I needed to address the elephant.

> M: I know this all sounds rather full-on, and dynamic supervision is often full-on, but I want you to know my stance as your supervisor. Congruently enough, I try to hold a mindful stance as much as I can in supervision, or what Freud called "evenly suspended attention," and see what happens. There is no judgment in this room. Your stories, your mistakes, your confusions, your emotions, your successes, your perceived failures, your moments of pride—they are all, for me, fascinating data. They are all part of a puzzle that you and I are working on, and we need as many pieces as we can find. That's why it's so important to say whatever is on your mind or in your heart, because whatever is there right now is probably another piece of the puzzle. All of your stories will be held in loving care, including the ones you are most embarrassed or ashamed about. Here's a good rule of thumb: If you have some experiences or thoughts in your therapy with Chloë, and you say to yourself, "Oh, I don't want to talk to Mark about that," then that is probably the first thing we should talk about in the next supervision session.

In being mindful of Pippa's anxieties, I had asked my internal representation of Pippa about what she would like to hear, and the response I "heard" had something to do with me "holding" her in loving care. After my short talk about fascination, collaborative puzzle work, nonjudgment, holding, and loving care, my feelings of anxiety (my internal Pippa) seemed to deliquesce and so did the anxieties

of the real Pippa seated in front of me. For the first time since we met that day she seemed relaxed. I felt at this point that we had finally "met" each other.

> M: Pip, you seem a bit more, I don't know…relaxed, than you were when you came in. How are you going?
> P: I was kind of wound up about talking to you about doing dynamic supervision. I know I want to do this, but there is a part of me that says, "No! You don't!" and I had all this irrational anxiety shit flying around me.
> M: Well, we can certainly talk about your flying irrational shit in supervision.
> P: [laughing and smiling] That'll be great! You and me "talkin' shit."
> M: I think it will be brilliant.

And right there, we have resonance.

The Future of Supervision

I am hopeful that researchers and practitioners in applied sport and performance psychology will pay increasing attention to the issues of supervised practice. The limited literature on supervision in sport and performance psychology, in stark contrast to the clinical and counseling fields, suggests that academics and practitioners in our field may not be adequately investigating, discussing, debating, and researching what should be a central feature of professional development for current and future practitioners. As sport and performance psychologists, we all help others on their intrapersonal, interpersonal, and performance journeys. But what of our own journeys? I am sure we could all use some assistance there, too. Supervision can help us pack our bags, ensure we have all (or most) of the kit we think we need (e.g., theoretical frameworks, interpersonal skills), point us in new directions (e.g., formulating cases from perspectives other than our dominant maps of service), and remind us that it is the process of traveling with presence, attunement, and resonance that aids us in assisting our clients' arrivals at what we hope are happier places than where they started their journeys with us.

Sport and performance psychology is a relatively newcomer to the helping professions family. This cousin may not be the black sheep of the family, but it is a bit on the "wild side." Sport and performance psychologists deliver services in their offices and clinics like much of the rest of the family, but they are also out there in the real and messy world of sport competition, performing arts, and other performance domains (e.g., business, medicine).

They work with their clients on pool decks, in rehearsal venues, on 20-hour international flights, in locker rooms, on practice fields, on stage, in hotels, in recording studios, and in a whole host of other places (and often at odd hours of the day or night). They often have to deal with other members of sporting and performance cultures who are not their clients (e.g., coaches, orchestra conductors). They need a heightened sensitivity to cultural and subcultural norms, hierarchies, and patterns of communication, and to be effective in these various environments and cultures, sport and performance psychologists need to be looser and more flexible in their service delivery than many of their other cousins in the helping professions. The potential for falling into ethical quagmires and descending slippery slopes (e.g., dual relationships, boundary blurring, erotic attraction) is substantial when operating out in the seductive world of sport and performance. I can think of no better place than supervision to address the ethical delivery of service and the panoply of ethical conundrums sport and performance psychologists will inevitably face in their careers (see also Chapter 3, this volume).

The supervision landscape for applied sport and performance psychology is wide open. Many investigators and researchers in clinical and counseling psychology have shown us the myriad paths for professional development and training that can be traveled in supervision. I am cautiously hopeful that more and more sport and performance psychologists will pick one of those paths and see where it leads them. The history of supervision in sport and performance psychology has not been particularly bright, but the future has the potential to be brilliant.

References

Andersen, M. B. (1994). Ethical considerations in the supervision of applied sport psychology graduate students. *Journal of Applied Sport Psychology, 6*, 152–167.

Andersen, M. B. (2002). Training and supervision in sport psychology. In T. Wilson (Clinical and Applied Psychology Section Editor), *International encyclopedia of the social and behavioral sciences* (pp. 14929–14932). Oxford, England: Elsevier Science.

Andersen, M. B. (2005). Touching taboos: Sex and the sport psychologist. In M. B. Andersen (Ed.), *Sport psychology in practice* (pp. 171–191). Champaign, IL: Human Kinetics.

Andersen, M. B., & Mannion, J. (2011). If you meet the Buddha on the football field—Tackle him! In D. Gilbourne & M. B. Andersen (Eds.), *Critical essays in applied sport psychology* (pp. 173–192). Champaign, IL: Human Kinetics.

Andersen, M. B., & Tod, D. (2011). Professional pathways and territories in sport psychology. In T. Morris & P. Terry (Eds.), *The new sport and exercise psychology companion* (pp. 403–423). Morgantown, WV: Fitness Information Technology.

Andersen, M. B., Van Raalte, J. L., & Brewer, B. W. (1994). Assessing the skills of sport psychology supervisors. *The Sport Psychologist, 8*, 238–247.

Andersen, M. B., Van Raalte, J. L., & Brewer, B. W. (2000). When sport psychology consultants and graduate students are impaired: Ethical and legal issues in graduate training and supervision. *Journal of Applied Sport Psychology, 12*, 134–150.

Andersen, M. B., Van Raalte, J. L., & Harris, G. (2000). In M. B. Andersen (Ed.), *Doing sport psychology* (pp. 167–179). Champaign, IL: Human Kinetics.

Andersen, M. B., & Williams-Rice, B. T. (1996). Supervision in the education and training of sport psychology service providers. *The Sport Psychologist, 10*, 278–290.

Barney, S. T., Andersen, M. B., & Riggs, C. A. (1996). Supervision in sport psychology: Some recommendations for practicum training. *Journal of Applied Sport Psychology, 8*, 200–217.

Bernard, J. M., & Goodyear, R. K. (1998). *Fundamentals of clinical supervision*. Boston: Allyn & Bacon.

Bradley, L. J., & Gould, L. J. (2001). Psychotherapy-based models of counselor supervision. In L. J. Bradley & N. Ladany (Eds.), *Counselor supervision: Principles, process, and practice* (pp. 147–180). Philadelphia: Brunner-Routledge.

Carr, C. M., Murphy, S. M., & McCann, S. (1992, October). *Supervision issues in clinical sport psychology*. Workshop presented at the annual conference of the Association for the Advancement of Applied Sport Psychology, Colorado Springs, CO.

Domingo, P., & Terwin, I. (2010). *My first forty years...and counting* (2nd ed.). London: Weidenfeld & Nicolson.

Epstein, M. (1995). *Thoughts without a thinker: Psychotherapy from a Buddhist perspective*. New York: Basic Books.

Feltz, D. L. (1987). The future of graduate education in sport and exercise science: A sport psychology perspective. *Quest, 39*, 217–223.

Freud, S. (1912/1958). Recommendations to physicians practicing psychoanalysis. In J. Strachey (Ed. & Trans.), *The standard edition of the complete psychological works of Sigmund Freud* (Vol. 12, pp. 111–120). London: Hogarth. (Original work published 1912)

Gardner, F. E. (Ed.). (2009). Mindfulness- and acceptance-based approaches to sport performance and well-being [Special issue]. *Journal of Clinical Sport Psychology, 3*, 291–395.

Gardner, F. E., & Moore, Z. E. (2004). A mindfulness-acceptance-commitment-based approach to athletic performance enhancement: Theoretical considerations. *Behavior Therapy, 35*, 707–723.

Gardner, F. E., & Moore, Z. E. (2007). *The psychology of enhancing human performance: The mindfulness-acceptance-commitment approach*. New York: Springer.

Huffington, A. S. (2002). *Maria Callas: The woman behind the legend*. New York: Cooper Square Press.

Iacobini, M. (2008). *Mirroring people*. New York: Farrar, Straus, & Giroux.

Iacobini, M., Woods, R. P., Brass, M., Bekkering, H., Mazziotta, J. C., & Rizzolatti, G. (1999). Cortical mechanisms of human imitation. *Science, 286*, 2526–2528.

Kurpius, D. J., & Morran, D. K. (1988). Cognitive-behavioral techniques and interventions for application in counselor supervision. *Counselor Education and Supervision, 27*, 368–376.

Langer, E. J. (1990). *Mindfulness*. Cambridge, MA: Da Capo Press.

Linehan, M. M., Schmidt, H., Dimeff, L. A., Craft, J. C., Kanter, J., & Comtois, K. A. (1999). Dialectical behavior therapy for patients with borderline personality disorder and drug-dependence. *American Journal on Addiction, 8*, 279–292.

Lubker, J., & Andersen, M. B. (in press). Ethical issues in supervision: Client welfare, practitioner development, and professional gatekeeping. In J. C. Watson, II & E. F. Etzel (Eds.), *Ethical issues in sport, exercise, and performance psychology*. Morgantown, WV: Fitness Information Technology.

Morris, T., Alfermann, D., Lintunen, T., & Hall, H. (2003). Training and selection of sport psychologists: An international review. *International Journal of Sport and Exercise Psychology, 1*, 139–154.

Parent, J. (2005). *Zen golf: Mastering the mental game*. New York: HarperCollinsWillow.

Petitpas, A. J., Brewer, B. W., Rivera, P., & Van Raalte, J. L. (1994). Ethical beliefs and behaviors in applied sport psychology: The AAASP ethics survey. *Journal of Applied Sport Psychology, 6*, 135–151.

Rogers, C. R. (1992). The necessary and sufficient conditions of therapeutic personality change. *Journal of Consulting and Clinical Psychology, 60*, 827–832.

Siegel, D. J. (2006). An interpersonal neurobiology approach to psychotherapy: How awareness, mirror neurons and neural plasticity contribute to the development of well-being. *Psychiatric Annals, 36*, 248–258.

Siegel, D. J. (2007). *The mindful brain: Reflection and attunement in the cultivation of well-being*. New York: Norton.

Siegel, D. J. (2010). *The mindful therapist. A clinician's guide to mindsight and neural integration*. New York: Norton.

Silva, J. M., III, Lerner, B., & Metzler, J. (2007). *Training professionals in the practice of sport psychology*. Morgantown WV: Fitness Information Technology.

Tod, D. (2007). The long and winding road: Professional development in sport psychology. *The Sport Psychologist, 21*, 94–108.

Tod, D., Andersen, M. B., & Marchant, D. B. (2009). A longitudinal examination of neophyte applied sport psychologists' development. *Journal of Applied Sport Psychology, 21*(Suppl.), S1–S16.

Tod, D., Andersen, M. B., & Marchant, D. B. (2011). Six years up: Applied sport psychologists surviving (and thriving) after graduation. *Journal of Applied Sport Psychology, 23*, 93–109.

Tod, D., Marchant, D. B., & Andersen, M. B. (2007). Learning experiences contributing to service-delivery competence. *The Sport Psychologist, 21*, 317–334.

Van Raalte, J. L., & Andersen, M. B. (2000). *Supervision I: From models to doing*. In M. B. Andersen (Ed.), *Doing sport psychology* (pp. 153–165). Champaign, IL: Human Kinetics.

Van Raalte, J. L., & Andersen, M. B. (2007). When sport psychology consulting is a means to an end(ing): Roles and agendas when helping athletes leave their sports. *The Sport Psychologist, 21*, 227–242.

Von Normann, A. (Producer), & Rosi, F. (Director). (1984). *Carmen* [Motion Picture]. France: Gaumont.

Watson, J. C., II, Zizzi, S. J., Etzel, E. F., & Lubker, J. R. (2004). Applied sport psychology supervision: A survey of students and professionals. *The Sport Psychologist, 18*, 415–429.

Winstone, W., & Gervis, M. (2006). Countertransference and the self-aware sport psychologist: Attitudes and patterns of professional practice. *The Sport Psychologist, 20*, 495–511.

Yalom, I. D. (1980). *Existential psychotherapy*. New York: Basic Books.

Zizzi, S. J., & Andersen, M. B. (2010). An Eastern philosophical approach. In S. J. Hanrahan & M. B. Andersen (Eds.), *Routledge handbook of applied sport psychology: A comprehensive guide for students and practitioners* (pp. 194–202). London: Routledge.

PART 6

Future Directions

CHAPTER
40

Sport and Performance Psychology:
A Look Ahead

Kirsten Peterson, Charles Brown, Sean McCann, *and* Shane Murphy

Abstract

As editor of this Handbook, I felt it was necessary to have a concluding chapter that discussed some of the main themes of the book and also looked ahead, anticipating the potential pitfalls and challenges facing sport and performance psychology in the years to come. To get a diversity of opinions on such intriguing issues, I contacted three leading figures in the field and asked them to answer a series of questions I had developed that addressed the future development of the field. The focus of this Handbook is on performance, so I contacted individuals with unquestioned credentials in that area. Each of them is comfortable moving among the academic, research and applied fields. Sean McCann is senior sport psychologist with the U.S. Olympic Committee and has provided services at numerous World Championships, national events, and Olympic Games. Kirsten Peterson is his counterpart in Australia, leading the sport psychology program in the High Performance Division at the Australian Institute of Sport. And Charlie Brown is a leader in performance psychology, working with clients on performance issues and moving the field ahead via such projects as the groundbreaking book he co-authored with Kate Hays in 2004, *You're On! Consulting for Peak Performance*. I hope you enjoy the "conversation" presented in this final chapter, which gives us the rare opportunity to peek inside the lives and experiences of true experts in sport and performance psychology.

Key Words: Sport and performance psychology, high performance, applied psychology, peak performance consultation

Question 1

In looking at the diversity of topics covered in this Handbook, and at the amount of interesting research that has been generated across these many topics, it is apparent that sport and performance psychology has grown into a vibrant, dynamic and multidisciplinary field. What aspect of the field's development has impressed you most over the past two decades?

Kirsten Peterson

If I cast an eye back 20 years ago, that would put us in 1991. I was in graduate school, in the middle of my doctoral studies, very excited about the idea of combining my master's education and interest in sport psychology with my doctoral degree work in counseling psychology, which was a rather radical proposition at the time. Most sport psychology students were still coming through sport science and kinesiology programs, being trained primarily as researchers. On the other side of things, there were maybe a handful of psychology programs that officially embraced the field of sport psychology as part of their curriculums. Sport was considered to be too frivolous a niche for the serious business of training psychologists. I was the only graduate student in my particular counseling psychology department who was interested in sport psychology, which made me a bit of a novelty. I was lucky, in that my graduate advisor was personally interested in sport psychology, so was willing to engage in a quid pro quo relationship—I taught her about sport and she taught me about counseling psychology. At the same time, I was positively challenged as I learned about the counseling process, and I found an unexpected affinity for the area of career development while developing my clinical skills in the college counseling center.

Those years, for me, felt like the beginnings of the period of acceptance of the field of applied sport psychology. During my 1989–1990 internship with the U.S. Olympic Committee's (USOC) sport psychology department, the applied side of our field was at best tolerated and at worst joked about by the other "harder" sport scientists. I recall that time as one during which we sport psychs all worked hard to justify our existence, selling our wares to coaches one at a time, and asserting our presence and right to conduct research projects side by side with the physiologists and biomechanists. We did important applied work, but the ideas of embedding ourselves with teams, travelling to competitions, and doing long-term work were still foreign concepts—even to ourselves.

I look now at our field and see a world of difference. The Association for Applied Sport Psychology (AASP) was born in 1986 as was the American Psychological Association (APA)'s Exercise and Sport Psychology Division (also established in 1986). Both organizations have grown tremendously in size and scope. We actually have a certification process for our field—not ideal but getting there—and we stand next to other sport science disciplines without having to justify our presence. The proliferation of journals and books in our field is staggering. We have been further buoyed by the emergence of a focus on positive psychology which, like sport psychology, focuses efforts on the wellness and self-actualization side of the human experience spectrum. At the same time, we have the whole realm of performance coaching and performance psychology that have cemented psychology's shift from a focus on returning to baseline functioning to an acceptance of the field's role in assisting people in reaching their potential.

Athletes and coaches have embraced the field as well. Sport psychology at the USOC has moved far from my internship days. Demand for dedicated sport psychology assistance continues to outstrip supply. This trend is also evident in terms of psychology credentials issued at the Olympic Games, moving from a single token presence to the entire USOC sport psychology staff (plus several outside consultants) having Games' access to their teams. In my current role as head of the performance psychology team at the Australian Institute of Sport (AIS), I see similar acceptance and demand placed upon members of our team. Sport psychology is alive and well, which bodes well for our applied future, at least.

Charlie Brown

The breadth of change within the field has been truly impressive within the past two decades, as practitioners and researchers have widened their perspectives both internally and externally. Two examples of this broadening of perspective are attention to systemic factors impacting performance (an internal focus) and the growing application of performance principles beyond traditional sport (an external focus).

When I started my respecialization in sport psychology during the mid 1990s, I was struck by the narrowness of perspective and the absence of attention to broader contextual factors. The majority of research was based on college students and youth athletes, with little attention to older athletes. A literature search with the keywords "significant other" and "sport" produced articles on teammates and coaches, but no mention of spouses, partners, or family members. When parents were occasionally referenced in the literature, they were typically characterized as factors interfering with the coach and team dynamics. As an older athlete myself, an experienced family/systems therapist, and a person who routinely worked with triathletes whose ages ranged from the mid 20s to 40s, the void screamed to be filled.

By contrast, we now have research and theories that address performance through the lifespan and also address broad contextual factors (national governing bodies, cultural expectations, media coverage, etc.) impacting performance. Today's elite and professional performers tend to be older, have serious relationships, families, and lives outside of performance. If a practitioner is to be effective with these individuals, he or she must be mindful of this broader system, engage and recruit resources whenever possible, and navigate the challenges of the performance domain.

As the field began expanding its tunnel vision on collegiate and youth athletes, the real excitement started as external perspectives broadened the field to include performance in other contexts. The research with youth, collegiate, and Olympic athletes has laid a solid foundation for documenting how we can impact a person's ability to perform under pressure. We now have established evidence that these principles and techniques are applicable across performance domains. For me, this broadening of perspective has been analogous to the shift from believing the earth is flat (a limited focus on athletics) to a round world with unlimited possibilities.

Sean McCann

Even though the environment of the Olympic Committee means that we are working with experienced, sophisticated coaches and athletes, I continue to be amazed at the changes in the awareness and perception of sport psychology by our customers. Back in the late 1980s and early 1990s, much of the work consisted of group presentations to teams in order to "expose them" to sport psychology. When preparing these presentations, I would spend a good amount of time thinking of compelling arguments to encourage coaches and athletes to consider working on sport psychology performance issues. Twenty years ago, part of your role as a sport psychologist was to be a salesman for the "product" of sport psychology. We expended this energy on selling, in large part because our customers either didn't know what sport psychology was, didn't know how it could help them, or worst of all, had a negative perception of sport psychology. The most common negative perception was that sport psychology was where you went if you were a screw-up, or a head case, or a choker. Over time, the field has been able to change these negative perceptions for most of our potential customers.

By the turn of the century, the need to sell sport psychology had already been greatly reduced, and in the last 10 years, the main challenge has been in trying to meet the expectations of customers. Here at the USOC, one of the drivers of this change has been the prior exposure of key decision-makers to sport psychology. In the last 5 years, I have had the pleasure of seeing past athlete clients become national team coaches, sport executive directors, and high-performance managers for the national team. It has been an interesting opportunity to work with the same person as an athlete and then as a coach. I've even had the fascinating experience of working with an Olympian who went on to a successful career at the USOC and who became my direct supervisor. My experience with these former athlete customers is that they do a wonderful job of utilizing sport psychology effectively with the athletes for whom they are responsible. As long as our professionals continue to do good, ethical work and have a positive impact, more and more of our customers will do the sales work for us down the road.

I see the increased awareness of sport psychology in many surprising places, from mentions in a variety of media sources, to the reactions of people on airplanes. In the past, when seatmates on flights asked me what I did, they would often respond with a comment such as "So, you help them deal with losing, or that kind of thing?" At best, the conversation would end up with the person saying something like, "Wow, that really sounds pretty interesting." These days, I am more frequently asked a question such as, "My nephew is thinking of that as a career, what advice do you have?" I wish I had a better response to the question, but the nature of the question indicates that the general public has heard of sport psychology, knows roughly what sport psychologists do, and sees it as a potential career. The overall impact of these changes in perception and awareness is that we can shift our focus from establishing footholds to establishing best practices in applied work.

The second major change I have observed is the shifting geography within the field of applied sport psychology. In particular, the centers of cutting-edge research in applied sport psychology appear to be moving out of North America. Although I am not so parochial as to believe that applied sport psychology is a North American invention (the early Soviet work, the founding of the International Society for Sports Psychiatry [ISSP] earlier than the Association for Applied Sport Psychology [AASP] or APA Division 47 are obvious counterarguments), there have been some significant shifts in the field. Early in my career, a great percentage of the leading lights in applied sport psychology research were based in the United States and Canada. Over the last 15 years, we have seen many of the strongest sport psychology research programs face budget cuts and elimination from their universities. The relative paucity of grants for pure sport research versus the availability of grants for health or medical research seems to be driving many of the best young researchers in North America into areas other than sport psychology. On the other hand, in Europe and Australasia, government funding for applied sport research is still available and a new generation of brilliant young researchers in applied sport psychology has emerged. I saw the strength of this trend while on a recent review committee for the annual AASP conference. The percentage of excellent research-based symposia from Europe and the dearth of this type of work from North America was shocking to me. I believe that the greatest percentage of new sport psychology knowledge (and sport science knowledge, generally), will not come from the Americas. I suppose, since much of this trend is due to the dearth of funding for sport psychology research and the drive for faculty to acquire funding first and foremost, that North America might simply be 15 years ahead of the rest of the world in this trend. If this is true (and I hope it isn't), then the field of sport psychology will be in danger of becoming a profession without a thriving science base. For now, however, I am very excited by all of the excellent work begun by a new generation of academics from all over the world.

Question 2

Your own work in sport and performance psychology is the very definition of "where the rubber meets the road." It demands that you keep up with the latest developments in the field and apply them to performers who are at the cutting edge of excellence. What research do you most need to help your clients improve performance?

Charlie Brown

As our world becomes more global with Internet technologies and instantaneous communication, the challenge becomes not only gaining access to information, but also filtering through the plethora of information available online. I rely on the sage advice of USOC sport physiologist, Randy Wilber, in evaluating research: "It must be applicable, practical and scientifically valid" (personal communication, 2010). My research needs also vary according to context—whether I am attempting to intervene at a programmatic or individual level.

If I am attempting to gain entry to a new performance domain, I usually need programmatic research that identifies key factors that improve performance. It is particularly valuable if the data demonstrates that the improvement has been achieved in a practical (translation: cost-effective) manner. Qualitative studies with highly successful performers, such as Dan Gould's work with Olympic champions on factors influencing Olympic success, are much more effective at facilitating entry into a new performance domain than is a study indicating statistical improvement in a youth soccer team.

If I am intervening at an individual level, I need solid research that generates pragmatic principles of intervention. The research should have strong metrics, such as physiological measurements and quantitative improvement. When dealing with elite performers, I consider my work to be ongoing single-case research. Each elite client is an *N of 1* study. Each is unique, typically operating far outside of the statistical norm and is usually cautious about changing those actions that have served as foundations for his or her success. I need research that generates solid principles of performance, with which the client and I can explore whether and how these principles might be applied to his or her unique situation.

At a very specific level, I would like to have more research on maximizing recovery. In my experience, elite performers usually have no difficulty training or working hard; their biggest challenge is being able to recover from the hard work. With greater demands being placed on performers (longer hours, more performances, fewer resources), recovery is increasingly important in all performance domains.

Sean McCann

All applied scientists at institutions such as the Olympic Training Center love research that focuses on elite athletes. The problem is that this research is hard to come by: It draws on an overly narrow slice of the population of athletes, it is difficult to conduct research with athletes in elite environments, and applications to other athletes and performers may be limited. Given this reality, the research that helps me most is the work that attempts to explain the common challenges for all athletes. This is research that provides a theoretical framework and potential solutions to the challenge. One great example is the work by Sian Beilock and colleagues on the mechanisms of choking. Using a simple and elegant design to sort through the various possibilities, the findings that explain how choking interferes with performance have been very helpful in my work. By addressing the cognitive and perceptual shifts that produce choking, we can learn directly from the research and begin to impact performance very quickly.

Another example of research on common challenges is the broad body of excellent work on athlete transitions from sport. Although much of this work has focused on a collegiate population, I believe it also can be applied effectively to the world of professional and Olympic athletes. The research indicates that a universal sense of loss and of getting lost occurs during the period after participation in elite sport, which may continue for a number of years. I've found that individual athletes are surprised to hear that others experience the same issues, and there is a sense of relief when they discover they are not alone. With some recent public examples of post sport career athletes going through tragic crises, I hope the findings in this area get more attention.

The other broad area of research I am finding increasingly useful in my applied work is the expanding knowledge of how the brain works. In particular, I have found it very useful to be able to explain to clients why and how anxiety evolves and how attention and focus can be manipulated. Both of these areas affect almost every serious athlete, and most athletes I work with benefit from the information. Part of the benefit is an increased understanding of the interaction between physiology and psychology, which makes sense for most athletes. The other primary benefit is that opening up the black box of the brain helps athletes understand that some specific performance issues will benefit from specific psychological work. Somehow, motivation to enhance mental skills is increased when athletes understand the how and why of their own brains.

Kirsten Peterson

Staying current with the research in our field has become increasingly challenging, with the proliferation of journals and sources of information available. At the same time, I have found it very useful to branch out by reading research in associated performance fields to see how they address issues of feedback, motivation, and elite performance skills.

Often, the applied research I need is the kind not yet conducted, or it is being done but not going to press. As an example, during my tenure at the USOC, I worked closely with combat sport athletes. Their daily challenge was the reality of training with some of their fiercest competitors. Each season concluded with the selection of a World or Olympic team, and suddenly these individual sport competitors were expected to become a team, to support and encourage each other. Intuitively, this switch made sense, but pragmatically, individuals on the team struggled with the idea of team building and more often rejected the premise out of hand. It was too easy to keep doing what they were used to doing, on their own, distrusting others' help (particularly their training partners, who were there to help them prepare, but who were often the runners up in that class). I recall combing the literature for examples of team building initiatives for individual sport athletes (or even individuals from other walks of life) with little success. The USOC was in the habit of holding themed coach education events, and I was fortunate enough to attend one in which coaches of individual sports came together to discuss common issues and present on best practice solutions. Although this may not be research in the traditional sense, I obtained wonderful examples of actual and successful team building initiatives going on with other individual sports, and I was able to question the architects of those programs, usually coaches, regarding their set-up and the conditions that promoted success.

Another area of value to me is research on elite performance conducted with actual elite performers. I have gained tremendous insight from the work of Dan Gould and colleagues, for example, which looks at how elite athletes develop their talent. When the rubber hits the road, it is also most useful to obtain information from Olympic champions themselves. I find that my clients—elite athletes—are discerning in their willingness to learn from me, even in the area of sport psychology. I must offer something that makes a difference. Often, that difference comes in the form of knowledge passed on from others who are like them—be they World or Olympic champions. Elite athletes find value in hearing about how other athletes succeeded, but it can be even more valuable when those athletes are willing to share their failures, the lessons learned, and the mistakes that were made and coped with. This can be very inspiring for athletes to hear and learn from, as they recognize the universality of the struggle to be one's very best.

I have also derived a lot of value from resources about elite performance in the business world. Unsurprisingly, there is much overlap between the worlds of sport and business, with the common need to perform at a high level under pressure. Books such as *Good to Great* by Jim Collins have helped me articulate to coaches and teams the concepts of building a high-performance culture and learning to be comfortable with change. Books by high-performing leaders can be useful for coaches and athletes since concepts such as continuous improvement, adapting to the need for different skills as you move up the performance environment ladder, and dealing with increasing potential for isolation at the top are shared and transferrable.

Question 3

What has surprised you about being a sport and performance psychologist?

Sean McCann

Well, since the day I made it to the USOC to work for an eccentric but passionate and committed Australian (who nowadays asks me to contribute to his latest editorial projects), I knew the work was going to be fun. And that has certainly continued to be true, virtually every day for the last 20 years. What has surprised me is that the work is so frequently meaningful and moving, and that the relationships developed are so often deep and long-lasting. For example, I cannot think of another setting in which I would have the privilege of meeting a junior athlete, working with him at age 16, then continuing a relationship with this same athlete through his retirement from sport 15 years later. During that span, I've seen him work through the challenges of teenage impulse control issues and resulting family conflict, failing at two Olympic Trials and succeeding at a third, relationship issues, marriage, and parenthood. When I began, I never realized that one of the most satisfying aspects of the job would be the opportunity for relationships that last longer than those of a Freudian analyst!

In addition to longevity, the aspect of the work that has surprised me is how frequently we address deep, meaningful, and moving issues. Of course, athletes and other performers are not immune to the complicated real-world issues that affect us all and that demand our best clinical and counseling skills, and the work on these "heavy" issues is often what I think about long after the workday is done. Although my work doesn't involve a steady stream of serious clinical issues, the blend of pure performance issues and mixed counseling/clinical/performance issues is very satisfying. I also find that working with athletes on clinical or counseling issues is often different from such work in other settings. Although elite athletes suffer just as much as the rest of us in experiencing psychological distress, an athlete's instinct for action helps move treatment along with more urgency than in other settings I am familiar with. This is very rewarding for the sport and performance psychologist. It reminds me of the coach's comment that, "When I was coaching with an all-pro quarterback my IQ went up 30 points. At least, that's how it seemed in the papers." Similarly, when working with great athletes, it's easier to be a good clinician.

Even in the performance realm, I've found that it is the individual triumphs, the comeback stories and personal bests—rather than the gold medal at the Olympics—that have moved me and stayed with me the longest. When a long-dominant World Cup performer wins an Olympic medal, the emotion that rises to the surface for me is often relief rather than pure elation. There is so much pressure and expectations these days for "favorites" that performing well

at the Games is the psychological equivalent of running a marathon in 90-degree heat. It is more of a brutal test of fortitude and survival than an opportunity to showcase an amazing talent.

On the other hand, for those athletes I have known through good times and bad, through injury and rehab, conflicts and resolution, getting through all that and coming out the other side makes me most thankful for my job. To have the privilege of being one of the few people in the world to know what a rough journey it has been for a team or for an individual athlete, and to understand how close to the precipice they have been, how vulnerable that team or athlete was, is to know how remarkable the performance is. When you know that you have been a support through those tough times, there is a special pride in watching a strong performance at the Olympics. Some of my favorite and most moving moments have simply been looking the athlete in the eye after that performance and both of us smiling in the knowledge of what a long hard trip it has been and how wonderful to end up here.

Kirsten Peterson

When I first heard about sport psychology back in the early 1980s, I was shocked that such a field existed. Excited, too, and convinced that it was what I really wanted to do—counsel athletes to help them be their very best. I was then surprised to discover how few people actually thought I would be able to make a go of it. Especially some of the graduate programs I applied to, who let me know in no uncertain terms that there was no market for what I wanted to do, but that I could always be a researcher. I am even more surprised to reflect upon my own reaction to that, which was to simply ignore them, which seems almost irrational as I look back. What made me think that I knew more than the scientists and experts in the field? Chalk it up to youthful naïveté, but ignore them I did.

Once in the field, working as a sport psychologist for the USOC, I was surprised by the lack of structure inherent in travelling on the road with teams. I had trained as a counseling psychologist used to working in an office for the traditional 50-minute hour, and even though I was intellectually aware that settings and modes of interaction would be different, I was unprepared for how that would make me feel: uncomfortable, unsure, and vaguely guilty, as if I was doing something wrong. Why wasn't I busier all day? What would people think of me if they saw me just standing or sitting around? I remember sharing this with my supervisor at the time, Sean McCann, and having him laugh and tell me that I was just bad at being lazy. Being cool with doing nothing for sometimes long periods of time is the occupational reality of an on-the-road sport psychologist. Recognizing that every situation is a chance to learn something useful about the people you are working with and that a psychologist can be very proactive with clients were not skills shared with me in graduate school. Learning to be good at "being lazy" meant getting out of my own head long enough to develop my observational skills; it meant getting out of my head long enough to think about where things were likely to happen and plant myself in that spot rather than this spot; it meant watching the athletes I worked with long enough to begin to recognize when might be a time to approach, when it was time to "conveniently" walk by, and when it was time to let well enough alone. It was certainly not a time to be surprised at making mistakes (and hopefully learning from them) along the way.

A more personal surprise is how difficult it has been to be a mother and a sport psychologist at the same time. I had my now 12-year-old child while working full-time, at a time when taking leave for childbirth and care was not a fashionable or functional idea in the United States. I was back at work 5 weeks later, resigned to the idea that it would be hard going for that first year, when my daughter required the most care. Getting through that year was one of the hardest things I have ever done. What was surprising in all this, however, was the near constant feeling of strain being a mother had on my job. I have since read more about the hormonal and brain chemistry shifting that literally rewires mothers to react to events in their lives in quantitatively different ways post childbirth, but at the time, I just thought it was bloody hard. Travel became harder (especially in airports and on airplanes, where other people's children were ever present), but it was also about the fact that my child did not stop needing a mother after that first year. Shocking, but true. Nor did I get over wanting to be a mother. This taught me to be opportunistic in shaping my work life in the directions I desired, but it was always (and continues to be) a struggle.

I am consistently surprised at what athletes are capable of. I remember being shocked as a young professional when I met my first "big time" athlete, a multiple Olympian training at the Olympic Training Center, and found how down to earth he was. That is a bona fide reality about athletes; they are all human beings as well. Some of them appear to have "it" all figured out. Most, however, have the same foibles, insecurities, hang-ups, and quirks as the rest of us, but find a way to do great things in their sports despite it all. It's a wonderful thing that defies prediction and part of what makes sport so enjoyable to watch and be a part of. As a sport psychologist, it's in part figuring out with the athlete which foibles to exploit and which ones to control that makes the job interesting.

Charlie Brown

There have been a number of pleasant surprises: seeing an athlete progress from a preteen with incredible dreams to actually fulfilling those dreams; having parents express their gratitude years later when I had been uncertain as to my impact; and encountering a welcome reception (sometimes even a hunger) for performance tools in other performance domains. But perhaps my biggest surprise is how indoctrinated I have been in the culture of therapy, and how challenging it was (and at times still is) to shift my mindset to work effectively within the culture of consulting, concentrating on performance.

In recent years, there has been growing attention to the importance of cultural sensitivity. The primary emphasis in the literature has been on sensitivity to groups of different race, religion, ethnicity, or sexual orientation. These efforts encourage awareness of the attitudes, values, customs, and expectations of groups that are different from one's reference group, and mindfulness that relationship and communication difficulties easily occur when interacting with a different culture. I find the concept of culture helpful in understanding the unexpected struggles that I have experienced in being a performance psychologist. It is also helpful when dealing with the tension that I have observed in the ubiquitous "research versus practice" debates within the field.

I spent my first two and a half decades of professional life immersed in the culture of therapy in a private practice context. This is a culture that worships confidentiality. No one should ever know of your involvement with a client or patient without the client's explicit consent. Services are delivered in a setting chosen by the professional, again with the goal of confidentiality being a primary objective. Financial compensation is based on time spent working on behalf of a client or patient at a previously agreed upon hourly rate. There are no bonuses for achieving results rapidly; in fact, there is a financial disincentive. When a client improves more slowly and requires more hours of direct service, the practitioner receives more income from that client.

Immersed in that culture for my first 25 years of practice, it all seemed logical and I excelled in it. People had problems; they did not want others to know their business. An hourly rate is fair and equitable. As declared by the Holy Creed of the Insurance UCR (usual, customary, and reasonable charges), all therapists and therapy are equal; services differ only in duration.

As I began consulting, I encountered what I now recognize as a serious case of culture shock. In contrast to therapy, consultation is a culture in which my presence is known: We work on the client's turf, people see me coming and going; the client often announces my involvement to others, I observe the client in action in the midst of his or her co-workers, we may meet over a meal or coffee. There is no way to hide it—yep, we're working together. In contrast to the stigma often associated with therapy, some clients even express pride in my being a new and valued resource to their team.

I adapted fairly well to the client's expectations of confidentiality. The culture of therapy is clear that confidentiality was the decision of the client, who could choose to waive the right of secrecy. And yes, there are times while consulting that a client is dealing with personal difficulties and confidentiality is essential. Before committing to any consulting relationship, I go to great lengths to clarify my role and expectations regarding what information can be shared and with whom. But, truth be told, I have been far more concerned about confidentiality than my clients, and I had to work on becoming comfortable with consulting in public arenas.

Adapting to the norms of financial compensation within the culture of consulting has been an unexpected challenge. Businesses and organizations don't organize their operations around hourly sessions. They want to get the job done, and they want a fixed fee for achieving those results so they can budget accordingly. The concept of one fixed fee for addressing a client's need is akin to blasphemy in the culture of therapy. I had to learn to do business proposals with cost estimates that include charges for unexpected problems that require additional time. I can accept my good fortune if I am able to achieve success more rapidly than anticipated, but have yet to take the step where the contract includes financial incentive for exceptional performance on my part. I intellectually know it makes good business sense to operate in this fashion, but I have been surprised by the ongoing mindfulness and effort required.

Question 4

A fundamental assumption of this Handbook is that the theories, methods, and interventions developed in sport psychology can be applied, with some modifications, in many areas of performance. Chapter authors have discussed the psychology of performance in areas such as sport, business, dance, theater, music, physical activity and exercise, the military, medicine, education, organizational management, and supervision. What is your approach when working with performers in fields other than sport?

Charlie Brown

My approach is actually fairly consistent in both sport and nonsport performance domains. I consider any venture into a performance setting as entering a foreign culture, whether it is the culture of a specific athletic team, a dance troupe, or a medical setting. First and foremost, I enter as an anthropologist rather than a missionary. A missionary enters a culture with "the answer." The missionary's role is to convert the natives to the superior knowledge, insight, or wisdom that the missionary brings. If the natives do not embrace the teachings of the missionary, they are often labeled as naïve, uneducated, or resistant. By contrast, an anthropologist seeks first to understand the culture and its values, attitudes, customs, and traditions. An anthropologist respects the culture and recognizes that the client has typically established a degree of expertise on being effective within that context. Within this framework, my role is to be a collaborative resource to the client, who is ultimately the expert on if and how the principles and techniques that I offer can be effective.

I am an advocate of making contextually intelligent decisions. As I enter any system, I attempt to "join through the hierarchy," making certain that I acknowledge and develop relationships with individuals at the highest position of influence within the system first, then build relationships throughout the organization. In my anthropologist's role, I am continually observing the system to create a contextual map for navigating it. I like to use the SPAM acronym in organizing my efforts: What is the formal and informal *structure* of the system? What are the *patterns* of interactions and decision-making? What are the *attitudes* and values of the different individuals? And what are the *means* of influence available to different individuals within the system? When I begin to intervene within the system, this mental map will guide my decisions as to how and with whom I direct my efforts, as well as the language and rationale that I use.

Often a client has requested my presence because of a specific problem or concern. I attempt to fully understand the concern and to identify the "pain" that the client is experiencing. At the same time, my conversations tend to be solution focused: How might I best serve as a resource? How would we know that my involvement was being effective? What have you attempted in the past to improve the situation? I sometimes surprise clients by being more interested in *exceptions* to the problem rather than hashing over why things are not working. I am guided by my grandfather's sage advice: You learn more from the one time you get it right than from the 99 times you get it wrong.

When I eventually offer suggestions, it is in a collaborative fashion. I share with the client that the principles of performance tend to be universal, but they must always be customized to the individual and the unique aspects of the situation. We then set about the business of tailoring those principles to fit the individual and the performance context. The process is founded on respect and collaboration, regardless of the performance domain.

Kirsten Peterson

I think that my work in sport psychology has informed me greatly as I have branched into work in other performance arenas. It is admittedly a small portion of my work experience, so I will speak primarily of my work with coaches and sport staff.

I have found it most useful when working with high performers who are not athletes to do the same thing I would when working within a new sport. I watch and listen. A lot. I also ask a lot of questions to make sure I understand their perspectives and roles.

With coaches in particular, it has been important for me to understand their histories as athletes, which can often yield a great deal of insight into their strengths and struggles as coaches. It is not uncommon for a talented athlete to decide (or be convinced) to become a coach. This transition can be difficult, and even talented athletes can fail if they aren't able to learn the skills and adapt to the different responsibilities inherent in this role. Too many coaches fall back on coaching in the way that they were coached, rather than developing a style that meshes best with their particular personality. Moreover, sticking to one style—no matter what—misses the point of understanding and appreciating the individuality of the athletes they now work with. New coaches in particular can also suffer from the change from active participant in their sport

to someone with substantially less control over the outcome. Coaches will often continue to see the outcome of their performers as their goal as well, without appreciating the fact that they, as coach, cannot actually hold themselves directly accountable to that goal. In addition to listening and watching a coach work to see how he or she interacts with the environment, I discuss the concept of control with them and see where he or she sits with regard to understanding his or her role in that context. This can be the time to help them focus on the specific coaching behaviors that they do actually control, be it organizing training, running the session, delegating responsibility, clearly communicating to their athletes, and so on. For some coaches, this can be one of those concepts that is easy to grasp on an intellectual level, but difficult to implement. Pragmatically, performance outcomes are often the benchmarks set by the public and sport programs to measure coaching success. So, how does a coach not focus on outcome? In this scenario, unless I acknowledge and support the reality of outcome in a way the coach can hear and appreciate, our work together may go nowhere.

I have found that it can be a particular challenge for male coaches to coach female athletes. In this instance, I have found that my own gender can be a useful tool, as I reflect with the coach about how particular behaviors they might consider appropriate and effective might land on me. In addition, this is an area in which I can point to literature and research to help the coach learn about the key differences in how girls and women think, process emotions, or interact as compared to men. Depending upon the maturity of the women in the team and the receptivity of the coach, this can be an opportunity for the athletes to teach the coach directly as well.

For head coaches, especially, this might also be the first time they have managerial responsibilities for others, which can also be a novel experience. Elite athletes often thrive when they are selfish and can narrow their life focus to what they need to do as individuals to reach their peak performance. This myopic focus can hurt a coach who has to learn to delegate authority, respond to the needs of a host of other individuals, and in general take a "bigger picture" look, as the CEO of his or her team. Getting to these issues requires good dialogue and feedback from others on the team, such as athletes, staff, and assistant coaches. Effective coaching also requires planning for who will take specific roles, and coaches must ask themselves—how will I get back to Big Picture planning? In addition to more staff and supervisory responsibilities, elite head coaches must also be able to integrate and work in an effective manner with a host of sport science service providers. Many coaches are distrustful of a team of "outsiders" coming in to work with their athletes; they don't know what to expect from them and can't easily evaluate their effectiveness. This is an area where I would consider bringing in an experienced coach who could share his or her own best practice experiences in how to positively exploit the resources of a sport science team.

Sean McCann

Being a sport psychologist for Olympic sport is helpful when moving out of sport altogether, since there are so many different Olympic sports and so many different challenges. I learned very early in my career that athletes in every sport make a point of emphasizing that their sport is different and has special challenges. Although using a story from another sport can be useful for making a point, I have seen too many sport psychology professionals make the mistake of using too many examples from another sport, resulting in athletes responding with attitudes such as "We aren't football players. He didn't get really get what it is that makes our sport so hard." From experiences such as these, I have learned that even during the first interactions with a new client, when the urge to "sell" your ideas is greatest, one can never skip past the initial stage of listening and collecting data. Otherwise, it is very easy to risk alienating the new client.

I have worked with performers in non-Olympic sports, particularly with auto racers. I also have some experience working with performers in other domains altogether, but the majority of my non-Olympic consulting has been with people in the business world. Although I have found a great deal of openness to and curiosity about the sports world from executives and managers, I am very wary of bringing up sport examples unless I am completely confident that the client first sees me as someone who understands his or her personal challenges, as well as the challenges of business today. I was given some great advice by a mentor in business consulting who told me I should get as comfortable with the *Financial Times* and the *Wall Street Journal* as I am with the sports section of the *Denver Post* or the *Boston Globe*. This means a comfort with language, terminology, and an awareness of the current environmental changes and trends that cut across all businesses. In addition, I take advantage of Google and other search options to learn as much as I can about the business and what people are saying about the business that I will be working with.

Question 5

I'm handing you the patented Murphy family crystal ball. Gazing into it, what do you see as the most exciting or interesting changes in sport and performance psychology come 2020?

Kirsten Peterson

Technology has changed our field in ways I couldn't have imagined even 5 years ago. With Skype and other forms of communication technology exploding in popularity, it is becoming easier to maintain regular contact with athletes and coaches around the world (accounting for time differences, of course). Texting has replaced the reminder phone call and has become also a favorite method of quick check-in, particularly with younger athletes. Although long-distance education has been around for decades, I can foresee a time when sport psychologists could regularly do even their educational sessions with teams from remote locations and from their laptops. The gap between an athlete's performance and visual feedback of that performance has become almost instantaneous. This, coupled with the portability of feedback options on devices like iPods and iPads, opens up a world for sport psychologists looking for ways to increase athlete self-awareness of their mental states, with the visual cues of a recent performance providing relevant and timely feedback.

I hope to see much more integration of sport psychology into the work of all the sport sciences. Organizations such as the USOC and the AIS have embraced the concept of interdisciplinary cooperation in the servicing of athletes, but much siloing of our disciplines continues to persist. Psychology has been integrated well into the field of nutrition, acknowledging the necessity of an interdisciplinary approach when dealing with disordered eating, and we work well with sports medicine in the area of injury and rehabilitation. I would like to see this concept embraced across the whole of sport science, both in terms of how we all do our applied work, but also in how we approach research.

An interesting example of the benefits of this cross-fertilization occurred at the AIS as a result of a speaking visit by Carol Dweck, Stanford University psychologist and leading researcher in the area of motivation. Fortuitously, her talk was heard by one of our physiology staff, who was inspired to look at how Dweck's concepts of learning versus fixed mindset could change and possibly improve how lab physiologists talked to athletes during physiological testing. The two disciplines collaborated on a protocol over the course of a cycling camp and found that what athletes heard in the interest of encouragement over the course of the camp influenced not only their immediate results on the tests, but their rate of improvement over the course of the camp. Athletes who were addressed in ways that suggested they could learn and adapt to get better at the particular test gave more effort and felt better about their results than did those who were told that their abilities were static. It was a useful wake-up call for physiologists to become aware of their influence—for excellence or passivity—on athlete testing.

Finally—and this is more of a hope than an expectation—I would like to see our applied training models for sport and performance psychology adapt to the realities of the profession in terms of how we are preparing students for satisfying and ethical careers in sport and performance psychology. I have enjoyed reading the position paper on this subject from Division 47, which talks in part about the areas of expertise a sport and performance psychologist should have, and which goes well beyond the "mental skills for athletes" courses of my sport psychology training. Sport and performance psychologists must be great consultants, quickly figuring out how to partner effectively with a client who often has no notion of what we do. In my consultation with colleagues and staff, I spend a lot of my time talking to them about how to manage the politics and power structures inherent in the sport organizations with which they are interfacing. In a number of instances, I have found that this aspect of doing business can be what derails or facilitates the sport psychology consultant's chances for success, irrespective of the quality of work going on with athletes and coaches. Sport and performance psychologists need to be competent psychologists in their base areas of expertise, but also knowledgeable and skilled in the area of psychological and emotional performance enhancement. On-the-road ethics is a course needing to be written and taught.

Charlie Brown

There will be growing pains as the third generation of sport psychologists emerges to lead the field. The first generation's members were rebels who broke from the traditions of their existing cultures and ventured into uncharted territory. Their primary concern was an applied focus in real-world situations. Success within this applied culture was achieved by improving performance. The second generation attempted to understand and organize what the first generation was doing, and to formalize the methodology of the first generation so that others could learn and replicate the process. These efforts were largely within an academic culture. Within this culture, the "currency" of success is academic publications, approval, and recognition by others within that culture. Success requires delineating the uniqueness of the field of study, demonstrating that it is clearly different from other institutional programs and concepts. If the second generation is effective, it establishes organizations that formalize the work of the first-generation rebels. Academic departments are formed, which in turn generate students and graduates. Those graduates who seek to return to operate in the applied culture of the original rebels give rise to the third generation. The third generation is concerned with effectiveness in a free-market, applied culture. Success within this culture is determined not by peers or organizations, but by clients. Clients must believe they will benefit from services and that the benefit is worth the compensation the consultant requests. Where the second generation focused on uniqueness, the third generation is acutely aware of commonalities. They draw knowledge from any and all disciplines that help them be more effective with clients. If the third generation is successful, clients will perceive the field as having sufficient value to produce a steady demand, such that individuals can support themselves financially by providing applied services.

As my friend and former APA President Ron Fox once advised, "Our ancestors swinging from tree to tree knew that if you want to make any progress, you've got to let go of what you've been holding on to." I predict that the field will let go of insisting that sport, exercise, and performance be melded together. Although commonalities exist related to physiology and activity, three areas with distinctly different applied goals will evolve. Sport psychology will focus on the developmental benefits of sport, such as character development, leadership, life skills, and team building. Exercise psychology will address issues of developing and maintaining a healthy and active lifestyle. Performance psychology will emerge as the field specializing in helping individuals achieve and sustain performance in pressure situations. Performance may be in any domain—sport, performing arts, business, or high-risk occupations. But the central concept is *performance* rather than the area or domain in which the performance occurs.

As the third generation emerges and performance psychology gains greater recognition, performance psychology will become assimilated into all cultures that address performance issues. If a professional is seeking to help an individual perform under pressure, there will be interest in the principles of performance psychology. Individuals in other helping professions will either seek collaboration with performance psychologists or pursue education in the principles and techniques of performance psychology.

In the midst of these evolutionary changes, continuing advances in telecommunication will alter the manner in which services are delivered. Video consultation will be commonplace, web-based technologies will provide instant feedback on performance issues, and educational services will be increasingly web-based. While the high-tech changes will facilitate information and communication, the technology will paradoxically produce a greater demand for "high-touch" interactions. The core of effective performance psychology services will be the personal relationship that the psychologist has with the client. Psychologists who are able to maintain a sense of personal connectivity with clients in the midst of warp speed technological changes will thrive.

These changes will produce major challenges for our existing organizations and institutions. In the free market culture of 2020, it is clearly a global economy where services can be delivered regardless of location. Our professional organizations will lead the way to establish national licensing standards, as it becomes increasingly evident that state-based efforts are not appropriate for telecommunication and global services.

Academic institutions will have major challenges as the economy drives a shift in the criteria for success within the academic culture. Historically, the key to success within the culture of academia has been "managing up." Professors attempt to establish their value to the hierarchy of an institution through scholarly presentations and publications. With diminishing financial resources, the most successful institutions will shift focus to a faculty member's success at "managing down"—addressing what the clients (i.e., students) want and need. There will always be a need for quality research, but, in 2020, the areas of research will be directed by what will help applied practitioners be more effective.

The needs of practice will guide research, which in turn will facilitate relevant and meaningful research guiding practice.

Sean McCann

For the profession of applied sport and performance psychology, I anticipate a formal recognition of the skills and competencies necessary to be an effective professional in this area. I believe the general consensus is tending toward a blended training of traditional applied psychology and performance enhancement theory and skill building. I believe that, in North America, doctoral-level training and licensure will be a requirement for employment at an institution, and I believe there will be increasing numbers of institutional positions in sport psychology. If these predictions are correct, the challenge for current and future educators and students in the field is to make the passage from applicant for graduate school to placement in a job as efficient, economically feasible, and effective as possible. This is certainly not true now.

Currently, too many stakeholders are focused on protecting their own status quo rather than making things better for the next generation. I believe examples of individuals who have changed their thinking and promoted a reasonable training model (such as John Silva at the AASP 25th anniversary conference), will help lead toward a sustainable path for new students. This will create challenges for programs that do not support this path and for individuals who have gone down a different training path. I believe, however, that a focus on the skills and competencies needed to be an effective professional will suggest that we need to make these difficult changes if we want to be excellent. And wouldn't it be ironic for a field that focuses on excellence to accept anything less than that for our training?

Final Comments from Shane

This final chapter turned out to be everything I had hoped—absorbing, insightful, provocative, and honest. My sincerest thanks are extended to Sean, Kirsten, and Charlie for having the courage to respond to my questions in such a thoughtful and straightforward manner. I admit that I deliberately chose questions that were designed to challenge. It's not often that we get the chance see in print the thoughts of those who are out in the "real world" of sport and performance psychology, working with the most elite of performers, concerning controversial issues such as training, education, and applied research. It was fascinating to hear Charlie's thoughts on the possible development of three separate fields of sport, exercise, and performance psychology; to ponder Sean's comments on the future of sport and performance psychology education and training; and to consider Kirsten's powerful example of the influence of a sport psychologist's theory and research on the actual testing and assessment of elite athletes. Their comments reinforce the essential relationship between informed practice and thoughtful research that forms the foundation of our field and lies at the heart of this Handbook. I can't think of a better note on which to end.

INDEX

Note: Page numbers followed by "*f*", "*t*", and "*n*" refer to figures, tables and notes, respectively.

A

AASP. *See* Association for Applied Sport Psychology
AASs. *See* anabolic-androgenic steroids
Abdou, Angie, 36
Abdul-Jabbar, Kareem, 707
ABQ. *See* Athlete Burnout Questionnaire
absorption, as conscious state, 139
acceptance, in performance psychology, 26
acceptance and commitment therapy, 125
acculturation, 421–23
achievement goals
   antisocial behavior and, 369
   of master athletes, 502
   moral behavior and, 368–69
   prosocial behavior and, 369
achievement goal theory (AGT)
   intrinsic goals in, 87
   leadership and, 329
   motivation and, 85
   performing arts and, 87–88
achievement motivation, 28
ACSM. *See* American College of Sports Medicine
ACT. *See* attentional control theory
ACTH. *See* adrenocorticotropic hormone
action-focused coping, 185
active listening, 27
actor-partner independence model (APIM), 409, 412–13
   actor effects in, 412
   interpersonal processes in, 412
   intrapersonal processes in, 412
   partner effects in, 412
acting, emotional expression in, 103
adaptation to transitions model, 514
adaptive approaches to competition model, 160
adolescents. *See also* youth development; youth sport
   in Canada, talent development for, 436
   physical activity for, 661–62
   sports expertise for, 436–37
   talent development among, in U.S., 436

Adolescents Training and Learning to Avoid Steroids (ATLAS), 554–55
adrenocorticotropic hormone (ACTH), 178
adults
   imagery by, 222
   physical activity for, 662–63, 669–71
affect
   emotion compared to, 155
   positive, 159
   self-efficacy from, 275–76
affective cycle of injury rehabilitation model, 595
age. *See also* age-related decline, in sports performance; master athletes; older athletes
   moral behavior and, 377
agents. *See* sports agents
age-related decline, in sports performance. *See also* older athletes
   compensation explanation for, 496–98
   cross-sectional trends for, 495–96, 495*f*
   deliberate practice and, 501
   for females, 494
   future research directions for, 508–9
   in golf, 497–98
   longitudinal trends for, 495–96, 495*f*
   mean age of peak performance and, 494
   motivation and, across lifespan, 501–8
   preserved differentiation account for, 499–500
   psychomotor expertise for, 498
   selective maintenance explanation for, 498–99
   selective optimization with compensation principle for, 498
   trends in, 494–96
aggression
   age as influence on, 377
   as antisocial behavior, 365
   gender and, 376
   hostile, 365
   instrumental, 365
   through modeling, 264
   morality and, 365

scenario approach for, 366–67
   in sport psychology, 8
agility, SPI and, 73–74
AGT. *See* achievement goal theory
AHA. See American Heart Association
Alekseev, Antoli, 12
Ali, Muhammad, 63
Almost Perfect Scale-Revised (APS-R), 295
American College of Sports Medicine (ACSM), 239
American Heart Association (AHA), 239
American Physical Education Review, 5
American Psychological Association (APA), 27
   Ethics Code for, 46–48
amotivation, 236
AN. *See* anorexia nervosa
anabolic-androgenic steroids (AASs), 545
   controlled studies for, 551*t*
   institutional ban on, 546
   medical consequences of, 550–52
   psychiatric consequences of, 550–52
analytical intelligence, 64
ancillary APEDs, 553
Andersen, Mark, 393, 693
Anderson, W. G., 4
Angell, Frank, 6
anger, 33–34
anorexia nervosa (AN), 637
   overexercise and, 625
anterior attentional system, 178
antisocial behavior
   achievement goals and, 369
   aggression as, 365
   measures of, 366
   research on, 380
Antonelli, Fernanando, 12
Antonelli, Ferruccio, 12
anxiety
   attentional bias and, 177–78
   attention and, 177
   audiences as influence on, 98
   causes of, 97–98

anxiety (*Cont.*)
    cognitive function and, 177
    in competitive sports, 174–77
    coping strategies for, 98–99
    critical factors for, 174
    environmental factors for, 97–98
    from expectations, 98
    feelings of exposure and, 98
    interpersonal factors for, 97–98
    management of, 98–99
    modeling as influence on, 258–59
    multidimensional theory for, 99
    music as therapy for, 99
    neural mechanisms for, 178–80
    from perfectionism, 90
    in performing arts, 97–99
    regulatory attentional control, 177–78
    self-talk and, 202
    state, 99
    training with, 185–86
    trait, 99
    visuomotor control and, 180–82
Anxiety Sensitivity Index, 623
APA. *See* American Psychological
    Association
APEDs. *See* appearance and performance
    enhancing drugs
APIM. *See* actor-partner independence
    model
appearance and performance enhancing
    drugs (APEDs)
    ancillary, 553
    blood doping and, 546
    body image disturbances and, 549–50
    conceptual foundations of, 548–50
    definition of, 545
    factors for use of, 553–54
    for fat burning, 552–53
    history of, 546–47
    illicit use of, 554
    interventions for, 554–55
    IOC guidelines for, 546, 556
    legal use of, 554
    medical consequences of, 550–52
    nonsteroidal, 553
    polypharmacy and, 548–49
    psychiatric consequences of, 550–52
    pyramiding and, 548
    scope of, 547–48
    stacking and, 548
    for weight loss, 552–53
applied sport psychology, 25–26
    in feminist sport psychology, 396
    future practices for, 41–42
    MST in, 26
    nontraditional forms of, 396
    perfectionism and, 300–301
    PST in, 26
    traditional forms of, 396
APS-R. *See* Almost Perfect Scale-Revised
Arab Americans, 421
    women in sports for, 425
Armstrong, Lance, 63, 627

artists. *See* performing artists
association, in pain management, 625
Association for Applied Sport Psychology
    (AASP), 16–17, 51–52
    certification program for, 17, 51
    ethnicity and performance guidelines
        under, 431
Association for Sport Psychology in
    Germany, 12
Association for the Advancement of
    Physical Education, 4
ASTQS. *See* Automatic Self-Talk
    Questionnaire for Sport
ATHENA. *See* Athletes Targeting
    Health Exercise and Nutrition
    Alternatives
Atherton, Mike, 127
Athlete Burnout Questionnaire (ABQ), 565
athletes. *See* coach-athlete relationships;
    elite athletes; master athletes; older
    athletes
Athletes Targeting Health Exercise
    and Nutrition Alternatives
    (ATHENA), 555, 652
athletic identity, 517
athletics, sports compared to, 336
ATLAS. *See* Adolescents Training and
    Learning to Avoid Steroids
attachment theory
    goal-corrected partnerships and, 410
    internal working models in, 409
    peer relationships and, 409–10
    secure attachments in, 409
attention
    anterior system, 178
    anxiety and, 177
    appropriateness of focus, 121
    attentional control theory, 144n10
    bias in, 177–78
    brain function and, 178
    capacity theory for, 120
    concentration and, 118–19
    as concentration of mental activity, 118
    definitions of, 118–19, 144n2
    distraction and, 145n17
    emotional regulation and, 163
    emotions as influence on, 159
    external focus of, 120
    filter theory for, 119–20
    internal focus of, 120
    multidimensional nature of, 118
    performance and, 121–23
    performance psychology and, 34
    PFC and, 178
    posterior system, 178
    processes for, 118
    regulatory attentional control, 177–78
    selective, 118–19
    self-talk and, 201
    spotlight metaphor for, 120–21
    unconscious factors for, 121
    voluntary, 178
attentional bias, 177–78

attentional control theory (ACT),
    144n10
    central executive functions in, 179
    emotions and, 159
    inhibition in, 179–80
    QE and, 182–83
    self-talk and, 201
    shifting in, 179–80
    stimulus-driven attentional control
        systems in, 179
    top-down control systems in, 179
attention training, somatics and,
    589–90
attunement, supervision and, 729–30
audiences
    anxiety and, as influence on, 98
    engagement of, 35
    interaction, 35
    performance psychology and,
        35, 103
    performing arts influenced by, 82
auditory imagery, 218
Australia, sport psychology in, 10
autocratic coaching behaviors, 316
automaticity, 98, 144n7
Automatic Self-Talk Questionnaire for
    Sport (ASTQS), 194
autonomy
    as basic psychological need, 237
    in CET, 234
    in SDT, 241
autonomy orientation, 237
autonomy-supportive leadership, 329,
    334–35, 338
    SDT and, 334
    in youth development, 455
awareness. *See* consciousness

B

Balague, Gloria, 13, 15
ballet, career length for, 38
Bandura, Albert, 665
Barber, Heather, 393
Barnard, Frederick, 250
basic needs support, motivation and, 88
basic psychological needs theory, 236–37,
    242–44
    autonomy in, 237
    competence in, 237
    motivation in, 242
    relatedness in, 237
basketball
    moral disengagement in, 371
    self-modeling in, 256
Bauman, Jim, 17
BEDs. *See* binge eating disorders
behavioral choice theory, 667
behavior epidemiology, framework for,
    660–61
behavior setting theory, 441
Belichick, Bill, 328
Bend It Like Beckham, 425
Bergstrom, J. A., 5

Between a Rock and a Hard Place
  (Ralston), 630–31
Beyond Boredom and Anxiety
  (Csikszentmihalyi), 629
bias. *See* attentional bias
binge eating disorders (BEDs), 637–38
bioecological perspective, 485–86
  direct effects in, 485
  exosystems in, 485
  indirect effects in, 485
  microsystems in, 485
bioinformational theory, 164
  imagery and, 227
biopsychosocial model of challenge and
  threat, 160
biopsychosocial model of injury
  rehabilitation, 595
Bird, Evelyn, 14
birth order, 484
birthplace bias, 441
blended families, 489–90
Bliese, Paul, 608
blindsight, 134
blood doping, 546
BMI. *See* body mass index
BN. *See* bulimia nervosa
bodily kinesthetic intelligence, 64
the body
  dualistic approach to, 586–88
  embodiment and, 588
  tension and, 585
  theoretical overview of, 583
body image
  APEDs and, 549–50
  BMI and, 91
  during childhood development, 636
  for dancers, 91
  definition of, 389
  EDs and, societal pressures and, 646
  for ideal feminine body, 389
  MD and, 639–40
  social physique anxiety and, 389
  women's sport and, 389–90
body mass index (BMI), 91
Bolt, Usain, 63
The Bone Cage (Abdou), 36
Bonica, John, 621
Boring, E. G., 25
Bouet, Michel, 12
boundary issues, ethics codes and,
  55–59
  BIRG and, 57
  conflicts of interest and, 59
  NSBCs, 57–58
  slippery slope for, 57
Boviner, Sherry Lyn, 14
Bowlby, John, 400, 405
Bowman, Bob, 127
Bowman, Scotty, 328
boxing, sport psychology for, 9
brain function
  ACTH, 178
  attention and, 178

CRF, 178
HPA axis, 178
imagery and, 219
neural mechanisms in, 178–80
SAM axis in, 160
Brandfonbrener, Alice, 82
Bredemeier, Brenda, 395
Brief Fear of Negative Evaluation Scale, 623
British Society of Sports Psychology, 12
Brown, Charlie, 742–45, 747–49, 751–52
Brown, David, 16
Brown, Paul, 8
Bryan, W. L., 5
bulimia nervosa (BN), 637
  overexercise and, 625
Bull, Deborah, 121–22
Bündchen, Giselle, 424
burnout
  antecedents of, 570–71
  avoidance strategies, 568–71
  characteristics of, 567–68
  in coaches, 570–71
  cognitive-affective model of, 571–72
  consequences of, 568–70
  definition of, 563–65
  depression and, 566
  disengagement and, 576
  energetic processes for, 577
  engagement and, 562–64
  fatigue and, 565–66
  future research applications for, 577–78
  JDR model for, 576–77
  job-person congruity and, 575
  job person fit and, 575
  from job stress, 566
  manifestations of, 567
  measurement of, 563–65
  metaphors for, 569
  motivational processes for, 577
  negative training stress response model
    for, 572
  from overtraining, 566–67
  PEE and, 564
  perfectionism and, 301
  from performance, 37
  recognition of, 563–65
  reduction strategies for, 574–77
  removal strategies for, 574–77
  SDT and, 573–74
  self-report measures for, 565
  SET and, 571
  sport commitment model for, 573
  sport devaluation and, 564
  stress-recovery perspective for, 572–73
  unidimensional identity development
    and external control model for, 573
business, as performance domain
  coaching in, 39
  competition in, 32
  cooperation in, 313
  group cohesion in, 318–19
  leadership in, 317
  morality in, 378

performance coaches for, 695f
as research focus, 25
role relationships in, 314–15
team building strategies in, 320–21
teams in, 310
teamwork in, 311
Butt, Dorcas Susan, 15

C
Cagigal, Jose-Maria, 12
Canada
  sport psychology in, 13
  talent development in, for
    adolescents, 436
Canadian Psychological Association
  (CPA), 49
Canadian Society for Psychomotor
  Learning and Sports Psychology, 12
capacity theory, for attention, 120
career completion, 37–38. *See also*
  retirement
career transitions, 437
  adaptation to transitions model for, 514
  assistance for, 519–21
  athletic identity and, 517
  conceptual frameworks for, 514–15
  counseling strategies for, 519
  early developmental factors and,
    517–18
  enhancement strategies for, 519
  environmental factors for, 514–15
  ethical considerations for, 521
  exploratory behavior engagement
    and, 517
  healthy, 515–18
  individual reactions to, 518–19
  LDI model for, 515, 519
  Olympic self-image and, 518
  organizational support for, 518
  planning for, 517
  psychological foreclosure and, 520
  psychological reactions to, 518–19
  resources for, 517–18
  self-awareness and, 519–20
  situational foreclosure and, 520
  social support for, 517–18
  sport-specific factors for, 515
  in stage models of grief and loss, 514
  support strategies for, 519
  theoretical frameworks for, 514–15
  whole person approach to, 515, 520–21
caring climates, 456
Caring Climate Scale, 352
Carlile, Forbes, 10
Carlile, Ursula, 10
Carroll, Pete, 14
CART-Q. *See* Coach-Athlete
  Relationship-Questionnaire
Casals, Pablo, 38
catastrophe model, 176
catastrophic injury, 602–3
catastrophizing, 619
Cattell, James, 6

causality orientations theory (COT), 237
  in sports settings, 246n1
CBAS. *See* Coaching Behavior Assessment
    System
CBQ. *See* Coaching Behavior
    Questionnaire
CBT. *See* cognitive-behavioral therapy
certification programs, AASP, 17
CET. *See* cognitive evaluation theory
CFQ. *See* Coaching Feedback
    Questionnaire
CFS. *See* chronic fatigue syndrome
challenge states, 160, 161*f*
Challenging Athletes Minds for Personal
    Success (CHAMPS), 18
championships, 494
CHAMPS. *See* Challenging Athletes
    Minds for Personal Success
change blindness, 143
childhood development
  body image during, 636
  perfectionism during, 301–3
children. *See also* youth development;
    youth sport
  imagery by, 222
  physical activity for, 661–62, 668–69
  self-talk with, 205
  sports expertise for, 436–37
choking
  competitive sports anxiety and, 174–75
  definition of, 174
  distraction theories for, 175
  emotional role in, 154
  self-focus theories for, 174–75
  in theory of reinvestment, 138
chronic fatigue syndrome (CFS), 566
chronic pain, 627
Clarke, Darren, 40
classification systems
  categorical models of, 528–29
  dimensional models of, 528–29
  in *DSM-IV*, 529
  MCS-SP, 529–34
Client-Centered Therapy (Rogers), 406
clinical psychologists, 27
closed-door racism, 424
clutch performances, 175–77
  definition of, 175
CMRT. *See* cognitive-
    motivational-relational theory
Coach-Athlete Relationship-Questionnaire
    (CART-Q), 403
coach-athlete relationships
  CART-Q, 403
  closeness in, 403
  co-orientation in, 403
coaches. *See also* performance coaches
  attitudes of, 348–49
  burnout in, 570–71
  CBQ, 196
  coach-athlete relationships, 403–4
  EDs and, 643–44
  education for, 353–56

efficacy beliefs of, 282, 349
female, 349–51, 387
injury and, 608
leadership behaviors for, 316
meditational model of leadership
    for, 329
moral behavior among, 372–74
moral behavior of, through ratings,
    367–68
opinions of, 348–49
performance, 685
personal philosophies of, 355–56
self-talk by, 204
sports psychologists and, 681–83
thoughts of, 348–49
youth development influenced by,
    454–56
coaching.
  active listening in, 27
  autocratic behaviors, 316
  burnout from, 570–71
  capabilities necessary for, 358
  CBQ, 196, 331–32
  CFQ, 330–31
  cognitive-meditational coaching
      leadership model, 345–46
  contemporary journals on, 343–44
  as context-specific, 347, 355
  definitions of, 344
  democratic behaviors, 316
  development of, as science, 344–45
  early literature on, 343
  education for, 353–56
  effective behaviors for, 347–48
  for elite athletes, 348
  empathy in, 27
  executive, 39
  expertise in, 354
  future directions in, 358–60
  GROW model, 356
  through hard leadership, 336
  knowledge in, 358
  for life skills, 351–53
  negative experiences during, 352
  performance psychology and, 27–28
  personal experiences with, 353–54
  personal philosophy as influence on,
      355–56
  personal qualities for, 358
  positive feedback in, 316
  psychology of, 344, 357–58
  quantitative methods for, 345
  as reflection in action, 355
  as reflection on action, 355
  reframing in, 27
  research on, 347, 357–58
  as retrospective reflection on
      action, 355
  SDT and, 346
  self-reflection in, 356
  self-talk in, 204
  social support in, 316
  through soft leadership, 336

for special populations, 349–51
  techniques in, 27
  theories for, 345–47
  training and instruction in, 316
  women, 349–51
Coaching Behavior Assessment System
    (CBAS), 330
Coaching Behavior Questionnaire (CBQ),
    196, 331–32
Coaching Feedback Questionnaire (CFQ),
    330–31, 331*f*
Coakley, Jay, 353
cocktail party phenomenon, 119
cognitive-affective model, 571–72
cognitive-behavioral therapy
    (CBT), 26
  performance psychology and, 35
  in sport psychology, 28
cognitive evaluation theory (CET),
    234–35
  autonomy in, 234
  competence in, 234, 244–45
cognitive function
  anxiety and, 177
  emotions and, 159
  negative emotions and, 159
Cognitive Interference Test, 194
cognitive-meditational coaching leadership
    model, 345–46
cognitive-motivational-relational theory
    (CMRT), 155–57
  central tenets of, 157
  core relational themes in, 156*t*
  primary appraisal in, 156
  secondary appraisal in, 156
cognitive self-modeling, 275
cohesion. *See* group cohesion
Coleman, Michelle, 18
collaboration, with teammates, 73
collaborative learning. *See* dyads,
    learning in
collective self-efficacy, 284–86
  contexts for, 285
  group cohesion and, 288
  limitations of, 286
  predictive effects of, 285
  transferable nature of, 285
Collins, Jim, 745
commitment. *See* functional commitment;
    obligatory commitment
communication
  cultural, 427
  of performance strategies, 427–28
compensation explanation, 496–98
competence
  as basic psychological need, 237
  in CET, 234, 244–45
  ethical codes and, 51–53
  moral behavior through, 372–73
  pressure and, 35–36
  in SDT, 244–45
competition
  adaptive approaches model, 160

biopsychosocial model of challenge and threat, 160
in business, 32
ego orientation and, 32
goal orientation and, 32
in high-risk domains, 32
performance psychology and, 31–33
siblings as, 484–85
tanking against, 32
task orientation and, 32
competitive self-efficacy, 278
competitive sports anxiety, 174–77
catastrophe model for, 176
choking and, 174–75
during clutch performances, 175–77
directional perspectives on, 175
ego and, 174
perceived control in, 176
PET for, 176
primary appraisals in, 176
QE and, 182–83
secondary appraisals in, 176
self-focus theories and, 174–75
three-dimensional conceptualization of, 176
transactional perspective on, 176
worry as part of, 176
complex families, 83
Comprehensive Soldier Fitness (CSF), 33
concentration
ACT and, 125
attention and, 118–19
automatic monitoring systems for, 123
on controllable factors, 125
definition of, 118
as deliberate, 123–24
distraction and, 145n17
focus as part of, 125
future research on, 128
hyperaccessibility and, 123
loss of, by performers, 122–23
mental practice in, 127
mindfulness training for, 125
one thought principle in, 124
outward focus in, 125
performance goal specification with, 125–26
pre-performance routines for, 126–27
principles of, 123–25, 124f
self-talk and, 124, 202
simulation training for, 127–28
techniques for, 125–28
trigger words for, 127
visualization in, 127
concussion, 600–602
confidence-based imagery, 226
confidentiality
disclosure standards, 54–55
ethical codes for, 53–55
for sports psychologists, 678
conflict management
by performance coaches, 697f
by sport psychologists, 685–86

congruence hypothesis, 332–33
conscientiousness, 96
emotional regulation and, 165
conscious awareness, learning and, 135–39
consciousness
absorption and, 139
academic evolution of, 131
analytic processes, 133
attention and, 136
control and, limitations of, 136–37
early views on, 132
as evolutionary adaptation, 140
flow and, 139, 145n19
for Freud, 132
fringe of, 132
global workplace theory and, 133
hypothesis testing for, 136
implicit learning and, 140–41
instance theory and, 137
intuitive processes and, 133
for James, 131–32
marginal perceptions of, 142–43
mind-body problem and, 132
optimum performance and, 139–40
phenomenal, 144n3
processing information and, 132–33
states of, 133–35
stream of, 132
suppression of, 139
theory of reinvestment and, 137–39, 145n14
thought suppression and, 135
unconscious awareness compared to, 134–35
working memory and, 132–33
conscious processing hypothesis, 137
constrained action hypothesis, 145n15
consultation
client attitudes toward, 40–41
in performance psychology, 27–28, 38–41
for performing artists, 39
in sport psychology, 38–41
contextual intelligence, 30, 64
knowing your environment and, 72
continuous tracking, 140
control
perceived, 176
regulatory attentional, 177–78
controlled orientation, 237
controlling behaviors, in youth development, 455
control process theory, 201–2
cooperation, in teamwork
in business, 313
in military, 313–14
in sports, 312–13
coping models, 254–55
coping self-efficacy, 278
coping strategies
action-focused, 185
for anxiety, 98–99
automaticity as, 98, 144n7

emotional regulation compared to, 161–62
emotion-focused, 162
for injury, 92
modeling in, 254–55
overlearning as, 98
problem-focused, 162
self-efficacy as, 257
in theory of reinvestment, 137
corticotrophin-releasing factor (CRF), 178
COT. See causality orientations theory
Coubertin, Pierre de, 5
counseling
client variables in, 540–41
counselor variables in, 540
cultural variables in, 541–42
evidence-based approach to, 535–39
intervention targets in, 536–37
MAC approach to, 537
for Pdy, 537–38
for performers in distress, 535–39
for PI, 538
psychologists, 27
for PT, 538–39
for PTSD, 537
setting variables for, 539–40
counterfactual thinking, 167
countertransference, 413n2
CPA. See Canadian Psychological Association
creative intelligence, 64
creativity
ego strength and, 101
mental illness and, 101
performing art psychology and, 101
types of, 101
crew resource management (CRM), 322
CRF. See corticotrophin-releasing factor
CRM. See crew resource management
CSF. See Comprehensive Soldier Fitness
Csikszentmihalyi, M., 629
Cullen, Florence Patricia, 14
cultural communication, 427–28
in counseling, 541–42
cultural intelligence, 65
culture
acculturation and, 421–23
for Arab Americans, 421
counseling influenced by, 541–42
definition of, 419
emotional regulation influenced by, 165
enculturation and, 421–23
generational status and, 422
immigration as influence on, 422
institutional, 88–89
performance psychology influenced by, 31
in U.S., 420
worldview influenced by, 423
culture, performance and
AASP guidelines for, 431
challenges to, 423–24
communication strategies, 427–28

culture, performance (*Cont.*)
crossing over and, 423–24
as exchange, 428–29
gender as influence on, 425–26
historical issues with, 421
integrated approaches to, 427–31, 430*f*
leadership cultivation with, 429–30
for Muslim cultures, 425
race logic and, 424
racism and, 424–25
self-awareness of, 420–23
selling out and, 423–24, 429
sensitive stereotyping of, 419
SES and, 419, 423, 426–27
social isolation and, 419
targeted mentoring and, 429
tokenism and, 423–24, 429
within-group variability of, 419
xenophobia and, 424–25
Cumbee, Frances, 14

D

Daly, John, 62, 78
dancers
AGT and, 85
basic needs support for, 88
BMI and, 91
culture of tolerance among, for pain, 92
disordered eating among, 91
EDs among, 639
homonegativism towards, 392
imagery for, in performing arts
psychology, 93–95, 225
injury and, 92–93
pain management among, 620
pain management for, 92–93
passion in, 85
peer relationships among, 407
SDT and, 85–86
Davis, Shani, 424
Day, Phyllis, 14
debilitative and facilitative competitive
state anxiety model, 160
Deci, Edward, 234
decision-making models. *See also*
professional judgment and
decision-making
ethics in, 49–51
for multiple relationships, 56
Decision Specific Reinvestment Scale,
145n16
DeFrantz, Anita, 387
deliberate play
expertise from, 477
investment years of, 339
sampling years for, 339
specializing years of, 339
sport and, 336
transition to deliberate practice, 338–39
in youth sport, 439
deliberate practice
deliberate play transition to, 338–39
expertise and, 437–38, 477

for older athletes, 501
within performing arts, 82–85
in talent development, 437–38, 477–78
in youth sport, 439
De Lima, Vanderlei, 122
democratic coaching behaviors, 316
depression
burnout and, 566
motivation and, 159
Depression Anxiety and Stress Scale, 623
Descartes, Rene, 131
Deutsch, Morton, 312
developmental lifespan model, for talent
development, 479
developmental model of sport
participation (DMSP), 435–36,
438–39
postulates for, 438*t*
recreational outcomes in, 444
stages of, 442–44
talent development and, 479
DHT. *See* dihydrotesterone
*Diagnostic and Statistical Manual of Mental
Disorders, Fourth Edition
(DSM-IV)*, 529
dihydrotesterone (DHT), 545
dinitrophenol (DNP), 552
disengagement, 576
disordered eating. *See also* body image;
body mass index
cultural influences on, 91
among dancers, 91
future research on, 91–92
prevalence rates for, 90–91
Disposable Heroes, 627
dissociation, in pain management, 625
distraction, 145n17
theories, 175
distress, 528–29
counseling for performers with, 535–39
DLPFC. *See* dorsal lateral prefrontal
cortex
DMSP. *See* developmental model of sport
participation
DNP. *See* dinitrophenol
Dorfman, Harvey, 40
dorsal lateral prefrontal cortex (DLPFC), 178
Drogba, Didier, 603
dropouts, from sport, 443
drug use. *See* anabolic-androgenic
steroids; appearance and
performance enhancing drugs;
dihydrotesterone; human growth
hormone
*DSM-IV. See Diagnostic and Statistical
Manual of Mental Disorders,
Fourth Edition*
dual relationships. *See* multiple
relationships, ethics codes and
Duda, Joan, 15
dyadic friendships, 401
dyads, learning in, 256–57
IOR and, 256

E

early specialization, in sports, 440
for elite athletes, 443
eating disorder not otherwise specified
(EDNOS), 637–38
eating disorders (EDs)
AN, 625, 637
BED, 637–38
BN, 625, 637
body dissatisfaction and, 647–48
coaches as influence on, 643–44
by competitive level of sport, 643
among dancers, 639
dietary restraints and, 648
EDNOS, 637–38
education about, 651
among elite athletes, 638–39
female athlete triad and, 639
future research applications for, 649–50
identification of, 653–54
integrated training environment and, as
intervention, 652
internalization of body ideal and, 647
interventions for, 650–54
for male athletes, 643–44
modeled behaviors as influence on,
648–49
moderators of, 649
negative affect and, 648
parents as influence on, 643–44
peer influences on, 643–44
performance environment and, 640–44
Petrie and Greenleaf model for, 645–46
prevention programming for, 652–53
risk factors for, 635
societal pressures and, for body
image, 646
sociocultural approach to, 635, 644–50
sport environment and, 640–44
sport-specific pressures and, 646–47
sport type and, 642–43
subclinical, 638
treatment strategies for, 653–54
ecological theory, 483
EDNOS. *See* eating disorder not
otherwise specified
EDs. *See* eating disorders
education
for coaching, 353–56
modeling applications for, 261
perfectionism in, 296–97
physical activity interventions, 668–69
self-talk in, 206
for sport psychologists, 689
EEG. *See* electroencephalography
egalitarian sports, 336–38
elite compared to, 338
ego orientation
competition and, 32
competitive sports anxiety and, 174
for moral behavior, 368–69
perfectionism and, 31
EI. *See* emotional intelligence

electroencephalography (EEG), 144n8
elite athletes. *See also* older athletes
  coaching for, 348
  early specialization for, 443
  EDs among, 638–39
  expertise for, 443
  personality for, 96
  self-confidence for, 100
  self-esteem for, 100
elite sports, 336–38
  egalitarian compared to, 338
Els, Ernie, 277
Emmons, Matthew, 118
emotions. *See also* emotional regulation
  affect compared to, 155
  anger, 33–34
  attentional control theory
      and, 159
  attention influenced by, 159
  in biopsychosocial model of challenge
      and threat, 160
  cardiovascular responses to, 160
  choking and, 154
  CMRT and, 155–57, 156t
  cognitive functioning and, 159
  core relational themes for, 156t
  debilitative and facilitative competitive
      state anxiety model, 160
  definitions of, 155–56
  emotional expression compared
      to, 103
  in groups, 157–58
  during high performance, 75
  IZOF and, 158
  mental health models for, 158
  mirror neurons and, 157–58
  mood compared to, 155
  motivation and, 159
  perceptions of, 160
  performance and, 33–34, 158–60
  in PETTLEP model, 221
  positive, 159, 161, 461
  regulation of, 33
  in resonance performance model, 34
  self-efficacy from, 276
  social purpose of, 168
  in sports environments, 154
  TCTSA and, 160
  threat states and, 160
  youth development influenced by,
      461–62
emotional contagion, 157
emotional expression, 102–3
  for actors, 103
emotional fitness, 33
emotional intelligence (EI), 33–34, 65
  shaping one's environment and, 73
  SPI and, 78
Emotional Intelligence (Goleman), 33
emotional regulation
  attention deployment in, 163
  in bioinformational theory, 164
  cognitive change and, 163–65

conscientiousness and, 165
coping strategies compared to, 161–62
costs of, 166–67
counterfactual thinking and, 167
cultural differences in, 165
ethnicity as influence on, 165
future research applications for, 168
goal setting with, 163
imagery and, 164
models for, 162–63
modifications in, 163
physiological effects of, 166
process model for, 162f
reappraisal in, 164–65
relaxation techniques for, 164
response modulation in, 165, 168
self-control and, 166–67
self-esteem and, 165
self-talk and, 163–64
in sports, 154
working memory and, 165
emotion-focused coping, 162
empathy, in coaching, 27
emulation, 252
enculturation, 421–23
engagement, burnout and, 562–64
entertainment sports, 336–37
environmental knowledge, 73–74
EOSE. *See* estimations of the other
      person's self-efficacy
Espenschade, Anna, 9, 14
Essais de psychologie sportive
      (Coubertin), 5
estimations of the other person's
      self-efficacy (EOSE), 288
ethics, codes of
  acculturation model for, 49
  in APA, 46–48
  boundary issues and, 55–59
  competency standards in, 51–53
  for confidentiality, 53–55
  decision-making models, 49–51
  definitions of, 48
  for informed consent, 53–55
  main features of, 59–60
  multiple relationships and, 55–59
  in performance psychology, 39
  privacy issues in, 55
  PST and, 47
  for psychological services
      delivery, 55
  for psychologists, 48
  risk management in, 49
  in sport psychology, 39
  for steroid use, 555–56
  in training, 51–53
  values and, 49
ethnicity
  acculturation and, 421–23
  for Arab Americans, 421
  definition of, 419
  emotional regulation influenced by, 165
  enculturation and, 421–23

generational status and, 422
immigration as influence on, 422
performance psychology influenced
      by, 31
in U.S., 420
worldview influenced by, 423
ethnicity, performance and
AASP guidelines for, 431
challenges to, 423–24
communication strategies, 427–28
crossing over and, 423–24
as cultural exchange, 428–29
definition of, 419
gender as influence on, 425–26
historical issues with, 421
integrated approaches to,
      427–31, 430f
leadership cultivation with,
      429–30
for Muslim cultures, 425
race logic and, 424
racism and, 424–25
self-awareness of, 420–23
selling out and, 423–24, 429
sensitive stereotyping of, 419
SES and, 419, 423, 426–27
social isolation and, 419
targeted mentoring and, 429
tokenism and, 423–24, 429
within-group variability of, 419
xenophobia and, 424–25
ethnic sports, 428
European Federation of Sport Psychology,
      12, 15
excellence, as focus, in performance
      psychology, 30–31
executive coaching, 39
exercise dependence, 640
exhaustion. *See* burnout; physical and
      emotional exhaustion
exosystems, 485
expectations
  anxiety from, 98
  mental skills with, 31
  of self, in performance psychology, 31
expertise, in sports. *See also* talent
      development
  for adolescents, 436–37
  career transitions and, 437
  for children, 436–37
  in coaching, 354
  from deliberate play, 477
  deliberate practice and, 437–38, 477
  developmental models for, 437–39
  DMSP and, 435–36, 438–39, 438f
  early specialization and, 440
  for elite athletes, 443
  performance coaches and, 702–3
  performance psychology and, 37
  personal development and,
      443–44
  psychomotor, 498
  sampling approach to, 440–41

expert modeling, 254
explicit monitoring hypothesis, 175
extended focus, 34
extraversion, 96
extrinsic motivation, 235–36
   external regulation in, 236
   introjected regulation in, 236
   moral behavior and, 369

F

fair play, 378
   attitudes for, 373
Fair Play for Kids program, 459
family, as influence. *See also* parents, as
      influence; siblings
   on asset development, 489
   bioecological perspective on, 485–86
   blended, 489–90
   complex, 83
   differentiation for, 83
   integration for, 83
   motivation from, 88–89
   in performance psychology, 37
   on physical activity, 669
   as social support, 488–89
   stage parents, 83
   on talent development, 83–84, 485–87
fatal injury, 602–3
fat burning drugs, 552–53
   female use of, 552
fatigue
   CFS, 566
   psychological, 565
Faul, Bill, 10
Favre, Brett, 63, 493
Fazio, Rob, 18
fear of failure, 370
Fear of Pain Questionnaire III, 623
Federer, Roger, 63
feedback
   in coaching, 316
   SDT and, 241
   from self-talk, 199
   in youth development, 455
feedforward, 255
Feltz, Deborah, 15–16
female athlete triad, 639
female coaches, 349–51, 387. *See also*
      women
   communication styles of, 350
   lesbian stereotypes of, 391–92
females. *See* women
feminism, 385–86
   herstory as term, 386–87, 397n1
   praxis in, 386
   sport psychology under, 394–97
feminist sport psychology, 394–97
   applied sport psychology and, 396
   career experiences in, 395–97
Ferrante, Alfred, 16
Ferrer-Hombravella, Jose, 12
figure-skating, self-modeling for, 255
filter theory, for attention, 119–20

cocktail party phenomenon and, 119
first-person perspective (1PP), 215–16
The First Tee program, 450, 452–53, 459
Fitt's Law, 218
Fitz, G. W., 4
flow state, 14
flow theory
   consciousness and, 139, 145n19
   high performance delivery and, 77
   optimal performance and, 711–12
   in performing arts, 89
   PFC involvement and, 145n21
   in sport psychology, 28
FMPS. *See* Frost Multidimensional
      Perfectionism Scale
focus
   in concentration, 125
   extended, 34
   self-focus theories, 174–75
FOLQ. *See* Functions of Observational
      Learning Questionnaire
French Society of Sports Psychology, 12
Freud, Sigmund, 132, 400
   transference for, 411
Freudenberger, Herbert, 563
friendships
   components of, 401
   dyadic, 401
   nonreciprocal, 402
   reciprocal, 402
   in youth development, 452–53
Fritz, Harry, 12
Frost, Reuben, 12
Frost Multidimensional Perfectionism
      Scale (FMPS), 295–96
FSTQ. *See* Functions of Self-Talk
      Questionnaire
Fullerton, Hugh, 8
functional commitment, 504
Functions of Observational Learning
      Questionnaire (FOLQ), 259–60
Functions of Self-Talk Questionnaire
      (FSTQ), 193, 202

G

Gallwey, Timothy, 30
game reasoning, 458–59
games, 494
gamesmanship, 138
games with rules, 439
gate control theory, 621
Gates, Bill, 64, 328
Gay Games, 392–93
GCT. *See* goal contents theory
gender. *See also* males; women; women's
      sport
   aggression by, 376
   definition of, 384
   ethnicity and, performance influenced
      by, 425–26
   ideology, 384–85
   master athletes and, 503
   modeling by, 260

moral behavior and, 376
   perfectionism by, 302
   physical activity by, social roles for, 388
   self-esteem by, 100
   socialization, 385
   sports and, 387–94
gender identity, 384
gender similarities hypothesis, 302
gender socialization, 385
generational status, 422
Germany
   Olympic Games in, 603
   sport psychology in, 7–8
Geron, Emma, 12, 14–15
Gibson, James, 585
Gibson, Kirk, 708–9
Giesecke, Minnie, 14
Giges, Burt, 9
Gill, Diane, 15, 394–95
girls
   gender equity in sports and, 388
   participation in team sports by, 386
   under Title IX legislation, 349, 386–88
   as tomboys, 388
Girls on the Run program, 450, 464
global self-esteem, 460
global workplace theory, 133
goal contents theory (GCT),
      237, 242–43
goal-corrected partnerships, 410
goal orientation
   competition and, 32
   intrinsic, 87
goal setting
   with emotional regulation, 163
   intrinsic, 87
   self-talk and, 199
   in shaping one's environment, 72
   in sport psychology, 28
   in team building strategies, 320
Goleman, Daniel, 33
golf
   age-related decline in skills, 497–98
   QE training for, 183–85
Gomez, Scott, 423
Good to Great (Collins), 745
Gould, Dan, 13, 744–45
Gower, David, 136, 138
Graf, Steffi, 62
Graves, B.C., 8
Green, Barry, 30
Gregory, Sean, 601
Grenville, Kate, 136
Gretzky, Wayne, 62, 78
grief and loss. *See* stage model of grief
      and loss
Griffith, Coleman, 7–9, 11, 25–26
group cohesion
   in business, 318–19
   collective self-efficacy and, 288
   in military, 319
   in sports, 318
   teamwork and, 318–19

GROW model, for coaching, 356
Gulick, Luther, 4
gymnastics
    modeling for, 260
    self-modeling for, 255

H

habituation, 585
Hall, G. Stanley, 6
Hall, Ruth, 395
Handbook of Applied Psychology, 11
hanging out, 52
Hanna, Thomas, 584
Hantuchova, Daniela, 127
hard leadership, 336
Harlow, Harry, 400
harmonious passion, 86, 370–71, 504
Harris, Dorothy, 13–15
Hayes, Martin, 121
Hays, Kate, 46
head injury, 600–602
healthy perfectionism, 295
healthy weight management (HWM), 652
hegemonic femininity, 389
hegemonic masculinity, 392
Henderson, Robert, 8
Henry, Franklin, 9
hero worship, 57
herstory, as feminist term, 386–87, 397n1
Heyman, Steve, 16
hGH. *See* human growth hormone
high performance, delivery of
    adjustments within, 76–77
    control of environment during, 76
    emotional states during, 75
    evaluations of, 77–78
    flow and, 77
    improvement assessment after, 77–78
    measurement criteria for, 77–78
    mental toughness and, 76
    opportunity assessment with, 76
    planning in, 74–77
    preparation in, 74–77
    under pressure, 76
    purposefulness in, 74–75
    success definitions for, 74
    trusting oneself with, 76
    what-if scenarios and, 75
Hillary, Edmund, 273
hockey
    self-modeling in, 256
    team building strategies in, 319–20
Holmes, Joseph, 8
Holyfield, Evander, 364
homonegativism, in sport, 390–94
    inclusive environments and, 392–93
    lesbian stereotypes, 387, 390
    against LGBT populations, 390
    in male sports contexts, 392
    social identity theory and, 392–93
    in women's sport, 390–92
homophobia, 390
hooks, bell, 385

hostile aggression, 365
HPA axis. *See* hypothalamic-
        pituitary-adrenal axis
Hubbard, Alfred W., 11, 14
human factor psychology, 11
human growth hormone (hGH),
        546–47
humility, 74
HWM. *See* healthy weight management
hydrocodone, 626
hyperaccessibility, 123
hyperalgesia, 619
hypnosis, in sport psychology, 9–10
hypothalamic-pituitary-adrenal (HPA)
        axis, 178

I

ideal body
    for males, 636
    for women, 389, 636
identified regulation, 236
identity
    athletic, 517
    gender, 384
    sexual, 384
identity foreclosure, 539
    athletic identity and, 517
illness, from performing, 37–38
imagery
    ability, 222–24, 227–28
    by adults, 222
    alternative outcomes of, 224–25
    antecedents, 227
    applied model of, 225–26, 225–26f
    auditory, 218
    bioinformational theory and, 227
    through brain imaging techniques, 216
    brain reorganization and, 219
    by children, 222
    confidence-based, 226
    controllability of, 222
    for dancers, 93–95, 225
    definitions of, 214–17
    emotional regulation and, 164
    Fitt's Law and, 218
    functional equivalence and, 217–18
    function of, 213
    improvement methods for, 229
    internal visual, 215–16
    interventions, 219–28
    key characteristics of, 214–17, 214t
    kinesthetic modality of, 216
    mental, 275
    meta-imagery, 223
    metaphorical, 95
    motor, 217
    motor learning and, 213
    for musicians, 93–95
    observational learning and, 95
    olfactory, 218
    in performing arts psychology,
        93–95
    personal meaning in, 226–27

perspective of, 215–216
PETTLEP model of, 94, 220–22, 220t
physical evidence of, 228–29
physical performance influenced by,
        218–19
plasticity and, 218
as pre-performance preparation, 94
self-report measures for, 229
with self-talk, 199
SIQ, 94
skill-based, 226
teacher's influence on, 94–95
as top-down knowledge-driven
        process, 215
triggers for, 217
triple-code model of, 226–27
visual, 218
vividness of, 222
imaginal experiences, 276
immersive virtual environment
        technology, 265–66
immigration, 422
impersonal orientation, 237
implicit learning
    consciousness and, 140–41
    continuous tracking and, 140
    motor learning in, 141–42
Imus, Don, 424
independence fostering, 483
individual zones of optimal functioning
        (IZOF), 158, 714–715
industrial-organizational psychology,
        27, 29
information acquisition, for SPI, 68–69
informed consent
    disclosure standards, 54–55
    ethical codes for, 53–55
    multiple relationships and, 56
Ingram, Anne, 14
inherent self-talk, 204, 207
inhibition, in ACT, 179–80
inhibition of return (IOR), 256
injury
    affective cycle of rehabilitation
        model, 595
    biopsychosocial model of, 595
    burnout and, from performance, 37
    catastrophic, 602–3
    chronic pain and, 627
    coaches' response to, 608
    concussion, 600–602
    coping strategies for, 92
    in culture of risk, 604–5
    fatal, 602–3
    future research applications for,
        605–7
    to head, 600–602
    integrated model of psychological
        response to sport injury and
        rehabilitation, 595–96
    interventions for, 607–9
    management, 609
    mind-body link with, 606

injury (*Cont.*)
  multidisciplinary service delivery for, 609–10
  musculoskeletal, 596–600
  normalization of, 604
  performance psychology and, 603–4
  in performing arts, 37–38, 92–93
  physicians' treatment of, 608
  psychologists and, 608–9
  psychophysiological model of injury risk, 594
  research literature for, 593–94
  retirement as result of, 516–17
  in return to sport model, 596
  service delivery for, 609
  sport ethic and, 604
  in sport psychology, 25
  with sports medicine therapists, 608
  in stage model of grief and loss, 594–95
  stress-injury model, 594
innate talent theory, 478
inspiration, in performing arts psychology, 101–2
instance theory, 137
institutional cultures, motivation through, 88–89
instrumental aggression, 365
instrumental competencies, 528
integrated model of psychological response to sport injury and rehabilitation, 595–96
integrated regulation, 236
intelligence. *See also* superior performance intelligence
  analytical, 64
  bodily kinesthetic, 64
  contextual, 30, 64, 72
  creative, 64
  cultural, 65
  EI, 33–34, 65, 73, 78
  interpersonal, 64
  intrapersonal, 64
  linguistic, 64
  logical, 64
  multiple, 64–65
  musical, 64
  naturalistic, 64
  organizational, 65
  personal, 65
  physical, 65
  social, 65
  spatial, 64
  in sport psychology, as measure, 8
  triarchic model, 64
  types of, 64–67
internal visual imagery, 215–16
International Bureau of Sport Pedagogy, 8
International Coaching Federation, 39
International Congress of the Psychology and Physiology of Sport, 5
International Olympic Committee (IOC), 546, 556

International Society for Mental Training and Excellence, 16
International Society of Sport Psychology (ISSP), 12, 15
interpersonal intelligence, 64
interpersonal leadership, 455–56
interventions
  in anxiety management, 98–99
  for APED use, 554–55
  for EDs, 650–54
  efficacy-based, 286–87
  imagery, 219–28
  for injury, 607–9
  for moral behavior, 377–78
  for physical activity, 667–72
  for self-talk, 197–200, 208
  in team building strategies, 322, 322*f*
  in youth development, 460–61
intrapersonal intelligence, 64
intra-team rivalry, 338
intrinsic goals, 87
intrinsic motivation, 234
  moral behavior and, 369
introjected regulation, 236
introversion, 96
investment years, 339
IOC. *See* International Olympic Committee
IOR. *See* inhibition of return
I-PPRS. *See* Psychological Readiness to Return to Sport Scale
Isner, John, 128
Israeli Society for Sport Psychology and Sociology, 15
ISSP. *See* International Society of Sport Psychology
It's Not about the Bike (Armstrong), 627
IZOF. *See* individual zones of optimal functioning

J
Jacobson, Edmund, 9
Jaeger, Andrea, 62, 78
James, LeBron, 424
James, William, 4, 6, 131–32, 135, 180, 184
Japan, sport psychology in, 7–8, 10
Jastrow, Joseph, 6
JDR model. *See* job demand-resources model
Jennings, Gabriel, 707
Jennings, Jason, 256
Jia Zhambo, 118
job demand-resources (JDR) model, 576–77
job-person congruity, 575
job person fit, 575
job stress, burnout from, 566
Johanson, Albert, 8
Johnson, Earvin "Magic," 63
Johnson, Michael, 63, 78
Jones, Graham, 28–29

Jordan, Michael, 62, 309
Jordan, Payton, 10
Judd, Charles, 6

K
Kasper, Gran Franco, 387
kinesiology
  for performance psychology, early training in, 47
  for sport psychology, early training in, 47
kinesthesia, 216
Kinsey, Alfred, 400
Klein, Melanie, 400
knowing your environment
  contextual intelligence and, 72
  controllable elements, 71–72
  uncontrollable elements, 72
knowing yourself, 67–68
koczi (coaching), 344
Korobkhov, Gabriel, 10
Krane, Vikki, 393, 395
Kubler-Ross, Elizabeth, 594

L
Laird, Donald, 8
Landers, Daniel, 15
Laver, Rod, 131
Lawther, John, 8, 12
Layman, Emma McCloy, 14
LDI model. *See* life development intervention model
leadership
  in business, 317
  for coaches, 316
  interpersonal, 455–56
  LSS, 316, 333
  in military, 317–18
  multidimensional model for, 316–17, 316*f*
  person-focused, 317
  task-focused, 317
  teamwork and, 316–18
  transformational, 332
  in youth development, 452–53
leadership, in sports, 316–17
  AGT and, 329
  autonomy-supportive, 329, 334–35, 338
  behaviors in pursuit of excellence, 340*f*, 340*t*
  CBQ, 331–32
  CFQ for, 330–31, 331*f*
  congruence hypothesis for, 332–33
  definition of, 328
  dimensions of, 333*t*
  in ego-involving climates, 334
  future directions for, 340–41
  hard, 336
  LSS, 316, 333
  meditational model of, 329–32, 329*f*
  models of motivation and, 335*f*
  multidimensional model of, 332, 332*f*, 345–46

soft, 336
  in task-involving climates, 334
  types of, 335–39
Leadership Behavior Description
    Questionnaire, 328
Leadership Scale for Sports (LSS), 316
  revisions to, 333
  situational consideration behaviors
    in, 333
learning
  conscious awareness and, 135–39
  in dyads, 256–57
  implicit, 140–41
  motor, 141–42
  observational, imagery and, 95
  self-efficacy and, 278
  for sport performance, 143–44
learning models, 254
learning self-efficacy, 278
lesbian, gay, bisexual, and transgender
    (LGBT) populations
  coming out process for, 393
  homonegativism against, 390
  under NCAA policy, 393
  sport psychology for, 393–94
lesbian, women's sport and, 387
lesbian stereotypes, women's sport and
  as coaches, 391–92
  homonegativism and, 387, 390
  team climate and, 390
Levitt, Eugene, 16
Lewis, Carl, 63
LGBT populations. See lesbian, gay,
    bisexual, and transgender
    populations
liberal feminism, 385
life development intervention (LDI)
    model, 515, 519
life skills
  CHAMPS and, 18
  coaching for, 351–53
  self-talk as part of, 206
linguistic intelligence, 64
listening. See active listening
Loehr, Jim, 13
logical intelligence, 64
Lombardi, Vince, 328
Lorenz, Konrad, 585
Lortie, Louis, 122
Loughran, Roger, 125
LSS. See Leadership Scale for Sports

M
MAC approach. See mindfulness-
    acceptance-commitment approach
Mahut, Nicolas, 128
maladaptive perfectionism, 31
males
  aggression among, 376
  EDs among, 643–44
  ethnicity and, performance influenced
    by, 425–26
  hegemonic masculinity, 392

ideal body for, 636
  internalization of body ideal for, 647
  MD in, 640
  modeling for, 260
  moral behavior for, 376
  perfectionism among, 302
  self-esteem for, in performance
    psychology, 100
Maltz, Maxwell, 12
managerial grid approach, 320
marginal perceptions of consciousness
  change blindness and, 143
  for outcome feedback, 142–43
  sport applications for, 143
  subjective thresholds in, 142–43
Martin, Jeffrey, 18
Marxist feminism, 385
masculinity, hegemonic, 392
Maslow, Abraham, 12. See also self-
    actualization, theory of
master athletes, 494
  achievement goals of, 502
  gender as influence on, 503
  relative age for, 503
  self-determination of, 502–3
master's sport
  functional commitment in, 504, 505t
  obligatory commitment in, 504–6, 505t
  social influences on, 507–8
  social networks and, 507
mastery experiences, 275–76
mastery models, 254–55
Matsui, Mitsuo, 7–8
Matuszak, John, 626
May, Jerry, 13, 15, 40
McCallaugh, Penny, 15
McCann, Sean, 743–46, 750–52
McCloy, C. H., 11
McGill Pain Questionnaire (MPQ), 623
McGinley, Paul, 122
MCS-SP. See Multilevel Classification
    System for Sport psychology
MD. See muscle dysmorphia
mediating variable framework model,
    664–65, 664f
mediation, perfectionism and, 298
medicine. See also sports medicine
  modeling applications with, 262
meditational model of leadership,
    329–32, 329f
  assessment for, 330
  CFQ in, 330–31, 331t
  coach behaviors in, 329
  players' perceptions in, 330
Meichenbaum, Donald, 528
memorization, 102
  PETTLEP model and, 102
memory. See also working memory
  overshadowing and, 145n13
mental health model, 158
mental illness, creativity and, 101
mental imagery, 275. See also cognitive
    self-modeling

mental practice, 127
mental skills training (MST), 26
mental toughness, 30, 64
  high performance delivery and, 76
  optimal performance and, 713–14
  pressure and, 36
Mental Toughness 48 (MT48), 716
mentoring. See targeted mentoring
meta-imagery, 223
meta-perception theory, 288
metaphorical imagery, in sports, 95
method acting, 34
Michels, Rinus, 328
microsystems, 485
Miles, Walter, 8–9
military, sport and performance
    psychology for
  in basic training, 33
  cooperation in, 313–14
  early applications of, 8–9
  emotional fitness in, 33
  group cohesion in, 319
  leadership in, 317–18
  OTAS and, 313
  role relationships in, 315
  team building strategies in, 321–22
  teams in, 310–11
  teamwork in, 309, 311
Mills, C. Wright, 584
mind-body problem, consciousness
    and, 132
mindfulness
  in concentration, training for, 125
  in performance psychology, 26
  SPI and, 75
  supervision and, 727–32
mindfulness-acceptance-commitment
    (MAC) approach, 537
mind-to-muscle relaxation, 164
Minnesota Multiphasic Personality
    Inventory (MMPI), 623
MIPS. See Multidimensional Inventory of
    Perfectionism in Sports
MIQ-R. See Movement Imagery
    Questionnaire-Revised
MMPI. See Minnesota Multiphasic
    Personality Inventory
modeling, performance and
  aggression through, 264
  anxiety influenced by, 258–59
  by athletes, 259–60
  conceptual approaches to, 251–53
  coping, 254–55
  dyad learning, 256–57
  educational applications for, 261
  emulation and, 252
  expert, 254
  gender differences in, 260
  for gymnasts, 260
  health behavior applications for,
    263–64
  immersive virtual environment
    technology for, 265–66

modeling, performance (*Cont.*)
learning, 254
mastery, 254–55
medical applications for, 262
model-observer similarity,
257–58, 266
motivation influenced by, 258
for music, 262
observation technology for, 264–66
for performing arts, 262
in physical activity domains, 253–57
point-light display in, 252
psychological behaviors influenced by,
257–59
research for, 260–64
self-efficacy and, 251, 257–58
self-modeling, 255–56, 275
self-regulation and, 252, 259
in sports domains, 253–57
for teachers, 261
theoretical approaches to, 251–53
verbal instructions compared,
253–54
video-based, 262–63, 265
virtual, 265–66
web-based, 262–63
momentary intentions, 120
Montana, Joe, 63
mood, emotion compared to, 155
moral behavior
achievement goals and, 368–69
age as influence on, 377
antecedents for, 368–72
attitudes for, 365
through character-building, 372–73
among coaches, 372–74
through coach ratings, 367–68
through competency, 372–73
by competitive level, 365
context characteristics for, 376–77
effectiveness of, 372–73
ego orientation for, 368–69
extrinsic motivation and, 369
through fair play attitudes, 373, 378
fear of failure and, 370
by gender, 376
individual differences, 458–59
intentional acts as part of, 366
interventions for, 377–78
intrinsic motivation and, 369
mechanisms for, 380
moral atmosphere for, 374
motivational climates for, 373–74
motivation types for, 369–71
negative consequences and, 364
through observation, 368
parental influences on, 374–75
passion and, 370–71
physical activity-based interventions
and, 459
of referees, 375–76
through relational support, 373
scenario approach for, 366–67

SDT and, 369–70
self-regulatory efficacy and, 371–72
through self-reports, 366–67
social antecedents of, 372–76
social approval for, 375
social contextual factors for, 457–58
as social goals, 369
in sports, 366–68
sportspersonship orientations, 365
task orientation for, 368–69
among teammates, 372–74, 379
moral disengagement, 371
moral functioning, 365
moral identity, 371
morality, 378–79
aggressive behavior and, 365
broad views of, 365
future research directions for, 379–81
mechanisms for, 380
in performing arts, 379
social contextual factors for, 457–58
in workplace, 378
youth development and, 456–59
moral judgment, 365
moral reasoning, 365
Morgan, William, 16
motivation. *See also* flow theory; self-
determination theory
achievement, 28
AGT and, 85
basic needs support and, 88
in basic psychological needs theory, 242
burnout and, 577
depression and, 159
emotional climate for, 88
emotions and, 159
extrinsic, 235–36, 369
through institutional cultures, 88–89
intrinsic, 234, 369
meta-theory of, 234
modeling as influence on, 258
moral behavior and, 369–71, 373–74
in older athletes, across lifespan,
501–8
parental influences on, 88–89,
374–75
passion and, 85–86
in performing arts, 85–89
quality of, 234
SDT and, 85–86
from self-talk, 202
for sport performance, 241–42
types of, in SDT, 235*f*
in youth development, 462–63
Motivation Orientation in Sport
questionnaire, 258
motor imagery, 217
motor learning, 141–42
imagery and, 213
Movement Imagery Questionnaire-
Revised (MIQ-R), 216
Movement Specific Reinvestment Scale,
138–39, 145n16

MPCI. *See* Multidimensional
Perfectionism Cognitions
Inventory
MPI. *See* Multidimensional Pain
Inventory
MPQ. *See* McGill Pain Questionnaire
MPS. *See* Multidimensional Perfectionism
Scale
MST. *See* mental skills training
MT48. *See* Mental Toughness 48
multidimensional anxiety theory, 99
Multidimensional Inventory of
Perfectionism in Sports (MIPS),
295–96
multidimensional model of sport
leadership, 332, 332*f*, 345–46
Multidimensional Pain Inventory
(MPI), 623
Multidimensional Perfectionism
Cognitions Inventory (MPCI),
295–96
Multidimensional Perfectionism Scale
(MPS), 295–96
Multilevel Classification System for
Sport psychology (MCS-SP),
529–34
PD in, 530–31
Pdy in, 531–32, 537–38
PI in, 532–33, 538
PT in, 533–34, 538–39
multiple intelligences, 64–65
multiple relationships, ethics codes and,
55–59
conflicts of interest and, 59
decision-making models for, 56
informed consent and, 56
objectivity assessment in, 56
peer consultation for, 57
risk management and, 56–57
standards for, 58–59
Munich Olympics, 603
Murphy, Shane, 15–16
muscle dysmorphia (MD), 639–40
gender differences in, 640
muscle guarding, 623
muscle-to-mind relaxation, 164
musculoskeletal injury, 596–600
antecedents for, 596–97
rehabilitation phase for,
598–600
return to sport transition after, 600
music
modeling applications with, 262
as therapy, 99
musical intelligence, 64
musicians
AGT and, 85
imagery for, in performing arts
psychology, 93–95
passion for, 85
perfectionism within, 90, 297–298
SDT and, 85–86
Muslim cultures, women's sports in, 425

N

Nadal, Rafael, 126
Naismith, James, 4
NASPSPA. *See* North American Society for the Psychology of Sport and Physical Activity
National Collegiate Athletics Association (NCAA), 52
　LGBT policy, 393
national governing bodies (NGBs), 16
naturalistic intelligence, 64
Navratilova, Martina, 62, 78
NCAA. *See* National Collegiate Athletics Association
negative acute pain, 619
negative emotions
　cognitive functioning and, 159
　threat states and, 161
　youth development and, 461
negative self-talk, 192, 194–95
negative training pain, 619
negative training stress response model, 572
negative warning pain, 619
nested agendas, 703*f*
neuroticism, 96
The New Psychology (Scripture), 4
NGBs. *See* national governing bodies
Nideffer, Robert, 13, 29, 34
Niiler, Herbert, 7
9/11, 603
nocebo response, 628
nonreciprocal friendships, 402
non-sexual boundary crossings (NSBCs), 57–58
　purposeful, 57
nonsteroidal APEDs, 553
North American Society for the Psychology of Sport and Physical Activity (NASPSPA), 12
NSBCs. *See* non-sexual boundary crossings

O

obligatory commitment, 504–6, 505*t*
Observational Assessment for Teamwork in Surgery (OTAS), 313
observational learning, 251–53
　imagery and, 95
　neurophysiological perspective for, 252–53
obsessive passion, 86, 370, 504
O'Gara, Ronàn, 123–24
Ogilvie, Bruce, 9, 15
Oglesby, Carole, 15, 394
older adults, physical activity for, 663–64, 663*t*, 671
older athletes. *See also* master athletes
　compensation explanation for, 496–98
　deliberate practice for, 501
　motivation for, across lifespan, 501–8
　passion model for, 503–4
　preserved differentiation account for, 499–500

psychomotor expertise for, 498
selective maintenance explanation for, 498–99
selective optimization with compensation principle for, 498
skills retention mechanisms for, 496–500
olfactory imagery, 218
Olsen, Morgan, 11
Olympic Games
　IOC, 546
　in Munich, Germany, 603
　sport psychology in, 26
　sports psychology and, 15–16
Olympic self-image, 518
On Death and Dying (Kubler-Ross), 594
1PP. *See* first-person perspective
one thought principle, in concentration, 124
openness to experience, 96
optimal performance. *See also* peak performance, as concept
　characteristics of, 713
　definition of, 708–12, 708*f*
　flow and, 711–12
　future research directions for, 720–22
　ideal performance states and, 714–15
　ideal state for, 716
　IZOF and, 714–15
　mental toughness and, 713–14
　peak experience and, 708–9
　psychological preparation for, 716–20, 717*f*
　psychological profile for, 712–16
optimization, 498
　selective, 517
optimum performance, consciousness and, 139–40
organismic integration theory, 235–36
　extrinsic motivation in, 235–36
organizational intelligence, 65
organizational psychology, 206
organizational support, 518
Orlick, Terry, 17
OTAS. *See* Observational Assessment for Teamwork in Surgery
other-efficacy, 283
Otto, Jim, 605, 627
Oudejans, Raul, 185
overexercise, 625
overidentification, with client, 57
overlearning, 98
over-recruitment, 585–86
overshadowing, 145n13
overtraining, burnout from, 566–67
overuse, from performance, 37
oxycodone, 626

P

PAC axis. *See* pituitary-adreno-medullary axis
Pace, Edward A., 6
pain

assessment of, 622–23
as barrier to rehabilitation, 624–25
biology of, 621–22
biopsychology of, 621–22
chronic, 627
gate control theory for, 621
muscle guarding and, 623
negative acute, 619
negative training, 619
negative warning, 619
through observation, 622–23
from overexercise, 625
from performance extremes, 627
positive training, 619
psychological factors for, 622
psychological interventions for, 623–26
psychological testing for, 623
scale measures for, 623
scientific principles of, 621–23
self-report measures for, 622
telephone line theory of, 621
tolerance of, 628–31
Pain and Negative Affect Scale, 623
Pain Anxiety Symptom Scale, 623
Pain Catastrophizing Scale, 623
pain management
　association in, 625
　catastrophizing in, 619
　coping strategies for, 619–20
　among dancers, 620
　dissociation in, 625
　for fatigue, 619
　hyperalgesia and, 619
　mental training for, 624
　in pain sport matrix, 625–26
　in performing arts, 92–93
　psychological interventions for, 623–26
　psychological perspectives on, 626–27
　sport ethic and, 620
pain sport matrix, 625–26
pain tolerance, 628–31
　through absorption in work, 629
　through altered consciousness, 629–30
　duration of, 630
　goal focus of, 629
　nocebo response, 628
　placebo analgesia response, 628
　in survival contexts, 630–31
Paralympic movement, 607
parents, as influence
　on EDs, 643–44
　on moral behavior, 374–75
　on motivation, 88–89
　stage parents, 83
　on talent development, 480–83, 488–89
　on youth development, 453–54
parental motivational climate, 374–75
parental relationships, in sport, 404–6
　belief systems as influence on, 405
　demographic factors for, 404
　parent-child attachment in, 405–6
　in performance contexts, 406

research on, 404–6
parental relationships, in sport (*Cont.*)
   role modeling hypothesis in, 404
parent-child attachment, 405–6
parenting styles, 488–89
passion
   for dancers, 85
   harmonious, 86, 370–71, 504
   moral behavior and, 370–71
   motivation and, 85–86
   for musicians, 85
   obsessive, 86, 370, 504
   in older athletes, 503–4
   SDT and, 86
Paynter, Richard, 9
PCDEs. *See* psychological characteristics
   for developing excellence
PCQ. *See* Performance Classification
   Questionnaire
PCT. *See* perceptual control theory
PD. *See* performance development
Pdy. *See* performance dysfunction
PE. *See* physical education
peak experience, 708–9
peak performance, as concept, 14, 710–11.
   See also optimum performance
   flow state in, 14
   mean age of, 494
   training interventions for, 47
PEE. *See* physical and emotional
   exhaustion
peer acceptance, 452–53
peer modeling. *See also* dyads, learning in
   for youth development, 451–52
peer relationships, in sport, 401–3
   dyadic friendships and, 401
   EDs and, 643–44
   in performance contexts, 402–3
   research for, 401
   youth development influenced by,
   451–52
peer tutoring. *See* dyads, learning in
Pele, 62
perceived control, 176
perceptual control theory (PCT), 280
perfectionism. *See also* disordered eating
   in academic performance, 296–97
   adaptive, 31, 301
   anxiety from, 90
   applied psychology implications,
   300–301
   in aptitude tests, 297–98
   Big Five trait dimensions, 95–96
   burnout and, 301
   during childhood development, 301–3
   concerns for, 294–95
   as domain-specific, 303
   ego orientation and, 31
   future research applications for, 301–3
   gender differences with, 302
   healthy, 295
   in laboratory tasks, 297–98
   maladaptive, 31

measurement methodology for, 295–96
mediation and, 298
multidimensional models of, 295*f*
in music competitions, 297–98
within musicians, 90
origins of, 90
parental influence on, 302
in performance psychology, 31,
   296–300
within performing arts, 89–90
as personality disposition, 294
in sports, 298–300
strivings for, 294–95
unhealthy, 295
Performance Classification Questionnaire
   (PCQ), 536
performance coaches
   in business context, 695*f*
   client perspectives on, 697–98
   conflict management by, 697*f*
   evidence testing for, 698–99
   expertise development by, 702–3
   goals of, 694–95
   knowledge base for, 693–96
   knowledge transfer for, 696–97
   nested agendas for, 703*f*
   PJDM and, 701–2
   professionalism of, 699–701
   sport psychologist compared to, 685
performance development (PD), 530–31
performance dysfunction (Pdy), 531–32
   counseling for, 537–38
performance impairment (PI), 532–33
   counseling for, 538
performance perfection, 31. *See also*
   high performance, delivery of;
   optimum performance
performance psychology. *See also* coaching;
   ethics; high performance, delivery
   of; modeling, performance and;
   performing arts, performance
   psychology in; self-confidence,
   performance psychology and;
   self-esteem, performance
   psychology and
   from 1890 to 1920, 4–6
   from 1920–1940, 6–9
   from 1940–1965, 9–12
   from 1965–1980, 12–15
   from 1980–1989, 15–17
   from 1990 to present, 17–18
   acceptance in, 26
   applied sport psychology and, 25–26
   attention and, 34, 121–23
   audience as influence in, 35, 82, 103
   CBT strategies and, 35
   common features of, 24–25
   competition and, 31–33
   confidentiality in, 53–55
   consultation in, 27–28, 38–41
   credibility in, 41
   cultural influences on, 31
   definition of, 24–25

emotions and, 33–34, 158–60
ethics in, 39
ethnicity as influence on, 31
excellence as focus in, 30–31
expectations of self, 31
expertise development and, 37
extended focus in, 34
family as influence in, 37
generalists in, 39
high standards-setting in, 30–31
hypnosis in, 9–10
informed consent in, 53–55
injury and, 603–4
journals for, 18
kinesiology training in, 47
mental components of, 25
military applications for, 8–9
mindfulness in, 26
as new psychology, 4
peak performance concepts, 14
perfectionism in, 31, 296–300
positive psychology in, 26
pressure in, 35–36
privacy issues in, 55
process as focus in, 25
psychotherapy systems and, 25–27
roles in, 39–40
roots of, 25–28
self-efficacy and, 274–75
self-talk and, 196–200
somatic practices in, 590
specialists in, 39
sport psychology as influence on, 28–29
temporal dimensions of, 25, 34–35
training and, 38–39
performance termination (PT), 533–34
   counseling for, 538–39
performing, as performance domain. *See
   also* dancers; musicians; talent;
   talent development
   burnout from, 37
   career completion and, 37–38
   challenges to, 37–38
   consequences of, 36–37
   contextual intelligence for, 30
   development of, 37–38
   emotions in, 33–34, 158–60
   illness from, 37–38
   injury from, 37–38, 92–93
   method acting in, 34
   overuse in, 37
   recovery from, 38
   as research focus, 25
performing arts, performance psychology
   in, 104*f. See also* dancers;
   musicians; talent development
   AGT and, 87–88
   anxiety and, 97–99
   audiences as influence on, 35, 82, 103
   creativity and, 101
   deliberate practice in, 82–85
   disordered eating and, 90–92
   emotional expression in, 102–3

expertise in, 82–85
flow and, 89
imagery in, 93–95
injury and, 37–38, 92–93
inspiration and, 101–2
memorization in, 102
modeling applications for, 262
morality in, 379
motivation in, 85–89
pain and, 92–93
perfectionism and, 89–90
personality and, 95–97
presence, 89
psychological skills for, 93–95
purpose of, 81–82
SDT and, 85–87
self-confidence in, 99–100
self-esteem in, 99–100
sports compared to, 81–82
talent in, 82–85
performing artists. *See also* talent; talent development
concentration loss for, 122–23
consultation for, 39
counseling for, 535–39
mental toughness for, 30
resilience for, 30
sport psychology for, 29–30
personality
for elite athletes, 96
measurement approaches to, 96–97
perfectionism and, 294
performing arts and, 95–97
in sport psychology, as measure, 8
personal vision, 68–69
in shaping one's environment, 72
person-focused leadership, 317
persuasion. *See* verbal persuasion, self-efficacy from
PET. *See* processing efficiency theory
Peterson, Kirsten, 741–42, 745–47, 749–51
Petrie and Greenleaf model, for EDs, 645–46
PETTLEP model. *See* Physical, Environment, Task, Timing, Learning, Emotion, and Perspective model
PFC. *See* prefrontal cortex
Phelps, Michael, 62, 127
phenomenal consciousness, 144n3
Phillipe, Jean, 5
Physical, Environment, Task, Timing, Learning, Emotion, and Perspective (PETTLEP) model
emotions in, 221
for imagery, 94, 220–22, 220t
memorization and, 102
Physical Activities Guidelines for Americans, 464, 466
physical activity
for adolescents, 661–62
for adults, 662–63, 669–71

behavioral choice theory for, 667
behavioral theories for, 665–67
for children, 661–62, 668–69
community interventions for, 669
correlates of, 661–64
family interventions for, 669
gender roles for, 388
health benefits of, 464
intervention guidelines, 667–72
mediating variable framework model for, 664–65, 664f
modeling domains for, 253–57
moral behavior and, 459
for older adults, 663–64, 663t, 671
psychological theories for, 665–67
school-based interventions for, 668–69
sedentary behavior change, 672
social cognitive theory for, 665
theory of planned behavior and, 662, 665–66, 671f
TTM for, 666–67, 666t
physical and emotional exhaustion (PEE), 564
physical education, 238
physical intelligence, 65
physicians, 608
PI. *See* performance impairment
pituitary-adreno-medullary (PAC) axis, 160
PJDM. *See* professional judgment and decision-making
placebo analgesia response, 628
planned behavior. *See* theory of planned behavior
Plato, 191
playing, sports compared to, 338
point-light display, 252
police psychology, 29
political somatics, 584
polypharmacy, 548–49
Portal, Dewitt, 9
positive affect, 159
positive emotions
cognitive functioning and, 159
threat responses and, 161
youth development and, 461
positive ethics, 49
positive psychology, 26, 33
positive self-review, 255
positive self-talk, 192, 194–95
positive training pain, 619
positive youth development, 449
posterior attentional system, 178
posttraumatic stress disorder (PTSD), 537
powerlifting, 642
PowerPlay program, 453
PPI. *See* Psychological Performance Inventory
praxis, in feminism, 386
pre-event routines, 126–27
prefrontal cortex (PFC)
attention and, 178
DLPFC, 178

flow theory and, 145n21
pre-performance routines, 35
for concentration, 126–27
superstitions in, 126–27
presence, 89
supervision and, 728–29, 731
preserved differentiation account, 499–500
pressure
competence and, 35–36
high performance delivery under, 76
mental toughness and, 36
in performance psychology, 35–36
resilience and, 36
self-efficacy and, 36
Price, Claude E., 5
primary appraisals
in CMRT, 156
in competitive sports anxiety, 176
priming, 143
Principles of Psychology (James, W.), 4
privacy, ethical codes for, 55
problem-focused coping, 162
problem-solving self-efficacy, 278
processing efficiency theory (PET), 176
self-talk and, 201–2
professional judgment and decision-making (PJDM), 701–2
progressive relaxation, 9
propinquity, 425
Prosocial and Antisocial Behavior in Sport Scale, 367
prosocial behavior, 365–66
achievement goals and, 369
measures of, 366
PST. *See* psychological skills training
psychodynamic theory, 406–7
psychological characteristics for developing excellence (PCDEs), 478–79, 486–87
Psychological First Aid, 603
psychological foreclosure, 520
Psychological Performance Inventory (PPI), 716
Psychological Readiness to Return to Sport Scale (I-PPRS), 600
psychological skills training (PST)
in applied sport psychology, 26
ethics and, 47
for supervision, 727
psychologists
ethics codes for, 48
injury and, 608–9
multiple relationships and, ethics codes for, 58–59
psychology. *See also* applied sport psychology; performance psychology; sport psychology
of coaching, 344, 357–58
human factor, 11
of human performance, 527–28
industrial-organizational, 27, 29
military applications of, 8–9

psychology (*Cont.*)
  organizational, 206
  police, 29
  positive, 26
  sport psychology influenced by, 28
  sports applications for, 6–9
  for women's sport, 388–89
Psychology of Coaching (Griffith), 7
Psychology of Sport: The Behavior Motivation, Personality, and Performance of Athletes (Butt), 15
psychomotor expertise, 498
psychomotor testing, in sport psychology, 8
psychotherapy
  CBT, 26
  performance psychology and, 25–27
  solution-focused techniques in, 26
PT. *See* performance termination
PTSD. *See* posttraumatic stress disorder
public safety applications, of sport psychology, 29. *See also* police psychology
Puni, A. C., 9–10
pyramiding, 548

Q

quiet eye (QE), 181–85
  ACT and, 182–83
  action-focused coping and, 185
  competitive sports anxiety and, 182–85
  mechanisms for, 184
  research support for, 184–85
  training for, 183–85

R

race logic, 424
racism
  closed-door, 424
  propinquity and, 425
  stacking and, 424–25
Radcliffe, Paula, 127
radical feminism, 385
Radvanovsky, Sondra, 38
Raiport, Gregory, 13
Ralston, Aron, 630–31
Ravizza, Ken, 13
reciprocal determinism, 665
reciprocal friendships, 402
reciprocal social relationships, 486
recovery
  from performance, 38
  in sport psychology, 25
Reddy, Camiolo, 602
referees, moral behavior of, 375–76
reflection in action, 355
reflection on action, 355
reframing, 27
Regis, John, 214
regulatory attentional control, 177–78
Reilly, Ray, 13
Re-Injury Anxiety Inventory (RIA), 600
reinvestment. *See* theory of reinvestment

Reinvestment Scale, 145n16
relatedness
  as basic psychological need, 237
  in SDT, 245
relation-inferred self-efficacy (RISE), 284
relationships
  APIM for, 409, 412–13
  attachment theory and, 409–10
  countertransference in, 413n2
  among dancers, 407
  future research on, 407–11
  internal working models for, 409
  interpersonal, in team-building, 320
  multiple, ethics codes and, 55–59
  parental, in sport, 404–6
  among peers, in sport, 401–3
  reciprocal social, 486
  role, 314–15
  secure attachment in, 409
  social, in youth development, 451–56
  sport psychologist-athlete, 406–7
relationship building, with SPI, 74
relative age effect, 441
relaxation
  for emotional regulation, 164
  mind-to-muscle, 164
  muscle-to-mind, 164
  progressive, 9
  with self-talk, 199
resilience
  for performing artists, 30
  pressure and, 36
  self-efficacy and, 275
resonance performance model, 34
  supervision and, 730–32
resonance theory, 34
retirement. *See also* career transitions
  external factors for, 516
  injury as reason for, 516–17
  voluntary, 516
retrospective reflection on action, 355
return to sport model, 596
rhythmic stereotypes, 439
RIA. *See* Re-Injury Anxiety Inventory
RISE. *See* relation-inferred self-efficacy
risk management
  in ethical decision-making models, 49
  multiple relationships and, 56–57
Rodionov, Albert, 12
Rodriguez, Alex, 63
Roethlisberger, Ben, 605
Rogers, Carl, 406
role experimentation, 517
role modeling hypothesis, 404
role relationships
  in business, 314–15
  in military, 315
  teamwork and, 314–15
Rotella, Bob, 13, 40
rough and tumble play, 439
Rousseau, Paul, 5
Rudik, P. A., 7–8
Rushell, Brent, 13

Russia, sport psychology in, 7–8, 10, 13
Ruth, Babe, 8, 63, 309
Ryan, Richard, 234

S

Sage, G. H., 18
SAM axis. *See* sympathetic-adreno-medullary axis
sampling years, 339
Sanders, Doug, 122
Scanlan, Tara, 15
schema systems, 181
Schulte, Robert Werner, 7
Schumacher, Michael, 63
Schwank, Walter, 12
Scott, Walter Dill, 6
Scripture, E. W., 4–6, 18
SDI. *See* self-determination index
SDT. *See* self-determination theory
Seashore, Carl, 6
secondary appraisals, in CMRT, 156
The Secret River (Grenville), 136
secure attachments, 409
sedentary behavior change, 672
selective attention, 118–19
selective maintenance explanation, 498–99
selective optimization with compensation principle, 498
  talent development and, 517
Seles, Monica, 40
the self, expectations of, 31
self-actualization, theory of, 12
self-belief, with SPI, 69
self-confidence, performance psychology and
  for elite athletes, 100
  in performing arts, 99–100
  self-talk and, 202
Self-Consciousness Scale, 145n16
self-control, 166–67
self-determination index (SDI), 238
self-determination theory (SDT), 85–87
  amotivation and, 236
  applications for, 243
  autonomy support in, 241
  autonomy-supportive leadership and, 334
  basic psychological needs theory and, 236–37, 242–44
  for burnout, 573–74
  CET in, 234–35
  coaching and, 346
  competence in, 244–45
  component theories of, 234–37
  cooperation and, 241–42
  COT in, 237
  in dance, 85–86
  development of, 234
  feedback and, 241
  future directions for, 245–46
  GCT and, 237, 242–43
  intrinsic motivation in, 234

master athletes and, 502–3
moral behavior and, 369–70
motivation and, 85–86, 235f
in music, 85–86
organismic integration theory and,
235–36
passion and, 86
in PE contexts, 238
relatedness in, 245
SDI in, 238
sport performance and, 237–43
youth development and, 463
self-efficacy
from affective states, 275–76
for coaches, 282, 349
cognitive self-modeling and, 275
collective, 284–86
competitive, 278
coping, 278
as coping strategy, 257
diverse forms of, 277–79
from emotional state, 276
empirical evidence of, 274–75
EOSE, 288
explanatory mechanisms for, 274–75
future applications for, 287–88
generality in, 273–74
from imaginal experiences, 276
for interpersonal tasks, 281–83
interventions for, 286–87
learning, 278
levels of, 273
limitations of, 279–81
from mastery experiences, 275–76
meta-perception theory and, 288
modeling and, 251, 257–58
other-efficacy, 283
PCT and, 280
personal agency within, 280
personal performance and, 274–75
from physiological condition, 276
pressure and, 36
problem-solving, 278
from psychological states, 275
referents in, 283–84
research applications for, 286–87
resilience and, 275
RISE, 284
for role performance, 283
sources of, 274f, 275–77
spirals and, 277
strength of, 273
in task-involving climates, 277
for teachers, 281–82
as theory, 264
from verbal persuasion, 275–76
from vicarious influences, 275
self-esteem, performance psychology and,
99–100
for elite athletes, 100
emotional regulation and, 165
by gender, 100
global, 460

in performing arts, 99–100
self-focus theories, 174–75
explicit monitoring hypothesis, 175
theory of reinvestment as, 175
self-image. See Olympic self-image
self-modeling, 255–56
in basketball, 256
cognitive, 275
feedforward and, 255
in figure skating, 255
in gymnastics, 255
in hockey, 256
performance benefits, 255–56
positive self-review, 255
in volleyball, 255
in weight lifting, 256
self-perceptions, in youth development,
460–61
self-presentational efficacy, 279
self-reflection, in coaching, 356
self-regulation
with modeling, 259
in social cognitive theory, 252
self-regulatory efficacy, 278–79, 371–372
moral behavior and, 371–72
self-talk, 124, 127
ACT and, 201
antecedents of, 195–96
anxiety control with, 202
attention and, 201
characteristics of, 198
with children, 205
by coaches, 204
concentration from, 202
control process theory and, 201–2
debilitative effects of, 192
definitions of, 192
description of, 194–95
in educational contexts, 206
emotional regulation and, 163–64
experimental evidence for, 203–4
experimental studies for, 197–200
facilitative effects of, 192
features of, 194–95
feedback from, 199
field studies for, 196–97
functions of, 200–204
future applications for, 207–8
goal setting and, 199
imagery with, 199
inherent, 204, 207
as instructional, 192
interventions for, 197–200, 208
in life-skills development, 206
long-term implications for, 204–6
matching hypotheses for, 198
measurement of, in literature,
193–94
mechanisms of, 200–204
mental skills packages for, 199
as mental strategy, 192, 207–8
methodological approaches to, 193
motivation from, 202

negative, 192, 194–95
in organizational psychology, 206
paradigms for, 192–93
performance and, 196–200
personal factors for, 195
PET and, 201–2
positive, 192, 194–95
relaxation techniques with, 199
research designs for, 199
research questions for, 192–93
situational factors for, 195–96
socio-environmental factors for, 196
in theory of reinvestment, 138
Self-Talk and Gestures Rating Scale
(STAGRS), 194
Self-Talk Questionnaire (S-TQ), 193
Self-Talk Use Questionnaire (STUQ), 193
Seligman, Martin, 26, 33, 687. See also
positive psychology
selling out, 423–24, 429
sensitive stereotyping, 419
serial reaction time task (SRTT), 144n6
SES. See socioeconomic status
SET. See social exchange theory
sex, definition of, 384
sexual identity, 384
sexual orientation, 384
SFQS. See Sport Friendship
Quality Scale
Shanky, Bill, 173
shaping one's environment, 72–73
collaboration and, 73
EI and, 73
goal-setting in, 72
personal vision in, 72
team creation in, 72–73
shifting, in ACT, 179–80
siblings
birth order and, 484
competition and rivalry among, 484–85
in ecological theory of, 483
as stressor, 484
talent development influenced by,
483–85
Silva, John, 16
simulation training, for concentration,
127–28
SIOP. See Society for Industrial-
Organizational Psychology
SIQ. See Sport Imagery Questionnaire
situational foreclosure, 520
situation selection, 163
skill-based imagery, 226
skill-building activities, in youth
development, 450
Slaughter, Mary Hoke, 14
Smith, A. L., 451
Smith, M. D., 457
Smith, Ron, 13
SMTQ. See Sport Mental Toughness
Questionnaire
Sobers, Garry, 124
soccer moms, 83

social cognitive theory, 264–65
  for physical activity, 665
  self-regulation in, 252
social environment, talent development
    and, 84–85
social exchange theory (SET), 571
social goals, 369
social identity theory, 392–93
social intelligence, 65
socialist feminism, 385
social networks, 466
  master's sport and, 507
social physique anxiety, 389
social support
  for career transitions, 517–18
  in coaching, 316
  density in, 517–18
  family as influence on, 488–89
  in youth development, 451
Society for Industrial-Organizational
    Psychology (SIOP), 29
socioeconomic status (SES), 419, 423,
    426–27
soft leadership, 336
somatics, 581–84. *See also* the body
  attention training and, 589–90
  blending in, 589
  centering in, 588
  entering in, 588
  extending in, 589
  facing in, 588
  in performance enhancement practices,
    589–90
  performance psychology interventions
    and, 590
  political, 584
  sitting in, 589–90
  standing practices, 590
  visual thinking in, 587
  in whole body approach, 587–88
Sorenstam, Annika, 63
spatial intelligence, 64
specializing years, 339
SPI. *See* superior performance intelligence
Spielberger State-Trait Anxiety
    Inventory, 623
spirals, self-efficacy and, 277
sports. *See also* competitive sports anxiety;
    expertise, in sports; leadership, in
    sports; pain sport matrix; women's
    sport
  athletics compared to, 336
  change blindness and, 143
  coach-athlete relationships in, 403–4
  cooperation in, 312–13
  COT in, 246n1
  deliberate play and, 336
  early specialization in, 440
  EDs by, 642–43
  egalitarian, 336–38
  elite, 336–38
  emotional regulation in, 154
  entertainment, 336–37

ethnic, 428
female herstory in, 386–87
gender and, 387–94
group cohesion in, 318
homonegativism in, 390–94
learning primers for, 143–44
marginal perceptions of consciousness
    and, applications for, 143
masters, 504–7
metaphorical imagery in, 95
modeling in, 253–57
moral behavior in, 366–68
moral disengagement in, 371
moral identity in, 371
parental relationships in, 404–6
peer relationships in, 401–3
perfectionism in, 298–300
performance environments for,
    variability of, 154
performing arts compared to, 81–82
playing compared to, 338
siblings as competition, 484–85
soccer moms, 83
team building strategies in, 320
teams in, 310
teamwork in, 311
Title IX legislation for, 349, 386–88
sport attraction, 573
Sport Behavior Inventory, 367
sport commitment model, 573
sport devaluation, 564
sport entrapment, 573
sport ethic, 604
  pain management and, 620
sport evangelist myth, 353
Sport Friendship Quality Scale (SFQS),
    401
Sport Imagery Questionnaire (SIQ), 94,
    260
Sport Mental Toughness Questionnaire
    (SMTQ), 716
Sport Motivational Climate Scale, 352
Sport Multidimensional Perfectionism
    Scale (Sport-MPS), 295–96
sport performance
  assessment methods for, 239–43
  autonomy support in, 241
  cooperation in, 241–42
  motivation promotion for, 241–42
  objective measures of, 240
  research for, 239–43
  SDT and, 237–39
The Sport Psychologist, 394–95
sport psychologist-athlete relationships,
    406–7
  for females, 407
  psychodynamic theory for, 406–7
sport psychologists
  athlete relationships with, 406–7
  coaches and, 681–83
  collegial support for, 688
  confidentiality for, 678
  conflict management for, 685–86

consultation structure for, 677–78,
    688–89
continuing education for, 689
educational training for, 677
effectiveness strategies for, 687–89
failure of, 686–87
isolation of, 685
journaling for, 687
management for, 679–81
organization for, 679–81
as part of high-performance team,
    678–84
performance coach compared
    to, 685
role definition for, 685–86
self-awareness for, 687
sports agents and, 18
success of, 686–87
support staff for, 679–81
technology for, 689
sport psychology. *See also* applied sport
    psychology; elite athletes; ethics
  from 1890 to 1920, 4–6
  from 1920–1940, 6–9
  from 1940–1965, 9–12
  from 1965–1980, 12–15
  from 1980–1989, 15–17
  from 1990 to present, 17–18
  achievement motivation in, 28
  aggression measures within, 8
  applied, 41–42
  in Australia, 10
  for boxing, 9
  in Canada, 13
  CBT in, 28
  common features of, 24–25
  confidentiality in, 53–55
  consultation in, 38–41
  credibility in, 41
  definitions of, 24–25
  early experiments in, 4
  feminist, 394–97
  flow theory in, 28
  generalists in, 39
  in Germany, 7–8
  goal setting in, 28
  graduate programs for, 13–14
  hypnosis in, 9–10
  informed consent in, 53–55
  injury in, 25
  intelligence measures in, 8
  in Japan, 7–8, 10
  kinesiology training for, 47
  in laboratories, 6–9
  for LGBT populations, 393–94
  literature about, 11, 16
  mainstream psychology as
    influence on, 28
  mental components of, 25
  military applications for, 8–9
  as new psychology, 4
  under NGBs, 16
  in Olympic Games, 26

performance psychology influenced by, 28–29
for performing artists, 29–30
personality measures in, 8
privacy issues in, 55
process as focus in, 25
psychomotor testing in, 8
public safety applications for, 29
recovery in, 25
roles in, 39–40
in Russia, 7–8, 10, 13
specialists in, 39
in Sweden, 14
temporal dimensions of, 25
training and, 38–39
in training process, 14, 17
transference in, 411–12
in U.S., 7–8, 11
youth development and, 449–50
Sport Psychology in Practice (Andersen), 47, 393
sports agents, sports psychologists and, 18
sports education, graduate programs for, 13–14
sports medicine, 11
therapists, 608
sportspersonship orientations, 365
spotlight metaphor, for attention, 120–21
criticisms of, 121
SRTT. *See* serial reaction time task
stacking, 424–25
APEDs and, 548
stage model of grief and loss, 514
for career transitions, 514
injury rehabilitation and, 594–95
stage parents, 83
Stagg, Amos Alonzo, 4
Stagner, Ross, 8
STAGRS. *See* Self-Talk and Gestures Rating Scale
Staley, Seward, 11
standards-setting. *See also* expectations
mental skills in, 31
in performance psychology, 30–31
state anxiety, 99
Stengel, Casey, 328
stereotypes. *See* rhythmic stereotypes; sensitive stereotyping
steroid use, 555–56
modern media influences on, 556
Sterrett, Jack, 8
stimulus-driven attentional control systems, 179
S-TQ. *See* Self-Talk Questionnaire
stream of consciousness, 132
stress, siblings as source of, 484
stress-injury model, 594
stress-recovery perspective, for burnout, 572–73
stretching yourself, 68–69
STUQ. *See* Self-Talk Use Questionnaire
success

celebration of, 71
high performance delivery and, 74
Suinn, Richard, 13, 15–16
Sullivan, Harry, 400
Summitt, Pat, 328
superior performance intelligence (SPI)
agility and, 73–74
data analysis of, 66
EI and, 78
environmental knowledge, as dimension of, 73–74
facets of, 65–67
foundations for, 63–64
framework for, 67t
future applications for, 78–79
high performance delivery and, as dimension of, 74–78
humility and, 74
information acquisition for, 68–69
interviews for, 66
knowing your environment, as dimension of, 71–72
knowing yourself, as dimension of, 67–68
mindfulness and, 75
personal vision and, 68–69
relationship building with, 74
sampling participants for, 66
self-belief with, 69
shaping one's environment, as dimension of, 72–73
stretching yourself in, 68–69
study findings for, 66–67
sustaining yourself, as dimension of, 69–71
superstitions, 126–27
criteria for, 127
supervision
attunement and, 729–30
definition of, 725–26
future research on, 735–36
history of, 726–27
intake sessions for, 732–35
meta-supervision and, 731
mindfulness and, 727–32
models of, 727
presence and, 728–29, 731
PST model for, 727
resonance and, 730–32
sustaining yourself
celebrating successes while, 71
failure recovery, 70–71
life balance with, 70
perspective in, 69–70
switching off, 71
Sweden, sport psychology in, 14
switching on/off, 124, 126
in sustaining yourself, 71
sympathetic-adreno-medullary (SAM) axis, 160
systems psychology, 27, 678–79

T
taekwondo

moral disengagement with, 371
weight restrictions with, 642
talent
definition of, 477
as multidimensional construct, 83
in performing arts, 82–85
in sports, 82–85
teachers as influence on, 83
talent development
athletic identity and, 517
bioecological perspective on, 485–86
birth order as influence on, 484
in Canada, among adolescents, 436
career transitions and, 437
by creative type, 84
deliberate practice in, 437–38, 477–78
developmental lifespan model for, 479
developmental models for, 437–39
developmental roles in, 481–82
DMSP and, 479
during early years, 480–81
family as influence on, 83–84, 485–87
family support in, 83–84
independence fostering in, 483
initiation roles in, 480–81
innate talent theory and, 478
investment roles in, 482–83
during later years, 482–83
mastery roles in, 482–83
during middle years, 481–82
models for, 477–80
parental role in, 480–83
parental styles as influence on, 488–89
PCDEs, 478–79, 486–87
process of, 435
pyramid approach to, 436
reciprocal social relationships in, 486
role experimentation and, 517
sampling roles in, 480–81
selective optimization and, 517
siblings as influence on, 483–85
social environment and, 84–85
specializing roles in, 481–82
stage parents and, 83
teachers as influence on, 83
in U.S., among adolescents, 436
tanking, 32
targeted mentoring, 429
task-focused leadership, 317
task orientation
competition and, 32
for moral behavior, 368–69
TCTSA. *See* theory of challenge and threat states in athletes
teachers
imagery development by, 94–95
modeling applications for, 261
self-efficacy for, 281–82
talent development influenced by, 83
Teaching Personal and Social Responsibility Model, 450, 453
teams. *See also* teamwork
in business, 310

teams (*Cont.*)
    collective self-efficacy for, 284–86
    in military, 310–11
    moral behavior within, 372–74, 379
    in sports, 310
team building strategies, 323*f*
    in business, 320–21
    CRM in, 322
    group goal setting, 320
    in hockey, 319–20
    individual role involvement in, 320
    interpersonal relationships in, 320
    intervention development in, 322, 322*f*
    managerial grid approach to, 320
    in military, 321–22
    in sports, 320
Team Up For Youth, 350
teamwork
    action processes for, 319
    in business, 311
    cooperation in, 312–14
    correlates of, 312–14, 312*f*
    definitions of, 310–11
    framework for, 311–12
    group cohesion and, 318–19
    interpersonal processes for, 319
    as intuitive value, 309
    leadership and, 316–18, 316*f*
    locomotion and, 311–12
    maintenance and, 311–12
    in military, 309, 311
    role relationships and, 314–15
    in sports, 311
    team building strategies for,
        319–22, 323*f*
    transition processes for, 319
telephone line theory, of pain, 621
Test of Performance Strategies
        (TOPS), 193
theory of challenge and threat states in
        athletes (TCTSA), 160
theory of planned behavior, 596
    physical activity and, 662, 665–66, 671*f*
theory of reinvestment, 137–39
    choking in, 138
    conscious processing hypothesis in, 137
    development of, 145n14
    gamesmanship in, 138
    Movement Specific Reinvestment
        Scale, 138–39
    problem-focused coping strategies in, 137
    process goals in, 138
    as self-focus theory, 175
    self-talk in, 138
theory of self-actualization. *See* self-
    actualization, theory of
third-person perspective (3PP), 215–16
Thornhill, William, 136
Thought Occurrence Questionnaire for
        Sport (TOQS), 193–94
threat states, 160–61, 161*f*
3PP. *See* third-person perspective
Tissie, Phillipe, 5

Title IX legislation, 349, 386–88
    criticism of, 387
TMS. *See* transcranial magnetic
        stimulation
Tog, 406–7
tokenism, 423–24, 429
tomboys, 388
top-down control systems, in ACT, 179
TOPS. *See* Test of Performance
        Strategies
TOQS. *See* Thought Occurrence
        Questionnaire for Sport
Torre, Joe, 328
Torres, Dana, 493
Tracy, David F., 9, 11
training
    with anxiety, 185–86
    with coaching, 316
    ethical codes for, 51–53
    peak performance, 47
    performance psychology and, 38–39
    QE, 183–85
    sport psychology and, 38–39
    sport psychology in, 14
    standards for, development of, 17
trait anxiety, 99
transcranial magnetic stimulation
        (TMS), 144n6
transference, 411–12
transformational leadership, 332
transtheoretical model (TTM),
        666–67, 666*t*
triarchic model of intelligence, 64
trigger words, 127. *See also* self-talk
triple-code model of imagery, 226–27
Triplett, Norman, 4–5, 18
TTM. *See* transtheoretical model
Tyson, Mike, 364

U
unconscious awareness
    blindsight and, 134
    consciousness compared to, 134–35
    unconscious-thought effect, 134
unconsciousness, global workplace theory
        and, 133
unconscious-thought effect, 134
Unestahl, Lars-Eric, 14, 17
unhealthy perfectionism, 295
unidimensional identity development
        and external control model, for
        burnout, 573
Unitas, Johnny, 605, 627
United States (U.S.)
    culture in, 420
    ethnicity in, 420
    sport psychology in, 7–8, 11
    talent development in, for
        adolescents, 436
    Title IX legislation in, 349
U.S. Olympics Committee (USOC), 13.
        See also Olympic Games
    sport psychology and, 15–16

V
values, 49
Vanek, Mirsoluv, 12
verbal persuasion, self-efficacy from,
        275–76
video-based modeling, 262–63, 265
virtual modeling, 265–66
virtues, 49
visual imagery, 218
visualization, 127
visuomotor control, 180–82
    QE in, 181–82
    schema systems for, 181
Vividness of Movement Imagery
        Questionnaire-2 (VMIQ-2), 215
VMIQ-2. *See* Vividness of Movement
        Imagery Questionnaire-2
volleyball, self-modeling for, 255
voluntary attention, 178
voluntary retirement, 516
vulnerability, personal, 103

W
WADA. *See* World Anti-Doping Agency
Waitley, Denis, 15
Walton, Sam, 328
Warner, Pop, 8
Watching Dance project, 103
Watson, Tom, 493
web-based modeling, 262–63
    coaching applications with, 265
weight lifting, 256
Weiss, Maureen, 15
Weiss, W. M., 454
Welch, Jack, 328
Wenz, Betty, 13, 15
what-if scenarios, 75
Whitmore, John, 356
whole body approach, 587–88
whole person approach, to career
        transitions, 515, 520–21
Williams, Jean, 15
Williams, Serena, 127, 423
Williams, Tom, 364
Williams, Venus, 423
Winter, Bud, 9
Witmer, Lightner, 6
Wolfe, Harry Kirke, 6
women. *See also* feminism
    age-related decline for, in sports
        performance, 494
    aggression among, 376
    coaching of, 349–51
    EDs among, 643–44
    ethnicity and, performance influenced
        by, 425–26
    female athlete triad, 639
    hegemonic femininity, 389
    ideal body for, 389, 636
    internalization of body ideal for, 647
    MD in, 640
    modeling for, 260

moral behavior for, 376
perfectionism among, 302
self-esteem for, in performance
　　psychology, 100
in sport psychologist-athlete
　　relationships, 407
Title IX legislation for, 349, 386–88
Women and Sports from Myth to Reality
　　(Oglesby), 394
women's sport
　　body image and, 389–90
　　female coaches and, 349–51, 387
　　feminist sport psychology and, 394–97
　　gender equity barriers for, 387
　　herstory in, 386–87, 397n1
　　homonegativism in, 390–92
　　lesbian labeling in, 387
　　in Muslim cultures, 425
　　physical health benefits of, 388
　　psychology of, 388–89
　　Title IX legislation for, 349, 386–88
Wooden, John, 49, 328
Woods, Tiger, 63, 126
working memory, 144n1
　　consciousness and, 132–33
　　emotional regulation and, 165
World Anti-Doping Agency (WADA),
　　546–47
worry, in competitive sports anxiety, 176
wrestling, 642
Wundt, Wilhelm, 6, 7

X

xenophobia, 424–25

Y

Yao Ming, 423
Yates, Dorothy, 9, 11, 14
YBRS. *See* Youth Behavior Risk Survey
YES-2. *See* Youth Experiences Scale
Young, Olive G., 14
Youth Behavior Risk Survey (YBRS),
　　547, 553–54
youth development. *See also* youth sport
　　assets in, 450
　　autonomy-supportive behaviors in, 455
　　behavioral development with, 449–51
　　caring climates for, 456
　　coaches as influence on, 454–56
　　competence information in, 455
　　components of, 449
　　controlling behaviors in, 455
　　emotions as influence on, 461–62
　　family belief systems as influence on, 453
　　features of, 450
　　friendships in, 452–53
　　future research on, 465–66
　　historical references for, 448–49
　　informational feedback in, 455
　　interpersonal, 450
　　interpersonal leadership in, 455–56
　　interventions in, 460–61
　　leadership in, 452–53
　　moral development in, 456–59
　　motivations in, 462–63
　　parental influence on, 453–54
　　PCDEs and, 486–87
　　peer acceptance in, 452–53
　　peer influence on, 451–52
　　peer modeling for, 451–52

personal, 450
physical assets in, 463–65
positive, 449
psychological assets in, 459–63
psychosocial behavior promotion in,
　　449–51
SDT and, 463
self-perceptions in, 460–61
through skill-building activities, 450
social assets in, 451–59
social relationships as part of, 451–56
social support in, 451
sport psychology and, 449–50
Teaching Personal and Social
　　Responsibility Model for,
　　450, 453
Youth Experiences Scale (YES-2), 352
youth sport. *See also* expertise, in sports;
　　talent development
　　behavior setting theory and, 441
　　birthplace bias in, 441
　　community size as influence on, 442
　　contexts for, 441–42
　　deliberate play in, 439
　　deliberate practice in, 439
　　developmental activities in, 439–40
　　dropouts from, 443
　　games with rules in, 439
　　personal development for, 443–44
　　positive development settings for, 442t
　　relative age affect in, 441
　　rhythmic stereotypes in, 439
　　rough and tumble play in, 439
　　in underpopulated settings, 441–42
Yuasa, Yasuo, 586